Consumer Behavior
Eighth Edition

▲▲▲

Consumer Behavior
Eighth Edition

▲▲

James F. Engel
Eastern College

Roger D. Blackwell
The Ohio State University

Paul W. Miniard
Florida International University

The Dryden Press
Harcourt Brace College Publishers

Forth Worth · Philadelphia · San Diego · New York · Orlando · Austin
San Antonio · Toronto · Montreal · London · Sydney · Tokyo

Acquisitions Editor	Lyn Hastert
Developmental Editor	Paul Stewart
Project Editor	Doug Smith
Art Director	Terry Rasberry
Production Manager	Ann Coburn
Permissions Editor and Photo Researcher	Elizabeth Banks
Product Manager	Lisé Johnson
Marketing Assistant	Sam Stubblefield
Director of Editing, Design, and Production	Diane Southworth
Publisher	Elizabeth Widdicombe
Copy Editor	Donna Regan
Indexer	Leslie Leland Frank
Compositor and Color Separator	Colortype
Text Type	10/12 Palatino
Cover Image	Private Collection/Superstock©

Address for Editorial Correspondence
The Dryden Press, 301 Commerce Street, Suite 3700, Forth Worth, TX 76102

Address for Orders
The Dryden Press, 6277 Sea Harbor Drive, Orlando, FL 32887
1-800-782-4479, or 1-800-433-0001 (in Florida)

ISBN: 0-03-098464-5

Library of Congress Catalog Number: 94-70806

Printed in the United States of America

4 5 6 7 8 9 0 1 2 3 039 10 9 8 7 6 5 4 3 2 1

The Dryden Press
Harcourt Brace College Publishers

THE DRYDEN PRESS SERIES IN MARKETING

Preface

▲▲▲

It is hard for us to believe that *Consumer Behavior* had its birth some 26 years ago in 1968. At that time, the subject was in its infancy and this would be its first text book. None of us could imagine that the field would have so rich a youth.

Although consumer behavior studies now benefit from universal establishment in the market curriculum, new opportunities continue to present themselves. We still face the never-ending challenge of making practical sense out of a subject that has diverse roots in economics and the behavioral sciences. Our basic purposes remain unchanged from the first edition:

1. To explore and evaluate a rapidly growing body of published and unpublished research
2. To advance generalizations and propositions from the evidence
3. To assess the practical significance of what has been learned
4. To pinpoint areas where research is rapidly evolving
5. To make the field of consumer behavior exciting, interesting, and relevant to both students and faculty

Our primary perspective continues to lie in marketing applications, although we fully acknowledge changing paradigms that have greatly broadened the perspective of the field. In particular, the postmodern research paradigm has had an enriching influence that has established the study of consumption behavior as a legitimate discipline in and of itself. You will see reflections of this paradigm throughout the book.

From the outset in 1968 we have used a model of consumer behavior as a basic method of exposition. It has changed over the years, however, and we have modified this edition to encompass the growing knowledge of consumption behavior. We continue to receive feedback that a model is helpful in the field and helps guide applications in both research and strategy.

We are grateful to the many users of previous editions who have helped us rethink our objectives. We especially acknowledge the following colleagues who gave significant help as this edition was conceived and developed; M. Wayne Alexander, Moorhead State University; Kenneth R. Lord, State University of New York at Buffalo; Susan Spiggle, the University of Connecticut; Stuart Van Auken, California State University at Chico; Newell D. Wright, Virginia Polytechnic Institute and State University.

As always, we approach this subject from one dominant point of view: " How helpful is a given concept, theory, or technique beyond the classroom?" As our knowledge and experience have grown over these decades, so has the richness of our applications.

Here are some of the changes that long-time users of *Consumer Behavior* will notice in this edition:

1. A revamped order of topics placing the essential practical issues of market segmentation and global marketing up front, followed by a focus on the stages of consumer decision process.

2. A greatly expanded consideration of postmodern research contributions. For the first time we have added a chapter on consumption in response to the rapid growth of research in this important area.

3. A continued commitment to uncover helpful consumer research examples and applications from all parts of the world. This has been made possible because two members of our team have extensive international involvement.

4. Expanded commitment to explore the ethics of consumer influence. It seems that the frequency of abuses grows even more rapidly than knowledge in the field. Readers also will notice extensive changes within all chapters. A substantial portion of the textbook is new because we have not stepped away from our long-standing commitment to be fully up-to-date with the burgeoning scholarship within this field of study.

We continue to expand the supplementary materials designed to help the classroom needs of instructors. A new series of accompanying videos will be of great interest to many. In addition, we offer a computerized test bank containing nearly 2,000 multiple-choice, true/false, and essay questions, plus color transparencies and transparency masters for classroom use. We also offer an instructor's manual containing teaching suggestions, chapter outlines, and answers to the end-of-chapter questions. Finally, many have chosen to use our companion casebook, *Contemporary Cases in Consumer Behavior*, Fourth Edition by Roger Blackwell, Tina Blackwell, and W. Wayne Talarzyk.

In the seventh (25th anniversary) edition we acknowledged the contributions of more than 60 colleagues over the years who have been of such great help. Once again, we want to let each of you know how much we appreciate you. Your influence lives on. We also express our appreciation to the staff of

Management Horizons, a division of Price Waterhouse, for the help provided from the very beginning.

John Antil, University of Delaware
April Atwood, University of Washington
Kenneth Baker, University of New Mexico
John Bennett, University of Northern Colorado
Gordon Bruner, Southern Illinois University, Carbondale
Steven Burgess, The University of Witwatersrand
Robert Burnkrant, Ohio State University
Peter Chadraba, University of West Oshkosh
Robert Coleman, Kansas State University
Sayeste Daser, Wake Forest University
Rohit Deshpande, University of Texas, Austin
Peter Dickson, Ohio State University
Peter DiPaulo, University of Missouri, St. Louis
Michael Dorsch, Valdosta State College
Hershey Friedman, Brooklyn College
David Gardner, University of Illinois, Urbana/Champaign
Peggy Gilbert, Southwest Missouri State University
James Ginter, Ohio State University
John Grabner, Ohio State University
Donald Granbois, Indiana University
Paul Green, University of Pennsylvania
Nessim Hanna, Northern Illinois University
Betty Harris, University of Southwestern Louisiana
Salah S. Hassan, George Washington University
Douglass Hawes, University of Wyoming
Gail Hudson, Arkansas State University
Wesley Johnston, Georgia State University
Benoy Joseph, Cleveland State University
Harold Kassarjian, University of California, Los Angeles
Inder Khera, Wright State University
Tina Kiesler, University of Southern California
Philip Kotler, Northwestern University
Jim Leigh, Texas A&M University
Larry Lepisto, Central Michigan University
Roger Leyton, University of New South Wales
JoAnn Linrud, Mankato State University
Ken Lord, SUNY, Buffalo
Deanna Mader, University of Louisville
James McNeal, Texas A&M University
Dan McQuiston, Butler University

Lee Meadow, Bentley College
Allan R. Miller, Towson State University
Don Norris, Miami University
Terry O'Brien, Northern Illinois University
J. Paul Peter, University of Wisconsin, Madison
Richard Pollay, University of British Columbia
Robert Pratt, Avon Products
John Schouten, University of Portland
Dan Sherrell, Louisiana State University
Deepak Sirdeshmukh, Ohio State University
Doug Stayman, Cornell University
W. Wayne Talarzyk, Ohio State University
Robert Tamilia, University of Quebec
B. Venkatesh, Burke Marketing Research
Angelina Villarreal, Miller Brewing Company
Tillie Voegtli, University of Missouri, St. Louis
Hugh Wales, University of Illinois (emeritus)
Malcolm White, California State University, Sacramento
Tommy E. Whittler, University of Kentucky, Lexington
Ron Willett, Indiana University
Robert Woodruff, University of Tennessee

We have benefited from a long and fruitful relationship with The Dryden Press. We extend special thanks to Lyn Hastert, executive editor; Lisé Johnson, senior product manager; Paul Stewart, development editor; Doug Smith, project editor; Ann Coburn, production manager; Terry Rasberry, art director; and Elizabeth Banks, permissions editor and photo researcher.

Finally, to Sharon and Tina, thanks for being genuine partners in every sense of the word.

James F. Engel, Philadelphia, Pennsylvania
Roger Blackwell, Columbus, Ohio
Paul W. Miniard, Miami, Florida

September 1994

About the Authors

▲▲

James F. Engel (Ph.D., University of Illinois, Urbana; B.S., Drake) has a distinguished name in the study of consumer behavior. He was honored by his peers in 1980 as the founder of the field when he was named one of the first two Fellows of the Association for Consumer Research. He received a similar citation with the prestigious Paul D. Converse Award of the American Marketing Association. These honors were given in recognition of his pioneering research that first appeared in 1960, his role as senior author of this textbook, and other forms of leadership.

He presently is Distinguished Professor of Marketing and Director of the Center for Organizational Excellence at Eastern College, St. Davids, Pennsylvania, where he moved in 1990. Professor Engel has shifted his emphasis from consumer goods marketing to the application of nonprofit marketing principles to religious organizations worldwide. He has served as a consultant and management development specialist with hundreds of organizations in more than 60 countries.

Roger D. Blackwell (Ph.D., Northwestern; B.S., Missouri) is professor of marketing at The Ohio State University where he has taught since 1965. He is a well-known author whose works include several casebooks also published by The Dryden Press. He is in frequent demand as a business consultant and speaker in the area of the impact of changing environments on marketing strategy for companies such as IBM, AT&T, CheckPoint, and The Limited. He serves on the board of directors for several firms in retailing, consumer services, manufacturing, and management consulting.

Dr. Blackwell was recipient of the 1984 Marketing Educator of the Year Award given by Sales and Marketing Executives International. He also has received numerous awards for outstanding teaching at Ohio State, including the Alumni Award for Distinguished Teaching in 1988.

Paul W. Miniard (Ph.D., M.A., B.S., University of Florida) is professor of marketing at Florida International University. He has previously been a tenured member of the faculties at the University of South Carolina and The Ohio State University. Over his career, he has received a number of undergraduate and graduate teaching awards.

Dr. Miniard is well known through his published research in the area of consumer behavior, which has appeared in such leading journals as *Journal of Consumer Psychology, Journal of Consumer Research, Journal of Marketing Research,* and *Journal of Experimental Social Psychology.* He also serves as a consultant and expert witness in areas involving consumer behavior. In 1992, Dr. Miniard visited the University of International Business and Economics in Beijing, China, to help set up a course in consumer behavior.

Brief Contents

Contents

▲▲▲

xiii

Consumer Behavior
Eighth Edition

▲▲▲

PART I

Introduction and Overview

▲▲

What is consumer behavior all about? Why should it receive such widespread recognition as the key to modern marketing success? As an academic discipline? As a field of research? And how does this exciting field create a dynamic blend of economics, marketing, psychology, and other related behavioral science disciplines? These and many other questions are considered in the first chapter, which builds a framework of essential principles and concepts.

It is important at the outset to discover how organizations develop strategies based on an understanding of consumer behavior. One of the challenges is to discover how groups of consumers **(segments)** differ from the total and to meet their unique needs with products and services designed for them. Market segmentation is the subject of Chapter 2 which also reviews major demographic trends and the ways in which they affect marketing strategy.

No introduction to the field would be complete, however, without an examination of global market segments and strategies. You will be introduced to the broad forces that shape international competition in Chapter 3. You will quickly grasp the challenges faced when we "think globally."

Let your mind range far and wide as you read these chapters. Ask yourself how the content speaks to your life and career. There is no field you could study that comes closer to daily life. Welcome to what we hope will be a real adventure for you.

CHAPTER 1

The Consumer:
Perspectives and Viewpoints

▲▲▲▲▲▲▲▲▲▲▲▲▲▲▲▲▲▲▲▲▲▲▲▲▲▲▲▲▲▲▲▲▲▲▲▲▲

"A Flight into the Unknown" —
The Dilemma of the Indian Frequent Flier

"I would call it a cannon ball run—full of risks, adventure, and improbabilities." These are the words of a regular flier on Indian Airlines, the vast and, until recently, only domestic airline in India. Crashes, frequent flight delays and cancellations, hijackings, and notoriously poor ground and inflight service led another long-suffering customer to observe that "flying the main airline is like flying on the unknown."

These are typical of the opinions uncovered in a 1993 study of frequent domestic fliers undertaken by Quantum Market Research in the four largest cities in India. To sum it up, "the customer is not king." Respondents believe that Indian Airlines takes them completely for granted:

- "If you are working for a government concern, you don't get sacked. You do what you want. You needn't treat passengers well. You can reply rudely. You can do anything."

- "If they could put us on a conveyor belt and move us, they would."

- "Their attitude is, 'You got a ticket? Get in at one end and get out at another. Just don't bother us.'"

- "Flight timings suit the needs of the pilot more than the needs of the traveller."

- "We joke about the air crashes. We say, if we die, our kin will get 2 million rupees from the government."

- "They have no value for human life. If they compromise today [safety, maintenance, crew training, traffic control] and get away with it they think that since nothing happened yesterday let us do it again. That is the attitude."

With such problems as these, why keep on flying? That's simple—*no real choice*. In the words of another customer, "It's like a bridge over a wide river. No matter how dangerous the bridge, what would you do? Take the bridge . . . or swim?"

Adapted from "Battling for the Domestic Sky," Destination Traveler *(May 1993), 57–68. © 1993 by Cross Section Publications (P) Ltd., New Delhi, India. All rights reserved.*

What's Consumer Behavior All About?

The story of the long-suffering Indian frequent flier is interesting reading, isn't it? It could be repeated in almost every country, demonstrating that people face very similar challenges in the everyday world of buying and consuming. The fact is that much of life focuses in this commonplace arena, and this alone makes consumer behavior a fascinating subject for anyone who is interested in how people cope with everyday existence.

It is not surprising that a large and expanding field of research has emerged focusing on consumer behavior. We define **consumer behavior** as *those activities directly involved in obtaining, consuming, and disposing of products and services, including the decision processes that precede and follow these actions.*

This subject can be approached from several perspectives, all of which are considered in this book: (1) consumer influence; (2) postmodern; and (3) intercultural. As you will see, these categories overlap to some extent.

Consumer Influence Perspective

Consumer behavior is of particular interest to those who, for various reasons, desire to influence or change that behavior, including those whose primary concern is marketing, consumer education and protection, and public policy. The dominant research perspective is *logical positivism,* in which the objectives are twofold: (1) to understand and predict consumer behavior, and (2) to discover cause-and-effect relationships that govern persuasion and/or education.[1]

Marketing

Nobody has greater interest in consumer motivation and behavior than entrepreneurial business people. Not surprisingly, potential competitors long viewed Indian Airlines as a "sitting duck waiting for the kill" but were banned from entering this government-protected market. The clouds over the air began to give way in 1986 when the government allowed limited service to begin. Matters improved even further in 1990 when private airlines, referred to as air taxi services, were given greater latitude in competing with Indian Airlines.

The most prominent of these new entries, East West Airlines, "put the smile back into flying" (Figure 1.1). Quantum market researchers found these to be the most important elements in its positive image[2]:

Service: excellent, warm, friendly, service with a smile attitude

Crew: classy, elegant, sophisticated, polished, refined, well trained

Connections: limited, not extensive or expansive

Timeliness in departure: a mixed picture of positive and negative

Even though it was small and restricted in its schedule, East West made a substantial dent in the Indian Airline bottom line. Its market share has declined by 10 percent; its load factor (the percentage of seats occupied) experienced a similar decline from 76.6 to 70.7, and financial losses have burgeoned.[3]

Figure 1.1   East West Airlines Customer Service Wounds a Competitor

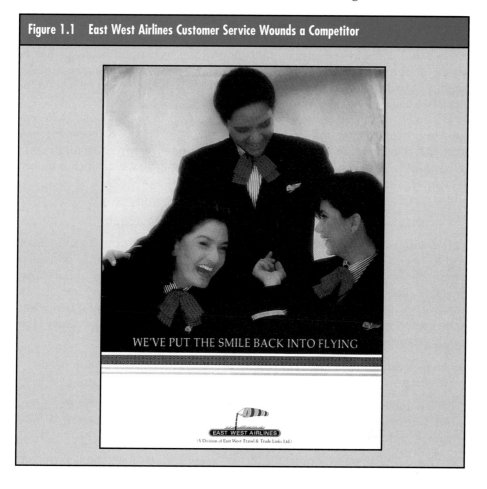

Unfortunately, parliament passed the Air Corporation Act in 1993, which re-established the virtual monopoly of Indian Airlines on its routes. Strict enforcement by the office of the Directorate General of Civil Aviation has severely curbed the profit potential of East West and other start-up airlines.[4]

Between 1990 and 1993, we have a great example of the *marketing concept* at work—the process of planning and executing the conception, pricing, promotion, and distribution of ideas, goods, and services to create exchanges that satisfy individual and organizational objectives.[5] The key element in this definition is the exchange between the customer and the supplier. Each party gives something of value to the other, with the goal of satisfying their respective needs, and in the process, both parties gain.

In marketing, *the consumer is king,* a fact that the management of Indian Airlines seemed to disregard. As Peter Drucker put it in 1954, "There is one valid definition of business purpose: *to create a customer*" [italics ours].[6] Peters and Austin[7] drove this point even more firmly home in their influential book *A Passion for Excellence:* "There are only two ways to create and sustain superior performance over the long haul. First, take exceptional care of your customers . . . via superior service and superior quality. Second, constantly innovate. That's it."

It should come as no surprise that the study of consumer behavior has its strongest historic roots in marketing. As Belk[8] put it, the underlying research issue is: "What arrangement of the marketing mix will have what effects on the purchase behavior of what types of consumers?"

It is important to understand that, until recently, *the buying process has been of more concern to marketers than the consumption process and has set the research agenda of the field.* Furthermore, marketers are not interested in research just for the purpose of understanding. Rather, consumer research must have distinct managerial relevance before it will be taken seriously.

Consumer Education and Protection

Others also want to shape and influence consumer behavior but do so in an effort to help the consumer buy wisely. The consumer economist, in particular, would be very interested in examining the attitudes and behavior of the Indian frequent fliers in terms of whether they make the best choices in view of their motivations and goals. Furthermore, the service deficiencies would be viewed with great concern in the context of consumer welfare. Here are some issues that might be raised:

1. Is the airline guilty of denying consumer rights to the information needed to make an informed choice?

2. What are the consequences of the Air Corporation Act of 1993 on the rights of consumers to have access to air service that meets basic expectations for safety and reliability?

3. What can be done to compel the airline to give full redress when consumer rights are violated?

Through education, the consumer can be taught how to detect the presence of deception and other abuses and be made aware of remedies that exist and opportunities for redress. Also, anyone can benefit from greater insight into money-saving strategies. Educational programs must be based on research into motivation and behavior if they are to be relevant in the real world of consumer life. Not surprisingly, consumer economists and home economists now rank among the most serious students of consumer behavior.[9]

The marketer and the consumer economist often take adversarial positions when analyzing the same behavior. Nevertheless, both desire to change that behavior when it is perceived from their perspective as being beneficial to do so. The only difference is in their respective agendas.

Public Policy

Education alone will not guarantee consumer welfare. The cornerstone of a free-enterprise economy is the right of any consumer to make an informed and unrestricted choice from an array of alternatives. When this right is curtailed because of business abuse, societal consensus affirms that government has the duty to influence consumer choice by restrictions in monopoly power and by curbing deception and other unfair trade practices. Unfortunately, many within India believe that parliament and its government took an entirely opposite agenda and acted in opposition to consumer interests to artificially restore Indian Airline's profitability.[10]

Consumer protection legislation and regulation all too often are based on the opinions of a small group of advocates. The outcome can be ineffective or even counterproductive activity. There now is growing awareness that greater reliance must be placed on consumer research if consumer protection is to function as intended.[11]

Postmodern Perspective

Until recently, most published consumer research was marketing motivated and hence embraced the research paradigm of **positivism,** in which rigorous empirical techniques are used to discover generalizable explanations and laws. Now, there is a growing movement within the field to supplement positivism with **postmodernism**—a form of inquiry that embraces different goals and methods.[12] As a result, the field of consumer research has been enriched and expanded in exciting ways.

The waters parted, in effect, in the early 1980s through the influence of Morris B. Holbrook and Elizabeth C. Hirschman.[13] Holbrook, in particular, tackled the managerial dominance of the field by calling for a new and broader research agenda that examines "all facets of the value potentially produced when some living organism acquires, uses, or disposes of any product that might achieve a goal, fulfill a need, or satisfy a want."[14] In other words, it is equally important to use consumer research to *understand consumption behavior* without any intent of *influencing it.*

Other voices quickly joined in the call for a new focus on *ownership and consumption* and the meanings that these processes convey to all of life.[15] The pre-purchase decision and buying processes, so important to marketers, are of far less importance than consumption in this context.

This broadened perspective has led to a recent growth in published research on such experiential aspects of the consumption experience as sensation seeking, emotional arousal, and fantasizing.[16] Methodology has moved beyond positivism to such diverse options as ethnography, semiotics, hermeneutics, literary criticism, and historicism to achieve a broader understanding of the impact of consumption on all aspects of life.[17]

If we were to analyze the travel-related behavior of the upper-class Indian professional from this point of view, here are some issues that might emerge:

1. To what extent is flying a part of a consumption ritual—a formal behavioral system undertaken for self-expression?

2. In what ways are mobility and time-saving, two values epitomized by flying, destructive of traditional Indian cultural and value systems?

3. What long-lasting effects will the consumer culture have on traditional ways of life?

There is no question that postmodernism is having an impact on the field, although the literature currently is relatively small. You will notice this impact especially in Chapter 8 (the many forms of expression surrounding consumer behavior) and Chapter 12 (consumer behavior as a form of self expression).

Global Intercultural Perspective

If one were to examine the literature, it would be easy to assume that consumer research is of primary importance only in North America, Europe, and Japan. A quick look at the ads in Figure 1.2 tells you that nothing could be further from the truth. On all continents, there is a striving toward economic development and greater self-sufficiency. As disposable income increases, a rising standard of living becomes a dominant motivation.

Astute entrepreneurs everywhere are discovering the gains that can be made when a concerted effort is made to understand prospective consumers and meet their needs with culturally relevant alternatives. Here are just a few examples.

- A vogue word in China today is "Huoli 28," the Chinese pronunciation for "Power 28," which almost instantaneously has become the most popular detergent in that country. Through television, radio, and newspaper advertising, sales increased by 10 times when Huoli 28 was launched in the 1980s, resulting in a substantial profit.

- The world's only scented children's footwear (strawberry, watermelon, and chocolate among others) is produced by the Calzados Dolphitos plant in

Figure 1.2 Evidence of a Growing Consumer Culture Worldwide — Russia, Nepal, Kenya, France, Thailand, and India

My Nepal, my pride

Discover the taste in Surya Luxury Kings

SURYA
LUXURY KINGS

Because you deserve the best

a little
luxury
every
day

Cussons

VANIA. ETRE BIEN VOUS VA SI BIEN.

vania *pocket*

Figure 1.2 continues on page 10.

Figure 1.2   (continued)

Santiago, Chile. Sales have more than doubled since the product was launched in 1986.[18]

● Procter & Gamble is gaining market inroads in Russia by offering brands featuring such previously unheard of benefits as dandruff control.[19]

It is accurate to state that basic consumer needs and decision processes are universal. Nevertheless, there are major cultural differences in the ways in which motivation and behavior are carried out in practice. Turn to Consumer in Focus 1.1 and discover the lessons learned by AT&T when an attempt was made to introduce its "I Plan" advertising campaign into Slavic cultures. The need for accurate consumer research becomes even greater when cultural boundaries are crossed.

Consumer in Focus **1.1**

Thumbs Down on AT&T's "Thumbs Up"

The "thumbs up" sign used in AT&T's "I Plan" campaign presented a problem when it had to be translated into other languages. To most Americans, "thumbs up" signifies positive affirmation. But to Russians and Poles, the fact that a person's palm was visible gave a print ad from N. W. Ayer an entirely different, even offensive meaning.

That's when the unusual expertise of YAR communications came in. YAR, one of a handful of agencies that specializes in translations, reshot the graphic element of the ad so that only the back of the person's hand was seen, thereby conveying the intended meaning to Russians and Poles.

"The AT&T example shows there's more to translating ads than simply putting English words into another tongue," says Yuri Radzievsky, YAR president. "Sometimes we can't translate something appropriately. In every market it is a new creation."

Source: Riccardo A. Davis, "Many Languages — 1 Ad Message," Advertising Age (September 1993), 80. Reproduced by special permission.

The Perspective of this Book

Since the first edition, we have tried to be eclectic in the best sense of the word and to reflect a broad orientation. Nevertheless, we approach the subject of consumer behavior from a marketing point of view. Our primary concern is phasing consumer research into marketing strategy. Increasingly, however, the other perspectives have changed our outlook. We welcome and affirm the enrichment that is taking place.

Right Thinking about the Consumer

Four significant principles underlie all that we say and do in these coming pages.

The Consumer Is Sovereign

With much hoopla, BIC Corp. introduced Parfum BIC, a $5 flask of perfume, to the supermarkets and drugstore chains in the United States, where it has achieved such success with its pens, shavers, and other products. It was withdrawn within a year after running up an $11 million loss.[20] It was almost totally ignored by its target market. According to one analyst, "Perfume is hardly as disposable and utilitarian as a bag of razors. Fragrance is an emotional sell to women. But the BIC package wasn't even feminine. It looked like a cigarette lighter."[21]

As this example demonstrates, the failure rate for new product introductions has been astonishingly high for decades, and it has not diminished in this era of supposedly sophisticated marketing. Kuczmarski & Associates studied the success rates for 11,000 new products launched by 77 different companies and found that only 56 percent are still on the market 5 years later.[22] Group EFO Ltd. reports even more discouraging figures. Only 8 percent of new product concepts offered by a group of 112 leading manufacturers and retailers reached the market, and 83 percent of those that did failed to meet marketing objectives.[23]

Why is this failure rate so high? The answer is simple and straightforward— *a new product must satisfy the customer's needs, not the needs and expectations of a management team.* The bottom-line issue is indifference to the basic principle that *the consumer is sovereign.* He or she is not an unthinking pawn to be manipulated at will by the commercial persuader.

Consumer behavior, as a rule, is purposeful and goal-oriented. Products and services are accepted or rejected on the basis of the extent to which they are perceived as relevant to needs and lifestyle. The individual is fully capable of ignoring everything the marketer has to say.

It is astonishing to realize that a viewer watching 30 hours of television a week in the United States will be bombarded by more than 35,000 commercials a year.[24] But, as you learn in Chapter 14, those in the audience are amazingly adapt at screening out (zap) anything that they do not want to see.

Furthermore, exactly the same thing is happening in Moscow, even in the face of great hunger for anything American. Having been weaned on propaganda and distrust of the media, professional-class Muscovites proved to be highly skeptical of advertising messages. As a case in point, a harried yuppie with his car telephone was dismissed as being unstable, hyperactive, and frivolous.[25]

It all comes down to the simple point: *Understanding and adapting to consumer motivation and behavior is not an option—it is an absolute necessity for competitive survival.* Consider these strong words from the editors of *Fortune* in the lead article of a 1993 special edition on the "tough new consumer":

> **MEET THE NEW CONSUMER.** And smile when you do—*because this is your boss* [italics ours]. It may not be the person you thought you knew. Instead of choosing from what you have to offer, the new consumer tells you what he [sic] wants. You figure out how to supply it.[26]

Understanding Consumer Motivation and Behavior through Research

Long before the onset of modern marketing, entrepreneurial enterprises used multiple ways to discern what their buyers wanted. Most ran small enterprises and knew their customers intimately, even to the point of designing or offering a custom product. They demonstrated that motivation and behavior *can be un-*

derstood sufficiently accurately to reduce substantially the risks of marketing failure. Today's research methodology, properly used, lowers that risk even further. Therefore, ignorance is no excuse whatsoever.

Influencing Consumer Behavior

Here is a fundamental principle that underlies all that is said in this book: *Consumer sovereignty presents a formidable challenge, but skillful marketing can affect both motivation and behavior if the product or service offered is designed to meet consumer needs and expectations.* A sales success occurs because demand either exists already or is latent and awaiting activation by the right marketing offering.

Much of the solution lies with management who move beyond the confines of their desk and office and seek active contact with consumers at the grassroots. A case in point is the Honda North America team, which recovered from its shock when the Accord was toppled from market dominance by the Ford Taurus. This management team became proactive in a vital and effective way.

Social Legitimacy of Consumer Influence when Shaped by a Proper Ethical Sensitivity

Consumer needs are real, and there is undeniable benefit from products or services that offer genuine utility. The consumer benefits while, at the same time, the economic system is energized. Leo Bogart, a well-known marketing strategist, stated it well over two decades ago:

> Apart from what a specific advertising [marketing] campaign does for a specific product, there is a broader combined effect of the thousands of advertising exhortations that confront every consumer, a constant reminder of material goods and services not yet possessed. That effect at the level of individual motivation is felt as a constant impetus toward more consumption, toward acquisition, toward upward mobility. At the collective level, it is felt in the economic drive to produce and to innovate which fuels our economic system.[27]

Reality is something quite different, however. Fraud and manipulation abound, thus giving rise in 1960 to development of the Consumer Bill of Rights and its propagation and enforcement by the burgeoning consumerism movement in the United States.[28] Take time to read the Consumer Bill of Rights (Figure 1.3). Even though it is discussed at length in Chapter 24, it is important to grasp its scope and essence at this point.

Rights are absolute, inviolable, and non-negotiable. Outright deception, low product quality, nonresponse to legitimate complaints, pollution, and other actions are nothing less than violation of legitimate rights and must be viewed as such.

There has been a shift in national consciousness, leading to increased stridency in demands for moral and ethical behavior in business, professions, and

---

Figure 1.3   Consumer Bill of Rights

The Consumer Bill of Rights

1. *The Right to Safety*—protection against products or services that are hazardous to health and life.
2. *The Right to be Informed*—provision of facts necessary for an informed choice; protection against fraudulent, deceitful, or misleading claims.
3. *The Right to Choose*—assured access to a variety of products and services at competitive prices.
4. *The Right to be Heard (Redress)*—assurance that consumer interests receive full and sympathetic consideration in formulation and implementation of regulatory policy, and prompt and fair restitution.
5. *The Right to Enjoy a Clean and Healthful Environment.*
6. *The Right of the Poor and Other Minorities to Have Their Interests Protected.*

---

politics. Manufacturers and retailers are increasingly faced with vigorous protest when actions go against social consensus.

To take just one example, consumer backlash was unleashed after statistics showed a fourth straight drop in average longevity among African-Americans, attributable, at least in part, to higher instances of tobacco- and alcohol-related illnesses. As a result, G. Heileman Brewing Co. was forced by public pressure to withdraw PowerMaster, its high-potency malt liquor aimed at inner-city consumers. Similarly, R. J. Reynolds dropped plans to market Uptown, a menthol cigarette aimed primarily at this segment.[29]

Consumer Research as a Dynamically Evolving Field of Inquiry

Consumer research as a systematic area of behavioral science inquiry in the form in which we know it today began to come into its own in the late 1950s and early 1960s. This is far more than an historic anecdote, however, because it emerged in response to major shifts in the economy of the Western world and in the broader environment at that time. Of even greater importance, *these underlying factors continue to shift in ways that intensify the challenge of consumer research and marketing strategy.*

In this section, we clarify the forces that have molded the growth of consumer research to the mature discipline that it is today. To help you understand something of what has happened in this century, we summarize with a broad brush the main impact of these determinants in three periods: (1) the pre–World War II era; (2) the post–World War II era through the late 1980s; and (3) the contemporary scene (the last 6 years).

You will quickly see that today's challenges are demanding ones indeed. Each generation builds on the shoulders of its predecessors, but it is now apparent that some of the conventional wisdom is under siege. Where does it go from here? Who knows for sure? Welcome aboard.

Dominant Forces Shaping Consumer Research

The analysis of consumer behavior has its initial roots in economic theory and later in marketing. Its content and methodology are shaped by these essential considerations: (1) the factors that move an economy from being *production-driven* to *market-driven*, and (2) the level of sophistication with which human behavior is understood in psychology and other behavioral sciences.

Move from Production Orientation to Market Orientation

Imagine, if you will, the challenges facing Henry Ford in the great days of the early 1900s when the remarkable product of that era, the Model T, swept the market. You are familiar with his famous saying — *"you can get it in any color as long as it is black."* If a consumer researcher from today were to move backward in a time warp to 1916, he or she would never find a job. "Who needs research? We can sell all that we make."

However, move Henry Ford forward in time to 1995. He would have no way to cope with the marketing pressures of a management team facing the competitive challenge of moving the Taurus to premier status. His management skills and understanding so suitable for an earlier era would be totally obsolete today. If he were alive today he would, among *many other things*, need a crash course in consumer behavior.

The complexity of management challenges faced is almost unimaginable as an economy moves from being production-driven to market-driven, characterized by mega competition and high technology. *At the bottom of this challenge is the imperative to have readily accessible and valid, practical information about consumer motivation and behavior.* Furthermore, this must be accompanied by real skill in moving from research to strategy.

There are five environmental factors that shape the magnitude of the marketing challenge faced in an economy and specific industries at any point in time:

1. Extent to which the supply of valid products and services exceeds consumer demand

2. Ability to communicate with customers quickly and accurately at long distances

3. Existence of multiple avenues through which products and services can be distributed quickly and economically

4. Extent to which the supplier of goods and services has the power and freedom to induce distributors to comply with overall marketing strategy

5. Economic growth both domestically and globally

We trace in the next few pages how these factors work themselves out.

Behavioral Science Sophistication

Consumer research is a multidisciplinary field. Consequently, its growth and vitality will be at least proportional to that of other behavioral sciences. Although
space does not permit a lengthy review, it is safe to say that behavioral science
theory and research were given real impetus during World War II. But the sophistication today is quantum leaps ahead of what it was then.

   The number of subfields within psychology alone has grown fourfold from a
handful in 1950 (social, industrial, clinical, and so on), and the same can be said
of other disciplines. Furthermore, the universality of advanced computerized
data analysis has facilitated research and information exchange that would not
even have been conceptualized a decade ago.

Pre–World War II Era

Figure 1.4 captures, in a nutshell, the situation in the prewar era, using the factors that we isolated earlier. If the vibrancy of the 1920s had persevered, it is
likely that sophisticated mass marketing would have leaped forward. Production was the greatest problem earlier in the decade, but this began to change as
competition intensified. Suppliers began to discover that competitive advantage
could not be maintained without such basic information as the product features
prospective buyers want, the advertising media they read, and the effectiveness
of persuasive marketing efforts. But all this was curbed by the economic crisis of
the Great Depression, which was ended only when the war began.

   Few marketers turned to psychology and the other behavioral sciences in
those days, although conventional marketing research began to be quite visible.
One main exception was the entry of learning theorist John B. Watson into the
advertising world. He was the founder of what is still known as *behaviorism.*
From this theoretical paradigm, he theorized with some justification that repetitive advertising would reinforce a response and lead to firm purchasing habits. Today's emphasis on repetition of brand name rests on this foundation
(Figure 1.5).

Post–World War II Era

The situation now changed dramatically. Productive capacity quickly far exceeded demand, and suppliers faced no choice but to adopt the *marketing concept.* Furthermore, the behavioral sciences quickly moved to center stage in a
changing society. All this brought about astonishing change (Figure 1.6).

Figure 1.4   Dominant Conditions in the Pre–World War II Era

Environmental Factors Affecting the Marketing Challenge

- Demand for consumer goods in most industries exceeded supply (except during the Great Depression), and *production* offered the greatest challenge.

- Ability to communicate at long distances through advertising was growing, especially with the onset of radio.

- Distribution channels were mostly small and locally owned, although supermarkets and chain stores made their debut during the 1930s.

- The seller faced no limitations in persuading distributors to sell products, especially where demand was stimulated by advertising.

- Economic growth was vital during the 1920s but seriously blunted until the onset of World War II, making this era atypical in many ways.

Status of the Behavioral Sciences

- Relatively limited in growth and impact until World War II.

- Somewhat more theoretical than empirical, although research began to grow at the end of the period.

It will be most helpful if we sketch the "prevailing wisdom" that guided the search for competitive advantage during much of this period. In particular, it is helpful to focus on the early 1960s, which saw the launch of the field of consumer research. From this, you will quickly grasp the issues marketers struggled with and the hunger they had for relevant information. Here are the foundational principles guiding much of marketing strategy at that time[30]:

- An entrepreneurial commitment to new product development is the key to differential advantage.

- Advertising, especially television and other forms of mass persuasion, will succeed in building sales.

- Mass marketing power will succeed in pulling products through the channels of distribution, with the result that suppliers take command in the channel.

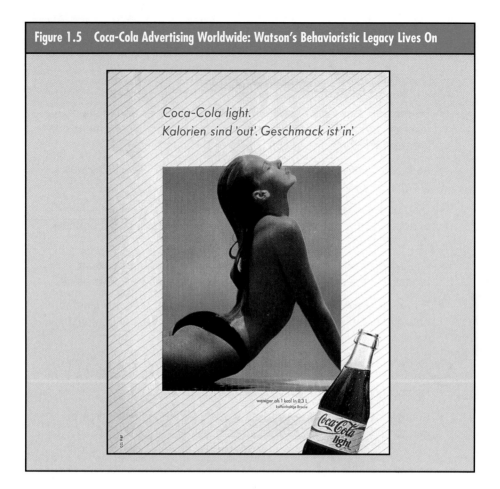

Figure 1.5   Coca-Cola Advertising Worldwide: Watson's Behavioristic Legacy Lives On

- Ongoing product development, accompanied by mass advertising, will build brand loyalty.
- Concentration on the domestic market will yield greatest returns.

The consumer research agenda of that period focused heavily on how to motivate consumers to become loyal buyers. Priority was placed on isolating the attributes that people expect a product to have if it is to meet their needs and expectations. Large advertising campaigns were undertaken with the objectives of increasing awareness of product benefits and creating positive attitudes. A good example appears in Consumer in Focus 1.2, which shows you how the Armour Company tackled its marketing challenges in the 1960s.

Companies today still face the same problems as Armour, and the research approach, although often more sophisticated, is similar. What this demonstrates is that a solid foundation of methodology and understanding was built and remains in place today, although other strategic issues have assumed greater priority.

Figure 1.6   Post–World War II Era — Consumer Research Is Born

---

Environmental Factors Affecting the Marketing Challenge

- Although consumers emerged from the war with pent-up demand and plenty of money, competitive growth soon led to the situation that productive capacity outstripped demand, thus motivating a widespread turn to the marketing concept.

- Television emerged as the "great salesperson." When combined with the other burgeoning media, the mass communications age hit full speed.

- Distribution underwent a virtual revolution with the emergence of shopping centers and discount houses. For the first time, potential buyers could purchase with convenience and ease.

- Manufacturers were able to use advertising and mass media power to pull new products through the channels of distribution, and distributors had little choice but to comply with supplier wishes.

- Economic growth burgeoned with only temporary downturns, and the Western world experienced an unprecedented period of wealth and buying power.

Status of the Behavioral Sciences

- Growth in the physical sciences generated a corresponding recognition that growth in human potential must match technological potential.

- Application of behavioral sciences to the challenges of human behavior and human potential accelerated.

- Notable contributions were appearing in such fields as perception and information processing, attitude research, problem-solving behavior, learning, diffusion of innovations, group influence, and personal influence.

Big Brother Is upon Us — The Freudian Invasion

Marketers were hungry for new insights, and a new fad burst on the scene — **motivation research.** Led by its chief proponent, Ernest Dichter,[31] the world of Sigmund Freud and psychoanalysis found its way to the marketplace. And the critics went wild! Vance Packard ignited fears of *Hidden Persuaders,*[32]

1.2   Consumer in Focus

Never Underestimate the Power of a Hot Dog

In 1962, the Armour Company, one of the largest meat packers, placed a series of 12 ads in *Better Homes and Gardens* magazine. The objective was to increase subscriber knowledge and brand preference for Armour as a company and for specific products. A "before and after" survey design was used, in which 350 people were first surveyed to find their awareness and preference prior to advertising exposure and were surveyed again after the series of 12 ads ran over a one year period. "Never Underestimate the Power of a Hot Dog" was one in this series.

Overall awareness of the Armour brand jumped ten percent. Brand preference, in turn, jumped an average of four percent, although it differed from product to product. But, of greater importance, the image of Armour sharply improved on those benefits which count the most including:

Products consistently good	+18.7%
Value for the money	+16.6
Concerned with consumers	+13.5
Improving their products	+12.0
Quality of products	+10.5

Source: Roger D. Blackwell, James F. Engel, and David T. Kollat, *Cases in Consumer Behavior* (New York: Holt, Rinehart & Winston, 1969), 75–81.

and the world was never the same. The behavioral sciences had gained a foothold.

The goal of the motivation researchers was to uncover hidden/nonrecognized motivations through use of guided interviewing, similar in some ways to what takes place in the clinic. Advertisers, in particular, jumped on this bandwagon and began to take consumer motivation seriously.

One widely reported finding from the motivation research era was that *women bake cakes out of the unconscious desire to give birth.* Yes, you read this correctly, and Pillsbury capitalized on this with its long-running campaign theme "nothin' says lovin' like somethin' from the oven" (Figure 1.7).

Quite understandably, public voices rose to combat what they perceived to be seditious ways of influencing behavior. These were accelerated by a widely reported claim that consumers could be appealed to *subliminally,* using psychometric methods without their awareness, and induced to respond as the advertiser intends (see Chapter 14 for more on this). A brave new world indeed!

Figure 1.7 "Nothin' Says Lovin' Like Somethin' from the Oven" — Freud Lives On!

Matters were made worse as reports became public that much of the uproar had been stimulated through quackery and fraud. Despite the furor (or perhaps because of it), the door was opened widely to legitimate behavioral science inquiry, and this was the entry point for many of us who were the first players in what was to become the field of consumer research as we know it now.[33]

New Field of Study Emerges

Consumer behavior soon emerged in its infancy as a distinct field of study during the 1960s through the influence of such writers as Newman,[34] Katona,[35] Ferber,[36] Howard,[37] and Engel.[38] Suddenly, the behavioral sciences became the "in thing" in the schools of business. Marketers, in particular, borrowed rather indiscriminately from social psychology, sociology, anthropology, or any other field that might relate to consumer behavior in some way, no matter how remotely.

Remember from the discussion thus far that marketers of that era were primarily concerned with how to stimulate a buying decision through product innovation and mass communication. Figure 1.8 gives you a quick feel for important issues that were addressed at that time and the theories or methods that were found to be most applicable.

Although this borrowing process was counterproductive at times, it also was necessary for a field of study in its infancy. Soon, this unfocused inquiry gave way to something far different with publication of what Holbrook[39] has referred to as the "landmark syntheses." Serious attempts were made by Nicosia,[40] Howard and Sheth,[41] and Engel, Kollat, and Blackwell[42] to integrate what was known about consumer motivation and behavior in the form of systematic models of decision making and choice.

The first edition of this book in 1968 was the trigger for rapid development of other texts,[43] and courses in consumer behavior quickly burgeoned throughout the Western world. The numbers of active researchers increased geometrically from the initial handful. A major catalytic influence was formation of the Association for Consumer Research in 1969. The literature has grown sharply, and the *Journal of Consumer Research* (first published in 1974) stands as a premier source. Consumer research also appears in many other sources such as *Journal of Marketing, Journal of Marketing Research, Psychology and Marketing, Journal of Consumer Marketing,* and *Journal of Consumer Psychology.*

The Contemporary Scene

There is growing consensus that the most developed countries are facing an era of change that may equal or exceed that of the industrial revolution more than 200 years ago.[44] As Tom Peters put it,

---

Figure 1.8   The Baby Is Born — Early Contributions of Behavioral Sciences to Practical Marketing Issues

1. Facilitating the development of new products as the key to differential advantage:
   - Diffusion of Innovations
   - Models of Human Problem-Solving Behavior and Choice
   - Measurement of Lifestyles and Needs

2. Discovering and responding to the multiple sources of influence on consumer choice:
   - Models of Interpersonal Influence and Word-of-Mouth Communication
   - Reference Group Theory
   - Social Class and Stratification

3. Creating more effective advertising and promotional campaigns:
   - Motivation Theories
   - Models of Attitude Formation and Change
   - Perception and Information Processing
   - Cognitive Dissonance and Post-Purchase Information Search

4. Developing brand loyalty:
   - Theory of Cognitive Dissonance
   - Quantitative Models (Bernoulli, Markov Chain, and Learning) of Brand Loyalty and Brand Shifting

---

No company's edge is commanding anymore. No transformation, no matter how dramatic, provides each five years' safety against the wildly gyrating forces at work. In today's fast-changing world, where we don't even know the names of next month's competitors, let alone their cost structure, no one has a safe lead. For the foreseeable future, organizations must learn to cherish change and to take advantage of constant tumult as much as they have resisted change in the past.[45]

Environmental Turmoil

You will recall that we earlier identified five major environmental factors that shape the essence of marketing strategy (p.15–16). Each is undergoing dramatic change, with the unsettling outcome that tried and true practices are eroding in potency. It is crucially important that we grasp the basic dynamics of what is taking place, because consumer research finds itself on some new playing fields.

Continued, Sustained Economic Growth No Longer Assumed

The 1990s represent quite a departure from those that preceded them. Economic growth has slowed to a crawl; large industries have seen their markets dwindle; layoffs have become a way of life. Consumers have been forced to cut back on consumption and sharply modify their lifestyles. Many experts speculate that we are in an era worldwide in which economic growth will slow or even stagnate. This means that the marketing engine that thrives in times of growth will have to change in some dramatic ways, which we highlight in the following sections.

Productive Capacity Outstripping Demand

The first of the environmental factors mentioned earlier that shape marketing activity is *the extent to which the supply of valid products and services exceeds consumer demand.* Western countries are facing an unprecedented deluge of new products and services as technology escalates. During 1992, almost 17,000 new products were introduced in the United States alone, an increase of 33 percent in 5 years.[46] There are now nearly 200 cereal brands in America, 220 types of cigarettes in Holland, and 100 perfumes in Argentina.[47] Need we say more? Consumers are overwhelmed with options.

The implications are drastic: *What this means is that an entrepreneurial commitment to new product development is no longer a sure key to differential advantage.* Mobile competitors respond almost instantaneously, quickly nullifying gains:

- *Matching competitive innovations and promoting new benefits.* This is done by national manufacturers and by distributors with their own private brands.[48] The net result is a glut of competing brands, all of which are perceived by the consumer to be essentially similar.

- *Price cuts.* Most shocking of all in recent years was the 50¢ price cut by Philip Morris USA on its Marlboro cigarette brand.[49] Within 1 week, its sales had increased 26.2 percent, mostly at the expense of the Winston brand, which dropped 45.7 percent. But this is just one example of a common trend. The pet food industry, for example, is under siege through a barrage of coupons and price deals and outright price cuts.[50]

Changes in Consumer Motivation and Behavior

When brands offer essentially the same features and compete mostly on price, the category has degenerated to the **commodity product** status—no brand has a competitive edge. This is demonstrated conclusively in an international study by BBDO, a major advertising agency, which showed that "nearly two-thirds of consumers worldwide believe that there are no relevant or discernible differences between rival brands across a broad range of products."[51]

What this means is that brand preference is declining and price is taking its place as the main factor in a wide range of buying decisions.[52] Carefully thought-through, reasoned decisions (referred to in Chapter 4 as **extended problem solving**) are giving way to **low involvement behavior,** defined in Chapter 4 as behavior in the situation in which all brands are basically similar and the final choice is made on the basis of price or special incentive.

Take time to read the story of Cheryl Morrisey in Consumer in Focus 1.3, and you will see that the 1990s are a far cry from the heydays of the 1960s when mass advertising could be counted on to build brand differentiation and loyalty.

Mass Markets Seldom Exist

Markets that were large and homogeneous are increasingly breaking into smaller and smaller segments identified by different buyer needs and expectations. Furthermore, television, the great sales medium of earlier decades, has also seen its market fragment as cable programming and local options proliferate to reach smaller and smaller special interest segments. Similar fragmentation is taking place in radio as well as print media.

What this means is that marketers must contend with small, rapidly changing segments of highly selective buyers intent on receiving genuine value at the lowest price. The dilemma is that the old ways of winning an acceptable market share, especially mass advertising, are coming up wanting.

Consumer in Focus   1.3

It's Not Worth Paying a Premium Any More

Cheryl Morrisey is, to put it mildly, a careful shopper. To stick to her monthly food budget of $250, the suburban Dallas mother of three spends hours each week clipping coupons, scanning ad supplements, and making lists before heading out to shop. And except for a handful of items, such as Northern bath tissue and Kraft Miracle Whip salad dressing, Morrisey buyers whatever brand is cheapest. She says, "I don't see a whole lot of difference. Soap is soap. If I have a coupon, all the better."

Shoppers like Morrisey — and there are growing numbers of them — are giving packaged-good makers fits. Jolted by the recession and its aftershocks and more interested in thrift than in the conspicuous consumption that defined the 1980s, they don't have much use for products that don't give them values — that mix of price, quality, and image.

Source: "Brands on the Run," Business Week (April 19, 1993), 26. Reproduced by special permission.

Shift of Balance of Economic Power to Distributors

Who would have envisioned 20 years ago that the mega shopping malls would be commonplace and that Wal-Mart and other "mega retailers" would dominate the scene? And few would have suspected that diminished brand preference would give retailers the upper hand in many situations. But that is exactly what has taken place. The only recourse for many is to push the product through channels with special incentives. Indeed, it can cost $10,000 or more just to buy shelf space in some supermarkets with what is called "slotting allowances."

Once distribution is attained, the battle now intensifies in the form of sales promotion—couponing, sampling, special displays, and so on. This, in turn, can become competitively ruinous. Is it any wonder that increasing numbers of marketers are searching for better distribution alternatives?

Enhancing Consumer Value Added: Marketing's New Challenge

You have seen in the previous pages that consumer sovereignty, a bedrock premise of marketing, has become even more a driving force in the contemporary economy. It is an oversimplification to state that consumers want more for their dollar and are becoming immune to the influences and attractions of an earlier era. As Jacob[53] put it, *"The only defense against this trend is to strip out costs permanently by focusing on what adds value for the customer and eliminating what doesn't"* [italics ours].

As we see it, there are several key factors that will determine success or failure in meeting this new challenge: (1) getting close to the consumer; (2) individualized marketing; (3) priority commitment to customer satisfaction and retention; and (4) a renewed focus on brand equity.

Getting Close to the Consumer

Yes, a contemporary "industrial revolution" is underway, and as never before, it is crucial to understand and respond appropriately to the consumer as the "new boss."[54] As Jack Welch, Jr., the Chair of General Electric Co., put it, "The key is to recapture the art of thinking small: Satisfying customers, getting faster communications, moving with more agility, all these things are easier when one is small. And these are all the characteristics one needs in a fast-moving global environment."[55]

Corporate bureaucracy is crumbling as entrepreneurial responsibilities are being assigned to those on the firing line.[56] These managers, in turn, are increasingly forced to have direct, meaningful contact with consumers. In short, consumer research is no longer the sole responsibility of those in the obscure and technologically sophisticated environs of the "research department."

At times, it will continue to be necessary to consult professionals and mount formal research investigations that can be complex and costly. We will give many examples of these throughout the book. However, there is no question that some of the best research is done as managers move outside the executive suite. When this is done sensitively and perceptively, research becomes an attitude, and the benefits are real. Tom Peters[57] calls for marketers to become obsessed with learning from and listening to their customers, and he recommends that they be in the field at least 25 percent of their time.

To take one example, Eastman Kodak executive Raymond H. DeMoulin was in a Tokyo fish market early one morning when he observed a photographer trying to pry open a film container with his teeth while holding his camera. This observation quickly gave rise to a product change so that it now is possible to open containers of Kodak film with one hand.[58]

DeMoulin was doing consumer research that morning, even though he had no clipboard with him and engaged in no computerized analysis of data. He made enlightened use of observation, which then was blended with experience and intuition (creative insight) to build practical, workable marketing strategy.

There are three foundations for marketing decisions: (1) experience, (2) intuition, and (3) research; none is complete without the other. Frequently, however, consumer research is often ignored—with unfortunate consequences. To illustrate limitations on experience and intuition, consider the outcomes when marketing experts and complete marketing novices were asked to predict the interests and opinions of American consumers. The predictive accuracy of these hunches was very low, and experts did no better than novices.[59] Need we say more?

What this says is that *all managers must become astute analysts of consumer motivation and behavior.* What you are about to learn, in short, will be an important part of the "arsenal" needed for survival on the firing line.

Individualized Marketing

Marketers are desperately searching for ways to overcome the decline of advertising power, erosion of brand preferences, and resulting ruinous retail price competition. A genuine breakthrough is occurring through a return to a time-tested concept—an individualized, one-on-one relationship with the customer.

For many decades, it has been a commonplace policy to design an entirely different marketing strategy for smaller units or segments within a market that differ in meaningful ways from other groups. This strategy is known as market segmentation. The 18- to 24-year age group becomes the target, for example, and different strategies are used for those who are older. These niches are becoming smaller and smaller as marketers struggle to gain a foothold.

You will find examples of segmentation research and strategies in the next chapter and throughout the book as we unfold the complex of influences on consumer behavior. But the challenge is to even further enter into a personal relationship with the customer who has become lost in the mass marketing of this century. Rapp and Collins coined a new name for a very old strategy—**individualized marketing.**[60] Here is what they meant:

> . . . a very personal form of marketing that recognizes, acknowledges, appreciates, and serves the interests and needs of selected groups of consumers whose individual identities are or become known to the advertiser [marketer].[61]

In one sense, there is little new here. Yet individualized marketing has come to take on an all new meaning in the past decade—data-base marketing.[62] Through use of warranty cards and other means, names of individual customers or prospects are acquired and used. The individual, as a microsegment, then becomes the target for **direct marketing** through such media as direct mail or telemarketing.

Direct marketing is only the beginning, however. The next step is customized marketing, which involves ongoing research dialogue between buyer and seller, with full customization of product, price, promotion, and distribution. With the imminent widescale introduction of interactive video, no one can predict the future marketing possibilities.

Individualized marketing is becoming so important that Philip Kotler, internationally recognized leader in marketing thought, predicted that future marketers will place primary reliance on customer data bases to compete globally.[63] Don't fail to read how Nestle turned away from a ruinous competitive battle at point of sale and launched genuine consumer partnership relationships through individualized marketing (Consumer in Focus 1.4).

Priority Commitment to Customer Satisfaction and Retention

In the past two decades, American and West European marketers have learned a costly lesson as they were badly beaten in the product-and-service quality war with Japan—*it is much more difficult to win a new customer than to retain an existing customer.* Incontrovertible evidence shows that sustainable market share comes primarily through a commitment to the ongoing priority focus on customer satisfaction and retention, leadership in quality, and service.[64]

Toyota has attained a 43 percent market share in Japan and the number 1 import position in the United States by "total dedication to continuous improvement."[65] Everything is done to ensure that the customer is completely satisfied, and this is the key to retaining that customer over time.

Renewed Focus on Brand Equity

"Brands have value in the marketplace. They are company assets that need to be managed like any other asset. Marketers realize that the more consumers equate quality with their brands, the more they will buy."[66] These are the words of David Smallen, vice president of Total Research Corp., on finishing a survey in which consumers ranked 190 brands in 55 product categories.

The common practice of outright price war and cutbacks in advertising is little more than a form of *marketing roulette,* which is destined to reduce brand eq-

Consumer in Focus | **1.4**

Nestlé Breaks through Marketplace Clutter with Individualized Marketing

On a global scale, Nestle group management at their headquarters in Vevy, Switzerland, is seeking to radically redefine what packaged goods marketing is all about.

Their top executives recognize that the power of traditional brand advertising is waning. But they have refused to join the stampede toward discounting of advertised brands as the only way to compete with economy-priced store brands.

Instead they have decided to make their key to success a program for building credibility around what they do and who they are. Nestle's Peter Brabeck says bluntly, "You can triple advertising spending, but if you can't establish a credible communication link with consumers, they won't act."

Now Nestle Baby Foods in France is breaking through the cluster of the marketplace with individualized marketing, by moving into the lives and activities of prospects and customers as a genuinely helpful, caring, trusted companion. Fabienne Petit, the marketing director, told us that she has a passion . . . for making life better for parents of babies.

In all media advertising, direct mail, and packaging, parents are invited to call the toll-free number for its free baby-nutrition counseling service, "Allo Nestle Diététique." Nestle maintains and constantly updates a data base of 220,000 new mothers with the names and addresses extracted from maternity records. The first mailing contains a reply card on which the new mother can fill in baby's name and indicate interest in receiving further mailings. This file is then used to send six direct-mail packages, personalized with the first name of the baby at key stages in development.

The most recent market research survey of 1,000 mothers showed an approval rating of 97% for the Nestle direct mail. The results keep getting better. Now, the Nestle share of market has climbed to more than 43%—close to a 24-point rise in less than seven years, while being outspent 7–1 in advertising.

Source: "Nestle Banks on Databases," (an extract from Beyond Maxi-Marketing by Stan Rapp and Thomas I. Collins), Advertising Age (October 25, 1993), 16 ff. Reproduced by special permission.

uity and ultimately to lead to a crumpling market share. Consumers simply do not purchase brands that they either do not recognize or do not trust, no matter how much sales promotion is put behind them.

As a result, maintenance and strengthening of brand equity cannot be disregarded. Extensions of preferred brand names is another common strategy. A good example is licensing the McDonald's Corp. to Mattel Toys. It makes far more sense to use an existing brand name than to create equity from scratch.

Another recommended strategy is to target existing customers according to Dr. Larry Light, a distinguished graduate student with this author team in the 1960s and chair of the Coalition for Brand Equity.[67] He noted, "We examined over 30 years of research into the psychology of advertising. Advertising plays a critical role in reinforcing the buying behavior, enabling us to convert a buyer into a loyalist."[68]

Fasten Your Seat Belt

It has been more than 30 years since the field of consumer research was born as we now know it. Now, we find ourselves with two new frontiers: (1) the second industrial revolution in the business word, and (2) the postmodern challenge of understanding consumer behavior from its broader perspective as an important part of life in its own right.

We tackle these challenges from a sophisticated base of theory and methodology, which is rapidly expanding in directions never envisioned in the early 1960s. The field is dynamic and exciting, and one thing is for sure—*all of us are daily participants as active players in all that is going on* in the world of consumer behavior.

Summary

Research into consumer motivation and behavior has assumed significance in contemporary societies worldwide. In the past 30 years, a large and growing multidisciplinary field of study has emerged. The central concern of businesses, consumer economists, and others is to find more effective strategies to influence and shape that behavior. As a result, consumer research is of premier importance in this applied world.

Others have a more holistic perspective referred to as *postmodernism* and are focusing efforts on studies of consumption to understand how humans think and behave in this important life activity. When we factor in the more recent expansion of inquiry across cultural borders, the result is a rich and growing field of research.

The perspective of this book is primarily, although not exclusively, that of the field of marketing. As a result, our central concern is the practical relevance of principles and findings to business strategies. Everything done by marketers and others attempting to influence consumer behavior rests on four essential premises:

1. The consumer is sovereign. The consumer has full capability to screen out all attempts at influence, with the outcome that everything done by the business firm must be adapted to consumer motivation and behavior.

2. Consumer motivation and behavior can be understood through research. Perfect prediction is not possible, but strategic outcomes are notably improved through properly undertaken and used research.

3. Consumer behavior can be influenced through persuasive activity that takes the consumer seriously as being sovereign and purposeful.

4. Consumer persuasion and influence has socially beneficial outcomes as long as legal, ethical, and moral safeguards are in place to curb attempts at manipulation.

When these premises are disregarded, the consequences almost always are negative. We gave examples of the outcomes of both right and wrong thinking about the consumer. We further demonstrated that consumer research, properly conceived and interpreted, provides essential input for marketing strategies. Finally, research also serves as the basis for consumer education and protection and furnishes important information for public policy decisions.

Review and Discussion Questions

1. Contrast the consumer influence and postmodern perspectives in consumer research. How would the agendas of researchers from these two perspectives differ in an analysis of the decision processes and consumption behavior undertaken by new home purchasers?

2. Assume that new home buyers are studied in Chicago; New Orleans; Nairobi, Kenya; and Sao Paulo, Brazil. In each case, the target market segment is the upper-middle class. What differences would you anticipate from one culture to the next?

3. Review Consumer in Focus 1.4. If you were to take a postmodern perspective in consumer research, what issues would you address in understanding mothers and their new babies?

4. Which of the following decisions should be considered legitimate topics of concern in the study of consumer behavior: (a) selecting a college, (b) purchasing a life insurance policy, (c) smoking a cigarette, (d) selecting a church to join, (e) selecting a dentist, (f) visiting an auto showroom to see new models, or (g) purchasing a college textbook.

5. Examine current advertisements for consumer products and select one for a new product. Will this product succeed in the long run in the consumer marketplace? What factors determine success?

6. A family has just come into the local office of a lending agency, asking for a bill consolidation loan. Payments for a new car, television, stereo, bedroom set, and central air conditioning have become excessive. The head of the family does not have a steady source of income, and real help is now needed. Is this an example of purposeful consumer behavior, or has this family been manipulated into making unwise purchases?

7. If it is true that motivations and behavior can be understood through research, is it also true that the marketer now has greater ability to influence the consumer adversely than would have been the case in an earlier era?

8. What contributions does the analysis of consumer behavior make to the field of finance? Of production? Of real estate? Of insurance? Of top management administration?

9. Would it be equally necessary to understand consumer behavior if the economic system were not one of free enterprise? In other words, is the subject matter of this book only of interest to those in capitalistic systems, or does it also have relevance for socialism and for communism where it still exists?

10. Consumer protection is an important issue. What areas of consumer behavior appear to be most in need of increased regulation and consumer education?

Endnotes

1. The dominance of logical positivism in consumer research has been under sharp attack in recent years. See, for example, Julie L. Ozanne and Laurel Anderson Hudson, "Exploring Diversity in Consumer Research," in Elizabeth C. Hirschman and Morris B. Holbrook, eds., *Postmodern Consumer Research* (Newbury Park, CA: Sage, 1992), 1–9; Bobby J. Calder and Alice M. Tybout, "Interpretive, Qualitative, and Traditional Scientific Empirical Consumer Behavior Research," in Hirschman and Holbrook, *Postmodern*, 199–208; John F. Sherry, Jr., "Postmodern Alternatives: The Interpretive Turn in Consumer Research," in Thomas S. Robertson and Harold J. Kassarjian, eds., *Handbook of Consumer Behavior* (Englewood Cliffs N.J.: Prentice-Hall, 1991), 548–591; Richard J. Lutz, "Presidential Address: Positivism, Naturalism and Pluralism in Consumer Research: Paradigms in Paradise," in Thomas K. Srull, ed., *Advances in Consumer Research* 16 (Provo, Utah: Association for Consumer Research, 1989), 1–8; and Craig J. Thompson, William B. Locander, and Howard R. Pollio, "Putting Consumer Experience Back into Consumer Research: The Philosophy and Methods of Existential Phenomenology," *Journal of Consumer Research* 16 (September 1989), 133–146.

2. "Battling for the Domestic Sky," *Destination Traveler* (May 1993), 67–68.

3. "Closing Down the Skies," *Business World* (June 1993), 38.

4. Ibid.

5. *Marketing News* (March 1, 1985), 1.

6. Peter F. Drucker, *The Practice of Management* (New York: Harper & Row, 1954), 37.

7. Tom Peters and Nancy Austin, *A Passion for Excellence* (New York: Random House, 1985), 4.

8. Russell W. Belk, "ACR Presidential Address: Happy Thoughts," in Melanie Wallendorf and Paul Anderson, eds., *Advances in Consumer Research* 14 (Provo, Utah: Association for Consumer Research, 1986), 2.

9. See E. Scott Maynes and ACCI Research Committee, eds., *The Frontier of Research in the Consumer Interest* (Columbia, Mo.: University of Missouri, American Council on Consumers Interests, 1988).

10. "Closing Down the Skies."

11. For an especially influential statement, see Maynes, *Frontier.*

12. The most definitive source on this subject is Sherry, "Postmodern Alternatives."

13. Morris B. Holbrook and Elizabeth C. Hirschman, "The Experiential Aspects of Consumption: Consumer Fantasies, Feelings, and Fun," *Journal of Consumer Research* 9 (September 1982), 132–140.

14. Morris B. Holbrook, "What is Consumer Research?" *Journal of Consumer Research* 14 (June 1987), 130.

15. Melanie Wallendorf and Eric J. Arnoud, "My Favorite Things: A Cross-Cultural Inquiry," *Journal of Consumer Research* 14 (March 1988), 531.

16. For an interesting and entertaining review, see Russell W. Belk, Melanie Wallendorf, and John Sherry, Jr., "The Sacred and the Profane in Consumer Behavior: Theodicy on the Odyssey," *Journal of Consumer Research* 16 (June 1989), 1–38.

17. For more background see Sherry, "Postmodern Alternatives" and Hirschman and Holbook, eds., *Postmodern Consumer Research.*

18. "When the Shackles Come Off," *Business Week/Enterprise 1993,* 80.

19. Valerie Reitman, "P&G Uses Skills It Has Honed at Home to Introduce Its Brands to the Russians," *Wall Street Journal* (April 14, 1993), B1.

20. "Flops," *Fitness Week* (August 16, 1993), 79.

21. "Flops," 80.

22. "Flops," 76–77.

23. Cyndee Miller, "Survey: New Product Failure is Top Management's Fault," *Marketing News* (February 1, 1993), 2.

24. "Getting Inside Their Heads," *American Demographics* (August 1989), 20.

25. "The Hidden Persuadees," *The Economist* (March 23, 1991), 79.

26. "Meet the New Consumer," *Fortune* (special edition on "The Tough New Consumer," Autumn/Winter, 1993), 6–7.

27. Leo Bogart, "Where Does Advertising Research Go from Here?" *Journal of Advertising Research* 9 (March 1969), 10.

28. For a fascinating history, see Robert J. Lampman, "JFK's Four Consumer Rights: A Retrospective View," in Maynes, *The Frontier of Research,* 19–36.

29. Frank Rose, "If It Feels Good, It Must Be Bad," *Fortune* (October 21, 1991), 92.

30. We acknowledge our debt here to William Weilbacher for confirming much of our thinking. See William M. Weilbacher, "Yesterday's Realities are Today's Myth," *Advertising Age* (June 7, 1993), 20.

31. Ernest Dichter was a prolific writer. Perhaps the most representative of his contributions is *The Strategy of Desire* (New York: Doubleday, 1960).

32. Vance Packard, *The Hidden Persuaders* (New York: Mackay, 1957).

33. Jim Engel's first publications addressed a major challenge at motivation research. See James F. Engel, "Motivation Research—Magic or Menace?" Parts I and II, *Michigan Business Review* 13 (March and May, 1961), 259–265 and 25–28.

34. Joseph Newman, *On Knowing the Consumer* (Ronald Press, 1963).

35. George Katona, *The Powerful Consumer* (New York: McGraw-Hill, 1960).

36. Robert Ferber's writings ranged from advanced statistical techniques to applications of principles of psychology and economics to various phases of consumer behavior. He was coeditor with Hugh G. Wales of an important early book, *Motivation and Market Behavior* (Homewood, Ill.: Richard D. Irwin, 1958).

37. John A. Howard, *Marketing Management Analysis and Planning,* rev. ed. (Homewood, Ill.: Richard D. Irwin, 1963).

38. James F. Engel, David T. Kollat, and Roger D. Blackwell, *Consumer Behavior,* 1st ed. (New York: Holt, Rinehart and Winston, 1968).

39. Morris B. Holbrook, "What Is Consumer Research?" *Journal of Consumer Research* 14 (June 1987), 130.

40. Francesco M. Nicosia, *Consumer Decision Processes* (Englewood Cliffs, N.J.: Prentice-Hall, 1966).

41. John A. Howard and Jagdish N. Sheth, *The Theory of Buyer Behavior* (New York: John Wiley & Sons, 1969).

42. Engel, Kollat, and Blackwell.

43. For an especially fine review of the field as it stands today, see Thomas S. Robertson and Harold H. Kassarjian, *Handbook of Consumer Behavior* (Englewood Cliffs, N.J.: Prentice-Hall, 1991). There are may textbooks, each of which makes a contribution in its own right: Henry Assael, *Consumer Behavior and Marketing Action,* 3d ed. (Boston: Kent Publishing Co., 1987); Del I. Hawkins, Roger J. Best, and Kenneth A. Coney, *Consumer Behavior — Implications for Marketing Strategy,* 5th ed. (Homewood, Ill.: BPI/Irwin, 1992); John C. Mowen, *Consumer Behavior,* 2d ed. (New York: Macmillan, 1990); J. Paul Peter and Jerry C. Olson, *Consumer Behavior — Marketing Strategy Perspectives,* 3d ed. (Homewood, Ill.: Richard D. Irwin, 1993); Michael R. Solomon, *Consumer Behavior,* 2d ed. (Boston: Allyn and Bacon, 1994); William L. Wilkie, *Consumer Behavior* (New York: John Wiley & Sons, 1986).

44. To grasp the broad scope and dimensions of this revolution, it is worth reading the December 13, 1993, edition of *Fortune* entitled "Managing in the Era of Change."

45. Tom Peters, "There Are No Excellent Companies," *Fortune* (April 27, 1987), 382.

46. "Shoot Out at the Check-Out," *The Economist* (June 5, 1993), 69.

47. Ibid., 70.

48. Distributor (private) brands are booming in both Europe and North America. See "The Eurosion of Brand Loyalty," *Business Week* (July 19, 1993), 22; and Julia Liesse, "Private Label Nightmare," *Advertising Age* (April 12, 1993), 1–5.

49. Ira Teinowitz, "Marlboro Price Promo Smoking RJR's Winston," *Advertising Age* (June 14, 1993), 3.

50. Julie Liesse, "Price War Bites a Pet Food Ad $," *Advertising Age* (April 5, 1993), 12.

51. "Shoot Out at the Check-Out," 69.

52. Gary Levin, "Price Rises as Factor for Consumers," *Advertising Age* (November 8, 1993), 37.

53. Rahul Jacob, "Beyond Quality and Value," *Fortune* special edition on "The Tough New Consumer" (Autumn/Winter 1993), 8.

54. "Meet the New Consumer," 6.

55. "Jack Welch on the Art of Thinking Small," *Business Week* (Enterprise 1993 edition), 212.

56. For an excellent analysis of the forms that this is taking, see John A. Byrne, "How Entrepreneurs Are Reshaping the Economy: Introduction,"; and Mark Maremont, "Summing Up," *Business Week* (Enterprise 1993 edition), 11–18 and 243–247.

57. Tom Peters, *Thriving on Chaos* (New York: Alfred A. Knopf, 1987).

58. "Why Kodak Is Starting to Click Again," *Business Week* (February 23, 1987), 134.

59. Stephen J. Hoch, "Who Do We Know? Predicting the Interests and Opinions of the American Consumer," *Journal of Consumer Research* 15 (December 1988), 315–324.

60. Stan Rapp and Tom Collins, *The Great Marketing Turnaround — The Age of the Individual and How to Profit from It* (Englewood Cliffs, N.J.: Prentice-Hall, 1990).

61. Ibid., 37.

62. Susan Krafft, "The Big Merge," *American Demographics* (June 1991), 44–48.

63. Thomas E. Caruso, "Kotler: Future Marketers Will Focus on Customer Data Base to Compete Globally," *Marketing News* (June 8, 1992), 21.

64. Two books shed particularly valuable light on the issue of quality. See Jan Carizon, *Moments of Truth* (Cambridge, Mass.: Ballinger, 1987); and Peters, *Thriving on Chaos.*

65. Alex Taylor III, "Why Toyota Keeps Getting Better and Better and Better," *Fortune* (November 19, 1990), 66–79.

66. Nancy Ten Kate, "Brand Names Can be Prime Assets," *American Demographics* (December 1991), 20.

67. See Melanie Wells, "Brand Ads Should Target Existing Customers," *Advertising Age* (April 26, 1993), 47; and Larry Light, "At the Center of It All Is the Brand," *Advertising Age* (March 29, 1993), 22.

68. Wells, "Brand Ads Should Target Existing Customers," 47.

CHAPTER 2

Market Segmentation and Demographic Analysis

▲▲

L. A. Gear Steps to the Front

L.A. Gear was the stock to own in the late 1980s, starting from $3 a share in 1987 and soaring to $50 by 1989. Its success came from selling a basic athletic shoe, not fundamentally different from Nike, Asics, Fila, and others. But this head-to-head strategy soon piled up masses of excess shoes in inventory and big losses, when compared to the successes of Nike and Reebok, both of which had far more advertising firepower. And the stock plummeted back to $7 by 1994.

When Mark Goldston, age 38 and author of *The Turnaround Prescription*, took charge of the company in the 1990s, he focused on market segments in which he could execute a flanking strategy around his better financed competitors. First segment for focused activity was children's shoes.

Goldston developed children's lines to provide affordable, quality footwear with fun, fashionable designs. The segmentation approach worked. The company was highly successful with *L.A. Lights*™ and *Light Gear*™ collections, shoes with lights that turn on when pressure is exerted in the sole. In 1994, L.A. Gear announced it had sold 4.5 million pairs of children's lighted shoes in one year, a runaway success so hot the company has difficulty manufacturing enough of the shoes. Segmentation of the children's market was extended with young girls' fashions that include extras such as floral embroidery, rhinestones, and removable charms. Boys' shoes feature breathable mesh panels, molded eyelets, and printed linings. Infants' shoe construction includes the patented *Bendables*™ outsole, designed to provide the flexibility recommended by pediatricians.

The company also developed a new product line for the high-quality athletic segment. In 1994, *L.A. Tech*®, the company's most technologically advanced product line, introduced innovative new technologies including the *Flak*™

Figure 2.A   L.A. Gear Targeted the Market in Shoes for Children

cushioning system, which uses material in the heel and forefoot similar to that found in bulletproof vests and high-performance hockey and football protective pads.

L.A. Gear is also using a new CAD/CAM system to produce 100 new styles for special segments of the shoe market. Taking advantage of the booming interest in rock climbing, shoes with the serrated wedge-tread of a rock-climbing boot were introduced, called *Gravity Gear™*. The *Kombat Gear™* line of "grunge" style boots was marketed to youthful segments, as well as designs that look like ski boots. Appealing to very specific market segments at lightning speed with the help of a sophisticated, state-of-the-art CAD/CAM system is the core of the strategy that helped turn around L.A. Gear with a profit in 1994, the first in years. In describing the niche approach to markets, COO Goldston says, "It's not hard core. It's innovation and fun."

Source: Based on L.A. Gear 1993 Annual Report (April 1994); and Damon Darlin, "Getting Beyond a Market Niche," Forbes *(November 22, 1993), 107–109.*

The study of consumer behavior focuses on how individuals decide to buy and use goods and services, as you learned in the first chapter of this book. Organizations rarely can afford to develop strategies based on the behavior of any one individual, however. Instead, organizations must base their strategies on the behavior of many individuals who behave in similar ways.

In Consumer in Focus 2.1, you can see how country music fans have become an important market segment, replacing rock music to some degree. At Denim & Diamonds, the clientele is of mixed ages. There is a preponderance of young consumers, but customers range from 21 to 60 years. As the young become older and richer, however, they often switch to something more mellow than rock. Although these consumers vary in their demographics, they behave in similar ways and thus provide the market target for a marketing strategy directed to this specific market segment. Garth Brooks appears to have learned well how to use his major in marketing and advertising to reach this segment.

Many tasks face consumer analysts, regardless of whether the consumer influence, postmodern, or intercultural perspective is adopted. One task is to understand how groups of consumers (segments of the total) vary from other consumers and how these behavioral differences affect segmented marketing programs of profit or nonprofit organizations. Another task is to understand how changes in behavior of specific segments lead to shifts in the behavior of the total market. First, let's take a closer look at the concept of market segmentation in understanding consumer behavior. Then we focus on understanding demographic trends and how they affect marketing programs for the future.

Market Segmentation

Market segmentation is the process of so designing or featuring a product or service that it will make a particularly strong appeal to some identifiable subpart of a total market. The alternative is called market aggregation or mass marketing, in which all consumers are offered identical products or services.

2.1	**Consumer in Focus**

Marketing to the Country Segment

The seats are covered in cowhide, pictures of the Judds and Hank Williams, Jr., grace the walls. The patrons, some 500 strong, are mostly outfitted in cowboy hats and Wrangler jeans. On the dance floor, an army of cowboy boots is stomping out a Texas two-step as Garth Brooks' song "Unanswered Prayers" blares from the disc jockey's booth.

A cowboy bar in Dallas? A honky-tonk in Nashville? Nope. It's Denim & Diamonds in trendy Santa Monica, one of the hot spots in the Los Angeles area. Less than a year ago, Denim & Diamonds was a disco playing Top 40 hits. Rock's out, country's in. "Country is much better to dance to, and besides, it's more sentimental. It's much easier to listen to." And not just in Santa Monica. Over the last few years, country music has taken over the airwaves and the record charts, as well as the best-seller lists.

Right in the eye of this popular storm is an Oklahoman named Garth Brooks. He used to watch the rock group Queen and figured there was no reason he couldn't do those kinds of theatrics in country. "Garth is like Led Zeppelin meets Roy Rogers," says James Bowen of Liberty Records. In 1 week, Brooks' records sold nearly 340,000 units, putting $500,000 in his wallet.

Brooks represents the new breed of country music entertainer. He was a marketing and advertising major in college, and the training shows—and it's not just in his stage antics. Brooks' ticket prices last year were $15, about half what the Rolling Stones charged on their last tour. "The less people pay at the gate, the more they'll spend inside," says Brooks. "That's just simple logic. I believe in the Wal-Mart school of business. The less people pay for a product that they are happy with, the happier they are with it." He pays attention to quality as well, selling T-shirts at $8.50 that are 100 percent cotton, about the heaviest weight you can buy. Brook says, "That shirt is an advertisement on someone's back. So we want to give people something that's going to last." Good quality at a reasonable price. What more can you ask from the entertainment industry—or any other business?

Source: Based on Lisa Gubernick and Peter Newcomb, "The Wal-Mart School of Music," Forbes: (March 2, 1992), 72–76.

Segmentation and Consumer Satisfaction

In developing economies, the mass market or identical product strategy is often used effectively. As you observed in the last chapter, Henry Ford lowered costs tremendously and dominated the market with standardized "black" cars in what was then a developing country. Eventually, the market evolved to the point Chevrolet could offer product variations (such as automatic starters and other colors), even with higher prices, to appeal to different segments of the market. In many areas of the world, the pent-up demand for basic products is so great that the most effective strategy is to provide basic functional benefits at the lowest possible price. That usually means a standardized product, produced at low cost in long, homogeneous production runs and sold through basic distribution channels with few services.

Mass marketing becomes less effective in economies in which most consumers already own the functional or core benefits. Segmentation offers variations in functional benefits and more attention to hedonic needs. Figure 2.1 shows how the German company AOK appeals to the lifestyles of two different

Figure 2.1   Appealing to Different Segments of the Market

segments, with the headline "For each type of sport, a different type of nutrition [diet] is needed."

The need for segmentation arises because people vary so much from other people. If all humans were identical in their preferences and behavior, there would be no need for market segmentation. Every product would be identical. Because people differ so much in their motivations, needs, decision processes, and buying behavior, ideally products would be custom-tailored to each user to give maximum satisfaction to consumers. There exist some individually developed products or services, such as custom-tailored clothing, beauty care, landscaping services, and architectural plans for custom-designed homes, but they are often so high priced that they cannot compete with more standardized products.

Effective marketing programs usually require an approach between extreme segmentation (custom-designed products that match each individual's behavior) and mass marketing (standardized products that please almost no consumers). The analytical goal is to measure consumer behavior and place each person into a group (segment) that will *minimize the variance in behavior between each member* of the segment and *maximize the variance between segments.*

There are few mass markets left in industrially advanced societies; there are only variations in the size of segments, caused by several factors:

1. *Affluence*—which permits consumers to afford products that reflect variations in their individual preferences and behavior

2. *Sophisticated consumer measurement and data bases*—which permit product designers and marketing strategists to understand variations in consumer decision making and behavior

3. *Custom manufacturing*—which permits production processes to be computer-controlled and tailored to smaller production runs without corresponding increases in costs

4. *New forms of distribution*—which permit innovations in multichannel retailing such as direct marketing that permit distribution to be closely related to computer data bases about the nature of market segments

Segmentation and Profitability

Segmentation is an important tool for increasing profitability. Increased profitability occurs when the economic value to consumers is higher than the cost of creating the value. For example, a computer program might be adapted to the special needs of some users. If the costs of adaptation were expensive but caused the program to be worth hundreds or even thousands of dollars of value to many users, the higher price that could be charged compared to a standardized product might yield millions of dollars of additional profitability. That is precisely how several billionaires have created their fortunes in the computer industry.

The goal of a segmented strategy is to fire a rifle shot, not a shotgun blast, at the market. Such pinpoint accuracy was difficult in an era of mass marketing. This process is just as important for nonprofit organizations as businesses.[1] Often nonprofit organizations make the mistake of trying to treat everyone the same but they would be more effective to make a segmented offering in their fund raising and other activities. The ability exists now, however, to measure and identify groups within the broader market that are sufficiently homogeneous to warrant separate products or marketing programs. Doing this increases the profitability or effectiveness of the organization to the extent that the economic benefits provided consumers exceed the costs of the segmentation process.

Criteria for Choosing Segments

Evaluating and choosing market segments involves matching market opportunities with marketing programs. Four criteria to help accomplish this process include measurability, accessibility, substantiality, and congruity.

Measurability refers to the information obtainable about the size, nature, and behavior of a market segment. Consumers may behave in similar ways, but if there is no way of measuring the people who have such similar behavior, it is difficult to formulate and implement a marketing mix. Much of this book is about methods of measuring consumer behavior.

Accessibility or reachability is the degree to which segments can be reached. Allstate Insurance experienced rapid growth in the decades following World War II, for example, because the typical Sears customer was an excellent target for suburban auto and home insurance. Allstate had a differential advantage in access to these customers through Sears stores. As the target market changed, Allstate had to change its locations from Sears stores to neighborhood offices. Competitive insurance companies also changed and often used direct mail to target the prime customers.

Substantiality refers to the size of market segments. Usually, the larger the segment, the more attractive. Sometimes, small firms prefer small segments because of the decreased likelihood of competing with large firms.

Congruity refers to how well members of a market segment fit together. Congruity is a measure of the appropriateness of the classification in explaining the behavior of the group. Congruity is helpful in predicting the nature of response to marketing programs by segments. The goal is to find groups of customers with intrasegment congruity also congruous with the firm's ability to market the product.

Market Strategy Decisions

Once the market has been segmented properly in terms of the four criteria, the firm has three options: (1) concentrated (single segment) marketing, (2) differentiated (multisegment) marketing, and (3) undifferentiated marketing.

Concentrated Marketing

In concentrated marketing, the primary focus is on a single segment. Clothing firms such as Laura Ashley concentrate on a specific market target with fashions that appeal to some women but not others. Ritz-Carlton concentrates on the luxury hotel segment, with service quality so good that it won the Malcolm Baldrige award. Red Roof Inns also provides good service but concentrates on the budget motel segment with dependably clean rooms at a low price and achieves the highest occupancy rate in the industry. Both hotel chains follow a concentration strategy; they just concentrate on different segments.

The goal in concentrated or niche marketing is to dominate a segment. Jerry Garcia of the Grateful Dead said it well: "You do not merely want to be considered just the best of the best. You want to be considered the only ones who do what you do."

Differentiated Marketing

An alternative approach is to concentrate on two or more segments, offering a **differentiated marketing** mix for each. There is a distinct trend toward multiple product offerings targeted at different segments. Hotel chains such as Marriott offer a portfolio of hotels for differentiated segments with names such as Marriott Resorts, Courtyard, Residence Inn, Fairfield Inn, and J. W. Marriott.

Differentiated or multisegment strategies were the key to growth at The Limited, Inc. In the 1970s and 1980s, The Limited appealed to young, moderately affluent, fashion-oriented women. As this market segment matured, so did The Limited, with more sophistication, higher price points, and slightly larger sizes. To continue growth of the corporation, The Limited Express (now Express) was developed to reach the same segment The Limited originally reached. Lane Bryant, Lerner, Henri Bendel, Victoria's Secret, and other chains were acquired to reach different market targets with a differentiated appeal. Male segments also became target markets with Structure and Abercrombie & Fitch.

There is no question that differentiated marketing offers the potential benefit of enhanced market position and access to more of the market, but it is not without its disadvantages. One of the greatest dangers lies in the loss of the core market unless precautions are taken. Chevrolet is a case in point. Generations of North Americans were raised to identify the Chevrolet as one of three cars (Chevrolet, Ford, and Plymouth) that provide safe, dependable, and affordable transportation for the "average family." The Chevy was quite different from other General Motors brands and had a clear identity. The Chevrolet line was greatly expanded in the early 1980s, with models offered at nearly all price ranges. In so doing, Chevrolet lost its traditional mass-market and low-price appeal and saw its core market dwindle because of inroads from imports and Ford Taurus. There is always the danger of blurring the established image in core markets unless precautions are taken. No product can be all things to all people as both Chevrolet and, more recently, The Limited illustrate.

Undifferentiated Marketing

Some manufacturers conclude that the best approach is to market products without creating a separate marketing strategy for specific market targets. This tactic worked well for Toyota, Nissan, Mazda, and Honda when they first introduced their products, but over time they needed more differentiated approaches. The problem with **undifferentiated marketing** is that it is often difficult to maintain market position if the needs of buyers are varied and they have the income to allow these variations in their purchases. As affluence increases, consumers buy products more suited to the specifics of their market segment.

Bases for Segmentation

Many bases or variables can be used to segment a market, including the following categories: (1) geographic, (2) demographic, (3) psychographic, and (4) behavioral. Segmentation requires the understanding or estimation of buyer preferences and responsiveness to the marketing mix with measurement techniques such as conjoint analysis.[2] Marketing programs are often based on observable covariates of behavior such as demographic or psychographic variables. Demographic variables are examined in this chapter and the next and psychographic variables in Chapter 13. As you study the rest of the book, you will find that much of it relates to behavioral variables, which are used in benefit segmentation or other methods of segmentation.

Behavioral variables frequently used for segmentation include (1) benefit, (2) extent of use and loyalty, and (3) usage situation. Consumers choose different brands of wine or cola for different usage situations or occasions, for example.[3] Often, the competitive mix leaves gaps in customer satisfaction, thus defining an opportunity to fill the competitive gap through benefit segmentation — a customer-driven response to an unmet need.[4] For example, research has shown that body shape (thin, obese, and so on) can be treated as an end benefit by consumers and that this benefit can be used to segment consumers into targets for food products and product imagery in communications programs.[5] Many organizations target the heavy users of the product, often referred to as the heavy half.

Uses of Segmentation in Marketing Strategy

One of the most common uses of segmentation is in *product positioning*, which refers to the ways in which consumers think of the product or identify a product with a defined set of attributes. Segmentation finds many uses in *promotional strategy*, especially in designing the basic appeal to show how the company offering delivers expected benefits and in selecting the specific media most useful in reaching the targeted market segments. *Distribution strategy* considers segmentation in many ways. Lifestyle affects how and where consumers prefer to buy. Busy working consumers may prefer in-home purchase and respond to direct marketing in catalogs or direct selling by firms such as Longaberger, Avon, Home Shopping Network, or L. L. Bean. Retailing outlets, in turn, are designed to appeal to increasingly narrow segments, as is demonstrated by the example of The Limited mentioned earlier. *Price policy* is similarly affected by segmentation as income affects ability to pay. Lifestyle, social class, and other variables may have an effect on willingness of consumers to spend and their emphasis on value or low price.

The zenith in segmentation may be found in direct marketing. Multichannel retailers are turning to direct marketing with stunning results. Through database management and sophisticated computer software, it may be nearly possible to reach the goal of a "segment of one."[6] Through a record of complete information on customer characteristics and preferences, highly tailored, personalized appeals can be made to buyers who otherwise are indifferent to retail advertising. Spiegel, as an example, offers a separate catalog tailored to the needs of its African-American consumers. Some firms direct market products and services for American Express platinum cardholders that are different from those for gold or green cardholders.

The simple truth of market segmentation is this: Effective marketing strategy requires that every element of the marketing mix fits together to deliver a coordinated and integrated appeal to the right group of customers. Competition is too tough today to expect anything less to be successful. Efficiency in segmentation strategy depends on the determination of ways of classifying customers in terms of behavioral congruity rather than descriptive, static characteristics. The complexity of consumer behavior makes this a difficult task and one that is constantly changing. Peter Dickson has advanced the use of segmentation in marketing strategy by relating consumer behavior to deep benefit segmentation, as shown in Figure 2.2.

Back to the Future

Most organizations have reward systems primarily based on past performance in the execution of strategies for existing markets or market segments. Organizations often give little more than superficial attention to the need to anticipate markets of the future — to monitor continuously and select dynamic market segments for adaptive marketing strategy.

Marketing is a process through which organizations change themselves to offer what people will buy. But what will people buy in the future? What segments of the market will become more important in the future? Which segments will decrease in their profit potential? That is the subject of the remainder of this chapter.

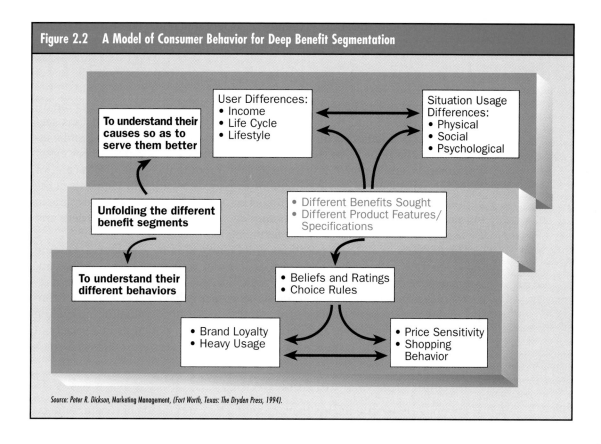

Figure 2.2   A Model of Consumer Behavior for Deep Benefit Segmentation

Source: Peter R. Dickson, Marketing Management, (Fort Worth, Texas: The Dryden Press, 1994).

Planning for Change

Unless management acts, the more successful a firm has been in the past, the more likely it is to fail in the future. Why? Because of the basic psychological principle that people tend to repeat behavior for which they have been rewarded. It is natural, therefore, for organizations to continue strategies that have made them successful in the past. Successful strategies must fit an environment that is constantly changing. Marketing programs that have been successful in the past will continue to be so only to the degree that the environment remains the same in the future. Frequently, the future arrives before managers are willing to give up the present.

Consumer analysts have the responsibility for monitoring and interpreting the environment and how it may change in the future. It is a role of increasing importance in most organizations. It is also a role of profound importance in understanding how the entire economy or society functions. These two roles are sometimes described as micromarketing and macromarketing.

Macroanalysis of Trends and Demographics

Will more food or less be required to feed the population of a country in the future? And what should be its fat and cholesterol content among various segments of the population? Will politicians of the future need to appeal to the affluent or to the poor to be elected? Should health care be provided for every consumer or only some? If it is impossible to provide the same health care for everyone, what level of service should be provided for different segments of the population? How large will the segments be of people who spend their time in museums, at sporting events, or at home "cocooning" around their gardens and TV sets or "fortressing" in their exurban neighborhoods?

The answers to all these questions will be provided by consumers. Finding those answers is the subject of macroanalysis of consumer behavior. The answers may be discovered with logical positivist research or with postmodern research. Macromarketing applications of consumer behavior focus on determining the aggregate performance of marketing in society, evaluating marketing from society's perspective, and understanding the consequences in a society of marketing actions and transactions.

Consumer Analysis and Social Policy

Many policy issues are related to macromarketing and trends in consumer decisions. If a tax cut is proposed, how will consumers spend such reductions? What policies would cause consumers to save more and spend less on current consumption? If the white population of the United States has low birthrates in combination with high birth and immigration rates among minorities, what will be the effect on Social Security when most of the older (white) retirees are supported by young minority members of the work force? Should consumers be encouraged to buy remarketed homes, cars, clothing, and sports equipment instead of new, thereby using less natural resources but diminishing the need for human workers in factories that manufacture new products? Should consumers be encouraged or allowed to make decisions that cause the work force of a nation to be primarily producers of services rather than manufactured goods?

You will not find the answers to these questions in this book, unfortunately. The reason is that we don't know the answers. Consumer analysts have focused mostly on micromarketing research, even though the field of consumer behavior had its birth in such questions in the pioneering work of George Katona.[7] There is a reawakening of interest in what Katona called behavioral economics and what is now called psychological economics. But frankly, not much is yet known. Perhaps you, as a reader of this book, will generate research that will be included as answers to these questions in future editions.

Microapplications of Trend Analysis

Micromarketing analysis of consumer trends has the goal of improving programs of profit and nonprofit organizations. Trend analysis focuses on discovering marketing opportunities that arise from changes in the environment for purposes such as developing new or modified products, changing distribution channels, and improving communications with consumers.

Demographic analysis of micromarketing programs is used in two different ways. Demographics are used as *descriptors* of market segments. This usage underlies the pages you just read on segmentation. In this application, markets match demographic profiles with consumer behavior in applications such as matching viewer profiles with usage segments when selecting media.

The other usage of demographics is in trend analysis. In this application, consumer analysts attempt to understand how demographic trends affect consumption and how to adapt marketing strategy to these changes. The rest of the chapter focuses on such changes, although they also relate to profiles of current market segments.

Enhanced Shareholder Value and the Criticality of Growing Profits

The chief financial goal of well-managed corporations is **enhanced shareholder value** (ESV). The ability of a company to provide job security for its employees and satisfaction for its customers is dependent on ESV. ESV is dependent on the ability to grow profits consistently in the long term and to communicate its ability to do so to the financial community.[8] ESV reflects long-term strategies of a company—such things as investment in new products, joint ventures, and major capital investment.[9] But where should these investments be made? That is a question for marketing strategists, especially those who understand consumer markets.

ESV occurs because firms know how to grow their earnings in good times and bad. When financial markets believe a firm is likely to grow in the future, the firm often achieves a high price/earnings (PE) ratio. Companies such as Starbuck's Coffee and Lone Star Steaks had PE ratios greater than 100 in 1994 because people believed in such companies' ability to grow profits in the future. ESV does not refer only to stock prices, however, but to long-term value defined broadly. If you are a successful student of consumer behavior, you should be prepared to show the company how to grow its profits in the future.

Can firms achieve the goal of a long-term, market-driven approach based on understanding consumer markets? Research by Narver and Slater[10] indicated that profitability is correlated with market orientation. Consider also the example of ConAgra, a diversified company with more than $20 billion of sales. The company defines its business as helping to feed people better in a world expected to have 8.5 billion people to feed by the year 2025. The company has a strong commitment to environmentally sustainable forms of economic progress over the long haul, with the goal of better than a 20 percent return on equity. The company emphasizes convenient, value-oriented foods with one of the most advanced and cost-efficient, shelf-stable grocery sales and distribution systems in the nation. ConAgra is a leading producer and marketer of frozen prepared foods, many of which appeal to changing lifestyles and demographic trends. Its Healthy Choice line of low-fat and cholesterol-free foods revolutionized supermarket competition. The company has grown in a fairly flat, fiercely competitive industry because managers know what consumers are looking for and deliver consistent quality that meets consumers' needs and expectations. Patio and Chun King are two good examples of applying consumer research to build sales to ethnic market segments, introducing Patio microwave burritos and Chun King microwave egg rolls.

Marketing has been central to ConAgra's business philosophy for years. In its annual report, the firm explained, "When we use the term, we are talking about marketing in its broadest sense; it's much more than the eye-catching packages and the memorable advertising campaigns that get so much attention. We focus on the entire marketing process of determining what our customers or consumers need, then providing the right product or service at an appropriate price/value relationship—and in a timely, consistent, and dependable manner." The results? If you bought 10,000 shares of ConAgra in 1975 at $3, by 1992 you would have owned 135,000 shares due to stock splits and your $30,000 investment would have grown to more than $6 million. Plus dividends along the way. That illustrates well the concept of ESV.

You do not need a marketing career to benefit from understanding changing markets and market segmentation. The key to increasing one's net worth is to buy stocks in companies that respond well to changes in the marketplace. Peter Lynch makes the point that people who understand consumer behavior make more money in the stock market than professional stock pickers who rely on financial numbers. Fortunes have been made in stocks such as The Gap, Body Shop, The Limited, and Ben & Jerry's with Lynch's principle, "If you like the store, chances are you'll love the stock."[11]

Customer satisfaction, job security, social responsibility, personal prosperity, and ESV—they all go together. But only if some person in the organization knows how to analyze market segments to grow profits of the firm. You should be one of those persons by the time you finish this chapter.

3 M's of Profit Growth

Three major ways of increasing profits exist in which the study of consumer trends plays a major role. The three ways of growing profits can be thought of as the 3 M's:

1. More markets

2. More market share

3. More margin

In this chapter and the next, we mainly examine the first M—markets. Later chapters discuss the second M—gaining market share. The third M—margin—involves strategies to reduce costs or to increase the price that can be obtained for a product. Cost reduction is mostly outside the scope of our present study. Logistics or physical distribution management analyzes ways to reduce costs. Logistics is related to consumer behavior because of its emphasis on defining and delivering customer satisfaction.[12] The ability to increase prices is a topic for consumer analysis because consumer perceptions of value are directly related to pricing strategies.

More Markets

Finding growth segments of people involves analysis of geographical growth areas, enlarging age groups, intercultural changes, new sources of income, global opportunities to replace declining domestic markets, and other trends. Consumer trend analysis also includes reaching growth segments sooner or more effectively than competitors. Consumer trend analysis is important in industrial marketing or business-to-business marketing as well as consumer firms because industrial demand is ultimately derived from consumer demand. Consumer analysis can reveal industrial products and services needed by growth firms producing and marketing consumer goods.

Firms may find growth opportunities by focusing on overall market trends and moving aggressively between industrial and consumer marketing. Service-Master is a rapidly growing service firm with sales of several billion dollars. Ten years ago, most profit revenues were from business services, but after a decade of responding to changing markets, the company now receives more than a fourth of its income from consumer services and products. The process occurred because the company focused on health care, education, child care, and home care, all services heavily influenced by demographic trends. Initially, ServiceMaster's expertise was mostly in management services to the firms in these growing industries, but over the years, the company extended these areas of expertise through divisions such as Terminix termite and pest control services, TruGreen and ChemLawn lawn services, Merry Maids home cleaning franchises, and American Home Shield appliance repair or replacement. In its annual report, ServiceMaster described this process as the "2 × 5" approach to markets—doubling the customer base every 5 years.

Changing Structure of Consumer Markets

Firms that fail to plan generally plan to fail. Planning, however, requires facts—a basis for assumptions about the future. How will these facts change in the future? What are the trends in market conditions? Markets have four main components:

1. People and their needs
2. Ability to buy
3. Willingness to buy
4. Authority to buy

In the following pages, we examine the first of these components—people. Ability to buy is examined in Chapter 9. Authority to buy is analyzed in Chapter 19 under the topic of family and household trends. Willingness to buy is covered in many chapters. In this chapter, the focus is on people—forecasting how many potential consumers are likely to exist and how their needs relate to age and other demographic factors.

People: Foundation of Market Analysis

People are the foundation of market analysis. How many will there be? What will be the age distribution? Where will they live? These issues involve the study of demographics, defined as the size, structure, and distribution of a population. When combined with data on purchasing power or wealth, this type of analysis is called economic demographics, the study of the economic characteristics of a nation's population. Much of North America and Europe are characterized by slow population growth, but if a firm can concentrate on growing segments or take share from competitors, a firm can still grow when the total market is slowing in growth or even declining.

Population trends are reliably predictable compared with many other variables in the study of consumer behavior. Population demographics move more like celestial mechanics. There are unknowns, such as natural calamities, wars, and medical problems such as plagues in ancient times or AIDS in modern times. Ordinarily, though, populations of geographic areas are reasonably predictable.

Births are the most important of the three variables (births, deaths, and net immigration) that determine the population of a country. Births are also the most volatile. Before making population projections, we need to know how many babies will be born in the future.

What Causes Babies?

Birthrates are determined by four variables. First is *age distribution* of the population. Second is *family structure* involving facts such as proportion of people who are married, proportion of women employed outside the home, and average age when people get married. The third cause of births is *social attitudes* toward family and children. Finally, birthrates are affected by *technology*, such as availability and cost of contraception.

Basic Concepts

Several terms are used to describe and project future populations.[13] The **birth-rate** (also called crude birthrate) is the number of live births per 1,000 population in a given year. The **fertility rate** (also called general fertility rate) is the number of live births per 1,000 women of childbearing age (defined as 15 to 44 years). Fertility rates are sometimes stated as age-specific rates (such as 30- to 39-year-old women) to facilitate comparison over time or to see differences in fertility at different ages. **Completed fertility rate** is the total number of children ever born to women of a specific age group. In 1910, the completed fertility rate for women aged 50 to 54 years was 4.1 but by 1990 had dropped to less than 3.0 and is expected to continue to decline in the 1990s.

The **total fertility rate** (TFR) is the average number of children that would be born alive to a woman during her lifetime if she were to pass through all her childbearing years conforming to the age-specific fertility rates of a given year. Although it is a synthetic number and might seem complex, TFR is the most useful indicator of fertility because it answers the simple question: How many children are women having currently? In many developing countries, the number is more than 6.0. Currently, in the United States, it is about 1.8 children. TFR is even lower in Europe and some other developed countries. A replacement rate is a fertility rate of 2.1 children, the number required for a couple to replace the current population, with allowance for some infant mortality.

The number of babies born in any year is a product of the fertility rate (generally declining in most countries) times the number of women of childbearing age (generally increasing). The result is increasing population in the United States and most countries but at a declining growth rate. The birthrate is as high as 52 per 1,000 in Kenya but as low as 10 per 1,000 in Denmark, where population is now decreasing annually. In the United States, the birthrate dropped from historical levels of 25 to 30 per 1,000 to about 15 or 16 in the latter part of the 1980s. Despite an increase in the number of older mothers in recent years, nearly 60 percent of babies are born to mothers in their twenties.

Birthrates should not be confused with natural increase, which is the surplus of births over deaths in a given time period. An even more important concept is **growth rate** caused by natural increase and net migration, expressed as a percentage of the base population. The growth rate takes into account all components of population growth. Although the world's growth rate is about 1.7 percent, the United States is at 0.9 and is projected to decline to about 0.6 by the year 2000. Trends and projections of these concepts are shown in Figure 2.3.

Future Fertility

Forecasting births in future decades is difficult. Although fecundity, the physiologic capability of couples to reproduce, is fairly predictable, fertility, which is actual reproductive performance, is more difficult. The solution to the problem of forecasting babies—and thus, total population—is to provide several

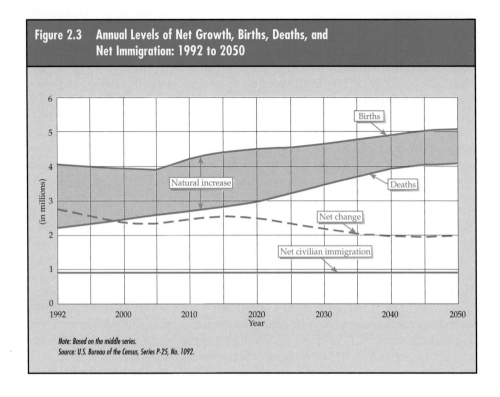

Figure 2.3   Annual Levels of Net Growth, Births, Deaths, and Net Immigration: 1992 to 2050

Note: Based on the middle series.
Source: U.S. Bureau of the Census, Series P-25, No. 1092.

projections based on different fertility assumptions. The Census Bureau calls these Series I (highest) assuming 2.7 children per woman, Series II (middle) assuming 2.1 children, and Series III (lowest) assuming 1.7. Before 1993, fertility had been at the low level for about 15 years, but in the 1990s a dramatic increase occurred, to almost 2.1. Is this just a temporary move representing what columnist Ellen Goodman called the "now or never club" or is it a fundamental change toward higher fertility? The answer makes a big difference in projections of future population, as you can see in Figure 2.4.

Family size has been dramatically affected by attitudes and behavior toward contraception, a trend that is reasonably permanent considering that the leading method of contraception in the United States is now sterilization.[14] After the age of 36 years, most women are no longer fertile because half have been surgically sterilized and 11 percent have impaired fecundity, according to the National Center for Health Statistics.

Order Effects

Order effects can affect consumption even when total births remain constant. First-order (firstborn) babies generate more economic impact than higher-order (second, third, fourth, and so on) babies. First-order babies may generate $1,500

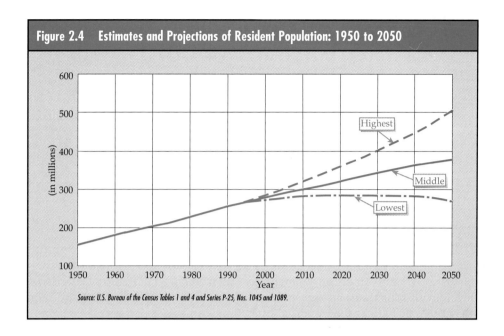

Figure 2.4 Estimates and Projections of Resident Population: 1950 to 2050

Source: U.S. Bureau of the Census Tables 1 and 4 and Series P-25, Nos. 1045 and 1089.

of retail sales, for example, compared with less than half of that for higher-order babies. More than 40 percent of all children are firstborn today, compared with 25 percent in the 1960s.

Order effects can be important in development of marketing programs. Eastman Kodak benefits from first-order babies when their happy parents buy cameras and take massive quantities of pictures. Higher-order children may be lucky to get one picture at graduation. One-child families, on the other hand, are better able to afford nice restaurants and products such as personal computers, new clothing instead of hand-me-downs, and services such as private education, ballet school, and sports lessons.

You might ask if parents will have enough money to buy all these nice things for their children. The answer is more likely to be yes if they only have one child. One reason only-children have such a disproportionately high achievement rate is the simple fact of resource constraints. A family with only one child has more economic and temporal resources — money and time — to spend on a child's development, education, and health than the same family would if there were more than one child.

Childlessness has become more prevalent. Some of the "baby busters" are those who have made a deliberate decision not to have children; others simply delay the decision for economic or personal reasons until the opportunity to have children is diminished. The fastest-growing household type among white households during the 1990s is married couples without children. The consumption effect is more spending power available for travel, luxury products that pamper one's self, adult education and self-development services, and savings and retirement planning.

Ethnic Variations

Small variations in fertility produce large differences in population. For 1995, the Census Bureau projects the following total fertility rates per 1,000 women:

American Indian	2,900
Hispanic origin	2,650
Black	2,459
Asian	2,326
White (non-Hispanic)	1,800

White women typically have babies at older ages than other ethnic groups. Therefore, white families have fewer babies in total. By 1990, about 66 percent of births to African-American women were to women who were not married, a level about four times as high as that of white women (19 percent) and more than twice as high as that reported by Latino women (26 percent).

About 66 percent of all births currently are non-Hispanic white. Using the Census Bureau middle-level assumptions, that percentage is expected to fall to 61 in 2000, 56 in 2010, and 42 in 2050. All other race and ethnic groups would increase their share of births.

About three-quarters of the population was non-Hispanic white in 1992, and this segment is expected to contribute only 30 percent of the total population growth between 1992 and 2000 and nothing to population growth after 2030, because the segment will be declining in size. The black population is projected to almost double from 32 million in 1992 to 62 million in 2050. After about 2005, more blacks than non-Hispanic whites would be added to the population each year. The Hispanic population would rise from 24 million in 1992 to 81 million in 2050, contributing 33 percent of the nation's growth from 1992 to 2000 but 57 percent of the growth from 2030 to 2050. The Asian and Pacific Islander population is expected to continue to be the fastest-growing group, rising from 9 million in 1992 to 13 million in 2000 and 41 million in 2050. Each year after 2002, this Asian segment would add more people to the population of the United States than would the non-Hispanic white group.

Life Expectancy

Life expectancy has increased dramatically in most countries. Nearly a century ago, the average American died at age 47 years. Today, a newborn can expect to live 75 years. White females have the longest life expectancy at 79.3 years and black males the shortest at 66 years. Black females have a life expectancy of 74.5 years and white males a life expectancy of 72.6 years. Keep in mind that these numbers reflect infant mortality, which you have already survived.

Immigration

Immigration represents 25 percent of annual growth in the United States. Legal net immigration was about 530,000 per year in the 1980s, increased to 700,000 during 1992 to 1994, and is projected to be about 880,000 thereafter. Undocumented migrants boost the numbers somewhat. As for fertility, the Census Bureau makes high and low series projections for immigration that range from 350,000 per year to 1,375,000, depending on legal immigration and possible changes in emigration. If low series fertility projections occur in the future, then immigration would be a much higher proportion of the total population increase.

Most Likely Scenarios

No one knows exactly what number of consumers will exist in the future, because the results will be affected by fertility, deaths, and immigration. The Census Bureau calculates projections based on high, middle, and low assumptions for each of these three components. The three most likely scenarios are shown in Table 2.1, which is the basis for discussion of changing segments in the following pages. Perhaps you will find it fascinating to look at all the numbers in that table, but don't be discouraged if it does not fascinate you; we'll provide explanations in the text of most of the trends.

The U.S. population is projected to grow from 260 million in 1994 to 274 million in 2000 and 382 million in 2050. These projections are based on the middle series. If low fertility rates actually occur, the Census Bureau projects population of 268 million in 2000 and 275 million in 2050. The high series projects population at 281 million in 2000 and 508 million in 2050.

This is a good point for you to make your own assumptions. Do you believe fertility rates will be low, middle, or high in the future? Calculations based on your assumptions are shown in Table 2.1. If you manage an organization, would you recommend investing money in new plants and products under the assumption of lots more consumers in the future? Or less? Those are the kinds of decisions that depend on your understanding of the population component of consumption.

NAFTA Markets

With the passage of the Free Trade Agreement (FTA) in 1989 and the North American Free Trade Agreement (NAFTA) in 1993, marketers in the United States, Canada, and Mexico have freer access to the consumers of other countries. Intermarket segmentation, explained in the next chapter, will be increasingly possible on the basis of age, lifestyle, or other variables across the boundaries of each of the countries. Marketers expect to find higher average income in the United States and Canada, but higher population growth and improving economic conditions in Mexico. In the rest of this chapter, the focus is on U.S. market segments, but marketing will increasingly be directed to segments that cut across NAFTA boundaries.

Table 2.1   **Projections of the Population by Age, Sex, Race, and Hispanic Origin: 1995 to 2010 (in thousands as of July 1; includes Armed Forces overseas)**

Age, Sex, Race, and Hispanic Origin	Lowest Series			Middle Series			Highest Series		
	1995	2000	2010	1995	2000	2010	1995	2000	2010
Total Population	260,715	268,108	278,078	262,754	274,815	298,109	264,685	281,306	317,895
Younger than 5 years old	19,165	17,438	16,356	19,553	18,908	19,730	19,949	20,448	23,640
5–19 years old	55,779	58,493	55,662	56,144	59,740	61,278	56,492	60,957	67,122
20–24 years old	17,672	17,647	20,118	17,885	18,161	21,061	18,091	18,660	21,974
25–34 years old	40,469	36,310	36,028	40,844	37,416	38,367	41,214	38,524	40,655
35–44 years old	42,296	43,995	36,782	42,500	44,662	38,853	42,726	45,461	41,191
45–54 years old	30,956	36,632	42,305	31,082	37,054	43,737	31,196	37,465	45,253
55–64 years old	21,042	23,626	34,134	21,153	23,988	35,378	21,238	24,257	36,260
65 years and older	33,335	33,968	36,694	33,594	34,886	39,705	33,778	35,534	41,790
16 years and older	199,881	207,677	222,829	201,294	211,976	234,650	202,602	216,006	245,437
White, total	216,151	220,092	223,922	217,511	224,594	237,412	218,811	229,063	251,352
Black, total	32,900	34,642	37,419	33,147	35,525	40,429	33,368	36,307	42,947
Hispanic, total	25,926	28,693	33,828	26,522	30,602	39,312	27,073	32,343	44,328
American Indian, Eskimo, and Aleut, total	2,241	2,383	2,658	2,247	2,409	2,772	2,250	2,422	2,833
Asian and Pacific Islander, total	9,422	10,991	14,079	9,849	12,287	17,496	10,257	13,514	20,763

Source: U.S. Bureau of the Census, Current Population Reports, Series P-25, No. 1092.

As you examine the data in the next few pages, keep in mind that although many trends in the United States and Canada are similar, Canada has about one-tenth of the U.S. population. Many trends in Mexico are affected by its younger and faster-growing population. These variations are shown in Table 2.2.

Throughout NAFTA markets, the trend is toward more education and the emerging importance of women in the labor force. Women make up the majority (about 52 percent) of all Canadian university students, as is true in the United States. The majority of Canadian families are dual-earner families, and 54 percent of women aged 25 years and older are in the labor force.

Changing Ages of Markets

The changing age distribution in North America affects consumer behavior and effective marketing in many ways. Understanding market changes permits fore-casting what kind of products will be bought and consumed as well as related behaviors, attitudes, and opinions.[15] To help you get an overall picture of the

Table 2.2	Projected Population of NAFTA Markets, Selected Statistics				
	Total Population (millions)	Annual Growth Rate (prior 10 years)	65 Years and Older (%)	Total Fertility Rate (no. children)	Life Expectancy (years)
Canada					
1993	27.7	1.0	12.0	1.84	78.0
2000	29.9	1.2	12.8	1.80	70.1
Mexico					
1993	90.4	2.1	4.1	3.25	72.6
2000	102.9	1.9	4.0	2.79	75.0
United States					
1993	258.1	.9	12.7	2.05	75.8
2000	275.3	1.0	12.7	2.07	76.4

Source: U.S. Bureau of the Census, International Data Base.

next few pages, refer to Figure 2.5, which graphically shows the changes in population expected from 1990 to 2000. As you read the following pages, look for ways demographics affect a firm's segmentation strategy currently as well as changes needed in the future.

Children as Consumers

The number of young children may decline during the 1990s, but their importance as consumers won't decline. Using the low series of population projections (see Table 2.1), the number of children younger than 5 years will decline by several million between 1995 and 2010, and the high series projects only a small increase. Under either assumption, however, the high proportion of first-order babies will generate high demand for quality products and services. In addition to higher-quality products, parents may expect more information about the product. Parents probably will pay for designer labels, shop more at specialty stores, and have higher expectations during usage of products.

Children don't sign checks, but they do have a big influence on spending. A couple whose oldest child is younger than 6 years old spends 10 percent more money in total than the average couple without children. A couple whose oldest child is aged 6 to 17 years spends 24 percent more, and a couple whose oldest child is aged 18 years or older spends 36 percent more.[16] On average, children influence 17 percent of family spending in many product categories, with some categories such as fruit snacks influenced 80 percent of the time by children.[17]

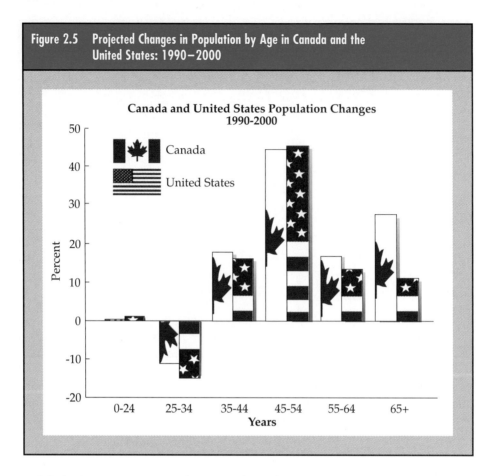

Figure 2.5   Projected Changes in Population by Age in Canada and the United States: 1990–2000

Marketing programs emphasize style and attractiveness when clothing and other products are consumed by only one child. Durability and timelessness of style become more important when products are "handed down." JC Penney added designer clothes and discarded "hard lines" such as tires and auto supplies to create a fashion image that appeals to children and parents who can afford and are willing to buy fashionable clothing.

Second-use stores and informal trading networks develop to achieve multiple use of clothing and other products by children—in various families. Conversely, in contrast to "hand-me-downs" in the same family, some products—such as diapers or other consumables—are more likely to be disposable, even in the face of environmental concerns about such products. Hotel chains such as Hyatt have targeted children to reach parents with a program called Camp Hyatt. Hyatt formed a Camp Hyatt Kids Council, for kids ages 7 to 12 years, which told the firm, among other things, to have fun things to do besides just jumping on beds. Trends are important to study because kids love new things, whether they be songs, dances, food, toys, or computer games.

Research methods adapted to understanding children are needed to prevent errors in marketing strategies based on outmoded assumptions. TV advertisers, for example, often buy TV programs for "kids 2 to 11 years" because that was the traditional definition. Yet, these age groups have little in common. The most popular children's shows are no longer on Saturday morning but on weekday evenings. Segmenting wisely is just as important in the youth market as in older markets.[18] Focus groups can be useful in studying children if moderators tune in properly and refine how to talk with kids on their own terms. Techniques include role playing and simulated shopping. The key is knowing how kids think. Does crunchy mean the same thing to a child as an adult? If kids are younger than 7 years, it's "crunchy" if they can hear it. You can't ask young children what foods they have eaten in the past month, because they often don't know what a month is. Peer pressure is one of the toughest obstacles; it can easily color kids' answers. One way to diminish peer pressure is to give children some anonymity by talking to them without the presence of other children in the room. If boys and girls are in the same room, differences in their reactions to products get muddled, so it is usually best to separate the sexes.[19]

McNeal points out that a customer, potentially worth $100,000 to a retailer during a lifetime, starts her or his buying career as a child. Children learn to be consumers by going through five stages: (1) observing, (2) making requests, (3) making selections, (4) making assisted purchases, and (5) making independent purchases. Children's first purchases may be clumsy, and they may interfere with the normal flow at checkout stations. But they give businesses a golden opportunity to encourage the bonding that could last a lifetime[20] (see Consumer in Focus 2.2).

Consumer in Focus **2.2**

Did You Get Your Skippies Today?

"Skippies" (school-aged kids with purchasing power) spend billions of dollars each year. Marketers who want to attract them must understand them. With more working moms and single-parent families, children are taking more accountability for their own diets, making more purchases without parental consent. By age 10, they are visiting stores 270 times a year. According to James U. McNeal's book *Kids as Customers*, kids between ages 4 and 12 spend $9 billion per year and influence parents' spending of $75 billion.

One promising trend: Kids who shop for food are eating healthier, eating more fruits and vegetables rather than junk food. Nutrition ideas by school lunch programs and health-conscious parents are leading kids to eat better. "Skippies" are savvy when it comes to purchasing but the possibilities are very much alive for selling nutrition if kids are creatively targeted.

Source: "Kids as Consumers," Futurist 28 (January–February 1994), 49.

Rise of Teenagers

The number of teenagers will increase during much of the 1990s, creating a growing market for clothing, music and entertainment, fast food, gasoline, and other products. In 1993, annual spending of teenagers was estimated at $89 billion by Teenage Research, a commercial research organization. However, perhaps as much as another $150 billion of purchasing power may be created by the 75 percent of teenagers who claim that they urge their parents to buy products and services for the home. Also, grocery marketers are now directing ads to teenagers, who are increasingly given the task of buying the family groceries in dual-income families. Research by Tootelian and Gaedeke[21] indicated that what teens like best about shopping is being with their friends and that companies should focus some of their marketing efforts on opinion leaders within teen groups.

Young Adults from the Baby Bust

Young adults are declining rapidly as a result of the Baby Bust from 1965 to 1980. Figure 2.5 showed that 25- to 34-year-old consumers will decline about 10 percent in Canada and 15 percent in the United States. Because age 25 to 34 years is the time when families usually form, bear young, and often buy their first home and their first new car, declining sales of these products and related products are to be expected. This is also the age when young families borrow heavily to duplicate the kind of standards of living their parents achieved. They use credit cards to support their "habit" of homes, microwaves, VCRs, and similar consumer goods. They often buy from value-oriented retailers such as Wal-Mart, Target, Kmart, and Odd Lots. Despite their declining numbers, baby busters are an important market segment. Consumer in Focus 2.3 describes how to reach these consumers, sometimes called Generation X.

Baby Boomers and Muppies

The most important year of the decade may be 1996 because that is when baby boomers start to hit age 50 years. Baby boomers is a term given to the cohort of people born in huge numbers after World War II. The soaring fertility lasted through 74 million births by 1964, which will continue to have an effect on markets and all other aspects of society for decades. In the 1980s, marketers focused on Yuppies—young urban professionals—because of their discretionary income and their influence on market trends. Today, Yuppies have become Muppies—middle-aged urban professionals—creating even more profitable markets.

Baby boomers delayed getting married and having children, but eventually they entered the trap and brought with them a permanent propensity to consume. They know what they want—quality products that are aesthetically pleasing, personally satisfying, natural, and, if possible, noncaloric. Products and services for baby boomers must be available in convenient and value-oriented distribution channels, such as off-price but quality retailers and catalogs. Baby

Consumer in Focus **2.3**

Marketing to the Baby Bust Generation

Busters were raised in times of oil crises and stagflation with low confidence in the future. They had fewer siblings than baby boomers, were less likely to be raised in a two-parent household, and if they did have both parents at home, were more likely to be raised by two working parents. Busters are pragmatic and exhibit greater signs of being individuals who are ambitious, selfish, and determined to succeed financially. The baby busters are dedicated, better-educated, diligent, and valued contributors. They are willing to work but are not into workaholism and are not willing to make the sacrifices demanded of their predecessors.

Busters are heavy consumers and trendsetters; many are compulsive shoppers. They are brand aware but not loyal, susceptible to the allure of well-known brands, and likely to buy imports. They are suspicious of unsubstantiated product claims. Silly or derogative advertising is apt to put them off. Marketers must make products available, accessible, and easy to use and operate. Twist tops will win over needing bottle openers or corkscrews.

Do not use political, economic, or business leaders as marketing endorsers because more busters can identify the judge on "People's Court" than can name the Chief Justice of the Supreme Court. Rather, current sports stars and entertainment figures will be recognizable.

Source: Summarized from Paul Herbig, William Koehler, and Ken Day, "Marketing to the Baby Bust Generation," Journal of Consumer Marketing 10, No. 1 (1993), 4–9.

boomers buy more and save less than past generations, spending on products that past generations would have considered luxuries, such as consumer electronics, second cars, and household services. When they were young, the instrument of choice for purchases was the credit card. Increasingly, it is cash. Banks and other financial institutions will make their money not so much from credit cards as from asset accumulation products, bought by baby boomers with an increasing awareness of the need to prepare for future retirement.[22]

The lifestyle decisions of Baby Boom consumers are influenced greatly by trends in marriage, divorce, and consumption during the 1980s. They don't need a new car, but if they buy one, it will be higher quality than what they accepted as young adults. It may also be one that restores some of the "youth" they don't want to concede to the next generation. The Infiniti ad in Figure 2.6 shows a Muppie being challenged by a young consumer on the highway, but the Muppie accelerates and pulls ahead of the younger driver. When baby boomers buy homes or products for the home, they also face less immediacy and more ability to finance quality. Instead of a split-level preferred in younger years, they want a nicer but perhaps smaller home, along with a second home that might someday be used for retirement.[23]

The 45- to 55-year-old and 55- to 64-year-old age groups are projected to grow by millions of consumers during the 1990s. By the end of the decade, many of

Figure 2.6   Appealing to Aging Baby Boomers

them will be empty-nesters, families whose children have not only left home but have also left the university. They have small families at home, are often at the height of their careers and earning power, have low or no mortgages to pay, and have generally reduced family responsibilities. The key to understanding the empty-nesters is freedom, because they already have an adequate inventory of housing products, cars, clothing, and such products. They not only have the freedom to spend on what they want; they have the freedom to withhold until they receive precisely what they want. In Figure 2.7, Jaguar appeals to a heritage that people want but could not afford until later in life.

Empty-nesters indulge in luxury travel, restaurants, and the theater—which often means they need more fashionable clothing, jewelry, and department stores. They watch their waistlines and diets and are good prospects for spas, health clubs, cosmetics, beauty parlors, and healthier foods. As they approach retirement, they purchase condominiums and begin to take more frequent but less expensive vacations. They are a prime prospect for financial products oriented toward asset accumulation and retirement income.

Many of the families of the baby boomers will be transgenerational couples, of mixed ages. Either the husband or the wife may be substantially younger in age than the other. Such spouses choose each other because of similarity in values, lifestyles, and interests rather than chronologic age. Notice the ad for Dewar's in Figure 2.8, (see page 67), in which the ages are listed as 50 and 33 years. Marketers sometimes employ celebrities who appeal to many ages. Elton John is such an example, with a top recording in 18 of the past 20 years. Spokespersons such as Dick Clark and Bill Cosby also appeal to a wide variety of age segments.

Young-Again Market

Another rapid growth segment is the "young-again" market, consumers who have accumulated lots of chronologic age but who feel, think, and buy young. Other terms to describe this segment include maturity market, seniors, and elderly. We have chosen the young-again (YA) phrase to describe a major part of the maturity market in the United States and Canada that is chronologically older but has attitudes and economic resources highly attractive to marketers.

Cognitive age is the age one perceives one's self to be. The cognitive age concept is applicable to people of all ages but has been studied most frequently in the context of mature adults. Cognitive age is measured in terms of how people feel and act, express interests, and perceive their looks. Cognitively younger "older" women, for example, manifest higher self-confidence and greater fashion interests, are more work-oriented, and have greater participation in entertainment and culturally related activities.[24] In a study of several methods of measuring cognitive age, Stephens[25] found that the age decade scale works best. Consumers are asked to complete statements such as "most of the time, I feel (look, have interests of, do) like I'm in my . . . (teens, 20s, 30s, . . . , 90s)." She found cognitive age to be useful in conjunction with chronologic age for better targeting of segments, more effective creative content, and more efficient media selections. Ads for Duracell feature stars such as Dick Clark, Nolan Ryan, and Bob Hope, people who are cognitively young even through chronologically old (Figure 2.9, on page 68).

Figure 2.7   An Appeal to Waiting for the Best

From a heritage of inspired design and engineering, comes the best Jaguar ever built.

They are some of the most coveted automobiles of all time. The 1961 E-type. The 1954 XK-140. The 1936 SS-100—automobiles that created the indelible tradition of Jaguar design and engineering excellence. Today, that tradition is carried forward by the 1992 XJS.

Through the years, Jaguar has pioneered technological innovations such as monocoque construction, four-wheel disc brakes, and fully independent suspension—achievements reflected today in the best sporting Jaguar ever built.

Now, computers and robotics are part of a highly advanced manufacturing process. New quality assurance procedures and sophisticated electronic controls exist side-by-side with the time-honored art of handcrafting wood and leather.

For its owner, the reward is a car of sensuous beauty and enviable performance. Its interior is an environment of unparalleled luxury and convenience. Race-bred handling and agile response create a relationship between driver and car at once confident and exhilarating.

And for 1992, even Jaguar's warranty has been enhanced, to four years/50,000 miles. For the nearest dealer, who can provide details on the limited warranty and Jaguar Royal Charter Care, call 1-800-4-JAGUAR.

J A G U A R

A   B L E N D I N G   O F   A R T   A N D   M A C H I N E

Older families have more to spend, but they need to spend less. Moschis[26] concluded older people are thrifty and careful with the money they spend. They need to be careful because inflation causes prices to increase, but not necessarily their income. They have experience with shopping and ability to wait to find

Figure 2.8   Appeal to Transgenerational Families

good value. They may respond more to coupons and be willing to shift their buying to off-peak times if given an adequate incentive to do so. Nevertheless, with home mortgages paid off or nearly so, no more college educations to finance, and an ample inventory of basic appliances and furnishings, mature

Figure 2.9 Chronologically Old or Cognitively Young?

HE RUNS LIKE HE'S ON DURACELL.

DURACELL® BATTERIES. NOTHING LASTS LONGER.

families are especially good prospects for luxury goods, travel-related goods and services, health care, and a wide range of financial services.

People who are now retiring have lived their lives in decades of economic expansion that has often given them a comfortable, even affluent retirement. On per-capita after-tax basis, consumers aged 65 to 69 years have high levels of discretionary income.

Market segmentation is especially important in the maturity market.[27] Most often, this is done on the basis of age, income, or work (retirement) status. Consumption patterns vary substantially between the retired and those still working.[28] Other useful segmentation variables are health, activity level, discretionary time, and engagement with society. Gender is also an important segmentation variable. Women greatly outnumber men because of greater life expectancy and more than 60 percent are not married. Many are widows who typically experience inability to earn an income, inadequate and often dangerous housing, and social and economic rejection.[29]

Older consumers use the mass media more than younger consumers do and have less interpersonal contact. They may need special services such as delivery or telephone shopping, and may be more loyal to firms that emphasize good service and value. In a comprehensive literature review of information processing among older consumers, Ross[30] found many problems with the media because of declining sensory abilities. Older consumers are likely to be newspaper readers and AM radio listeners. They are more likely to shop at department or other traditional stores than in discount stores. Older consumers are pretty much like younger segments in their brand loyalty and shopping behavior[31] and respond equally well to young or older role models, at least for age/neutral products such as coffee.[32]

Marketing to the Young-Again Market

The current YA or mature market is a cohort influenced by the Great Depression and World War II. The resulting emphasis was on saving and conservative consumption. The mature market of the future, however, has experienced mostly prosperity since World War II and a willingness to spend as long as credit cards are not over their limit. YA markets are "experience" markets rather than "things" markets because they already have enough things, as well as the maturity of attitude that does not associate things with happiness. The YA market therefore places more emphasis on experiences such as travel, activities with persons in similar situations, and staying in touch. Segmenting or predicting purchases within the YA market may not be so much based on product/ service attributes as on the amount of life satisfaction experienced by mature consumers.[33]

Differences in consumption between older consumers and younger consumers go beyond attitudes. Some differences are physical. Eyes don't see as well, creating the need for larger print and bright colors rather than pastels or earth tones. Shiny paper in packaging or print ads should be avoided. TV commercials with visual changes every few seconds are annoying. Legs do not move as fast or as high, creating physical vulnerability that creates a booming home security market. Hands have less flexibility, causing doorknobs to be replaced with levers. Phones need larger buttons as well as volume controls.

Three qualities are especially important in products purchased by mature markets: comfort, security, and convenience. Young people may stuff their feet into high-heeled shoes that are trendy. Older people want to be comfortable in their clothing, as well as in the furniture in their homes and in their feelings about the institutions handling their assets. They are less willing to take risks, whether they be physical, social, or financial. Thus, need for security is higher than with other markets and rewarding to the marketers who understand this need. Convenience is also a price for which the mature market will reward marketers. They want a computer that is easy to understand, even more than most people. They want to go to stores where they are sure they will find what they expect. They don't want to struggle with the frustration of automated teller machines too complex to operate. Some banks recognize these trends and provide personal assistance at teller machines with heavy concentrations of mature customers. Some stores and shopping malls provide convenient, dependable bus or van service between their facilities and concentrations of mature customers. Among the "young old," there is a sensitivity to revealing one's age. Consequently, an ad that blasts out in pictures or words that the product is for 60-year-olds won't work. Nor will advertising that is obviously directed to 30-year-olds. The most effective way to get around that problem is to create affinities between the product and some interest of the mature generation. Walker and Macklin[34] conducted research that indicates, for example, that grandparenting is an important affinity, and stressing the role of grandparenting as central to life is an effective appeal. Dychtwald, a gerontologist specializing in marketing, explains:

> Quaker Oats is now very cleverly launching a campaign to get Quaker Oats viewed as a nutritious product for old people. They don't say, "Quaker Oats is good for you if you're old." What they say is, "Eating Quaker Oats lowers your cholesterol level." That's an affinity. That's an issue that anyone over the age of 50 is going to land right on. For 19-year-olds, it's invisible. They don't worry about their cholesterol levels.[35]

Consequences of a Slow-Growing, Older Consumer Base

North America and most other industrialized areas are becoming old — really old. Although the United States has more than 12 percent of its population older than the age of 65 years and Canada has 10.4 percent, that is young compared with Sweden, which has nearly 17 percent older than age 65 years.[36] All European countries are older than the United States and Canada. Between 1990 and 2000, the population older than 90 years is projected to increase 50 percent in the European community and even 70 or 80 percent in countries such as Belgium and Germany.[37] The challenge for consumer analysts is to understand what this means, not only for products purchased by older consumers but for labor and retirement policies, political elections, family structures, health care, and many other areas of life.

The impact on the rest of consumers will also be substantial. As younger people are surrounded by older consumers and realize that life is going to last much longer than it used to, they may spend more money on health and appearance products and spend more time on healthier activities. Look at Figure 2.10 and you will see how Morningstar Farms satisfies these demands. The ad features

Figure 2.10   Good Taste and Good Health: Baby Boomers' Choice

A Delicious Way To Cut Down On Meat Without Cutting Down Your Options.

Crumble up our Breakfast Patties to prepare delicious Italian dishes like lasagna.

When you take something away, you usually have less. But the way we see it, now you have more. Because Morningstar Farms® offers you a way to eat less meat while giving you more delicious ways to enjoy your favorite meat dishes.

Made with wholesome grains and vegetable protein, these meatless foods are a healthier way to eat because they have no animal fat and zero cholesterol. Yet they taste so much like meat, you can enjoy your favorite meals the way you always have. Microwave them in minutes just the way they are, or use them to prepare delicious dishes for breakfast, lunch and dinner.

With our Breakfast Links, you can still enjoy your favorite morning meals.

Morningstar Farms has the most complete line of meatless products, including Grillers® Breakfast Links, Breakfast Patties and Breakfast Strips. Look for them in your supermarket's frozen breakfast section. They're a delicious way to prove that less can be more.

MORNINGSTAR FARMS®

There are as many ways to top Grillers as there are to top hamburgers.

Make It Meatless & SAVE $1.20

For your free Morningstar Farms recipe booklet, plus coupons worth $1.20 for Morningstar Farms products, send a postcard to: *Meatless Favorites, Morningstar Farms, P. O. Box 6018, Dept. VT, Worthington, OH 43085.*   Worthington Foods, Inc.

Limit one per family.   Allow 8 weeks for delivery.

products people love to eat but without the cholesterol or fat by being meatless. As Mickey Mantle is reported to have said, "If I'd known I was going to live so long, I'd have taken better care of myself."

Slow growth in population creates high value in retaining current customers instead of attaining new customers. With fewer new consumers to attract, marketing budgets shift from advertising to training to emphasize good service that retains customers. Retailers such as Nordstrom have achieved great success by emphasizing good service as a customer retention strategy. More resources also go to consumer affairs departments or other programs for soliciting and handling complaints.[38] Defensive marketing encourages complaints because higher economic value results from settling complaints quickly, and the savings may justify the additional costs associated with compensating dissatisfied customers. Economic models help calculate these trade-offs.[39]

The need to retain customers is increasingly recognized in *relationship marketing,* a marketing strategy that seeks to establish an ongoing relationship with customers rather than emphasize individual transactions. A central element in relationship marketing is trust between the partners. Relationship marketing goes beyond market segmentation by determining which customers are most important to the future of the seller and making sure those customers are delighted with all aspects of the firm. Carl Sewell, a Cadillac dealer in Dallas, Texas, observes that a customer should be viewed as a potential profit center of several hundred thousand dollars in a lifetime rather than the profit generated from just one transaction.[40]

One form of relationship marketing is network marketing, a relationship to the customer operated by several noncompetitive organizations. Other forms of relationship marketing involve strategic alliances between various members of the distribution channel. A good example of network marketing is found in the travel industry in the form of frequent traveler programs. Major airlines use them to create loyalty but also to track the behavior of the best customers—who are also the best customers of hotels, rental car companies, marketers of upscale consumer goods, and credit cards. The more a customer buys from the airline, the more likely the customer is to buy from a hotel and use a credit card. A firm's success is determined not only by its own marketing program but by the quality of the relationship network to which the firm belongs.[41]

Changing Geography of Demand

The search for growing segments in a slow-growth society almost always leads to specific geographic areas. Where people live and earn their money is critical to understanding consumer demand. We finish this chapter with a brief look at the geography of demand in North American markets. Sometimes this is called **geodemography**—the study of demand related to geographic areas.

State and Provincial Markets

Market trends vary substantially between states and provinces. The states gaining the most population recently are California, Texas, and Florida. Florida passed Pennsylvania to become the fourth most populous state.

What will the future bring? These projections are shown in Table 2.3 Such projections are based on the components of change: births, deaths, and net

| Table 2.3 | Total Population in Thousands by State, 1990 to 2010; Absolute Change and Percent Change for 1990 to 2000, and 2000 to 2010 |

	1990	2000	2010	1990–2000		2000–2010	
				Change	Percent	Change	Percent
U.S. total	249,891	267,747	282,055	17,856	7.1	14,308	5.3
Alabama	4,181	4,410	4,609	229	5.5	199	4.5
Alaska	576	687	765	111	19.3	78	11.4
Arizona	3,752	4,618	5,319	866	23.1	701	15.2
Arkansas	2,427	2,529	2,624	102	4.2	95	3.8
California	29,126	33,500	37,347	4,374	15.0	3,847	11.5
Colorado	3,434	3,813	4,098	379	11.0	285	7.5
Connecticut	3,279	3,445	3,532	166	5.1	87	2.5
Delaware	666	734	790	68	10.2	56	7.6
District of Columbia	614	634	672	20	3.3	38	6.0
Florida	12,818	15,415	17,530	2,597	20.3	2,115	13.7
Georgia	6,663	7,957	9,045	1,294	19.4	1,088	13.7
Hawaii	1,141	1,345	1,559	204	17.9	214	15.9
Idaho	1,017	1,047	1,079	30	2.9	32	3.1
Illinois	11,612	11,580	11,495	−32	−0.3	−85	−0.7
Indiana	5,550	5,502	5,409	−48	−0.9	−93	−1.7
Iowa	2,758	2,549	2,382	−209	−7.6	−167	−6.6
Kansas	2,492	2,529	2,564	37	1.5	35	1.4
Kentucky	3,745	3,733	3,710	−12	−0.3	−23	−.06
Louisiana	4,513	4,516	4,545	3	0.1	29	0.6
Maine	1,212	1,271	1,308	59	4.9	37	2.9
Maryland	4,729	5,274	5,688	545	11.5	414	7.8
Massachusetts	5,880	6,087	6,255	207	3.5	168	2.8
Michigan	9,293	9,250	9,097	−43	−0.5	−153	−1.7
Minnesota	4,324	4,490	4,578	166	3.8	88	2.0
Mississippi	2,699	2,877	3,028	178	6.6	151	5.2
Missouri	5,192	5,383	5,521	191	3.7	138	2.6
Montana	805	794	794	−11	−1.4	0	0.0
Nebraska	1,588	1,556	1,529	−32	−2.0	−27	−1.7
Nevada	1,076	1,303	1,484	227	21.1	181	13.9
New Hampshire	1,142	1,333	1,455	191	16.7	122	9.2
New Jersey	7,899	8,546	8,980	647	8.2	434	5.1
New Mexico	1,632	1,968	2,248	336	20.6	280	14.2
New York	17,773	17,986	18,139	213	1.2	153	0.9
North Carolina	6,690	7,483	8,154	793	11.9	671	9.0
North Dakota	660	629	611	−31	−4.7	−18	−2.9
Ohio	10,791	10,629	10,397	−162	−1.5	−232	−2.2
Oklahoma	3,285	3,376	3,511	91	2.8	135	4.0
Oregon	2,766	2,877	2,991	111	4.0	114	4.0
Pennsylvania	11,827	11,503	11,134	−324	−2.7	−369	−3.2
Rhode Island	1,002	1,049	1,085	47	4.7	36	3.4
South Carolina	3,549	3,906	4,205	357	10.1	299	7.7
South Dakota	708	714	722	6	0.8	8	1.1
Tennessee	4,972	5,266	5,500	294	5.9	234	4.4
Texas	17,712	20,211	22,281	2,499	14.1	2,070	10.2
Utah	1,776	1,991	2,171	215	12.1	180	9.0
Vermont	562	591	608	29	5.2	17	2.9
Virginia	6,157	6,877	7,410	720	11.7	533	7.8
Washington	4,657	4,991	5,282	334	7.2	291	5.8
West Virginia	1,856	1,722	1,617	−134	−7.2	−105	−6.1
Wisconsin	4,808	4,784	4,713	−24	−0.5	−71	−1.5
Wyoming	502	489	487	−13	−2.6	−2	−0.4

Note: Numbers may not add to totals due to rounding.
Source: Bureau of the Census, Current Population Reports, Series P-25, No. 1017.

migration. California and Florida each gained more than 2 million persons through net immigration in the 1980s, and Texas gained more than 1.2 million. Those three states accounted for more than half of national population growth in the past decade. Almost half the migrants to California are from another country.[42] Marketers can find segments of growth even in states with declining population. An example is the 35- to 54-year-old age cohort, which is increasing in every state.

There are pitfalls associated with concentrating only on growth. Alaska was the fastest growing state in the 1980s and is projected to grow rapidly during the 1990s. Alaska, along with Wyoming, is also one of the least populous states, with only 576,000 people in 1990. This illustrates the trap to avoid of chasing the trend but ignoring the substance. A 10 percent market share in a no-growth market such as Ohio or Michigan may be preferable to a high market share in a rapid-growth but minuscule state such as Alaska or Nevada. Also, the costs of doing business in areas where the infrastructure is already paid for may be lower than in areas with rapidly expanding population.

Canada

Although Canada is the world's largest country at 3.9 million square miles, about 80 percent of all Canadians live within 200 kilometers of the United States–Canada border. This geography creates a market about 4,000 miles long and 125 miles wide. The fact that Canadian consumers are in a horizontal string in contrast to U.S. population clusters is a logistics problem in Canada compared with U.S. retailing that forms distribution circles oriented to urban clusters. Some U.S. distribution centers circle over major Canadian markets, especially Ontario. It often is more efficient to supply Canadian markets from those efficient high-volume distribution circles than from Canada's thin linear supply line. As a consequence, Canadian firms that operate in the northern United States and use those cities as distribution points to Canada may have lower costs than firms operating solely in Canada. Higher distribution costs, higher labor costs, and more developed social programs add to the challenge Canadian firms face in the freer-trade environment of the 1990s.[43] These realities create opportunities for U.S. firms, as you can see in Consumer in Focus 2.4.

The rural areas to the north contain 80 percent of Canada's land but only about 1 percent of the population. The largest market in Canada is a 750-mile megalopolis stretching from Quebec City southwestward through Montreal, Ottawa, Toronto, and the Niagara Peninsula to Windsor. The cities in this area contain about 40 percent of the population, income, and retail sales in Canada. Toronto is Canada's largest city with a population of 3.9 million. The moderate climate and highly developed resource and service industries of British Columbia provide a good base for future growth. The eastern provinces continue to grow the slowest.

Consumer in Focus   **2.4**

Tapping Canadian Markets

Selling hockey sticks to Canada may evoke the "carrying coals to Newcastle" irony, but Bending Branches, a Minneapolis-based company, attributes nearly half its exports to Canadian markets. "The volume is great," says president Dale Kicker, "although it's become difficult with the value of the dollar floating up and down." There are more predictable vexations — government bureaucracy, paperwork, the expense of customs brokerage and freight costs. But Kicker's 22-employee company is typical of the small U.S. businesses that plunge into the Canadian market intuitively, without getting advice on importing, exporting, or setting up a Canadian branch from federal, state, and provincial agencies or private sources of information.

Underserved niche markets in Canada embrace U.S. business, particularly when they cut through the red tape at the border and deliver on time. Some of the fastest growing market segments for exports to Canada include pollution control and equipment, computer software and services, computers and peripherals, and automotive parts and service equipment.

Source: Excerpts from Albert Warson, "Tapping Canadian Markets," Inc. (March 1993), 90–91.

Cities and Consumer Analysis

Cities are the most important unit of analysis in most marketing plans as well as fundamental in determining the prosperity of nations. The forces that create the health of cities are their markets, jobs, technology, transplants (of prosperity to suburbs and exurbs), and capital.[44] Suburbs have grown rapidly, but today **exurbs** — areas beyond the suburbs — are experiencing the fastest growth. Fast-growing counties are often nonmetropolitan or rural but adjacent to suburban or metropolitan areas.

Cities are a fundamental unit of analysis in consumer research, especially in the design of promotional programs. Advertising media are usually bought on a geographic basis — usually cities or the areas surrounding a city reached by the TV signals of the city, called the area of dominant influence (ADI) or designated marketing area (DMA). Some national magazines such as *Time* and *Business Week* sell regional advertising sections on a state or city basis. Print media are moving toward editions based on geographic areas as specific as zip codes.

Analyzing City Data

The analysis of consumer trends by cities requires use of standardized definitions. For example, which city do you believe is largest: San Jose or San Francisco? Columbus or Boston? If you picked San Jose and Columbus, you were correct because the question referred to cities. If the question had referred to metropolitan areas, San Francisco and Boston would have been the better answers. If you asked which metropolitan area had the largest population in the last census, the answer would be New York, but if you asked which had the largest increase in population in the past decade, the answer would be Orlando. Such comparisons of market attractiveness would not be useful without standardized definitions.

The metropolitan statistical area (MSA) is defined as a free-standing metropolitan area, surrounded by nonmetropolitan counties and not closely related with other metropolitan areas. A **primary metropolitan statistical area (PMSA)** is a metropolitan area that is closely related to another city. A grouping of closely related PMSAs is a **consolidated metropolitan statistical area (CMSA)**.

Megalopolis

More than one-third of the people in the United States live in the country's 22 megalopolises or CMSAs. The biggest of these are huge areas made up of many counties and two or more smaller metropolitan areas. The largest of them all is New York–Northern New Jersey–Long Island, with an estimated population of 18 million in 1990. Even though New York City itself has declined in population, the rest of the counties in the CMSA have grown.

The Los Angeles–Anaheim–Riverside CMSA gained more than 1 million people from 1980 to 1990 to give it a population of 14.5 million, well ahead of third-ranking Chicago–Gary–Lake County. When implementing marketing strategies, it is useful to consider that because of the amount of income in metropolitan areas, reaching the New York–Newark–Jersey City CMSA is a market larger than Canada or six of the European Common Market countries.[45]

Cities are especially important for ethnic marketing. More than half of all Americans lived in the 50 largest metro areas in 1990 but more than 70 percent of Asians and Hispanics lived in those areas. Most new immigrants settle in urban areas. New York is the most popular destination, but 37 other metropolitan areas in the United States receive at least 2,000 immigrants a year. Specific cities often attract immigrants from some countries more than others. Illinois has five times as many Polish immigrants as the rest of the United States.

Collecting and Analyzing Demographic Data

You have now studied several major demographic variables, the foundation of market analysis. When you plan a marketing research project or are responsible for a marketing plan to reach consumers, it is likely that demographic analysis of market segments will be your starting point. Where do you find the data to make such analyses? There are so many sources that it is usually safe to assume data exist somewhere on the topic—if only you can figure out where!

Census Data

The most important source of demographic data in Canada is Statistics Canada. In the United States, it is the Bureau of the Census of the U.S. Department of

Commerce. The Census Bureau has become "customer oriented" in recent years and provides a wide variety of publications, newsletters, and data bases in formats ranging from CD-ROM to hard copies. Most of these can be found in a good research library and can be purchased reasonably from the Census Bureau or Government Printing Office.

Consumer analysts pay close attention to the Current Population Reports, known as the "P" series, based on a monthly survey of 60,000 households. On a national basis, the "P-20" series provides reports on marital status, households and families, geographic residence and mobility, fertility, school enrollment, educational attainment, persons of Hispanic origin, and other demographic topics. The "P-23" reports are special studies about such groups as blacks, youth, women, and older people. The "P-27" reports provide data about the farm population, and the "P-60" series reports on consumer income, classified by variables such as race, ethnic origin, age, sex, and education. The "P-25" series is of particular value to marketing planners because it provides projections of the future U.S. population.

In Canada, statistics provide comprehensive market data. Canadian Social Trends provides data on major social indicators as well as trends in income, population, crime, education, housing, and other variables. The most current data are reported in Statistics Canada Daily or on a weekly basis in Informat.

Private Data Firms

Explosive growth has occurred among private firms providing analyses of demographic and economic data. Several of them have formed a consortium of firms to pay for assembly of census data by zip codes. These firms, in return, receive the right to use and sell census data in their form before it becomes available publicly. Private firms often provide specialized analyses to match the general data with specific needs of marketers. Sales Management's *Survey of Buying Power (SBP)*, published in July of each year, contains data on population; effective buying income; and retail sales for all metropolitan areas, states, counties, and cities in the United States and for most metropolitan areas, provinces, counties, and cities in Canada. *American Demographics* publishes a directory each year about where to find demographic information, and individual issues carry advertisements for private data firms.

Demographics and Segmentation

Demographic data are just a beginning point in the measurement of market segments and trends in the marketplace. But they are the essential foundation of market analysis. Without people, there can be no markets. Firms increasingly must analyze their internal records to enhance their data bases about customers. Three key benefits of adding data to internal files include (1) customer profiling that gives direction to marketing, (2) customer segmentation for finding the most profitable customers, and (3) the additional income that can be achieved from list rental.[46]

Although much of the study of consumer behavior involves individual consumers, marketing strategy usually involves many consumers or segments of the total market. That is why this chapter and the next focus on segmentation, one of the most important concepts in the lexicon of marketing. Segmentation is the key to marketing strategy in current markets, but is also essential to understanding markets of the future.

Summary

Market segmentation is a process of so designing or featuring a product or service that it will make a particularly strong appeal to some identifiable subpart of a total market. The alternative is called market aggregation or mass marketing, a process in which all consumers are offered identical products or services.

Evaluating and choosing market segments toward which an organization's resources are to be directed is a process of matching market opportunities with marketing programs. Four criteria for choosing segments include measurability, accessibility, substantiality, and congruity. Measurability refers to the degree to which information is available or obtainable about the size, nature, and behavior of a market segment. Accessibility or reachability refers to the degree to which a given segment can be differentially reached. Substantiality refers to the size of market segments. Congruity refers to the degree to which the members of a market segment fit together. The goal is to find groups of customers with intrasegment congruity also congruous with the firm's ability to market the product.

Once the market has been segmented properly in terms of the four criteria, the firm has three options: (1) concentrated (single segment) marketing, (2) differentiated (multisegment) marketing, and (3) undifferentiated marketing. Many variables or bases can be used to segment a market. Some of these bases include the following categories: (1) geographic, (2) demographic, (3) psychographic, and (4) behavioral. Segmentation analysis plays an essential role in all phases of marketing strategy. Common uses of segmentation include product positioning, promotional strategy, distribution strategy, and price policy. Through data-base management and sophisticated computer software, marketers may come closer to the goal of a "segment of one."

Consumer analysts have responsibilities for monitoring the environment for both macromarketing and micromarketing reasons. Analysis of changing segments is important to this process. Macromarketing applications focus on determining the aggregate performance of marketing in society. Micromarketing analysis focuses on the marketing programs of specific organizations.

The primary financial goal of business firms is ESV. The financial community attributes such value to a company's stock to the degree that the company is perceived to be able to increase profits in the future. Thus, a major role for consumer analysts is to determine trends to help a corporation increase profits in the future. This can be achieved through the 3 M's—more markets, more market share, and more margin.

Population projections involve three variables: births, deaths, and net immigration. Of these, births are usually the most important determinant of population trends and the most difficult to forecast. Births are determined by four variables: age distribution, family structure, social attitudes toward family and children, and technology. These variables contribute to declining fertility in industrialized countries such as the United States and Canada, although NAFTA partner Mexico is experiencing rapid growth in population.

The population base of the United States and Canada is still growing but at a declining rate. It may peak at around 250 to 270 million in the United States and at around 28 million in Canada, depending on fertility assumptions. During the 1990s, both countries will see more first-order babies, more teenagers, more aging baby boomers (but fewer consumers in the 24- to 35-year-old age category), a new era of expanding empty-nesters, and an enormous increase in the YA or mature markets. Each of these categories offers attractive market opportunities for firms that recognize the specialized needs of each segment. Mexico will experience somewhat different trends because of the youth of its population.

A large part of consumer market analysis involves geodemography, the study of demand as it is related to geography. In the United States, population is expanding rapidly in some states—notably California, Texas, and Florida—with slow growth in the Midwest. In Canada, Ontario is the largest market but population growth in all provinces is slow as a result of decreased fertility and immigration rates.

Review and Discussion Questions

1. Why does market segmentation exist? Is the use of market segmentation strategies by organizations harmful or helpful to consumers and to society?

2. What are some of the most common bases used for market segmentation?

3. What criteria for selecting segments should be used by an organization using market segmentation strategies?

4. Distinguish between macromarketing and micromarketing. How does the work of consumer analysts vary between these two fields?

5. Is the concept of ESV (enhanced shareholder value) a socially defensible objective for business corporations? Wouldn't society be better off by focusing on the needs of society and giving the money shareholders receive to poor consumers?

6. How does the concept of ESV compare with traditional goals such as market share, profitability, and sales?

7. "Analysis of consumer trends is obviously important for firms marketing consumer products but of limited value to industrial marketers." Evaluate this statement.

8. Will there be more or fewer births in the future in the United States? What variables should be considered in answering this question?

9. Assume a marketer of major appliances is interested in the effects of the baby boomers on demand for the company's products. What are your conclusions,

and what, if any, research should be conducted to answer the question more fully?

10. "Maturity markets are growing in number very rapidly, but they are of little interest to marketers because they have little money compared with younger markets." Analyze this statement.

11. What are the main similarities and the main differences in the population structures of the United States, Mexico, and Canada? Why should consumer analysts in these countries have an interest in understanding consumer markets in the other countries?

12. "Cities are the key to marketing plans." How would you evaluate this statement?

13. Find and interview a firm that specializes in the analysis of consumer trend or demographic data. How are such analyses used by marketing organizations?

Endnotes

1. James W. Harvey, "Benefit Segmentation for Fund Raisers," *Journal of the Academy of Marketing Science* 18 (Winter 1990), 77–86.

2. Paul E. Green and Abba M. Krieger, "Segmenting Markets with Conjoint Analysis," *Journal of Marketing* 55 (October 1991), 20–31.

3. Joel S. Dubow, "Occasion-Based vs. User-Based Benefit Segmentation: A Case Study," *Journal of Advertising Research* 32 (March–April 1992), 11–18.

4. For a helpful discussion of this strategy and its rationale, see David W. Stewart, "Consumer Self-Selection and Segments of One: The Growing Role of Consumers in Segmentation," in Rebecca H. Holman and Michael R. Solomon, eds., *Advances in Consumer Research* 18 (Provo, Utah: Association for Consumer Research, 1991), 179–186. For some helpful examples, see Renee Zabor, "An Application of Segmentation Research in the Travel and Leisure Industry: The Case of Hilton Hotels," in Holman and Solomon, *Advances,* 176–177; and Ronald Hoverstad, Charles W. Lamb, Jr., and Patrick Miller, "College Benefit Segmentation Analysis: Approach and Results," in Thomas R. Srull, *Advances in Consumer Research* 16 (Provo, Utah: Association for Consumer Research, 1989), 332–338.

5. Martin R. Lautman, "End-Benefit Segmentation and Prototypical Bonding," *Journal of Advertising Research* 31 (June–July 1991), 9–18.

6. Jan Larson, "A Segment of One," *American Demographics* (December 1991), 16–17.

7. George Katona, *Psychological Economics* (New York: Elsevier Scientific Publishing, 1975).

8. For more information on this topic, see Alfred Rappaport, *Creating Shareholder Value: The New Standard for Business Performance* (Glencoe, Ill.: Free Press, 1986).

9. J. Randall Woolridge, "Competitive Decline: Is a Myopic Stock Market to Blame?" *Journal of Applied Corporate Finance* 1 (Spring 1988), 26–36.

10. John C. Narver and Stanley F. Slater, "The Effect of a Market Orientation on Business Profitability," *Journal of Marketing* 54 (October 1990), 20–35.

11. Peter Lynch, *Beating the Street* (New York: Simon & Schuster, 1993).

12. Bernard J. LaLonde, Martha C. Cooper, and Thomas G. Noordewier, *Customer Service: A Management Perspective* (Oak Brook, Ill.: Council of Logistics Management, 1988); and Martha C. Cooper, Daniel E. Innis, and Peter R. Dickson, *Planning for Logistics* (Oak Brook, Ill.: Council of Logistics Management, 1992).

13. Definitions in this section are based on Arthur Haupt and Thomas T. Kane, *Population Handbook* (Washington, D.C.: Population Reference Bureau, 1985).

14. "Fertility of American Women," Series P-20, No. 427 (Washington, D.C.: U.S. Government Printing Office, 1988).

15. Joseph O. Rentz and Fred D. Reynolds, "Forecasting the Effects of an Aging Population on Product Consumption: An Age-Period-Cohort Framework," *Journal of Marketing Research* 28 (August 1991), 355–360.

16. Thomas G. Exter, "Big Spending on Little Ones," *American Demographics* 14 (February 1992), 6.

17. James U. McNeal, "The Littlest Shoppers," *American Demographics* 14 (February 1992), 48–53.

18. Horst Stipp, "New Ways to Reach Children," *American Demographics* 15 (August 1993), 50–56.

19. Betsy Spethmann, "Focus Groups Key to Reaching Kids," *Advertising Age* (February 10, 1992).

20. James U. McNeal and Chyon-Hwa Yeh, "Born to Shop," *American Demographics* 15 (June 1993), 34–39.

21. Dennis H. Tootelian and Ralph M. Gaedeke, "The Teen Market: An Exploratory Analysis of Income, Spending, and Shopping Patterns," *Journal of Consumer Marketing* 9 (Fall 1992).

22. Roger D. Blackwell and Margaret Hanke, "The Credit Card and the Aging Baby Boomers," *Journal of Retail Banking* 9 (Spring 1987), 17–25.

23. For additional examples, see Dale Blackwell and Roger Blackwell, "Yuppies, Muppies and Puppies: They Are Changing Real Estate Markets," *Ohio Realtor* (August 1989), 11–15.

24. Robert E. Wilkes, "A Structural Modeling Approach to the Measurement and Meaning of Cognitive Age," *Journal of Consumer Research* 19 (September 1992), 292–301.

25. Nancy Stephens, "Cognitive Age: A Useful Concept for Advertising?" *Journal of Advertising* 20 (December 1991), 37–48.

26. George Moschis, "Marketing to Older Adults," *Journal of Consumer Marketing* 8 (Fall 1991), 33–41.

27. Paula Fitzgerald Bone, "Identifying Mature Segments," *Journal of Consumer Marketing* 8 (Fall 1991), 19–32.

28. Thomas Moehrle, "Expenditure Patterns of the Elderly: Workers and Nonworkers," *Monthly Labor Review* 113 (May 1990), 34–41.

29. Benny Barak, "Elderly Solitary Survivors and Social Policy: The Case for Widows," in Andrew Mitchell, *Advances in Consumer Research* (1984), 27–30.

30. Ivan Ross, "Information Processing and the Older Consumer: Marketing and Public Policy Implications," in Mitchell, *Advances*, 31–39.

31. Nark D. Uncles and Andrew S. C. Ehrenberg, "Brand Choice among Older Consumers," *Journal of Advertising Research* 30 (August–September 1990), 19–22.

32. Alan J. Greco and Linda E. Swayne, "Sales Response of Elderly Consumers to Point-of-Purchase Advertising," *Journal of Advertising Research* 32 (September–October 1992), 43–53.

33. Elaine Sherman and Philip Cooper, "Life Satisfaction: The Missing Focus of Marketing to Seniors," *Journal of Health Care Marketing* 9 (March 1988), 69–71.

34. Mary Walker and M. Carole Macklin, "The Use of Role Modeling in Targeting Advertising to Grandparents," *Journal of Advertising Research* 32 (July–August 1992), 37–44.

35. Ken Dychtwald, quoted in Curtis Hartman, "Redesigning America," *Inc.* 10 (June 1988), 59–69.

36. Barbara Boyle Torrey, Kevin Kinsella, and Cynthia M. Taeuber, *An Aging World* (Washington, D.C.: Bureau of the Census, 1987), 7.

37. "1992: Europe's Year of the Elderly," *Market: Europe* (February 1993), 8–9.

38. For details, see Roger D. Blackwell, "The Rising Importance of Consumer Affairs Departments," *Mobius: Journal of Consumer Affairs Professionals* (Fall 1990).

39. Claes Fornell and Birger Wernerfelt, "Defensive Marketing Strategy by Customer Complaint Management: A Theoretical Analysis," *Journal of Marketing Research* 24 (November 1987), 337–346.

40. Carl Sewell, *Customers For Life* (New York: Doubleday Currency, 1990).

41. Blackwell and Hanke, "The Credit Card and the Aging Baby Boomers."

42. "Growth Isn't Always Good for Business," *American Demographics* 15 (July 1993), 20–21.

43. Randall Litchfield, "Competitiveness and the Constitution," *Canadian Business* (August 1991), 18.

44. Jane Jacobs, *Cities and the Wealth of Nations* (New York: Random House, 1984).

45. "Megalopolis," *American Demographics* 6 (January 1984), 50–51.

46. Thomas Kobak, "How to Unmask Your Customers," *American Demographics* 15 (July 1993), 52–55.

CHAPTER 3

Global Consumer Markets: Structure and Strategy

▲▲

The Jaegermeister Invasion

Many might think it nearly impossible to import and sell a German medicinal-like cordial to rowdy U.S. college crowds. But not Sidney Frank, an eager U.S. distributor. All it took was product repositioning, promotion, and vision.

While visiting a New York City bar in the 1970s, Frank got his first taste of Jaegermeister, a thick, auburn cordial, which, according to even its most loyal fans, tastes like a concoction of licorice, herbs, and Vicks Formula 44. Europeans have been sipping warm Jaegermeister after their meals for almost 60 years. Its 56 herbs and spices are touted to aid digestion. Its 35 percent alcohol content definitely aids relaxation.

Enthusiastic about the cordial, Frank visited the Jaegermeister distillery located in Wolfenbuettel, Germany. There he persuaded the Mast family, who owns the brand, to grant him distribution rights for the southeastern portion of the United States. After bringing the product home, Frank quickly found that he would have to adapt the product to the U.S. market if he wanted to sell a significant volume of the cordial. Southerners certainly did not want to drink a warm liquor during sweltering months.

Frank had the good fortune of visiting a bar in New Orleans that was serving cold shots of Jaegermeister from a bottle they were keeping in the freezer. It was a hit. Frank showed other bars how to serve the drink cold, and sales soon were Wunderbar! By 1985, Frank had the distribution rights for the rest of the United States and a desire to get the Jaegermeister message out on a national basis. After one failed advertising campaign, he tried selling Jaegermeister with help from the one thing he thought would interest young men the most—young women. The Jaegerettes were born.

The first Jaegerette worked in a New York bar spraying samplings of Jaegermeister into the mouths of willing patrons. Soon she hired other Jaegerettes to help her. Frank now employs 400 Jaegerettes nationwide, each earning $25 per hour, costing $1 million annually. Roughly $5 million goes to other promotional materials, such as T-shirts, Frisbees, and pennants handed out by the Jaegerettes at Jaegermeister parties. Frank is rapidly expanding distribution to include niche markets, such as rock 'n' roll clubs, black nightclubs, and gay bars. For the latter, Frank is now hiring Jaegerdudes.

Some critics say this method of promotion is unsophisticated. Frank does not seem to mind. Jaegermeister sales jumped more than 30 percent to 350,000 cases, in 1992 ranking it as the nation's fourth imported cordial, behind Kahlua, Bailey's Irish Creme, and Grand Marnier. As for Sidney Frank Importing Co., it had revenues of $42 million last year, 80 percent of which came from hefty Jaegermeister sales. With eager assistance of college students and Yuppies nationwide, Frank has transformed a German medicinal cordial into a trendy new drink. Even the critics admit, ice-cold Jaegermeister is really hot.

Source: Based on Christopher Palermi, "Meet the Jaegerettes," Forbes (February 15, 1993), 108–112.

Global Marketing Strategy

In the last chapter, you learned how to analyze how consumers behave as segments of a total market. Only domestic segments were examined, although "domestic" segments include Canada, Mexico, and the United States since NAFTA took effect at the beginning of 1994. In this chapter, we broaden the horizon to examine global market segments and how to reach them with global marketing strategies.

Ethnocentricity, or focusing on one's own way of doing things with little sensitivity or interest in the ways of the rest of the world, is a disease that infects many people, including those that manage many American organizations. However, ethnocentric managers are becoming increasingly an endangered species.

Perhaps no manager should be promoted to a position of major responsibility in a contemporary organization if that individual cannot "think globally." Thinking globally involves the ability to understand markets beyond one's own country of origin with respect to

1. Sources of demand

2. Sources of supply

3. Methods of effective management and marketing

Consumer in Focus 3.1 illustrates each of these three elements and shows how Liebert International continues to succeed by thinking globally.

The globalization of marketing requires managers of all types to understand the broad forces that characterize contemporary markets. The forces affecting globalization and international competition have been identified by Michael Porter to include the following:

1. *Growing similarity of countries*—in terms of available infrastructure, distribution channels, and marketing approaches

2. *Fluid global capital markets*—national capital markets are growing into global capital markets because of the large flow of funds between countries

3. *Technological restructuring*—the reshaping of competition globally as a result of technological revolutions such as in microelectronics

4. *Integrating role of technology*—reduced cost and increased impact of products have made them accessible to more global consumers

5. *New global competitors*—a shift in competition from traditional country competitors to emerging global competitors.[1]

Some countries have more experience in these areas than others. The Netherlands is such a country. It has a history of global trading and operations stretching over 400 years, as Figure 3.1 shows. The Dutch East India Co. dominated the world economically for many years, and Holland was the second largest owner of U.S. investments until recently. It is no wonder that companies such as Unilever, Shell, KLM, and Phillips have achieved global success.

Importance of Global Thinking in Marketing

Emergence of the multinational enterprises (MNE) or corporations with operations in multiple countries makes it essential that managers have the ability to "think globally." Corporations such as Coca-Cola, IBM, Gillette, Nestle, Sony, and Unilever derive more than 50 percent of their sales outside their country of domicile. Figure 3.2 examines how firms such as Wal-Mart, The Body Shop, and the 3M Co. implement global thinking to expand profits.

Globalization is not limited to large corporations. Small, relatively obscure companies with specialized "niches" or market segments that transcend national boundaries are likely to export and be successful. In fact, 80 percent of the 100,000 U.S. companies that export are small businesses.[2] Because of their size, small firms tend to be flexible and adapt to local markets well. The Brooklyn Brewery, a small New York brewery, found much success in Japan because of a gimmick its Japanese distributor developed. By flying the beer to Tokyo versus shipping it by boat and dating each bottle, Brooklyn Brewery positioned its beer as "fresh from the brewery." This attribute impressed the Japanese consumer so much that the beer now sells for $15 per bottle.[3]

Exporting is the form of global business most commonly discussed because it has been practiced for hundreds of years; however, global sourcing has proved profitable for companies in recent decades. Resource capabilities may emphasize labor costs in one country, raw materials in another, and information technologies in still others. The Limited can be classified as a global company

| 3.1 | **Consumer in Focus** |

Liebert Growth Leaps with Global Thinking

Prosperity for firms and individuals increasingly is based on the ability to think globally. An interview with Karsten Boerger, president of Liebert International, examines the type of global thinking needed to survive and prosper in a global economy.

Liebert is the leading global producer of computer support systems for environmental control and site monitoring. It is also the world's leading supplier of precise power distribution, power protection, and voltage regulation equipment for computer, industrial, and telecommunications applications.

"If we were not a global company, we would be a much smaller company," said Boerger at Liebert's headquarters in Columbus, Ohio. As CEO of Liebert International, Boerger has seen export sales grow from $5 million to about $50 million in 10 years, with global sales accounting for close to 50 percent of total Liebert sales.

Boerger explains, "Liebert associates know that international business is important to their jobs, so they go the extra mile for global exports." That sometimes means 10-day production schedules for export to China instead of the slower pace acceptable for domestic markets. Boerger adds, "Our employees have not seen the recession our competitors have, because of our ability to compete in international markets."

All three components of global thinking as described in this chapter are apparent at Liebert. Future and present managers can learn from Liebert's global success.

First, effective managers must be able to implement effective global marketing strategies, including selling in other countries. Liebert's Hong Kong office provides an example of the results of Boerger's change from selling through distributors around the world to going directly to most of its global markets. In 1987, Liebert Hong Kong Limited, headed by Roger Chen, U.S.-educated and Liebert-trained, replaced the local distributor. The office soared from $600,000 sales to $19.5 million in 1992, with a staff of nearly 50 people. This office supports and coordinates with offices in Beijing, Shanghai, Chengdu, Guangzhou, Seoul, Taipei, and others. This approach is consistent with the strategy of Liebert's parent, Emerson Electric, for increasing commitment to Asia/Pacific markets.

Global sales are also strengthened by the freedom Liebert gives its foreign offices to make decisions based on local situations. Liebert believes in recruiting outstanding people from its international markets to run its global offices. It places a great deal of trust in them and supports them with the rest of its global manufacturing and service force.

Continued

because of its sourcing procedures. Clothing designs are conceived in Italy and other countries, the garments are produced in Asia and Eastern Europe by local manufacturers, and shipped over global logistics networks to the United States, where they are distributed to more than 3,600 retail outlets including The Limited, Express, Victoria's Secret, Abercrombie and Fitch, Lerner, Lane Bryant, and Henri Bendel. A company that sources globally can be considered a global company even if it never sells a product outside its country of domicile.

Consumer in Focus, Continued **3.1**

Boerger points out that Liebert does not try to implement a standardized approach around the globe. Liebert International is run with few universal rules because every country has different ways of doing things — different power requirements, different shipping methods, and so forth. Instead of trying to sell standard American products to other countries, Liebert designs products that fit the special requirements of each country. U.S. product engineers, for example, go to Japan to be sure that U.S.-made products have the correct Japanese legend or Japanese gauges. This may be one of the most important principles to learn from Liebert's approach to global thinking.

Liebert also sources globally by manufacturing in several countries, including Italy, the United Kingdom, and Ireland. "If you are not manufacturing in the European Community, you are out of business," Boerger observes. However, European manufacturers face high wages, heavy social welfare costs, 6-week vacations, and 37 1/2-work weeks, and thus, decreased cost-efficiency. Although manufacturing in Liebert's U.S. plant is very efficient, fluctuations in the dollar and local requirements create a need for global manufacturing plants.

Liebert's global sourcing practices allow U.K. managers to get help from Liebert's Taiwan purchasing person to buy components that are cheaper and better than European components. Liebert's sourcing includes working with an Indian firm that has developed such sophisticated design engineering and computer software that it can provide designs for Liebert products better and far more quickly than California suppliers.

The third area of global thinking that can be observed at Liebert is its ability to absorb the best in management and marketing methods, process engineering, and product improvements from around the world. When Liebert personnel compete with the best manufacturers and marketers in every part of the world, it helps to know about different cultures and speak different languages. Liebert is strong in Japan, so it knows about the latest Japanese advances in products and processes, something a nonglobal firm would find difficult. Boerger observes, "We benefit greatly by adopting the best from the best competitors throughout the world."

There is one important caveat in this process, however. Boerger points out that a global competitor must be careful not to add every feature from every part of the world. "To do so would price us out of the market . . . there is no such thing as a global product for our firm. Maybe for a TV or radio but not in our company, or even in cars. We must produce the right product specifically for each country."

Source: Excerpted from S. Hassan and R. Blackwell, "How Liebert Grows by Thinking Globally," Global Marketing Perspectives and Cases (1994), 9–11.

The corporate cultures of today's successful organizations also are increasingly global. Volkswagen in Germany recently appointed a president from the United States and a Spanish purchasing director. The president of Coca-Cola came from Cuba. IBM appointed an American to head its European Division, which includes Africa and the Middle East, and General Motors turned to Canada and Germany for leadership to rejuvenate the firm. Global managers must be able to learn a new language quickly, speak at least two languages

Figure 3.1   Global Companies Do Well in an Environment That Understands Global Business

Sources: Courtesy of Netherlands Foreign Investment Agency

fluently, understand the structure and culture of any country in the world, and work effectively with people from any country. Consumer analysts can play a key role in this process by identifying structural, cultural, and ethnic differences and similarities among markets in different countries.

Global market analysis starts with understanding markets on a global basis in terms of the people, their needs, their ability to buy, and their willingness to spend. Today's consumers choose not only from products made in many countries, but from ideas, advertisements, and friends representing a diversity of nations and cultures. Their willingness to buy is also affected by cultural, ethnic, and motivation variables. Because consumer analysts must help design strategies to reach these consumers, the following pages show how to analyze

---

Figure 3.2   Going Global: Different Strokes for Different Folks

Global Sources of Demand: Wal-Mart Sells to Mexico

- Many were surprised when Wal-Mart, the all-American retailer, announced it would be opening retail locations in Mexico. In a joint venture with CIFRA, SA, a Mexican counterpart, Wal-Mart took its winning Sam's Wholesale Club concept south of the border. It appears under the name Club Aurrera, named after CIFRA's phenomenally sucessful hypermarket chain.

- If it is true that one of the largest obstacles for a U.S.-based company to succeed in a foreign country is lack of familiarity with the market, a joint venture with an established local force largely eliminates a foreign business's biggest problem. Wal-Mart saw this global expansion as a way to expand profits, and others are following suit. Among the companies that have either recently entered or expanded their presence in Mexico are McDonald's, Kentucky Fried Chicken, Colombo Yogurt, Blockbuster Video, Wendy's, and Domino's Pizza.

Gobal Sources of Supply: The Body Shop Shops the Globe

- The Body Shop, a cosmetic company dedicated to the research, development, manufacturing, and distribution of healthy beauty care products for men and women, was founded in 1976 by Ms. Anita Roddick and was housed in a small store in Brighton, England. Almost 20 years and more than 800 locations later, The Body Shop has become a global success.

- One characteristic that makes The Body Shop a truly unique company is its sourcing procedures. Its global concern extends beyond selling in foreign markets; it includes sourcing in Third World countries. Roddick and her team search throughout the world for new beauty secrets, which often takes them to remote ends of the world. For example, The Body Shop uses Brazil nut oil gathered and extracted by South American tribes. It also uses a variety of natural ingredients harvested and partially processed by various groups throughout Third World countries.

Continued

Figure 3.2   Continued

Global Management and Marketing: 3M Employs the World

- European expansion often requires a "Euromanager," who can manage cultural diversity, understand foreign markets, and is willing to travel or take temporary assignments in other countries to increase his or her understanding of a foreign market.

- Claire-Noelle Bigay is one of those Euromanagers. As one of a new European "core team" for 3M, she spends more than one-third of her time traveling outside France. Her colleagues are a Dutch woman in Germany, a Belgian, an Italian, and two Britons who all communicate in English, yet are fluent in at least one other language. 3M has learned to breed such managers successfully as a result of its "top management's internationalism."

- Reorganization at 3M has consisted of two steps. First, the company has shifted most strategic and operational responsibility to 19 product divisions, or Business Centres, with European responsibilities rather than to national subsidiaries as was done in the past. This allows all European and American units to report to one boss with global responsibilities. Second, the remaining geographic responsibilities have been shifted away from the smaller countries to several new European "regions". This allows greater efficiency in functions such as logistics and information technology.

Sources: Roger D. Blackwell, Kristina S. Blackwell, and W. Wayne Talarzyk, "Wal-Mart in Mexico," in Contemporary Cases in Consumer Behavior, (Fort Worth: The Dryden Press, 1993), 436–441; Blackwell, Blackwell, and Talarzyk, "The Body Shop," in Contemporary Cases in Consumer Behavior, 17–25; "Here, There and Everywhere," Financial Times (November 10, 1993).

---

variables cross-culturally. The last part of the chapter examines marketing opportunities in some specific countries of the world beyond North America.

Structure of Global Markets

The world population is approximately 5.4 billion and growing at the rate of about 1.7 percent annually.[4] That represents a decline from a 2.04 percent growth rate in the 1960s and reversal of two centuries of increasing growth rates.

Demographers expect the growth rate to continue to decline to between 1.4 and 1.5 percent in the year 2000 and zero toward the end of the twenty-first century. Even though the rate is declining, the numbers added are still growing about 83 million people each year and will increase to abut 86 million people added each year in the 1990s, peaking at 89 million added in the year 2000 when the world's population is estimated by the United Nations to be about 6.1 billion. After that, the numbers added each year are projected to decline but will still produce a world population of 10.2 billion by the last decade of the twenty-first century, when population in absolute numbers should begin to decline.[5]

The population of a country is affected by natural growth variables of fertility and death rates as well as migration rates. Birthrates are declining in industrialized nations. The primary reasons are higher educational attainment, urbanization, rising standards of living, legal abortion, more effective methods of contraception, widespread sterilization, increased labor force participation of women, high divorce rates, and delayed marriage and childbearing. Emigration from developing countries to developed countries is increasing rapidly. The best-educated and relatively affluent segments of the population are often the ones who emigrate.

Important global population trends can be summarized as

1. Prolonged below-replacement fertility in developed nations

2. Rapid growth despite falling fertility in developing nations

3. Rapid urbanization in less-developed countries (LDC) with unprecedented migration from poor LDCs to more affluent industrialized nations

Fast- and Slow-Growth Markets

Growth-oriented firms, striving for enhanced shareholder value (ESV), depend on consumer analysts to find the most promising global market segments in which the firm should commit resources to achieve its growth objectives. This process requires, but is not limited to, accurate projections of world population trends. Let's examine where the growth markets are—and are not—focusing first on population growth. We will later add the important variable of ability to buy to the market attractiveness equation.

Birth Dearth

The ability to buy has been concentrated historically in North America, Europe, and Japan. However, these affluent countries are expecting either a decline or slight increase in population in the next decade. Industrialized countries such as the United States, Canada, Israel, and Australia are projected to decline from 15 percent of the world's population in 1985 to barely 5 percent in the year 2100.[6] Table 3.1 shows that population in the European Common Market is expected to increase slightly between 1993 and 2010. Actual decline in population

Table 3.1	World Population Growth (Population in Millions)		
	1993	**2010**	**Percentage Change**
United States	258.3	298.6	15.6
Western Europe			
Austria	7.9	8.2	3.8
Belgium	10.1	10.1	0.0
Denmark	5.2	5.2	0.0
France	57.7	58.8	1.9
Germany	81.1	78.2	−3.6
Greece	10.5	10.9	3.8
Italy	57.8	56.4	−2.4
Luxembourg	0.4	0.4	0.0
Norway	4.3	4.5	4.7
Sweden	8.7	9.0	3.4
United Kingdom	58.0	59.9	3.3
Eastern Europe			
Bulgaria	9.0	8.9	−1.1
Hungary	10.3	10.4	1.0
Poland	38.5	41.3	10.7
Other developed countries			
Australia	17.8	20.9	17.4
Canada	28.1	32.7	16.4
Japan	124.8	130.4	4.5
New Zealand	3.4	3.9	14.7
Developing countries			
Bangladesh	113.9	164.8	44.7
Brazil	152.0	185.6	22.1
China	1,178.5	1,397.8	18.6
Guatemala	10.0	15.8	58.0
Hong Kong	5.8	6.3	8.6
India	897.4	1,166.2	30.0
Indonesia	187.6	238.8	27.3
Israel	5.3	6.9	30.2
Mexico	90.0	118.5	31.7
Philippines	64.6	85.5	32.4
South Africa	39.0	55.9	43.3
Singapore	2.8	3.2	14.3
Uruguay	3.2	3.5	9.4

Source: 1993 World Population Data Sheet, The Population Bureau, Inc. (1993).

is projected in some European countries, and Japan is projected to increase about half the rate of the United States and Canada. Slow population growth was one of the reasons stimulating the formation of the European Community.

Fast-Growth Populations

Some countries are projected to grow rapidly. These countries can be identified in Table 3.1 by examining their population percentage changes and the changing rank of countries shown in Table 3.2.

The fastest growing country in the world is India. If current trends continue, India will surpass China as the most populous country in the world in the next century. Kenya is the fastest growing country by percentage increase, rising approximately 4.2 percent annually. Although Kenya is relatively small in size, its 1988 population of 23 million is expected to quadruple by the year 2025. Kenya is a land of economic potential because of its abundance of export commodities such as coffee and tea. However, as a consumer market, it does have some problems. With the average woman bearing about eight children in her lifetime, just keeping up with the basic needs of a surging population will strain already limited resources.

Another fast-growing country is Bangladesh, the ninth most populous nation in the world and growing rapidly. Between 1983 and 2000, 52 million people are projected to be added to Bangladesh's population. That is roughly equivalent to a country with the population of France being added to a state the size of Georgia.

The dramatic effect of the growth rates of developed and developing countries is indicated in Table 3.2. In 1950, only 8 of the 15 most-populated countries were developing countries. Currently, the number is 10, and by the year 2050, it is projected to be 13, and only 3 of the 30 most-populated countries will be industrialized countries.

The changing rank of developing countries will produce some dramatic changes over the next few decades. By the year 2025, Iran and Ethiopia will join the list of the 15 largest countries, whereas Japan is expected to drop from seventh to twentieth. Perhaps the greatest changes for consumer analysts to monitor are countries such as Nigeria and Pakistan, which were thirteenth and fourteenth in 1950 but which are expected to move to third and fourth place by the year 2050. Among Latin American countries, Brazil is expected to retain its rank as one of the ten largest countries in the future.

Finding countries with the largest populations is not the only challenge facing companies wanting to expand their profits. From a market perspective, the greatest challenge for the "rich" countries that hope to have growing markets for their products in the future is to assist the "poor" countries in developing themselves to where they also are rich enough to be economically strong markets.

Table 3.2	Countries Ranked by Population Size: 1950, 1987, 2025, and 2050		
1950	**1987**	**2025**	**2050**
1. **China**	1. **China**	1. **China**	1. **India**
2. **India**	2. **India**	2. **India**	2. **China**
3. Soviet Union	3. Soviet Union	3. Former Soviet Union	3. **Nigeria**
4. United States	4. United States	4. **Indonesia**	4. **Pakistan**
5. Japan	5. **Indonesia**	5. **Nigeria**	5. Former Soviet Union
6. **Indonesia**	6. **Brazil**	6. United States	6. **Brazil**
7. **Brazil**	7. Japan	7. **Brazil**	7. **Indonesia**
8. United Kingdom	8. **Nigeria**	8. **Pakistan**	8. United States
9. West Germany	9. **Bangladesh**	9. **Bangladesh**	9. **Bangladesh**
10. Italy	10. **Pakistan**	10. **Iran**	10. **Iran**
11. **Bangladesh**	11. **Mexico**	11. **Ethiopia**	11. **Ethiopia**
12. France	12. **Vietnam**	12. **Mexico**	12. **Philippines**
13. **Nigeria**	13. **Philippines**	13. **Philippines**	13. **Mexico**
14. **Pakistan**	14. West Germany	14. **Vietnam**	14. **Vietnam**
15. **Mexico**	15. Italy	15. Japan	15. **Kenya**
16. Spain	16. United Kingdom	16. **Egypt**	16. **Zaire**
17. **Vietnam**	17. France	17. **Turkey**	17. **Egypt**
18. Poland	18. **Thailand**	18. **Zaire**	18. **Tanzania**
19. **Egypt**	19. **Turkey**	19. **Kenya**	19. **Turkey**
20. **Philippines**	20. **Egypt**	20. **Thailand**	20. Japan
21. **Turkey**	21. **Iran**	21. **Tanzania**	21. **Saudi Arabia**
22. **South Korea**	22. **Ethiopia**	22. **Burma**	22. **Thailand**
23. **Ethiopia**	23. **South Korea**	23. **South Africa**	23. **Uganda**
24. **Thailand**	24. Spain	24. **Sudan**	24. **Sudan**
25. **Burma**	25. **Burma**	25. **South Korea**	25. **Burma**
26. East Germany	26. Poland	26. France	26. **South Africa**
27. **Argentina**	27. **South Africa**	27. United Kingdom	27. **Syria**
28. **Iran**	28. **Zaire**	28. Italy	28. **Morocco**
29. Yugoslavia	29. **Argentina**	29. West Germany	29. **Algeria**
30. Romania	30. **Colombia**	30. **Uganda**	30. **Iraq**

Note: Developing countries are shown in boldface.
Source: Bureau of the Census, World Population Profile, 1987 (Washington, D.C.: U.S. Department of Commerce, 1987), 5.

Economic Resources and Market Attractiveness

The most attractive markets are countries that are growing both in population and in economic resources. Economic resources, or ability to buy, can be measured in various ways. Per capita income is an important indicator, although there are problems, such as the currency with which it will be measured and the purchasing power of income within a country. One of the most valid indicators is "hours required to purchase" standard consumer goods. For example, consumers might require 11 hours at an average wage to purchase a standard television receiver in the United States but as much as 11 months in some developing countries. Unfortunately, such data are not readily available for market analysis purposes.

A useful indicator of "ability to buy" is a country's Gross National Product (GNP) or Gross Domestic Product (GDP) per capita. Even though the statistic does not reflect variations in distribution between countries, per capital GNP or GDP is a commonly accepted indicator of market attractiveness. These data for some major countries are presented in Table 3.3.

Three other indicators of market attractiveness are natural increase (percentage increase in population each year considering births and deaths), life expectancy, and urban population (as a percentage of total population). Market indicators are shown in Table 3.3, where data are presented for the countries appearing in Table 3.1. Data for additional countries are available from the Population Reference Bureau.

The search for both population growth and ability to buy increasingly takes consumer analysts to the Pacific Rim. Hong Kong, Singapore, Malaysia, and South Korea have much higher population growth rates than Europe and relatively high incomes. China and India are attracting the interest of world marketers because of the size of the population bases and the rapidity of their growth. Although low GNP is a disadvantage when selling in these countries, it is an advantage to those firms sourcing in these countries.

Cultural Analysis of Global Markets

After market structures are examined, consumer analysts must focus on cultural analysis. This involves the ability to understand and be effective in communicating with the core values of a society. Ethnographic analysis of marketing focuses on the interactive processes of exchange with particular attention to the subtle nuances and orderliness of the selling process.[7] Hawrysh and Zaichkowsky[8] showed how ethnographic information can also be useful in business negotiation processes. By understanding the different styles, habits, and skills of each party involved, negotiation strategies are more likely to be successful.

Marketing practitioners need cultural empathy, defined as the ability to understand the inner logic and coherence of other ways of life. Cultural empathy includes restraint not to judge the value of other ways of life. Consumer analysis focuses on "meaning systems" of consumers in a nation that are intelligible within the cultural context of that country.

Global strategies should be adapted to meaning systems of the market rather than attempting to change the market to the customary marketing programs of

Table 3.3	Market Data for Selected Major Countries, 1993		
Country	Natural Increase (%/Yr)	Life Expectancy (Yrs)	Per Capita GNP (US$)
United States	0.8	75	22,560
Western Europe			
Austria	0.2	76	20,380
Belgium	0.2	76	19,300
Denmark	0.1	75	23,660
France	0.4	77	20,600
Germany	−0.1	75	23,650*
Greece	0.1	76	6,230
Italy	0.0	77	18,580
Luxembourg	0.3	76	31,080
Norway	0.4	77	24,160
Sweden	0.3	78	25,490
United Kingdom	0.3	76	16,750
Eastern Europe			
Bulgaria	−0.2	71	1,840
Hungary	−0.2	70	2,690
Poland	0.3	71	1,830
Other developed countries			
Australia	0.8	77	16,590
Canada	0.8	77	21,260
Japan	0.3	79	26,920
New Zealand	1.0	75	12,140
Developing countries			
Bangladesh	2.4	53	220
Brazil	1.5	67	2,920
China	1.2	70	370
Guatemala	3.1	63	930
Hong Kong	0.7	78	13,200
India	2.1	59	330
Indonesia	1.7	59	610
Israel	1.5	76	11,330
Mexico	2.3	70	2,870
Philippines	2.5	64	740
South Africa	2.6	64	2,530
Singapore	1.3	74	12,890
Uruguay	0.9	73	2,860

*Former West Germany only.

Source: 1993 World Population Data Sheet, The Population Bureau, Inc. (1993).

the firm. For example, firms in the United States typically spend about 3 percent of sales on advertising. In nations such as Australia, the advertising/sales ratio is typically between 7 and 8 percent, in Sweden about 5 percent, in Mexico a little more than 5 percent, and in Canada between 4 and 5 percent.[9] An American company entering Australia may underbudget for advertising according to local practices.

The marketplace is changing rapidly. Global marketers find it useful to track global trends to predict and better understand how consumers in various parts of the world will be changing. Table 3.4 lists some of the trends shaping the world. See how many ideas you can formulate as to how the global marketplace might change in the next decade and how as a marketer these changes would affect your marketing strategies.

Cross-Cultural Analysis

Cross-cultural analysis is the systematic comparison of similarities and differences in the material and behavioral aspects of cultures. Anthropologists have developed techniques to catalog similarities and differences among peoples of various cultures. Remarkable similarities are found in the methods people use to handle common problems among societies located so far apart that they could not possibly have come into contact with each other.

Cross-cultural research methodology involves standard research techniques adapted to the special requirements of different languages, structural characteristics of the societies, and values of the investigator. Cross-cultural studies in anthropology often focus on social organization, child rearing, belief systems, and similar topics. In marketing, the elements studied are more likely to be distribution systems, beliefs about sales and pricing activities, and communications channels.

All cross-cultural studies are either descriptive or analytical in nature. Descriptive studies describe structural components and are used to contrast or compare societies, whereas analytical or functional studies attempt to deduce general principles of behavior that apply in one or more cultures.[10]

Cultural analysis assists researchers in understanding the consumer behavior of diverse nations and diverse groups within a nation. In Africa, for example, tribal cultures within countries such as Zambia, Nigeria, Zimbabwe, and South Africa may be more significant than differences that exist between these countries. Many of the ethnic influences cut across national boundaries established by white colonists with little regard for cultural or tribal boundaries. Cross-cultural analysis provides an approach for understanding such situations.

Cross-cultural analysis of values is receiving more attention in consumer behavior because of the value of cross-cultural research in market segmentation and development of global marketing strategy. Schopphoven[11] showed that a promotional strategy can be developed to address a specific value orientation and thus allow targeted consumers to identify themselves with a particular

Table 3.4	Trends Shaping the Global Marketplace

1. The West will continue its concern for personal health and physical culture, but the developing countries will adopt the bad habits of the richer nations including smoking and high-fat diets.

2. The gap between rich and poor countries will widen in the next decades because populations in poor countries will continue to increase faster than their incomes.

3. The technology gap between developed and developing countries will widen. This will aggravate trade between countries of the Northern and Southern hemispheres.

4. People in industrialized countries will increase mobility in terms of residences, jobs, and occupations in the next decade.

5. The proportion of illiterate adults in developing countries will drop from 39 percent in 1985 to 28 percent by 2000, although the absolute number will increase by 10 million people.

6. By 2000, many or most of the Eastern European countries will be associate members of the EC.

Source: Excerpted from "50 Trends Shaping the World," The Fururist 25 (September-October 1991).

product. Consumer research can also help firms make strategic decisions about a specific country or market based on the commonalities and differences between the various markets. Kentucky Fried Chicken chose to test market its breakfast menu in Singapore because research showed that breakfast was becoming an eating occasion of growing importance in Singapore. Positive research can stimulate interest in other markets. Consumer behavior increasingly must be researched and discussed in international terms.[12]

An outline for conducting cross-cultural studies from a marketing perspective is shown in Table 3.5. This outline can be used by a marketing organization to determine if unmet needs exist for which a company might adapt or develop new products. The information gathered by use of this outline also helps develop a successful marketing program to meet those needs.

Can Marketing Be Standardized?

Can one marketing program be used in all or at least many countries? Or must marketing programs be modified for each country? If marketing programs must be modified to each culture, firms will fail if they do not develop specific products, promotions, and organizations for each country. Enormous economies are achieved, however, if the marketing program is standardized.

Is consumer behavior subject to cultural universals? Erik Elinder answered this question affirmatively and advanced the position that advertising can be

Table 3.5 Outline of Cross-Cultural Analysis of Consumer Behavior
Determine Relevant Motivations in the Culture
What needs are fulfilled with this product in the minds of members of the culture? How are these needs presently fulfilled? Do members of this culture readily recognize these needs?
Determine Characteristic Behavior Patterns
What patterns are characteristic of purchasing behavior? What forms of division of labor exist within the family structure? How frequently are products of this type purchased? What size packages are normally purchased? Do any of these characteristic behaviors conflict with behavior expected for this product? How strongly ingrained are the behavior patterns that conflict with those needed for distribution of this product?
Determine What Broad Cultural Values Are Relevant to This Product
Are there strong values about work, morality, religion, family relations, and so on, that relate to this product? Does this product connote attributes that are in conflict with these cultural values? Can conflicts with values be avoided by changing the product? Are there positive values in this culture with which the product might be identified?
Determine Characteristic Forms of Decision Making
Do members of the culture display a studied approach to decisions concerning innovations or an impulsive approach? What is the form of the decision process? On what information sources do members of the culture rely? Do members of the culture tend to be rigid or flexible in the acceptance of new ideas? What criteria do they use in evaluating alternatives?
Evaluate Promotion Methods Appropriate to the Culture
What roles does advertising occupy in the culture? What themes, words, or illustrations are taboo? What language problems exist in present markets that cannot be translated into this culture? What types of salesmen are accepted by members of the culture? Are such salesmen available?
Determine Appropriate Institutions for This Product in the Minds of Consumers
What types of retailers and intermediary institutions are available? What services do these institutions offer that are expected by the consumer? What alternatives are available for obtaining services needed for the product but not offered by existing institutions? How are various types of retailers regarded by consumers? Will changes in the distribution structure be readily accepted?

standardized.[13] Elinder's question and the validity of his answer have intrigued marketers since Elinder first raised the issue. It was a major topic addressed in the first edition of this text more than 20 years ago and has become more important because of increased global competition facing marketers. The debate was intensified by a controversial article by Ted Levitt describing the globalization of the marketplace.[14]

The need for globalized marketing strategies arises not only from market characteristics but also from technological and organizational characteristics. To compete, a firm must use technology that is not limited to national borders and people operating in worldwide organizations. Measures of marketing efficiency must now include global market share, requiring firms to understand their market niche in terms of customer types, not geodemographic segments.

As the European Community (EC) fine tunes functioning as a single market, firms are increasingly defining market segments to consist of similar types of customers and cultures throughout Europe rather than groups within a specific country. But as more businesses treat the EC as one common market, will the cultural identities of each country disappear? Will the French become more or less French if treated as a generic European? The answer depends on whether a firm's marketing strategies are based on the similarities of consumers or the differences among consumers.

Intermarket Segmentation

Many firms that have been successful in global marketing have focused on intermarket segmentation. Segments have historically been regarded as intramarket divisions of the total market as discussed in Chapter 2. Global firms, however, increasingly find it profitable to focus on intermarket segments.

Intermarket segments are groups of customers who transcend traditional markets often defined by geographic boundaries such as nations or regions of the world. Intermarket segments consist of people who have similar patterns of behavior regardless of where they live. Firms are considered to have a strategic focus involving intermarket segmentation when their strategies focus on similar customer behavior wherever it is found in the world rather than on national boundaries as definitions of markets.[15]

Intermarket segmentation plays a key role in understanding the similarities as well as the differences between consumers and countries that become the foundation of marketing standardization. Marketing organizations want such standardization in international marketing programs.[16] A study of 27 MNEs, including companies such as General Foods, Nestle, Coca-Cola, Procter & Gamble, Unilever, and Revlon, found that 63 percent of the total marketing programs could be rated as "highly standardized."[17] People are basically the same around the globe. They vary in specific traits, often influenced by structural elements such as economic resources, urbanization, and population age. The challenge is to build the core of the marketing strategy on the universals rather than on the differences.

An example of this strategy would be the focus on the desire to be beautiful. In a sense, young women in Tokyo and in Berlin are sisters not only "under" the skin but "on" their skin, lips, fingernails, and even in their hair styles. Consequently, Fatt[18] stated that they are likely to buy similar cosmetics with similar appeals. If they could, Fatt believed, the women of Moscow would follow suit, and some of them do. Appeals to such images as mother and child, freedom from pain, and glow of health are examples of appeals that may cut across many boundaries.

Boss and Eskada illustrate well how two German companies accomplish intermarket segmentation in the apparel industry. Both appeal to affluent, design-conscious people who are concerned about their appearance and constitute a basis for global segmentation. Whereas Boss offers clothing for men and Eskada for women, both have similar product quality and positioning. Men who buy Boss can be found in the same type of stores, reading the same type of advertisements in globally distributed magazines, expecting the same type of fit and service, and buying at the same price points, whether they live in Munich, London, New York, Mexico City, or Hong Kong. Furthermore, the behavioral differences between men buying Boss and Sears suits in New York are probably greater than the behavioral differences between men buying Boss in New York and men buying Boss in Hong Kong. These men are similar enough to constitute an intermarket segment.[19] Similarly, Eskada is able to identify intermarket segments based on similarities among its customers worldwide. That segment is targeted with a unified marketing strategy whether women in the segment live in Munich, New York, or Hong Kong. Figure 3.3 shows how BMW, like Boss and Eskada, targets customers around the globe with appeals to attract global intermarket segments. Similar appeals work for similar market segments worldwide. The German ad copy translates, "What are you wearing this summer?" This appeal to fashion consciousness is an appropriate offer to the affluent in any nation.

The underlying factors associated with the strategies of such successful "niche" or intermarket segmentation firms were identified in a study by

Figure 3.3   Intermarket Segment Marketing

WAS TRAGEN SIE DIESEN SOMMER?

Simon.[20] Characteristics that are associated with intermarket segmentation success include the following:

1. Combine strategic focus with geographic diversity.

2. Emphasize factors such as customer value.

3. Blend technology and closeness to customers.

4. Rely on their own technical competence.

5. Create mutual interdependence between the company and its employees.

Localization Based on Differences

True localization of marketing strategies would argue for different products and ads in every country of the world. Although this is economically inefficient and impractical, it is necessary to examine the needs and wants of specific markets and to adapt products, packaging, and advertising based on the differences between markets and the consumer behavior patterns of the target markets. Therefore, going global and acting local has become the choice of many marketers.

Although Pepsi is basically the same around the world, it had to adapt slightly to the market when it entered India. Pepsi will "Indianize" its soft drinks by adopting the prefix Lehar, meaning "wave" in Hindi, which will coordinate with the "wave" advertising. Before Japanese cars were introduced into the U.S. market, the cars had to be redesigned so that the steering wheels were on the left side of the car. How many Americans would have bought Hondas had the steering wheel been on the "wrong" side? You might think that medicines would be the same around the world because they are used for the same human species. Yet, it is not uncommon to see the same medicine dispensed according to local preferences: capsules in the United States and Canada, tablets in England, injections in Germany, and suppositories in France. Read Consumer in Focus 3.2 to see how McDonald's Corp. has achieved success in the global marketplace through both standardized and localized marketing practices.

Global Advertising Effectiveness

In a global business environment, many firms turn to advertising to communicate with new consumers around the world. This can either be done through globalized or localized advertising campaigns. Global campaigns focus on sending the same message to consumers around the world. Localized campaigns adapt messages to the norms of the different cultures addressed in a particular market.

Global advertising agencies can be efficient in implementing globalized advertising campaigns that relay the same message to each market regardless of

Consumer in Focus **3.2**

McDonald's Is the Same Yet Different around the World

McDonald's Corp. opened its 13,400th location in 1993, marking yet another "McMilestone" in the firm's 33-year history, during which it grew from a single hamburger joint to a household word across the country and around the world. In recent years, McDonald's has focused its marketing efforts on foreign market expansion, with 40 percent of its sales arising from its global locations outside the United States.

McDonald's is committed to growing foreign sales. It now has 4,400 restaurants outside of the United States, with more than 1,000 in Japan, 275 in Latin America, 3 in China, and 3 in Moscow. Other locations include Saudi Arabia, Oman, and Iceland. Although McDonald's has stayed true to its basic theme of good-tasting, consistent, fast food during its globalization, it has had to deal with differences among consumers and business conditions in new markets. It has either adapted wisely to local conditions or helped change the local conditions to promote better business opportunities.

McDonald's Overcomes Differences

Perhaps the most significant event in McDonald's history occurred in 1990 when Moscow became the new home for the world-famous Golden Arches. Fast food took on new meaning as enthusiastic patrons waited $2\frac{1}{2}$ hours for their "Beeg Maks" even as staffers served an average of 5,000 sandwiches an hour. But even after this hectic pace, the Soviet staffers served up salty, golden fries and polite smiles, a result of training, McDonald's style. For Soviet consumers used to frowning, unfriendly retail clerks, this was a welcome change and a reason to revisit McDonald's.

Among the reasons for its success, McDonald's executives point to the firm's commitment to local communities. Because many of the food supplies needed for the traditional McDonald's hamburger and fries were not available in Moscow, it built a $50 million food factory in Moscow and taught Soviets how to produce the potatoes needed for good fries. These steps ensured consistency among McDonald's meals from store to store and country to country, a key to its long-term success. It also aided in the development of this foreign market as a long-term investment, a key to McDonald's continued worldwide growth. McDonald's helped create a successful marketing environment by training staff and teaching a new generation of suppliers.

McDonald's Adapts to Differences

Although McDonald's has always sold its "taste of the U.S.," it found that to be successful in certain markets, it would have to adapt to some of the local tastes. Thus, it offers McSpaghetti in the Philippines because of the popularity of the dish. Rice, the staple food of most Asian countries, is offered in many of its Asian locations, including China and Japan.

McDonald's will face an interesting challenge when it begins to enter India in 1995. As India anxiously awaits the arrival of the Golden Arches, McDonald's is fine-tuning its plan to open 20 Indian locations. The challenge is catering to the market's taste's, roughly 80 percent of which are Hindu and do not eat beef. So McDonald's plans on offering beefless Big Macs.

Sources: American Marketplace (March 31, 1988), 9, 49; "No Fast Food in Moscow," Columbus Dispatch (July 21, 1990), 2H; McDonald's Corp. 1991 and 1992 Annual Reports; and Valerie Reitman, "India Anticipates the Arrival of the Beefless Big Mac," Wall Street Journal, October 20, 1993, B1.

geographical location. This strategy has worked well for John Deere. The tractor is used and perceived similarly in most markets and lends itself well to a global strategy with a uniform image worldwide. But Nestle found difficulties in promoting its Nescafe line to consumers in different cultures because the definition of coffee is different for many people. Japan has a tea culture. France, Germany, and Brazil like ground coffee; the United Kingdom has embraced instant coffee. Nestle decided to sell "coffee-ness" around the world rather than selling coffee. By selling the aroma and feelings associated with "coffee-ness" and allowing consumers to decide what coffee means to them, Nescafe has overcome cultural differences and linked Nescafe advertising in 50 countries.

Some advertising messages and specific product characteristics tend to be suited better than others for a globalized advertising approach. These characteristics are summarized as follows:

1. The communications message is based on similar lifestyles.

2. The appeal of the ad is to basic human needs and emotions.

3. The product satisfies universal needs and desires.[21]

Although global advertising campaigns might be effective for some products and firms, others need to recognize cultural differences and adapt their campaigns accordingly.[22] Nivea failed to consider that what is appropriate, acceptable, and allowed in one country may not be in another. A Nivea print ad was published in the United States and was ultimately banned from further publication due to what in the United States was considered to be indecent exposure. The same message and image had been used in Germany, however, without any controversy. McCain Foods, the distributor of a highly successful brand of frozen French-fried potato, decided to adapt its advertising to the local tastes and norms of the specific markets. Television commercials seen in Germany show the potatoes served at the dinner table with a glass of beer nearby. If the same ad were shown in France, it would be ineffective because wine is the usual drink with meals.

MNEs are faced with the trade-off between the efficiencies of standardized advertising and the effectiveness and cultural sensitivity of localized campaigns. Consumer in Focus 3.3 focuses on American Express television ads that combine common footage with local (country-specific) variations.

Some global advertising, although uniform in its message throughout the world, uses language or stereotypes to keep the feeling associated with the product distinctive. Figure 3.4A and B shows how two different European apparel companies have tried to keep their European flare in their U.S. ads. Using words from another language in an ad violates the reader's grammatical norms, and therefore, attracts attention.[23] Although foreign text may catch the attention of a reader, it might also cause miscommunication if the words are not understood. The foreign text and stereotypes do, however, help create a glamorous "European" image for their products.

Consumer in Focus **3.3**

AmEx Euro Ads: A Global Message with Local Flair

American Express believes in localizing of its global advertising campaigns. It will begin running television ads that combine common footage with local (country specific) variations.

The commercial features a young photographer who is on her way to a photo shoot when her equipment is sent out on the wrong flight to an unknown destination. She is faced with paying a high rental fee to rent photo equipment, which she charges on her AmEx card.

The second (local portion) of the ad takes place in a restaurant when she tells a friend of her mishap, but the restaurant scene is different in each country the commercial airs. Different women play the role of the photographer in different countries and local props are used to localize the restaurant scene. For example a blue-eyed blonde in a German *Gasthof* may be featured in Germany, while a woman with olive skin in an Italian *trattoria* might be featured in the Italian version.

Initial research indicates the "localization" of the ads does not adversely affect the delivery of a universal message or the global image of American Express. The solution to the question of globalization or localization in advertising for American Express is a "multi local approach."

Source: Laurel Wentz, "New Euro Ads Get Localized Element," *Advertising Age* (November 25, 1991), 28.

Overcoming Language Problems

Language problems must be overcome to standardize marketing programs. In a Paris hotel, a sign suggests that guests "Please leave your values at the desk." In Bangkok, a dry cleaner's advertising suggested customers "Drop your trousers here for best results." In an Acapulco hotel, the concerns of customers about water purity were probably not relieved by a sign that stated, "The manager has personally passed all the water served here." A Zurich hotel signs says, "Because of the impropriety of entertaining guests of the opposite sex in the bedroom, it is suggested that the lobby be used for this purpose." In a Norwegian cocktail lounge, the message may have been a bit confused by a sign that says, "Ladies are requested not to have children in the bar."

If you need quality dental care in Hong Kong, you might find it at a dentist who advertises tooth extractions "using the latest Methodists." The phrase "Come alive with Pepsi" experienced problems when it was translated into German ads as "Come alive out of the grave" and in Chinese as "Pepsi brings your ancestors back from the grave." Coors used a slogan in English as "Turn It Loose," but the phrase in Spanish became "Suffer from Diarrhea." When Frank Perdue's "It Takes a Tough Man to Make a Tender Chicken" was translated into Spanish, it became "It Takes a Sexually Stimulated Man to Make a Chicken Affectionate." And Budweiser's "King of Beers" became "Queens of Beers" in

Figure 3.4 (a) Foreign Language Creates Image and Attention (b) Creating an Image by Using Stereotypes of Country of Origin

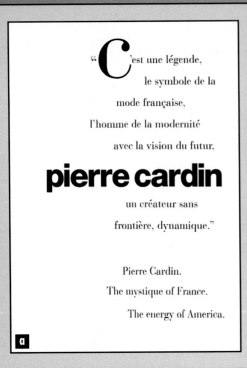

Spanish because the Spanish word for beer, *cerveza,* has a feminine ending.[24] Linguistics techniques borrowed from cross-cultural methodologies are helpful to marketers in overcoming such problems.

Back-Translation

A useful technique for overcoming language problems is back-translation. In this procedure, a message (word or a series of words) is translated from its original language to the translated language and back to the original by several translators. This process may be repeated several times, with the translated versions being interchanged with the original among the translators. The purpose of the iterations is an attempt to achieve conceptual equivalency in meaning by controlling the various translation biases of translators.[25]

Marketing research questionnaires often need to be translated into additional languages. This process can be more reliable with back-translation. Sometimes, however, it is necessary to use scales other than verbal or quantitative. Figure 3.5

Figure 3.5 Cross-Cultural Questionnaire for Holiday Inn

The "Faces" game

Dear guest to round off your stay we'd like you to play a Faces game indicate the face which corresponds most closely to your own expresslon In each of Ihe situations mentioned below. Please hand this in Reception (or if you prefer, mail to the Public Relations Officer, Holiday Inns, P. O. Box 4280, Johannesdurg 2000).

What was your facial reaction to the following aspects of vour stay?

Die „Gesiggies"spletjie

Bleste gas om u kuiertjie af te rond wil ons graag hê dat u die „Gesiggies" -speietjie speel. Dui dle gesiggie aan met die uitdrukking wat naaste kom aan u eie in elk van die situasies hieronder. Gee dit asseblief by Ontvangs in (of, as u verkies, pos dit aan die Skakelbeampte, Holiday Inns. Posbus 4280, Johannesburg 2000).

Wat was u gesig se reaksie op elk van die volgende aspekte van u verblyf?

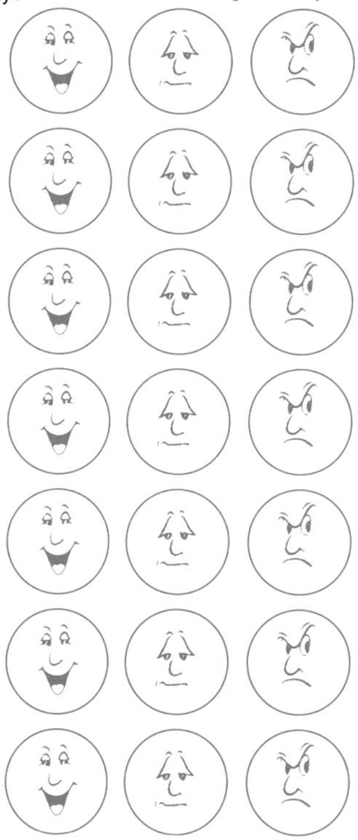

Making your reservation	Bespreking
Reception desk service	Die diens by die ontvangstoonbank
Standard of room	Gehalte van die kamer
Food	Kos
Restaurant service	Restourantdiens
Bar service	Kroegdiens
Hospitality	Gasvryheid

Other remarks/Ander opmerkings --

Name/Naam --

Address/Adres --

Room No./Kamer No. ----------- Date/Datum --

Holiday Inn stayed at/Holiday Inn verblyf in --

Source: Courtesy of the South African division of Holiday Inns. Reprinted by permission.

shows an example from Holiday Inn in which questions are given in English and Afrikaans and also nonverbally with smiling or unhappy faces.

Brand Names

Brand names should be evaluated from a cross-cultural perspective even if currently used only in domestic markets. "Thinking globally" includes considering the possibility that the brand will someday be extended to other countries, as well as making it more appealing to diverse cultures within the current country. Coined names are increasing in popularity among Fortune 500 companies because they do not need to be translated and avoid awkward translation. This makes names like Exxon and Xerox very effective in a global market.

The steps that should be used for a cross-cultural approach, in addition to legal search, in finding an English name acceptable on a global basis include the following:

1. Does the English name of the product have another meaning, perhaps unfavorable, in one or more of the countries where it might be marketed?

2. Can the English name be pronounced everywhere? For example, Spanish and some other languages lack a "k" in their alphabets, an initial letter in many popular U.S. brand names.

3. Is the name close to that of a foreign brand, or does it duplicate another product sold in English-speaking countries?

4. If the product is distinctly American, will national pride and prejudice work against the acceptance of the product?[26]

Global brands can have substantial advantages for creating awareness for a product or brand worldwide. As consumer travel between countries, global

Table 3.6 Who Makes the Best?		
Product	**Country**	**% Choosing**
Men's clothes	Italy	35
Televisions	Japan	59
Cars	Germany	49
Washing machines	Germany	46
Cosmetics	France	53
Photograph film	Japan	48
Sports equipment	United States	33

Source: ESOMAR seminar, 1993.

brands are easily recognized and often trusted. Global brands often have help-ful associations as well. The image of being global often adds legitimacy to the brand in addition to the association of being competitive and having staying power. A country association to a brand occurs frequently. Grey Poupon is French mustard, Steiff is German stuffed animals, and Levi's is American jeans.[27] If a country has the perception in the mind of consumers to produce the best product in a specific category, a distinct country-of-origin association and ad-vantage is created. Table 3.6 shows from which countries consumers perceive the best products to originate, and Figure 3.6A and B shows how advertisers have used the country of origin or country association to appeal to new car and watch buyers.

Although global brands often work well, many companies are realizing that globalization is not an all-or-nothing proposition. There are many parts to a brand: the name, symbol, slogan, and associations. Many marketers including Coca-Cola are finding that although they have a global brand, not all portions of the brand are global. Diet Coke is sold in the United States whereas the same product is sold as Coca-Cola Light in Europe due to restrictions on using the word *diet* when no medicinal connotation is intended. Aaker indicates that it is

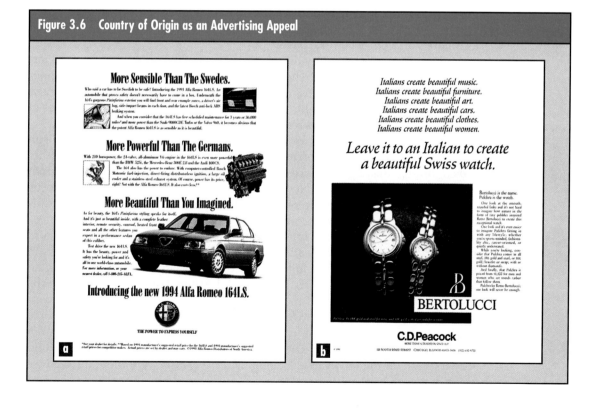

Figure 3.6 Country of Origin as an Advertising Appeal

important to globalize those elements for which there is a payoff in cost or impact but to let other elements of a product's brand equity be customized to local markets.

There are many other ways companies can prepare for increasing globalization of marketing. For example, Pizza Hut restaurants in Brussels have menus available in several languages. By keeping separate menus in a clearly marked rack, the process for both the customer and restaurant personnel, who may not be able to speak all the languages, is simplified. Visual language is another solution to the problem of cross-cultural communications. Many European hypermarkets and grocery stores solve the language problem by using scales that have pictures of products being weighed rather than words. Consumers from any country need only push the button with the correct picture to determine the weight and price of their produce.

Research Methodology for Cross-Cultural Analysis

Consumer behavior has borrowed from disciplines such as anthropology, linguistics, and sociology to obtain needed methodology for cross-cultural studies. This is reflected in the increased application of standard marketing research techniques on a cross-cultural basis.

Multiattribute methodology dominates much of the consumer behavior literature, as you will see in later chapters. Berger, Stern, and Johansson[28] demonstrated that it can be used across cultures in comparing American and Japanese car buyers. Japanese respondents tend to answer more in intermediate ranges of the scales, whereas Americans respond more at the extreme ends of scales.

Focus groups, a traditional form of consumer research, are also applicable on a global basis. Global focus groups take place in multiple locations and are linked through the use of video conference centers. BMW sends executives from Munich to its ad agency in New York via video technology to watch focus groups. It also enables them to interact with consumers around the world during focus groups without extensive travel.

Psychographic studies are often used for market segmentation and are also useful in cross-cultural applications. Boote[29] demonstrated their usefulness in a cross-cultural study in the United Kingdom, Germany, and France. Using an approach based on Rokeach's instrumental value scales, Boote found the methodology (coupled with Z-methodology factor analysis) useful in discovering substantial differences between those three countries, belying what some believe to be a homogeneous common market. Germans scored high on an "appearance-conscious" segment, whereas the French scored high on an "outside interest" in the environment segment. The British were more directed toward home interests.

Participant-observer studies involve an investigator or team of investigators living in intimate contact with a culture. The investigator makes careful and comprehensive notes of observations about the culture. Data collection includes records of what is observed, interviews with "key" informants, and perhaps structured questionnaires, attitude scales, and projective tests.

Content analysis is a technique for determining the values, themes, role prescriptions, norms of behavior, and other elements of culture. Analysis is based on objective materials produced by the people of a culture in the ordinary course of events.[30] Usually the content studied is verbal in nature, such as newspaper or magazine stories. It could be derived from advertisements or any other objective material, such as art, products, or even the garbage discarded by consumers. Some of the more interesting of these approaches are described in Webb's *Unobtrusive Measures.*[31]

Content analysis is used in domestic marketing studies as well as crossnationally, often concerning advertising themes. Pollay[32] conducted a contentanalytic study of American advertising during the past 80 years. He found that American advertising has become more focused, is more forceful, and attempts fewer total value appeals. One study based on content analysis, Naisbitt's book *Megatrends*, became a bestseller. Many global methodologies are not fundamentally different from domestic marketing research, but consumer analysts equipped for the future can be expected to understand how to conduct research on a global basis, including techniques used for cross-cultural analysis.

Global Marketing Strategies

Business without borders will probably not be the reality, but global relationships between MNEs are a reality facing consumer analysts and marketing strategists. Consumer analysts, perhaps more than other individuals in an organization, need to be on the "cutting edge" of knowledge about how global markets are changing, including the interenvironmental elements as well as the intraenvironmental elements, and how to reach global market segments.

What are some of the specifics of how consumer analysts and their knowledge of cultural norms can benefit an organization? Look at Figure 3.7, which displays the meaning of gestures used throughout the world. After you have read each one, ask yourself if this is the meaning you intend to communicate when you are in that country.

Figure 3.7   International Gesture Dictionary

International Gesture Dictionary

Gestures Using the Face

Eyebrow Raise: In Tonga, a gesture meaning "yes" or "I agree." In Peru, means "money" or "Pay me."

Blink: In Taiwan, blinking the eyes at someone is considered impolite.

Wink: Winking at women, even to express friendship, is considered improper in Australia.

Eyelid Pull: In Europe and some Latin American countries, means "Be alert" or "I am alert."

Ear Flick: In Italy, signifies that a nearby gentleman is effeminate.

Ear Grasp: Grasping one's ears is a sign of repentance or sincerity in India. A similar gesture in Brazil—holding the lobe of one's ear between thumb and forefinger—signifies appreciation.

Nose Circle: The classic American "okay" sign—the fingers circle—is placed over the nose in Colombia to signify that the person in question is homosexual.

Nose Tap: In Britain, secrecy or confidentiality. In Italy, a friendly warning.

Nose Thumb: One of Europe's most widely known gestures, signifying mockery. May be done double-handed for greater effect.

Nose Wiggle: In Puerto Rico, "What's going on?"

Cheek Screw: Primarily an Italian gesture of praise.

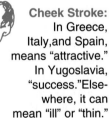

Cheek Stroke: In Greece, Italy, and Spain, means "attractive." In Yugoslavia, "success." Elsewhere, it can mean "ill" or "thin."

Source: Reprinted from the book Do's and Taboos Around the World — A Guide to International Gift-Giving published by Parker Pen U.S.A. Limited. To obtain a copy of the complete book, contact John Wiley and Sons, Inc., 608 Third Avenue, New York, New York 10158.

Network marketing is increasingly global in scope. News reports indicate that corporate alliances between firms in different countries increased 47 percent annually during the past decade, and a survey of U.S.-based companies reported some 12,000 in which American firms owned 10 to 50 percent equity position in a foreign firm.[33] These networks are required for access to markets as well as resources. Such alliances may be essential for global dominance. This was apparently the motivation in an alliance between DuPont, the largest American chemical firm, and Phillips, the largest Dutch electronics firm. They needed each other in a joint venture to develop optical disc products, expected to be a $4 billion market. In centrally planned economies such as China, a local partner may be legally required to do business in the alien system.

In this final section of the chapter, we briefly spotlight some of the opportunities for consumer analysts seeking growth opportunities for organizations that are increasingly global in their operations.

Consumer Behavior in Developing Countries

Population is growing rapidly in Africa, some Asian countries, and in Latin America. But most also have low incomes. Great care must, therefore, be used to design effective marketing strategies for developing countries.

What are the most important attributes of the developing countries? Youthfulness is one, specifically a large number of babies. In the last chapter, we examined declining fertility in North America, but in some developing countries, women bear seven or eight children. The ten countries with the highest birth rates in the world (in order) are Kenya, Pakistan, Saudi Arabia, Egypt, the Philippines, Peru, South Africa, India, Venezuela, and Brazil.

Most developing countries are predominantly rural. Despite their rural nature, consumers are usually dependent on other countries for food supplies. Often, other countries are also responsible for educating the nation's youth. Although in many parts of the world, television has been blamed for contributing to societal problems, Brown[34] indicates that attention should be focused on the prosocial effects of entertainment television programs in developing countries.

Observe in Figure 3.8 how companies use the strong appeal of the mother/child relationship in the African culture. Rama margarine uses subtle humor to position itself as South Africa's favorite margarine, something that even mothers and daughters can agree on. Johnson & Johnson has positioned its marketing strategy for the African market as well. The photograph communicates the love and concern of a mother for her baby without the need for words. The copy, however, features an economy appeal by saving 20 cents. Also, however, Johnson & Johnson has positioned itself as concerned about all children in the culture by donating 20 cents to the Child Welfare Fund with each purchase. This ad provides a useful example of effective strategy based on an understanding of the economic and cultural realities of the African market.

Figure 3.8 Advertising Appeals Based on African Culture

Source: Johnson & Johnson Company, Africa.

Cultural sensitivity is especially needed in developing countries because pictures may be much more important than words. As an example, one marketer attempted to export the firm's detergent to a Middle Eastern country. Advertising for the detergent featured dirty clothes piled on the left and clean clothes stacked on the right. Reading right to left, as consumers in the Middle East frequently do, the message was clear: Soap soiled the clothes.

Consumer Behavior in the Pacific Rim

The Pacific Rim provides some of the most attractive markets for growth-oriented marketing strategies. The area includes many low-income but fast-growing population bases in Southeast Asia, as well as some of the most affluent markets in the world, such as Japan, Singapore, and Australia (refer to Tables 3.1 and 3.3, pages 92, 96). Singapore is a center of logistics for the Pacific Rim, and its airport is a key element in its logistical network. In fact, it is also advertised as a tourist attraction in Figure 3.9

India

As a country projected to become the largest in the world, India is attracting worldwide interest among marketers. Although poor by Western standards, the

Figure 3.9   Singapore's Changi Airport Is a Key in the Logistics Network and a Destination Spot

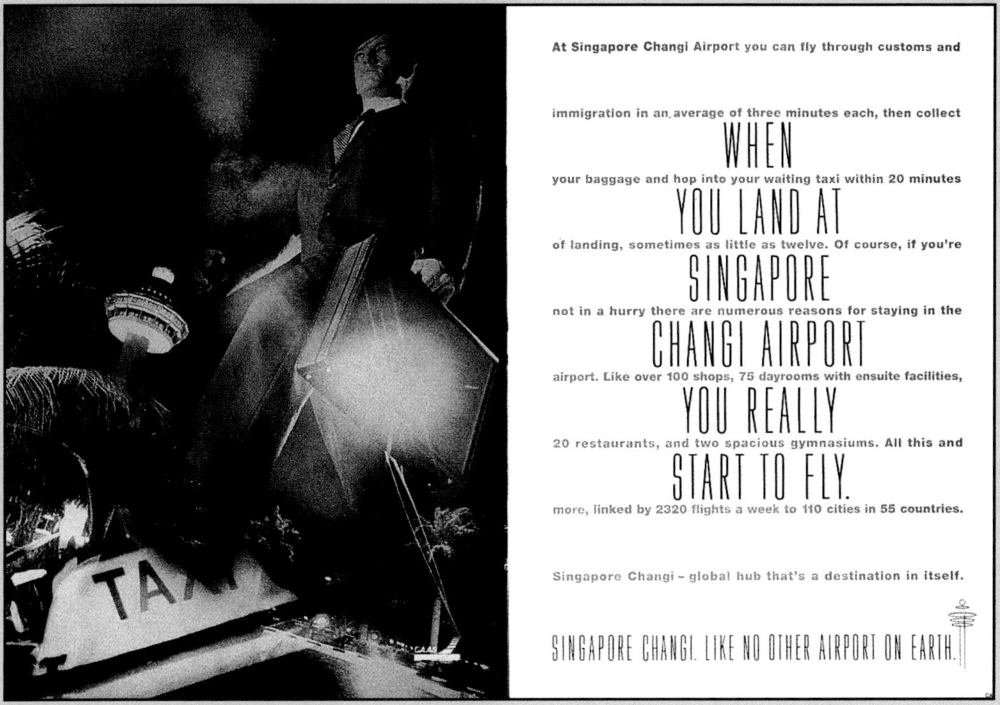

At Singapore Changi Airport you can fly through customs and immigration in an average of three minutes each, then collect

WHEN

your baggage and hop into your waiting taxi within 20 minutes

YOU LAND AT

of landing, sometimes as little as twelve. Of course, if you're

SINGAPORE

not in a hurry there are numerous reasons for staying in the

CHANGI AIRPORT

airport. Like over 100 shops, 75 dayrooms with ensuite facilities,

YOU REALLY

20 restaurants, and two spacious gymnasiums. All this and

START TO FLY.

more, linked by 2320 flights a week to 110 cities in 55 countries.

Singapore Changi – global hub that's a destination in itself.

SINGAPORE CHANGI. LIKE NO OTHER AIRPORT ON EARTH.

(For more information, see Roger Blackwell, From the Edge of the World, The Ohio State University Press, Columbus, Ohio, 1994)

attractiveness of India is based on its infrastructure; well-developed legal system; and large numbers of well-educated doctors, engineers, and others needed for growth of a thriving middle class. India is a country with growth in national income and productivity but major problems caused by its large debt, shortage of foreign exchange, and unsettling coalitions of government.[35] Even though facing a period of uncertainty, the long-run future of the market is promising for global marketers.

The middle class is the key to understanding India's consumer markets. Although the government does not publish statistics on this politically sensitive subject, some economists estimate the number at 7 to 12 percent of the population or a market range from 60 million to 100 million, larger, for example, than that of West Germany and France.[36] McDonald's expansion into India is based on the size of the middle class.[37] Consequently, the demand for consumer goods is rising rapidly. Yearly car sales have tripled since 1980, sales of motorbikes and scooters have more than tripled in recent years, and production of consumer durables in general is rising at the rate of 20 percent annually. Movie theaters have doubled in the past decade. The middle-class family with a yearly income of about $1,400 does not live in luxury but may be buying a television; a radio; appliances such as an electric iron and clocks; and a respectable wardrobe of shoes, jewelry, and silk saris. Consumer purchases are often deliberate, with the wife acting as information gatherer but with long discussions and interaction about the best choice.

South Korea

Ability to buy has increased at an astounding rate in South Korea. Annual per capita GNP soared from $120 in 1965 to $6340 in 1991. Private consumption in recent years has been growing at an annual rate of 5.5 percent. Soaring income and plummeting birthrates; good health care; a high regard for religious values; and a young, increasingly well-educated population give South Korea many strengths on which to build.

A key element in the success of Korea has been export capabilities, strongly assisted by governmental policies. The most successful car ever to be imported into the North American market is Hyundai, first in Canada and later in the United States. Consumers in North America might not have heard of Korean firms such as Daewoo, a massive industrial firm, but they are quickly entering the market and having substantial success.

Australia

Australia is a market similar in characteristics to European and North American markets. High income and an older population are characteristics shared with other industrialized economies.[38]

Australia has a well-developed infrastructure and plenty of room to grow. At one time, immigration was mostly European, but in recent years, nearly 50 percent of immigration has been Asian. Marketers find the nation attractive because it also has a well-developed advertising and marketing research support system, and as sailing enthusiasts and *Crocodile Dundee* fans both can attest, the influence of Australia on the rest of the world is considerable.

China

China is the largest nation in the world. The pent-up demand of a billion consumers excites marketers all over the world. In the past, most of China's imports have been industrial goods, but new government priorities caused marketers to begin to consider the potential for consumer markets, even with concerns about human rights and political instabilities. China is in the process of creating a market-based economy from one that had been a planned Communist country for decades. The country ran an $18.3 billion trade surplus with the United States in

1992. It bought $7.5 billion in U.S. exports, which translated into jobs for thousands of Americans.[39]

What do Chinese consumers want to buy most? Refrigerators top the list in a study made in two of China's largest cities, Beijing (with a population of 9.5 million) and Guyangzhou (with a population of 7 million). Washing machines are equally wanted, although television sets are the electrical appliance most often owned. Chinese consumers are also interested in cameras and radio/cassette recorders. With increasing salaries of urban workers and the rise of new entrepreneurs in China's special economic areas, more people are now able to consider a broader array of consumer goods.[40]

In recent years, more than 1 million Chinese have become *dakuan*, or dollar millionaires, with approximately 5 percent of the population declared as affluent in terms of Chinese standards. Li Xiaohua went from being a cook in a Beijing restaurant in the 1970s to a business tycoon with a Rolex watch and two Mercedes-Benzes today. He is just one example of a country full of success stories, yet most citizens still live in crowded cities or poor farming villages. The shift to more of a market-driven system is producing enormous change and conflict in China, which raises major questions about the proper role of marketing activities. Some of the ways the culture is changing are highlighted in Consumer in Focus 3.4.

Japan

Although Japan is smaller in land area than California, its 123 million people consume more goods and services than any other country in the world, except the United States. Its population is also aging more rapidly than in any other country because of the highest longevity in the world, as you saw in the previous chapter.

Land is perhaps the most scarce and valuable natural resource in Japan, which also lacks petroleum and other natural resources. Yet is main assets are its culture and people, which have contributed to the development of its powerhouse economy. Japanese people love their culture. Although some young adults are questioning the strict work and family ethics of their elders, there still exists a very strong Japanese traditional lifestyle and aesthetic sense. The Japanese have integrated high technology into their traditional lifestyles. Nishikawa concludes that the fundamental philosophy for product designing and marketing in Japanese enterprises is to adapt high-tech products to the culture of the countries in which they are sold.[41]

Opportunities for non-Japanese firms will increase in the future perhaps as never before because of the emphatic shift in the Japanese economy to consumer goods. Wealth and economic power have been accumulated by efforts to stimulate export of goods, but a combination of accumulated affluence, world pressure to encourage more imports by Japan, and the relative inefficiency of consumer goods distributed in Japan is creating the opportunity for European

3.4	**Consumer in Focus**

The Me Generation Is Alive and Well in China

When we think of China we tend to think of pandas, The Great Wall, wonderful food, studious children, a strong work ethic, and mysterious spirituality. Marketers are now thinking of China's latest product . . . its Me Generation.

If you visit J.J.'s on a Friday night, you will see young men and women, all fashionably dressed, dancing up a storm in the heart of old Shanghai. Young business people sit at small tables by the dance floor and talk on their cellular phones in between sips of their cocktails. This young generation is eager and willing to take advantage of the economic reforms occurring in China, and they are also eager to enjoy their new sense of freedom by seeking their fortunes, mates, and own identities. Although still aware of the limitations that surround them, they choose to ignore the presence of the Communist regime.

As with the Me Generation of other developed countries, this group is shedding some of its parents' traditional views on life, happiness, and security. The parents of Pang Rui, an 18-year-old student, wanted him to become a teacher or a doctor, and thus secure. But Pang wants to be free to earn his fortune in a job that he likes.

Another young woman, Zhao Li, decided to quit her state-assigned job as an interpreter. Instead, she joined a foreign-owned public relations company for four-times her previous salary. Soon thereafter she was able to move into her own two-room apartment. Her outlook is becoming common among her peers. The Chinese Me Generation is marrying later, and they are choosing their own spouses. "It used to be that Communist Party membership was important," said Wang Zhixiong, a Guangdong researcher. "Now people's tastes favor money, professional ranking, and appearances."

Source: Sandra Burton, "A New Me Generation," Time (November 29, 1993), 39.

and North American consumer goods firms to export more to Japan in the future.

Limited space does not permit close examination of the Japanese market; however, Table 3.7 examines how Americans and Japanese view each other. Americans were asked about their feelings toward the Japanese on the specific attributes shown in the table, while the Japanese were asked about their view of Americans on each attribute. Japanese culture has received much attention in other places.[42] We will look, however, at how advertising is affected by consumer behavior in Japan.

Japanese Advertising

The purpose of advertising is the same in Japan as it is in the West—to stimulate consumption. In Japan, however, upsetting, outspoken opinions are not welcome. Advertising reflects a concern for harmony to the extent that Westerners often fail to understand the message of a particular advertisement. The

Table 3.7	Americans and Japanese: How They See Each Other		
Attribute		**American View**	**Japanese View**
Which of the following do you admire the most about Japan (asked of American respondents)/America (for Japanese respondents)?			
1. Form of Government		23%	63%
2. Freedom of Expression		27	89
3. Variety of Lifestyles		25	86
4. Industriousness		88	27
5. Educational Institutions		71	48
6. Leisure Time Available to Workers		15	88
7. Respect for Family Life		75	87
8. Treatment of Women		20	68
Which of the following words describe what people in Japan (asked of Americans)/in America (asked of Japanese) are like?			
1. Friendly		59%	64%
2. Competitive		94	50
3. Devoted to Fair Play		35	43
4. Lazy		4	21
5. Crafty		68	13
6. Poorly Educated		12	21
Which country will be the strongest economic power 10 years from now?			
1. United States		51%	14%
2. Japan		27	35
3. Other		11	30

Source: "Japan in the Mind of America, America in the Mind of Japan," Time (February 10, 1992), 16–23.

underlying idea is that the more the advertisement pleases customers, the more likely it is to move the product.

Japanese consumers react more to beautiful background scenery, a star of the entertainment world, or the development of a story than to product recommendations. Among younger consumers especially, the presence of American pop culture in advertising is influential in the buying decision. Japanese viewers dislike garrulous and argumentative sales talk; product information should be short and conveyed with song that sets a mood. The great majority of Japanese TV commercials are directed toward affective rather than cognitive components of attitude. This is an important point for foreign manufacturers more accustomed to the American hard-sell advertisements. Japanese advertising is more likely to develop a story, describe the expression of people, and enhance poetically the mood of the product. The product message comes at the end of the commercial, almost as an afterthought to the rest of the commercial.

Commercials in Japan constructed around a comparison of products are virtually nonexistent. Commercial practices are based, at least at the visible level, on the principle of respect for one another. Attacking and putting down a rival openly is avoided. Comparative advertising is not permitted by the Advertising Code, which explains, "Let us avoid slandering, defaming and attacking others."[43] Marketing programs in Japan are strongly influenced by Confucianism, which places high value on self-esteem, reciprocity, and harmony. Rudeness is intolerable even to the point that polite lies are acceptable rather than the expression of contradictory opinions. From Buddhism, values are also derived, leading to a need for simplicity and a dominant aesthetic sense as well as loyalty and satisfaction in interpersonal relationships.[44]

Latin America

As U.S. companies become more familiar with trading with Mexico and understanding the Mexican markets because of NAFTA taking effect in 1994, there will occur a natural migration of interest further south to Central and South American countries. The most attractive market segments include those of Brazil, Venezuela, Colombia, Argentina, and Chile.

Although most Latin American countries have high population growth rates and large markets of young consumers, some have promising income growth rates as well. Brazil is the tenth largest country in the world but also has one of the largest rich–poor gaps of any major country in the world. More than 10 million of its 150 million population represent an attractive high-income segment. American culture is becoming very popular in Brazil with the arrival of more American newspapers, magazines, automobiles, and fast food restaurants. The acceptance of American culture is occurring in Chile as well, with American fast food restaurants and food courts appearing in malls almost as frequently as Chilean wines appear in U.S. stores. Some grocery stores in Chile and Peru rival the biggest and best found in the United States, with more than 50 checkout registers and oversized American-style snack food aisles. In fact, when a drug lord was recently killed in Colombia, he was shot at Medellin in the southern hemisphere's largest center, among Hallmark, Liz Claiborne, and other American companies.

Consumer analysts note that low reported per capita income levels often hide substantial market segments with high income levels. Although most consumers in Latin American countries might not be able to afford luxury or even mass market items, intermarket segmentation helps identify existing segments that can afford many items such as appliances, cars, clothing, travel, and specialty food items. Tables 3.1 and 3.3 (pages 92 and 96) give specific information about some of these countries.

Communist–Capitalist Continuum

Communism challenged capitalism for half a century as a viable method of organizing society and markets. It crumbled rapidly in recent years. When a new flag was raised in Moscow in 1992, it symbolized much more than a change from one nation to another. It symbolized change from centralized control of the Soviet republics and, in reality, many other countries throughout the world, to decentralized nations representing a continuum of approaches to government and market control. Although bastions of communism remain in places, such as Cuba and North Korea, other nations such as China had begun the trek toward more market control, whereas Russia and other former Soviet republics as well as most of Eastern Europe were steaming ahead to something other than central planning.

Russia and the Republics

Russia and other former members of the Union of Soviet Socialist Republics offer some of the most challenging markets in the world. Together they are a huge market, industrially developed in some ways, with enough spending power to represent one of the great growth markets of the future. The "iffy" part of the scenario is whether that spending power can change from one market centrally planned for the production of industrial and defense goods to one capable of producing and distributing large amounts of consumer goods and services in a market-driven economy.

The change in direction was stimulated by policies advocated by Mikhail Gorbachev and his advocacy of *glasnost* and *perestroika*—the opening up of society.[45] In these restructured economies, the goal is to achieve market-directed production with an emphasis on more consumer goods. In the long run, market efficiencies and higher motivation should lead to a higher standard of living if the society can survive the suffering and starvation associated with the transition. There was no entrepreneurial culture under either the Communists or the czars. Developing such a culture is essential in a market-driven society, but achieving that quickly enough to prevent collapse of the production and distribution of essential products as food and energy is an issue of monumental proportions.

Advertising is both a blessing and a bane in Russia and the former Soviet republics. On the one hand, there are few consumer goods to buy. Even the Russian products, whose poor quality was a staple of Russian humor, are not very available. Yet, on the other hand, the sudden opening of market possibilities and the lure of hard currency have led to the appearance of advertisements in most of the media for these virtually nonexistent products. A general euphoria about advertising has given way to a recognition of many problems: the absence of a precise advertising policy, the shortage of specialists, and the lack of a code of ethical norms for advertising. They have resulted in television viewers in the former Soviet Union being bombarded with low-quality advertising and rejection by consumers on the basis that the gap between advertising and real life is too great.[46]

The market structure of the former U.S.S.R. is complicated. There are two, or more, main groups separated more or less as Slavic and non-Slavic. European-oriented Russia has provided leadership and much of the population. At the same time, there is a tremendous increase in the Muslim republics of Central Asia and their high birthrates. In Russia and most Eastern European countries, a high proportion of women is employed in the labor force, often in the professions. That fact, and the traditional system of labor-intensive distribution (reflecting a political philosophy that emphasizes labor rather than capital), has created a massive demand for labor-saving appliances and services.

Shopping is usually an arduous and time-consuming activity. Shortages and high prices are characteristics of the buying environment. Coffee has skyrocketed in price. Toilet paper is chronically in short supply, requiring consumers to use substitutes such as newspaper ripped in square pieces. Laundry soap has virtually disappeared except for a few luxury brands.

About 65 percent of Soviet households have a refrigerator, 55 percent have a washing machine, 38 percent have a television, and 40 percent have a radio. With one of the lowest ownership levels of refrigerators of any country in the world and one of the most advanced technological capacities in such areas as nuclear engineering and theoretical physics, significant opportunities surely exist for growth. These often occur from joint ventures and other market development strategies with firms from other countries, one such example being the Moscow McDonald's success story.

Youth lead the way to change in most societies. In Russia and other republics of the Confederation, this principle appears to be true. Western consumer goods such as jeans and boomboxes dramatized alternative lifestyles before *perestroika*. Rock lyrics and ads for Western beauty products offer teenagers formulas to express their search for love in much the same way this intermarket segment (teenagers) does throughout the world. To some extent, the intensity of Soviet youth culture is owed, as in many other developing countries, to relatively recent massive migration to the cities.

Eastern Europe

Eastern European economies are opening up for trade with the rest of the world, some with much more success than others. Hungary has been among the most receptive to a market economy, especially for tourism and other industries that bring hard currency quickly. Poland generates high interest in the United States for trading relationships, but the country suffers from massive debt along with severe shortages and sweeping price hikes. Slovakia, the Czech Republic, and Romania have stimulated interest among many global firms as offering significant opportunities for companies that serve consumers well and can develop market-oriented strategies. Consumer in Focus 3.5 examines the Warsaw Marriott, a successful joint venture in Poland.

The attractiveness of Eastern European markets for global marketers is the similarity with preferences of Western consumers. The most-desired durable

Poland's First Western Icon

Poland is a gray country. In nearly every block of every city in every village, visitors' eyes see little except gray, deteriorating buildings housing families, shops, and factories. There is one shining exception. Although new construction is beginning to be spotted in various places, the Warsaw Marriott was the first Western icon.

It is easy to spot the shiny, new Warsaw Marriott. It has been the hub of business as well as much political activity since it opened. The lobby buzzes with different languages and sounds of alliances being formed. Nearly every topic in business or politics can be overheard in nearly every language of the world with many Germans, an abundance of Japanese business people, and a sampling of many other industrial powers of the world present. It is the closest one could come to a real world, modern version of the Inter-Galactic Bar in the movie *Star Wars!*

The $65 million hotel was a welcome sign of commitment and future investment in Poland. It is the perfect example of a global strategic alliance done well; in fact it was the first joint venture under Polish law. Under the agreement and joint venture contract No. 001, Marriott owns 25% of the hotel, with Ilbau, an Austrian construction firm, owning 25% and LOT airlines owning 50%.

Even though the building and all of its amenities are impressive, the physical attributes are outshined by the level of service offered by enthusiastic Warsaw Marriott employees. The majority of the over 1000 employees are native Poles with no hotel experience. Marriott executives felt that those with previous hotel and restaurant experience probably had the wrong type of experience. Although they did not have many of the skills needed to perform their hotel duties, they did possess the natural hospitality and verbal skills needed to make the Warsaw Marriott run as smoothly as (if not more smoothly than) its Western counterparts.

The hotel valets, bellboys and waitpersons are eager to tell their guests how proud they are to work at the Marriott. One young man joined the Marriott team and was working at the front desk. In almost perfect English he told how he had left a job as a doctor to work for Marriott. At first glance, it might be assumed the career change occurred only because of the higher wages and perks, including 2 free meals per day, uniforms, shoes and free language lessons, offered by the hotel. But such an assumption would be wrong. The real reason for working for a well-managed, Western firm is opportunity to learn and the ability to embrace change.

Source: Kristina Blackwell, "Poland: Star in the East," in Roger Blackwell, ed., From the Edge of the World (Columbus, Ohio: The Ohio State University Press, 1994), 71–72.

products in Eastern Europe are Western cars (58 percent), video recorders (42 percent), and microwaves (35 percent), and the most-wanted nondurables are perfume and athletic shoes. Television viewing is the most frequent leisure-time activity, but 85 percent of East Europeans shop every day, spending an average of 2 hours a day.[47]

Companies such as Procter & Gamble are now significant marketers in countries such as Hungary, Poland, and the Czech Republic. Products include

Pampers disposable diapers and Blend-a-Med toothpaste in Hungary, Vidal Sassoon Wash & Go shampoo and Pampers in Poland, and Vizir and Ariel laundry detergents in the Czech Republic through the acquisition of a leading producer of detergents and cleaning products. All brands are backed by TV advertising from international advertising agencies with creative strategies that avoid authoritarian approaches that might offend sensitivities of consumers developed in the past 40 years. Unlike marketing in North America, all advertising for Procter & Gamble carries the P&G logo and emphasizes corporate identity to develop a degree of credibility for future product introductions.

European Single Market

The EC or EU became a free internal market in 1993. People, money, and goods began to move across borders without passports, exchange controls, or customs, thus making Europe a larger single market than the United States.[48]

As you saw earlier in this chapter, population growth slowed or has become nonexistent in Europe. But from Euro-stagnation of the early 1980s, countries have unified economically in an attempt to develop efficiencies and growth in the 1990s in a way that became the pattern for the North American Free Trade Agreement (NAFTA). In Europe, factories become more efficient as they serve a market of 344 million people expected to purchase $4 trillion in goods and services. Greater efficiencies in the physical movement of goods and the financial movement of funds are some of the results of the single market. The result is also tougher competition for many firms as companies take a Europe-wide approach to marketing.

The EC consists of 12 members: Britain, Ireland, Denmark, Germany, France, Spain, Portugal, Italy, Greece, Belgium, the Netherlands, and Luxembourg. Some of the benefits of the EC have been extended to the seven members of the European Free Trade Association (EFTA) consisting of Austria, Finland, Iceland, Liechtenstein, Norway, Sweden, and Switzerland, possibly setting the stage for those countries' full integration into the common market. If all the countries that have expressed interest in joining the EC were to do so, the number of members would be about 25.

Increasingly, business managers and some consumers are referring to themselves as "we Europeans" rather than the national identity. Borders between countries may have only a sign noting the country but featuring the EC symbol prominently. Firms are beginning the do the same. Notice the point-of-purchase sign for Miele (a European appliance manufacturer) in Figure 3.10, which carries the EC emblem. Also, notice that the company has chosen words to describe its product that can be readily understood by consumers regardless of whether their first language is German, Dutch, English, or a romance language.

The largest market in the world is now the EC. The dominant force in that market is Germany, which receives its importance not only for its role in the EC but also for its favorable position to trade with Eastern Europe and the

Figure 3.10   Euromarketing by Miele

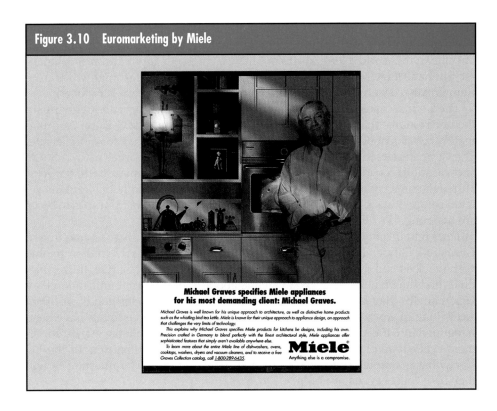

**Michael Graves specifies Miele appliances
for his most demanding client: Michael Graves.**

Michael Graves is well known for his unique approach to architecture, as well as distinctive home products such as the whistling bird tea kettle. Miele is known for their unique approach to appliance design, an approach that challenges the very limits of technology.

This explains why Michael Graves specifies Miele products for kitchens he designs, including his own. Precision crafted in Germany to blend perfectly with the finest architectural style, Miele appliances offer sophisticated features that simply aren't available anywhere else.

To learn more about the entire Miele line of dishwashers, ovens, cooktops, washers, dryers and vacuum cleaners, and to receive a free Graves Collection catalog, call 1-800-289-6435.

Miele

Anything else is a compromise.

former Soviet republics. Although Brussels is the capital city of the EC, from a marketing perspective Berlin may become the capital of all of Europe. For this reason, we conclude this chapter with a closer look at the economic power that is emerging as a new world superpower, alongside the United States and Japan.

Germany

Germany has undergone drastic changes in almost every measurable area including population, average income, average age, even geographical size of the country. Consumer analysts forecast growth in other countries; reunification achieved it almost instantly. The German economy and corporations have had to adjust to the addition of 17 million people to increase its population base to roughly 78 million, 20 million stronger than the next largest European country, Italy, with 58 million.

The German form of capitalism is somewhere between the Japanese form, which promotes business, and the American form, which regulates business. The blend of business, government, and unions based on a structured value system has created a standard of living that is among the highest in the world and a quality of life for the masses of workers that would be the envy of most of the elite in the world. Germans do not have as high per capita income as Japanese but have large homes, excellent food, world-class cars, fast highways, environmentally concerned cities ringed by green forests, and very good beer!

The German market has created its high standard of living without giving up the one resource that Japanese and Americans have the least: leisure. Approximately 80 percent of American workers would trade lower pay for more leisure. The Germans already have the leisure with a standard work week of 37 1/2 hours and vacations mandated by law at 4 weeks but that are commonly 6 to 8 weeks, although some changes in this structure may be required to help Germany remain competitive in the global marketplace. Leisure products from spas to boats are booming.

Does reunification translate into a liability or an opportunity for marketing in Germany? Former East Germany could be characterized as 17 million people with the need and desire to buy everything. Under Communist rule, they sometimes had the money but lacked available goods to buy. Since reunification they lack many of the resources needed to satiate their appetite for goods, but they are willing to work to gain resources to spend. As Eastern Germans have been integrated into the reunified economy, they become a large, viable market for almost every type of product from cars to fresh fruit. Trade barriers of the EC somewhat guarantee they won't buy too many Toyotas. The question is will they buy Volkswagens or Fords?

Germany has made economic sacrifices in the short term to invest in its long-run future, which include a new labor supply made up of people with similar values and good positioning for market dominance in other Eastern European countries. Figure 3.11 shows an ad sponsored by the Economics Ministry of the Federal Republic of Germany to further the understanding of the New Federal States of Germany and its goals and stimulate investment in its future. In the long run, it will be recognized that culture and language form a bond among people that not even walls can destroy. It is values that make a country wealthy, not its natural resources.

Global Thinking — A Final Perspective

Perhaps the most important aspect of global thinking is not knowledge of how to sell in other countries or how to source in other countries, but the ability to understand marketing and management globally, to adopt the best methods from around the globe, and to avoid the worst. A study of firms that are successful around the world — Coca-Cola, Unilever, Toyota, and Aldi — helps to achieve this goal.

Aldi is a family-owned grocery chain based in Germany that operates in many countries including the United States. It is a niche player, however, and its

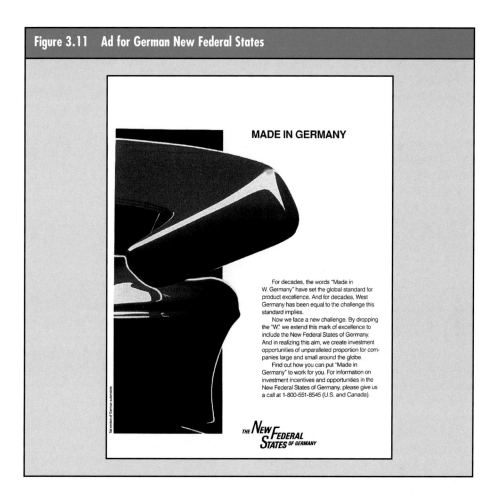

Figure 3.11 Ad for German New Federal States

niche is the cost-sensitive segment, whether that be in the cities of the United States or the rural villages of the Benelux. How does a firm keep its prices dramatically lower than the competition throughout the world? By unrelenting pressure to lower costs. Look at Figure 3.12 and you will see a shopper selecting a shopping cart in an Aldi supermarket. There is an interesting detail. She must first place a coin into the cart before taking it. The coin is refunded when the cart is returned from the parking lot. A small idea but think of the reduction in labor costs (from pushing the carts back from the parking lot), reduction in theft, and reduction in maintenance costs because the carts are not left out in bad weather. Perhaps the idea would not work in affluent suburbs of the United States—but that's not Aldi's market segment, although it does attract some members of this group. Too often American business managers have been ethnocentric or simply

Figure 3.12 Cost Reduction with Coin-Operated Shopping Carts

unaware of management and marketing solutions around the world. Consumer analysts need the skills to lead the way in understanding behavior on a cross-cultural basis.

Summary

Consumer behavior analysts are increasingly required to understand buying and consumption decisions on a global basis. Population growth is slowing so rapidly in industrialized countries that consumer analysts must find and understand the cultures of new markets that have both population vitality and ability to buy to be attractive market segments for global marketing organizations.

The fastest-growing country in the world in population is India. African countries such as Kenya and Nigeria have rapid population growth but low income. The search for markets that have both population growth as well as good or improving economic conditions often leads to the Pacific Rim.

Cross-cultural analysis is the systematic comparison of similarities and differences in the behavioral and physical aspects of cultures. Cross-cultural analysis provides an approach to understanding market segments both across national boundaries and between groups within a society. The process of analyzing markets on a cross-cultural basis is particularly helpful in deciding which elements of a marketing program can be standardized in multiple nations and which elements must be localized.

Major changes in markets are caused by the continuum of change found in countries that formerly were Communist and are now moving toward capitalism. Russia and its fellow republics provide a hope for huge markets in the future because of the size of the nations and the historic base of technology, although currently there is enormous suffering and struggle caused by the inefficiencies of the distribution system. Eastern European countries provide some of the best opportunities for purchase of Western products and services produced and marketed by global marketing organizations.

The EU is now the largest market in the world with 344 million people in 12 countries. The addition of EFTA creates more market opportunities, and potentially this market could encompass as many as 25 countries. The economic powerhouse of this area and increasingly the world is reunified Germany. Germany has solved one of the classic consumption problems. Not only has it achieved a high level of economic resources for its citizens, approaching the level of the United States and Japan, Germany has achieved the goal of providing leisure by developing an economy that achieves productivity levels that permit large amounts of leisure time.

Review and Discussion Questions

1. Is it really necessary to "think globally" in the study of consumer behavior? Why?

2. Which countries of the world will provide the best consumer markets in the next 5 to 10 years? In the next 10 to 30 years? Why?

3. How do you reconcile the belief that India represents an attractive market when Table 3.3 reports such a low per capita GNP?

4. Assume that a soft drink marketer wanted to enter the Russian market. Prepare a set of recommendations for doing so.

5. Assume that a manufacturer of shoes wishes a market analysis on how to enter the most profitable markets in Africa. What should be included in the report?

6. Assume that a French manufacturer of women's apparel is seeking to expand markets by exporting to Canada or the United States. What would you recommend for maximum effectiveness?

7. What is meant by the term *cross-cultural analysis?* Why is it important for marketers?

8. What are the opportunities for trade or joint ventures in Russia or other former Soviet republics? What are the main elements that you would include in a market analysis of such ventures?

9. "If a firm were entering Europe now, it should probably place its headquarters in Berlin." Evaluate this statement.

Endnotes

1. Michael E. Porter, ed., *Competition in Global Industries* (Cambridge, Mass.: Harvard Business School Press, 1986).

2. "Three Small Businesses Profit by Taking on the World," *Wall Street Journal* (November 8, 1990), B2.

3. Ibid.

4. *1991 World Population Data Sheet*, Population Reference Bureau, Inc. (1991).

5. Thomas W. Merrick, "World Population in Transition," *Population Bulletin* 41 (April 1986), 3.

6. Ben J. Wattenberg, *Birth Dearth* (New York: Pharos Books, 1987).

7. Robert Prus, *Pursuing Customers: An Ethnography of Marketing Activities* (Newbury Park, Calif.: Sage Publications, 1989).

8. Brian Mark Hawrysh and Judith Lynne Zaichkowsky, "Cultural Approaches to Negotiations: Understanding the Japanese," *European Journal of Marketing* 25 (1991), 51.

9. Charles F. Keown, Nicolas Synodinos, Laurence Jacobs, and Reginald Worthley, "Can International Advertising Be Standardized?" World Congress of the Academy of Marketing Sciences, Barcelona, 1987. For a macroeconomic perspective on this issue, see Seymour Banks, "Cross-National Analysis of Advertising Expenditures," *Journal of Advertising Research* 26 (April–May 1986), 11–23.

10. An introduction to cross-cultural methods is found in R. W. Bristin, W. J. Lonner, and R. M. Thorndike, *Cross-Cultural Research Methods* (New York: John Wiley & Sons, 1973); and Walter J. Lonner and John W. Berry, *Field Methods in Cross-Cultural Research* (Beverly Hills, Calif.: Sage Publications, 1986).

11. Iris Schopphoven, "Values and Consumption Patterns: A Comparison between Rural and Urban Consumers in Western Germany," *European Journal of Marketing* 25 (1991), 20–35.

12. James Wills, Coskun A. Samli, and Laurence Jacobs, "Developing Global Products and Marketing Strategies: A Construct and a Research Agenda," *Journal of the Academy of Marketing Science* 19 (Winter 1991), 7.

13. Erik Elinder, "How International Can European Advertising Be?" *Journal of Marketing* 29 (April 1965), 7–11.

14. Theodore Levitt, "The Globalization of Markets," *Harvard Business Review* 61 (May–June 1983), 92–102. For the contrasting perspective, see Yoram Wind, "The Myth of Globalization," *Journal of Consumer Marketing* 3 (Spring 1986), 23–26.

15. Salah Hassan and Roger Blackwell, *Global Marketing Perspectives and Cases* (Forth Worth, TX: The Dryden Press, 1993), 53–57.

16. Robert D. Buzzell, "Can You Standardize Multinational Marketing?" *Harvard Business Review* 46 (November–December 1986), 102–113; Theodore Levitt, "The Globalization of Markets," *Harvard Business Review* 61 (May–June 1983), 92–102; "Multinationals Tackle Global Marketing," *Advertising Age* (June 25, 1984), 50ff. Also see "Marketers Turn Sour on Global Sales Pitch Harvard Guru Makes," *Wall Street Journal* (May 11, 1988), 1.

17. Ralph Z. Sorenson and Ulrich E. Wiechmann, "How Multinationals View Marketing Standardization," *Harvard Business Review* 53 (May–June 1975), 38–56. Also see William H. Davidson and Philippe Haspeslagh, "Shaping a Global Product Organization," *Harvard Business Review* 60 (July–August 1982), 125–132.

18. Arthur Fatt, "The Danger of 'Local' International Advertising," *Journal of Marketing* 31 (January 1967), 60–62.

19. Hassan and Blackwell, *Global Marketing Perspectives and Cases.*

20. H. Simon, "Lessons from Germany's Midsize Giants," *Harvard Business Review* (March–April 1992), 115–123.

21. Roger Blackwell, Riad Ajami, and Kristina Stephan, "Winning the Global Advertising Race: Planning Globally, Acting Locally," *Journal of International Consumer Marketing* 3 (1991), 108.

22. For an in-depth description of what can go wrong in global market situations, see David Ricks, *Big Business Blunders: Mistakes in Multinational Marketing* (Homewood, Ill.: Dow Jones-Irwin, 1983). A valuable guide to avoiding global blunders is found in Vern Terpstra and Kenneth David, *The Cultural Environment of International Business* (Cincinnati, Ohio: South-Western Publishing, 1985).

23. Hassan and Blackwell, *Global Marketing Perspectives and Cases.*

24. Kevin Lynch, "Adplomacy Faux Pas Can Ruin Sales," *Advertising Age* (January 15, 1979), S-2ff; and "When Slogans Go Wrong," *American Demographics* 14 (February 1992), 14.

25. Richard W. Brislin, "Back-Translation for Cross-Cultural Research," *Journal of Cross-Cultural Psychology* 1 (September 1970); Oswald Werner and Donald T. Campbell, "Translating, Working through Interpreters and the Problems of Decentering," in Raoul Naroll and Ronald Cohen, eds., *A Handbook of Method in Cultural Anthropology* (Garden City, N.Y.: National History Press, 1970), 298–420.

26. Walter P. Margulies, "Why Global Marketing Requires a Global Focus on Product Design," *Business Abroad* 94, (January 1969), 22.

27. David A. Aaker, *Managing Brand Equity* (New York: The Free Press, (1991), 263–269.

28. Karen A. Berger, Barbara B. Stern, and J. K. Johansson, "Strategic Implications of a Cross-Cultural Comparison of Attribute Importance: Automobiles in Japan and the

United States," in *Proceedings of the American Marketing Association Educators' Conference* (Chicago: American Marketing Association, 1983), 327–332.

29. Alfred S. Boote, "Psychographic Segmentation in Europe," *Journal of Advertising Research* 22 (December 1982), 19–25.

30. For details of this methodology, see Bernard Berelson, *Content Analysis in Communications Research* (New York: Free Press, 1952); and Klaus Krippendorff, *Content Analysis* (Beverly Hills, Calif.: Sage Publications, 1980).

31. Eugene J. Webb et al., *Unobtrusive Measures* (Chicago: Rand McNally, 1966).

32. Richard W. Pollay, "The Identification and Distribution of Values Manifest in Print Advertising 1900–1980," in Robert E. Pitts, Jr., and Arch G. Woodside, eds., *Personal Values and Consumer Psychology* (Lexington, Mass.: Lexington Books, 1984), 111–135.

33. "Business Without Borders," *U.S. News & World Report* 104 (June 20, 1988), 48–53.

34. William J. Brown, "The Use of Entertainment Television Programs for Promoting Prosocial Messages," *Howard Journal of Communications* 3 (Winter–Spring 1992), 253–266.

35. "Caged, a Survey of India," *The Economist* 319 (May 4, 1991).

36. Anthony Spaeth, "A Thriving Middle Class Is Changing the Face of India," *Wall Street Journal* (May 19, 1988), 22.

37. Valerie Reitman, "India Anticipates the Arrival of the Beefless Big Mac," *Wall Street Journal* (October 20, 1993), B1.

38. Grame Hugo, *Australia's Changing Population: Trends and Implications* (Oxford: Oxford University Press, 1987).

39. Bruce W. Nelan, "Watch Out for China," *Time* (November 29, 1993), 36–39.

40. Jerry Stafford, "Vast China Market Just Waiting to Be Researched," *Marketing News* 20 (September 12, 1986), 1.

41. Tohru Nishikawa, "New Product Development: Japanese Consumer Tastes in the Area of Electronics and Home Appliances," *Journal of Advertising Research* 30 (2) (1990), 30.

42. The classic book to understand Japanese culture for business persons is probably William Ouchi, *Theory Z* (New York: Addison-Wesley, 1981).

43. This section abstracted from Dentsu Incorporated, *Marketing Opportunity in Japan* (London: McGraw-Hill, 1978), 84–114. Dentsu is one of the largest advertising agencies in the world.

44. Walter A. Henry, "Impact of Cultural Value Systems on Japanese Distribution Systems," in Pitts and Woodside, *Personal Values and Consumer Psychology*, 255–270.

45. Mikhail Gorbachev, *Perestroika: New Thinking for Our Country and the World* (New York: Harper & Row, 1988).

46. Svetlana Kolesnik, "Advertising and Cultural Politics," *Journal of Communications* 41 (Spring 1991), 46–54.

47. "Perestroika: The Consumer Signals," *Euromarketing Insights* 2 (February 1991), 4.

48. For statistical information on the European Community, see sources such as Brian Morris, Klaus Boehm, and Maurice Geller, *The European Community* (Berlin: Walter DeGruyter & Co., 1991); Secretariat of The Economic Commission for Europe, *Economic Survey of Europe* (New York: United Nations Publication, 1991); Alan Tillier, *Doing Business in Today's Western Europe* (Chicago: NTC Business Books, 1992).

PART II

Consumer Decision Processes

▲▲

The chapters in this section introduce you to the important subject of the nature of decision processes that shape buying and consumption behavior. The goal is to help you develop a comprehensive grasp of (1) the complexities of decision processes and (2) the many resulting implications for strategy.

Chapter 4 is of special importance because it presents an overview of a model of consumer decision process behavior which is used throughout the book. It gives a broad picture of the primary variables and factors which must be understood by any serious student in the field. Take special time to understand this model as it is presented, because it provides the structure around which this book is organized.

Chapter 5 focuses on the first two stages in decision processes — **need recognition and search for information.** The nature of determinants of need recognition are discussed first. Then our focus shifts to the role and characteristics of both internal and external information search.

Information acquisition, of course, is just an initial step in the process of evaluating various alternatives to satisfy activiated need. **Pre-purchase Alternative Evaluation** is the subject of Chapter 6. The heart of this process is comparison of alternatives against **evaluative criteria** (desired product/service attributes). The chapter describes how evaluative criteria are formed and the ways in which evaluation is undertaken in extended problem solving (EPS), limited problem solving (LPS), and habitual decision making.

Chapter 7 focuses on **purchase.** As you are already aware, purchases can be made in many different ways, ranging from use of interactive video to an instore visit. The variety of purchasing options has grown rapidly in recent years and there are many implications for marketing strategy.

As Chapter 8 explores the last three stages in consumer decision processes— **consumption, post-purchase alternative evaluation,** and **divestment.** You will be exposed to the broad field of consumption research, a relative newcomer to this field, and you will be fascinated with its broad and often unexpected scope. Decision making does not stop with consumption, however, because there is likely to be continued evaluation of the product or service leading to a response of **satisfaction** or **dissatisfaction.** No subject in consumer research has greater implications for customer retention, one of the greatest marketing challenges. Finally, you will be introduced to the emerging subject of product divestment which takes the form of outright disposal, recycling, or remarketing.

Consumer Decision Processes

▲▲▲▲▲▲▲▲▲▲▲▲▲▲▲▲▲▲▲▲▲▲▲▲▲▲▲▲▲▲▲▲▲▲▲

Focusing on the Focus Group

One of the most popular forms of consumer research today is the *focus group*. A skilled moderator guides a group ranging from 8 to 12 people *focusing* on the purchase and use of a product or service. The in-depth insights generated in this way find major use in marketing strategy around the world.

We have the privilege of listening in for a moment on one of the sessions. A group of eight married women between the ages of 28 and 35 years are sitting around a table, all of whom also work full-time in the managerial and professional ranks. Their subject? Attitudes and feelings when the time comes to take their car in for new tires or minor service such as wheel alignment or a brake job. Your role is simply to listen and interpret what you see and hear. See if you can isolate some commonalities in the decision-process behavior reported by each person.

Taking the car in: Nothing I hate more!

These words summed it up when the moderator asked, "How did you feel the last time you had to take your car in for brakes or some other kind of routine maintenance?"

Sally: "I felt like a complete jerk. This clown leers at me asking, 'What can I do for you lady?' I known darn well he was thinking, 'Another bimbo to rip off.'"

Joanne: "Yeah, I know what you mean. I never know what to say. All I hear is a kind of a squeal coming from the rear. How do I tell him that?"

Gail:	"We're sitting ducks for these characters. What if I needed new tires? I don't understand anything about them. What's worse, my husband knows less than I do. So why do I have to do this?"
Moderator:	"Not a very pleasant experience, huh? Well, let's think about the last time you had to get your car fixed. What happened to make you take this step?"
Mary Anne:	"I have a little sticker on the windshield that tells me when I should get my next oil change. It was about 2 months late when I saw it, but it reminded me I had better do something."
Sarah:	"I hit a mammoth pothole on I-76. I knew I was in trouble when the car started pulling hard to the right."
Dottie:	"My husband said, 'Take the d— thing to the garage and have that headlight replaced before some cop tickets you!" (laughter)
Debi:	"My husband could care less. But I'm kind of a car nut. I stick by those maintenance intervals right down to the exact mile. I want that car to run perfectly all the time."
Moderator:	"So, just how did you decide where to take your car?"
Joanne:	"I always take it to the dealer. At least I feel the job is done right most of the time."
Janice:	(interrupting) "...to the dealer? No way! Those car jockeys charge you an arm and a leg, and what do you get for it? I go to Kmart, Pep Boys, or someplace like that where I get a decent service guarantee for the lowest price."
Dottie:	"You can guess what I do—just follow my husband's orders. We would have World War II if I made that choice." (groans from around the room)
Sarah:	"We have a neighborhood guy who usually is there when I need him. At least he treats me like a human being."
Gail:	"Oh, I don't know. Maybe the nearest place that has a name I recognize."
Debi:	"The first thing I do is ask around the office and find out where I can go to avoid hassles. And, you know, I have a great place. I've come to know the guys there, and I trust them."
Gail:	"Boy, let me have that name." (another chorus of agreement)
Moderator:	"Will you shop around to find a place you want?"

Figure 4A   Insights from a Focus Group

Janice:	"I sure will if I have the time. And I look for one that has been in business for awhile."
Many voices:	"I agree." "You can learn a lot from just looking at a place." "I pay a lot of attention to how they answer questions on the phone."
Moderator:	"OK, just for the fun of it, let's design a car repair place where we would like to go. What would you make sure that it has?"
Everyone:	"Decent coffee." "Friendly people." "It will be clean and nice." "A woman at the front." "A darn good guarantee that I could trust." "A car to use while I am waiting." "Someone who takes the time to explain to me what must be done and stands behind it."

Mary Anne:	"You know what I hate the most about places like this? The girlie magazines. And there's no way I would go in the ladies' room without a can of Lysol."
Sally:	"I feel the same way you do. But my biggest hang-up is the time it takes. I have to cool my heels for an hour or two, and I haven't got that kind of time. Either give me a loaner car or do something to make it easy to leave the car and be on my way."
Gail:	"I don't really want to leave the car for an oil change. A short wait is no big deal. But please—get rid of the talk shows on TV while being watched by some woman fighting with her kids running around the room. Have a quiet place something like an office reception area with the latest papers, including the *Wall Street Journal.* And have a decent cup of coffee! None of that crud that has fried on the burner for 10 hours."
Dottie:	"My great concern is that I know the car will be fixed right. I don't want to wind up stalled on some freeway. It's got to be done right!" (general agreement)
Joanne:	"How about having a woman design the public areas and maybe even have a decently dressed guy or woman up front?"
Moderator:	"Would you be willing to pay a premium price for such services?"
Everyone:	"Absolutely." "Yes, once I recover from my shock that they are willing to do these things." "You bet."
Moderator:	"What do you do if you've had a bad experience?"
Sally:	"Yell at the kids I guess. Actually, I just make a decision never to go near that place again." (many voices of agreement)
Debi:	"I'll do a lot more than that. I'll be back in a minute to complain and stick with it until they make it right."
Sarah:	"You can bet my friends will know about it. We'll hit those suckers where it hurts the most—in the cash register."

Everyone has a concept or "model" of consumer behavior that hypothesizes those forces motivating and shaping it. A model provides a map that makes sense out of what otherwise could be a bewildering maze without clear direction and outcomes. It would appear that the management of Direct Tire Sales had a very accurate model of the decision process of working women who are seeking automotive service (see Consumer in Focus 4.1).

Consumer in Focus　**4.1**

Retreading the Consumer

Of course Direct Tire Sales loans customers cars while theirs are being repaired. And fixes flats for free on all tires purchased. And guarantees linings and pads on brake jobs for the life of the car.

But what excites customers about this independent tire dealer and auto service firm is the customer lounge: The room is spotless, a high-tech coffee pot burbles in one corner, and the magazine rack features publications like *Newsweek, Discover,* and *Cosmopolitan.* It even has an aquarium. And no girlie calendars featuring Miss Drive Train. Sales employees wear a tie as part of their uniform, and "Yes sir," and "Yes ma'am" with all the polish of a West Point cadet.

Are appearances everything? No, just the beginning. "When I asked them how I could get home, they said they would pay for the cab," recalls one customer, a hardened management consultant. "That's never happened to me before." Such astonished customers don't mind paying a 10% to 15% premium; on the contrary, they come back again.

Source: Rahul Jacob, "How to Retread Customers," Fortune ("The Tough New Consumer" special edition, 1993), 23. Reproduced by special permission.

It is the purpose of this chapter to help you develop a model of consumer decision processes. This is a challenge, because it is necessary to isolate correctly the steps most people follow when decisions are made, as well as the system of internal and external forces that interact and affect how the consumer thinks, evaluates, and acts. Otherwise, everything done in marketing is likely to fall seriously short of potential.

Nature of Decision Processes

Think for a moment of the many interrelated decisions that consumers make many times each day:

- Purchase options

    Whether to buy or save

    When to buy

    What to buy, both product category and brand

    Where to buy

    How to pay

- Consumption options

  Whether to consume or not

  When to consume

  How to conusme

- Divestment options

  Outright disposal

  Recycling

  Remarketing (resale of used items)

Over the years, researchers and specialists have produced many studies and theories regarding human choice behavior. John Dewey's conceptualizations of decision-process behavior as problem solving have been especially influential.[1] By problem solving, we refer to thoughtful, consistent action undertaken to bring about need satisfaction.

As you have seen, many factors can shape the final outcome, including internal motivations and such external influences as social pressures and marketing activities. Somehow individuals sort through all these factors and make decisions that are logical and consistent for them. Consider these words by Ajzen and Fishbein[2]:

> Generally speaking . . . human beings are usually quite rational and make systematic use of the information available to them . . . people consider the implications of their actions before they decide to engage or not engage in a given behavior.

At times, consumer problem solving involves careful weighing and evaluation of utilitarian (or functional) product attributes. Often the term *rational decision making* is used when this is the case. At other times, *hedonic (emotion-driven) benefits* will dominate, and the consumption object is viewed symbolically in terms of sensory pleasures, daydreams, or aesthetic considerations.[3] Buying and consumption generally reflect a mixture of both the utilitarian and the hedonic.

The problem-solving perspective encompasses all types of need-satisfying behavior and a wide range of motivating and influencing factors. Broadly speaking, consumer decision making has the following stages:

1. *Need recognition*—a perception of difference between the desired state of affairs and the actual situation sufficient to arouse and activate the decision process.

2. *Search for information*—search for information stored in memory (internal search) or acquisition of decision-relevant information from the environment (external search).

3. *Pre-purchase alternative evaluation*—evaluation of options in terms of expected benefits and narrowing the choice to the preferred alternative.

4. *Purchase*—acquisition of the preferred alternative or an acceptable substitute.

5. *Consumption*—use of the purchased alternative.

6. *Post-purchase alternative evaluation*—evaluation of the degree to which the consumption experience produced satisfaction.

7. *Divestment*—disposal of the unconsumed product or its remnants.

Consumer Decision-Process Model

We now tackle the issue of developing a model of consumer decision-making process that will provide a comprehensive frame of reference for the discussion in forthcoming chapters. A model is nothing more than a replica of the phenomena it is designed to represent. It specifies the building blocks (variables) and the ways in which they are interrelated (a solid arrow for a direct relationship and a broken arrow for an indirect or feedback relationship). Models of this type offer several advantages:

1. Explanations are provided for behavior. It is possible to grasp visually what happens as variables and circumstances change.

2. A frame of reference is provided for research. Gaps in knowledge and understanding become readily apparent, and research priorities can be established. It also is possible to relate individual research projects to one another.

3. A foundation is provided for management information systems. Proper use of a model discloses the kinds of information required to understand differing consumer decision processes and provides essential insights for marketing strategy.

Variables That Shape Decision Making

Consumer decision making is influenced and shaped by many factors and determinants, which fall into these three categories: (1) individual differences; (2) environmental influences; and (3) psychological processes. A summary follows of the many variables under these headings. Although each is covered in depth in later chapters, the discussion here provides you with a broad overview.

Individual Differences

There are five major categories of individual differences that affect behavior: (1) consumer resources; (2) knowledge; (3) attitudes; (4) motivation; and (5) personality, values, and lifestyle.

Consumer Resources

Each person brings three resources into every decision-making situation: (1) time, (2) money, and (3) information reception and processing capabilities. Generally, there are distinct limits on the availability of each, thus requiring some careful allocation. Chapter 9 will provide many guidelines as you assess the implications of limited resources on consumer motivation and behavior.

Knowledge

Knowledge is defined in Chapter 10 as the information stored in memory, and it encompasses a vast array such as the availability and characteristics of products and services; where and when to buy; and how to use products. Assessing the levels of knowledge among those in a target market segment is important. One main goal of advertising and selling is to provide relevant knowledge and information, which often are needed in decision making, especially under extended problem solving.

Attitudes

Behavior is strongly influenced by attitudes toward a given brand or product. An attitude is simply an overall evaluation of an alternative, ranging from positive to negative. Once formed, attitudes play a directive role on future choice and are difficult to change. Nevertheless, attitude change is a common marketing goal (Chapter 11).

Motivation

Psychologists and marketers alike have conducted considerable research to determine what takes place when goal-directed behavior is energized and activated. As we will discover at many points, especially Chapter 12, needs and motives affect all phases of decision processes in major ways.

Personality, Values, and Lifestyle

Individuals differ in many ways that affect decision processes and buying behavior. This broad category discussed in Chapter 13 encompasses what has come to be known as *psychographic research* to probe into those individual traits, values, beliefs, and preferred behavior patterns that characterize a market segment.

Environmental Influences

Consumers live in a complex environment. Their decision-process behavior is influenced by (1) culture, (2) social class, (3) personal influence, (4) family, and (5) situation.

Culture

Culture, as used in the study of consumer behavior, refers to the values, ideas, artifacts, and other meaningful symbols that help individuals communicate, interpret, and evaluate as members of society. A marketer with a defective knowledge of culture is doomed. Chapters 17 and 18 provide a comprehensive overview of cultural issues from both a global and ethnic perspective.

Social Class

Social classes are divisions within society composed of individuals sharing similar values, interests, and behaviors (Chapter 19). They are differentiated by socioeconomic status differences ranging from low to high. Social class status often leads to differing forms of consumer behavior (for example, the types of alcoholic beverages served, the make and style of car driven, and the styles of dress preferred).

Personal Influence

As consumers, our behavior often is affected by those with whom we closely associate. This is what we mean by *personal influence* discussed in Chapter 20. We often respond to perceived pressure to conform with the norms and expectations provided by others. Also, we value those around us for their counsel on buying choices. This influence can take the form of observation of what others are doing, with the result that they become a comparative reference group. When we actively seek advice from another, however, that person can serve as an influential or opinion leader.

Family

Since the field of consumer research was founded in the post–World War II era, the family has been a focus of research. You will learn in Chapter 19 that the family often is the primary decision-making unit, with a complex and varying pattern of roles and functions. Cooperation and conflict often occur simultaneously with interesting behavioral outcomes.

Situation

It is obvious that behavior changes as situations change. Sometimes, these changes are erratic and unpredictable, such as a job layoff. At other times, they can be predicted by research and capitalized on in strategy. Marketers often capitalize on situational influences, particularly in retail settings, to influence consumer behavior. Following the initiative of Belk and others in the 1970s,[4] situation now is treated as a research variable in its own right (Chapter 21).

Psychological Processes

Finally, those who wish to understand and influence consumer behavior must have practical grasp of three basic psychological processes: (1) information processing, (2) learning, and (3) attitude and behavior change.

Information on Processing

Communication is a bottom-line marketing activity. Therefore, consumer researchers long have been interested in discovering how people receive, process, and make sense of marketing communications. Studies in this important field have underscored our foundational principle of *consumer sovereignty—people see and hear what they want to see and hear.* Information processing research, discussed in Chapter 14, addresses ways in which information is transformed, reduced, elaborated, stored, recovered, and received.

Learning

Anyone attempting to influence the consumer is trying to bring about learning —the process by which experience leads to changes in knowedge and behavior. The marketing significance of learning theory became apparent when one of its leading proponents, John B. Watson, entered the advertising field in the 1930s. Learning theory (Chapter 15) has even greater practical relevance today, especially for those products and services bought on the basis of relatively little reflection and evaluation.

Attitude and Behavior Change

Changes in attitude and behavior are an important marketing objective. This process reflects basic psychological influences that have been the subject or decades of intensive research. Chapter 16 reviews this literature from the perspective of designing effective promotional strategies.

Decision-Process Behavior

Now we pull all influences together and build a model of the process of decision-process behavior. The best way to understand how this process works is to think in terms of an actual purchase situation, namely, that of a hybrid mountain/racing bike named the "Cross Sport." See Consumer in Focus 4.2. This story is especially interesting because of the fact that the manufacturer seemed to misdiagnose the decision process and made some unfortunate strategic errors.

Need Recognition

The initial stage in any decision-making process is need recognition, discussed in Chapter 5 and shown in Figure 4.1. This occurs when an individual senses a difference between what he or she perceives to be the *ideal* state of affairs compared with the *actual* state of affairs at any point in time. In other words, it is a state of desire that initiates a decision process that in turn occurs through the interaction of *individual differences* such as values and needs and *environmental influences,* especially social interaction.

A major source of problem recognition is need arousal, especially when that need is related to self-image. Motives represent enduring predispositions to behave toward certain goals. The potential buyer here could have been motivated by many factors such as commitment to physical fitness, a desire to have the very latest, and so on.

Consumer in Focus   **4.2**

Know Thy Customer, Obey What You Hear

Huffy Corp., the successful $700 million bike maker, did careful research before it launched a new bicycle it dubbed the Cross Sport, a combination of the sturdy mountain bike popular with teenagers and the thin-framed, nimbler racing bike. Huffy conducted two separate series of market focus groups in shopping malls across the country, where randomly selected children and adults viewed the bikes and ranked them. The bikes met with shoppers' approval.

So far so good. In the summer of 1991, Cross Sports were shipped out to mass retailers, such as the Kmart and Toys "R" Us chains, where Huffy already did most of its business. That was the mistake.

As Richard L. Mole, Huffy president and chief executive, explains the company's slipup, the researchers missed one key piece of information. These special hybrid bikes, aimed at adults and, at $159, priced 15% higher than other Huffy bikes, needed individual sales attention by the sort of knowledgeable salespeople who work only in bike specialty shops. Instead, Huffy's Cross Sports were supposed to be sold by the harried general salespeople at mass retailers such as Kmart. Results: "It was a $5 million mistake." By 1992, the company had slashed Cross Sport production 75% and recorded an earnings drop of 30%.

Source: Christopher Power, "Flops," Business Week (August 16, 1993), 79. Reproduced by special permission.

One could also speculate about environmental influences. One could be kids who persuade, "Come on mom, get rid of that old bike." Or neighbors with whom pressure for fitness becomes a war in which the most committed wins. Therefore, need recognition is likely to be multifaceted and complex.

Search for Information

The next step following need recognition is internal search into memory to determine whether enough is known about available options to allow a choice to be made without further information search. External search usually will be required when this is not the case. Internal and external search, depicted in Figure 4.2, are discussed in Chapter 5. External search proved to be a necessity among potential buyers of the Huffy Cross Sports, many of whom found themselves thwarted by inadequate information at point of sale.

Figure 4.2 shows that propensity to engage in external search is affected by individual differences and environmental influences. For example, some potential buyers in almost any product class are cautious and unwilling to act without extensive and detailed information, whereas other shoppers make purchases without even comparing alternatives. Furthermore, search can be stimulated by situational influence, an example being the breakdown of a trusted exercise bike. One also could imagine that conflict with the family could lead the potential buyer to prove his or her point.

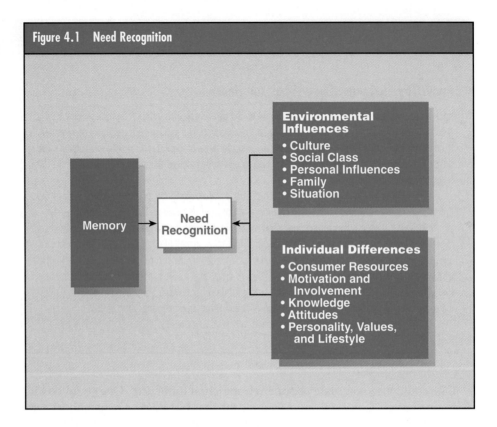

Figure 4.1   Need Recognition

What sources are used when search is undertaken? We put these into two categories in Figure 4.3: (1) marketer-dominated, and (2) other. By marketer-dominated, we refer to anything that the supplier does for purposes of information and persuasion. This can include advertising and point-of-sales materials.

But it certainly does not stop there. Among those sources that are not dominated by the marketer, *word-of-mouth* from others is by far most important. If the Cross Sports bike caught on, it could become quite the subject for discussion in the neighborhood. "What do you think of it?" "How much did it cost?" As we will see in Chapter 24, the success or failure of a new product is often determined right at this point.

Others who are in active information search will turn to objective product rating sources such as *Consumer Reports*. If the Cross Sport were to be rated poorly here and in other similar publications, its future could be doomed.

Information Processing

Now, what happens as the consumer is exposed to information during external search? To answer this question in a preliminary manner, we turn to the impor-

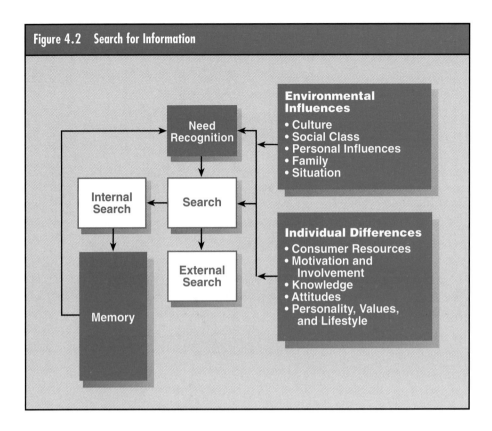

Figure 4.2   Search for Information

tant subject of information processing covered in Chapter 14, which includes these steps in Figure 4.3:

1. *Exposure.* As a first step, information and persuasive communication must reach consumers where they happen to be. Once exposure occurs, one or more of the senses are activated and preliminary processing commences.

2. *Attention.* After exposure, the next step is to allocate (or not allocate) information-processing capacity to the incoming information. Attention is most likely to be attracted when the incoming message and its content are considered to be relevant. Consumers frequently ignore commercial persuasion at this stage and exercise their capabilities of selective attention.

3. *Comprehension.* If attention is attracted, the message is further analyzed against categories of meaning stored in memory. The marketer hopes that accurate comprehension will be the outcome.

4. *Acceptance.* The goal is to modify or change existing beliefs and attitudes. If the incoming message is not screened out at this stage as being unacceptable (a common outcome), we can conclude that acceptance has taken place.

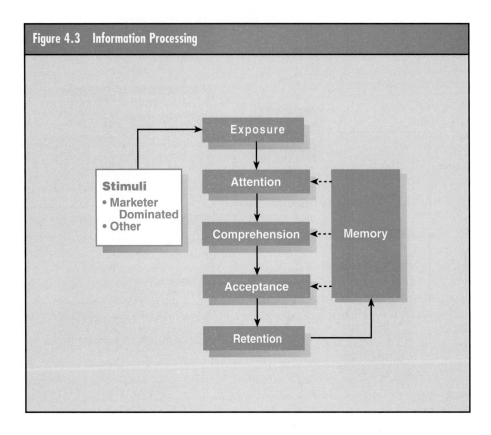

Figure 4.3   Information Processing

Further, there is a good chance of at least some changes occurring if there has been acceptance within the system or structure.

5. *Retention.* Finally, the goal of any persuader is for this new information to be not only accepted but also stored in memory in such a way that it is accessible for future use. But as you learn in Chapter 14, this is by no means a certainty.

You will recall the importance of brand equity from Chapter 1. A favorable impression or image certainly enhances the probability of successful communication. Huffy apparently has a high level of acceptance, and there is every reason to think that its advertising and sales material would be considered if prepared properly.

But favorable brand equity will not be sufficient in and of itself—*attention will be attracted and held only if the information is pertinent for the individual in terms of his or her motivations and needs.* Everybody sifts through the barrage of competing messages and selects only a tiny subset that will be further processed. Much commercial persuasion falls by the wayside at this stage as consumers exercise their capabilities of selective information processing.

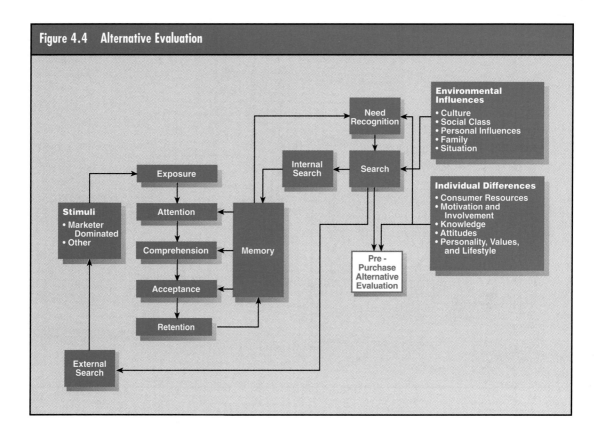

Figure 4.4   Alternative Evaluation

Pre-purchase Alternative Evaluation

The prospective bike purchaser now will examine the Huffy Cross Sports in terms of the product attributes offered as compared with his or her own standards and specifications. This is what we mean by pre-purchase alternative evaluation discussed in Chapter 6 (Figure 4.4), which makes use of *evaluative criteria* — the standards and specifications used by consumers to compare different products and brands.

In other words, these criteria are the desired outcomes from purchase and consumption and are expressed in the form of preferred attributes. In turn, they are shaped and influenced by individual differences and environmental influences. As such, they become a product-specific manifestation of an individual's needs, values, lifestyles, and so on.

We can only speculate as to the nature of the findings from consumer interviews. One likely consideration for many is "durability in rough use" — an attribute not possessed by racing bikes. Others might place primary importance on "ease of shifting" or "light weight." One thing is sure, however—management seriously underestimated consumers' needs for relevant information and

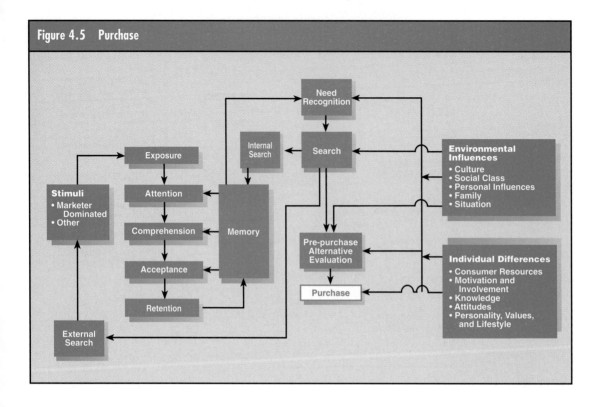

Figure 4.5   Purchase

hence imperiled the chances for success. They seemed to miss the point that buyers are not likely to have their needs met by untrained salespeople in a mass merchandising outlet.

Purchase

Purchase (Figure 4.5) most often takes place in some type of retail outlet, although our discussion in Chapter 7 demonstrates the remarkable growth of various forms of in-home shopping. Often, as we see in this case, a prospect will require contact with a highly skilled salesperson. The point is that deliberation and evaluation is not necessarily done once the person is at the counter.

Consumption and Post-consumption Alternative Evaluation

The next stages in the decision-process model are discussed together in Chapter 8, because it is obvious that consumption and post-purchase alternative evaluation are closely related (Figure 4.6). As we mentioned earlier, consumption has not traditionally been much concern to marketers whose primary objective has been to close the sale. Now there has been a dramatic competitive shift toward customer satisfaction and retention. Huffy management could have learned a

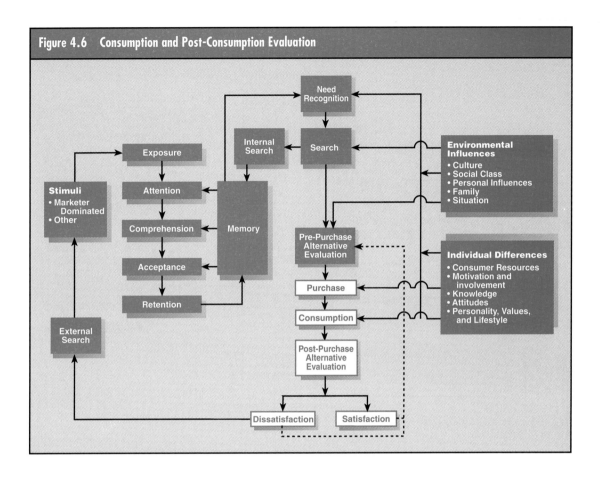

Figure 4.6 Consumption and Post-Consumption Evaluation

great deal by examining how new purchasers use their bikes. What do they like best? What suggestions do they have for product modification? It is especially important to probe into reasons why they are returned.

Here is the important question: *Are buyers' expectations met?* If expectations are matched by perceived performance, *satisfaction* is the outcome. The feedback arrow in Figure 4.6 demonstrates the important role of satisfaction in future alternative evaluation and choice.

When the alternative is perceived as falling short in significant ways, dissatisfaction is the result. Sometimes, it is possible to experience such doubts even before trial simply because of the presence of unchosen alternatives with desirable features. Often known as *postdecision regret,* this can be an incentive for further information search, as the dotted feedback arrow in Figure 4.6 indicates.

A product's failure to perform will not be accepted easily by the buyers, especially when the purchase has high perceived importance. Complaints and efforts to achieve redress are common. The quality of postsale service can make a great difference.

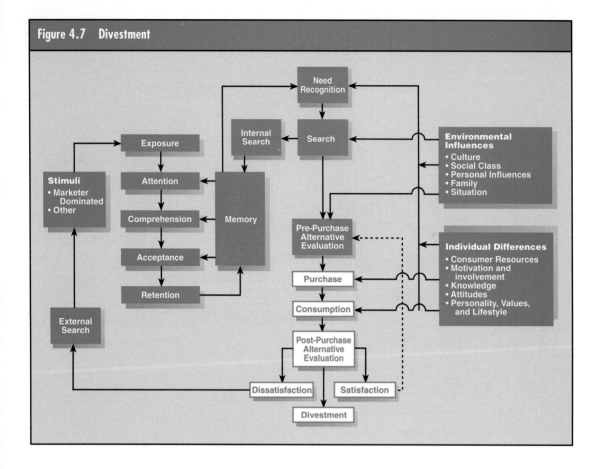

Figure 4.7   Divestment

Divestment

Divestment is the last stage in our consumer decision-process model (Figure 4.7). The consumer now faces the options of outright disposal, recycling, or re-marketing (sale on the used market). As you learn in Chapter 8, the latter two options are growing in importance.

Types of Decision Processes

The extent to which each of the stages in Figure 4.7 is followed in the precise form and sequence suggested here can vary, however, from one situation to the next. Sometimes consumers undertake a complex decision process requiring substantial amounts of time and energy. More common, however, are rather simplistic processes in which relatively little time and effort are devoted to the decision.

Decision-Process Continuum

One way to think about these variations is to imagine a continuum of decision-making complexity ranging from high to low (Figure 4.8). In situations in which consumers are making a decision for the first time, actions must be based on some form of problem solving. When this process is very complex, it is called *extended problem solving (EPS). Limited problem solving (LPS),* however, represents a lower degree of complexity. For convenience, we refer to the process along the middle of the continuum as *midrange problem solving.*

In Figure 4.8, we allow for the fact that most consumer purchases are made on a repeated basis. When this is the case, the individual may engage in problem solving once again. Alternatively, he or she may greatly simplify the decisions by foregoing any deliberation of purchase alternatives and simply choosing the same brand purchased previously. What this represents is habitual decision making, the least complex of all decision processes.

Initial Purchase

When the initial decision was made by EPS, enduring buying patterns are often established on brand loyalty. However, limited problem solving leads to inertia-based habits—it's easier to do the same thing over again than switch. The reasons for these distinctions will become more clear as we proceed.

Extended Problem Solving

When the decision process is especially detailed and rigorous, extended problem solving generally is a necessity. Certainly, most prospective buyers of the Huffy bike engaged in EPS. Furthermore we have evidence from the focus

Figure 4.8 Consumer Decision-Process Continuum

Extended Problem Solving (EPS)	Midrange Problem Solving	Limited Problem Solving (LPS)	
High	Degree of Complexity		Low

Decision-Making Processes for Repeat Purchases

Extended Problem Solving (EPS)	Midrange Problem Solving	Limited Problem Solving (LPS)	Habitual-Decision Making
High	Degree of Complexity		Low

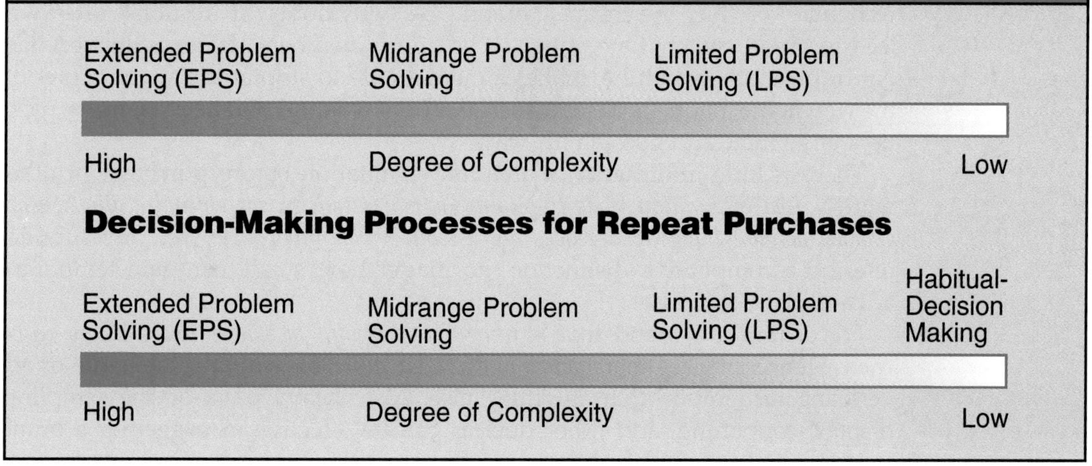

group data at the beginning of the chapter that female users of automobile repair services experience real doubts and fears. They are open to information from various sources and are motivated to undertake the effort to make "the right choice." Also, EPS also is commonly used by consumers purchasing automobiles, expensive clothing, stereo equipment, and other major products or services for which the costs and risks of a wrong decision are high.

When EPS is activated, all six stages in the decision process are likely to be followed, although not necessarily in any precise order. It is likely that many alternatives will be evaluated and a wide variety of information sources consulted. Furthermore, the decision on how and where to make the purchase also may require additional search and evaluation.

In short, *thought and evaluation precede the act of purchase and use because of the importance of making the right choice.* The process of analysis and reflection, however, does not cease after purchase and use. If the item purchased is perceived as falling short of expectations, the outcome can be substantial and often vocal dissatisfaction. The desired outcome is satisfaction expressed in the form of positive recommendations to others and intention to repurchase should the occasion arise.

Limited Problem Solving

We now approach the other extreme of the decision-making continuum (LPS) and arrive at what Harold Kassarjian has humorously depicted as the consumer who is "muddling through."[5] In most situations, consumers have neither the time, the resources, nor the motivation to engage in EPS. It is far more common to simplify the process and sharply reduce the number and variety of information sources, alternatives, and criteria used for evaluation.

Take time to read Consumer in Focus 4.3, which allows us to listen once again to the dialog in a focus group but with quite a different product category—toothpaste.

Choice often is made by following a simple rule such as "buy a brand that I recognize" or "buy the cheapest brand."[6] A "why not try it" response often will lead to brand switch. One of our focus group members squeezes the very last out of his toothpaste tube, makes a mental note to stop at the supermarket on the way home, happens to see a special on a new brand that he recognizes, picks up a large tube, and goes on his way.

There is little information search and evaluation before purchase. In other words, *need recognition leads to buying action; extensive search and evaluation are avoided because the purchase does not assume great importance.* Yet, any supplier offering a competitive distinction, no matter how small, can gain temporary advantage.

For example, a brand that is *recognized at point of sale* is more likely to be tried. Hence, market share often is dictated more by winning the battle of advertising recognition than anything else. Also, heavy point-of-sale sampling, display, couponing, and other devices can be effective in triggering a brand switch.

Buying Toiletries—Get It over with Fast

Eleven men younger than the age of 40 years are participating in a focus group on a topic that no one thinks is too exciting—brand preferences for bath soap and toothpaste. Our moderator has just asked, "Which brand of toothpaste do you prefer to buy?" Six different brands were mentioned. Then he asked, "Would you buy another brand if your favorite is not available?"

Ed:	"Yes. There are a couple of other brands that are just as good. All I care is that it has fluoride."
Brad:	"What difference does it make? Toothpaste is toothpaste."
Sam:	"Yeah, I'd buy something else, but there's no way that I would pay more, no matter what it is."
Rick:	"Sure. I like to shift brands once in awhile just to try something new. I get tired of the same old thing."
Moderator:	"OK, what if a new brand is available two-for-one at the same price of the other brands? Would you be likely to try it?"
Greg:	"Sure, as long as it isn't some weirdo thing from Mars."
Bill:	"I agree with that. I would probably try it if I recognize the company or brand name. Why not?"
Fred:	"You bet—low price is what I want."
Moderator:	"What I am hearing is that low price is probably the most important thing and that you are willing to try different brands."
Everyone:	Many expressions of agreement.

Midrange Problem Solving

As we have noted, EPS and LPS are extremes on a decision-process continuum, but many decisions range somewhere in between. An example is a couple who are deciding which movie to see. A minimum amount of information usually is required to know what is playing, which is easily found in the daily paper. Because several options look promising, there is a need to evaluate which option to choose. Often the basis is the recommendation of a friend or critic. All this can be accomplished quickly with only minimal deliberation.

Repeat Purchases

Thus far, we have not addressed the issue of what happens when the buying process is repeated over time. There are two possibilities: (1) repeated problem solving, and (2) habitual decision making.

Repeated Problem Solving

Repeat purchases often require continued problem solving. Several factors can lead to this outcome, one of the most important being dissatisfaction with the previously bought alternative. A brand switch is likely. But continued problem solving also is required when retail stock has been depleted or circumstances change in some other way. Now the buyer must weigh the consequences of investing time and energy in finding another alternative.

Habitual Decision Making

It is far more likely that repeat purchases will be made on the basis of habits or routines that are formed to enable the consumer to cope more effectively with the pressures of life. Habitual behavior takes different forms, depending on the decision process followed in the initial purchase: (1) brand or company loyalty, or (2) inertia. You will enjoy Ellen Goodman's dilemma of becoming an "enslaved, dazed consumer" (Consumer in Focus 4.4).

Brand or Company Loyalty

Recall the dilemma expressed by many women when compelled to have their car repaired. A strong desire was expressed to find an outlet that would offer the services they most wanted, and furthermore, most would gladly reward that company with continued use over time. This is what we mean by brand or company *loyalty*. It occurs when it is important to find an alternative that meets needs, and the resulting loyalty can be highly resistant to change.

   Any marketer covets high loyalty and does everything possible to maintain it. Anyone who tries to dislodge loyal purchasers of a brand of 35mm film such as Fuji could face a tough challenge indeed. This loyalty is often based on both the high involvement nature of photography to many and a belief that Fuji offers the truest color and picture quality. Such buyers have no incentive to change unless there is a real and demonstrable competitive breakthrough.

Inertia

Toothpaste is a product category in which there is limited brand loyalty per se. Where any degree of loyalty does exist, it mostly consists of several brands, all of which are about equal. Buying habits of this type are based on *inertia* and are unstable. Although there is no incentive to switch, this may occur quite readily when prices are lowered or another brand is bannered as offering something new.

Special Categories of Buying Behavior

Two other forms of buying behavior do not neatly fit into the problem-solving continuum and thus should be considered as special cases: (1) impulse buying, and (2) variety seeking.

Consumer in Focus **4.4**

Freedom of Choice Enslaves Dazed Consumer

The woman is standing in the drugstore suffering from acute "consumeritis." This attack has been brought on by the excess of choices on the shelf before her. Its chief symptom is mental paralysis, the total inability to make a decision.

She came here on a quest for a refill of shampoo. But when her usual brand was no longer available, she was tossed willy-nilly into the chaos of the modern day world of shampoos.

What did she want after all? Which of the three-dozen options lined up before her would make the dead follicles that grow out of her busy head come alive? A moisturizing formula? A body-building protein? A mysterious chemical soup of Elastin? Collagen? Keratin? Balsam?

She was compelled by the labels to ask herself some penetrating questions. Was she the sort of person who needed her pH balanced? Or would she prefer her pH a bit off of kilter? Should she put essential fatty acids in her scalp? Did she want shampoo with a pectin extract? Or isn't that what she uses to make jelly?

This proliferation of personal products had turned shopping into a decision-making marathon. The competing claims of manufacturers had produced an information glut.

Informed consumers are propelled into examining their bodies in ever more minute detail. Does my skin need intensive care or not? Do I have plaque on my teeth or not? Ridges on my nails? Split ends on my hair? Am I normal or dry?

One thing is clear to the woman lathering the body-building protein into her scalp: What the advertisers call brand loyalty is a low-level consumer protest movement. It's our way of cutting through the bouts of decision-making, avoiding the barrages of useless information. It's a defense against the need to waste energy differentiating things that barely differ.

Source: Ellen Goodman, "Freedom of Choice Enslaves Dazed Consumer," Copyright 1987, The Boston Globe Newspaper Company/Washington Post Writer's Group. Reprinted with permission.

Impulse Buying

The so-called impulse purchase (an unplanned spur-of-the-moment action triggered by product display or point-of-sale promotion)[7] is the least complex form of LPS but differs in some important ways. Here are its characteristics[8]:

1. A sudden and spontaneous desire to act accompanied by urgency

2. A state of psychological disequilibrium in which a person can feel temporarily out of control

3. The onset of conflict and struggle that is resolved by an immediate action

4. Minimal objective evaluation—emotional considerations are dominant

5. A lack of regard for consequences

Although there is an absence of the careful reasoning characteristic of EPS, there is not the indifference that accompanies LPS. A high sense of emotional involvement and urgency, in effect, short-circuits the reasoning process and motivates immediate action.

Variety Seeking

Consumers will often express satisfaction with their present brand but still engage in brand switching. The reason? Activation of variety seeking as a motive. Variety seeking is seen most often when there are many similar alternatives and frequent brand shifts and high purchase frequency.[9] When variety seeking seems likely, there is merit in appeals such as that illustrated in Figure 4.9—"Want a little spice in life?" or "Tired of the same old thing?"

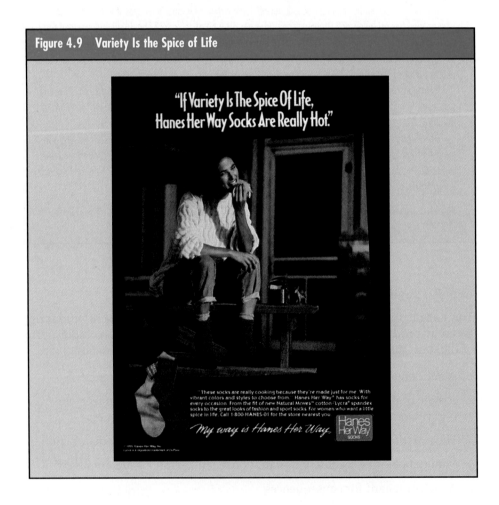

Figure 4.9   Variety Is the Spice of Life

Factors Influencing the Extent of Problem Solving

Extended problem solving is most often undertaken when three major conditions are met: (1) There is a high degree of *involvement* (personal relevance) accompanying the purchase; (2) the alternatives are differentiated in relevant ways; and (3) there is sufficient time available for deliberation.

Degree of Involvement

The degree of *personal involvement* is the most important factor that shapes the type of decision-process behavior that will be followed. Following the definition of John Antil, "Involvement is the level of perceived personal importance and/or interest evoked by a stimulus (or stimuli) within a specific situation."[10] To the extent that it is present, the consumer acts with deliberation to minimize the risks and to maximize the benefits gained from purchase and use.

Involvement is best conceived as a function of person, object, and situation. The starting point always is with the person—underlying motivations in the form of needs and values. It is activated when the object (a product, service, or promotional message) is perceived as being instrumental in meeting important needs, goals, and values. But as we will see, the perceived need-satisfying significance of the object will vary from one situation to the next. Therefore, all three factors (person, object, and situation) must be taken into account.

Involvement, then, is a reflection of strong motivation in the form of high perceived personal relevance of a product or service in a particular context, and it also takes the form of a continuum ranging from low to high. Involvement becomes activated and felt when intrinsic personal characteristics (needs, values, self-concept) are confronted with appropriate marketing stimuli within a given situation.[11] Furthermore, it seems to function in comparable ways across cultures, although the specific products and modes of expression will vary somewhat.[12]

Are the focus group participants highly involved in the process of finding an acceptable outlet for automobile service? The answer to this is a resounding *yes.* They know that having the repair done right is important. And they have all kinds of fears that they will make the wrong choice. To top it off, they are repelled by people and conditions once they get there. Can we blame them?

Determinants of Involvement

Research on the factors that generate high or low involvement is extensive. Therefore, we only highlight some main points here.

Personal Factors

Without activation of need and drive, there will be no involvement, and it is strongest when the product or service is perceived as enhancing self-image.[13] When that is the case, involvement is likely to be enduring and to function as a stable trait, as opposed to being situational or temporary.[14]

Product Factors

Products or brands also become involving if there is some perceived risk in purchase and use. In 1960, the late Raymond Bauer advanced this important proposition: "Consumer behavior involves risk in the sense that any action of a consumer will produce consequences which he cannot anticipate with anything approximating certainty, and some of which are likely to be unpleasant."[15]

Many types of perceived risk have been identified, including physical (risk of bodily harm), psychological (especially a negative effect on self-image), performance (fear that the product will not perform as expected), and financial (risk that outcomes will lead to loss of earnings).[16]

As one would logically expect, the greater the perceived risk, the greater the likelihood of high involvement. When perceived risk becomes unacceptably high, there is motivation either to avoid purchase and use altogether or to minimize risk through the search and pre-purchase alternative evaluation stages in extended problem solving. Interestingly, middle-class consumers in India and in the United States ranked exactly the same products as being high and low in risk.[17]

Situational Factors

Whereas enduring involvement can be considered as a stable trait, situational (or instrumental) involvement changes over time. It is operational on a temporary basis and wanes once purchasing outcomes are resolved. This is often the case with fads such as trendy clothing items in which involvement is high initially but quickly diminishes once the item is worn and fashions begin to change.

There also are times when an otherwise uninvolving product takes on a different degree of relevance because of the manner in which it will be used.[18] For example, there can be a big difference between the perceived importance of a brand of hand soap purchased for home use as opposed to that given as a gift.

Finally, involvement can increase when social pressures are felt. Zaichkowsky demonstrated, for example, that consumers react quite differently when they purchase wine for ordinary personal consumption as opposed to wine that will be served at a dinner party.[19]

Outcomes of High and Low Involvement

When involvement is high for any of the reasons mentioned earlier, here are the usual outcomes:

1. EPS is usually initiated, accompanied by pre-purchase alternative evaluation.[20] Consumers are motivated to search for relevant information and to process it thoroughly.[21]

2. Highly involved consumers are more likely to be influenced by strength of the selling appeals in advertising and promotion (referred to as *argumentation*) as opposed to the way in which the appeal is expressed and visualized.[22] When this occurs, it is said that *message involvement* has been activated. Notice the ad for Sanyo washers that appeared in a general purpose publication in Thailand (Figure 4.10). The selling points would

Figure 4.10 How Will You Process This Ad? It All Depends on Level of Involvement

be of greatest interest for those experiencing high *message involvement,* whereas these same points would be largely disregarded by consumers experiencing low message involvement. Instead, other aspects of the message become more influential when message involvement is low. Thus, involvement has important implications for persuasion strategy.

3. Consumers are more likely to notice differences in the attributes offered by various products or brands, and a common outcome is greater brand loyalty.

Extent to Which Alternatives Are Perceived to Be Different

As you would expect, EPS is more probable to the extent that choice alternatives are seen as being differentiated.[23] The more similar they are perceived to be, however, the greater the likelihood of LPS or some form of midrange problem solving.

Time Availability

Returning to our first focus group at the beginning of the chapter, the person in need of auto repair probably will act differently if forced by circumstances to make a quick decision. "Any port in the storm," as they say, if you need to keep your car on the road. As a general rule, therefore, EPS is followed when time pressures are low.

Consumer Mood as an Important Moderating Variable

It would be a mistake to conclude our discussion of EPS without recognizing consumer mood as an important factor that can strongly influence the information processing and evaluation that takes place.[24] It appears that mood can function in two opposing ways.

First, one stream of evidence has demonstrated that positive affect can increase the information-processing load and lead people to avoid that strain. Hence, they will respond by reducing the length and complexity of the decision process.[25] But Mano[26] discovered that mood can have exactly the opposite effect as well. Until there is further clarifying research, all we can conclude is that consumer mood must be taken into consideration as we diagnose and predict consumer behavior.

Limited Problem Solving: The Marketer's Greatest Challenge

Ask yourself this question: In the past month, how often have you engaged in information search and alternative evaluation for the products and services you have purchased? For most of us, we would mention very few because of the simple fact that most of our purchases are "everyday" and "mundane" and are undertaken by LPS or habit.[27] This fact was clearly noted some years ago by distinguished advertising strategist Leo Bogart:

> *Perhaps the main contribution that advertising research can make to the study of communications is in the domain of inattention to low-key stimuli, as exemplified by the ever increasing flow of unsolicited and unwanted messages to which people are subject in our over communicative civilization.*[28]

Dental floss is a good example. Almost everybody agrees that this product category represents the extreme of low involvement. Few want to invest any time in replenishing supply, and until very recently, all brands were pretty much the same. Most people would move right from need recognition to purchase of one of the available brands with a minimum of thought and evaluation. This presents quite a marketing challenge. Read the story in Consumer in Focus 4.5 of how W. L. Gore & Associates broke through limited problem-solving behavior with their new "Glide" brand.

Need Recognition

In the case of dental floss, this product is a useful aid in hygiene and is a regular part of life for many people in the Western world. Need recognition is quite routine and represents little more than an "out-of-stock situation."

Search

When involvement is low, motivated information search before shopping, if undertaken at all, is often confined to such strategies as scanning the ads for price specials. It would be a mistake to conclude, however, that advertising and other types of sales effort are without influence. It is common for shoppers to truncate point-of-purchase search by confining themselves to brands they know. Therefore, an unknown brand is doomed. Management at W. L. Gore & Associates wisely built brand equity and trial through one of the most trusted of all information sources—the family dentist.

Pre-purchase Alternative Evaluation

When consumers engage in LPS, pre-purchase alternative evaluation consists of little more than an assurance that each competitive alternative "qualifies" in terms of the expected benefit(s). Dental floss users expect little more than quick cleaning between the teeth without shredding. We now see *noncompensatory alternative evaluation* in which an option will be eliminated if it falls short or fa-

4.5	**Consumer in Focus**

"Glide" — the Giant Killer

W. L. Gore & Associates, the maker of Gore-Tex fabrics, created a new product in a tired category, dental floss. Then, instead of advertising massively, Gore used niche marketing and data-base technology to create customer enthusiasm.

The company's technicians applied their lessons in creating strong fibers to make a superslick floss. The product, called Glide, doesn't snap, slash gums, or shred between the teeth. Well and good, but how to take on floss giants Johnson & Johnson and Gillette Co.'s Oral-B division? John Spencer, the Gore manager responsible for Glide, went for word of mouth in his launch last year. Six months before he hit drugstores, he sent samples to dentists for them to hand out free to patients. "The response was incredible," Spencer says.

Because patients liked the floss, many dentists started buying it. To capture customer names for future product launches, Gore at first sold to the public only through an 800 number. In some instances, enthusiasts ordered cases by phone. As a result, Glide had a wide reputation and a core of dedicated users before it hit the stores.

Source: Zachary Schiller, "How to Get Closer to Your Customers," Business Week *(Enterprise/1993 edition), 45.*

vored if it rates especially well. This is commonly done at the point of sale and is confirmed as the product is used or consumed.

Purchase

Consumers engaged in LPS rarely will shop widely for an item and expect it to be available at the most convenient places. Point-of-purchase advertising and display now becomes crucial. A "shelf-talker" sign reads: "New Glide is here — cleans your teeth as slick as can be and won't snap or shred." A buyer remembers hearing about Glide from a friend or an ad and comes to the conclusion, "why not try it."

Consumption, Post-purchase Evaluation, and Divestment

Product trial is the most important objective for any marketer facing this decision process. Most product evaluation takes place *after purchase*. Satisfaction, in turn, should lead to habitual use out of inertia more than anything else. If a competitor comes along with a better deal, and W. L. Gore is certain to face immediate competitive response, why not shift brands? Finally, divestment options usually are either outright disposal or recycling. Most of the products that fall into this category have little or no remarketing value.

Repurchase Behavior

The most likely outcome, is brand loyalty motivated by inertia. It is common to have a set of acceptable brands and to make a continued choice on the basis of lowest price. Brand switching will readily occur, however, if one of the alternatives differs notably from others either in terms of price or new features.

Diagnosing Consumer Behavior

This chapter has covered a wide range of material. Now, it is important to give you another guide for strategic thinking, this time a set of questions that will help in formulating diagnostic marketing research. This set of questions is in Figure 4.11.

The greatest research challenge lies in measuring involvement, our most critical determining variable.[29] Zaichkowsky[30] has designed a useful involvement inventory (Figure 4.12). You might try this inventory yourself across a variety of products. Notice that her scale items mostly measure the product importance di-

---

Figure 4.11   Diagnosing the Consumer Decision-Making Process

Motivation and Need Recognition

1. What needs and motivations are satisfied by product purchase and usage? (i.e., What *benefits* are consumers seeking?)
2. Are these needs dormant or are they presently perceived as felt needs by prospective buyers?
3. How involved with the product are most prospective buyers in the target market segment?

Search for Information

1. What product- and brand-related information is stored in memory?
2. Is the consumer motivated to turn to external sources to find information about available alternatives and their characteristics?
3. What specific information sources are used most frequently when search is undertaken?
4. What product features or attributes are the focus of search when it is undertaken?

Continued

Figure 4.11 Continued

Alternative Evaluation

1. To what extent do consumers engage in alternative evaluation and comparison?
2. Which product and/or brand alternatives are included in the evaluation process?
3. Which product evaluative criteria (product attributes) are used to compare various alternatives?
   a. Which are most salient in the evaluation?
   b. How complex is the evaluation (i.e., using a single attribute as opposed to several in combination)?
4. What are the outcomes of evaluation regarding each of the candidate purchase alternatives?
   a. What is believed to be true about the characteristics and features of each?
   b. Are they perceived to be different in important ways, or are they seen as essentially the same?
5. What kind of decision rule is used to determine the best choice?

Purchase

1. Will the consumer expend time and energy to shop until the preferred alternative is found?
2. Is additional decision-process behavior needed to discover the preferred outlet for purchase?
3. What are the preferred models of purchase (i.e., retail store, in the home, or in other ways)?

Outcomes

1. What degree of satisfaction or dissatisfaction is expressed with respect to previously used alternatives in the product or service category?
2. What reasons are given for satisfaction or dissatisfaction?
3. Has perceived satisfaction or dissatisfaction been shared with other people to help them in their buying behavior?
4. Have consumers made attempts to achieve redress for dissatisfaction?
5. Is there an intention to repurchase any of the alternatives?
   a. If no, why not?
   b. If yes, does intention reflect brand loyalty or inertia?

mension. Follow the scoring directions at the bottom—the higher the score, the greater the involvement. A maximum possible score is 140. Zaichkowsky found a mean score of 89.55 across 15 categories, with automobiles and calculators emerging as most involving and instant coffee, bubble bath, and breakfast cereals as least.

As you observe and try to explain the behavioral situations encountered every day in marketing, keep these points in mind:

1. Remember the continuum of initial purchase decision-process possibilities ranges from full-scale EPS on the one extreme to impulse buying (a "Why not try it?" response reflecting LPS) on the other. Similarly, habitual decision making also is a continuum, with brand loyalty on one end and inertia on the other.

Figure 4.12   Personal Involvement Inventory

(insert name of object to be judged)

important	__:__:__:__:__:__:__	unimportant*
of no concern	__:__:__:__:__:__:__	of concern to me
irrelevant	__:__:__:__:__:__:__	relevant
means a lot to me	__:__:__:__:__:__:__	means nothing to me*
useless	__:__:__:__:__:__:__	useful
valuable	__:__:__:__:__:__:__	worthless*
trivial	__:__:__:__:__:__:__	fundamental
beneficial	__:__:__:__:__:__:__	not beneficial*
matters to me	__:__:__:__:__:__:__	doesn't matter*
uninterested	__:__:__:__:__:__:__	interested
significant	__:__:__:__:__:__:__	insignificant*
vital	__:__:__:__:__:__:__	superfluous*
boring	__:__:__:__:__:__:__	interesting
unexciting	__:__:__:__:__:__:__	exciting
appealing	__:__:__:__:__:__:__	unappealing*
mundane	__:__:__:__:__:__:__	fascinating
essential	__:__:__:__:__:__:__	nonessential*
undesirable	__:__:__:__:__:__:__	desirable
wanted	__:__:__:__:__:__:__	unwanted*
not needed	__:__:__:__:__:__:__	needed

*Indicates item is reverse scored.
Items on the left are scored (1) low involvement to (7) high involvement on the right. Totaling the 20 items gives a score from a low of 20 to a high of 140.
Source: Judith L. Zaichkowsky, "Measuring the Involvement Construct," Journal of Consumer Research 12 (December 1985), 350.

2. Consumers will differ from one to the next. One may be motivated by high involvement to engage in EPS, whereas this is not always the case with others. Recognize multiple segments with differing motivations and decision-process behavior.

3. In some instances, you will not have sufficient information to allow a proper diagnosis, in which case marketing research probably is needed.

Summary

The purpose of this chapter has been to introduce you to the nature of consumer decision making and the influences on this process. First, we introduced you in a general way to the complex set of factors that influence and shape decision-process behavior. The first of these is *individual differences:* (1) consumer resources; (2) knowledge; (3) attitudes; (4) motivation and involvement; and (5) personality, values, and lifestyle. The second is *environmental influences,* including (1) culture; (2) social class; (3) personal influence; (4) family; and (5) situation.

Then we provided a model of consumer decision process that encompasses the following stages: (1) need recognition; (2) search for information; (3) pre-purchase alternative evaluation; (4) purchase; (5) consumption; (6) post-purchase alternative evaluation; and (7) divestment.

Next, we examined the ways in which decision processes differ. EPS can be viewed as one end of a problem-solving continuum. It is characterized by intensive search for information and complex alternative evaluation. The opposite end of this continuum is anchored by LPS. Here, there is far less motivation to search widely for information and to engage in alternative evaluation.

When the occasion arises for repeat purchases, however, many consumers quickly develop habitual decision processes. On occasion, they are brand loyal and stay with their initial choice. This occurs mainly when there is high perceived involvement. When this is not the case, however, habits are built on inertia. If a consumer has no reason to switch, a repurchase will be made. But the consumer also is prone to switch if there is incentive to do so. Once again, there is low involvement and little commitment to one alternative versus another.

Finally, we focused on ways in which decision-process behavior can vary, and these are the important determining factors: (1) the extent to which alternatives are differentiated in significant ways; (2) the presence or absence of restricting time pressures; and (3) the degree of involvement—perceived relevance of the purchase in the context of important needs and motivations.

The remaining chapters in Part 2 of the book flesh out the six stages of the decision-making process. Part 3 concentrates on individual differences. We move from there to psychological processes in Part 4 and consider the ways in which information processing and learning affect the outcomes, with special focus on influencing attitudes and behavior. Part 5 takes a more general perspective and concentrates on environmental influences and marketing strategies. And the book concludes in Part 6 with marketing issues and ethical responsibility.

Review and Discussion Questions

1. There are some who argue that consumers really do not pursue any kind of decision process but make their selections more or less randomly without any apparent reasoning. What is your position on this issue? Why?

2. In speaking of the problems that might result from psychological analysis of consumer behavior, one critic stated many years ago, "Much of it seems to represent regress rather than progress for man in his struggle to become a rational and self-guiding being." His point is that marketing persuaders now have new tools that enable them to manipulate the consumer and to circumvent his or her processes of reasoning. Comment.

3. Define the terms *extended problem solving* and *limited problem solving*. What are the essential differences? What type of decision process would you expect most people to follow in the initial purchase of a new product or brand in each of these categories: toothpaste, flour, men's cologne, carpeting, toilet tissue, bread, light bulbs, a 35mm camera, a sports car?

4. Referring once again to Question 3, is it possible that decision-process behavior could differ widely from one consumer to another in purchasing each of these items? Explain.

5. How might a manufacturer of automatic washers and dryers use a decision-process approach to better understand how consumers purchase these products?

6. Which of the following types of products do you think are most likely to be purchased on the basis of brand loyalty and on the basis of inertia: laundry detergent, motor oil, lipsticks, shoe polish, soft drinks, lawn care products (fertilizers, and so on), and spark plugs?

7. Assume you are responsible for marketing a new and previously unknown brand of 35mm slide film. You are up against Kodak and Fuji, both of which have built substantial brand loyalty. What strategies could you suggest to make market inroads?

8. Assume you have been called in as a marketing consultant to suggest an advertising strategy for a new brand of dry cat food. Which of the types of decision-process behavior discussed in this chapter do you believe is likely with most prospective buyers? Why do you say this? What difference will this make in marketing strategy?

Endnotes

1. John Dewey, *How We Think* (New York: Heath, 1910).

2. Icek Ajzen and Martin Fishbein, *Understanding Attitudes and Predicting Social Behavior* (Englewood Cliffs, N.J.: Prentice-Hall, 1980).

3. Elizabeth C. Hirschman and Morris B. Holbrook, "Hedonic Consumption: Emerging Concepts, Methods, and Propositions," *Journal of Marketing* 46 (Summer 1982), 92–101.

4. For significant early writings on this subject, see Russell W. Belk, "An Exploratory Assessment of Situational Effects in Buyer Behavior," *Journal of Marketing Research* 11 (May 1974), 156–173; Russell W. Belk, "Situational Variables and Consumer Behavior," *Journal of Consumer Research* 2 (December 1975), 157–164. Also Gordon R. Foxall, *Consumer Choice* (London: Macmillan, 1983), 86–97.

5. Harold E. Kassarjian, "Consumer Research: Some Recollections and a Commentary," in Richard J. Lutz, ed., *Advances in Consumer Research* 13 (Provo, Utah: Association for Consumer Research, 1986), 6–8.

6. Wayne D. Hoyer, "Variations in Choice Strategies across Decision Contexts: An Examination of Contingent Factors," in Lutz, *Advances,* 23–26.

7. Francis Piron, "Defining Impulse Purchasing," in Rebecca H. Holman and Michael R. Solomon, eds., *Advances in Consumer Research* 18 (Provo, Utah: Association for Consumer Research, 1991), 512.

8. Dennis W. Rook and Stephen J. Hoch, "Consuming Impulses," in Elizabeth C. Hirschman and Morris B. Holbrook, eds., *Advances in Consumer Research* 12 (Provo, Utah: Association for Consumer Research, 1985), 23–27.

9. Itamar Simonson, "The Effect of Purchase Quantity and Timing on Variety-Seeking Behavior," *Journal of Marketing Research* 27 (May 1990), 150–162; Wayne D. Hoyer and Nancy M. Ridgway, "Variety Seeking as an Explanation for Exploratory Purchase Behavior: A Theoretical Model," in Thomas C. Kinnear, ed., *Advances in Consumer Research* 11 (Provo, Utah: Association for Consumer Research, 1984), 114–119.

10. John H. Antil, "Conceptualization and Operationalization of Involvement," in Kinnear, *Advances,* 204.

11. Richard L. Celsi and Jerry C. Olson, "The Role of Involvement in Attention and Comprehension Processes," *Journal of Consumer Research* 15 (September 1988), 210–224.

12. See James Sood, "A Multi Country Research Approach for Multinational Communication Strategies," *Journal of International Consumer Marketing* 5 (1993), 29–50; Dana L. Alden, Wayne D. Hoyer, and Guntelee Wechasara, "Choice Strategies and Involvement: A Cross-Cultural Analysis," in Thomas K. Srull, ed., *Advances in Consumer Reasearch* 16 (Provo, Utah: Association for Consumer Research, 1989), 119–125.

13. Meera P. Venkatraman, "Investigating Differences in the Roles of Enduring and Instrumentally Involved Consumers in the Diffusion Process," in Michael J. Houston, ed., *Advances in Consumer Research* 15 (Provo, Utah: Association for Consumer Research, 1988), 299–303.

14. Robin A. Higie and Lawrence F. Feick, "Enduring Involvement: Conceptual and Measurement Issues," in Srull, *Advances,* 690–696.

15. Raymond A. Bauer, "Consumer Behavior as Risk Taking," in *Dynamic Marketing for a Changing World* (Chicago: American Marketing Association, 1960), 389.

16. See George Brooker, "An Assessment of an Expanded Measure of Perceived Risk," in Kinnear, *Advances,* 439–441; John W. Vann, "A Multi-Distributional, Conceptual Framework for the Study of Perceived Risk," in Kinnear, *Advances,* 442–446.

17. Kanwar, "The Influence of Perceived Risk."

18. Russell W. Belk, "Effects of Gift-Giving Involvement on Gift Selection Strategies," in Andrew Mitchell, ed., *Advances in Consumer Research* 9 (Ann Arbor, Mich.: Association for Consumer Research, 1981), 408–411.

19. Judith L. Zaichkowsky, "Measuring the Involvement Construct," *Journal of Consumer Research* 12 (December 1985), 341–352.

20. Hoyer, "Variations in Choice Strategies across Decision Contexts," 23–26.

21. J. Craig Andrews, "Motivation, Ability, and Opportunity to Process Information: Conceptual and Experimental Manipulation Issues," in Houston, *Advances,* 219–225.

22. Richard E. Petty, John T. Cacioppo, and David Schumann, "Central and Peripheral Routes to Advertising Effectiveness: The Moderating Role of Involvement," *Journal of Consumer Research* 10 (September 1983), 135–144.

23. Giles Laurent and Jean-Noel Kapferer, "Measuring Consumer Involvement Profiles," *Journal of Marketing Research* 22 (February 1985), 41–53.

24. Consumer research was strongly influenced in 1980 by the finding that feelings and mood *(affective responses)* operate independently from cognitive responses. See Robert Zajonc, "Feeling and Thinking: Preferences Need No Inferences," *American Psychologist* 35 (February 1980), 151–175. This was followed by an influential article by Mitchell and Olson. See Andrew Mitchell and Jerry Olson, "Are Product Attribute Beliefs the Only Mediator of Advertising Effects on Brand Attitudes?" *Journal of Marketing Research* 18 (August 1981), 318–322.

25. Meryl Paula Gardner, "Mood States and Consumer Behavior: A Critical Review," *Journal of Consumer Research* 12 (December 1985), 281–300.

26. Haim Mano, "Emotional States and Decision Making," in Marvin E. Goldberg, Gerald Gorn, and Richard W. Pollay, eds., *Advances in Consumer Research* 17 (Provo, Utah: Association for Consumer Research, 1990), 577–589.

27. Among the first to challenge the consumer research field with this observation were Richard W. Olshavsky and Donald H. Granbois. See "Consumer Decision-Making—Fact or Fiction?" *Journal of Consumer Research* 6 (September 1969), 93–100.

28. Leo Bogart, "Where Does Advertising Research Go from Here?" *Journal of Advertising Research* 9 (March 1969), 6.

29. See Laurent and Kapferer, "Measuring Consumer Involvement Profiles." Also J. Craig Andrews, Srinivas Durvasula, and Syed H. Akhter, "A Framework for

Conceptualizing and Measuring the Involvement Construct in Advertising Research," *Journal of Advertising* 19 (November 1990), 27–40; Judith L. Zaichkowsky, "Issues in Measuring Abstract Construct," in Goldberg, Gorn, and Pollay, *Advances*, 616–618.

30. Zaichkowsky, "Measuring the Involvement Construct."

CHAPTER 5

Need Recognition and Search

▲▲▲

Do Consumers Need Fax Machines?

Do you own a fax machine? Odds are you don't. Less than 1 percent of American households have fax machines. Contrast that with the 99 percent of American corporations that own one. Almost 60 percent of small- to mid-sized businesses—those with 5 to 99 employees—are equipped with fax.

Why don't you want a fax machine? "Don't need it" is a common reply. And this represents a major challenge to the fax industry. As the business market reaches saturation, future growth will heavily depend on stimulating consumer demand. And stimulating demand will require showing consumers how a fax machine could make their lives easier, more productive, and more entertaining.

Fax Interactive, a company offering fax services, has a couple of ideas about the types of services that consumers might want. One is a stock portfolio service that provides up-to-the-minute news and information on the market. Another service could focus on "triggering events." A subscriber would identify certain topics of interest, and when something happens related to those topics, he or she would automatically receive a fax with detailed information.

Another company, DataFax Communications Corp., plans to provide services where callers can request airline schedules, daily updates on their favorite soap operas, horoscopes, real estate information, recipes from food manufacturers, health information, movie schedules, weather updates . . . the list goes on. The company is also developing interactive fax games.

According to DataFax president Norberto Blumenscweig, "The key will be to begin offering all of these services simultaneously. The fax manufacturers want to be able to offer the consumer a package of several services as an enticement to buy the fax machine. If you only have one or two things available, it's not going to work."

Source: Excerpted in part from Kristine J. Tegethoff, "Fax Appeal," Link (March 1992), 22–25, 36–39.

The future of fax machines, as is the case for all goods and services, ultimately depends on whether consumers perceive them as fulfilling consumption needs. It is the activation and recognition of consumption needs that leads the consumer into a decision-making process that will determine product purchase and consumption. Accordingly, we label the first stage of the decision-making process as **need recognition** — defined as the perception of a difference between the desired state of affairs and the actual situation sufficient to arouse and activate the decision process. The first part of this chapter is devoted to this crucial stage of decision making.

Once need recognition has occurred, the consumer may then engage in a search for potential need satisfiers. These search activities constitute the second stage of decision making, called **search,** which is defined as the motivated activation of knowledge in memory or acquisition of information from the environment. After discussion of need recognition, the remainder of this chapter is devoted to search.

Need Recognition

The simple diagram appearing in Figure 5.1 illustrates what happens during need recognition. Need recognition essentially depends on how much discrepancy exists between the actual state (the consumer's current situation) and the desired state (the situation the consumer wants to be in).[1] When this discrepancy meets or exceeds a certain level or threshold, a need is recognized. For example, a consumer currently feeling hungry (actual state) and wanting to eliminate this feeling (desired state) will experience need recognition if the discrepancy between the two states is of sufficient magnitude. However, if the discrepancy is below the threshold level, need recognition will not occur.

It is necessary to point out that the presence of need recognition does not automatically activate some action. This will depend on a couple of factors. First, the recognized need must be of sufficient importance. A hungry consumer may not think that the rumblings in her or his stomach merit action at this point in time. Second, consumers must believe that a solution to the need is within their means. If need satisfaction is beyond a consumer's economic or temporal re-

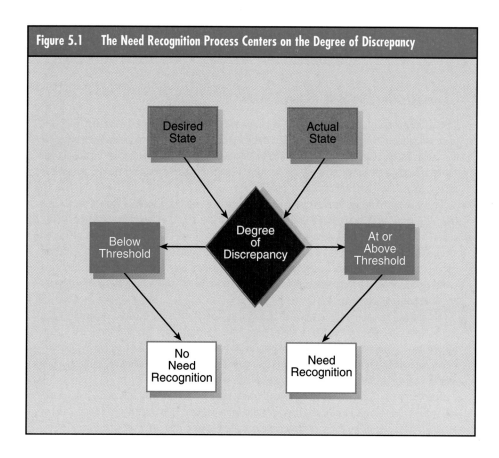

Figure 5.1   The Need Recognition Process Centers on the Degree of Discrepancy

sources (see Chapter 8), for instance, action is unlikely. As described in Consumer in Focus 5.1, only a slight improvement in consumers' abilities to satisfy their needs can make a world of difference to some industries.

Need Activation

A need must first be "activated" before it can be "recognized." A host of factors will influence the likelihood that a particular need will be activated. Such factors operate by altering the person's actual and/or desired states.

Time

As anyone who has gone too long since their last meal well knows, the simple passage of time can be a potent activator of consumption needs. Similarly, the time since the smoker's last cigarette is a major influence on her or his need to light up again. In both cases, time gradually deteriorates the consumer's actual

5.1	**Consumer in Focus**

Consumers Needing Help to Buy Homes

Interest rates continue to favor home buyers, but home sales are sluggish in many communities. That's because half of American families cannot afford a median-priced home in their own communities, according to a Census Bureau report. Among families who already own their home, 42 percent don't make enough money to handle a median-priced mortgage payment, 12 percent have too much debt, and 8 percent lack the cash for the down payment and closing costs.

Only 9 percent of renter families qualify for a median-priced mortgage under 1991 conditions. A few years ago, legislators tightened the Federal Housing Administration's underwriting program to stem the tide of loan defaults. "There's some thought that some of those reforms went too far and were too stringent," says Duane McGough, director of the Department of Housing and Urban Development's division of housing and demographic analysis. Now federal housing analysts are poring over the data, seeking the best ways to assist more people in buying homes. They have studied the effect of changes in mortgage interest rates and down-payment subsidies.

But different groups need different kinds of assistance. Interest rates, for example, apparently mean little to renters. A 6 percent variation in interest rates, from 3 percent above the current rate to 3 percent below it, results in no statistically significant change in the number of renters who are able to buy a house. The reason is that many renters lack equity and cash as well as income. For current owners, an interest rate drop of 1 percent enables almost 800,000 more of them to qualify.

Small down-payment subsidies could have a dramatic effect for some. With as little as $2,500, 1.6 million families and unrelated individuals could afford a down payment on a median-priced home. Most of those who need help with a down payment are already homeowners who presumably have some equity. Renters would need a subsidy of at least $5,000 before a significant number would be able to afford a home.

The fact that so many people are tantalizingly close to qualifying has not gone unnoticed. The National Association of Home Builders is among several that support looser mortgage programs. "If you were able to require a 2.5 percent down payment—that's half the minimum FHA payment—we think you could sell another 150,000 to 170,000 homes a year," says David Crowe, the association's assistant staff vice president for housing policy.

Source: Excerpted from Tibbett Speer, "Helping Renters Make the Down Payment," American Demographics (December 1993), 21–22.

state until it becomes sufficiently discrepant from the desired state to trigger need recognition.

Time can influence the desired state as well. As consumers grow older, they often experience changes in their tastes and values, which, in turn, alter their desired state. Whereas many baby boomers get a haircut as soon as their hair starts touching their ears, in their younger days need recognition did not occur even though their hair was touching their shoulders!

Changed Circumstances

Needs will often be activated due to changes in one's life. Many students discover on graduation and starting a new job that their current wardrobe needs to be expanded for them to function more comfortably within their work environment, particularly when there exist strong expectations within the firm as to what represents appropriate attire. Changes within the family can also trigger need recognition. The birth of a child, for instance, results in modified requirements for food, clothing, furniture, and housing.

Product Acquisition

The acquisition of a product may, in turn, activate the need for additional products. It is not uncommon to find that acquiring new furnishings will affect perceptions of the desirability of existing carpeting, wall coverings, and so on. Similarly, buying a new home will usually require the purchase of additional products, particularly for first-time buyers. It is for this reason that new home buyers are an important target market for many companies.

Product Consumption

Actual consumption itself can trigger need recognition. In many buying situations, a need is recognized simply because of an out-of-stock situation. The last slices of bread were toasted for breakfast, and more bread will be needed for tonight's dinner. Thus, need recognition occurs because of an anticipated need in the immediate future resulting from a change in the actual situation.

Individual Differences

Bruner[2] has proposed that consumers may differ in whether need recognition results from changes in the actual state versus the desired state. At one extreme are consumers (called **actual state types**) for whom need recognition is triggered typically by changes in the actual state. Consumers at the other extreme (called **desired state types**) usually experience need recognition produced by changes in the desired state. For example, actual state types tend to recognize a need for clothing only when their clothing does not perform satisfactorily. Desired state types, however, will frequently experience need recognition as a result of their desires for something new.

Marketing Influences

Thus far, our focus has been on factors that have an effect on need recognition but that are largely beyond a company's ability to influence in some advantageous way. This need not always be the case, as companies have at their disposal a variety of ways that can affect consumer need recognition. Indeed, stimulating consumers' awareness of their needs is often an important objective that, when neglected, can have unfavorable consequences for companies and entire

| 5.2 | **Consumer in Focus** |

Furniture: An Industry in Need of Need Recognition

In 1992, U.S. furniture-store sales totaled about $33.5 billion, up less than 4 percent since 1989. Consumers spent a smaller percentage of their 1992 disposable income on furniture than they did in 1980. In the 1970s, they bought dinettes once every 12 to 13 years. Today, the average replacement rate is once every 21 years.

Consumers have been blasé about furniture, in part because furniture makers have done little to court them. "The auto industry has convinced Americans to buy $25,000 cars that they throw away every three years, but the furniture industry still sells bedroom sets that people pass down to their kids," grouses Larry Spangler, vice-president for advertising at Thomasville Industries.

Just like Ford and Chrysler, furniture makers bring out new models every year. Now, after years of inept marketing and unimpressive sales, furniture marketers are banding together to try to inspire people to redecorate more often. Part of the effort is built around a planned weekly TV show called "Haven," to be hosted by Joy Philbin, wife of talk-show personality Regis Philbin. Products featured on the show will come from the 165 furniture makers and 3,500 retailers who are members of the Home Furnishings Council. During each program, a toll-free number will flash across the screen to encourage viewers to call in and learn more about particular pieces of furniture.

" 'Haven' isn't going to be a 'Lifestyles of the Rich and Famous,' " says Robert Nightengale, director of the furniture council. "We want to reach all people and reverse the trend of consumer spending on home furnishings."

Source: Adapted from Teri Agins, "Furniture Firms Try Show Biz to Woo Public," Wall Street Journal (November 12, 1993), B1, B6.

industries. Such is the case for furniture makers, as described in Consumer in Focus 5.2.

How can companies stimulate need recognition? Sometimes it will suffice to simply remind consumers of a need. Consumers browsing a retailer's aisles may encounter a display that reminds them of a previously recognized but since forgotten purchase need. In a similar way, a dentist may send patients who are overdue for a checkup and cleaning a simple reminder, such as the one appearing in Figure 5.2, of their need to schedule an appointment.

Another example of how companies can attempt to influence need recognition appears in Figure 5.3. Many parents may not recognize that plaque can be a problem even for very young consumers. Instead, they may incorrectly perceive the baby's actual state as being healthier than it actually is. For these consumers, the ad in Figure 5.3, if believed, should cause them to recognize that the actual state is discrepant from the desired state, thus causing need recognition.

Product innovations are another source of need recognition, which was certainly the case when Reebok came out with its pump athletic shoe. This innova-

Figure 5.2   Reminding Consumers of Their Needs Can Activate Need Recognition

tion changed the ideal state of many teenagers, leading them to view their current pair of shoes as inadequate. The same basic principle applies to Whirlpool's innovation for refrigerators, shown in Figure 5.4.

A basic distinction among efforts to activate need recognition is whether they attempt to stimulate primary or selective demand. An example of the former is the milk industry's advertising campaign to strengthen the primary demand for this product. Ads targeted at young consumers show a milk-drinking youngster maturing into an attractive young adult. Other ads tell older consumers they should drink milk "because you're not a kid anymore." Marketing activities that focus on primary demand are, in essence, attempting to elicit **generic need recognition.**

Selective need recognition, however, occurs when the need for a specific brand within a product category (selective demand) is stimulated. Consider persons owning a credit card charging 12 percent interest for outstanding balances

Figure 5.3 This Ad Attempts to Activate Need Recognition by Educating Consumers about the Actual State

Figure 5.4 Product Innovations can Activate Need Recognition by Changing about the Actual State

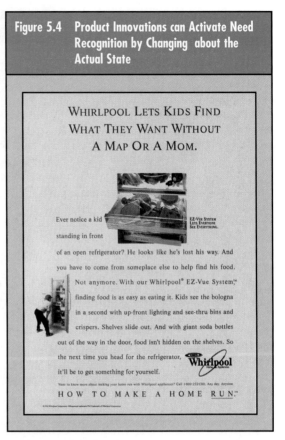

and feeling quite satisfied with this rate. They then see an ad for a competitor's credit card offering an 8 percent interest rate. Suddenly, they feel a bit uncomfortable. Their perceptions of the desired state begin to change. They wonder why they should pay their current card 12 percent when someone else is offering a lower rate. Thus, the ad has prompted both a redefinition of the desired state and selective need recognition for the advertised brand.

Search

Once need recognition has occurred, the consumer may then engage in a search for potential need satisfiers. **Search,** the second stage of the decision-making process, can be defined as the motivated activation of knowledge stored in memory or acquisition of information from the environment. This definition suggests that search can be either internal or external in nature. **Internal search** involves the retrieval of knowledge from memory, whereas **external search** consists of collecting information from the marketplace.

Internal Search

Search of an internal nature first occurs following need recognition (Figure 5.4). Internal search is nothing more than a memory scan for decision-relevant knowledge stored in long-term memory (see Chapter 10).[3] If this scan reveals sufficient information to provide a satisfactory course of action, external search is obviously unnecessary. Many times a past solution is remembered and implemented. For example, one study reports that many consumers needing an auto repair service relied on their existing knowledge in making their choices.[4] Only 40 percent turned to external search.

Whether consumers rely solely on internal search will heavily depend on the adequacy or quality of their existing knowledge. First-time buyers are obviously unlikely to possess the necessary information for decision making. Even experienced buyers may need to undertake external search. Experienced buyers may find their knowledge to be inadequate for product categories characterized by large interpurchase times (the amount of time between purchase occasions) during which there are significant product changes in terms of prices, features, and new brands and stores. Even if product changes have been minimal, internal search is hindered by large interpurchase times due to problems of forgetting. Nor may existing knowledge be sufficient when the present consumption problem is perceived to be different from those in the past.

The degree of satisfaction with prior purchases will also determine the consumer's reliance on internal search. If the consumer has been satisfied with the results of previous buying actions, internal search may suffice.[5] Such is the case with habitual decision making, in which the consumer simply remembers to buy the same brand as before.

External Search

When internal search proves inadequate, the consumer may decide to collect additional information from the environment. External search that is driven by an upcoming purchase decision is known as **pre-purchase search.** This type of external search can be contrasted with another type called **ongoing search,** in which information acquisition occurs on a relatively regular basis regardless of sporadic purchase needs.[6] For example, a consumer subscribing to automotive magazines would reflect an ongoing search activity. These same magazines might also be examined during pre-purchase search but only when the consumer is in the market for a new car.

The primary motivation behind pre-purchase search is the desire to make better consumption choices. Similarly, ongoing search may be motivated by desires to develop a knowledge base that can be used in future decision making. Ongoing search, however, may also occur simply because of the enjoyment derived

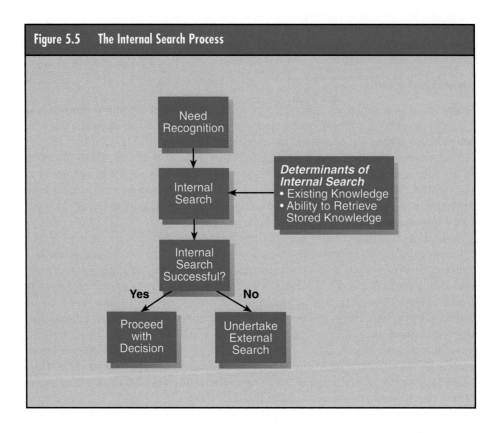

Figure 5.5   The Internal Search Process

from this activity. There is no denying that many consumers enjoy ongoing search for its own sake. Consumers may browse through a mall, without having specific purchase needs, simply because it is "fun" to them. One study reports that enjoyment was the driving force behind consumers' ongoing search for both clothing and personal computers.[7]

Note that ongoing search should affect the need for pre-purchase search. Consumers active in ongoing search seem likely to possess greater amounts of decision-relevant information in memory, thereby lowering the amount of pre-purchase search necessary for decision making.

Dimensions of Search

Table 5.1 indicates that consumer search can be characterized along three main dimensions: degree, direction, and sequence. **Degree** represents the total amount of search. Search degree is reflected by the number of brands, stores, attributes, and information sources considered during search as well as the time taken in doing so. **Direction** represents the specific content of search. The emphasis here

Table 5.1	Dimensions of Consumer Search

Degree of Search
- How many brands are considered?
- How many stores are visited/contacted?
- How many attributes are considered?
- How many information sources are used?
- How much time is spent on search?

Direction of Search
- Which brands are considered?
- Which stores are visited/contacted?
- Which attributes are considered?
- Which information sources are used?

Sequence of Search
- In what order are brands considered?
- In what order are stores visited/contacted?
- In what order is product attribute information processed?
- In what order are information sources used?

is on the particular brands and stores involved during search rather than simply the number. The third dimension, **sequence,** represents the order in which search activities occur.

Degree of Search

Consumers often engage in very little external search before a purchase, even for major expenditures involving furniture, appliances, and automobiles.[8] Indeed, significant numbers of consumers make major purchases after shopping at a single retailer and/or considering only one brand. Consumer in Focus 5.3 provides further testimony to just how limited consumer search may be.

The fact that consumers sometimes engage in minimal search has led some to suggest that purchase can occur without being preceded by a decision process.[9] The problem with this view is that it fails to consider the role of internal search. As noted earlier, internal search alone may sometimes suffice in making purchase decisions. That consumers choose to rely on their existing knowledge would seem inadequate for suggesting that decision making has not occurred.

The degree of search is directly related to the type of decision-making process. Differences in search as a function of the decision process are summarized in

| 5.3 | **Consumer in Focus** |

Consumer Search during Grocery Shopping

How much search do consumers undertake while grocery shopping? It would appear to be rather minimal based on the amount of time they stand in front of the shelving that displays the product. In one study, observers recorded the amount of time invested by consumers while making their purchase decisions within 4 different product categories: cereal, coffee, margarine, and toothpaste. On average, consumers took less than 12 seconds in making each decision. And nearly half spent 5 seconds or less.

After placing their selection in the cart, shoppers were approached by the observer and questioned about their choice. Fewer than 1 in 4 shoppers reported making a price comparison between their chosen brand and a competitive brand. Indeed, more than 40 percent did not even bother to check the price of the brand placed in their cart. Perhaps most surprising was the fact that less than half of the shoppers were aware they had chosen a brand that was being offered by the grocer at a reduced price.

Source: Peter R. Dickson and Alan G. Sawyer, "The Price Knowledge and Search of Supermarket Shoppers," Journal of Marketing 54 (July 1990), 42–53.

Table 5.2. An extended problem-solving process will usually entail a considerable amount of search. The consumer may consider several brands, visit several stores, consult friends, and so on. At the other extreme is the habitual decision process. Here the consumer minimizes search time and effort by considering only one brand (the brand last purchased) and one attribute (brand name). Other sources of information are ignored. Uncertain, however, is the number of stores shopped, which may range from one (if the consumer is also store loyal) to several. Search under a limited problem-solving process falls between these two extremes.

The amount of search related to a particular product can vary greatly from one consumer to the next. Consequently, it is possible to segment consumers based on their level of search. A study of new car purchasers, for instance, identified the following six segments[10]:

1. A low-search group, representing 26 percent of the respondents, with below-average activity on all search dimensions, especially out-of-store search activities.

2. A purchase-pal-assisted search group, representing 19 percent of the respondents. A purchase pal is someone known to the consumer who is perceived as having some expertise and who helps during the search process.

3. A high-search group, with only 5 percent of the respondents, characterized by above-average activity on all search factors.

Table 5.2	Differences in the Degree of Search as a Function of the Decision-Making Process			
		Decision-Making Process		
Nature of Search		Extended Problem Solving	Limited Problem Solving	Habitual
Number of brands		Greater	Fewer	One
Number of stores		Greater	Fewer	Unknown
Number of attributes		Greater	Fewer	One
Number of external information sources		Greater	Fewer	None
Amount of time		Larger	Smaller	Minimal

4. A high-self-search group, representing 12 percent of the respondents, who are above average on all out-of-store search activities in addition to the total number of visits to different car dealers.

5. A retail-shopper group comprising about 5 percent of respondents.

6. A moderate-search group, accounting for 32 percent of the respondents, characterized by moderate activity on all search factors, although slightly above average on out-of-store search activities and slightly below average on number of visits to car dealers.

Segmentation based on the degree of search can provide some insight into how search affects purchase behavior. Suppose that a car maker found that the segment characterized by very high levels of search was much more likely to buy one of the company's cars than segments that undertake less search. What implications does this finding suggest? Obviously, this segment would represent an attractive target relative to the remaining segments, given its demonstrated propensity to buy the company's products. Moreover, the company should also consider the possibility of enhancing consumers' search efforts, perhaps through advertising the potential advantages of search activity, because doing so should increase the likelihood that consumers will buy one of the company's offerings. Figure 5.5 presents two different advertisements that attempt to encourage consumer search.

Even when markets are segmented on some other basis, it is still desirable to understand the search behavior of each segment. Segments that engage in considerable external search generally will be easier to reach. Marketers can feel more confident about the potential payoff of investments in advertising and

Figure 5.6 Ads That Encourage Consumer Search

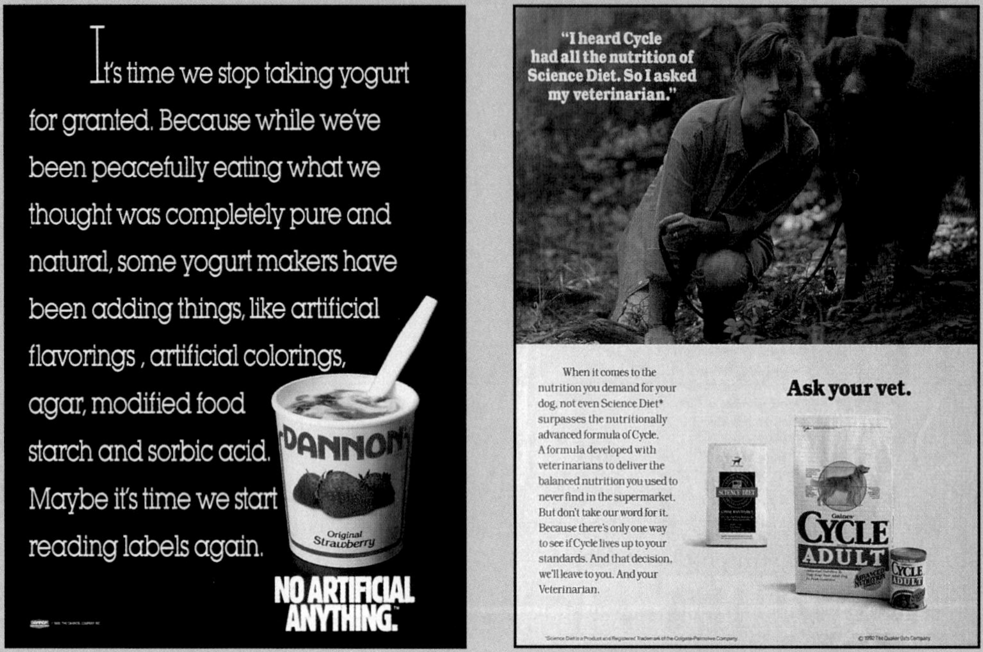
It's time we stop taking yogurt for granted. Because while we've been peacefully eating what we thought was completely pure and natural, some yogurt makers have been adding things, like artificial flavorings, artificial colorings, agar, modified food starch and sorbic acid. Maybe it's time we start reading labels again.
DANNON
Original Strawberry
NO ARTIFICIAL ANYTHING.
"I heard Cycle had all the nutrition of Science Diet. So I asked my veterinarian."
When it comes to the nutrition you demand for your dog, not even Science Diet* surpasses the nutritionally advanced formula of Cycle. A formula developed with veterinarians to deliver the balanced nutrition you used to never find in the supermarket. But don't take our word for it. Because there's only one way to see if Cycle lives up to your standards. And that decision, we'll leave to you. And your Veterinarian.
Ask your vet.
SCIENCE DIET
CYCLE
ADULT

in-store information. In contrast, such investments can be wasted on segments that rely on internal search. For these segments, free samples or substantial and well-publicized price discounts may be required to attract consumers.

Direction of Search

Although it is important to understand how much consumers search before the purchase, it is equally if not more vital to examine the direction of the search. As discussed in greater detail in Chapter 6, knowing which brands consumers considered during decision making would be very useful in understanding the consumer's view of a firm's competitive set. Distribution decisions could benefit from information about which stores are visited.

Marketers are especially interested in the specific product attributes that consumers examine during search. Attributes receiving attention during search might be emphasized more strongly in promotional materials unless they represent areas of product weaknesses. The emphasis consumers place on price during search can affect a company's pricing strategies. For example, grocery

Table 5.3	Sources of Information		
		Impersonal	**Personal**
Commercial		Advertising In-store information	Salespeople
Noncommercial		General purpose media	Social others

executives are more likely to respond to a competitor's price cuts for "high-visibility" items (soda, milk, bananas) as the amount of price comparison shopping increases.[11]

The particular information sources used during search will also influence marketing strategy. Table 5.3 indicates that information sources can be classified in terms of their source (personal versus impersonal) and type (commercial versus noncommercial). Each of these major sources is discussed subsequently.

Advertising

Once consumers recognize a need, they generally become more receptive to advertising, which they previously might have ignored completely. Ads are then often consulted for informational purposes. Although the informational role of advertising varies between products and consumers, the following are illustrative findings:

1. Consumers make considerable use of TV ads for information on style and design.[12]

2. About 50 percent of those interviewed in one study actually purchased a product after seeing a magazine ad or a commercial for it. Information on price reduction was a major sales trigger.[13]

3. There is a distinct segment of the American public that relies heavily on advertising. They are likely to be male, young, single, and employed.[14]

4. Print and TV ads were found to be the primary information sources used in the purchase of small electrical appliances and outdoor products.[15]

The effects of advertising can be difficult to discern through questioning. People typically do not remember much about advertising unless it clearly stands out as decisive. A more definitive test is to do a field experiment, such as advertising in one market and not in another. This is expensive and methodologically demanding, but many companies will do it simply because there is no better way.

In-Store Information

Many buying decisions are actually made at the point of purchase. It has been reported that two-thirds of all food purchase decisions are made in the grocery store.[16] Consequently, in-store information can have a strong influence on consumer decision making. At least 40 percent of the buyers of housewares mentioned using in-store displays.[17] The informativeness of displays should increase sharply in the future as computerization becomes more common. Revlon and Estée Lauder introduced computerized displays when they discovered that consumers often want answers to questions that might be embarrassing to raise with a potentially ill-informed sales clerk. Hence, the display allows immediate feedback to these questions.

Package labels are often consulted (see Consumer in Focus 5.4), and at times, the effects of this information source can be substantial. For example, nutritional labeling tends to improve consumer perception of such attributes as "wholesome" and "tender."[18] It has also been found that strictly promotional terms such as "sweet" and "succulent" leave people with an assurance of quality comparable with that of the more-detailed nutritional data. This shows how easy it is for deception to take place.

However, there is evidence that sometimes labels are misperceived, used only in part, or disregarded altogether.[19] This is a particularly disturbing finding when the content consists of safety warnings or precautions. Moreover, consumers with lower socioeconomic status make less use of package information and vice versa—just the opposite of what policy makers usually intend.[20]

Salespeople

Several situations exist in which personal selling still plays an important role, even in this era of mass merchandising. It becomes especially crucial when there is the necessity of some type of point-of-sale negotiation and information exchange between buyer and seller. The energy-use labeling program for major appliances, for instance, was found to be ineffective without the input from sales personnel to explain just what the ratings meant.[21] The druggist remains an important information source on various aspects of health care and medication usage.[22]

Consumers' reliance on the opinions of salespeople should be considered in developing promotional strategy. A basic decision confronting marketers is the relative emphasis they should place on **push** versus **pull** strategies. A pull strategy involves the manufacturer creating product demand by appealing to the ultimate consumer, who, in turn, will encourage the channel to carry the product. Under a push strategy, manufacturers focus their selling efforts on the channel, which is then responsible for attracting consumers. This latter strategy makes more sense when the salesperson represents an important source of information.

Consumer in Focus **5.4**

Food Labels and Consumer Search

If you think that consumers don't pay much attention to food labels, think again. On average, over one-third always read ingredient or nutritional information, although this varies across consumers. Women are more likely than men to read labels. Older consumers also make greater use of labels than younger ones.

Food labels are particularly important for products making a first impression. Nearly 80 percent of consumers report that they always or sometimes read labels prior to purchasing a food item for the first item. Many consumers also indicate that label information can influence what they buy. For instance, one-third report that their cereal purchases are influenced by what appears on the label.

Source: William Mueller, "Who Reads the Label?" American Demographics 13 (January 1991), 36–41. Reprinted with permission.

General Purpose

The mass media frequently contain items of interest to those in the midst of the decision process. Some purchasers of houseware items, for example, reported that editorial articles in magazines and newspapers proved helpful.[23] Governmental agencies also generate a wealth of consumer-relevant information.

Various product-rating agencies have risen to the forefront in recent years, the most widely known being Consumers' Union, which publishes *Consumer Reports.* Several manufacturers have found, frequently to their dismay, that ratings by such agencies can have a potent effect, especially if the ratings are negative.[24]

Social Others

As discussed in Chapters 20 and 21, social others such as friends and family can serve as significant sources of information. In a survey by J. D. Power and Associates, an automotive market research firm, two-thirds of new car buyers reported that their decision concerning which make of car to buy was most strongly influenced by their social contacts.[25]

Sequence of Search

The final search dimension, sequence, focuses on the order of search activities. Researchers have been particularly interested in the order in which product-attribute information is acquired.[26] When confronted with a set of brands described along several attributes, consumers may follow a **brand search sequence** (often referred to as **processing by brand**), in which each brand is examined along the various attributes before the search proceeds to the next brand. Alternatively, an **attribute search sequence** (or **processing by attribute**) may occur, in which brand information is collected on an attribute-by-attribute basis. For example, a consumer might first examine each brand's price, followed by an inspection of each brand's warranty. The sequence in which product-attribute information is acquired is an important property of the decision rules we consider in the following chapter.

The information source consumers consult at the beginning of external search may partly determine their purchase behavior. A study of consumers' appliance shopping behavior reports that those buying from Sears were most likely to begin their search process by consulting either newspaper ads or catalogs.[27] Purchases made at furniture stores, however, were most likely to start with discussing the situation with a friend or relative. Different sources can guide the consumer along different purchase paths.

Determinants of Search

A considerable amount of research has accumulated regarding the variety of factors that influence search. Some of these determinants are discussed next.

Situational Determinants

The manner in which situational forces can affect consumer decision making is considered in Chapter 22. As we note there, the information environment will play a significant role in shaping consumer behavior. External search is obviously constrained by the availability and quantity of information in the marketplace. Even the format in which information is presented can alter search behavior, as reflected by consumers' greater use of unit price information when presented in lists rather than in the standard tags on the grocer's shelf.[28]

Time pressures are another source of situational influence.[29] A refrigerator stuffed with food that breaks down beyond repair affords the consumer little time to pursue an extensive and deliberate search. Similarly, the person searching a new city for an upcoming move typically will have only a few days to locate living quarters.

Product Determinants

Features of the product can affect consumer search. The degree of product differentiation is very important.[30] If consumers believe that all brands are essentially the same, there is little need for extensive search. As brands become more distinct, the potential payoff from search grows larger. How-ever, such perceived differences must also be coupled with an uncertainty as to which brand is "best." For example, if consumers believe that a given brand offers the lowest prices, they are unlikely to undertake price comparisons regardless of how much difference they perceive in the prices of competing brands.

Product price is another factor.[31] Higher prices will create greater concerns about the financial risks involved with the purchase, which in turn leads to greater search.

The stability of a product category may affect search. Experienced consumers can rely more heavily on their existing knowledge for categories (milk, garden hoses, cigarettes) that change relatively little over time. In contrast, unstable categories characterized by product innovations or price changes (personal computers, electronic games) may require consumers to "update" their knowledge through search.[32]

Consumer search may also vary between goods and services. Because consumers may perceive greater risk in buying services than goods, they may adopt somewhat different information search patterns to reduce perceived risk. In one study of this possibility, consumers relied more heavily on personal sources of information for decisions involving services.[33]

Retail Determinants

The retail environment will also influence consumer search. The distance between retail competitors can determine the number of stores consumers shop during decision making. Fewer stores will be visited as distance increases.

The similarity among retailers is another source of influence. Search is more likely when consumers perceive important differences across retailers.[34] This is particularly true when retailers differ in the prices charged for products.[35] Again, however, there must also be uncertainty about which store is best before perceptions of store differences will affect search.

Consumer Determinants

Characteristics of the consumer strongly determine search behavior. Some of the more important determinants are discussed subsequently.

Knowledge

Knowledge can have both inhibiting and facilitating effects on search behavior. It can allow the consumer to rely more heavily on internal search during decision making, thereby lowering the need for pre-purchase search. Consequently, knowledge or prior purchase experience is often found to have a negative relationship with external search.[36]

Alternatively, knowledge can enhance search, primarily by enabling more effective use of newly acquired information. When consumers feel more confident about their ability to judge products, they will typically acquire more information.[37] Research has, therefore, found that knowledge may be related positively to external search.[38]

These positive and negative influences may combine to produce an inverted-U relationship between knowledge and external search.[39] Consumers possessing extremely limited knowledge (such as first-time buyers) may feel incompetent to undertake an elaborate search and analysis. Instead, they may try to solve their consumption problem by relying on others. For example, in the "purchase-pal" car buying segment described earlier in the chapter, these inexperienced and unconfident consumers depended very heavily on the opinions of others (perhaps dad) in making their decisions. Similarly, many first-time appliance buyers may decide to place their faith in the salesperson of a trusted retailer.

Greater pre-purchase search should occur for moderately informed consumers. They will possess sufficient knowledge to explore and understand the information environment. However, their knowledge is not so great that they feel comfortable relying heavily on memory. In contrast, a stronger reliance on memory may take place for those possessing high levels of relevant knowledge. Internal search may uncover most if not all information desired for decision making, thus leading to little pre-purchase search for very knowledgeable consumers.[40]

Involvement

Search will also depend on the level of consumer involvement with the product and decision process. Product involvement, which reflects a more enduring interest in the product than that stimulated by purchase requirements, should strongly influence ongoing search.[41] Pre-purchase search, by contrast, will depend more heavily on consumers' involvement with the purchase decision stemming from their perceptions of the economic and psychological risks associated with product purchase. In both cases, higher involvement should lead to greater search.[42]

As one example of how involvement can influence consumer search, consider soup. It should come as no surprise that this product is rather uninvolving for many consumers. This lack of involvement is reflected by how little patience consumers have in locating what they want. According to Anthony Adams, vice president of marketing research at Campbell Soup Co., "After about 45 seconds, we find that consumers just give up." The company therefore streamlined its soup selections to facilitate shoppers locating what they want as quickly as possible.[43]

One tactic that consumers frequently use for low-involvement purchases is the use of product trial as a "substitute" for pre-purchase search. Such is the case for many of the new products that find their way onto the grocer's shelves. Given the relatively low cost of these items, consumers will often decide that the most efficient use of their resources is to simply "buy it and try it." However, when consumers are highly involved with the purchase decision, a substantial amount of search may be undertaken to develop the conviction desired by consumers that they are making a good choice.

Beliefs and Attitudes

Search behavior, just like purchase behavior, is affected by consumers' beliefs and attitudes. For many consumers, shopping is a dreaded chore to be minimized whenever possible. Others hold very different attitudes, as exemplified by those consumers who proudly wear T-shirts proclaiming "Born to shop!" Generally speaking, consumers engage in more search as their attitudes toward shopping become more favorable.[44]

In the case of repeat purchases, consumer satisfaction with their prior choices may determine the perceived need for search while making their current choices. If the prior choice was satisfactory, consumers become less motivated to search. This simple fact goes a long way in explaining why grocery shoppers spent so little time in making the decisions described earlier in Consumer in Focus 5.3.

When prior choices turn out to be less than satisfying or when consumers are making an initial purchase decision within the product category, at least some degree of search will be needed. In such cases, product attitudes can be important because search will tend to focus initially on brands with high prior attractiveness.[45]

The beliefs held by consumers are also important determinants.[46] Perceptions regarding the costs versus benefits of search play a major role in guiding search.[47] Consumers will usually invest more effort into search when the perceived benefits of this activity grow and the costs decline.

This cost-benefit view of search plays an important role in Wilkie and Dickson's model of appliance shopping behavior reproduced in Figure 5.7. Following need recognition (called "precipitating purchase circumstance" in their model), the consumer is seen as developing some preliminary specifications for the product purchase (for example, must be under $400). A store is then visited, perhaps because it is currently promoting sale prices. At this point, a salesperson might influence the consumer to modify her or his initial specifications. If the "best" alternative (that is, the one coming closest to meeting the consumer's specifications) available at the store is exactly what the consumer wants, search will end and purchase takes place. If not, the consumer must then decide on the relative costs versus benefits of continued search.

Demographic Characteristics

Research indicates that search may be related to several demographic characteristics.[48] Age is often negatively related to search.[49] Older consumers can call on their greater experience. They may also be more brand loyal than their younger counterparts.

Higher-income consumers search less than lower-income consumers. Higher-income consumers presumably value their time more highly, which increases search costs. Higher costs will reduce search.[50]

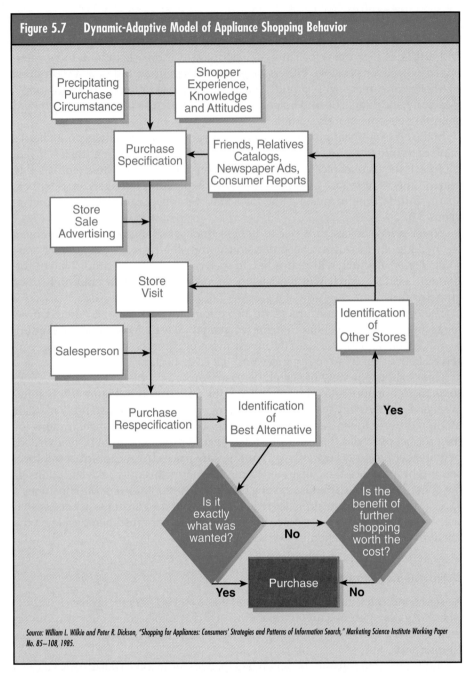

Figure 5.7   Dynamic-Adaptive Model of Appliance Shopping Behavior

Source: William L. Wilkie and Peter R. Dickson, "Shopping for Appliances: Consumers' Strategies and Patterns of Information Search," Marketing Science Institute Working Paper No. 85–108, 1985.

A positive relationship usually occurs between education and search. More educated consumers may have greater confidence in their ability to use search effectively. Such confidence will enhance search behavior.[51]

There are basically two main approaches to measuring the search activities of consumers when making their purchase decisions: retrospective questioning and observation.[52] The most popular method, retrospective questioning, involves simply asking consumers to recall their search activities during decision making. This can be done through surveys and store exit interviews. Also, specifically designed warranty registration cards can be useful for this purpose.

Although this method finds widespread use, it suffers from the obvious limitation of reliance on recall. Unless the purchase is highly involving and recently made, it is probable that many details of the search process will be forgotten.

One way to overcome consumers' imperfect memory for their search behavior is to use an observational approach.[53] Evidence indicates that the incidences of actual information seeking are higher when they are observed than when indicated by a reliance on retrospective questioning.[54] Nonetheless, the observational method is not without its own set of limitations. Researchers can observe what consumers do within a specific store. But what about when consumers leave the store? Observational techniques are extremely limited in their potential to provide information about many aspects of consumer search, such as consulting with friends and reading relevant materials.

In addition to measuring what sources of information consumers consult during decision making, it is also useful to examine the extent to which consumers rely on a particular source. Consider two consumers, both of whom consult the same source (for example, a salesperson) during search. Suppose, however, that one consumer relies on the source's advice, whereas the other ignores this advice. Search measures that only capture whether consumers search a particular source without also gauging whether consumers use the source will provide an incomplete picture of the role information sources play during consumer decision making. For this reason, it is recommended that consumers be asked to report both what sources they consult and how useful and influential they found each source to be.[55]

Summary

The decision process begins when a need is activated and recognized because of a discrepancy between the consumer's desired state and actual situation. Need recognition can be triggered by several factors. Changes in one's personal circumstances, such as the birth of a child, can activate new needs. Marketers can also influence the likelihood of need activation through advertising and product innovations.

Search for potential need satisfiers will occur following need recognition. If an internal search of memory provides a satisfactory solution to the consumption problem, it will be unnecessary for consumers to seek information from their environment. Often, however, some degree of external search will be necessary. Just how much search will occur varies across consumers and depends on a host of situational, marketplace, and consumer characteristics.

Not all external search is driven by an immediate purchase need. Indeed, some consumers continually engage in ongoing search activities as a result of their involvement with the product category.

Understanding consumer search can be useful in developing marketing strategy. How much consumers search and the particular sources consulted during search can help shape a firm's pricing, promotion, and distribution strategies.

Review and Discussion Questions

1. What are the basic strategies available for companies seeking to influence need recognition?

2. Discuss how need recognition triggered your last soft drink purchase. Was this different from need recognition leading to the purchase of new shoes? What role, if any, do you feel marketing efforts played in both situations?

3. Suppose you were faced with the situation confronting the furniture industry, as described in Consumer in Focus 5.2. Drawing on the chapter discussion of need recognition, what would you recommend?

4. What effect is ongoing search likely to have on consumers' use of internal search during decision making?

5. Explain how each of the following factors might affect consumer search: (a) brand loyalty, (b) store loyalty, (c) uncertainty about which brand best meets consumers' needs, and (d) the importance consumers place on paying a low price.

6. Consider two alternative target segments that differ only in their propensity for information search. One segment undertakes a substantial amount of external search during decision making. In contrast, consumers in the remaining segment are far less active in their search behaviors. Which segment, if either, would be a better target market? Assuming both were targeted, how should marketing activities differ in pursuing each segment?

7. A recent study has classified consumers into one of three segments based on how much search they did when making their purchase decisions. For each segment, the percentage buying your brand versus competitive brands was examined. The results appear below.

	Percentage Buying:	
Amount of Search	Your brand	Competitors' brands
Minimal	3	97
Moderate	9	91
Extensive	17	83

What implications do these results carry for marketing strategy?

8. The results of a consumer research project have just arrived on your desk. This study examined whether target consumers' brand preferences at the time of need recognition carried over to actual purchase. Consumers just beginning their decision process were asked about their preferences for the company's brand and two competitors. These results, as well as each brand's share of purchases, are presented below.

Brand	Consumers' Preference at Time of Need Recognition	Share of Purchases
Company's brand	50%	30%
Competitor A	30%	50%
Competitor B	20%	20%
Total	100%	100%

What conclusions would you reach from this information?

Endnotes

1. Sirgy has used the concept of congruity to predict the strength of need recognition. See M. Joseph Sirgy, "A Social Cognition Model of Consumer Problem Recognition," *Journal of the Academy of Marketing Science* 15 (Winter 1987), 53–61.

2. Gordon C. Bruner II, "The Effect of Problem Recognition Style on Information Seeking," *Journal of the Academy of Marketing Science* 15 (Winter 1987), 33–41; Gordon C. Bruner II, "Problem Recognition Styles and Search Patterns: An Empirical Investigation," *Journal of Retailing* 62 (1986), 281–297; Gordon C. Bruner II, "Recent Contributions to the Theory of Problem Recognition," in Robert F. Lusch et al., eds., *1985 AMA Educators' Proceedings* (Washington, D.C.: American Marketing Association, 1985), 11–15.

3. Internal search has received relatively little attention in the consumer behavior literature. For exceptions, see James R. Bettman, *An Information Processing Theory of Consumer Choice* (Reading, Mass.: Addison-Wesley, 1979), 107–111; Gabriel J. Biehal, "Consumers' Prior Experiences and Perceptions in Auto Repair Choice," *Journal of Marketing* 47 (Summer 1983), 87–91. For research on how the adequacy of internal search will affect external search, see Girish Punj, "Presearch Decision Making in Consumer Durable Purchases," *Journal of Consumer Marketing* 4 (Winter 1987), 71–82.

4. Biehal, "Consumers' Prior Experiences and Perceptions in Auto Repair Choice."

5. Geoffrey C. Kiel and Roger A. Layton, "Dimensions of Consumer Information Seeking Behavior," *Journal of Marketing Research* 18 (May 1981), 233–239.

6. Peter H. Bloch, Daniel L. Sherrell, and Nancy M. Ridgway, "Consumer Search: An Extended Framework," *Journal of Consumer Research* 13 (June 1986), 119–126.

7. Ibid.

8. John D. Claxton, Joseph N. Fry, and Bernard Portis, "A Taxonomy of Prepurchase Information Gathering Patterns," *Journal of Consumer Research* 1 (December 1974), 35–42; David H. Furse, Girish N. Punj, and David W. Stewart, "A Typology of Individual Search Strategies among Purchasers of New Automobiles," *Journal of Consumer Research* 10 (March 1984), 417–431; Joseph W. Newman, "Consumer External Search: Amount and Determinants," in Arch G. Woodside, Jagdish N. Sheth, and Peter D. Bennett, eds., *Consumer and Industrial Buyer Behavior* (New York: North-Holland, 1977), 79–94.

9. Richard W. Olshavsky and Donald H. Granbois, "Consumer Decision Making— Fact or Fiction?" *Journal of Consumer Research* 6 (September 1979), 93–100.

10. Furse, Punj, and Stewart, "A Typology of Individual Search Strategies among Purchasers of New Automobiles." Also see David F. Midgley, "Patterns of Interpersonal Information Seeking for the Purchase of a Symbolic Product," *Journal of Marketing Research* 20 (February 1983), 74–83.

11. Joel E. Urbany and Peter R. Dickson, "Consumer Information, Competitive Rivalry, and Pricing in the Retail Grocery Industry," working paper, University of South Carolina, 1988.

12. Michael A. Houston, "Consumer Evaluations and Product Information Sources," in James H. Leigh and Claude R. Martin, Jr., eds., *Current Issues and Research in Advertising* (Ann Arbor, Mich.: University of Michigan Graduate School of Business, 1979), 135–144.

13. *A Study of Media Involvement* (New York: Magazine Publishers' Association, 1979).

14. "Whirlpool Corporation," in Roger D. Blackwell, James F. Engel, and W. Wayne Talarzyk, *Contemporary Cases in Consumer Behavior,* rev. ed. (Hinsdale, Ill.: Dryden Press, 1984), 365–388.

15. "Study Tracks Housewares Buying, Information Sources," *Marketing News* (October 14, 1983), 16.

16. Judann Dagnoli, "Heinz Marketing Gets $100M Boost," *Advertising Age* (September 16, 1991), 3, 45.

17. "Study Tracks Housewares Buying, Information Sources."

18. Edward H. Asam and Louis P. Bucklin, "Nutritional Labeling for Canned Goods: A Study of Consumer Response," *Journal of Marketing* 37 (April 1973), 32–37.

19. Gary T. Ford and Philip G. Kuehl, "Label Warning Messages in OTC Drug Advertising: An Experimental Examination of FTC Policy-Making," in James H. Leigh and Claude R. Martin, Jr., eds., *Current Issues and Research in Advertising* (Ann Arbor, Mich.: University of Michigan Graduate School of Business, 1979), 115–128; Lorna Opatow, "How Consumers 'Use' Labels of OTC Drugs," *American Druggist* 177 (March 1978), 10ff; Jo-Ann Zybtniewski, "Keeping Pace with the Nutrition Race," *Progressive Grocer* 59 (July 1980), 29.

20. James McCullough and Roger Best, "Consumer Preference for Food Label Information: A Basis for Segmentation," *Journal of Consumer Affairs* 14 (Summer 1980), 180–192.

21. John D. Claxton and C. Dennis Anderson, "Energy Information at the Point of Sale: A Field Experiment," in Jerry C. Olson, ed., *Advances in Consumer Research* 7 (Ann Arbor, Mich.: Association for Consumer Research, 1980), 277–282.

22. "Public Goes on Strong 'Self-Medication Kick,'" *Marketing News* (June 27, 1980), 1.

23. "Study Tracks Housewares Buying, Information Sources."

24. Mark G. Weinberger and William R. Dillon, "The Effects of Unfavorable Product Rating Information," in Jerry C. Olson, ed., *Advances in Consumer Research* 7 (Ann Arbor, Mich.: Association for Consumer Research, 1980), 528–532.

25. Cited in Bloch, Sherrell, and Ridgway, "Consumer Search," 121.

26. See James R. Bettman and Jacob Jacoby, "Patterns of Processing in Consumer Information Processing," in Beverlee B. Anderson, ed., *Advances in Consumer Research* 3 (Ann Arbor, Mich.: Association for Consumer Research, 1976), 315–320; James R. Bettman and Pradeep Kakkar, "Effects of Information Presentation Format on Consumer Information Acquisition Strategies," *Journal of Consumer Research* 3 (March 1977), 233–240; James R. Bettman and C. Whan Park, "Effects of Prior Knowledge and Experience and Phase of the Choice Process on Consumer Decision Processes: A Protocol Analysis," *Journal of Consumer Research* 7 (December 1980), 243–248; Itamar Simonson, Joel Huber, and John Payne, "The Relationship between Prior Brand Knowledge and Information Acquisition Order," *Journal of Consumer Research* 14 (March 1988), 566–578.

27. William L. Wilkie and Peter R. Dickson, "Shopping for Appliances: Consumers' Strategies and Patterns of Information Search," Marketing Science Institute Working Paper No. 85-108, 1985.

28. J. Edward Russo, "The Value of Unit Price Information," *Journal of Marketing Research* 14 (May 1977), 193–201; J. Edward Russo, Gene Krieser, and Sally Miyashita, "An Effective Display of Unit Price Information," *Journal of Marketing* 39 (April 1975), 11–19.

29. Sharon E. Beatty and Scott M. Smith, "External Search Effort: An Investigation across Several Product Categories," *Journal of Consumer Research* 14 (June 1987), 83–95; William L. Moore and Donald R. Lehmann, "Individual Differences in Search Behavior for a Nondurable," *Journal of Consumer Research* 7 (December 1980), 296–307.

30. James A. Muncy, "Involvement and Perceived Brand Similarities/Differences: The Need for Process Oriented Models," in Marvin E. Goldberg, Gerald Gorn, and Richard W. Pollay, eds., *Advances in Consumer Research* 17 (Provo, Utah: Association for Consumer Research, 1990), 144–148.

31. Kiel and Layton, "Dimensions of Consumer Information Seeking Behavior."

32. Joel E. Urbany and Peter R. Dickson, "Information Search in the Retail Grocery Market," working paper, Ohio State University, Columbus, Ohio, 1987.

33. Keith B. Murray, "A Test of Services Marketing Theory: Consumer Information Acquisition Activities," *Journal of Marketing* 55 (January 1991), 10–25.

34. Calvin P. Duncan and Richard W. Olshavsky, "External Search: The Role of Consumer Beliefs," *Journal of Marketing Research* 19 (February 1982), 32–43.

35. Joel E. Urbany, "An Experimental Examination of the Economics of Information," *Journal of Consumer Research* 13 (September 1986), 257–271.

36. Beatty and Smith, "External Search Effort"; Kiel and Layton, "Dimensions of Consumer Information Seeking Behavior"; Moore and Lehmann, "Individual Differences in Search Behavior for a Nondurable"; Joseph W. Newman and Richard Staelin, "Prepurchase Information Seeking for New Cars and Major Household Appliances," *Journal of Marketing Research* 9 (August 1972), 247–257; Girish N. Punj and Richard Staelin, "A Model of Consumer Information Search Behavior for New Automobiles," *Journal of Consumer Research* 9 (March 1983), 366–380; Joel E. Urbany, Peter R. Dickson, and William L. Wilkie, "Buyer Uncertainty and Information Search," *Journal of Consumer Research* 16 (September 1989), 208–215.

37. Duncan and Olshavsky, "External Search."

38. Merrie Brucks, "The Effects of Product Class Knowledge on Information Search Behavior," *Journal of Consumer Research* 12 (June 1985), 1–16; Jacob Jacoby, Robert W. Chestnut, and William A. Fisher, "A Behavioral Process Approach to Information Acquisition in Nondurable Purchasing," *Journal of Marketing Research* 15 (November 1978), 532–544; Urbany, Dickson, and Wilkie, "Buyer Uncertainty and Information Search."

39. Bettman and Park, "Effects of Prior Knowledge and Experience and Phase of the Choice Process on Consumer Decision Processes"; Julie L. Ozanne, Merrie Brucks, and Dhruv Grewal, "A Study of Information Search Behavior during the Categorization of New Products," *Journal of Consumer Research* 18 (March 1992), 452–463.

40. Knowledge can also affect the sequence of search. See Simonson, Huber, and Payne, "The Relationship between Prior Brand Knowledge and Information Acquisition Order."

41. Bloch, Sherrell, and Ridgway, "Consumer Search."

42. Beatty and Smith, "External Search Effort"; Judith Lynne Zaichkowsky, "Measuring the Involvement Construct," *Journal of Consumer Research* 12 (December 1985), 341–352. For research on how involvement's influence may vary between functional versus expressive products, see Banwari Mittal, "Must Consumer Involvement Always Imply More Information Search?" in Thomas K. Srull, ed., *Advances in Consumer Research* 16 (Provo, Utah: Association for Consumer Research, 1989), 167–172.

43. Patricia Braus, "What Is Good Service?" *American Demographics* 12 (July 1990), 36–39.

44. Beatty and Smith, "External Search Effort"; Punj and Staelin, "A Model of Consumer Information Search Behavior for New Automobiles."

45. Simonson, Huber, and Payne, "The Relationship between Prior Brand Knowledge and Information Acquisition Order."

46. Duncan and Olshavsky, "External Search"; Deborah Roedder John, Carol A. Scott, and James R. Bettman, "Sampling Data for Covariation Assessment: The Effect of Prior Beliefs on Search Patterns," *Journal of Consumer Research* 13 (June 1986), 38–47.

47. Urbany, "An Experimental Investigation of the Economics of Information." Also see Narasimhan Srinivasan and Brian T. Ratchford, "An Empirical Test of a Model of External Search for Automobiles," *Journal of Consumer Research* 18 (September 1991), 233–242.

48. For a brief review of the literature concerning demographics and search, see Beatty and Smith, "External Search Effort."

49. Catherine A. Cole and Siva K. Balasubramanian, "Age Differences in Consumers' Search for Information: Public Policy Implications," *Journal of Consumer Research* 20 (June 1993), 157–169.

50. John, Scott, and Bettman, "Sampling Data for Covariation Assessment"; Urbany, "An Experimental Investigation of the Economics of Information."

51. Duncan and Olshavsky, "External Search."

52. For an example of measuring consumer search in laboratory settings, see Merrie Brucks, "Search Monitor: An Approach for Computer-Controlled Experiments Involving Consumer Information Search," *Journal of Consumer Research* 12 (November 1988), 117–121.

53. Peter R. Dickson and Alan G. Sawyer, "The Price Knowledge and Search of Supermarket Shoppers," *Journal of Marketing* 54 (July 1990), 42–53; Wayne D. Hoyer, "An Examination of Consumer Decision Making for a Common Repeat Purchase Product," *Journal of Consumer Research* 11 (December 1984), 822–829; Joseph W. Newman and Bradley D. Lockman, "Measuring Prepurchase Information Seeking," *Journal of Consumer Research* 11 (December 1975), 216–222.

54. Newman and Lockman, "Measuring Prepurchase Information Seeking."

55. Jeff Blodgett and Donna Hill, "An Exploratory Study Comparing Amount-of-Search Measures to Consumers' Reliance on Each Source of Information," in Rebecca H. Holman and Michael R. Solomon, eds., *Advances in Consumer Research* 18 (Provo, Utah: Association for Consumer Research, 1991), 773–779.

CHAPTER 6

Pre-purchase Alternative Evaluation

▲▲▲▲▲▲▲▲▲▲▲▲▲▲▲▲▲▲▲▲▲▲▲▲▲▲▲▲▲▲▲▲▲▲▲▲▲

Businesses' Green Appeals for Consumers' Changing Environmental Concerns

The importance consumers attach to environmental considerations is changing. At the outset of the 1980s, environmental issues were not a major concern for most consumers. Today it's a different story. In some surveys, environmental concerns rank as high as the fourth most important issue among Amercan consumers.

These attitudinal changes are affecting consumer behavior. Research indicates that one-third of consumers regularly check product labels for environmental information. And they want more. In a survey of women aged 21 to 54 years, 85 percent reported that product labels do not contain enough environmental information.

These changing attitudes have not gone unnoticed by businesses. What some have called "green marketing," businesses have begun catering to environmentally concerned consumers. Many of these green appeals have come in the form of new packaging. L'eggs, the world's largest maker of women's hosiery, has replaced its famous plastic egg container with an environmentally friendly cardboard package. McDonald's has discontinued using plastic foam cartons in favor of paper wraps.

Companies are also changing what comes inside the package. Manufacturers of disposable diapers, for instance, have reformulated their products to ease the demands they place on landfill space. Battery companies have reduced the amount of mercury in their products in order to make them more environmentally friendly (see Figure 6.1). And the Safe Brands Corp. is marketing its Sierra brand of antifreeze, which is made with propylene glycol instead

Figure 6.1   Appealing to Consumers' Environmental Concerns

of ethylene glycol, as less toxic and environmentally safer than conventional antifreeze.

Sources: Leah Rickard, "'Safer' Antifreeze Frosts Prestone Over Claims in Ads," Advertising Age *(October 4, 1993), 64; Howard Schlossberg, "Latest Trend: Targeting Consumers According to Environmental Beliefs,"* Marketing News 26 *(January 6, 1992), 5; Howard Schlossberg, "Americans Passionate about the Environment? Critic Says That's 'Nonsense',"* Marketing News 25 *(September 16, 1991); 8; Howard Schlossberg, "Survey: Consumers More Aware, Still Want More Info,"* Marketing News 25 *(December 9, 1991), 6.*

The chapter opener aptly illustrates that the importance consumers place on product features in evaluating choice alternatives affects a company's product offerings and marketing focus. This chapter examines the third stage of our consumer decision-making model, pre-purchase alternative evaluation. **Pre-purchase alternative evaluation** can be defined as the process by which a choice alternative is evaluated and selected to meet consumer needs. Although we have presented search and pre-purchase alternative evaluation as "separate" stages for pedagogical reasons, you should recognize that the two stages are intricately intertwined during decision making. The acquisition of product information from the environment, for instance, will normally lead to some evaluation (for example, "these prices are too high") that may then guide subsequent search (for example, "let's check the store across the street").

The complexity of pre-purchase alternative evaluation will vary dramatically depending on the particular process consumers follow in making their consumption decisions. When decision making is habitual in nature, this decision-making stage will simply involve the consumer forming an intention to repurchase the same product as before. Similarly, consumers lacking the knowledge needed for selecting an appropriate medicinal product may rely on the pharmacist's recommendations rather than try to decide for themselves. Under this scenario, pre-purchase alternative evaluation consists of the rather simple decision rule, "Buy what the expert recommends."

Sometimes pre-purchase alternative evaluation will be quite complex, as is the case for many of the high-priced durable goods that we purchase. In its most complex form, pre-purchase alternative evaluation will take the form depicted in Figure 6.2. Decisions must be made initially about which choice alternatives to consider and the evaluative criteria (that is, dimensions or attributes) to use in judging the alternatives. The relative performance of the considered alternatives along the evaluative criteria must then be judged. A decision rule is then

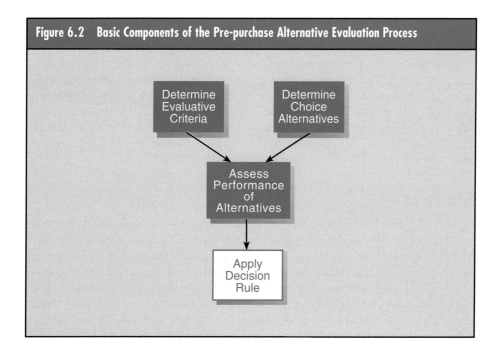

Figure 6.2 Basic Components of the Pre-purchase Alternative Evaluation Process

applied to these judgments to select a particular alternative. In the following sections, we examine more fully these components of the pre-purchase alternative evaluation process.

Evaluative Criteria

Evaluative criteria are nothing more than the particular dimensions or attributes that are used in judging the choice alternatives. Evaluative criteria come in many forms. In purchasing a car, consumers may consider factors such as safety, reliability, price, brand name, country of origin (where it is made), warranty, and gas mileage. The consumer may also consider evaluative criteria more hedonic in nature, such as the feelings that come from owning (such as prestige and status) and driving (such as exhilaration and excitement) the car. Although it is beyond the scope of this text to provide a detailed review of the various evaluative criteria used by consumers, a couple deserve special comment.

Price

Certainly one of the more important evaluative criteria is price. Indeed, we have all experienced situations in which our product choice was heavily affected by pricing considerations. Nonetheless, there is considerable variation in the importance of price across both consumers and products.[1] Consequently, consumers' price sensitivity may often be useful for market segmentation.

Nonetheless, the importance of price is often overrated. When supermarket shoppers were asked the price of an item they had just placed in their shopping basket, less than half of them could do so. Similarly, less than half were aware they had chosen a product offered at a reduced price.[2] Nor are consumers always looking for the lowest possible price or even the best price-to-quality ratio. Other factors such as convenience or brand name may assume greater importance.[3]

Brand Name

Figure 6.3 presents a display from the makers of Boar's Head meat that consumers encountered at the deli section of their local supermarket. Of particular relevance here is the statement, "The name you can trust for the nutrition of your family." Implicit in such an appeal is the idea that a product's brand name is important to consumers when making their purchase decisions. Indeed, brand name frequently emerges as an important evaluative criterion, as it did in a study of purchasing behavior involving dress shirts and suits.[4] It also proved to be significant in choosing over-the-counter drugs.[5] In these cases, the brand

Figure 6.3   A Trusted Brand Name Can Enhance Consumers' Product Evaluations

name appears to serve as a surrogate indicator of product quality. The potential for brand name to influence consumers' product evaluations has been well documented.[6]

The importance consumers place on brand name may depend on their ability to judge quality. For example, in the case of headache and cold remedies, the average consumer cannot judge purity and quality. Consequently, brand name becomes especially crucial as a surrogate indicator of quality. It is such a dominant factor with many consumers that they will pay more for aspirin when it carries a well-known brand name, even though they are aware that government regulations require all aspirin products to contain the same basic therapeutic formulation.[7]

Brand name can also be influential when the name is seen as a status symbol, and consumers are motivated by such considerations. For some consumers, having the Rolex name on a watch is just as important as any physical feature of the product itself. The Marlboro ad, appearing in Figure 6.4, promotes the product based on the symbolic value of the brand name.

Country of Origin

In this age of intensifying international competition and the loss of many manufacturing jobs to cheaper foreign labor, it is not surprising that the country in which a product is produced has become an important consideration among many American consumers.[8] Some companies have tried to capitalize on this concern by emphasizing that their product is "Made in the U.S.A." (Figure 6.5). Others have taken this one step further by advertising not only that the product is "American-built" but also that the manufacturer is "American-owned."

Salience of Evaluative Criteria

The concept of **salience** reflects the notion that evaluative criteria often differ in their influence on consumers' product selections. Some criteria will have a greater impact than others. A pleasant retail atmosphere may be a nice amenity,

Figure 6.4 Appealing to Consumers' Brand Consciousness

but the prices charged by the retailer will usually carry more weight in consumers' decisions about where to shop.

Similarly, as illustrated in Consumer in Focus 6.1, consumers can differ from one another in the salience they attach to various evaluative criteria. You might recall from Chapter 2 the concept of benefit segmentation, in which a market is divided based on the benefits sought from product consumption. Recognize that this type of segmentation is only useful when consumers differ in the salience they place on evaluative criteria.

Salience refers to the *potential* influence each dimension may exert during the comparison process. Whether this potential influence materializes depends on how consumers perceive the alternatives under consideration to perform along an evaluative criterion. Take airline travel as an example. An airline's ability to provide safe passage is of obvious importance to consumers. However, because most consumers perceive all airlines as providing relatively safe travel, safety is not a deciding factor in selecting a carrier. Similarly, consumers may rate price as a very important attribute, but if all brands cost the same amount, the impact of price essentially drops out. Salient attributes that actually influence the

Figure 6.5   Promoting Country of Origin as a Reason to Buy

Reasons for Choosing a Supermarket: Americans versus Canadians

What evaluative criteria do consumers use in selecting a supermarket? The answer depends on what consumers you are talking about. American and Canadian shoppers recently were asked to indicate what they look for when making their supermarket choices. The results appear below:

Rankings for U.S. Shoppers	Rankings for Canadian Shoppers
#1 Cleanliness	#1 Good produce department
#2 Low prices	#2 Low prices
#3 Prices clearly labeled	#3 Good variety/selection
#4 Pleasant employees	#4 Pleasant employees
#5 Freshness date on products	#5 Good meat department
#6 Good produce department	#6 Convenient location
#7 Short wait for checkout	#7 Prices clearly labeled
#8 Good meat department	#8 Money-saving specials
#9 Convenient location	#9 Short wait for checkout
#10 Unit pricing signs on shelves	#10 Fresh deli and bakery selections

Interestingly, store cleanliness ranked as the #1 reason for selecting a supermarket among American shoppers, although this evaluative criterion did not make the top ten for Canadian shoppers. In light of recent news stories alleging unsanitary practices within the meat department of some U.S. supermarkets, this sensitivity to cleanliness among Americans is understandable. On the other hand, variety and selection ranked third among Canadians, but failed to make the top ten for Americans.

Source: "Why Canadians Like U.S. Food," American Demographics (November 1993), 25–26.

evaluation process (that is, attributes on which alternatives differ in their performance) are known as **determinant attributes**.[9]

An important aspect of understanding consumer decision making involves identifying the particular evaluative criteria consumers use when deciding among purchase alternatives. It is also necessary to assess the relative salience of these criteria. We will return to these issues during our coverage of the multi-attribute attitude models in Chapter 11.

Determinants of Evaluative Criteria

The particular evaluative criteria used by consumers during decision making will depend on several factors. Some of these are discussed next.

Situational Influence

Situational factors will often have an important influence on an evaluative criterion's salience.[10] Location convenience, for example, often assumes greater importance in the selection of a fast-food restaurant when the consumer is pressed for time than when time is not a factor. Similarly, many consumers will select a prestigious brand of liquor when it is to be served at a party but will opt for a less prestigious (and less expensive) brand for their own private use.

Similarity of Choice Alternatives

The similarity or comparability of alternatives from which consumers choose can vary substantially. A consumer deciding how to spend a tax refund may be considering such diverse alternatives as buying a new wardrobe, taking a vacation, or putting the money in the bank. Much greater similarity among choice alternatives will exist, however, for decisions about which brand to purchase within a product category.

Decisions involving noncomparable alternatives may require the consumer to use more abstract evaluative criteria during pre-purchase alternative evaluation.[11] Consider, for instance, the consumer faced with choosing between a refrigerator, a television, and a stereo. These alternatives share few concrete attributes (price is an exception) along which comparisons can be made directly. Comparisons can be undertaken, however, using abstract dimensions such as necessity, entertainment, and status.

Consumers' reliance on price during decision making can be affected by the similarity of choice alternatives. If, for instance, consumers believe that all lawn care companies will provide essentially the same basic service and benefits, they will depend much more heavily on price differences in making a choice. In general, price becomes more important in the absence of meaningful product differentiation. For this reason, those seeking a higher price for their product relative to competitors must continuously work at keeping consumers from perceiving all brands as offering essentially the same thing. One example of how this might be done is the ad appearing in Figure 6.6, which proclaims that "Contrary to popular belief, all flours are not created equal."

Motivation

As discussed more fully in Chapter 12, a basic distinction in understanding motivation is whether consumers are driven by utilitarian versus hedonic considerations. The presence of such motivations will determine the type of evaluative criteria likely to be used during pre-purchase alternative evaluation. Utilitarian motivations during the purchase of athletic shoes could lead to examination of a shoe's price and construction, whereas hedonic motivations might lead to consideration of the feelings that come from product ownership and usage (such as the person who buys Nike to project a desirable image).

Figure 6.6   One Company's Attempt to Foster Perceived Differentiation

Involvement

Consumers' involvement with a decision will influence the number of evaluative criteria used in pre-purchase alternative evaluation. A greater number of evaluative criteria are likely to enter into the decision as involvement increases.[12]

Involvement may also influence the relative salience of evaluative criteria. One study of the evaluative criteria used by Iowa farmers in selecting a retail outlet for supplies found that highly involved decision makers were more concerned with service attributes, whereas those less involved focused on low price and a retailer's size and reputation.[13]

Knowledge

Knowledge can have several effects on consumers' use of evaluative criteria. Well-informed consumers will have information stored in memory about the dimensions useful for comparing choice alternatives. This information is much less likely to exist in the memory of novices. Consequently, novices will be much more susceptible to external influences that attempt to shape the particular criteria used during decision making.[14] For example, advertisements that suggest the evaluative criteria that consumers should consider are likely to be more effective in this regard for first-time buyers.

Knowledge can also determine consumers' use of particular evaluative criteria. Consumers may rely much more heavily on brand name or others' recommendations, for instance, when they lack the knowledge necessary for directly evaluating product quality.

Determining Choice Alternatives

Not only must consumers decide on the criteria to use in pre-purchase alternative evaluation, they must also determine the alternatives from which choice is made. These alternatives define what is known as the **consideration set** (also known as the **evoked set**).[15] As suggested by the information presented in Table 6.1, the consideration set will typically contain only a subset of the total number

Table 6.1	Average Size of Consumers' Consideration Sets by Product Category		
Product Category	Average Consideration Set Size	Product Category	Average Consideration Set Size
Analgesic	3.5	Insecticides	2.7
Antacid	4.4	Laundry detergent	4.8
Air freshener	2.2	Laxative	2.8
Bar soap	3.7	Peanut butter	3.3
Bathroom cleaner	5.7	Razors	2.9
Beer	6.9	Shampoo	6.1
Bleach	3.9	Shortening	6.0
Chili	2.6	Sinus medicine	3.6
Coffee	4.0	Soap	4.8
Cookies	4.9	Soda	5.1
Deodorant	3.9	Yogurt	3.6
Frozen dinners	3.3		

Source: John R. Hauser and Birger Wernerfelt, "An Evaluation Cost Model of Consideration Sets," Journal of Consumer Research 16 (March 1990), 393–408.

of alternatives available to the consumer. Recognize that these results represent the average size of the consideration set. Thus, some consumers will have even larger consideration sets, whereas the consideration sets for other consumers will be smaller. Some consumers, such as those extremely loyal to a particular brand, will have only one brand in their consideration set.

Gaining entry into the consideration set is a top priority. Failure to do so means that a competitor's offering will be purchased. Marketers must, therefore, take steps to see that their products gain consideration during decision making. Examine the ad appearing in Figure 6.7. Notice how it plays on consumers' fears about making a mistake during decision making as a means of gaining consideration.

Another tactic used by companies for gaining consideration, as exemplified by Figure 6.8, is to offer incentives. Automobile manufacturers sometimes offer consumers gifts or money to simply test drive their cars. Coupons can play essentially the same role.

Figure 6.7   Gaining Consideration: A Necessary Prerequisite for Purchase

Constructing the Consideration Set

Suppose you were hungry and decided to eat out tonight. In this instance, there are at least two ways you could go about constructing a consideration set. You could undertake external search, such as scanning the restaurants listed in the yellow pages, mentally noting those worth further consideration. A more likely scenario, however, would involve an internal search through memory, which is likely to yield several possibilities. In the latter situation, the consideration set would depend on your recall of alternatives from memory (that is, the **retrieval set**).[16]

Obviously, consumers cannot construct a consideration set based on an internal search of memory without prior knowledge of at least some alternatives. Yet, in the case of first-time buyers for some product categories, consumers may lack

---

Figure 6.8   Offering Incentives to Gain Purchase Consideration

knowledge about what alternatives are available to choose from. When this occurs, the consideration set may be developed in any one of several ways. The consumer might talk to others, search through the yellow pages, consider all brands available at the store, and so on. Thus, external factors such as the retail environment have a greater opportunity to affect the consideration set of less knowledgeable consumers.[17]

The manner in which the consideration set is constructed can shape marketing strategy. Consider those situations in which consumers construct a consideration set based on an internal memory search. When this occurs, the odds of a given offering being chosen are dependent on its being recalled from memory. Accordingly, when consideration sets are based on internal search, it is very important that consumers are able to *recall* the company's offering. As we shall see in Chapter 15, there are several ways a company can influence consumers' ability to remember the company's name. Chapter 15 also discusses the possibility of undermining the competition by inhibiting the recall of competitive offerings.[18]

At other times, *recognition* rather than recall becomes more important in determining the consideration set. Take the consumer who quickly scans the shelf at a grocery store to determine what is available and makes a choice among those brands that are recognized (that is, look familiar) by the consumer. Recognition of alternatives available at the point of purchase would therefore determine the consideration set. Beyond making sure its offering is available at the store, a company would also want to teach consumers about what its product packaging looks like so that it could be easily recognized.

Is the evaluation and choice of a given alternative affected by what other alternatives are included in the consideration set? Several studies have reported an **attraction effect** in which a given alternative's attractiveness is enhanced when an inferior alternative is added to the set of choice alternatives.[19] Although the robustness of this effect is not well understood, it does suggest the possibility that a product might benefit from encouraging consumers to consider weaker offerings.

Assessing Choice Alternatives

Another component of the pre-purchase alternative evaluation process involves judging the performance of choice alternatives along salient evaluative criteria. As reported in Consumer in Focus 6.2, consumers may often be limited in their ability to evaluate choice alternatives "accurately."[20] Such limitations are a cause for concern among those involved with consumer protection (see Chapter 25).

Consumer in Focus **6.2**

Can Consumers Tell the Difference between Cheap and Expensive Ties?

Can you tell the difference between a cheap $3 necktie and an expensive designer tie? If you can, you are in the minority. Reporters at the *Washington Post* asked attorneys, office workers, and others passing the newspaper's office to identify whether a tie was cheap or expensive. Each person was handed five low-priced ties and four expensive ties, including a Georgio Armani tie priced at $67.50. Participants were allowed to touch and inspect the ties except for peeking at the label.

On average, people accurately classified five of the nine ties, which is about the same level of accuracy as would be expected if people made their judgments by flipping a coin. Of the 82 people who participated, only one person accurately identified all nine ties . . . and he confessed he stuck out his neck and made some lucky guesses!

In many cases, consumers already have stored in memory judgments or beliefs about the performance of the choice alternatives under consideration. The ability to retrieve this information may strongly affect which alternative is eventually chosen.[21] However, consumers lacking such stored knowledge will need to rely on external information in forming beliefs about an alternative's performance.

The Use of Cutoffs

In judging how well an alternative performs, consumers may often use cutoffs.[22] A **cutoff** is simply a restriction or requirement for acceptable attribute values. One example is price. Consumers are likely to have a fairly defined range of prices they are willing to pay. A price that falls outside of this range or zone will be viewed as unacceptable.[23]

Cutoffs are used for many evaluative criteria other than price. A consumer may refuse to consider generic soft drink brands. Another may reject any soft drink exceeding a certain number of calories. Still another may insist that the drink contain some amount of real fruit juices.

The cutoffs used by consumers during decision making will obviously have a strong influence on the final choice. Consequently, it is important for marketers to understand the presence and nature of cutoffs. A brand that fails to meet a cutoff may be rejected regardless of how well it performs on other dimensions.

The Use of Signals

Judgments about choice alternatives can depend on the presence of certain cues or signals. Earlier in the chapter, we noted that consumers may often rely on brand name in judging the quality of over-the-counter drugs. Warranties might also be interpreted as signals of product quality.[24] In evaluating different types of carpeting, consumers may feel limited in their ability to assess the relative quality of different carpets. Consequently, they may use the warranty as a quality cue. When this occurs, companies offering a strong warranty (Figure 6.9) may gain a competitive advantage. In some cases, however, a company may sell itself short by failing to offer a stronger warranty. Read Consumer in Focus 6.3 to learn about one such situation.

Another type of cue consumers might use for judging product quality is price. Consider the lesson learned by one cosmetics manufacturer that introduced a new line of very low-priced cosmetics. Sales were virtually nonexistent, and the line was eventually withdrawn from the market. However, when essentially the same line was later reintroduced at a higher price, sales took off. Why? Because consumers used price as a signal of quality and were unwilling to run the risk of wearing low-quality cosmetics.

Figure 6.9   A Strong Warranty Can Increase Perceived Product Quality

Consumer in Focus   **6.3**

Is Whirlpool Missing the Signal?

Which brand of washing machines is best? To answer this question, *Consumer Reports* rated 16 brands along numerous dimensions: load capacity, water and energy efficiency, how well the machine could handle unbalanced loads, and so on. As reported in the February 1991 issue, products of the Whirlpool Corp. received the best ratings. In addition to selling washers that carry the Whirlpool name, the company also makes the washers that sell under the Sears' Kenmore and KitchenAid brand names. All three brands were at the top of the ratings.

But what if consumers are unaware of the *Consumer Reports* ratings? How might they go about judging quality? As we noted in the chapter, a product's warranty can serve as a signal of quality. And this is where Whirlpool may be missing the signal. Consider the following warranty information based on a fact sheet developed by the manufacturer of the Amana brand which rested upon its washers being displayed by the retailer.

	Transmission		Nontransmission		Cabinet Rust
	Labor	Parts	Labor	Parts	
Amana	5 Years	10 Years	1 Year	2 Years	5 Years
Frigidaire	1 Year	5 Years	1 Year	1 Year	1 Year
GE/Hotpoint	1 Year	5 Years	1 Year	1 Year	1 Year
Kenmore	1 Year	5 Years	1 Year	1 Year	1 Year
Maytag	1 Year	10 Years	1 Year	2 Years	5 Years
Whirlpool	1 Year	5 Years	1 Year	1 Year	1 Year

Based on this information, consumers may come to very different conclusions about which brand is best than implied by the *Consumer Reports* ratings. One can only wonder about how many sales Whirlpool may be losing because of the weak signal conveyed by its warranty.

Source: "Washing Machines," Consumer Reports (February 1991), 112–117.

The use of price as a signal of quality has been substantiated repeatedly.[25] Even so, price may have little influence on perceived quality in some situations and for some consumers. For instance, price may have little signaling power when consumers are able to easily judge product quality or rely on other signals (for example, brand name, image of the store carrying the product) to infer quality.

Recognize that although higher-priced offerings benefit when consumers perceive a price–quality relationship, this perception is not desirable from the perspective of those offering lower-priced products. The challenge for low-priced competitors, then, is to undermine consumers' use of price as an indicator of quality. In the camera film market, the Konica Imaging USA Co. tried to steal share from the higher-priced market leader, the Eastman Kodak Co., through an ad campaign themed "Why pay the price if you can't see the difference?" In one commercial, a man on a stretch rack is stretched more and more as he repeatedly fails to guess correctly what pictures are taken with what film.[26]

Selecting a Decision Rule

The final element of the pre-purchase alternative evaluation process is the decision rule. **Decision rules** represent the strategies consumers use to make a selection from the choice alternatives.[27] Decision rules can range from very simplistic procedures that require little time and effort to very elaborate ones that involve considerably more time and processing effort on the part of the consumer.

When choice is habituated, the decision rule is very simple: Buy the same brand as last time. Even when choice is not habituated, consumers may use simplistic decision rules such as "buy the cheapest" or "buy the brand my spouse likes." This is because consumers continually make trade-offs between the quality of their choice (that is, buying the "best" brand) and the amount of time and effort necessary to reach a decision. In many cases, consumers will follow decision rules that yield a satisfactory (as opposed to optimal) choice while minimizing their time and effort. These simplistic decision rules are more likely to occur for repetitive product choices that are relatively low in importance or involvement.[28]

At other times, however, consumers are more highly motivated during decision making. Consequently, they will use more elaborate or complex decision rules that require greater processing effort. A fundamental distinction between these more complex rules is whether they involve a compensatory versus a noncompensatory procedure.

Noncompensatory Decision Rules

Noncompensatory decision rules are characterized by the fact that a product's weakness on one attribute *cannot* be offset by its strong performance on another attribute. Consider snack foods. Manufacturers have the capability of meeting consumers' desires for healthier snacks by cutting the amount of oil and salt in the products. But eliminate too much of these ingredients and the snacks taste lousy. Although the reformulated product will score high marks on nutritional considerations, this strength cannot overcome the weakness in the product's taste. According to Dwight Riskey, a psychologist and vice president of market research at Frito-Lay, "Consumers won't sacrifice taste for health in snacks."[29]

The simplistic decision rules described earlier further illustrate the potential for consumer decision making to follow a noncompensatory strategy. For instance, a brand that is more expensive than other brands would not be chosen no matter how well it performs on other evaluative criteria when the decision rule is "buy the cheapest." That is, the brand's weakness in price is not compensated by its favorable performance in other attributes. Three types of noncompensatory rules are lexicographic, elimination by aspects, and conjunctive.[30]

Lexicographic

Under this decision strategy, brands are compared initially on the most important attribute. If one of the brands is perceived as superior based on that attribute, it is selected. If two or more brands are perceived as equally good, they are then compared on the second most important attribute. This process continues until the tie is broken.

To illustrate this rule, consider the information presented in Table 6.2. This table contains attribute-performance ratings (from excellent to poor) for four different food item brands and attribute-importance rankings (in which "1" is the most important). Which brand would be chosen under the lexicographic rule?

The answer is brand A. A comparison on the most important attribute, taste, produces a tie between brands A, B, and D. This tie is broken on the next most important attribute, price, because brand A has the highest rating of the three brands. Notice, however, what would happen if the attribute-importance rankings were slightly different. For instance, if price were more important, brand C would then be chosen.

The concepts of processing by brand (PBB) and processing by attribute (PBA), originally introduced in the discussion of search sequence in Chapter 5, are also relevant here. Recall that in PBB, information is acquired for one brand at a time. The person who learns all about one brand before learning about the next is processing by brand. PBA involves gathering of information about a particular attribute of the various brands. The person comparing brands on taste, then on price, and so forth, is processing by attribute.

Decision rules differ in whether they require PBB or PBA. The lexicographic procedure involves PBA because brands are compared on one attribute at a time.

Table 6.2	Hypothetical Ratings for Illustrating Decision Rules				
		Brand Performance Ratings			
Attribute	Importance Ranking	Brand A	Brand B	Brand C	Brand D
Taste	1	Excellent	Excellent	Very Good	Excellent
Price	2	Very Good	Good	Excellent	Fair
Nutrition	3	Good	Good	Poor	Excellent
Convenience	4	Fair	Good	Good	Excellent

Elimination by Aspects

This rule closely resembles the lexicographic procedure. As before, brands are first evaluated on the most important attribute. Now, however, the consumer imposes cutoffs. The consumer may, for example, use cutoffs such as "must be under $2" or "must be nutritious."

If only one brand meets the cutoff on the most important attribute, it is chosen. If several brands meet the cutoff, then the next most important attribute is selected and the process continues until the tie is broken. If none of the brands are acceptable, the consumer must revise the cutoffs, use a different decision rule, or postpone choice. Once again, processing by attribute is required.

Returning to Table 6.2, choice based on elimination by aspects would depend on the particular cutoff values imposed by the decision maker. Suppose the minimum acceptable values for taste and price were "excellent" and "very good," respectively. Brand A would again be chosen. But if the cutoff for taste was lowered to "very good" and the cutoff for price was raised to "excellent," then brand C would be selected.

Conjunctive

Cutoffs also play a prominent part in the conjunctive decision rule.[31] Cutoffs are established for each salient attribute. Each brand is compared, one at a time, against this set of cutoffs. Thus, processing by brand is required. If the brand meets the cutoffs for *all* the attributes, it is chosen. Failure to meet the cutoff for *any* attribute leads to rejection. As before, if none of the brands meet the cutoff requirements, a change in either the cutoffs or the decision rule must occur. Otherwise, choice must be delayed.

To illustrate the conjunctive choice rule, assume that the consumer insists that the brand receive a rating of at least "good" on each attribute. In Table 6.2, brand A is rejected because of its inadequate rating (that is, does not meet the cutoff requirement of "good") on convenience, whereas brand C is inadequate on nutrition. Brand D is eliminated by the unacceptable price rating. Only brand B meets all the cutoff requirements and therefore would be evaluated as an acceptable choice.

Compensatory Decision Rules

Did you notice the plight of poor brand D in Table 6.2? Despite its excellent ratings in three of the four salient attributes (including the most important attribute), brand D never emerged as the top brand. Why? Because of its poor price performance. Indeed, none of the noncompensatory strategies permitted the brand's poor rating on price to be offset by its otherwise excellent performance.

This is not the case for compensatory decision rules. Under a compensatory strategy, a perceived weakness of one attribute may be offset or compensated for by the perceived strength of another attribute. Two types of compensatory rules are the simple additive and weighted additive.

Simple Additive

Under this rule, the consumer simply counts or adds the number of times each alternative is judged favorably in terms of the set of salient evaluative criteria. The alternative having the largest number of positive attributes is chosen. The use of a simple additive rule is most likely when consumers' processing motivation or ability is limited.[32]

Weighted Additive

A more complex form of the compensatory rule is the weighted additive. The consumer now engages in more refined judgments about the alternative's performance than simply whether it is favorable or unfavorable. The relative salience of relevant evaluative criteria is also incorporated into the decision rule. In essence, a weighted additive rule is equivalent to the multiattribute attitude models that will be described in Chapter 11.

Phased Decision Strategies

Phased decision strategies involve the sequential use of at least two different decision rules as a means of coping with many choice alternatives.[33] Phased strategies typically consist of a two-stage process. In the initial stage, one type of rule is used as a screening device to help narrow down the choice set to a more manageable number. A second decision rule is then applied to the remaining alternatives to make the final choice. For example, a consumer confronted with many brands might first eliminate those above a certain price from contention. The remaining brands would then be evaluated across several salient attributes.

Constructive Decision Rules

Many of the choice situations consumers encounter can be handled by simply retrieving the appropriate decision rule from memory. Stored rules are more likely to exist in memory as the consumer accumulates experience in making such choices. However, when consumers lack such experience, they may find it necessary to construct their decision rules at the time of choice.[34] That is, consumers build a constructive decision rule using "fragments" of rules that are available in memory that can accommodate the choice situation.

Affect Referral

A special type of decision rule is known as affect referral.[35] This rule assumes that the consumer has previously formed attitudes or overall evaluations toward each choice alternative. Rather than judging alternatives on various evaluative criteria, the consumer simply retrieves these attitudes from memory. The alternative having the most favorable attitude is then chosen. In essence, attitude serves as the single evaluative criterion used in decision making.

Marketing Implications

At this point, it is useful to stop and consider what all this means for the practitioner. What value does knowledge about the particular decision rule consumers use during pre-purchase alternative evaluation have for the development of marketing strategies?

Fundamentally speaking, marketers need to understand decision rules because these rules have an impact on consumer choice. An understanding of the decision rule (or rules) used by a company's customers, which is the rule that leads to the choice of the company's product, that may suggest actions that maintain or facilitate customers' use of this rule. For instance, if customers use a lexicographic rule with product quality being the most important attribute, the company may find it profitable to implement an advertising campaign stressing the importance of product quality and the quality of the company's product. This understanding may also indicate actions that should be avoided because of their potential to change the customer's decision rule and possibly her or his choice. For example, when the customer's decision rule is simply "buy the same brand as last time," the marketer should avoid conditions that may trigger a change in the decision rule, such as a noticeable decline in product quality, significant price increases, or an out-of-stock situation.

The manner in which attribute information is organized and presented may also be important.[36] Presenting information about various brands' performance on one attribute at a time, although appropriate for decision rules that require processing by attribute, would discourage the use of rules requiring consumers to process by brand. Conversely, a brand-based presentation format would favor rules that involve processing by brand.

Even knowledge that consumers do not have a well-defined decision strategy (meaning that a constructive method is used) can be useful. Consumers who are uncertain about how they should make their decision may be receptive to those, such as salespeople, offering some guidance. Informative advertisements and brochures may also be well received by these consumers.

Understanding consumers' decision rules is also important in the development of attitude-change strategies.[37] This can be demonstrated by returning to Table 6.2 (page 223). Suppose that brand C improved its taste perception from "very good" to "excellent." This change makes considerable sense if consumers use a lexicographic process in making their evaluation, because it would lead to brand C being chosen. Suppose, however, that consumers use a conjunctive rule with cutoffs of "good." Improving the product's taste would be of little value because its nutritional rating of "poor" is unacceptable. Instead, it would be critical to enhance the brand's nutritional performance.

Recognize that changing consumers' decision rules provides marketers with another mechanism for influencing consumer choice. In some cases, this might involve changing the relative importance of salient evaluative criteria. For instance, assuming a lexicographic rule, the maker of brand C in Table 6.2 might consider altering the relative importance consumers attach to taste and price. A lexicographic rule with price being the most important attribute would lead to the selection of brand C, whereas this type of rule with taste being most important results in brand A being chosen.

Changing the cutoffs is another mechanism for altering the decision rule. As illustrated by the example considered in the prior discussion of the elimination by aspects decision rule, changes in the minimum acceptable values for taste and price resulted in the selection of different brands from Table 6.2.

It may sometimes be desirable to encourage a change in the type of decision rule. In Table 6.2, for instance, brand B would want consumers using a lexicographic decision rule to switch to a conjunctive decision rule with a cutoff value of "good" for each attribute. Unfortunately, little is known about the likelihood of getting consumers to switch their decision strategies.

Summary

Pre-purchase alternative evaluation represents the decision-making stage in which consumers evaluate alternatives to make a choice. Other than for habitual decision making, during this stage, consumers typically (an exception being when decision making is habitual in nature) must (1) determine the evaluative criteria to use for judging alternatives, (2) decide which alternatives to consider, (3) assess the performance of considered alternatives, and (4) select and apply a decision rule to make the final choice.

Consumers may use several different evaluative criteria, including price, brand name, and country of origin, in making their decision. These criteria will usually vary in their relative importance or salience. Price may be a dominant dimension in some decisions and yet rather unimportant in others. The salience of evaluative criteria depends on a host of situational, product, and individual factors.

Consumers must determine the set of alternatives from which a choice will be made (that is, the consideration set). Sometimes the consideration set will depend on the consumer's ability to recall from memory viable alternatives. On other occasions, an alternative will be considered if it is recognized at the point of purchase. When consumers lack prior knowledge about choice alternatives, they must then turn to the environment for assistance in forming their consideration set.

Consumers may often rely on their existing knowledge for judging how well alternatives perform along the salient evaluative criteria. Otherwise, external search will be required to form these judgments. The cutoffs or ranges of acceptable values that consumers impose for evaluative criteria will strongly determine whether a given alternative is viewed as acceptable. Also, consumers may use certain signals or cues in forming their judgments. Such is the case when price is used to infer product quality.

Finally, the strategies or procedures used for making the final choice are called decision rules. These rules may be stored in memory and retrieved when needed. Alternatively, they may be constructed to fit situational contingencies.

Decision rules vary considerably in their complexity. They may be very simple (for example, buy what I bought last time). They can also be quite complex, as suggested by the weighted additive decision rule. Another important distinction is between compensatory and noncompensatory decision rules. Noncompensatory rules, such as lexicographic, elimination by aspects, and conjunctive, do not permit product strengths to offset product weaknesses. In contrast, compensatory rules do allow product weaknesses to be compensated by product strengths.

Review and Discussion Questions

1. What are evaluative criteria? What criteria did you use when you purchased your last pair of shoes? How did these differ, if at all, from those used by others in your family?

2. In the chapter, we indicate that offering incentives is one way for a product to gain consideration during consumer decision making. How else might a product try to enter the consideration set?

3. A restaurant is trying to decide on the appropriate method for assessing consumers' consideration set in deciding where to eat out. One person has argued for a recall method in which consumers are asked to remember the names of restaurants without any memory cues. Another person recommends a recognition method in which consumers are given a list of local restaurants and asked to circle the appropriate names. Which method would you recommend? Would your answer change if consumers normally consulted the yellow pages in making the decision?

4. Consider the company that currently offers a product warranty quite similar to the warranties offered by competitors but is considering the merits of increasing the warranty coverage to make it superior to the competition. A market study was therefore undertaken to examine consumer response to an improved warranty. College students were shown the product accompanied by either the original warranty or the improved warranty. The results indicated that students did, in fact, perceive the improved warranty as much stronger and that the product quality was rated higher when the product was paired with the improved warranty. Although the company viewed these results as very encouraging, concerns were raised about the appropriateness of using college students, most of whom have yet to make a purchase in the product category at this point in their life. Consequently, the study was replicated using older consumers who had made at least two purchase decisions in the product category. As before, the improved warranty was seen as providing much better coverage. However, judgments of product quality were not affected by the warranty. How can you explain this difference between the two studies' findings about the warranty's influences on perceived product quality? Also, what recommendations would you make to the company about whether it should offer the improved warranty?

5. Would you expect a price–quality relationship for each of the following product classes: hand soap, toilet paper, panty hose, men's shirts, china and glassware, and gasoline? Why?

6. Identify which decision rule would lead to the selection of each of the brands in the following table.

7. Why is it important to understand the decision rules consumers use during pre-purchase alternative evaluation?

Attribute	Importance Ranking	Performance Ratings		
		Brand A	Brand B	Brand C
Price	1	Excellent	Very Good	Very Good
Quality	2	Poor	Very Good	Good
Convenience	3	Poor	Average	Good

Endnotes

1. Andre Gabor and C. W. J. Granger, "Price Sensitivity of the Consumer," *Journal of Advertising Research* 4 (December 1964), 40–44; Joel Huber, Morris B. Holbrook, and Barbara Kahn, "Effects of Competitive Context and of Additional Information on Price Sensitivity," *Journal of Marketing Research* 23 (August 1986), 250–260.

2. Peter R. Dickson and Alan G. Sawyer, "The Price Knowledge and Search of Supermarket Shoppers," *Journal of Marketing* 54 (July 1990), 42–53.

3. Huber, Holbrook, and Kahn, "Effects of Competitive Context and of Additional Information on Price Sensitivity"; Kent B. Monroe, "Buyers' Subjective Perceptions of Price," *Journal of Marketing Research* 10 (February 1973), 70–80.

4. David M. Gardner, "Is There a Generalized Price–Quality Relationship?" *Journal of Marketing Research* 8 (May 1971), 241–243.

5. J. F. Engel, D. A. Knapp, and D. E. Knapp, "Sources of Influence in the Acceptance of New Products for Self-Medication: Preliminary Findings," in R. M. Haas, ed., *Science, Technology and Marketing* (Chicago: American Marketing Association, 1966), 776–782.

6. William B. Dodds, Kent B. Monroe, and Dhruv Grewal, "Effects of Price, Brand, and Store Information on Buyers' Product Evaluations," *Journal of Marketing Research* 28 (August 1991), 307–319; Durairaj Maheswaran, Diane M. Mackie, and Shelly Chaiken, "Brand Name as a Heuristic Cue: The Effects of Task Importance and Expectancy Confirmation on Consumer Judgments," *Journal of Consumer Psychology* 1 (1992), 317–336; Akshay R. Rao and Kent B. Monroe, "The Effect of

Price, Brand Name, and Store Name on Buyers' Perceptions of Product Quality: An Integrative Review," *Journal of Marketing Research* 26 (August 1989), 351–357.

7. Engel, Knapp, and Knapp, "Sources of Influence."

8. For research on how this attribute can affect product evaluations, see Johnny K. Johansson, Susan P. Douglas, and Ikujiro Nonaka, "Assessing the Impact of Country of Origin on Product Evaluations: A New Methodological Perspective," *Journal of Marketing Research* 22 (November 1985), 388–396; Sung-Tai Hong and Robert S. Wyer, Jr., "Effects of Country-of-Origin and Product-Attribute Information on Product Evaluation: An Information Processing Perspective," *Journal of Consumer Research* 16 (September 1989), 175–187; Sung-Tai Hong and Robert S. Wyer, Jr., "Determinants of Product Evaluation: Effects of the Time Interval between Knowledge of a Product's Country of Origin and Information about Its Specific Attributes," *Journal of Consumer Research* 17 (December 1990), 277–288.

9. Mark I. Alpert, "Identification of Determinant Attributes: A Comparison of Methods," *Journal of Marketing Research* 8 (May 1971), 184–191.

10. Peter R. Dickson, "Person-Situation: Segmentation's Missing Link," *Journal of Marketing* 6 (Fall 1982), 56–64; Kenneth E. Miller and James L. Ginter, "An Investigation of Situational Variation in Brand Choice Behavior and Attitude," *Journal of Marketing Research* 16 (February 1979), 111–123.

11. James R. Bettman and Mita Sujan, "Effects of Framing on Evaluation of Comparable and Noncomparable Alternatives by Expert and Novice Consumers," *Journal of Consumer Research* 14 (September 1987), 141–154; Kim P. Corfman, "Comparability and Comparison Levels Used in Choices among Consumer Products," *Journal of Marketing Research* 28 (August 1991), 368–374; Michael D. Johnson, "Consumer Choice Strategies for Comparing Noncomparable Alternatives," *Journal of Consumer Research* 11 (December 1984), 741–753; Michael D. Johnson, "Comparability and Hierarchical Processing in Multialternative Choice," *Journal of Consumer Research* 15 (December 1988), 303–314; Michael D. Johnson, "The Differential Processing of Product Category and Noncomparable Choice Alternatives," *Journal of Consumer Research* 16 (December 1989), 300–309; C. Whan Park and Daniel C. Smith, "Product-Level Choice: A Top-Down or Bottom-Up Process?" *Journal of Consumer Research* 16 (December 1989), 289–299.

12. Michael L. Rothschild, "Advertising Strategies for High and Low Involvement Situations," in John C. Maloney and Bernard Silverman, eds., *Attitude Research Plays for High Stakes* (Chicago: American Marketing Association, 1979), 74–93; Michael L. Rothschild and Michael J. Houston, "The Consumer Involvement Matrix: Some Preliminary Findings," in Barnett A. Greenberg and Danny N. Bellenger, eds., *Contemporary Marketing Thoughts* (Chicago: American Marketing Association, 1977), 95–98.

13. Dennis H. Gensch and Rajshekhar G. Javalgi, "The Influence of Involvement on Disaggregate Attribute Choice Models," *Journal of Consumer Research* 14 (June 1987), 71–82.

14. Bettman and Sujan, "Effects of Framing on Evaluation of Comparable and Noncomparable Alternatives by Expert and Novice Consumers"; Peter Wright and

Peter D. Rip, "Product Class Advertising Effects in First-Time Buyers' Decision Strategies," *Journal of Consumer Research* 7 (September 1980), 176–188.

15. For research on consideration sets, see Joseph W. Alba and Amitava Chattopadhyay, "Effects of Context and Part-Category Cues on Recall of Competing Brands," *Journal of Marketing Research* 22 (August 1985), 340–349; Juanita J. Brown and Albert R. Wildt, "Consideration Set Measurement," *Journal of The Academy of Marketing Science* 20 (Summer 1992), 235–243; John R. Hauser and Birger Wernfelt, "An Evaluation Cost Model of Consideration Sets," *Journal of Consumer Research* 16 (March 1990), 393–408; Frank R. Kardes, Gurumurthy Kalyanaram, Murali Chandrashekaran, and Ronald J. Dornoff, "Brand Retrieval, Consideration Set Composition, Consumer Choice, and the Pioneering Advantage," *Journal of Consumer Research* 20 (June 1993), 62–75; Prakash Nedungadi, "Recall and Consumer Consideration Sets: Influencing Choice Without Altering Brand Evaluations," *Journal of Consumer Research* 17 (December 1990), 263–276; John H. Roberts and James M. Lattin, "Development and Testing of a Model of Consideration Set Composition," *Journal of Marketing Research* 28 (November 1991), 429–440.

16. Alba and Chattopadhay, "Effects of Context and Part-Category Cues on Recall of Competing Brands."

17. Joseph W. Alba and J. Wesley Hutchinson, "Dimensions of Consumer Expertise," *Journal of Consumer Research* 13 (March 1987), 411–454.

18. For research on recall inhibition, see Alba and Chattopadhyay, "Effects of Context and Part-Category Cues on Recall of Competing Brands"; Joseph W. Alba and Amitava Chattopadhay, "Salience Effects in Brand Recall," *Journal of Marketing Research* 23 (November 1986), 363–369. Also see Paul W. Miniard, H. Rao Unnava, and Sunil Bhatla, "Investigating the Recall Inhibition Effect: A Test of Practical Considerations," *Marketing Letters* 2 (January 1991), 27–34.

19. Joel Huber, John W. Payne, and Christopher Puto, "Adding Asymmetrically Dominated Alternatives: Violations of Regularity and the Similarity Hypothesis," *Journal of Consumer Research* 9 (June 1982), 90–98; Joel Huber and Christopher Puto, "Market Boundaries and Product Choice: Illustrating Attraction and Substitution Effects," *Journal of Consumer Research* 10 (June 1983), 31–44; Barbara Kahn, William L. Moore, and Rashi Glazer, "Experiments in Constrained Choice," *Journal of Consumer Research* 14 (June 1987), 96–113; Sanjay Mishra, U. N. Umesh, Donald E. Stem, Jr., "Antecedents of the Attraction Effect: An Information-Processing Approach," *Journal of Marketing Research* 30 (August 1993), 331–349; Yigang Pan and Donald R. Lehmann, "The Influence of New Brand Entry on Subjective Brand Judgments," *Journal of Consumer Research* 20 (June 1993), 76–86; Srinivasan Ratneshwar, Allan D. Shocker, and David W. Stewart, "Toward Understanding the Attraction Effect: The Implications of Product Stimulus Meaningfulness and Familiarity," *Journal of Consumer Research* 13 (March 1987), 520–533; Itamar Simonson, "Choice Based on Reasons: The Case of Attraction and Compromise Effects," *Journal of Consumer Research* 16 (September 1989), 158–174.

20. For additional research in this domain, see Noel Capon and Deanna Kuhn, "Can Consumers Calculate Best Buys?" *Journal of Consumer Research* 8 (March 1982), 449–453; Catherine A. Cole and Gary J. Gaeth, "Cognitive and Age-Related

Differences in the Ability to Use Nutritional Information in a Complex Environment," *Journal of Marketing Research* 27 (May 1990), 175–184.

21. Gabriel Biehal and Dipankar Chakravarti, "Information Accessibility as a Moderator of Consumer Choice," *Journal of Consumer Research* 10 (June 1983), 1–14; Gabriel Biehal and Dipankar Chakravarti, "Consumers' Use of Memory and External Information in Choice: Macro and Micro Perspectives," *Journal of Consumer Research* 12 (March 1986), 382–405; John G. Lynch, Jr., Howard Marmorstein, and Michael F. Weigold, "Choices from Sets Including Remembered Brands: Use of Recalled Attributes and Prior Overall Evaluations," *Journal of Consumer Research* 15 (September 1988), 169–184.

22. For research on cutoff usage, see Barton Weitz and Peter Wright, "Retrospective Self-Insight on Factors Considered in Product Evaluations," *Journal of Consumer Research* 6 (December 1979), 280–294; Peter L. Wright and Barton Weitz, "Time Horizon Effects on Product Evaluation Strategies," *Journal of Marketing Research* 14 (November 1977), 429–443.

23. Susan M. Petroshius and Kent B. Monroe, "Effects of Product-Line Pricing Characteristics on Product Evaluations," *Journal of Consumer Research* 13 (March 1987), 511–519.

24. William Boulding and Amna Kirmani, "A Consumer-Side Experimental Examination of Signaling Theory: Do Consumers Perceive Warranties as Signals of Quality?" *Journal of Consumer Research* 20 (June 1993), 111–123.

25. Dodds, Monroe, and Grewal, "Effects of Price, Brand, and Store Information on Buyers' Product Evaluations"; Gary M. Erickson and Johnny K. Johansson, "The Role of Price in Multi-Attribute Product Evaluations," *Journal of Consumer Research* 12 (September 1985), 195–199; Michael Etgar and Naresh K. Malhotra, "Determinants of Price Dependency: Personal and Perceptual Factors," *Journal of Consumer Research* 8 (September 1981), 217–222; Zarrel V. Lambert, "Product Perception: An Important Variable in Price Strategy," *Journal of Marketing* 34 (October 1970), 68–76; Irwin P. Levin and Richard D. Johnson, "Estimating Price–Quality Tradeoffs Using Comparative Judgments," *Journal of Consumer Research* 11 (June 1984), 593–600; Kent B. Monroe, "The Influence of Price Differences and Brand Familiarity on Brand Preferences," *Journal of Consumer Research* 3 (June 1976), 42–49; Petroshius and Monroe, "Effects of Product-Line Pricing Characteristics on Product Evaluations"; Rao and Monroe, "The Effect of Price, Brand Name, and Store Name on Buyers' Perceptions of Product Quality."

26. Riccardo A. Davis, "Konica Snaps at Kodak over Price," *Advertising Age* (September 20, 1993), 49.

27. For a detailed discussion of decision rules, see James R. Bettman, *An Information Processing Theory of Consumer Choice* (Reading, Mass.: Addison-Wesley, 1979), Chapter 7.

28. Wayne D. Hoyer, "An Examination of Consumer Decision Making for a Common Repeat Purchase Product," *Journal of Consumer Research* 11 (December 1984), 822–829. Also see Wayne D. Hoyer and Steven P. Brown, "Effects of Brand Awareness on Choice for a Common, Repeat-Purchase Product," *Journal of Consumer Research* 17 (September 1990), 141–148.

29. Robert Johnson, "In the Chips," *Wall Street Journal* (March 22, 1991), B1–B2.

30. For a discussion of other forms of noncompensatory rules, see Bettman, *An Information Processing Theory of Consumer Choice*, 181–182.

31. For a study of the conjunctive decision rule, see David Grether and Louis Wilde, "An Analysis of Conjunctive Choice: Theory and Experiments," *Journal of Consumer Research* 10 (March 1984), 373–385.

32. Joseph W. Alba and Howard Marmorstein, "The Effects of Frequency Knowledge on Consumer Decision Making," *Journal of Consumer Research* 14 (June 1987), 14–25.

33. Denis A. Lussier and Richard W. Olshavsky, "Task Complexity and Contingent Processing in Brand Choice," *Journal of Consumer Research* 6 (September 1979), 154–165.

34. Biehal and Chakravarti, "Consumers' Use of Memory and External Information in Choice"; James R. Bettman and Michael A. Zins, "Constructive Processes in Consumer Choice," *Journal of Consumer Research* 4 (September 1977), 75–85.

35. Peter Wright, "Consumer Choice Strategies: Simplifying vs. Optimizing," *Journal of Marketing Research* 12 (February 1975), 60–67. Also see Bettman, *An Information Processing Theory of Consumer Choice*; Amitava Chattopadhyay and Joseph W. Alba, "The Situational Importance of Recall and Inference in Consumer Decision Making," *Journal of Consumer Research* 15 (June 1988), 1–12.

36. For research relevant to this issue, see James R. Bettman and Michael A. Zins, "Information Format and Choice Task Effects in Decision Making," *Journal of Consumer Research* 6 (September 1979), 141–153.

37. Peter L. Wright, "Use of Consumer Judgment Models in Promotion Planning," *Journal of Marketing* 37 (October 1973), 27–33.

CHAPTER 7

Purchase

▲▲▲▲▲▲▲▲▲▲▲▲▲▲▲▲▲▲▲▲▲▲▲▲▲▲▲▲▲▲▲▲▲▲▲▲▲▲

Shopping from Your Living Room

Cathy Burke, a 55-year-old secretary in Kearney, New Jersey, is one satisfied customer. A few days ago, the mail carrier delivered a $50 pink pants suit and a $40 Kenneth Jay Lane *faux* gold-and-seed-pearl necklace that she purchased from home shopping channel QVC. She loves them. Burke has bought about 200 items from the network over the past 5 years.

Gabe Doppelt, 33, editor-in-chief of *Mademoiselle* magazine, says she has been "obsessed with television shopping for years." An avowed insomniac, she watches television all night. Among her purchases: everything from Ninja Turtle toothbrushes to throw pillows to wrap dresses. Does the editor of a hot fashion magazine actually wear dresses she bought on TV: "Hell, yeah," says Doppelt. "I wear them all the time."

No wonder many industry executives are saying that the business of retailing will never be the same. The ultimate vision: a sort of video mall where shoppers will browse through channels as through individual stores, ask for information and advice, and pay — all without leaving the comforts of home.

Source: Adapted from Laura Zinn, "Retailing Will Never Be the Same," Business Week (July 26, 1993), 54. Reproduced by special permission.

The world of purchasing behavior has changed dramatically. Shoppers are experiencing some real modifications in the way they make purchases. The numbers who are willing to "graze the malls" have dropped sharply.[1] In fact, a Harris poll showed that 47 percent of those interviewed are spending less time shopping outside the home than they did just a few years ago.[2]

Retailers are being forced by shoppers to rethink their business and to offer customers what they expect in the way of service, assortments, and sales assistance.[3] Gone are the days when the options largely consisted of the corner store and friendly downtown department emporium. The imminent onset of interactive electronic media will allow anyone literally to scan the world and order at their ease and convenience.

Purchase is the fourth major stage in our model of consumer decision processes (Figure 7.1). But as we see in this chapter, purchase requires a decision-making process of its own. You will soon discover that many creative marketers are making some of their greatest competitive gains by focusing on innovations that facilitate the purchase process. Remember the shopping and buying experiences of Cathy Burke and Gabe Doppelt. These provide just a taste of the revolutionary changes that are now taking place.

Purchase Decision-Making Process

Several issues must be contended with in the process of purchase: (1) whether to buy; (2) when to buy; (3) what to buy, (4) where to buy; and (5) how to pay.

First, not all purchase intentions are fulfilled, because the consumer always faces the option of aborting the process at this point. A host of factors could intervene, and here are some examples:

- *Changed motivations*—activated need is fulfilled in other ways or other needs become dominant.

- *Changed circumstances*—economic considerations or other factors make a purchase at this point unwise.

- *New information*—previous alternative evaluation is shown to be deficient.

- *Desired alternatives are no longer available*—unanticipated shortages.

The timing of a purchase is also a consideration. Some products, for example, are bought mostly on a seasonal basis. Air conditioners in northern climates, Christmas gifts, and Caribbean cruises are examples. Others, such as detergents and frozen foods, are often purchased only when stock is depleted.

Next, buying intentions often are left open-ended, thus necessitating further information search on what alternative to select. This is a major motivation for shopping behavior. As we discover in the next section of the chapter, there is a continuum ranging from fully planned purchases to unplanned purchases. Obviously, the dynamics will be sharply different.

As we have seen, the consumer also faces burgeoning options on where to buy. In-home shopping, for example, has seen remarkable growth in most of the developing countries of the world. Many retailing establishments have been forced into direct marketing to complement their normal activities. Hence, the

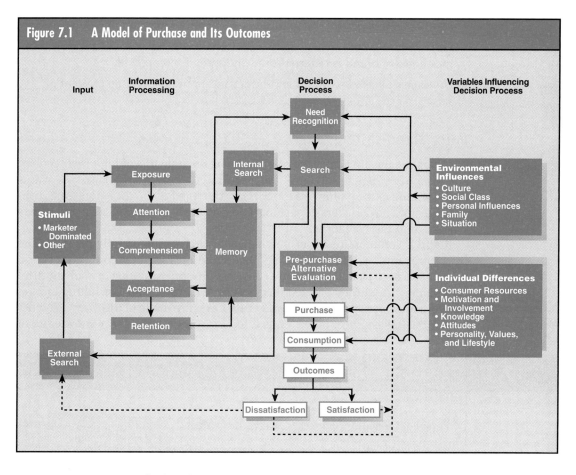

Figure 7.1 A Model of Purchase and Its Outcomes

growing importance of "data-based marketing" at both the manufacturer and retailer level.[4] Sears, Roebuck & Co. has the astonishing figure of 44 million household accounts in its customer data base.[5]

Finally, the consumer must decide how to pay. Other chapters document the relentless trend away from cash payment to the use of credit cards and other forms of delayed payment.

The focus of this chapter is on two of these issues: (1) what to buy, and (2) where to buy. The discussion continues in Chapter 21, which explores how consumer research is used in retailing strategy.

Choosing the Right Alternative

When asked to do so after pre-purchase alternative evaluation, it often is possible for consumers to articulate their purchase intentions, and these fall into three categories which appear on the following page:

- *Fully planned purchase*—both product and brand are chosen in advance.

- *Partially planned purchase*—there is an intention to buy a given product, but the choice of brand is deferred until shopping is completed.

- *Unplanned purchase*—both the product and brand are chosen at point of sale.

Fully Planned Purchase

On occasion, this first category of intention is the outcome of high involvement and extended problem solving—the buyer knows exactly what he or she wants and is willing to shop until it is found. Consumer in Focus 7.1 demonstrates conclusively that most buyers of personal computers are knowledgeable purchasers who fall into this category.

It also is common for lower involvement purchases to be fully planned. The buyer prepares a shopping list beforehand and plans to buy both product and brand. The store visit, then, mostly consists of routine scanning of shelves. A recent nationwide survey of 4,200 shoppers by Willard Bishop Consulting Ltd. revealed that 61 percent of supermarket purchases are made in this way.[6] Whether or not this takes place, however, is affected by two factors: (1) knowledge of

---

| **7.1** | **Consumer in Focus** |

Personal Computer Shoppers "Know Their Stuff"

Whether they're shopping or just browsing, most consumers of PC products know what they want before they even walk in the door, according to a new study conducted by Directions for Decisions, Inc. More than 85 percent of those surveyed said they considered themselves knowledgeable about PCs, and at least 60 percent said they're often asked for buying advice.

These folks were also experienced at buying PCs. More than three-quarters said they had purchased PCs before, and 64 percent were involved in purchasing microcomputers, peripherals, or software for their companies.

Armed with that kind of knowledge, most shoppers have a clear idea of what PC products they want before they walk into the store, and they aren't likely to change their minds. For example, 60 percent of the buyers interviewed knew the specific brand of PC they wanted, and at least 87 percent bought that brand. The study also revealed that the shoppers weren't big on impulse buying, with only 12 percent of them making an unplanned purchase.

More evidence that shoppers have their minds made up was shown in the low percentage who said they turned to salespeople for help. Only a quarter of the respondents said they usually use salespeople as a source of information. Most of the shoppers said they usually get the scoop from computer publications (60 percent) or friends and relatives (45 percent).

Source: Cyndee Miller, "Study Says PC Shoppers Are Knowledgeable and Experienced," Marketing News (September 27, 1993), 5.

store layout and design, and (2) time pressures that restrict browsing and in-store decision making.[7]

Partially Planned Purchase

It also is correct to view category 2 (product only) as a planned purchase even though choice of brand is made at point of sale. Shopping now can become an important form of information search, especially when involvement is high.[8] When involvement is low, however, the decision rule often is "buy one of the brands I already consider to be acceptable." The final decision now may hinge on promotional influences such as price reductions or special display and packaging.[9]

Unplanned Purchase

Now we face a dilemma. Can we consider a purchase to be unplanned when a conscious intention was not articulated before the act of buying? Or is this strictly a matter of "impulse" or whim? This issue was first addressed empirically in 1967 by David T. Kollat, a member of the original author team of this book.[10] Because some estimate that up to 50 percent of purchases are made in this way,[11] it is important to understand the underlying dynamics.

It is important to note Kollat's important distinction, first of all, that a purchase can be planned in one sense even though a definite intention is not expressed verbally or in writing on a shopping list.[12] This is because shoppers often make intentional use of product display in mass merchandising outlets as a surrogate shopping list. In other words, display provides a reminder of a need, and a purchase is triggered. Active processing of in-store information also can trigger new needs.[13]

There is growing evidence, however, that a true impulse action is something quite different, characterized by a unique set of influences. Consider Rook's clarification:

> Impulse buying occurs when a consumer experiences a sudden, often powerful and persistent urge to buy something immediately. The impulse to buy is hedonically complex and may stimulate emotional conflict. Also, impulse buying is prone to occur with diminished regard to its consequences.[14]

When defined in this way, some impulse purchasing is not based on consumer problem solving and is best viewed from an hedonic or experiential perspective.[15] According to Rook's research, impulse buying can have one or more of these characteristics:

1. *Spontaneity.* It is unexpected and motivates the consumer to buy now, often in response to direct point-of-sale visual stimulation.

2. *Power, compulsion, and intensity.* There can be motivation to put all else aside and act immediately.

3. *Excitement and stimulation.* These sudden urges to buy are often accompanied by emotions characterized as "exciting," "thrilling," or "wild."

4. *Disregard for consequences.* The urge to buy can be so irresistible that potentially negative consequences are ignored.[16]

Impact of Situational Influence

Situational influence can have a strong influence on fulfillment of purchase intentions. Although we discuss this subject in more detail in Chapter 22, it is necessary at this point to acknowledge the marketing implications.

Many situational factors, such as weather and temporary unemployment, are beyond the influence of the marketer or retailer, but this is not always the case by any means. Marketers have direct control over display, product promotion and exposure, price reductions, store atmospherics, and out-of-stock conditions, to mention only a few. The most important point here is to be aware of the manner in which these situational considerations can affect choice and to avoid such unfortunate situations as out-of-stock and inadequate display.[17]

Choosing the Source of Purchase

At one point in time, a large percentage of shopping and buying was done at home through use of the itinerant peddler. As convenient and inexpensive transportation methods became commonplace, however, the retail store gained ascendancy. The pendulum has swung once again in recent years to the point at which both retailing and in-home buying are vigorous competitors. An interesting marketing challenge is presented.

Retail Shopping and Purchasing

For at least the past century, shopping in retail stores has been a great American pastime. Although in-home shopping is making unquestioned inroads and exact figures are impossible to come by,[18] our best estimate is that about 90 percent of all consumer purchases in terms of total value still are made through visits to a retail outlet or catalog, showroom, or vending machine.

As recently as 1987, about 70 percent of Americans visited a large shopping mall in a given week. Furthermore, about a third of these were men.[19] Why do people shop? In a landmark study published in 1972, Tauber showed that consumers engage in this activity for both personal and social motives described in Table 7.1. One obvious primary motivation is information acquisition.[20] Until recently, there really has been no other alternative for those who want to discover and evaluate a full range of options.

But the motivations for shopping are more diverse. Indeed, shopping has almost become a way of life in and of itself for some. Here are just some of the

Table 7.1 Why Do People Shop?

Personal Motives

Role Playing
   Many activities are learned behaviors, traditionally expected or accepted as part of a certain position or role in society — mother, housewife, husband, or student.

Diversion
   Shopping can offer an opportunity for diversion from the routine of daily life and thus represents a form of recreation.

Self-Gratification
   Different emotional states or moods may be relevant for explaining why (and when) someone goes shopping. Some people report that often they alleviate depression by simply spending money on themselves. In this case, the shopping trip is motivated not by the expected utility of consuming, but by the utility of the buying *process* itself.

Learning about New Trends
   Products are intimately entwined in one's daily activities and often serve as symbols reflecting attitudes and lifestyles. An individual learns about trends and movements and the symbols that support them when the individual visits a store.

Physical Activity
   Shopping can provide people with a considerable amount of exercise at a leisurely pace, appealing to people living in an urban environment. Some shoppers apparently welcome the chance to walk in centers and malls.

Sensory Stimulation
   Retail institutions provide many potential sensory benefits for shoppers. Customers browse through a store looking at the merchandise and at each other; they enjoy handling the merchandise, the sounds of background music, the scents of perfume counters or prepared food outlets.

Social Motives

Social Experiences Outside the Home
   The marketplace has traditionally been a center of social activity and many parts of the United States and other countries still have market days, country fairs, and town squares that offer a time and a place for social interaction. Shopping trips may result in direct encounters with friends (e.g., neighborhood women at a supermarket) and other social contact.

Communications with Others Having a Similar Interest
   Stores that offer hobby-related goods or products and services such boating, collecting stamps, car customizing, and home decorating provide an opportunity to talk with others about their interests and with sales personnel who provide special information concerning the activity.

Peer Group Attraction
   The patronage of a store sometimes reflects a desire to be with one's peer group or a reference group to which one aspires to belong. For instance, record stores may provide a meeting place where members of a peer group may gather.

Status and Authority
   Many shopping experiences provide the opportunity for an individual to command attention and respect or to be waited on without having to pay for this service. A person can attain a feeling of status and power in this limited master – servant relationship.

Pleasure of Bargaining
   Many shoppers appear to enjoy the process of bargaining or haggling, believing that with bargaining, goods can be reduced to a more reasonable price. An individual prides himself in his ability to make wise purchases or to obtain bargains.

Source: Excerpted from Edward M. Tauber, "Why Do People Shop?" Journal of Marketing 36 (October 1972), 46–59. Reprinted from the Journal of Marketing published by the American Marketing Association.

reasons frequent shoppers give: alleviating loneliness, dispelling boredom, shopping as a sport (that is, beating the system), spoils of the hunt (shopper as "the great provider"), escape, fantasy fulfillment, and relieving depression.[21]

Things have changed sharply since the middle 1980s. Although the number of shopping malls increased 22 percent between 1986 and 1989, the number of shoppers going to malls each month rose only three percent.[22] The data in Table 7.2 reveal a drop in average shopping mall usage each month. The main reasons seem to be diminishing leisure time, increased stress levels in life, and economic fears.

There also is a group that, to put it mildly, is not enamored with shopping. McNeal and McKee[23] found a substantial segment, consisting of 20 percent of the population, who will avoid the marketplace whenever possible. Antishopping seems to be a part of a generally negative world view. Moreover, such consumers are largely oblivious and nonresponsive to marketing efforts designed to lure them into the retailing net.

Enhancing Relationship Marketing at the Retail Level

All retailers endeavor to create an environment at point-of-sale in which a mutually beneficial exchange takes place between buyer and seller. The contemporary term for this is **relationship marketing,** a concept discussed at length in Chapter 1. Fruitful exchange and creation of a loyal customer base is accomplished through the following means: (1) a focus on consumer value added; (2) personal selling; (3) sales promotion; and (4) data-based marketing.

Consumer Value Added

The editors of *Fortune* put the marketing challenge this way in a special 1993 issue on *The Tough New Customer:*

> The menu mentality is dead. Instead of choosing from what you have to offer, the new consumer tells you what he [*sic*] wants. You figure out how to supply it. Buyers have been spoiled and, like a bulldog that's tasted steak, will never again be happy with what used to satisfy them.[24]

Americans have become purposeful shoppers with high expectations for *total value received.* High-quality merchandise is assumed, but this is only one dimension of the value sought by today's customers. Furthermore, it is increasingly difficult to gain competitive advantage in that arena.

Total value is enhanced when quality is matched by a consistent policy of everyday low prices (EDLP), a concept pioneered by Wal-Mart Stores and Toys "R" Us. A study by Grey Advertising Agency revealed that only one-third of consumers compare prices today, compared with more than 50 percent in 1991.[25] What this means is that there is a reduction of "store hopping" in favor of rewarding those outlets that offer the best combination of quality and lowest prices on a consistent basis.

Table 7.2   Shoppers Are a Dwindling Species

Spare Hours

Compared to five years ago, do you personally feel you have less free time, more free time, or about the same free time you had back then?

More free time	21%
About the same	25%
Less free time	54%
Not sure	0%

At Leisure

Now which of these do you enjoy doing the most in your free time — watching TV, spending time with your family, going to movies, outdoor activities, shopping, or just relaxing at home?

Watching TV	7%
Spending time with your family	23%
Going to the movies	2%
Outdoor activities	23%
Shopping	6%
Just relaxing at home	36%
Not sure	3%

Time at the Store

Compared to five years ago, are you spending more time than you were then, less time, or about the same time shopping?

Spending more time	18%
About the same time	34%
Spending less time	47%
Not sure	1%

A Pleasure or a Pain?

Now which one of these, if you had to choose, best describes how you feel about shopping?

Shopping gives me a real sense of pleasure and excitement	16%
While shopping sometimes is a chore, mostly I like doing it	20%
Even though from time to time it's a pleasure, mostly it's something I do because I have to	48%
I get no pleasure from shopping	15%
Not sure	1%

Where the Shoppers Are

Compared to five years ago, are you shopping more, less, or about the same amount . . .

	More	Less	About same	Not sure
In department stores	20%	36%	43%	1%
In specialty stores, which concentrate on a particular line of products, such as electronics, clothing, and toys	23%	38%	38%	1%
From catalogs and mail-order sources	25%	34%	37%	4%

Who's the Best?

Now, if you had to say, which of these three—department stores, specialty stores, or catalogs—do you think offers the best of each of the following?

	Department Stores	Specialty Stores	Catalogs	Not sure
Overall service	52%	30%	15%	3%
Quality of merchandise	43%	38%	15%	4%
Variety of merchandise	64%	11%	23%	2%
Value for the money	56%	17%	25%	2%
Quality of sales people	47%	38%	10%	5%

Big-Store Mistakes

As you know, many well-known department stores have either gone out of business or are having financial trouble. Which one of these do you think is the main reason for this: They lost touch with their customers, their prices were too high, they opened too many stores, or they have poor management?

Lost touch with customers	14%
Prices too high	26%
Opened too many stores	23%
Poor management	33%
Not sure	4%

Happy Holidays?

During this holiday season, do you think you will be buying as much as you did a year ago, will you be buying more, or will you be buying less than you did last year?

Buying as much	29%
Buying more	17%
Buying less	54%
Not sure	0%

Survey of 1,255 adults conducted Nov. 9–13 for *Business Week* by Louis Harris & Associates, Inc. Results should be accurate to within three percentage points.

Source: Business Week/Harris Poll, "Shoppers Are a Dwindling Species," *Business Week* (November 26, 1990), 144. Used by special permission.

High quality accompanied by EDLP is by no means confined to the North American market. Kmart has invaded Prague by positioning itself right beside the city's communist-built Maj department store, which also is owned by Kmart's parent company.[26] In so doing, it has generated enormous mass appeal. Furthermore, the antiquated distribution system in Japan is being blown apart virtually overnight by the emergence of stores resembling Wal-Marts. Read Consumer in Focus 7.2 (next page) to discover how this retailing revolution has come about.

| 7.2 | **Consumer in Focus** |

Revolution in Japanese Retailing

Even when its economy was booming, Japan had one glaring problem: a distribution system as labyrinthine as a shogun's palace. Everything a consumer bought—made in Japan or imported, whether personal computer, razor, ball bearing, or man's suit—had to wend through the books of as many as a half-dozen middlemen. A bottle of 96 aspirin tablets costs $20, and not just because of the strong yen.

At long last, the system is breaking down. Pinched by 3 years of recession and weary of subsidizing the low prices they see for Japanese goods elsewhere, Japanese consumers are getting fed up. A recent poll cosponsored by Gallup found that price, not quality, now determines most purchases in Japan.

This stingy attitude is forcing retailers and manufacturers to look for ways to cut prices. One sure method is to find shortcuts through the distribution maze. Suddenly, stores resembling Wal-Marts and Price Clubs are sprouting all over Japan. Upstart specialty retailers who buy factory remainders and overstocks are thriving.

Daiei Inc., a department store chain, has opened a wholesale membership club called Kou's in the port city of Kobe. In the first year, 146,000 people joined the club, which offers up to 80 percent discounts on everything from coach bags to refrigerators to salad oil. Most of the savings stem from Daiei's willingness to bypass customary distribution routes. One of the best deals at Kou's is a pack of 12 Spalding Magna Plus golf balls, which the company buys directly from the manufacturer in the United States. The result: At Kou's, the package, the same one available in the United States, sells for $26.80; anywhere else in Japan, it costs $72. (In U.S. discount stores, it goes for as low as $19.99.)

Two other elements must be added to round out the total value concept—*service* and *atmosphere*. Fletcher Music Centers, Inc., in Clearwater, Florida, provides a good illustration of what we mean.[27] At one point, it sold only keyboard instruments but suffered greatly because of the long decline in the market for organs and pianos. It has doubled its sales, however, by focusing on meeting the musical, physical, and social needs of its primary customers—retirees. Every aspect of customer service has been revamped—from designing Fletcher's own electronic organ with oversize print and controls to making a genuine social event out of free group lessons.

Although Chapter 22 discusses these dimensions of customer value added in depth, you get a very good overall sense of the value-added concept by reading Consumer in Focus 7.3, which tells the story of how Men's Wearhouse has profited by sharpening its competitive weapons.

Personal Selling

Although much of retailing is characterized today by self-selection without the intervention of a salesperson, personal selling still plays a significant role. After all, marketing is a process of exchange in which buyer and seller are mu-

Consumer in Focus   **7.3**

Enhance Customer Value through Retail Reengineering

Many consumers simply want everything. But at Men's Wearhouse, a discount clothing chain, customers do not have to pass up good service just because they're shopping at a discount retailer. Prices are 20 percent to 30 percent below those of department stores, which is what draws customers the first time. But the company sees a huge opportunity in delighting customers with niceties like free pressing and realteration for the life of any suit bought in the store. CEO George Zimmer insists salesmen call 15 days after a suit is sold to make sure it fits right.

Enter just about any Men's Wearhouse location and a salesman will walk up to you and introduce himself by name—and ask you yours. The service is like a good restaurant's, usually unobtrusive until you need it. The store offers a wide selection of suits from well-known brands like Halston to private labels. Says Kurt Barnard, a retail consultant: "Value today is a huge assortment, a very pleasurable shopping experience, and moderate pricing."

Source: Rahul Jacob, "Beyond Quality & Value," Fortune (Autumn–Winter special edition, 1993), 11. Reproduced by special permission.

tual beneficiaries.[28] Exchange becomes most intimate and, hopefully, beneficial when both parties are engaged face-to-face in what has come to be known as **dyadic interaction** (that is, a two-person group). This is especially true in high-involvement extended problem-solving situations in which the buyer seeks additional information and the benefits of negotiation.

What makes a salesperson effective? This question has been asked for decades, and answers still are elusive. A faculty research team from the University of Wisconsin undertook an in-depth analysis of 116 published and unpublished studies in an effort to isolate factors that predict sales performance.[29] The data showed, first of all, that enduring personal characteristics such as aptitude variables and personal/physical traits have some relationship to performance, but the correlations are not strong. Of greater importance are skill levels and motivation—characteristics that can be influenced through increased training and experience.

What this means is that sales success is not primarily dependent on such attributes as personality, temperament, age, and appearance. The determinant factors fall into two categories: (1) the relationship during the transaction, and (2) the persuasion strategies used.[30]

Buyer–Seller Relationship

The salesperson's ability to win a buyer's confidence and successfully complete a negotiation process is affected by four main variables: (1) perceived knowledge and expertise; (2) perceived trustworthiness; (3) customer knowledge; and (4) adaptability.

(1) Perceived Knowledge and Expertise. A commercial spokesperson's ability to exert persuasive influence will be affected by his or her perceived expertise. Woodside and Davenport[31] varied the exhibited expertise of a music store salesperson who encouraged customers to purchase a tapedeck cleaning kit. When the salesperson was seen as knowledgeable, two-thirds bought the product, but this dropped to only 20 percent when there was admission of unfamiliarity with the product. The implications for sales training should be obvious.

(2) Perceived Trustworthiness. A buyer's prior beliefs about a seller's trustworthiness affect the entire negotiation process. Schurr and Ozanne[32] reported that high levels of perceived trustworthiness accompanied by a corresponding image of bargaining toughness led to significantly more positive outcomes in terms of buyer–seller agreement as well as buyer willingness to make concessions. Do not fail to note, however, that a stance of bargaining toughness that is not accompanied by perceived trustworthiness will have a decided boomerang effect.

(3) Customer Knowledge. Several recent studies have demonstrated a positive correlation between sales performance and the elaborateness of the customer knowledge base possessed by the salesperson.[33] Knowledge structures, in turn, appear to have two components: (1) category structures, and (2) script structures. Category structures contain the information needed to describe and classify different types of customers, including knowledge about traits, motives, and behavior. Scripts, however, embody information about sequences of events and actions encountered in sales situations that can guide salesperson behavior in similar situations.

(4) Adaptability. A sophisticated customer knowledge structure, in turn, seems to be related to adaptability. With this structure in place, a salesperson is enabled to respond to customer needs and expectations.

Persuasion Strategies

In recent years, behavioral scientists outside the field of marketing have been motivated to examine the influence strategies that are most effective in dyadic interaction.[34] Of these, the book by Robert B. Cialdini gives the most helpful practical insights. Among the many that he finds to be effective are (1) reciprocation; (2) reject and retreat; (3) foot-in-the-door; (4) contrast; and (5) scarcity.[35]

Compensating for the Right Things

Salespeople traditionally have been compensated in three basic ways: (1) straight salary; (2) commission on sales; or (3) a combination of salary and commission. Salary is the preferred mode when salespeople perform a variety of functions such as consultation and after-sales service. Commission, however, is favored when the objective is to maximize sales volume.

These compensation schemes are increasingly proving to be inadequate in today's marketing environment, which places a premium on customer retention and satisfaction.[36] If sales volume alone is the criterion, the salesperson will be encouraged to **highspot**—that is, to focus only on hot prospects and securing the sale. Straight salary, in turn, may not provide sufficient incentive to close the sale. Therefore, we suggest that serious consideration be given to adjustment of commission schemes to reflect both sales/profitability and satisfaction as measured by retention and survey.

Sales Promotion

You will recall the most common new product purchasing scenario when the customer is motivated to avoid the rigor of extended problem solving:

Exposure to advertising ⟶ *Recognition at point of sale* ⟶ *Trial*

Limited problem solving, then, is often activated by point-of-sale exposure through **sales promotion,** which has been defined as "those marketing activities other than personal selling, advertising, and publicity that stimulate consumer purchasing and dealer effectiveness."[37] Well over $30 billion is invested in sales promotion each year, and this figure is growing rapidly.

Sales Promotion Methods

The most common methods used to stimulate a "why not try it" response include (1) display and advertising; (2) price incentives; (3) premiums; and (4) sampling.

(1) Display and Advertising. If there is to be point-of-sale recognition of a new brand or product, it must be displayed in such a way that attention is attracted. And this is increasingly true worldwide. Eye-level display is the ideal sought by all but achieved mostly by those who can afford to pay premium fees known as **slotting allowances.** This was the key to success when Procter & Gamble introduced its premium detergent Ariel Microsystem in the major cities in India.[38]

Other favored options include end of aisle and cash register locations. Also, nothing attracts attention more readily than a **shelf talker**—an ad placed on the shelf or within the product display in a way that the brand name stands out.

(2) Price Incentives. As we have repeatedly stressed, consumers expect low prices. There is no question that sales volumes can be increased in the short run through an outright price reduction or through offering a *deal* such as a coupon. Such incentives work best under the following conditions:[39]

- Price incentives are used infrequently and at widely spaced intervals. They are not a cure-all for declining sales.

- Brand loyalty is low or nonexistent.

- The brand is relatively new.

- Incentives are not used as an alternative to advertising.

Price incentives, however, can be dangerous if used on a regular basis. First, the effects are often only temporary brand shifts that reverse as competitors retaliate. Furthermore, the net impact may be to induce the consumer to stock up at this point and reduce future purchases, thus interrupting cash flow from normal sales patterns. Finally, price incentives, once initiated, are difficult or impossible to reverse, thus resulting in an endless cycle of competitive retaliation. These are the major reasons why so many are turning to "everyday low pricing" as discussed earlier.

(3) Premiums. A premium is some type of merchandise or service offered either free or at a bargain price to induce purchase of another product or service offering. It is important that the premium be perceived as an enhancement to the product in question. Otherwise, only a short-term trial use will occur. A good example is the offer of the popular 3-in. raisin figures for just 99¢ with proof of purchase of California raisins. These figures have almost become a kind of cult symbol and clearly bring the product to mind every time they are seen.

(4) Sampling. Sampling is an expensive way to introduce a new brand or product but often proves to be necessary. This is especially true when scent, taste, consistency, or other attributes can only be communicated through a small-scale trial. At other times, it is used as a massive form of competitive retaliation. Procter & Gamble has held its competitors at bay for years with this tactic, but to say the least, it requires "deep pockets." The risks and huge costs of a backfire, however, are a distinct limit to this strategy in the current cost-conscious era.

Sampling can be a good strategy in non-Western countries where trial may be the only way to change entrenched buying habits. Gillette Co. introduced its Presto razors in India by giving them away free of charge to spectators at cricket matches and consumers in shops.[40] The reason? It was necessary for the Indian man to discover the unique benefits of disposable blades—an unknown feature until Gillette entered the market.

Importance of Integrated Marketing

The methods discussed here never can stand by themselves. Instead, sales promotion must be viewed as only one component in an **integrated marketing campaign.** Each component ranging from packaging, price, advertising, sales promotion, and so on must be thought through from this broader perspective if there is to be optimum return on investment. Success in this important objective may be one of the primary factors that differentiate market survivors from those who fall by the wayside.

Database Marketing

Retail distributors also are being forced into contemporary strategies of relationship marketing. The goal is an ongoing personalized contact and continued patronage based on sharpened ability to meet individual customer needs with precision. For this to take place, customer names must be collected and placed in a data base that contains a wealth of information about each person. Furthermore, there must be a commitment to ongoing interaction with each customer that goes far beyond the usual casual contact when a sale is consummated.

Bloomingdale's, a large department store chain, has experienced real success with mailings to a carefully managed data base of credit cardholders and other prospects to increase sales of its furniture lines.[41] Those who have recently moved, for example, receive a 24-page catalog of newest offerings. Others receive target mailings that highlight new options that are consistent with preferences and lifestyle, information collected for each person.

We are surprised how many retailers fail to grasp the significance of this important step. Newer specialty stores are becoming expert at building customer relationships, and established outlets that lag behind the trend are failing to see clear warning signs of future customer attrition.

In-Home Shopping and Purchasing

A growing percentage of consumer shopping and buying activity now takes place in the home. Strategies used to reach the consumer in his or her home are referred to as direct marketing. *Direct Marketing* magazine estimates that nearly two-thirds of U.S. advertising dollars are undertaken to generate a direct response, including home and retail sales.[42] Between 1986 and 1992, the volume of direct mail alone increased by 60 percent, and expenditures rose by 99 percent.[43]

Direct marketing also is growing rapidly in most developing countries of the world. Focusing only on mail-order statistics, 1990 sales in 17 countries in Europe and Asia totaled nearly $60.6 billion, as compared with almost $151 billion in the United States and Canada.[44] It may come as a surprise to learn that direct marketing is surging in such unexpected countries as India. Be sure to read Consumer in Focus 7.4, which explains the rapid changes taking place.

There have been a number of studies profiling the in-home buyer.[45] Although estimates vary, we think it is safe to conclude that at least 60 percent of U.S. consumers have ordered from catalog, direct mail, or telephone sources in the past year. As Table 7.3 shows, direct mail purchase is dominant, followed closely by telephone.

Compared with the general population, in-home shoppers differ in these ways:

- They are somewhat younger with slightly higher household incomes.

- They are somewhat above average in terms of education and income.

- They are more likely to live in a smaller town or rural area.

- Items most frequently ordered are apparel, magazines, home accessories, home maintenance and kitchen equipment, and home office supplies.

- Most are active retail shoppers who shop at home for reasons other than deliberate avoidance of the store or shopping mall.

Here are some of the factors that have contributed to the rapid growth of this phenomenon:

| **7.4** | **Consumer in Focus** |

Direct Marketing—A Key to Success in India's Competitive Marketplace

Indian companies are quickly coming to recognize that the increasingly competitive marketplace is forcing them to opt for direct marketing to retain customers and gain new ones. This is happening for many reasons. First, today's consumers are far more exposed to advertising than a generation ago. They are more educated. And disposable income is getting squeezed by a growing set of wants.

On the other hand, there are far more brands in various product categories for consumers to choose from than there were a mere 5 years ago. And consumers have far less time at their disposal than the previous generation. So they put off purchases, leading advertisers to strive harder to get their attention.

Trikaya Grey Direct was set up as a division of Trikaya Grey Advertising in 1989. Division manager Ajay Row reports that people are beginning to trust the mail as a medium and that they are no longer awed by it. "We have had response rates of 65 percent for enquiries and responses with cheques of between 12.5 and 14.5 percent," he claims.

Already, products like Real Value's Ceasefire fire extinguishers and Eureka Forbes's vacuum cleaners owe their success in large measure to direct marketing. While the bulk of effort so far concentrates on direct mail, industry sources believe that telemarketing and mail order marketing will catch on as well.

Source: Austin Lobo, "Customized Communication," Business India (May 24–June 6, 1993), 98–99.

- Changing consumer lifestyles resulting from greater emphasis placed on leisure, the number of working wives, and demand for more services and conveniences in shopping
- Availability of credit, especially credit cards
- Problems encountered when shopping (examples are congested parking lots, inadequate parking, uninformed sales personnel, long lines, and in-store congestion during peak hours)
- Trend toward a greater focusing of life within the circle of home and family (often referred to as *cocooning*)

The in-home shopper offers a unique opportunity to the marketer, because there is evidence that people may be more likely to buy when they are most contented. Studies by Retail Planning Associates show, for example, that those who have just finished a meal at home are 25 percent more likely to buy clothing than a person who is hungry.[46]

Table 7.3 In-Home Purchasing Patterns	
Mode of Purchasing	**Adult Population Who Are Users (%)**
Mail order	45
Direct mail	10
Catalog	33
Telephone	33
Television	9
Magazine or newspaper	4

Source: *1992–1993 Statistical Fact Book.*

Direct-Marketing Methods

There are six ways in which consumers are reached to stimulate a direct response: (1) direct selling, (2) direct-mail ads, (3) direct-mail catalogs, (4) telemarketing, (5) direct-response ads, and (6) interactive electronic media. All these offer the unique benefit of precise segmentation.

Direct Selling

Direct selling is defined as any form of face-to-face contact between salesperson and a customer away from a fixed retail location. Although accurate statistics are hard to come by,[47] direct personal selling now accounts for about 2 percent of all general merchandise sales and mostly takes place in a home, a workplace, or some other form of nonretail location.

Mary Kay Cosmetics, Inc., has achieved a significant share of the cosmetics industry by concentrating exclusively on in-home presentations and sales.[48] All presentations are made to groups invited by a hostess. This situation adds social influence to the powerful benefit of first-hand observation of the personal effects of skin care. A definite segment of the market prefers this method over a similar presentation in a department store.

Direct-Mail Ads

Shopping in response to direct-mail appeals has been shown to meet real consumer needs. The most often-cited benefits are "availability of merchandise," "convenience," "low price," and "better quality." This may fall on deaf ears to many readers who often assume wrongly that direct mail is an unwanted invasion into the home. Polls consistently show that well over half welcome direct mail, open it, and read it, although this declines as education and income increase. If you still are skeptical, do not fail to read Consumer in Focus 7.5, which reveals the popularity of direct mail in Great Britain.

Direct-Mail Catalogs

Catalog buying has experienced dramatic growth in recent years, although it peaked during the recent recession. In a comprehensive recent survey undertaken by Impact Resources, about 20 percent of those surveyed use catalogs regularly.[49] And those who do differ sharply from those who do not:

- Women outnumber men by 58 percent compared with 42 percent.
- Catalog purchasers are, on the average, 3 years younger than their counterparts.
- Catalog shoppers are better educated—more than two-thirds have attended college.
- Larger percentages of catalog shoppers use every type of home technology such as VCRs and home computers.
- The catalog shopper also spends more time and money on leisure events.
- Far smaller percentages of catalog shoppers prefer department stores (25 percent compared with 42 percent).
- High quality is a more important motivator to the "cataloger."

This type of purchasing has become so popular that some marketers now are offering their catalogs for sale at prices ranging from $1 to $5. Moreover, it has

---

7.5   Consumer in Focus

Direct Mail Is a Winner in Great Britain

A survey by the Direct Mail Information Service shows that the "Brits" are avid fans of direct mail. Far from throwing out anything that does not have a personal stamp, four out of five agree that "I sift through any mail I receive and read what interests me." About four in ten claim to enjoy reading direct mail largely based on its usefulness as a source of product information.

Readers also respond as buyers. Once again, four in ten responded to direct mail in the last 12 months. Moreover, six out of ten reported that at least one member in their household made a direct mail purchase in that period. Nevertheless, nearly three-quarters identified some of the mail they receive as junk. This term was used for "things I don't want or am not interested in" as well as unsolicited items.

The survey also revealed strong evidence that the reception a mailing will get is influenced by a number of factors: using a creative treatment that is appropriate both for the product and for the target; the degree to which a person usually responds; and the underlying attitudes a person has to direct mail.

Source: Adapted from "The Medium and the Message," Direct Marketing (January 1994), 27–28. Used by special permission.

been discovered that between 5 and 15 percent of those who buy a catalog actually order merchandise, versus only 2 percent who receive them through the mail.[50]

Telemarketing

Nearly 20 percent of direct-response orders now are triggered by a telephone call (referred to as **outbound telemarketing**), and a vast majority of Fortune 500 companies are using this method profitably.[51] Homes can be targeted with great demographic precision using census data available within geographic zip codes. Also, real personalization can be achieved if the caller is skillful and sensitive.

Inbound telemarketing, on the other hand, refers to the use of an 800 number to place orders directly. An AT&T survey disclosed that the most frequently purchased items in the order of importance are clothing and accessories, records and tapes, housewares and cookware, and books and educational materials. The heaviest users are found among the younger and better-educated families with higher incomes and children at home.[52]

There is no question that there is a public backlash against unwanted and insensitive telemarketing calls. Here are some insights that will prove helpful[53]:

- Telemarketing works much better with present customers as opposed to "cold contacts." This assumes that a customer data base is in place that enables you to know and understand the prospects' interests and preferences.

- Best results are achieved when the offer is a timely response to changing events. "Mr. Smith, the NASDAQ stock average is setting records every day, and now is a good time to update your portfolio."

- Call at convenient times. We doubt that anyone will be overjoyed to discuss their stock portfolio in the middle of dinner after a long day.

- Avoid cliché beginnings — "Hello, Mary — How are you?" And so on. These are a quick signal to many that a turnoff is needed, especially when you do not even know the other person.

- State your offer and benefit at the outset. You will only have a very short time to attract and hold the prospect's attention.

Direct-Response Ads

About 20 percent of in-home purchases are stimulated each year by newspaper, magazine, and yellow pages ads that call for a direct response such as return of an order form. But big growth in this category is occurring in TV home shopping both in the United States and abroad. With the startling news of a merger between QVC and Home Shopping Network on July 12, 1993, a mega-shopping network was born that will be available to 60 million viewers — two-thirds of all U.S. television-owning homes.[54] Furthermore, there is rapid growth in 30- to 60-minute time purchases known as **infomercials.**

A survey undertaken by Impact Resources showed relatively few demographic differences between TV shoppers and their counterparts, the only real exception being that this group is somewhat younger.[55] But as one would expect, they are more interested in technology and are frequent TV viewers. Also, they are above-average users of the other forms of home shopping discussed above.

The "on-screen sell" seems to work well with a variety of products, especially when there is a need for demonstration. Eastman Kodak Co. introduced its new Cameo zoom lens camera in December 1993 on the QVC shopping network, and 9,700 were sold in just 70 minutes.[56] Kodak also benefited from pitching some related company products at the same time.

Interactive Electronic Media

We have saved the "glamour child" of home shopping until the last — **interactive electronic media.** Most observers believe that we are at the very dawn of radically changed lifestyles brought about through a revolution in information technology. Here is the scenario: For those who are willing to pay the price, it will be possible to have nearly immediate access over cable television to virtually unlimited worldwide sources of programming, information, communication, and so on. All it will require is a simple keyboard entry.[57]

The availability of nearly instantaneous two-way communication offers consumer benefits, including convenience and opportunity to plan purchases through immediate access to needed information. The disadvantage has been the necessity of purchasing specialized equipment that, until recently, appears to have been too costly for most consumers. Also, there has been some understandable reluctance from those who are not familiar with computer hardware and software. But new technology is about to change all this.

Interactivity will take place in three ways[58]:

- *Video on demand (VOD).* Viewers make the choice of the programming they want from among the available options.

- *Store it in a box.* Much as viewers can presently do with a VCR, information is stored and chosen for viewing at some future point.

- *Simulcast.* Viewers interact by entering their choices and opinions and controlling the programming itself. By this means, you could second-guess an NFL quarterback or order more information during a documentary.

It would appear that the simulcast is the retailer's dream. It will be no problem whatsoever to shop the world, interact with a salesperson, and dicker and negotiate right in the living room. A video catalog channel may be a reality much as it presently is on such subscription interactive services as Prodigy or CompuServe.

As of this writing, technology is still developing. Nonetheless, fully interactive video should become a reality for many in the next 5 years, although its full growth and maturity may require 10 years or more.

Direct Marketing's Growing Impact

An inexplicable bias against direct marketing in some circles in the past is now rapidly changing. Many leading advertising agencies finally have entered this field. In part, this is a belated recognition that many efforts to reach the prospective consumer, especially through media advertising, are not much more than background noise.

The fact is that marketers are becoming fully aware that it is increasingly difficult to reach a target audience without the interference of a barrage of competitive efforts. As a result, many are placing growing reliance on a combination of direct-marketing methods.

Summary

This chapter examines the act of purchase that encompasses the following related decisions: (1) whether to buy; (2) when to buy; (3) what to buy; (4) where to buy; and (5) how to pay. First, purchase is a function of two factors: (1) purchase intentions, and (2) environmental influences and/or individual differences. Often, purchases are fully planned in the sense that there is intention to purchase both product and brand. At other times, intention encompasses only the product, with the choice of brand reserved for further deliberation at point of sale.

The so-called unplanned purchase is discussed at length. It was stressed that a purchase intention is not always consciously articulated, in which case product display provides a "surrogate shopping list." But many items also are bought purely on the basis of impulse, which can be spontaneous and hedonic in motivation.

A purchase can be made either at a retail outlet of some type or in the home. Retail outlets prosper in part because shopping has intrinsic value in and of itself. Often, there is a need for further information collection and evaluation through contact with a competent salesperson. The fruitfulness of this interaction depends on the relationship established and the persuasion strategies used. The factors that differentiate successful salespersons from their counterparts are (1) perceived knowledge and expertise; (2) perceived trustworthiness; (3) knowledge of their customer; and (4) adaptability. Also, it is important to ensure that compensation methods encompass the development of customer satisfaction and retention, not merely the ability to close a sale.

Most retail purchasing, however, takes place under limited problem solving in which there is low brand loyalty and propensity to shift brand choices. The goal here is to induce trial. The most common methods used to stimulate a "why not try it" response are (1) display and advertising; (2) price incentives; (3) premiums; and (4) sampling.

But there is also a dramatic growth of buying through direct mail, telephone, cata-logs, and other nonretail sources. Strategies designed to reach the in-home buyer are referred to as direct marketing. Among those discussed in this chapter are (1) direct selling, (2) direct-mail ads, (3) direct-mail catalogs, (4) telemarketing, (5) direct-response ads, and (6) interactive electronic media. All these offer the unique benefit of precise segmentation, and every sign points to continued rapid growth, especially as technology is developed to bring interactive electronic media to a mass market.

Review and Discussion Questions

1. Many, if not most, shoppers at supermarkets do not have a detailed shopping list. Does this mean that most of their purchases are unplanned and impulsive?

2. You are the marketing manager for a manufacturer of specialty electronic items such as tiny lamps that illuminate only the page of a book and a line of watches designed for runners. Would you seek to sell these items through retail stores or would you be inclined to try direct marketing (either alone or in combination with retail distribution)? Why?

3. Would your answer to question 2 differ if the product line consisted mostly of costly "upscale" women's fashion accessories (for example, gloves, scarves)?

4. Given the diverse reasons why many consumers genuinely enjoy shopping, how would you capitalize on this phenomenon if you are marketing a high-quality ice cream line?

5. A large furniture retailer is experiencing very low retention of present customers, and complaints are increasing. Management suspects that some salespeople are "highspotting"—that is, focusing only on "hot prospects" and largely ignoring those who have questions and need help. How would you solve this problem? Would a change of compensation away from 100 percent commission help?

6. Why would you say that many conventional marketers have been hesitant to enter into direct marketing? What case would you make for direct marketing to a book publisher? A distributor of French wines?

7. Many contend that interactive electronic media will revolutionize consumer buying patterns. Although it is too early to arrive at a definitive judgment, what is your opinion? What advantages are offered? Will traditional retail shopping become largely obsolete?

Endnotes

1. Chip Walker, "Strip Malls; Plain but Powerful," *American Demographics* (October 1991), 48–51.

2. "Shoppers Are a Dwindling Species," *Business Week* (November 26, 1990), 144.

3. "Retailing: Who Will Survive?" *Business Week* (November 26, 1990), 134–144.

4. Laura Loro, "Data Bases Seen as 'Driving Force,'" *Advertising Age* (March 18, 1991), 39.

5. Arnold Fishman, "The Database Marketing 250," *Direct Marketing* (September 1990), 26.

6. Cyndee Miller, "P-O-P Gains Followers as 'Era of Retailing' Dawns," *Advertising Age* (May 14, 1990), 2.

7. C. Whan Park, Easwar S. Iyer, and Daniel C. Smith, "The Effects of Situational Factors on In-Store Grocery Shopping Behavior: The Role of Store Environment and Time Available for Shopping," *Journal of Consumer Research* 15 (March 1989), 422–433.

8. Alain d'Asdtous, Idriss Bensouda, and Jean Guindon, "A Re-Examination of Consumer Decision Making for a Repeat Purchase Product: Variations in Product Importance and Purchase Frequency," in Thomas K. Srull, *Advances in Consumer Research* 16 (Provo, Utah: Association for Consumer Research, 1989), 433–438.

9. For a careful analysis of the impact of retail promotions, see Rodney G. Walters, "Assessing the Impact of Retail Price Promotions on Product Substitution, Complementary Purchase, and Interstore Sales Displacement," *Journal of Marketing* 55 (April 1991), 17–28.

10. David T. Kollat and Ronald P. Willett, "Customer Impulse Purchasing Behavior," *Journal of Marketing Research* 4 (February 1967), 21–31.

11. Joe Agnew, "P-O-P Displays Are Becoming a Matter of Consumer Convenience," *Marketing News* (October 9, 1987), 14.

12. Kollat and Willett, "Customer Impulse Purchasing Behavior."

13. Park, Iyer, and Smith, "The Effects of Situational Factors."

14. Dennis W. Rook, "The Buying Impulse," *Journal of Consumer Research* 14 (September 1987), 191.

15. Morris B. Holbrook and Elizabeth C. Hirschman, "The Experiential Aspects of Consumer Behavior: Consumer Fantasies, Feelings, and Fun," *Journal of Consumer Research* 9 (September 1982), 132–140.

16. Rook, "The Buying Impulse."

17. For more detail, see Gordon R. Foxall, *Consumer Choice* (London: Macmillan Press, 1983), 86–97.

18. For a careful analysis, see Robert A. Peterson and Gerald A. Albaum, "Nonstore Retailing in the United States" (unpublished paper), August 1993.

19. Betsy Morris, "As a Favored Pastime, Shopping Ranks High with Most Americans," *Wall Street Journal* (July 30, 1987), 1ff.

20. Jack A. Lesser and Sanjay Jain, "A Preliminary Investigation of the Relationship between Exploratory and Epistemic Shopping Behavior," in Robert F. Lusch et al., eds., *1985 AMA Educators' Proceedings* (Chicago: American Marketing Association, 1985), 75–81.

21. Morris, "As a Favored Pastime."

22. "Retailing: Who Will Survive?" *Business Week* (November 26, 1990), 135.

23. James U. McNeal and Daryl McKee, "The Case of Antishoppers," in Lusch et al., *1985 AMA Educators' Proceedings*, 65–68.

24. "Meet the Tough New Consumer," *Fortune* (Autumn–Winter special issue, 1993), 6, 7.

25. Rahul Jacob, "Beyond Quality & Value," *Fortune* (Autumn–Winter special issue, 1993), 10.

26. Laura Zelenko, "Attention, Comrade Shoppers: Kmart Invades Prague," *American Demographics* (January 1993), 21–22.

27. Susan Greco, "The Art of Selling," *Inc.* (June 1993), 73.

28. It was Wroe Alderson who first characterized marketing as a negotiation process. See Wroe Alderson, *Marketing Behavior and Executive Action* (Homewood, Ill.: Irwin, 1957). This was then clarified by Bagozzi and others as a process of exchange. See Richard P. Bagozzi, "Marketing as Exchange," *Journal of Marketing* 39 (October 1975), 32–39.

29. Gilbert A. Churchill, Jr., Neil M. Ford, Steven W. Hartley, and Orville C. Walker, Jr., "The Determinants of Salesperson Performance: A Meta-Analysis," *Journal of Marketing Research* 22 (May 1985), 103–118.

30. This categorization has its roots in Peter H. Reingen and Arch G. Woodside, *Buyer–Seller Interactions: Empirical Research and Normative Issues* (Chicago: American Marketing Association, 1981).

31. Arch G. Woodside and William Davenport, Jr., "The Effect of Salesman Similarity and Expertise on Consumer Purchasing Behavior," *Journal of Marketing Research* 11 (May 1974), 198–203. Also see Paul Busch and David T. Wilson, "An Experimental Analysis of a Salesman's Expert and Referent Bases on Social Power in the Buyer–Seller Dyad," *Journal of Marketing Research* 13 (February 1976), 3–11.

32. Paul H. Schurr and Julie Ozanne, "Influences on Exchange Processes: Buyers' Preconceptions of a Seller's Trustworthiness and Bargaining Toughness," *Journal of Consumer Research* 11 (March 1985), 939–953.

33. Siew Meng Leong, Paul S. Busch, and Deborah Roedder John, "Knowledge Bases and Salesperson Effectiveness: A Script-Theoretic Analysis," *Journal of Marketing Research* 26 (May 1989), 164–178; Harish Sujan, Mita Sujan, and James R. Bettman, "Knowledge Structure Differences between More Effective and Less Effective Sales People," *Journal of Marketing Research* 25 (February 1988), 81–86; and David M. Syzmanski, "Determinants of Selling Effectiveness," *Journal of Marketing* 52 (January 1988), 64–77.

34. See Robert B. Cialdini, *Influence Science and Practice*, 3rd ed. (New York: HarperCollins, 1993); Kathleen Kelley Reardon, *Persuasion in Practice* (Newbury Park, Calif.: Sage Publications, 1991); Robert C. Prus, *Making Sales* (Newbury Park, Calif.: Sage Publications, 1989).

35. Cialdini, *Influence Science and Practice.*

36. Ira Sager, "IBM Leans on Its Sales Force," *Business Week* (February 7, 1994), 110.

37. *Marketing Definitions: A Glossary of Marketing Terms* (Chicago: American Marketing Association, 1960), 20.

38. Anil Wanvari, "The Great Indian Giveaway," *BusinessWorld* [India] (June 2–15, 1993, 106–110.

39. James F. Engel, Martin R. Warshaw, and Thomas Kinnear, *Promotional Strategy,* 8th ed. (Homewood, Ill.: Irwin, 1994).

40. Wanvari, "The Great Indian Giveaway."

41. "Customer Rapport," *Direct Marketing* (January 1994), 46.

42. This estimate is based on annual statistics published in *Direct Marketing.*

43. "International Direct Mail Trends," *Direct Marketing* (October 1993), 93.

44. Arnold Fishman, "International Mail Order," *Direct Marketing* (October 1991), 36.

45. See, for example, Peterson and Albaum, "Nonstore Retailing in the United States"; Martin P. Block and Tamara S. Brezen, "A Profile of the New In-Home Shopper," in Rebecca Holman, ed., *Proceedings of the 1991 Conference of the American Academy of Advertising* (New York: Rebecca H. Holman, D'Arcy Masius Benton & Bowles, Inc., 1991), 169–173; Paul I. Edwards, "Home Shopping Boom Forecast in Study," *Advertising Age* (December 15, 1986), 88.

46. "Home Shopping. Is It a Revolution in Retailing—or Just a Fad?" *Business Week* (December 16, 1986), 68.

47. A special issue (vol. 2, no. 2) of the *Journal of Marketing Channels* is devoted to this subject.

48. "Mary Kay Cosmetics, Inc. (A)," in James F. Engel and W. Wayne Talarzyk, *Cases in Promotional Strategy,* rev. ed. (Homewood, Ill.: Irwin, 1983), 3–10.

49. Harvey D. Braun, "The Catalog Shopper of the '90s," *Direct Marketing* (March 1993), 15–16.

50. James R. Lumpkin and John R. Hawes, "Retailing without Stores: An Examination of Catalog Shoppers," *Journal of Business Research* 13 (1985), 139–151.

51. "Behavior and Attitudes of Telephone Shoppers," *Direct Marketing* (September 1987), 50ff.

52. Ibid.

53. Engel, Warshaw, and Kinnear, *Promotional Strategy.*

54. Laura Zinn, "Retailing Will Never Be the Same," *Business Week* (July 26, 1993), 54–59.

55. Harvey D. Braun, "Guess Who's Watching," *Direct Marketing* (July 1993), 21–23.

56. Riccardo A. Davis, "QVC Clicks for Kodak Cameras," *Advertising Age* (January 17, 1994), 17.

57. See Rebecca Pirrito, "Taming the TV Beast," *American Demographics* (May 1993), 34–39; Rachel Kaplan, "Video on Demand," *American Demographics* (June 1992), 38–43.

58. Pirrto, "Taming the TV Beast."

CHAPTER 8

Consumption, Satisfaction, and Divestment

▲▲

Gillette Responds to a Market Need

Jill Shurtleff has shed blood in the line of duty. Or more precisely, her legs have. The only female industrial designer in Gillette Co.'s shaving division, Shurtleff was handed a key assignment five years ago: Take a fresh look at the women's shaving market, a niche that had long been neglected at male-oriented Gillette. Shurtleff decided to ignore existing products and start with a clean slate. She began with a basic question: How do women shave?

The short answer from Gillette researchers was: very differently from men. The average American woman shaves nine times more surface area than a man, repeats the process 2.5 times a week, and changes blades 10 times a year. And unlike men, who shave in front of a well-lit mirror, most women perform their ritual in a slippery, often poorly lit tub or shower. Women also have parts of the body they can't see well, such as underarms and backs of thighs. Not surprisingly, Gillette found that most women complained about nicks and cuts and viewed shaving as an unpleasant chore.

Gillette and its rivals had long marketed women's razors. "The general approach was to take a man's razor, change the handle a bit, color it pink, and say, 'Here Honey, this is for you,'" says John M. Darman, director of new shaving products at Gillette. Most women shunned the so-called women's razors, opting instead to use hubby's razor or cheap disposables made for men.

Source: Mark Maremont, "A New Equal Right: The Close Shave," Business Week *(March 29, 1993), 58–59. Reproduced by special permission.*

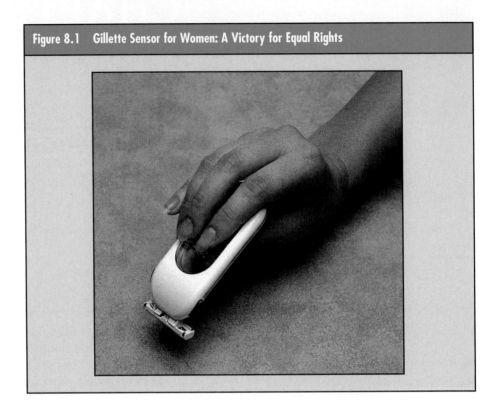

Figure 8.1   Gillette Sensor for Women: A Victory for Equal Rights

Gillette produced a $100 million product winner for 1993 and a 60 percent market share by producing the Sensor for Women, a flat-handled shaver designed to align the cartridge with the hand (see Figure 8.1). This simple solution provided the tactile control needed to help women meet their shaving needs. In short, Gillette Co. demonstrated that a proper understanding of how products are *consumed* can lead to extraordinary *satisfaction* and brand loyalty—coveted outcomes in today's atmosphere of hypercompetition.

This chapter explores the last three stages in the consumer decision process, *consumption, post-purchase alternative evaluation,* and *divestment* (Figure 8.2). The decision process does not stop with consumption. First, there is likely to be continued evaluation of the product or service once it is consumed, leading to a response of satisfaction or dissatisfaction. The probability of repurchase often is determined at this point. Finally, a divestment decision must be made— outright disposal of unconsumed product or remnants, recycling, or remarketing (exchange activities that facilitate second-time ownership and usage of a product).[1]

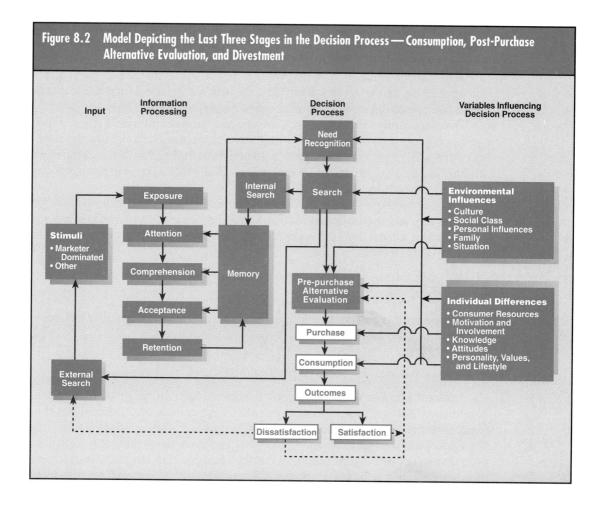

Figure 8.2 Model Depicting the Last Three Stages in the Decision Process—Consumption, Post-Purchase Alternative Evaluation, and Divestment

Consumption of Products and Services

Decision to Consume or Not to Consume

The act of purchase normally is followed by consumption or use. But the consumer then must decide how this is to be done. There are several options including

- Usage at the earliest convenient opportunity
- Short-term storage in anticipation of later usage opportunities
- Long-term storage with no specific or anticipated use in mind

Another possible decision-making option is to abort the consumption process. This can happen, first of all, through the influence of unanticipated situational factors such as a job layoff, disagreement among family members that the right decision was made, new information that suggests that the choice made is inappropriate, and so on. It is likely that the product will be returned if it is possible to do so or disposed of in other ways discussed later in the chapter.

The consumption process also can be aborted because of **buyer's regret.** Have you ever come to a decision under high-involvement conditions, say, the selection of a college or university, only to experience doubts that you did the right thing? You think, perhaps, of several other schools that also were good options and find yourself troubled.

You are now experiencing *buyer's regret* motivated by post-decision doubt (or dissonance), a common initial outcome that can occur with or without a prior judgment of satisfaction or dissatisfaction. Here are the circumstances that can activate this response:

- A certain threshold of dissonance-motivated tension is surpassed.
- The action is irrevocable.
- There are other unchosen alternatives with qualitatively dissimilar but desirable attributes.
- The choice is made entirely by free will or volition (that is, you have not been constrained by social or parental pressures).[2]

You now are motivated to do something to reduce this dissonance, and you have two basic options: (1) confirmation of your choice, or (2) conclusion that you have made an unwise decision.[3]

One of the best ways to underscore that you have done the right thing is to search for supportive information, especially that provided by the manufacturer through ads or new buyer instructions. There is evidence that confirms that buyers experiencing regret indeed are more receptive to these types of materials.[4]

It makes marketing sense to take pains to reinforce the wisdom of choice by stressing product superiorities and other sources of uniqueness once again. A good place to do this is in owner manuals. Warranties can be helpful for this purpose. In other words, the buyer may need reassurance that he or she acted wisely. Doubts often can be counteracted if this can be put into buyers' hands quickly. A personal letter or telephone call from the manufacturer or dealer also is an effective strategy.

The other option, concluding that a bad choice has been made, is painful and can have negative consequences for the marketer. At the very least, a repurchase is unlikely, and it is quite possible that the product will be returned. Even more critical is the possibility of negative word of mouth.

Bear in mind that these doubts usually are transitory and do not, as yet, signify dissatisfaction. They are an entirely normal consequence when there are attractive unchosen alternatives. There is no need for them to degenerate into dissatisfaction when it is so easy to provide reinforcement through a personal word or literature.

Consumption Research

As you will recall from Chapter 1, there is growing recognition that *customer satisfaction and retention* hold the keys to entrepreneurial success in mature marketing environments. In other words, changing times are forcing a return to the time-tested concept of a more intimate, one-on-one relationship with the customer, referred to as **relationship marketing.**[5]

How can relationship marketing be established and retained without ongoing research into the ways in which people live and behave in the everyday world of consumption? Jill Shurtleff at Gillette Co. asked just the right question: "How do women shave?" In earlier years, the research question was more likely to be phrased, "How can we get people to buy the new product?"

Interest in consumption, however, goes well beyond the marketing sphere. Consider these words of Russell W. Belk, prominent postmodern researcher, in his presidential address to the Association for Consumer Research:

> [W]e have tended to examine consumer behavior in isolation from other aspects of our existence. One key to gaining a better sense of balance in consumer research would seem to involve relating consumer behavior to the rest of human behavior. . . . In a world so full of wondrous things, both natural and humanly created, there is much to engage us—both as consumers and as consumer researchers. . . . And yet we have spent (some might say squandered) the first couple of decades of consumer research on what Saul Bellow calls "the dog-food level of things."[6]

We agree that it is valid and worthwhile to examine levels of attachment to and meanings associated with object ownership without placing priority on marketing implications. Therefore, consumption research falls into two primary categories: (1) profit-motivated consumption research and entrepreneurial gain, and (2) postmodern consumption research.

Profit-Motivated Consumption Research

Before the past two centuries, suppliers and customers engaged in face-to-face relationships, and the supplier had little choice but to understand consumption patterns. Customized production for a single customer was often necessitated, and this is still seen in some parts of the world today. Satisfaction was an essential for maintenance of a productive relationship. But the mass marketing era weakened this link.

For most of the twentieth century, competitive advantage has been gained through new product development, mass distribution, and sale. The driving purpose for marketing research was to find ways to attract new customers and trigger a *buying response.* What people did with the product and the extent of satisfaction gained through use were issues pushed into the background during the mass marketing heydays.

Mass marketing became the province of large organizations, but sheer size has come to be a major hindrance in the current era. As Pizza Hut's marketing chief Robert Perkins observed, we must return marketing to the nineteenth century when every merchant knew their customers by name.[7] We can no longer rely on large sample marketing research to reveal customer preferences; it is time to enter the home to dialog, observe, and experience the world as the consumer does. This is precisely the step Black & Decker took in creating its Quantum line of power tools for the serious home improvement "do-it-yourselfer" (Consumer in Focus 8.1).

8.1	Consumer in Focus

The World of "Mr. Super-Fixer-Upper"

You've seen this guy, and admit it, you hate him. Meet Mr. Super-Fixer-Upper, a growing breed in the ever-expanding ever more sophisticated world of home improvement. The real-life DIYer, as he is known in the trade, wants more than a run-of-the-mill $25 electric screwdriver but doesn't need a $300 professional-quality miter saw either. Tool giant Black & Decker took on the Japanese — and Sears — to go after this expanding niche market.

What exactly were serious DIYers looking for? To gather intelligence on this new group, B&D gave Field-work Atlanta, an independent research firm, a tightly specified assignment: Find 50 male homeowners, ages 25 to 54, who own more than six power tools. From June to September 1991 they were questioned about the tools they used and why they had picked particular brands. B&D marketing executives hung out with them in their homes and around their workshops. They watched how the 50 used their tools and asked what they liked or disliked about certain ones, how the tools felt in their hands, and even how they cleaned up their work space when they were finished.

The B&D people tagged along on shopping trips too, monitoring what DIYers bought and how much they spent. On occasion executives even took an industrial psychologist with them on home visits, hoping this would tell them even more about what the customer wants. For example, instead of asking, "What kind of projects do you do?" the exec learned to say, "What was your first project, and how did you feel about doing it?" This prompted DIYers to discuss things at greater length. In particular, they were more frank about why they favored particular brands.

By the end of 1991, initial research was fortified by interviewing hundreds of Black & Decker customers who had mailed in warranty cards, asking them similar questions. The conclusion: Black & Decker could give these customers everything they wanted and more. With meticulous attention to detail, the company created Quantum, a line of 18 power tools that it hopes will capture the minds and wallets of the advanced DIYer.

Source: Susan Caminiti, "A Star is Born," Fortune (Autumn–Winter 1993), 45–46.

The benefits from this common sense approach to consumer research are legion, and here are some examples:

- Procter & Gamble Co. was surprised to discover how Russians use detergents. It was found that detergents typically are stored in cramped bathrooms; therefore, the box must be able to sustain water damage. Also, Russians tend to soak their clothes for hours in the tub to overcome weak strength of local detergents. Many also boil clothes after washing them.[8]

- A leading manufacturer of scissors, Fiskar, found that its conventional line of scissors worked well for 25- to 45-year-olds but sold poorly in other age segments. Therefore, a spring-action mechanism was added to take pressure off weakened or arthritic hands. This simple modification led to a tenfold gain in sales in 1992.[9]

- Research by *Decorating Remodeling* magazine has uncovered new insights into the role of kitchens in family life. The "dream kitchen" must provide for six different functions: (1) a central area for food preparation; (2) a mud room for coats and boots; (3) a dining area; (4) a study; (5) climate-controlled storage for food; and (6) a butler's pantry. It would take up about 600 square feet, more than one-third of total floor space in most homes.[10]

- Ease of use is becoming more important as products become more complex. The Sharp Electronics Corp. is developing a VCR that talks with users during programming to make it more user-friendly. The company also found that the controls on its "Half-Pint" microwave ovens were far too complex for those aged 65 years or older. As a result, pre-programmed keys were added for common dishes.[11]

This kind of customer intimacy is increasingly being recognized as a definitive way to hold market share under competitive onslaught. This is particularly important when multinational brands invade the markets in developing countries such as India. Vivek Burman, managing director of vast manufacturing complex Dabur India, is confident that "we can give any foreign brand a run for its money." To protect its dominance in the health tonic, hair oil, and digestive candy market, the company is doing everything possible to stress historic ties with traditional Indian medicine. In Burman's words, "We want to assert that foreign brands can be no more than pretenders to this position."[12]

Postmodern Consumption Research

An interesting event took place in the summer of 1986 that has now become known as the *consumer behavior odyssey.* A group of consumer researchers worked together over a period of several weeks traveling across America with the purpose of observing ordinary people as they buy and consume products and services in everyday life.[13] To our knowledge, this was the first application of ethnographic methods combined with more traditional methods on such a wide scale. The data output included 800 pages of field notes and journals, 137 videotapes, 12 audiotapes, and 4,000 photographs.[14]

The odyssey, more than any other factor, served to accelerate interest in postmodern consumer research. The emerging data on consumption can be organized into these categories: (1) sacred versus profane consumption, and (2) compulsive consumption.

Sacred versus Profane Consumption

It is important here to grasp exactly what postmodern researchers mean when they use the words *sacred* and *profane*. Belk, Wallendorf, and Sherry[15] put it this way:

> We take the sacred in the realm of consumption to refer to that which is regarded as more significant, powerful, and extraordinary than the self. The profane, by contrast, is ordinary and lacks the ability to induce ecstatic, self-transcending, and extraordinary experiences.[16]

8.2	**Consumer in Focus**

Consumption Becomes Sacred — Notes from the Odyssey

Sacralization may be accomplished in part by imposing one's own identity on possessions through transformations. The urge to change, customize, or just symbolically appropriate, as with photographs, appears to be strong, as illustrated in this comment by a woman who was renovating the house she shares with her husband and children:

> The first day that we were able to be here, which was just two minutes after settlement I guess, we ran in. My husband's stepfather came and photographed inside and outside, and [then we also took pictures of] stages of changes as we redid last summer. It's just fun to get those out and remember how, oh, it was awful.

The photographs are a remembrance of the time when this was a profane house. The celebration of such sacralizing transformation is common. A teen-aged male described his months-long work altering his first automobile to make it just the way he wanted it. He ritually cares for the finished car with twice-a-week baptismal washings and a once-a-week anointing with wax.

An elderly informant explained that she and her husband had spent much of their adult lifetimes fixing their home just the way they wanted it. They then purchased a second farm home that they renovated extensively, including putting in a lake. Furniture pieces made from walnut trees removed from the lake site were given to each of their three children as symbols of the transformation of the farm into a singularized home. "It was so much fun to do. Even though you didn't make them yourself, you felt like you were responsible for them."

Source: Russell W. Belk, Melanie Wallendorf, and John F. Sherry, Jr., "The Sacred and the Profane in Consumer Behavior: Theodicy on the Odyssey," Journal of Consumer Research 16 (June 1989), 14–15. Reproduced by special permission.

Their point is that consumption often has meanings that move far beyond the realm of everyday needs. The sacred dimension reflects transcendence of ordinary mundane existence. For an interesting discussion of sacred consumption, be certain to read Consumer in Focus 8.2.

Can you identify domains of sacred consumption in your life? Here are some clues:

- *Significant places,* especially in the home. What comes to mind first? For many, it will be the kitchen. This will come as no surprise to marketers. Consider these words from Cap Hendrix, executive vice president of Thermador, Inc., a maker of high-priced ranges: "The kitchen is the heart of the home. It's really about nurturing, and that is the woman's domain."[17] Also, products such as cognac can take their association with special times and intimate friendships (Figure 8.3).

Figure 8.3 Cognac—A Product that Becomes Sacred for Many

- *Tangible items.* It could be anything—a special piece of clothing, a treasured gift, a pet.

It is important to understand that marketers do not create this sacralization; it happens uniquely in the life of each of us through the following means: (1) ritual, (2) pilgrimage, (3) quintessence, and (4) collecting.

A *ritual* is a set of repetitive, expressive, symbolic behaviors that occur in fixed sequence.[18] Through rituals, possessions become transformed and imbedded with one's personal identity. Here are some of the ways in which this happens[19]:

- *Exchange.* The intent here is to pass something of yourself on to another person. The object then becomes transformed beyond its physical properties.

- *Possession.* Most of us will take pride in discussing, comparing, and showing off possessions. As this takes place, the item "becomes mine" and, in a sense, I take on its properties. CompuServe is well aware of the "sophisticated world citizen" qualities offered by the opportunity to communicate globally within a few seconds (Figure 8.4).

- *Times.* Holidays, sporting events, special meals.

- *Grooming.* Because goods are perishable in nature, meaning often must be renewed and recaptured on a repeated basis. Certainly, this is the explanation of the pampering of a car by a true fanatic.

- *Divestment.* Often, there is a great sorrow or sense of loss associated with the wearing out of a treasured item. It is not merely a matter of physical disposal, because there also must be an emotional divestment.

Pilgrimage is one common form of sacred consumption. Pilgrimage requires a journey to a consumption site where sacredness is experienced. Once this happens, the place can become a treasured shrine. Apparently, this explains the power of Graceland, the home of the late (?) Elvis Presley. It also explains why several of the team associated with this book love to return to Le-Bec-Fin Restaurant in Philadelphia. It is seldom that a meal can take on elements of the sacred, but we can give testimony that it happens.

Sacralization also takes place through *quintessence*, whereby the object is exactly what it should be—precisely right. Belk, Wallendorf, and Sherry[20] cited the examples of the Mont Blanc pen and the Swiss Army knife, each of which serves as a kind of *talisman with a soul of its own.* This may seem a little remote or strange, but most of us have treasured possessions that, for some reason or another, have precisely this quality, even though we cannot fully explain why it has taken place. Does this explain the near cult status of Godiva chocolate products (Figure 8.5)?

Collecting is yet another common consumption ritual. One of three Americans are collectors, and the "odyssey" sheds meaningful light on the commonplace

Figure 8.4   Join CompuServe and Become a World Citizen

consumer practice.[21] First, collections can become addictive and compulsive, even though the process seldom is begun purposely. Collections soon serve as part of one's extended self-concept, and this explains why profane to sacred conversions occur the moment an item is entered into the collection. The process often continues over a long period for the reason that continual acquisition gives a sense of power and progress. The paradoxical outcome is both a simultaneous desire for and fear of completing a collection.

Compulsive Consumption

For the first time, the field of consumer research is acknowledging that consumption behavior can take forms and directions that are decidedly counterproductive. The term **compulsive consumption** refers to those practices that,

Figure 8.5 Godiva—A Sacred Item?

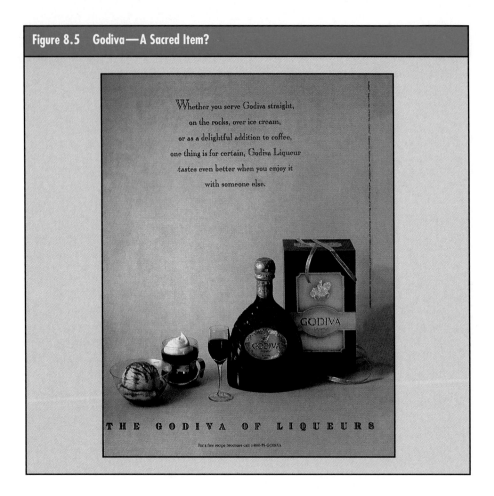

although undertaken to bolster self-esteem, are inappropriate, excessive, and disruptive to the lives of those who are involved.[22] The gratifications received usually are temporary, and common outcomes include profound guilt and helplessness.

Gambling is one common form of compulsive consumption, especially because lotteries are now available in nearly every locality. Evidence shows that heavy lottery players have less income but much higher levels of fantasy regarding outcomes than do light players. Much of the motivation centers around sensation seeking and risk taking.[23]

Shopping addiction is another form of compulsive consumption. The so-called shop-a-holic finds release in this behavior in much the same ways as alcoholics or drug addicts.[24] The unique element here, however, is that the addiction is to the *process of buying* and not the possession of the items. Shopping addicts often give testimony to the fact that the things purchased rarely serve any useful purpose.

Business as a whole has a mixed record when it comes to addressing these issues. The usual response is to ignore that such behavior takes place, although the alcoholic beverage industry is to be commended for its "drink, don't drive" campaigns. We wish that the same level of social responsibility could be exhibited by cigarette manufacturers, who deny the incontrovertible truth of decades of evidence and continue to encourage the dangerous practice of addictive smoking.

Post-consumption Alternative Evaluation

The process of alternative evaluation does not cease once the sale has been made and the product has been consumed, especially when involvement is high. Postpurchase alternative evaluations can take one of two forms — customer satisfaction or dissatisfaction (CS/D). The marketing literature today is flooded with research and commentary on this issue, far more than it was even a decade ago. There are several reasons for the priority placed on CS/D:

1. Emergence of customer retention as a dominant marketing objective in view of the formidable expense and difficulty of attracting new prospects

2. The undisputed fact that customer satisfaction is the key to customer retention

3. The central competitive role of product and service quality in forming the CS/D response

In our opinion, meeting the stringent demands of customer satisfaction is the greatest challenge facing marketers today.

Consumer Satisfaction/Dissatisfaction

Everyone enters into a purchase with certain expectations about what the product or service will do when it is used, and satisfaction is the hoped-for outcome. Satisfaction is defined here as a *post-consumption evaluation that a chosen alternative at least meets or exceeds expectations*. In short, it has done at least as well as you hoped it would. The opposite response is dissatisfaction.

The pressures of consumerism and growing public disdain for shoddy levels of quality have brought this subject to the forefront in consumer research in the past decade. The response, not surprisingly, has been an increasingly militant swell of customer outrage against seemingly calloused companies and the

| 8.3 | **Consumer in Focus** |

Simple Apology for Poor Service Is in Sorry State

I'm sorry to have to report that apologies have all but disappeared from America's commercial discourse.

In airports, hotels, restaurants, stores and offices across the country, consumers complain that even when service people make flagrant mistakes, they simply refuse to say they are sorry. In some cases, the expression of quick and sincere regrets could prevent a letter-writing campaign, an insurance claim or even a lawsuit.

"It's tragic that one of the fundamental human niceties has vanished," says Richard Whiteley, vice chairman of Forum Corp., a Boston service quality consultant. "Organizations are larger and moving faster, and people just don't have the time for that kind of personal interaction."

The near extinction of the basic apology is the result of several recent cultural changes, including the litigation explosion and a diminishing sense of personal responsibility for the mistakes made by other parts of a large company. If the accounting department made the mistake, the customer-service people might think, "I didn't make the mistake, why should I apologize?"

Growing time and productivity pressures also contribute to the decline of service civility. "With new technology, clerks are getting very good at processing," says Mr. Whiteley. "They process customers the way data, meat or cheese are processed."

Consumers must also take a share of the blame. As consumers have learned to be more alert to their rights, more people have bought into the notion that the squeakier the wheel, the better the grease. Saying "I'm sorry" to customers who retort, "You should be," also dissuades service people from apologizing.

Some companies say they don't encourage apologies because they fear that such expressions will be interpreted as false substitutes for corrective action. "'I'm sorry' might be creeping out of the vocabulary because it normally indicates that you're not really doing anything about the problem," says Colson Turner, vice president of customer service for New York Telephone Co.

Most customers understand that accidents happen, even the best-laid plans sometimes go awry, and no one's perfect. They say they are prepared to accept misfortune at the hands of a service provider if someone simply acknowledges that a wrong has been done. "We can all be soothed by someone saying they're sorry," says Letitia Baldrige, author of the *Complete Guide to the New Manners for the '90s.* "An apology is like mommy kissing your hurt finger."

Source: Cynthia Crossen, "Simple Apology for Poor Service Is in Sorry State," Wall Street Journal (November 29, 1990), B1 and B3.

individuals who represent them at point of sale. Take time to read Cynthia Crossen's penetrating analysis in Consumer in Focus 8.3.

Expectancy Disconfirmation Model

Richard Oliver[25] spearheaded research on this subject with his expectancy disconfirmation model. Briefly, this theory postulates that satisfaction or dissatisfaction is the outcome of a comparison of pre-purchase expectations against actual outcomes, and it has been consistently validated in empirical research.[26]

Consumers enter into a purchase with expectations of how the product will actually perform once it is used, and these fall into three categories:

1. *Equitable performance*[27]—a normative judgment reflecting the performance one ought to receive given the costs and efforts devoted to purchase and use

2. *Ideal performance*[28]—the optimum or hoped-for "ideal" performance level

3. *Expected performance*[29]—what the performance probably will be

Category 3, expected performance, is most often used by consumers in arriving at a CS/D judgment, because this is the logical outcome of the pre-purchase alternative evaluation process.

Once the product or service has been purchased and used, outcomes are compared against expectancies, and a judgment is made. Most researchers view this CS/D judgment as a subjective evaluation of the difference between expectancy and outcomes.

Others have shown that consumers make use of two basic criteria in arriving at this judgment. The first is an objective product-performance evaluation.[30] But consumers also experience differentiated emotions in the consumption experience as well as *affective* (pro/con) responses to the product as a whole and to its components.[31] Unless both the cognitive and affective elements are taken into account, the measurement process will be incomplete. We concur that both dimensions must be taken into account if the measurement process is to be valid.

The CS/D judgment takes one of three different forms:

- Positive disconfirmation—performance is better than expected.

- Simple confirmation—performance equals expectations.

- Negative disconfirmation—performance is worse than expected.

Positive disconfirmation leads to a response of satisfaction, and the opposite takes place when disconfirmation is negative. Simple confirmation implies a more neutral response that is neither extremely positive nor negative. The outcome directly affects repurchase intentions; the greater the positive disconfirmation, the better. Negative disconfirmation is the worst case outcome.

To take an example, a young executive jogger develops knee pain that is diagnosed as a result of improper foot movement (pronation) and stride. She is given the choice of six different shoes that will minimize the problem. She has tried each on and makes a selection, believing that the problem will be solved. Her beliefs with respect to the chosen brand represent the pre-purchase expectation, and it is positive. If actual running experience equals or exceeds that expectation, the outcome will be one of relative satisfaction. When this is not the case, there will be dissatisfaction.

High levels of satisfaction with a previously owned brand are often accompanied by some dissatisfaction after repurchase.[32] It appears that failure to exceed that high expectation can lead to mild dissatisfaction. At other times, however, those with poor prior experience are pleasantly surprised and indicate even higher levels of satisfaction than do their previously satisfied counterparts.[33]

Consumer Response to Dissatisfaction

How extensive is dissatisfaction? What do consumers do when it occurs? Are complainers different from those who do not complain? These questions have been thoroughly researched in recent years.

Complaints

Evidence over the years has demonstrated the frequency of dissatisfaction to range from about 20 percent to about 50 percent of buyers, depending on type of product, with an average of approximately one-third. Several studies have shown the main forms that dissatisfaction can take,[34] and a recent study by Singh[35] suggested three different categories:

1. Voice responses — seeking redress from the seller

2. Private responses — negative word-of-mouth communication

3. Third-party responses — taking legal action

These studies can be misleading, however, because they report only the complainers. There is solid evidence that the majority never complain or seek redress. In fact, Day and colleagues[36] have shown that only one-third do so and are more likely instead to boycott or to complain to others.

Dissatisfaction, in fact, often is a poor predictor of complaint behavior. Oliver[37] has shown that the percentage of complaints among the dissatisfied directed toward the retailer range from 23 to 40 percent, and only 5 percent complain directly to the manufacturer. In his research, only 15 percent of variance in complaint behavior is explained by the satisfaction/dissatisfaction dimension.

Two main determinants of complaint behavior are cultural values and personal attitudes surrounding this type of action.[38] Yet, LeClaire[39] found that Chinese will overcome the traditional values of social harmony, moderation, and face-saving and engage in complaints if they feel strongly aggrieved.

Here are additional factors that will affect whether a complaint will be made:[40]

- Significance of the consumption event—product importance, price, social visibility, and time required in consumption

- Knowledge and experience—number of previous purchases, product knowledge, perception of ability as a consumer, and previous complaining experience

- Difficulty of seeking redress—time, disruption of routine, and costs

- The perceived probability that complaining will lead to retribution or some other postivie outcome.[41] For example, they will readily complain when a warranty is offered.

Characteristics of Complainers

The type of person who complains and seeks redress tends to be younger, with higher-than-average income and education.[42] Also, they are positive about consumerist activities in general, prefer a lifestyle that demonstrates difference and individuality,[43] and experience little hesitancy in letting their problems be known.[44]

They do not keep these concerns to themselves. More than half share their experiences with friends and relatives, and evidence indicates that negative word of mouth can have a major influence on the buying behavior of others.[45]

Response to Complaints

What type of response can be expected when a complaint is registered? Overall, research studies indicate that 55 to 60 percent are resolved to the consumer's satisfaction.[46] In a recent study, for example, Cobb, Walgren, and Hollowed[47] found a 58 percent response rate to complaint letters. Most were in the form of a personal letter. The greatest response came from pizza and snack manufacturers, whereas only one-fourth of clothing firms replied.

There is sufficient convincing evidence to support the principle that making a sincere effort to rectify problems will noticeably increase consumer assurance that the firm really cares. Not surprisingly, satisfaction and intent to repurchase are strengthened in the process.[48]

Retaining the Customer

As we have stressed repeatedly, customer retention should receive even greater priority than new customer solicitation. First, it generally is less expensive to hold onto present customers than to attract new ones. Furthermore, customer loss can be disastrous in mature markets that are experiencing little real growth. Therefore, customer loyalty based on genuine and ongoing satisfaction is one of the greatest assets a firm can acquire. Here are some of the ways in which marketers can strengthen their customer relationship.

Make Individualized Marketing a Reality

As we have repeatedly stressed, business today must "downsize" in its approach to the consumer even to the point of creating a one-on-one touch through a data-base system. In this way, it is possible to meet customer needs and expectations in such a way that satisfaction will be optimized. This is precisely what the fast-food division of PepsiCo Inc., Pizza Hut, is doing through a system that contains electronic profiles of 9 million customers who have gotten deliveries of pizza.[49] As a result, "you can target the relevant message to the right customer," said marketing executive Robert Perkins.[50]

Institute a Total Quality Control Policy

The Strategic Planning Institute of Cambridge, Massachusetts, has analyzed the performance of nearly 2,600 businesses over 15 years using such criteria as market share, return on investment, and asset turnover. Referred to as Profit Impact of Market Strategy (PIMS), this research led to one incontrovertible conclusion: *Financial performance is tied directly to perceived quality of a company's goods and service.*[51]

Total quality control (TQC) is an operating philosophy that has its roots in the late 1970s when the Japanese took seriously the teachings of W. Edwards Deming on this crucial subject.[52] Deming called for a total commitment to excellence from top management exemplified by an effective system of quality circles (groups of employees regularly meeting to help solve problems), an employee suggestion system, wide use of statistical quality control principles, a goal of "zero defects," and constant training programs.

Toyota Motors is frequently cited as the premier example of a company that has built dominant market position by following the slogan of *kaizan — constant improvement.*[53] Taylor[54] pointed out that

> Extensive interviews with Toyota executives in the U.S. and Japan demonstrate the company's total dedication to continuous improvement. What is often mistaken for excessive modesty is, in fact, an expression of permanent dissatisfaction—even with exemplary performance. So the company is simultaneously restructuring its management, refining its already elegant manufacturing processes, planning its global strategy for the 21st century, tinkering with its corporate culture, and even becoming a fashion [automotive styling] leader.

There has been an unfortunate period of Japan bashing until recently, blaming the inroads of Japanese products into the American market on unfair trade practices. Most balanced commentators take quite an opposite viewpoint, however, and point with devastating accuracy to the extent to which Japan has beaten the United States at its own game. TQC is the reason this has happened. Fortunately, executives in most industries have recognized this point and are responding creatively.[55]

A commitment to quality, however, is no small undertaking. It all begins with top management, who must leave their offices, be close to the customer, and be accessible to operations in all phases. Employee turnover must be reduced, and incentives must be given for innovation and change.[56]

This can be both risky and costly, but competitive survival is at stake. All readers are painfully aware of widespread layoffs as one firm after another either goes out of business entirely or is totally restructuring in the hopes of regaining lost market position. But today's competitive world is forcing everyone to face these harsh realities.

Introduce an Early Warning Satisfaction Feedback System

By the time a customer shows up as a cancellation, it normally is too late for retention measures to do much good. What is needed, then, is an "early warning system" that indicates problems with sufficient lead time for corrective actions to be taken. Ongoing surveys of consumer satisfaction lie at the heart of this warning system.

Many companies monitor quality and performance using an internally based technical perspective but miss a basic point: Quality is meaningful only if monitored through the eyes of the consumer. A case in point is the financial services company that enforced a standard response time to consumer inquiries of 14 to 21 days only to find that 60 percent of customers expected seven-day responses.[57]

So here is the basic principle: Learn what the customer expects in quality and performance and monitor customer response continually. There are many ways that this can be done ranging from putting management on the road to focus groups and regular surveys. It is an excellent idea, in fact, to appoint and empower all salespeople to be relationship managers.[58] Consumer in Focus 8.4 shows you what can be learned through use of an ongoing competitive satisfaction scorecard.

Build Realistic Expectations

Remember that satisfaction is based on an assessment that pre-purchase expectations were fulfilled. Consider what might happen if a consumer purchased a cellular car telephone on the basis of its offer of "clearest reception in the entire metropolitan area," only to find some real geographic limits on its use. Even if all other brands have exactly the same problem, this company created an erroneous expectation through its promotion. Widespread dissatisfaction is altogether likely, and the blame lies with the advertising claim. The bottom line? Avoid exaggeration—the consumer might actually believe what you are saying and hold you accountable.

8.4	**Consumer in Focus**

Retailers Who Keep Score Know What Shoppers Value

Last Christmas season [1992], the busiest "busy" season in recent memory, the first National Shoppers Study was sponsored by Arena Systems, a manufacturer of software for retail point-of-sale systems.

Nine hundred shoppers were interviewed in 41 states immediately after they have finished shopping at a quality store (a broad cross-section of stores qualified). Their fresh specific reactions were obtained before time could blur the experience. Respondents rated 21 separate dimensions of shopping: from price to atmosphere, from how they were treated to how knowledgeable the store employees were. Six themes emerged:

1. Time appears to be the major factor that shapes reactions to shopping experiences. Three of the five most highly rated dimensions are related to time: the time it took to pay for purchases; the total amount of time spent in the store; and the amount of time needed to pay with a credit card.

2. Other efficiencies also proved to be very important. These included having enough open lanes and available cash registers; the quality of the signs in the store and the ease of finding things; the quality and informativeness of the receipt given to shoppers; and the knowledge of employees working at the store.

3. How shoppers are treated at the store also figures prominently in the evaluation. Are employees making an effort or going through the motions? Can shoppers get help when they need it?

4. Of course, price has major bearing on shoppers' ratings. To a great extent, shoppers preselect stores based on price image. In addition to prices themselves, price-related factors play a role: displays offering special prices and how clearly prices are marked on items.

5. The physical attributes of the store can also significantly raise or lower a store's evaluation. Atmosphere and roominess have a bearing on evaluation.

6. Shoppers' positive attitudes about what technology can do figure in a store's evaluation. Is the store using modern technology to the advantage of shoppers? Are the employees able to use the cash registers easily?

Source: Joe Peritz, "Retailers Who Keep Score Know What Their Shoppers Value," Marketing News (May 24, 1993), 9.

Provide Guarantees

"Quality comes first with us." This now is a common advertising message, but consumers often greet it with the bored response, "Oh yeah? Prove it!" Therefore, product guarantees are growing at "fever pitch." Although there is evidence that warranties and guarantees have greater effects on product evaluations for new brands,[59] all companies can benefit from creative use of this strategy.

Provide Information on Product Use

Product designers should be aware of the ways in which the product fits into a consumer's lifestyle. How is it used? It should be designed and promoted in such a way that performance will be adequate under conditions actually experienced in the home. For example, buyers often use electric toasters for English muffins, rolls, and other types of baked goods as well as for bread. If the toaster will not properly handle these items, unconfirmed expectancies and dissatisfaction are likely.

Solicit Customer Feedback

A customer feedback system is an absolute imperative. As we saw earlier, most who are dissatisfied will never complain or communicate directly with you. Consumer feedback must, first of all, be solicited. Such simple actions as providing ready access through an 800 phone number can make a real difference.

Equally important, feedback must reach all levels of management and serve as input for constant improvement. Someone within the enterprise, however, has to be responsible for hearing the consumer's voice with responsibility to hear complaints and cool down an irate customer. A Consumer Affairs Department must have clout, and this comes only if these stipulations are met:

1. A direct reporting line to top management,

2. Power to give redress on the spot and to take other forms of action necessary to remedy damages which might have been done, and

3. Access to all decision-making units within the company with top management-backed power to oversee changes to remedy deficiencies in quality and service.

The first step is to establish a guiding policy that all complaints are taken seriously. In the late 1980s, there was widespread public furor over the Audi 5000 model. There was a devastating exposé on the CBS "60 Minutes" program of an alleged problem with engine surge that was reported to have caused death and injuries. The consistent response of Audi management was that the car was not at fault. They claimed instead that the blame lay with the drive who hit the accelerator instead of the brake.

Although there was opinion and evidence to the contrary, management stuck to this position for a long period of time. Finally, a recall was ordered and a minor transmission modification was made. Unfortunately, public confidence in Audi plummeted, and the future of the Audi 5000 model was doomed. Later evidence exonerated the company, incidentally.

What was the problem here? It was a total disregard of customer relations. The greatest sin was passing the buck to the consumer. What did the company have to gain by stonewalling on this issue? Absolutely nothing! An immediate and apologetic recognition that something was seriously wrong accompanied by a recall might have headed off the outrage. The point, of course, is that widespread dissatisfaction can prove fatal.

We wish we could be optimistic that business will accept the counsel given here. Unfortunately, data provided by Fornell and Westbrook argue to the contrary.[60] After an extensive review of the way in which customer complaints are handled, they concluded that organizational willingness to listen and respond decreases as the numbers of complaints increase. We see few signs of real change. We have more to say about this distressing problem in Chapter 25.

Reinforce Customer Loyalty

Bergiel and Trosclair have demonstrated the benefits of a very simple application of instrumental learning theory.[61] They found that the loyalty of insurance customers could be reinforced by occasional reminders that their company still is interested in them. All it takes is a periodic letter affirming the commitment of both the company and the broker.

Divestment

The problem of product divestment after consumption has always been with us, but only recently has it emerged as a focus of serious research and marketing strategy largely because of serious environmental concerns. Broadly speaking, research can be divided into three major categories: (1) outright disposal; (2) recycling; and (3) remarketing.

Outright Disposal

As we have discovered, it is common to form real psychological bonds and ties with items which have come to assume the status of being *sacred*.[62] Yet, nothing can be designed to last forever, and the dimensions of sacred versus profane inevitably change as life scripts change.[63] Therefore, disposal in some form ultimately becomes a necessity.

When an object has become sacred, disposal often involves a ritual with varying degrees of formality. Many of us have treasured childhood possessions which currently are unused yet still are displayed prominently as icons of the past—teddy bears, Scouting awards, etc. Perhaps this is not disposal in a final sense, but it does represent a form of divestment.

Recycling

Recycling, of course, has become commonplace, especially as municipalities, counties, and other governmental units have made it mandatory in some areas.

When an option exists to comply or not comply, estimates of compliance range from as low as 25 percent to 90 percent or more. As a general rule, compliance varies inversely with age.

There has been remarkable growth in sales of used items even to the point where used cars often outsell their new counterparts on dealers' lots. This is an example of what we mean by **remarketing:**

Flea markets and garage sales are now a common occurrence in America. Several flea markets describe themselves as the "nation's largest." One such institution, found in Fort Lauderdale, Florida, reportedly brings 40,000–50,000 buyers to the market to purchase apparel, consumer electronics, and a wide array of other goods. Covering a huge area, this market has evolved in a pattern analogous to the emergence of department stores nearly a century ago.

Also, remarketing advertising media are commonplace including the classified section of newspapers, shoppers' newspapers, and computer bulletin boards. If current growth continues, such sources could quickly rival their traditional counterparts in terms of influence on buyer behavior.

Summary

This chapter examines the last three stages in the consumer decision process—(1) consumption, (2) post-purchase alternative evaluation, and (3) divestment. It was pointed out that interest in consumption (as opposed to the act of purchase) is relatively recent. It has been stimulated among marketers in large part by the everyday imperatives of *individualized marketing*. The need today is customer retention, and this requires intimate knowledge of how products are used, consumed, and disposed of.

The greatest contributor to consumption research, however, is the growing postmodern research thrust in the field of consumer research. Consumption rather than purchase is the primary variable, and research is undertaken to discover the meaning of consumption in everyday life. Much has been learned about how products take on special meaning and become sacred through rituals, pilgrimage, and other means.

Decision-process behavior does not cease once a purchase is consummated, however. Further evaluation takes place in the form of comparing product or service performance against expectations. The outcome is one of satisfaction or dissatisfaction. Satisfaction serves to reinforce buyer loyalty, whereas dissatisfaction can lead to complaints, negative word of mouth, and attempts to seek redress through legal means.

This means that customer retention becomes a crucial part of marketing strategy. We stress how this can be done through such tactics as creating realistic expectations, ensuring that product and service quality meet expectations, monitoring satisfaction and customer-retention levels, offering guarantees, and meeting dissatisfaction head-on by quick and appropriate response.

Review and Discussion Questions

1. You are the product manager for a line of kitchen utensils that include silverware, cutting knives, and aluminum cooking ware. Competition has become ruinous, and market share is diminishing. It has been suggested that your staff follow the lead of Black & Decker (Consumer in Focus 8.1) and spend extensive time studying actual in-home usage of these products. How would you suggest that this research be undertaken? What kinds of insights do you think could be gained?

2. Research has been completed that reveals the extent to which today's computers along with their "bells and whistles" have taken on certain dimensions of the *sacred*. This seems to happen through the rituals of *exchange* and *possession*. Why do you think that this happens? Does it have any implications for marketing strategy?

3. Some products become sacred through *quintessence*—that is, a particular item is so "precisely right" that it becomes a talisman. Once this happens, there is a special tie between object and consumer. Do you think that "building sacredness through quintessence" can be done successfully through marketing strategy?

4. Remarketing is a growing way to dispose of items that have fulfilled their purpose. What types of products do you think are the best candidates for remarketing? Which ones would be less suitable? Why do you say this?

5. The brand manager for a laundry detergent has read about the phenomenon of buyer regret and asks the company marketing research department to undertake a survey to see if this happens when laundry products are purchased. Do you feel that research would disclose widespread buyer regret when purchasing and using this product? Would your answer be different if the product is a compact disc stereo system featuring an all-new speaker system design? Why?

6. Review the situation facing Audi Motors after the disclosure of widespread problems with engine surge in Audi 5000 models with automatic transmission. What might have been done differently to meet this problem? Make a case to management justifying your conclusions.

7. What influences do advertising and selling efforts have in forming buyer expectations? What advice can you give to an advertising manager if you are asked to suggest ways in which promotional strategy could help increase buyer satisfaction?

8. "Come to White Fence Farm where we offer the world's best chicken." This claim has been heard for many years on Chicago radio. Would you recommend its continuation from the perspective of consumer satisfaction? What are the possible dangers?

9. You are asked to recommend ways of getting small portable appliance designers and engineers to take quality seriously from the consumer's perspective. What would you suggest?

10. A manufacturer of do-it-yourself lawn care items is interested in understanding what happens to former customers. The issue is what brands they are now using, and why. What kind of research would you undertake to answer this question?

Endnotes

1. Roger D. Blackwell, "Toward a General Theory of Remarketing: Macro and Micro Marketing Implications in an Age of Reconsumption" (unpublished working paper, May 17, 1993).

2. Jack W. Brehm and Arthur R. Cohen, *Explorations in Cognitive Dissonance* (New York: Wiley, 1962), 300.

3. The literature here is dated. For an excellent review and clarification see Michael S. Latour, "Buyer's Regret," unpublished paper, College of Business and Public Administration, Old Dominion University, 1992.

4. Ronald E. Milliman and Phillip J. Decker, "The Use of Post-Purchase Communication to Reduce Dissonance and Improve Direct Marketing Effectiveness," *Journal of Business Communication*, 27 (Spring 1990), 159–170.

5. Stan Rapp and Tom Collins, *The Great Marketing Turnaround—The Age of the Individual 1How to Profit from It* (Englewood Cliffs, N.J.: Prentice-Hall, 1990).

6. Russell W. Belk, "ACR Presidential Address: Happy Thought," in Melanie Wallendorf and Paul Anderson, eds., *Advances in Consumer Research* 14 (Provo, Utah: Association for Consumer Research, 1987), 1.

7. Christopher Power, "How to Get Closer to Your Customers," *Business Week* (Enterprise 1993 edition), 44.

8. Valerie Reitman, "P & G Uses Skills it Has Honed at Home to Introduce its Brands to the Russians," *Wall Street Journal* (April 14, 1993), B1.

9. Jan Larson, "Fiskars Adapts Its Scissors to Older Market," *American Demographics* (December 1992), 24.

10. Susan Krafft, "The Heart of the Home," *American Demographics,* (June 1992), 46–50.

11. Charles D. Schewe, "Get in Position for the Older Market," *American Demographics* (June 1990), 40.

12. Arunava Sinha and Shiv Taneja, "Fighting the Aliens," *Business Today* [India] (June 7–21, 1993), 61–62.

13. Many who participated in the odyssey have written self reflective reports. See, for example, Melanie Wallendorf, Russell Belk, and Deborah Heisley, "Deep Meaning in Possessions: The Paper," in Michael Houston, ed., *Advances in Consumer Research* 15 (Provo, Utah: Association for Consumer Research, 1988), 528–530; Morris B. Holbrook, "From the Log of a Consumer Researcher: Reflections on the Odyssey," in Wallendorf and Anderson, *Advances,* 365–369; and Harold H. Kassarjian, "How We Spent Our Summer Vacation: A Preliminary Report on the 1986 Consumer Behavior Odyssey," in Wallendorf and Anderson, *Advances,* 376–377.

14. John F. Sherry, Jr., "Postmodern Alternatives: The Interpretive Turn in Consumer Research," in Thomas S. Robertson and Harold H. Kassarjian, eds., *Handbook of Consumer Behavior* (Englewood Cliffs, N.J.: Prentice-Hall, 1991), 566.

15. Russell W. Belk, Melanie Wallendorf, and John F. Sherry, Jr., "The Sacred and the Profane in Consumer Behavior: Theodicy on the Odyssey," *Journal of Consumer Research* 16 (June 1989), 13.

16. Belk, Wallendorf and Sherry, "Theodicy on the Odyssey."

17. Krafft, "The Heart of the Home," 50.

18. Dennis W. Rook, "The Ritual Dimension of Consumer Behavior," *Journal of Consumer Research* 12 (December 1985), 252.

19. For more insight into the forms that rituals can take, see Grant McCracken, "Culture and Consumption: A Theoretical Account of the Structure and Movement of the Cultural Meaning of Consumer Goods," *Journal of Consumer Research* 13 (June 1986), 76–84.

20. Belk, Wallendorf, and Sherry, "Theodicy on the Odyssey."

21. Russell W. Belk, Melanie Wallendorf, John Sherry, Morris Holbrook, and Scot Roberts, "Collectors and Collecting," in Houston, *Advances*, 548–553.

22. Ronald J. Faber, Thomas C. O'Guinn, and Raymond Krych, "Compulsive Consumption," in Wallendorf and Anderson, *Advances*, 132–135.

23. Alvin C. Burns, Peter L. Gillett, Marc Rubinstein, and James W. Gentry, "An Exploratory Study of Lottery Playing, Gambling Addiction and Links to Compulsive Consumption," in Gerald A. Gorn and Richard W. Pollay, eds., *Advances in Consumer Research* 17 (Provo, Utah: Association for Consumer Research, 1990), 298–305.

24. Thomas C. O'Guinn and Ronald J. Faber, "Compulsive Buying: A Phenomenological Explanation," *Journal of Consumer Research* 16 (September 1989), 151–155.

25. The basic source is Richard L. Oliver, "A Cognitive Model of the Antecedents and Consequences of Satisfaction Decisions," *Journal of Marketing Research* 17 (November 1980), 460–469.

26. There have been many studies validating Oliver's theoretical model. One of the most recent is Ruth N. Bolton and James H. Drew, "A Multistage Model of Customers' Assessments of Service Quality and Value," *Journal of Consumer Research* 17 (March 1991), 375–384. For a thorough review of earlier evidence, see Richard L. Oliver and Wayne S. DeSarbo, "Response Determinants in Satisfaction Judgments," *Journal of Consumer Research* 14 (March 1988), 495–507; and David K. Tse and Peter C. Wilton, "Models of Consumer Satisfaction Formation: An Extension," *Journal of Marketing Research* 25 (May 1988), 204–212.

27. Robert B. Woodruff, Ernest R. Cadotte, and Roger L. Jenkins, "Modeling Consumer Satisfaction Using Experience-Based Norms," *Journal of Marketing Research* 20 (August 1983), 296–304.

28. Morris B. Holbrook, "Situation-Specific Ideal Points and Usage of Multiple Dissimilar Brands," in Jagdish N. Sheth, ed., *Research in Marketing* 7 (Greenwich, Conn.: JAI Press, 1984), 93–112.

29. M. Leichty and Gilbert A. Churchill, Jr., "Conceptual Insights into Consumer Satisfaction with Services," in Neil Beckwith et al., eds., *Educators' Conference Proceedings* (Chicago: American Marketing Association, 1979), 509–515.

30. Gilbert A. Churchill, Jr., and Carol Suprenant, "An Investigation into the Determinants of Customer Satisfaction," *Journal of Marketing Research* 19 (November 1983), 491–504. Also Peter C. Wilton and David K. Tse, "A Model of Consumer Response to Communication and Product Experiences," in Larry Percy and Arch G. Woodside, eds., *Advertising and Consumer Psychology* (Lexington, Mass.: Lexington Books, 1983), 315–332.

31. See Lalita A. Manrai and Meryl P. Gardner, "The Influence of Affect on Attributions for Product Failure," in Holman and Solomon, *Advances,* 249–254; Laurette Dube and Bernd H. Schmitt, "The Processing of Emotional and Cognitive Aspects of Product Usage in Satisfaction Judgments," in Holman and Solomon, *Advances,* 52–56; and Laurette Dube-Rioux, "The Power of Affective Reports in Predicting Satisfaction Judgments," in Goldberg, Gorn, and Pollay, *Advances,* 571–576.

32. Robert A. Westbrook and Joseph W. Newman, "An Analysis of Shopper Dissatisfaction for Major Household Appliances," *Journal of Marketing Research* 15 (August 1978), 456–466.

33. Stephen A. LaTour and Nancy C. Peat, "The Role of Situationally Produced Expectations, Others' Experiences, and Prior Experience in Determining Consumer Satisfaction," in Jerry C. Olson, ed., *Advances in Consumer Research* 7 (Ann Arbor: Association for Consumer Research, 1980), 588–592.

34. See, for example, Steven Brown and Richard F. Baltramini, "Consumer Complaining and Word of Mouth Activities: Field Evidence," in Thomas K. Srull, ed., *Advances in Consumer Research* 16 (Provo, Utah: Association for Consumer Research, 1989), 9–16.

35. Jagdip Singh, "Consumer Complaint Intentions and Behavior: Definition and Taxonomical Issues," *Journal of Marketing* 52 (January 1988), 93–107.

36. Ralph L. Day, Klaus Brabicke, Thomas Schaetzle, and Fritz Staubach, "The Hidden Agenda of Consumer Complaining," *Journal of Retailing* 57 (Fall 1981), 86–106.

37. Richard L. Oliver, "An Investigation of the Interrelationship between Consumer Dissatisfaction and Complaint Reports," in Wallendorf and Anderson, *Advances* 14, 218–222.

38. Ralph L. Day, "Modeling Choices among Alternative Responses to Dissatisfaction," in Thomas C. Kinnear, ed., *Advances in Consumer Research* 11 (Provo, Utah: Association for Consumer Research, 1984), 496–499.

39. Kenneth LeClaire, "Chinese Complaints Behavior," *Journal of International Consumer Marketing* 5.4 (1993), 73–92.

40. Day, "Modeling Choices."

41. Diane Halstead and Cornelia Droge, "Consumer Attitudes Toward Complaining and the Prediction of Multiple Complaint Responses," in Holman and Solomon, *Advances,* 210–216; Stephen P. Brown and Richard F. Baltramini, "Consumer

Complaining and Word of Mouth Activities: Field Evidence," in Srull, *Advances*, 9–16; and George John and John R. Nevin, "The Role of Information Uncertainty, Disconfirmation and Disclosure Regulations as Determinants of Consumer Satisfaction and Complaint Behavior," in Terrance L. Shimp, ed., 1986 *Educators' Proceedings* (Chicago: American Marketing Association, 1986), 68–73.

42. Michelle N. Morganowsky and Hilda Mayer Buckley, "Complaint Behavior: Analysis by Demographics, Lifestyle, Consumer Values," in Wallendorf and Anderson, *Advances*, 223–226.

43. Kathy J. Cobb, Gary C. Walgren, and Mary Hollowed, "Differences in Organizational Responses to Consumer Letters of Satisfaction and Dissatisfaction," in Wallendorf and Anderson, *Advances*, 227.

44. Marcia L. Richins, "An Investigation of Consumers' Attitudes towards Complaining," in Andrew Mitchell, ed., *Advances in Consumer Research* 9 (Ann Arbor: Association for Consumer Research, 1982), 502–506.

45. Brown and Baltramini, "Consumer Complaining and Word of Mouth Activities."

46. Cynthia J. Grimm, "Understanding and Reaching the Consumer: A Summary of Recent Research. Part II—Complaint Response Satisfaction and Market Impact," *Mobius* (Fall 1987), 18.

47. Cobb, Walgren, and Hollowed, "Differences in Organizational Responses."

48. Denise T. Smart and Charles L. Martin, "Manufacturer Responsiveness to Consumer Correspondence: An Empirical Investigation of Consumer Perceptions," *Journal of Consumer Affairs* 26 (Summer 1991), 104–128.

49. Power, "How to Get Closer to Your Customers," 44.

50. Power, "How to Get Closer to Your Customers," 56.

51. John R. Hauser and Robert L. Klein, "Without Good Research, Quality Is a Shot in Dark," *Marketing News* (January 4, 1988), 1–2.

52. For a valuable summary of Deming's methods, see Mary Walton, *The Deming Management Method* (New York: Dodd, Mead, & Company, 1986).

53. Lex Taylor III, "Why Toyota Keeps Getting Better and Better and Better," *Fortune* (November 19, 1990), 66.

54. Taylor, "Why Toyota Keeps Getting Better," 67.

55. See, for example, Frank Rose, "Now Quality Means Service Too," *Fortune* (April 22, 1991), 98–110; and Gilbert Fuchsberg, "Gurus of Quality Are Gaining Clout," *Wall Street Journal* (November 27, 1990), B1.

56. See Patricia Sellers, "What Customers Really Want," *Fortune* (June 4, 1990), 58–66.

57. William Band, "Performance Metrics Keep Customer Satisfaction Programs on Track" *Marketing News* (May 28, 1990), 12.

58. Lawrence A. Crosby, Kenneth R. Evans, and Deborah Cowles, "Relationship Quality in Services Selling: An Interpersonal Influence Perspective," *Journal of Marketing* 54 (July 1990), 68–81.

59. Daniel E. Innis and H. Rao Unnava, "The Usefulness of Product Warranties for Reputable and New Brands," in Holman and Solomon, *Advances,* 317–322.

60. Claes Fornell and Robert A. Westbrook, "The Vicious Cycle of Consumer Complaints," *Journal of Marketing* 48 (Summer 1984), 68–78.

61. Blaise Bergiel and Christine Trosclair, "Instrumental Learning: Its Application to Consumer Satisfaction," *Journal of Consumer Marketing* 2 (Fall 1985), 23–28.

62. Belk, Wallendorf, and Sherry, "Theodicy on the Odyssey."

63. Melissa Martin Young, "Disposition of Possessions During Role Transitions," in Rebecca H. Holman and Michael R. Solomon, eds., *Advances in Consumer Research* 18 (Provo, Utah: Association for Consumer Research, 1991), 33–39.

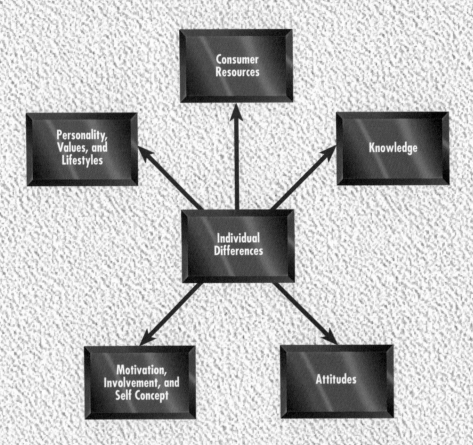

PART III

Individual Differences

▲▲▲

No two people are created the same. Certainly this is the case in consumer behavior. Which individual differences, however, are most crucial based on research and marketing experience? What are the implications for strategy? These are the issues covered in Part III.

We begin in Chapter 9 with a discussion of differences among individuals in terms of the *resources* they bring to purchase and consumption decisions. A person with an income of $95,000 will have substantially different responses as compared with someone who barely scrapes by on $20,000. But this is only one example of what we mean by resources because you will discover that consumers also differ in such critical resources as *time* and *information processing capacity.*

Individuals also differ in other fundamental ways. Chapter 10 focuses on *knowledge* and *awareness.* Chapter 11 introduces you to the important subject of consumer *attitudes* and the effects on behavior. Chapter 12 explores the always fascinating subject of *motivation* and *self concept.*

The final section of Part III, Chapter 13, deals with *personality, values,* and *lifestyle.* Lifestyle is an important summary concept which finds widespread use in consumer research. As you will discover, lifestyles are the patterns of living that are the outcomes of many other variables and influences—especially motivation and personality. You will find the discussion here to be both interesting and of practical significance in marketing strategy.

CHAPTER 9

Consumer Resources

▲▲▲▲▲▲▲▲▲▲▲▲▲▲▲▲▲▲▲▲▲▲▲▲▲▲▲▲▲▲▲▲▲▲▲▲▲▲▲

Colleges Join the Hunt for Affluent Consumers

When the first few colleges started calling, David Alpern was flattered. "This is great, people want me to come," thought the 17-year-old high school senior in the affluent Los Angeles suburb of La Canada. The thrill was short-lived. Once Mr. Alpern heard that his classmates were getting the same treatment from tuition-hungry schools, "the meaning kind of lessened," he said. "Colleges are trying to get as many people as they can. All they care about are the numbers."

Freshman enrollment has dropped in recent years, and the dismal statistics have made many colleges increasingly aggressive about seeking students who can pay full or close to full tuition. The expression *a student of value* used to mean a valedictorian, student body president, or varsity athlete. Now, the phrase means a student who can pay.

To find students who can pay, a growing number of schools are relying on **geodemographics** — information culled from census data, mailing lists, and even product warranties to target students living in well-off neighborhoods, who get bombarded with school literature and personal telephone calls. DePauw University in Greencastle, Indiana, breaks out three top socioeconomic categories that the school's marketers use to profile potential students. One is the "young suburbia" bracket. The other two are "blue-blood estates" and "furs-and-station wagons." Should colleges admit students based on their ability to pay tuition? For more and more financially strapped colleges these days, the answer is a reluctant "yes."

Summarized from Sarah Lurman, "A 'Student of Value' Means a Student Who Can Pay the Rising Cost of College," Wall Street Journal (January 5, 1994), B1; and Sarah Lurman, "The Tradition of Need—Blind Admissions Is Starting to Die," Wall Street Journal (January 5, 1994), B1.

Willie Sutton, the infamous bank robber, said, "I go where the money is . . . and I go there often." So do marketers, whether the product is cars, clothing, or the colleges described in the opening scenario. Knowledge, attitudes, personality—these are all determinants of individual purchase decisions including whether to "buy" a college education, but certainly no individual characteristic affects purchasing any more than the amount of resources that individual has.

Explaining why purchase outcomes vary between individuals usually involves analysis of groups of consumers—the segmentation process you studied in Chapter 2. In Chapters 2 and 3, our focus was on population trends—the number of people in domestic and global markets. The search for growing market segments must also analyze ability. Who has high income to spend on consumer products and services? Which segments are growing the fastest? What products and services do these segments value most? Where, when, and how do they buy?

Focusing on these micromarketing questions does not negate the macro issues or the social importance of studying people in poverty. That social issue is similar to the ethical and social dilemma posed in the opening scenario. For marketers, however, reality lies in the truism that it is easier to sell to people with money than to people without money.

| 9.1 | **Consumer in Focus** |

Consumers' Resources Buy Beauty

Of the 40 percent of American women who color their hair, almost half do it themselves, generating a $500 million market. During a recession, however, women become more cautious with their discretionary income. Those who used to rely on professionals turn to home products. If not exclusively, at least as maintenance between less frequent salon visits.

As companies strive to keep their edge on the competition, favorite products are continually reevaluated and improved in the areas of shade selection, application ease, smell, and conditioning effect on the hair. At the same time, the industry is coming up with innovative new products that infiltrate traditional salon territory at a fraction of the cost. One recent introduction that goes directly after the salon dollar is L'Oreal's Color Weaving kit, which provides both highlights and low lights for the kind of dimensional color previously available only from a professional. At a retail cost of about $10, the kit offers a realistic alternative to the salon where prices for comparable services range from $40 to $350 for a top colorist.

Economic factors aside, the most obvious reason for at-home coloring's popularity is convenience. "We're aware that time is a women's most precious commodity." says Karen Freeman, assistant vice president of marketing at L'Oreal. "So our at-home products are designed to give quick, easy, and consistent results in 40 minutes, compared with salon services, which can take up to three hours." For women who don't have time to eat lunch, much less schedule—and keep—an appointment with a salon, the at-home option simply makes a whole lot of sense.

Source: Excerpts from L. J. Kavanaugh, "The Business Side of Beauty," Working Woman (January 1992), 72.

Resources can be of many types. In Consumer in Focus 9.1, as you read about the "business side of beauty" you will see that consumers are concerned about time as well as money, because buying beauty requires both. In this chapter, key resources of consumers are analyzed in the categories of (1) economic, (2) temporal, and (3) cognitive (ability to process and use information).

Economic Resources

"Money is what I need" echo the lyrics of a popular song. Credit cards also suffice. No other variable is as important in understanding what people buy as money. "Money is what I should study" could well be the theme song of every student of consumer behavior. Nearly every marketing research survey includes income as one of the key variables in explaining consumer behavior.

In an earlier era, barter—the trading of goods for goods—was common. Barter is still important in less-developed societies and to a degree in the underground economies of all societies. There exists a substantial "informal economy" in which people barter or purchase goods and services in ways that may escape record keeping and taxation. The "heavy users" of the informal economy are affluent, well educated, and comparatively young.[1]

Consumption is an important recent concern in the study of consumer behavior, as we indicated in Chapter 1, and was among the first variables to be analyzed in the study of consumer behavior, as early as 1672. The first studies with a reasonable statistical basis were published by Ernest Engel in 1857. The relationships between income and expenditures became popularized as Engel's Laws of Consumption. They contained propositions about the relationship between family income and the proportion spent on categories such as food, clothing, lodging, and "sundries" (education, health, recreation, and so forth).[2] Over time, basic expenditures change, depending on economic development of the country or income of individual families (Figure 9.1). Since the early part of this century, the proportion of budgets spent on food and clothing has dropped dramatically, leaving money for upgraded housing and for the broad category of "other," similar to Engel's "sundries." It is this latter category that makes marketing dynamic and understanding consumers challenging. Less-developed countries of the world generally have a pattern of consumer expenditures more like the left side of Figure 9.1.

Measuring Economic Resources

Marketing involves exchange of economic resources, but measuring economic resources is complex. The objective is to define variables that mean the same for everyone and that permit comparisons over time or across market segments. Marketing organizations usually develop their own definitions of income to use in questionnaires. Questions need to be simple to understand by respondents

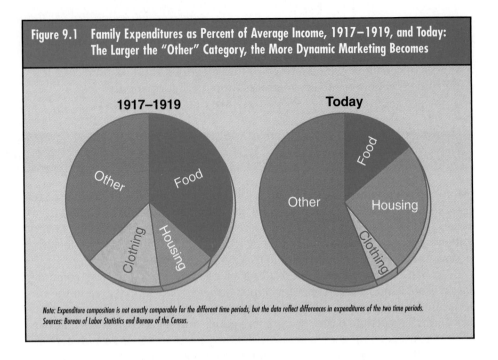

Figure 9.1   Family Expenditures as Percent of Average Income, 1917–1919, and Today: The Larger the "Other" Category, the More Dynamic Marketing Becomes

Note: Expenditure composition is not exactly comparable for the different time periods, but the data reflect differences in expenditures of the two time periods.
Sources: Bureau of Labor Statistics and Bureau of the Census.

but precise enough to provide reliable and valid data for analysis. They need to be close enough to standard definitions to be compared with census data or reference surveys by governmental agencies.

Income

The Census Bureau defines income as money from wages and salaries as well as interest and welfare payments. The latter two are often underreported. Official measures of income do not include other kinds of compensation such as employer or government benefits. Attempts to estimate the cash values of these benefits are difficult and raise consumer income substantially. Yet the failure to include them underreports changes in income in recent years. Similarly, if workers receive contractual rights to pensions in the future, no income is reported until such pensions are received, causing current income to be understated. The Census Bureau tries to equalize the rental value of a home to its owner by inputting a value to income for the home but ignores the mortgage tax subsidy that homeowners receive compared with renters. Changes in size of families, a rising number of nonfamily households, changing tax laws, and other variables create problems that consumer researchers should consider when analyzing data based on income measures.[3]

Gross Domestic Product and Gross National Product

Consumer analysts, the media, and government policy makers need a single, easily understood measure of the economic condition of the nation. Since 1941, the Commerce Department has published the **gross national product (GNP)**, a measure of total goods and services produced or provided by the U.S. economy, valued at market prices. It measures the nation's economic health and, when reported as per capita GNP, the economic health of consumers. Since 1992, however, the **gross domestic product (GDP)** has been used more often. GDP includes goods and services produced by foreign companies operating in the United States. GNP did not include these goods and services but did include goods and services produced by U.S. residents and corporations in other countries. GDP is a more accurate gauge of what a nation's economy is actually doing. Production of Ford of Europe as a wholly owned subsidiary, for example, was included in GNP but is excluded in GDP. Honda in the United States is part of GDP. Gross state product (GSP) reflects the same concept as GDP at a state level.

Consumer Confidence

Consumers drive the economy, accounting for more than two-thirds of all economic activity in economies such as the United States and Canada. Consumption is heavily influenced by what consumers believe will happen in the future. Current income is the primary determinant of products such as food at home, but consumer confidence about future income is essential in understanding purchases of automobiles, major appliances, and other durable goods. Consumer confidence is a main factor influencing whether consumers will increase their debt levels or defer spending to pay off debt.

Measures of consumer confidence are important to marketers making decisions such as inventory levels, staffing, or promotional budgets. During late summer, for example, retailers closely examine consumer confidence about future economic conditions to place inventory orders for the holiday selling season. The months of November and December account for more than half the sales or profits of many types of retailers. If inventories are too low, sales will be missed. If inventories are too high, price cuts may be needed so early in the season and so deep that few profits will be realized. Thus, consumer confidence is an important variable in the marketing decisions of retailers, their suppliers, and the entire economy.

Two organizations are well known for their surveys of consumer confidence. The Conference Board survey of 5,000 households is conducted by mail and asks respondents to look 6 months ahead and focuses on the availability of jobs. The University of Michigan survey, which tends to be less volatile, questions 500 households a month by telephone about such things as family finances and overall business conditions. The types of questions asked in these two surveys are displayed in Figure 9.2.

Whose Income?

Consumer behavior focuses on individuals, yet economic resources are often shared with others, in families or households. Consumer surveys usually ask entirely about individual behavior, except in the demographic section, where

Figure 9.2 Two Measures of Consumer Confidence

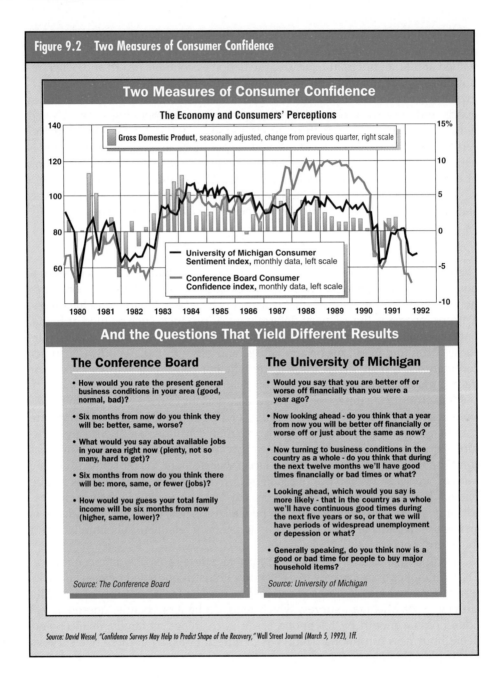

Two Measures of Consumer Confidence

The Economy and Consumers' Perceptions

Gross Domestic Product, seasonally adjusted, change from previous quarter, right scale

University of Michigan Consumer Sentiment index, monthly data, left scale

Conference Board Consumer Confidence index, monthly data, left scale

And the Questions That Yield Different Results

The Conference Board

• How would you rate the present general business conditions in your area (good, normal, bad)?

• Six months from now do you think they will be: better, same, worse?

• What would you say about available jobs in your area right now (plenty, not so many, hard to get)?

• Six months from now do you think there will be: more, same, or fewer (jobs)?

• How would you guess your total family income will be six months from now (higher, same, lower)?

Source: The Conference Board

The University of Michigan

• Would you say that you are better off or worse off financially than you were a year ago?

• Now looking ahead - do you think that a year from now you will be better off financially or worse off or just about the same as now?

• Now turning to business conditions in the country as a whole - do you think that during the next twelve months we'll have good times financially or bad times or what?

• Looking ahead, which would you say is more likely - that in the country as a whole we'll have continuous good times during the next five years or so, or that we will have periods of widespread unemployment or depession or what?

• Generally speaking, do you think now is a good or bad time for people to buy major household items?

Source: University of Michigan

Source: David Wessel, "Confidence Surveys May Help to Predict Shape of the Recovery," Wall Street Journal (March 5, 1992), 1ff.

resource questions usually ask for family or household income. When conducting marketing research, you may need to adjust family or household data by the number of members to determine per capita income.

Where Is the Income?

Where would you go to find consumers who have the income to buy your product? The answers might be based on geography, age, household size, occupation, racial or ethnic characteristics, or other variables. The primary source for data on income, savings, and wealth is the *Survey of Current Business* published by the Bureau of Economic Analysis (BEA) and the *Current Population Survey (CPS)* published by the Bureau of the Census.

A frequently used basis for targeting income segments is geographic area. Suburban areas or certain metropolitan counties contain consumers with high incomes. Table 9.1 shows the variation that exists between states. The Bureau of Economic Analysis reports that although average per capital personal income for Americans was $13,245 in a recent year, substantial variation exists. Income in the richest state, Connecticut, was more than twice that of the poorest state, Mississippi. Furthermore, even though the growth rate is expected to be slower in the future, Connecticut is still projected to be the best market target in the year 2000, based on per capita personal income. You can examine the trends for other states in Table 9.1. Private data services sell similar data with current estimates for specific areas such as nine-digit zip codes.

Identifying Market Potential

Total consumption or market potential may be identified by analyzing income and its allocation to product category by demographic segments. This type of information is shown in Table 9.2 (pages 302 and 303) and reveals that expenditures vary greatly by variables that may be useful in defining market segments. Although numbers change some from year to year, the relationships between spending and other variables are fairly stabile.

Who Has Buying Power?

It is much easier to hit a bull's-eye when you can see the target. That is why marketers place so much emphasis on knowing who has the buying power and how they are spending their money.

You may have questioned why so much attention in marketing is concentrated on husband and wife consuming units rather than single households or why marketers seem to emphasize consumers aged 45 to 54 years so heavily. Examination of Table 9.2 quickly reveals the answer. Consuming units with the reference person aged 45 to 54 years average several thousand more dollars income to spend and save. Analysis of age segments shows that the 45- to 54-year age group spends almost the same on food at home as the 35- to 44-year age group but considerably more for food away from home, as well as somewhat more for alcoholic beverages, apparel, and some other categories. The younger group, however, spends more on housing. Consumers older than 65 years spend considerably more on health care.

Table 9.1 Per Capita Personal Income Projected to 2000

Region, Division, and State	Personal Income Per Capita		Average Annual Change (%)	
	1988	2000	1979–1988	1988–2000
United States	**$13,245**	**$15,345**	**1.53**	**1.23**
Northeast	**15,432**	**17,635**	**2.69**	**1.12**
New England	**16,205**	**18,154**	**3.41**	**0.95**
Maine	12,126	14,014	2.87	1.21
New Hampshire	15,449	17,363	3.69	0.98
Vermont	12,305	14,193	2.38	1.20
Massachusetts	16,736	18,694	3.69	0.93
Rhode Island	13,540	15,555	2.54	1.16
Connecticut	18,500	20,503	3.39	0.86
Middle Atlantic	**13,738**	**15,904**	**1.54**	**1.23**
New York	15,470	17,852	2.58	1.20
New Jersey	17,780	19,932	3.42	0.96
Pennsylvania	13,028	15,173	1.39	1.28
Midwest	**12,840**	**14,938**	**0.92**	**1.27**
East North Central	**13,042**	**15,098**	**0.93**	**1.23**
Ohio	12,486	14,531	0.96	1.27
Indiana	11,937	14,031	0.80	1.36
Illinois	14,126	16,131	1.01	1.11
Michigan	13,288	15,361	0.91	1.22
Wisconsin	12,490	14,575	0.82	1.29
West North Central	**12,362**	**14,562**	**0.89**	**1.37**
Minnesota	13,378	15,508	1.41	1.24
Iowa	11,777	13,849	0.14	1.36
Missouri	12,414	14,592	1.33	1.36
North Dakota	10,255	12,461	−0.49	1.64
South Dakota	10,244	12,330	−0.07	1.56
Nebraska	11,882	14,322	0.54	1.57
Kansas	12,645	14,986	0.70	1.43
South	**11,885**	**13,975**	**1.57**	**1.36**
South Atlantic	**12,927**	**15,009**	**2.27**	**1.25**
Delaware	14,217	15,747	2.14	0.86
Maryland	15,727	17,665	2.72	0.97
District of Columbia	17,149	19,823	1.88	1.21
Virginia	14,189	16,345	2.72	1.19
West Virginia	9,393	10,921	0.19	1.26
North Carolina	11,481	13,481	2.33	1.35
South Carolina	10,372	12,304	1.83	1.43
Georgia	12,262	14,297	2.60	1.29
Florida	13,340	15,496	2.01	1.26
East South Central	**10,340**	**12,272**	**1.39**	**1.44**
Kentucky	10,304	12,178	0.97	1.40
Tennessee	11,138	13,192	1.84	1.42
Alabama	10,318	12,247	1.49	1.44
Mississippi	8,936	10,631	0.91	1.46
West South Central	**11,122**	**13,206**	**0.41**	**1.44**
Arkansas	9,812	11,594	1.11	1.40
Louisiana	9,876	11,680	0.08	1.41
Oklahoma	10,700	12,937	0.00	1.59
Texas	11,716	13,851	0.41	1.41
West	**13,811**	**15,844**	**1.02**	**1.15**
Mountain	**11,694**	**13,698**	**0.73**	**1.33**
Montana	10,364	12,474	−0.06	1.56
Idaho	10,119	12,181	0.14	1.56
Wyoming	10,956	12,898	−1.93	1.37
Colorado	13,220	15,311	1.00	1.23
New Mexico	10,037	11,949	0.57	1.46
Arizona	12,029	13,926	1.38	1.23
Utah	9,791	11,605	0.37	1.43
Nevada	14,076	15,855	0.55	1.00
Pacific	**14,566**	**16,607**	**1.10**	**1.10**
Washington	13,228	15,316	0.56	1.23
Oregon	11,953	13,908	0.21	1.27
California	15,070	17,113	1.26	1.06
Alaska	15,302	16,765	−0.56	0.76
Hawaii	13,449	15,219	1.13	1.04

Source: Bureau of Economic Analysis, Survey of Current Business, May 1990.

Life cycle effects are readily observable in Table 9.2. Husband and wife consumer units with older children have more income than other families. Single persons and single parent consuming units spend dramatically lower amounts on most items although relatively less on housing. Expenditures are higher than income among single parent consumers, indicating the distressed economic situation of this market segment.

Relationships between income and spending are revealed most readily by examining expenditures by quintiles of income. Notice in Table 9.2 the dramatic differences in income between the lowest quintile and the highest quintile. For some products such as food at home, the differences are relatively minor. The top 20 percent spend nearly five times as much as the lowest quintile, however, for food away from home. The top quintile spend more than five times as much as the lowest 20 percent does for apparel and seven times as much for vehicle purchases. You can easily understand why marketers place so much emphasis on the "up market."

Targeting the Up Market

The up market, generally defined as the upper quintile or quartile of income, is likely to be dual-income households and time constrained (especially when children are present) and emphasizes quality in the product preferences. This segment is a particularly important target for products such as men's wear, furniture, electronic and home entertainment, home furnishings, tableware, domestics, fine jewelry and tools, hardware, and building materials.[4] For many luxury goods, the up market accounts for well over half of all sales. The highest end of the up market is sometimes described as "super affluents," defined as income levels greater than $50,000, $75,000, or even more than $100,000.

High quality and good service dominate the purchase decisions of the up market. Department stores such as Nordstrom and Dillard's have grown rapidly by excelling in service to upscale consumers. Specialty stores are also primary beneficiaries of the purchasing power of the up market but so are some discount stores, such as factory outlet stores that provide high-quality goods at value prices. The importance of service in many businesses was the theme in an influential book by Albrecht and Zemke, *Service America.*[5] Lawn maintenance, beauty salons, and many other rapidly growing service industries derive most of their growth from the service-oriented up market.

Communicating to the up market is more print-oriented than to other market segments. Readership of local weekday and Sunday newspapers is higher. So is readership of many magazines, creating effectiveness for ads such as those shown in Figure 9.3 (page 304). Notice the ad for Mont Blanc, which assumes that its up-market target will understand copy in German, Spanish, and English. The Godiva ad uses phrases such as "far-too-civilized" and "imaginative coatings" to communicate with an up-market target willing to pay $25 per pound for chocolate truffles. The up market watches television less and listens to radio less than other segments, although up-market consumers have a higher concentration subscribing to cable television and listening to public television and radio.

Line No.	Characteristic	Income before Taxes[1]	Total Expenditures	Food, Total	Food at Home Total[2]	Cereal, Bakery Products	Meats, Poultry, Fish, Eggs	Dairy Products	Fruits and Vegetables	Food away from Home	Alcoholic Beverages
1	All consumer units	33,901	29,614	4,271	2,651	404	709	294	429	1,620	297
	Age of reference person:										
2	Under 25 years old	14,319	16,745	2,528	1,410	225	356	154	177	1,118	252
3	25 to 34 years old	34,032	29,280	4,272	2,529	382	662	301	389	1,742	370
4	35 to 44 years old	41,871	36,446	5,405	3,324	522	879	369	527	2,080	354
5	45 to 54 years old	48,413	38,137	5,184	3,147	462	889	333	496	2,037	360
6	55 to 64 years old	38,285	31,945	4,217	2,639	381	729	286	430	1,578	260
7	65 to 74 years old	22,723	22,564	3,466	2,364	370	611	251	439	1,102	217
8	75 years old and over	16,247	15,782	2,548	1,864	301	485	213	359	684	81
	Region of residence:										
9	Northeast	36,953	31,026	4,506	2,673	435	764	302	446	1,833	355
10	Midwest	31,535	27,675	3,977	2,456	392	601	281	380	1,522	261
11	South	31,706	28,062	4,091	2,589	376	743	274	408	1,502	250
12	West	37,167	33,131	4,695	2,974	436	730	335	509	1,721	358
	Size of consumer unit:										
13	One person	18,057	17,569	2,283	1,267	197	311	145	217	1,015	262
14	Two or more persons	40,119	34,234	5,032	3,180	484	861	351	510	1,852	310
15	Two persons	36,955	30,648	4,184	2,541	369	673	273	442	1,643	349
16	Three persons	40,124	34,389	4,897	2,999	465	835	323	458	1,898	273
17	Four persons	46,196	38,806	5,869	3,754	563	1,038	419	581	2,115	302
18	Five or more persons	40,965	38,269	6,583	4,552	739	1,209	530	696	2,031	264
	Single consumers:										
19	No earner	10,327	12,744	1,880	1,383	224	355	169	250	497	80
20	One earner	22,746	20,499	2,517	1,202	182	285	131	196	1,315	367
	Consumer units of two or more persons:										
21	No earner	18,556	19,529	3,546	2,718	412	774	282	477	827	180
22	One earner	31,661	29,407	4,397	2,959	453	805	332	490	1,438	249
23	Two earners	46,013	37,581	5,235	3,134	477	823	348	500	2,101	353
24	Three or more earners	56,122	45,513	6,799	4,130	624	1,164	454	612	2,668	389
	Husband and wife consumer units:										
25	Total	44,460	37,134	5,376	3,353	514	887	372	546	2,023	318
26	Husband and wife only	40,579	32,937	4,447	2,686	389	698	286	482	1,760	350
	Husband and wife with children:										
27	Oldest child under 6	43,046	36,075	4,610	3,030	456	740	380	478	1,580	295
28	Oldest child 6 to 17	47,983	40,839	6,241	3,877	636	999	449	599	2,364	247
29	Oldest child 18 or over	49,638	41,798	6,631	3,984	608	1,158	409	589	2,647	342
30	One parent, at least one child under 18	20,302	21,653	3,641	2,588	399	761	283	362	1,053	134
31	Single person and other	21,255	20,092	2,762	1,636	246	440	182	269	1,126	292
	Occupation of reference person:										
32	Self employed workers	42,939	36,072	5,044	3,011	450	743	333	534	2,033	363
	Wage and salary earners:										
33	Managers and professionals	53,812	42,802	5,446	2,986	456	730	333	500	2,459	437
34	Technical, sales, and clerical	36,388	31,383	4,440	2,579	410	672	288	405	1,861	327
35	Service workers	22,908	23,205	3,822	2,546	360	796	261	385	1,277	246
36	Construction workers/mechanics	35,872	29,925	4,401	2,838	424	797	312	420	1,563	290
37	Operators, fabricators, and laborers	30,249	26,455	4,126	2,653	407	729	308	388	1,474	284
38	Retired	18,614	19,284	3,043	2,194	345	588	240	389	849	163
	Income before taxes:										
39	Complete reporters of income[1]	33,901	30,487	4,367	2,725	414	725	307	438	1,642	314
	Quintiles of income:										
40	Lowest 20 percent	5,981	13,464	2,343	1,726	257	502	194	279	617	127
41	Second 20 percent	14,821	18,986	3,306	2,303	344	652	256	374	1,003	190
42	Third 20 percent	26,073	26,144	3,945	2,577	391	690	284	411	1,368	306
43	Fourth 20 percent	40,868	36,151	5,199	3,140	480	801	358	500	2,058	371
44	Highest 20 percent	81,594	57,597	7,033	3,875	597	980	440	624	3,159	575
45	Incomplete reporting of income	(¹)	24,903	3,880	2,347	366	642	242	395	1,533	225

[1] Income values derived from "complete income reporters" only. Represents[1] the combined income of all consumer unit members 14 years old and over during the 12 months preceding the interview. A complete reporter is a consumer unit providing values for at least one of the major sources of income. [2] Includes items not shown separately.

Table 9.2 Average Annual Income and Expenditures of U.S. Consumer Units, Continued

| Total | Housing | | | | Apparel and Services | Transportation | | | Health Care | Personal Insurance and Pensions | Other Expenditures[5] | Personal Taxes |
	Shelter	Fuel, Utilities, Public Services	Household Operations, Furnishings[3]	Housekeeping Supplies		Vehicle Purchases	Gasoline, Motor Oil	All Other Transportation[4]				
9,252	5,191	1,990	1,648	424	1,735	2,111	995	2,045	1,554	2,787	4,567	3,172
4,886	3,059	983	666	178	1,201	1,916	711	1,241	360	967	2,682	799
9,888	5,944	1,799	1,773	370	1,722	2,196	1,013	1,967	1,030	2,903	3,919	3,169
11,335	6,621	2,208	1,998	507	2,347	2,682	1,197	2,425	1,487	3,811	5,403	4,288
11,208	6,239	2,493	1,988	488	2,245	2,553	1,316	2,836	1,727	4,317	6,391	4,585
9,457	4,901	2,247	1,810	499	1,622	2,215	1,048	2,262	1,846	3,462	5,555	3,884
6,849	3,328	1,920	1,172	430	1,270	1,535	758	1,612	2,300	1,033	3,521	1,384
5,871	2,834	1,586	1,136	315	638	528	385	852	2,197	268	2,413	1,634
10,341	6,262	2,105	1,576	396	1,877	1,812	884	2,159	1,504	2,883	4,705	3,767
8,289	4,307	1,950	1,605	428	1,641	2,162	988	1,920	1,482	2,582	4,371	2,411
8,303	4,339	2,031	1,540	392	1,683	2,333	1,035	1,871	1,669	2,621	4,207	2,817
10,895	6,592	1,853	1,951	499	1,792	1,990	1,053	2,364	1,506	3,215	5,261	4,044
6,143	3,847	1,246	831	219	980	971	499	1,152	1,014	1,233	3,032	1,739
10,446	5,707	2,275	1,961	502	2,024	2,549	1,186	2,387	1,761	3,383	5,156	3,734
9,253	4,989	2,044	1,744	477	1,596	2,491	1,002	2,208	1,862	3,018	4,682	3,848
10,600	5,890	2,279	1,966	465	2,150	2,432	1,208	2,392	1,759	3,385	5,291	3,428
12,176	6,701	2,502	2,416	556	2,356	2,572	1,393	2,735	1,705	4,157	5,541	4,451
11,343	6,173	2,640	1,972	557	2,624	2,871	1,409	2,423	1,546	3,397	5,809	2,908
4,936	2,784	1,279	658	216	561	409	281	632	1,457	107	2,401	380
6,881	4,502	1,225	932	221	1,226	1,318	633	1,473	741	1,927	3,415	2,563
6,476	3,062	1,872	1,136	406	1,094	1,191	606	1,290	2,096	310	2,741	1,398
9,598	5,156	2,196	1,788	459	1,788	2,344	1,008	1,827	1,668	2,398	4,129	2,609
11,430	6,434	2,256	2,224	515	2,142	2,866	1,279	2,651	1,670	4,319	5,636	4,637
12,385	6,750	2,855	2,164	616	2,903	3,117	1,742	3,568	1,945	4,963	7,700	4,988
11,173	6,060	2,377	2,190	546	2,117	2,777	1,288	2,609	1,963	3,858	5,657	4,301
9,746	5,120	2,157	1,941	527	1,644	2,641	1,066	2,380	2,131	3,397	5,136	4,480
12,937	7,281	2,104	3,093	458	2,222	2,537	1,180	2,252	1,614	3,892	4,537	3,921
12,510	7,021	2,482	2,444	564	2,452	2,918	1,396	2,705	1,733	4,472	6,166	4,537
11,035	5,837	2,763	1,792	643	2,580	2,930	1,682	3,280	2,252	4,107	6,961	3,974
7,788	4,458	1,781	1,216	333	1,763	1,232	646	1,243	779	1,380	3,047	1,418
6,733	4,068	1,469	937	258	1,177	1,301	633	1,366	1,095	1,483	3,252	1,868
10,933	6,139	2,411	1,863	520	2,007	2,413	1,132	2,380	2,121	4,077	5,601	3,596
13,355	7,925	2,303	2,580	548	2,612	3,220	1,187	2,967	1,659	5,101	6,818	6,025
9,826	5,727	1,961	1,706	433	1,916	2,292	1,066	2,270	1,321	3,155	4,773	3,463
7,543	4,168	1,734	1,303	337	1,589	1,014	874	1,558	1,267	1,794	3,499	1,591
8,851	4,997	1,972	1,501	381	1,385	2,538	1,317	2,071	1,285	3,087	4,699	3,197
7,597	4,108	1,867	1,265	357	1,452	2,274	1,209	1,955	1,175	2,531	3,850	2,453
6,309	3,026	1,753	1,167	363	959	1,152	604	1,310	2,096	522	3,126	1,379
9,325	5,208	1,961	1,704	451	1,801	2,154	998	2,084	1,563	3,142	4,740	3,172
4,905	2,741	1,291	639	235	813	670	471	754	1,041	296	2,044	333
6,178	3,343	1,652	860	324	1,112	1,209	721	1,266	1,371	907	2,729	513
7,975	4,405	1,893	1,288	388	1,443	1,960	1,011	1,850	1,580	2,224	3,851	2,099
10,644	5,917	2,171	2,026	530	2,103	2,961	1,271	2,607	1,672	3,999	5,326	3,632
16,898	9,621	2,795	3,704	779	3,530	3,963	1,514	3,933	2,149	8,265	9,738	9,263
8,939	5,087	2,162	1,380	310	1,451	1,851	978	1,832	1,503	642	3,602	(¹)

[3]Includes household equipment. [4]Includes other vehicle expenses and public transportation. [5]Includes entertainment, personal care, reading, education, tobacco smoking supplies, cash contributions, and miscellaneous expenditures.

Figure 9.3   Ads Targeted to the Up Market

Source: Courtesy of Mont Blanc; Godiva.

What will consumer analysts primarily be studying in the future? At least half their time will be spent in understanding what the affluent want to buy. The reason for this provocative statement is that the wealthiest 20 percent of U.S. families now command 50 percent of after-tax family income. Thus, assuming this trend continues, at least half the activity of consumer analysts will have to be spent studying the affluent. Perhaps more than half because the spending behavior of the poor is much more predictable and the financial rewards for serving the affluent, despite the difficulty of doing so, are so much greater.

The trend toward affluence is very important in understanding market opportunities in industrialized countries. Table 9.3 displays the dramatic shift in income that occurred during the past decade in the United States. Inequality grew sharply, with most of the increase in median family income concentrated in the top quintile. Most of the gains arose from the entry of wives as second earners rather than from changes in incomes of established workers. Such changes create enormous changes in consumption and opportunities for people who understand the changes. Food preparation shifted from homes to restaurants and microwaves and even to "personal chefs" who come to the home

Table 9.3	Average After-Tax Family Income		
Income Category	Annual Household Incomes (after-tax, in 1990 dollars)		
	1980	1990	% Change
Richest 1%	$213,675	$399,697	87.1
Richest 5%	100,331	151,132	50.6
Richest fifth	58,886	78,032	32.5
Next richest fifth	32,075	34,824	8.6
Middle fifth	24,031	24,691	2.7
Next poorest fifth	16,088	16,123	0.2
Poorest fifth	7,357	6,973	−5.2

Source: U.S. Center on Budget & Policy Priorities.

weekly and prepare customized menus for affluent consumers. Booming markets for child care and home cleaning created opportunities for entrepreneurs and "nanny gate" problems for politicians.

In Canada, caution characterizes many affluent (and other) consumers because of inflation, decreased purchasing power, unemployment, and slower economic growth. The latter part of the 1980s saw improvement in these trends, leading to more willingness to buy and optimism about markets of the future, but concern exists about Canadian retailing due to the goods and services tax (GST), prompting many affluent (and other) Canadian consumers to go south of the border for shopping.

Targeted Affluents

Selling to super affluents involves upscale products and retailers as well as high levels of service. Even the dream of becoming a "millionaire" is more attainable for many Americans, and most make their millions themselves rather than inheriting it. Typically, the super affluent are entrepreneurs who own their own businesses. Many are physicians, dentists, or consultants. The average age is 57 years, and most are likely to live in California, New York, Texas, or Illinois. Millionaires are often considered to be the market for yachts, Rolls-Royces, and so forth, but, in fact, these products are more likely to be purchased by corporations. Millionaires do not spend their fortunes on luxury goods; they are more likely to have a Sears credit card than American Express, Neiman-Marcus, Saks Fifth Avenue, or Lord & Taylor cards. They buy few home furnishings and appliances (because they already have them), but they do spend large amounts on services, travel, and college tuitions.[6] Consumer in Focus 9.2 shows how Steiff sells toys to an intermarket affluent segment globally.

| 9.2 | **Consumer in Focus** |

Targeting the Affluent Market

A 1928 stuffed bear—a teddy bear—sold at a recent London auction for $86,000. It was a Steiff.

Known for their exquisite design, meticulous manufacturing, and rich materials, antique Steiff toys typically fetch around $5,000 at auction. The German company, founded in 1880, is the world's oldest toy maker. For the past 30 years, Steiff toys, distinguished by a *knopf im ohr,* "button in ear," have been distributed in the U.S. through an importer. Recently Steiff formed a wholly owned subsidiary to build visibility in the discriminating marketplace to ensure Steiff's legendary craftsmanship is not lost in a sea of plastic Ninja Turtles.

With prices as high as $295 for a black bear and $345 for a teddy bear, Steiff says it is catering to a "knowledgeable, sophisticated, above-average-income consumer." When asked if Steiff might be considered the Mercedes-Benz of the toy market, the managing director replies, "No. With all respect to the fatherland, we are the Rolls-Royce of toys."

Source: Excerpts from Michael Konik, "Menagerie Marketing," Profiles (June 1992), 9.

Macroeconomic effects of social policies targeted toward the affluent provide important concerns for consumer analysis. The Omnibus Budget Reconciliation Act of 1993 increased the highest marginal tax rates from 31 percent to 39.6 percent. Many consumers offset the tax increase by reducing spending, saving, and investment, generally undesirable social effects. When an Atlanta attorney found his tax bill increased by $16,000, he decided to postpone investment in the construction of a new restaurant. As a result, workers are not needed to build the restaurant nor are new jobs created for restaurant personnel.[7] The intended $27 billion collected from a "soak-the-rich" policy might seem a desirable way to reduce the national deficit but also has potentially greater negative effects by creating unemployment or recession. It is the task of consumer analysts to understand these related effects.

Targeting the Down Market

Throughout the world, the great majority of consumers are low income. In Canada, Europe, the United States, and other industrialized countries, most customers are middle income, but even in these countries, the numbers of consumers in the "down market" are substantial. But even stores that appeal to the down market need to be attractive and stylish and treat people with respect. Sanford Goodkin explained, "Nobody wants to be reminded that they are not rich. Successful discounters have made their mark by convincing customers that they are smart and special, not poor riffraff."[8]

Value-oriented retailers have experienced rapid growth—and enormous enhanced shareholder value (ESV)—by providing good products at reasonable prices to the down market as well as higher-income segments. The key is service that is reliable and respectful to consumers even though it is a basic, no-frills approach. McDonald's has used this recipe for success throughout the world. Wal-Mart became the largest retailer in the United States (and has entered Mexico) with two basic themes. One theme, "Every Day Low Price," might naively be thought to be most important, but its other theme, "Treat Every Customer as a Guest," is more important in understanding the success of Wal-Mart. A policy of treating customers with respect is also more difficult to understand and duplicate by competitors.

Firms that treat the down market with respect and good service also attract some of the up market and much of the mass market. An example is All For One, a division of Consolidated Stores, shown in Figure 9.4. This chain buys "close-outs" from manufacturers or other retailers that have excess inventories or are in financial difficulty. It sells brand name merchandise for one price, currently a dollar. There have always been stores such as this, but the difference between All For One and many of its competitors is that the stores are light and bright, very clean and attractive, are planned for logistical efficiency, provide good service, and are sometimes located in shopping centers

Figure 9.4   All For One: Designed for Value Shoppers

willing to rent at low prices because of excess space. And because the inventory is ever-changing, consumers find different products to keep the enthusiasm alive.

Another firm that targets the down market but attracts other segments is Aldi, a grocery store chain with low prices, basic levels of product selection, and appeal to the economical shopper. This privately held German firm is believed to be the largest grocery retailer in the world, with stores in many countries, including the United States. The typical Aldi store avoids computers, scanners, service desks, or other items that add costs and slow handling of merchandise, although it typically pays 40 to 50 percent higher wages than other supermarkets to avoid turnover in personnel. Aldi does not usually have listings in telephone directories to keep costs low enough to achieve the prices shown in its newspaper advertisement in Figure 9.5. Aldi (as well as Wal-Mart, Food Lion, and other firms) uses an every day low price (EDLP) policy rather than a high–low price policy, in which some advertised prices are very low and used as "loss leaders" to attract people to other prod-ucts that are priced high. Supermarkets such as Byerly's in Minneapolis and Stew Leonard's in Connecticut appeal to affluent consumer segments with wide selections of premium produce, bakery goods, meats, and other prod-ucts displayed on the "perimeter" of the store and sold with many special services. Aldi's, in contrast, locates in rural or low-income areas, emphasizes core food items usually with only one (often a store) brand, charges for bags, accepts no credit cards or coupons, and provides an absolute minimum of service. Both firms are highly successful— with strategies appropriate to their target markets.

As consumer resources change through economic cycles, responsive marketers can profit even from economic adversity. During a recession, good marketers focus on attributes that provide value for customers at the lowest price. Well-financed firms can expand market share by maintaining advertising when competitors are forced to lower their promotional activities. Well-financed firms may be able to demand better terms from vendors or for retailing space, further benefiting from recessionary economic conditions. During a recession, Campbell Soup Co. observed consumers shifting from higher-priced foods such as ready-to-serve soups toward cheaper cook-at-home products. Campbell took cream of broccoli soup out of a higher-end Gold Label can, cut the price, and packed it in the familiar red-and-white can, promoted as a base for homemade meals. It sold more than 55 million cans and became the most successful new soup since 1935. Campbell also scored big by packing favorite soups in family-size, 26-ounce cans, permitting a cut in unit price.[9]

Back-to-the-basics marketing is the key to reaching down-market consumers, including the 40 percent of U.S. households that earn less than $25,000. They are likely to be young or old and single or divorced. The poorest Americans spend heavily on education, prescription drugs, and tobacco. They are heavy users of products such as malt liquor, pancake syrup, whole milk, and laxatives. They are light users of dishwasher detergent, white wine, Diet Pepsi, skimmed milk, and Grey Poupon mustard.[10]

Figure 9.5   Aldi's Appeals to Economical Shoppers

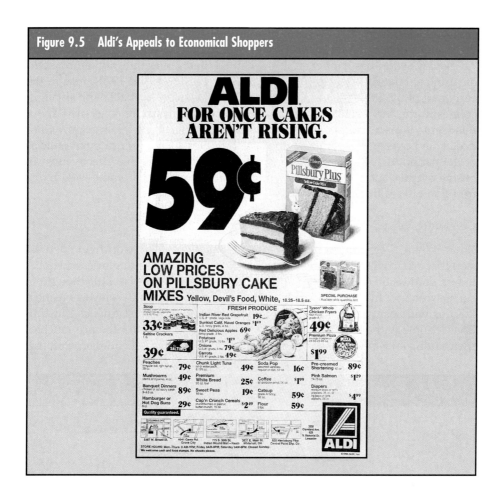

Poverty

The field of consumer behavior is also concerned about the consumption of "nonmarkets"—people such as the homeless and other disadvantaged consumers who have needs but few economic resources. If the number of impoverished people in a society is increasing, it is difficult to market "as usual" to those who still have money for two reasons. First, the attitudes of people with money will be affected negatively, probably leading to increased frugality in buying decisions and decreased willingness to take on debt for durable goods. Second, if the number of impoverished people is increasing, increased demand for services causes rises in crime, government services, and other variables that lead to higher tax rates and decreased consumption among the general consumer market.

Furthermore, even the impoverished buy many basic products and services. Many retailers operate profitably by accepting food stamps, offering realistic credit policies, using high-security procedures, and in other ways adapting to the realities of serving the poor. What is the trend concerning poverty? Figure 9.6 displays what has happened in the United States over time and among ethnic groups. Poverty decreased substantially in the 1960s and 1970s, rose in the early part of the 1980s, decreasing to less than 13 percent by 1990, with small increases in the early part of the 1990s. Consumer analysts are concerned about this segment for reasons beyond its attractiveness as a market. Future growth or decline in poverty will be determined by variables such as educational policies of the nation, value systems of consumers, global competitive effectiveness of business firms, and the degree to which economic policies promote wealth distribution or wealth creation.

Consumer Behavior in a Depression

What if there were to be a major depression, similar to the worldwide depression that occurred in the years following 1929? Some marketing researchers believe a depression could occur,[11] although most researchers give little thought to such a scenario. In the event of a severe depression, Cornish[12] believes business failures will soar. Cash will be king because people distrust financial institutions. People will decide it is smart to be thrifty, which will influence much of their saving and spending behavior. Born-again savers will mend their clothing,

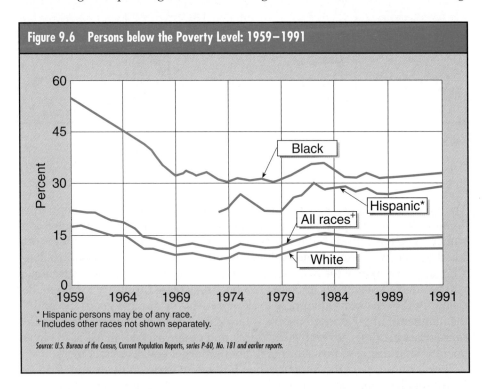

Figure 9.6 Persons below the Poverty Level: 1959–1991

* Hispanic persons may be of any race.
+ Includes other races not shown separately.

Source: U.S. Bureau of the Census, Current Population Reports, series P-60, No. 181 and earlier reports.

grow their own vegetables, and repair products instead of buying new ones. Buying things secondhand will become more popular. Sales of "big ticket" goods such as cars and services will drop faster than those of less-expensive items, dramatically reducing the standard of living of both the rich and the poor, but the rich will be better able to maintain their usual lifestyles.

Other Economic Resources

Other economic resources besides income affect consumer behavior. The most important are wealth (net worth) and credit.

Wealth, measured by assets or net worth, is correlated with income. The government and private research organizations collect many statistics on income but relatively few about assets or net worth. Thus, it is more difficult to target consumers based on wealth. The primary variation is that older consumers tend to have a larger proportion of wealth than younger consumers. The primary asset of most Americans is their home—about 60 percent of total assets but only 9 percent of the assets of households with a net worth of more than $1 million. Millionaires are more likely to have their assets in stocks, bonds, and certificates of deposit. Although homes may appreciate, they are not readily available as a source of cash unless marketers can show consumers how to obtain a secondary mortgage. In today's environment, such loans may be tax advantages.

Wealthy families spend their money on services, travel, interest, and investments more than do their less wealthy neighbors. Their expenditures on home furnishings, appliances, entertainment equipment, and similar products are not particularly high because wealthy families are usually in later stages of the life cycle and not concerned with furnishing new homes or making additional purchases of major equipment. They are an important market target for services because they place a premium on time. Improved customer service, immediate availability, trouble-free operation of products, and dependable maintenance and repair services are highly valued. They are willing to pay the price for services that assure product performance and limit inconvenience. They are also the market target for products and services to enhance the physical self, especially to maintain and restore youthfulness: cosmetics, skin care products, health foods, vitamins, cosmetic surgery, spas, hair stylists, clothing consultants, exercise facilities, and diet and health programs. They are attractive targets for products and services that secure and protect individuals and property: sensing devices, home protection systems, security guards, protected residential areas, insurance of various kinds, fire and burglar protection, financial security plans, air and water purifiers, and sanitation products. They are also major supporters of the arts and community organizations.

Targeting wealthy consumers is difficult. Usually marketers use income as a proxy for wealth. Government data are available from the Federal Reserve Board's Survey of Consumer Finances or the Census Bureau's Survey of Income and Program Participation. Donnelley Marketing Information Services of

Stamford, Connecticut, keeps a master file of 82 million households that can be used to predict the overall affluence of a household. The annual Disposabl e Income and Net Worth Report from CACI of Fairfax, Virginia, shows how to find households with a high net worth by looking at the age of the householders, income distributions, and other factors.[13]

Credit extends the income resource, at least for a period of time. Actually, because the cost of credit must be subtracted from the consumer's total resource availability, credit reduces the ability to buy goods and services in the long run. Nevertheless, Americans are increasingly willing to use credit for temporary expansion of their economic resources. Americans are most willing to borrow for cars, for medical bills, or for educational reasons. Younger households and those with higher incomes are more willing to borrow, no matter what the reason.[14]

Consumers' use of credit has an effect on the economic condition of a nation as well as specific expenditures. The 1980s in America was a boom time of consumer spending, stimulated by tax cuts and baby boomers setting up households but facilitated by credit. In 1980, total household debt was equal to about 70 percent of total household income, but by 1990, household debt approached 90 percent of household income. The need to pay off this debt, as well as declining values in commercial and residential real estate caused by overbuilding during the 1980s, means that consumer spending is much slower in the 1990s than the previous decade.[15]

Time and Change in Spending

Time and change will surely prove how firm a foundation is found in spending patterns. Knowing how consumers spend their money is basic to making major macroeconomic policy decisions, as well as to understanding the microeconomic implications of marketing opportunities for individual firms.

There is a close relationship between consumption and economic variables, such as employment. The Office of Technology Assessment (OTA) of the U.S. government projects personal consumption expenditures in the year 2005, based on demographic, economic, lifestyle, and technological variables.[16]

Early in the history of this country, Americans grew their own food. As manufacturing developed to reflect spending and production in the country, a specialized agricultural industry developed in which most of the nation derived employment from either farming or manufacturing. Today, employment is much less derived from growing food and much more concentrated in its processing and serving. The OTA study shows, for example, that the number of scientists, lawyers, and computer professionals involved in supplying Americans with food is roughly equal to the number of farmers. In other areas, services that were once purchased, such as movies, are now provided at home through videocassette recorders. At the same time, services that once were provided at home such as child care, cooking, and cleaning are now purchased. Shifting such services from unpaid categories to measured production of goods and services accounts for much of the increase in GDP in recent years.

Environmental Scanning

Marketing organizations need systematic and timely information about the environment as it currently exists as well as projections of trends. This activity is called environmental scanning and involves information internal to the organization, such as the cognitive maps used by executives in making decisions, as well as external variables relating to the present or projected resources of consumers. When precise projections are not possible, many organizations use scenario development to compare alternative futures and how these alternative scenarios affect planning. Some large corporations place such responsibility with staff departments, usually in marketing research or strategic planning. Research indicates, however, that environmental scanning is most effective when it is done by line managers who must also take responsibility for the decisions to be made with the scanning output.[17]

Other effects of economic resources on consumer buying could be analyzed. We'll stop the discussion of economic resources now, however, and examine one of the other major resources that facilitate and shape consumer decisions.

Temporal Resources

Consumer resources consist of two budget constraints: money budget and time budget. Income and wealth are critical variables, as we just read, but to understand consumer behavior fully, marketers must also examine how consumers spend their time budgets.[18] Although high incomes might allow some segments to buy more of everything, they cannot conceivably do more of everything. Doing more things requires an additional resource: time. Whereas money budgets have no theoretical expansion limits, time has an ultimate restraint. It is a zero-sum game. Scarcity creates value. For affluent consumers, the chief concern becomes buying more time rather than more products.

Many consumers value leisure time as highly as they value money because of their increasing lack of time. The most time-crunched Americans are women, parents, and minorities. Almost half of American workers say they would give up a day's pay to get an extra day off.[19] Are you one of these time-crunched consumers? Table 9.4 shows questions used to measure time crunch. **Timestyles** refers to how consumers allocate time among various activities.

Consumer time budgets traditionally were naively regarded as having two components: work and leisure. This conceptualization is shown in the upper portion of Figure 9.7. A more contemporary conceptualization is shown in the lower portion. Here, consumer time budgets are divided into three blocks: "paid time," "obligated time," and "discretionary time." Lane and Lindquist[20] used a similar classification system including income-producing time, committed (obligated and nonobligated) time, and uncommitted (planned and unplanned) time. It is only the latter block of discretionary or uncommitted time that can be

Table 9.4 Are You Time-Crunched?	
If you agree with more than three statements on the list below, consider yourself time-crunched.	
	Americans Who Agree with Selected Statements (%)
1. I often feel under stress when I don't have enough time	43
2. When I need more time, I tend to cut back on my sleep	40
3. At the end of the day, I often feel that I haven't accomplished what I set out to do	33
4. I worry that I don't spend enough time with my family or friends	33
5. I feel that I'm constantly under stress—trying to accomplish more than I can handle	31
6. I feel trapped in a daily routine	28
7. When I'm working long hours, I often feel guilty that I'm not at home	27
8. I consider myself a workaholic	26
9. I just don't have time for fun anymore	22
10. Sometimes I feel that my spouse doesn't know who I am anymore	21

Source: John P. Robinson, "Your Money or Your Time," American Demographics 13 (November 1991).

truly regarded as leisure time. Voss[21] concluded, "Leisure is a period of time referred to as discretionary time. It is that period when an individual feels no sense of economic, legal, moral, or social compulsion or obligation, nor of physiological necessity. The choice of how to utilize this time period belongs solely to the individual." Products and services classified by their time properties may be called time goods, and the time properties of goods have important marketing implications. Activities are known as *substitutes* if each can satisfy the same need and *complements* if they are engaged in jointly to satisfy a broader need.

An additional complication in defining leisure occurs when individuals are paid for activities they might otherwise choose as discretionary activities. Artists, professors, and professional athletes may be examples of individuals who are fortunate to be paid for activities they would otherwise choose as leisure activities. Perhaps students might even view reading textbooks such as this one as leisure rather than obligated or paid activities! Then again, perhaps they might not.

Time budgets are similar to money budgets in the sense they are influenced by other persons in the household or family, referred to as the dyadic nature of time use for married individuals. For husbands and wives, *divergent* timestyles are dominated by *individual* activities, whereas timestyles dominated by com-

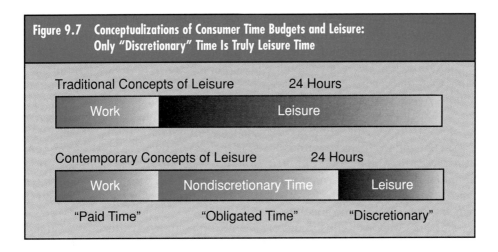

Figure 9.7 Conceptualizations of Consumer Time Budgets and Leisure: Only "Discretionary" Time Is Truly Leisure Time

Traditional Concepts of Leisure   24 Hours

| Work | Leisure |

Contemporary Concepts of Leisure   24 Hours

| Work | Nondiscretionary Time | Leisure |

"Paid Time"   "Obligated Time"   "Discretionary"

mon activities are *convergent*. Anderson, Golden, Umesh, and Weeks[22] found that employment outside the home affects the wife's activity mix much more than it affects her husband's.

Time-Using Goods

Some products and services require the use of time with the product. Examples would be watching television, skiing, fishing, golfing, or playing tennis, all of which are usually classified as leisure-time activities. They fall in the category of time budgets called "discretionary time" or leisure.

Will consumers buy products that require the use of time? The answer depends on their time usage in a typical 24-hour day. Paid time or work, for example, usually increases as people earn more income. This may be caused by spouses entering the work force, promotions that occur most to workers who work most, overtime pay, or any activities that cause income and time worked to increase together.

Statistics that indicate shorter work weeks are often misleading if they are based on payroll data. Payroll statistics include both full-time and part-time workers, which distorts the averages for all workers in times of increasing proportions of part-time workers. Payroll records do not distinguish second jobs, which understates the real work week for many consumers. The main increases in leisure time have been associated with earlier retirement as well as an increased number of holidays and length of vacations rather than reducing the hours worked in a normal week.[23] Statistics that indicate shorter work weeks can also be misleading if they fail to report increases in obligated time.

Even if people do have more free time, as some diary studies indicate, millions of consumers psychologically perceive a "time famine" and devote most of their gains in free time to watching television.[24] Perceived time pressure can have negative effects—such as poor nutrition—but can be overcome to some extent with consumer knowledge or education.[25]

Nondiscretionary or obligated time is a major block of nonmarket (nonwork) time that affects consumer purchases of time goods. Nondiscretionary time includes physical obligations (sleeping, commuting, personal care, and so forth), social obligations (which increase with urbanization and the rising proportion of professional and white-color occupations), and moral obligations. Physical and social obligations increase with increasing income. Americans spend more time traveling today than they did 10 years ago, especially those in high-income households. Men who earn more than $35,000 travel 12 hours a week compared with low-income men who travel 8 hours. High-income women travel 2 hours a week more than low-income women.[26]

Harried American consumers cope with time-crunched lifestyles in many ways. The Hilton Time Values Study, described in Consumer in Focus 9.3, found that cutting back on sleep to "make" more time was true for 38 percent. Although Americans are facing a time–money dilemma, they have little ability to change their situations. For a marketer such as Hilton Hotels, this dilemma represents a market opportunity, as Consumer in Focus 9.3 describes. Other ways of coping may not result in the purchase of time goods. For example, "gross national housework" time is declining. People, especially women, are simply spending less time doing housework.[27] Some gender reversal is also occurring. In 1965, women were doing "hard core" housework or cleaning at a ratio of 5:1 compared with men, but that has been reduced to a 2:1 margin today.[28] Consumer decision making takes time. Some activities involved in decision making are shown in Figure 9.8. The amount of time consumers are willing to spend in shopping activities—price comparison, for example—should be (negatively) related to wage rates according to economic theory, although subjective factors such as enjoyment of shopping may also influence the amount of time consumers are willing to devote to buying activities.[29]

Consumers may earn high incomes but live in time poverty. Such consumers require a lot of value from the limited hours available for leisure or discretionary activities. They may be willing to pay more money to enjoy their leisure time, thereby expanding market potential for such things as air travel, expensive sports equipment to maximize their enjoyment, top-notch exercise facilities, instruction to increase their exercise effectiveness, and so forth. They are likely to switch from less-intense or less-active leisure activities such as fishing to more active sports such as racquetball or squash. This was shown in a study of leisure-time satisfactions in which highly educated and high-income men (presumably busier) were more likely to derive satisfaction from tennis than from golf.[30]

The 41 million households that take one or more vacation trips per year spend an average of $3,000 a year on personal travel, but the 19 million frequent-traveling households (three or more personal trips and at least one international

Hilton Targets Time-Crunched Consumers

The Hilton Hotels Corporation commissioned the Hilton Time Values Survey, a telephone survey of 1,010 adults age 18 years and older. It focused on America's values and attitudes toward time and the reasons behind people's behavior.

The study disclosed that finding enough time for both work and personal lives has become so critical for most working Americans that nearly two-thirds say they would be willing to take less pay to get more time off. Working women, particularly those with children, feel the time crunch more than men. During the 1990s, respondents indicate spending time with family and friends will become more important than making money. More people (77 percent) selected "spending time with family and friends" than any other priority. More emphasis on "having free time" was the choice of 66 percent and "pursuing personal experiences such as traveling for pleasure and pursuing hobbies" was chosen by 59 percent. "Making money" came in fifth place (61 percent), and "spending money on material possessions" came in last (29 percent). People in the eastern states placed more emphasis on making money than in the more-relaxed western states.

Other findings that reveal America's current time-crunch attitudes include the following:

Thirty-three percent said they are unlikely to be able to make time for their ideal weekend.

Twenty-one percent said they don't have time for fun anymore.

Thirty-three percent said they don't accomplish what they set out to do each day.

Thirty-eight percent report cutting back on sleep to "make" more time.

Twenty-nine percent constantly feel under stress.

Thirty-one percent worry they don't spend enough time with family and friends.

Twenty percent report calling in sick to work at least once during the past 12 months when they simply needed time to relax.

As a response to the study, Hilton created the BounceBack Weekend to be an affordable, stress-relieving getaway. In essence, Hilton enables its guests to buy the free time they need in the form of a getaway weekend. Starting at $65 per night, BounceBack Weekends include free Continental breakfast for everyone in the party and kids stay free in their parents' room. The program emphasizes that consumers gain freedom from daily routine and the other time-crunch problems that rob them of their leisure hours. Families get a chance to step off the treadmill and gain new energy and perspective. Michael Ribero, Hilton's senior vice president for marketing, reported that the concept has proved so popular that Saturday has become Hilton's highest occupancy night.

Source: Materials courtesy of Hilton Hotels & Resorts.

Figure 9.8   Consumer Activities, All of Which Involve the Expenditure of Time

Pre-Purchase	Purchase	Post-Purchase

• Information gathering
  – Conversation
  – Misc. media use
    (e.g. *Consumer Reports*)
  – Browsing, window
    shopping
  – Other advertising
    (e.g. billboard)
 	
• Search for "time-saving"
  features
 	
• Comparison shopping
	• Buying
	  – By mail/telephone
	  – In the store
	  – Form of payment
	    (e.g., cash, check,
	    credit card)
	
	• Related travel time and
	  waiting in line
		• Information gathering and
		  learning on how to use
		  product
		
		• Filling out warranty forms
		
		• Repairs and maintenance
		
		• Actual use of the product
		  and continued use of the
		  product
		
		• Disposing of product (pre-
		  sorting aluminum and
		  plastic, driving to the city
		  dump, etc.)

Source. John P. Robinson and Franco M. Nicosia, "Of Time, Activity, and Consumer Behavior: An Essay on Findings, Interpretations, and Needed Research," Journal of Business Research 22 (1991), 171–186.

---

trip per year) spend $4,000 a year.[31] Middle-aged consumers have the least amount of leisure, but as they move toward retirement and become empty-nesters, they begin to add to their budgets for leisure while at the same time they begin to decrease their budgets for necessary expenses.

Time-Saving Goods

Consumers can gain leisure time (discretionary time) by decreasing nondiscretionary time expenditures. Fortunately for marketers, this may be done through the purchase of goods and services.

The purchase of services is one way to increase leisure or to have more discretionary time. Hiring either a neighborhood teenager or ChemLawn may free the consumer for either more work (which might increase income) or more non-market time to pursue leisure activities. Child care, housecleaning, restaurants, and a wide array of other services are direct substitutes for time obligations and are among the fastest growing markets in industrialized economies. Table 9.5 discloses consumers are using time-saving strategies more today than in previous years. More than 60 percent of consumers report saving time by taking

Table 9.5	Saving Time		
Consumers Are Increasing Time-Saving Activities			
Percent of adults who "often or sometimes" choose time-saving activities, by type of activity, 1986–1991.			
Type of Activity		**1986**	**1991**
Housecleaning Put Off		64	74
Eat in Fast-Food Restaurants		59	70
Purchase Take-Out Food		48	60
Shop in Convenience Stores		44	56
Prepare Frozen Dinners/Foods		30	42
Shop by Mail, Computer, or Phone		22	29
Pay for Housekeeping		12	14

Source: "Time Savers," American Demographics 13 (February 1992), 10.

home meals, eating at fast-food restaurants, or simply postponing tasks such as housecleaning.

The purchase of durable and nondurable goods is another way to have more leisure or discretionary time. Dishwashers and microwave ovens are examples of how time-saving attributes create enormous market opportunities. Nondurables are also affected, because it is difficult to introduce new food products today that are not microwavable. Not only does this affect food industries, it also profoundly affects packaging products. Convenience stores and disposable products illustrate more market developments created by consumers' desire to buy time. A comprehensive review of the literature and an econometric study of consumption related to time concluded

> The rises in the prices of male and female time relative to other prices (annual increases of 6.1 percent and 6.5 percent in the prices of male and female time, respectively, versus annual 4.8 percent increases in the implicit price index for personal consumption expenditures) combined to alter American consumption patterns over the 30-year period from one in which nondurables played a large role to one in which durables and, increasingly, services play important roles. Unless some structural change occurs to disturb these results, increasing prices of time will continue to alter American consumption patterns.[32]

Polychronic Time Use

Polychronic time involves combining activities simultaneously, such as eating while watching television or working with a laptop computer while traveling on an airplane. By combining activities, individuals use their time resources to accomplish several goals at the same time. This concept has also been called "dual time usage" and contrasts with performing only one activity at a time (**monochronic time** use). Computers make some of these things possible. Figure 9.9 shows how one firm sells polychronic time experiences.

Many products are marketed to enrich the time budgets of consumers through polychronic time usage. Drive-through cleaners, supermarkets offering planned assortments of food to simplify a consumer's need to plan and prepare meals, the addition of racks to facilitate reading while using exercise bikes, or the addition of beepers to allow medical or dental patients to shop in nearby stores while waiting for appointments are just a few innovations facilitated by consumers' use of polychronic time.[33] Cellular phones were accepted rapidly, probably because they appealed to people with high incomes and the need for polychronic time usage.

Figure 9.9   Time Savings

A pragmatic approach to elegance. Some people need all the room our First Class provides. Others insist on a measure of understated luxury. Our priority is the best utilization of our passengers' time, so we have no quarrel with either view. Time is everything. swissair +

Swissair is a partner in the Delta, USAir and Air Canada frequent flyer programs.

Time Prices

Some advertisers feature the "time price" of a product. Such ads may state that the product requires only 2 hours to install. Convenience due to a nearby location is also an attempt to reduce the time price. Some shopping malls announce the best ways to enter and exit the mall to attract shoppers unwilling to pay the time price of traffic congestion. New malls may have a comprehensive regional plan to prevent such problems. Harried consumers—those who feel rushed and pressured for time—visit fewer stores and make few comparisons by considering fewer brands and attributes than those who are relaxed shoppers.[34] Consumer mood can affect perceptions of time or time prices. Consumer in Focus 9.4 shows how to implement mood-inducing strategies to affect perceptions. Music, for example, can influence consumers' perceptions of time passage. Music may operate in ways contrary to popular wisdom, however, because music

Consumer in Focus   9.4

Mood-Inducing Strategies to Enhance Subjective Time Judgments

Consumer behavior involves the use of products, time, and space. When making temporal judgments, consumers are frequently influenced by situational conditions that may mediate their subjective evaluations. Momentary conditions, such as mood, play a critical role in time use and allocation. Mood generally is thought of as a mild affective state that may influence cognitive processes such as evaluation, memory, and decision strategies. Consumers are more likely to recall positive information when they are in a good mood and negative information when they are in a bad mood. Research indicates that mood, especially positive mood, is a powerful determinant in time perception and orientation. Specifically, consumers in a positive mood state tend to underestimate the time of events and have more of a future orientation in their views and plans. Consumers in a negative mood state overestimate the time involved in events.

Marketing strategy for time-related products should be tied closely to strategies designed to enhance consumers' moods. If consumers enter into an activity in a good mood, they are more likely to evaluate things positively. The mood induced during the prearrival stages of leisure or recreation activities (such as parking at sports events) is an important source of leisure benefits and satisfaction. Minor changes in physical surroundings, use of music, or advertising appeals may influence consumers' mood at the point of purchase and their perception of shopping time, working time, driving time, the duration of service encounters, and subsequent evaluation of these events. Communication strategies in which time properties are featured, such as ads for microwave ovens and retort pouch cooking, should be embedded in a proper mood-inducing advertising environment, to produce the desired perception. For products such as insurance and savings programs, inducing a positive mood is associated with willingness to delay gratification and suffer immediate costs for the promise of larger, long-term rewards.

Source: Summarized from Jacob Hornik, "The Role of Affect in Consumers' Temporal Judgments," Psychology & Marketing 10 (May–June 1993), 239–255.

may cause people to overestimate the amount of time required to shop or to wait on hold on a telephone.[35]

Product attributes may communicate the ability to reduce the time price of the product. Examples include new "dry" deodorants, quick-dry paint, higher-horsepower lawn mowers, and the Concorde airplane, which, although it has a high price in economic resources, is the cheapest plane in the air in temporal resources.

Some marketers offer a **time guarantee** (TG), defined as a promise by the seller that assures customers they will not have to devote an unreasonable amount of time to getting product and service problems resolved. Any unusual problems would be handled at locations and times convenient to the customer. Koerner Ford in Rochester, New York, offers a TG that assures customers that if a problem with the vehicle is not fixed right the first time, the dealership will send a mechanic to the home or work location at times convenient to the customer to solve the problem. In a study of this offer, 63 percent of customers of the dealership rated the TG as very important, although most wanted it as an included service rather than something for which customers would pay extra.[36]

The Times, They Are a Changin'

Consumers are changing the way they spend their time. Although some activities are stable, there are major changes, especially in the area of communications, such as interpersonal conversations. For men between 25 and 44 years, Juster[37] found that time on the telephone has almost doubled recently, and the gap between the sexes has narrowed. In other areas of time budgets, television viewing was increasing in prior years but now appears to be declining.

In a study comparing today's time budgets with those of the past, Hawes[38] found that women are spending less time in housework because of their entry to the labor force but men are spending more time doing things around the home.

Analysis of temporal resources in marketing is a contemporary recognition of the principle Benjamin Franklin in 1748 told a young tradesperson, "Remember that time is money." Franklin also commented, "Dost thou love Life? Then do not squander Time; for that's the stuff Life is made of."

Cognitive Resources

Walking through a supermarket in the mid-1990s, you may see a lot of consumers looking up and down the shelves, picking up products and comparing labels, spending minutes or even hours in the store, and often looking a bit confused. This is not a few form of ritual shopping behavior; it is an illustration that consumers have another resource from which they must spend to buy products and services. The other activity is information processing or spending cognitive resources.

Cognitive resources represent the *mental capacity available for undertaking various information-processing activities.* Just as marketers compete for consumers' money and time, so also do marketers compete for cognitive or information processing. Marketers need to get the attention of consumers, and in today's marketplace, such a task may be difficult.

Capacity is a limited resource. We are able to process only a certain amount of information at a time. Capacity size is often described in terms of a chunk, which represents a grouping or combination of information that can be processed as a unit. Depending on which source one chooses to draw on, capacity varies from four or five chunks to as many as seven.[39] It has been rumored that the telephone company selected seven-digit phone numbers because of the difficulties many consumers would have with more numbers. Consistent with this, learning declines as the number of words in a sentence increases beyond seven.[40]

The allocation of cognitive capacity is known as **attention.** Attention consists of two dimensions: direction and intensity.[41] *Direction* represents the focus of attention. Because consumers are unable to process all the internal and external stimuli available at any given moment, they must be selective in how they allocate this limited resource. Some stimuli will gain attention; others will be ignored.

Intensity, however, refers to the amount of capacity focused in a particular direction. Consumers will often allocate only the capacity needed to identify a stimulus (for example, another car ad) before redirecting their attention elsewhere. On other occasions, consumers may pay enough attention to understand the basic gist of the ad. Sometimes consumers may give the ad their complete concentration and carefully scrutinize the message, such as a consumer in the market for a new car who is reading an automobile ad.

The fact that capacity is a limited resource carries several important implications concerning how consumers process information and make product choices. Some of these are discussed subsequently. An information-intensive environment creates a need for better management of cognitive processing. This is just as true for an individual consumer as it is for a business in which the value of knowledge as an asset may be better recognized. Widespread adoption of computers and telecommunications technology generally involves an increase in the *speed* with which information is transmitted as well as an increase in the *amount* of information that can be stored and processed in a given unit of time.[42] Consumers who know how to assemble and organize information can achieve more goods and services for themselves, just as surely as can those who have more economic or temporal resources. These decisions will be based on consumer estimations of the value of the information as well as time constraints of the consumers.[43] An example of this is shown in Consumer in Focus 9.5. Marketers who know how to facilitate the search process gain competitive advantage over those who do not.

| 9.5 | **Consumer in Focus** |

Allocating Cognitive Resources

As a recent graduate taking a new job, Monika needs a car. Because she recognizes that there are over 300 makes and models on the market, she used a prescreening process to limit her consideration set to relatively few cars. But even so her task is formidable. Because this purchase may be the most expensive thus far in her life, she knows that her decision should be based on good information but time spent on searching for information will cost her dearly.

She can become well informed by reading *Consumer Reports, Car & Driver, Road & Track*, and other magazines; she can seek the advice of friends, neighbors, and colleagues; and she can pay close attention to advertising. She can even visit a showroom, test-drive some cars, argue with a salesperson, and faint from sticker shock. A manufacturer or car dealer will want to understand Monika's behavior to invest in better communications to provide information she needs to choose *that marketer's* car.

For time allocation, Monika wishes to maximize the value she can obtain from the information sources within the constraints imposed by her job. Sources can have value even when the information obtained does not favor the brand of car she is evaluating (negative information). Mathematical models can be used to predict the order of selection of information sources. Time constraints will affect how Monika allocates effort to positive versus negative information. Information search can be for a specific brand, for example the Miata. Monika will decide whether to add that brand to her consideration set or continue the search for other brands. As her consideration set evolves, some brands may be added and others deleted.

Monika must decide *which* sources to search — does *Consumer Reports* give enough information to justify the time commitment (and cost)? If a source is to be searched, Monika must decide *when* to search that source — should she read *Consumer Reports*, then go to the showroom, or should she go to the showroom, then read *Consumer Reports?* Once at a source, she must decide *how long* she should search it — when is long enough with a car salesperson? All three decisions (which, when, how long) are interrelated.

Source: Excerpts from John R. Hauser, Glen L. Urban, and Bruce D. Weinberg, "How Consumers Allocate Their Time when Searching for Information," Journal of Marketing Research 30 (November 1993), 452–466.

Gaining Attention

Gaining the consumer's attention represents one of the most formidable challenges a marketer may face. Consumers are bombarded continually by many stimuli that compete for their limited capacity. Estimates of the number of ads consumers encounter in a typical day range in the hundreds and are likely to increase as marketers continue to develop new avenues for reaching consumers (for example, the use of ads in rental videos, or video displays in shopping carts or at the checkout area of a store). A major determinant of an ad's success, then, is the likelihood of its gaining the consumer's attention.

Gaining attention at the point of purchase can be equally important. The use of eye-catching displays can be instrumental in helping a product stand out from

Consumer in Focus **9.6**

Gaining Attention with Point-of-Purchase Displays: Olympia Brewing Company

Point-of-purchase (POP) displays are often used by marketers for attracting consumers' attention in a retail environment that is increasingly "cluttered" with new products. The Olympia Brewing Co. conducted a study to determine the effects of POP displays on purchase behavior. The research involved both food and liquor stores located within two California cities. Some of the stores received a display, but others did not (these latter stores provided a baseline for comparing the results for stores with displays). Also, two types of POP displays were tested: motion displays (those with some movement being generated by the display) versus static displays (those without movement).

Sales in the stores were then monitored over a 4-week period. The results (numbers represent the increase in sales over stores without displays) are presented as follows:

	Static Display	Motion Display
Food Store	18%	49%
Liquor Store	56%	107%

These findings clearly reveal the effectiveness of POP displays in generating sales. The presence of a display produced an average sales increase of more than 50 percent. The greater effectiveness observed for liquor stores relative to food stores suggests that the impact of POP displays is facilitated when consumers are already inclined toward purchasing the product (it seems safe to believe that those visiting the liquor store were so inclined). Further, the use of movement generated nearly three times the sales of the static display in food stores and nearly twice the sales in liquor stores.

the clutter of brands squeezed onto a retailer's shelf (Consumer in Focus 9.6). Packaging can serve a similar function. Achieving a "louder voice on store shelves" was a major consideration in designing the cans for the various Coca-Cola brands.

Consequently, it is very important for marketers to understand what factors may influence the focus of attention. When you read Chapter 14 (*Information Processing*), you will find there are many stimuli at the marketer's disposal for gaining attention.

Shallow Attention

Many products are simply not important enough to consumers to warrant a "large" investment of their limited cognitive resources. These products can be called low-involvement products. In many respects, consumers are "cognitive misers," as they attempt to find acceptable rather than optimal solutions for many of their consumption needs. Thus, the cognitive demands required by an elaborate decision-making process are such that consumers will devote the needed capacity (as well as the time) for only a few products. Simplistic decision strategies (as discussed in Chapter 7) that lower the demands on capacity are more common.

This same barrier occurs for marketing communications. Even if one can succeed in gaining attention, consumers may not devote the amount of attention desired. Research indicates that failure to achieve an adequate degree of attention can reduce learning. For example, in a typical shadowing study, subjects wearing headphones receive a different message in each ear.[44] Subjects are then asked to "shadow" one of the messages, that is, repeat aloud the content. Despite hearing two different messages simultaneously, subjects can easily shadow one of them, although this task requires nearly all their cognitive capacity.

The interesting question is what can be recalled about the message that is not shadowed. Some aspects of this message are absorbed, such as whether it contained human speech versus a nonspeech sound (for example, buzzing) or when the sex of the speaker changed during the message. However, recall of message content is nonexistent. Even changes from normal speech to a nonsense speech sound (for example, normal speech played backward) escape detection. These findings suggest that stimuli that fail to receive a sufficient amount of capacity are unlikely to leave a lasting impression on the consumer.

Persuasion as well as learning can depend on the amount of capacity allocated to a communication.[45] If consumers are unwilling or unable to devote the attention necessary for carefully evaluating an ad's claims, then persuasion can depend more heavily on reactions to the ad's executional features.[46] However, such features may have little influence when the claims receive the attention necessary for a thoughtful evaluation of their validity. We return to this issue in Chapter 16.

Danger of Exceeding Cognitive Capacity

Because capacity is limited, it is possible that the demands of the information environment may sometimes exceed this capacity. The Federal Trade Commission, for instance, once developed a proposal for increased disclosure of nutritional information within food advertisements. A fundamental flaw with the proposal was that it required the presentation of more information than could be processed within the time made available.[47]

What happens when the demands of the information environment exceed cognitive capacity? This question has led to a considerable amount of research and debate concerning the potential for information overload. Some have speculated that increased disclosure of product information may have undesirable effects. If the information "load" (that is, the amount of information) in a choice environment exceeds capacity, then consumers might become confused and make poorer choices.

In an early study of overload by Jacoby and colleagues,[48] they concluded that

> it would appear that increasing package information load tends to produce: (1) dysfunctional consequences in terms of the consumer's ability to select that brand which was best for him, and (2) beneficial effects upon the consumer's degree of satisfaction, certainty, and confusion regarding his selection. In other words, our subjects felt better with more information but actually made poorer purchase decisions.

This study and a similar investigation sparked a heated controversy.[49] Critics contended that the Jacoby studies overstated their findings and suggested that the data did not reflect overload as a result of increased product information, a conclusion that seems justified. This is not to say that overload cannot occur, only that the Jacoby studies did not demonstrate that more product information led to poorer decisions.

The information overload controversy has continued, although with somewhat different players.[50] Jacoby now maintains that information overload, although possible, is unlikely because consumers will stop processing information before they are overloaded.[51] However, a study suggests that consumers may be unable to stop short of overloading themselves when faced with a sufficiently rich information environment.[52]

The right amount of information will depend on factors such as involvement, situation, and personality or other variables as they vary between market segments. A consumer may allocate considerable amounts of information processing, for example, to a food product in a supermarket that attracts attention with a colorful display at a convenient location with a label that speaks of cholesterol, calories, fat, or other variables. A consumer with a heart problem that generates high involvement in the product category and an ample time budget may allocate a great deal of cognitive activity (and time) to consideration of alternatives. This consumer may eventually also allocate his or her money budget to the product that is successful in winning the consumer's cognitive budget.

Summary

Consumers possess three primary resources that they use in the exchange process of marketing. These resources are economic, temporal, and cognitive. Practically speaking, this means that marketers are competing for consumers' money, time, and information processing. A consumer's perception of available resources may affect the willingness to spend time or money for products. Thus, measures of consumer confidence may be useful in forecasting future sales by product category.

Buying is affected greatly by consumers' income. Affluence is a variable of major interest to marketers. The upper quintile or quartile or up market is often the focus of marketing programs. This group makes proportionately high purchases of products such as apparel, furniture, electronic and home entertainment, home furnishings, tableware, domestics, fine jewelry, tools, hardware, and building materials. Department stores are particularly strong competitors for affluent customers but so are some off-price retailers and specialty stores. These customers are reached relatively more effectively with print media, although they also have higher ownership of cable television. Americans have expressed a high propensity to use credit, which extends the income resource, at least for a period of time. The down market is also important, especially in difficult economic conditions. This market segment is attracted by lower prices and basic assortments but still expects to be treated with respect and good service.

The second main consumer resource is time. Products and services classified by their time properties may be called time goods. Time-using goods require the use of time with the product and include products such as attending a museum, watching television, and other activities often classified as leisure activities. Time-saving products allow consumers to increase their discretionary time, often through the purchase of services or goods that reduce the time required in other activities. Polychronic time usage involves more than one simultaneous activity and may be used to enhance consumers' time budget. A contemporary conceptualization of time budgets includes paid time, obligated time, and discretionary time (or leisure). Situational or momentary events may induce moods that affect consumers' subjective time perceptions.

The third main type of consumer resource is cognitive capacity. The allocation of cognitive capacity is known as attention. Because this capacity is limited, people must be selective in what they pay attention to and how much attention is allocated during information processing. Gaining the consumer's attention is a major hurdle for marketers. Similarly, gaining "enough" attention can be equally challenging, particularly when the product is of limited importance. Finally, there is the possibility of consumers becoming "overloaded" when the information environment exceeds their cognitive capacity.

Review and Discussion Questions

1. Why is "perception" of economic resources a variable as important in explaining consumer behavior as actual resources?

2. Describe the relationships that can be expected between income and the purchase of major product categories.

3. When conducting marketing research, how should income be measured?

4. If a consumer goods manufacturer is seeking growth opportunities that may be expected from rising affluence, what advice would you provide?

5. What is meant by the term *GDP?* How does it differ from GNP?

6. How might the relationship between time budgets and economic budgets affect the marketing strategy of a major retailer?

7. A retailer has just completed a study of the effects caused by the amount of shelf space given a product and where the product is located in the store. Whereas both the amount of space and location had significant effects on the sales for some items

(for example, cookies), such effects were not observed for other items (for example, milk). How can you explain these differences?

8. Consider the manufacturer interested in determining which of two alternative ads would be most effective. Initially, target consumers were shown one of the ads along with several other ads and later tested for recall. The results revealed no difference in recall between the ads. However, in a later field test in which target consumers encountered the ads in a "real world" setting, major differences were observed in the ads' effectiveness. How can you account for these inconsistencies between the two studies?

9. What is your opinion about the information-overload controversy? Do you believe overload can occur? Do you believe it will occur?

Endnotes

1. Kevin F. McCrohan and James D. Smith, "Consumer Participation in the Informal Economy," *Journal of the Academy of Marketing Sciences* 13 (Winter 1987), 62–67.

2. Ernest Engel, "Die Productions and Consumptionsverhaltnisse des Konigreichs Sacksen," *Zeitschrift des Statistichen Bureaus des Koniglich Sachsischen Ministeriums des Innern*, Nos. 8–9 (November 22, 1857), 8.

3. Martha Farnsworth Riche, "New Definitions of Income," *American Demographics* 12 (November 1990), 14–15.

4. Mandy Putnam, *The Up Market* (Columbus, Ohio: Management Horizons, Division of Price Waterhouse, 1988).

5. Karl Albrecht and Ron Zemke, *Service America* (Homewood, Ill.: Dow Jones-Irwin, 1985).

6. Thomas J. Stanley and George P. Moschis, "America's Affluent," *American Demographics* 6 (March 1984), 28–33.

7. "Wealthy Taxpayers Cut Back on Good Life to Cushion Tax Rise," *Wall Street Journal* (January 11, 1994), A1.

8. "Real Estate, Retail Outlook," *American Marketplace* (July 4, 1991), 133.

9. "Seizing the Dark Day," *Business Week* (January 13, 1992), 26–28.

10. Jan Larson, "Reaching Downscale Markets," *American Demographics* 13 (November 1991), 38–41.

11. Ravi Batra, *The Great Depression of 1990* (New York: Random House, 1988).

12. Edward Cornish, "Start of Another Depression?" *Futurist* 10 (January–February 1988), 2ff.

13. Joe Schwartz, "How to Find the Affluent," *American Demographics* 11 (June 1989), 22.

14. David E. Bloom and Todd P. Steen, "Living on Credit," *American Demographics* 9 (October 1987), 22–29.

15. James W. Hughes, "Understanding the Squeezed Consumer," *American Demographics* 13 (July 1991), 44–49.

16. Office of Technology Assessment, *Technology and the American Economic Transition: Choices for the Future* (Washington, D.C.: U.S. Government Printing Office, 1988).

17. Charles Stubbart, "Are Environmental Scanning Units Effective?" *Long Range Review* 12 (1987), 133–143.

18. This conceptual framework is developed originally in Justin Voss and Roger Blackwell, "Markets for Leisure Time," in Mary Jane Slinger, ed., *Advances in Consumer Research* (Chicago: Association for Consumer Research, 1975), 837–845; and Justin Voss and Roger Blackwell, "The Role of Time Resources in Consumer Behavior," in O. C. Ferrel, Stephen Brown, and Charles Lamb, eds., *Conceptual and Theoretical Developments in Marketing* (Chicago: American Marketing Association, 1979), 296–311.

19. John P. Robinson, "Your Money or Your Time," *American Demographics* 13 (November 1991), 22–26.

20. Paul M. Lane and Jay D. Lindquist, "Definitions for the Fourth Dimension: A Proposed Time Classification System," in Kenneth D. Bahn, ed., *Developments of Marketing Science* 11 (Blacksburg, Va.: Academy of Marketing Science, 1988), 38–46.

21. Justin Voss, "The Definition of Leisure," *Journal of Economic Issues* 1 (June 1967), 91–106.

22. Wilton Thomas Anderson, Linda L. Golden, U. N. Umesh, and William A. Weeks, "Timestyles: Role Factor Influences on the Convergence and Divergence of Couples' Complementary and Substitute Activity Patterns," *Psychology and Marketing* 9 (March–April 1992), 101–122.

23. Geoffrey H. Moore, "Measuring Leisure Time," *The Conference Board Record* (July 1971), 53–54.

24. John P. Robinson and Franco M. Nicosia, "Of Time, Activity, and Consumer Behavior: An Essay on Findings, Interpretations, and Needed Research," *Journal of Business Research* 22 (1991), 171–186.

25. David L. Mothersbaugh, Robert O. Herrmann, and Rex H. Warland, *Journal of Consumer Affairs* 27 (Summer 1993), 106–126.

26. John P. Robinson, "Americans on the Road," *American Demographics* 11 (September 1989), 10.

27. "How Americans Use Time," *Futurist* (September–October 1991), 23–27.

28. Robinson and Nicosia, "Of Time, Activity, and Consumer Behavior."

29. Howard Marmorstein, Dhruv Grewal, and Raymond P. H. Fishe, "The Value of Time Spent in Price-Comparison Shopping: Survey and Experimental Evidence," *Journal of Consumer Research* 19 (June 1992), 52–61.

30. Douglass K. Hawes, W. Wayne Talarzyk, and Roger D. Blackwell, "Consumer Satisfaction from Leisure Time Pursuits," in Mary J. Slinger, *Advances*, 822.

31. Blayne Cutler, "Where Does the Free Time Go?" *American Demographics* 12 (November 1990), 36–39.

32. W. Keith Bryand and Yan Wang, "American Consumption Patterns and the Price of Time: A Time-Series Analysis," *Journal of Consumer Affairs* 24 (1990), 280–308.

33. Carol Felker Kaufman, Paul M. Lane, and Jay D. Lindquist, "Exploring More than 24 Hours a Day: A Preliminary Investigation of Polychronic Time Use," *Journal of Consumer Research* 18 (December 1991), 392–401.

34. Aida N. Rizkalla, "Consumer Temporal Orientation and Shopping Behavior: The Case of Harried vs. Relaxed Consumers," in Robert L. King, ed., *Retailing: Its Present and Future* 4 (Charleston, S.C.: Academy of Marketing Science, 1988), 230–235.

35. James J. Kellaris and Robert J. Kent, "The Influence of Music on Consumers' Temporal Perceptions: Does Time Fly When You're Having Fun," *Journal of Consumer Psychology* 1 (1992), 365–376.

36. Eugene H. Fram and Andrew J. DuBrin, "The Time Guarantee in Action: Some Trends and Opportunities," *Journal of Consumer Marketing* 5 (Fall 1988), 53–60.

37. F. Thomas Juster, "A Note on Recent Changes in Time Use," in F. Thomas Juster and Frank P. Stafford, eds., *Time, Goods, and Well-Being* (Ann Arbor: University of Michigan, 1985), 316–317.

38. Douglass K. Hawes, "Time Budgets and Consumer Leisure-Time Behavior: An Eleven-Year-Later Replication and Extension," in Melanie Wallendorf and Paul Anderson, eds., *Advances in Consumer Research* 14 (Provo, Utah: Association for Consumer Research, 1987), 543–547.

39. Herbert A. Simon, "How Big Is a Chunk?" *Science* 183 (February 1974), 482–488; George A. Miller, "The Magical Number Seven, Plus or Minus Two: Some Limits on Our Capacity for Processing Information," *Psychological Review* 63 (March 1956), 81–97.

40. Alexander J. Wearing, "The Recall of Sentences of Varying Length," *Australian Journal of Psychology* 25 (August 1973), 156–161.

41. Scott B. MacKenzie, "The Role of Attention in Mediating the Effect of Advertising on Attribute Importance," *Journal of Consumer Research* 13 (September 1986), 174–195.

42. Rashi Glazer, "Marketing in an Information-Intensive Environment: Strategic Implications of Knowledge as an Asset," *Journal of Marketing* 55 (October 1991), 1–19.

43. John R. Hauser, Glen L. Urban, and Bruce D. Weinberg, "How Consumers Allocate Their Time when Searching for Information," *Journal of Marketing Research* 30 (November 1993), 452–466.

44. For example, see E. C. Cherry, "Some Experiments on the Recognition of Speech with One and Two Ears," *Journal of the Acoustical Society of America* 25 (1953), 975–979.

45. Anthony G. Greenwald and Clark Leavitt, "Audience Involvement in Advertising: Four Levels," *Journal of Consumer Research* 11 (June 1984), 581–592.

46. See, for example, Scott B. MacKenzie and Richard J. Lutz, "An Empirical Examination of the Structural Antecedents of Attitude-toward-the-Ad in an Advertising Pretesting Context," *Journal of Marketing* 53 (April 1989), 48–65; Richard E. Petty and John T. Cacioppo, *Communication and Persuasion: Central and Peripheral Routes to Attitude Change* (New York: Springer/Verlag, 1986).

47. James R. Bettman, "Issues in Designing Consumer Information Environments," *Journal of Consumer Research* 2 (December 1975), 169–177.

48. Jacob Jacoby, Donald Speller, and Carol Kohn Berning, "Brand Choice Behavior as a Function of Information Load," *Journal of Marketing Research* 11 (February 1974), 63–69.

49. Jacob Jacoby, Donald Speller, and Carol Kohn Berning, "Brand Choice Behavior as a Function of Information Load: Replication and Extension," *Journal of Consumer Research* 1 (June 1974), 33–42; J. Edward Russo, "More Information Is Better: A Reevaluation of Jacoby, Speller, and Kohn," *Journal of Consumer Research* 11 (November 1974), 467–468; William L. Wilkie, "Analysis of Effects of Information Load," *Journal of Marketing Research* 11 (November 1974), 462–466; Jacob Jacoby, Donald E. Speller, and Carol A. K. Berning, "Constructive Criticism and Programmatic Research: Reply to Russo," *Journal of Consumer Research* 1 (September 1975), 154–156; Jacob Jacoby, "Information Load and Decision Quality: Some Contested Issues," *Journal of Marketing Research* 15 (November 1977), 569–573.

50. Debra L. Scammon, "Information Load and Consumers," *Journal of Consumer Research* 4 (December 1977), 148–155; Naresh K. Malhotra, "Information Load and Consumer Decision Making," *Journal of Consumer Research* 8 (March 1982), 419–430; Naresh K. Malhotra, Arun K. Jain, and Stephen W. Lagakos, "The Information Overload Controversy: An Alternative Viewpoint," *Journal of Marketing* 46 (Spring 1982), 27–37; Naresh K. Malhotra, "Reflections on the Information Overload Paradigm in Consumer Decision Making," *Journal of Consumer Research* 10 (March 1984), 436–440.

51. Jacob Jacoby, "Perspectives on Information Overload," *Journal of Consumer Research* 10 (March 1984), 432–435.

52. Kevin Lane Keller and Richard Staelin, "Effects of Quality and Quantity of Information on Decision Effectiveness," *Journal of Consumer Research* 14 (September 1987), 200–213.

CHAPTER 10

Knowledge

▲▲

Compaq's Challenge of Creating Consumer Knowledge

Compaq Computer Corp. has crafted a reputation for selling solid personal computers with strong service at attractive prices. In the business PC market, Compaq is a big name. Unfortunately, Compaq's latest target, the consumer home market, knows little about that reputation.

The home market has boomed as PC prices have fallen. According to Link Resources Corp., sales are expected to reach 5 million PCs this year, an 11 percent increase. It's a varied market: people who bring work home, home-based businesses, kids. But it is wide open—just 31 percent of U.S. homes have a PC.

In courting the home market with its new Presario brand, Compaq must win over consumers who have far more familiarity with Packard Bell, Apple Computer's Macintosh Performa, and IBM Personal Computer's PS/1. "We're many points below IBM and Apple"—and Packard Bell, the longtime leader in the consumer market—"in general brand awareness," acknowledges Michael Baldwin, senior vice-president-management supervisor at Ammirati & Puris, New York, Compaq's ad agency.

Part of Compaq's efforts to close this gap involved an estimated $15 million fourth-quarter ad blitz. Compaq is getting its message across in other ways, including point-of-purchase materials and a 10-city media tour to promote home computing.

Will it work? Jim Garrity, director of marketing communications, thinks so. He explains, "Given the tough times some of our competitors have fallen upon, we see a unique opportunity to go in and capture a perceptual leadership."

Source: Adapted from Bradley Johnson, "Compaq Puts $15M behind Presario Launch," Advertising Age (September 13, 1993), 12.

Figure 10.1 Companies Often Try to Influence Consumer Behavior by Providing Information That Affects Consumer Knowledge

As the chapter opener reveals, influencing consumer knowledge is a common marketing objective, and understandably so. Obviously, it is difficult to sell an unknown product, especially when consumers have the option of choosing a more familiar one. Consequently, companies are constantly sending information to consumers in the hope that such information will be accepted and acted on. One example of how MCI attempts to create knowledge that will lead consumers to select MCI as their long distance telephone company is the promotion piece appearing in Figure 10.1. This figure also contains a newspaper insert that poses the question, "Did you know this?" which is followed by information intended to create favorable knowledge about the advertised pharmacy. Additional advertisements designed to influence consumer knowledge are presented in Figure 10.2.

Figure 10.2 Additional Examples of Companies Trying to Expand Consumer Knowledge

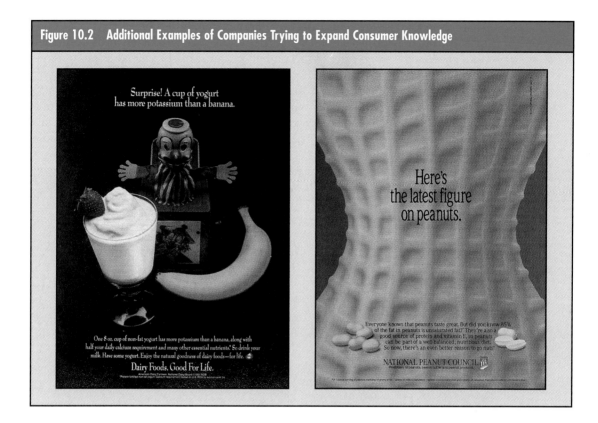

More generally, it is important for companies to acquire a thorough understanding of what consumers know (or don't know) for one simple reason—what consumers buy, how much they will pay,[1] where they buy, and when they buy depends on the knowledge they possess about these basic decisions. Such understanding may lead to discovering significant gaps in consumer knowledge that, when filled in, will increase the likelihood of product purchase. Consider what happened when CBS's "60 Minutes" aired a segment that moderate consumption of red (but not white) wine reduces the risk of heart disease. Sales of red wine skyrocketed 40 percent. Wine World Estates later placed tags on its red wine bottles carrying excerpts from the program. This promotion was especially significant because it represented the first time that the government approved any claim about the benefits of moderate drinking.[2]

In addition to identifying gaps in what consumers know, marketers must also be on the lookout for errors in consumer knowledge. It is not at all uncommon to discover that a hefty number of consumers are misinformed and thus hold inaccurate knowledge. This inaccurate knowledge, typically referred to as **misperception,** may pose a significant barrier to the success of a business. A retailer that charges the same prices as a competitor but is misperceived as being more expensive is at a disadvantage.

When misperceptions exist that undermine the product's attractiveness to consumers, corrective actions will be necessary. An excellent example of one company's efforts to combat inaccurate knowledge is provided by Lever Brothers, the maker of Dove soap. The company had identified several undesirable

Figure 10.3   One Company's Effort to Eliminate Product Misperception

Consumer in Focus **10.1**

Consumer Knowledge and Public Policy

How well prepared are today's high school seniors who will shortly become full participants in the world of consumption? Answering this question is obviously important to public policy makers concerned with consumer education. And based on the findings of a recent study, it would appear they have good reason to be concerned.

Consumer Federation of America, the nation's largest consumer advocacy organization, and American Express sponsored a study in which seniors took a test of their consumer knowledge. The test covered six areas: consumer credit, checking/savings, auto insurance, housing rental, food purchasing, and car purchasing. Multiple questions were developed for each area, and each question was presented in a multiple-choice format with four answers. Consequently, chance alone would lead to a score of 25 percent.

The average score for the entire test was 42 percent. Seniors scored the highest (50 percent) on car buying, the lowest (36 percent) on checking/savings. In comparison, adults averaged 16 percentage points higher on a similar test. The report concluded that "high school seniors are not well prepared for the world of consumption." Apparently, the same could be said for many adults as well.

Source: Student Consumer Knowledge: The Results of a Nationwide Test. *Sponsored by Consumer Federation of America and American Express, 1991.*

misperceptions about its product and responded by mailing target households a packet that contained, among other things, the brochure appearing in Figure 10.3. These misperceptions were listed inside the brochure, followed by an explanation as to why each was incorrect.

Understanding consumer knowledge is also important to public policy makers (see Consumer in Focus 10.1). Governmental agencies such as the Federal Trade Commission may commission a survey of consumer knowledge to help guide policies aimed at protecting the "uninformed" consumer. When consumers are judged to lack sufficient information to make an "informed choice," policy makers may enact legislation that requires the disclosure of appropriate information. Such was the motivation behind the government requiring the cigarette industry to replace the original warning required by law ("The Surgeon General has determined that cigarette smoking is dangerous to your health") with a series of warning labels describing specific dangers (for example, "Smoking causes lung cancer, heart disease, emphysema, and may complicate pregnancy") that are rotated periodically. At other times, consumers may hold inaccurate knowledge as a result of deceptive or misleading advertising. Corrective advertising may then be ordered by government agencies to remedy this erroneous knowledge.[3]

At a general level, **knowledge** can be defined as the information stored within memory. The subset of total information relevant to consumers functioning in the marketplace is called **consumer knowledge.** This chapter addresses three basic questions about consumer knowledge: What do consumers know? How is knowledge organized in memory? How can knowledge be measured? Questions concerning the processes and factors that govern how external information is transferred to memory (that is, becomes knowledge) and retrieved are deferred until later chapters on information processing (Chapter 14) and learning (Chapter 15). Similarly, the role played by knowledge during the cognitive processes that shape consumer decision making is described in subsequent chapters as well.[4]

Content of Knowledge

A fundamental question that arises in a proper consumer analysis is "What do consumers know?" The answer to such a question rests on understanding the contents of memory. Cognitive psychologists have suggested that there are two basic types of knowledge: declarative and procedural.[5] **Declarative knowledge** involves the subjective facts that are known (for example, that eggs, flour, and water are ingredients for making a cake), whereas **procedural knowledge** refers to the understanding of how these facts can be used (knowing how these ingredients are actually combined in making a cake). These facts are subjective in the sense that they need not correspond to objective reality. For instance, a consumer may believe price is an indicator of quality even when the two are truly unrelated.

Declarative knowledge is divided into two categories: episodic and semantic.[6] **Episodic knowledge** involves information that is bounded by the passage of time. It is used for answering the question, "When did you last buy some clothes?" **Semantic knowledge,** however, contains generalized knowledge that gives meaning to one's world. It is the knowledge you would use, for example, in describing a videocassette recorder.

Although these distinctions provide a general basis for categorizing knowledge content, a more useful typology is needed for the marketing practitioner. Although consumer researchers have largely ignored the development of such a typology,[7] our experience suggests that marketers will often find it useful to examine consumer knowledge within three general areas: product knowledge, purchase knowledge, and usage knowledge.

Product Knowledge

Product knowledge is a conglomerate of many different types of information. It would encompass

1. Awareness of the product category and brands within the product category
2. Product terminology (for example, "floppy disk" in computers)
3. Product attributes or features
4. Beliefs about the product category in general and specific brands

Table 10.1	The Ten Most Familiar Brand Names in America	
#1	Campbell's Soup	98%
#2	Hallmark Greeting Cards	97%
#3	United Parcel Service	97%
#4	Hershey's	97%
#5	McDonald's	97%
#6	Sears	97%
#7	Kmart	96%
#8	7 Up	95%
#9	Coca-Cola	95%
#10	Kodak	95%

Note: Brand rankings based on percentage of adults who had any opinion about theme.
Source: Total Research Corp., as cited in Diane Crispell and Kathleen Brandenburg, "What's in a Brand?"
American Demographics (May 1993), 26–32.

In general, marketers are most interested in consumers' knowledge about their brand and competitive offerings. This information is provided by two types of analyses: awareness analysis and image analysis.

Awareness Analysis

A common approach to assessing brand awareness is the "top-of-the-mind" awareness measure. As the name suggests, consumers are asked to recall all the brands that are applicable to the probe. The probe might be very general, such as a question asking you to name all the toothpaste brands you can remember. Alternatively, the probe might limit the set of relevant brands by defining a particular benefit or usage situation (for example, the brands that would be best suited for someone going on a date). Those brands familiar to the consumer comprise the **awareness set.**

Suppose we polled American consumers to determine the most familiar brand names. What brands do you think would make the top ten? The answer, according to the findings of the Total Research Corp., can be found in Table 10.1.

Making consumers familiar with a brand's name has long been recognized as an essential prerequisite for building a brand image. Consumer in Focus 10.2 provides an illustration of these concerns within the pharmaceutical industry.

Beyond serving as the foundation for creating a brand image, brand name awareness serves as the gateway for entry into the consumer's consideration set (see Chapter 6). Consumers cannot consider what they are unaware of. Not only can awareness affect the odds of gaining consideration, it may also serve as a basis for choice itself.[8] Consequently, some consumers buy familiar brands even if they believe the product has no advantage. The Roper organization reports that

10.2	**Consumer in Focus**

Prescription Drugs Catch the Branding Fever

Creating brand name awareness and image has become a major concern to pharmaceutical companies. Through direct-to-consumer advertising, promotions, and educational programs, a growing number of companies are working to ensure that their products' names, unknown to most patients until their doctors prescribe them, become familiar to and valued by consumers.

According to Kathy Franolich, VP-marketing for the advertising research company VNU, "There's a big move on among pharmaceutical companies to create brand identities for their products. We're beginning to see a lot of money being spent to advertise in the consumer press, much more than is spent in the medical press in many cases." Upjohn Co. started a $10 million-plus print campaign for Depo-Provera prescription birth control injections that will cover more than 25 magazines, including *Modern Bride, Newsweek, People,* and *Rolling Stone.*

"Companies are trying to create a franchise," explains Avi Dan, executive vice-president of the consumer division of the health care agency Lally, McFarland & Pantello, New York. "If a company can make its brand known before there is a low price generic alternative, consumers are more likely to stay with the branded product." Once a drug patent expires and generics become available, a brand loses 50 percent to 60 percent of sales the first year; up to 80 percent is lost within the first few years. "Smart manufacturers are starting to build equity in consumers' minds before this might happen," says Mr. Dan.

Source: Excerpted from Emily DeNitto, "Branding Fever Strikes among Prescription Drugs," Advertising Age (November 22, 1993), 12.

just half of Americans think that specific brands of mayonnaise are different or better than others and worth a higher price. But 62 percent know what brand of mayonnaise they want when they enter the store. Another 22 percent look for a well-known brand offering the best price. The same pattern applies to many products, including beer, coffee, and soap.[9]

Although examining consumers' awareness of brand names is an important part of understanding their product knowledge, it is just the beginning step. A more enriched appreciation of a brand's standing comes from consideration of the brand's image.

Image Analysis

Each brand within the awareness set is likely to have a set of associations between itself and other bits and pieces of information that are stored in memory. Crest may be strongly associated with decay and cavity prevention. Rolex and Mercedes-Benz are likely to be linked with prestige. McDonald's is the home of the golden arches and Ronald McDonald. Goodyear has the blimp.

Consumer in Focus   **10.3**

Logos Can Help a Company's Image . . . or Hurt

Corporate and brand logos are a very visible reflection of a marketer's image. And yet, a new study commissioned by a corporate identity and design firm, the Schechter Group, found consumers' opinions of companies can actually be hurt by these logos.

"People assume that when they do a logo, take a name and dress it up, it's going to improve their image," said CEO Alvin Schechter. "But it's not true. In more cases, it downgrades their image rather than upgrades it."

In the study, consumers were exposed to 24 company names, printed on cards in standard black type. If they recognized the company, they were asked to rank it on being "trustworthy and reputable," "offering quality products and services," "having products and services for the 1990s," and "offering a product or service I would use." The same group of consumers was later exposed to each company's color logo and asked to rank them on the same attributes. Differences in a company's ranking when the logo was present or absent indicated the logo's effect on company image.

Ten logos in the study hurt their company's images. Three logos provided improvements and 11 more had statistically neutral effects. Of 48 other logos studied in 1991 and 1992, 8 detracted from their company's images, whereas 19 improved them and 21 proved neutral. Among the logos tested in the current study, the images of Borden, IBM, and Mercedes-Benz of North America were enhanced the most by their logos. At the other end, the logos for American Express, GM's Oldsmobile, and British Airways detracted the most from perceptions of their corporate reputations.

Source: Adapted from Gary Levin, "Study: Some Logos Hurt Image," Advertising Age (September 13, 1993), 40.

And for many consumers, the name Nike activates the advertising slogan "Just do it."

Each of these brands will possess additional associations beyond those mentioned. It is the entire array of associations that defines a brand's image. These associations may involve the brand's physical properties and attributes as well as the benefits and feelings that come from product consumption. Brand associations may also include symbols (such as the drum-playing rabbit in the Energizer battery ads), persons (for example, Michael Jordan and Gatorade), advertising campaigns and slogans, logos (see Consumer in Focus 10.3), and so on. The first step, then, of an image analysis is to identify the particular associations that define a brand's image. Such associations can be identified usually by consumers' responses to the question, "What comes to mind when you think about [brand name]?"

Not all associations will be linked to the same degree to a brand. Accordingly, the second step of an image analysis is to assess the strength of a brand's associations. Although both Clydesdale horses and Spuds, the spotted dog, may be symbols associated with Budweiser, the former association is likely to be much stronger given the greater frequency and time period this association has been made in Budweiser advertising.

Let's consider an example of how information about the strength of association between a brand and specific attributes could be collected and used. Suppose we were commissioned by bank A to assess the consumers' images of their bank and two competitors' banks. For simplicity, our example will focus on four specific attributes. In practice, many more attributes or dimensions may be used.

Figure 10.4 contains the results of the image analysis that represent consumers' average ratings of the three banks along scales representing each of the four attributes. Rather than aggregating the data across all respondents, it is useful to separate the respondents into different groups. First, we would want to consider the findings based on bank A's customers. These are presented in the top half of the figure. In an absolute sense, the results indicate that bank A's customers generally hold favorable beliefs about the bank. Even so, there is room for improvement (assuming that consumers desire a bank to fall in the extreme left response category of each attribute scale), particularly in the areas of the speed of service and the personnel's friendliness toward customers. To the extent these attributes are important, improvements in them should enhance the bank's ability to retain customers.

A comparison of the three banks' ratings also carries implications for customer retention. For example, bank B receives very poor ratings. Consequently, this bank would pose little threat to bank A's customer base without substantial changes in its image. Bank C, however, represents a much more serious competitive threat, as it receives very similar ratings to bank A. Further, those areas in which bank C is deficient might easily be improved. Bank A should, therefore, be much more sensitive to the threat posed by bank C and may wish to undertake activities that would help further differentiate the two banks within the minds of their current customers.

The benefits of this image analysis extend beyond their implications for customer retention. Indeed, it can also assist the development of customer-recruitment programs that focus on converting competitive users into our users. For this, we need to examine the findings based on competitive users. Ideally, this would be done for each competitor's customer base, as different competitive customers may hold very different beliefs. In our example, we consider the results based on bank B's customers, which are summarized in the bottom half of Figure 10.4.

These results indicate both opportunities and constraints for bank A in attempting to attract bank B's customers. Bank B holds a substantial location advantage. If this perceived advantage is false, in the sense that these customers hold a misperception of bank A's convenience (for example, they may be unaware of a nearby brand office), then correcting this misperception would be critical. However, if this disadvantage is real, bank A may be forced into build-

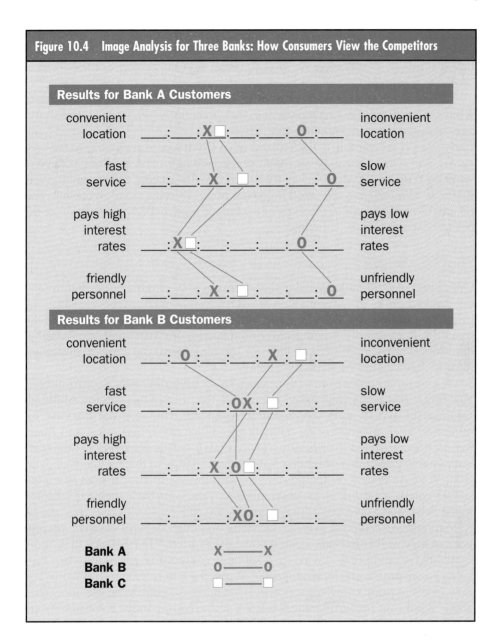

Figure 10.4 Image Analysis for Three Banks: How Consumers View the Competitors

ing one or more branch offices to attract these customers. Alternatively, bank A may try to offset this location disadvantage by building their image on other attributes.

The approach used in our bank example is incomplete in that it does not provide needed information about the importance consumers place on the various attributes. There are, however, other approaches at the marketer's disposal that yield such information. Indeed, some of these techniques can even identify a brand's "ideal" positioning or image. These alternative approaches are presented in Chapter 11.

Companies may also find it useful to probe for a deeper understanding of what a brand's associations represent in the consumer's psyche as part of an image analysis. Beyond knowing that Clydesdales are strongly associated with Budweiser, it is desirable to understand what Clydesdales symbolize to the consumer. For some, they may represent power, strength, and tradition: "They're working horses . . . that's the way they used to deliver beer." Others might view them as symbolizing the working-class man: "Strong, hard working, and proud." The end result of this type of probing is an enriched appreciation of the brand's meaning to the consumer.[10]

Price Knowledge

One aspect of product knowledge that deserves to be singled out is that involving product prices. An examination of what consumers know about an absolute price (for example, the price of a 1-lb. can of Maxwell House coffee) and a relative price (for example, whether this brand costs more than another or whether one store charges more than another for the same item) can provide important information for guiding marketing actions.

One example comes from a proprietary study undertaken by a consumer service firm. Consumers were asked to estimate the price of this service. Although users of the service gave very accurate estimates, this was not the case for nonusers. Their average price estimate was twice the actual price, and many nonusers exaggerated the price by a factor of 3 or 4. This discovery of nonusers' unfavorable price misperceptions resulted in a change in the company's advertising strategy. A new campaign centering around the theme "It's not as expensive as you might think" was soon launched. This same basic theme is reflected in the Seiko and Volvo ads appearing in Figure 10.5.

Marketing executives' pricing decisions may also depend on their perceptions of how well informed consumers are about prices.[11] Marketers will be more motivated to hold prices down and respond to competitive price cuts when they believe consumers are knowledgeable about the prices charged in a market. Low levels of price knowledge, however, enable marketers to be less concerned about significant price differences relative to the competition. If consumers are largely uninformed about relative price differences, marketers may exploit this ignorance through higher prices.

Purchase Knowledge

Purchase knowledge encompasses the various pieces of information consumers possess that are germane to acquiring products. The basic dimensions of pur-

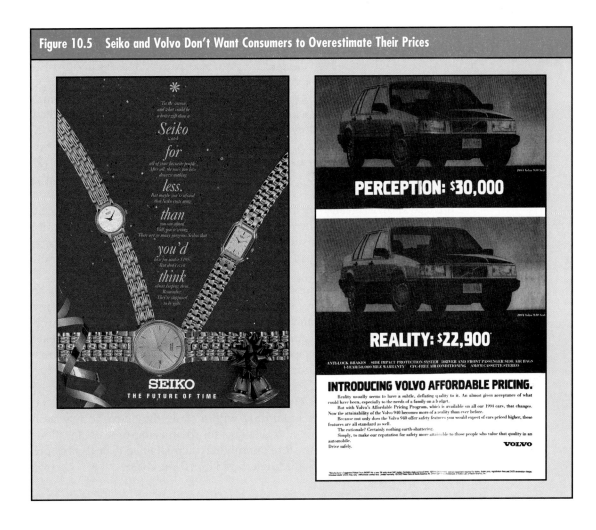

Figure 10.5   Seiko and Volvo Don't Want Consumers to Overestimate Their Prices

chase knowledge involve information concerning the decisions of where the product should be purchased and when the purchase should occur.

Where to Buy

A fundamental issue consumers must address during decision making is where they should purchase a product. Many products can be acquired through very different channels. Cosmetics, for example, may be purchased by visiting a retail store, ordering from a catalog, or contacting a field representative of a cosmetic firm that uses a sales force (such as Avon or Mary Kay).

Because a given channel may consist of multiple competitors, the consumer must further decide which one to patronize. A consumer who has chosen to buy her cosmetics from a retailer can pick from several different department stores, mass merchandisers, and specialty stores.

Decisions of where to buy depend on purchase knowledge. As in our prior discussion of product knowledge, awareness and image are important components of purchase knowledge. Low levels of patronage, for instance, may simply be caused by a lack of store awareness among target consumers. Alternatively, it may reflect deficiencies in store image. The store may be seen as inferior to the competition in one or more key areas (for example, breadth of offering, price, convenience, availability of salespeople). Recognize that the image analysis described earlier can be easily adapted to examining consumers' knowledge about retailers.

Purchase knowledge also includes the information consumers have about the location of products within the retail environment. One aspect of this location knowledge involves the consumer's information about which stores carry which products. One objective of the ad appearing in Figure 10.6 is to create this type of knowledge.

Another dimension concerns the knowledge about where the product is actually located within the store. In a study of the latter, shoppers were shown floor plans of a supermarket and asked to identify the location of various products.[12] Shoppers were more accurate for products placed on peripheral or exterior aisles than for those items located along central or interior aisles. Accuracy was also greater for smaller stores and for shoppers reporting higher levels of store patronage.

Knowledge about the location of products in a store can affect purchase behavior.[13] When consumers are unfamiliar with a store, they have to rely more heavily on in-store information and displays for identifying product locations. This increased processing of in-store stimuli may activate needs or desires previously unrecognized, thereby leading to unplanned purchases.

When to Buy

Consumers' beliefs about when to buy is another relevant component of purchase knowledge. Consumers who know that a product is traditionally placed on sale during certain times of the year may delay purchasing until such times.[14] Knowledge about when to buy can be a very important determinant of purchase behavior for new innovations. Many consumers will not immediately acquire new products because they believe that prices may drop over time.

Usage Knowledge

Usage knowledge represents our third category of consumer knowledge. Such knowledge encompasses the information in memory about how a product can be used and what is required to actually use the product. A consumer might

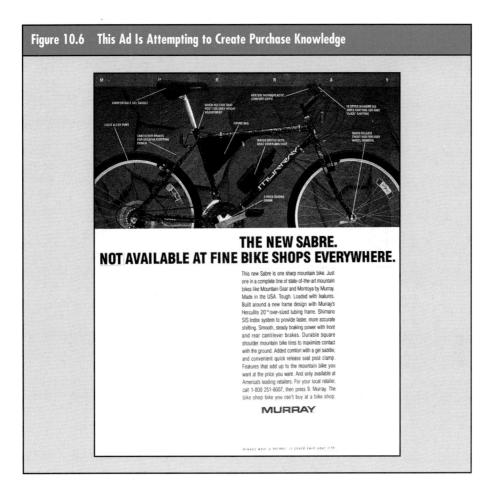

Figure 10.6   This Ad Is Attempting to Create Purchase Knowledge

know what a power saw can be used for but still lack the knowledge about how to operate the product.

The adequacy of consumers' usage knowledge is important for several reasons. First, consumers are certainly less likely to buy a product when they lack sufficient information about how to use it. Marketing efforts designed to educate the consumer about how to use the product are then needed. For example, some consumers avoid making conference calls simply because of a lack of knowledge about how to do so. One way of overcoming this barrier, shown in Figure 10.7, is to provide consumers with the necessary information on a plastic card that can be stored for future reference.

A similar barrier to purchase occurs when consumers possess incomplete information about the different ways or situations in which a product can be used. The discovery of aspirin's potential to reduce heart attack risks prompted Bayer to inform consumers of this new use. The Chex cereal ad shown in Figure 10.8

Figure 10.7   Creating Knowledge about How to Use a Service

seeks to expand consumers' usage knowledge by providing the recipe for making a party mix. Similarly, the Morton Salt ad also appearing in Figure 10.8 describes additional uses for the product beyond cooking and eating. Such efforts are quite common, as businesses often identify and promote new product uses to enhance demand, particularly in the case of mature products. To learn about how influencing consumers' usage knowledge has paid off for one industry, read Consumer in Focus 10.4.

Note, however, that care must be taken in selecting new uses. A major concern is that a new use may, in fact, lower a product's attractiveness to consumers. For example, Avon used a multiple-usage positioning for its bath oil, Skin-So-Soft. In addition to describing its use as an after-shower moisturizer, Avon also suggested that it could remove tar spots on automobiles. Some consumers may be less than enthusiastic about using a skin moisturizer that can also remove tar from a car.

Figure 10.8   Expanding Consumers' Knowledge about Different Ways to Use a Product

Even if inadequate usage knowledge does not prevent product purchase, it can still have detrimental effects on consumer satisfaction. A misused product may not perform properly, causing the customers to feel dissatisfied. Even worse, misuse may lead to bodily injury, such as accidents involving hand-held power saws.[15]

One final point before moving to the next topic. In considering how businesses attempt to increase consumer knowledge, our focus has been rather narrow in the sense that the examples have revolved around companies providing information about their products. Yet it is important to recognize that businesses may sometimes find it advantageous to educate consumers about topics that are unrelated to their products. The Coca-Cola Co. published a pamphlet, *How to Talk to a Company and Get Action,* which explained what a consumer should do in approaching companies with a complaint or a request. The pamphlet did not refer directly to any of Coca-Cola's products. Even so, the company realized some important benefits.

10.4	**Consumer in Focus**

Olive Oil Sales Benefit from New Advertising Focus on Product Uses

Olive oil is making a comeback. After more than 3 years of flat or minimal growth, sales volume gains are hitting double digits. Olive oil recently passed corn oil to become the No. 2 pourable oil after vegetable oil. The comeback is attributed to increased advertising that highlights the product's versatility, as well as a virtual freeze on prices.

"Nobody in the olive oil business had been doing much by way of advertising or marketing," says Michael Besso, director of marketing for Bertolli USA, the market share leader. "But we've gone back to basics. We're spending a lot of money and, quite candidly, we're kicking some butt. Before, we said, `Eat well, live long, be happy.' Today we're using recipes and photos of prepared meals to show people this is what you can do with olive oil."

David Tourville, marketing director for Filippo Berio, adds that his company "has been quite successful in getting consumers to use olive oil in more varied ways. The industry as a whole has been working to get olive oil use beyond the special occasion."

Source: Excerpted from Emily DeNitto, "Olive Oil Sales Climb Out of the Pits with Advertising Touting Versatility," Advertising Age (September 6, 1993), 8.

One benefit stems from the reality that many unhappy customers never bother to make a complaint. Instead, they just take their business elsewhere. Studies suggest that around two-thirds of these dissatisfied customers switch brands without letting the company know why. By educating consumers on how to complain, Coca-Cola hopes that more of them will do so. This should at least provide the company with the opportunity to take corrective actions that will help retain customers.

Also, many consumers gave Coca-Cola high marks for sponsoring the publication. Half of those who read the pamphlet reported feeling more confident about the company. And 15 percent claimed they would purchase more of the company's products.[16]

Organization of Knowledge

In this section, we consider how the various pieces of information within memory are structured or organized. Although there are many theories about memory organization, the literature largely favors the view of memory being organized in the form of an **associative network**.[17] According to this associative network concept, memory consists of a series of nodes (representing concepts) and links (which represent associations between nodes). Figure 10.9 displays a simplified

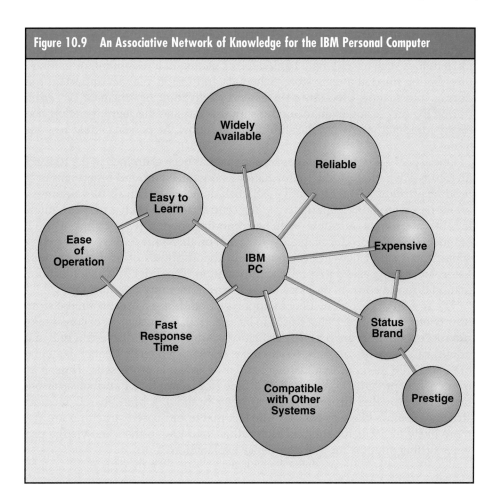

Figure 10.9 An Associative Network of Knowledge for the IBM Personal Computer

associative network that might exist for an IBM personal computer. Recognize that the image analysis discussed earlier in the chapter attempts to identify the various nodes that are linked to the node representing the brand name.

The combination of various nodes within memory leads to more complex units of knowledge. A link between two nodes forms a **belief** or **proposition,** such as "IBM is an expensive brand." These beliefs will differ in the strength of the association between the two nodes. Thus, the consumer may strongly believe that IBM is an expensive brand but be far less convinced about the ease of learning how to operate an IBM.

These propositions or beliefs, in turn, can be combined to create a high-order knowledge structure called a **schema.**[18] Schemata are likely to exist for most brands familiar to the consumer. Schemata can also occur at various levels of abstraction. For example, consumers may possess a schema for a specific brand of automobile (for example, Mercedes-Benz) as well as the general concept of automobile.

One type of schema, known as a **script,** contains knowledge about the temporal action sequences that occur during an event.[19] Most of us have scripts for activities such as making a bank deposit, dining in a restaurant, or getting a prescription filled at a drug store. Schemata and scripts play an important role during information processing. In essence, activation of schemata or scripts during the processing of an incoming stimulus reduces the cognitive effort necessary for identifying what the stimulus is and how the person should respond to it.

One aspect of knowledge organization that has been examined in the research literature is whether product information is organized around brand names or product attributes. The associative network depicted in Figure 10.9 assumes a brand-based structure. Alternatively, the central node of such a network might involve a product attribute with surrounding nodes representing various brands within the product category. Research on this issue will typically expose subjects to a set of new information about the attributes of fictitious brands.[20] Later, subjects are asked to recall the information. The order in which this information is retrieved from memory is used to infer memory organization.[21]

The weight of current evidence supports a brand-based organizational structure.[22] Some have argued that this is to be expected, because most of consumers' product experiences are brand-specific (for example, an ad discussing only one brand).[23] Consistent with this, research has shown a tendency to organize information within memory in a manner similar to how it is processed.[24] Thus, if information is presented one brand at a time (for example, all attributes for one brand are provided before turning to other brands), a brand-based memory structure is more likely to emerge. The fact that brand-based structures are also more likely to occur for subjects high rather than low in their knowledge provides further support for this experience explanation.[25]

Measuring Knowledge

Consumer researchers have used a variety of approaches for measuring consumer knowledge. Some studies have relied on the amount of purchase or usage experience as an indicator of knowledge.[26] The assumption is that greater experience translates into greater knowledge. Although product experience is obviously a rich source of information, consumers can possess some level of knowledge even though they have never used a particular product. Further, different types of experiences can create different types of knowledge. For these reasons, then, experience represents an imprecise indicator of knowledge.[27]

Perhaps the most obvious manner of measuring knowledge is to assess directly the contents of memory. Measures of **objective knowledge** are those that tap what the consumer actually has stored in memory.[28] This is by no means an easy task, given the vast array of relevant knowledge that consumers may possess. Indeed, our prior discussion of knowledge content provides some indication of the different pieces of information that may comprise consumer knowledge.

Figure 10.10 lists some of the questions that might be used in measuring consumers' objective knowledge. These questions represent various aspects of consumers' product, purchase, and usage knowledge. Which of them should be

---

Figure 10.10　Measuring Objective Knowledge

Product Knowledge Measures

1. *Terminology*
   What is meant by the following terms?
   a. Basic
   b. Terminal
   c. CPU
2. *Attributes*
   What product features are important to you in deciding which brand of refrigerator to buy?
3. *Brand Awareness*
   List all of the brands of coffee you can remember.
4. *Product Beliefs*
   How fattening are potatoes?
   Which tastes better, Coke or Pepsi?
   How much does a McDonald's Big Mac cost?

Purchase Knowledge Measures

1. *Store Beliefs*
   Which stores carry JVC televisions?
   Which grocer offers lower prices, Big Bear or Kroger?
2. *Purchase Timing*
   Are some times better than others during the year for buying a new car?

Usage Knowledge Measures

1. *Usage Operation*
   Describe the steps involved in creating a data file on a personal computer.
2. *Usage Situations*
   What are the different ways a person can use baking soda?

used will depend on the objective of the research. A study focusing on whether advertising has been successful in communicating a new product use would focus on usage knowledge. Research intended to aid pricing decisions, however, would focus on consumers' price knowledge.

A final option for assessing knowledge is to use measures of **subjective knowledge**.[29] These measures, as reflected by those appearing in Figure 10.11, tap consumers' perceptions of their own knowledgeability. In essence, consumers are asked to rate themselves in terms of their product knowledge or familiarity.

Unlike measures of objective knowledge, which focus on specific pieces of information that may be known to consumers, subjective knowledge measures center around the consumers' impressions of their total knowledge and familiarity. Thus, a consumer may feel very familiar with aspirins and still be unaware of the product's benefits in reducing the risks of heart attacks.

Research has revealed that subjective and objective knowledge measures, although related, are not substitutable.[30] That is, some people overestimate their knowledge, while others underestimate what they know. Apparently, subjective measures are affected by one's self-confidence such that people who are self-confident may overreport their level of knowledge.

In general, marketers will be most interested in what consumers actually know. As we have already seen, information about consumers' brand awareness and how they perceive the brand (that is, its image) can be very useful in formulating marketing activities. Implications for marketing action are also afforded by understanding the contents of consumers' purchase and usage knowledge.

Figure 10.11   Measuring Subjective Knowledge

1. How knowledgeable are you about personal computers?
   very knowledgeable __:__:__:__:__:__ very unknowledgeable

2. Rate your knowledge of personal computers, as compared to the average consumer.
   one of the most knowledgeable __:__:__:__:__:__ one of the least knowledgeable

3. How familiar are you with personal computers?
   very familiar __:__:__:__:__:__ very unfamiliar

4. If you were going to buy a personal computer today, how comfortable would you feel making such a purchase based on what you know about personal computers?
   very comfortable __:__:__:__:__:__ very uncomfortable

This is not to say that measuring consumers' subjective knowledge is worthless. Subjective measures may be preferable when one is interested in anticipating the likelihood that consumers will search the environment for new information during decision making. This is because external search is less likely when consumers perceive themselves as possessing adequate amounts of information, regardless of how much they truly know. Conversely, even consumers who actually possess a high level of knowledge may search if they believe their knowledge is inadequate. Thus, subjective measures may outperform objective measures in forecasting consumers' propensity to acquire new information from their environment.[31]

Summary

Consumer knowledge consists of the information stored within memory. Marketers are particularly interested in understanding consumer knowledge. The information consumers hold about products will greatly affect their purchasing patterns. Awareness and image analyses are very useful for exploring the nature of product knowledge. Marketers should also consider purchase knowledge in terms of the beliefs consumers hold about where and when purchases should occur. Usage knowledge is another content area worthy of consideration. Expanding such knowledge can be a significant avenue for increasing sales.

Some attention has been given to understanding how consumer knowledge is organized within memory. Present findings suggest that memory is organized in the form of an associative network, with brand names serving as a central node for structures involving product knowledge.

Finally, consideration was given to alternative methods for measuring knowledge. Purchase or usage experience, while certainly related to knowledge, does not necessarily provide an accurate indication of just how much information consumers possess. Objective knowledge measures attempt to assess the actual contents of memory. Subjective knowledge measures, however, ask people to indicate how knowledgeable they perceive themselves to be.

Review and Discussion Questions

1. What is meant by the terms *product knowledge, purchase knowledge,* and *usage knowledge?* Give an example of how each might influence consumer behavior.

2. Consider the following set of results from an image analysis in which the customers of a competitive food product (brand A) rated their own brand, your brand (B), and another competitor (brand C).

good tasting <u>C</u> : <u>A</u> : <u>B</u> : <u> </u> : <u> </u> : <u> </u> poor tasting

high in nutrition <u>C</u> : <u> </u> : <u> </u> : <u>A</u> : <u>B</u> : <u> </u> : <u> </u> low in nutrition

expensive <u>C</u> : <u> </u> : <u> </u> : <u>A</u> : <u> </u> : <u>B</u> : <u> </u> inexpensive

easy to cook <u> </u> : <u>B</u> : <u>A</u> : <u> </u> : <u> </u> : <u> </u> : <u>C</u> difficult to cook

What conclusions can you make based on this information?

3. Describe how advertising strategies may differ depending on consumer knowledge.

4. A grocer recently completed a study of consumers who patronize the store. One of the more intriguing findings was that the amount spent during a shopping trip depended on the number of times a consumer had shopped at the store. Consumers spent significantly more money when it was only their first or second trip. How can you explain this finding?

5. You have been asked to develop some brochures that describe a fairly sophisticated and technically oriented product. Results of market research indicate that the two primary target markets hold very different beliefs about how much product knowledge they possess. One segment perceives itself as very knowledgeable, whereas the other thinks it is quite ignorant about the product. What implications does this difference in perceived knowledge carry for developing the brochures?

6. A recent market study suggests that consumers have very limited knowledge about the prices charged by your product and competitors. When asked to give a specific price, most were unable or unwilling to do so. Moreover, the average error of those giving a price was plus or minus 25 percent. What conclusions can you draw from these results about consumers' price sensitivity during decision making?

7. A recent survey of various target markets reveals important differences in both their level of product knowledge and use of friends' recommendations during decision making. Consumers having limited knowledge relied heavily on others' recommendations, whereas knowledgeable consumers did not. How can you explain this difference?

Endnotes

1. Akshay R. Rao and Wanda A. Sieben, "The Effect of Prior Knowledge on Price Acceptability and the Type of Information Examined," *Journal of Consumer Research* 19 (September 1992), 256–270.

2. Carole Sugarman, "Wine's Benefits, Risks Argued on Labels," *The State* (November 10, 1992), 4D.

3. William L. Wilkie, Dennis L. McNeill, and Michael B. Mazis, "Marketing's 'Scarlet Letter': The Theory and Practice of Corrective Advertising," *Journal of Marketing* 48 (Spring 1984), 11–31.

4. A comprehensive and advanced discussion of how knowledge affects various cognitive processes can be found in Joseph A. Alba and J. Wesley Hutchinson, "Dimensions of Consumer Expertise," *Journal of Consumer Research* 13 (March 1987), 411–454.

5. John R. Anderson, "A Spreading Activation Theory of Memory," *Journal of Verbal Learning and Verbal Behavior* 22 (1983), 261–295.

6. Endel Tulving, "Episodic and Semantic Memory," in Endel Tulving, ed., *Organization of Memory* (New York: Academic Press, 1972).

7. For an exception, see Merrie Brucks, "A Typology of Consumer Knowledge Content," in Richard J. Lutz, ed., *Advances in Consumer Research* 13 (Provo, Utah: Association for Consumer Research, 1986), 58–63.

8. Wayne D. Hoyer and Steven P. Brown, "Effects of Brand Awareness on Choice for a Common, Repeat-Purchase Product," *Journal of Consumer Research* 17 (September 1990), 141–148.

9. Diane Crispell and Kathleen Brandenburg, "What's in a Brand?" *American Demographics* (May 1993), 26–32.

10. For an interesting discussion of image analysis, see Sal Randazzo, "Build a BIP to Understand Brand's Image," *Marketing News* 25 (September 16, 1991), 18.

11. Joel E. Urbany and Peter R. Dickson, "Consumer Information, Competitive Rivalry, and Pricing in the Retail Grocery Industry," (working paper, University of South Carolina, 1988).

12. Robert Sommer and Susan Aitkens, "Mental Mapping of Two Supermarkets," *Journal of Consumer Research* 9 (September 1982), 211–215.

13. C. Whan Park, Easwar S. Iyer, and Daniel C. Smith, "The Effects of Situational Factors on In-Store Grocery Shopping Behavior: The Role of Store Environment and Time Available for Shopping," *Journal of Consumer Research* 15 (March 1989), 422–433.

14. For research on how consumer knowledge about deals affects purchase behavior, see Aradhna Krishna, "The Effect of Deal Knowledge on Consumer Purchase Behavior," *Journal of Marketing Research* 31 (February 1994), 76–91.

15. For an example of research concerning product safety knowledge, see Richard Staelin, "The Effects of Consumer Education on Consumer Product Safety Behavior," *Journal of Consumer Research* 5 (June 1978), 30–40.

16. Judith Waldrop, "Educating the Customer," *American Demographics* 13 (September 1991), 44–47.

17. John R. Anderson, *The Architecture of Cognition* (Cambridge, Mass.: Harvard University Press, 1983).

18. For an evaluation of the schema concept, see Joseph W. Alba and Lynn Hasher, "Is Memory Schematic?" *Psychological Bulletin* 93 (March 1983), 203–231.

19. Research on consumer scripts can be found in George John and John C. Whitney, "An Empirical Investigation of the Serial Structure of Scripts," in *AMA Educators'*

Conference Proceedings (Chicago: American Marketing Association, 1982), 75–79; Ruth Ann Smith and Michael J. Houston, "A Psychometric Assessment of Measures of Scripts in Consumer Memory," *Journal of Consumer Research* 12 (September 1985), 214–224; John C. Whitney and George John, "An Experimental Investigation of Intrusion Errors in Memory for Script Narratives," in Alice M. Tybout and Richard P. Bagozzi, eds., *Advances in Consumer Research* 10 (Ann Arbor, Mich.: Association for Consumer Research, 1983), 661–666.

20. An example of studying memory structure for existing knowledge can be found in J. Edward Russo and Eric J. Johnson, "What Do Consumers Know about Familiar Products?" in Jerry C. Olson, ed., *Advances in Consumer Research* 7 (Ann Arbor, Mich.: Association for Consumer Research, 1980), 417–423.

21. For an excellent discussion of the methodological limitations of this approach and alternative methods for testing memory structure, see John G. Lynch, Jr., and Thomas K. Srull, "Memory and Attentional Factors in Consumer Choice: Concepts and Research Methods," *Journal of Consumer Research* 9 (June 1982), 18–37.

22. Gabriel Biehal and Dipankar Chakravarti, "Information — Presentation Format and Learning Goals as Determinants of Consumers' Memory Retrieval and Choice Processes," *Journal of Consumer Research* 8 (March 1982), 431–441; Russo and Johnson, "What Do Consumers Know about Familiar Products?"

23. Eric J. Johnson and J. Edward Russo, "The Organization of Product Information in Memory Identified by Recall Times," in H. Keith Hunt, ed., *Advances in Consumer Research* 5 (Chicago: Association for Consumer Research, 1978), 79–86.

24. Biehal and Chakravarti, "Information — Presentation Format and Learning Goals as Determinants of Consumers' Memory Retrieval and Choice Processes"; Johnson and Russo, "The Organization of Product Information in Memory Identified by Recall Times"; Thomas K. Srull, "The Role of Prior Knowledge in the Acquisition, Retention, and Use of New Information," in Richard P. Bagozzi and Alice M. Tybout, eds., *Advances in Consumer Research* 10 (Ann Arbor, Mich.: Association for Consumer Research, 1983), 572–576.

25. Eric J. Johnson and J. Edward Russo, "Product Familiarity and Learning New Information," *Journal of Consumer Research* 11 (June 1984), 542–550.

26. Examples of experience-based measures can be found in James R. Bettman and C. Whan Park, "Effects of Prior Knowledge and Experience and Phase of the Choice Process on Consumer Decision Processes: A Protocol Analysis," *Journal of Consumer Research* 7 (December 1980), 234–248; Jacob Jacoby, Robert W. Chestnut, and William A. Fisher, "A Behavioral Process Approach to Information Acquisition in Nondurable Purchasing," *Journal of Marketing Research* 15 (November 1978), 523–544; Kent B. Monroe, "The Influence of Price Differences and Brand Familiarity on Brand Preferences," *Journal of Consumer Research* 3 (June 1976), 42–49; Joseph W. Newman and Richard Staelin, "Prepurchase Information Seeking for New Cars and Major Household Appliances," *Journal of Marketing Research* 9 (August 1972), 249–257.

27. See Merrie Brucks, "The Effects of Product Class Knowledge on Information Search Behavior," *Journal of Consumer Research* 12 (June 1985), 1–16; Catherine A.

Cole, Gary Gaeth, and Surendra N. Singh, "Measuring Prior Knowledge," in Richard J. Lutz, ed., *Advances in Consumer Research* 13 (Provo, Utah: Association for Consumer Research, 1986), 64–66; Fred Selnes and Kjell Gronhaug, "Subjective and Objective Measures of Product Knowledge Contrasted," in Richard J. Lutz, ed., *Advances in Consumer Research* 13 (Provo, Utah: Association for Consumer Research, 1986), 67–70.

28. Examples of objective knowledge measures can be found in Brucks, "The Effects of Product Class Knowledge on Information Search Behavior"; Richard L. Celsi and Jerry C. Olson, "The Role of Involvement in Attention and Comprehension Processes," *Journal of Consumer Research* 15 (September 1988), 210–224; Akshay R. Rao and Kent B. Monroe, "The Moderating Effect of Prior Knowledge on Cue Utilization in Product Evaluations," *Journal of Consumer Research* 15 (September 1988), 253–264; Selnes and Gronhaug, "Subjective and Objective Measures of Product Knowledge Contrasted"; Mita Sujan, "Consumer Knowledge: Effects on Evaluation Strategies Mediating Consumer Judgments," *Journal of Consumer Research* 12 (June 1985), 31–46.

29. Examples of subjective knowledge measures can be found in Brucks, "The Effects of Product Class Knowledge on Information Search Behavior"; Johnson and Russo, "Product Familiarity and Learning New Information"; Arno J. Rethans, John L. Swasy, and Lawrence J. Marks, "Effects of Television Commercial Repetition, Receiver Knowledge, and Commercial Length: A Test of the Two-Factor Model," *Journal of Marketing Research* 23 (February 1986), 50–61; Selnes and Gronhaug, "Subjective and Objective Measures of Product Knowledge Contrasted."

30. Brucks, "The Effects of Product Class Knowledge on Information Search Behavior"; Cole, Gaeth, and Singh, "Measuring Prior Knowledge"; Selnes and Gronhaug, "Subjective and Objective Measures of Product Knowledge Contrasted."

31. Selnes and Gronhaug, "Subjective and Objective Measures of Product Knowledge Contrasted."

CHAPTER 11

Attitudes

▲▲▲▲▲▲▲▲▲▲▲▲▲▲▲▲▲▲▲▲▲▲▲▲▲▲▲▲▲▲▲▲▲▲▲▲▲▲▲

The Power of Positive Attitudes

In Chapter 10, you learned about the ten brands that are most familiar to American consumers. But is a familiar brand also a well-respected brand? Not necessarily. In the same study by the Total Research Corporation that identified the most familiar brands, consumers were also asked to rate brands on a 10-point scale, with 10 meaning outstanding, extraordinary quality. The brands having the highest perceived quality were

#1	Disney World/Disneyland	8.5
#2	Kodak Photographic Film	8.3
#3	Hallmark Greeting Cards	8.2
#4	United Parcel Service	8.2
#5	Fisher-Price Toys	8.1
#6	Levi's Jeans	8.0
#7	Mercedes-Benz Automobiles	8.0
#8	Arm & Hammer Baking Soda	8.0
#9	AT&T Long-Distance Telephone	7.9
#10	IBM Personal Computers	7.9

A comparison of these results with those presented in Chapter 10 (see Table 10.1) reveals some important differences. Although Campbell's Soup ranked #1 in terms of familiarity, it did not make the top ten for perceived quality. In fact, only three of the ten most familiar brand names made the top-ten list of perceived quality. The point is that a familiar brand name does not translate necessarily into a respected brand name.

Source: Diane Crispell and Kathleen Brandenburg, "What's in a Brand?" American Demographics *(May 1993), 26–32.*

In the prior chapter you learned why it is important for businesses to understand what consumers know and don't know. Equally important is the need to understand what consumers like and dislike. These likes and dislikes are called **attitudes.** More formally, attitude can be defined as simply an overall evaluation. As illustrated by the chapter opener, these attitudes play an important part in determining a product's standing among consumers.

Attitudes usually play a major role in shaping consumer behavior. In deciding which brand to buy or in which store to shop, consumers will typically select the brand or store that is evaluated most favorably. Consequently, in building an understanding of why consumers do or do not buy a particular product or shop at a certain store, attitudes can be quite useful. This is especially true when attitudes are linked to the knowledge consumers possess about a product or store, as we shall see later in the chapter when we discuss attitude models.

Attitudes can also be useful to marketers in many others ways. They are often used for judging the effectiveness of marketing activities. Consider an advertising campaign designed to increase sales by enhancing consumers' attitudes. Relying solely on sales for evaluating the campaign's success can be potentially misleading as sales are affected by many factors beyond advertising (for example, a competitor who slashes prices in response to the campaign). Consequently, it is possible for advertising to have a positive impact on attitudes without influencing sales. If, however, the ads failed to have the desired effect on attitudes, it would probably be necessary to revise the campaign.

Attitudes can help evaluate marketing actions even before they are implemented within the marketplace. A packaging decision is one example. Establishing which version of several alternative packages evoked the most favorable attitudes from consumers could prove quite useful in making the final selection.

As discussed in Consumer in Focus 11.1, attitudes can also be used to segment markets and choose target segments. One approach to segmentation involves dividing the market based on how favorable consumers are toward the product. All other things being equal, a firm would target the segment holding favorable attitudes, because these consumers should be more responsive to the product offering than those possessing less favorable attitudes. Even if some other base is used to segment a market (for example, geographic), one should still attempt to examine the relative favorability of various segments toward the product. The barriers to success become smaller as a segment's liking for a product grows larger.

Consumer in Focus **11.1**

Segmenting the Mature Market Using Consumer Attitudes

When the oldest baby boomers hit age 50 in 1996, the mature market will explode. Between 1990 and 2000, the number of Americans aged 50 years and older will grow by 12 million, whereas the number of 18- to 34-year-olds will shrink to 9 million.

Unfortunately, most businesses targeting mature Americans go about it all wrong, say Carol Morgan and Doran Levy, authors of *Segmenting the Mature Market*. Their study of 3,000 people aged 50 years and older shows that segmenting older consumers by age, race, income, or location is simplistic and ineffective. These characteristics do not reflect the powerful role individual differences play in older consumers' behavior.

In their study, attitudes rather than traditional demographics were used to segment the mature market. By asking questions on retirement, financial planning, attitudes toward food, and attitudes toward health, more than 1,000 pieces of information were collected from each respondent. These results were combined with information on the respondents' investment behavior, purchasing patterns, residence, demographics, and media usage.

Morgan believes that attitudinal segmentation is far more useful than traditional segmentation. "I was continually struck by the differences between segments that rested on attitudes, from use of cosmetics to political party, food habits, to miles driven in a car," she says. "Obviously, joining attitudes with demographics and behavior is key."

Source: Adapted from Gabrielle Sandor, "Attitude (Not Age) Defines the Mature Market," American Demographics (January 1994), 18–21.

Product attitudes are one of many different types of attitudes that marketers concern themselves with. Attitudes toward health and fitness, for instance, can carry potent implications for many industries, including cigarettes, exercise equipment, and diet foods. In the realm of persuasion, the attitudes formed toward an advertisement should also be considered as they can determine the ad's effectiveness (see Chapter 16).[1] A major study by the Advertising Research Foundation indicates that viewers' liking of a TV commercial is an important predictor of the ad's success in the marketplace.[2] Although this chapter's discussion and examples focus heavily on product attitudes, you should remember that these are only a part of the total picture.

Thus, an understanding of consumer attitudes can be beneficial in several ways. Fortunately, decades of attitude research have yielded a wealth of information on which we can draw. Unfortunately, the amount of information necessary for even a basic appreciation of attitudes cannot fit within the constraints of a conventional textbook chapter. Consequently, we have devoted two chapters to this topic. In this initial chapter, we explore some of the fundamental issues relevant to attitudes, such as their components and properties, as well as how they can be used to predict consumer behavior. Chapter 16 builds on this foundation and focuses on the variety of tactics available for influencing attitudes.

The Components of Attitude

As represented in Figure 11.1, attitude has traditionally been viewed as consisting of three components: cognitive, affective, and conative. A person's knowledge and beliefs about some attitude object reside within the **cognitive** component. The **affective** component represents a person's feelings about the attitude object. The **conative** component refers to the person's action or behavioral tendencies toward the attitude object.

A more contemporary view of attitude is reflected within Figure 11.2. From this perspective, attitude is viewed as being distinct from its components, with each component being related to attitude. Both the cognitive component (beliefs) and the affective component (feelings) are conceptualized as determinants of attitudes. In other words, a person's overall evaluation of an attitude object is seen as being determined by the person's beliefs and/or feelings about the atti-

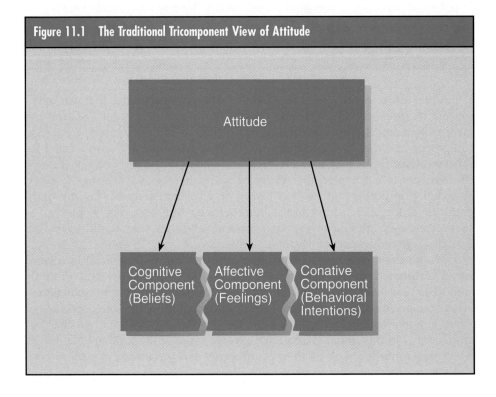

Figure 11.1   The Traditional Tricomponent View of Attitude

Attitude

Cognitive Component (Beliefs)

Affective Component (Feelings)

Conative Component (Behavioral Intentions)

tude object.[3] For some products, attitudes will depend primarily on beliefs. Consumers' attitudes toward a vacuum cleaner, for instance, may be driven primarily by their perceptions about the product's functional benefits, such as how well it cleans and how easy it is to use.

For other products, however, feelings may be the primary determinant of attitudes. Amusement parks, ballets, movies, music, and sporting events are valued for the feelings they evoke during consumption. It is also possible for both beliefs and feelings to influence attitudes. A consumer's overall evaluation of

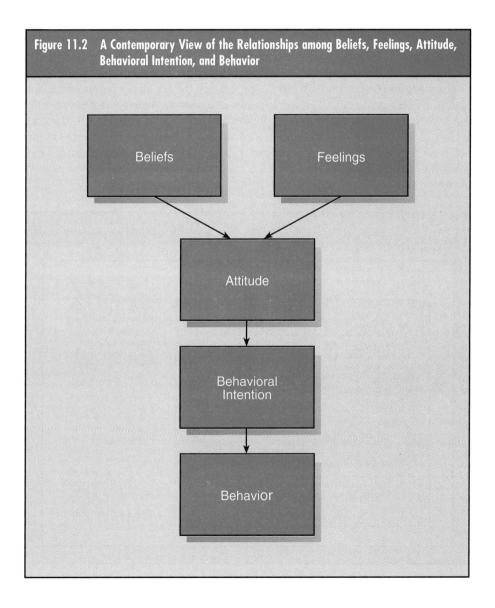

Figure 11.2 A Contemporary View of the Relationships among Beliefs, Feelings, Attitude, Behavioral Intention, and Behavior

a car can depend on beliefs about the car's dependability and gas efficiency as well as the feelings of prestige and fun that come from owning and driving the car.

Thus, according to the perspective diagrammed in Figure 11.2, there are two fundamental ways that attitudes are formed: through beliefs, and through feelings about the attitude object. Identifying the manner in which attitudes are formed is important because it provides guidance to those interested in influencing consumers' attitudes. Consider, for example, the ad appearing in Figure 11.3. It attempts to create favorable beliefs by pointing out that the product is fat-free. At the same time, it acknowledges the importance of feelings by emphasizing how consumption of the advertised product will eliminate the guilty feelings that may be experienced when eating regular eggs. We consider more fully the topic of influencing attitudes later in the chapter, as well as in Chapter 16.

Unlike the cognitive and affective components, the conative component is not seen as a determinant of attitudes. Instead, attitudes are viewed as determining the conative component. That is, a person's behavioral intentions will depend on her or his attitudes. Consequently, consumers' intentions to perform some behavior (such as purchasing a product) should increase as their attitudes become more favorable.

Figure 11.3   Egg Beaters Emphasizes "Fat Free, Guilt Free" to Create Favorable Attitudes

The fact that, within Figure 11.2, behavioral intention lies closest to behavior indicates that behavior is expected to be more highly related to behavioral intention than to attitudes, beliefs, or feelings.[4] For this reason, when one is interested in predicting behavior, behavioral intention should be measured because it should yield the most accurate prediction of future behavior.[5] We return to this issue later in our discussion of using attitudes and intentions to predict consumer behavior. Next, however, we turn our attention to the properties of attitudes.

The Properties of Attitudes

Attitudes can vary along several dimensions or properties. One such dimension is **valence.** Valence refers to whether the attitude is positive, negative, or neutral. A person may like Coke and Pepsi, dislike Shasta cola, and be fairly indifferent toward RC cola.

Attitudes can differ in their **extremity** (that is, the intensity of the liking or disliking). Extremity represents the idea that there can be varying degrees of favorability. Thus, although some consumers may hold a positive attitude toward both Coke and Pepsi, they may be much more favorable toward one brand than another.

Attitudes can also differ in their **resistance.**[6] Resistance is the degree to which an attitude is immune to change. Whereas some attitudes are highly resistant to change, others may be much more vulnerable. Many a manufacturer and retailer has been left "holding the bag" after an abrupt shift in consumers' attitudes about what is trendy. Similarly, changes in consumers' health attitudes have been bad news for some industries (cigarettes) but good news for others (exercise and sporting equipment and clothing). Consequently, businesses can benefit from tracking consumer attitudes over time as one way of anticipating potential changes in product demand and shopping behavior.[7]

Understanding attitude resistance is also important for developing both defensive and offensive marketing strategies. Defensive strategies focus on keeping current customers, whereas offensive strategies seek to recruit new customers. From a defensive perspective, knowledge about the resistance of current customers' attitudes sheds light on their potential vulnerability to competitive attacks, such as a competitor using comparative advertising. In some cases, efforts may be warranted to enhance resistance.[8] From an offensive perspective, recruiting new customers will be easier when doing so requires changing their attitudes, and these attitudes are less resistant to change.

Persistence is another property of attitudes. Persistence reflects the notion that attitudes may gradually erode simply due to the passage of time. Thus, both positive and negative attitudes may move toward a more neutral valence as time goes by.[9] Companies may therefore find it desirable to develop and support activities designed simply to maintain consumers' favorable attitudes toward their products.

Finally, not all attitudes are held with the same degree of **confidence.** Confidence represents a person's belief that her or his attitude is correct.[10] Some attitudes may be confidently held, whereas others may exist with a minimal degree of confidence. Attitudes based on direct experience with a product, for instance, are usually held with more confidence than those derived from indirect experience, such as those that might be formed after seeing an ad for a new product.[11]

Understanding the degree of confidence associated with an attitude is important for two basic reasons. First, it can affect the strength of the relationship between attitudes and behavior.[12] Confidently held attitudes will usually be relied on more heavily to guide behavior. When confidence is low, consumers may not feel comfortable with acting on their existing attitudes. Instead, they may search for additional information before committing themselves. Second, confidence can affect an attitude's susceptibility to change. Attitudes associated with greater confidence are more resistant to change.[13]

Using Multiattribute Attitude Models to Understand Consumer Attitudes

Although it is certainly important for businesses to know whether consumers hold favorable or unfavorable attitudes toward their products, it is also imperative for them to understand the basis or reasons for these attitudes. Knowing that consumers dislike your product does not tell you why this is so, or how you might go about overcoming this unfavorable evaluation.

Traditionally, consumer researchers have focused on the cognitive component of attitude in explaining the reasons behind favorable or unfavorable evaluations. From this perspective, attitude is seen as depending on a person's beliefs about the attitude object. Within multiattribute attitude models, these beliefs typically involve perceived associations between the attitude object and various features or attributes.

In addition to beliefs about an object's attributes, multiattribute attitude models also consider the salience of the attributes. **Salience** represents the importance assigned to an attribute. A product's attributes can vary substantially in how important they are to consumers when forming their product attitudes. In evaluating soup, the color of the label on the can will be considered far less relevant than the taste of the soup inside.

Although several different multiattribute attitude models have been proposed in the literature, we limit our focus to two versions.[14] After describing these different models, we discuss some of the benefits they can offer marketers.

The Fishbein Model

Fishbein's formulation is perhaps the most well-known multiattribute model.[15] Symbolically, it can be expressed as

$$A_o = \sum_{i=1}^{n} b_i e_i$$

where

A_o = attitude toward the object,
b_i = the strength of the belief that the object has attribute i,
e_i = the evaluation of attribute i, and
n = the number of salient attributes.

The model therefore proposes that attitude toward a given object (such as a product) is based on the summed set of beliefs about the object's attributes weighted by the evaluation of these attributes. To illustrate the model's properties and operations, consider the situation in which the model is used to understand consumers' preferences for three brands of running shoes. The first step would be to discover the target market's salient attributes. The most obvious and popular approach for identifying salient attributes is to ask consumers which ones they use in evaluating brands within the product category. The assumption is made that the person is aware of these salient attributes and will state them when asked. Those attributes receiving the most frequent mention or highest ranking are considered to be the most salient.

Sometimes, however, consumers may not divulge their true feelings.[16] People may distort their answers because of concerns over what others may think of them. For instance, consumers may underreport their use of price because they do not want to appear cheap.

One proposed remedy is to elicit a third-person response through some type of projective question.[17] An example would be, "What product features do most of the people around here consider to be important in buying a dishwasher?" Response biases presumably are minimized by making respondents believe that they are not revealing their personal opinions.

Returning to our running shoe example, assume that the following attributes are identified:

- whether the shoe is shock absorbent to permit running on hard surfaces
- whether it is priced less than $50
- durability of the shoe
- how comfortable it is to wear
- whether it is available in a desired color
- amount of arch support

Next, the appropriate b_i and e_i measures would be developed. The e_i component, representing the evaluation of an attribute, is typically measured on a 7-point evaluative scale ranging from "very good" to "very bad," such as

Buying running shoes priced at less than $50 is

very good __:__:__:__:__:__:__ **very bad**
$$+3 \ +2 \ +1 \ \ 0 \ \ -1 \ -2 \ -3$$

This would be done for each of the six salient attributes identified previously.

The b_i component represents how strongly consumers believe that a particular brand of running shoes possesses a given attribute. Beliefs are usually measured on a 7-point scale of perceived likelihood ranging from "very likely" to "very unlikely." For example,

How likely is it that brand A running shoes are priced at less than $50?

very likely __:__:__:__:__:__:__ **very unlikely**
$$+3 \ +2 \ +1 \ \ 0 \ \ -1 \ -2 \ -3$$

For each brand, it would be necessary to assess consumers' beliefs for each attribute. Given three brands and six attributes, a total of 18 belief measurements would be necessary.[18]

Let us further assume that a survey containing these measures is administered to a sample of white-collar men earning more than $50,000 a year. An average response could then be calculated for each b_i and e_i measure. A set of hypothetical results appear in Table 11.1. It is important to keep in mind while interpreting these results that the b_i and e_i scales range from a maximum score of +3 to a minimum of −3.

In this example, durability and comfort are evaluated as the most desirable product attributes, followed by shock absorbent and arch support, with color a relatively minor although still salient consideration. Unlike the remaining attributes, low price (less than $50) receives a negative score for this high-income

Table 11.1 Hypothetical Results for Fishbein's Multiattribute Model

Attribute	Evaluation (e_i)	Beliefs (b_i) Brand A	Brand B	Brand C
Shock absorbent	+2	+2	+1	−1
Price less than $50	−1	−3	−1	+3
Durability	+3	+3	+1	−1
Comfort	+3	+2	+3	+1
Desired color	+1	+1	+3	+3
Arch support	+2	+3	+1	−2
Total $\Sigma b_i e_i$ score		**+29**	**+20**	**−6**

sample. This does not mean that price is unimportant. Rather, it indicates that low price is viewed as an undesirable characteristic. This result is quite possible for a sample that perceives a price–quality relationship.

Findings involving brand beliefs suggest that brand A is viewed favorably by the sample because it receives a positive rating on all desired attributes. Indeed, brand A attains maximum ratings on both durability and arch support. The sample also believes that it is very unlikely (-3) that brand A costs less than $50. Given that low price is undesirable, this perception works in favor of brand A.

As a rule of thumb, marketers want consumers to perceive their brand as (1) possessing desirable attributes (when e_i is positive, b_i should be positive) and (2) not possessing undesirable attributes (when e_i is negative, b_i should be negative). Both strategies are commonly used in advertising for creating favorable attitudes. The ad presented in Figure 11.4 informs consumers about the automobile's features and how these meet or surpass the features of more expensive

Figure 11.4 Communicating the Presence of Desirable Attributes Can Create Favorable Attitudes toward the Product

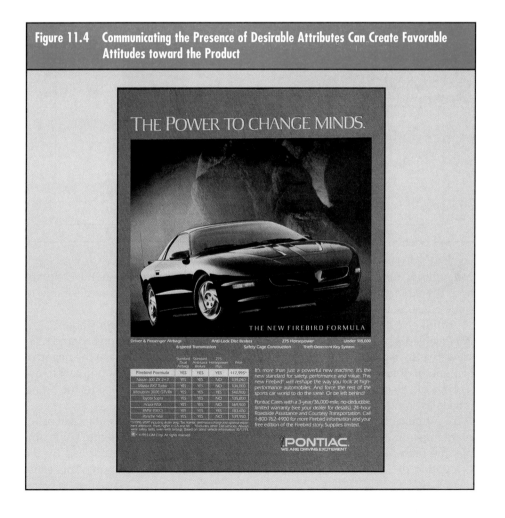

Figure 11.5 Communicating the Absence of Undesirable Attributes Can Also Create Favorable Attitudes

competitors, whereas the ad in Figure 11.5 announces that, unlike the competition, the advertised brand does not contain an attribute that is undesirable to some consumers.

Although brand B outperforms brand A on comfort and color in Table 11.1, it is perceived as inferior to brand A on the remaining dimensions. Brand C is viewed as low-priced, a perception that undermines attitude, given the negative evaluation of low price. The sample also believes that brand C is unlikely to absorb shock, be durable, or provide arch support. On the positive side, the brand is seen as somewhat comfortable and having a desired color.

To estimate the attitude toward each brand using the $\Sigma b_i e_i$ formula, each belief score must first be multiplied by the corresponding evaluation score. For example, the brand A belief score of $+2$ for shock absorbency is multiplied by the evaluation of $+2$, which produces a value of $+4$ for this attribute. This same process is repeated for each of the five remaining attributes. This produces a total $\Sigma b_i e_i$ score of +29 for brand A. For brands B and C, the $\Sigma b_i e_i$ values are +20 and −6, respectively.

The score for brand A is very good, considering that the maximum score, given the current set of evaluations, is +36. The maximum score is derived by assuming the "ideal" belief score (+3 or −3, depending on whether the attribute is positively or negatively evaluated) and combining it with the existing evaluation scores.

The Ideal-Point Model

A unique and important aspect of the ideal-point model is that is provides information concerning an "ideal brand" as well as information concerning how existing brands are viewed by consumers.[19] The model can be represented symbolically as

$$A_b = \sum_{i=1}^{n} W_i \, | \, I_i - X_i |$$

where

A_b = attitude toward the brand,
W_i = the importance of attribute i,
I_i = the "ideal" performance on attribute i,
X_i = the belief about the brand's actual performance on attribute i, and
n = the number of salient attributes.

Under the ideal-point model, consumers are asked to indicate where they believe a brand is located on scales representing the various degrees or levels of salient attributes. Consumers would also report where the "ideal" brand would fall on these attribute scales. As indicated in Consumer in Focus 11.2, consumers may have very different notions about what the ideal brand should contain. According to the model, the closer a brand's actual rating is to the ideal rating, the more favorable the attitude.

As an illustration, suppose we were to apply the model to soft drinks. Assume that the following attributes are identified as salient dimensions underlying soft drink attitudes:

- sweetness of taste
- degree of carbonation
- number of calories
- amount of real fruit juices
- price

| 11.2 | **Consumer in Focus** |

Regional Differences in the Ideal Product

One of the reasons businesses vary their product offerings from one geographic region to another is because of regional differences in what consumers would prefer in their ideal product. For years, Maurice Bessinger has relied on a mustard-based barbecue sauce to satisfy the taste buds of his Southern customers. In search of new customers, Mr. Bessinger decided to target Northeasterners. Doing so required a product change that might strike some Southerners who have spent a lifetime with the mustard-based sauce as heretical. The new sauce, "Yankee Red," contains honey and . . . tomato paste.

Advertising for "Yankee Red B-B-Q Sauce: World's Best!" appeared in *Yankee* magazine, published in Boston. "It's a test," says Mr. Bessinger from his Piggie Park headquarters in Cayce, South Carolina, the capital of mustard-based sauce. "We're going to start a national promotion very soon. We want to bring some Yankee money south."

Source: Adapted from Pat Berman, "Barbecue King Hopes Yankees Will See Red," The State (December 8, 1993), D1.

Next, we would develop a scale representing various levels of an attribute for each salient dimension. Using sweetness as an example, the scale could look like

$$\text{very sweet taste } \underline{\ :\ :\ :\ :\ :\ :\ } \text{ very bitter taste}$$
$$\phantom{\text{very sweet taste }}\ 1\ \ 2\ \ 3\ \ 4\ \ 5\ \ 6\ \ 7$$

Consumers would then indicate their ideal or preferred taste by placing an "I" in the appropriate response category. This would be followed by ratings of where various brands fall along this taste continuum (that is, the X_i from the model equation). Consumers would also provide ratings of attribute importance on a scale such as

$$\text{not at all important } \underline{\ :\ :\ :\ :\ :\ :\ } \text{ extremely important}$$
$$\phantom{\text{not at all important }}\ 0\ \ 1\ \ 2\ \ 3\ \ 4\ \ 5\ \ 6$$

Unlike the bipolar coding scheme used for the Fishbein multiattribute model, unipolar coding is used for quantifying responses to the ideal-point model scales. Unipolar coding is necessary for importance measures, because a brand's performance on an unimportant attribute should not affect attitude. For this reason, we assign a zero to the "not at all important" response category. However, bipolar coding could be used for the ideal and actual brand ratings. Given that the difference between the ideal and actual brand ratings is converted to an absolute value, either coding scheme will produce the same results. We prefer unipolar coding because most people find it easier to work with mathematically.

The Fishbein and ideal-point models use very different approaches in measuring beliefs. The ideal-point model's belief measure focuses on perceptions of the brand's location along an attribute continuum. The Fishbein belief measure assesses the perceived likelihood that the brand is located at a single point on the continuum. For instance, the Fishbein counterpart to the ideal-point taste belief measure presented above might be "How likely is it that the soft drink has a very sweet taste?" Although it is clear what consumers mean when they indicate that it is very likely that the drink tastes very sweet, less apparent is what consumers mean when they report that it is very unlikely the product has a very sweet taste. This may indicate that they believe the taste is actually bitter. It may also indicate that they perceive the product to have neither a sweet nor a bitter taste. Either of these possibilities could lead to the same "unlikely" response on the Fishbein measure. Thus, the ideal-point measure can be more useful for understanding consumers' beliefs.

The models also differ in their measurement of attribute salience. Fishbein calls for an evaluation of the attribute (how good or bad), whereas the ideal-point model uses an importance measure. The two measures are not equivalent. Measures of importance can sometimes provide an incomplete picture of consumer motivation. This is because some attributes can be important for very different reasons. An attribute may be important because consumers want the product to have the attribute. In contrast, an attribute may be important because consumers do not want the product to possess the attribute. For example, "carbonation" in a soft drink may be very desirable for many consumers, but for those preferring an uncarbonated drink, it would be rather undesirable. Both segments are likely to rate carbonation as "important," although for very different reasons.

Note that this potential limitation with importance measures is avoided by measures that require evaluations of the attributes.[20] When an attribute is important and desirable, consumers will respond on the side of the evaluation scale anchored by "very good." If an attribute is important because it is undesirable, responses will move to the other side of the scale anchored by "very bad." When consumers really don't care whether the product possesses an attribute, their responses should fall on the midpoint of the scale. In general, measures of attribute evaluation are more informative because they capture both the importance and the desirability of an attribute.

Fortunately, this potential limitation is not a problem for the ideal-point model. This is because information about attribute desirability is provided by where the consumer locates the ideal performance of a product along the attribute continuum. For example, if carbonation is important because consumers prefer an uncarbonated drink, they should place their ideal points along the low end of the carbonation continuum.

Continuing our soft drink example, suppose we found the results presented in Table 11.2. The first column specifies the attributes and the continuum (for example, sweet to bitter) along which the ideal (the third column) and actual

Table 11.2	Hypothetical Results for the Ideal-Point Multiattribute Model				
				Beliefs (X_i)	
Attribute	Importance (W_i)	Ideal Point (I_i)		Brand A	Brand B
Taste:					
sweet (1) — bitter (7)	6	2		2	3
Carbonation:					
high (1) — low (7)	3	3		2	6
Calories:					
high (1) — low (7)	4	5		4	5
Fruit juices:					
high (1) — low (7)	4	1		2	2
Price:					
high (1) — low (7)	5	5		4	3
Total $\Sigma W_i \mid I_i - X_i \mid$ score				16	29

brand (the fourth and fifth columns) ratings were taken. Attribute-importance ratings appear in the second column.

In this example, taste is the most important attribute, and carbonation is the least important. The ideal-point ratings indicate that the ideal soft drink would be sweet-tasting, somewhat carbonated, fairly low in calories, very high in fruit juices (in actuality, we would probably use a scale of juice content ranging from 0 percent to 100 percent), and toward the low side on price (again, we might use a different scale, such as one containing specific price points). Brand A is perceived as being very close to the ideal brand. Brand B also performs well on some attributes (for example, calories) but suffers on others (such as carbonation).

Total brand attitude scores are estimated by first taking the difference between the ideal and actual brand ratings on an attribute. For taste, brand A has a difference of 0 (2 − 2), and the difference for brand B is −1 (2 − 3). This difference is converted to an absolute value, as indicated by the symbol surrounding $I_i - X_i$ in the model equation and multiplied by the importance score. This operation would produce scores of 0 for brand A (0 × 6) and 6 for brand B (1 × 6) on the taste attribute. We would then repeat this process for the remaining attributes and sum the scores. For brand A, the total score is 16, and brand B's score is 29. Unlike Fishbein's multiattribute model, in which higher scores are preferred, lower scores are better under the ideal-point model. In fact, the best score a brand can receive is 0, which would indicate that the brand matches perfectly the ideal attribute configuration.

Benefits of a Multiattribute Analysis

A major attraction of multiattribute attitude models stems from their substantial diagnostic powers. That is, they provide richer insights into the reasons behind consumers' choices than afforded by measures of overall evaluations and behavioral intentions. One example of the type of diagnostic analyses provided by multiattribute models was presented in the image analysis section of Chapter 10. As we illustrated with the bank image example, examining consumers' beliefs can be very useful for identifying both undesirable misperceptions (such as when consumers incorrectly perceive your brand as more expensive than another) and the relative competitive threat posed by competitors. It can also reveal the perceptual obstacles one must overcome in recruiting competitors' customers. You might want to return to this example in Chapter 10 and review it one more time to better appreciate how it fits within a multiattribute perspective.

Another way of thinking about the marketing implications of a multiattribute analysis is represented by the simultaneous importance–performance grid shown in Figure 11.6.[21] A brand is classified into one of eight cells. This classification depends on the attribute's importance (high versus low), the brand's performance on the attribute (good versus poor), and a competitive brand's performance on the attribute (good versus poor). Marketing implications are then drawn for each cell. For example, when a company's brand is truly superior to competitors on an important attribute, this provides a competitive advantage that should be exploited, such as through a comparative advertising campaign.

Poor performance by all brands on an important attribute signals a "neglected opportunity." By enhancing our brand's performance on this attribute, we could turn this into a competitive advantage. Poor performance by all brands on an unimportant attribute, however, represents little opportunity. Improving the brand's performance would have little, if any, impact on consumer choice as long as the attribute remained unimportant to consumers.

A multiattribute analysis can also provide the information necessary for some types of segmentation. For example, one might find it useful to segment consumers based on the importance they place on various attributes. Marketing activities will differ considerably when target consumers are primarily concerned with buying at a low price rather than buying the highest quality.

Another benefit of a multiattribute analysis is its usefulness for new product development.[22] Discovering that current offerings fall short of the ideal brand would reveal an opportunity for introducing a new offering that more closely resembles the ideal. A multiattribute model has also been used successfully by the Lever Brothers company to forecast the market shares of products such as Tone moisturizing soap and Coast deodorant soap before their market introduction.[23]

Figure 11.6	The Simultaneous Importance-Performance Grid

Attribute Importance	Our Performance	Competitor's Performance	Simultaneous Result
High	Poor	Poor	Neglected Opportunity
		Good	Competitive Disadvantage
	Good	Poor	Competitive Advantage
		Good	Head-to-Head Competition
Low	Poor	Poor	Null Opportunity
		Good	False Alarm
	Good	Poor	False Advantage
		Good	False Competition

Source: Alvin C. Burns, "Generating Marketing Strategy Priorities Based on Relative Competitive Position," Journal of Consumer Marketing 3 (Fall 1986).

Attitude Change Implications

From a multiattribute model perspective, there are several ways to change consumer attitudes.[24] Returning to Table 11.2, suppose we wanted to increase consumers' attitudes toward brand B relative to brand A. Can you identify the different ways for doing this? They are (1) changing beliefs, (2) changing attribute importance, and (3) changing ideal points.

Changing Beliefs

As reflected by the ad appearing in Figure 11.7, companies often attempt to change consumers' beliefs about their products in the hope that this will en-

Figure 11.7   IBM Designed This Ad to Change Consumers' Beliefs about Its Services

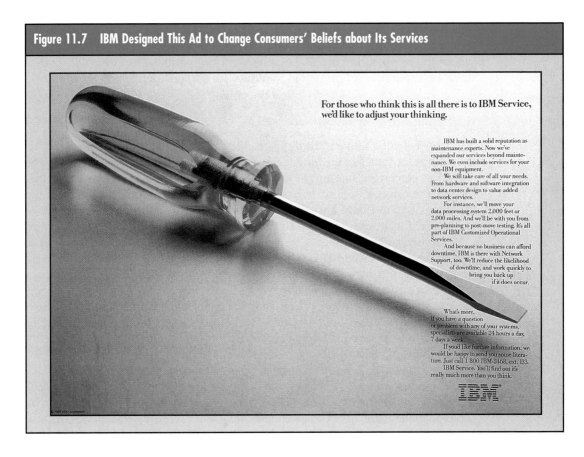

For those who think this is all there is to IBM Service, we'd like to adjust your thinking.

IBM has built a solid reputation as maintenance experts. Now we've expanded our services beyond maintenance. We even include services for your non-IBM equipment.

We will take care of all your needs. From hardware and software integration to data center design to value added network services.

For instance, we'll move your data processing system 2,000 feet or 2,000 miles. And we'll be with you from pre-planning to post-move testing. It's all part of IBM Customized Operational Services.

And because no business can afford downtime, IBM is there with Network Support, too. We'll reduce the likelihood of downtime, and work quickly to bring you back up if it does occur.

What's more, if you have a question or problem with any of your systems, specialists are available 24 hours a day, 7 days a week.

If you'd like further information, we would be happy to send you some literature. Just call 1 800 IBM-2468, ext. 133.

IBM Service. You'll find out it's really much more than you think.

hance consumers' attitudes. In this ad, IBM is trying to persuade those who do not fully appreciate the full range of support services provided by the company.

Returning to Table 11.2, a change in the belief for brand B along any of the attributes except the brand's calories has the potential to improve attitudes. Because the brand belief for calories perfectly corresponds to the ideal point, any change here would only hurt attitudes. For the remaining attributes, any belief change in the direction of the ideal point would make the brand more attractive to consumers.

Recognize that the need to modify the product offering to change consumers' beliefs will depend on the accuracy of these beliefs. When consumers hold undesirable beliefs because they have misperceived the offering (for example, consumers who overestimate product price), efforts should focus on bringing these beliefs into harmony with reality. If, however, consumers are accurate in their perceptions of a product's limitations, it may be necessary to implement product changes.

Also recognize that brand B may be able to have an adverse influence on consumers' beliefs about brand A. Research indicates that comparative advertising (such as the ads presented earlier in Figures 11.4 and 11.5), which touts the advantages of the advertised brand over a competitor, can undermine beliefs about the competitor's brand.[25] Consequently, if feasible, brand B could undertake a comparative ad campaign to reduce consumers' perceptions of brand A.

Changing Attribute Importance

Another way of altering attitudes is to change the importance consumers attach to various attributes in forming their overall evaluations. Depending on how the brand is perceived, one might wish either to increase or to decrease an attribute's importance. Research has demonstrated the potential to enhance the salience of an attribute already viewed as somewhat important.[26] Nonetheless, as a general rule, changing an attribute's importance is more difficult to accomplish than changing beliefs.

For brand B in Table 11.2, what changes in attribute importance would you recommend and in what direction (that is, an increase or decrease in importance)? In answering this question, you need to consider how each brand is perceived relative to the ideal performance. When the beliefs for both brands match the ideal point, little is to be gained by altering the attribute's importance. No matter what importance is attached to fruit juices, the relative preference between brands A and B will not change given the current set of beliefs.

When, however, brand A is seen as closer to the ideal point for a particular attribute than brand B, decreasing the attribute's importance is to brand B's advantage. Such is the case for taste, carbonation, and price. Anything that can be done to make these attributes even less important to consumers will help reduce preferences for brand A relative to brand B.

Increasing attribute importance is desirable when the competitor's brand is farther from the ideal point than your offering. In Table 11.2, brand A is farther than brand B from the ideal point along the calories dimension. Consequently, enhancing the importance of calories would benefit brand B.

Another variant of changing the attribute importance approach to attitude change involves efforts to add a new attribute. That is, a company may try to create salience for an attribute that is currently unimportant. Flame broiling is unimportant to many consumers in selecting a fast-food burger restaurant, although Burger King's advertising has attempted to alter this feeling. Adding a new attribute to the set of salient attributes essentially amounts to increasing the importance of something that previously was nonsalient.

Changing Ideal Points

Another option for changing attitudes suggested by the ideal-point model involves altering consumers' preferences about what the ideal product would look like on each attribute. For example, in buying a television set, would your ideal brand be low-priced, moderately priced, or expensive? Many consumers would place their ideal point somewhere other than on the expensive end. In an effort to persuade consumers that their ideal brand should be expensive, Curtis-Mathes ran a campaign centered around the theme "The most expensive television set in America. And darn well worth it!"

There are several ideal-point changes in Table 11.2 that would help brand B. If consumers preferred either a more bitter taste, less carbonation, or a higher price, attitudes toward brand B would increase. Such changes could also decrease attitudes toward brand A, depending on whether they broadened the gap between perceptions of brand A's performance and the ideal performance.

Changes for the remaining attributes, calories and fruit juices, would not be attractive to brand B. Given that brand B is seen as having the ideal amount of calories, altering the ideal point would be self-destructive. And although it is true that attitudes toward brand B would improve if consumers preferred a little less fruit juice in their beverage, this change would produce the same attitudinal impact for brand A. Because both brands are perceived as being the same on this attribute, any change in the preferred level of fruit juices cannot alter consumers' relative brand attitudes.

Estimating the Attitudinal Impact of Alternative Changes

As you have seen, there are many alternative changes that one might consider implementing to increase how much consumers like brand B relative to its competitor. Decisions about which changes to pursue should depend on several considerations. Some changes will be discarded because they will require product modifications that are prohibitively expensive to implement or that are virtually impossible to accomplish (such as greatly improving product quality while maintaining a price lower than the competitor's).

Consumer resistance to change should also be considered, as some changes may be more likely than others. A belief based on inaccurate product information about the brand's price can be corrected fairly easily. In the absence of an actual product change, it may be nearly impossible to change beliefs derived from actual consumption about the taste of Spam. Nor should one underestimate how difficult it can be to change attribute importance and ideal points. An airline with a poor safety record may wish that consumers place less importance on safety in selecting a carrier, but it would be impossible for the company to actually accomplish this (not to mention the negative publicity that would accompany any effort to do so). Generally speaking, it is difficult to have a major impact on attribute importance and ideal points. Consequently, these typically should be taken as a given.

Another consideration in deciding which changes should be implemented is the potential attitudinal payoff that each change might deliver. A multiattribute model can help estimate this payoff. Let's go back to brand B in Table 11.2 one last time. Can you identify the one change that, if successful, would have the most favorable attitudinal impact from brand B's point of view?

Changing the ideal point for carbonation from 3 to 6 would be the single best change. The total multiattribute score for brand B would drop from 29 to 20 (remember, lower total scores are better for the ideal-point model). This same change would increase the total score for brand A from 16 to 25. This is the only single change that would give brand B a more favorable total score than brand A.

The next best change would involve shifting the ideal point for taste from 2 to 3. The new total scores for brands A and B would be 22 and 23, respectively. This process would continue for each of the possible changes, thus yielding information about their relative attitudinal impact. All else being equal, those changes offering the greatest impact should be pursued.

The Importance of Feelings in Understanding Consumer Attitudes

Thus far, we have focused exclusively on how an examination of the cognitive component can be used for understanding the reasons behind consumer attitudes. However, as indicated in Figure 11.1, attitudes may depend on the affective component, representing the feelings associated with the attitude object, as well as the cognitive component. When, in fact, attitudes are based at least in part on feelings, then considering only the cognitive component will lead to an incomplete appreciation of the factors influencing attitudes.

Consumers experience feelings that will affect their attitudes in a variety of contexts. Feelings occur during consumption of many products.[27] Indeed, some consumption experiences are valued primarily for their ability to induce certain feelings, whether it be the tranquility that comes from listening to the waves caress the shore at a tropical resort or the thrills induced while skydiving.

Even for products whose consumption is relatively free of emotion (such as the plastic garbage bag), feelings in the form of frustration and regret may still be experienced if the product fails to perform properly (the garbage bag that busts, leaving quite a mess to be picked up). Accordingly, then, feelings have been shown to play an important role in determining consumers' post-consumption evaluations.[28]

Beyond understanding the feelings experienced during product consumption, it is also necessary to understand the feelings evoked by advertising. Some ads may amuse us; others may annoy us. As discussed more fully in Chapter 14, these feelings may strongly shape the attitudes formed after processing an advertisement.[29]

Fortunately, a considerable amount of effort has been given to the development of feeling measures.[30] One illustration of how such feelings could be measured appears in Figure 11.8. In this example, consumers would indicate how of-

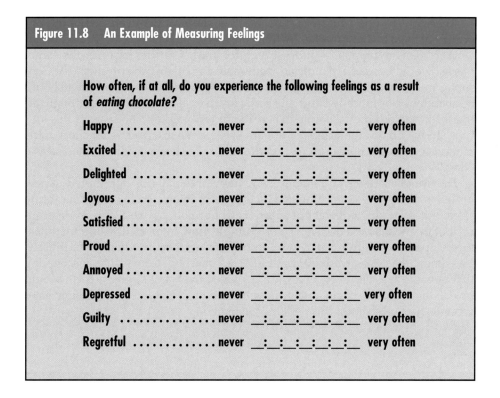

Figure 11.8 An Example of Measuring Feelings

How often, if at all, do you experience the following feelings as a result of *eating chocolate?*

Happy . . . . never __:__:__:__:__:__ very often

Excited . . . . never __:__:__:__:__:__ very often

Delighted . . . . never __:__:__:__:__:__ very often

Joyous . . . . never __:__:__:__:__:__ very often

Satisfied . . . . never __:__:__:__:__:__ very often

Proud . . . . never __:__:__:__:__:__ very often

Annoyed . . . . never __:__:__:__:__:__ very often

Depressed . . . . never __:__:__:__:__:__ very often

Guilty . . . . never __:__:__:__:__:__ very often

Regretful . . . . never __:__:__:__:__:__ very often

ten they experience positive and negative feelings during product consumption. Recognize that Figure 11.8 contains only a small subset of the feelings that might be relevant. In their study of how feelings influence advertising effectiveness, Edell and Burke examined more than 60 different types of feelings (see Table 14.1 in Chapter 14).[31]

Using Attitudes and Intentions to Predict Consumer Behavior

In many situations, companies are concerned with forecasting consumer behavior. Suppose a company had just developed a new product and was interested in determining whether there is sufficient demand in the marketplace to warrant introduction. One approach to making this determination involves introducing the product into one or more test markets. Depending on these results, a more informed judgment about the product's potential could then be made.

Alternatively, one could examine whether the product even merits the opportunity to go to a test market by first considering consumers' attitudes and intentions. This approach is quite straightforward. Consumers from the target market would be asked to indicate their interest in buying the product (see Consumer in Focus 11.3). If few consumers express an interest, the product should be abandoned or modified and retested. However, if consumers are strongly attracted to the product, it's time to consider a test market. The costs of this attitude study will run thousands of dollars. Even so, such a price is far short of the millions one might spend on test markets, only to discover that a "star" was a "dog."

The use of attitudes and intentions to forecast demand is not limited to new products. Producers of existing products are also interested in predicting future sales. Indeed, knowledge about future consumption can be a critical determinant of many business decisions. For example, how interested would manufacturers operating at full capacity be in expanding their production facilities if they knew that sales were going to increase sharply? Conversely, discovering that demand was about to level off after several years of strong growth would reveal the need to begin exploring alternative avenues for achieving sales growth (such as stealing competitors' customers).

11.3   Consumer in Focus

Forecasting the Success of New Products

How accurate are attitudes and intentions in forecasting whether a new product will be successful? Very accurate, according to Doug Hall, president of Richard Saunders International, a market research company located in Cincinnati, Ohio. In 1991, Richard Saunders joined forces with another research company, Marketing Intelligence Service in Naples, N.Y., to see if they could predict the success of 500 new products sold through supermarkets.

Each month, Marketing Intelligence Service compiles a list of the 35 to 45 most significant new packaged goods. Then Richard Saunders randomly recruits a group of 400 to 500 women who make most of the supermarket buying decisions in their households. The women gather in a hotel meeting room to see pictures and hear descriptions of the products. The women then type their reactions into a computer, including whether they would be interested in buying the product.

By using data from Information Resources, a company in Chicago that tracks supermarket sales, it was possible to estimate whether the scores based on how interested the women were in buying the products could forecast a new product's success. These scores predicted in 89 percent of the cases whether the product would go on to find a lot of buyers.

Source: Adapted from Trish Hall, "Telling the 'Yeas' from the 'Nays' in New Products," New York Times (December 9, 1992), B1.

Fortunately, the predictive accuracy of attitudes and behavioral intentions has long been a main area of inquiry in the social sciences, with research dating back to the early 1930s.[32] Much has been learned during this time about factors that can influence the extent to which attitudes and behavioral intentions will predict behavior. Such knowledge enables us to anticipate when forecasts based on attitudes and behavioral intentions are likely to be most accurate. Accordingly, we now consider some of these factors.

The Effect of Time Interval

Generally speaking, attitudes and intentions are likely to be very good predictors when they are measured at a time relatively close to when the behavior is to occur. One demonstration of how well intentions predict behavior is provided by polls taken less than 2 weeks before the 1992 presidential election. These polls, which essentially ask voters to indicate who they intend to vote for, were used to project whether a state would go for George Bush or Bill Clinton. These projections appear in the first part of Figure 11.9. Note that some states were classified as "too close to call" because voters were evenly split between the candidates.

Now consider the actual results of the presidential race, shown in the second part of Figure 11.9. Comparison of the two figures reveals that the polls accurately forecasted every state that was projected to go for Bush or Clinton. Thus, given a relatively short time interval between measurement and the behavior, intentions yielded extremely accurate predictions.

Most companies, however, are interested in using attitudes to forecast behaviors that are somewhat distant in time. Retailers, for instance, place their orders for the Christmas buying season many months in advance.

The need to assess attitudes well in advance of behavior works against the predictive accuracy of attitudes and intentions. Attitudes and intentions are not static. They can change as a result of unexpected circumstances and situational influences.[33] A sudden budget crunch can lead to the postponement of a previously planned purchase, or an unanticipated increase in financial resources can result in purchases that were not seriously contemplated before this increase. The subsequent introduction of new products and brands can also influence previously formed attitudes and intentions.

The earlier example of the 1992 presidential race can also be used to illustrate that attitudes and intentions can change, sometimes rather dramatically, over time. Consider Figure 11.10, which displays the results for the 1988 presidential race between George Bush and Michael Dukakis. A comparison of this figure with the results for the 1992 presidential race (Figure 11.9) reflects a substantial change in voters' opinions about George Bush over the 4 years.

This potential for change suggests that the ability to predict future behavior will depend on the time interval between when attitudes and intentions are measured and when the to-be-predicted behavior actually occurs. As this time

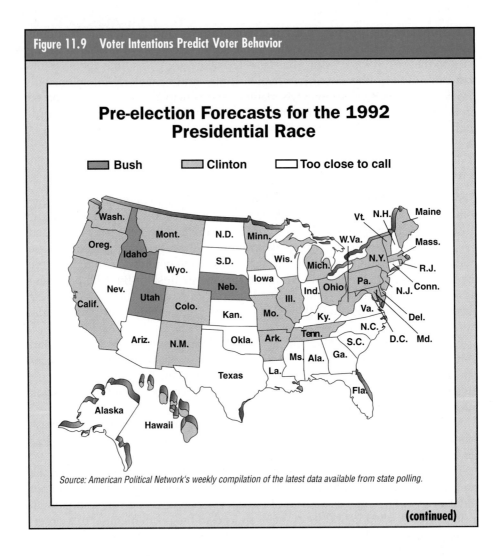

Figure 11.9   Voter Intentions Predict Voter Behavior

Pre-election Forecasts for the 1992 Presidential Race

☐ Bush   ☐ Clinton   ☐ Too close to call

Source: American Political Network's weekly compilation of the latest data available from state polling.

(continued)

interval increases, the opportunity for change becomes greater. Generally speaking, the shorter the time interval, the better the prediction.[34]

Even a relatively short time interval does not necessarily ensure accurate prediction. Unanticipated circumstances, such as out-of-stock conditions or an attractive in-store promotion by an alternative brand, can intervene. In such situations, it is unreasonable to expect that attitudes and intentions measured before this new information will provide a strong prediction of behavior.

Social Influences on Behavior

Behavior is sometimes affected by pressures from the social environment more than by personal attitudes. We have all probably experienced situations in

Figure 11.9   Voter Intentions Predict Voter Behavior (continued)

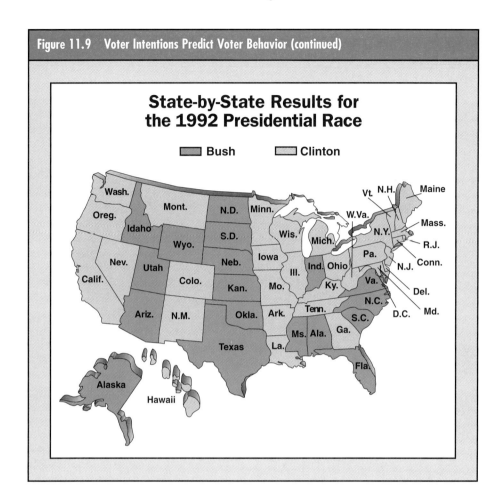

which we did something not because of our personal desires but because of social influences (such as the person who refrains from smoking when accompanied by nonsmokers). In these situations, attitudes may not prove predictive of behaviors that are determined more heavily by social influences.

The potential influence of both attitudes and social influences is explicitly recognized in Fishbein and Ajzen's theory of reasoned action,[35] which is diagrammed in Figure 11.11. According to the theory, the immediate antecedent of behavior is the intention to perform the behavior. The theory further proposed that behavioral intentions are determined by one or both of two possible factors: attitudes and subjective norm, the latter representing perceived social influence.

Thus, the theory recognizes that sometimes only attitudes will determine intentions whereas at other times social influences will dominate intentions and that, in some instances, both attitudes and subjective norms will be influential. Understanding the relative importance of attitudes and subjective norms in determining intentions and ultimately behavior can prove quite useful in devising

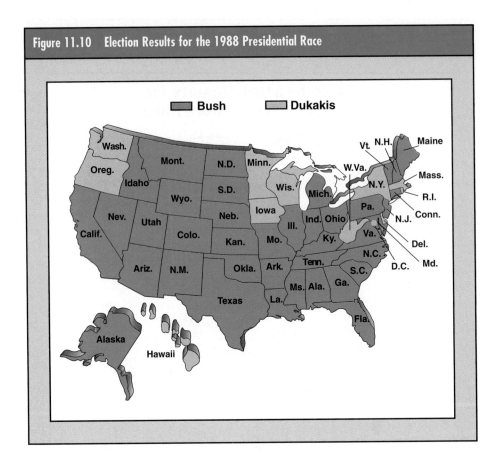

Figure 11.10 Election Results for the 1988 Presidential Race

effective behavioral influence strategies. For example, when social pressures are a dominant force, influencing behavior might require altering the person's beliefs about what social others expect. Such efforts would hold little promise, however, if social others have minimal influence on behavior.

The theory of reasoned action has received a substantial amount of empirical attention.[36] For the most part, this research has been quite supportive.[37]

Volitional Control

Volitional control represents the degree to which a behavior can be performed at will. Many behaviors are under our complete volitional control. For instance, you have control over whether you will continue to read the rest of this sentence.

In contrast, some behaviors are not under a person's complete volitional control. A person may intend to rent a particular movie at the video store only to discover that all copies have been rented for the evening. Similarly, a smoker may intend to quit but is unable to do so if habit proves more powerful than

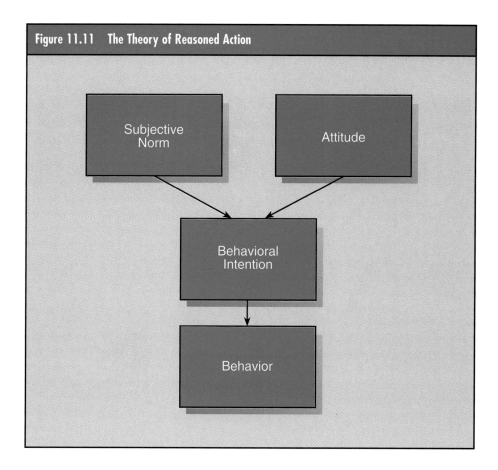

Figure 11.11   The Theory of Reasoned Action

willpower. As a behavior becomes more dependent on factors outside a person's control, the less the behavior is under volitional control. The presence of these uncontrollable factors can therefore interfere with the person's ability to do what he or she intended to do. When this occurs, intentions will become less accurate predictors of behavior.

The importance of volitional control has lead Ajzen to propose the theory of planned behavior, which is shown diagrammatically in Figure 11.12.[38] Similar to the theory of reasoned action presented in Figure 11.11, the theory of planned behavior proposes that attitude and subjective norm are determinants of behavioral intention. Unique to the theory of planned behavior is the introduction of perceived behavioral control.

As the name implies, **perceived behavioral control** represents a person's belief about how easy it would be to perform the behavior. When people believe they lack the resources or opportunities to perform a behavior (in other words, when perceived behavioral control is low), they are unlikely to form strong intentions to perform the behavior. Accordingly, perceived behavioral control is

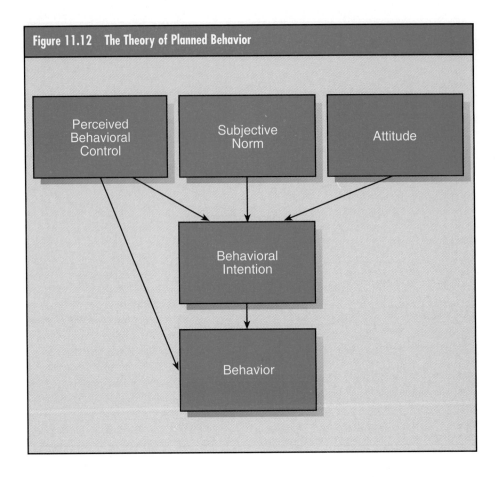

Figure 11.12 The Theory of Planned Behavior

Perceived Behavioral Control

Subjective Norm

Attitude

Behavioral Intention

Behavior

thought to directly influence intention, as shown by the arrow between control and intention in Figure 11.12. Similarly, even if one intends to do something, he or she may be unable to do so if the behavior is not under volitional control. Accordingly, perceived behavioral control is represented in Figure 11.12 as also being related directly to behavior.

The findings from several studies have been very supportive of the usefulness of including perceived behavioral control as a determinant of intention and behavior.[39] Research also indicates that any incremental accuracy in predicting behavior provided by perceived behavioral control depends on the degree of volitional control one has over the behavior.[40] For behaviors that are high in volitional control, intentions alone will suffice in predicting behavior.

The Role of Direct Experience

Attitudes are frequently formed as a result of direct contact with the attitude object. Consumers who enjoy a pleasant shopping trip to a retailer are likely to develop favorable attitudes toward the retailer. In contrast, a product that fails to perform as expected can easily lead to negative attitudes.

Recognize, however, that attitudes can be formed even in the absence of actual experience with an object. For example, many consumers have never driven a Mercedes-Benz or vacationed in Hawaii, but they still hold favorable attitudes toward this car and state as a vacation spot. Similarly, product attitudes may be formed even when consumers' experience with the product is limited to what they saw in an ad.

As noted earlier in the discussion of attitude properties, attitudes based on direct experience are usually held with more confidence. Research has shown that consumers are more confident about their product attitudes when based on actual product usage than when based on advertising alone.[41] We also noted earlier that confidently held attitudes are more likely to be relied on in guiding behavior.

Consequently, the attitudes of consumers who have purchased and consumed a product should prove more predictive of their future purchase behaviors than those lacking such experiences. Similarly, attitudes should be more indicative of a new product's potential when consumers are allowed actually to use the product as opposed to only being shown pictures or nonfunctional prototypes of the product. New product research may require the production of prototypes, even at high cost, and a simulated shopping context to achieve the greatest success in forecasting demand.

Attitude Accessibility

Before the attitudes stored in memory can influence behavior, they must first be retrieved from memory. However, simply because information is available in memory does not necessarily mean that it is always accessible. Indeed, only a fraction of this available information is actually accessible at any given moment. **Accessibility** represents the likelihood that information can be retrieved from memory. From this perspective, greater attitude accessibility should strengthen the attitude–behavior relationship.[42]

The Importance of Measurement

Earlier in the chapter we illustrated how one could measure the beliefs (in the section on multiattribute attitude models) and feelings (Figure 11.8) that underlie consumers' attitudes. Missing, however, have been examples of how one might measure attitudes and intentions. Figure 11.13 fills this void by presenting some alternative measures of attitude and intention.

Suppose we wanted to predict whether consumers will buy a Mercedes-Benz automobile. Would the attitude or intention measures presented in Figure 11.13 provide the best prediction of this purchase behavior, and why? As indicated in our earlier coverage of attitude components, a measure of the intention to buy a Mercedes-Benz should yield more accurate predictions than an attitude measure

---

Figure 11.13   Alternative Measures of Attitude and Intention

Attitude Measures

1. How much do you like Mercedes-Benz?

   like very much __:__:__:__:__:__:__ dislike very much

2. How favorable is your overall opinion of Mercedes-Benz?

   very favorable __:__:__:__:__:__:__ very unfavorable

3. Mercedes-Benz is

   good __:__:__:__:__:__ bad

   appealing __:__:__:__:__:__ unappealing

   pleasant __:__:__:__:__:__ unpleasant

4. Indicate how strongly you agree with the following statement:

   "I really like Mercedes-Benz."

| Strongly agree | Somewhat agree | Slightly agree | Neither agree nor disagree | Slightly disagree | Somewhat disagree | Strongly disagree |

Intention Measures

1. Do you intend to buy a Mercedes-Benz?

   definitely intend to buy __:__:__:__:__:__:__ definitely do not intend to buy

2. How likely is it that you would buy a Mercedes-Benz?

   very likely __:__:__:__:__:__:__ very unlikely

3. What is the probability that you would buy a Mercedes-Benz?

   0% 10% 20% 30% 40% 50% 60% 70% 80% 90% 100%

4. Indicate how strongly you agree with the following statement:

   "I intend to buy a Mercedes-Benz."

| Strongly agree | Somewhat agree | Slightly agree | Neither agree nor disagree | Slightly disagree | Somewhat disagree | Strongly disagree |

---

that assesses how much consumers like this particular brand of automobile. The simple fact is that someone may like a Mercedes-Benz very much but still not buy such a car due to a lack of need (the person just bought a new car) or ability (the person can't afford it). A measure of product liking would not register these purchase constraints. In contrast, consumers lacking the need or ability to buy would report that they do not intend to purchase a Mercedes-Benz.

Moreover, regardless of whether one is using attitudes or intentions to forecast behavior, the accuracy of such forecasts will heavily depend on the degree of measurement correspondence between what is being measured and what is being predicted. **Measurement correspondence** refers to how well a measure captures the action, target, time, and/or contextual elements that make up the to-be-predicted behavior.[43] Greater correspondence leads to more accurate predictions. Unfortunately, the importance of measurement correspondence is sometimes underappreciated, as illustrated in Consumer in Focus 11.4. Consequently, we now turn our attention to each of the elements that determine the degree of correspondence.

Consumer in Focus   11.4

Attitude Measures Receive Bad Press

It is not uncommon to find reports that, on the surface, seem to cast doubt on the relationship between consumers' attitudes and their behavior in the marketplace. NPD, a market research firm, has been tracking Americans' food attitudes and eating habits for more than a decade. These surveys report rather dramatic changes in attitudes with little corresponding effect on behavior. For example, although the number of consumers expressing concerns about French fries increased by nearly 40 percent between 1985 to 1989, the number eating fries at least once every 2 weeks dropped by only 7 percent. Similarly, the number of consumers who discourage fried chicken consumption more than doubled in a 4-year period. Actual consumption declined by less than 10 percent.

What can account for these discrepancies between changes in attitudes and behaviors? According to Lois Kaufman, a vice president of Environmental Research Associates, "People lie consistently." She adds, "People's behaviors are going to lag behind what they say."

There is certainly some truth to Kaufman's observations. People may distort or hide their true feelings, particularly when the topic is heavily value laden such as alcohol and tobacco consumption, environmentalism, and nutrition. In many cases, however, the culprit is simply that the attitude measure did not correspond very well to the behavior of interest. The fact that consumers are becoming more concerned about the nutritional properties of French fries need not imply that they will eat them less often. There are alternative ways these concerns may be expressed such as changing how French fries are prepared (switching to a cholesterol-free oil) or eating fewer fries per consumption occasion. As discussed in the chapter, accurate prediction of specific behaviors (eating French fries less often) requires the use of specific measures that correspond to the behavior (asking the consumer whether he or she intends on eating fries less often).

Sources: Howard Schlossberg, "Americans Passionate about the Environment? Critics Say That's 'Nonsense,'" Marketing News 25 (September 16, 1991), 8; Becky Townsend, "Consumers Don't Always Do What They Say," American Demographics 13 (April 1991), 12–13.

Action refers to the *specific* behavior of interest (for example, buying, using, borrowing). It is imperative that measures accurately represent the action element, because failure to do so can be very detrimental to their predictive accuracy. If one wants to predict whether consumers will purchase a product, the measure should focus on their opinions toward buying the car, not simply on whether they like the car. In general, measures that omit the action element will be inferior to measures that specify the action element in forecasting behavior.

Target elements can be very general (buying *any* automobile) or very specific (buying a Mercedes). The degree of target specificity depends on the behavior of interest. For instance, the trade association for the automobile industry is primarily concerned with purchases of all automobiles. In contrast, General Motors would be more interested in purchases of its own models.

Time focuses on the time frame in which the behavior is to occur. Suppose that on Monday you were asked about your intention to buy soft drinks. You report a favorable intention because you plan to purchase soft drinks on Wednesday, your normal day for grocery shopping. However, on Tuesday, you are asked to indicate which, if any, soft drinks you purchased since the day before. The apparent inconsistency between attitudes and behavior that would occur is simply caused by the failure to specify this important timing factor. A more appropriate measure would have assessed your intention toward buying soft drinks within the next 24 hours.

The remaining element, context, refers to the setting in which the behavior is to occur. Soft drinks can be purchased in a variety of settings, such as a grocery store, vending machine at school, restaurant, and movie theater. If one is interested in predicting vending machine purchases, the measure must incorporate this contextual element.

Summary

An analysis of consumer attitudes can yield both diagnostic and predictive benefits. Identifying receptive market segments, evaluating current and potential marketing activities, and forecasting future behaviors are some of the main ways in which attitudes can assist marketing decision making.

Attitudes are defined as an overall evaluation. Attitudes can vary along several properties, including valence, extremity, resistance, persistence, and confidence.

Attitudes depend on two basic factors: beliefs and feelings. As such, understanding why consumers hold certain attitudes requires examining the underlying beliefs and feelings consumers have about the attitude object. One approach to examining the former is represented by multiattribute attitude models, which focus on consumers' beliefs about a product's attributes. Such models can also provide useful insight into the potential payoff of alternative attitude change strategies. Two types of multiattribute attitude models are the Fishbein and ideal-point models. A main advantage of the ideal-point model is that it identifies consumers' preferred or ideal configuration of product attributes.

In addition to helping one understand consumer behavior, attitudes and especially behavioral intentions are also useful in predicting consumer behavior. However, the accuracy of these predictions will depend on several factors, such as time interval, volitional control, and the degree of measurement correspondence.

Review and Discussion Questions

1. A marketing research study undertaken for a major appliance manufacturer disclosed that 30 percent of those polled plan on purchasing a trash compactor in the next 3 months and 15 percent plan on purchasing a new iron. How much confidence should be placed in the predictive accuracy of these intention measurements? More generally, will predictive accuracy vary across products? Why or why not?

2. You are interested in predicting whether a person will purchase a new Chrysler from the Bob Caldwell dealership in the next month. Someone suggests the following phrasing for the intention measure: "How likely is it that you will buy a new automobile soon?" Why is this measure unlikely to predict the behavior of interest?

3. In January 1993, before market introduction, Mr. Dickson conducted a survey of consumers' attitudes toward his new product. The survey revealed that 80 percent of those interviewed have favorable attitudes toward the product. The product was introduced in June 1994, and product sales have been very low. What explanations can you offer for this discrepancy between the attitude survey and product sales?

4. To determine which of two alternative celebrities should be used as the endorser for an upcoming ad campaign, a company assessed how much target consumers liked each celebrity. Based on these results, one of the celebrities was selected and the campaign was launched. Shortly thereafter, the campaign was withdrawn, as it proved ineffective. Interestingly, when the campaign was reintroduced using the celebrity who was liked less, it was found to be quite effective. How can you explain the greater effectiveness of the less-liked endorser?

5. A recent survey using measures of attribute importance shows that "high price" was rated the most important of all attributes. Your boss asks you whether this means consumers will avoid a high-priced brand. How would you respond? Would your answer be different if the survey had a measure of attribute evaluation?

6. Consider the following results for a TV set, based on Fishbein's multiattribute model:

Attribute	Evaluation	Brand Belief
Clear picture	+3	+2
Low Price	+2	−1
Durable	+3	+1
Attractive cabinet	+1	+3

First, calculate the overall attitude score. Second, calculate the maximum overall score a brand could receive given the current set of attribute evaluations. Third, describe the product's strengths and weaknesses as perceived by consumers.

7. Using the multiattribute results presented in Question 6, identify all possible changes that would enhance brand attitude. Which change would lead to the greatest improvement in attitude?

8. Discuss the trade-offs between multiattribute attitude models, measures of attitude toward a product, and measures of purchase intentions in terms of (a) their relative predictive power and (b) their usefulness in understanding consumer behavior.

9. Assume a company is trying to decide which consumer segments represent its best bet for future expansion. To help in this decision, the research department has collected information about segment members' product attitudes. The results show the following average attitude scores on a 10-point scale ranging from "bad product" (1) to "good product" (10):

Segment A   8.2

Segment B   7.5

Segment C   6.1

Based on this information, it has been proposed to target segment A. Do you agree? What problems might exist with making this decision based on the current information?

Endnotes

1. Scott B. MacKenzie, Richard J. Lutz, and George E. Belch, "The Role of Attitude toward the Ad as a Mediator of Advertising Effectiveness: A Test of Competing Explanations," *Journal of Marketing Research* 23 (May 1986), 130–143; Andrew A. Mitchell and Jerry C. Olson, "Are Product Attribute Beliefs the Only Mediators of Advertising Effects on Brand Attitudes?" *Journal of Marketing Research* 18 (August 1981), 318–332; Paul W. Miniard, Sunil Bhatla, and Randall L. Rose, "On the Formation and Relationship of Ad and Brand Attitudes: An Experimental and Causal Analysis," *Journal of Marketing Research* 27 (August 1990), 290–303.

2. Cyndee Miller, "Study Says `Likability' Surfaces as Measure of TV Ad Success," *Marketing News* 25 (January 7, 1991), 6, 14. Also see Cyndee Miller, "Researchers Balk at Testing Rough Ads for `Likability,' " *Marketing News* 25 (September 2, 1991), 2.

3. Rajeev Batra and Olli T. Ahtola, "Measuring the Hedonic and Utilitarian Sources of Consumer Attitudes," *Marketing Letters* 2 (1990), 159–170; Mark P. Zanna and John K. Rempel, "Attitudes: A New Look at an Old Concept," in Daniel Bar-Tal and Arie Kruglanski, eds., *The Social Psychology of Knowledge* (New York: Cambridge University Press, 1988), 315–334.

4. For research on the intention–behavior relationship, see Donald H. Granbois and John O. Summers, "Primary and Secondary Validity of Consumer Purchase Probabilities," *Journal of Consumer Research* 4 (March 1975), 31–38; Paul W. Miniard, Carl Obermiller, and Thomas J. Page, Jr., "A Further Assessment of Measurement Influences on the Intention–Behavior Relationship," *Journal of Marketing Research* (May 1983), 206–212; David J. Reibstein, "The Prediction of Individual Probabilities of Brand Choice," *Journal of Consumer Research* 5 (December 1978), 163–168; Paul R. Warshaw, "Predicting Purchase and Other Behaviors from General and Contextually Specific Intentions," *Journal of Marketing Research* 17 (February 1980), 26–33.

5. Research indicates that measuring the perceived likelihood of performing a behavior rather than the intention to perform a behavior can enhance predictive accuracy. See Paul R. Warshaw and Fred D. Davis, "Disentangling Behavioral Intention and Behavioral Expectation," *Journal of Experimental Social Psychology* 21 (1985), 213–228. Interestingly, research suggests that simply measuring behavioral intention may affect the likelihood of the behavior being undertaken. See Vicki G. Morwitz, Eric Johnson, and David Schmittlein, "Does Measuring Intent Change Behavior?" *Journal of Consumer Research* 20 (June 1993), 46–62.

6. For an excellent discussion and review of the literature concerning attitude resistance, see Alice H. Eagly and Shelly Chaiken, *The Psychology of Attitudes* (Fort Worth, Texas: Harcourt Brace Jovanovich, 1993).

7. For a discussion of different ways to track attitudes, see Matthew Greenwald and John P. Katosh, "How to Track Changes in Attitudes," *American Demographics* 9 (August 1987), 46–47.

8. One way of enhancing resistance is suggested by inoculation theory. See William J. McGuire, "Inducing Resistance to Persuasion: Some Contemporary Approaches," in L. Berkowitz, ed., *Advances in Experimental Social Psychology* 1 (San Diego, Calif.: Academic Press, 1964), 191–229.

9. An exception is the "sleeper effect" in which attitudes become more extreme over time. See A. R. Pratkanis, A. G. Greenwald, M. R. Leippe, and M. H. Baumgardner, "In Search of Reliable Persuasion Effects: III. The Sleeper Effect Is Dead. Long Live the Sleeper Effect," *Journal of Personality and Social Psychology* 54 (1988), 203–218.

10. Ida E. Berger, "The Nature of Attitude Accessibility and Attitude Confidence: A Triangulated Experiment," *Journal of Consumer Psychology* 1 (1992), 103–124.

11. Russell H. Fazio and Mark P. Zanna, "On the Predictive Validity of Attitudes: The Roles of Direct Experience and Confidence," *Journal of Personality* 46 (June 1978),

228–243; Lawrence J. Marks and Michael A. Kamins, "The Use of Product Sampling and Advertising: Effects of Sequence of Exposure and Degree of Advertising Claim Exaggeration on Consumers' Belief Strength, Belief Confidence, and Attitudes," *Journal of Marketing Research* 25 (August 1988), 266–281; Robert E. Smith and William R. Swinyard, "Attitude–Behavior Consistency: The Impact of Product Trial Versus Advertising," *Journal of Marketing Research* 20 (August 1983), 257–267.

12. Berger, "The Nature of Attitude Accessibility and Attitude Confidence"; Fazio and Zanna, "On the Predictive Validity of Attitudes"; Smith and Swinyard, "Attitude–Behavior Consistency."

13. Marks and Kamins, "The Use of Product Sampling and Advertising."

14. Discussion of additional multiattribute models can be found in Frank A. Bass and W. Wayne Talarzyk, "Attitude Model for the Study of Brand Preference," *Journal of Marketing Research* 9 (February 1972), 93–96; Jagdish N. Sheth and W. Wayne Talarzyk, "Perceived Instrumentality and Value Importance as Determinants of Attitudes," *Journal of Marketing Research* 9 (February 1973), 6–9; Milton J. Rosenberg, "Cognitive Structure and Attitudinal Affect," *Journal of Abnormal and Social Psychology* 53 (November 1956), 367–372; Olli T. Ahtola, "The Vector Model of Preferences: An Alternative to the Fishbein Model," *Journal of Marketing Research* 12 (February 1975), 52–59. For general reviews of multiattribute models, see Richard J. Lutz and James R. Bettman, "Multi-Attribute Models in Marketing: A Bicentennial Review," in Arch G. Woodside, Jagdish N. Sheth, and Peter D. Bennett, eds., *Consumer and Industrial Buying Behavior* (New York: North-Holland, 1977), 137–149; William L. Wilkie and Edgar A. Pessemier, "Issues in Marketing's Use of Multi-Attribute Models," *Journal of Marketing Research* 10 (November 1973), 428–441.

15. Martin Fishbein, "An Investigation of the Relationships between Beliefs about an Object and the Attitude toward That Object," *Human Relations* 16 (August 1963), 233–240; Martin Fishbein and Icek Ajzen, *Belief, Attitude, Intention, and Behavior: An Introduction to Theory and Research* (Reading, Mass.: Addison-Wesley, 1975); Icek Ajzen and Martin Fishbein, *Understanding Attitudes and Predicting Social Behavior* (Englewood Cliffs, N.J.: Prentice-Hall, 1980).

16. See, for example, Ernest Dichter, *The Strategy of Desire* (New York: Doubleday, 1960).

17. For an application of this technique, see Robert L. Thornton, "Selling the Hard Goods the Soft Way: American Versus Foreign Cars," *Journal of Consumer Marketing* 1 (1983), 35–44.

18. Evidence suggests that the order in which beliefs are measured (by attribute across brands versus by brand across attributes) can be important. See Eugene D. Joffe and Israel D. Nebenzahl, "Alternative Questionnaire Formats for Country Image Studies," *Journal of Marketing Research* 21 (November 1984), 463–471.

19. Examples of model application can be found in James L. Ginter, "An Experimental Investigation of Attitude Change and Choice of a New Brand," *Journal of Marketing Research* 11 (February 1974), 30–40; Donald R. Lehmann, "Television Show Preference: Application of a Choice Model," *Journal of Marketing Research* 8 (February 1972), 47–55.

20. Joel B. Cohen, Martin Fishbein, and Olli T. Ahtola, "The Nature and Uses of Expectancy-Value Models in Consumer Attitude Research," *Journal of Marketing Research* 9 (November 1972), 456–460.

21. Alvin C. Burns, "Generating Marketing Strategy Priorities Based on Relative Competitive Position," *Journal of Consumer Marketing* 3 (Fall 1986), 49–56.

22. For research on the model's usefulness in new product development, see Morris B. Holbrook and William J. Havlena, "Assessing the Real-to-Generalizability of Multiattribute Attitude Models in Tests of New Product Designs," *Journal of Marketing Research* 25 (February 1988), 25–35.

23. "Lever Brothers Uses Micromodel to Project Market Share," *Marketing News* (November 27, 1981).

24. For an empirical demonstration, see Richard J. Lutz, "Changing Brand Attitudes through Modification of Cognitive Structure," *Journal of Consumer Research* 1 (March 1975), 49–59.

25. Paul W. Miniard, Randall L. Rose, Michael J. Barone, and Kenneth C. Manning, "On the Need for Relative Measures When Assessing Comparative Advertising Effects," *Journal of Advertising* 22 (September 1993), 41–58; Cornelia Pechmann and S. Ratneshwar, "The Use of Comparative Advertising for Brand Positioning: Association versus Differentiation," *Journal of Consumer Research* 18 (September 1991), 145–160; Randall L. Rose, Paul W. Miniard, Michael J. Barone, Kenneth C. Manning, and Brian D. Till, "When Persuasion Goes Undetected: The Case of Comparative Advertising," *Journal of Marketing Research* 30 (August 1993), 315–330.

26. Scott B. MacKenzie, "The Role of Attention in Mediating the Effect of Advertising on Attribute Importance," *Journal of Consumer Research* 13 (September 1986), 174–195.

27. William J. Havlena and Morris B. Holbrook, "The Varieties of Consumption Experience: Comparing Two Typologies of Emotion in Consumer Behavior," *Journal of Consumer Research* 13 (December 1986), 394–404; Elizabeth C. Hirschman and Morris B. Holbrook, "Hedonic Consumption: Emerging Concepts, Methods, and Propositions," *Journal of Marketing* 46 (Summer 1982), 92–101; Morris B. Holbrook, "Emotion in the Consumption Experience: Toward a New Model of the Human Consumer," in Robert A. Peterson, Wayne D. Hoyer, and William R. Wilson, eds., *The Role of Affect in Consumer Behavior* (Lexington, Mass: Heath, 1986), 17–52; Morris B. Holbrook and Elizabeth C. Hirschman, "The Experiential Aspects of Consumption: Consumer Fantasies, Feelings, and Fun," *Journal of Consumer Research* 9 (September 1982), 132–140.

28. Haim Mano and Richard L. Oliver, "Assessing the Dimensionality and Structure of the Consumption Experience: Evaluation, Feeling, and Satisfaction," *Journal of Consumer Research* 20 (December 1993), 451–466; Richard L. Oliver, "Cognitive, Affective, and Attribute Bases of the Satisfaction Response," *Journal of Consumer Research* 20 (December 1993), 418–430; Robert A. Westbrook, "Product/Consumption-Based Affective Responses and Postpurchase Processes," *Journal of Marketing Research* 24 (August 1987), 258–270; Robert A. Westbrook and Richard L. Oliver, "The Dimensionality of Consumption Emotion Patterns and Consumer Satisfaction," *Journal of Consumer Research* 18 (June 1991), 84–91.

29. Marian Chapman Burke and Julie A. Edell, "The Impact of Feelings on Ad-Based Affect and Cognition," *Journal of Marketing Research* 26 (February 1989), 69–83; Julie A. Edell and Marian Chapman Burke, "The Power of Feelings in Understanding Advertising Effects," *Journal of Consumer Research* 14 (December 1987), 421–433; Thomas J. Olney, Morris B. Holbrook, and Rajeev Batra, "Consumer Responses to Advertising: The Effects of Ad Content, Emotions, and Attitude toward the Ad on Viewing Time," *Journal of Consumer Research* 17 (March 1991), 440–453; Douglas M. Stayman and Rajeev Batra, "Encoding and Retrieval of Ad Affect in Memory," *Journal of Marketing Research* 28 (May 1991), 232–239.

30. Applications of various feeling measures in consumer contexts can be found in Chris T. Allen, Karen A. Machleit, and Susan Schultz Kleine, "A Comparison of Attitudes and Emotions as Predictors of Behavior at Diverse Levels of Behavioral Experience," *Journal of Consumer Research* 18 (March 1992), 493–502; Edell and Burke, "The Power of Feelings in Understanding Advertising Effects"; Havlena and Holbrook, "The Varieties of Consumption Experience: Comparing Two Typologies of Emotion in Consumer Behavior"; John P. Murry, Jr., John L. Lavosticka, and Surendra N. Singh, "Feeling and Liking Responses to Television Programs: An Examination of Two Explanations for Media-Context Effects," *Journal of Consumer Research* 18 (March 1992), 441–451.

31. Edell and Burke, "The Power of Feelings in Understanding Advertising Effects."

32. Richard Tracy LaPiere, "Attitudes vs. Actions," *Social Forces* 13 (December 1934), 230–237.

33. For research on how unexpected situations can influence the attitude–behavior relationship, see Joseph A. Cote, James McCullough, and Michael Reilly, "Effects of Unexpected Situations on Behavior-Intention Differences: A Garbology Analysis," *Journal of Consumer Research* 12 (September 1985), 188–194.

34. Ajzen and Fishbein, *Understanding Attitudes and Predicting Social Behavior;* E. Bonfield, "Attitude, Social Influence, Personal Norms, and Intention Interactions as Related to Brand Purchase Behavior," *Journal of Marketing Research* 11 (November 1974), 379–389.

35. Ajzen and Fishbein, *Understanding Attitudes and Predicting Social Behavior;* Fishbein and Ajzen, *Belief, Attitude, Intention, and Behavior.* Alternative variations of the theory of reasoned action can be found in Paul W. Miniard and Joel B. Cohen, "Modeling Personal and Normative Influences on Behavior," *Journal of Consumer Research* 10 (September 1983), 169–180; Paul R. Warshaw, "A New Model for Predicting Behavioral Intentions: An Alternative to Fishbein," *Journal of Marketing Research* 17 (May 1980), 153–172.

36. For reviews, see Ajzen and Fishbein, *Understanding Attitudes and Predicting Social Behavior;* Fishbein and Ajzen, *Belief, Attitude, Intention, and Behavior;* Michael J. Ryan and E. H. Bonfield, "The Fishbein Extended Model and Consumer Behavior," *Journal of Consumer Research* 2 (September 1975), 118–136; Blair H. Sheppard, Jon Hartwick, and Paul R. Warshaw, "The Theory of Reasoned Action: A Meta-Analysis of Past Research with Recommendations for Modifications and Future Research," *Journal of Consumer Research* 15 (December 1988), 325–343.

37. One concern with the theory of reasoned action has centered around the question of how to separate the influence of attitudes and social others. See Paul W. Miniard and Joel B. Cohen, "Isolating Attitudinal and Normative Influences in Behavioral Intentions Models," *Journal of Marketing Research* 16 (February 1979), 102–110; Paul W. Miniard and Joel B. Cohen, "An Examination of the Fishbein-Ajzen Behavior Intention Model's Concepts and Measures," *Journal of Experimental Social Psychology* 17 (July 1981), 309–339; Miniard and Cohen, "Modeling Personal and Normative Influences on Behavior"; Michael J. Ryan, "Behavioral Intention Formation: A Structural Equation Analysis of Attitudinal and Social Influence Interdependency," *Journal of Consumer Research* 9 (December 1982), 263–278.

38. Icek Ajzen, "From Intentions to Actions: A Theory of Planned Behavior," in J. Kuhland and J. Beckman, eds., *Action Control: From Cognitions to Behavior* (Heidelberg: Springer-Verlag, 1985), 11–39.

39. For a review, see Icek Ajzen, "The Theory of Planned Behavior," *Organizational Behavior and Human Decision Processes* 50 (1991), 179–211.

40. Thomas J. Madden, Pamela Scholder Ellen, and Icek Ajzen, "A Comparison of the Theory of Planned Behavior and the Theory of Reasoned Action," *Personality and Social Psychology Bulletin* 18 (February 1992), 3–9.

41. Marks and Kamins, "The Use of Product Sampling and Advertising"; Smith and Swinyard, "Attitude–Behavior Consistency."

42. Berger, "The Nature of Attitude Accessibility and Attitude Confidence"; Ida E. Berger and Andrew A. Mitchell, "The Effect of Advertising on Attitude Accessibility, Attitude Confidence, and the Attitude–Behavior Relationship," *Journal of Consumer Research* 16 (December 1989), 269–279; Russell H. Fazio, Martha C. Powell, and Carol J. Williams, "The Role of Attitude Accessibility in the Attitude-to-Behavior Process," *Journal of Consumer Research* 16 (December 1989), 280–288.

43. The literature is greatly indebted to the following article for its contribution concerning the importance of measurement correspondence: Icek Ajzen and Martin Fishbein, "Attitude–Behavior Relations: A Theoretical Analysis and Review of Empirical Research," *Psychological Bulletin* 84 (September 1977), 888–918. For an empirical demonstration, see James Jaccard, G. William King, and Richard Pomazal, "Attitudes and Behavior: An Analysis of Specificity of Attitudinal Predictors," *Human Relations* 30 (September 1977), 817–824.

CHAPTER 12

Motivation and Self-Concept

▲▲▲▲▲▲▲▲▲▲▲▲▲▲▲▲▲▲▲▲▲▲▲▲▲▲▲▲▲▲▲▲▲▲▲▲▲

You Just Can't Talk to These Kids

Mizuhu Arai knows what she likes. A 20-year-old uniformed office worker by day, at night she assembles a decidedly casual look—loafers, a sweater, Levi's 501s, and a black parka. Shopping with a beige L.L. Bean bag over her shoulder, she prefers bargain outlets to the high-priced designer boutiques that flourished in the 1980s. "I don't like to be told what's trendy," Arai says. "I can make up my own mind."

That's bad news for marketers who would rather make it up for her. Arai is one of 8.1 million young Japanese, aged 18 to 21, dubbed the "baby boomer juniors." Mostly the children of Japan's baby boomers, they spend almost $33 billion a year, according to ad agency Dentsu, Inc.

But marketers often sound downright baffled by the juniors. "They don't listen to us," complains Kenichi Mizorogi, cosmetics-development manager at $4.7 billion Shiseido Co. Mizorogi and other marketers spent the 1980s spotting the must-have fads and styles that the twentysomethings [sic] of the last decade—called *shinjinrui*, or new breed—happily snapped up. In the late 1980s, for example, Shiseido launched its Perky Jean line of makeup with the ad message, "Everyone is buying it." Says Mizorogi: "That would never work now."

So what's come over Junior? In a survey, Dentsu has found Junior puts a big premium on individuality, rather than price tags and labels. Fully 94% say they buy what they like, even if it is not a famous brand. Instead of fads and flash, they want value, simplicity, and practicality. "Compared with the *shinjinrui*, who just played and hopped on trends, the juniors aren't a consumer society," says sociologist Yashushi Matsumoto of Nagoya University.

"You can't fool them," advises Dentsu marketing researcher Chiaki Yamaguchi. Instead, you have to convince them — a tougher task in any market.

Source: Karen Lowry Miller, "You Just Can't Talk to These Kids," Business Week *(April 19, 1993), 104, 106. Reproduced by special permission.*

An interesting story, isn't it? Here you have a graphic illustration of what happens when marketers fail to understand what motivates the consumer. The purpose of this chapter is to help keep you from joining the ranks of "baffled marketers" who have only themselves to blame for their dilemma.

A person can be said to be motivated when his or her system is energized (aroused), made active, and behavior is directed toward a desired goal. The marketing challenge is to discover the primary motivating influences and to design strategies that both activate and satisfy felt needs. Those who have done this with the "baby boom juniors" have prospered. Sanyo Electric Co. has responded by stripping unwanted gadgetry and controls from its product lines. Furthermore, sales tripled when a "jeans-washing" mode was added to its washing machine line.[1]

This chapter explores some foundational concepts and theories of motivation. We begin with a discussion of the dynamics of the motivation process and the central importance of need activation and satisfaction. You will discover the important role played by self-concept. We then turn to some major needs that affect consumer behavior, various approaches to measurement and evaluation, and the primary implications for marketing strategy.

Dynamics of the Motivation Process

An overview of the motivation process[2] appears in Figure 12.1. You will notice that everything starts with need recognition (or activation). A **need** is activated and felt when there is a sufficient discrepancy between a desired or preferred state of being and the actual state. As this discrepancy increases, the outcome is activation of a condition of arousal referred to as **drive**. The stronger the drive, the greater the perceived urgency of response. Alert marketers will do everything possible to provide products or services that are effective in reducing this state of arousal.

Over time, certain behavior patterns are recognized as more effective than others for need satisfaction, and these come to function as **wants**. A college student studying for a final examination says to her roommate, "I'm thirsty."

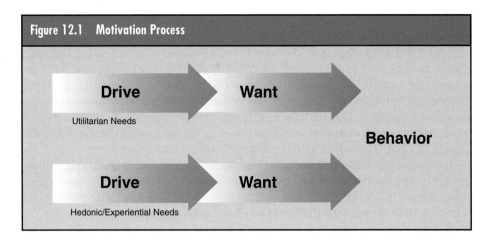

First, she perceives discomfort, *felt need,* that is recognized as thirst. This activated need leads to *drive* (arousal). A can of Diet Coke (her favorite beverage) from the machine down the hall is the thing that she most *wants,* and she behaves accordingly.

Felt Need

Felt need can be activated in different ways, one of which is entirely physiological, thirst or hunger being examples. The human being also possesses the capacity for thinking about a person or object not present at the immediate time or imagining the desirable consequences of a particular action. This thought process in itself can be arousing. All of us, for example, can feel hunger at times just by thinking about a favorite food. Finally, arousal can be triggered by outside information. You become hungry when your eye is stopped by a point-of-sale display announcing a special low price for Dove Bars.

Figure 12.1 illustrates that felt needs can be classified into two broad categories based on the benefits expected through purchase and use: (1) utilitarian needs, and (2) hedonic/experiential needs.[3] **Utilitarian needs** lead to consideration of objective, functional product attributes or benefits, whereas **hedonic/experiential needs** encompass subjective responses, pleasures, daydreams, and aesthetic considerations.[4]

It is common for utilitarian and hedonic needs to function simultaneously in a purchase decision. For example, a potential buyer compares European luxury cars on such objective dimensions as head room, rear seat room, acceleration, and automatic locking systems. Hedonic benefits, however, can include such subjective considerations as a sense of status and prestige derived from owning a top-of-the-line car and the sheer sense of pleasure in driving. Alternative evaluation now becomes more spontaneous and holistic, focusing on overall symbolism, as opposed to specific features.[5]

We doubt that you have learned much that is new here except, possibly, the terminology that is used. All of us are fully aware that we are motivated by both objective and subjective considerations. Yet, a reading of much of the literature in this field in the period ranging from the 1960s to early 1980s could have led you to the conclusion that consumers act in a semiautomatic, nonemotional manner, weighing purely cognitive factors such as price and performance in arriving at a decision. This distorted perspective probably reflects the aversion of most researchers at that time to the excesses of the motivation research era discussed in Chapter 1 when the "Freudian invasion" took place.

Fortunately, common sense now prevails. In fact, we have returned, without recognizing it, to the balanced and once-influential perspective of marketing pioneer Melvin Copeland, who claimed as early as 1924 that consumers are motivated by both rational (utilitarian) and emotional motives.[6]

Motivational Role of Involvement

You will recall from Chapter 4 that the concept of *involvement* (the level of personal importance or interest evoked by a stimulus in a given situation)[7] is of major significance in understanding and explaining consumer behavior. This term was first popularized in marketing circles by Krugman in 1965 and has generated considerable interest since that time.[8] To the extent that it is present, the consumer is motivated to act with deliberation to minimize risks and to maximize the benefits gained from purchase and use.

Involvement, then, is a reflection of strong motivation in the form of high perceived personal relevance of a product or service in a particular context. Depending on the perceived linkage between the individual's motivating influences and the benefits offered by the object, it is a continuum ranging from low to high. Involvement becomes activated and felt when intrinisic personal characteristics (needs, values, self-concept) are confronted with appropriate marketing stimuli within a given situation.[9]

Influence of Affect

When a person is motivated, there can be quite a range of accompanying feelings, emotions, and moods that also function to shape behavioral outcomes. These influences now are referred to as **affect**—positive or negative feeling states[10]—and influence consumer behavior in different ways:

1. Positive affect (that is, a good mood) speeds up information processing and reduces the decision time in selecting appropriate products.[11]

2. Activated mood leads to recall of products with positive associations.

3. Emotions can serve to activate a state of drive.[12]

The basic marketing principle here is familiar and obvious: "You have a better chance of winning them if you make them feel good." There is no end to exam-

Figure 12.2   Emotions Are a Powerful Selling Appeal

ples that could be cited. For example, what feelings do you think are evoked by the ad in Figure 12.2, even though you may not understand French? This ad might even warm the heart of a cheese hater. And do you remember the role of a female-oriented atmosphere in attracting women to take their car for service into the once-dreaded lair of the grease monkeys (Chapter 4)?

It is well known that people develop emotional attachments to brands. As the research documented in Consumer in Focus 12.1 reveals, this may be the reason why Campbell Soup has had such a remarkable record of sales success over many decades.

Be careful, however, when working cross-culturally to make sure that the emotional symbols used convey the intended meaning. Take time to read Consumer in Focus 12.2, which documents the significant role that affect generated by careful landscaping can play in selling houses to Asian-Americans.

12.1   Consumer in Focus

Campbell Soup—A "Nutritional Scarf"

Campbell Soup Company has used *emotional sonar* [an interactive computer program designed to measure emotions] to gain insight into how its core consumer groups form emotional bonds with the brand. It surveyed people who buy more than 100 cans of Campbell soup a year. "We want to understand the brand's essence," says Anthony Adams, Campbell's vice president of marketing research. "These are people who would put an 'I Love Campbell's' bumper sticker on their car. What makes them want to do that?"

The research showed that one of the things that keeps core customers coming back to Campbell is the brand's nurturing image. They helped Campbell develop its latest generation of ads. In one, a chilly little boy is served a bowl of soup and wrapped in a scarf by his mom. A nurturing mother, a child, and warmth are all part of Campbell's imagery. They are summed up in the symbol of the scarf. "Soup is like a nutritional scarf," says Adams. "It warms you, whether you are physically or psychologically cold."

Source: Rebecca Piirto, "Mind Games," American Demographics (December 1991), 54.

12.2   Consumer in Focus

Using The "Wind and the Water" to Attract Asian Homeowners

Imagine a curving path leading to a house nestled in the hills. In the backyard glistens an ornamental pool. The house doesn't sound like it would be hard to sell to anyone. But it is especially appealing to Asian homebuyers. These qualities, along with many others, translate into *feng shui*—literally, "the wind and the water."

Rooted in China's centuries-old agrarian culture, *feng shui* (pronounced "fung shoy") often guides many Asians' beliefs about good and bad luck in a home. "If it's a good *feng shui* environment, then more Asians will buy it," says Marsha Golangco, a real estate marketer in Alamo, California.

Ponderosa Homes, a San Francisco Bay area developer, sought Golangco's cross-cultural advice when designing several subdivisions. Ponderosa minimized the number of "T" intersections, rejected rectangular front lawns in favor of kidney-shaped lawns, and planted shrubs, Japanese maples, and evergreen pear trees. They also added rounded rocks to each yard.

These changes influence *chi,* which many Asians believe is an invisible energy current. *Chi* represents an important part of *feng shui* beliefs. "Vicious, harmful *chi* travels on a straight line," Golangco says, "Beneficial, gentle *chi* travels on a curved, irregular path."

Source: Dan Fost, "Asian Homebuyers Seek Wind and Water," American Demographics (June 1993), 23–24.

Figure 12.3 Does This Ad Create a Need?

Dashing.

The forecast for this holiday season calls for delicious accumulations of Godiva® Chocolate. Imagine, all those golden boxes being opened in a flurry of excitement. Then the momentary silence as those legendary chocolates with their enchanted fillings are experienced with sheer delight. It's a delectable prediction that can be shared with family and friends. So, don't let the season drift by without the magical gift of Godiva.

For more information about Godiva chocolates, call 1-800-732-7333, in NY 1-212-951-2888. Godiva Chocolatier, 701 Fifth Avenue, New York, New York 10022.

Can Needs Be Created?

Here is a question that has been debated in marketing classrooms probably since the first course was taught in 1904 at the University of Michigan: *Can marketers create needs?* More specifically, can the famous European confectioner, Godiva Chocolatier, somehow manipulate consumers to respond by creating a need for its expensive product line through the ad in Figure 12.3? If so, some serious ethical questions are raised.

There are critics who argue vigorously that marketers are manipulating the unwary consumer by inducing them to buy things they do not need. Consider these words from Cheryl Russell and Thomas G. Exter:

> Perhaps the most notorious example of a created need is the ad campaign that made an entire nation conscious of morning breath. But some products cannot be construed as necessary by any stretch of most people's imaginations. Here, the method is to cajole people into giving themselves a treat. L'Oréal's "I'm worth it" campaign for premium hair coloring is a prime example.[13]

We contend, in rebuttal, that a need for these products already existed, even though it may have been dormant and largely unrecognized; it is not created by the marketer. We suspect that many already were concerned about "morning breath" and its effect on personal relations. Therefore, a need existed long before marketer's got wind of it. What marketing communication accomplished, however, was to position a mouthwash brand in the most favorable light in terms of potential to overcome the problem. In other words, *skillful marketing can stimulate a want or desire for a product or service,* but this will not happen unless a need already exists.

So, where is the great manipulatory power alluded to by Russell and Exter? Nothing has been done in the examples cited to circumvent an uninhibited freedom of choice. The charges aimed at marketers seem to represent little more than a personal opinion regarding the products cited. Each generation of critics (as well as business executives) must relearn a historically validated principle: *Marketing efforts succeed by satisfying existing needs, not by creating needs.*

Unity and Stability of Motive Patterns

One of the fundamental premises of human behavior is that people behave in a purposeful and consistent manner. This implies that needs and motivations are integrated in a meaningful way. In the course of this century, authorities have come to agree that self-concept provides this unification.[14] The late Carl R. Rogers[15] defined self-concept in this way:

> *The self-concept, or self-structure, may be thought of as an organized configuration of perceptions of the self which are admissible to awareness. It is composed of such elements as the perceptions of one's characteristics and abilities; the percepts and concepts of the self in relation to others and to the environment; the values and qualities which are perceived as associated with experiences; and objectives, goals and ideals which are perceived as having positive or negative valence.*

A central motive is to enhance this view of one's self. As a result, striving toward self-esteem has a direct influence on values, goals, and objectives. As the "baby boomer juniors" in Japan proved, consumers engage in information processing and buying behavior that is consistent and *congruent* with their self-image. Therefore, it is probable that advertising appeals congruent with self-image will be more effective in terms of brand memory, brand attitude, and purchase intentions.[16]

Research motivated by congruity theory was especially prevalent during the Freudian invasion in the motivation research days of the 1950s. Attempts were made to capitalize on or change existing brand images to stress the match between self-image and brand image. Upwardly mobile, status-conscious executives, for example, allegedly were more prone to buy Buicks, which were positioned on the market as the car for the "person on the move." This led to great interest in studies of brand image, which continue to this day.

Several consumer research studies were then undertaken to examine the congruency hypothesis rigorously.[17] On the basis of a thorough review of the evidence, however, Sirgy[18] came to the conclusion in the early 1980s that the correlations, although generally positive, were sufficiently low to suggest that marketers have little to gain by attempts to measure self-concept. This led to a virtual moratorium on this avenue of research, which was heeded for well over a decade.

Part of the reason for Sirgy's conclusion is the obvious fact that most consumer products fall into the category of the mundane and unimportant.[19] It is hard to imagine congruity between a preferred brand of toilet paper or motor oil and self-concept.

The interest in self-concept was reignited in the later 1980s, however, when the postmodern research perspective emerged.[20] The breakthrough came when product consumption was substituted for buying behavior and purchase as the principal variable.[21] But you must remember that postmodern researchers have interests that often are unrelated to those of marketers. The primary focus of the research reviewed in this section is to discover ways in which individuals use goods and services to construct and maintain their social reality.[22] Nevertheless, you will also discover some interesting marketing insights.

Broader View of Self-Concept

This vein of consumer research acknowledges that self-concept now is viewed in a much broader manner as having multiple dimensions.[23] Figure 12.4 illustrates these dimensions and the behavioral outcomes that have been identified:

- *Ideal self* (the self I aspire to be)
- *Real self* (the way I think I actually am)
- *Self in context* (the way I see myself in different social settings)
- *Extended self* (self as incorporated into objects and artifacts that assume importance)

Self-Expression in the Daily Life of the Consumer

Postmodern consumer researchers are plowing new ground and have identified multiple ways in which the self-concept works itself out in the daily life of the consumer: (1) transcendence; (2) self-monitoring; (3) fantasy; and (4) self-gift giving.

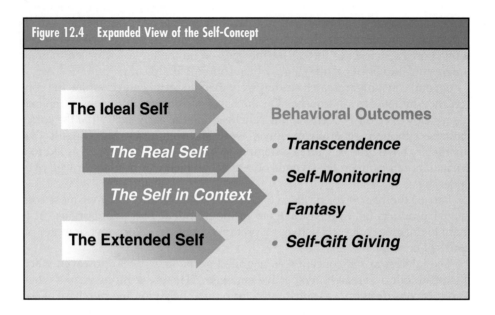

Figure 12.4   Expanded View of the Self-Concept

The Ideal Self

The Real Self

The Self in Context

The Extended Self

Behavioral Outcomes

- *Transcendence*
- *Self-Monitoring*
- *Fantasy*
- *Self-Gift Giving*

Transcendence

Russell Belk[24] contends that "we are what we have" and that there is an extended self-concept that encompasses possessions. This allows us to *transcend* our existence as biologic beings and to assign unique, often sacred[25] meanings to our possessions. In so doing, our sense of self is spatially enlarged and enriched.[26]

We agree that possessions in most cultures play the important role of helping us learn who we are, where we have been, and where we are going. Certainly, the designers of the Cross pen ad in Figure 12.5 were well aware of this aspect of human nature. Notice how effectively the words capitalize on the emotional linkages with something as seemingly mundane as a pen.

Possessions also play the important role of linking a person with his or her past. Objects often are acquired to preserve memories and to serve as a permanent nostalgic benchmark of a different time. Indeed, it is not an overstatement that such objects can take on sacred dimensions. Preservation of the past also can be a potent advertising appeal (Figure 12.6).

The point is that objects take on characteristics that go far beyond their utilitarian features. As a result, deep and complex attachments can be assigned to products in some very surprising ways. Ahmed Mills in Bombay, India, for example, makes a cooking oil marketed under the brand name Postman. It has successfully fought off competition from Bombay Oil Mills' Saffola brand by reassuring users that it had stood the test of time for 60 years. "Mothers . . . they're always right."[27]

Figure 12.5   A Quality Pen Has Rich Meaning

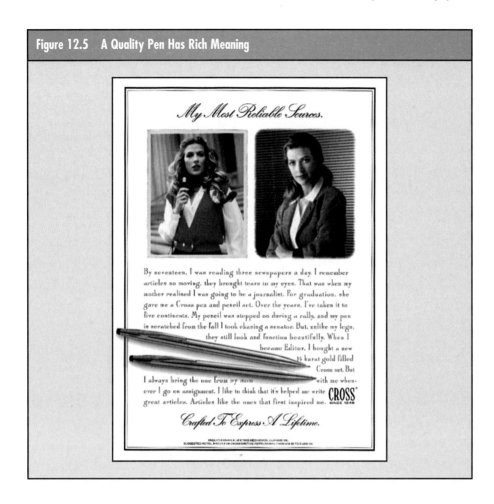

But who would have guessed that Levi's 501 jeans ever would have become a cultural icon? These jeans have come to possess a surprisingly rich image as the following list details.[28]

- *Confidence:* "I don't have to worry about what I'm wearing."
- *Magic:* "I can do anything in them."
- *Personalization:* "Jeans are me."
- *Mnenomic value:* "Jeans are my companion, and what great memories I have had."
- *Continuity:* "I can trust my jeans—they last forever."
- *Ceremonial rites:* "I always will remember breaking these jeans in, and I treasure wearing my mother's favorite jeans."

Figure 12.6   Power of Nostalgia

Self-Monitoring

Most people are well aware of the varying expectations in social contexts and will modify behavior accordingly. This is what we mean by **self-monitoring**,[29] which has three forms of expression: (1) concern for social appropriateness of behavior; (2) attention to social comparison as cues for appropriate self-expression; and (3) the ability to modify self-presentation and expression across situations.[30]

Low self-monitors are more prone to guide their behavior from their own personal dispositions, feelings, and interests and hence are more consistent. Those in this category are much more likely to respond to the appeal in Figure 12.7 by "taking the crowd with you" rather than following it. High self-monitors, however, will be more responsive to appeals that reflect the image of the self they strive to be in social situations (Figure 12.8).

Figure 12.7 "Don't Follow the Crowd"

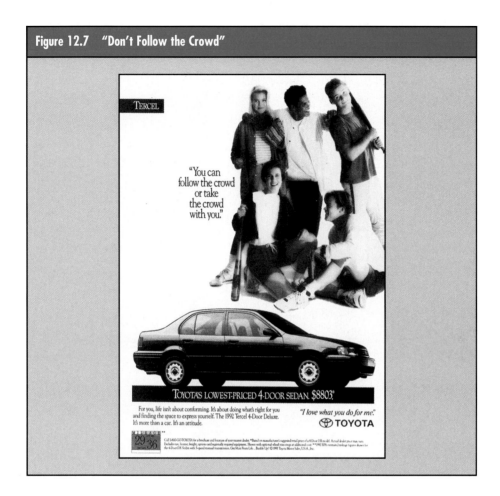

Fantasy

Another form of monitoring is comparison of real self with ideal self. One of the most common outcomes is fantasy and daydreaming. If taken to extremes, this can be dysfunctional, but there is no question that fantasy can be a powerful selling appeal. What do you think of the imagery in the Obsession ad in Figure 12.9?

Self-Gift Giving

For many years, McDonald's Corp. prospered with the advertising theme, "You deserve a break today" in recognition that self-gift giving is a common phenomenon. A self-gift bolsters self-esteem through an indulgence justified by deserving behavior. As Mick and DeMoss[31] have discovered, self-gifts are premeditated and usually take the form of a high-involvement product or service.

Figure 12.8   Responding to the Expectations of Others

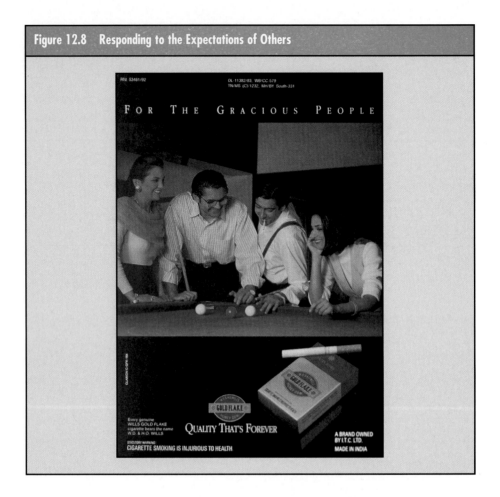

FOR THE GRACIOUS PEOPLE

QUALITY THAT'S FOREVER

Every genuine
WILLS GOLD FLAKE
cigarette bears the name
W.D. & H.O. WILLS

STATUTORY WARNING:
CIGARETTE SMOKING IS INJURIOUS TO HEALTH.

A BRAND OWNED
BY I.T.C. LTD.
MADE IN INDIA

Understanding Consumer Needs

Need is a variable of central importance to those whose intent is to influence consumer behavior. If needs can be measured and understood, it is possible to position marketing efforts more effectively in the context of consumer goals.

Challenge of Measurement

Several methodologic approaches to measurement are possible, including (1) scaled activity, interest, and opinion (AIO) questions; (2) motivation research methods (in-depth guided interviews and projective tests); (3) focus groups; (4) qualitative research; and (5) ethnography.

Figure 12.9   Obsession — Fantasy!

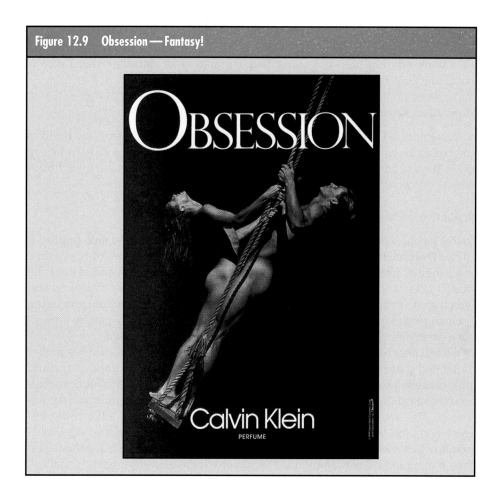

Scaled AIO Questions

A common approach makes use of a series of scaled agree-disagree questions covering varying areas of possible motivation and interest. Often these are referred to as AIO or psychographic questions. Basic needs and motivations are often uncovered by searching for a common pattern of interest across various questions.

Psychographic questions were used in a study of American college students, and here are three concerns that proved to be strongly correlated[32]: (1) how to overcome performance stress on the campus; (2) how to get better grades; and (3) how to be free from financial worries when I graduate.

The common denominator here is a fear of future financial insecurity, which is expressed by strong motivation to get better grades (mentioned as being of major importance by more than half of the students). Not surprisingly, more than 10 percent of students responded positively to direct marketing appeals for a book offering help in getting better grades—an unusually high direct-marketing response.

Motivation Research Methods

We have referred to the so-called Freudian invasion several times—the motivation research era in marketing that was mostly confined to the 1950s and early 1960s. It was characterized by fairly widespread use of methods borrowed from clinical psychology, including depth interviews and projective tests.

Depth Interviews

One of the most common motivation research methods is the so-called **depth** (or guided) **interview**.[33] Only a small sample is interviewed (50 or less) one at a time in a lengthy, unstructured session. Some early advocates contended that the guided interview enables researchers to plumb all levels of consciousness and even the unconscious, thus moving beyond the scope of conventional marketing research methods. It was alleged that the marketer has much to gain by appealing to motivating influences that cannot be consciously expressed.

We still hear this claim, and here is an example. A clinically trained researcher contended that people in one European country disdain consumption of fluid milk because of unfavorable childhood imagery. The proposed solution, supposedly based on in-depth, guided interviews, was to associate milk with motherhood. This was accomplished by nature-like packaging and advertising imagery, complete with rolling hills, suggesting a most obvious part of the female anatomy as viewed at the time of birth. Plausible? Well, sales did increase. Perhaps a more logical explanation is that greatly increased advertising enhanced name recognition.

Few today would contend that in-depth interviewing has such magic qualities. First of all, probing into the unconscious is difficult over a period of many months, let alone a 1-hour interview. But of much greater importance, there is consensus that the most deeply hidden drives and desires have little to do with why people buy.[34]

Nevertheless, the use of unstructured, probing questions has survived to this day and is experiencing a revival. The reason for this resurgence is growing awareness that the typical structured survey is too inflexible to probe into those individualized responses that often reveal the most about motivation. We agree that it is possible to learn more, at times, from 40 guided interviews than from much larger samples with rigid questioning techniques.

Projective Tests

Projective tests are another import from the counseling clinic. They are based on the accurate assumption that people can avoid direct questions and give evasive

Consumer in Focus **12.3**

Mind Games

Americans buy things for strange and unexpected reasons. For example, one ordinary household cleaning product has a strong appeal to women who want revenge on their boyfriends.

A few years ago, the McCann-Erickson advertising agency wanted to find out why Raid roach spray out-sold Combat insecticide disks in certain markets. In interviews, most users agreed that Combat is a better product because it kills roaches without any effort on the user's part. So the agency asked the heaviest users of roach spray—low-income Southern women—to draw pictures of their prey. The goal was to get at their underlying feelings about this dirty job.

All of the 100 women who participated in the agency's interviews portrayed roaches as men. "A lot of their feelings about the roach were very similar to the feelings they had about the men in their lives," says Paula Drillman, executive vice president at McCann-Erickson. They said that the roach, like the man in their life, only comes around when he wants food.

The act of spraying roaches and seeing them die was satisfying to this frustrated powerless group. Setting out Combat disks may have been less trouble, but it just didn't give them the same feeling. "These women wanted control," Drillman says. "They used the spray because it allowed them to participate in the kill."

Source: Rebecca Piirto, "Beyond Mind Games," American Demographics (December 1991), 52.

answers. At other times, they may not know what their motivation is. Many methods still are in common use (cartoons, incomplete sentences, and other variations). For an interesting example, see Consumer in Focus 12.3.

Focus Groups

At other times, people are asked to discuss their motivations and behavior in small groups referred to as focus groups. Groups of about ten people are brought together for a session that usually does not exceed 1 hour in length. The interviewer, a skilled discussion leader, lets conversation flow naturally but guides it in such a way that pertinent issues are covered. The group setting provides a relaxed atmosphere, and the thoughts of one person stimulate those of others. Participants soon find themselves talking freely about their concerns. The outcome is often a richer yield of information than is possible through structured questionnaires.

Qualitative Research

The postmodern input to the understanding of consumer behavior has come about, in part, through a family of techniques referred to by Hirschman[35] as

interpretive research. Included among these is **qualitative research**, which centers on how meaning is generated in communication messages.[36] This is done through analysis of the ways in which message elements (signs, symbols, and icons) are combined to create meaning. As Holbrook[37] noted, primary emphasis is placed on the researcher's personal, subjective, and introspective inputs as an important part of the analysis.

Here is an example of interpretive research used to clarify the advertising meaning of a very familiar symbol, the teddy bear named Snuggle.[38] Lever Brothers Co. built a $300 million fabric softener brand through the charms of this little bear and wanted to further capitalize on this potent symbol. Here are the words of Carol Moog, a psychologist who made use of semiotics:

> The bear is an ancient symbol of aggression, but when you create a teddy bear, you provide a softer, nurturant side to that aggression. As a symbol of tamed aggression, the teddy bear is the perfect image for a fabric softener that tames the rough texture of clothing. To keep the magic, it has to be just Snuggle and the viewer communicating. The teddy bear acts as a bridge between the consumer's rational and more instinctual, emotional side.[39]

What do you think of this interpretation? Admittedly, it is subjective and open to challenge, but insights of this type lie far beyond the realm of surveys. We think this is plausible and welcome the richness to be found when we move beyond the confines of our traditional research boundaries.

Ethnography

The methods presented thus far all focus primarily on verbal or written responses to questions of various types. There is growing interest in more naturalistic methods that concentrate on observation and interpretation of behavior as it happens.[40] Among the most popular in recent years has been the tried-and-true staple of cultural anthropologists — **ethnography**.

As you discover in Consumer in Focus 12.4, the guided interview is supplemented by participant observation of buying and consumption behavior.[41] Inquiry is directed less by specific hypotheses and more by a determined attempt to understand what's taking place from a wide-ranging, interdisciplinary perspective.

Classification of Needs

For nearly 100 years, psychologists and marketers alike have tried their hand at classifying needs. Some of their lists are quite lengthy and exhibit creative ingenuity. It is still common today to find detailed enumeration of needs as classified by Murray in 1938,[42] McClelland,[43] McGuire,[44] and others.

The only contribution of this nature that has stood the test of time, however, was proposed by Abraham Maslow,[45] and it is worthy of discussion. Maslow as-

Consumer in Focus **12.4**

Socks, Ties, and Videotape

It may be useful to hear what consumers say, but it's essential to keep track of what they do. Sometimes the only way to find out why people really make specific purchase decisions is to catch people in the act and ask them. Says Allison Cohen, a psychologist and director of account planning for the Ally & Gargano agency in New York City, "You can get a more honest answer if you catch them off guard."

This form of direct observation is called ethnography. It's a technique borrowed from anthropology, and it helps market researchers identify the motivations that lie beneath the surface of the rational mind.

Today, a video camera is the consumer ethnographer's best friend. Allison Cohen has used ethnography to study products as diverse as Tampax tampons and Swiss chocolates, and she won't go anywhere without a video camera in tow. Typically, she'll go into someone's home, poke through their pantry, record the brands she finds, and interview the occupants.

In a study for a Swiss chocolate manufacturer, Cohen went into the homes of "chocoholics" to see how chocolate fit into their lives. "We saw some aberrant behavior in otherwise sane people," she says. Chocoholics hid their stashes in lingerie drawers, in freezers, on top of china cabinets, and under sofas. They ate chocolate in the same way other people drink wine — using domestic brands like Snickers every day and hoarding Godiva chocolates to savor only on special occasions or after a particularly bad day.

Source: Rebecca Piirto, "Socks, Ties, and Videotape," American Demographics (September 1991), 6.

sumed that needs are organized in such a way as to establish priorities and hierarchies of importance among them (referred to as **prepotency**). His classification of needs ranging from lowest to highest order appears in Figure 12.10.

Maslow's hierarchy can be summarized into three categories: (1) survival and safety; (2) human interaction, love, and affiliation; and (3) self-actualization (competency, self-expression, and understanding). Each higher-order need is presumed to be largely dormant until lower-level needs are satisfied.

A distinguished pioneer in consumer research, the late economist George Katona, confirmed that need hierarchies are reflected in consumer behavior.[46] He observed that previously ignored desires exert themselves most frequently after a purchase has satisfied a predominant (and perhaps lower-order) need. This can help explain why an older, successful business or professional person in his or her 50s can move away from status as a dominant motive into a more leisurely pursuit of art and music.

Few researchers today would accept that lower-order needs somehow cease functioning once there is a satisfactory level of fulfillment in the sense that Maslow implied. Furthermore, actions can be impelled by a combination of needs across the hierarchy. Finally, there is great variation in hierarchies across

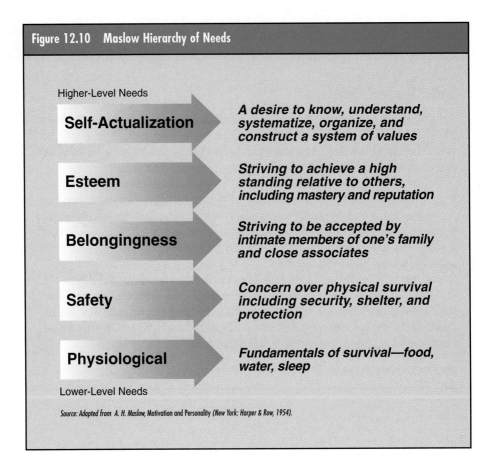

Figure 12.10   Maslow Hierarchy of Needs

Higher-Level Needs

Self-Actualization — *A desire to know, understand, systematize, organize, and construct a system of values*

Esteem — *Striving to achieve a high standing relative to others, including mastery and reputation*

Belongingness — *Striving to be accepted by intimate members of one's family and close associates*

Safety — *Concern over physical survival including security, shelter, and protection*

Physiological — *Fundamentals of survival—food, water, sleep*

Lower-Level Needs

Source: Adapted from A. H. Maslow, Motivation and Personality (New York: Harper & Row, 1954).

cultures. Therefore, the Maslow perspective is accepted more as a helpful general principle than a determining rule of behavior.

Role of Specific Needs

The more recent literature has concentrated on specific needs that can be isolated and explained empirically. An example is **need for cognition**. Although everyone engages in thinking, there are real differences in the extent to which individuals exhibit a desire to know, understand, systematize, and prioritize. This is what we mean by need for cognition, which recently has attracted the attention of consumer researchers.[47]

This has given rise to interesting practical applications. For example, those high in this need are more influenced by the quality of ad arguments than their counterparts, and their attitudes, once formed, are more persistent over time.[48]

Some Clues for Marketing Strategy

Our central objective has been to establish and reinforce the principle that marketers must accept needs as given. They are not likely to be created or modified by any type of marketing effort. Therefore, the goal always is to position a product or service within a target market as a valid and useful alternative for need satisfaction. This is the cardinal tenet of consumer sovereignty. There are several additional ways, however, to sharpen marketing impact.

Interpret Research with Caution

People have a tendency to give socially acceptable answers to questions probing their motivations, especially in such sensitive areas as sexual behavior.[49] Therefore, make every attempt to determine whether actions match the words. Focus groups can be useful in this context, for the reason that people have a tendency to be more open when they sense that others are being candid. Analysis of response patterns thus allows a researcher to infer the true state of affairs. Unless this can be done, there always is the possibility of being misled by surface answers. Also, participant observation may provide important clues on what really is taking place.

Be Alert to the Possibility of Motivational Conflict

It is common for several needs to function in a given situation. Kurt Lewin[50] put forth the theory that some forces produce movement toward a goal object (he refers to this as approach), whereas others bring about avoidance. Hence, conflicts can occur, especially when involvement is high.

It frequently is possible for a skillful marketer to anticipate and overcome conflict. Here is an example: A female executive is attracted to a previously unknown brand of leisure clothing advertised in a catalog received through direct mail. Although she is very interested in purchasing several items (approach), she is fearful about sizes and quality (avoidance). Her action will be dictated by a trade-off between these two forces, and one outcome may be no purchase. This conflict could easily be anticipated and diminished by a personalized service backed by a money-back guarantee.

Be Prepared to Provide Socially Acceptable Reasons for Choice

The most important buying motive may be one that, for varying reasons, the consumer does not want to acknowledge consciously. When that is the case, it can be wise to give a set of reasons that are more acceptable. The consumer

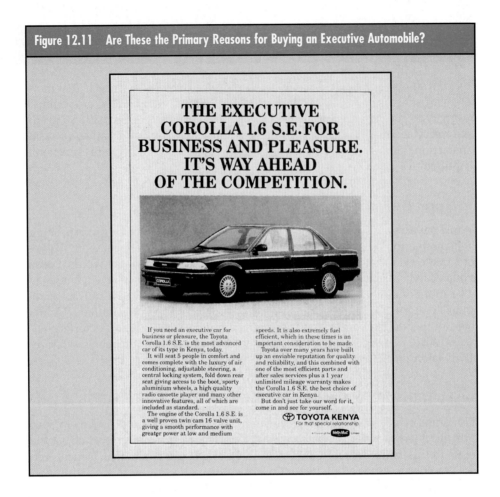

Figure 12.11   Are These the Primary Reasons for Buying an Executive Automobile?

thus is allowed to attribute a greater degree of objectivity or rationality to the choice.

Do you feel that the mechanical and technical details mentioned in the Toyota Kenya ad (Figure 12.11) are of central importance for all who are considering buying an executive car? (The Corolla 1.6 S.E. is considered luxury in Kenya.) It is far more probable that the real motivation is the prestige and power associated with the privilege of owning and driving a luxury car.

Exercise Caution when Marketing Cross-Culturally

In a general sense, needs are universal, but priorities and means of expression and satisfaction can vary sharply. In many parts of Africa, for example, overly conspicuous consumption is frowned on. Self-esteem in India is derived more from group acceptance than from individual factors. All this says is to avoid the trap of **ethnocentrism**—using your cultural lens to evaluate others. This can be the kiss of death in cross-cultural marketing.

Summary

This chapter examined, albeit briefly, the complex subject of motivation. Our purpose has been to identify the ways in which consumer behavior is activated, energized, and directed.

Need is a central variable in motivation. We defined need as a perceived difference between an ideal state and the present state, sufficient to activate behavior. When need is activated, it gives rise to drive (energized behavior), which is channeled toward certain goals that have been learned as incentives. These needs fall into two basic categories: (1) utilitarian (functional, practical benefits) or (2) hedonic (subjective and emotional benefits).

Involvement (perceived relevance or pertinence) is an important factor in understanding motivation. Involvement refers to the degree of perceived relevance in the act of purchase and consumption. When it is high, there is motivation to acquire and process information and a much greater likelihood of extended problem solving.

The self-concept as the unifying force in motivation was explored at length. The self was shown to be multifaceted consisting of the real self (the way I see myself), the ideal self (the way I would like to be), the extended self (I am what I own and use), and the self in context (I am a different person from one situation to the next). As a general rule, the consumer behaves in ways that are congruent or consistent with self, but consumer researchers have just begun to uncover the richness of resulting behavior.

It was pointed out that measurement of motivation always poses a challenge. A variety of methods was explored including (1) scaled AIO questions; (2) motivation research methods (in-depth guided interviews and projective tests); (3) focus groups; (4) qualitative research; and (5) ethnography.

The most important implication is to accept these motivations as given and to find ways to present a product or service as a valid means of drive satisfaction. Many examples were given of how to identify needs through research and then capitalize on them through skillful use of the marketing mix.

Review and Discussion Questions

1. Can needs be changed by marketing efforts? Why or why not?

2. Differentiate between utilitarian and hedonic needs. How might these be expressed in purchase and use of a compact disc player? An electric can opener? Expensive perfume?

3. For which of these product categories would you expect high involvement for most buyers? A moped? Dry dog food? Lawn care products? A home computer? Dishwashing detergent? What reasons can you give?

4. Self-concept is said to be the source of motive integration and prioritizing. What is the self-concept? What is meant by the principle of congruence?

5. Would it be helpful for the marketing manager of a new line of detergents to have some insight into the self-concept of the average consumer, assuming this were possible through research?

6. What is meant by the concept of hierarchy of effect? Contrast the economies of Germany and Haiti. What differences would you expect in priorities within the need hierarchy as discussed by Maslow?

7. To what extent do you think that need for cognition influences the following types of buying behavior: soft drinks, lawn care products, eye makeup, motor oil, wine, choice of restaurant, and ballpoint pens?

8. Based on your own experience, would you agree that categories of needs are the same everywhere in the world? If so, how do you explain the widespread differences in buying behavior?

9. A survey was taken on college campuses throughout Scandinavia asking for beer brand preferences. When asked for the reasons, the most common answers were "flavor" and "price." If you were the brand manager for a brewery marketing in these countries, would you accept these findings as valid?

Endnotes

1. Karen Lowry Miller, "You Just Can't Talk to These Kids," *Business Week* (April 19, 1993), 106.

2. For a classic source on theories of motivation, see David C. McClelland, *Personality* (New York: William Sloane, 1951).

3. See Brian T. Ratchford and Richard Vaughn, "On the Relationships between Motives and Purchase Decisions: Some Empirical Approaches," in Thomas K. Srull, ed., *Advances in Consumer Research* 16 (Provo, Utah: Association for Consumer Research, 1989), 293–299; T. C. Srinivasan, "An Integrative Approach to Consumer Choice," in Melanie Wallendorf and Paul Anderson, eds., *Advances in Consumer Research* 14 (Provo, Utah: Association for Consumer Research, 1987), 96–101; William J. Havlena and Morris B. Holbrook, "The Varieties of Consumption Experience: Comparing Two Typologies of Emotion and Consumer Behavior," *Journal of Consumer Research* 13 (December 1986), 394–404; Roberto Friedman and V. Parker Lessig, "A Framework of Psychological Meaning of Products," in Richard J. Lutz, ed., *Advances in Consumer Research* 13 (Provo, Utah: Association for Consumer Research, 1986), 338–342; Morris B. Holbrook and Elizabeth C. Hirschman, "The Experiential Aspects of Consumption: Consumer Fantasies, Feelings, and Fun," *Journal of Consumer Research* 9 (September 1982), 132–140.

4. Elizabeth C. Hirschman and Morris B. Holbrook, "Hedonic Consumption: Emerging Methods and Propositions," *Journal of Marketing* 46 (Summer 1982), 92–101; Holbrook and Hirschman, "The Experiential Aspects of Consumption."

5. Srinivasan, "An Integrative Approach to Consumer Choice."

6. Melvin Copeland, *Principles of Merchandising* (Chicago: A. W. Shaw, 1924), Chapters 6–7.

7. Paraphrasing the definition given by John H. Antil, "Conceptualization and Operationalization of Involvement," in Thomas C. Kinnear, ed., *Advances in Consumer Research* 11 (Provo, Utah: Association for Consumer Research, 1984), 204.

8. Herbert Krugman, "The Impact of Television Advertising: Learning without Involvement," *Public Opinion Quarterly* 29 (Fall 1965), 349–356.

9. See Richard L. Celsi and Jerry C. Olson, "The Role of Involvement in Attention and Comprehension Processes," *Journal of Consumer Research* 15 (September 1988), 210–224.

10. Joel B. Cohen and Charles S. Areni, "Affect and Consumer Behavior," in Thomas S. Robertson and Harold H. Kassarjian, eds., *Handbook of Consumer Behavior* (Englewood Cliffs, N.J.: Prentice-Hall, 1991), 191. Also, see Carl Obermiller and April Atwood, "Feelings and about Feeling-State Research: A Search for Harmony," in Marvin E. Goldberg, Gerald Gorn, and Richard W. Pollay, eds., *Advances in Consumer Research* 17 (Provo, Utah: Association for Consumer Research, 1990), 590–593; Haim Mano, "Emotional States and Decision Making," in Goldberg, Gorn, and Pollay, *Advances,* 577–584; Mary T. Curren and Ronald C. Goodstein, "Affect and Consumer Behavior: Examining the Role of Emotions on Consumers' Actions and Perspectives," in Rebecca H. Holman and Michael R. Solomon eds., *Advances in Consumer Research* 18 (Provo, Utah: Association for Consumer Research, 1991), 624–626; Meryl Paula Gardner and John Scott, "Product Type: A Neglected Moderator of the Effects of Mood," in Goldberg, Gorn, and Pollay, *Advances,* 585–589.

11. Rajeev Batra and Douglas M. Stayman, "The Role of Mood in Advertising Effectiveness," *Journal of Consumer Research* 17 (September 1990), 202–214; Haim Mano, "Emotional States and Decision Making," in Goldberg, Gorn, and Pollay, *Advances,* 577–589; and Meryl Paula Gardner, "Effects of Mood States on Consumer Information Processing," *Research in Consumer Behavior* 2 (May 1987), 113–135.

12. John C. Mowen, *Consumer Behavior,* 2nd ed. (New York: Macmillan, 1990), 150.

13. Cheryl Russell and Thomas G. Exter, "Mad Money," *American Demographics* (July 1993), 28.

14. See, for example, Lynn R. Kahle, "The Relationships among Consumer Attitudes, Self-Concept, and Behaviors: A Social Adaptation Approach," in Jerry Olson and Keith Sentis, eds., *Advertising and Consumer Psychology* 3 (New York: Praeger, 1986), 121–131; and Keith Sentis and Hazel Markis, "Brand Personality and the Self," in Olson and Sentis, *Advertising and Consumer Psychology,* 132–148.

15. Carl R. Rogers, *Client-Centered Therapy* (Boston: Houghton Mifflin Company, 1951), 492.

16. George M. Zinkhan and Jae W. Hong, "Self Concept and Advertising Effectiveness: A Conceptual Model of Congruency, Conspicuousness, and Response Mode," in Holman and Solomon, *Advances*, 348–354.

17. For a helpful review, see J. Paul Peter, "Some Observations on Self-Concept in Consumer Behavior Research," in Jerry C. Olson, ed., *Advances in Consumer Research* 7 (Ann Arbor, Mich.: Association for Consumer Research, 1980), 625–626.

18. M. Joseph Sirgy, "Self-Concept in Consumer Behavior: A Critical Review," *Journal of Consumer Research* 9 (December 1982), 287–300.

19. Joel B. Cohen, "An Over-Extended Self?" *Journal of Consumer Research* 16 (June 1989), 125–128.

20. See Amy Morgan, "The Evolving Self in Consumer Behavior: Exploring Possible Selves," in Leigh McAlister and Michael L. Rothschild, eds., *Advances in Consumer Research* 20 (Provo, Utah: Association for Consumer Research, 1993), 429–432.

21. Morris B. Holbrook, "Patterns, Personalities, and Complex Relationships in the Effects of Self on Mundane Everyday Consumption: These Are 495 of My Most and Least Favorite Things," in John H. Sherry, Jr., and Brian Sternthal, eds., *Advances in Consumer Research* 19 (Provo, Utah: Association for Consumer Research, 1992), 417–423.

22. Michael R. Solomon, "The Imperial Self," in Goldberg, Gorn, and Pollay, *Advances*, 68–70.

23. See Beth Ann Walker, "New Perspectives for Self-Research," in Sherry and Sternthal, *Advances*, 664–665.

24. Russell W. Belk, "Possessions and the Extended Self," *Journal of Consumer Research* 15 (September 1988), 139–168.

25. Russell W. Belk, Melanie Wallendorf, and John H. Sherry, Jr., "The Sacred and the Profane in Consumer Behavior: Theodicy on the Odyssey," *Journal of Consumer Research* 16 (June 1989), 1–38.

26. Russell W. Belk, "The Role of Possessions in Constructing and Maintaining a Sense of Past," in Goldberg, Gorn, and Pollay, *Advances*, 669–676.

27. Charabala Annuncio, "The Good News Oil," *Advertising and Marketing* [India] (May 1993), 108–110.

28. Michael R. Solomon, "Deep-Seated Materialism: The Case of Levi's 501 Jeans," in Lutz, *Advances*, 619–622.

29. See Mark Snyder, "Selling Images Versus Selling Products: Motivational Foundations of Consumer Attitudes and Behavior," in Srull, *Advances*, 306–311; Jacques Nantel and William Strahle, "The Self-Monitoring Concept: A Consumer Behavior Perspective," in Lutz, *Advances*, 703–710; Mark Snyder, "Self Monitoring of Expressive Behavior," *Journal of Personality and Social Psychology* 34 (1974), 526–537.

30. Nantel and Strahle, "The Self-Monitoring Concept."

31. David G. Mick and Michelle DeMoss, "Self Gifts: Phenomenological Insights from Four Contexts," *Journal of Consumer Research* 17 (December 1990), 322–333.

32. Unpublished survey undertaken by Management Development Associates, Wheaton, Ill., 1987.

33. For an interesting history of the motivation research era, see Sidney J. Levy's comments in *ACR Newsletter* (March 1991), 3–6.

34. Rebecca Piirto, "Beyond Mind Games," *American Demographics* (December 1991), 54.

35. Elizabeth C. Hirschman, ed., *Interpretive Consumer Research* (Provo, Utah: Association for Consumer Research, 1989).

36. Bobby J. Calder and Alice M. Tybout, "Interpretive, Qualitative, and Traditional Scientific Empirical Consumer Behavior Research," in Hirschman, *Interpretive Consumer Research,* 199–208.

37. Morris B. Holbrook, "Seven Routes to Facilitating the Semiological Interpretation of Consumption Symbolism and Marketing Imagery in Works of Art: Some Tips for Wildcats," in Srull, *Advances,* 337–447.

38. Ronald Alsop, "Agencies Scrutinize Their Ads for Psychological Symbolism," *Wall Street Journal* (June 11, 1987), 25.

39. Ibid.

40. See Richard J. Lutz, "Positivism, Naturalism and Pluralism in Consumer Research: Paradigms in Paradise," in Srull, *Advances,* 1–8.

41. For further examples and explanations, see Neil M. Alperstein, "The Verbal Content of TV Advertising and Its Circulation in Everyday Life," *Journal of Advertising* 19 (November 1990), 15–22; Laurel Anderson Hudson and Julie L. Ozanne, "Alternative Ways of Seeking Knowledge in Consumer Research," *Journal of Consumer Research* 14 (March 1988), 508–521.

42. A. H. Murray, *Explorations in Personality* (New York: Oxford University Press, 1938).

43. David C. McClelland, *Personality* (New York: William Sloane, 1941).

44. William J. McGuire, "Psychological Motives and Communication Gratification," in J. G. Blumer and C. Katz, eds., *The Uses of Mass Communications: Current Perspectives on Gratification Research* (New York: Sage, 1974), 167–196.

45. A. H. Maslow, *Motivation and Personality* (New York: Harper & Row, 1954).

46. George Katona, *The Powerful Consumer* (New York: McGraw-Hill, 1960), 132.

47. For a review, see Sharon Shavitt, "Individual Differences in Consumer Attitudes and Behavior," in Srull, *Advances,* 51–55.

48. Curtis P. Haugtvedt and Richard E. Petty, "Need for Cognition and Attitude Persistency," in Srull, *Advances,* 33–36.

49. Diane Crispell, "Sex Surveys: Does Anyone Tell the Truth?" *American Demographics* (July 1993), 9–10.

50. Kurt Lewin, *A Dynamic Theory of Personality* (New York: McGraw-Hill, 1935).

CHAPTER 13

Personality, Values, and Lifestyle

▲▲

Because It's There

From the Swiss village of Zermatt, a first glance at the Matterhorn is chilling. There are higher peaks nearby, but none stands so stark, so imposing as the defiant 14,692-ft. granite pyramid. No one says so brashly: "I dare you."

As many as 2,000 people a year climb the Matterhorn during a short summer season from mid-July to mid-September. A corps of 75 expert guides has made the adventure relatively safe for adults in good physical condition. You can hire one to make the 2-day ascent for about $480 at the Bergfuhrerburo alpine guide office on Dorfstrasse, Zermatt's main street.

Guides say men and women from 30 to 45 years are the best candidates because they have greater combined mental and physical strength than younger people. But there's no upper limit on age. One man climbed the Matterhorn at the age of 90 years. The climb itself takes 2 days, starting with a hike to the base camp. "Going down was very tough. I ran out of energy. Mental strength got me down," says Patricia Ruiz, a former IBM executive based in Paris who prepared by jogging up the steps to the top of the Eiffel Tower every day for 6 months.

The Matterhorn can be unforgiving. Each year, the mountain claims 10 to 20 lives of those who failed to respect the safety rules. "One mistake, and you are down," over the edge, says a guide who has scaled the mountain more than 200 times. Anyone who can run 10 k has the basic endurance to make the ascent, but not without a week or two of special training at high altitude. Guides recommend a minimum of 3 days hiking in the surrounding mountains and 1 day training with a guide on snow and ice.

The worst candidates, guides say, are those who seek to prove something to others. The best are those who are driven by awe of the mountain and a reverence for nature. Ask any mountain guide to take you to the top, and he'll first look into your eyes and see which type you are. A guide explains, "I can usually tell standing in the office if someone can make it or not."

Source: Excerpted from Gail Schares, "A Peak Experience," Business Week *(June 1, 1992), 118.*

Relevance of Individuals for Marketing Programs

Do you wish you had the ability of the Matterhorn guide to look into the eyes of an individual and know if that person could make the climb? What is the guide looking for? Physical characteristics? Age? Gender? No, although they may have some effect. The guide is looking for something more determinant of behavior. That "something" might be called personality. Behavior is also related to values, as we saw in the opening scenario, when the guide described reverence for nature as a determinant of success. Whether the individual is successful is also a function of the person's lifestyle, as we also saw when the opening scenario referred to a person's jogging up stairs. These variables, which explain why a person wants, buys, and uses a product, are the topic of this chapter.

Consumer analysts might wish they could look into a consumer's eyes, as the Swiss guide does, and tell if the consumer will buy Fords or Chevrolets. In the absence of such ability, consumer analysts must use other methodologies to predict the effects of internal or individual variables on behavior.

No one is like anyone else. A fingerprint check will quickly cure all doubts, should there be any. Even for such behaviors as choosing the clothing one wears, decorating a home, or pursuing leisure activities, few if any people have exactly the same preferences. Yet there must be some way to appeal to the needs of people at more than one at a time. The solution is to focus on the personality, values, and lifestyle of consumers *to identify core market segments,* as we studied in Chapter 2. Another reason for studying individual variables is *to make communications programs relevant to consumers.*

Relevant advertising can be achieved with a message that has an especially strong appeal to market segments with similar personality, values, or lifestyles. Marketing communications are "relevant" when consumers respond by saying "That product or that ad is for me." The product or message fits what I believe (values), the way I normally behave (personality), and my situation in life (lifestyle). These variables are not necessarily more important than other variables you have studied—resources, knowledge, motivation, attitudes, and so forth. However, lifestyles and the underlying personality or values they reflect are frequently more visible. Even personality is more visible than is motivation or knowledge. We speak in everyday terms of the nature of an individual as his or her "personality."

Figure 13.1 Appealing to Consumer Individuality

Marketing communications hope to evoke the response in an individual that the communicator truly understands her or him. Notice in Figure 13.1 how Waterman positions its product as a reflection of the individuality of consumers.

Personality

Personality has many meanings. In consumer studies, **personality** is defined as *consistent responses to environmental stimuli.*[1] An individual's personality provides for orderly and coherently related experiences and behavior. Personality is the particular pattern of organization that makes one individual unique and different from all others. Personality provides a consistency of responses based on *enduring, inner psychological characteristics.*

Three major theories or approaches to the study of personality have been used in consumer research: psychoanalytic, socio-psychological, and trait-factor. Personality is sometimes related to the self-concept or the ideal self that individuals would like themselves to be, including Maslow's hierarchical theory in which people seek to achieve their fullest potential of self-actualization.[2]

Psychoanalytic Theory

Psychoanalytic theory posits that the human personality system consists of the id, ego, and superego.[3] The id is the source of psychic energy and seeks immediate gratification for biological and instinctual needs. The superego represents societal or personal norms and services as an ethical constraint on behavior. The ego mediates the hedonistic demands of the id and the moralistic prohibitions of the superego. The dynamic interaction of these elements results in unconscious motivations that are manifested in observed human behavior.

Psychoanalytic theory served as the conceptual basis for the motivation-research movement described in Chapter 12 but was also the forerunner of lifestyle studies. According to the philosophy of motivation researchers such as Dr. Ernest Dichter, consumer behavior is often the result of unconscious consumer motives, which can be determined through indirect assessment methods such as projective and related psychological techniques. The motivation-research movement produced some extraordinary findings such as these often-related examples: A man who buys a convertible sees it as a substitute mistress; a woman is very serious when baking a cake because, unconsciously, she is going through the symbolic act of giving birth; and men want their cigars to be odoriferous to prove their masculinity.[4]

These examples are interesting and perhaps even useful. They are subject to serious questions of validity, however. Certainly, one must go further to gain a thorough, in-depth understanding of personality and consumer decision making. A consumer's personality is a result of more than subconscious drives. Yet, a great deal of advertising is influenced by the psychoanalytic approach to personality, especially its heavy emphasis on sexual and other deep-seated biological instincts.

Socio-Psychological Theory

Socio-psychological theory recognizes the interdependence of the individual and society. The individual strives to meet the needs of society, whereas society helps the individual to attain his or her goals. The theory is therefore not exclusively sociological or psychological but rather the combination of the two. This theoretical orientation is associated with Adler, Horney, Fromm, and Sullivan.[5] Socio-psychological personality theory differs from psychoanalytic theory in two important respects. First, social variables rather than biological instincts are considered to be the most important determinants in shaping personality. Second, behavioral motivation is directed to meet those needs.

An example of socio-psychological personality theory is the Horney paradigm. This model suggests that human behavior results from three predominant, interpersonal orientations: compliant, aggressive, and detached. Questions designed to measure these variables are referred to as a CAD scale. Compliant people are dependent on other people for love and affection and are said to move toward others. Aggressive people are motivated by the need for power and move against others. Detached people are self-sufficient and independent and move away from others.[6] In Figure 13.2, the ad for Quaker Oats appeals to the compliant, interpersonal needs of a hug and encourages consumers "to do the right thing."

Figure 13.2   Quaker Oats Appeals to the Need for a Hug

When people are reconsidering and perhaps reconstructing their self-concept, they may become receptive to goods, services, or ideas that they formerly would have considered unnecessary, such as cosmetic plastic surgery. Schouten[7] found that such purchases are important to both the maintenance and the development of a stable, harmonious self-concept.

Trait-Factor Theory

Trait-factor theory is a quantitative approach to personality. This theory postulates that an individual's personality is composed of definite predispositional attributes called traits. A **trait** is defined as any distinguishable, relatively enduring way in which one individual differs from another. Examples of such traits might be sociability, relaxed style, amount of internal control. Scale statements to measure such traits are shown in Table 13.1. Traits can also be considered individual difference variables.[8]

Three assumptions delineate the trait-factor theory. It is assumed that traits are common to many individuals and vary in absolute amounts among individuals. Thus, such traits might be useful to identify market segments. It is fur-

---

Table 13.1   Test Items in the Modified Personality Instrument

Sociable
   I am always glad to join a large gathering.
   I consider myself a very sociable, outgoing person.
   I find it easy to mingle among people at a social gathering.
   When I am in a small group, I sit back and let others do most of the talking.
   I have decidedly fewer friends than most people.
   I am considered a very enthusiastic person.

Relaxed
   I get tense as I think of all the things lying ahead of me.
   Quite small setbacks occasionally irritate me too much.
   I wish I knew how to relax.
   I shrink from facing a crisis or a difficulty.

Internal Control
   Sometimes I feel that I don't have enough control over the direction my life is taking.
   Many times I feel that I have little influence over the things that happen to me.
   What happens to me is my own doing.
   Becoming a success is a matter of hard work; luck has nothing to do with it.
   Getting a good job depends mainly on being in the right place at the right time.

Source: Kathryn E. A. Villani and Yoram Wind, "On the Usage of 'Modified' Personality Trait Measures in Consumer Research," Journal of Consumer Research 2 (December 1975), 223–228.

ther assumed that these traits are relatively stable and exert fairly universal effects on behavior regardless of the environmental situation. It follows directly from this assumption that a consistent functioning of personality variables is predictive of a wide variety of behavior. The final assumption asserts that traits can be inferred from the measurement of behavioral indicators.

Several standard psychological inventories exist such as the California Psychological Inventory or the Edwards Personal Preference Scale (EPPS). Such tests are widely used for psychological testing and are sometimes applied to marketing applications. Borrowing standard scales that were designed for clinical purposes may produce poor results, however, when applied to marketing.[9] Modified tests, such as those shown in Table 13.1, are more likely to be useful for consumer research.[10]

Trait-factor theory has been the primary basis of marketing personality research. The typical study attempts to find a relationship between a set of personality variables and assorted consumer behaviors such as purchases, media choice, innovation, fear and social influence, product choice, opinion leadership, risk taking, and attitude change. Personality has been found to relate to specific attributes of product choice.[11] Research also indicates that people can make relatively good judgments about other people's traits and how these relate to such choices as automobile brands, occupations, and magazines.[12]

Predicting Buyer Behavior

Predicting consumer behavior has been the objective of most personality research, at least until very recently. The rich literature on personality in psychology and other behavioral sciences has enticed marketing researchers to theorize that personality characteristics should predict brand or store preference and other types of buyer activity. These studies generally fall into two classifications: (1) susceptibility to social influence, and (2) product and brand choice.

Much of the consumer researchers' interest in personality was stimulated by Evans,[13] an early researcher who attempted to test the assumption that automobile buyers differ in personality structure. A standard personality inventory, the EPPS, was administered to owners of Chevrolets and Fords. There were only a few statistically significant differences between the two groups. Using a discriminant analysis, he was able to predict correctly a Ford or Chevrolet owner in only 63 percent of the cases, not much better than the 50 percent that would be expected by chance. Using 12 objective variables, such as age of car, income, and other demographics, he made a correct prediction in 70 percent of the cases. Evans concluded that personality is of relatively little value in predicting automobile brand ownership.

Several other studies investigated the hypothesis that personality could be directly related to product choices, and a few of these reported some relation between product use and personality traits. Most found only very small amounts of variance in product choice explained by personality. Looking back from today's vantage point, it is not surprising that these studies found little relationship between personality and product choice. After all, personality is but one variable in the process of consumer decision making. If any relationship were to be established, dependent variables such as intention would be better candidates than would behavior.

Even if personality traits were found to be valid predictors of intentions or behavior, would they be useful as a means of market segmentation? A positive answer would require that the following circumstances prevail:

1. People with common personality dimensions must be homogeneous in terms of demographic factors such as age, income, or location so that they can be reached economically through the mass media. This is necessary because data are available on media audiences mostly in terms of demographic characteristics. If they show no identifiable common characteristics of this type, there is no practical means of reaching them as a unique market segment.

2. Measures that isolate personality variables must be demonstrated to have adequate reliability and validity. The difficulties in this respect have been extensive.

3. Personality differences must reflect clear-cut variations in buyer activity and preferences, which, in turn, can be capitalized on meaningfully through modifications in the marketing mix. In other words, people can show different personality profiles yet still prefer essentially the same product attributes.

4. Market groups isolated by personality measures must be of a sufficient size to be reached economically. Knowledge that each person varies on a personality scale is interesting but impractical for a marketing firm, which, of necessity, must generally work with relatively large segments.

The evidence to date falls short of these criteria, and personality has not been demonstrated convincingly as a useful means of market segmentation. There is no reason to assume, for example, that individuals with a given personality profile are homogeneous in other respects; nor does it seem reasonable to expect that they have enough in common to be reached easily through the mass media without attracting many nonprospects.

Research on personality has failed to explain more than about 10 percent of variance in behavior, even in the most conclusive studies. Procter & Gamble conducted many studies in the 1970s using personality as a segmentation variable. They approached these studies with care, diligence, and the best resources available. After 3 years of effort, the attempt was abandoned because the brand and advertising managers could not generate results that allowed them to develop marketing strategies any more effectively than with other methodologies.

Research with the greatest ability to predict consumer behavior usually involves specific scales. Specific scales are developed for specific products or buying behavior. Naturally, they will predict behavior better because they are so closely related to the behavior. Unfortunately, this causes such scales to lack generalizability—not to be useful for other products or other buying situations. More generalized scales or "pure" scales are derived from psychological tests with a history of validity and reliability evidence to support them. Although they have better support for use from a theoretical and methodological perspective, they generally do not predict consumer behavior as well as more specific scales.

The failure of personality measures to predict consumer behavior has stimulated development of more recent approaches. One approach is to study the personality of brands, rather than of people. The second approach is to relate personality measures to mediating variables or stages within the decision process, such as need recognition. The third approach is to develop broader, more behavioral concepts that are likely to be better targets for market segmentation—namely, lifestyles, discussed later in the chapter.

Brand Personality

For marketing applications, it may be more effective to analyze brand personality, as part of the brand's overall image. Brand personality refers to the communication of product attributes and the perceptions of those attributes received by consumers about specific brands.[14] The assumption is dropped that people have consistent patterns (drives or traits) that guide their decisions to all brands or consumption situations. Rather, brands have consistent responses evoked to them by consumers responding to the brands.

Brands have three dimensions. One dimension is *physical attributes*, such as the color, price, or ingredients. Tang is an orange powder that costs 98 cents, for example. A second dimension is *functional attributes,* or the consequences of using a brand. Lemon-fresh Pledge polishes the consumer's furniture and repels dust. Both of these types of attributes are objectively verifiable. The third dimension is their *characterization,* their personality as perceived by consumers. Brands may be characterized as modern or old-fashioned, or lively or exotic, just as people are characterized. The Obsession brand of fragrance may be erotic to some consumers or pornographic to others, whereas the Poison brand of fragrance may evoke a perception of danger. These elements, mediated by the information processing of individuals interacting with the brand, are transformed into a consumer's head as making the brand "appropriate for me" or "not appropriate for me," or possibly, "me for it."[15]

When consumers buy products, they often want more than functional or tangible attributes provided by the product. They also want a good experience, a good emotional response from usage of the product, or the hedonic benefits of consumption. Although subjective and intangible, emotional responses also evoke physiological reactions that can be measured with physiological research methods.[16]

There are attempts to profile categories of emotional responses to brands found among consumers. The Mehrabian-Russell category of emotions represents three dimensions. The constructs of pleasure, arousal, and dominance define emotions in terms of continuous dimensions; this is called the PAD paradigm. A more extensive list was developed by Plutchik[17] to include fear, anger, joy, sadness, disgust, acceptance, expectancy, and surprise. Although the indices of these approaches are correlated, research by Havlena and Holbrook[18] indicates that the Mehrabian-Russell PAD approach explains more about the emotional character of consumption experiences than does the approach of Plutchik.

Personality and Decision Making

Personality can help explain how consumers behave in various stages of the decision process. This is more effective than attempting to explain behavioral outcomes with personality. The most promising of this research focuses on the relationship between personality and information-processing variables. Sometimes the variable of personality is called "learning styles," referring to the way people absorb and retain information and/or skills. Cognitive styles may influence the way consumers make decisions about innovative products.[19] The learning styles of eight consumer segments identified by Sproles and Sproles are described in Table 13.2.

The personality variable of **need for cognition** (Ncog) appears to be related to how advertisements may influence the formation of attitudes toward a consumer product. Ncog is a measure of the extent to which an individual intrinsically enjoys performing effortful information-processing-related activities. More simply, Ncog is an *individual's tendency to enjoy thinking*. Marketing experiments by Haugtvedt and associates[20] indicate that individuals high in Ncog are more influenced by the quality of arguments contained in an ad than are individuals low in Ncog. Individuals low in Ncog are more influenced by peripheral advertising stimuli such as endorser attractiveness than are individuals high in Ncog.

Understanding personality variables such as need for cognition may be useful in several ways. Individuals with low need for cognition (Ncog) may require more repetitions before an ad is more effective. Individuals with high Ncog may need fewer repetitions but may need longer ads or ones with higher amounts of information. Individuals with high Ncog may rely more on newspapers and magazines for news, with television perhaps more useful for low Ncog individuals. Although it is difficult to segment the market by the Ncog variable, understanding the type of individuals attracted may help design the communications program with greater effectiveness than not considering personality variables. Haugtvedt and associates[21] have demonstrated the usefulness of personality

Table 13.2   Individual Learning Styles and Consumer Decision Making

Consumer Styles

1. Perfectionistic, High-Quality-Conscious Consumer: Consumer searches for the best quality in products. Systematic, analytical learning styles with highly goal-oriented behavior.

2. Brand-Conscious, Price-Equals-Quality Consumer: Consumer is oriented toward buying the more expensive, well-known national brands. Choosing known brands is an expedient strategy for making consumer choices requiring little thinking and learning.

3. Novelty- and Fashion-Conscious Consumer: Consumer likes new and innovative products and gains excitement from seeking out new things. Involved in serious, observation-centered learning as well as passive, accepting learning.

4. Recreational and Shopping-Conscious Consumer: Consumer finds shopping a pleasant activity and shops just for the fun of it. Learning favors involvement in and enjoyment of shopping, especially among younger consumers who engage in shopping as a social experience with peers.

5. Price-Conscious, Value-for-Money Consumer: Consumer has particularly high consciousness of sale prices and lower prices in general. Learning is active and concrete, fact-oriented learning, perhaps by shopping several stores and enjoying the details of learning characteristics and prices of products.

6. Impulsive, Careless Consumer: Consumer tends to buy at the spur of the moment and to appear unconcerned about how much he or she spends or to search for "best buys." Strongly oriented toward nonadaptive, struggling learning. Engages in less planning or information seeking and does not want to be bothered with the learning process.

7. Confused by Overchoice Consumer: Consumer perceives too many brands and stores from which to choose and who likely experiences information overload in the market. Becomes confused or mentally overloaded when trying to learn too much about too many different brands or products and overwhelmed in a complex multichoice market.

8. Habitual, Brand-Loyal Consumer: Consumer repetitively chooses the same favorite brands and stores. Serious learner whose habitual consumer behavior may come from careful learning experiences that have led to positive outcomes, thus reinforcing this repeated behavior.

Source: Elizabeth Kendall Sproles and George B. Sproles, "Consumer Decision-Making Styles as a Function of Individual Learning Styles," Journal of Consumer Affairs 24 (Summer 1990), 134–147.

variables such as Ncog in consumer decision making, however, especially in the area of attitude formation and change, a topic for discussion in later chapters. Other personality variables such as self-esteem have attracted interest in recent years as helpful in explaining information processing and persuasion.[22]

Risk taking may also influence how some consumers will respond to marketing activities such as offering new products[23] or selling through catalogs or responding to risky situations in advertising. Risk, as defined in personality research, is more than just uncertainty about outcomes. It is a personal expectation that a loss will occur. The greater a person's certainty for the loss, the more that person is a risk taker.[24]

Some consumers are described as "Type T," for "thrillseekers." They have a higher than average need for stimulation and become bored easily. They are predisposed to pursue adventure and are likely to list success and competence as their goals in life in contrast to risk avoiders, who list happiness as their first choice.[25] Risk takers are more likely to end up with health hazards such as those involving alcohol, drugs, and reckless driving but are more likely to be self-motivated and well adjusted. Some advertising on television and other media contains appeals to fast driving, hang gliding, bungee jumping, or other risks. Such ads are directed to the thrillseeking market segment, believed to be about 25 percent of the American population, whereas most ads exhibit a less risky appeal.

Future consumer research seems headed toward more emphasis on understanding the perceptions and responses of consumers in the consumption experience. An example is the process of **self-monitoring.** Snyder[26] describes this trait as the degree to which individuals are influenced by internal versus external cues. Low self-monitoring individuals are especially sensitive and responsive to inner feelings, attitudes, and beliefs and view their behavior influenced primarily by internal cues such as personal beliefs and values. In contrast, high self-monitors are less sensitive to internal beliefs and values. They view behavior as stemming primarily from a pragmatic view of what external, situational cues define as socially appropriate action. They are sensitive to the expression and self-presentation of relevant others in social situations, using these cues as guidelines for monitoring (regulating and controlling) their own verbal and nonverbal self-presentation.

Current research also focuses on how consumers interact with sales personnel as a dyad. Such interactions may determine activities such as planned and impulse purchasing and product/store situations.[27] Fine and Schumann[28] have shown that there is an interactive effect between the self-monitoring of customers and salespersons. More positive outcomes are more likely when the self-monitoring levels of the dyad partners are different. Research such as this, which examines elements of the decision-making process, appears more useful than attempts to relate buying to the older, more general personality research based on assumptions of pervasive traits or temperaments. Fortunately, as we see in the next few pages, concepts more comprehensive than personality are available for managerial questions facing marketing organizations.

Personal Values

Values provide another explanation of why consumers vary in their decision making. Values represent consumer beliefs about life and acceptable behavior. Values express the goals that motivate people and appropriate ways to attain those goals. The enduring nature of values and their central role in personality structure have caused them to be applied to understanding many consumption situations, including product choice, brand choice, and market segmentation. Burgess[29] has shown that the concept of values is implicit or explicit in many of the psychological theories of Freud, Jung, Fromm, Adler, Horney, Erikson, Dichter, and others.

Values can be either personal or social. Because our concern in this chapter is on individual consumers, the focus is on *personal values*. When we study culture in Chapter 17, the focus will be on *social values*—shared beliefs that characterize a group of people such as Americans or African-Americans. *Social values define "normal" behavior for a society or group whereas personal values define "normal" behavior for an individual.* Remember as you read the next few pages, however, that the values of groups to which you belong (social values) will have a major influence on your personal values. Values describe goals and ways to accomplish them, many of which are derived from the society into which a consumer is born.

The values that dominate a nation are its *national character*. Clark[30] describes national character as enduring personality characteristics found among the populations of nations. Have you ever wondered why the people of some countries are rich and others poor? If you said natural resources, read Consumer in Focus 13.1 and consider how the relationship between values and prosperity may

Consumer in Focus   13.1

Why Are People Rich or Poor?

Why is one country rich and another poor? If you think back to a high school geography class, perhaps someone told you the wealth of a country is based on natural resources. Although there are a few temporary exceptions in the oil-rich countries of the Middle East, the natural resource theory doesn't hold up when you visit countries such as Argentina, Brazil, and Nigeria—or even Russia.

The countries with the highest per capita natural resources are among the poorest in the world. Countries with almost no natural resources, not even farmland—such as Switzerland and Japan—are among the richest in the world. Don't you find it interesting that the largest food company in the world—Nestle—is based in one of the world's smallest countries? So are some of the world's most powerful banks, pharmaceutical and equipment manufacturing firms.

The reason resource-starved countries such as Switzerland, Japan, and Singapore rank among the richest in the world is their values. That principle probably holds for organizations and individuals as well. The difference between a Wal★Mart and its competitors is not its products or prices, for those can be found in other stores; it is values—of its management and employees. In the case of Wal★Mart, many of those values can be traced directly to its founder, Sam Walton. Probably anyone in any country can be prosperous, but not without understanding values such as those of the Swiss.

Source: Excerpts from Roger D. Blackwell, From the Edge of the World: Global Lessons for Personal and Professional Prosperity (Columbus: The Ohio State University, 1994), 110–111.

apply to individuals and corporations as well as countries. Lee Kuan Yew, the highly effective leader of his country, explains, "Singapore is an immigrant society. Our values are those which assure survival, security, and success." By choosing these values, Singapore has become the "economic miracle of the Orient."[31]

Personal values reflect the choices an individual makes from the variety of social values or value systems to which that individual is exposed. Your values concerning work ethic and social interaction, for example, may determine how much time you have spent studying this text for the examination. The consequences of your values may affect your grade in this course but, more important, will affect the outcomes you achieve throughout life. Although individuals are influenced by social values of groups to which they belong (nation, religion, family, and so forth), individuals pick and choose from social values to develop their own personal values. This process is illustrated in Figure 13.3. Notice how this ad for Nike emphasizes that individuals are free to develop values different from those of their own families. As this ad indicates, a consumer's personal values are ultimately indicated not by statements, but by decisions.

Figure 13.3   Personal Values Reflect an Individuals's Own Decisions

THE BODY YOU HAVE IS THE BODY YOU INHERITED, BUT **YOU MUST DECIDE WHAT TO DO WITH IT.** YOU MUST DECIDE IF YOU WANT STRENGTH, DECIDE IF YOU WANT AGILITY. YOU MUST DECIDE IF YOU WANT ABSOLUTELY EVERYTHING THAT COMES FROM CROSS-TRAINING, AND ABSOLUTELY ONE SHOE TO DO IT IN. BECAUSE THE NIKE CROSS-TRAINER LOW HAS INHERITED ITS OWN SET OF STRENGTHS, ITS OWN KIND OF RESILIENCE. IT HAS ALSO INHERITED A GOOD DEAL OF CUSHIONING, STABILITY, AND TRUE, INTELLIGENT FIT. SO THANK YOUR MOTHER FOR WHAT YOU HAPPENED TO BE BORN WITH. BUT THANK YOURSELF FOR WHAT YOU ACTUALLY DO WITH IT.

Source: Courtesy of Nike.

Rokeach Value Scale

Measurement of values for consumer research often uses the Rokeach Value Scale (RVS). Rokeach believed values are concerned both with the *goals (end-state or terminal elements) and the ways of behaving (instrumental components) to obtain goals.* He defined a value as an enduring belief that a specific mode of conduct or end-state of existence is personally or socially preferable to an opposite or converse mode of conduct or end-state of existence.[32] The RVS is a series of goals and ways of behaving people are asked to rank in importance. These can be analyzed by gender, age, ethnicity, or whatever variable might be of interest in market segmentation. The values identified by Rokeach are the following[33]:

Terminal (Desirable End-States)	Instrumental (Modes of Conduct)
A comfortable life	Ambitious
An exciting life	Broad-minded
A sense of accomplishment	Capable
A world at peace	Cheerful
A world of beauty	Clean
Equality	Courageous
Family security	Forgiving
Freedom	Helpful
Happiness	Honest
Inner harmony	Imaginative
Mature love	Independent
National security	Intellectual
Pleasure	Logical
Salvation	Loving
Self-respect	Obedient
Social recognition	Polite
True friendship	Responsible
Wisdom	Self-controlled

Several studies have linked personal values to brand choice, product usage, or market segmentation.[34] In a study of car buying, Vinson, Scott, and Lamont[35] found consumption-related variables are related to family-oriented core values that stimulate motivation. With low-involvement products such as deodorants, Pitts and Woodside[36] found that individuals who preferred Right Guard over Arrid, for example, were consumers with high importance on the RVS measuring "mature love." Most of the applications in the past used the RVS to describe the differences between segments defined *a priori* on demographic or other variables. More recently, consumer analysts are using values as the criterion for segmenting the population into homogeneous groups of individuals who share a common value system.[37]

Schwartz Value Scale

The Schwartz Value Scale (SVS) focuses on value systems or the universal content and structure of values. It challenges the simple Rokeach classification of instrumental and terminal values and identifies the structure of motivational factors. Based on empirical studies from 35 countries, the Schwartz theory proposes that *values are transituational goals that serve the interest of individuals or collectives of people and express one of ten universal motivations or value types.*[38] These motivations or value types are the guiding principles in consumers' lives. The meaning of an individual value is reflected in the pattern of its intercorrelation with other values with an analytical technique called smallest space analysis (SSA). Values serve *individual* interests for achievement, self-direction, and stimulation. *Collective* interests may be related as motivational types representing benevolence, conformity, and security. *Mixed* interests such as "a world of beauty," a "world at peace," wisdom, and mature love are described in the SVS as universalism.[39] The SVS has been used to understand why some consumers prefer banks instead of competitive financial institutions as well as to compare brand preferences between market segments.[40]

Understanding personal values helps to understand individual answers to the question, "Is this product for me?" Values are particularly important in the need-recognition stage of consumer decision making but affect consumers in determining evaluative criteria, answering the question, "Is this brand for me?" Values influence the effectiveness of communications programs as consumers ask, "Is this situation (portrayed in the ad) one in which I would participate?" Values are enduring motivations or the "ends" people seek in their lives. In a sense, marketing often provides the "means" to reach these ends.

Laddering

Understanding how values determine market demand can be facilitated by a technique called **laddering**. Laddering refers to in-depth probing directed toward uncovering higher-level meanings at both the benefit (attribute) level and the value level. Laddering seeks to uncover the *linkages between product attributes, personal outcomes (consequences), and values* that serve to structure components of the cognitive network in a consumer's mind.[41]

Figure 13.4 shows the attributes provided by wine coolers (carbonation, crisp, expensive, label, bottle, less alcohol, filling, smaller size) and how the consequences of those benefits (refreshing, thirst-quenching, more feminine, avoid negatives of alcohol, impress others, and so on) relate to the values (self-esteem, accomplishment, belonging, family life) of varying market segments. Any of

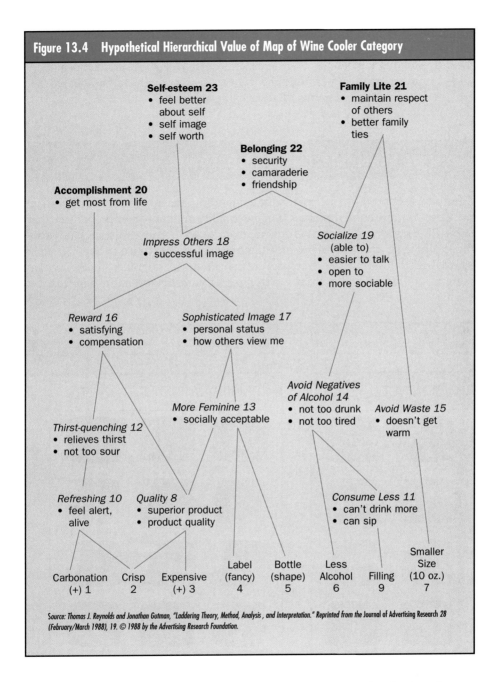

Figure 13.4   Hypothetical Hierarchical Value of Map of Wine Cooler Category

Source: Thomas J. Reynolds and Jonathan Gutman, "Laddering Theory, Method, Analysis , and Interpretation." Reprinted from the Journal of Advertising Research 28 (February/March 1988), 19. © 1988 by the Advertising Research Foundation.

these perceptual maps of the value structures could lead to developing alternative marketing strategies. Although the attributes might be the same, the image that should be developed for those with the self-esteem value would emphasize impressing others, perhaps with a sophisticated image, whereas the other image would be developed for the family life value, emphasizing socializing without the negatives of alcohol. Additional analysis may indicate the size of segments, the degree of overlap between segments, appeals that can be used to appeal to the widest number of consumers, and the level of abstraction that should be used in advertising and other elements of advertising strategy.[42]

Lifestyle Concepts and Measurement

Lifestyle is a popular concept for understanding consumer behavior, perhaps because it is more contemporary than personality and more comprehensive than values. Lifestyle marketing attempts to relate a product, often through advertising, to the everyday experiences of the market target. Notice in the TV storyboards of Figure 13.5 how an ice cream product recognizes that everyday patterns of Friday and Saturday are different. Drumstick probably believes con-

Figure 13.5   An Advertiser Adapts to Variations in Lifestyle

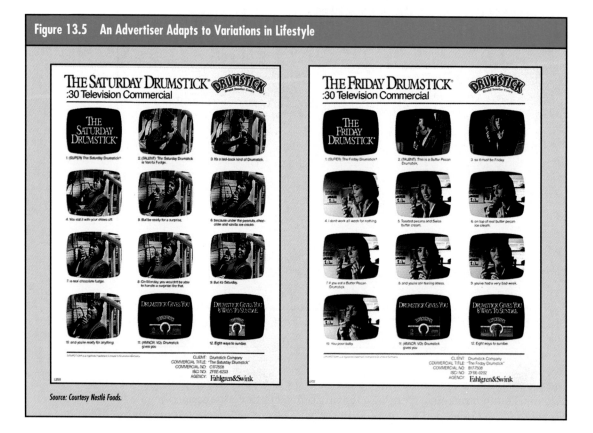

Source: Courtesy Nestlé Foods.

sumers will identify with its product because the company identifies with the lifestyles of its consumers.

Lifestyle is a summary construct defined as *patterns in which people live and spend time and money.* Lifestyles reflect a person's activities, interests, and opinions (AIOs). People use constructs such as lifestyles to construe the events happening around them and to interpret, conceptualize, and predict events as well as to reconcile their values with events. George Kelly has noted that such a construct system not only is personal but also continually changes in response to a person's need to conceptualize cues from the changing environment to be consistent with his or her own values and personality.[43]

Values are relatively enduring; lifestyles change more rapidly. Lifestyle researchers must, therefore, place attention on currency and flexibility in research methods and marketing strategies. Some of the most effective advertisers track trends in lifestyles of key market targets and reflect those lifestyles in their ads. Look at Figure 13.6 and you will see how some advertisers attempt to appeal to market segments that reflect changing lifestyles. Clothing changes to reflect changing lifestyles and Purex relates its product to each of these lifestyles. Consumers in many segments are concerned about both fat and taste and this lifestyle is reflected in the for Simple Pleasures Light. The lifestyles of many smokers have been changed because of changes in social attitudes and this is incorporated into the ad for Wrigley's gum. Lifestyles include the leisure activities that are part of the creative strategy of the Nintendo ad shown in Figure 13.6.

If you are studying consumer behavior, you should recognize the differences between your own lifestyle and the lifestyles of other people. The responsibility of effective communicators is to understand the lifestyles of the audience, not just themselves. Perhaps you are thinking, do differences really exist? Look carefully at Table 13.3, which shows current lifestyles and value of the consumers in the United States. The table also shows lifestyle statements of advertising agency personnel.

Psychographics

Psychographics is an operational technique to measure lifestyles. Psychographics provide quantitative measures and can be used with the large samples needed for definition of market segments. In contrast, soft or qualitative research techniques such as focus-group interviews or in-depth interviews may provide richer insights or ideas for creative strategy even though they do not provide quantitative estimates. Analysis of psychographic data tends to be of two types, shown in Figure 13.7 (page 452). Techniques for classifying and segmenting consumers are shown on the left side of that figure involving multivariate analysis of associative, interdependent data. The right side of Figure 13.7 lists four multivariate procedures for analysis of dependence used for associating psychographic items with other market-related variables.[44]

Figure 13.6 Appeals to Changing Lifestyles

Table 13.3   Lifestyles of the Public and Advertising Agency Employees

Lifestyle Activity, Interest, Opinion	Ad Agency Employees	Public
I went bowling last year.	46%	30%
I bought a lottery ticket last year.	75	61
I want to look different from others.	82	62
There's too much sex on prime-time TV.	50	78
TV is my primary form of entertainment.	28	53
I went to a bar or tavern in the past year.	91	50
There should be a gun in every home.	9	32
My favorite music is classic rock.	64	35
My favorite music is easy listening.	27	51
Couples should live together before marriage.	50	33
My greatest achievements are still ahead of me.	89	65

Source: "Study: The Customer Ain't Me," Advertising Age (January 20, 1992).

Psychographics are more comprehensive than demographic, behavioral, and socioeconomic measures. Emanuel Demby,[45] a researcher generally credited with inventing the term, explains:

> The use of psychological, sociological, and anthropological factors, such as benefits desired (from the behavior being studied), self-concept, and lifestyle (or serving style) to determine how the market is segmented by the propensity of groups within the market—and their reasons—to make a particular decision about a product, person, ideology, or otherwise hold an attitude or use a medium.

Psychographics is a term often used interchangeably with AIO measures, or statements to describe the activities, interests, and opinions of consumers. Some researchers use the A to stand for attitudes, but activities are a better measure of lifestyles because they measure what people do. AIO components are defined by Reynolds and Darden[46] as follows:

> An *activity* is a manifest action such as viewing a medium, shopping in a store, or telling a neighbor about a new service. Although these acts are usually observable, the reasons for the actions are seldom subject to direct measurement. An *interest* in some object, event, or topic is the degree of excitement that accompanies both special and continuing attention to it. An *opinion* is a spoken or written "answer" that a person gives in response to stimulus situations in which some "question" is raised. It is used to describe interpretations, expectations, and evaluations—such as beliefs about the intentions of other people, anticipations concerning future events, and appraisals of the rewarding or punishing consequences of alternative courses of action.

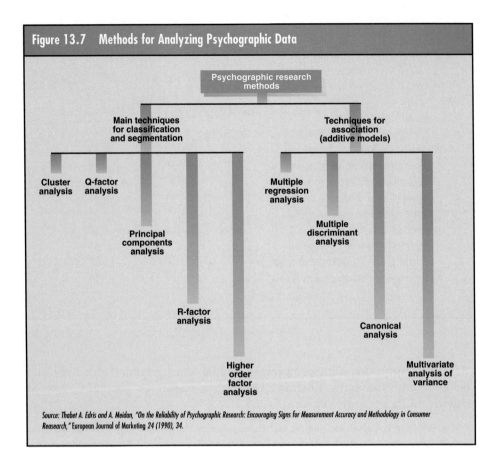

Figure 13.7 Methods for Analyzing Psychographic Data

Source: Thabet A. Edris and A. Meidan, "On the Reliability of Psychographic Research: Encouraging Signs for Measurement Accuracy and Methodology in Consumer Reasearch," European Journal of Marketing 24 (1990), 34.

Examples of each category are shown in Table 13.4. Demographics are also included in most psychographic or AIO studies.

AIO Statements

AIO statements may be general or specific. In either type, consumers are usually presented with Likert scales (named after the researcher who popularized the method of response) in which people are asked whether they strongly agree, agree, are neutral, disagree, or strongly disagree. Statements can be administered in person, by phone, or by mail. An efficient form of administration is with mail panels such as those operated by Market Facts of Chicago or NFO of Toledo.

General and Specific AIOs

AIO statements may refer to general activities and motivations or they may be specific. The specific approach focuses on statements that are product specific and that identify brands associated with the product or brand.

Table 13.4	AIO Categories of Lifestyle Studies		
Activities	**Interests**	**Opinions**	**Demographics**
Work	Family	Themselves	Age
Hobbies	Home	Social issues	Education
Social events	Job	Politics	Income
Vacation	Community	Business	Occupation
Entertainment	Recreation	Economics	Family size
Club membership	Fashion	Education	Dwelling
Community	Food	Products	Geography
Shopping	Media	Future	City size
Sports	Achievements	Culture	Stages in life cycle

Source: Joseph T. Plummer, "The Concept and Application of Life Style Segmentation," Journal of Marketing 38 (January 1974), 34. Reprinted from the Journal of Marketing published by the American Marketing Association.

One study concerned with health care services included both general and specific statements.[47] The study was concerned with predicting what types of consumers were likely to bring malpractice suits. Because attitude theory indicates that consumers try to behave in a way that will achieve consistency between their behavior and attitudes, it was necessary to determine specific attitudes toward physicians as well as toward malpractice. Thus, statements such as the following were included: "I have a great deal of confidence in my own doctor; about half of the physicians are not really competent to practice medicine; most physicians are overpaid; and in most malpractice suits, the physician is not really to blame."

In this study, respondents who indicated that they have a great deal of confidence in their doctors also reported a much lower likelihood of bringing a malpractice suit. Respondents agreeing with the statements that physicians are not really competent and that they are overpaid and disagreeing with the statement that physicians are not really to blame in malpractice suits were more likely to file a malpractice suit.

Analysis of this study also showed that respondents who agreed with general AIO statements such as "I generally do exercises" and "I am sick a lot more than my friends are" were found also to be more likely to bring malpractice suits. Such findings demonstrate how both general and specific AIOs can be used to profile consumers and relate their lifestyles to behavior.

Market Segmentation

Psychographic studies are used to develop an in-depth understanding of market segments. Sometimes marketers use psychographics to define segments, but a better practice is to avoid definition of the segments through AIOs in favor of using AIOs to better understand segments that have been defined with more traditional variables.

AIO statements can be analyzed by cross-tabulating each statement on the basis of variables believed important for market segmentation strategies, such as gender and age. Factor analysis or other multivariate techniques may be used to group the statements into a more parsimonious format. Factor analysis is a mathematical technique for examining the intercorrelation between statements in an attempt to determine common or underlying factors that explain observed variation.[48]

Such techniques often reveal factors such as the "traditional" segment or the "modern" segment or perhaps the "frugal" segment or the "natural" segment or group within a segment defined by other variables. General Foods identified a health-conscious segment of consumers through psychographics to reposition its Sanka brand of decaffeinated coffee. Previously, decaffeinated coffee was associated with elderly persons. Through psychographics, General Foods targeted active achievers of all ages, using advertising appealing to interests of adventurous lifestyles. The ads featured people in lifestyles such as running the rapids in a kayak with the copy line that Sanka "Lets you be your best."

Psychographic analysis allows marketers to understand consumer lifestyles of the core customers in order to communicate more effectively with people in that segment. The analysis may also lead to efforts to position new or existing products closely to consumers in a lifestyle segment, perhaps more effectively than if the segment were described only by demographics. The idea is to go beyond standard demographics to position the product in line with the activities, hopes, fears, and dreams of the product's best customers.

The "healthy" market segment is an example of a lifestyle that attracts many marketers currently. ConAgra brought out the Healthy Choice brand of food and became almost an instant success. McDonald's introduced the McLean sandwich with much less success. Kentucky Fried Chicken changed its name to KFC, dropping the word *fried*, which many people consider an unhealthy way to cook. Even the image of Col. Harland Sanders' face was changed from brown ink to blue to fit changing lifestyles.[49] Worthington Foods found that many of the people who most enjoyed eating eggs need to avoid fat and cholesterol. The result was a new product called Better 'n Eggs, shown in Figure 13.8. The objective in psychographic segmentation is to develop a marketing program that is consistent in all its elements with many of the AIOs of the target market. Advertising in such programs often emphasizes the lifestyle elements rather than product attributes and may use models or celebrities that communicate to the specific lifestyle concerns of the audience, as Consumer in Focus 13.2 shows.

VALS and the Nine American Lifestyles

A widely used approach to lifestyle marketing is the values and lifestyle (VALS) and its most recent form, VALS II. The original program was developed by Mitchell at SRI and defined "nine American lifestyles." They are shown in Table

Figure 13.8 An Appeal to Healthy Lifestyles

13.5, along with typical demographics and buying patterns. Another approach, called Monitor, is available from Yankelovich, Skelly, and White, although the SRI or VALS approach appears to be used more by marketers.[50] We examine VALS more closely.

The VALS system defines a typology of three basic categories of consumer values and lifestyles, with nine more-detailed types. SRI describes consumer market segments as need-driven, outer-directed, or inner-directed.

Need-driven consumers exhibit spending driven by need rather than preference and are subdivided into survivors and sustainers, the former among the most disadvantaged people in the economy.

Outer-directed consumers, who are divided into three subgroups, are the backbone of the marketplace and generally buy with awareness of what other people will attribute to their consumption of that product.

Inner-directed consumers are divided into four subgroups. They comprise a much smaller percentage of the population (see Table 13.5). Their lives are

13.2	**Consumer in Focus**

Dieting Lifestyles Are Found in Many Sizes

Brooke Shields is appearing in commercials for Ultra Slim-Fast, a departure for the diet brand, which usually uses older, chubbier stars, such as Tommy Lasorda and Willard Scott. By using Ms. Shields, who shed a dozen pounds in 8 weeks, Slim-Fast is hoping to tap into a new segment for the diet industry: those who don't need to drop 30 to 50 pounds. The advantage of using Ms. Shields is that consumers can identify with her predicament. She gained a modest amount of weight by nibbling too much.

Competition is heating up in the segment of the diet business that targets people who want just a fine-tuning as opposed to a total overhaul. Weight Watchers, a unit of H. J. Heinz, began running ads with former network anchorwoman Kathleen Sullivan, showing her losing 8½ pounds in about 2 weeks. Nestle's Sweet Success is also growing fast.

Marketing experts feel the casting of Ms. Shields is an inspired choice. "Think of using Brooke Shields in terms of market segmentation," says Steven E. Permut, president of Marketing Sciences. "The first tier of people you have to sell the Slim-Fast program to is obvious. That's the easy part. Then, after that group is saturated, you look for other high-potential targets. That segment may be smaller in number perhaps, but there hasn't been promotion to this new group. Ms. Shields represents someone who is youthful, attractive and in excellent health."

Source: Excerpted from Kevin Goldman, "Slim-Fast Ads Use Brooke Shields to Appeal to the Low-Fat Dieter," Wall Street Journal (January 10, 1994), B3.

directed more toward their individual needs than toward values oriented to externals. Although their numbers are small, they may be important as trend setters or groups through whom successful ideas and products trickle down. This segment is growing rapidly, whereas the number of need-driven consumers is declining and outer-directed is holding steady.

Advertising agencies and marketing organizations use the VALS system to segment markets and communicate more effectively with segments. At one time, Merrill Lynch Pierce Fenner & Smith used an advertising campaign featuring a herd of galloping bulls with the slogan "Bullish on America." With the help of Young & Rubicam advertising agency, the theme was shifted to reach the achievers target audience, who are upwardly mobile and self-motivated. As a result, the thundering herds were replaced in the ads by a lone bull that wandered through the canyons of Wall Street or huddled in a cave where it found shelter while Merrill Lynch and its achiever customers were described as "A breed apart."

At Clairol, ads were developed for the inner-directed segment to make them feel in charge of their own lives with the theme "Make it happen" and for the outer-directed group the reassurance of "Sells the most, conditions the most." At General Foods, the belonger woman was the target for Jell-O ads that show women in the provider role who don't make just Jell-O for their families, they

Table 13.5 VALS Lifestyle Segmentation

Percentage of Population (Age 18 and Over)	Consumer Type	Values and Lifestyles	Demographics	Buying Patterns
Need-Driven Consumers				
4%	Survivors	Struggle for survival Distrustful Socially misfitted Ruled by appetites	Poverty-level income Little education Many minority members Many live in city slums	Price dominant Focused on basics Buying for immediate needs
7	Sustainers	Concern with safety, security Insecure, compulsive Dependent, following Streetwise, determination to get ahead	Low income Low education Much unemployment Live in country as well as cities	Price important Want warranty Cautious buyers
Outer-Directed Consumers				
35%	Belongers	Conforming, conventional Unexperimental Traditional, formal Nostalgic	Low to middle income Low to average education Blue-collar jobs Tend toward noncity living	Family Home Fads Middle and lower mass markets
10	Emulators	Ambitious, show-off Status conscious Upwardly mobile Macho, competitive	Good to excellent income Youngish Highly urban Traditionally male, but changing	Conspicuous consumption "In" items Imitative Popular fashion
22	Achievers	Achievement, success, fame Materialism Leadership, efficiency Comfort	Excellent incomes Leaders in business, politics, etc. Good education Suburban and city living	Give evidence of success Top of the line Luxury and gift markets "New and improved" products
Inner-Directed Consumers				
5%	I-Am-Me	Fiercely individualistic Dramatic, impulsive Experimental Volatile	Young Many single Student or starting job Affluent backgrounds	Display one's taste Experimental fads Source of far-out fads Clique buying
7	Experiential	Drive to direct experience Active, participative Person-centered Artistic	Bimodal incomes Mostly under 40 Many young families Good education	Process over product Vigorous, outdoor sports "Making" home pursuits Crafts and introspection
8	Societally Conscious	Societal responsibility Simple living Smallness of scale Inner growth	Bimodal low and high incomes Excellent education Diverse ages and places of residence Largely white	Conservation emphasis Simplicity Frugality Environmental concerns
2	Integrated	Psychological maturity Sense of fittingness Tolerant, self-actualizing World perspective	Good to excellent incomes Bimodal in age Excellent education Diverse jobs and residential patterns	Varied self-expression Esthetically oriented Ecologically aware One-of-a-kind items

Source: Reprinted with permission of Macmillan Publishing Company from Arnold Mitchell, Nine American Lifestyles: Who We Are and Where We Are Going (New York: Macmillan, 1983). Copyright © 1983 by Arnold Mitchell.

"Make some fun." A comprehensive approach to apply VALS segments and demographics with varied eating situations was applied at the Max & Erma's restaurant chain, described in Consumer in Focus 13.3.

VALS and LOV

VALS gained rapid acceptance and widespread usage in marketing. Nevertheless, it has its limitations. Consumers are not "pure" in their type of lifestyle. Respondents are given a score that reflects the degree to which they share similar responses on lifestyles other than their primary lifestyle. Because VALS is a proprietary data base, some consumer researchers also criticize the act that researchers do not have full information on the factor loadings or rotations or the explained variance, causing them to revert to the more basic approaches based on the academic value studies of Rokeach and Schwartz.

An alternative to VALS is the list of values (LOV) approach, developed by Kahle.[51] Typically, respondents are asked to rank a list of values derived from the RVS. Marketers use the top-ranked value to assign consumers to segments.

13.3	**Consumer in Focus**

Max & Erma's Customers

By 1994, Max & Erma's had grown to a chain of 27 casual, family-oriented dinner restaurants based in the Midwest with locations in Akron, Canton, Chicago, Cleveland, Columbus, Dayton, Detroit, Lexington, and Pittsburgh. The restaurant is targeted to consumers who seek a casual, contemporary, sophisticated, adult dining experience conducive to relaxation and fun. Major competitors include T.G.I. Friday's, Dalts, Houlihan's, Bennigans, and Chi-Chi's.

The firm grew rapidly in the late 1970s and the early 1980s, along with rapid growth in the restaurant industry. Losses were experienced in the 1980s, however, and the restaurant undertook extensive research to understand its core customers and to develop an effective marketing program.

Customers had previously been defined as the "18 to 45" age group with an emphasis on singles, but the firm felt the need for additional variables that would explain the individuals who were the core customers. A survey of 400 frequent customers (more than twice a month) was conducted to measure demographics, lifestyle variables, (specifically VALS categories), and situation variables.

Using VALS categories, the Max & Erma core customer was described as 38 percent "inner-directed" in contrast to only 20 percent of the population. They typically hold managerial or professional jobs, often with two professional incomes. They eat out a lot, will try anything, and are sophisticated and nonconformist. They care more about their personal tastes than status or what other people think. They like a wide choice of offbeat menu items that would make a "belonger" really uncomfortable.

The Max & Erma segment also contains more (38 percent) "achievers" than the population (31 percent). They are success oriented with a high education. They work hard, are motivated by good service,

Continued

Kahle, Beatty, and Homer[52] compared VALS with LOV and found that the LOV approach predicted consumer behavior better than VALS. Used alone, VALS appears better than LOV, but when demographic data are included with LOV, the latter approach is more effective.[53] When LOV is augmented with measures of more general values—such as materialism—the predictive power is further improved.[54] Recent research by Kamakura and Novak[55] incorporates the more conceptual approach of Schwartz to *define market segments* (rather than use *a priori* segments) *on the basis of the latent value systems* of market segments. This extension of the LOV approach reflects the multiple values that affect an individual's buying behavior. Although the traditional top-rank approach with LOV identifies more but smaller segments, the Kamakura-Novak approach provides a richer understanding of the activities and interests of the segments.

Global Lifestyles

The emergence of the European Community and the North American Free Trade Agreement (NAFTA) and the rising importance of globalization require that

---

Consumer in Focus, Continued   **13.3**

view value more in terms of quality than price, and have a high level of self-confidence. "Belongers" were more likely to choose the traditional offerings of Shoney's, Bob Evans, and other restaurants than Max & Erma's.

Individuals were also described by the situation in which they choose Max & Erma's. These occasions were convenience (24.8 percent), fun (20.4 percent), dates (19.6 percent), regulars (12.4 percent), fast (9.7 percent), families (7.9 percent), and business (4.2 percent). Max & Erma's was much stronger in the fun, dates, and regulars categories and much lower than other restaurants in the fast, families, and business situations.

A marketing plan was implemented targeted toward the key segments. The menu was tailored to inner-directed customers with "name your own burger," "top your own pasta," and "build your own sundae" items. Individualized local store programs of special promotions, coupons, and direct mail were used. The achievers were targeted for less formal occasions. An extensive TV advertising program was developed featuring a well-known achiever attorney and his respected but more inner-driven wife, who is also an attorney. They both are shown in TV ads eating frequently at Max & Erma's. Appeals emphasized time convenience, relaxed fun, and quality menu items. An extensive training program for store management and waiters was also implemented to ensure high levels of customer satisfaction. Menus evolved to contain ethnic and tasty items that reflect changing lifestyles.

The results: The firm achieved a turnaround in same-store sales at a time when industry sales were flat or declining. Profits were dramatically higher and generated the cash flow and debt capacity to open additional restaurants. The company attributed the success to its total marketing and operational program based on a thorough understanding of the individual characteristics of its target of core customers.

marketing strategy increasingly be planned on a global basis. Rather than sell internationally, however, firms are using the intermarket segmentation approach described in Chapter 3 to reach segments of the population—in whatever country they may be. VALS and other approaches have been used to identify lifestyle segments across country borders.[56] The VALS typology has been used successfully to segment Canadian markets in a study reported by Ian Pearson.[57]

One of the most comprehensive studies of values on a wide range of topics in Europe was recently published by Ashford and Timms[58] and deserves careful study by anyone interested in the values of Europeans. This study shows how values vary between Western European countries as well as changes during the past decade. The study shows that the overwhelming majority in each country say that they are happy. There are no significant differences between men and women in any of the countries surveyed, but some countries enjoy higher levels of happiness than others. A few of the specific differences between countries are shown in Table 13.6, reflecting underlying values in these nations.

Table 13.6 Western European Values									
	GB	**NI**	**RI**	**WG**	**N**	**B**	**F**	**I**	**S**
	(Percent Who Support)								
Support equal rights for men and women	60	60	58	54	68	49	58	44	60
Support equal rights for natives and immigrants	43	33	28	27	59	24	30	15	14
Support equal rights for able bodied and handicapped	86	91	85	65	81	64	79	63	62
Think a woman needs children for fulfillment	19	29	24	34	11	41	68	62	45
Support abortion where woman is not married	33	15	8	21	29	25	24	23	27
Support abortion when child may be physically handicapped	76	49	32	79	60	75	83	77	68
More emphasis on family life is a good thing	88	92	94	87	67	84	89	93	88
Work is most important thing in my life	8	12	12	8	8	9	4	9	6
I take a great deal of pride in my work	83	79	77	17	26	34	15	30	48
Most important aspect of job is good pay	68	74	73	73	71	71	54	72	78
Most important aspect is good job security	57	62	61	73	41	39	35	61	62
Support ecology movement, nature protection	92	89	94	97	95	93	91	92	90
Support anti-nuclear energy movement	56	57	85	72	68	74	64	67	76
Agree country's economic system needs fundamental change	75	83	86	28	27	42	59	76	73
Economy will be healthier if government allows more freedom for individuals to do as they wish	44	41	51	32	41	28	45	41	41
Confidence in Parliament	46	46	50	50	53	42	43	32	41

GB Great Britain; NI Northern Ireland; RI Republic of Ireland; WG West Germany; N Netherlands; B Belgium; F France; I Italy; S Spain.

Source: Sheena Ashford and Noel Timms, What Europe Thinks: A Study of Western European Values (Aldershot: Dartmouth, 1992), various pages.

Multiple Measures of Individual Behavior

As you have seen in this chapter, several measures of individual behavior are used in the analysis of consumer behavior. Personality has an effect on buying; lifestyles have more. Certainly economic resources such as income and time, described in Chapter 9, are also very important. Probably the concept that is currently receiving the most interest in consumer research is values. Understanding all these concepts helps us understand why one individual buys and uses products differently from another. Using some or all of these measures may provide a way of defining market segments that gives the firm you work for the competitive edge over the firm that fails to understand such concepts. If you understand these concepts well, perhaps like the Swiss guide in the opening scenario of this chapter, you will be able to look into a consumer's eyes and predict that individual's behavior!

Summary

Purchase decisions vary between individuals because of unique characteristics possessed by each individual. One such variable is called personality. Personality is defined as consistent responses to environmental stimuli. Three major theories or approaches to the study of personality include psychoanalytic, socio-psychological, and trait-factor. Newer approaches to the use of personality include brand personality and more recent attempts to relate personality to elements of consumer decision making and information processing, such as the need for cognition.

Personal values also explain individual differences among consumers. Rokeach developed the RVS and identified values as terminal and instrumental, or the ends to which behavior is directed and the means of attaining those ends. Schwartz developed the SVS, which identifies the value system that underlies motivations and which appears to have broad generality across disparate cultures. A useful technique for relating values to attributes of products is called laddering and is helpful in segmenting markets and developing product and communications strategies to reach those markets.

Lifestyles are patterns in which people live and spend time and money. Lifestyles are the result of the total array of economic, cultural, and social life forces that contribute to a person's human qualities.

People develop constructs with which to interpret, predict, and control their environment. These constructs or patterns result in behavior patterns and attitude structures that minimize incompatibilities and inconsistencies in a person's life. Psychographics or AIOs measure the operational form of lifestyles. AIO stands for activities, interests, and opinions, and may be either general or product-specific. VALS and LOV are alternative approaches to understanding values and lifestyles.

The practical solution to marketing mix problems often involves looking at multiple measures of individual characteristics. In addition to personality and lifestyle, such measures include economic resources such as money and time, as well as demographic measures such as age or nature of the household. All these variables may interact with the usage situation for the product.

Review and Discussion Questions

1. Clearly distinguish between the following terms: lifestyles, psychographics, AIO measures, personality, benefits.

2. Explain the difference between a general lifestyle measure and a specific lifestyle measure. Give two examples of each for a research project involving a soft drink.

3. What is the basis for the VALS system? How might it be used by a marketing organization?

4. Describe the trait-factor theory of personality and assess its importance in past and future marketing research.

5. Should a restaurant segment its market by lifestyle, income, situation, or some other variable? Explain your answer.

6. Assume that you have recently been employed by a large department store and have been asked to prepare an analysis of the market for furniture in your city. The president of the store is interested in doing a psychographic study and has asked you to prepare a questionnaire. Be sure to indicate the specific content of the questionnaire, some sample questions, the method of data collection, and methods of analysis.

7. Assume that you are developing an advertising program for an airline. How would you use laddering to assist in the development of the program?

8. How might personal values be used to segment markets for financial services? Could similar approaches be used in less-developed countries as well as industrialized markets?

Endnotes

1. H. Kassarjian, "Personality and Consumer Behavior: A Review," *Journal of Marketing Research* (November 1971), 409–418.

2. For descriptions of major personality theories, see Walter Mischel, *Introduction to Personality: A New Look* (New York: CBS College Publishing, 1986); and Larry Hjelle and Daniel Ziegler, *Personality Theories: Basic Assumptions, Research and Applications* (New York: McGraw-Hill, 1987).

3. For a marketing view of psychoanalytic theory, see W. D. Wells and A. D. Beard, "Personality and Consumer Behavior," in Scott Ward and T. S. Robertson, eds.,

Consumer Behavior: Theoretical Sources (Englewood Cliffs, N.J.: Prentice-Hall, 1973).

4. The classic example of this literature is Ernest Dichter, *Handbook of Consumer Motivations* (New York: McGraw-Hill, 1964). For a recent example of motivation research by Dr. Dichter, see the "Swan Cleaners" case in Roger D. Blackwell, James F. Engel, and W. Wayne Talarzyk, *Contemporary Cases in Consumer Behavior* (Chicago: Dryden, 1990), 135–142.

5. For a more complete explanation of this approach, see C. S. Hall and G. Lindzey, *Theories of Personality* (New York: John Wiley & Sons, 1970), 154–155.

6. J. B. Cohen, "An Interpersonal Orientation to the Study of Consumer Behavior," *Journal of Marketing Research* 4 (August 1967), 270–278; J. B. Cohen, "Toward an Interpersonal Theory of Consumer Behavior," *California Management Review* 10 (1968), 73–80. Also see Jon P. Noerager, "An Assessment of CAD: A Personality Instrument Developed Specifically for Marketing Research," *Journal of Marketing Research* (February 1979), 53–59.

7. John W. Schouten, "Selves in Transition: Symbolic Consumption in Personal Rites of Passage and Identity Reconstruction," *Journal of Consumer Research* 17 (March 1991), 412–423.

8. A good introduction to the theory and techniques of this approach is found in A. R. Buss and W. Poley, *Individual Differences: Traits and Factors* (New York: Halsted Press, 1976).

9. Raymond L. Horton, "The Edwards Personal Preference Schedule and Consumer Personality Research," *Journal of Marketing Research* 11 (August 1974), 335–337.

10. Kathryn E. A. Villani and Yoram Wind, "On the Usage of 'Modified' Personality Trait Measures in Consumer Research," *Journal of Consumer Research* 2 (December 1975), 223–226.

11. Mark I. Alpert, "Personality and the Determinants of Product Choice," *Journal of Marketing Research* 9 (February 1972), 89–92.

12. Paul E. Green, Yoram Wind, and Arun K. Jain, "A Note on Measurement of Social-Psychological Belief Systems," *Journal of Marketing Research* 9 (May 1972), 204–208.

13. F. B. Evans, "Psychological Objective Factors in the Prediction of Brand Choice: Ford Versus Chevrolet," *Journal of Business* 32 (1959), 340–369.

14. Joseph T. Plummer, "How Personality Makes a Difference," *Journal of Advertising Research* 24 (January 1985), 27–31.

15. Ibid., 29.

16. James A. Muncy, "Psychological Responses of Consumer Emotions: Theory, Methods and Implications for Consumer Research," in Susan P. Douglas et al., *1987 AMA Educators' Conference Proceedings* (Chicago: American Marketing Association, 1987), 127–132.

17. Robert Plutchik, *Emotion: A Psychoevolutionary Synthesis* (New York: Harper & Row, 1980).

18. William J. Havlena and Morris B. Holbrook, "The Varieties of Consumption Experience: Comparing Two Typologies of Emotion in Consumer Behavior," *Journal of Consumer Research* 13 (December 1986), 394–404.

19. Gordon R. Foxall and Seema Bhate, "Cognitive Style and Personal Involvement as Explicators of Innovative Purchasing of 'Healthy' Food Brands," *European Journal of Marketing* 27 (1993), 5–16.

20. Curt Haugtvedt, Richard E. Petty, John T. Cacioppo, and Theresa Steidley, "Personality and Ad Effectiveness: Exploring the Utility of Need for Cognition," *Advances in Consumer Research* 16 (Provo, Utah: Association for Consumer Research, 1988).

21. Curtis P. Haugtvedt and Richard E. Petty, "Personality and Persuasion: Need for Cognition Moderates the Persistence and Resistance of Attitude Changes," *Journal of Personality and Social Psychology* 63 (1992), 308–319; and Curtis P. Haugtvedt, Richard E. Petty, and John T. Cacioppo, "Need for Cognition and Advertising: Understanding the Role of Personality Variables in Consumer Behavior," *Journal of Consumer Psychology* 1 (1992), 239–260.

22. D. J. O'Keefe, *Persuasion: Theory and Research* (Newbury Park, Calif.: Sage, 1990).

23. V. W. Mitchell and P. Boustani, "Market Development Using New Products and New Customers: A Role for Perceived Risk," *European Journal of Marketing* 27 (1993), 17–32.

24. Robert N. Stone and Frederick W. Winter, "Risk: Is It Still Uncertainty Times Consequences?" in Russell W. Belk et al., eds., *1987 AMA Winter Educators' Conference Proceedings* (Chicago: American Marketing Association, 1987), 261–265.

25. Frank Farley, "The Big T in Personality," *Psychology Today* 20 (May 1986), 44ff.

26. M. Snyder, "Self-Monitoring Processes," in L. Berkowitz, ed., *Advances in Experimental Social Psychology,* 12th ed. (New York: Academic Press, 1979), 85–129. Also see M. Snyder and K. G. DeBono, "Understanding the Function of Attitudes: Lessons from Personality and Social Behavior," in A. R. Pratkanis, S. J. Breckler, and A. G. Greenwald, eds., *Attitude Structure and Function* (Hillsdale, N.J.: Lawrence Erlbaum Associates, 1989) 339–359.

27. Patricia M. Anderson, "Personality, Perception and Emotional-State Factors in Approach-Avoidance Behavior in the Store Environment," in Terence A. Shimp et al., eds., *1986 AMA Educators' Conference Proceedings* (Chicago: American Marketing Association, 1986), 35–39.

28. Leslie M. Fine and David W. Schumann, "The Nature and Role of Salesperson Perceptions: The Interactive Effects of Salesperson/Customer Personalities," *Journal of Consumer Psychology* 1 (1992), 285–296.

29. Steven M. Burgess, "Personal Values and Consumer Research," *Research in Marketing* 11 (1992).

30. Terry Clark, "International Marketing and National Character: A Review and Proposal for an Integrative Theory," *Journal of Marketing* 54 (October 1990), 66–79.

31. Roger D. Blackwell, *From the Edge of the World: Global Lessons for Personal and Professional Prosperity* (Columbus: The Ohio State University Press, 1994), 119–137.

32. Milton Rokeach, *The Nature of Human Values* (New York: Free Press, 1973), 5. Also see M. Rokeach and S. J. Ball-Rokeach, "Stability and Change in American Value Priorities, 1968–1981," *American Psychologist* 44 (May 1989), 773–784.

33. Rokeach, *The Nature of Human Values*, 57–58.

34. K. G. Grunert, S. C. Grunert, and S. E. Beatty, "Cross-Cultural Research on Consumer Values," *Marketing and Research Today* (February 1989), 30–39; J. M. Munson and E. F. McQuarrie, "Shortening the Rokeach Value Survey for Use in Consumer Research," *Advances in Consumer Research* 15 (Association for Consumer Research, 1988), 381–386; S. W. Perkings and T. J. Reynolds, "The Explanatory Power of Values in Preference Judgments Validation of the Means-End Perspective," *Advances in Consumer Research* 15 (Association for Consumer Research, 1988), 122–126; G. Roehrich, P. Valette-Florence, and B. Rappachi, "Combined Incidence of Personal Values, Involvement, and Innovativeness on Innovative Consumer Behavior," in *Is Marketing Keeping Up with the Consumer? Lessons from Changing Products, Attitudes and Behavior* (Vienna, Austria: ESOMAR, 1989), 261–279; D. K. Tse, J. K. Wong, and C. T. Tan, "Towards Some Standard Cross-Cultural Consumption Values," *Advances in Consumer Research* 15 (Association for Consumer Research, 1988), 387–395; P. Valette-Florence and A. Jolibert, "Social Values, A.I.O. and Consumption Patterns: Exploratory Findings," *Journal of Business Research* 20 (March 1990), 109–122.

35. Donald E. Vinson, Jerome E. Scott, and Lawrence M. Lamont, "The Role of Personal Values in Marketing and Consumer Behavior," *Journal of Marketing* 41 (April 1977), 44–50.

36. Robert E. Pitts and Arch G. Woodside, "Personal Values and Market Segmentation: Applying the Value Construct," in R. E. Pitts and A. G. Woodside (1984), 55–67.

37. Wagner A. Kamakura and Jose Alfonso Masson, "Value Segmentation: A Model for the Measurement of Values and Value Systems," *Journal of Consumer Research* 18 (September 1991), 208–218.

38. S. H. Schwartz and L. Sagiv, "Identifying Culture-Specifics in the Content and Structure of Values," *Journal of Cross-Cultural Psychology* 23 (1992).

39. S. H. Schwartz, "Universals in the Content and Structure of Values: Theoretical Advances and Empirical Tests in 20 Countries," *Advances in Experimental Social Psychology* 25 (1992); and S. H. Schwartz and W. Bilsky, "Toward a Theory of the Universal Structure and Content of Values: Extensions and Cross-Cultural Replications," *Journal of Personality and Social Psychology* 58 (1992), 878–891.

40. Steven M. Burgess and Roger D. Blackwell, "Personal Values and South African Financial Services Brand Preference," *South African Journal of Business Management* 25 (1994).

41. Thomas J. Reynolds and Jonathan Gutman, "Advertising Is Image Management," *Journal of Advertising Research* 24 (February–March 1984), 27–36.

42. Thomas J. Reynolds and Jonathan Gutman, "Laddering Theory, Method, Analysis, and Interpretation," *Journal of Advertising Research* 28 (February–March 1988), 11–31.

43. George A. Kelly, *The Psychology of Personal Constructs* (New York: W. W. Norton, 1955). Also see Fred Reynolds and William Darden, "Construing Life Style and Psychographics," in William D. Wells, ed., *Life Style and Psychographics* (Chicago: American Marketing Association, 1974), 71–96.

44. Thabet A. Edris and A. Meidan, "On the Reliability of Psychographic Research: Encouraging Signs for Measurement Accuracy and Methodology in Consumer Research," *European Journal of Marketing* 24 (1990), 23–41.

45. Emanuel H. Demby, "Psychographics Revisited: The Birth of a Technique," *Marketing News* (January 2, 1989), 21.

46. Reynolds and Darden, "Construing Life Style," 87.

47. This research is summarized from Roger Blackwell and Wayne Talarzyk, *Consumer Attitudes toward Health Care and Malpractice* (Columbus, Ohio: Grid Publishing, 1977), Chapter 5.

48. Introductions to factor analysis are available in Joseph Hair et al., *Multivariate Data Analysis* (Tulsa: PPC Books, 1979); and George H. Dunteman, *Introduction to Multivariate Analysis* (Beverly Hills, Calif.: Sage Publications, 1984).

49. "Kentucky Fried Chicken Redesigns for New Image," *Marketing News* (March 18, 1991), 6.

50. Rebecca Holman, "A Values and Lifestyles Perspective on Human Behavior," in Pitts and Woodside, eds., *Personal Values and Consumer Psychology,* 35–54; Sonia Yuspeh, "Syndicated Values/Lifestyles Segmentation Schemes: Use Them as Descriptive Tools, Not to Select Targets," *AMA Marketing News* 18 (May 25, 1984), 1ff; James Atlas, "Beyond Demographics," *Atlantic Monthly* (October 1984), 49–59.

51. Lynn R. Kahle, *Social Values and Social Change: Adaptation to Life in America* (New York: Praeger, 1983).

52. Lynn R. Kahle, Sharon E. Beatty, and Pamela Homer, "Alternative Measurement Approaches to Consumer Values: The List of Values (LOV) and Values and Life Styles (VALS)," *Journal of Consumer Research* 13 (December 1986), 405–409. See also S. M. Burgess, "Personal Values and Consumer Behaviour: An Historical Perspective," Working paper #89/7 (Johannesburg: Business Economics Research Group of the University of Witswatersrand, 1989); and Matthew Perri III, "Application of the List of Values Alternative Psychographic Assessment Scale," *Psychological Reports* 66 (July 1990), 403–406.

53. Thomas P. Novak and Bruce MacEvoy, "On Comparing Alternative Segmentation Schemes: The List of Values (LOV) and Values and Life Styles (VALS)," *Journal of Consumer Research* 17 (June 1990), 105–109.

54. Kim P. Corfman, Donald R. Lehmann, and Sarah Narayanan, "Values, Utility, and Ownership: Modeling the Relationships for Consumer Durables," *Journal of Retailing* 67 (Summer 1991), 184–204.

55. Wagner A. Kamakura and Thomas P. Novak, "Value-System Segmentation: Exploring the Meaning of LOV," *Journal of Consumer Research* 19 (June 1992), 119–132.

56. Arnold Mitchell, "Nine American Lifestyles: Values and Societal Change," *The Futurist* 18 (August 1984), 4–13.

57. Ian Pearson, "Social Studies," *Canadian Business* 58 (1985), 67–73.

58. Sheena Ashford and Noel Timms, *What Europe Thinks: A Study of Western European Values* (Aldershot: Dartmouth Publishing Company Limited, 1992).

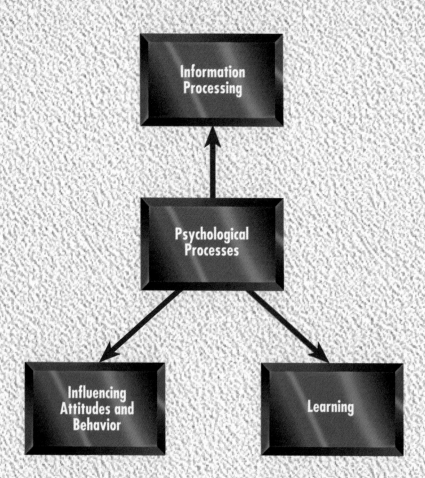

PART IV

Phychological Processes

▲▲

N ow our focus shifts to three central psychological processes that shape all aspects of consumer motivation and behavior: (1) **information processing** (Chapter 14), (2) **learning** (Chapter 15), and (3) **attitude and behavior change** (Chapter 16).

The information processing arena has attracted droves of behavioral sciences researchers in the last three decades, including many who specialized in consumer behavior. This is understandable because this subject focuses on ways in which information is received, processed, and used in daily life. Nothing could be of greater practical significance. Chapter 14 covers a wide range of topics and issues in this field. You will find rewards from perseverance here because the concepts developed are used in the chapters that follow.

Chapter 15 addresses the subject of learning. Certainly no single chapter can do justice to such a broad field of inquiry, but you are introduced to various theories and concepts that have proved to have the greatest practical relevance for understanding the consumer.

Can consumer attitudes and actions be influenced? The answer obviously is yes, and much of the key lies in an understanding of persuasion. This is the subject of Chapter 16. A broad range of literature is reviewed from the perspective of principles and strategies that offer the greatest practical payout.

CHAPTER 14

Information Processing

▲▲▲▲▲▲▲▲▲▲▲▲▲▲▲▲▲▲▲▲▲▲▲▲▲▲▲▲▲▲▲▲▲▲▲▲▲

Flying without an Airplane: Swissair's Ad Campaign Grabs Attention

Nudity still shocks, but a European ad campaign demonstrates that beyond capturing attention, bare bodies can be good for the bottom line. Swissair, Switzerland's national airline, launched a new business class with a campaign showing a naked, carefree man flying through the skies. The first ads showed only his legs, followed at intervals by other parts of his body, until the whole man appeared in the last ads. The man's derriere was shown, but there weren't any frontal glimpses. The campaign ran in magazines in Europe, North Africa, and Turkey, in European newspapers, and on television in the United Kingdom.

The campaign is a rare departure from traditional airline advertising, which tends to show smiling hostesses serving happy customers trays of food. "We created something unconventional and unique," says Konrad Korsunsky, Swissair advertising manager. "We created a renaissance person—not only a man flying totally unencumbered, without hassle, with freedom to move. Passengers understood the message. We will be doing this sort of advertising again."

And no wonder. "The response was incredible," says Mr. Korsunsky. He claims the campaign resulted in "solidly booked seats, even though capacity in business class was increased by 30%."

Source: Adapted from Lisa Bannon and Margaret Studer, "Two Ads Show Benefits of Overexposure," Wall Street Journal (June 17, 1993), B6.

As you discover later in the chapter, Swissair's advertising campaign is but one example of how companies try to get consumers to process the information conveyed by their advertising messages. Because consumers' reactions to advertising will depend on the manner in which it is processed, an understanding of information processing can be very useful. **Information processing** refers to the process by which a stimulus is received, interpreted, stored in memory, and later retrieved. As you will see, an appreciation of information-processing principles and findings can yield some important lessons for those interested in influencing consumer behavior. Although advertising is perhaps the greatest beneficiary of what we know about how people process information, these lessons can be applied to many areas of communication, including personal selling, package design, branding, training of salespeople, and even consumer behavior classrooms.

Information processing can be broken down into five basic stages (Figure 14.1), based on the information-processing model developed by William McGuire.[1] These stages can be defined as follows:

1. **Exposure:** the achievement of proximity to a stimulus such that an opportunity exists for one or more of a person's five senses to be activated

2. **Attention:** the allocation of processing capacity to the incoming stimulus

3. **Comprehension:** the interpretation of the stimulus

4. **Acceptance:** the persuasive impact of the stimulus

5. **Retention:** the transfer of the stimulus interpretation and persuasion into long-term memory

Figure 14.1 indicates that a stimulus must be present and available for processing before the first stage of information processing, exposure, can occur. After exposure, the consumer may pay attention to or "process" the stimulus. During this processing, the consumer will attach meaning to the stimulus, which is the comprehension stage.

The next stage, acceptance, is of critical concern in the realm of persuasive communication. Although the consumer may accurately understand what a salesperson or advertisement is saying, the critical question addressed at this stage is whether the consumer actually believes this information.

The final stage, retention, involves the transfer of information into long-term memory. Note, however, that memory also influences prior stages as well. For example, the consumer who remembers an upcoming birthday of a family member is more likely to pay attention to gift ads. Similarly, the interpretation of stimuli depends on stored knowledge and prior experiences.

An important implication of this information-processing model is that a stimulus must pass through each of the stages before it reaches memory. Consequently, the effectiveness of persuasive communications will hinge on their ability to survive all the information-processing stages. This is not an easy task. In one study involving 1,800 TV commercials, only 16 percent of those exposed to an ad could remember the advertised brand.[2] Similarly, according to some day-after recall tests, an average of only 24 percent of those people exposed to a television ad can give a sufficient response to reflect that retention of the ad has oc-

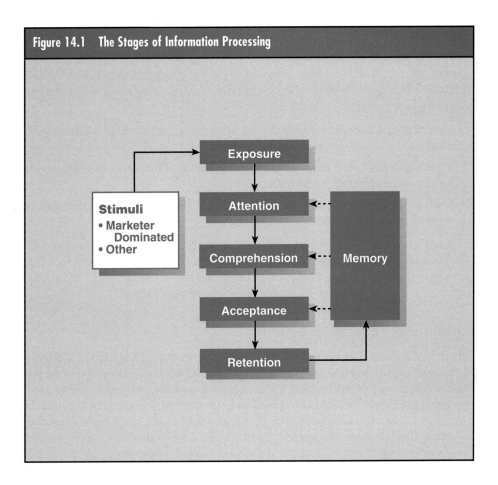

Figure 14.1   The Stages of Information Processing

curred 24 hours after exposure.[3] One benefit you should derive from this chapter is a better appreciation of the factors that influence the likelihood of a stimulus, such as an ad, passing through the separate stages of information processing.

Exposure

Information processing begins when patterns of energy in the form of stimulus inputs reach one or more of the five senses. **Exposure** occurs from physical proximity to a stimulus that allows the opportunity for one or more senses to be activated. This requires the communicator to select media, either interpersonal or mass, that reach the target market.[4]

Threshold Levels

Given exposure to a stimulus of sufficient strength, a person's sensory receptors are activated and the encoded information is transmitted along nerve fibers to the brain. This activation is called a **sensation,** which is affected by the following three thresholds[5]:

1. **Lower or absolute threshold:** the minimum amount of stimulus energy or intensity necessary for sensation to occur

2. **Terminal threshold:** the point at which additional increases in stimulus intensity have no effect on sensation

3. **Difference threshold:** the smallest change in stimulus intensity that will be noticed by an individual

Some consumer researchers maintain that stimuli must attain at least the lower or absolute threshold before they can have an impact on the person. Others argue that stimuli below the lower threshold can be influential. This controversial concept has become known as **subliminal persuasion.**

Subliminal Persuasion

Much of the interest in subliminal persuasion can be traced back to the late 1950s when Jim Vicary, the owner of a failing research business, claimed that he had discovered a way of influencing consumers without their conscious awareness. He reported Coca-Cola sales increased by 18 percent and popcorn sales grew by 52 percent when the words *DRINK COKE* and *EAT POPCORN* were flashed on a movie theater screen at speeds that escaped conscious detection. However, when an independent replication of the study failed to show any effects, Vicary confessed to fabricating the results in the hope of reviving his business.[6]

For years, the subject lay dormant until Wilson Bryan Key contended in a popularized book that erotic subliminal cues are implanted in advertisements (for example, the juxtaposition of ice cubes in a liquor ad) designed to appeal to subconscious sex drives.[7] Today, the use of subliminal stimuli is quite prevalent. Consumers spend millions of dollars each year on self-help tapes containing subliminal messages. Horror films have included subliminals in the form of death masks and other scary images to enhance their ability to frighten viewers. Retailers have incorporated subliminal messages within their in-store music designed to motivate employees and undermine shoplifting. Even some resorts have tried subliminals to help vacationers relax.[8]

Despite their prevalent use, the power of subliminal stimuli is still a strongly contested issue. There is some research to suggest that subliminal stimuli can be influential.[9] In a typical study, subjects are exposed to stimuli for very brief amounts of time (in the milliseconds). Exposure is so brief that subjects are unable to identify these stimuli in subsequent recognition tasks. Even so, subjects evaluate these previously seen but unrecognized stimuli more favorably than similar stimuli encountered for the first time. Such findings support the possibility of influencing attitudes without conscious cognitive activity.

Others, however, have challenged the effectiveness of subliminal stimuli. In the words of Timothy Moore[10]:

> A century of psychological research substantiates the general principle that more intense stimuli have a greater effect on people's behavior than weaker ones. . . . Subliminal stimuli are usually so weak that the recipient is not just unaware of the stimulus but is also oblivious to the fact that he/she is being stimulated. As a result, the potential effects of subliminal stimuli are easily nullified by other on-going stimulation in the same sensory channel whereby attention is being focused on another modality.

Stated differently, why should one choose a weak method of persuasion when much more effective methods exist?

Weber's Law

It is often important to understand whether a change in some marketing stimulus (such as price) will be perceived by consumers. A retailer who promotes a special sale, for instance, will be disappointed unless consumers perceive the discounted price to be sufficiently lower than the normal price. Similarly, claims of product improvement will be ineffective when consumers fail to perceive a difference between the old and new versions.

In these situations, the **difference threshold**, representing the smallest change in stimulus intensity that will be noticed, is quite relevant. This threshold must be met in attempting to generate perceptions of change. According to Weber's law, as expressed in the following equation, the actual amount of change necessary to reach the difference threshold will depend on the initial starting point.

$$K = \frac{\Delta I}{I}$$

where

K = a constant that differs across the various senses,
ΔI = the smallest change in stimulus intensity necessary to produce a just noticeable difference (JND), and
I = the stimulus intensity at the point where the change occurs.

Weber's law suggests that, as the strength of the initial stimulus intensity increases, a greater amount of change is necessary to produce a just noticeable difference. Let's consider price changes as an example. Some managers believe that a 15 percent price reduction is necessary for attracting consumers to a sale.[11] Assuming K equals 15 percent, then a discount of at least $15 would therefore be needed for a $100 item before consumers would perceive a real cost savings.

This same $15 discount, however, would not be effective for a $150 item ($15/$150 = 10 percent, which is less than the needed 15 percent). In this instance, a discount of at least $22.50 would be necessary.[12]

In some situations, a business may not wish to meet or exceed the difference threshold. Consumers have complained about chips that were cut 8/1000 of an inch too thick or thin. To stay beneath this difference threshold, quality-control engineers at Frito-Lay measure the thickness of chips to 36/1000 of an inch for flat chips and 91/1000 for Ruffles, the company's brand of ridged potato chip.[13]

Also, companies are sometimes interested in changing their products or prices without consumers noticing such changes. Price increases and reductions in product size (such as a shrinking candy bar) are changes that, if possible, should be undertaken without activating the just noticeable difference.

Attention

Not all the stimuli that activate our sensory receptors during the exposure stage will receive additional processing. Because of limitations in our cognitive resources, as discussed in Chapter 9, it is impossible for us to process all the stimuli available at any given moment. Consequently, the cognitive system is constantly monitoring sensory inputs, selecting some of these for further processing. This screening occurs at a preconscious level and is referred to as **preattentive processing.**[14] Those stimuli that pass through this screening process enter into the second stage of the information processing model, **attention.** Attention can be defined as the allocation of processing capacity to a stimulus.

One of the biggest challenges facing a company is getting consumers to pay attention to what the company has to say and what it has to sell. It is indeed quite some challenge. Some have estimated that the typical consumer will encounter about 300 ads each day.[15] The average television viewer sees more than 100 commercials in a day. The average home receives 216 pieces of junk mail annually.[16] Unfortunately, many of these ads will fail to capture the attention necessary for them to have an influence (see Consumer in Focus 14.1).

The challenge is no less formidable in the retail environment. A typical supermarket will contain between 18,000 to 20,000 products. Standing out on the grocer's shelf and grabbing the consumer's attention has become an even more important consideration in designing the product's packaging. Moreover, "packaging has to do that from 5 feet away at 3 miles an hour," says Frank Malfa, graphics design director at Pepperidge Farm.[17]

Although life would be much easier for companies if consumers paid attention to all the ads and products they encounter in the marketplace, the reality is that consumers are quite selective in what they attend to. Some ads and packages will break through the clutter; many will not. Given this reality of selective

Consumer in Focus   **14.1**

When Commercials Come On, Viewers Turn Off

In 1953, market researchers found that water consumption rose during television commercial breaks. Ever since then, advertisers have speculated about what else viewers do during this time besides using the bathroom. With the introduction of remote-control devices, advertisers have become even more suspicious that no one is watching their commercials. New data from the Roper Organization partially confirm their fears.

Nearly half of all adults say they often get up and do something else during commercials, according to Roper's 1993 survey. Fewer than one in four say they often stay in their seats. One-third frequently talk to others in the room without paying attention to the commercials. One-quarter switch to another channel, and one in seven turn the sound down.

The restless urge increases with income. Fifty-one percent of adults with household incomes of $50,000 or more leave their sets during breaks, compared with 39 percent of those with household incomes less than $15,000. Viewers with at least some college education are more likely to find something else to do than are those with less education. Older watchers are more likely than younger viewers to stay in their seats during commercial breaks. Just 37 percent of those aged 60 years and older leave the room, compared with 51 percent of those younger than 30 years.

Television commercials have their fans, too. About 22 percent of Americans say they often sit and watch commercials, and 14 percent frequently discuss them with other people in the room. Twenty-six percent say they are frequently amused by commercials, and 17 percent are often interested in learning about products and services. Even so, only 9 percent of viewers say they almost never leave their seats during commercials.

Source: Excerpted from Judith Waldrop, "And Now, a Break from Our Sponsor," American Demographics (August 1993), 16, 18.

attention, it is important to understand what factors influence the consumer's allocation of this limited resource, particularly for those seeking to attract the consumer's attention. Such factors can be grouped into two major categories: personal or individual determinants and stimulus determinants.

Personal Determinants of Attention

Personal determinants refer to those characteristics of the individual that influence attention. For the most part, these factors are not under the marketer's control. Rather, their existence should be recognized and viewed as constraints against which strategy should be evaluated.

Need/Motivation

Everyone is well aware from daily life that physiological needs have a strong influence on those stimuli that receive attention and those that do not. Hungry people, for example, are far more receptive to food stimuli than they would be on other occasions. Consumer economists have long contended that the worst time for food shopping is when one is hungry because of the sharp increase in purchasing.

The nature of consumers' need states at the time of exposure to advertising should affect the emphasis placed on an ad's attention-getting properties. If it is possible for an ad to reach consumers when their needs are activated, less emphasis on enhancing an ad's ability to gain attention is warranted because the consumer is already motivated to process the ad. Unfortunately, this can be difficult to achieve because the time span of consumer decision making is often quite small.[18] More often than not, it will be advantageous to develop advertising that contains stimuli (such as those described shortly) that enhance attention.

Attitudes

According to **cognitive consistency theories**, such as balance theory and congruity theory, people strive to maintain a consistent set of beliefs and attitudes (hence the name cognitive consistency).[19] Inconsistency in this cognitive system is believed to induce adverse psychological tension. Consequently, people are viewed as being receptive to information that maintains or enhances consistency, while avoiding information that challenges their beliefs and attitudes.

The principle of cognitive consistency suggests that attitudes may also influence the attention given to marketing communications. Consumers possessing unfavorable attitudes may allocate little attention, such as an avid antismoker exposed to the cigarette industry's campaign of "smokers' rights." However, smokers should be much more attentive to these messages. Thus, attitude can be a facilitator when consumers hold favorable feelings toward the product but may serve as a barrier when consumers are negative.[20]

Adaptation Level

An important tendency people share is to become so habituated to a stimulus that it is no longer noticed—that is, they develop an **adaptation level** for the stimulus. Consider, for example, the couple who moves from a quiet, small town to an apartment in the middle of New York City. Initially, they will find the noise levels to be very disturbing and will suffer through many nights of restless sleep. Eventually, however, they will grow accustomed or become adapted to the noise.

This same phenomenon occurs in marketing. Advertising is especially likely to fall victim to adaptation. Many products are familiar, and it is often difficult to say much that is really new. This can place some real demands on the design and format of the message. Similarly, repeated exposure to an ad may not be effective as consumers become habituated to this stimulus. A strategy of repetition must, therefore, be carefully conceived because of the danger of habituation.

Although adaptation level frequently represents a barrier between marketers and consumers, marketers can also use it to their advantage. The use of unique product packaging, for instance, can help a product stand out on the shelf. Similarly, an advertising tactic for gaining attention is to include stimuli within an ad that deviate from the consumer's adaptation level. The use of the phrase "A bad ad" in the advertisement appearing in Figure 14.2 is contrary to what consumers expect to see in an ad. As described subsequently, some of the stimulus factors that help capture attention do so because they capitalize on adaptation.

Span of Attention

The amount of time we can focus our attention on a single stimulus or thought is quite limited. You can easily demonstrate this to yourself by testing just how

Figure 14.2   Deviating from Consumers' Adaptation Level Can Help Capture Their Attention

long you are able to concentrate on a particular thought before your mind begins to "wander." In an advertising context, the use of shorter commercials is one way to overcome consumers' limited attention spans.[21]

Stimulus Determinants of Attention

The second set of factors influencing attention, **stimulus determinants,** are characteristics of the stimulus itself. They represent "controllable" factors in the sense that they can be manipulated to gain and/or increase attention.[22] Consequently, they are often used by companies competing for the consumer's attention.

Size

In general, the larger the stimulus, the more likely it will attract attention. Increasing a print ad's size will enhance the odds of gaining the consumer's attention.[23] A similar relationship holds for the size of the illustrations or pictures within an ad.[24]

The likelihood of a product being noticed in a store can depend on the size or amount of shelf space allocated to the product. This can be particularly important for impulse items, whose sales may depend partly on how much space they receive.[25]

Color

As so nicely illustrated by the ad presented in Figure 14.3, the attention attracting and holding power of a stimulus may be sharply increased through the use of color.[26] In a field study involving newspaper advertising, one-color ads produced 41 percent more sales than did their black-and-white counterparts.[27] Color ads cost more, so their incremental effectiveness must be weighed against the additional expense.

Moreover, some colors may be more attention-getting than others. Did you know that red cars get more speeding tickets than cars of any other color? Further testimony to the power of red comes from the fact that companies placing ads in the yellow pages are encouraged to use this color as a way of attracting attention.

Intensity

Greater stimulus intensity often produces more attention. Loud sounds and bright colors, for instance, can enhance attention. Radio and television commercials may begin with a loud noise to attract attention. Brightly colored print ads are quite common.

Contrast

People have a tendency to attend more closely to those stimuli that contrast with their background. The presentation of stimuli that are inconsistent or contrast

Figure 14.3   The Right Colors Can Grab Attention

with one another creates a perceptual conflict that enhances attention. Contrast is used in the ad presented in Figure 14.4 by combining arctic and tropical birds and landscapes into a single scene.

Techniques based on the contrast principle appear in a variety of forms in advertising. For example, a black-and-white ad preceded by color ads may be more noticed because of contrast. Similarly, a TV ad that is louder than the programming that preceded it may also attract greater attention. Note that both examples follow from adaptation level. Consumers become adapted to color ads only or to a certain volume that, when violated, attracts their attention.

Position

Stimuli may also be more noticeable simply because of certain locational properties. Grocery vendors know this very well and compete for such prime grocery

Figure 14.4   Ads with Contrasting Stimuli Can Attract Attention

locations as end of the aisle and shelves located near eye level. Similarly, impulse items are strategically located near cash registers.

Position can also be important for print media. Greater attention is given to ads located in the front rather than back part of the magazine, on right-hand pages rather than left-hand pages, and on the inside front, inside back, and outside back covers.[28] Presumably, these effects are due to the manner in which consumers typically flip through magazines.

Position within the printed page itself can also affect attention. A rule of thumb in advertising is that the upper left-hand corner of the page is the most likely corner to receive attention, whereas the lower right-hand corner is least likely.[29]

Position in broadcast advertising has received less attention in research, although it is a generally accepted rule that commercials perform better when

Figure 14.5 An Ad Design That Encourages Proper Eye Movement

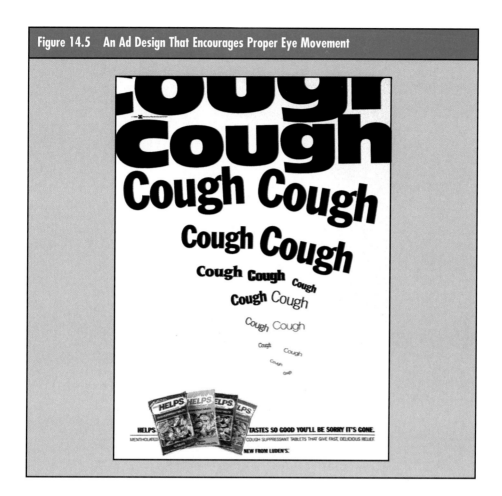

included as part of the regular program rather than during the "clutter" of a program break.[30] Commercials at the beginning and end of a program suffer from the clutter of announcements and other distracting nonprogram material.

Directionality

The eye will tend to follow any signs within the stimulus that indicate directionality. Examples would be arrows or pointing devices. Examine the ad in Figure 14.5. Notice how it directs the eye to the brand name and package.

Movement

Stimuli in motion elicit greater attention than stationary stimuli. Even quasi- or perceived motion, as suggested by the shattering glass that is featured in the ad presented in Figure 14.6, can enhance attention.

Figure 14.6   Attracting Attention with Quasimotion

[MEMOREX AUDIO EQUIPMENT.   JUST BREAKING.]

Isolation

Isolation, which involves presenting a few stimuli in a relatively barren perceptual field, can also attract attention. The use of isolation in print advertising means that, rather than completely filling the ad with information and pictures, a substantial portion of the ad will remain "unused," such as the ad appearing in Figure 14.7.

Novelty

Unusual or unexpected stimuli (such as those that deviate from one's adaptation level) attract attention. Advertisers understand the value of novelty and frequently rely on it for gaining attention, as illustrated by Figure 14.8. Other applications include the use of "pop-ups" in print ads (such as the two-page Dodge ad in which a paper truck would pop up when the ad was opened), 3-D

Figure 14.7   Gaining Attention with Isolation

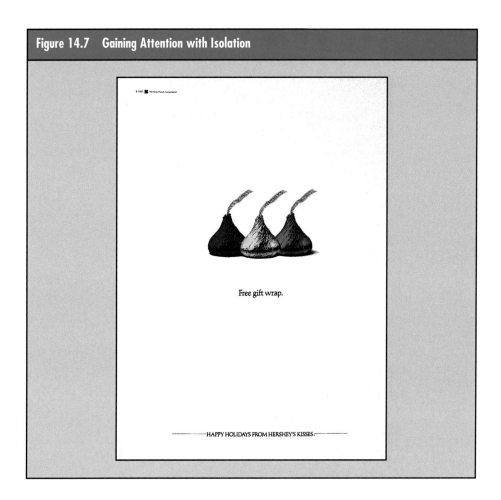

Free gift wrap.

HAPPY HOLIDAYS FROM HERSHEY'S KISSES.

ads, and print ads that play music thanks to a microchip activated by opening the ad.[31]

"Learned" Attention-Inducing Stimuli

Some stimuli attract our attention because we have been taught or conditioned to react to them. A ringing phone or doorbell, for example, typically elicits an immediate response from the person. Ringing phones or wailing sirens are sometimes included in the background of radio and TV ads to capture attention.

Attractive Spokesperson

A common attention-grabbing device is to use an attractive model or celebrity as a spokesperson.[32] It is nearly impossible to watch TV for any length of time or

Figure 14.8   Attracting Attention with Novelty

flip through most magazines without encountering at least one ad with an attractive person. One company, in an effort to break through the clutter of products on supermarket shelves, developed a line of common grocery products (cereal, trash bags, light bulbs) named Star Pak, which features the faces of some very famous movie stars (Marilyn Monroe, Clark Gable) on the product packaging.[33]

One danger of using a spokesperson is that it can backfire when consumers perceive it as inappropriate for the product being advertised. Models attired in bathing suits, although seen as appropriate endorsers for suntan products, may evoke unfavorable reactions when used to promote furniture.

Scene Changes

Another technique for capturing attention is the use of rapid-fire scene changes, which can cause an involuntary increase in brain activity.[34] In some Pontiac commercials, the viewer is exposed to a large number of scenes that last no longer than 1 1/2 seconds, with some scenes as short as 1/4 of a second. However, there is some concern that quick-cut commercials may be less memorable and persuasive than slower paced ads.[35]

Attracting Attention: A Precaution

As we have already pointed out, capturing the consumer's attention represents a major challenge to marketers. This will only become more difficult as consumers are bombarded with increasing numbers of products and promotions. Very often, marketers will have little choice but to rely on stimulus factors as bait for the consumer's attention.

We must be sensitive, however, to the fact that the use of stimulus factors is not without risk. A stimulus that dominates viewers' attention, while leaving the remaining message ignored, is self-defeating. The marketer must try to use stimuli that capture attention initially but that do not inhibit processing of the entire message. Whenever possible, stimuli should be used that help reinforce the brand name or product positioning as well as gain attention.

Comprehension

Comprehension, the third stage of information processing, is concerned with the interpretation of a stimulus. It is the point at which meaning is attached to the stimulus. This meaning will depend on how a stimulus is categorized and elaborated in terms of existing knowledge.

Stimulus Categorization

Stimulus categorization involves classifying a stimulus using concepts stored in memory.[36] Consumers' behavior can be affected by how they categorize marketing stimuli. Toro introduced a lightweight snowthrower named Snow Pup, which proved unsuccessful because the name led consumers to categorize the product either as a toy or as not powerful enough for the job. Changing the name (to first Snowmaster and then Toro) reversed this problem and made the product a success.[37]

Research also indicates that how a stimulus is categorized may influence how the stimulus is evaluated.[38] To the extent that the concepts used during categorization are associated with particular feelings and attitudes, these feelings and attitudes may transfer over to the newly classified stimulus. Thus, stimulus categorization can be quite important.

Companies often try to influence how consumers will categorize their products. Consider, for example, how the ad appearing in Figure 14.9 encourages consumers to categorize Chrysler as the "minivan company." In doing so,

Figure 14.9   Chrysler Wants Consumers to Categorize Its Company in a Certain Way

The Minivan Company.

*One automotive company
has earned that title.*

*The company that in 1984
invented the minivan.*

*The company responsible for such
technological innovations
as the first minivan airbag
and the first built-in child seat.*

*The company that has sold
more minivans than all other
companies combined.*

*The Minivan Company.
It has a more formal name:*

The Chrysler Corporation.

Ask any of the three million owners who've helped make Chrysler The Minivan Company.™

**Ask the woman
who baby-sits in one.**

**Ask the family who used to be
in a Honda commercial.**

**Ask the family
that owns six.**

**Ask the engineer who hadn't
owned an American car
in over ten years.**

**Ask the magazine that took
one to the Arctic Circle.**

**Ask the family who survived
a collision in one.**

Dodge Caravan and Plymouth Voyager were this country's first minivans.
Ten years later, they're still America's first choice. And no one else even comes close.
The McDonough clan can tell you why. They own six Chrysler minivans.

With our minivan airbag, rear shoulder belts and our anti-lock brakes,' America has chosen us for the safest of reasons.
Ask the Cartwrights, who ran right into a concrete abutment. And walked away with only a few bumps and bruises.

Thanks to Town & Country, Chrysler minivans have been selected for the most luxurious of reasons, as well.
Just ask David Tarnosky. His '92 Town & Country is the first American vehicle he's owned since 1979.

And our choice of lengths, seating options and built-in child seats' have made us a natural for growing families everywhere.
Three million owners can tell you why.

*Call 1-800-876-MINIVAN and tell us your story.
Maybe we'll use it, too.*

To buy or lease, see your Dodge or Chrysler Plymouth Dealer.

Chrysler hopes to achieve a prominent position in the consumers' mind when thinking about minivans. Similarly, in an ad for the Champion Trans-Van motor home, consumers were told "Call it a first car, second car, custom van, vehicle or motor home." The ad therefore attempted to broaden the product's appeal by encouraging consumers to use multiple categories during the categorization process.

Stimulus Elaboration

Another aspect of comprehension is the degree of elaboration that occurs during stimulus processing. **Elaboration** refers to the amount of integration between the new information and existing knowledge stored in memory or, as some have described it, the number of personal connections made between the stimulus and one's life experiences and goals.[39] Elaboration falls along a continuum ranging from low to high (or shallow to deep).[40]

Consumer researchers have typically focused on elaboration in the form of semantic or verbal elaboration. The amount and nature of elaboration during ad processing, for example, is often measured by asking subjects to write down the thoughts that occur while viewing the ad.[41] As discussed later under the acceptance stage, the persuasive impact of a stimulus can depend heavily on these thoughts.

Images may also occur during stimulus elaboration. **Imagery** is a process by which sensory information and experiences from long-term memory are represented in short-term memory.[42] An image may range from a single sensory dimension (visualizing a chocolate cake) to a combination of sensory dimensions (such as imagining the smell and taste of the cake as well).

Stimulus Organization

Are there principles or rules governing the manner in which people organize incoming stimuli? This question is the domain of an area known as **Gestalt psychology**, which focuses on how people organize or combine stimuli into a meaningful whole. Three principles of stimulus organization are considered here.

Simplicity

People have a strong tendency to organize their perceptions into "simple" patterns. That is, people will opt for simple perceptions even when more complex perceptions can be derived from the stimulus. This principle is illustrated in Figure 14.10. Suppose you were asked to connect the dots in stimulus A. Most people would form a circle (B), even though the more complex pattern of two squares (C) can also be derived. In a similar way, consumers may come to a more simplistic interpretation of a message than is actually communicated.

Figure and Ground

People tend to organize their perceptions into two major patterns. The first is **figure,** which represents those elements within a perceptual field that receive

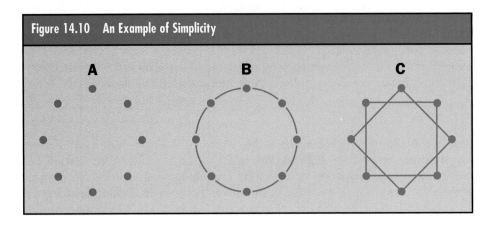

Figure 14.10   An Example of Simplicity

the most attention. The remaining, less meaningful elements that comprise the background are referred to as **ground.** Previous experience exerts a strong effect on what will be figure and what will be ground. The more familiar object tends to stand out. A familiar face, for example, can usually be recognized in a crowd. Similarly, the familiar brand symbol will stand out, thus underscoring the value of repetitive advertising.

The importance of the figure-ground principle in an advertising context is illustrated by consumers' reactions to the television commercials featuring James Garner and Mariette Hartley for Polaroid cameras. The commercials built on verbal sparring by a married couple, and there was no question that people liked them. However, many of those surveyed named Kodak as the brand being advertised. For these consumers, Garner and Hartley became the figure while the product became ground, just the reverse of the advertiser's intent.

Closure

Another useful principle from Gestalt psychology is **closure,** which refers to our tendency to develop a complete picture or perception even when elements in the perceptual field are missing. Because of this drive to "fill in" the missing parts, the presentation of an incomplete stimulus provides marketers with a mechanism for increasing the effort and involvement that occur during information processing.[43]

Closure is a very popular technique in advertising. A classic example is the Salem musical jingle of "You can take Salem out of the country, but you can't take the country out of Salem." In the initial stages of the campaign, this jingle was strongly established in the consumer's mind. Subsequently, a new ad was developed that ended with that part of the jingle up to the word "but." According to all reports, the campaign was quite successful.

Closure can be used in many other ways. Kellogg's, for instance, has developed ads as well as billboards in which either the bottom portion or last couple of letters of their name are missing. The ad appearing in Figure 14.11 uses the closure principle by obscuring a considerable portion of the word *improvement*. Sometimes ads will present a partial picture of the product itself. Playing the soundtrack of well-known TV commercials may also evoke closure as the listener reproduces the visual portion.[44] Heavy viewers of MTV probably have a similar experience when the song from a familiar music video is played on the radio. This possibility, called "imagery transfer" by some, is further explored in Consumer in Focus 14.2.

Personal Determinants of Comprehension

Comprehension, like attention, is influenced by many stimulus and personal factors. We first consider how personal factors can affect comprehension.

Motivation

Just as a person's motivational state during information processing can influence attention, so too can it exert an effect on comprehension. In a classic study,

Figure 14.11   The Use of Closure in Advertising

NO ROOM FOR IMPROVEMENT

When your biscuits have 100% real buttermilk and Pillsbury's best flour, it's tough to make them any better. So we made them bigger. Pillsbury's Grands! Biscuits. Our biggest, fluffiest, most delicious biscuits ever.

14.2	Consumer in Focus

How Closure Helps Radio Advertising Reinforce Television Advertising

The results of a new study from Statistical Research Inc. (SRI) reveal that radio advertising may magnify the impact of an advertiser's TV advertising by prompting listeners to recall segments from a TV commercial previously seen by consumers. Repeated exposure to the TV commercial builds a mental association between the sight and sound elements in the ad. When consumers later hear a radio ad that replays the sound elements, they mentally activate the images initially contained in the visual portion of the TV commercial. The study found that the likelihood of image transfer was greater for younger persons.

"This is a fantastic study for radio in general and national network radio in particular," asserts Dr. Tom Evans, VP-research for Westwood One Radio Networks. "It proves the power of the word to generate images. The increase in recent years of new media has not dulled the human mind's ability to recall images."

The study's results show that advertisers who "want to increase GRPs can do it with radio at a lower cost," says Bill McClenaghan, senior VP-research and development for ABC Radio Networks. "The advertiser can get more bang for the buck using radio to supplement TV schedules."

Source: Adapted from Rhody Bosley, "Radio Study Tells Imagery Potential," Advertising Age (September 6, 1993), R3.

subjects who differed in the amount of elapsed time since their last meal were asked to describe what they saw in an "ambiguous" picture. As expected, subjects were more likely to categorize the stimulus as some type of food-related object the longer it had been since they had last eaten.[45]

Motivation can also influence the elaboration that occurs during comprehension.[46] When a stimulus is perceived as personally relevant (that is, the stimulus is seen as having some usefulness for need satisfaction), more elaborate processing should occur. An ad featuring a product that is irrelevant to a consumer's needs will typically be processed in a very shallow fashion. The relatively few thoughts that are generated during processing will focus more on the ad (for example, thoughts about the ad's executional properties) than the product. In contrast, when consumers are more motivated during ad processing, they will engage in more thinking, especially about the advertised product (such as the thoughts about the benefits of owning the product).

Knowledge

The knowledge stored in memory is obviously a major determinant of comprehension.[47] Categorization of a stimulus depends heavily on knowledge. The novice perceives a gold coin; the expert sees a rare and valuable St. Gaudens $20 gold coin in MS-65 condition (a grade for coins in near-perfect shape).

Knowledge also enhances consumers' ability to understand a message. Unlike the expert, the novice may have difficulty with understanding the terminology (did you know what MS-65 meant?) and the significance of message

Figure 14.12 The "Broken B" Stimulus: Prior Conceptions Affect Current Perceptions

claims. Knowledgeable consumers are more likely to recognize faulty logic and erroneous conclusions. Knowledgeable consumers are also more likely to elaborate on message claims, whereas unknowledgeable consumers may focus on nonclaim cues (background music, pictures, and so on) within the message.[48] Finally, greater knowledge reduces the odds of consumers making incorrect interpretations during message processing.

Expectation or Perceptual Set

Comprehension will often depend on prior conceptions or expectations of what we are likely to see. Suppose that you were asked to identify the stimulus shown in Figure 14.12. Many people would probably perceive the number 13, whereas others may interpret it as the letter B. However, what if before encountering this stimulus, you first viewed either four different capital letters or four pairs of digits? Research shows that those led to expect digits will report "13," whereas those who are primed to anticipate letters will report "B."[49]

This same phenomenon is often observed in marketing. In a classic study, consumers were asked to taste and rate various beers. These ratings were attained under both "blind" (no brand identification) and "labeled" (brands were identified) conditions. When the brands were unlabeled, the ratings were essentially the same for all brands. That is, consumers did not differentiate among the brands. However, significant rating differences emerged when the brands were labeled. Thus, the expectation created by the brand label was powerful enough to alter consumers' perceptions of the products.[50]

Expectations can also influence how consumers process information provided by a salesperson. In one study, subjects engaged in much more careful consideration of the information supplied by a salesperson who deviated from their expectations of the "typical" salesperson than in that supplied by one who matched their expectations.[51]

Stimulus Determinants of Comprehension

The actual physical properties of a stimulus play a major role in shaping how it is interpreted. The Apple computer company learned the hard way about the importance of size. Many consumers found it difficult to believe that the Apple IIc, the trimmer version of the Apple IIe, was more powerful, because of its smaller size. A new promotional program was developed to combat this perception (the basic theme being "It's a lot bigger than it looks"), and sales increased.

The color of a stimulus can serve as an important cue in consumers' perceptions. Orange, for instance, is seen as being cheap. To convey the idea that it sold inexpensive hot dogs, Wienerschnitzel, a 350-outlet hot dog chain, modified the colors at a store to include orange. When sales rose 7 percent, every store in the chain was redone.[52] Appliance makers have discovered that consumers will perceive the product as being lighter in weight when colored with pastel rather than darker colors. Manufacturers of laundry soaps and cold capsules recognize the benefits of including colored granules as a visual reinforcement for product claims.

Similarly, comprehension can depend on a product's packaging and brand name. A grocery store discovered that the practice of prepackaging fresh fish with a plastic wrap led consumers to perceive the product as being older and not as fresh. Many consumers interpreted the packaging to mean that the fish had been frozen. Consequently, a seafood bar was added where unwrapped fish were displayed on crushed ice. Sales for the wrapped fish remained constant, but total sales, including those generated by the seafood bar, nearly doubled.

The impact of a product's brand name on how it is perceived by consumers is illustrated by Wendy's single hamburger. Although their single contains as much meat as a Whopper or Quarter Pounder and more than the Big Mac, its name fails to convey its size. Wendy's introduction of The Big Classic hamburger was intended to overcome this problem.[53] Additional illustrations of how a product's name can influence consumer perception are presented in Consumer in Focus 14.3.[54]

Linguistics

A rather substantial body of literature comprises the area known as **psycholinguistics**, the study of psychological factors involved in the perception of and response to language. Listed next are findings that reflect the potential contribution psycholinguistics can make to understanding and enhancing message comprehension[55]:

1. Words used frequently in everyday language are more easily comprehended and remembered.[56]

2. Negative words such as *not* or *never* are less easily comprehended.[57]

3. The potential for misunderstanding is greater for passive sentences (for example, "The product was developed by Company X") than for active sentences (for example, "Company X developed the product").[58]

Psycholinguistics can also play a useful role in the creation of brand names. Name Lab, a company that assists businesses in picking the right names for their

Consumer in Focus **14.3**

Is the Name to Blame?

In the immortal words of William Shakespeare, "A rose by any other name would smell as sweet." But would it? The experience of many businesses would suggest otherwise. Buncan MacRae, owner of the Yesterday's Tavern and Grill restaurant in Columbia, South Carolina, had a spicy dish called "Spanish chicken and rice" that would not sell. According to MacRae, after changing the name to "Lowcountry chicken and rice," the dish became so popular it "flew out of the window."

Bill Bricker and Ed Hensley have a similar story. In 1984, they began selling one of the richest organic manures available on the market. The source of this manure? Crickets, and lots of them. Two billion crickets played their part in the manufacturing process during the past year.

Originally, the product was named "CC-84." The CC stood for cricket crap, and the 84 represented the year they began selling it. Unfortunately, for those unfamiliar with the name's origins, the product was more likely to be perceived as a chemical than an organic fertilizer. Sales were dismal. In the words of Bricker's wife, "It was a bomb."

The name was changed to "Gotta Grow," but sales remained unchanged. One of Bricker's friends, an advertising salesman, then suggested a new name: "Kricket Krap." Once given this distinctive and memorable name, the product started selling. However, some were less than enthusiastic about the new name. The telephone company refused to list the full name in the phone book. Instead, it was listed as "Kricket #¢*?."

Source: "Fertilizer By Any Other Name Doesn't Sell as Well, By Jiminy," The State (September 28, 1991), 9A.

products, has developed such names as Acura, Compaq, Sentra, and ZapMail through the use of "constructional linguistics," a method in which basic word parts or morphemes (the smallest meaningful unit in a language) are combined to form the desired meaning.

Order Effects

Suppose that you and a friend were each given a list of the same personality traits describing a hypothetical individual, but the order of the traits on the lists were exactly opposite. Would different orderings cause a difference in how much you and your friend liked this person? According to Asch's research, the answer is yes.[59]

There are two main types of order effects. One is **recency**, in which stimuli appearing at the end of a sequence are given more weight in the resulting interpretation. Alternatively, a **primacy** effect can occur. Primacy is consistent with the notion of "first impression" such that stimuli appearing at the beginning are given more weight. Unfortunately, it is presently impossible to predict which effect will emerge in a particular situation. Thus, for ads or salespeople presenting multiple product claims, it will be necessary to test whether a particular ordering of the claims might prove most effective.

The order in which stimuli are presented can be important in other ways as well.[60] Consider the salesclerk in a clothing store who is helping a customer interested in buying a suit and a sweater. Which one should the salesperson try to sell first?

Sales personnel are often instructed to sell the more expensive item first, and for good reason. Perceptions of a product's expensiveness can be affected by the price of the product initially purchased. By starting with the suit, the sweater will seem less expensive. In contrast, starting with the sweater can make the price of the suit appear all the more expensive.[61]

Context

The **context**, or surrounding situation in which the stimulus occurs, will in part determine what is comprehended.[62] In Chapter 22 you will learn how context operates in communication situations, such as when the particular magazine or television program in which the ad appears affects how consumers respond to the ad.

The retail environment also represents a potential source of context effects. In the early 1980s, Levi jeans expanded distribution into mass merchandisers such as Sears and JC Penney's. Department stores viewed the move as damaging the brand's fashion image and threatening to their markups. Consequently, many stores turned to other jeans manufacturers for a replacement, and Lee jeans benefited considerably. Frito-Lay experienced undesirable context effects when displays for its new Cheetos "Paws," a corn snack in the shape of a cheetah's foot, were located near the pet food aisle. In the words of one confused consumer, "Are Paws for my cat or for me?"[63]

Miscomprehension

You might remember our discussion in Chapter 10 about misperception, a commonplace market phenomenon in which consumers hold inaccurate knowledge. The origins of such misperceptions can be traced back to the comprehension stage of information processing. Unfortunately, the meanings consumers attach to stimuli may often differ from those desired by marketers. Research suggests that a substantial number of people have some misunderstanding of what they view on TV, whether it is news, a regular program, or advertising.[64] Consequently, accurate comprehension of a message, even a relatively simple one, cannot be assumed.

Why does miscomprehension occur? In some cases, the consumer can be faulted, such as when inadequate attention is allocated to the stimulus during processing. At other times, however, miscomprehension may arise because of ambiguity in the stimulus itself. Consider the retailer that advertises "Lowest prices guaranteed." What does this mean to you? It could mean that the retailer is claiming lower prices than the competition. It may also mean that the retailer's prices are the lowest it has offered all year. There is even another possible meaning. When Montgomery Ward made this claim in newspaper ads, the company was referring to its policy of matching competitors' prices. If customers found the same item at a lower price than they paid at Montgomery Ward within 30 days of purchase, they would be refunded the difference.[65]

Miscomprehension can also occur because of misleading information. In a Tropicana orange juice ad, Olympic decathlon winner Bruce Jenner was shown squeezing oranges into the product carton. However, Tropicana is not squeezed directly into the carton. It is pasteurized and sometimes frozen first. Similarly, an ad for Jartran do-it-yourself moving trucks placed the trucks of its competitor, U-Haul, in the background. The result was that the U-Haul trucks looked small. Both the Tropicana and Jartran ads were ruled misleading.

Acceptance

Acceptance, the fourth stage of information processing, focuses on the persuasive effect of a stimulus. This persuasiveness may be reflected by influencing knowledge, attitudes, and even behavior itself.

Suppose that an advertisement successfully captures attention and is accurately understood by viewers. Will persuasion occur? Not necessarily. The simple fact is that message comprehension is not the same as message acceptance. Consumers may understand perfectly all that is being communicated, but they may not agree with the message for any number of reasons. Indeed, many if not most consumers are very skeptical of advertising claims. One study reports that more than 70 percent of consumers do not believe ads that use test results to support claims of product superiority.[66]

A key question, then, is what determines how much, if any, acceptance will occur during information processing. Research has shown that acceptance may heavily depend on the thoughts that occur during the comprehension stage.[67] Such thoughts are often referred to as **cognitive responses**.

Cognitive Responses

Consider a knowledgeable consumer who is highly motivated while processing an ad that contains several claims about a product that the consumer anticipates buying very soon. This consumer may engage in considerable thinking about the claims' validity. The nature of these cognitive responses will determine the acceptance of the claims. Of particular importance are those responses called support arguments and counterarguments. **Support arguments** are thoughts that are favorable to the claims. **Counterarguments** are thoughts that oppose the message claims. Acceptance is enhanced as support argumentation increases but is reduced by greater counterargumentation.

Consumers may often be unmotivated or unable to consider carefully an ad's claims about the product. When this occurs, acceptance may depend more heavily on the cognitive responses evoked by an ad's executional elements.[68] For example, the favorable thoughts evoked by a picture in an ad may lead to more positive attitudes toward the product, even when the picture is irrelevant to the product. You will learn more about this possibility in the persuasion through communication section of Chapter 16.

Cognitive responses provide a valuable complement to standard attitude measures in evaluating communication effectiveness. Although standard attitude measures can reveal whether a communication leaves a favorable or unfavorable impression on the viewer, they often fail to reveal the reasons for this impression. If an ad flops, is it because of an ineffective spokesperson, the absence of compelling arguments, or poor visuals? Standard attitude measures may not answer such questions. Cognitive responses can give insights into these various concerns.

Nonetheless, cognitive responses are not without their limitations. One concern is that focusing solely on cognitive thoughts is overly restrictive. Accordingly, researchers have explored the role of affective responses during information processing and persuasion.[69]

Affective Responses

Although an ad's persuasiveness may often depend on cognitive responses, there are also times when an ad's impact will depend on how it makes us feel. **Affective responses** represent the feelings and emotions that are elicited by a stimulus. Consider the ad appearing in Figure 14.13. Not only may the picture of the snorkeling dog gain attention via its novelty, but it may also evoke a favorable affective response in the form of a humorous feeling.

Affective responses can take any one of several different forms, as suggested by the diversity of feelings appearing in Table 14.1. Notice, however, that this variety of feelings can be classified into one of three primary dimensions: upbeat, negative, and warm. Generally speaking, upbeat and warm feelings will enhance acceptance, whereas negative feelings will reduce acceptance.

Research has been very supportive of the importance of affective responses during the acceptance stage of information processing.[70] For example, one study reports that both cognitive and affective responses were useful in predicting the attitudes formed after ad exposure.[71]

In developing effective communications, advertisers must consider the particular cognitive and affective responses that are likely to occur during information processing. Because acceptance depends on the favorability of these responses, the ad should only contain elements that evoke positive thoughts and feelings. Elements that elicit undesirable responses should be modified or elim-

Figure 14.13   This Ad Seeks to Evoke a Favorable Affective Response

inated from the ad. In Chapters 15 and 16, we consider more carefully how advertisers try to influence affective and cognitive responses through their use of certain advertising elements.

Retention

The final stage of information processing is **retention,** which involves the transfer of stimulus interpretation and persuasion into long-term memory. Although much of what we know about memory comes from the cognitive psychology literature, consumer researchers have become increasingly interested in this area.

Physiological Properties of the Human Brain

The human brain is divided into left and right hemispheres, which are connected by a large fiber tract known as the corpus callosum. Interestingly, the hemispheres differ in the types of cognitive operations performed during information processing. The left brain is viewed as the center for logical, abstract, and

Table 14.1 Types of Feelings		
Upbeat	**Negative**	**Warm**
Active	Angry	Affectionate
Adventurous	Annoyed	Calm
Alive	Bad	Concerned
Amused	Bored	Contemplative
Attentive	Critical	Emotional
Attractive	Defiant	Hopeful
Carefree	Depressed	Kind
Cheerful	Disgusted	Moved
Confident	Disinterested	Peaceful
Creative	Dubious	Pensive
Delighted	Dull	Sentimental
Elated	Fed-up	Touched
Energetic	Insulted	Warm-hearted
Enthusiastic	Irritated	
Excited	Lonely	
Exhilarated	Offended	
Good	Regretful	
Happy	Sad	
Humorous	Skeptical	
Independent	Suspicious	
Industrious		
Inspired		
Interested		
Joyous		
Light-hearted		
Lively		
Playful		
Pleased		
Proud		
Satisfied		
Stimulated		
Strong		

Source: Julie A. Edell and Marian Chapman Burke, "The Power of Feelings in Understanding Advertising Effects," *Journal of Consumer Research* 14 (December 1987), 424, Table 1.

conceptual thinking, whereas the right brain focuses on creative, intuitive, and imaginal thinking. Also, the right brain is involved with the processing of pictorial or visual information. Both hemispheres assist in processing verbal or semantic information, although differences do exist in the particular types of operations performed by each.[72]

Evidence for these distinctions comes from "split-brain" persons (those who have lost the corpus callosum). In such cases, the two hemispheres operate as independent units because the absence of the corpus callosum eliminates communication between the hemispheres. Consequently, it is possible to present stimuli so that only one hemisphere "receives" the information. If, for instance, a pair of scissors is processed by only the left hemisphere and the person is asked to identify the object, he or she can easily respond with the semantic concept of "scissors." However, when this same object is processed by the right hemisphere, the person is unable to give the answer.

People differ in the relative dominance of the two hemispheres. Some people are left-brain-dominated, whereas others are right-brain-dominated. In one test of hemispheric dominance, people are visually presented the word *red* in blue letters. They are then asked to verbalize the color of the letters. The left brain says red, whereas the right brain says blue. Whatever response finally emerges gives an indication of the hemispheres' relative dominance.

Advertisers have been particularly interested in examining how each hemisphere responds while consumers are processing advertising messages. Consumer in Focus 14.4 describes the benefits yielded by brain wave research for one company.[73] Some personnel consultants have also advocated the value of understanding hemispheric dominance in the recruitment and utilization of employees.[74]

Multiple-Store Theory of Memory

In addition to these physiological characteristics of memory, important psychological differences exist in the structure and functioning of memory. One influential viewpoint, presented in Figure 14.14, is that memory consists of three different storage systems: (1) sensory memory, (2) short-term memory, and (3) long- term memory.[75]

Sensory Memory

In sensory memory, incoming information receives an initial analysis based largely on such physical properties as loudness and pitch. Visual processing at this stage is referred to as **iconic** and auditory processing as **echoic**. It takes place virtually instantaneously, with iconic processing requiring only 1/4 second.[76]

Short-Term Memory

Once the stimulus passes through sensory processing, it enters short-term memory, which is viewed as the "workbench" for information-processing activities.

14.4	**Consumer in Focus**

Hemispheric Research and Advertising Effectiveness

In order to gain further insights into how their advertising messages are being processed by the brain, some advertisers use electroencephalograms (better known as EEGs), which trace electrical activity within the brain. Research on EEGs and advertising during the past decade or so has shown that emotional slice-of-life commercials tend to be processed mostly in the right hemisphere. More logical ads, such as product demonstrations, are handled predominantly by the left hemisphere.

That knowledge can help spot blunders that might turn an otherwise memorable commercial into a forgettable one. Neuro-Communication Research Laboratories Inc., a company that uses brainwave analysis to evaluate ads, cites a commercial in which a father and daughter were speaking. The father's affection produced a high level of processing activity in the right hemisphere. But just as the viewer was being drawn into that emotional scene, the commercial quickly cut to product information. And, deep inside the brain, that caused trouble.

The EEG showed the right hemisphere was still highly active, making it difficult for the brain to process words. Linguistic processing usually requires roughly equal activity in both the left and right hemispheres. In short, the timing may have muddled the message.

Source: Excerpted from Michael J. McCarthy, "Mind Probe," Wall Street Journal (March 22, 1991), B3.

In effect, it combines sensory input with the contents of long-term memory so that categorization and interpretation can take place.

Short-term memory is limited in several respects. First, it can hold only a limited amount of information at any given point in time. It has been estimated that this capacity is limited to as little as four and perhaps up to seven units of information.[77]

Short-term memory is also limited in how long information can exist without efforts to keep it activated. Suppose you were shown a phone number just long enough to process it and then were prevented from rehearsing the number. How much time would have to elapse before the number faded away? Information is typically lost in 30 seconds or less without rehearsal.[78]

Long-Term Memory

Long-term memory is viewed as an unlimited, permanent storehouse containing all our knowledge. We have already examined two key properties of long-term memory, content and organization, in Chapter 10.

Given that marketers often attempt to implant information within the consumer's mind, it is very important for us to understand how retention takes place. That is, what factors influence the amount of retention that occurs during information processing? The answer to this question can be found in Chapter 15, under the topic of cognitive learning.

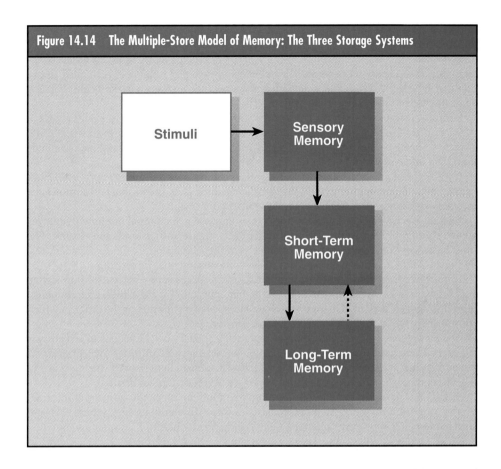

Figure 14.14 The Multiple-Store Model of Memory: The Three Storage Systems

Stimuli → Sensory Memory → Short-Term Memory → Long-Term Memory

Summary

A model of the stages information passes through while being processed by consumers was presented in this chapter. This information-processing model consists of five stages: exposure, attention, comprehension, acceptance, and retention.

Exposure can be defined as the achievement of proximity to a stimulus such that an opportunity exists for activation of one or more of the five senses. Such activation results when a stimulus meets or exceeds the lower threshold: the minimum amount of stimulus intensity necessary for sensation to occur. Efforts to influence consumers with stimuli below the lower threshold are known as subliminal persuasion. Current evidence indicates that subliminal stimuli have, at best, minimal effects and suggests that fears of their persuasiveness are unfounded.

Attention represents the allocation of processing capacity to the incoming stimulus. Because of definite limitations in this capacity, consumers are very selective in what they pay attention to. Gaining the consumer's attention will often be a major hurdle. An understanding of what factors influence attention can be very useful in jumping this hurdle. Attention is affected by two main types of determinants: personal and stimulus. Personal determinants are individual characteristics such as motivation, attitudes, adaptation level, and span of attention. The net effect of personal influences is to make attention highly selective. Personal determinants are best viewed as constraints and barriers against which strategy should be evaluated.

Stimulus factors are characteristics of the stimulus itself. Size, color, intensity, contrast, position, directionality, movement, isolation, novelty, learned attention-inducing stimuli, attractive spokesperson, and scene changes can influence attention. These factors can be used by marketers in competing for the consumer's valuable attention.

Comprehension is concerned with the interpretation of the stimulus. Successful marketing will often depend on understanding the meaning consumers attach to stimuli such as price, packaging, and brand names, as well as advertising.

Gestalt psychology has uncovered several important principles about how people organize stimuli into a meaningful whole: simplicity, figure and ground, and closure. The most basic level of comprehension involves stimulus classification. Once classified, further elaboration may occur in the form of semantic or imaginal processing.

Comprehension is influenced by several factors. A consumer's level of knowledge and motivation or involvement and her or his expectations are critical determinants. Stimulus factors, such as the linguistic characteristics of a stimulus or the order in which stimuli are processed, can also affect comprehension.

The acceptance stage of information processing focuses on the extent to which persuasion occurs in the form of new or modified knowledge and attitudes. Acceptance will depend on the particular cognitive and affective responses experienced during processing. Acceptance is more likely as these responses become more favorable.

The final stage of information processing, retention, involves the transfer of information to long-term memory. Memory consists of three different storage systems: (1) sensory memory, (2) short-term memory, and (3) long-term memory.

Review and Discussion Questions

1. How can the concept of information processing be useful in understanding why ads are "successful" or "unsuccessful"?

2. Do you believe there are situations in which advertisers should consider the use of subliminal cues? Why or why not?

3. A retailer of computer goods is puzzled by consumers' response to her recent fall sale. There was only one purchase of the $3,000 model (sale priced at $2,750). The $1,000 model (sale priced at $875), despite having only half the $250 savings offered by the more expensive model, sold out. How can you explain these results?

4. Listed below are a set of recommendations for designing yellow pages ads that appeared in the September 1993 issue of *Link*, a trade magazine for the yellow pages industry:

   a. Use color wisely. Don't feel compelled to put every image or block of text into color. And don't just 'colorize' your existing ad.

b. Incorporate material from other media. If you advertise in other media, use the images from these ads in your yellow pages to create an integrated marketing approach.

c. Beat the ho-hum pattern on the page. Use irregular borders to draw users away from your cookie-cutter competitors. Also, notice how copy is arranged in most ads—and do the opposite.

d. Use an illustration wherever appropriate. A visual image is an essential eye-catcher. Use something with a contemporary feel, and avoid dated clip art.

e. Use more 'yellow space.' Cluttered ads confuse and repel users. Words with little space around them are more attractive and are more likely to be read.

What principles for gaining attention are reflected in these recommendations?

5. Many critics contend that too much advertising today is gimmicky and cute. The argument is that creative people are carried away by flashy attention-attracting devices and are forgetting that good advertising must sell. How would you respond to this criticism?

6. How does adaptation level create a barrier for advertising? How can it be used to increase advertising effectiveness?

7. A recent study reveals that a particular ad was much more effective in magazine A than in magazine B, even though the readership of the two magazines is virtually identical. How can you explain this finding?

8. Two consumers are exposed to the same ad. One is in the market for this product, but the other is not. How might these two consumers differ in their processing of this ad?

Endnotes

1. William J. McGuire, "Some Internal Psychological Factors Influencing Consumer Choice," *Journal of Consumer Research* 2 (March 1976), 302–319.

2. Harry W. McMahan, "TV Loses the 'Name Game' but Wins Big in Personality," *Advertising Age* 51 (December 1, 1980), 54.

3. "To Burke or Not to Burke?" *TV Guide* 29 (February 7, 1981), 3.

4. For a detailed review of the principles of media selection, see James F. Engel, Martin R. Warshaw, and Thomas C. Kinnear, *Promotional Strategy*, 4th ed. (Homewood, Ill.: Richard D. Irwin, 1979), Chapter 13.

5. See W. N. Dember, *The Psychology of Perception* (New York: Holt, Rinehart and Winston, 1961), Chapter 2.

6. Walter Weir, "Another Look at Subliminal 'Facts,'" *Advertising Age* (October 15, 1984), 46.

7. Wilson Bryan Key, *Subliminal Seduction: Ad Media's Manipulation of a Not-So-Innocent America* (Englewood Cliffs, N.J.: Prentice-Hall, 1972). Also see Wilson

Bryan Key, *Media Sexploitation* (Englewood Cliffs, N.J.: Prentice-Hall, 1976). Key's claims have been strongly challenged. See Jack Haberstroh, "Can't Ignore Subliminal Ad Charges," *Advertising Age* (September 17, 1984), 3, 42, 44; Weir, "Another Look at Subliminal 'Facts.'" Research continues in this area and can be found in Ronnie Cuperfain and T. Keith Clark, "A New Perspective on Subliminal Advertising," *Journal of Advertising* 14 (July 1985), 36–41; Myron Gable, Henry T. Wilkens, Lynn Harris, and Richard Feinberg, "An Evaluation of Subliminally Embedded Sexual Stimuli in Graphics," *Journal of Advertising* 16 (1987), 26–31; Philip M. Merikle and Jim Cheesman, "Current Status of Research on Subliminal Perception," in Melanie Wallendorf and Paul Anderson, eds., *Advances in Consumer Research* 14 (Provo, Utah: Association for Consumer Research, 1987), 298–302.

8. Jo Anna Natale, "Are You Open to Suggestion?" *Psychology Today* (September 1988), 28, 30.

9. Jon A. Krosnick, Andrew L. Betz, Lee J. Jussim, and Ann R. Lynn, "Subliminal Conditioning of Attitudes," *Personality and Social Psychology Bulletin* 18 (April 1992), 152–162; Robert B. Zajonc and Hazel Markus, "Affective and Cognitive Factors in Preferences," *Journal of Consumer Research* 9 (September 1982), 123–131. Also see Punam Anand and Morris B. Holbrook, "Reinterpretation of Mere Exposure or Exposure of Mere Reinterpretation," *Journal of Consumer Research* 17 (September 1990), 242–244; Punam Anand, Morris B. Holbrook, and Debra Stephens, "The Formation of Affective Judgments: The Cognitive-Affective Model Versus the Independence Hypothesis," *Journal of Consumer Research* 15 (December 1988), 386–391; Timothy B. Heath, "The Logic of Mere Exposure: A Reinterpretation of Anand, Holbrook, and Stephens (1988)," *Journal of Consumer Research* 17 (September 1990), 237–241; Chris Janiszewski, "Preconscious Processing Effects: The Independence of Attitude Formation and Conscious Thought," *Journal of Consumer Research* 15 (September 1988), 199–209; Chris Janiszewski, "The Influence of Print Advertisement Organization on Affect toward a Brand Name," *Journal of Consumer Research* 17 (June 1990), 53–65; Carl Obermiller, "Varieties of Mere Exposure: The Effects of Processing Style and Repetition on Affective Response," *Journal of Consumer Research* 12 (June 1985), 17–31; Yehoshua Tsal, "On the Relationship between Cognitive and Affective Processes: A Critique of Zajonc and Markus," *Journal of Consumer Research* 12 (December 1985), 358–362.

10. Timothy E. Moore, "Subliminal Advertising: What You See Is What You Get," *Journal of Marketing* 46 (Spring 1982), 38–47.

11. Albert J. Della Bitta and Kent B. Monroe, "A Multivariate Analysis of the Perception of Value from Retail Price Advertisements," in Kent B. Monroe, ed., *Advances in Consumer Research* 8 (Ann Arbor, Mich.: Association for Consumer Research, 1980), 161–165.

12. Research on price thresholds can be fo505und in Sunil Gupta and Lee G. Cooper, "The Discounting of Discounts and Promotion Thresholds," *Journal of Consumer Research* 19 (December 1992), 401–411.

13. Robert Johnson, "In the Chips," *Wall Street Journal* (March 22, 1991), B1–B2.

14. For research on preattentive processing and its influence on stimulus evaluation, see Chris Janiszewski, "Preattentive Mere Exposure Effects," *Journal of Consumer Research* 20 (December 1993), 376–392.

15. Michael J. McCarthy, "Mind Probe," *Wall Street Journal* (March 22, 1991), B3.

16. Janny Scott, "Propaganda Holds Sway in Society," *The State* (July 27, 1992), 1A, 5A.

17. Laura Bird, "Romancing the Package," *Adweeks's Marketing Week* (January 21, 1991), 10, 11.

18. National Advertising Bureau, *How America Shops and Buys* (June 1983), 23.

19. For a discussion of cognitive consistency theories, see William J. McGuire, "The Current Status of Cognitive Consistency Theories," in Joel B. Cohen, ed., *Behavioral Science Foundations of Consumer Behavior* (New York: Free Press, 1972), 253–274.

20. For research on how general attitudes toward advertising can affect attention, see Ronald C. Goodstein, "Category-based Applications and Extensions in Advertising: Motivating More Extensive Ad Processing," *Journal of Consumer Research* 20 (June 1993), 87–99.

21. For research on the effect of using shorter commercials, see Surendra N. Singh and Catherine A. Cole, "The Effect of Length, Content, and Repetition on Television Commercial Effectiveness," *Journal of Marketing Research* 30 (February 1993), 91–104.

22. For an interesting discussion of how an ad's executional elements can affect attention, see Deborah J. MacInnis, Christine Moorman, and Bernard J. Jaworski, "Enhancing and Measuring Consumers' Motivation, Opportunity, and Ability to Process Brand Information," *Journal of Marketing* 55 (October 1991), 32–53.

23. Adam Finn, "Print Ad Recognition Readership Scores: An Information Processing Perspective," *Journal of Marketing Research* 25 (May 1988), 168–177.

24. Ibid.

25. Keith K. Cox, "The Effect of Shelf Space upon Sales of Branded Products," *Journal of Marketing Research* 7 (February 1970), 55–58.

26. Finn, "Print Ad Recognition Readership Scores."

27. Larry Percy, *Ways in Which the People, Words and Pictures in Advertising Influence Its Effectiveness* (Chicago: Financial Institutions Marketing Association, July 1984), 19.

28. Finn, "Print Ad Recognition Readership Scores."

29. Sandra E. Moriarty, *Creative Advertising: Theory and Practice* (Englewood Cliffs, N.J.: Prentice-Hall, 1986). For research indicating that changes in the position of elements within an ad can also influence the ad's persuasiveness, see Janiszewski, "The Influence of Print Advertisement Organization on Affect toward a Brand Name."

30. For research on advertising clutter, see Peter H. Webb, "Consumer Initial Processing in a Difficult Media Environment, *Journal of Consumer Research* 6 (December 1979), 225–236. Also see Michael L. Ray and Peter H. Webb, "Three Prescriptions for Clutter," *Journal of Advertising Research* 26 (February–March 1986), 69–77.

31. Joe Agnew, "Musical Whiskey Ad to Chime in Time for Christmas," *Marketing News* 21 (October 9, 1987), 24–25; "Oh, What a 3-D Feeling from Toyota," *Marketing News* 21 (October 23, 1987), 9.

32. For research in this area, see M. Wayne Alexander and Ben Judd, Jr., "Do Nudes in Ads Enhance Brand Recall?" *Journal of Advertising Research* 18 (February 1978), 47–50; Michael J. Baker and Gilbert A. Churchill, Jr., "The Impact of Physically Attractive Models on Advertising Evaluations," *Journal of Marketing Research* 14 (November 1977), 538–555; M. Steadman, "How Sexy Illustrations Affect Brand Recall," *Journal of Advertising Research* 9 (March 1969), 15–18; Lynn R. Kahle and Pamela M. Homer, "Physical Attractiveness of the Celebrity Endorser: A Social Adaptation Perspective," *Journal of Consumer Research* 11 (March 1985), 954–961.

33. Joe Agnew, "Shoppers' Star Gazing Seen as Strategy to Slash Supermarket Shelf Clutter," *Marketing News* 21 (January 16, 1987), 1, 16.

34. David H. Freedman, "Why You Watch Some Commercials — Whether You Mean To or Not," *TV Guide* (February 20, 1988), 4–7.

35. McCarthy, "Mind Probe."

36. Advanced discussions of categorization in the context of consumer information processing can be found in Joseph W. Alba and J. Wesley Hutchinson, "Dimensions of Consumer Expertise," *Journal of Consumer Research* 13 (March 1987), 411–454; Kunal Basu, "Consumers' Categorization Processes: An Examination with Two Alternative Methodological Paradigms," *Journal of Consumer Psychology* 2(1993), 97–122; Joel B. Cohen and Kunal Basu, "Alternative Models of Categorization: Toward a Contingent Processing Framework," *Journal of Consumer Research* 13 (March 1987), 455–472.

37. J. Neher, "Toro Cutting a Wide Swath in Outdoor Appliance Marketing," *Advertising Age* 50 (February 25, 1979), 21.

38. David M. Boush and Barbara Loken, "A Process-Tracing Study of Brand Extension Evaluation," *Journal of Marketing Research* 28 (February 1991), 16–28; Joan Meyers-Levy and Alice M. Tybout, "Schema Congruity as a Basis for Product Evaluation," *Journal of Consumer Research* 16 (June 1989), 39–54; Mita Sujan, "Consumer Knowledge: Effects on Evaluation Strategies Mediating Consumer Judgments," *Journal of Consumer Research* 12 (June 1985), 16–31.

39. Herbert Krugman, "The Measurement of Advertising Involvement," *Public Opinion Quarterly* 30 (March 1966), 583–596. Also see David Glen Mick and Claus Buhl, "A Meaning-based Model of Advertising Experiences," *Journal of Consumer Research* 19 (December 1992), 317–338.

40. Fergus I. M. Craik and Robert S. Lockhart, "Levels of Processing: A Framework for Memory Research," *Journal of Verbal Learning and Verbal Behavior* (December 1972), 671–684; Anthony G. Greenwald and Clark Leavitt, "Audience Involvement in Advertising: Four Levels," *Journal of Consumer Research* 11 (June 1984), 581–592.

41. For example, see Jerry C. Olson, Daniel R. Toy, and Philip A. Dover, "Do Cognitive Responses Mediate the Effectiveness of Advertising Content on Cognitive Structure?" *Journal of Consumer Research* 9 (December 1982), 245–262; Peter Wright, "The Cognitive Processes Mediating Acceptance of Advertising," *Journal of Marketing Research* 10 (February 1973), 53–62.

42. Deborah J. MacInnis and Linda L. Price, "The Role of Imagery in Information Processing: Review and Extensions," *Journal of Consumer Research* 13 (March 1987),

473–491. Also see Paula Fitzgerald Bone and Pam Scholder Ellen, "The Generation and Consequences of Communication-Evoked Imagery," *Journal of Consumer Research* 19 (June 1992), 93–104.

43. James T. Heimbach and Jacob Jacoby, "The Zergarnik Effect in Advertising," in M. Venkatesan, ed., *Proceedings of the Third Annual Conference* (Urbana, Ill.: Association for Consumer Research, 1972), 746–758.

44. Julie A. Edell and Kevin Lane Keller, "The Information Processing of Coordinated Media Campaigns," *Journal of Marketing Research* 26 (May 1989), 149–163.

45. Robert Levine, Isidor Chein, and Gardner Murphy, "The Relation of the Intensity of a Need to the Amount of Perceptual Distortion," *Journal of Psychology* 13 (January 1942), 283–293.

46. Richard L. Celsi and Jerry C. Olson, "The Role of Involvement in Attention and Comprehension Processes," *Journal of Consumer Research* 15 (September 1988), 210–224.

47. Alba and Hutchinson, "Dimensions of Consumer Expertise."

48. Richard E. Petty and John T. Cacioppo, "The Elaboration Likelihood Model of Persuasion," in Leonard Berkowitz, ed., *Advances in Experimental Social Psychology,* vol. 19 (New York: Academic Press, 1986), 123–205.

49. Jerome S. Bruner and A. Leigh Minturn, "Perceptual Identification and Perceptual Organization," *Journal of General Psychology* 53 (July 1955), 21–28.

50. Ralph I. Allison and Kenneth P. Uhl, "Influence of Beer Brand Identification on Taste Perception," *Journal of Marketing Research* 1 (August 1964), 36–39.

51. Mita Sujan, James R. Bettman, and Harish Sujan, "Effects of Consumer Expectations on Information Processing in Selling Encounters," *Journal of Marketing Research* 23 (November 1986), 346–353.

52. Randall Lane, "Does Orange Mean Cheap?" *Forbes* (December 23, 1991), 144–146.

53. "'Classic' Marketing Meets Whopper of a Challenge," *Marketing News* 21 (June 5, 1987), 22f.

54. Research on the interpretation of brand names containing mixtures of letters and numbers can be found in Teresa Pavia and Janeen A. Costa, "The Winning Number: Consumer Perceptions of Alpha-Numeric Brand Names," *Journal of Marketing* 57 (July 1993), 85–98.

55. For a general discussion of the role of psycholinguistics in advertising copy, see Larry Percy, "Psycholinguistic Guidelines for Advertising," in Andrew Mitchell, ed., *Advances in Consumer Research* 9 (Ann Arbor, Mich.: Association for Consumer Research, 1982), 107–111. Also see Karen Ann Hunold, "Verbal Strategies for Product Presentation in Television Commercials," in Michael J. Houston, ed., *Advances in Consumer Research* 15 (Ann Arbor, Mich.: Association for Consumer Research, 1988), 256–259.

56. Leo Postman, "Effects of Word Frequency on Acquisition and Retention under Conditions of Free-Recall Learning," *Quarterly Journal of Experimental Psychology* 22 (May 1970), 185–195.

57. Philip B. Gough, "The Verification of Sentences: The Effect of Delay on Evidence and Sentence Length," *Journal of Verbal Learning and Verbal Behavior* 5 (October 1966), 492–496; Dan I. Slobin, "Grammatical Transformation and Sentence Comprehension in Childhood and Adulthood," *Journal of Verbal Learning and Verbal Behavior* 5 (June 1966), 219–227.

58. Percy, "Psycholinguistic Guidelines for Advertising."

59. Solomon E. Asch, *Social Psychology* (Englewood Cliffs, N.J.: Prentice-Hall, 1952), Chapter 8.

60. See, for example, Frank R. Kardes and Gurumurthy Kalyanaram, "Order-of-Entry Effects on Consumer Memory and Judgment: An Information Integration Perspective," *Journal of Marketing Research* 29 (August 1992), 343–357.

61. Robert B. Cialdini, *Influence: How and Why People Agree to Things* (New York: William Morrow, 1984).

62. For research on how context can affect the way products are perceived, see Robert E. Kleine III and Jerome B. Kernan, "Contextual Influences on the Meanings Ascribed to Ordinary Consumption Objects," *Journal of Consumer Research* 18 (December 1991), 311–324.

63. Robert Johnson, "In the Chips."

64. Jacob Jacoby and Wayne D. Hoyer, "Viewer Miscomprehension of Televised Communication: Selected Findings," *Journal of Marketing* 46 (Fall 1982), 12–26. Also see in this same journal issue Gary T. Ford and Richard Yalch, "Viewer Miscomprehension of Televised Communication: A Comment," 27–31; Richard W. Mizerski, "Viewer Miscomprehension Findings Are Measurement Bound," 32–34; Jacob Jacoby and Wayne D. Hoyer, "On Miscomprehending Televised Communication: A Rejoinder," 35–43. For an update, see "Warning: This Story Will Be Miscomprehended," *Marketing News* 21 (March 27, 1987), 1, 34. For research involving print communication, see Jacob Jacoby and Wayne D. Hoyer, "The Comprehension/Miscomprehension of Print Communication: Selected Findings," *Journal of Consumer Research* 15 (March 1989), 434–443.

65. Francine Schwadel, "Lowest-Price Claims in Ads Stir Dispute," *Wall Street Journal* (August 12, 1988), B1.

66. This figure comes from a study by Needham, Harper, and Steers as cited by Stephen J. Hoch and Young-Won Ha, "Consumer Learning: Advertising and the Ambiguity of Product Experience," *Journal of Consumer Research* 13 (September 1986), 221–233.

67. Rajeev Batra and Michael L. Ray, "Affective Responses Mediating Acceptance of Advertising," *Journal of Consumer Research* 13 (September 1986), 234–249; George E. Belch, "The Effects of Television Commercial Repetition on Cognitive Response and Message Acceptance," *Journal of Consumer Research* 9 (June 1982), 56–63; Amitava Chattopadhyay and Joseph W. Alba, "The Situational Importance of Recall and Inference in Consumer Decision Making," *Journal of Consumer Research* 15 (June 1988), 1–12; Anthony G. Greenwald, "Cognitive Learning, Cognitive Response to Persuasion and Attitude Change," in Anthony G. Greenwald, Timothy C. Brock, and Thomas M. Ostrom, eds., *Psychological Foundations of*

Attitudes (New York: Academic Press, 1968), 147–170; Manoj Hastak and Jerry C. Olson, "Assessing the Role of Brand-Related Cognitive Responses as Mediators of Communication Effects on Cognitive Structure," *Journal of Consumer Research* 15 (March 1989), 444–456; David Glen Mick, "Levels of Subjective Comprehension in Advertising Processing and Their Relations to Ad Perceptions, Attitudes, and Memory," *Journal of Consumer Research* 18 (March 1992), 411–424; Jerry C. Olson, Daniel R. Toy, and Philip A. Dover, "Do Cognitive Responses Mediate the Effects of Advertising Content on Cognitive Structure?" *Journal of Consumer Research* 9 (December 1982), 245–262; Arno J. Rethans, John L. Swasy, and Lawrence J. Marks, "Effects of Television Commercial Repetition, Receiver Knowledge, and Commercial Length: A Test of the Two-Factor Model," *Journal of Marketing Research* 23 (February 1986), 50–61; Daniel R. Toy, "Monitoring Communication Effects: A Cognitive Structure/Cognitive Response Approach," *Journal of Consumer Research* 9 (June 1982), 66–76; Peter Wright, "The Cognitive Processes Mediating Acceptance of Advertising," *Journal of Marketing Research* 10 (February 1973), 53–62.

68. Scott B. MacKenzie and Richard J. Lutz, "An Empirical Examination of the Structural Antecedents of Attitude-toward-the-Ad in an Advertising Pretesting Context," *Journal of Marketing* 53 (April 1989), 48–65; Paul W. Miniard, Sunil Bhatla, Kenneth R. Lord, Peter R. Dickson, and H. Rao Unnava, "Picture-based Persuasion Processes and the Moderating Role of Involvement," *Journal of Consumer Research* 18 (June 1991), 92–107; Petty and Cacioppo, "The Elaboration Likelihood Model of Persuasion."

69. There are also some reasonable questions about the extent to which cognitive responses or, more generally, verbalizations of mental processes can fully reflect the content and activities that occur during processing. See Richard E. Nisbett and Timothy D. Wilson, "Telling More than We Can Know: Verbal Reports on Mental Processes," *Psychological Review* 84 (May 1977), 231–259; Peter Wright, "Message-Evoked Thoughts: Persuasion Research Using Thought Verbalizations," *Journal of Consumer Research* 7 (September 1980), 151–175; Raymond J. Smead, James B. Wilcox, and Robert E. Wilkes, "How Valid Are Product Descriptions and Protocols in Choice Experiments?" *Journal of Consumer Research* 8 (June 1981), 37–42.

70. David A. Aaker, Douglas M. Stayman, and Michael R. Hagerty, "Warmth in Advertising: Measurement, Impact, and Sequence Effects," *Journal of Consumer Research* 12 (March 1986), 365–381; Batra and Ray, "Affective Responses Mediating Acceptance of Advertising"; Marian Chapman Burke and Julie A. Edell, "The Impact of Feelings on Ad-Based Affect and Cognition," *Journal of Marketing Research* 26 (February 1989), 69–83; Julie A. Edell and Marian C. Burke, "The Power of Feelings in Understanding Advertising Effects," *Journal of Consumer Research* 14 (December 1987), 421–433; Meryl Paula Gardner, "Mood States and Consumer Behavior: A Critical Review," *Journal of Consumer Research* 12 (December 1985), 281–300; Morris B. Holbrook and Rajeev Batra, "Assessing the Role of Emotions as Mediators of Consumer Responses to Advertising," *Journal of Consumer Research* 14 (December 1987), 404–420; Thomas J. Olney, Morris B. Holbrook, and Rajeev Batra, "Consumer Responses to Advertising: The Effects of Ad Content, Emotions, and Attitude toward the Ad on Viewing Time," *Journal of Consumer Research* 17 (March 1991), 440–453; Douglas M. Stayman and Rajeev Batra, "Encoding and Retrieval of Ad Affect in Memory," *Journal of Marketing*

Research 28 (May 1991), 232–239; Patricia A. Stout and John D. Leckenby, "Measuring Emotion Response to Advertising," *Journal of Advertising* 15 (1986), 35–42; Mita Sujan, James R. Bettman, and Hans Baumgartner, "Influencing Consumer Judgments Using Autobiographical Memories: A Self-Referencing Perspective," *Journal of Marketing Research* 30 (November 1993), 422–436; David M. Zeitlin and Richard A. Westwood, "Measuring Emotional Response," *Journal of Advertising Research* 26 (October–November 1986), 34–44.

71. Batra and Ray, "Affective Responses Mediating Acceptance of Advertising."

72. Flemming Hansen "Hemispheral Lateralization: Implications for Understanding Consumer Behavior," *Journal of Consumer Research* 8 (June 1981), 23–36; Chris Janiszewski, "The Influence of Nonattended Material on the Processing of Advertising Claims," *Journal of Marketing Research* 27 (August 1990), 263–278.

73. For research examining how hemispheric processing can influence advertising effectiveness, see the work of Chris Janiszewski cited in Endnotes 9, 14, and 72. Also see Michael L. Rothschild and Yong J. Hyun, "Predicting Memory for Components of TV Commercials from EEG," *Journal of Consumer Research* 16 (March 1990), 472–478.

74. Kevin McKean, "Of Two Minds: Selling the Right Brain," *Discover* 5 (April 1985), 30–40.

75. Lyle E. Bourne, Roger L. Dominowski, and Elizabeth F. Loftus, *Cognitive Processes* (Englewood Cliffs, N.J.: Prentice-Hall, 1979); Donald A. Norman, *Memory and Attention* (New York: John Wiley and Sons, 1969); Peter H. Lindsay and Donald A. Norman, *Human Information Processing* (New York: Academic Press, 1972); A. Newell and H. A. Simon, *Human Problem Solving* (Englewood Cliffs, N.J.: Prentice-Hall, 1972).

76. For more background, see Bourne, Dominowski, and Loftus, *Cognitive Processes*; Ulrich Neisser, *Cognitive Psychology* (New York: Appleton, 1966); Robert G. Crowsers, *Principles of Learning in Memory* (Hillsdale, N.J.: Lawrence Erlbaum, 1976); Hershel W. Leibowitz and Lewis O. Harvey, Jr., "Perception," *Annual Review of Psychology* 24 (1973), 207–240.

77. Herbert A. Simon, "How Big Is a Chunk?" *Science* 183 (February 1974), 482–488; George A. Miller, "The Magical Number Seven, Plus or Minus Two: Some Limits on Our Capacity for Processing Information," *Psychological Review* 63 (March 1956), 81–97.

78. Richard M. Shiffrin and R. C. Atkinson, "Storage and Retrieval Processes in Long-Term Memory," *Psychological Review* 76 (March 1969), 179–193.

CHAPTER 15

Learning

▲▲▲

Billions in Forgettable Ads

"You've Got the Right One Baby, Uh-Huh!"

"I Love What You Do for Me."

"WOW! What a Difference."

"You Never Get a Second Chance to Make a First Impression."

"Sometimes You've Gotta Break the Rules."

"Just Do It."

"A Mind Is a Terrible Thing to Waste."

America has a bad case of ad nauseam. On any given day the average American is exposed to about 300 ad messages. That is 9,900 a month or 109,500 a year.

Little wonder that the clutter has helped create a case of national amnesia: Some 80 percent of Americans can't remember the typical commercial one day after they have seen it, according to Mapes & Ross, a company in Princeton, N.J., that measures advertising effectiveness.

That probably isn't such a bad thing. But it has inspired researchers to probe deeper than ever into the recesses of the brain on a quest for the Holy Grail of advertising: the secrets to making commercials memorable and effective.

Source: Excerpted from Michael J. McCarthy, "Mind Probe," Wall Street Journal (March 22, 1991), B3.

Why do consumers appear to have such a poor memory for advertising? Does failure to remember advertising mean that the advertising is ineffective? Are there ways to enhance the memorability of advertising?

513

Answers to these and other important questions are founded in an understanding of how consumers learn. The significance of learning is captured by one simple but powerful observation: Consumer behavior is learned behavior. The tastes, values, beliefs, preferences, and habits that strongly influence consumers' shopping, purchase, and consumption behaviors are the result of prior learning. Consequently, an understanding of learning is an essential prerequisite for those responsible for diagnosing and influencing consumer behavior.

Learning is the process by which experience leads to changes in knowledge, attitudes, and/or behavior. This definition is quite broad in that it reflects the position of two major schools of thought about learning. One perspective on learning is known as the **cognitive approach**. Under this perspective, learning is reflected by changes in knowledge. Consequently, the focus is on understanding the mental processes that determine how people learn information (that is, how information is transferred to long-term memory).

In contrast, the **behaviorist approach** to learning is solely concerned with observable behaviors. Mental processes, which cannot be observed and, thus, must be inferred, are ignored under this approach. Rather, learning is shown by changes in behavior due to the development of associations between stimuli and responses.

Both approaches to learning are explored in this chapter. We begin with cognitive learning. This discussion is followed by an examination of two primary types of learning from the behaviorist perspective: classical and operant conditioning. Finally, we examine a hybrid type of learning, called vicarious learning, which combines elements of both the cognitive and behaviorist approaches.

Cognitive Learning

As indicated previously, mental processes are the focus under cognitive learning. These mental processes include a variety of activities ranging from the learning of information to problem solving. From this perspective, much of decision making can be viewed as cognitive learning in that such decisions essentially involve finding an acceptable solution to a consumption problem. Where should I spend my vacation? How should I go about selecting a physician for the surgery I require? What is the best strategy for allocating my savings across the many investment options in today's financial markets? All these represent problems that consumers must solve. Problem solving can also be important even after a purchase decision has been made. Trying to decipher the "easy-to-follow" instructions while assembling a product and understanding why a product breakdown occurs (Did I do something wrong or is this another instance of inferior craftsmanship?) are examples of post-purchase problem-solving activities in the consumer domain.

Although acknowledging the importance of problem solving, this section focuses instead on the learning of information for a very important reason.[1] Quite simply, the objective of many marketing activities is to "implant" particular information within the consumer's mind. Sometimes this information takes the form of a brand name, store location, or upcoming sale. At other times, marketers are interested in consumers retaining a particular image of their offering along one or more important dimensions (for example, the brand that claims to be the fastest and safest nonprescription relief available on the market).

Consequently, it is useful for us to understand how people learn information. Knowledge about those factors that influence cognitive learning can help marketers develop effective strategies for implanting the seeds of information within the garden of the mind. Two main determinants of learning are rehearsal and elaboration.

Rehearsal

Rehearsal involves the mental repetition of information or, more formally, the recycling of information through short-term memory. Some have described it as a form of inner speech.

Rehearsal serves two main functions. First, it allows for the maintenance of information in short-term memory. An example is when we mentally repeat a telephone number that we looked up just long enough for us to dial the number. Rehearsal is undertaken to keep the information activated long enough for the person to dial the number. The second function of rehearsal involves the transfer of information from short-term memory to long-term memory. Greater rehearsal increases the strength of the long-term memory trace, thereby enhancing the likelihood that the trace can be later retrieved.

Elaboration

The amount of **elaboration** (representing the degree of integration between the stimulus and existing knowledge) that occurs while a stimulus is processed will influence the amount of learning that takes place. At low levels of elaboration, a stimulus is processed in much the same form in which it is encountered. For instance, a person who wanted to remember a license plate numbered AJN-268 might encode this stimulus without any elaboration by simply repeating "A-J-N-2-6-8."

A more elaborate encoding of this license plate number could involve rearranging the letters into the name JAN, adding the numbers (which total 16), and then visualizing a 16-year-old girl named Jan. This, in fact, was the strategy a person reported using for remembering the license number of a car he witnessed leaving the scene of a bank robbery. After realizing he had seen the getaway car, he telephoned the police and gave them the license number. The suspects were apprehended, and he received a $500 reward.

Greater elaboration will generally lead to greater learning.[2] That is, the more a person elaborates on a piece of information (or the more "deeply" it is processed), the greater the number of linkages formed between the new information and information already stored in memory. This, in turn, increases the number of avenues or paths by which the information can be retrieved from memory. In essence, the memory trace becomes more accessible given the greater number of pathways (linkages) available for retrieval. Many of the techniques suggested by memory experts and performers for increasing one's ability to learn and remember new information rely on the benefits of elaboration.

Although we will soon explore the different methods advertisers can use to enhance the memorability of their messages, at this point it is useful to acknowledge the advantages afforded by advertising that encourages elaboration. Quite simply, ads that encourage elaboration will be more memorable than those that don't. How can ads encourage elaboration? Consider Figure 15.1. Notice how the ads link the company name (Bull) to words (lovable, flexible) likely to exist in memory. Another example is the radio ad for an automotive parts supplier called Kar Part Outlet. This ad encouraged listeners to elaborate on the name by having the spokesperson say, "Kar, as in what you drive; part, as in what you do to your hair; outlet, as in what you stick a plug in."

The amount of elaboration that occurs during information processing is strongly influenced by the person's motivation and ability.[3] Each of these is discussed next.

Motivation

A person's motivational state at the time of exposure to new information will have a considerable influence on what is remembered. Consider an automobile advertisement that is viewed by two consumers, one of whom is currently in the market for a new car. He or she would more actively process the ad, resulting in greater elaboration. Typically, the consumer more highly motivated during message processing will have greater learning than the less interested one.

This difference in learning depending on the level of motivation has been referred to as **directed** versus **incidental learning**.[4] Directed learning occurs when learning is the primary objective during information processing (such as the student reading this text in preparation for the upcoming exam). Incidental learning, however, represents learning that occurs even when learning is not a processing objective (the student flipping through a campus newspaper while waiting for class to begin). Although learning can take place even when the person is not deliberately trying to do so, greater retention occurs under directed learning.[5]

Ability

Knowledge is an important determinant of learning, as it enables the person to undertake more meaningful elaboration during information processing. In a classic study of how prior knowledge enhances learning, chess masters and

Figure 15.1   An Example of How Advertising Can Encourage Elaboration of the Company Name

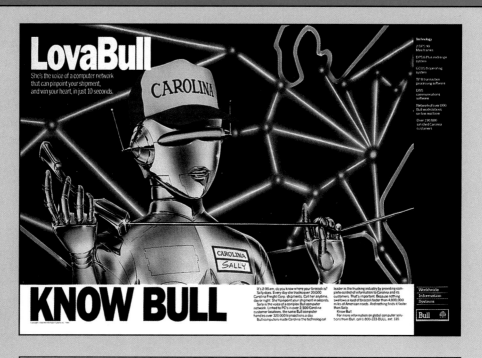

novices were shown chess games in progress.[6] The masters generally held a substantial advantage over novices in remembering the board positions of the chess pieces. Interestingly, this superiority disappeared when subjects were exposed to games in which the pieces were randomly organized. Thus, the beneficial effect of knowledge materialized only when the information conformed to the expert's knowledge structures and expectations (that is, when the pieces' placement "made sense").

Even when knowledge is high, ability to process may still be low. This is because ability depends on both individual and environmental factors.[7] A knowledgeable consumer may be unable to engage in much elaboration of an ad appearing on TV if the room is filled with distractions (such as a crying baby). Similarly, the aging process apparently reduces our learning abilities as suggested by a study reporting learning deficiencies among elderly consumers.[8]

Methods for Enhancing Retention

When consumers are both motivated and able to engage in rehearsal and elaboration during information processing, life for the marketer is much simpler. Efforts need be directed only toward ensuring that consumers are exposed to and accurately comprehend the information. However, consumers are often unwilling or unable to engage in much rehearsal or elaboration of marketing stimuli. When this happens, efforts are needed for enhancing the memorability of such stimuli. Some of the ways in which this may be achieved are described subsequently.

The Importance of Interrelations among Stimulus Elements

In a print ad for a brand of vodka, the copy reads, "SMOOTH AS ICE . . . Icy Cold. Icy Clear. Imported Icy Vodka of Iceland. Why can't everything in life be this smooth?" The ad picture shows a bottle with the brand name ICY that appears to be made of smooth clear ice. In this ad, the brand name, the copy, and the picture are all interrelated.[9]

The presence of interrelations among stimulus elements enhances the memorability of these elements.[10] Consumers will be more likely to remember the Icy Vodka name after processing the ad just described than if the ad copy and picture did not reinforce the icy concept.

Interrelations may enhance memory for several reasons. To the extent each advertising element activates the same basic concept, then the presence of multiple elements leads to repetition, which, as discussed shortly, will increase memory. Interrelations may also increase the number and strength of relations between a particular piece of information stored in memory and other stored information that, according to associative network models of memory (see Figure 10.9 in Chapter 10), should increase the likelihood of retrieving this piece of information.[11]

Another explanation involves the possibility that information can be stored in both semantic and visual forms.[12] Information stored in both forms essentially doubles the pathways that can be traveled within memory for retrieving the information, relative to storage in only one form.[13]

Accordingly, pictures that provide a visual image of the brand name, such as those presented in Figure 15.2, lead to greater memory of the names. This same basic principle is used by the sign promoting a candidate for a local school board that appears in Figure 15.3.

Note, however, that pictures need not necessarily lead to greater memory. This will depend on whether the nonpicture information itself is rich in visual imagery. For example, if the copy in an ad by itself evokes imagery, pictures have less to offer than when the ad copy elicits little imagery. Better recall has been found when pictures are added to low-imagery copy but not when they are included in an ad containing high-imagery copy.[14]

Use Concrete Words

Another way of gaining the memory advantage offered by visual imagery is through the use of concrete words. **Concrete words**, such as tree or dog, are those that can be visualized easily. In contrast, **abstract words**, such as democracy or equality, do not lend themselves to a visual representation. Research indicates that people exposed to a list of both concrete and abstract words will demonstrate greater retention of concrete words.[15]

The retention advantage of concrete words carries an important message for marketers. Far too often new products are introduced with rather abstract

Figure 15.2   Visual Representations Increase the Memorability of Brand Names

Figure 15.3   This Sign Encourages Visual Imagery Which Can Increase Voters' Memory of the Candidate's Name

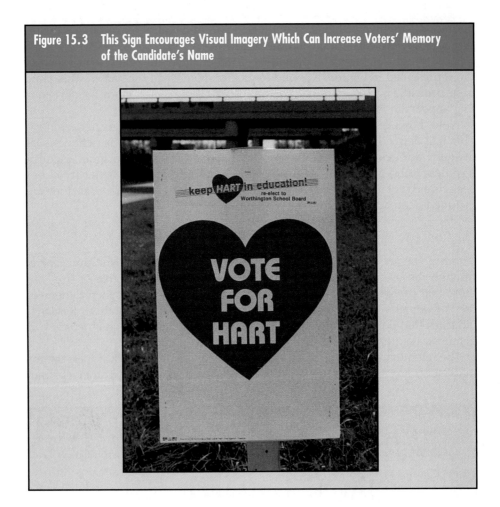

names. Consider, for instance, product names such as Actifed, Advil, Encaprin, and Nuprin, versus more concrete names such as Head and Throat, Easy-Off, or Scrub Free. This lesson was learned by the Matex Corp. with its Rusty Jones rust inhibitor product. Initially introduced as Thixo-Tex, the subsequent renaming of the product was one reason for sales climbing from $2 million to about $100 million in just a few years.[16]

Encourage Self-Referencing

Learning is greater when self-referencing occurs during information processing. **Self-referencing** involves relating the information to one's own self and experiences. In a typical study, subjects are exposed to a series of words and asked whether each word describes them. These subjects exhibit greater recall than others who perform different tasks during information processing (for example, identify a synonym for the word).[17]

This facilitating effect of self-referencing is attributed to a more elaborate encoding of the stimulus information. The representation of the self in memory is believed to be a complex, highly organized structure that is activated by self-referencing. The use of this richer structure during encoding should enhance the number and strength of potential linkages that can be made between stimulus and other stored information which in turn increases the likelihood of retrieval.

Research supports the potential for encouraging self-referencing through advertising copy. This activation of self-referencing was achieved by using the word *you* and copy that prompted subjects to retrieve prior relevant product experiences. As expected, recall of the information from the ad was greater when the copy encouraged self-referencing.[18]

Use Mnemonic Devices

Memory may also be enhanced through simple mnemonic devices such as rhymes and jingles.[19] Brim coffee tells us to "fill it to the rim with Brim," while Shout stain remover asks us to "Shout it out." And millions of consumers still remember the "I wish I were an Oscar Meyer wiener" jingle.

Time-Compressed Speech May Help

Technological advances have enabled advertisers to "compress" radio ads without distortion in speech or sound characteristics. For example, a 30-second ad can be reduced to 24 seconds. Initial research indicated that time-compressed ads can yield higher levels of recall than their longer counterparts, presumably because viewers are less likely to divert their attention elsewhere at this higher rate of information transmission.[20] More recent studies, however, have been less supportive.[21] These studies have found time-compressed ads to be either equally or less effective than normally paced ads. Additional work is necessary to establish if and when time compression will be beneficial.

Saying It Over and Over: The Value of Repetition

When consumers are motivated and able to engage in meaningful elaboration during message processing, then only a single exposure to an advertisement may be necessary for the desired effect. Additional exposures will be desirable, however, if either motivation or ability is low. For instance, when the communication conveys a large or complex set of information, consumers may be unable to comprehend fully the message during a single exposure, although this can depend on the type of medium in which the ad appears. Unlike radio and television ads, print ads can be processed at one's own rate and reprocessed if necessary. Thus, the additional opportunities for elaboration afforded by repetition may be more useful for ads appearing in broadcast than print media.

Repetition will also be more useful for some product categories than others. Many of the products consumers purchase at the grocery store engender relatively low levels of involvement. Consequently, motivation to process an ad intensively will typically be quite limited. Companies therefore use repetition as a form of externally imposed rehearsal.

For these reasons, then, repetition is an important tool for enhancing learning. In addition to repeating the same ad over and over, repetition can also be used within a single ad. Ralston-Purina used cats in TV commercials to repeat over and over the Meow Mix brand name. The same basic strategy was used in a television campaign for Rolaids antacid. The ads featured different persons being asked the question," How do you spell relief?" Every time the person spelled out "R-O-L-A-I-D-S."

The facilitating effect of repetition has been well substantiated.[22] The standard finding is that message learning will grow with additional exposures, although at a diminishing rate (that is, each successive exposure adds less than the preceding one). However, the effectiveness of repetition may depend on the level of competitive advertising. One study reports that repetition enhanced recall when competitive advertising was minimal or nonexistent. This effect disappeared, however, under higher levels of competitive advertising.[23]

It is also evident that too much repetition can have adverse effects. That is, after a certain number of repetitions, additional repetitions may reduce advertising effectiveness. This phenomenon is called **advertising wearout**[24] and is the topic of Consumer in Focus 15.1.

Wearout can occur for two reasons. First, consumers may simply quit attending to an ad after a certain number of exposures. Alternatively, consumers may continue to pay attention, but they become more argumentative as a result of the tedium of seeing the same ad over and over.[25]

One possible solution to the wearout problem is to use ads that differ in their executional strategies but that carry the same basic message.[26] The ad campaign for Energizer batteries featuring the drum-banging pink bunny consists of more than 20 commercials (see Figure 15.4). Not to be outdone, competitor Duracell has developed more than 40 spots in which different battery-operated toys are shown to run longer when powered by a Duracell battery.[27] Although additional expenses are incurred from the production of multiple ads, this cost may be a worthwhile investment for reducing the problems of advertising wearout.

Forgetting

Before reading past this sentence, stop and write down all the brands of toothpaste you can remember. Once you have done this, consider the following set of toothpaste brands: Aim, Aquafresh, Check Up, Close Up, Colgate, Crest, Gleem, Pearl Drops, Pepsodent, Sensodyne, Topco, Topol, Ultrabrite, and Zact. It is probably safe to wager that you did not recall all the brands just listed. It is also

Consumer in Focus **15.1**

When Ads Wear Out Their Welcome

"April in Paris" may never be the same. Thanks to a commercial that has run over and over again for Maxwell House Rich French Roast coffee, the classic song and all-too-familiar sales pitch ("He spoke English like I spoke French") are chiseled into the minds of daytime television viewers. But for ad executives, a key question remains unanswered: Is this commercial still selling coffee?

Advertising has always relied on repetition to hammer a message home. But viewers simply don't watch commercials that are too familiar, and money spent to air them continually is wasted, says Karl Rosenberg, vice president of Research Systems Corp., an advertising testing firm. He argues agencies are playing it safe instead of smart by relying on ads that were once effective but are now just plain stale.

Researchers point to a multitude of overused ads such as the one for Kaopectate, in which a wife meets her husband's plane and his first words to her are about diarrhea. In a much-aired spot for "I Can't Believe It's Not Butter," violins swell as a couple falls in love with margarine. And then there are entire categories that have grown tired, such as ads for local car dealerships with the predictable balloon-filled showrooms and tuxedo-clad men touting rebates.

Mr. Rosenberg says his research on tired ads offers a rule of thumb: After a given commercial accumulates 1,000 gross ratings points—the sum of all the ratings that a commercial gets based on the programs in which it appears—it loses half its effectiveness. At the 1,000 mark, an ad has reached some 42 percent of all U.S. households with TV sets at least 10 times.

Source: Excerpted from Laura Bird, "Researchers Criticize Overuse of Ads," Wall Street Journal (January 3, 1992), B3.

probably a safe bet that you did not write down some brands that you "know" as reflected by your recognition of these names while reading the list.

Why, then, did you forget brands that are familiar to you? Two explanations have been offered for the lack of **retrieval**, defined as the process by which the contents stored in long-term memory are activated.

The Role of Decay

It is well known that forgetting and time go hand in hand. The ability to remember information decreases as the time since it was learned initially increases. According to decay theory, the strength of a memory trace will fade with the passage of time. Retrieval failure will occur when the trace lacks sufficient strength.

However, forgetting may differ even when the influence of time is held constant. For example, forgetting will be much lower when the time is spent sleeping than if the person spends the same time awake.[28] This suggests that forgetting is due to more than simply the passage of time.

Figure 15.4 Energizer Uses Multiple Ad Executions to Reduce Advertising Wearout

STONEHENGE, WILTSHIRE, ENGLAND. 7:53 A.M. STILL GOING. NOTHING OUTLASTS THE ENERGIZER.

MONUMENT VALLEY, UTAH. 5:32 P.M. STILL GOING. NOTHING OUTLASTS THE ENERGIZER.

The Role of Interference

According to interference theory, forgetting is caused by the learning of new information over time. One form of interference, where recently learned information inhibits the retrieval of previously learned information, is known as **retroactive inhibition**. Interference can also take the form of **proactive inhibition**, in which prior learning hinders the learning and retrieval of new information. Both forms of inhibition were detected in an advertising study that reported that recall of the information presented in an ad was impaired when subjects were also exposed to ads for competitive products that either preceded (proactive inhibition) or followed (retroactive inhibition) the ad to be remembered.[29]

From this perspective, information can be available in memory (the memory trace is of sufficient strength) and yet not be retrieved because of limitations in its accessibility. All of us have experienced situations in which we have tried unsuccessfully to remember something, only to have it "pop" into our mind some time later. Similarly, hypnosis has been used to facilitate the retrieval of "lost" memories. This distinction between availability and accessibility has been supported by research showing that information that appeared to be forgotten could, in fact, be subsequently retrieved when subjects were provided with certain retrieval cues.[30]

The issue of information accessibility is particularly important to marketers. The influence of advertising, for instance, can depend on the consumer's ability to retrieve information from an ad seen some time ago while shopping at a store. More generally, consumers' product attitudes[31] and choices[32] may heavily depend on what information is retrieved from memory.

Two major determinants of information accessibility are (1) the amount of information stored in memory within the same "content domain" and (2) the particular retrieval cues available at the time.[33] The more brand names a consumer "knows," for instance, the more difficulty he or she will have in retrieving a particular name due to the greater number of competing responses.

Retrieval can be enhanced by the cues present at the time of such activity. Retrieval cues can be either self-generated or externally generated. In trying to retrieve a particular brand name, one might try to reconstruct the situation in which the product was last seen or used. A picture of the celebrity spokesperson who is strongly associated with the product may also trigger retrieval of the brand name.

Retrieval cues can help overcome one of the challenges to advertising effectiveness that arises from the time delay that typically occurs between ad exposure and product choice. An ad may elicit a very positive reaction from consumers sitting in their living rooms but have little influence on consumers who fail to remember the ad when making their choices at the point of purchase. In such cases, enhancing the retrieval of the ad information would be desirable.

One method for increasing consumers' ability to remember advertising is the use of retrieval cues at the point of purchase. An example of this comes from the popular Quaker Oats' "Mikey" commercial for its Life brand of cereal. For many years, the company placed a picture of one of the commercial's scenes on the product package. This cue presumably served as a prompt to help consumers remember the ad. The same strategy has been used more recently by the Eveready Battery Co. Figure 15.5 shows how the packaging for its Energizer brand was gradually transformed, first using an insert with the pink bunny, and eventually portraying the rabbit on the package itself.

The wisdom of this strategy has been supported in both laboratory and field settings. As expected, the presence of such cues enhances recall of an ad's claims. Moreover, given the favorable nature of the recalled information, the cues also led to more positive brand evaluations.[34] Similarly, the Campbell Soup Co. reports that sales increased by 15 percent when point-of-purchase materials were directly related to television advertising.[35]

Although marketers typically are interested in enhancing consumers' abilities to retrieve information, there may be situations in which they wish to achieve just the opposite—that is, to reduce the retrieval of information. Consider the situation in which a consumer might normally consider four alternative brands during decision making. One approach a brand might adopt for gaining a competitive advantage would entail inhibiting the consumer's ability to recall one or more of the remaining brands. How could this inhibition be achieved?

Research suggests that increasing the salience of a brand (that is, its prominence in short-term memory) will interfere with the retrieval of other brands within the same product category.[36] For instance, increasing a brand's salience by exposure to an ad for that brand was found to lower the number of recalled brands, including those brands that consumers would consider buying with one

Figure 15.5   Eveready Battery Company Has Changed the Energizer Packaging to Include the Pink Bunny as a Retrieval Cue

exception—it did not inhibit recall of whichever brand was most preferred by consumers. This inability to undermine consumers' retrieval of their preferred brand does reduce the potential value of marketing efforts to induce interference.

Measures of Cognitive Learning

The two main approaches used to measure cognitive learning are recognition and recall. Whereas recognition measures provide the person with some type of cue to prompt memory, this is not the case for recall measures. For example, asking a student on an exam to define the concept of elaboration would represent a recall measure. A recognition measure would involve asking the student to identify the correct definition from a set of possible answers.

Recognition tests generally reflect greater learning than recall measures, although there are exceptions.[37] Similarly, forgetting appears to occur more slowly when measured by recognition. This "superiority" of recognition measures is attributable to the additional retrieval cues inherent in such measures.

The Use of Learning Measures in Advertising

Recognition and recall are often used to evaluate advertising effectiveness. Several measurement versions pose different degrees of retrieval difficulty.

Simple recognition measures involve presenting ads to people and asking them whether they remember seeing the ad previously.[38] This measure will yield the highest estimate of learning, because the presence of the original stimulus is a very strong retrieval cue. One problem with this approach is the potential for overestimating the amount of retention. People have been found to claim recognition of bogus ads that they could not possibly have seen before.[39]

Forced-choice recognition measures, however, offer a more realistic and informative appraisal of ad memory.[40] This approach focuses on the memorability of particular ad and brand elements, thus allowing a more detailed analysis of what is retrieved. Also, respondents are forced to choose among a set of fixed answers in responding to questions about a specific element, much like a multiple-choice exam.

Alternatively, recall measures may be used as indicators of learning.[41] Recall measures differ in their use of retrieval cues. **Aided recall measures** (for example, "Do you remember the brand of soft drink advertised during last night's broadcast of the Academy Awards?") provide such cues. **Unaided recall measures** (for example, "Name all the brands you have seen advertised during the past 24 hours") do not.

One of the most frequently used recall measures is the **demonstrated recall measure**. The day after an ad has aired, households in the area are contacted by telephone until a sufficient number of qualified persons (those who watched the program) are located. Each person is then asked to recall both the name of the advertised product and one copy point. On average, about 24 percent can provide this information.[42]

Learning Measures: Are They Appropriate Indicators of Advertising Effectiveness?

In the early stages of the product life cycle, establishing brand name awareness is a major objective. Measures that tap brand name learning are very useful in determining whether this objective is being achieved. Similarly, learning measures are valuable indicators for evaluating advertising aimed at educating consumers about the brand's properties or uses.

In contrast, learning measures may have very little to say about an ad's impact on consumer attitudes. The fact that consumers can *remember* the claims made in an ad does not mean that they *believe* the claims. Obnoxious ads can be very memorable, but they may also have a negative effect on viewers' attitudes. Consequently, recall alone may have very little relationship with attitude.[43] Thus, when an important objective of advertising is to influence product preferences, it is necessary to go beyond learning measures and assess consumer attitudes.

Another concern with using ad memory measures as indicators of ad effectiveness is when it is assumed that an ad must be remembered before it can have an influence. If a person is unable to recall an ad, has the advertising been wasted? We don't think so. It seems quite possible for advertising to have an effect without establishing a strong link in the consumer's mind between the product and the ad itself. Certainly all of us retain certain bits and pieces of product knowledge as a result of prior advertising and yet cannot identify the source of such knowledge.

Recognition or Recall: Which One?

When learning measures are appropriate, one is faced with the choice of whether to rely on recognition or recall measures. It has been suggested that this choice should be based on whether consumers rely on brand recognition or brand recall during decision making.[44] As you discovered in Chapter 6, consumers may construct their consideration sets (brands that receive purchase consideration) through either an internal or external search process. An internal search process requires the consumer to recall brand names from memory, whereas an external search process (such as scanning the yellow pages) simply requires the consumer to recognize a name. Recall measures become more appropriate when consumers rely on their memory for identifying brands worthy of purchase consideration.[45]

This decision can have a strong impact on the efficiency of advertising expenditures.[46] Dollars are likely to be wasted if only brand recognition is needed and brand recall is used as the advertising objective. This is because it will typically require fewer exposures (and hence dollars) to achieve a certain level of recognition than needed to reach the same level of recall.

Classical Conditioning

As noted in the beginning of the chapter, cognitive learning is but one of the ways in which learning occurs. The building of stimulus–response associations can also lead to learning. The development of these associations is the focus of classical conditioning.

For many, the term classical conditioning elicits thoughts of Pavlov and his dogs. Pavlov, the father of classical conditioning, demonstrated this type of learning through the following procedures. First, an existing stimulus–response relationship is selected, such as food, referred to as the **unconditioned stimulus** (US), which elicits salivation, referred to as the **unconditioned response** (UR). A new stimulus, called the **conditioned stimulus** (CS), such as a bell, is then paired repeatedly with the food. Eventually, the CS will elicit a response, called the **conditioned response** (CR), that is quite similar to the response originally generated by the US.

Figure 15.6 presents the basic classical conditioning framework within a product context.[47] In this example, a father–child situation that elicits favorable affective responses or feelings is paired with a product in the hope that these feelings can be conditioned to the product. This basic framework is illustrated by the ad appearing in Figure 15.7.

This simple principle of association between two objects or stimuli underlies much of today's advertising. A prime example is a scene from a Pepsi television

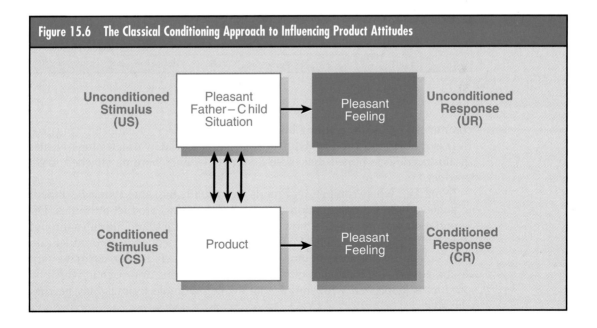

Figure 15.6 The Classical Conditioning Approach to Influencing Product Attitudes

Figure 15.7   Using Classical Conditioning in Advertising to Create Favorable Attitudes toward the Product

commercial featuring a young boy playing with a pack of exuberant puppies. By associating the product with the pleasurable and warm feelings elicited by this scene it is hoped that these favorable feelings become attached to the product.[48]

In markets where competitive brands are virtually the same, it may be difficult to achieve brand differentiation through emphasizing product attributes. Differentiation may be possible, however, by conditioning brand attitudes through stimuli that evoke favorable affective responses. Consequently, in product categories composed of fairly homogeneous offerings, such as beer, cigarettes, and liquor, advertising that relies on a classical conditioning approach in which the product is associated with stimuli that evoke favorable feelings may be most effective.

Classical conditioning need not be limited to using stimuli that, although rich in their ability to evoke desired feelings, are devoid of product-relevant meaning. In situations in which the product is associated with stimuli that convey product-relevant meaning, consumers' beliefs about the product may be affected.[49] Pairing an orange soft drink with a picture of orange slices, for example, may lead consumers to form more favorable beliefs about the product's attributes.[50] In a similar manner, Gallo's pairing of its product with a rich-tasting dessert in the ad appearing in Figure 15.8 may enhance consumers' perceptions of the wine's taste.

Determinants of Classical Conditioning

Simply pairing a US with a product (the CS) does not guarantee that classical conditioning will occur. Indeed, as described subsequently, several factors will influence the effectiveness of any efforts to induce conditioning.[51]

Figure 15.8   Using Classical Conditioning in Advertising to Create Favorable Beliefs about the Product's Taste

It's time for a change to Gallo.

THE WINE CELLARS OF
ERNEST & JULIO GALLO
CABERNET SAUVIGNON
OF CALIFORNIA

US Strength

The strength of the US will partly determine the amount of conditioning. By strength, we are referring to the intensity of the feelings elicited by the US. A stronger US can enhance conditioning. When the US is weak, it may not be possible to induce conditioning.

There is considerable diversity among stimuli in their strength. In an interesting study of "thrills" (tingling sensations that occur in response to emotionally arousing stimuli), respondents were asked to indicate how often they experienced thrills for a variety of stimuli. Virtually everyone reported thrills for music, two-thirds had experienced thrills while viewing a beautiful painting, whereas parades elicited thrills from only one-fourth of the respondents.[52]

Number of Pairings

Just as repetition can play a major role in cognitive learning, it will also influence the degree of classical conditioning. Conditioning has been found for product preferences after a single CS–US pairing.[53] Even so, additional pairings are likely to be needed for maximum effectiveness. Perhaps as many as 30 pairings may be required before the conditioning of product attitudes is maximized.[54]

CS–US Order

Conditioning can also depend on the order in which the CS and US are presented. There are three possible orders. **Forward conditioning** is when the CS precedes the US. **Backward conditioning** is when the US precedes the CS. Finally, presenting the CS and US at the same time is known as **simultaneous conditioning**.

Although conditioning may occur using any of these orders, forward conditioning appears to be the most effective.[55] This carries several implications for advertising practice. Suppose you were developing a TV ad that includes a well-liked musical tune. When should this tune (US) appear relative to the product (CS)? Superior results are expected when product presentation precedes rather than follows the tune or when the product is presented simultaneously with the tune.

Some media may be better suited for classical conditioning by virtue of allowing more control of the order in which the US and CS are processed.[56] Broadcast channels (TV, radio) provide such control, whereas print media (magazines, billboards) do not. Simply because the product is positioned at the top of a page with the US appearing at the bottom does not guarantee that the viewer will process these stimuli in the desired order. The US may easily be viewed first. For this reason, then, print media may be less effective avenues for classical conditioning advertising.

Familiarity

Prior familiarity or experience with a stimulus can undermine conditioning.[57] A well-known song, for instance, may be less effective than a tune created spe cifically for the product (although this weakness in using a popular song may be more than offset by other considerations, such as greater liking for the music).

Similarly, classical conditioning may be more effective for new products rather than existing ones. Support for this proposition comes from research showing greater conditioning for unfamiliar brands.[58]

Elaboration

The degree of cognitive elaboration during message processing may moderate the impact of classical conditioning.[59] Classical conditioning is believed to occur only under low levels of issue-relevant thinking, such as when consumers are relatively uninvolved during message processing. Presumably, the presence of extensive issue-relevant thinking will override any possible effects of classical conditioning. However, this possibility has yet to be tested.

Extinction

Extinction occurs when the CS no longer evokes the CR. A classically conditioned response does not simply disappear over time. Rather, it will disappear when the relationship between the CS and US is broken.

How is the CS–US relationship broken? One way is for the CS to be encountered without the US. Suppose a company uses classical conditioning in an ad by pairing music with the product. Encountering the product without the music will reduce the effectiveness of this ad. Accordingly, advertising that does not pair the product with the US will undermine advertising that does.

Many products, such as cars and clothing, are seen more frequently outside of commercials than other types of products, such as soaps and laundry detergents. These encounters encourage extinction because the CS (product) is seen without the US. Classical conditioning should therefore be better for less frequently encountered products.

Just as contact with the CS without the US will enhance extinction, so too will contact with the US without the CS. The Pepsi commercials featuring Hammer and his music suffer from this limitation. That is, many consumers will encounter Hammer and his music in situations in which Pepsi is not present. This will encourage extinction. Consequently, a "novel" US may often be preferable to familiar or popular ones, because the former is less likely to be encountered without the CS. Despite this limitation, the use of Hammer is very appropriate when we consider his strength as a US (that is, his ability to elicit very strong favorable reactions from many young consumers). Indeed, it is important to keep in mind that a stimulus, although deficient on one factor, can be very effective for inducing conditioning because of other factors that more than offset some limitation.

Generalization

Generalization occurs when, for an existing stimulus–response relationship, a new stimulus that is very similar to the existing one elicits the same response. In Pavlov's experiments, for instance, a noise that was very similar to the bell would evoke the salivation response.

Companies sometimes use generalization in the form of **family branding** by placing the same brand name on its different products. General Electric does so in the hope that consumers will generalize the favorable feelings developed toward one GE product to another.

There is currently a trend toward positioning new products as product-line extensions rather than developing separate brand identities.[60] Through consumer research, it was discovered that the Dole brand name, although traditionally associated with the fresh and canned fruit sections of a supermarket, could also work in the frozen section as well. This led to the launch of Dole Fruit & Juice Bars and other frozen desserts.[61] Other examples of this strategy include Crest Tartar Control, Duncan Hines cookies, Ivory shampoo, Cherry 7-Up, and Liquid Tide. Nabisco Brands also reaped the benefits of generalization when the company changed the name of its new offering from Apple Bars to Apple Newtons, a change that facilitated consumers connecting the product with the company's well-established Fig Newtons brand. This trend is driven primarily by financial considerations. The cost of establishing a new brand name has been estimated between $50 million to $150 million, an expense far greater than incurred by extending an established name to a new product.[62]

Recognize, however, that a family branding strategy may not always be the best course of action. Separate brand identities are desirable for a company wishing to market products of varying quality. Gallo Winery was concerned about the possibility that its new line of wine coolers would dilute the quality image of its wines' brand name. Consequently, the wine coolers were given a separate identity—Bartles & Jaymes. Interestingly, as discussed in Consumer in Focus 15.2, Gallo Winery has opted for a different strategy in its recent move toward marketing of more expensive wines.

In some cases, manufacturers try to encourage generalization through product packaging that is very similar to a leading competitor's packaging, as illustrated in Figure 15.9. This is the so-called me-too product. A soup manufacturer may produce a red and white can that is very similar to the Campbell's soup can. This use of generalization is intended to evoke the same favorable response that is typically associated with the Campbell's brand. Indeed, it is surprising just how often this form of generalization happens in the marketplace.

Consumer in Focus   **15.2**

Gallo Winery Faces the Challenge of Stimulus Generalization

For years, Gallo Winery has been trying to make a name for itself with the more expensive and prestigious varietal wines, those made from a specific variety of grape, like zinfandel. In fact, Gallo is now the largest producer of varietals, selling 8 million cases last year. But it is largely stuck in the low end of the high end, with fighting varietals, named for the rough-and-tumble niche of $3 to $5 wine.

In the last two years, Gallo has spent millions on advertising and marketing and has succeeded in carving out a respectable slice of the $5 to $7 range of varietals. But what the Gallo brothers have their hearts set on is the next level, the $8 to $10 bottles of cabernet, chardonnay, and merlot. Industry sales in this niche have grown 25 percent in the last year, while wine sales as a whole were flat. Yet the Gallos sell virtually nothing on this shelf.

It remains to be seen, however, whether premium wine can be made in multimillion-case volumes, as is the Gallo way. So far, the company's $5 to $7 line has received little more than middling reviews from the critics and publications that rule the premium wine business. Gallo must still show it can do more than trade screw caps for corks.

It all adds up to the biggest challenge of their 59-year careers for Ernest Gallo, the company's powerful and feared chairman, and his brother Julio, who is president. It is a challenge made all the harder by Ernest Gallo's insistence on labeling the winery's premium products with the Gallo name, a decision made against the advice of marketing experts inside and outside his company.

Marketing consultants say this is a triumph of ego over reason. They say Gallo could sell much more premium wine, and at higher prices, were it to use another name. "They should think like Honda," said Al Ries, chairman of Trout and Ries, a leading marketing firm in Greenwich, Conn. "When Honda wanted to come out with an expensive car, they didn't call it Honda, they called it Acura."

The conventional wisdom is that it is better to establish a high-end brand first and then let its prestige carry a lower-priced, higher-volume brand. That's what Mondavi winery did. But Ernest Gallo calls that a wrong-headed approach. "They're depreciating their image," he said. "We're increasing ours." In fact the company is phasing out the Gallo name from its jug wines in favor of a brand called Livingston vineyards. And next year, the Gallo name is set to appear on two new ultrapremiums, a cabernet sauvignon set at $60 and a chardonnay at $30. "Using a different brand name would not be any fun," says Ernest Gallo. "Where's the challenge?"

Source: Lawrence M. Fisher, "The Gallo Brothers Go for the Gold and Away from the Jugs," New York Times (November 22, 1992), B1.

Consumers may also generalize between competitive products that possess very similar names (for example, Muffler King versus Speedy Muffler King, Country Inn versus Cross Country Inn). Legal battles often result in such situations. The Adolph Coors Brewing Co., maker of Coors beer, brought suit against the soft drink manufacturer of Corr's Natural Beverages on grounds that

Figure 15.9   Using Product Packaging to Encourage Stimulus Generalization

the names are indistinguishable to a substantial number of consumers.[63] Similarly, McDonald's filed suits against McTravel Travel Services and McSleep Hotels for infringing on the company name.[64]

Discrimination

Discrimination is the process whereby an organism learns to emit a response to one stimulus but avoids making the same response to a similar stimulus. Using classical conditioning, discrimination can be encouraged by pairing a positive US with one product but not a competitive product. Conditioning should occur only for the product paired with the US. Even greater discrimination could be encouraged by pairing the competitor's product with a negative US.

Discrimination is obviously an important concept in marketing. As reflected by the ad shown in Figure 15.10, companies usually want consumers to distinguish between their products and those of competitors. When discrimination is

Figure 15.10   Canon Wants Consumers to Discriminate between Its Offering and Competing Brands

desired, it is typically best achieved through endowing the product with unique benefits or features. Although this may often be possible, sometimes it is not. As indicated by the beer label study described in Chapter 14 on information processing, consumers could not distinguish between various brands in blind taste tests.[65] When brands are fairly homogeneous, companies must search for other means of differentiating their products.

A classic marketing example of discrimination on dimensions other than the product's benefits is the Goodrich advertising campaign of many years ago. Goodrich had discovered that many consumers did not distinguish between its name and that of a major competitor, Goodyear. Indeed, when exposed to Goodrich advertising, some consumers mistakenly perceived it as advertising for Goodyear. Consequently, it became critical for Goodrich to combat this

15.3	**Consumer in Focus**

Rollerblade Wants Brand Name Discrimination

Rollerblade is not a verb or a noun, but a proper name for the company that has become America's trendiest vocabulary word. Since the Rollerblade name was coined in 1980 by two Minneapolis hockey players who developed a pair of in-line skates for off-season training, the name has become almost synonymous with the sport.

But by becoming too well known, the Minneapolis-based company that made in-line skating epitomize coolness could become too big for its skates and become a victim of the dreaded "genericide." To avoid becoming like a host of other words that were once company names but lost their trademark, Rollerblade Inc. is actively trying to avoid becoming the generic term for in-line skating.

If anyone uses Rollerblade in print as a general term or as a verb for in-line skating, the company sends a letter outlining correct usage, says spokesperson Mary Haugen. If an in-line skate manufacturer uses the term *Rollerblade* in any form with its product, it receives several warning letters and faces possible legal action.

It's "a great form of flattery when something becomes the word," but when a company loses its trademark, other companies can cash in on the name by using it to market their own products, says Michael Finn, communications manager for the U.S. Trademark Association. Finn also points out that if the courts were to declare *Rollerblade* a generic term for in-line skating "they will have lost a great marketing impetus."

Source: Excerpted from Carrie Goerne, "Rollerblade Reminds Everyone That Its Success Is Not Generic," Marketing News 26 (March 2, 1992), 1–2.

confusion. This was accomplished by using the well-known Goodyear blimp in the campaign slogan "We're the one without the blimp."

Discrimination is also very important in the domain of brand name protection (see Consumer in Focus 15.3). Marketers that fail to encourage brand name discrimination run the risk of losing their trademarks. Courts can rule that a name has passed into the public domain (that is, the trademark is revoked) when it has become so common or generic that it has lost its specific meaning. Examples of lost trademarks include aspirin, cellophane, corn flakes, cube steak, dry ice, escalator, kerosene, linoleum, raisin bran, shredded wheat, shuttle, thermos, and yo-yo.[66] Firms are sometimes hired to monitor a name's use in public and take appropriate actions when potential problems arise.

Operant Conditioning

While shopping at the grocery store, a consumer notices a new brand of cereal and decides to buy it. The next morning she gives it a try and is very satisfied with the taste. She likes it so much that she makes a mental note to pick up another box during her next shopping trip.

This simple example illustrates how learning can occur as a result of operant conditioning. This form of conditioning, also called instrumental learning, is concerned with how the *consequences* of a behavior will affect the frequency or probability of the behavior being performed again. The satisfaction experienced by the consumer while eating the cereal increased the odds of repeat purchase. However, repeat purchasing would be unlikely if the cereal failed to satisfy the consumer.

Figure 15.11 reveals that consequences can affect behavior (called the operant behavior in the jargon of this literature) in one of three ways. To illustrate these distinctions, consider a typical operant conditioning experiment in which a pigeon is placed in a cage containing a bar that, when pressed, produces some consequence. Under **positive reinforcement**, pressing the bar (the operant behavior) leads to receiving some positive stimulus such as food. Under **negative reinforcement**, bar pressing leads to the removal of some adverse stimulus such as stopping a low-level electrical shock. In both cases, the pigeon is more likely to repeat the behavior in the future. In contrast, **punishment** would reduce the odds of the behavior occurring again. In this case, pressing the bar would cause the appearance of an adverse stimulus.

Although there may be occasions when marketers will use punishers (for example, revoking a product warranty for failing to adhere to the maintenance schedule), reinforcement is the main focus of interest from a marketing perspective. In the following sections, we examine the various reinforcers available for modifying consumer behavior and factors that influence their effectiveness.

Reinforcement from Product Consumption

The degree to which reinforcement occurs as a result of product consumption is a critical determinant of whether the product will be purchased again. Products that deliver reinforcement are more likely to be repurchased. Repeat purchasing is unlikely when product use does not reinforce the consumer or, even worse, punishes the consumer (such as a lighter that explodes during use). The level of reinforcement provided by products can, and should, be monitored through the use of satisfaction measures, a topic considered earlier in Chapter 8.

Types of Product Reinforcement

Products differ in whether they provide positive or negative reinforcement.[67] For example, a consumer may eat candy because of the positive sensory experiences that result from this action. In contrast, eye drops might be used to remove the adverse feelings caused by burning, irritated eyes. It is possible for a product to deliver both positive and negative reinforcement. An air freshener can replace odors (negative reinforcement) with a refreshing smell (positive reinforcement).

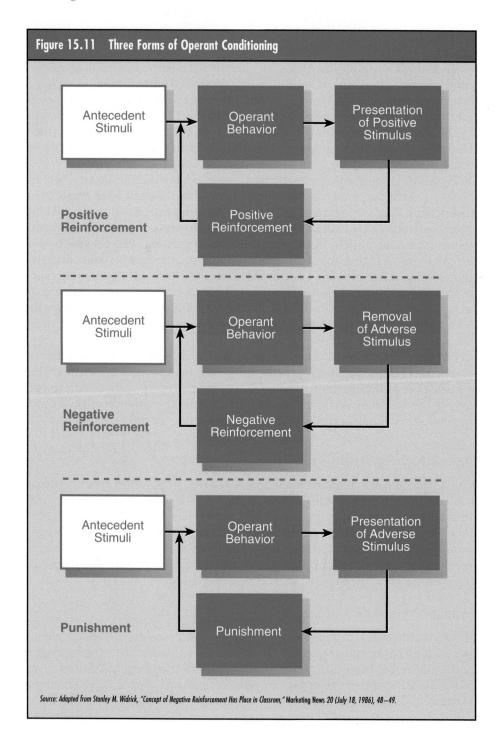

Figure 15.11 Three Forms of Operant Conditioning

Source: Adapted from Stanley M. Widrick, "Concept of Negative Reinforcement Has Place in Classroom," Marketing News 20 (July 18, 1986), 48–49.

The type of reinforcement provided by a product can influence consumer behavior. Consumers are less likely to enjoy buying and using negative reinforcement products. Consequently, they will often spend less time and effort in buying these products.[68] This, in turn, limits a product's opportunity to break through the clutter of competitive brands and gain the consumer's consideration.

Marketers of negative reinforcement products should recognize the existence of three distinct consumer segments for their product. Obviously, consumers currently experiencing the problem solved by the product are the primary segment. Consumers who formerly suffered from the problem comprise a segment that may be receptive to appeals that encourage product use to ensure that the problem will not recur. Even consumers who have not faced the problem may be a viable segment. It might be possible to encourage product use as a means of reducing the odds that consumers would ever experience the problem, such as those who take aspirin daily because of its potential for reducing heart problems.

Product Reinforcement without Product Purchase

According to one old saying, "You can't get something for nothing." Well, that's not always true. As shown in Figure 15.12, companies often offer consumers free samples of their product. When Duncan Hines was rolling out its new brand of cookies, target households received free samples in the mail. Similarly, when Coca-Cola developed the new versions of Coke, it arranged for packages containing single cans of the various brand extensions to be delivered to the consumer's doorstep. Food manufacturers also recognize the advantages of having someone pass out bite-sized servings of their products to shoppers strolling the aisles of supermarkets.

Why do companies incur the expense and trouble of doing this? Because it pays off. As suggested by the headline for the car ad shown in Figure 15.13, getting consumers to simply try a product, thereby enabling them to appreciate the reinforcement derived from consumption more fully, often enhances the odds of purchase.

Further support for the effectiveness of providing consumers a free product trial comes from research testing the impact of delivering free samples when rolling out a new product. Figure 15.14 (page 544) summarizes the findings based on eight new product introduction tests conducted by National Panel Diary, a market research firm, in which one group of consumers received a free sample while another group did not.[69] The impact of free samples is reflected by a comparison of the two groups. The top graph in Figure 15.14 represents the results involving initial or trial purchasing. As can be seen, nearly 50 percent more households receiving a free sample engaged in initial purchasing relative to control households (those not receiving a free sample). Moreover, as represented by the bottom graph in Figure 15.14, those who purchased after receiving the free sample were slightly more likely to buy it again.

Figure 15.12   Giving Consumers Free Samples Allows Them to Experience Product Reinforcement without Product Purchase

To estimate the impact of offering free samples on total market penetration, we need to multiply the trial rate times the repurchase rate for those who did or did not receive a free sample. Free samples yielded a total penetration of 5.7 percent after 6 months (trial rate of 16.0 percent times the repurchase rate of 35.7 percent) compared with a level of 3.6 percent (11.4 percent times 31.8 percent) when free samples were not used. Thus, by using free samples, market penetration was increased by nearly 60 percent ([5.7–3.6]/3.6).

Nonproduct Reinforcement

Although the degree of reinforcement a consumer experiences from using the product is critical, reinforcement can also be delivered in many other forms (see Consumer in Focus 15.4). Fast-food restaurants often use the tactic of includ-

Figure 15.13   This Ad Provides Testimony to the Benefits of Offering Free Product Trial

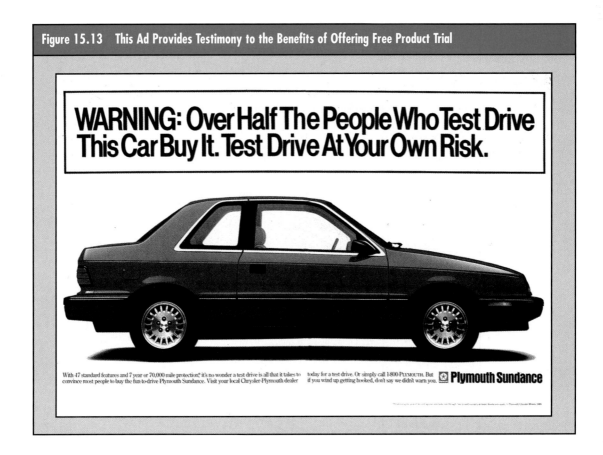

ing a small gift in children's meals for reinforcing the child, who, in turn, influences Mom and Dad. MCL, a cafeteria-style restaurant, provides parents with a token that the child can use in a machine that dispenses small toys. Even adults can be the target of such reinforcers. The Sunflower Chinese restaurant in Columbus, Ohio, often bestows complimentary chocolate mints to its regular patrons.

Reinforcing the Heavy User

To the extent that a company has decided to supplement the reinforcement from product consumption with additional reinforcers, special emphasis should be placed on heavy users when this segment exists. Heavy users are those consumers who account for a disproportionate amount of product consumption. All other things being equal, it is more desirable to attract and retain heavy users than moderate or light users.

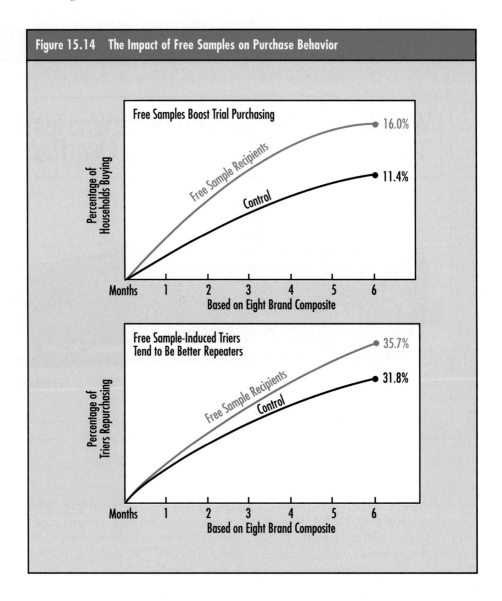

Figure 15.14 The Impact of Free Samples on Purchase Behavior

Consider the promotional program developed by Marriott for its chain of Fairfield Inns (see Figure 15.15). Frequent hotel users are offered a free night for staying and paying three nights. Harley Hotels also implemented a money-back program aimed at the heavy user in which the consumer receives $25 for every seven nights of usage. Consumers who often take to the skies find the frequent-flyer programs offered by airlines very attractive. Similarly, the Zayre Corp. introduced the "Frequent Z" points-for-purchase program. Customers earn points for their purchases, which can then be redeemed for catalog gift items.

Thanks for the Business

Perhaps one of the most underappreciated forms of reinforcement is to simply thank customers for their patronage. Many companies show this concern by sending new customers "thank you" notes. Similarly, the phrase "We thank you for your support" is a common component of the Bartles & Jaymes wine cooler commercials.

Evidence of the effectiveness of thank you notes comes from a study of new life insurance purchasers. Following each monthly payment, some of the customers received a letter thanking them for their recent payment. Less than 9 percent of this customer group canceled their policy during the 6-month test period. In contrast, the cancellation rate of those customers not receiving this reinforcement was 23 percent.

Additional testimony to the power of thanking customers comes from a jewelry store that employed this tactic. After experiencing a considerable drop in sales, some of the store's prior customers were contacted by phone and thanked for their business, whereas other customers were not. Although sales did not increase among those customers not receiving the verbal reinforcement, the customers who did receive the phone calls responded quite favorably. In fact, the store was able to completely reverse the sales decline during the test month.

Source: Blaise J. Bergiel and Christine Trosclair, "Instrumental Learning: Its Application to Customer Satisfaction," *Journal of Consumer Marketing* 2 (Fall 1985), 23–28; J. Ronald Carey, Steven H. Clicque, Barbara A. Leighton, and Frank Milton, "A Test of Positive Reinforcement of Customers," *Journal of Marketing* 40 (October 1976), 98–100.

According to Stanley M. Adler, president, "We believe this program will attract new shoppers to our stores while building greater loyalty among current customers."[70]

Schedules of Reinforcement

Different schedules of reinforcement produce different patterns of behavior. Laboratory studies of animal behavior suggest that learning occurs most rapidly when the desired response is always reinforced (**total reinforcement**). However, when the response is reinforced only part of the time (**partial reinforcement**), learning is more lasting (that is, more resistant to extinction). A partial reinforcement schedule can be either systematic (for example, every third response is reinforced) or random (for example, the first and second responses are reinforced, the third is not, the fourth is, and so on).

The relative effectiveness of total versus partial reinforcement has been examined in the context of bus ridership.[71] Coupons offered as rewards were just as effective in enhancing ridership when given on a partial (every third person) schedule as when given on a continuous schedule (every person). Because it was much cheaper to offer the coupons only part of the time, considerable

Figure 15.15 One Way of Reinforcing the Heavy User Is to Offer a Reward for Achieving a Certain Level of Usage

savings resulted from understanding the effectiveness of alternative reinforcement schedules.

This is not to say that partial reinforcement will always be the optimal strategy. Indeed, some have argued that partial reinforcement schedules may not work in many settings because the consumer may switch to another brand during the periods when the reinforcement is unavailable.[72] The best course of action is to examine empirically which schedule is best suited for a particular marketing situation.

Shaping

Shaping refers to the reinforcement of behaviors that must be performed before the desired response can be emitted.[73] An animal that was expected to perform a complex trick would never succeed if the trainer waited for the animal to do the complete trick before rewarding it. Instead, the trainer rewards the animal for each step leading to the trick.

Shaping principles can be used to a marketer's advantage.[74] A retailer can offer door prizes or loss leaders to encourage store entry, a behavior that must occur before the desired response of buying the retailer's products can be achieved. Similar tactics can be used by a car dealer offering free coffee and doughnuts for those visiting the showroom. The dealer might then give selected visitors a financial incentive for taking a test drive. Whatever the situation may be, shaping encourages marketers to think about what behaviors must precede the ultimate action of purchase and how these prerequisite behaviors can be encouraged through appropriate reinforcements.

As a result of prior association with reinforcers, **discriminative stimuli** can influence behavior even though they themselves do not provide reinforcement. Rather, they serve as cues about the likelihood that performing a particular behavior will lead to reinforcement. In marketing, discriminative stimuli can take the form of a brand or store name where the consumer has learned from prior experience that purchase behavior will be rewarded only when the distinctive cue is present. Examples of discriminative stimuli include such things as distinctive brandmarks (the Levi tag), store signs (50 percent off sale), and store logos (Kmart's big red K).[75]

Vicarious Learning

A special type of learning that incorporates aspects of both cognitive and behavioral learning theories is vicarious learning. **Vicarious learning** (also called **modeling**) can occur when an individual observes the actions of others and the consequences of those behaviors.[76] This form of learning underlies much of today's advertising. Household products often promote themselves through ads that show the consumer receiving positive outcomes from product purchase and usage. Laundry detergent ads, for example, show a homemaker being drowned in praise from her family because their clothes are bright and clean. Similarly, dishwashing detergent ads offer users the promise of being noticed for young-looking and smooth hands.

Advertising will sometimes promote the product by focusing on negative consequences that may occur from using the competitive brand. In one of Wendy's advertisements, competitors are shown asking their customers to "step aside" and wait in long lines.

Summary

In this chapter, we examined four main types of learning. Cognitive learning is concerned with the mental processes that determine the retention of information. Classical conditioning focuses on learning through association. Operant conditioning considers how behavior is modified by reinforcers and punishers. Vicarious learning deals with learning through observation.

The retention of information will depend on the degree of rehearsal and elaboration that occurs during information processing. These in turn are affected by many individual (such as motivation and ability) and stimulus (including pictures, concrete words, repetition, mnemonic devices, and time-compressed speech) characteristics. The fact that retention has occurred does not necessarily mean that the information can be retrieved. Retrieval failure may be caused by either decay or interference in the form of proactive or retroactive inhibition.

Marketers often rely on classical conditioning, particularly in advertising, for influencing consumer preferences. The effectiveness of conditioning depends on a host of variables, including the strength of the US, the number of CS–US pairings, the order of the CS–US pairing, familiarity with the CS and US, and the amount of elaboration during stimulus processing. Extinction, however, will occur when the CS–US association is broken.

Operant conditioning emphasizes the importance of reinforcement as a tool for influencing consumer behavior. The degree of reinforcement consumers experience during consumption strongly determines future purchase behavior. Marketers can also provide additional reinforcers to consumers through tokens of appreciation (gifts, thank you notes) for their patronage.

Review and Discussion Questions

1. In this chapter, we discuss many factors that can influence the memorability of ads. What do you perceive as the important principles that can be learned from this chapter for making advertising more memorable?

2. Consider the print ad for Isle of Capri casino, in which the copy says "Isle have fun. Isle get lucky. Isle get rich." Based on the chapter discussion of cognitive learning, explain why this ad may be effective at increasing consumer memory of the casino's name.

3. The product manager for a new brand of skin softener is considering two possible names: Soft Skin versus Dickson's Skin Moisturizer. What name would you select? Why?

4. A company is trying to decide which of two alternative print ads should be adopted for an advertising campaign to be used during the market introduction phase for a new ice cream product called Snowball. The only difference between the two ads is the type of picture that appears at the top of the ad. The picture for ad A shows the product sitting on top of snow and surrounded by a mound of snowballs. The

picture for ad B shows a cute little girl consuming the product. To help decide which ad should be used, a study was undertaken in which target consumers were exposed to either ad A or ad B. (Assume that the method used to expose consumers to the ad was both valid and realistic.) The results indicated that ad A produced greater brand recall, but ad B generated more favorable product attitudes. Given these results, which ad would you recommend be used for introducing the product to the market, and why? Second, how can you explain that one ad is better for recall while the other is better for attitude, given that the ads differed only in their picture?

5. Suppose you were developing a TV ad containing three main stimuli: (1) the product, (2) an attractive model, and (3) a well-liked musical jingle. Based on classical conditioning principles, what order would you recommend for structuring these stimuli within the commercial?

6. When is classical conditioning most appropriate for promoting products? What factors are likely to limit the effectiveness of classical conditioning advertising?

7. A coffee producer is planning a new promotion to cover a 6-week period in which a small gift is attached to the outside of the package. Should this gift be offered every week or every other week?

8. Figure 15.12, presented earlier in this chapter, displays the free samples offered by companies competing in three different product categories. Do you think that the effectiveness of free samples might differ across these products? If so, why? More generally, what factors might influence the effectiveness of free samples?

9. Find advertising examples for the following concepts: (1) vicarious learning, (2) generalization, and (3) discrimination.

Endnotes

1. For research on more complex forms of cognitive learning, see Robert J. Meyer, "The Learning of Multiattribute Judgment Policies," *Journal of Consumer Research* 14 (September 1987), 155–173; Peter Wright and Peter Rip, "Product Class Advertising Effects on First-Time Buyers' Decision Strategies," *Journal of Consumer Research* 7 (September 1980), 151–175.

2. Terry L. Childers and Michael J. Houston, "Conditions for a Picture-Superiority Effect on Consumer Memory," *Journal of Consumer Research* 11 (September 1984), 643–654; Fergus I. M. Craik and Endel Tulving, "Depth of Processing and the Retention of Words in Episodic Memory," *Journal of Experimental Psychology: General* 104 (September 1975), 268–294; Fergus I. M. Craik and Michael J. Watkins, "The Role of Rehearsal in Short-Term Memory," *Journal of Verbal Learning and Verbal Behavior* 12 (December 1973), 599–607; Meryl Paula Gardner, Andrew A. Mitchell, and J. Edward Russo, "Low Involvement Strategies for Processing Advertisements," *Journal of Advertising* 14 (1985), 4–12; Scott A. Hawkins and Stephen J. Hoch, "Low-Involvement Learning: Memory without Evaluation," *Journal of Consumer Research* 19 (September 1992), 212–225; Joel Saegert and

Robert K. Young, "Comparison of Effects of Repetition and Levels of Processing in Memory for Advertisements," in Andrew A. Mitchell, ed., Advances in Consumer Research 9 (St. Louis: Association for Consumer Research, 1982), 431–434.

3. Richard E. Petty and John T. Cacioppo, "The Elaboration Likelihood Model of Persuasion," in Leonard Berkowitz, ed., Advances in Experimental Social Psychology 19 (New York: Academic Press, 1986), 123–205.

4. Gabriel Biehal and Dipankur Chakravarti, "Information-Presentation Format and Learning Goals as Determinants of Consumers' Memory Retrieval and Choice Processes," Journal of Consumer Research 8 (March 1982), 431–441; Eloise Coupey and Kent Nakamoto, "Learning Context and the Development of Product Category Perceptions," in Michael J. Houston, ed., Advances in Consumer Research 15 (Provo, Utah: Association for Consumer Research, 1988), 77–82; James H. Leigh and Anil Menon, "Audience Involvement Effects on the Information Processing of Umbrella Print Advertisements," Journal of Advertising 16 (1987), 3–12; Barry McLaughlin, "Intentional and Incidental Learning in Human Subjects: The Role of Instructions to Learn and Motivation," Psychological Bulletin 63 (May 1965), 359–376.

5. Interestingly, recent research indicates that poorer learning may be advantageous in that people may believe more strongly in what they have learned. See Hawkins and Hoch, "Low-Involvement Learning."

6. William G. Chase and Herbert A. Simon, "Perception in Chess," Cognitive Psychology 4 (January 1973), 55–81. For a more general discussion, see Joseph W. Alba and J. Wesley Hutchinson, "Dimensions of Consumer Expertise," Journal of Consumer Research 13 (March 1987), 411–454.

7. Rajeev Batra and Michael Ray, "Situational Effects of Advertising: The Moderating Influence of Motivation, Ability and Opportunity to Respond," Journal of Consumer Research 12 (March 1986), 432–445; Danny L. Moore, Douglas Hausknecht, and Kanchana Thamodaran, "Time Compression, Response Opportunity, and Persuasion," Journal of Consumer Research 13 (June 1986), 85–99; James M. Munch and John L. Swasy, "Rhetorical Question, Summarization Frequency, and Argument Strength Effects on Recall," Journal of Consumer Research 15 (June 1988), 69–76.

8. Catherine A. Cole and Michael J. Houston, "Encoding and Media Effects on Consumer Learning Deficiencies in the Elderly," Journal of Marketing Research 24 (February 1987), 55–63. Also see Gary J. Gaeth and Timothy B. Heath, "The Cognitive Processing of Misleading Advertising in Young and Old Adults," Journal of Consumer Research 14 (June 1987), 43–54.

9. This example comes from Bernd H. Schmitt, Nader T. Tavassoli, and Robert T. Millard, "Memory for Print Ads: Understanding Relations among Brand Name, Copy, and Picture," Journal of Consumer Psychology 2 (1993), 55–82.

10. Jose Biron and Stewart J. McKelvie, "Effects of Interactive and Noninteractive Imagery on Recall of Advertisements," Perceptual and Motor Skills 59 (May 1984), 799–805; Childers and Houston, "Conditions for a Picture-Superiority Effect on Consumer Memory"; Julie A. Edell and Richard Staelin, "The Information Processing of Pictures in Print Advertisements," Journal of Consumer Research 10

(June 1983), 45–61; Michael J. Houston, Terry L. Childers, and Susan E. Heckler, "Picture-Word Consistency and the Elaborative Processing of Advertisements," Journal of Marketing Research 24 (November 1987), 359–369; James J. Kellaris, Anthony D. Cox, and Dena Cox, "The Effect of Background Music on Ad Processing: A Contingency Explanation," Journal of Marketing 57 (October 1993), 114–125; Kathryn A. Lutz and Richard J. Lutz, "Effects of Interactive Imagery on Learning: Application to Advertising," Journal of Applied Psychology 62 (August 1977), 493–498; Schmitt, Tavassoli, and Millard, "Memory for Print Ads."

11. Schmitt, Tavassoli, and Millard, "Memory for Print Ads."

12. Allan Paivio, "Mental Imagery in Associative Learning and Memory," Psychological Review 76 (May 1969), 241–263; Allan Paivio, Mental Representations: A Dual Coding Approach (New York: Oxford University Press, 1986).

13. Some uncertainty does exist over the validity of this explanation. See, for example, Childers and Houston, "Conditions for a Picture-Superiority Effect on Consumer Memory"; Deborah J. MacInnis and Linda L. Price, "The Role of Imagery in Information Processing: Review and Extensions," Journal of Consumer Research 13 (March 1987), 473–491.

14. H. Rao Unnava and Robert E. Burnkrant, "An Imagery-Processing View of the Role of Pictures in Print Advertisements," Journal of Marketing Research 28 (May 1991), 226–231.

15. Roberta L. Klatzky, Human Memory: Structures and Processes (San Francisco: W. H. Freeman, 1975), 230.

16. Hooper White, "Name Change to Rusty Jones Helps Polish Product's Identity," Advertising Age (February 18, 1980), 47–48.

17. See, for example, T. B. Rogers, N. A. Kuiper, and W. S. Kirker, "Self-Reference and Encoding of Personal Information," Journal of Personality and Social Psychology 35 (September 1977), 677–688; Polly Brown, Janice M. Keenan, and George R. Potts, "The Self-Reference Effect with Imagery Encoding," Journal of Personality and Social Psychology 51 (November 1986), 897–906.

18. Robert E. Burnkrant and H. Rao Unnava, "Self-Referencing: A Strategy for Increasing Processing of Message Content," Personality and Social Psychology Bulletin 15 (December 1989), 628–638. Also see Kathleen Debevec, Harlan E. Spotts, and Jerome B. Kernan, "The Self-Reference Effect in Persuasion: Implications for Marketing Strategy," in Melanie Wallendorf and Paul Anderson, eds., Advances in Consumer Research 14 (Provo, Utah: Association for Consumer Research, 1987), 417–420.

19. Richard F. Yalch, "Memory in a Jingle Jungle: Music as a Mnemonic Device in Communicating Advertising Slogans," Journal of Applied Psychology 76 (1991), 268–275.

20. Priscilla LaBarbera and James MacLachlan, "Time-Compressed Speech in Radio Advertising," Journal of Marketing 43 (January 1979), 30–36; James MacLachlan and Michael H. Siegel, "Reducing the Cost of TV Commercials by Use of Time Compressions," Journal of Marketing Research 17 (February 1980), 52–57.

21. Moore, Hausknecht, and Thamodaran, "Time Compression, Response Opportunity, and Persuasion"; Mary Jane Rawlins Schlinger, Linda F. Alwitt, Kathleen E. McCarthy, and Leila Green, "Effects of Time Compression on Attitudes and Information Processing," Journal of Marketing 47 (Winter 1983), 79–85.

22. For a general review, see Alan G. Sawyer, "The Effects of Repetition: Conclusions and Suggestions about Experimental Laboratory Research," in G. D. Hughes and Michael L. Ray, eds., Buyer/Consumer Information Processing (Chapel Hill, N.C.: University of North Carolina Press, 1974), 190–219. Research on repetition effects can be found in Batra and Ray, "Situational Effects of Advertising Repetition"; George E. Belch, "The Effects of Television Commercial Repetition on Cognitive Response and Message Acceptance," Journal of Consumer Research 9 (June 1982), 56–65; Arno J. Rethans, John L. Swasy, and Lawrence J. Marks, "Effects of Television Commercial Repetition, Receiver Knowledge, and Commercial Length: A Test of the Two-Factor Model," Journal of Marketing Research 23 (February 1986), 50–61; Surendra N. Singh and Catherine A. Cole, "The Effects of Length, Content, and Repetition on Television Commercial Effectiveness," Journal of Marketing Research 30 (February 1993), 91–104; Surendra N. Singh, Michael L. Rothschild, and Gilbert A. Churchill, Jr., "Recognition Versus Recall as Measures of Television Commercial Forgetting," Journal of Marketing Research 25 (February 1988), 72–80; Esther Thorson and Rita Snyder, "Viewer Recall of Television Commercials: Prediction from the Propositional Structure of Commercial Scripts," Journal of Marketing Research 21 (May 1984), 127–136.

23. Raymond R. Burke and Thomas K. Srull, "Competitive Interference and Consumer Memory for Advertising," Journal of Consumer Research 15 (June 1988), 55–68.

24. For research on advertising wearout, see Bobby J. Calder and Brian Sternthal, "Television Commercial Wearout: An Information Processing View," Journal of Marketing Research 17 (May 1980), 173–186.

25. Richard E. Petty and John T. Cacioppo, "Effects of Message Repetition and Position on Cognitive Responses, Recall, and Persuasion," Journal of Personality and Social Psychology 37 (January 1979), 97–109; Rethans, Swasy, and Marks, "Effects of Television Commercial Repetition, Receiver Knowledge, and Commercial Length."

26. Robert E. Burnkrant and Hanumantha R. Unnava, "Effects of Variation in Message Execution on the Learning of Repeated Brand Information," in Melanie Wallendorf and Paul F. Anderson, eds., Advances in Consumer Research 14 (Provo, Utah: Association for Consumer Research, 1987), 173–176; H. Rao Unnava and Robert E. Burnkrant, "Effects of Repeating Varied Ad Executions on Brand Name Memory," Journal of Marketing Research 28 (November 1991), 406–416.

27. Laura Bird, "Researchers Criticize Overuse of Ads," Wall Street Journal (January 3, 1992), B3.

28. John G. Jenkins and Karl M. Dallenbach, "Oblivescence during Sleep and Waking," American Journal of Psychology 35 (October 1924), 605–612.

29. Burke and Srull, "Competitive Interference and Consumer Memory for Advertising." Also see Carolyn L. Costley and Merrie Brucks, "Selective Recall and

Information Use in Consumer Preferences," Journal of Consumer Research 18 (March 1992), 464–474; Kevin Lane Keller, "Memory and Evaluation Effects in Competitive Advertising Environments," Journal of Consumer Research 17 (March 1991), 463–476.

30. Endel Tulving and Zena Pearlstone, "Availability Versus Accessibility of Information in Memory for Words," Journal of Verbal Learning and Verbal Behavior 5 (August 1966), 381–391.

31. Amitava Chattopadhyay and Joseph W. Alba, "The Situational Importance of Recall and Inference in Consumer Decision Making," Journal of Consumer Research 15 (June 1988), 1–12; Jolita Kisielius and Brian Sternthal, "Detecting and Explaining Vividness Effects in Attitudinal Judgments," Journal of Marketing Research 21 (February 1984), 54–64; Jolita Kisielius and Brian Sternthal, "Examining the Vividness Controversy: An Availability-Valence Explanation," Journal of Consumer Research 12 (March 1986), 418–431; Barbara Loken and Ronald Hoverstad, "Relationships between Information Recall and Subsequent Attitudes: Some Exploratory Findings," Journal of Consumer Research 12 (September 1985), 155–168.

32. Gabriel Biehal and Dipankar Chakravarti, "Information Accessibility as a Moderator of Consumer Choice," Journal of Consumer Research 10 (June 1983), 1–14; Gabriel Biehal and Dipankar Chakravarti, "Consumers' Use of Memory and External Information in Choice: Macro and Micro Perspectives," Journal of Consumer Research 12 (March 1986), 382–405.

33. John G. Lynch, Jr., and Thomas K. Srull, "Memory and Attentional Factors in Consumer Choice: Concepts and Research Methods," Journal of Consumer Research 9 (June 1982), 18–37.

34. Kevin Lane Keller, "Memory Factors in Advertising: The Effect of Advertising Retrieval Cues on Brand Evaluations," Journal of Consumer Research 14 (December 1987), 316–333. For additional research on retrieval cues, see Marian Friestad and Esther Thorson, "Remembering Ads: The Effects of Encoding Strategies, Retrieval Cues, and Emotional Response," Journal of Consumer Psychology 2 (1993), 1–24; Kevin Lane Keller, "Cue Comparability and Framing in Advertising," Journal of Marketing Research 28 (February 1991), 42–57; Keller, "Memory and Evaluation Effects in Competitive Advertising Environments."

35. Joseph O. Eastlack, Jr., "How to Get More Bang for Your Television Bucks," Journal of Consumer Marketing 1 (1984), 25–34.

36. Joseph W. Alba and Amitava Chattopadhyay, "Effects of Context and Part-Category Cues on Recall of Competing Brands," Journal of Marketing Research 22 (August 1985), 340–349; Joseph W. Alba and Amitava Chattopadhyay, "Salience Effects in Brand Recall," Journal of Marketing Research 23 (November 1986), 363–369. Also see Paul W. Miniard, H. Rao Unnava, and Sunil Bhatla, "Investigating the Recall Inhibition Effect: A Test of Practical Considerations," Marketing Letters 2 (January 1991), 290–303.

37. Endel Tulving and Donald M. Thompson, "Encoding Specificity and Retrieval Processes in Episodic Memory," Psychological Review 80 (September 1973), 352–373.

38. For a review of the literature on recognition measures, see Surendra N. Singh and Catherine A. Cole, "Forced-Choice Recognition Tests: A Critical Review," Journal of Advertising 14 (1985), 52–58.

39. Eric Marder and Mort David, "Recognition of Ad Elements: Recall or Projection?" Journal of Advertising Research 1 (December 1961), 23–25. For an interesting discussion of recognition measures, see Adam Finn, "Print Ad Recognition Readership Scores: An Information Processing Perspective," Journal of Marketing Research 25 (May 1988), 168–177.

40. Surendra N. Singh and Gilbert A. Churchill, Jr., "Using the Theory of Signal Detection to Improve Ad Recognition Testing," Journal of Marketing Research 23 (November 1986), 327–336; Singh and Cole, "Forced-Choice Recognition Tests"; Surendra N. Singh and Michael L. Rothschild, "Recognition as a Measure of Learning from Television Commercials," Journal of Marketing Research 20 (August 1983), 235–248; Singh, Rothschild, and Churchill, "Recognition Versus Recall as Measures of Television Commercial Forgetting."

41. There has been some criticism of recall measures' ability to provide an accurate assessment of the learning that occurs from emotional or feeling ads. See Hubert A. Zielske, "Does Day-After Recall Penalize 'Feeling' Ads?" Journal of Advertising Research 22 (February–March 1982), 19–22.

42. "To Burke or Not to Burke?" TV Guide 29 (February 7, 1981), 3ff.

43. Chattopadhyay and Alba, "The Situational Importance of Recall and Inference in Consumer Decision Making"; Loken and Hoverstad, "Relationships between Information Recall and Subsequent Attitudes." Note, however, that the relationship between recall and attitude is stronger when attitudes are not formed during ad processing but are formed at a later time based on retrieval of the ad information. For a discussion of this issue, see Reid Hastie and Bernadette Park, "The Relationship between Memory and Judgment Depends on Whether the Judgment Task Is Memory-Based or On-Line," Psychological Review 93 (June 1986), 258–268; Meryl Lichtenstein and Thomas K. Srull, "Processing Objectives as a Determinant of the Relationship between Recall and Judgment," Journal of Experimental Social Psychology 23 (March 1987), 93–118.

44. James R. Bettman, An Information Processing Theory of Consumer Choice (Reading, Mass.: Addison-Wesley, 1979).

45. For a discussion of advertising tactics to enhance brand recognition and recall, see John R. Rossiter and Larry Percy, "Advertising Communication Models," in Elizabeth C. Hirschman and Morris B. Holbrook, eds., Advances in Consumer Research 12 (Provo, Utah: Association for Consumer Research, 1985), 510–524.

46. Singh, Rothschild, and Churchill, "Recognition Versus Recall as Measures of Television Commercial Forgetting."

47. For an excellent translation of this literature into the marketing domain, see Frances K. McSweeney and Calvin Bierley, "Recent Developments in Classical Conditioning," Journal of Consumer Research 11 (September 1984), 619–631. For a recent review, see Terence A. Shimp, "Neo-Pavlovian Conditioning and Its

Implications for Consumer Theory and Research," in Thomas S. Robertson and Harold H. Kassarjian, eds., Handbook of Consumer Behavior (Englewood Cliffs, N.J.: Prentice-Hall, 1991), 162–187.

48. Walter R. Nord and J. Paul Peter, "A Behavior Modification Perspective on Marketing," Journal of Marketing 44 (Spring 1980), 36–47.

49. Chris Janiszewski and Luk Warlop, "The Influence of Classical Conditioning Procedures on Subsequent Attention to the Conditioned Brand," Journal of Consumer Research 20 (September 1993), 171–189.

50. Paul W. Miniard, Sunil Bhatla, Kenneth R. Lord, Peter R. Dickson, and H. Rao Unnava, "Picture-based Persuasion Processes and the Moderating Role of Involvement," Journal of Consumer Research 19 (June 1991), 92–107.

51. For a more detailed discussion of conditioning determinants, see Werner Kroeber-Riel, "Emotional Product Differentiation by Classical Conditioning," in Thomas C. Kinnear, ed., Advances in Consumer Research 11 (Provo, Utah: Association for Consumer Research, 1984), 538–543; McSweeney and Bierley, "Recent Developments in Classical Conditioning." For research on how conditioning may depend on conscious awareness of the CS–US relationship, see Chris T. Allen and Chris A. Janiszewski, "Assessing the Role of Contingency Awareness in Attitudinal Conditioning with Implications for Advertising Research," Journal of Marketing Research 26 (February 1989), 30–43.

52. Avram Goldstein, "Thrills in Response to Music and Other Stimuli," Physiological Psychology 8 (September 1980), 126–129.

53. Gerald J. Gorn, "The Effects of Music in Advertising on Choice Behavior: A Classical Conditioning Approach," Journal of Marketing 46 (Winter 1982), 94–101; Elnora W. Stuart, Terence A. Shimp, and Randall W. Engle, "Classical Conditioning of Consumer Attitudes: Four Experiments in an Advertising Context," Journal of Consumer Research 14 (December 1987), 334–349. Also see Chris T. Allen and Thomas J. Madden, "A Closer Look at Classical Conditioning," Journal of Consumer Research 12 (December 1985), 301–315; James J. Kellaris and Anthony D. Cox, "The Effects of Background Music in Advertising: A Reassessment," Journal of Consumer Research 16 (June 1989), 113–118; Terence A. Shimp, Eva M. Hyatt, and David J. Snyder, "A Critical Appraisal of Demand Artifacts in Consumer Research," Journal of Consumer Research 18 (December 1991), 273–283.

54. Kroeber-Riel, "Emotional Product Differentiation by Classical Conditioning."

55. McSweeney and Bierley, "Recent Developments in Classical Conditioning"; Stuart, Shimp, and Engle, "Classical Conditioning of Consumer Attitudes."

56. McSweeney and Bierley, "Recent Developments in Classical Conditioning."

57. Ibid.

58. Stuart, Shimp, and Engle, "Classical Conditioning of Consumer Attitudes"; Terence A. Shimp, Elnora W. Stuart, and Randall W. Engle, "A Program of Classical Conditioning Experiments Testing Variations in the Conditioned Stimulus and Context," Journal of Consumer Research 18 (June 1991), 1–12.

59. Anthony G. Greenwald and Clark Leavitt, "Audience Involvement in Advertising: Four Levels," Journal of Consumer Research 11 (June 1984), 581–592; Richard E. Petty and John T. Cacioppo, "The Elaboration Likelihood Model of Persuasion," in Leonard Berkowitz, ed., Advances in Experimental Social Psychology 19 (New York: Academic Press, 1986), 123–205.

60. "Firm: Consumers Cool to New Products," Marketing News 20 (January 3, 1986), 1ff.

61. Elinor Selame and Greg Kolligian, "Brands Are a Company's Most Important Asset," Marketing News 25 (September 16, 1991), 14, 19. For research on factors that may influence the success of brand extensions, see David A. Aaker and Kevin Lane Keller, "Consumer Evaluations of Brand Extensions," Journal of Marketing 54 (January 1990), 27–41; David M. Boush and Barbara Loken, "A Process-Tracing Study of Brand Extension Evaluation," Journal of Marketing Research 28 (February 1991), 16–28; Kevin Lane Keller, "Conceptualizing, Measuring, and Managing Customer-Based Brand Equity," Journal of Marketing 57 (January 1993), 1–22; Kevin Lane Keller and David A. Aacker, "The Effects of Sequential Introduction of Brand Extensions," Journal of Marketing Research 29 (February 1992), 35–50; Barbara Loken and Deborah Roedder John, "Diluting Brand Beliefs: When Do Brand Extensions Have a Negative Impact," Journal of Marketing 57 (July 1993), 71–84; C. Whan Park, Sandra Milberg, and Robert Lawson, "Evaluation of Brand Extensions: The Role of Product Feature Similarity and Brand Concept Consistency," Journal of Consumer Research 18 (September 1991), 185–193.

62. Selame and Kolligian, "Brands Are a Company's Most Important Asset," 19.

63. "Coors vs. Corr's," Time 123 (February 6, 1984), 51.

64. Diane Schneidman, "Use of 'Mc' in Front of Travel Firms' Names Leads to Lawsuits," Marketing News 21 (November 20, 1987), 17.

65. R. I Allison and K. P. Uhl, "Influence of Beer Brand Identification on Taste Perception," Journal of Marketing Research 1 (August 1964), 36–39.

66. Julia Keller, "These Are Not Q-Tips," Columbus Dispatch (April 10, 1987), G1.

67. Stanley M. Widrick, "Concept of Negative Reinforcement Has Place in Classroom," Marketing News 20 (July 18, 1986), 48–49; Stanley Widrick and Eugene H. Fram, "Identifying Negative Products: Do Customers Like to Purchase Your Products?" Journal of Consumer Marketing 1 (Fall 1983), 59–66.

68. Widrick, "Concept of Negative Reinforcement Has Place in Classroom."

69. Insights, NPD Research, Inc., 1979–1982.

70. "Zayre Launches 'Frequent Z' to Make Points with Shoppers," Marketing News 21 (November 20, 1987), 1.

71. Brian C. Deslauriers and Peter B. Everett, "The Effects of Intermittent and Continuous Token Reinforcement on Bus Ridership," Journal of Applied Psychology 62 (August 1977), 369–375.

72. Michael L. Rothschild and William C. Gaidis, "Behavioral Learning Theory: Its Relevance to Marketing and Promotions," Journal of Marketing 45 (Spring 1981), 70–78.

73. Nord and Peter, "A Behavior Modification Perspective on Marketing."

74. There has been some controversy over the application of shaping principles. See Nord and Peter, "A Behavior Modification Perspective on Marketing"; Rothschild and Gaidis, "Behavioral Learning Theory"; J. Paul Peter and Walter R. Nord, "A Clarification and Extension of Operant Conditioning Principles in Marketing," Journal of Marketing 46 (Summer 1982), 102–107.

75. Nord and Peter, "A Behavior Modification Perspective on Marketing."

76. Ibid.

CHAPTER 16

Influencing Attitudes and Behavior

▲▲

Michelin Seeks Young Buyers for Long-Term Relationship

For the past nine years, Michelin, through its famous baby ads, has positioned itself as one way consumers can reduce the threat of road hazards to themselves and their young passengers. Michelin says its baby ads have been effective—consumers equate Michelin tires with safety, quality, reliability, and dependability. But you won't see any babies in Michelin's latest marketing blitz. You won't see any tires either. At least not right away. The French tire maker is trying a different approach to reach a different kind of buyer—one that typically hasn't bought Michelins.

Michelin is thinking demographics. Lifestyles. That young, aspiring, pre-affluent buyer who is feeling angst about her or his wheels. "Current relationship on skids. Seeking advice," goes the copy for one of the new ads. "I used to feel like my 240SX convertible and I were one. I'd think a move, and we'd make it. Now, we don't have that close-as-skin feeling I love. Can we get it back?" Radio and television versions use the notion of recapturing paradise lost—suggesting that customers who buy Michelin high performance tires will see their cars recover flagging pep and nimbleness.

The marketing campaign is built around the final piece of Michelin's redesigned high-performance tire line called the XGT H4. Karen Brubaker, product manager for the tire, puts it this way: With the all-season XGT H4, Michelin is going after people who don't typically think of themselves as Michelin buyers, either because they are scared Michelin's reputation means premium prices or because they're gravitated to other high-performance brands.

The new "H" rated tire is aimed right at these young buyers. The typical buyer in the target market for the new tires drives a Saturn, a Pontiac Grand Am

GT, a Ford Mustang, or a Nissan 240SX. The company wants to get these young buyers in a long-term relationship. Michelin figures if it can get them now, they'll be back when they own more expensive sports cars. And this is a strategy that has worked. Michelin research shows it has the highest customer loyalty rate in the industry.

Source: Adapted from Stuart Drown, "Michelin Aiming New Ads at Different Kind of Buyer," The State *(April 2, 1994), B9–B10.*

Influencing consumers' attitudes and behavior is one of the most fundamental and yet challenging tasks confronting businesses. Companies invest billions of dollars each year in efforts designed to modify or reinforce how consumers think, feel, and act in the marketplace. Consequently, knowing how to influence consumers' attitudes and behavior is one of the most valuable skills a marketer can possess.

This chapter attempts to provide a foundation for such knowledge. You will discover that many of the concepts and ideas presented in previous chapters are very relevant to this discussion. We begin our journey with a consideration of the persuasive power of marketing communications.

Persuasion through Communication

Marketing communications, whether in the form of advertising, a salesperson's "pitch," a point-of-purchase brochure, or product packaging, represent a significant means for persuading consumers. The processes that underlie the persuasive impact of such communications were described in Chapters 14 (Information Processing) and 15 (Learning). Little attention, however, was given to understanding how persuasion can depend on certain elements of the communication, such as the source and types of claims. The persuasive impact of various message elements is explored in this section. But first, we consider a conceptualization known as the elaboration likelihood model that will help you better understand much of the material covered in this section of the book.

The Elaboration Likelihood Model of Persuasion

According to the **elaboration likelihood model** (ELM) developed by Petty and Cacioppo, the influence exerted by various communication elements will depend on the amount of issue-relevant thinking (such thinking is called elaboration) that occurs during processing.[1] When elaboration is high, the **central route** to persuasion is followed, in which only those message elements (called **arguments**) relevant to forming a "reasoned" opinion are influential. Conversely, the **peripheral route** to persuasion occurs under low levels of elaboration as elements (called **peripheral cues**) that are irrelevant to developing a reasoned opinion become influential. Both arguments and peripheral cues may have an effect under moderate levels of elaboration.

Elaboration, in turn, depends on the person's motivation and ability during message processing. A person motivated and able to elaborate will take the central route. The peripheral route is traveled when motivation or ability is lacking. Figure 16.1 provides a diagram of the basic model.

Research testing the ELM has been largely supportive of its validity.[2] In one such study, subjects were exposed to a series of print ads.[3] The properties of one of these ads, featuring a fictitious razor product, were systematically manipulated. Some versions of the razor ad listed strong arguments or claims about the product, whereas others contained weak arguments. Different product endorsers were also used in the ad versions. Some contained celebrity endorsers; other versions featured noncelebrity endorsers. Finally, subjects' involvement was also manipulated from low to high to vary the amount of elaboration that

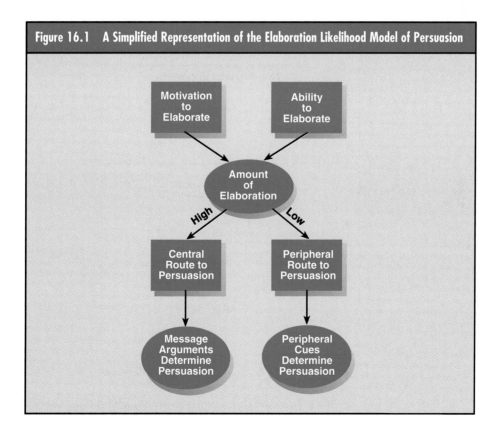

Figure 16.1   A Simplified Representation of the Elaboration Likelihood Model of Persuasion

occurred while processing the razor ad. Only those subjects assigned to the high-involvement condition were told that they would eventually make a choice among razors. As a consequence, high-involvement subjects should be motivated to think more carefully about the claims made in the razor ad.

Following ad exposure, all subjects completed measures assessing their attitudes toward the advertised brand, the results of which are presented in Figure 16.2. As predicted by the ELM, the influence of the message elements varied across involvement. The attitudes of high-involvement subjects were affected only by the differences in the message arguments. In contrast, low-involvement subjects' attitudes were influenced by both the strength of the arguments (al-

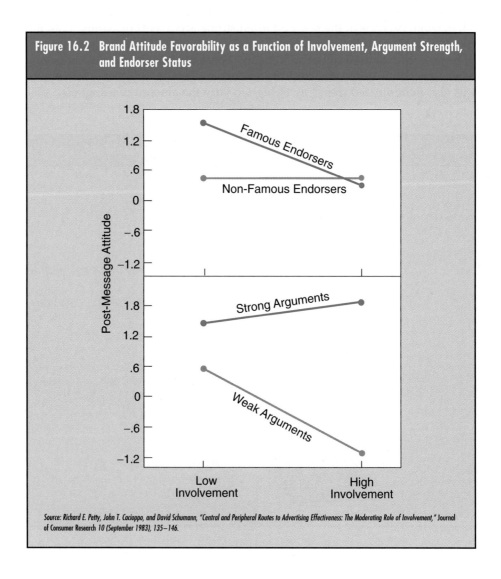

Figure 16.2 Brand Attitude Favorability as a Function of Involvement, Argument Strength, and Endorser Status

Source: Richard E. Petty, John T. Cacioppo, and David Schumann, "Central and Peripheral Routes to Advertising Effectiveness: The Moderating Role of Involvement," Journal of Consumer Research 10 (September 1983), 135–146.

though to a lesser extent than the attitudes formed under high involvement) and the celebrity status of the product endorser.

The ELM highlights the importance of anticipating how much thinking is likely to occur during message processing when developing effective communications. If consumers carefully consider the message's content, then the presence of compelling claims about the advertised brand is essential for developing favorable attitudes toward the brand. However, when consumers do not think carefully about the message claims, the strength of the ad claims becomes rather unimportant. Instead, the ad's persuasive impact will depend on whether it contains positive peripheral cues.

The Message Source as a Source of Persuasion

Suppose you were in the market for a new car. While visiting a car dealership, a salesman explains why you should buy from his lot rather than from one of his competitors. His salespitch includes many claims about the virtues of his cars, including the statement that they are the most reliable automobiles on the market. Would you believe him?

Now suppose you received the same basic information from a close friend who possessed considerable expertise in this area. Would you be any more likely to believe the information is valid? Chances are you would. Although the message remains unchanged, the difference in the source of the message could determine whether you believe it. Unlike your friend, the salesman has a vested interest in what he says. Consumers realize this, thus making them more skeptical about the information they receive.

As implied by the preceding example, certain source characteristics can enhance the persuasive impact of communications. A long-standing principle of persuasion is that a credible source (one that is perceived as knowledgeable and trustworthy) will usually enhance persuasion.[4] Physically attractive sources can be more persuasive.[5] The same is true for sources that are likeable,[6] hold celebrity status,[7] or are similar to the target audience.[8]

Recall from Chapter 5 the distinction made between personal and nonpersonal information sources. Whereas source effects for personal communications, in which the consumer receives information from another individual (doctor, friend, salesperson, and so on), are limited solely to the person transmitting the message, source effects for impersonal commercial communications, in which the information is transmitted by some advertising medium, are more complex. Consider an ad featuring someone endorsing a company's product that appears in a magazine. In this instance, source effects may stem from the magazine, the company sponsoring the ad, and the product endorser. A magazine perceived to be careful in screening out deceptive advertisers, for example, may enhance the ad's credibility.

Similarly, the reputation of the company sponsoring the message can be important. To illustrate this, consider the study in which subjects processed a comparative ad and then ranked the advertised brand relative to competitors. Before ad exposure, subjects received information that created either a positive or negative reputation for the advertiser. The study also varied the extremity of the claims made by the ad. Of 100 brands, the advertised brand was claimed to be either the top-rated brand in a taste test, the third best, the fifth best, or the twentieth best tasting brand. The results, displayed in Figure 16.3, show that the brand was ranked more favorably when the source possessed a positive reputation, particularly when the ad contained the most extreme claim of the brand tasting better than all other brands. We return to this study and its findings involving the extremity of ad claims later in the chapter when we examine message claims more closely.

Product Endorsers

When nonpersonal communications contain a product endorser (someone who appears in the ad on behalf of the product), source effects may also depend on the product endorser. Movie and rock stars, athletes (see Consumer in Focus 16.1 for a discussion of one famous athlete — Michael Jordan), doctors, veteri-

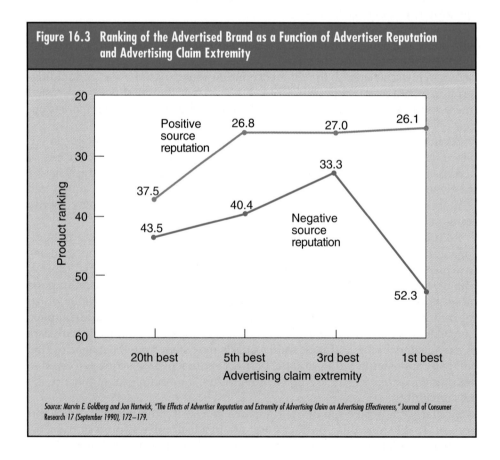

Figure 16.3 Ranking of the Advertised Brand as a Function of Advertiser Reputation and Advertising Claim Extremity

Positive source reputation: 26.8, 27.0, 26.1
37.5
Negative source reputation: 43.5, 40.4, 33.3, 52.3

Product ranking (y-axis): 20, 30, 40, 50, 60
Advertising claim extremity (x-axis): 20th best, 5th best, 3rd best, 1st best

Source: Marvin E. Goldberg and Jon Hartwick, "The Effects of Advertiser Reputation and Extremity of Advertising Claim on Advertising Effectiveness," *Journal of Consumer Research* 17 (September 1990), 172–179.

Consumer in Focus 16.1

Michael Jordan: Basketball Superstar and Consummate Product Endorser

In 1992, Chicago Bulls superstar Michael Jordan earned about $36 million for endorsing products, making himself the highest paid athlete in the world, according to a survey by *Forbes* magazine. A list of his major national endorsements appears below.

Company	Product	Estimated Annual Fee
Nike	Basketball shoes	$18 million*
McDonald's	Restaurants	$ 3 million
Quaker Oats	Gatorade	$ 2 million
Sara Lee	Hanes, Ball Park Franks	$ 3 to 4 million
General Mills	Wheaties	$ 2 to $3 million
Wilson Sporting Goods	Basketballs	Less than $1 million

*Includes profit from sales of Air Jordan line.

The sudden decision by Mr. Jordan to retire from basketball won't end his career as a celebrity endorser—at least not right away. But new campaigns will have to be devised putting him in the more passive role of retired athlete, sports marketing experts say.

Nearly all of the major companies that use Mr. Jordan in their commercials say they will retain basketball's greatest player. These advertisers include Nike, which built an entire line of basketball shoes around the star named Air Jordan; McDonald's, which, for the first time, created a hamburger named after an athlete, the McJordan; Gatorade; General Mills' Wheaties cereal and Ball Park Franks. "There is no one close to taking his place, and I don't mean just with scoring statistics," said Nova Lanktree, president of Lanktree Passport Celebrity Service in Northbrook, Ill., which supplies sports stars for commercials. "He doesn't have a peer when it comes to charisma and his impact with commercials and the game."

Source: Adapted from Kevin Goldman, "Is There Life after Basketball? Companies That Use Jordan Are About to Find Out," Wall Street Journal (October 7, 1993), B1, B8.

narians, teachers, technicians, and even ordinary consumers often appear in advertisements extolling the product's virtues. Such is the case for the White Step ad appearing in Figure 16.4, which uses Heather Locklear, one of the stars of "Melrose Place", as a product endorser.

Product endorsers may help determine the ad's persuasiveness in several ways. As indicated in Chapter 14, celebrities can serve as an attention-getting device. Also, product endorsers may shape consumers' interpretation of the ad and product through **meaning transfer**.[9] Meaning transfer is when the meaning conveyed by one object is transferred to another object. Thus, consumers may come to see a product as more powerful or more elegant simply because the product is associated with endorsers having these meanings. Endorsers can also serve as peripheral cues that, as discussed earlier, can enhance persuasion under the peripheral route. And to the extent that the product endorser is trusted by consumers, they may be more accepting of the ad claims.

Figure 16.4 Celebrity Endorsers Can Increase Advertising Effectiveness

In selecting an effective product endorser, companies should consider not only the endorser's characteristics but also how well the product and endorser fit together.[10] When the late John Houseman (who played the hard-nosed law professor on the TV series "Paper Chase") told us, on behalf of the Smith Barney investment firm, "We make money the old-fashioned way, we earn it," the ad raised the company's image and sales. The same could not be said of his appearance in a McDonald's spot.[11] Bill Cosby is very effective in promoting Jell-O food products and Kodak film, but he was far less persuasive when he appeared in a commercial for the E. F. Hutton investment company.[12]

Thus, the use of a celebrity endorser does not guarantee success. Indeed, celebrity endorsements have sometimes had embarrassing consequences for the sponsoring product. Such was the case when the beef industry developed an advertising campaign designed to stimulate beef consumption in which celebrities told consumers that beef was "Real food for real people." One of these celebrities was Cybill Shepherd. Imagine how the industry felt when it was later published that Cybill was a vegetarian.

Message Effects

Additional characteristics of the message beyond the source can play a significant role in the persuasion process. Of particular interest here are the claims and executional elements that comprise the communication.

Strength of Claims

The strength of message claims will strongly determine how much yielding occurs under the central route to persuasion. Strong claims will inhibit negative thoughts while encouraging positive thoughts. Just the opposite holds for weak claims.

What makes a claim strong? Relevancy is critical. Claims that focus on dimensions that carry little or no weight in the decision process lack relevancy. One industry study reports that relevancy was the most important determinant of new product advertising's success in persuading consumers to try the product.[13]

Another important characteristic is a claim's objectivity. **Objective claims** focus on factual information that is not subject to individual interpretations. **Subjective claims**, however, are ones that may evoke different interpretations across individuals. Consider a product's price or weight. Claims such as "low-priced" or "lightweight" would be considered subjective, inasmuch as what is low or light for one person may not be for the next. These same attributes could be expressed objectively by giving the actual price and weight.

Objective claims are preferred by consumers over subjective claims because they are more precise and more easily confirmed. Objective claims are perceived as more believable, reduce counterargumentation while increasing the number of support arguments, and create more favorable product beliefs and attitudes.[14]

The verifiability of claims can also be significant. Table 16.1 presents some examples of claims differing in their verifiability and objectivity. **Search claims** are those that can be accurately evaluated before purchase. **Experience claims** are those that can be fully evaluated only after product consumption. **Credence claims** differ from the prior two types in that accurate evaluation is beyond the consumer's capabilities. Consumers perceive search claims to be much more truthful than either experience or credence claims.[15]

Substantiation of claims is also important.[16] Consider the experience claim of great taste. This claim is more likely to be accepted if supported by credible taste-test findings than when such substantiation is lacking. Product demonstrations may also prove an effective way to substantiate claims. Read Consumer in Focus 16.2 to learn more about this.

Number of Claims

Not only may communications differ in the strength of their claims, they may also vary in the number of claims contained within the message. Such is the case for the two promotional pieces appearing in Figure 16.5. It seems rather obvious that consumers will be more likely to buy a product as the number of reasons for doing so increases, as long as the additional reasons are important to the consumer. But what if the additional reasons are unimportant? Will persuasion still be greater?

The answer depends on the amount of thinking consumers do during message processing. When consumers follow the central route to persuasion and carefully think about the message, then adding more claims about unimportant information does not help. However, under the peripheral route, claim quantity

Table 16.1	Claims That Differ in Their Objectivity and Verifiability	
	Objective	Subjective
Search	• We offer five styles of cedar chests	• We offer an extraordinary collection of jewelry
	• Our brand has no cholesterol	• There are a variety of attractive styles
Experience	• Our tent keeps you dry	• We offer delicious meals
	• Our test gives you results in 30 minutes	• Easy to use with professional results
Credence	• We invested over $5 billion in our long-distance network	• Our tire has been extensively tested
	• Our polish is used by 77 leading galleries and museums	• Our wine is naturally fermented

Source: Gary T. Ford, Darlene B. Smith, and John L. Swasy, "Consumer Skepticism of Advertising Claims: Testing Hypotheses from Economics of Information," Journal of Consumer Research 16 (March 1990), 433–441.

Product Demonstrations and Advertising Effectiveness

Product demonstrations have long been used by advertisers in their never-ending pursuit of persuading consumers. Some time ago GE wanted to convince people that they didn't have to rinse dishes before putting them into the company's dishwasher. To illustrate this point, a GE dishwasher was shown to polish off a 2-pound, three-layer chocolate cake—on the first rinse. The ad headline read, "GE Washers really take the cake."

Similarly, to demonstrate the strength of its corrugated paper, St. Regis built a bridge of the material. A 2.5-ton Rolls-Royce was then driven over it. To show its shoes are lightweight and able to stand up to shocks, Rockport uses ads that show a man running the New York marathon in them. "Some might be surprised to learn that a man actually ran a grueling 26-mile marathon in dress shoes," a voiceover says. "It will come as no surprise that they were Rockports." The ad closes with a shot of the man's foot as he crosses the line in his Rockports. The event really did happen. A Rockport employee laced up a pair of the company's shoes for the big run.

"When you have a story you can demonstrate, it makes sense to show it," said Rob Moorman, senior VP at Jordan, McGrath, Case & Taylor, Rockport's agency. "Plus, actually showing it adds authenticity." In a recent study by Research Systems Corp. (RSC) of 5,000 ads across 21 product categories, a significant relationship was found between the use of a demonstration in a TV spot and its ability to persuade. Twenty-one percent of the ads using a demonstration snagged an above-average mark in persuasion versus only 12 percent for those not using demonstrations. According to Mark Gleason, senior VP at RSC, "It's a lot easier to believe something that you see with your own eyes than it is to listen to someone telling you something. A picture's worth a thousand words."

Source: Adapted from Cyndee Miller, "Demonstrating Your Point: Showing How the Product Works Adds Authenticity," Marketing News (September 13, 1993), 2.

serves as a peripheral cue. Consequently, when thinking is limited during message processing, increasing the number of claims increases persuasion despite the fact that the additional claims involve only unimportant information.[17]

Message Sidedness

What may come as a surprise is that including some weak claims along with strong claims can enhance a message's persuasiveness. Two-sided messages (those including pros and cons) increase perceptions of advertiser truthfulness and believability relative to one-sided messages (those presenting only pros).[18]

Comparative Messages

Claims can also vary in their use of brand comparisons. Comparative advertising, in which the advertised brand is implicitly or explicitly compared against one or more competitors, is often used by new brands seeking to take business

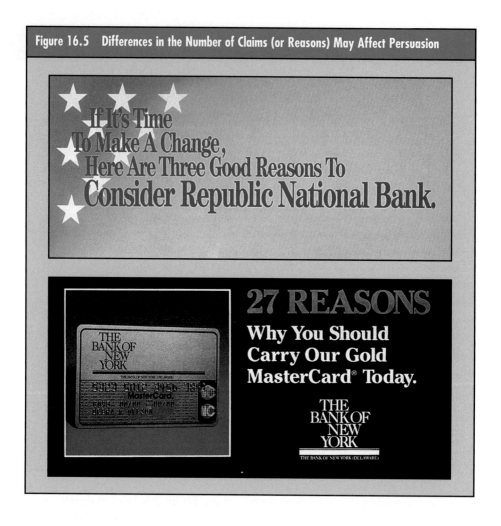

Figure 16.5   Differences in the Number of Claims (or Reasons) May Affect Persuasion

away from existing brands. It also is used by established brands, as evidenced by the advertising campaigns during the burger and cola wars. Although comparative ads have been shown to outperform noncomparative ads,[19] even in terms of producing greater sales,[20] this is not always the case. Sometimes comparative ads are no better or even worse than noncomparative versions.[21]

Affective Messages

Whereas informationally oriented messages attempt to evoke favorable cognitive responses during processing, affective messages are designed to elicit favorable affective responses. Such is the case for the ad presented in Figure 16.6. Similarly, the ad appearing in Chapter 15 (see Fig. 15.7) relied on a picture of a father and child sharing a loving moment to evoke favorable feelings. The March of Dimes has departed from its traditional institutional-style advertising

Figure 16.6   Affective Messages Try to Persuade through Feelings

in favor of "emotional response" ads for targeting less literate segments.[23] These new ads contained powerful visuals (such as a liquor label on a baby bottle filled with alcohol) with little or no copy. To the extent consumers experience favorable feelings when processing affective messages that become associated with the advertised product, then persuasion will be facilitated.[22]

Affective messages are not limited to simply affect-laden visuals. Many message elements are capable of evoking affective responses. Such responses may often occur for music. Similarly, ad copy that encourages consumers to retrieve memories about a favorable personal experience may have the same basic effect.[24]

Beyond enhancing persuasion, affective advertising may provide other potential advantages.[25] People may pay greater attention to emotional ads because of affect's role in guiding attention. Emotional ads may also increase the viewer's arousal, which, as discussed later, can enhance message processing.

Executional Elements

Although persuasion may often depend on what you say in your message, how you say it can be equally, if not more, important in many situations. Message execution must therefore be carefully considered in the development of persuasive communications. Indeed, executional elements such as visuals, sounds, colors, and pace can play a critical role during persuasion in several ways.

First, as covered in Chapter 14, executional elements can attract attention. These elements may also affect consumers' beliefs about the product and its attributes.[26] By using a peppery background in the ad shown in Figure 16.7, consumers who like peppercorn may form more favorable perceptions of the product's taste. Similarly, the Armstrong Tire Co. includes pictures of "Tuffy the Rhino" in its advertising to reinforce perceptions of the product's strength, durability, and toughness.[27] And General Motors has replaced the "Heartbeat of America" theme in its Chevy truck commercials with Bob Seger's "Like a Rock" to signal dependability and toughness.[28]

Finally, executional elements may influence attitudes without affecting beliefs about the product.[29] This is the case when these elements serve as peripheral cues that, while irrelevant to the product, may still affect consumers' post-communication attitudes.

The Influence of Attitudes toward the Ad

The ability of advertising to create favorable attitudes toward a product may often depend on consumers' attitudes toward the ad itself. Ads that are liked or evaluated favorably can lead to more positive product attitudes. Disliked ads may lower consumers' product evaluations. Attitudes toward the ad have been shown repeatedly to serve as a significant predictor of product attitudes.[30]

This is not to say that consumers must always like an ad for it to be effective.[31] There can be ads that are disliked but still successful. Indeed, advertisers sometimes make ads deliberately annoying in the hope that the message can break through the clutter. A good example is the "Mr. Whipple" commercials for Procter & Gamble's Charmin toilet tissue that began in 1968 and ran for 14 years.[32] Consumers reported that they couldn't stand watching the ads. Even so, the campaign was very effective in communicating the brand's softness positioning and certainly helped it become the dominant brand in its category.

Repetition Effects

Research on the persuasive effects of message repetition has produced a mixed set of findings. Indeed, the literature has reported that repetition has a positive,[33] negative,[34] null,[35] or inverted-U[36] (in which persuasion increases up to some point, beyond which persuasion declines) relationship with persuasion.

Perhaps the most promising explanation for how repetition affects persuasion is the two-stage attitude-modification process proposed by Cacioppo and

Figure 16.7 Executional Elements and Persuasion: Kraft Uses a Certain Background to Influence Consumers' Beliefs about the Product

Petty.[37] Early exposures are believed to provide the person with additional opportunities to evaluate the position advocated by the message. Once the person has fully evaluated the message's implications for her or his attitudes, the second stage takes over and tedium with the message becomes dominant. This tedium will lower message acceptance. The point at which tedium begins will depend on the amount of processing that occurs during prior exposures. If the ad is fully evaluated after one exposure, tedium will set in immediately. If such thinking does not occur until after many exposures, the negative impact of tedium is delayed.

Thus, according to this view, additional repetitions are needed only if the person is unable or unwilling to fully evaluate the message's position after a single exposure.[38] For example, an informationally complex television ad may require several exposures, especially when the consumer is not highly motivated to process the ad carefully.

Moreover, when additional repetitions are required, the effect of repetition will depend on the strength of the message. More repetition should produce more favorable thoughts about the advertised product for messages using strong claims. Just the opposite should occur for weak claims, in which repetition will increase the number of unfavorable thoughts.

Evidence germane to this view has been largely supportive.[39] Cacioppo and Petty's initial study focused on the acceptance of a message containing strong arguments in favor of increasing university expenditures.[40] Subjects were exposed to the message a low (once), moderate (three), or high (five) number of times. Agreement with the message increased from one to three exposures but then decreased after five exposures. This pattern was consistent with the cognitive response data. Favorable thoughts followed the same pattern, whereas unfavorable thoughts moved in the opposite manner (negative thoughts decreased from one to three exposures and increased after five exposures).

The role of message strength as a moderator of repetition effects has also been demonstrated. Whereas acceptance was greater after three exposures for a message presenting strong claims, acceptance was lower after three exposures for a message based on weak claims.[41] Finally, responses reflecting tedium have been found to increase in frequency and intensity with greater amounts of repetition.[42]

Consumer Considerations

Although marketers are able to enhance the persuasiveness of their communications by bringing together the appropriate blend of source and message elements, the ultimate impact of any communication will depend heavily on how consumers respond to it. These responses, in turn, are shaped by a multitude of consumer characteristics, such as the person's motivation or knowledge at the time of exposure. Consequently, the characteristics of the consumer at the time of exposure to a persuasive communication should be taken into account in designing the communication. In this section, we examine some of the more important consumer characteristics.

Motivation

There is a tremendous diversity in consumers' motivational states when they are receiving marketing communications. Sometimes, consumers will be highly motivated to carefully process and evaluate such communications. Quite often, however, this is not the case, as consumers either ignore or expend little cognitive effort during processing.

The importance of the consumer's motivational state during message processing was illustrated earlier in the chapter by Petty, Cacioppo, and Schumann's study (see Figure 16.2, page 562).[43] Recall that when their subjects were more strongly motivated to process the ad (the high-involvement condition), persuasion depended solely on the strength of the message claims. However, when this motivation was lacking (the low-involvement condition), the celebrity status of the endorser featured in the ad became influential.

The extent to which the product is purchased because of utilitarian versus hedonic considerations (see Chapter 12) is another important consideration in developing persuasive communications. If the product is purchased primarily for its utilitarian benefits (its ability to solve current problems or eliminate potential problems), informational appeals (how the product solves the problem and why it should be chosen over others) should be emphasized. Products that are bought primarily for their hedonic benefits (such as those that provide sensory gratification or intellectual stimulation) should rely more heavily on affective appeals.[44]

It is possible that both types of appeals will be necessary for promoting the product. Automobiles are a good example. Print ads are typically filled with considerable amounts of details and facts about the car's characteristics that can be processed at the consumer's leisure. Television ads, however, may focus on the sensory pleasures that come from driving the car.

Arousal

Physiological arousal, representing a person's degree of alertness along a continuum ranging from extreme drowsiness to extreme wakefulness, can moderate the persuasion process. Arousal presumably has both facilitating and inhibiting effects on the amount of elaboration during message processing. Little processing can occur when the person is drowsy. A certain level of arousal is, therefore, desirable. However, increases in arousal lead to more processing of internal cues sent by the nervous system, thereby reducing the cognitive capacity available for message elaboration. These considerations suggest an inverted-U relationship between arousal and elaboration. Elaboration should be stronger at moderate levels of arousal than when arousal is very low or very high.

Research has supported the persuasive role of arousal.[45] When arousal was moderate, attitudes formed following message processing depended only on the strength of the message claims. In contrast, attitudes formed under high arousal were based more heavily on the celebrity status of the product endorser.

Such findings indicate the need to consider the arousal level of consumers when exposed to persuasive communications. Message elements other than the product claims may play a much greater role in determining persuasion when arousal is very high. High arousal may characterize several situations in which consumers receive persuasive communications, such as sporting events, action-packed movies, and workout shows in which viewers actively participate.

Knowledge

As discussed in Chapter 10, consumer knowledge is a major determinant of consumer behavior. The same holds true in the realm of persuasion. When consumers are knowledgeable about the topic of some persuasive communication, they are better able to evaluate the strengths and weaknesses of the message claims. Consistent with this, knowledgeable consumers have been shown to respond more favorably as advertising content becomes more technical.[46] Just the opposite was observed for unknowledgeable consumers.

This line of reasoning carries important implications for communication strategy.[47] Because knowledgeable consumers already know the benefits of product ownership and usage, less emphasis on benefits relative to more technical features may be desirable. Camera ads aimed at experts, for instance, often emphasize technical product features. However, when target consumers lack such knowledge, communications that focus on easily understood product benefits are likely to be more successful.

Similarly, knowledgeable consumers are more likely to focus on information most relevant for evaluating a product's strengths and weaknesses. Those less informed may be more persuaded by information that is peripheral or less relevant. In one study, experts' evaluations of a camera were strongly affected by a description of the product's attributes but were unaffected by a label of the camera type (110 or 35mm SLR). The opposite was true for novices, as their product evaluations depended only on the product type label.[48]

Pre-existing Attitudes

The success of a persuasive communication will also depend on the pre-existing attitudes held by consumers before being exposed to the message. For example, consumers' attitudes about the trustworthiness of advertising in general may affect how they respond to an ad. Advertising effectiveness is likely to be diminished when consumers are generally skeptical of advertising claims.

Unfortunately for advertisers, a great number of consumers appear to be rather suspicious about the trustworthiness of advertising.[49] In one study, more than 70 percent of consumers reported that they do not believe ads that use test results to support claims of product superiority.[50]

Another indication of the pervasiveness of consumer skepticism toward advertising is provided by the study discussed earlier in the section concerning the effects of a message source. Return to Figure 16.3 (page 564) and look at the results for when the source had a positive reputation (the top line in the graph). Notice anything peculiar? Think about where the product was ranked according to the ad and where it was ranked by the consumers in this study. Look at the substantial difference between the two. For instance, even when the source had a positive reputation and the ad claimed the brand had the best taste, consumers still ranked the brand, on average, as the twenty-sixth best. Apparently, consumers' skepticism of advertising led to a substantial discounting of the ad claims.

Whether consumers hold pre-existing attitudes toward the topic of the message (typically the product is the topic) is also important. Sometimes the consumer will not have a pre-existing attitude, as would be so for a new product. When this occurs, advertising that intends to influence attitudes would encourage consumers to *form* favorable attitudes toward the product.

At other times, consumers will already possess attitudes, as is the case for familiar products. When consumers already hold favorable attitudes, advertising will hopefully *reinforce* these attitudes. However, consumers may hold attitudes that are less favorable than suggested by an ad. In this instance, advertising would face the challenge of trying to *change* attitudes toward a more favorable state.

In general, persuasive communications will be more successful when attitudes are being formed than when attitudes are being changed. Changing attitudes is more difficult because of the additional resistance that comes from the commitment to the existing attitude. Commitment will be stronger for attitudes anchored in a person's sense of self-worth or ego.[51] The stronger this commitment, the greater the resistance, as reflected by greater counterargumentation with the message.

Thus, in the case of mature brands that are very familiar to consumers, advertising may have limited influence on consumers' attitudes toward these brands. Nonetheless, advertising may still affect consumers' interest in these brands.[52] **Brand interest** represents the inquisitiveness or curiosity a consumer has about a brand. Greater interest in a brand may increase the odds of the brand gaining entry into the consideration set (see Chapter 6).

When consumers hold pre-existing attitudes toward the product, communications effectiveness will further depend on how these attitudes were formed initially. Consider the study in which initial attitudes were formed toward a brand of peanut butter by either providing subjects with some product information or allowing them actually to taste the product.[53] Afterward they were exposed to a communication favoring the product delivered by either a high- or low-credibility source. The impact of source credibility depended on the method of initial attitude formation. Source credibility affected postcommunication attitudes only when subjects did not first taste the product. Thus, attitudes based on direct experience proved more resistant to the message.

Finally, the favorability of pre-existing attitudes can also determine the relative effectiveness of different persuasive communications. Suppose you were trying to change the attitudes of consumers who currently hold a negative opinion of your product. Should you use a humorous ad to do so, or would a non-humorous ad be more effective? The nonhumorous ad has been shown to be more persuasive in this situation. However, when prior attitudes were initially favorable, the humorous ad was more effective.[54]

Mood

Another consumer characteristic that can influence persuasion is the consumer's mood state at the time of exposure to a communication. **Moods** refer to transient feelings (such as happiness and sadness) that exist at a particular time and place.[55] Research suggests that favorable moods can enhance persuasion, whereas unfavorable moods reduce persuasion.[56]

How can a communicator encourage favorable moods? One approach is to include within the communication certain executional elements that tend to evoke the desired mood state, as is commonly done in affective messages. A second approach is to place the communication in a context that encourages favorable moods. The program in which a commercial appears, for example, can affect the moods consumers bring to the communication situation.[57]

Personality Traits

A consumer's personality may also shape her or his responsiveness to persuasive communications. A person's **need for cognition**, representing an individual's tendency to undertake and enjoy thinking, is one such personality trait.[58] Persons scoring high on need for cognition measures are more influenced by message claims, whereas those having a low need for cognition display greater sensitivity to peripheral message cues such as source attractiveness.[59]

Self-monitoring has also been linked to persuasion. High self-monitoring persons are very sensitive to situational and interpersonal considerations. They are quite willing and adept at modifying their behavior to be the "right person in the right place at the right time." Low self-monitoring individuals do not modify their behavior in this way. Rather, they rely more heavily on their own internal feelings and attitudes to guide behavior.[60]

The relative effectiveness of appeals based on a product's image versus claims about a product's quality can depend on self-monitoring.[61] High self-monitors have been found to respond more favorably to image advertising, whereas advertising focusing on product quality was received more favorably by low self-monitors. Similar differences were also observed between high and low self-monitors in their willingness to try and how much they would pay for products associated with either an image or quality appeal. When Mercury abandoned its image-oriented advertising in favor of a new campaign emphasizing more substantive aspects of the cars themselves, the primary target market was low self-monitors.[62]

Product Considerations

Thus far, our discussion has largely neglected how characteristics of the product can affect persuasion strategy. However, just as characteristics of the target consumer should be taken into consideration when developing persuasion strategy, so too must various aspects of the product be taken into account.[63]

Stage in the Product Life Cycle

Persuasion strategy will vary over a product's life cycle. Gaining aware-ness and product trial are primary objectives for new products. Whereas build-ing favorable brand attitudes is critical during the growth stages, maintain-ing or reinforcing these attitudes is paramount when the product reaches maturity.

Product Experience

The impact of persuasive communications will depend on consumers' subse-quent experiences with the product. A poor tasting beverage is unlikely to be fa-vorably evaluated, no matter how much advertising tries to claim otherwise.

In some cases, however, consumers are limited in their ability to assess prod-uct performance accurately. Can consumers truly evaluate the benefits that may arise from taking a vitamin a day? And how do we know whether or not the per-son who repaired our car or TV took advantage of us by unnecessarily replac-ing parts that were in working condition?

Research suggests that the "ambiguity" of product experiences can shape the impact of prior advertising. In one study, advertising's potential to affect per-ceptions of product quality was examined for two products—polo shirts and paper towels.[64] After ad exposure, subjects were allowed to either visually in-spect different brands of polo shirts or actually test the water absorption prop-erties of various paper towel brands. The water test yielded clear evidence about the paper towels. Consequently, subjects based their product quality percep-tions on this evidence alone and ignored the advertising. In contrast, the am-biguous information provided by visually inspecting the shirts enabled adver-tising to exert a favorable influence.

Product Positioning

A major determinant of persuasion strategy is the particular positioning desired for a product. That is, what product image does the marketer wish to create in the consumer's mind? The answer to this question will strongly dictate the type of message one uses to influence consumers. A product built around a status po-sitioning will use very different messages from the product that competes based on price.

Relative Product Performance

Attention must also be given to the product's performance relative to competi-tive products in the areas representing the desired positioning. When the prod-uct is demonstrably superior to competitors, this advantage can be a potent sell-ing point. In the absence of such superiority, other tactics must be used for communicating the product offering.

The two ads appearing in Figure 16.8 illustrate this point. The apparent superiority of Zact over Topol in removing stains permits Zact to use a comparative ad making strong claims along this dimension. In contrast, the Topol ad attempts to convey the desired positioning without reference to competitors. Instead, an appropriate visual image (the model dressed completely in white with shining teeth) is combined with the claim that Topol "works more effectively."

The attractiveness of affective and informational appeals may depend on the relative performance of competing brands. Informational appeals may be of limited value when consumers perceive competing brands to be homogeneous in their product characteristics. Affective appeals may represent a more promising means for achieving differentiation in such settings.

Relative product performance is also important in determining whether peripheral advertising cues may influence consumers' brand choices.[65] Read Consumer in Focus 16.3 to find out how.

Figure 16.8 Different Brands Follow Different Advertising Strategies Depending on Their Relative Product Performance

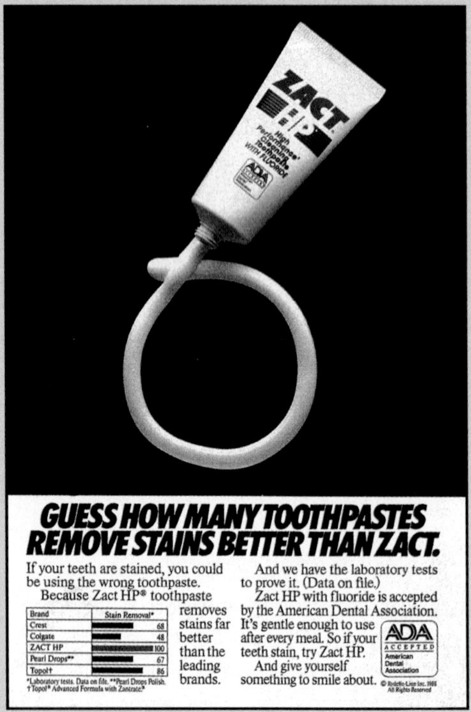

Consumer in Focus   **16.3**

Influencing Product Choice through Peripheral Advertising Cues

Recent research supports the potential for peripheral advertising elements that are devoid of product-relevant information to alter choice behavior under certain conditions. In this study, people looked at a series of print ads. One of the ads featured a brand of soft drink called Sunburst. For some individuals, the ad contained an attractive picture. For others, the ad contained an unattractive picture. Pretesting revealed both pictures were devoid of product meaning.

After viewing the ads, participants were given the results of a taste test in which others had tasted and rated Sunburst and two other brands along three important attributes. The study used three different taste test results: One version revealed the presence of a dominant brand other than Sunburst which received vastly superior ratings on all attributes; the second version reported virtually the same taste ratings for all brands; and in the final version, one brand received the best ratings on one of the three attributes used in the taste test, another brand was rated the highest on the second attribute, and the remaining brand received the best ratings for the third attribute. Participants were told to look over the taste test results and choose the brand they wanted for their free six-pack.

The results indicated that the peripheral pictures had a strong influence on the brand chosen unless the taste test results revealed a dominant brand. When the taste ratings were essentially the same for all three brands, thus indicating a lack of differentiation, Sunburst was chosen twice as often when it had previously been paired with the attractive picture in the ad compared to being paired with the unattractive ad picture. Similar results occurred even when the ratings revealed important brand differences without one brand being dominant. However, when the ratings indicated that Sunburst was dominated by another brand, choices were insensitive to the peripheral advertising cues.

Source: Paul W. Miniard, Deepak Sirdeshmukh, and Daniel E. Innis, "Peripheral Persuasion and Brand Choice," Journal of Consumer Research 19 (September 1992), 226–239.

Behavior Modification Techniques

Persuasive communications represent but one of the many weapons in the marketer's arsenal for influencing consumers' attitudes and behavior. In this section, we explore several additional techniques that have been successfully used for modifying human behavior.

Prompting

Prompting is nothing more than simply requesting some action from the person. Probably everyone who has ordered from a fast-food restaurant has encountered a prompt. Requests such as "Would you like to try our new Philly Beef and

Cheese?" or "Would you also like a side order of french fries?" are examples. Similarly, shoe salespeople will often ask the female customer preparing to purchase shoes if she is interested in a matching handbag. Prompts require the consumer to at least consider the product. Product purchase is thus more likely than it would be if the product were never considered.

Multiple Request Techniques

Whereas a simple prompt may be effective, preceding one's request with another request may be even better. That is, before asking a person what one is really interested in them doing (called the critical request), the person is first asked an initial request. **Multiple request techniques** involve making an initial request before the critical request.[66] Depending on the nature of the initial request, multiple request techniques may involve either foot-in-the-door or door-in-the-face.[67]

Foot-in-the-Door

Foot-in-the-door (FITD) represents a technique in which the initial request is a "reduced version" of the critical request. To illustrate, consider Freedman and Fraser's pioneering research that introduced FITD. The critical request involved asking homeowners to temporarily display a large, ugly sign reading "Drive Carefully" in their front yards. When homeowners were simply asked this request, 17 percent agreed to do so. Using FITD, in which an initial small request (placing a small sign advocating safe driving in their front windows) was made before the request of interest, 76 percent agreed to having the large sign in their front yard.[68]

The typical explanation offered for the FITD effect is derived from self-perception theory,[69] which maintains that individuals come to know their own attitudes, emotions, and other internal states partially from inferring them from observations of their own behavior. Getting a person to comply with an initial request produces a behavior that indicates favorableness toward the behavioral domain. For instance, agreeing to display a small sign implies that the person supports such behaviors. This favorableness results in greater compliance with a second request involving the same behavioral domain. In contrast, those asked to comply only with the second request have not undertaken the behavior generated by the first request. Consequently, they are less likely to do what is asked of them.

Marketing investigations of foot-in-the-door's usefulness for enhancing compliance have focused on behaviors such as answering surveys and donating to charity. Results have been largely supportive. Most studies have found FITD to be more effective than a straight request,[70] although a few have not.[71] The amount of delay between the first and second request, the magnitude of the requests, whether the person actually undertakes the initial request or only agrees to do so, the similarity in topics between the first and second request, and many other factors may influence the effectiveness of FITD.[72]

Door-in-the-Face

Door-in-the-face (DITF) is the flip side of foot-in-the-door. Under this approach, the person is first asked to do something of substantially greater magnitude than the critical request. In fact, this initial request is designed to be so extreme that the person will refuse. After this refusal, the second request is made. Research has shown DITF will often increase compliance relative to simply asking the second request alone.

Why does DITF work? One reason is perceptual contrast, whereby the second, small request is made to look even smaller when preceded by the initial, large request. Another reason is the **principle of reciprocity**, which essentially says that we should try to repay what others have done for us.[73] Thus, when someone makes a concession to us, we should reciprocate. The dramatic reduction between the first and second request is intended to create the perception that the requester is making a concession. In return, it is hoped that the person will reciprocate by now agreeing to the second request. Research indicates that such concession making is a necessary prerequisite for the DITF effect.[74]

The basic DITF strategy of large-then-smaller-request sequence underlies the retail store sales practice of "talking the top of the line."[75] The shopper is first shown the deluxe model. If the shopper buys this model, so much the better. If not, the salesperson can counteroffer with a less expensive model. When Brunswick used this approach by first showing customers the most expensive pool table, followed by the rest of the product line, the average sale was more than $1,000. However, starting customers with the least expensive table and working up produced an average sale of $550.[76]

The Principle of Reciprocity

As just noted, the principle of reciprocity provides a potential point of leverage for those attempting to influence behavior.[77] Religious groups, including the Hare Krishnas, have used this technique to enhance compliance with their requests for donations by first offering the person some gift, such as a flower. It also applies to marketing. Many charitable organizations often include a small gift in their direct mailings to increase the odds of consumers returning the favor in the form of a contribution (see Figure 16.9). Food companies often hire someone to stand in supermarket aisles and offer shoppers a taste of the product. The hope is that consumers will find it difficult to accept the sample without feeling a sense of obligation to buy the product. Similarly, the Amway Corp. instructs their salespeople to leave product samples with prospective customers for a couple of days. When the salesperson returns to collect the unused portion of the samples, reciprocity should lead consumers to feel more compelled to make a purchase.[78]

Figure 16.9   The Blinded Veterans Organization May Evoke Reciprocity by Offering Free Address Labels When Soliciting Contributions

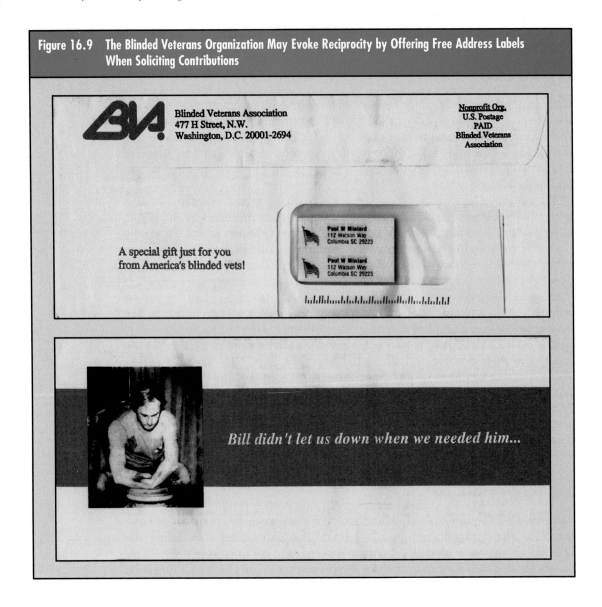

The Role of Commitment

The very act of making a commitment can have a strong influence on subsequent behavior. This effect is aptly demonstrated by research asking people to estimate the length of various lines.[79] One group was required to write down their estimates, sign their names, and turn the form in to the experimenter. A second group wrote their estimates on a "magic" writing pad that could be erased before others could see what they had written. A final group kept their judgments in their mind.

Participants were then given new evidence that challenged their initial estimates. The group who had turned in their original estimates to the experimenter showed the least amount of opinion change. The simple act of publicly committing themselves made them less willing to change their minds. Interestingly, the second group who made a private commitment also displayed less change than those who only made a mental note of their original estimates. Thus, the very act of writing something down, even though it was not made publicly available, caused a sense of commitment that carried over.

Gaining a person's commitment to an opinion or action is a very good way of enhancing the odds that he or she will behave in a consistent manner. Gaining commitment is the key element of the unethical "lowballing" procedure.[80] A car dealer, for example, might use this procedure by offering customers a great deal to gain their commitment to buying the car. Once the customer has agreed to do so, the deal is then changed. This can be done in a variety of ways. The salesperson might claim that he or she "forgot" to include the price of some option. Another story line is that the boss has canceled the deal because "we would be losing money." Some customers may walk away. Unfortunately, others will not. The act of committing to the purchase will lead them to complete the transaction despite this change in terms.

Earlier, we noted that the simple act of writing something down can enhance one's commitment. This observation helps explain the attractiveness of contests that require consumers to submit essays on "Why I like this product." Door-to-door sales companies have also discovered the magic of written commitment. They are able to reduce their cancellation rates (that is, customers who void the contract during the "cooling-off" period guaranteed by law) by simply having the customer, rather than the salesperson, complete the sales agreement form.[81]

Labeling

Labeling involves attaching some description to a person, such as "You are kind." Labels presumably lead people to view themselves in the manner implied by the label. This, in turn, should increase the likelihood that they will undertake behaviors that are consistent with the label. Research in this area has been very supportive across several behavioral domains, including voting, littering, and charitable actions.[82] However, the influence of labeling may be fairly short-lived. In one study, labeling had an effect on voting behavior that occurred 1 week after the label was attached but not on voting behavior 8 months later.[83]

Labeling appears to hold considerable promise, although further research is needed, particularly with respect to its effects on purchase behavior. Labeling could prove to be very useful in the realm of personal selling. The encyclopedia salesperson might describe prospective buyers with children as "concerned parents." Similarly, charitable organizations might wish to label potential donors as "generous and compassionate." Research does support the usefulness of advertising as a mechanism for labeling consumers.[84]

Incentives

Incentives encompass a broad range of promotional tools, including price discounts, premiums, contests, sweepstakes, rebates, and coupons. Incentives typically represent an important component of the overall product-promotion strategy. Indeed, for some companies, incentives are a vital ingredient to their success. Such is the case for Publishers Clearing House. Each year, the company mails forms to millions of consumers in which they can order magazines. Even if consumers don't order anything, they can still complete and return the form for a chance to win millions of dollars in the company's famous sweepstakes drawing. Entries number in the tens of millions, with about half of them containing subscription orders. There is little doubt that, without the allure of the sweepstakes, many consumers would not even bother opening the envelope, let alone place an order.

A similar success story can be told by General Motors in gaining entry into the highly competitive credit card market. As indicated by the ad appearing in Figure 16.10, consumers can earn discounts for buying GM vehicles when they use this card for making other purchases. Household Bank, issuer of the GM card, says accounts increased an incredible 86 percent between 1992 and 1993.[85]

Packaged goods manufacturers often rely on incentives in the form of coupons for influencing sales, distributing nearly 300 billion coupons in 1993.[86] To better understand how coupons affect purchasing behavior, consider Figure 16.11, which summarizes the results of four new product introduction tests.[87] The influence of coupons is reflected by comparing the purchase behaviors of those consumers who were sent coupons versus those who were not sent coupons.

The top graph in Figure 16.11 represents the findings involving initial or trial purchasing. As can be seen, coupons had a very strong effect on trial purchasing. More than twice as many households receiving a coupon made a trial purchase compared with those households not receiving the coupon.

What may come as a surprise are the findings involving repeat purchasing. The bottom graph in Figure 16.11 indicates that coupon-induced triers were *less* likely to repurchase the product than those who tried the product without the coupon inducement. Does this finding argue against the use of coupons? Not necessarily. In the present situation, coupons yielded a penetration level of 3.7 percent (trial rate of 15.1 percent times the repurchase rate of 24.8 percent), compared with a level of 2.3 percent when coupons were not used. The lower repurchase rate of coupon-induced triers is more than offset by the substantial boost in trial purchasing when coupons were used. This need not always be the case. Furthermore, even when coupons provide greater market penetration, this increase must be evaluated in terms of overall profitability. One company discovered, for example, that a 50-cent coupon on a tube of toothpaste yielded a $348,000 loss. However, a 40-cent coupon for the same item provided $147,000 in profits.[88]

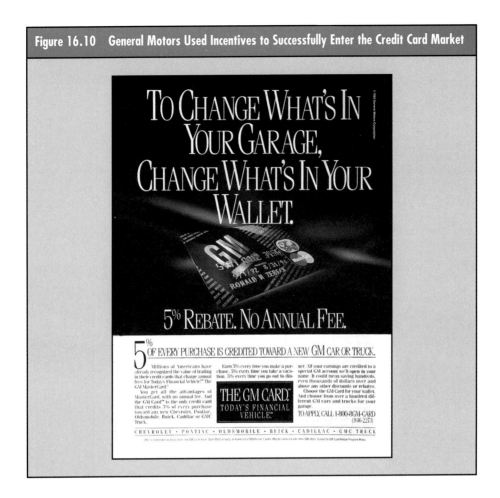

Figure 16.10   General Motors Used Incentives to Successfully Enter the Credit Card Market

Consistent with the repeat purchase results presented in Figure 16.11, a common finding in the literature is that repurchase rates are typically lower after a promotional purchase (a purchase induced by an incentive) than a nonpromotional purchase.[89] Why does this occur? One explanation is that consumers who purchase a product because of some incentive are less likely to attribute the purchase to favorable product attitudes than consumers who purchase without an incentive. As a result, consumers might hold less favorable product attitudes, which, in turn, could lead to lower loyalty and repeat purchase rates.[90] However, a recent test of this possibility did not find incentives to have a detrimental effect on product attitudes.[91]

Alternatively, lower repurchase rates after promotional purchases may have little to do with reduced attitudes and loyalty. Rather, it may simply be a reflection of the type of customers that are attracted by incentives.[92] There is a segment of consumers whose purchase decisions are dictated by whatever brand is

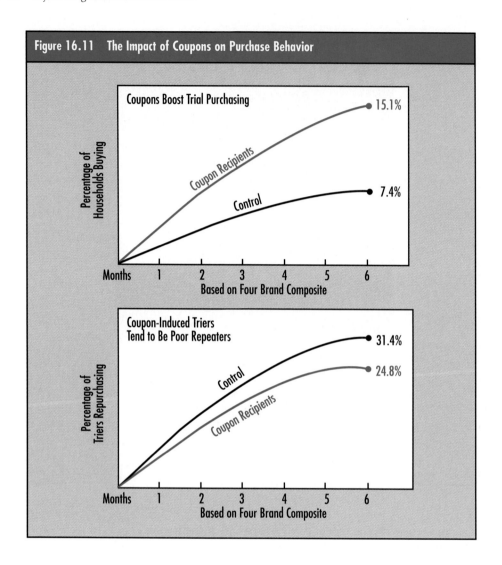

Figure 16.11 The Impact of Coupons on Purchase Behavior

offering the best deal. They will buy a given brand only as long as it provides the best deal. Since deals come and go, so do they.

Single versus Multiple Incentives

"Single-shot" incentives may often be inadequate for modifying long-run behavior. Rather, a series of incentives may be necessary to produce more lasting effects on purchasing behavior. Instead of offering consumers a single coupon, it may be more productive to provide a series of coupons to be used on successive purchase occasions. Each time customers purchase the product they become more accustomed to buying and consuming it. Hopefully, consumers will continue to do so once the incentive is removed.

The Coca-Cola promotional program used for introducing its new Coke formula was based on a multiple-application approach. Consumers were given both free samples (single cans of the product) and a set of coupons. The coupon with the largest discount had the earliest expiration date, whereas the smallest discount coupon had the latest expiration date. Note that this same basic strategy of declining coupon size is reflected in the material appearing in Figure 16.12.

This decline in the size of the discount is very desirable. It enhances the proportion of reinforcement received from the product versus that stemming from the coupon. The gradual reduction also increases the similarity of each purchase to the behavior ultimately desired (buying at regular price).

Potential Problems with Incentives

As you have seen, incentives can be very effective in boosting sales. Even so, this increase in sales may come at the expense of a company's bottom line. Kraft

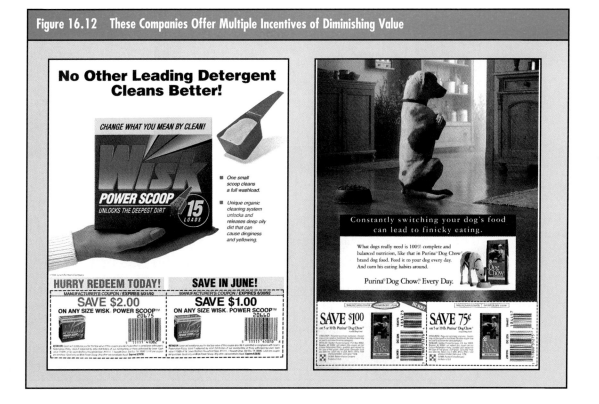

Figure 16.12   These Companies Offer Multiple Incentives of Diminishing Value

USA, for example, discovered that seven of every ten boxes of its macaroni and cheese sold during one of its promotional campaigns would have been sold *without* the promotion.[93] Unless the profits made on the incremental sales due to coupons covered the reduced profit on the remaining sales, Kraft lost money.

This same basic point can be made for Chrysler's rebate program for its minivans (see Figure 16.13). In the 2 months before the rebate, Chrysler was averaging nearly 30,000 sales per month. When the company began offering $1,000 rebates in mid-December, sales began to climb. In January, the last month rebates were offered, Chrysler sold nearly 64,000 minivans. Notice how the General Motors' minivan sales remained quite stable during this time, suggesting that the rebates had little impact on Chrysler's competitor. Where, then, did the increased Chrysler sales during December and January come from?

Perhaps these sales came from consumers who would have purchased a vehicle other than a minivan without the rebate. It is also possible that at least

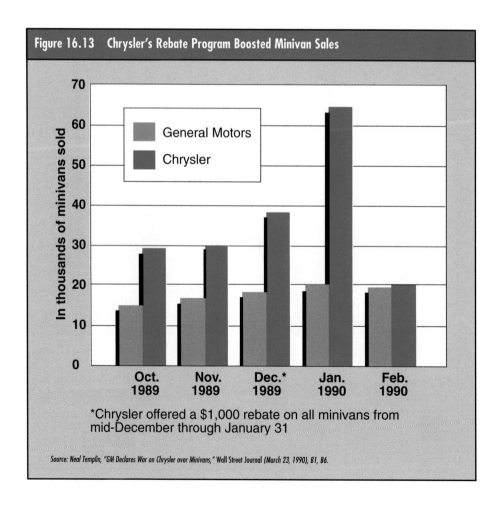

Figure 16.13   Chrysler's Rebate Program Boosted Minivan Sales

*Chrysler offered a $1,000 rebate on all minivans from mid-December through January 31

Source: Neal Templin, "GM Declares War on Chrysler over Minivans," Wall Street Journal (March 23, 1990), B1, B6.

some of these sales represented "accelerated" purchases. Consumers who were planning on buying a Chrysler minivan later in the year may have moved up their purchase plans to take advantage of the rebate offer. The fact that sales after the rebates ended were substantially below the sales levels before the rebates being offered is a strong indication that many consumers purchased vans earlier than they would have. Each of these accelerated purchases represents a loss in profits that must be weighed against the profits generated by incremental sales in evaluating the incentive program's profitability.[94] Another potential problem with incentives is that, if used too often, consumers may become conditioned to buy based simply on whatever product is offering the best deal (see Consumer in Focus 16.4). As Rothschild and Gaidis[95] point out,

> Purchase may become contingent upon the presence of a promotional tool. Removal of the promotion may lead to the extinction of purchase behavior. If long-term behavior toward the product is desired, promotional tools should not overshadow the product. In a marketing situation, it is paramount that reinforcement for purchase be derived primarily from the product, lest purchase become contingent upon a never ending succession of consumer deals.

Consumer in Focus 16.4

Consumers Wait for the Rebate

According to Jay Lewis, cruise industry consultant and president of Market Scope, "The auto industry taught the consumer to wait for a rebate. The cruise industry has taught the consumer to wait for the discount. You figure if you wait till the last possible moment, you get the best possible deal. That is how the consumer is thinking today."

And for good reason. Discounting in the cruise industry is averaging around 30 percent, with some cruise lines offering savings in the neighborhood of 50 percent.

But will consumers become conditioned to the lower rates? "I hope not," says Carol Morse, manager of Travel Is Fun. "Like the airlines, [cruise lines] can't keep undercutting their profit margin."

But once consumers have become conditioned to deals, weaning them is no easy matter. Automakers have been trying for several years to reduce their dependency on incentive programs, with little success. Ford, for example, tried to eliminate its direct-to-customer rebates in December 1990. Instead of offering discounts to consumers, Ford copied Japanese automakers, which typically offer discounts only to dealers.

The dealers are then free to pass on all the money, or use some of it to increase advertising, or keep some to boost their own profits. But the strategy didn't work. Ford was forced to resume customer incentives five months later because of sluggish sales. "In a way, incentive programs are like hard drugs," asserts Christopher Cedergren, an auto analyst at Auto Pacific Group Inc. "Once you get on, it's hard to get off."

Source: Excerpted in part from Krystal Miller, "Car Prices Start Turning Around as Firms Cut Rebates," Wall Street Journal (February 14, 1992), B1, B6; and Philip Stelly, Jr., "Winds of War Knock Wind Out of Sales for the Cruise Industry," Adweek (March 4, 1991), 2–3.

Summary

This chapter has attempted to convey some sense of the richness and complexity of the vast literature concerning how one might influence attitudes and behavior. A substantial amount of attention has been given to understanding persuasion through communication. From an information-processing perspective, persuasion depends on the cognitive (thoughts) and affective (feelings) responses that occur during message processing. These responses, in turn, are affected by several communication (such as the message source and claims) and consumer (including such things as the consumer's motivation, knowledge, and prior attitudes) characteristics.

According to the ELM, persuasion can be characterized as following one of two basic routes. Under the central route, consumers rationally evaluate the position advocated in a message. Consequently, the strength of message claims will determine the amount of acceptance. Persuasion in the absence of issue-relevant thinking is called the peripheral route. Other communication elements (peripheral cues) now become important determinants of persuasion.

Characteristics of both the consumer and the product should be taken into account in developing communication strategy. Consumers' motivation, knowledge, arousal, moods, personality traits, and existing attitudes can strongly affect the impact of persuasive communications. Similarly, the product's life cycle stage, the desired positioning, and the product's performance relative to competition will play major roles in shaping such activities.

In addition to persuasive communication, consumers' attitudes and behavior can be influenced through any one of several behavior modification techniques. Single (prompts) and multiple (foot-in-the-door and door-in-the-face) requests can be effective devices for shaping behavior. Evoking the principle of reciprocity (through a free gift) or commitment ("why I like this product" contests) can also be very useful in modifying behavior. Incentives such as coupons and rebates are often used by marketers to encourage purchase behavior.

Review and Discussion Questions

1. What is meant by central and peripheral routes to persuasion?

2. When is the source most likely to enhance the persuasive power of an advertisement?

3. Suppose you were faced with the choice between an ad that attempts to create favorable attitudes by making several strong claims about the product versus an ad devoid of such claims but filled with attractive visuals and favorable music. How might your preference for using a particular ad depend on (a) consumer's involvement at the time of ad exposure, (b) consumer's product knowledge at the time of ad exposure, and (c) the product's performance relative to competition?

4. A pretest of two alternative commercials found that consumers liked commercial A better than commercial B but that commercial B produced more favorable product

attitudes. Why might this difference occur? Which commercial would you select, and why?

5. In a laboratory study, it is discovered that a foreign make of automobile is regarded more favorably when advertising messages feature positive selling points as well as the fact that problems have existed in the past with respect to brake fade, door leaks and rattles, faulty ignition, and spark plug fouling. Would you, as the director of advertising research, recommend that this company use a two-sided campaign?

6. In the chapter, we noted that consumers' skepticism of advertising can reduce advertising effectiveness. How might advertisers modify their communications to minimize the adverse influence of consumer skepticism?

7. A local charitable organization is planning its annual door-to-door fund-raising campaign. What suggestions would you make as to how the organization might enhance the effectiveness of its solicitors?

8. A recent study revealed that 20 percent of target households receiving a discount coupon tried the product compared with a 10 percent trial rate among those target households not receiving the coupon. Repeat-purchase rates, however, were far greater among noncoupon trier households (30 percent) relative to coupon-induced triers (15 percent). First, how can you explain this pattern of results? Second, do these results support the use of coupons as a means for increasing the customer base? Justify your position.

9. Consider the following proposals for using price-off coupons during the market introduction of a new food snack purchased weekly:

	Week			
Proposal	1	2	3	4
A	50% off	No coupon	No coupon	No coupon
B	50% off	50% off	50% off	50% off
C	50% off	35% off	20% off	5% off
D	5% off	20% off	35% off	50% off

Under proposal A, for instance, consumers would be supplied with a 50 percent discount coupon in the first week but no coupons in the second, third, and fourth weeks. Which proposal is likely to generate the greatest number of customers in week 5 when coupons are no longer available? Why?

Endnotes

1. For summaries of the ELM and associated literature, see Richard E. Petty and John T. Cacioppo, *Communication and Persuasion: Central and Peripheral Routes to Attitude Change* (New York: Springer-Verlag, 1986); and Richard E. Petty and John T.

Cacioppo, "The Elaboration Likelihood Model of Persuasion," in Leonard Berkowitz, ed., *Advances in Experimental Social Psychology* 19 (New York: Academic Press, 1986), 123–205. A similar conceptualization is offered by Shelly Chaiken, "Heuristic Versus Systematic Information Processing and the Use of Source Versus Message Cues in Persuasion," *Journal of Personality and Social Psychology* 39 (November 1980), 752–766. Also see Alice H. Eagly and Shelly Chaiken, *The Psychology of Attitudes* (Fort Worth, Tex. Harcourt Brace Jovanovich, 1993).

2. For research and critiques beyond those cited in the preceding endnote, see Charles S. Areni and Richard J. Lutz, "The Role of Argument Quality in the Elaboration Likelihood Model," in Michael J. Houston, ed., *Advances in Consumer Research* 15 (Provo, Utah: Association for Consumer Research, 1988), 197–201; Mary J. Bitner and Carl Obermiller, "The Elaboration Likelihood Model: Limitations and Extensions in Marketing," in Elizabeth C. Hirschman and Morris B. Holbrook, eds., *Advances in Consumer Research* 12 (Ann Arbor, Mich.: Association for Consumer Research, 1985), 420–425; Curt Haugvedt, Richard E. Petty, John T. Cacioppo, and Theresa Steidley, "Personality and Ad Effectiveness: Exploring the Utility of Need for Cognition," in Michael J. Houston, ed., *Advances in Consumer Research* 15 (Provo, Utah: Association for Consumer Research, 1988), 209–212; Lynn R. Kahle and Pamela M. Homer, "Physical Attractiveness of the Celebrity Endorser: A Social Adaptation Perspective," *Journal of Consumer Research* 11 (March 1985), 954–961; Scott B. MacKenzie and Richard A. Spreng, "How Does Motivation Moderate the Impact of Central and Peripheral Processing on Brand Attitudes and Intentions?" *Journal of Consumer Research* 18 (March 1992), 519–529; Joan Meyers-Levy and Durairaj Maheswaran, "When Timing Matters: The Influence of Temporal Distance on Consumers' Affective and Persuasive Responses," *Journal of Consumer Research* 19 (December 1992), 424–433; Joan Meyers-Levy and Laura Peracchio, "Getting an Angle in Advertising: The Effect of Camera Angle on Product Evaluations," *Journal of Marketing Research* 29 (November 1992), 454–461; Paul W. Miniard, Peter R. Dickson, and Kenneth R. Lord, "Some Central and Peripheral Thoughts on the Routes to Persuasion," in Michael J. Houston, ed., *Advances in Consumer Research* 15 (Provo, Utah: Association for Consumer Research, 1988), 204–208; Paul W. Miniard, Sunil Bhatla, Kenneth R. Lord, Peter R. Dickson, and H. Rao Unnava, "Picture-based Persuasion Processes and the Moderating Role of Involvement," *Journal of Consumer Research* 18 (June 1991), 92–107; Richard E. Petty and John T. Cacioppo, "The Effects of Involvement on Responses to Argument Quantity and Quality: Central and Peripheral Routes to Persuasion," *Journal of Personality and Social Psychology* 46 (January 1984), 69–81; Richard E. Petty, John T. Cacioppo, and David Schumann, "Central and Peripheral Routes to Advertising Effectiveness: The Moderating Role of Involvement," *Journal of Consumer Research* 10 (September 1983), 135–146; S. Ratneshwar and Shelly Chaiken, "Comprehension's Role in Persuasion: The Case of Its Moderating Effect on the Persuasive Impact of Source Cues," *Journal of Consumer Research* 18 (June 1991), 52–62; and Richard F. Yalch and Rebecca Elmore-Yalch, "The Effect of Numbers on the Route to Persuasion," *Journal of Consumer Research* 11 (June 1984), 522–527.

3. Petty, Cacioppo, and Schumann, "Central and Peripheral Routes to Advertising Effectiveness."

4. For a general review, see Brian Sternthal, Lynn Phillips, and Ruby Dholakia, "The Persuasive Effect of Source Credibility: A Situational Analysis," *Public Opinion Quarterly* 42 (Fall 1978), 285–314; and Brian Sternthal and C. Samuel Craig, *Consumer Behavior: An Information Processing Perspective* (Englewood Cliffs, N.J.: Prentice-Hall, 1982), 295–304. Also see Danny L. Moore, Douglas Hausknecht, and Kanchana Thamodaran, "Time Compression, Response Opportunity, and Persuasion," *Journal of Consumer Research* 13 (June 1986), 85–99; Arch G. Woodside and J. William Davenport, Jr., "The Effect of Salesman Similarity and Expertise on Consumer Purchasing Behavior," *Journal of Marketing Research* 11 (May 1974), 198–202; and Chenghuan Wu and David R. Shaffer, "Susceptibility to Persuasive Appeals as a Function of Source Credibility and Prior Experience with the Attitude Object," *Journal of Personality and Social Psychology* 52 (1987), 677–688. We should note that less credible sources have on occasion been found to induce more persuasion. See Robert R. Harmon and Kenneth A. Coney, "The Persuasive Effects of Source Credibility in Buy and Lease Situations," *Journal of Marketing Research* 19 (May 1982), 255–260; and Brian Sternthal, Ruby Dholakia, and Clark Leavitt, "The Persuasive Effect of Source Credibility: Tests of Cognitive Response," *Journal of Consumer Research* 4 (March 1978), 252–260.

5. Michael J. Baker and Gilbert A. Churchill, Jr., "The Impact of Physically Attractive Models on Advertising Evaluations," *Journal of Marketing Research* 14 (November 1977), 538–555; Shelly Chaiken, "Communicator Physical Attractiveness and Persuasion," *Journal of Personality and Social Psychology* 37 (August 1979), 752–766; and Kahle and Homer, "Physical Attractiveness of the Celebrity Endorser."

6. Kahle and Homer, "Physical Attractiveness of the Celebrity Endorser."

7. Petty, Cacioppo, and Schumann, "Central and Peripheral Routes to Advertising Effectiveness."

8. Rohit Deshpande and Douglas M. Stayman, "A Tale of Two Cities: Distinctiveness Theory and Advertising Effectiveness," *Journal of Marketing Research* 31 (February 1994), 57–64; Woodside and Davenport, "The Effect of Salesman Similarity and Expertise on Consumer Purchasing Behavior."

9. Grant McCracken, "Who Is the Celebrity Endorser? Cultural Foundations of the Endorsement Process," *Journal of Consumer Research* 16 (December 1989), 310–321.

10. McCracken, "Who Is the Celebrity Endorser?"; Mary Walker, Lynn Langmeyer, and Daniel Langmeyer, "Celebrity Endorsers: Do You Get What You Pay For?" *Journal of Consumer Marketing* 9 (Spring 1992), 69–76.

11. Iris Cohen Selinger, "Celebrity Overexposure," *Adweek* (March 4, 1991), 12–13.

12. Ibid.

13. David Olson, "The Characteristics of High-Trial New-Product Advertising," *Journal of Advertising Research* 25 (October–November 1985), 11–16.

14. See William K. Darley and Robert E. Smith, "Advertising Claim Objectivity: Antecedents and Effects," *Journal of Marketing* 57 (October 1993), 100–113; Julie A. Edell and Richard Staelin, "The Information Processing of Pictures in Print

Advertisements," *Journal of Consumer Research* 10 (June 1983), 45–61; Gary T. Ford, Darlene B. Smith, and John L. Swasy, "Consumer Skepticism of Advertising Claims: Testing Hypotheses from Economics of Information," *Journal of Consumer Research* 16 (March 1990), 433–441; and Morris B. Holbrook, "Beyond Attitude Structure: Toward the Informational Determinants of Attitude," *Journal of Marketing Research* 15 (November 1978), 545–556.

15. Ford, Smith, and Swasy, "Consumer Skepticism of Advertising Claims."

16. James M. Munch, Gregory W. Boller, and John L. Swasy, "The Effects of Argument Structure and Affective Tagging on Product Attitude Formation," *Journal of Consumer Research* 20 (September 1993), 294–302.

17. Petty and Cacioppo, "The Effects of Involvement on Responses to Argument Quantity and Quality." Also see Joseph W. Alba and Howard Marmorstein, "The Effects of Frequency Knowledge on Consumer Decision Making," *Journal of Consumer Research* 14 (June 1987), 14–25.

18. For research on message sidedness, see Linda L. Golden and Mark I. Alpert, "Comparative Analysis of the Relative Effectiveness of One- and Two-Sided Communication for Contrasting Products," *Journal of Advertising* 16 (1987), 18–25; Michael A. Kamins and Lawrence J. Marks, "Advertising Puffery: The Impact of Using Two-Sided Claims on Product Attitude and Purchase Intention," *Journal of Advertising* 16 (1987), 6–15; Michael A. Kamins and Henry Assael, "Two-Sided Versus One-Sided Appeals: A Cognitive Perspective on Argumentation, Source Derogation, and the Effect of Disconfirming Trial on Belief Change," *Journal of Marketing Research* 24 (February 1987), 29–39; and Cornelia Pechmann, "Predicting When Two-Sided Ads Will Be More Effective than One-Sided Ads: The Role of Correlational and Correspondent Inferences," *Journal of Marketing Research* 29 (November 1992), 441–453.

19. Cornelia Droge and Rene Y. Darmon, "Associative Positioning Strategies through Comparative Advertising: Attribute Versus Overall Similarity Approaches," *Journal of Marketing Research* 24 (November 1987), 377–388; Gerald J. Gorn and Charles B. Weinberg, "The Impact of Comparative Advertising on Perception and Attitude: Some Positive Findings," *Journal of Consumer Research* 11 (September 1984), 719–727; Cornelia Pechmann and S. Ratneshwar, "The Use of Comparative Advertising for Brand Positioning: Association Versus Differentiation," *Journal of Consumer Research* 18 (September 1991), 145–160; Cornelia Pechmann and David W. Stewart, "The Effects of Comparative Advertising on Attention, Memory, and Purchase Intentions," *Journal of Consumer Research* 17 (September 1990), 180–191; and Mita Sujan and Christine Dekleva, "Product Categorization and Inference Making: Some Implications for Comparative Advertising," *Journal of Consumer Research* 14 (December 1987), 372–378.

20. Z. S. Demirdijian, "Sales Effectiveness of Comparative Advertising: An Experimental Field Investigation," *Journal of Consumer Research* 10 (December 1983), 362–364.

21. A brief review of these findings is presented in Gorn and Weinberg, "The Impact of Comparative Advertising on Perception and Attitude." Note, however, that

research reporting equivalent persuasion between comparative and noncomparative advertising may be limited by measures that are insufficiently sensitive to the persuasive impact of comparative advertising. See Paul W. Miniard, Randall L. Rose, Michael J. Barone, and Kenneth C. Manning, "On the Need for Relative Measurements in Assessing Comparative Advertising Effects," *Journal of Advertising* 22 (September 1993), 41–57; and Randall L. Rose, Paul W. Miniard, Michael J. Barone, Kenneth C. Manning, and Brian D. Till, "When Persuasion Goes Undetected: The Case of Comparative Advertising," *Journal of Marketing Research* 30 (August 1993), 315–330.

22. Surendra N. Singh and Catherine A. Cole, "The Effects of Length, Content, and Repetition on Television Commercial Effectiveness," *Journal of Marketing Research* 30 (February 1993), 91–104. For additional citations of research on the role of affective responses in persuasion, see Endnote 70 in Chapter 14.

23. "Emotional Response Is Evoked for March of Dimes Campaign," *Marketing News* 20 (November 21, 1986), 6.

24. Mita Sujan, James R. Bettman, and Hans Baumgartner, "Influencing Consumer Judgments Using Autobiographical Memories: A Self-Referencing Perspective," *Journal of Marketing Research* 30 (November 1993), 422–436.

25. Michael L. Ray and Rajeev Batra, "Emotion and Persuasion in Advertising: What We Do and Don't Know about Affect," in Richard P. Bagozzi and Alice M. Tybout, eds., *Advances in Consumer Research* 10 (Ann Arbor, Mich.: Association for Consumer Research, 1983), 543–548.

26. For research illustrating how executional elements in the form of pictures can influence consumers' product beliefs, see Miniard, Bhatla, Lord, Dickson, and Unnava, "Picture-Based Persuasion Processes and the Moderating Role of Involvement"; and Andrew A. Mitchell and Jerry C. Olson, "Are Product Attribute Beliefs the Only Mediators of Advertising Effects on Brand Attitudes?" *Journal of Marketing Research* 18 (August 1981), 318–332.

27. "Armstrong Retreads 'Tuffy the Rhino,'" *Marketing News* 21 (November 20, 1987), 16.

28. Raymond Serafin, "Chevy '80s 'Heartbeat' Yields to '90s Value Theme," *Advertising Age* (September 13, 1993), 60.

29. See, for example, Miniard, Bhatla, Lord, Dickson, and Unnava, "Picture-Based Persuasion Processes and the Moderating Role of Involvement"; and Andrew A. Mitchell, "The Effect of Verbal and Visual Components of Advertisements on Brand Attitudes and Attitude toward the Advertisement," *Journal of Consumer Research* 13 (June 1986), 12–24.

30. Interest in this area was largely sparked by the following two articles: Mitchell and Olson, "Are Product Attribute Beliefs the Only Mediators of Advertising Effects on Brand Attitudes?"; and Terence Shimp, "Attitude toward the Ad as a Mediator of Consumer Brand Choice," *Journal of Advertising* 10 (1981), 9–15. Additional research can be found in Amitava Chattopadhyay and Prakash Nedungadi, "Does Attitude toward the Ad Endure? The Moderating Effects of Attention and

Delay," *Journal of Consumer Research* 19 (June 1992), 26–33; Stephen P. Brown and Douglas M. Stayman, "Antecedents and Consequences of Attitude toward the Ad: A Meta-analysis," *Journal of Consumer Research* 19 (June 1992), 34–51; Marian C. Burke and Julie A. Edell, "Ad Reactions over Time: Capturing Changes in the Real World," *Journal of Consumer Research* 13 (June 1986), 114–118; Scot Burton and Donald R. Lichtenstein, "The Effect of Ad Claims and Ad Context on Attitude toward the Advertisement," *Journal of Advertising* 17 (1988) 3–11; Dena S. Cox and Anthony D. Cox, "What Does Familiarity Breed? Complexity as a Moderator of Repetition Effects in Advertisement Evaluation," *Journal of Consumer Research* 15 (June 1988), 111–116; Cornelia Droge, "Shaping the Route to Attitude Change: Central Versus Peripheral Processing through Comparative Versus Noncomparative Advertising," *Journal of Marketing Research* 26 (May 1989), 193–204; Julie A. Edell and Marian Chapman Burke, "The Power of Feelings in Understanding Advertising Effects," *Journal of Consumer Research* 14 (December 1987), 421–433; Meryl P. Gardner, "Does Attitude toward the Ad Affect Brand Attitude under a Brand Evaluation Set?" *Journal of Marketing Research* 22 (May 1985), 192–198; Larry G. Gresham and Terence A. Shimp, "Attitude toward the Advertisement and Brand Attitudes: A Classical Conditioning Perspective," *Journal of Advertising* 14 (1985), 10–17; Pamela M. Homer, "The Mediating Role of Attitude toward the Ad: Some Additional Evidence," *Journal of Marketing Research* 27 (February 1990), 78–86; Scott B. MacKenzie and Richard J. Lutz, "An Empirical Examination of Structural Antecedents of Attitude toward the Ad in an Advertising Pretesting Context," *Journal of Marketing* 53 (April 1989), 48–65; Scott B. MacKenzie, Richard J. Lutz, and George E. Belch, "The Role of Attitude toward the Ad as a Mediator of Advertising Effectiveness: A Test of Competing Explanations," *Journal of Marketing Research* 23 (May 1986), 130–143; Thomas J. Madden, Chris T. Allen, and Jacquelyn L. Twible, "Attitude toward the Ad: An Assessment of Diverse Measurement Indices under Different Processing 'Sets,'" *Journal of Marketing Research* 25 (August 1988), 242–252; Paul W. Miniard, Sunil Bhatla, and Randall L. Rose, "On the Formation and Relationship of Ad and Brand Attitudes: An Experimental and Causal Analysis," *Journal of Marketing Research* 27 (August 1990), 290–303; Mitchell, "The Effect of Verbal and Visual Components of Advertisements on Brand Attitudes and Attitude toward the Advertisement"; Banwari Mittal, "The Relative Roles of Brand Beliefs and Attitude toward the Ad as Mediators of Brand Attitude: A Second Look," *Journal of Marketing Research* 27 (May 1990), 209–219; Whan C. Park and S. Mark Young, "Consumer Response to Television Commercials: The Impact of Involvement and Background Music on Brand Attitude Formation," *Journal of Marketing Research* 23 (February 1986), 11–24; Singh and Cole, "The Effects of Length, Content, and Repetition on Television Commercial Effectiveness"; and Robert E. Smith, "Integrating Information from Advertising and Trial: Processes and Effects on Consumer Response to Product Information," *Journal of Marketing Research* 30 (May 1993), 204–219.

31. For a discussion of when ad liking may be more important in determining persuasion, see Larry Percy and John R. Rossiter, "A Model of Brand Awareness and Brand Attitude Advertising Strategies," *Psychology and Marketing* 9 (July–August 1992), 263–274.

32. John R. Rossiter and Larry Percy, *Advertising and Promotion Management* (New York: McGraw-Hill, 1987), 235.

33. J. Lee McCullough and Thomas Ostrom, "Repetition of Highly Similar Messages and Attitude Change," *Journal of Applied Psychology* 59 (June 1974), 395–397; and Carl Obermiller, "Varieties of Mere Exposure: The Effects of Processing Style and Repetition on Affective Response," *Journal of Consumer Research* 12 (June 1985), 17–30.

34. John T. Cacioppo and Richard E. Petty, "Central and Peripheral Routes to Persuasion: The Role of Message Repetition," in Linda F. Alwitt and Andrew A. Mitchell, eds., *Psychological Processes and Advertising Effects* (Hillsdale, N.J.: Lawrence Erlbaum, 1985), 91–111; and Singh and Cole,598 "The Effects of Length, Content, and Repetition on Television Commercial Effectiveness."

35. George E. Belch, "The Effects of Television Commercial Repetition on Cognitive Response and Message Acceptance," *Journal of Consumer Research* 9 (June 1982), 56–65; Arno J. Rethans, John L. Swasy, and Lawrence J. Marks, "Effects of Television Commercial Repetition, Receiver Knowledge, and Commercial Length: A Test of the Two-Factor Model," *Journal of Marketing Research* 23 (February 1986), 50–61; and Singh and Cole, "The Effects of Length, Content, and Repetition on Television Commercial Effectiveness."

36. John T. Cacioppo and Richard E. Petty, "Effects of Message Repetition and Position on Cognitive Response, Recall, and Persuasion," *Journal of Personality and Social Psychology* 37 (January 1979), 97–109; Bobby J. Calder and Brian Sternthal, "Television Commercial Wearout: An Information Processing View," *Journal of Marketing Research* 17 (May 1980), 173–186; and Gerald J. Gorn and Marvin E. Goldberg, "Children's Responses to Repetitive Television Commercials," *Journal of Consumer Research* 6 (March 1980), 421–424.

37. Cacioppo and Petty, "Central and Peripheral Routes to Persuasion." For discussions of alternative explanations, see Calder and Sternthal, "Television Commercial Wearout"; Obermiller, "Varieties of Mere Exposure"; Rethans, Swasy, and Marks, "Effects of Television Commercial Repetition, Receiver Knowledge, and Commercial Length"; Alan G. Sawyer, "Repetition, Cognitive Response and Persuasion," in Richard E. Petty, Thomas Ostrom, and Timothy Brock, eds., *Cognitive Responses in Persuasion* (Hillsdale, N.J.: Lawrence Erlbaum, 1981), 237–261; and Robert B. Zajonc and Hazel Markus, "Affective and Cognitive Factors in Preference," *Journal of Consumer Research* 9 (September 1982), 123–131.

38. Also see Punam Anand and Brian Sternthal, "Ease of Message Processing as a Moderator of Repetition Effects in Advertising," *Journal of Marketing Research* 27 (August 1990), 345–353; Rajeev Batra and Michael L. Ray, "Situational Effects of Advertising Repetition: The Moderating Influence of Motivation, Ability, and Opportunity to Respond," *Journal of Consumer Research* 12 (March 1986), 432–445; and Moore, Hausknecht, and Thamodaran, "Time Compression, Response Opportunity, and Persuasion."

39. For a dissenting point of view, see Belch, "The Effects of Television Commercial Repetition on Cognitive Response and Message Acceptance"; and Rethans, Swasy,

and Marks, "Effects of Television Commercial Repetition, Receiver Knowledge, and Commercial Length."

40. Cacioppo and Petty, "Effects of Message Repetition and Position on Cognitive Response, Recall, and Persuasion."

41. Cacioppo and Petty, "Central and Peripheral Routes to Persuasion."

42. Rethans, Swasy, and Marks, "Effects of Television Commercial Repetition, Receiver Knowledge, and Commercial Length."

43. Petty, Cacioppo, and Schumann, "Central and Peripheral Routes to Advertising Effectiveness." Also see Durairaj Maheswaran and Joan Meyers-Levy, "The Influence of Message Framing and Issue Involvement," *Journal of Marketing Research* 27 (August 1990), 361–367; Gerald J. Gorn, "The Effects of Music in Advertising on Choice Behavior: A Classical Conditioning Approach," *Journal of Marketing* 46 (Winter 1982), 94–101; Alan G. Sawyer and Daniel J. Howard, "Effects of Omitting Conclusions in Advertisements to Involved and Uninvolved Audiences," *Journal of Marketing Research* 28 (November 1991), 467–474; and David W. Schumann, Richard E. Petty, and D. Scott Clemons, "Predicting the Effectiveness of Advertising Variation: A Test of the Repetition-Variation Hypotheses," *Journal of Consumer Research* 17 (September 1990), 192–202.

44. For an expanded discussion of how persuasion tactics may depend on the type of motivation, see John R. Rossiter and Larry Percy, "Advertising Communication Models," in Elizabeth C. Hirschman and Morris B. Holbrook, eds., *Advances in Consumer Research* 12 (Provo, Utah: Association for Consumer Research, 1985), 510–524; and Rossiter and Percy, *Advertising and Promotion Management.*

45. David M. Sanbonmatsu and Frank R. Kardes, "The Effects of Physiological Arousal on Information Processing and Persuasion," *Journal of Consumer Research* 15 (December 1988), 379–385. Also see Surendra N. Singh and Gilbert A. Churchill, Jr., "Arousal and Advertising Effectiveness," *Journal of Advertising* 16 (1987), 4–10.

46. Rolph E. Anderson and Marvin A. Jolson, "Technical Wording in Advertising: Implications for Market Segmentation," *Journal of Marketing* 44 (Winter 1980), 57–66.

47. Joseph W. Alba and J. Wesley Hutchinson, "Dimensions of Consumer Expertise," *Journal of Consumer Research* 13 (March 1987), 411–454.

48. Mita Sujan, "Consumer Knowledge: Effects on Evaluation Strategies Mediating Consumer Judgments," *Journal of Consumer Research* 12 (June 1985), 31–46. Also see Alba and Marmorstein, "The Effects of Frequency Knowledge on Consumer Decision Making."

49. John E. Calfee and Debra Jones Ringold, "Consumer Skepticism and Advertising Regulation: What Do the Polls Show?" in Michael J. Houston, ed., *Advances in Consumer Research* 15 (Provo, Utah: Association for Consumer Research, 1988), 244–248. For a more general discussion of consumers' irritation with advertising,

see David A. Aaker and Donald E. Bruzzone, "Causes of Irritation in Advertising," *Journal of Marketing* 49 (Spring 1985), 47–57. Also see Richard W. Pollay and Banwari Mittal, "Here's the Beef: Factors, Determinants, and Segments in Consumer Criticism of Advertising," Journal of Marketing 57 (July 1993), 99–114. And for research on how personality variables are related to skepticism in advertising, see David M. Boush, Chun-Hyum Kim, Lynn R. Kahle, and Rajeev Batra, "Cynicism and Conformity as Correlates of Trust in Product Information Sources," *Journal of Current Issues and Research in Advertising* 5 (Fall 1993), 71–79.

50. This figure comes from a study by Needham, Harper, and Steers as cited by Stephen J. Hoch and Young-Won Ha, "Consumer Learning: Advertising and the Ambiguity of Product Experience," *Journal of Consumer Research* 13 (September 1986), 221–233.

51. C. W. Sherif, M. Sherif, and R. E. Nebergall, *Attitude and Attitude Change* (New Haven, Conn.: Yale University Press, 1961).

52. Karen A. Machleit, Chris T. Allen, and Thomas J. Madden, "The Mature Brand and Brand Interest: An Alternative Consequence of Ad-Evoked Affect," *Journal of Marketing* 57 (October 1993), 72–82.

53. Wu and Shaffer, "Susceptibility to Persuasive Appeals as a Function of Source Credibility and Prior Experience with the Attitude Object." Also see Lawrence J. Marks and Michael A. Kamins, "The Use of Product Sampling and Advertising: Effects of Sequence of Exposure and Degree of Advertising Claim Exaggeration on Consumers' Belief Strength, Belief Confidence, and Attitudes," *Journal of Marketing Research* 25 (August 1988), 266–281; and Robert E. Smith and William R. Swinyard, "Attitude-Behavior Consistency: The Impact of Product Trial Versus Advertising," *Journal of Marketing Research* 20 (August 1983), 257–267.

54. Amitava Chattopadhyay and Kunal Basu, "Humor in Advertising: The Moderating Role of Prior Brand Evaluation," *Journal of Marketing Research* 27 (November 1990), 466–476.

55. Meryl Paula Gardner, "Mood States and Consumer Behavior: A Critical Review," *Journal of Consumer Research* 12 (December 1985), 281–300.

56. Rajeev Batra and Douglas M. Stayman, "The Role of Mood in Advertising Effectiveness," *Journal of Consumer Research* 17 (September 1990), 203–214; Gerald J. Gorn, Marvin E. Goldberg, and Kunal Basu, "Mood, Awareness, and Product Evaluation," *Journal of Consumer Psychology* 2 (1993), 237–256; and Thomas K. Srull, "Memory, Mood, and Consumer Judgment," in Melanie Wallendorf and Paul Anderson, eds., *Advances in Consumer Research* 14 (Provo, Utah: Association for Consumer Research, 1987), 404–407. Interestingly, consumers' more favorable evaluations of gift-wrapped packages has been linked to gift-wrapping effects on moods. See Daniel J. Howard, "Gift-Wrapping Effects on Product Attitudes: A Mood-Biasing Explanation," *Journal of Consumer Psychology* 1 (1992), 197–224.

57. Marvin E. Goldberg and Gerald J. Gorn, "Happy and Sad TV Programs: How They Affect Reactions to Commercials," *Journal of Consumer Research* 14 (December 1987), 387–403.

58. John T. Cacioppo and Richard E. Petty, "The Need for Cognition," *Journal of Personality and Social Psychology* 42 (1982), 116–131.

59. Curtis R. Haugvedt, Richard E. Petty, and John T. Cacioppo, "Need for Cognition and Advertising: Understanding the Role of Personality Variables in Consumer Behavior," *Journal of Consumer Psychology* 1 (1992), 239–260. Also see Danny Axson, Susan Yates, and Shelley Chaiken, "Audience Response as a Heuristic Cue in Persuasion," *Journal of Personality and Social Psychology* 53 (1987), 30–40; Batra and Stayman, "The Role of Mood in Advertising Effectiveness"; Haugvedt, Petty, Cacioppo, and Steidley, "Personality and Ad Effectiveness"; J. Jeffrey Inman, Leigh McAlister, and Wayne D. Hoyer, "Promotion Signal: Proxy for a Price Cut?" *Journal of Consumer Research* 17 (June 1990), 74–81.

60. For a general review of self-monitoring, see Mark Snyder, "Self-Monitoring Processes," in Leonard Berkowitz, ed., *Advances in Experimental Social Psychology* 12 (New York: Academic Press, 1979), 85–128. For a recent study, see Sharon Shavitt, Tina Lowrey, and Sang-Pil Han, "Attitude Functions in Advertising: The Interactive Role of Products and Self-Monitoring," *Journal of Consumer Psychology* 1 (1992), 337–364.

61. Mark Snyder and Kenneth G. DeBono, "Appeals to Image and Claims about Quality: Understanding the Psychology of Advertising," *Journal of Personality and Social Psychology* 49 (September 1985), 586–597.

62. Edward F. Cone, "Image and Reality," *Forbes* (December 14, 1987), 226, 228.

63. For another perspective on how advertising strategy depends on the nature of the advertised product, see Percy and Rossiter, "A Model of Brand Awareness and Brand Attitude Advertising Strategies."

64. Hoch and Ha, "Consumer Learning."

65. Timothy B. Heath, Michael S. McCarthy, and David L. Mothersbaugh, "Spokesperson Fame and Vividness Effects in the Context of Issue-Relevant Thinking: The Moderating Role of Competitive Setting," *Journal of Consumer Research* 20 (March 1994), 520–534; Paul W. Miniard, Deepak Sirdesmukh, and Daniel E. Innis, "Peripheral Persuasion and Brand Choice," *Journal of Consumer Research* 19 (September 1992), 226–239.

66. A review of research on multiple request techniques can be found in Edward F. Fern, Kent B. Monroe, and Ramon A. Avila, "Effectiveness of Multiple Request Strategies: A Synthesis of Research Results," *Journal of Marketing Research* 22 (May 1986), 144–152.

67. For research involving another type of multiple request technique beyond those covered in the chapter, see Daniel J. Howard, "The Influence of Verbal Responses to Common Greetings on Compliance Behavior: The Foot-in-the-Mouth Effect," *Journal of Applied Social Psychology* 20 (1990), 1185–1196.

68. Jonathan L. Freedman and Scott C. Fraser, "Compliance without Pressure: The Foot-in-the-Door Technique," *Journal of Personality and Social Psychology* 4 (August 1966), 195–202.

69. Daryl J. Bem, "Self-Perception Theory," in Leonard Berkowitz, ed., *Advances in Experimental Social Psychology* 6 (New York: Academic Press, 1972), 1–62. Also see William DeJong, "An Examination of Self-Perception Mediation of the Foot-in-the-Door Effect," *Journal of Personality and Social Psychology* 37 (December 1979), 2221–2239. For a dissenting point of view, see Peter H. Reingen, "On Inducing Compliance with Requests," *Journal of Consumer Research* 5 (September 1978), 96–102; and Alice M. Tybout, Brian Sternthal, and Bobby J. Calder, "Information Availability as a Determinant of Multiple Request Effectiveness," *Journal of Marketing Research* 20 (August 1983), 280–290.

70. Chris T. Allen, Charles D. Schewe, and Gosta Wijk, "More on Self-Perception Theory's Foot Technique in the Pre-Call/Mail Survey Setting," *Journal of Marketing Research* 17 (November 1980), 498–502; Robert A. Hansen and Larry M. Robinson, "Testing the Effectiveness of Alternative Foot-in-the-Door Manipulations," *Journal of Marketing Research* 17 (August 1980), 359–364; Reingen, "On Inducing Compliance with Requests"; Peter H. Reingen and Jerome B. Kernan, "Compliance with an Interview Request: A Foot-in-the-Door, Self-Perception Interpretation," *Journal of Marketing Research* 14 (August 1977), 365–369; and Carol A. Scott, "Modifying Socially Conscious Behavior: The Foot-in-the-Door Technique," *Journal of Consumer Research* 4 (December 1977), 156–164.

71. David H. Furse, David W. Stewart, and David L. Rados, "Effects of Foot-in-the-Door, Cash Incentives, and Followups on Survey Response," *Journal of Marketing Research* 18 (November 1981), 473–478; Peter H. Reingen and Jerome B. Kernan, "More Evidence on Interpersonal Yielding," *Journal of Marketing Research* 16 (November 1979), 588–593; and Carol A. Scott, "The Effects of Trial and Incentives on Repeat Purchase Behavior," *Journal of Marketing Research* 13 (August 1976), 263–269.

72. Fern, Monroe, and Avila, "Effectiveness of Multiple Request Strategies."

73. Robert B. Cialdini, Joyce E. Vincent, Stephen K. Lewis, Jose Catalan, Diane Wheeler, and Betty Lee Darby, "Reciprocal Concessions Procedure for Inducing Compliance: The Door-in-the-Face Technique," *Journal of Personality and Social Psychology* 31 (February 1975), 206–215. For an alternative explanation, see Tybout, Sternthal, and Calder, "Information Availability as a Determinant of Multiple Request Effectiveness."

74. John C. Mowen and Robert B. Cialdini, "On Implementing the Door-in-the-Face Compliance Technique in a Business Context," *Journal of Marketing Research* 17 (May 1980), 253–258.

75. Robert B. Cialdini, *Influence: How and Why People Agree to Things* (New York: William Morrow, 1984), 57. This book is highly recommended reading for those interested in a well-written, interesting, and informative discussion of influence techniques.

76. John Vollbrecht, "To Get Volume Up, Sell Down," *Sales Management* (July 22, 1974), 29.

77. Also see Dennis T. Regan, "Effects of a Favor and Liking on Compliance," *Journal of Experimental Social Psychology* 7 (1971), 627–639.

78. Cialdini, *Influence.*

79. Morton Deutsch and Harold B. Gerard, "A Study of Normative and Informational Social Influences upon Individual Judgment," *Journal of Abnormal and Social Psychology* 51 (November 1955), 629–636.

80. Cialdini, *Influence,* 102–103.

81. Ibid., 86.

82. For research on this topic, see Chris T. Allen, "Self-Perception Based Strategies for Stimulating Energy Conservation," *Journal of Consumer Research* 8 (March 1982), 381–390; Trudy Kehret-Ward and Richard Yalch, "To Take or Not to Take the Only One: Effects of Changing the Meaning of a Product Attribute on Choice Behavior," *Journal of Consumer Research* 10 (March 1984), 410–416; Robert Kraut, "Effects of Social Labeling on Giving to Charity," *Journal of Marketing Research* 14 (November 1977), 509–516; Ellen M. Moore, William O. Bearden, and Jesse E. Teel, "Use of Labeling and Assertions of Dependency in Appeals for Consumer Support," *Journal of Consumer Research* 12 (June 1985), 90–96; and Alice M. Tybout and Richard F. Yalch, "The Effect of Experience: A Matter of Salience," *Journal of Consumer Research* 6 (March 1980), 406–413.

83. Tybout and Yalch, "The Effect of Experience."

84. Allen, "Self-Perception Based Strategies for Stimulating Energy Conservation."

85. John Waggoner, "Rebates, Discounts Give Credit-Card Use a Charge," *USA Today* (March 11, 1994), B1.

86. "Marketing Briefs," *Marketing News* 26 (January 31, 1994), 1.

87. *Insights,* NPD Research, Inc., 1979–1982.

88. Richard Gibson, "Marketers' Mantra: Reap More with Less," *Wall Street Journal* (March 22, 1991), B1-B2.

89. Joe A. Dodson, Alice M. Tybout, and Brian Sternthal, "Impact of Deals and Deal Retraction on Brand Switching," *Journal of Marketing Research* 15 (February 1978), 72–78; and Anthony N. Doob, J. Merrill Carlsmith, Jonathan L. Freedman, Thomas K. Landauer, and Soleng Tom, "Effect of Initial Selling Price on Subsequent Sales," *Journal of Personality and Social Psychology* 11 (April 1969), 345–350.

90. Dodson, Tybout, and Sternthal, "Impact of Deals and Deal Retraction on Brand Switching."

91. Scott Davis, J. Jeffrey Inman, and Leigh McAlister, "Promotion Has a Negative Effect on Brand Evaluations—Or Does It? Additional Disconfirming Evidence," *Journal of Marketing Research* 29 (February 1992), 143–148.

92. Scott A. Neslin and Robert W. Shoemaker, "An Alternative Explanation for Lower Repeat Rates after Promotion Purchases," *Journal of Marketing Research* 26 (May 1989), 205–213.

93. Gibson, "Marketers' Mantra."

94. For research on those consumer segments most likely to become incremental purchasers due to coupons, see Kapil Bawa and Robert W. Shoemaker, "Analyzing Incremental Sales from a Direct Mail Coupon Promotion," *Journal of Marketing* 53 (July 1989), 66–78.

95. Michael L. Rothschild and William C. Gaidis, "Behavioral Learning Theory: Its Relevance to Marketing and Promotions," *Journal of Marketing* 45 (Spring 1981), 70–78.

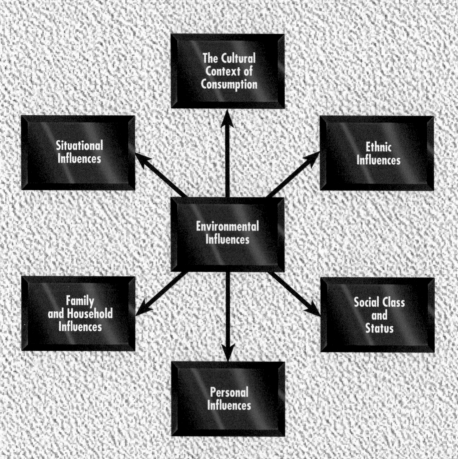

PART V

Environmental Influences

▲▲▲

No person is an island. This statement certainly is true in the study of consumer behavior. What makes you unique? Is your behavior caused mostly by genetic predispositions, by the environment, or by some combination that is uniquely you? Scientists from many disciplines disagree on the answers to such basic questions.

Nevertheless, it is clear that consumers are shaped by thier environment as they live and operate within it. While at the same time changing that environment through their behavior. The following chapters show you how this takes place by addressing the impact of environmental influences on purchase and consumption decisions.

Most fundamental of all is an understanding of the nature and meaning of culture which is the subject of Chapter 17. Chapter 18 extends the discussion by focusing more concretely on **ethnic influences of consumer behavior.** You will immediately grasp the importance of cultural insight in this era of globalized marketing. Also important is an understanding of **personal influence** (Chapter 20), **the family** (Chapter 21), and **situation** (Chapter 22).

Influence of Culture
on Buying and Consumption

▲▲▲▲▲▲▲▲▲▲▲▲▲▲▲▲▲▲▲▲▲▲▲▲▲▲▲▲▲▲▲▲▲▲▲▲▲▲

Is Anything Sacred?
Is Nothing Sacred?

If you can't stand the heat, stay out of the mosque. Last week at the Chanel couture collection, Herr Hauteness Karl Lagerfeld "borrowed" beautiful designs of Arabic script to adorn several low-cut evening gowns. But when Muslim leaders saw a photo of Claudia Schiffer overflowing in the Chanel dance dress, they were *not* amused. Seems the design is actually sacred phrases from the Koran.

In *France-Soir*, Moammar Gadhafi called the incident evidence of "a new Occidental crusade against Muslims in order to annihilate them." A boycott of Chanel was called for because of "Lagerfeld's disdain for the Koran."

In response, Lagerfeld has ordered the blasphemous bustier dresses removed from the Chanel collection. Arlette Theibault of Chanel says: "It was an unfortunate error and not intended as an insult."

Is anything sacred? Not in fashion. Christian crosses, priest frocks, and nunlike vestments are offered by Calvin Klein, Richard Tyler, and Donna Karan. Last year, Paris designer Jean-Paul Gaultier did a version of Hasidic chic, complete with clip-on curled sideburns. Industry observers say these sacrilegious styles reveal our search for deeper meaning and a retroactive guilt trip over the gluttonous '80s.

Source: Excerpts from "Chanel's Fashion Faux Pas: Koran Phrases as Decoration," USA Today (January 27, 1994), 3D.

Figure 17A Chanel Dress Causes Controversy

By Laurent Rebours, AP

BIG CONTROVERSY: Model Claudia Schiffer wears a low-cut dress printed with a passage from the Koran. Muslims were not amused.

Source: USA Today, January 27, 1994, 3D.

The study of consumer behavior historically focused on individual decision making—how consumers buy and use products to reflect their concept of self. That has been the approach of much of this book until now. However, Markus and Kitayama[1] show that it is often more relevant to *understand the interdependent self rather than the independent self.* Knowledge of group influences on self is important in a global economy because 70 percent of the world's consumers live in a *collectivist culture* rather than the *individualistic culture* of North America.[2]

In North America, a wide variety of group influences are likely to influence consumers. Culture, ethnicity, social class, family, and other personal influences are described in this and following chapters. An executive in Tokyo can look out his corporate window and know that most consumers will have similar beliefs about honor, family, religion, education, and work habits. Consequently, there is considerable homogeneity in incomes, cars, homes, and commuting patterns, all variables of importance in understanding consumer behavior.

When an executive in North America looks out the corporate window, she or he may see a wide array of languages, religions, and ethnic backgrounds. Both the United States and Canada have significant Asian-American or Asian-Canadian groups. Both countries have significant groups of African descent, although the influence is greater in the United States. Canada has a much larger French ethnic group, although the United States has some, principally in Louisiana. The United States and Canada are similar, although Canadian values are closer to European values than are U.S. values. There is enough cultural similarity between Canada, Mexico, and the United States, however, to cause Wal-Mart to operate retail stores in all three countries with a similar strategy.

This chapter discusses social influences on consumer behavior under the general rubric of culture to understand how culture affects consumption and buying. These concepts are foundational to understanding ethnicity in the following chapter. In Chapter 13, you studied the concept of personal values, but in this chapter, we analyze *social values* that become part of the personal values of consumers.

What Is Culture?

Culture refers to a set of values, ideas, artifacts, and other meaningful symbols that help individuals communicate, interpret, and evaluate as members of society. Culture does not include instincts, nor does it include idiosyncratic behavior occurring as a one-time solution to a unique problem.

Culture includes both abstract and material elements. **Abstract elements** include values, attitudes, ideas, personality types, and summary constructs, such as religion. **Material components** include such things as books, computers, tools, buildings, and specific products, such as a pair of Levi's 501 jeans or the latest CD by Mariah Carey or R.E.M. Material elements of culture are sometimes described as **cultural artifacts** or the material manifestation of culture, thereby restricting the use of **culture** to abstract concepts.

Culture provides people with a sense of identity and an understanding of acceptable behavior within society. Some of the more important attitudes and behaviors influenced by culture are the following[3]:

1. Sense of self and space

2. Communication and language

3. Dress and appearance

4. Food and feeding habits

5. Time and time consciousness

6. Relationships (family, organizations, government, and so on)
7. Values and norms
8. Beliefs and attitudes
9. Mental processes and learning
10. Work habits and practices

Values

Values are shared beliefs or group norms internalized by individuals, perhaps with some modification. **Norms** are beliefs held by consensus of a group concerning the behavior rules for individual members. Cultural or social values are those shared broadly across groups of people, whereas personal values, as you read in Chapter 13, are the terminal (goals) or instrumental (behavior) norms of individuals. Personal values may not be shared by all or even many of the members of the group, although one's family, religion, or national origin usually influences personal values, as we see in the section below. The social values described in this chapter are closely related to the personal values described in Chapter 13 and are sometimes measured with psychographic (AIO) or Rokeach (RVS) scales.[4]

Macroculture refers to values and symbols that apply to an entire society or to most of its citizens. The term *society* usually refers to large and complex, yet organized, social systems, such as a nation or perhaps even Western civilization. **Microculture** refers to values and symbols of a restrictive group, such as a religious, ethnic, or other subdivision of the whole. Microcultures are sometimes called subcultures, but we use the term *microculture* to avoid concern that calling ethnic groups *sub*cultures connotes inferiority.

Where Do People Get Their Values?

Socialization

The processes by which people develop their values, motivations, and habitual activity are called **socialization,** the process of absorbing a culture. From the time a baby looks up and begins cooing and smiling, he or she starts forming val-ues. Socialization continues throughout life, causing people to adopt values that influence consumption—such as thrift, pleasure, honesty, and ambition. These life forces also produce specific preferences—relating to choices of color, packaging, convenience, hours of shopping, and characteristic interactions with salespeople and many others. **Consumer socialization** is the acquisition of consumption-related cognitions, attitudes, and behavior. Early studies focused on how young people learned consumer skills, but today consumer socialization is recognized as a lifelong process.[5]

Culture Is Learned

Unlike animals, whose behavior is more instinctive, humans are not born with norms of behavior. Instead, humans learn their norms through imitation or by observing the process of reward and punishment in a society of members who adhere to or deviate from the group's norms. Norms learned early in life may be highly resistant to promotional effort by marketers. When an advertiser is dealing with deeply ingrained, culturally defined behavior (about food, sex, basic forms of clothing, and so on), it is easier to change the marketing mix to conform with cultural values than to try to change the values through advertising. As an example, eating dogs, horses, sheep eyes, or even live fish is normal and healthy behavior in some cultures. Advertising would have great difficulty, however, in convincing typical North American consumers to buy these products.

Culture Is Inculcated

Culture is passed from one generation to the next, primarily by institutions such as family, religion, and schools. Early lifetime experiences and peers also transmit values; this process is shown in Figure 17.1. Predicting the values that will affect consumer behavior in the future is based on understanding how these institutions are changing, a topic discussed later in this chapter.

Culture Rewards Socially Gratifying Responses

Culture develops and exists almost as if it were an entity in itself. Some anthropologists view culture as an entity serving humans in their attempts to meet the basic biological and social needs of society. When norms no longer provide gratification in a society, the norms are extinguished.

Culture Is Adaptive

Culture is adaptive. Marketing strategies based on values of society must also be adaptive. As change occurs in the traits that represent a society's ability to function, trends develop that provide marketing opportunities to those who spot the traits before competitors. As culture evolves, it may be possible to associate the benefits of a product or brand with new values or it may be necessary to change the product if that value is no longer gratifying in society. For

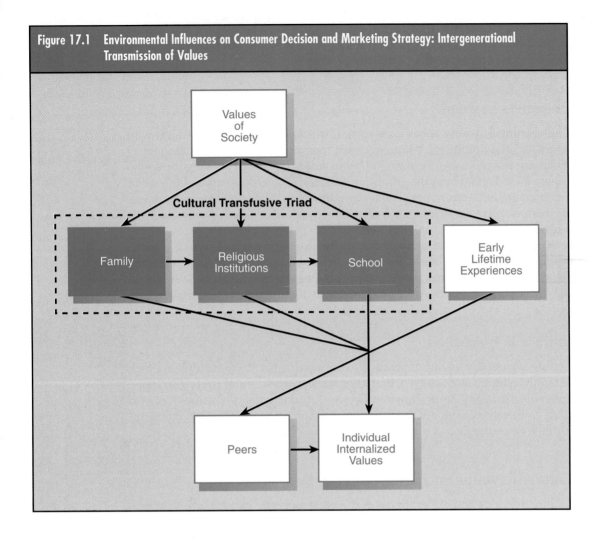

Figure 17.1   Environmental Influences on Consumer Decision and Marketing Strategy: Intergenerational Transmission of Values

example, meat and potatoes used to be desired foods in the mass American culture. When most consumers worked on a farm or in strenuous manufacturing and labor jobs, high-energy and high-calorie foods were valued and gratifying. As those jobs were replaced increasingly by white-collar and other sedentary careers, the beef industry had to change its appeal to lean beef with less calories, fat, and cholesterol. Worthington Foods extends this principle further and markets a wide variety of "meat analogues," such as "Grillers" and "Links," with no cholesterol and less fat—products that look and taste like meat but contain no animal fat.

How Culture Affects Consumer Behavior

Culture has a profound effect on why people buy. Culture affects the specific products people buy as well as the structure of consumption, individual decision making, and communication in a society.

Why People Buy Products

Consumers buy products to obtain *function, form, and meaning*. Marketers must give attention to all three variables, as they are defined by the cultural context of consumption.

When consumers buy a product, they expect it to perform a *function* — to clean clothes in the case of laundry detergent or to provide nutrition in the case of food. A high level of consumer satisfaction and loyalty occurs only if expectations are met consistently. As a consequence, firms today allocate significant resources to product-quality programs. They must also allocate resources to customer-contact programs to find out when functional expectations are not met or exceeded.

Appliances such as washing machines, as an example, may vary in function and form between cultures. In European cultures, washing machines are expected to last for decades. Highly efficient, front-loading machines costing more than $1,000 are marketed successfully by firms such as Miele, based in Germany. An example is shown in Figure 17.2. Yet, when Miele introduced this same level of quality in North America, it found only limited success because, in the American culture, appliances should be priced at a few hundred dollars and are not expected to have much quality.[6] Americans move more frequently than Europeans, have lower quality of repair services available, and expect the more-convenient but less-efficient cleaning ability of top-loading machines. Consequently, washing machines are almost a disposable product. When they break or if the consumer moves, they are often left behind or discarded. The cultural context of the consumer defines the meaning of quality in the function of the product.

Successful products must also meet expectations about *form*. Nutritional requirements in food might be met in many ways, but some forms are much preferred by customers. Foods are expected to be "hot" or "cold" or "crisp" or "tender" or "microwavable." Shushimi or fish served raw may be a special treat in Japan but unacceptable to the majority markets of North America. Veal might be a special treat for Americans of recent European descent but an anathema to a California vegetarian. A front-loading washing machine is a requirement for success in European markets but not desired in the United States. Such realities are determined by a consumer's culture.

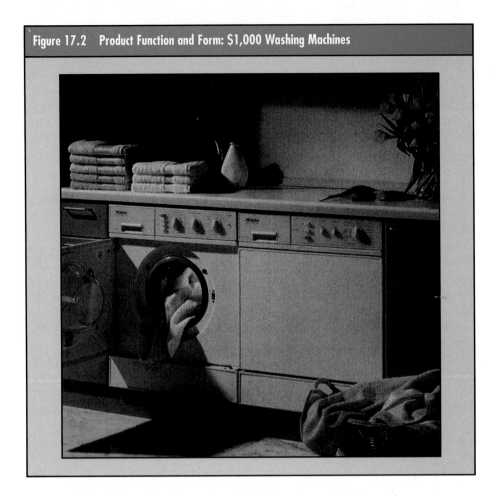

Figure 17.2   Product Function and Form: $1,000 Washing Machines

Products also provide *symbols of meaning* in a society.[7] Spinach may be associated with strength, possibly enticing children to eat an otherwise unappealing choice. Foods often represent symbols of family relationships, as in the case of a special recipe handed down through generations or associated with one's national or ethnic identity. Products sometimes are used in *ritual behavior,* as when certain foods are eaten during holidays or by candlelight for special occasions as you see in Figure 17.3. Occasionally, products become so much of a symbol in a society that they are an *icon,* as in the case of foods eaten especially in religious observances. Sometimes, the form of the product also acts as a symbol of the function, as the addition of "blue crystals" may do for a detergent that gets clothes "whiter."

The importance of values in understanding why people buy what they buy is described by Sheth, Newman, and Gross[8] in the concept *consumption values.*

Figure 17.3   Symbolic Associations with Products

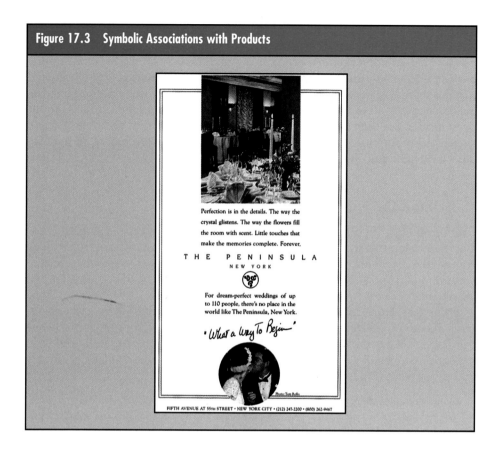

Consumer choice in this theory is influenced by functional value, conditional value, social value, emotional value, and epistemic value. These multiple values are considered to be independent of each other and influence how consumers make product or consumption choices as well as brands and other elements of consumer choice.

Structure of Consumption

Consumption is an increasing concern in the study of consumer behavior, as we have seen in previous chapters. Through the legal and governmental system, a nation's culture determines what suppliers can offer, the ways products can be marketed, and the degree to which consumers are allowed to act on their preferences. Shall countries put their resources into military, industrial, or consumer goods? Shall a nation produce good cars or good tanks? Good education or good health? Good computers or good music? And because insatiability of demand dictates there will never be enough goods for all, should these products be most available to the old or to the young? To which ethnic or religious groups? To the persons who are the best educated or to the members of the "right" families or to persons of the ruling party? Such choices are heavily affected by an individual's particular culture.

Individual Decision Making

Culture, along with other elements of the environment, affects all stages of consumer decision making. For example, American culture emphasizes individual, competitive behavior, whereas Japanese culture emphasizes conformity in consumption and production. Such values may affect both **need recognition** and **search.**

From the culture, products absorb meaning through advertising, fashion systems, retailing presentation, and many other ways not influenced by marketers but important to consumers in stages of need recognition or search. The individual consumer develops meaning through possession, exchange, grooming, and divestment rituals. McCracken[9] explains:

> Culture constitutes the phenomenal world in two ways. First, culture is the "lens" through which the individual views phenomena; as such, it determines how the phenomena will be apprehended and assimilated. Second, culture is the "blueprint" of human activity, determining the co-ordinates of social action and productive activity, and specifying the behaviors and objects that issue from both.

During alternative evaluation, some consumers place more weight on some product attributes than on others. The cause for such weights is often the culture to which the individual belongs. For example, some wealthy consumers may be found to place a great weight on low price, not because they lack money but because cultural values influence their choices. Conversely, a poor consumer may purchase an expensive pair of shoes because of personal or group values.

During purchase processes, the amount of price negotiation expected by both seller and buyer is culturally determined. In Greece and some Middle-Eastern countries, for instance, even the price of a physician's services is subject to negotiation.

Consumers' complaints or expressions of satisfaction may also be affected by cultural variables. Mexican-Americans, for example, are less likely than other consumers to complain about unsatisfactory service when they buy products. But they are more likely to protest delays in delivery, possibly because of a cultural value of obtaining things "today" or "right now."[10]

How Core Values Affect Marketing

Successful retailers know that a basic group of products is essential to the store's traffic, customer loyalty, and profits. These products are known as **core merchandise**. A group of values, called **core values**, also exists. These values are basic to understanding the behavior of people and can be helpful to marketers in several ways.

Core values define how products are used in a society. Not only do core values determine what foods should be eaten, but they also determine with what other foods they are appropriate, how they are prepared, and the time of day to eat them.

Core values provide positive and negative valences for brands and communications programs. "As American as apple pie" communicated well in America for Chevrolet, but negative valences would surely result from associating cars with other foods such as bird nest soup or monkey gland stew (which have positive valences in China or Africa, respectively). Marketers may use celebrity athletes or musicians such as Michael Jackson, Tonya Harding, or Magic Johnson to achieve positive valences to their brands, a successful strategy unless the image of the celebrity changes to produce negative valences.

Core values define acceptable market relationships. In Japan, the relationships between groups of firms—dating back to east and west dynasties—are so rigid and complex that outsiders have difficulty obtaining distribution unless they form a joint venture with one of the groups.

People in rich economies tend to assume that transactions probably will be completed as specified. If problems arise, they have agencies such as the Better Business Bureau, consumer protection agencies, and access to the legal system. In contrast, in poor countries, very little of this support structure may exist, and people may have little faith in trading with distant partners. Even when liberal laws exist, the social resources to protect economic transactions may not be available.

In peasant marketplaces, people develop long-term trading partnerships to provide reciprocating values to both buyers and sellers. These values include assured supply, reliable quality, employment of family members and neighbors, and price stability. In Haiti, trading partnerships are known as *pratik*. A buying *pratik* who knows that her selling counterpart is coming will wait at the proper place and time, refusing to buy from others the stock that she is sure her *pratik* is carrying. Similarly, a selling *pratik* will refuse to sell to others until she has met her *pratik* buyer. In Nigeria, similar partnerships are called *onibara* relationships; in Jamaica, they are "customers" rather than "higglers"; in the Philippines, such relationships are called *suki*. In Guatemala, growers bargain vigorously in the marketplace with middlemen with whom they do not have personal relationships. A *cliente* middleman, in contrast, will pay the prevailing price with no bargaining and will almost always buy the products unless he has absolutely no use for them. In return, the agricultural producer is expected to deliver the best produce to the *cliente* middlemen.[11]

These forms of networking are becoming much more important to understand with an increasing need for relationship marketing, a topic of more analysis in Chapter 22. *Relationship marketing refers to building long-term relationships with consumers rather than discrete exchanges.* Such relationships require a large element of trust between members of the distribution channel. In Japan, a company will often do business with small suppliers or distribution companies owned by former employees. In most Latin American countries, companies may be created or changed to serve family members or family friends to fulfill a position needed in the network. In the United States, where the culture favors impersonal relationships and equality, it may be more difficult to develop the trust needed for effective relationship marketing.[12]

Core values define ethical behavior. Recent years in the United States have been characterized as a "money culture" in which business executives operate principally on greed and Wall Street is "a den of thieves."[13] The ethical constraints on marketing behavior and executive action is a topic for you to consider in the final chapter of this book.

Core values affect these and many other marketing functions. You may remember from Chapter 3 the core values of various nations or from Chapter 13 how the values of nations such as Switzerland and Japan cause their inhabitants to be more prosperous than nations with far more natural resources but less-effective values. What, however, are the core values of North American societies that affect consumer decisions and marketing programs?

North American Core Values

Core values can be observed in Canada and the United States, even though both countries encompass values reflecting diverse national origins within their populations. Values are less rigid in North America, because these countries are so young compared with most Asian and European countries. First, we'll examine U.S. values and then compare the two countries. Many values described as American also apply in Canada, although there are important differences, as discussed in the second section. The term *American* includes Latin America as well, but in the following pages, we will restrict the discussion to only a part of America—the United States.

Some of the core values also apply to Mexican markets, although there are not yet sufficient data to allow in-depth discussion of consumer behavior in Mexico. The fact that emigration from Mexico to the United States is attractive to many people indicates acceptance of at least some U.S. values. Firms such as Wal-Mart and Amway have achieved success by translating marketing strategies based solidly on American values into the Mexican market. Consumer in Focus 17.1 provides more details of Amway's success in Mexico.

American Values: Their Influence on Consumers

The United States was an agrarian nation only two generations ago. Although it is now primarily urbanized and suburbanized, many core values are still traceable to the agrarian base. Daily living is now regulated more by the clock and

---

Consumer in Focus   **17.1**

Inspirational Marketing

"Amway is more than a company, it's a movement to help people help themselves," says Richard DeVos, founder of Amway, the world's second-largest door-to-door sales operation with $3.1 billion in retail sales. Amway manufactures and sells soap, cosmetics, vitamins, food products, and other household products as well as Coca-Cola machines, MCI service, clothing, and thousands of other items.

Although the average Amway distributor sells about $1,700 worth of goods a year, a few of the distributors at the top make really big money—$300,000 and more a year. The really big money is made not by selling goods so much as recruiting for Amway's sales force. In a world where many people find little satisfaction in the paychecks they receive, visions of financial independence are often compelling. But Amway goes a crucial step beyond mere money. It offers its recruits membership in a community of like-minded people—entrepreneurial, motivated, upwardly mobile—who believe in their country, in God, and in their family.

Amway rallies typically resemble a mix between a rock concert and a religious revival meeting. The evenings are kicked off with inspiring music—the theme from *Rocky* or *Chariots of Fire*—followed by much audience hand-holding, singing, swaying, and listening to testimonials. Some inspirational speeches last into the early morning hours. Hundreds of average working people are introduced, and many of them recount how they became successful and became better people with Amway. DeVos says, "We have two forms of reward in this world. One is recognition and the other is dollars. We employ them both in the Amway business."

The company has been successful in a number of other countries, including Canada (where it experienced legal problems) and Mexico. DeVos is convinced that motivating foreigners is no different from motivating people in the United States. "In Mexico, people will ride a bus for hours to come to an Amway meeting because Amway will give them a shot at success. Most of these people have believed for generations that they would never be anybody, because the rich guy on the hill told them they'd never be anybody. But the Amway business has come to symbolize for great numbers of people their chance to get out of their rut."

Source: Based on Paul Klebnikov, "The Power of Positive Inspiration," Forbes 148 (December 9, 1991), 244–249.

the calendar than by the seasons or degree of daylight. Most people are employees of large, complex organizations rather than farmers or shopkeepers. Goods and services are purchased rather than produced, with money or plastic rather than property as the denominator of exchange. Yet, many American values retain the agrarian base.

The origin of American values is described by Arensberg and Niehoff[14]:

> Where does this American character come from? . . . The values derived from life on the frontier, the great open spaces, the virgin wealth, and the once seemingly limitless resources of a "new world" appear to have affected ideas of freedom. Individualism seems to have been fostered by a commitment to "progress" which in turn was derived from expansion over three hundred years. Much of the religious and ethical tradition is believed to have come from Calvinist (Puritan) doctrine, particularly an emphasis on individual responsibility and the positive work ethic. Anglo-Saxon civil rights, the rule of law, and representative institutions were inherited from the English background; ideas of egalitarian democracy and a secular spirit sprang from the French and American Revolutions. The period of slavery and its aftermath, and the European immigration of three centuries, have affected the American character strongly.

What are the core values that provide appeals for advertising and marketing programs? Eight of the most basic are described in Table 17.1. After you have studied the table, refer to Consumer in Focus 17.1, and you will see how many of these values are manifested in the successful Amway strategy.

Sometimes advertisers are accused of appealing mostly to fear, snobbery, and self-indulgence. Would advertisers be effective if they continually based their advertising on such appeals? As you examine Table 17.1, you will see that such an approach would have limited appeal. Marketers are more successful when they appeal to core values based on hard work, achievement and success, optimism, and equal opportunity for a better material standard of living.

Order and cleanliness are keys to the success of firms such as McDonald's and Stew Leonard's, in Connecticut, which is probably the largest family-owned supermarket in the nation. Both firms appear to subscribe to the "rest room" theory of management: Firms that have dirty rest rooms are rarely successful. Sewell Cadillac in Texas has become America's largest Cadillac dealer by incorporating such values. One of the keys of this automobile company's success is a service area with floors scrubbed several times a day, literally clean enough to eat lunch off.[15]

Advertisers must understand values to avoid violating standards. Benetton, the Italian retailer, uses ads that reflect social issues. But most Americans never see some of Benetton's more provocative material. Figure 17.4 features some of these ads. In one, readers are presented with pastel-colored balloon-type images. A closer look reveals that they are condoms, part of a safe-sex blitz in which some stores give away condoms. In Europe, another ad displayed a white baby feeding at the breasts of a black woman. Although the advertisement was part of a long-running campaign stressing harmony among the races, the ad was

Figure 17.4 How Social Values Affect Advertising

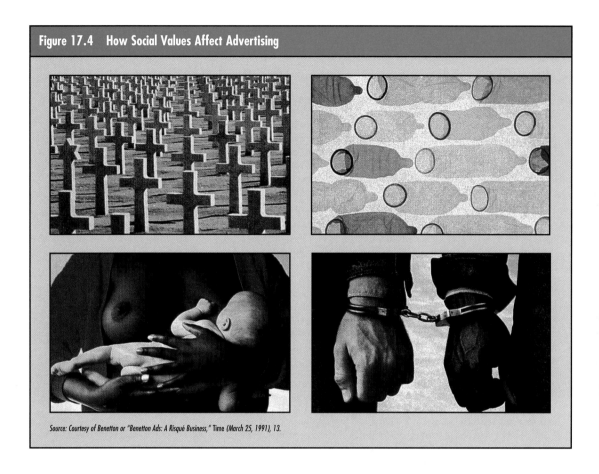

Source: Courtesy of Benetton or "Benetton Ads: A Risqué Business," Time (March 25, 1991), 13.

considered too provocative for use in the United States and Britain. In the midst of the Persian Gulf conflict, Benetton ran an ad in Europe with a lone Star of David in a cemetery full of white crosses. Many periodicals refused the ad on the basis that it was offensive to religion. Still another Benetton ad showed a black man and a white man chained together to promote the "united colors" theme. It was withdrawn in the United States after minority groups complained that the ad implied the black man was a criminal, and charged the company with racism.[16]

U.S. and Canadian Variations in Values

Canada and the United States share much communality, but their values and institutions vary in important ways. For one, there is less of an ideology of Canadianism than there is one of Americanism. The emphasis on individualism and achievement can be traced to the American Revolution, an upheaval that Canada did not support. Canada presents a more neutral, affable face that

Table 17.1 How Marketers Adapt to Core American Values

Material Well-Being

Americans believe in the marvels of modern comforts: swift and pleasant transportation, central heating, air conditioning, instant hot and cold water, and labor-saving devices of unending variety. It is almost a right to have such material things, and consumers reward Procter & Gamble, DuPont, McDonald's, and other firms who provide them. A familiar statement of core values says, "Cleanliness is next to godliness." As a consequence, marketers who expect to sell hotel space, food, or gasoline had better provide sanitary toilets and soft tissue.

Achievement and success are measured mostly by the quantity and quality of material goods. There is display value in articles that others can see: designer clothes, luxury personal cars, hot tubs, and personal computers for the children. Although rebellion against such values is expressed occasionally, well-being is fundamental to the American value system—one that marketers and politicians can count on year after year. As the popular movie *Wall Street* opined, "In America, greed is good."

Twofold Moralizing

Americans believe in polarized morality. Twofold judgments are the rule: moral-immoral, legal-illegal, civilized-primitive, secular-sacred. This is not the yin-and-yang duality of the Chinese but a classification of actions as good or bad. Consequently, the evaluation that public officials do "bad" things causes enormous problems, whereas this behavior would be accepted as normal in other parts of the world. Most Americans may personally accept nonmonogamous sexual relationships, but accusations against a politician can end a presidential campaign. Public personalities are considered ethical or unethical—not a little of both.

Marketing strategy is affected in many ways. Advertising that is "a little deceptive" is considered bad even if the overall message is largely correct. Salespeople in many countries are expected to give gifts to managers of client firms, but in North America, most corporations have policies that severely restrict or totally exclude the acceptance of gifts. In many countries, it would be considered immoral for a manager not to give preference in hiring to members of the manager's family or ethnic group. In North America, managers are expected to give jobs to the best-qualified person and to impose severe sanctions against preference toward family or ethnic members, even though such preference may be common in the manager's social relationships. Gambling is "wrong" and often a criminal activity but "right" if organized as a state lottery to benefit a good cause.

Work Is More Important than Play

Work is serious, adult business. People are judged by their work. When strangers meet, often the first topic of conversation is the kind of work each does. People are supposed to "get ahead" and "make a contribution" to society through their work.

While work is associated in American values with high or necessary purpose and grim effort, play is associated with frivolity, pleasure, and children. In other cultures, festivals and holidays and children having fun are the most important events in the society. In America, even socializing is often work-related. Advertisements for most products appeal more to work situations than to having fun or "play." Saturday morning television ads, however, appeal to play values because they are for children.

Time Is Money

Americans' view of time is different from that of many other cultures. In some countries, people actually distinguish between *hora Americana* versus *hora Mexicana* or *among Amelikan* versus *among Lao*. In doing so, they mean that American time is exact—that people are punctual, activities are scheduled, time is apportioned for separate activities, and the measure is the mechanical clock. Americans are often irritated when their people miss appointments or delivery schedules for promised orders. In some cultures, people have difficulty understanding the values that produce a need to keep hours or appointments precisely.

Effort, Optimism, and Entrepreneurship

Americans believe that problems should be identified and effort should be expended to solve them. With proper effort, one can be optimistic about success. Europeans sometimes laugh at their American friends who believe that for every problem there is a solution. When Americans find a problem, they form a committee or start a fund to solve it.

Continued

distinguishes it from its more exuberant and aggressive neighbor. Canadians have greater awareness of American media and institutions than conversely.

Canada and the United States have different situations and different histories. For example, law and order—enforced by the centrally controlled Northwest Mounted Police—tamed Canada's frontier much earlier than was the case in

Table 17.1 How Marketers Adapt to Core American Values, Continued

Effort, Optimism, and Entrepreneurship *continued*

This attitude is based on the concept that the universe is mechanistic, people are their own masters, and all is perfectible almost without limit. Thus with enough effort, people can improve themselves and manipulate the part of the universe around themselves. This viewpoint produces a certain intolerance for people who have failed to do so by those who have succeeded. A failure in life is a person who "didn't have the guts" to "make a go of it" and "get ahead." American heroes are "can-do" people. Advertising often depicts the same attitudes of rugged toughness, from pick-up trucks to the Marlboro Man.

In the American culture, effort is rewarded, competition is enforced, and individual achievement is paramount. Activist, pragmatic values rather than contemplative or mystical ones are the basis of American character. Entrepreneurship is one result of American values of effort and optimism. In such a competitive society, some people win and some people lose. And that is fine. Being the best is morally acceptable; more than acceptable, it is the goal. Football reflects American values, and Vince Lombardi said it well: "Winning is not everything, it is the only thing." In business, excellence and being number one is the goal.

Mastery over Nature

American core values produce a conquering attitude toward nature. In Buddhism and Hinduism, people and nature are one, and people work with nature rather than attempt to conquer it. In America, lack of water to grow crops is conquerable by irrigation. Chemicals are used to kill bugs and weeds with little regard for nature's balance. This conquering attitude toward nature appears to rest on at least three assumptions: that the universe is mechanistic; that people are the masters of the earth; and that people are qualitatively different from all other forms of life.

American advertising usually depicts people who are in command of the natural environment. It is the exception that proves the rule when an advertiser deviates from core values by saying, "It's not nice to fool Mother Nature." There are always people waiting by buy the latest product to reverse nature's battle to make men bald, old people wrinkled, and people overweight.

Egalitarianism

American core values support the belief that all people should have equal opportunities for achievement. This is more of a moral imperative than an actual condition, and many groups face discrimination by other groups and individuals. Yet the core values, codified legislatively and judicially, favor equality of all people, if those people accept the core values and behaviors of the social majority.

Americans often favor the "underdog," a trait that is difficult for people raised in some other cultures to understand. Open patterns of subordination, deference to royalty, or prestige based on variables other than personal achievement bother most Americans. People who receive advantages without "earning" them are objects of ridicule. Persons of inherited wealth are subjects of such ridicule in both advertising and television programming. Lee Iacocca became a folk hero in America partly because of his immigrant background and underdog "fighting the big boys" positioning.

Humanitarianism

An American trait of coming to the aid of the less fortunate is widespread. It expresses itself in the giving of donations to unknown individuals and groups; in the outpouring of aid to victims of famines, floods, and epidemics; in contributions of time and money to the Heart Association and countless other causes (with the exception, initially, of AIDS, which conflicted with other mainstream values); and in the rebuilding of factories and homes of conquered enemies after world wars.

In some countries, humanitarianism is more personal and related to kinship obligations, but in America, giving is more organized and depersonalized. In India and other countries, the recipients of almsgiving are usually seen with outstretched palm; in the United States, homeless recipients are more likely to be unseen and reached through a committee or a direct mailing list. For marketers, humanitarianism is not only a social responsibility but an important communications and marketing program. McDonald's, with its sponsorship of Ronald McDonald houses, youth organizations, and other community and national humanitarian programs, is a prime example.

the United States. Seymour Lipset, one of the most prolific analysts of Canadian-U.S. relationships, believes this is the reason why Canadians generally have more respect for law and order today than do U.S. citizens.[17] We summarize other differences between the values of the two countries, based on Lipset's research, in Table 17.2.

Table 17.2 Variations in Values between Canada and the United States

Canada	United States
More observance of law and order	Less observance
Emphasis on the rights and obligations of community	More emphasis on individual rights and obligations
Courts are perceived as an arm of the state	Courts perceived as a check on the powers of the state
Lawful society	Greater propensity to redefine or ignore rules
Use the system to change things	Employ informal, aggressive, and sometimes extra-legal means to correct what they think is wrong. "The greater lawlessness and corruption in the U.S. can also be attributed in part to a stronger emphasis on achievement"
Canadians find success in slightly bad taste	"Americans worship success"
Greater value of social relationships	Greater importance of work
	Higher commitment to work ethic
	Greater value of achievement (Goldfarb study)
Canadians more cautious	Americans take more risks
Corporate network denser in Canada. 1984—80% of companies on TSE controlled by 7 families. 32 families and 5 conglomerates control about 33% of all nonfinancial assets	100 largest firms own about 33% of all nonfinancial assets, few controlled by individuals
5 banks hold 80% of all deposits	Literally thousands of small banks in the United States
Anti-combines legislation weakly enforced	Business affected by anti-elitist and anti–big business sentiments
Favor partial or total government ownership	Strong antitrust laws
	Anti–big business, pro competition
Business leaders more likely to have privileged upbringing and less specialized education	Business leaders more likely to have a specialized education
Emphasis on social programs and government support	More laissez-faire
Canadian labor union density more than twice that of the American	
Fewer lobbying organizations in Canada even in proportion to smaller Canadian population. Since politicians toe party line, lobbying not as important	7,000 lobbying organizations registered with Congress— since Congresspersons can vote as they choose on a bill, lobbying can be effective

Source: Summarized from Seymour Martin Lipset, Continental Divide: The Values and Institutions of the United States and Canada (New York: Routledge, 1990).

Changing Values

Society's values change continuously, even though the core values are relatively permanent. Marketers must pay special attention to values in transition because they affect the size of market segments. Changes in values may alter responses

Table 17.3   Changing Values in Western Civilization

Traditional Values	New Values
Self-denial ethic	Self-fulfillment ethic
Higher standard of living	Better quality of life
Traditional sex roles	Blurring of sex roles
Accepted definition of success	Individualized definition of success
Traditional family life	Alternative families
Faith in industry, institutions	Self-reliance
Live to work	Work to live
Hero worship	Love of ideas
Expansionism	Pluralism
Patriotism	Less nationalistic
Unparalleled growth	Growing sense of limits
Industrial growth	Information/service growth
Receptivity to technology	Technology orientation

Note: Developed Western societies are gradually discarding traditional values and are beginning to embrace emerging new values on an ever-widening scale.
Source: Joseph T. Plummer, "Changing Values," Futurist 23 (January–February 1989), 10.

to advertising as well as responses to service offerings and preferred retailing formats. Some of the changes that are occurring in the 1990s have been identified in research at Young & Rubicam, shown in Table 17.3. They represent what Plummer calls a paradigm shift or a fundamental reordering of the way we see the world around us.[18]

Two types of forces explain both constancy and change in values. The first source of values is the triad of institutions: families, religious institutions, and schools. The second source is early lifetime experiences. Such experiences include wars, civil rights movements, and economic realities. Also, institutions such as government and the media transmit influences on values. Individuals internalize these values in a process affected by peers as well as by an individual's own decision and learning process (see Figure 17.1, page #000).

Changes in a society's values can be forecast on the basis of a **life-cycle explanation**, meaning that as individuals grow older, their values change. Therefore, the distinctive values seen now among young people will become like those of older ages in a few decades, and societal values in the future will be similar to today as younger people grow older and grow into the values of their parents. This is a theory of behavioral assimilation. **Generational change**, in contrast, suggests that there will be gradual replacement of existing values by those of young people who form the "leading" generation in value terms. When today's young people grow old, they will retain the values of their youth and replace societal values of today's older consumers.[19] Because you are probably young if you are reading this book, you hold the answer to these alternative explanations. About 30 years from now, will you be more like your peers or your parents?

Changing Institutions

The values of one generation are inculcated in the next primarily by family, religion, and education. This *cultural transfusive triad* plays a key role in understanding the values of a society, with help from media. As long as the triad institutions are stable, the values transmitted are relatively stable. When these institutions change rapidly, the values of consumers change, creating the need for corresponding changes in marketing and communications programs. Although the following changes are in the context of the United States, similar trends are occurring in many other countries.

Declining Family Influences

Family is the dominant transfusive agent of values in most cultures. Many changes are occurring in the family, examined more closely in Chapter 21. We look at only a few basic influences on values now.

Less time for in-home or parent–child influence is available for children. This is partly due to increased enrollments in preschool or day-care facilities. Among 3- to 4-year-olds, only 5.7 percent were enrolled in schools in 1965. Today that number is approaching 60 percent. In the past, children spent the first 6 formative years with their parents. Now, children must increasingly learn their values outside the family. Substitute parents, such as babysitters, schools, and the media, now transmit values to children. Today's parents may have extensive travel responsibilities and longer, irregular working hours. With both parents away from home much of the time, especially among the higher social classes, the values of children—who will eventually become our future leaders—depend more heavily on sources outside the family. An increase in illegitimate births from 5.3 percent in 1960 to a current rate of more than 26 percent and an increase in the proportion of children with single mothers from 8 percent to 22 percent also diminish the potential parental influence on children.

Increasing divorce rates contribute to decreased family influence as children are socialized in one-parent households. The divorce rate has more than doubled in the past 20 years; current estimates are that about half of all marriages formed in recent decades will end in divorce. Most children are now raised part of their lives in single-parent households. Divorced men typically remarry younger women. Therefore, the husband's children from his first marriage are likely to be older than the wife's first children, causing problems for reconstituted families of different ages.[20]

The isolated nuclear family or geographical separation of the nuclear family from grandparents and other relatives (extended family) contributes to decline in family influences on value transmission. Because of the increase in young people attending college, a larger percentage of families seek employment in areas far removed from where the family grew up; they therefore lose the influence of their extended families. This removes an important stabilizing or traditionalizing influence on values. The result may be a lack of heritage or a yearning for roots.

Communications and travel companies may benefit from families' geographical separation, provided they have effective marketing programs. Delta Airlines has developed a senior citizen program with ads that proclaim, "Attend weddings and family reunions and be sure to allow enough time to visit the grandchildren." Red Roof Inns has a program encouraging weekend rates for distant families and friends attending weddings.

How should businesses respond to the diminished influence of family? Some companies are reviewing their policies about job interference with family life; providing quality day-care centers for employees; encouraging families to travel out of town with executives; involving spouses in company seminars and newsletters; providing scholarships for employees' children; providing marital counseling; and in other ways recognizing the changing role of family life.

Changing Religious Influences

Judeo-Christian religious institutions historically played an important role in shaping the values of Western cultures. In recent years, these institutions have changed substantially.

Some religious groups necessarily grow at the expense of others. Catholics have risen from tiny levels in 1776 to a quarter of the U.S. population largely because of European immigration in the early 1900s and current immigration from Hispanic countries. Baptists have replaced Anglicans (Episcopalians) as the dominant Protestant group. More recently, rapidly growing groups, such as the Latter Day Saints (Mormons), have become a major influence on many of the values of their members. Non-Christian religions have gained influence in the United States, including many of the traditional Oriental religions and the New Age movement.

Groups declining in membership currently include moderate and liberal groups (Lutherans, Methodists, Presbyterians, Episcopalians, and others). The greatest gains in religious preference currently in the United States are among fundamentalists and among those with no religious preference.

Current trends in religious affiliation and attitudes are associated with the secularization of religious institutions—or loss of religious function. According to a thesis developed by Francis Schaeffer, religion has become compartmentalized and has lost some of its capacity to judge secular values and structure.[21] Although religion has weakened as an institutional influence in American society, it still is important for many individuals. For example, women are more likely than men to define success in religious terms.[22] Consumer in Focus 17.2 shows how Procter & Gamble has been influenced by religious belief or misunderstanding.

What are the effects of changing religious institutions on marketing? The answer seems to be that in coming years, values of consumers will be more personal, diversified, and pluralistic. Retailers report more inventory shrinkage if religious institutions decline because employees may no longer think stealing is wrong. If the traditional Judeo-Christian value system declines, firms need to recruit more selectively and to develop programs that inculcate values among employees.

17.2	**Consumer in Focus**

Cultural Values and Corporate Decisions

Procter & Gamble recently announced that its trademark man-in-the-moon logo would be modernized—to keep in step with fashion. Although P&G officials insisted that the make-over had absolutely nothing to do with Satanism charges, the new design restyled the curls in the man's beard, which, when held upside down before a mirror (perhaps in a graveyard, on a dark and stormy night) had clearly formed Beelzebub's favorite Lotto number: 666.

P&G made the switch several months after Burger King capitulated to a boycott led by Christian Leaders for Responsible Television (ClearTV) and placed big newspaper ads to announce that, of course, the company did not, never had, and never would support "anti-family, anti-Christian" TV shows. A spokesperson said Burger King would never sponsor NBC's "Saturday Night Live" because "you certainly don't know, because it's live, what might be said."

NBC has gotten the message. The network warned Universal Television, the producer of "Quantum Leap," that Universal would be liable for lost revenues if any advertisers pulled their spots from a planned episode dealing with homosexuality and suicide. (The show's time-traveling body-snatcher hero was due to inhabit the body of a despondent gay teenager.) NBC's unprecedented move came after advertisers had yanked spots from the NBC movie "Roe v. Wade" and an episode of ABC's "thirtysomething" that featured two men in bed together.

Source: "Slants & Trends," American Marketplace (October 10, 1991), 199.

Religious values are major influences on marketing, but what about the ability of marketing to affect religion? Can religious institutions use marketing methods to enhance effectiveness? The answer is yes. Much of the material presented in this textbook has been developed by Engel into a book specifically designed for religious organizations.[23] Religious institutions are doing consumer research and applying the results to marketing plans.[24]

Changing Educational Institutions

The third major institution that transmits values to consumers is education. The influence of education appears to be increasing, due partly to the increased participation of Americans in formal education and partly to the vacuum left by families and religious institutions. At the same time, there is concern about the nature of the increased influence.

A dramatic rise in formal education has occurred at all levels. The result is a highly educated work force. Today, one in four workers in the United States is a college graduate, up from about one in eight in 1970. Fewer women workers are college graduates compared with men, but currently more women are enrolled in colleges and universities than are men. Weekend MBA programs, "Night Owl" and "Early Bird" programs, and other innovations in university continuing education departments encourage higher levels of education, even among those beyond the usual college age.

Another trend in education involves the emergence and proliferation of new teaching methods. Previously, teaching often emphasized description and memorization. This approach to learning implicitly, if not explicitly, says, "This is the way things are; just learn it," with no latitude for questioning. There has been a gradual but steady trend away from these methods toward analytical approaches emphasizing questioning of the old and the formulation of new approaches and solutions. There is no one correct answer; new horizons are encouraged. The case method in business schools is an example of this analytical, questioning approach. Another effect is described in *The Closing of the American Mind*,[25] in which Bloom argues persuasively that American universities no longer provide much knowledge about values that arise from the great traditions of philosophy and literature.

Consumers who have been socialized in the new teaching environment may reject rigid definitions of right or wrong. Individuals, particularly younger consumers, are no longer willing to lead unexamined lives. This leads to aggressive consumerism, causing marketing organizations to revise their sales programs and product-information formats to provide answers when customers ask questions. Consumers may not complain to the firm but tell friends instead. Firms need complaint-management programs that seek out such complaints rather than just passively accept them. In a society in which new consumers are increasingly scarce, it may be profitable to compensate complaints of existing customers, even when compensation exceeds the product's profit margin.[26] Nordstrom department stores and Stew Leonard's grocery stores are examples of firms that prosper with liberal refunds and complaint handling.

These three institutions — family, religion, and school — all contribute to transmitting traditional values as well as creating receptivity for changed lifestyles.

Intergenerational Motivating Factors

Consumers are products of their environment. People strive as adults to achieve what they believe they were deprived of in early stages of life. As a result, consumer analysts can further understand the socialization process by studying early lifetime influences of groups of people who experience similar influences while growing up.

Cohort analysis is a method for investigating the changes in patterns of behavior or attitudes of groups called cohorts. A cohort is any group of individuals linked as a group in some way — usually by age. Cohort analysis focuses on actual changes in the behavior or attitudes of a cohort, the changes that can be attributed to the process of aging, and changes that are associated with events of a particular period, such as the Great Depression or the Watergate scandal.[27] Many marketing organizations have focused on the baby boomers, a group of consumers of similar age and experience, described in Chapter 2.

Pre-World War II Consumers

Millions of mature consumers experienced the Great Depression of the 1930s. Even more experienced the upheavals of World War II. The severity of these cataclysmic events profoundly and indelibly affected the people who lived through them. These events affected their values of security, patriotism, and the acquisition and protection of material goods. Such values reflect the deprivations that individuals experienced during the Depression and war.

Interpersonal Generation

The cohort of consumers who were children in the 1950s and 1960s — the Interpersonal Generation — express awareness and concern for other people. These early births after World War II who are now aging baby boomers manifest themselves in social concern on issues of civil rights and equal opportunity. Fashion is also more important. They were not interested in fashion in the sense of keeping up with the Joneses, as had been true of their parents, but fashion that emerged because of so much social contact and interpersonal awareness.

The Self Generation

The values of the last of the baby boomers emphasize the self — self-expression, self-realization, self-help, and do-it-yourself. Critical influences on this cohort include the energy crisis, inflation, feminism, and Watergate. Concern of the previous cohort was how to help others achieve the good life, but the most recent cohort is more concerned with the problem of maintaining the good lifestyle. You can see many of these values, likely to affect the 1990s, reflected in Table 17.3, page 627.

Self-interest and social concern are often blended on a personal basis. Consumers in today's cultural environment often express concern for the environment, not so much because it is socially correct behavior but because they must take responsibility for their own survival. Among other things, self-interest also emphasizes nutrition and health and perhaps how to cope with a midlife crisis. About 40 percent of Americans work out every day; a quarter take part in more than one sport; and wellness programs are increasingly supported by organizations as well as by individuals.[28] As a consequence, advertising frequently features such themes. Identification with healthy foods, personal appearance, and sports have surged in advertising usage for a broad array of products and services. The more sedentary may be motivated toward "cocooning" or "fortressing" in their suburban homes.

Firms that built their success on traditional values are changing. Notice how this is done by both McDonald's and Amway in Figure 17.5. McDonald's was built on what was often called junk food. Today, it is one of the fast-food industry's leaders in providing nutritional information and developing innovative products related to health concerns. Amway, stressing individual effort and success motivation described earlier in the chapter, also demonstrates its sensitivity to environmental issues, including an awareness of Native American ethnicity.

X-Generation

The most recent cohort of consumers are those emerging from colleges and universities currently who were born in the late sixties or seventies. Their childhood experiences included disco, seventies music, and the Iran cover-up. Their concerns are often federal deficits associated with an expanding tax and Social Security burden to provide for earlier generations. This causes some people to forecast a "generation war" as the X-generation faces the need to pay most of

Figure 17.5   Marketing Responses to Changing Values

Source: Courtesy of McDonald's and Amway.

their income to care for health and other needs of the skyrocketing numbers of older people.

Observers describe the X-generation as cynical, a result of being bombarded by the media during their youth by programs filled with violence, sexual abuse, and deviate behavior. Violent crime went from 16 per 10,000 people in 1960 to 76 per 10,000 in 1990, and homicide became the number two cause of death (after accidents) for their peers. X-ers listen to the cynical comedy of David Letterman and cynical commentary of Howard Stern and Rush Limbaugh, often rejecting the social concerns and political correctness of their parents and professors. They are faced with comments that only the best students will be recruited for careers with advancement potential and that the masses of the X-ers will be the first generation faced with jobs and lifestyles less than their parents. Many marketing organizations—managed probably by baby boomers—have difficulty in understanding how to appeal to the X-generation, as you can see in Consumer in Focus 17.3. Differences between the individualistic X-ers and their earlier baby boomer elders are shown in Table 17.4.

Consumer in Focus   **17.3**

Marketers Must Change to Fit Changing Cohorts

The Limited, known for its quick response to fashion shifts, doesn't quite understand the generational battles going on, according to Carol Farmer, a futurist and president of Carol Farmer Associates, speaking at the 1994 convention of the National Retail Federation. Nor do Ann Taylor Stores and Merry-Go-Round and other retailers who miss the changes in generational values.

There are five generations that make up today's society according to Farmer. The GI generation includes those age 69 and over. The silents are age 51 to 68; the boomers are age 33 to 50; generation X are age 12 to 32; and young children. Each generation has its own set of values and ideas.

The baby boomers made The Limited a major retailing force but boomers have different motivations than the X-ers. Boomers are idealists, nearing or experiencing midlife crises. They want to spend more time with their families and are less practical and materialistic than other generations. X-ers are made up of a group that is cynical and angry and are a mystery to retailers such as The Limited. Generation X doesn't have the buying power of the boomers but much of the marketing is directed at it.

Silents generally try to be generational peace keepers, Farmer believes, but trying to mix the boomers and X-ers in a single marketing strategy could be lethal. Instead, retailers need concepts that span the generations. "The Limited doesn't get the generational power struggle," she said. "You need to really reach these divisions (within a company) and decide what goes with whom." The Gap has been among the more successful speciality retailers catering to different generations, according to Farmer.

Source: Carol Farmer quoted in Barnet D. Wolf, "Wexner Missing Mark On Generations, Futurist Says," Columbus Dispatch (January 24, 1994), 8.

Table 17.4	Individualistic X-Generation Compared with Baby Boomers (Attitudes of high school seniors in 1975 and 1988)		
		1988	**1975**
How important is it to have a job that provides you with a chance to earn a good deal of money?		86%	72%
How likely do you think it is that you would stay married to the same for life? (percent very likely)		58	65
I enjoy the fast pace and changes of today's world.		57	41
Most people can be trusted. (percent agree)		23	35

Source: Institute for Social Research, University of Michigan, quoted in Cheryl Russel, "The Master Trend," American Demographics 15 (October 1993), 28–37.

National Culture

Culture has a profound impact on the way consumers perceive themselves, products they buy and use, purchasing processes, and the organizations from which they purchase. It is because of this impact that thinking seriously about buying and consumption requires serious thinking about culture and how it is inculcated. Methods of studying a nation's culture were described in Chapter 3 in the context of cross-cultural or global markets. Marketers are giving more attention, however, to understanding overall or macrocultures, whether for global marketing or domestic marketing.

Culture can be viewed as the collective mental programming of people in an environment. Culture represents the characteristics of people conditioned by the same institutions (cultural transfusive triad) and life experiences. Hofstede[29] found that four dimensions in culture are common among 66 countries:

Individualism versus collectivism. Individualism describes the relationship between an individual and fellow individuals, the collectivity which prevails in society. Countries such as the United States and the Netherlands display strong individualism whereas countries such as Taiwan have a high degree of collectivism or expectations that people should hold only opinions and behaviors sanctioned by their in-group.

Uncertainty avoidance. Uncertainty avoidance concerns the different ways in which societies react to the uncertainties and ambiguities inherent in life. Some societies need well-defined rules or rituals to guide behavior whereas others are tolerant of deviant ideas and behavior.

Power distance. Power distance reflects the degree to which a society accepts inequality in power at different levels in organizations and institutions. It can affect preferences for centralization of authority, acceptance of differential rewards, and the ways people of unequal status work together.

Masculinity–femininity. This factor defines the extent to which societies hold values traditionally regarded as predominantly masculine or feminine. Assertiveness, respect for achievement, and the acquisition of money and material possessions are identified with masculinity; and nurturing, concern for the environment, and championing the underdog are associated with a culture's score on femininity. The Hofstede analysis is used increasingly in marketing studies. McIntyre, Meloche, and Lewis[30] found Hofstede's conceptualization of culture to be useful in identifying environmentally sensitive segments of the market. Kaale[31] has shown how cultural understanding can improve the effectiveness of personal selling and has found it useful in management education programs.

Marketing is done in an environment of multicultural diversity. This requires an understanding of the culture and values of these markets. This chapter has focused on the macroculture of North America, principally the United States and Canada, setting a foundation for microcultures in the next chapter.

Summary

Culture is the complex of values, ideas, attitudes, and other meaningful symbols that allow humans to communicate, interpret, and evaluate as members of society. Culture and its values are transmitted from one generation to another. The core values of a society define how products are used, with regard to their function, form, and meaning. Culture also provides positive and negative valences for brands and for communications programs and defines the ideology of consumption.

Core values in America include material well-being; twofold moralizing; the concepts that work is more important than play and that time is money; effort-optimism-entrepreneurship; mastery over nature; egalitarianism; and humanitarianism. Canadian and U.S. values are more similar to each other than to most other countries but differ in significant ways.

The fundamental forces that form values include the cultural transfusive triad and early lifetime experiences. The former refers to the influence of the institutions of the family, religion, and schools. The latter refers to basic intergenerational influences, such as depressions, wars, and other major events. Contemporary consumers are oriented to self-fulfillment and satisfaction among baby boomers and cynical individualism among the X-generation.

Four dimensions of macrocultures have been identified by Hofstede. They are individualism versus collectivism, uncertainty avoidance, power distance, and masculinity–femininity.

Review and Discussion Questions

1. What is meant by the term *culture?* Why does this term create confusion about its meaning?

2. What are some of the factors in the *ideology of consumption?* Why should this concept be of concern to marketers?

3. Where do consumers get their values?

4. Examine the American core values described in this chapter. Consider how they might influence a marketer of consumer electronics products.

5. Select the topic of family, religious institutions, or schools, and prepare a report documenting the changes that are occurring in the institution you chose.

6. Describe ways in which advertising directed to consumers brought up during the Depression era might differ compared with that directed at consumers of the post-World War II era. What do you consider to be the most important changes that will occur in the future?

7. Describe values of the X-generation. What appeals or methods of marketing are likely to be effective with this market segment?

8. Select one of the dimensions of culture identified by Hofstede, and describe how it might be used in market segmentation.

Endnotes

1. Hazel Rose Markus and Shinobu Kitayama, "Culture and the Self: Implications for Cognition, Emotion, and Motivation," *Psychological Review* 98 (1991), 224–253.

2. Harry C. Triandis, "Cross-Cultural Studies of Individualism and Collectivism," in John Berman, ed., *Nebraska Symposium on Motivation* (Lincoln: University of Nebraska Press, 1989), 41–133.

3. Phillip R. Harris and Robert T. Moran, *Managing Cultural Differences* (Houston: Gulf Publishing Company, 1987), 190–195.

4. P. Valette-Florence and A. Jolibert, "Social Values, A.I.O., and Consumption Patterns," *Journal of Business Research* 20 (1990), 109–122.

5. George P. Moschis, *Consumer Socialization* (Lexington, Mass.: Lexington Books, 1987), 9.

6. "Miele," in Roger D. Blackwell, Kristina S. Blackwell, and W. Wayne Talarzyk, *Contemporary Cases in Consumer Behavior* (Hinsdale, Ill.: Dryden Press, 1993), 452–462.

7. James H. Leigh and Terrance G. Gabel, "Symbolic Interactionism: Its Effects on Consumer Behavior and Implications for Marketing Strategy," *Journal of Consumer Marketing* 9 (Winter 1992), 27–38.

8. Jagdish N. Sheth, Bruce I. Newman, and Barbara L. Gross, "Why We Buy What We Buy: A Theory of Consumption Values," *Journal of Business Research* 22 (1991), 159–170.

9. Grant McCracken, "Culture and Consumption: A Theoretical Account of the Structure and Movement of the Cultural Meaning of Consumer Goods," *Journal of Consumer Research* 13 (June 1986), 71–81.

10. Bettina Cornwell, Alan David Bligh, and Emin Babakus, "Complaint Behavior of Mexican-American Consumers to a Third-Party Agency," *Journal of Consumer Affairs* 25 (Summer 1991), 1–18.

11. Stuart Plattner, "Equilibrating Market Relationships" (paper presented to Society for Economic Anthropology Conference, University of California-Davis, April 6–7, 1984).

12. Angela da Rocha, Rebecca Arkader, and Antonio Barretto, "On Networks and Bonds: A Cultural Analysis of the Nature of Relationships," in David W. Cravens and Peter R. Dickson, eds., *Enhancing Knowledge Development in Marketing* (Chicago: American Marketing Association, 1993), 92–96.

13. William Taylor, "Crime? Greed? Big Ideas? What Were the '80s About?" *Harvard Business Review* (January–February 1992), 32–45.

14. Conrad M. Arensberg and Arthur H. Niehoff, "American Cultural Values," in James P. Spradley and Mihale A. Rykiewich, eds., *The Nacirema: Readings on American Culture* (Boston: Little, Brown and Company, 1980), 363–379. Table 17.1 builds on Arensberg and Niehoff.

15. Carl Sewell, *Customers for Life* (New York: Doubleday, 1990).

16. "Benetton Ads: A Risqué Business," *Time* (March 25, 1991), 13.

17. Seymour M. Lipset, *North American Cultures: Values and Institutions in Canada and the United States* (Orono, Maine: Borderlands, 1990), 6.

18. Joseph T. Plummer, "Changing Values," *Futurist* 23 (January–February 1989), 8–13.

19. Sheena Ashford and Noel Timms, *What Europe Thinks: A Study of Western European Values* (Aldershot: Dartmouth, 1992).

20. Karhyn A. Lond and Barbara F. Wilson, "Divorce," *American Demographics* 10 (October 1988), 23–26.

21. Francis A. Schaeffer, *How Should We Then Live?* (Old Tappan, N.J.: Fleming H. Revel Company, 1976).

22. "A Measure of Success," *American Demographics* 13 (April 1991), 9.

23. James Engel, *Contemporary Christian Communications* (Nashville, Tenn.: Thomas Nelson, 1979).

24. James F. Engel and H. Wilbert Norton, *What's Gone Wrong with the Harvest?* (Grand Rapids, Mich.: Zondervan Publishing House, 1975); Donald McGavran, *Understanding Church Growth* (Grand Rapids, Mich.: William B. Eerdmans, 1970).

25. Allan Bloom, *The Closing of the American Mind* (New York: Simon and Schuster, 1987).

26. Claes Fornell and Birger Wernerfelt, "Defensive Marketing Strategy by Customers' Complaint Management: A Theoretical Analysis, *Journal of Marketing Research* 24 (November 1987), 337–346.

27. Norval D. Glenn, *Cohort Analysis* (Beverly Hills, Calif.: Sage Publications, 1977).

28. Doris Walsh, "A Healthy Trend," *American Demographics* 6 (July 1984), 4–6.

29. Gert Hofstede, *Culture's Consequences: International Differences in Work-Related Values* (Beverly Hills, Calif.: Sage Publications, 1984).

30. Roger P. McIntyre, Martin S. Meloche, and Susan L. Lewis, "National Culture as a Macro Tool for Environmental Sensitivity Segmentation," in David Cravens and Peter Dickson, eds., *Enhancing Knowledge Development in Marketing* (Chicago: American Marketing Association, 1993), 153–159.

31. Sudhir H. Kaale, "The Cultural Domain of Cross-National Buyer–Seller Interactions," in Cravens and Dickson, *Enhancing Knowledge Development in Marketing*, 208–213.

CHAPTER 18

Ethnic Influences on Consumer Behavior

▲▲▲▲▲▲▲▲▲▲▲▲▲▲▲▲▲▲▲▲▲▲▲▲▲▲▲▲▲▲▲▲▲▲▲▲▲

Cultural Influences in the Marketplace

A young violinist steps to the front of the stage to perform with one of the world's great orchestras. At age 12, she has already captivated audiences, critics, and fellow musicians the world over with her astonishing technical facility and the depth and range of her musicality. When Zubin Mehta first heard her play at age 8, he was so impressed that he invited her to be guest soloist with the New York Philharmonic where she thrilled audiences playing the Paganini Concerto No. 1. In 1994, her talent was broadcast worldwide, airing on PBS's "Great Performances" series. Born in Philadelphia to Korean parents, her name is Sarah Chang.

Observers were probably no more surprised to learn that Sarah Chang is an Asian-American than they were when Kristi Yamaguchi represented America by winning the Olympic Gold Medal in figure skating nor when African-American Michael Jordan became America's most respected and highest paid athlete. Nor should observers have been surprised to learn that America's last two commanding generals of the Joint Chiefs of Staff have been General Colin Powell, an African-American of Jamaican cultural background, and General John "Shali" Shalikashvili, a Polish-born person of Georgian and German heritage.

Consumers are influenced when buying and consuming products by both **macroculture** discussed in the last chapter and **microculture**, referring to values and symbols of a restrictive group such as a religious, ethnic, or other subdivision of the whole. Remember that microcultures are frequently called *subcultures*, but we use the term *microculture* because calling ethnic groups *subcultures* might connote inferiority. The norms and values of specific groups or microcultures are called **ethnic patterns**, which affect many aspects of living, including buying and consumption of products.

The individuals you read about in the opening scenario may have been influenced slightly or extensively by the ethnic patterns of the microculture in which they were raised. That depends on the individual. They also may be a member of several ethnic groups, each with varying influence. Which influence will be greatest on a consumer such as Whoopi Goldberg? Her color (black)? Her religion (Jewish)? Her gender (female)? Or her income class (high)? And what are the effects on the more typical black woman. Audrey Murell says that being a "double minority" black woman means that it takes 10 months to earn what white women and black men make in 8 months and white men earn in 6 months.[1]

The products purchased by members of ethnic groups may be heavily influenced by the ability to buy. Asian minority groups earn more income than majority groups, but other minority groups earn less, as you can see in Table 18.1. If you are Jewish, Christian Scientist, or Episcopalian, you are also more likely to be more affluent than if you are Baptist or Pentecostal.

Ethnicity is a process of group identification in which people use ethnic labels to define themselves and others. A "subjectivist" perspective reflects ascriptions people make about themselves. An "objectivist" definition is derived from sociocultural categories. In consumer research, ethnicity is best defined as some combination of these, including the strength or weakness of affiliation that people have with the ethnic group.[2] To the degree that people in an ethnic group share common perceptions and cognitions that are different from those of other ethnic groups or the larger society, they constitute a distinct ethnic group or market segment.[3] Consumer behavior is a function of "felt ethnicity" as well as cultural identity, social surroundings, and product type.[4]

Multicultural Societies

Cultural diversity and equality of treatment may be highly valued in multicultural societies such as the United States and Singapore. In much of the world, however, ethnic differences may not be so valued. It may be culturally acceptable to assign work roles or differential status and rewards on the basis of culture. In Mexico, for example, indigenous Indians are not expected to be in management positions, which are controlled by European descendants. In Japan, it took an AT&T manager months to get Japanese managers to talk to key East Indian employees.[5]

The values and norms of an ethnic microculture may conflict with the values of the macroculture. Individuals exhibit a synthesis of the macroculture and perhaps several microcultures. It is important to keep in mind as you read this chapter that specific consumers may not reflect the values of the ethnic group with which they are commonly identified. To believe that a given individual necessarily accepts the values of any specific microculture would make the observer guilty of stereotyping.

Table 18.1　Median Income by Race and Hispanic Origin		
	Number of Households (1,000)	1991 Income ($)
White	81,675	31,569
Black	11,083	18,807
Asian, Pacific Islander	2,094	36,449
Hispanic	6,379	22,691
Source: U.S. Bureau of the Census, Current Population Reports, P60-180.		

Microcultures may be formed around nationality, religion, physical attributes, geographic location, or other factors. The gay/lesbian market could be considered a microculture, although marketing to this group is discussed later, in the chapter on family/household. Bikers or the Gray Panthers might even be an important ethnic group for some. Consumer in Focus 18.1 describes some of the advantages in business of belonging to a "tribe" or ethnic group.

Native American Culture

In a sense, the truly "American" culture is that of Native Americans, although marketers view Native Americans as a minority ethnic group in today's majority culture. Almost 2 million people in the United States identified themselves as American Indian in the 1990 census and more than 7 million claim some American Indian ancestry. The 1990 figure was 38 percent more than in 1980, a higher growth rate than for African-Americans (6 percent) but not as high as the growth rate for Hispanics (53 percent) or Asian (108 percent).[6]

After nearly a century of assimilation into white society, there is a resurgence of identification with Native American culture, both by Indians and *bahanas* (whites). Some American Indians dislike the idea of sharing their culture and spiritual practices with white people, but others welcome people of any race into their culture. The interest in Native American culture has increased consumer demand for products that reflect their ancient crafts and skills. The movie *Dances with Wolves* helped to stimulate demand for Native American literature and arts.

Other Nationality Groups

America is a montage of nationality groups. It has been called the greatest genetic pool of malcontents in the world, composed mostly of people or the descendants of people who were dissatisfied in their original nation and sought something better. England is the background nation for 26.34 percent of Americans, followed closely by Germany with 26.14 percent. The 50-million figure for English Americans is higher than the current population of England. The Irish are the third largest, with 17.77 percent, followed by African-Americans at 11.13

percent. Other nationality groups with significant numbers include French, Italian, Scottish, Polish, and Mexican, but recent figures register 54 countries represented with 100,000 or more American residents.

Some immigrants identify with much of their culture of origin; others do not. A variable closely associated with national ethnic identity is the language spoken at home. Two groups of Americans who often speak a language other than English are Chinese and Hispanics. Eighty-one percent of Chinese-Americans speak Chinese at home. About 43 percent of Hispanics speak Spanish at home, including Cuban-Americans at 92 percent and Mexican-Americans at 77 percent of the households.[7]

A key issue is the degree to which immigrants embrace traditional American core values. Some nationality groups contribute to the cultural diversity of North America more than others, but frequently the variables that lead to success for

---

18.1	**Consumer in Focus**

Ethnic and Religious "Tribes" Will Dominate the Business Future

"What's your tribe?" The answer to that question may define your business success in the coming years. A tribe is any group of people, spread out across the world, whose language, religion, or culture knits the members together to create a powerfully efficient business network. Members of these groups cut deals with each other, advance the group's interests alongside their own, trade privileged information, offer special opportunities and lower prices to other group members—and are rewarded by instant access to thousands of customers, distributors, investors, and suppliers who won't deal with outsiders.

Perhaps you belong to a close-knit ethnic group like the Armenians or the Jews, bound together by family ties and 3,000 year old traditions. Or maybe you're part of a religious tribe like the Mormons, whose congregants trade business cards as gleefully as they share their faith. Whatever your group, you should carefully nurture your ties with it, if you plan to succeed in the coming economy.

Unconditional group loyalty. What do Hasidic Jews and Jains—a sect of Indian ascetics—have in common? Both dominate major diamond markets because everyone knows everyone else. It's why Orthodox Jews are good in this business. If you break the rules, you risk being cast totally out.

"Shameless" love of gain. The strongest tribes teach their warriors to love financial gain without shame or guilt. While medieval Christians were told to admire the poor, the Talmud warned that, "Poverty is more painful than fifty lashes." The British were despised by other Europeans for their grubby commercialism—but England went on to dominate the world.

Mutual aid. Tribal loyalty demands that the strong help the weak, for the survival of the whole. Immigrant groups commonly admonish their members against taking business outside the community.

Flexibility. Jews often found themselves excluded or overwhelmed by the stronger resources of Gentiles. Unable to compete in the higher circles of industrial capitalism, they fixed their attention on many of the emerging niches of the developing world economy, for which they are now best known, such as diamonds, communications, fashion, retailing, entertainment, and the professions.

Source: Excerpts from Joel Kotkin, "Go Native!" Success (September 1993), 80.

majority Americans are the same as for immigrants who become nationality-market segments. When an immigrant family becomes American, the members often manifest and reinforce the work ethic that is at the core of American values.[8]

Religious Ethnic Groups

Religious groups have important influences on consumption. Mormons, for example, may refrain from purchasing tobacco, liquor, and other stimulants but may be prime prospects for fruit juices endorsed by Marie and Donnie Osmond. The *Christian Science Monitor* is not the best place for ads for Anacin or Tylenol. Seventh-Day Adventists limit their purchases of meat and may be prime targets for vegetable-based foods.

Born-again Christians are sometimes less materialistic and less interested in consumer goods than other Americans, have low use of credit, and have weaker-than-average preferences for national brands. They have higher per capita consumption, however, of automobiles and motorcycles, groceries and fast food, apparel stores, sporting goods, insurance, and products from hardware or fabric and pattern stores.[9]

Consumer in Focus 18.2 shows how some firms target evangelicals.

Consumer in Focus   18.2

Marketing to a Religious Ethnic Segment

A recent advertisement in the *Saturday Evening Post* appealed to readers to buy Dayspring greeting cards, "When You Want to Share Your Heart and God's Love," reflecting an increased amount of attention given by advertising to the large (59 million) consumer market segment comprising "evangelicals" or "born-again Christians."

Research generally indicates that highly religious people tend to be more moral, empathetic, conscientious, and consistent, more disciplined, responsible, dependent and social, more conservative and traditional, more submissive and trusting, less dominant, less prone to hold "feminist" positions, more insightful and mature, and more positive regarding their quality of life. They are better than average consumers of automobiles, motorcycles, grocery stores, fast-food and family restaurants, apparel, sporting goods, drug stores, insurance companies, hardware stores, and fabric and pattern stores.

Evangelicals are less likely to be reached by the business section, news section, or sports section of the local paper than are the general population. They are more likely to read publications such as *Guideposts*, *Moody Monthly*, or *Crossroads*, as well as *Reader's Digest*. They have heavy readership of *Time* and *Newsweek* but are less likely to read *Business Week*, *National Enquirer*, sports magazines such as *Sports Illustrated*, and skin magazines such as *Playboy*, *Playgirl*, and *Penthouse*.

Source: Excerpts from Stephen W. McDaniel and John J. Burnett, "Targeting the Evangelical Market Segment," Journal of Advertising Research 31 (August–September 1991), 26–33.

Jewish ethnicity is both religious and national and is an attractive market for many firms. Food products provide specific identification for kosher certification. Maxwell House coffee and Tetley tea have tried to appeal to Jewish consumers by featuring bagels in their ads. Star-Kist says, "Beautify a bialy with Star-Kist tuna salad surprise." Chef Boyardee promotes its macaroni shells with the line, "Treat your macaroni mayvin to real Italian taste."

Recent research has concentrated on differences in cognitive processing and other variables related to ethnicity. Hirschman[10] found that Jewish norms create more childhood information exposure than among other groups, more adult information seeking, consumption innovativeness, consumption information transfer, and more active memory capacity. Jewish consumers are more disposed toward sensory gratification and arousal compared with other nationality groups, as evidenced by the types of leisure activities they prefer and their motives for engaging in these activities. Jewish (and also Hispanic) consumers appear more oriented toward sensual behavior (for example, making love) in leisure activity than do other nationality groups that have been examined, and they differ substantially from Christians in product-salience rankings. The research by Hirschman clearly indicates that ethnicity (Jewish or otherwise) is a variable of large potential influence. The more an individual consumer identifies with the ethnic group, the greater the influence is likely to be.

Geographic Culture

Geographic areas in a nation sometimes develop their own culture. The Southwest area of the United States is known for casual lifestyles featuring comfortable clothing, outdoor entertaining, and active sports. The Southwest may also appear to be more innovative toward new products, such as cosmetic surgery, when compared with conservative, inhibited attitudes that characterize other areas of the nation. Climate, religious affiliations of the population, nationality influences, and other variables are interrelated to produce a core of cultural values in a geographic area.

The *Nine Nations of North America*, as conceived by Joel Garreau[11] cut across national, state, and provincial borders of North America. This conceptualization incorporates the culture of each area, as well as its climate, institutions, business organizations, and resources such as minerals and water. In Garreau's system, North America is described as consisting of the following areas: The Foundry (industrial Northeast); Dixie; Ectopia (northern Pacific Rim); Mexamericana (Southwest wealthy area); Breadbasket; Quebec; The Empty Quarter (Northwest Canada); the Islands; and New England.

The application of geographic values to marketing is explained by Kahle:[12]

> Contemporary marketing managers must also know that marketing activities often vary from one place to another. Because the underlying causes of success and failure in various places may not always be evident, understanding the values of various regions may provide an important clue to deciphering what sometimes seems like a regionally random pattern of successful expe-

riences in marketing both new and established products. For example, an advertisement promoting the capacity for self-fulfillment (e.g., "Set yourself free with Stouffer's") of a product may be more successful in the West than in the South. Security, on the other hand, may be a more successful appeal in the South than in comparably urbanized areas of the West (e.g., "Protect your home from break-ins with Electronic Touch Alarm"). For personal computers, an advertising campaign emphasizing how computers can help one accomplish his/her goals or emphasizing the computer attributes that facilitate accomplishment will probably be more effective in the East than in the South, and particularly in the West South Central.

The interests of marketers in the United States are most focused on three ethnic groups: African-Americans, Hispanics (Latinos), and Asian-Americans. The rest of the chapter is devoted to these market segments, as well as French-Canadians. Table 18.2 shows the number of people in each of these groups by geographic region, with detailed categories of some, as of the most recent census in the United States.

African-American or Black Culture

African-American or black culture refers to a common heritage rather than to a skin color. In the United States, the black heritage is conditioned by an American beginning in slavery, a shared history of discrimination and suffering, confined housing opportunities, and denial of participation in many aspects of the majority culture. Greater homogeneity in black markets than among white markets has been historically a valid assumption, although that may be challenged as well-educated black people achieve substantial separation in income and social status from other black people.[13] Some firms build appeals to the cultural heritage into their advertising as you can see in ads for McDonald's and Seagrams in Figure 18.1.

The African-American market is worthy of serious marketing attention. It has a population base of more than 30 million (and growing faster than the white population base, as you saw in Chapter 2) and buying power estimated as high as $280 billion.[14] If U.S. black consumers were considered a separate country, that country would rank as eleventh largest in the Free World. The African-American middle class is emerging as an important source of consumer buying power and influence. Despite the fact that African-Americans comprise 12.1 percent of the U.S. population and 11.3 percent of the readership of all magazines, on the average only 3.15 percent of the people shown in magazine advertising are black and only 7.5 percent of television ads include black actors. Blacks (and other minorities) are underrepresented, declining in representation, and frequently shown in stereotypical or menial roles.[15] The research of Whittler and others indicates that it makes sound economic sense for an advertiser to

Table 18.2   Resident Population, by Region, Race, and Hispanic Origin

Race and Hispanic Origin	Population (1,000)					Percent Distribution				
	United States	Northeast	Midwest	South	West	United States	Northeast	Midwest	South	West
Total	248,710	50,809	59,669	85,446	52,786	100.0	20.4	24.0	34.4	21.2
White	199,686	42,069	52,018	65,582	40,017	100.0	21.1	26.0	32.8	20.0
Black	29,986	5,613	5,716	15,829	2,828	100.0	18.7	19.1	52.8	9.4
American Indian, Eskimo, Aleut	1,959	125	338	563	933	100.0	6.4	17.2	28.7	47.6
American Indian	1,878	122	334	557	866	100.0	6.5	17.8	29.7	46.1
Eskimo	57	2	2	3	51	100.0	2.9	3.5	4.9	88.8
Aleut	24	2	2	3	17	100.0	8.1	8.1	11.5	72.3
Asian or Pacific Islander	7,274	1,335	768	1,122	4,048	100.0	18.4	10.6	15.4	55.7
Chinese	1,645	445	133	204	863	100.0	27.0	8.1	12.4	52.4
Filipino	1,407	143	113	159	991	100.0	10.2	8.1	11.3	70.5
Japanese	848	74	63	67	643	100.0	8.8	7.5	7.9	75.9
Asian Indian	815	285	146	196	189	100.0	35.0	17.9	24.0	23.1
Korean	799	182	109	153	355	100.0	22.8	13.7	19.2	44.4
Vietnamese	615	61	52	169	334	100.0	9.8	8.5	27.4	54.3
Laotian	149	16	28	29	76	100.0	10.7	18.6	19.6	51.0
Cambodian	147	30	13	19	85	100.0	20.5	8.8	13.1	57.7
Thai	91	12	13	24	43	100.0	12.9	14.2	26.0	46.8
Hmong	90	2	37	2	50	100.0	1.9	41.3	1.8	55.0
Pakistani	81	28	15	22	17	100.0	34.3	18.9	26.5	20.4
Hawaiian	211	4	6	12	189	100.0	2.0	2.6	5.8	89.6
Samoan	63	2	2	4	55	100.0	2.4	3.6	6.4	87.6
Guamanian	49	4	3	8	34	100.0	7.3	6.4	16.8	69.5
Other Asian or Pacific Islander	263	49	34	54	126	100.0	18.5	12.9	20.6	48.0
Other races	9,805	1,667	829	2,350	4,960	100.0	17.0	8.5	24.0	50.6
Hispanic origin*	22,354	3,754	1,727	6,767	10,106	100.0	16.8	7.7	30.3	45.2
Mexican	13,496	175	1,153	4,344	7,824	100.0	1.3	8.5	32.2	58.0
Puerto Rican	2,728	1,872	258	406	192	100.0	68.6	9.4	14.9	7.0
Cuban	1,044	184	37	735	88	100.0	17.6	3.5	70.5	8.5
Other Hispanic	5,086	1,524	279	1,282	2,002	100.0	30.0	5.5	25.2	39.4
Not of Hispanic origin	226,356	47,055	57,942	78,679	42,680	100.0	20.8	25.6	34.8	18.9

* Persons of Hispanic origin may be of any race.

Source: U.S. Bureau of the Census, 1990 Census of the Population, General Population Characteristics, United States (CP-1-1).

consider including black actors in advertisements for both black audiences and for mixed audiences.[16]

There is controversy about whether *black* or *African-American* is the preferred term of usage. More than 70 percent of black Americans prefer the term *black*, compared with 15 percent preferring African-American. After considering all the issues involved, Williams recommends the most prudent choice for marketers is the term *black/African-American*.[17] Structural influences shape African-American

Figure 18.1 Appeals to African-American Heritage

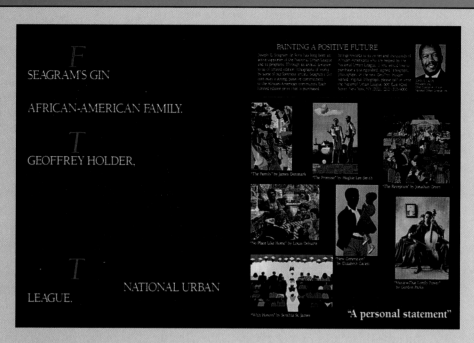

ethnic markets. They also inhibit some black consumer preferences or intentions. These structural influences include low income, educational deprivation, different family characteristics, and discrimination.

Income Deprivation

The African-American culture is sometimes associated with the low-income culture. This confusion is not difficult to understand because black consumers average less income than white consumers. About 33 percent of black families are below the poverty level, as defined by the U.S. Department of Commerce, compared with only about 11 percent of white families and 29 percent of Hispanic families. More white families fall below the poverty level in absolute terms, but the percentage of black families is larger.[18]

Two factors related to low income among black families are significant in the study of consumer behavior. First, there is the direct effect derived from reducing spending power. Consumers often must buy from stores that welcome food stamps; many products are not financially within the reach of poor consumers; and, to a large degree, income must be spent on the basics of life.

The second factor is the methodologic complexity of separating effects caused by low income from those due to being African-American. Some studies attempt to correct for the income differences when reporting black–white differences, but many report "differences" between black and white consumers that are mostly differences in income levels. If marketers do not recognize this problem, it is easy to minimize the importance of middle- and higher-income black market targets. There are more similarities than differences in black and white spending. Most of the differences are linked to African-Americans' lower incomes and concentrations in central cities.[19]

Educational Deprivation

Inadequate education places African-American consumers at a disadvantage not only in earning income but in acquiring consumer skills. Such skills must be learned on the street if not at school. Because of inadequate resources or by design, schools have often failed in helping black consumers master the educational skills needed for full participation in the market system.

Quality education can also provide a way out for black consumers. Some advertisers sponsor scholarship contests as you can see in Figure 18.2 featuring Sears and State Farm Insurance. Ads showing consumer durables and other expensive goods often use models portraying occupations that require education, knowing that many black customers recognize this is the best way to upward mobility and the middle-class lifestyle. The advantages of education are obvious in the Coors ad in Figure 18.3, but the U.S. Army ad also appeals to the need to overcome the difficulty of getting jobs faced by many black consumers. Research

Figure 18.2 Appeals to Education

by Qualls and Moore gives some indication, however, that the actors used in the ads must be consistent with the cognitive schema or expectations of the target market.[20]

Family Characteristics

The African-American culture is influenced by unique family characteristics, primarily a highly mobile family structure. A high proportion of families are headed by women, perhaps twice as high as for white families. Therefore, black women influence purchases and create subtleties of relationships an advertiser must understand and consider in devising advertisements. Only 38 percent of black children live with two parents compared with 80 percent of white children.[21]

The typical black family is much younger than the typical white family. The median age is about 5 years younger, a factor accounting for differences in preferences for clothing, music, shelter, cars, and many other products and activities.[22]

Figure 18.3 Appeals to Job Importance for Black Consumers

Discrimination

The effects of discrimination on the African-American culture are so massive and enduring that they cannot be ignored in the analysis of consumer behavior. Discrimination has been particularly restrictive on black consumption decisions in the area of housing.

As a result of years of discrimination, black consumers should have substantial skepticism toward white businesses. Affirmative action programs, about which substantial controversy exists concerning their effectiveness, have not achieved employment parity for African-Americans. A major factor in the underrepresentation of minorities in higher- and lower-status occupations is discrimination.[23] Many businesses contributed to limited employment opportunities as well as segregated residential patterns. They supported invisibility of blacks in the media until recent years. Today, firms that make a special effort to show sensitivity to the black culture, use black media wisely, and stand against discrimination may be able to turn a problem into an opportun-

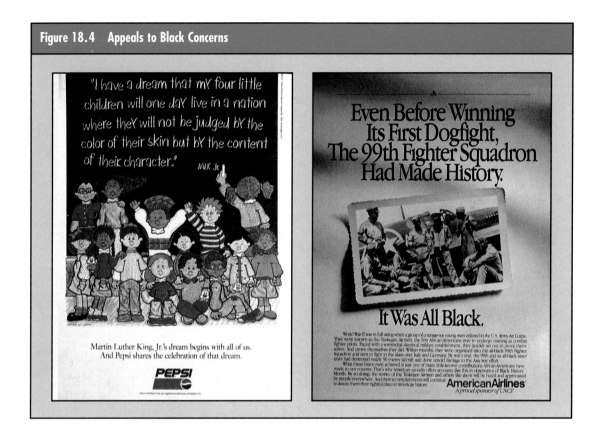

Figure 18.4 Appeals to Black Concerns

"I have a dream that my four little children will one day live in a nation where they will not be judged by the color of their skin but by the content of their character."

MLK Jr.

Martin Luther King, Jr.'s dream begins with all of us. And Pepsi shares the celebration of that dream.

PEPSI

Even Before Winning Its First Dogfight, The 99th Fighter Squadron Had Made History.

It Was All Black.

World War II was in full swing when a group of courageous young men enlisted in the U.S. Army Air Corps. They were known as the Tuskegee Airmen, the first African-Americans ever to undergo training as combat fighter pilots. Faced with a somewhat skeptical military establishment, they quickly set out to prove themselves. And prove themselves they did. Within months, they were organized into the all-black 99th Fighter Squadron and sent to fight in the skies over Italy and Germany. By war's end, the 99th and its all-black sister units had destroyed nearly 50 enemy aircraft and done untold damage to the Axis war effort.

What these brave men achieved is just one of many little-known contributions African-Americans have made to our country. That is why American proudly offers accounts like this in observance of Black History Month. By so doing, the stories of the Tuskegee Airmen and others like them will be heard and appreciated by people everywhere. And their accomplishments will continue **AmericanAirlines** to assure them their rightful place in American history. *A proud sponsor of UNCF*

---

ity. Notice how Pepsi and American Airlines attempt to build rapport with black consumers (Figure 18.4). These ads appeared in *Ebony* magazine.

Many companies target black consumers through public relations and special promotions. Kraft publishes a free booklet featuring African-American cooking. For several years, Budweiser has offered posters of "The Great Kings and Queens of Africa." Coca-Cola sponsors a "Share the Dream" scholarship program. American Airlines features ads with prominent black Americans such as Olympic runner Florence Griffith-Joyner and film maker Spike Lee. Most of these promotions are scheduled to appear around Black History Month in February.[24] Some of the most important of these programs encourage young African-Americans to become entrepreneurs or "kidpreneurs." Most of these programs combine an academic curriculum with hands-on experiences, making business skills both challenging and fun for children to learn.[25] White- or black-owned firms that hope to reach the black community in this mission must be prepared to invest human resources, often with the assistance of organizations active in this task. Table 18.3 lists some of these organizations as well as other ways to encourage "kidpreneurs."

Table 18.3 Developing African-American Kidpreneurs

How to Encourage Your Children in Business: Enroll Them in a Program

For help in finding programs, contact your local NAACP, Urban League, or National Business League. Also, check with social service organizations like the YWCA/YMCA and Boys and Girls Clubs. Colleges and universities often offer programs for children through their continuing education divisions. Many school districts, professional associations, and some churches also are beginning to sponsor programs. Experts say good programs for children should feature:

• Instructors who have owned and operated a business and/or
  business owners from the local community who work as mentors with students;
• A solid curriculum that explains business concepts in a way children can understand and relate to;
• Funding that includes money to finance start-ups so that children can gain hands-on experience owning and operating
  a business;
• An active, knowledgeable, committed program administrator and board of directors.

Start Your Own Program

Other concerned parents and business people probably will help you organize the effort. For advice and information about curriculum, training, and business publications for children, contact:

• National Foundation for Teaching Entrepreneurship (NFTE), 64 Fulton Street, Suite 700, New York, NY 10038; 212-233-1777.
• Education, Training and Enterprise Center (EDTEC), 309 Market Street, Suite 201, Camden, NJ 08102; 609-342-8277.
• AVS & Associates, 610 16th Street, Suite 302, Oakland, CA 94612; 510-251-2872.
• SWAYBO Inc., 3687 Dover Blvd. S.W., Atlanta, GA 30331; 404-691-4111.

Teach Your Children What You Know

If joining or starting a program just isn't feasible, consider what you can teach your children yourself:

• Help them read and understand articles in *Black Enterprise, The Wall Street Journal,* and *Fortune;*
• Introduce them to black business owners and explain why you patronize their establishments;
• On shopping trips, discuss retail prices vs. wholesale prices and how business owners make a profit;
• Get up to speed yourself. Order a copy of Emmanuel Modu's *The Lemonade Stand: A Guide to Encouraging the Entrepreneur in Your Child;* 1-800-438-TEEN.

Source: Adrienne S. Harris, "Hot Kidpreneur Programs," Black Enterprise 24 (February 1994), 182.

Marketing communications should recognize substantial differences in media patterns. None of the top 10 shows favored by blacks are among the top 20 with total viewers. When the top programs among majority audiences were "60 Minutes," "Roseanne," "Murphy Brown," "Cheers," "Designing Women," and "Home Improvement," the top programs among black viewers were "A Different World," "Fresh Prince of Bel-Air," "The Cosby Show," "In Living Color," "Roc," "Blossom," and "In the Heat of the Night."[26] It should not surprise you that blacks like shows that portray blacks positively but are turned off by shows that feature embarrassing racial stereotypes and situations. For example, the central black character in "Designing Women," ranked 50th by blacks but fifth overall, is an ex-convict. Of the top-rated shows in black households, most had black performers in prominent or starring roles. Certain networks do a better job of catering to black tastes. Of the top 10 shows among blacks, five are produced by NBC and three by Fox.

African-American Consumption Patterns

Do African-Americans differ in their consumption patterns from other market segments? The similarities are greater than the differences, especially among middle-income groups. Many differences in consumption are explained by income differences. Parks Sausage, a black-owned firm based in Baltimore, has achieved decades of success with products that sell to all segments of the market but also sells specialty products such as chitterlings that have an ethnic appeal. Parks' advertising is shown in Figure 18.5.

Many factors must be considered in developing marketing programs for the African-American. Several studies provide guidelines for developing effective programs.[27] Marketers must consider both cultural and structural elements. A fast-food chain, for example, in marketing research found lower per capita purchases of hamburgers among black customers than among white consumers. The chain's stores in predominantly black, inner-city areas, however, had the highest volume of any stores in the nation—apparently in conflict with market research. At first, executives were bewildered by the research findings. The answer lies, however, in the population-density ratios of the areas surrounding the store. Although the average per capita consumption was lower, so many people living in the neighborhood bought hamburgers that the store's total volume was surprisingly high.

Consumer research has focused on similarities and differences between white and black people in the United States, starting with early reviews by Bauer and Cunningham and others.[28] For the most part, these studies failed to control for socioeconomic status or other structural variables.[29] Often they were conducted in a single city quite a few years ago. Thus, for the consumer researcher, a dilemma exists. Which of the studies are still valid? Which were valid to begin with? It would be incorrect to disregard all of them because some—such as the evidence that African-Americans are loyal to specific brands—have been reported repeatedly.[30]

We solved the dilemma by reporting the findings about black and white differences in Table 18.4. Moschis consolidates many studies, focusing on the topic of black consumer socialization. Remember that some are based on early research that may not be true today. There is no easy way to determine which findings are still valid or which need modification. Nevertheless, they provide propositions about black consumer behavior and ways to reach black markets. The propositions can be considered as hypotheses helpful in the design of marketing programs.

Figure 18.5 Ethnic Appeal for a Specialty Product

Marketers are becoming more aware of the African-American market. Toy marketers are recognizing the growing importance of minority children as you can see in Consumer in Focus 18.3. Black kids are expected to grow from 14.8 percent of the market now to 16 percent of the market by 2010, Hispanic kids will grow from 13.3 percent to 18.6 percent, and Asian kids are expected to grow from 3.5 percent to 6.4 percent of the market.[31] Retailers such as J. C. Penney, Sears, and Montgomery Ward have all recently introduced merchandise targeted specifically to black and Hispanic consumers. Sears named its line of clothing for blacks Essence. Homeland is the brand for Montgomery Ward. Spiegel Inc. launched "E Style" catalogs of women's clothing, geared toward readers of *Ebony* magazine. Mass marketers Maybelline, Revlon, Procter & Gamble's Cover Girl, and L'Oreal are some of the cosmetics companies making special efforts to target women of color with products for dark skin tones rather than the ads of the past, which mostly featured all-American, blond, blue-eyed beauties.[32]

Table 18.4   Black Consumer Behavior

1. Socioeconomic deprivation leads black youths to behave differently from whites in an effort to upgrade their status. Black youths, in relation to their white counterparts, are more likely to
   a. have higher occupational aspirations
   b. have stronger desires for conspicuous consumption
   c. be more impatient regarding acquisition of socially conspicuous items
   d. be less likely to defer consumption gratifications

2. Black youths, compared with their white counterparts, are more likely to respond favorably to marketing stimuli. They tend to
   a. have more positive attitudes toward marketing stimuli
   b. be more susceptible to marketing practices

3. Black youths are more likely than white youths to use brand names when purchasing low involvement products.

4. The black youths' propensity to use brand name as a criterion in purchasing products declines with socioeconomic status.

5. White youths are more likely than their black counterparts to use price as a criterion when purchasing low involvement products.

6. Black girls in comparison with white girls are more likely to
   a. acquire greater independence than boys
   b. participate more in family purchasing decisions than boys

7. Black youths are more likely to have favorable orientations toward television than their white counterparts. Black youths are more likely than white youths to
   a. watch television
   b. evaluate television stimuli as being realistic
   c. use television for consumer information
   d. model after television characters

8. White youths are more likely than black youths to use newspapers for information about consumption.

9. Black youths are less likely than white youths to interact with parents about consumption matters.
   a. Black youths discuss consumption less frequently than white youths.
   b. Black youths are less likely to model after their parents' consumer behavior than white youths.

10. White youths are socialized into the consumer role earlier than black youths.

11. Different socialization processes operate among black and white youths.

12. Black adult consumers are more likely than their white counterparts to emphasize consumption. Blacks are more likely than whites to
    a. hold materialistic values
    b. spend a larger proportion of their available income on items of social status and social significance
    c. be innovators of socially conspicuous products
    d. have higher occupational aspirations

13. Blacks are more likely than whites to trade goods and services among family members.

14. Black consumers are not likely to interact with the marketplace as effectively and efficiently as white consumers. Blacks are less likely than whites to
    a. seek information
    b. consider a larger number of alternatives
    c. evaluate alternatives on a large number of objective attributes

15. Black/white differences in consumer behavior are contingent on the adult person's socioeconomic status. When social class is taken into account
    a. blacks are more likely to hold egalitarian sex role perceptions about household decisions
    b. black/white differences in consumer behaviors are greater among lower-class than higher-class adults

16. With increasing age, older black consumers are more likely to experience declining activity in consumption than older white consumers.

Source: George P. Moschis, Consumer Socialization (Lexington, Mass.: Lexington Books, 1987), 247–258.

| 18.3 | **Consumer in Focus** |

Marketing to Minority Kids

Toymakers are beginning to send messages of diversity. Patti Lewis, Tyco vice president, interviewed African-American mothers who said "they wanted a doll 'for our girls, not just a white doll in a different color. A doll that would help them appreciate how pretty they are. One they can identify with. One that says that blonde hair and blue eyes isn't the ideal.'" The result was Kenya, an ethnically authentic black hair-styling doll, which has sold 500,000 units in a little over a year.

Yia Eason of Olmec Toys, the nation's largest black-owned toy company, got into the field in 1985 when her son said he couldn't be a superhero because he wasn't white. Eason responded by creating Sun-Man, a superhero action figure, and the Bronze Bombers, miniature figures based on an Army unit that fought in World War I and II. In 1989, two years before Mattel introduced Shani, its ethnically correct black fashion doll, Olmec brought out Imani, a realistically sculpted "African-American Princess," followed by Consuelo Hispanic fashion doll. "When I started, I was told black people didn't want dolls that look black," Eason recalls. "That's changed totally."

Board games, software, and electronic games represent a natural next arena for grabbing what is called the "Cross Colors Generation" of young people who are attuned to the larger world of racial diversity and the technological explosion. Crayola has developed a collection of art supplies in realistic skin tones. Hasbro official Wayne Charness says, "It's a matter of marketers responding to the marketplace. Demand has always been there. People are just getting more savvy about developing and selling products that access different markets."

Source: Excerpts from Michelle Healy, "Consumers 'Hunger' for New Products," USA Today (December 10–12, 1993), A1.

Asian-American Culture

Asian-Americans are rapidly increasing as a desirable target for marketing organizations for two reasons. First, they are growing in number, as you saw in Chapter 2, and could reach 15 to 20 million by early next century. Second, Asian-Americans have higher incomes and more education and are more likely to own a business than other minorities.[33] As you saw in Table 18.1, at the beginning of this chapter, income of the Asian-American minority segment is higher than the majority (white) markets in the United States. Asian-Americans are usually defined to include Chinese, Japanese, Koreans, Vietnamese, Cambodians, Laotians, Filipinos, Asian Indians, Pakistanis, Hawaiians, Samoans, Guamanians, Fiji Islanders, and other Asians and Pacific Islanders living in the United States. Some immigrants from Hong Kong, looking for safety and refuge before the 1997 change of control, have brought not only their minds and skills but substantial amounts of capital to the United States and Canada. The rapid growth of Asian-Americans is caused by above-average fertility and a high rate of international immigration. The immigration rate is more than twice that of Hispanics.[34]

The Asian-American culture is characterized by hard work, strong family ties, appreciation for education, and other values that lead to success in entrepreneurship, technical skills, and the arts. The success also may bring conflict with more entrenched immigrants and other consumers. Japanese-Americans have a long history in America, including great suffering and discrimination associated with World War II. In recent years, immigration has been more extensive from other Asian countries than from Japan.

Retailing and advertising are two areas of marketing directly affected by national ethnic groups. Many cities contain large groups of relatively homogeneous nationality groups, creating the opportunity for stores featuring ethnic foods and other products. Staff may need to be bilingual. By making special appeals to Asians in their showrooms, Steinway now sells 15 percent of its product to Asian-Americans. National- and language-oriented media may promote greater loyalty among the readers and listeners, as well as provide excellent "cost-per-thousand" of concentrated market targets. Among Asian-Americans, 54 percent shop as a leisure activity compared with 50 percent of the general population. Asians also think quality is more important than price when they choose a store. They are far more likely to use technology such as automated teller machines, and many more own VCRs, CD players, microwave ovens, home computers, and telephone answering machines.[35]

Numbers are important to Asian-Americans, particularly the number 8, which symbolizes prosperity. Colors are also important, especially red. They believe that white envelopes should not be used around a holiday because white usually symbolizes death. Citibank effectively featured a dragon in one of its New Year's ads, instead of corks from champagne bottles, which are considered inappropriate. Celebrities, especially those of Asian background, can be very effective in appealing to Asian-American consumers. When Reebok featured tennis star Michael Chang in ads, shoe sales among Asian-Americans greatly increased.[36] Kellogg's featured Olympic gold medalist Kristi Yamaguchi on its cereal boxes, describing her as "California native" without reference to her Japanese ancestry.

Korean-Americans have substantially more education than other Asian groups and may respond better to communications than less educationally oriented groups. Koreans dominate the ownership of businesses, with ownership of more than 100 businesses per 1,000 population, far more than any other minority or nonminority population group.[37] Koreans not only have a higher rate of business ownership but also a higher rate of business success than nonminority consumers. A major study of Korean immigrants concludes that the values of hard work and merchant ability have been developed as a result of coming to America, rather than due to their Korean background.[38]

Marketers can increase their probability of success by adapting to the values and norms of ethnic market segments. As an example, in San Francisco, which has long been the capital of Asian-America, a Volkswagen dealer noticed that youthful, white consumers who once bought "Bugs" by the boatload, now were opting for more expensive German imports or cheaper cars from Japan. The dealer placed ads in the Asian yellow pages, mailed fliers to middle-class Asian neighborhoods, and sent his salespeople to visit shops and hangouts frequented by the Asian bourgeoisie.

Bringing Asian customers into the showroom, however, was the easy part. Persuading them to buy was where the real challenge began. Most intimidating was the Chinese value on tough bargaining over price. To the Chinese, this is simply a normal part of the business culture. But to someone more accustomed to American business—even a car salesperson—the exchange can seem downright cutthroat. "When the guy comes in here and makes a ridiculous offer on a car, you don't get mad," the dealer instructed his sales force. "You come back with something equally ridiculous and have a good laugh. Then start your real negotiation."

Another facet of the dealer's "Asian Sensitivity Training" focused on dealing with the family. The Chinese prefer shopping in large family groups, with buying decisions usually made by the family elders. The dealer explained to salespeople that although the car might be for a teenage schoolgirl or a middle-aged engineer, the successful sales approach may have to be directed to the grandfather or elderly uncle. To help things along, the dealer's 75-year-old father is often on hand to make the generational connection. Largely as a result of sales to Asian-Americans, the dealer boosted car sales from only 20 a month to more than 100, ranking among the top few VW dealers in America.[39]

Hispanic or Latino Culture

Although African-Americans are the largest minority group and Asian-Americans have the highest income, it is the Hispanic or Latino ethnic group currently that is increasing in interest to marketers. The rapid growth in numbers and the distinctiveness of a separate language capability attracts the attention of consumer analysts hoping to find growth markets for the future. Values of Hispanics can be compared with other minority and majority segments with the Rokeach Value System (RVS) described in the previous chapter and Chapter 13.[40]

Hispanics are the fastest-growing ethnic market in the United States, with buying power estimated as high as $100 billion and higher household income than blacks, as you saw in Table 18.1 at the beginning of the chapter. Between the 1980 and 1990 census, Hispanics increased from 14.6 million to 21.3 million. By 2015, experts believe Hispanics will outnumber African-Americans because of immigration and higher birthrates. The Hispanic market is 88 percent concentrated in cities, an attractive feature for media plans, distribution facilities, and other elements of marketing programs. The diversity in culture and other variables dictates that the Hispanic market be regarded as a heterogeneous set of wants and behaviors rather than the "Hispanic segment."[41]

Who Is Hispanic?

Language and identity, rather than national origin, are the key elements in Hispanic culture and may be of any color or racial group. An important question to be answered is whether the term *Hispanic* or *Latino* is more appropriate. It is a controversial question. The Census Bureau uses the term *Hispanic* to describe Americans whose origin was in the Spanish-speaking countries of the Western world. Most news media use the term *Hispanic* except in areas with large populations from Mexico and Central America where *Latino* is often used to refer to the local community. Many Spanish-speaking groups prefer terms indicating their country of origin, such as *Mexican-American, Puerto Rican,* or *Cuban-American*. Academic groups tend to prefer *Latino* over *Hispanic* as do poorer groups and recent immigrants, whereas affluent and older immigrants prefer the term *Hispanic*.[42] In these pages, the term *Hispanic* is mostly used to reflect usage in government statistics and the media but *Latino* may be preferable in marketing communications.

Hispanic consumers are often segmented into four groups. Mexicans are the largest segment, about 60 percent of all Hispanics. They are concentrated in the Southwest, and 53 percent were born in the United States. They tend to be young and have large families. Puerto Ricans are about 15 percent of all Hispanics. They are concentrated in the Northeast, especially in New York City. Most have arrived in the past 25 years, and many are now in middle age, with young children born in the United States. Cubans are about 7 percent of all Hispanics and are concentrated in the Southeast. Only 7 percent were born in the United States. Cubans are the oldest group, have fewer children, and are the aristocracy in terms of occupation, education, and income. Other Hispanics constitute 18 percent, heavily from Central America, and are dispersed geographically. They are 93 percent foreign-born and mostly young adults with few children.[43] Central American immigration is expected to contribute to future growth of the Hispanic market.

The diversity provides differences in values and motivations. Mexican-Americans are more likely to be assimilated into the U.S. culture, with less desire to return to Mexico. Cubans are more likely to consider themselves stranded in the host country. Although they may not want to return to Cuba, they are more likely than are other Hispanics to think of themselves as Hispanic first and American second.[44] Cuban average income is much higher than that of any other Hispanic group, roughly at or above the average American income. Puerto Ricans have the lowest average of any Hispanic group.

Language is often described as a unifying factor, but even this is not always true. An advertiser describing brown sugar in Spanish would need to say *azucar negra* in New York, *azucar prieta* in Miami, *azucar cafe* in California, *azucar morena* in South Texas, and *azucar pardo* in other U.S. areas. In New York, an insecticide company advertised to Puerto Ricans that its product would kill all *bichos* (bugs) without realizing that for Puerto Ricans the colloquial *bichos* is a reference to male genitals.

Culturally unaware marketers might assume that because Hispanics are bilingual, it would be adequate to communicate with them in English. About 94 percent speak Spanish in the home, and studies show that Hispanics think in Spanish—creating the need for marketers to communicate in Spanish-based forms to be most effective.[45]

There are also differences between Hispanics who identify closely with their subculture and those who do not. Webster found that Spanish-language Hispanics, or those who identify closely with their subculture, do not rely on printed sources of information as much as English-language Hispanics. However, Spanish-language Hispanics do rely greatly on in-store point-of-purchase displays, coupons, and word of mouth.[46]

Marketing to Hispanic Values

The Hispanic culture places a high value on quality. Many Hispanics emigrated from poorer countries. They seek status symbols that demonstrate that they have "arrived." For example, Bulova watches had an image in the Hispanic market of a "cheap American product." To counter this image, Bulova used Hispanic media to position its product as an expensive but affordable piece of jewelry. The revised advertisements emphasized Bulova's extensive line of 18-karat gold watches, because Hispanics view 14-karat as synonymous with gold-plated. Through these efforts, Bulova achieved a 40 percent share in the Spanish-speaking market. Pavion, which has a successful line of cosmetics for black consumers called Black Radiance, has now added Solo Para Ti (Only For You) for Hispanic women. All aspects of Solo Para Ti—products, promotions, and even the name—were designed with the Latino culture in mind. Hispanic women preferred products with high shine and in bright shades. Pavion is advertised on Spanish language TV and radio, and in-store promotions are in both Spanish and English.[47]

Coupons are thought to be not as effective with Hispanics as with non-Hispanic white and black consumers because of the stigma coupons have for people who came to this country poor. Hispanics are proud that they are now making a better living. They may not want to use coupons that are "for people who can't afford to pay the full price"[48]

Some products have made successful adaptations to the Hispanic market. Cudahy established a premium bacon called Rex, based on the strategy that a lean, premium bacon could sell in a 12-oz. size for prices comparable with the biggest competitor's (Farmer John) 16-oz. package. The package shouts the message, *"Vale su peso en carne."* Beer companies such as Budweiser and Miller have battled to sponsor community celebrations such as Cinco de Mayo and the Independence Day Fair because of their importance in the Spanish culture.

The family is extremely important in Hispanic culture and differs from non-Hispanic whites not only in values but also in size (larger) and age (younger).[49] Look at Figure 18.6 and you can see how Sears has incorporated these values into its advertising. The ad on the left shows classical golden elegance and quality for Christmas. The ad on the right stresses elegant clothes for children *para una ocasion especial* (for a special occasion—Christmas). Figure 18.7 also shows how family values dominate Goya, a thriving Hispanic food firm.

Avoiding Marketing Blunders

Failure to understand the Hispanic culture can lead to marketing blunders. Humberto Valencia has identified three main types: translation blunders, culture misunderstandings, and Hispanic idiosyncrasies.[50]

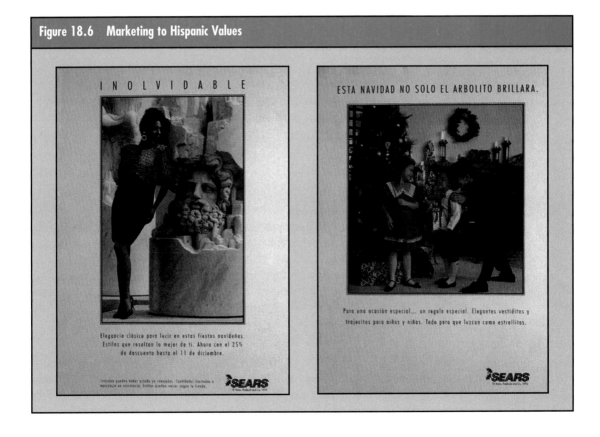

Figure 18.6   Marketing to Hispanic Values

Figure 18.7   Hispanic Family Values in Business

With roots in strong family ties, Hispanic business owners want their hard work and long hours to be passed on to future generations. One way of ensuring this is to bring children, siblings, and other relatives into the family business.

One family that has united to continue its founder's dream of a thriving business is the Unanue family of Goya Foods, Inc. As a Spanish immigrant in 1936, Prudencio Unanue bought the Goya name from a Spanish company and began to import native foods to New York City's Hispanic community. Over the years, the Goya product line and markets have expanded to about $500 million in sales with 1,800 employees.

"I love working with my family," says Andy Unanue, who directs purchasing and is one of the chairman's six children. "We're a typical close-knit Latino family. We treat everyone here like they're part of *grande familia Goya.*"

Whether passing on long-honed culinary skills or business savvy to younger family members, older Hispanics not only ensure the continued quality and profitability of their business but also keep the family together.

Source: Excerpts from "All in the Family," *Hispanic* (December 1993), 64.

Translation Blunders

Translation blunders occur in Hispanic markets just as they often do in global markets. One cigarette advertisement wanted to say "less tar," but the translation actually said the brand claimed to have "less asphalt." A beer company found that the radio commercial they hoped would say "less filling, delicious" incorrectly came across in Spanish as "filling, less delicious" merely because of the way it was sung. Even market researchers blunder when they ask for the *dama de la casa* (madam of the house) rather than the *senora de la casa* (lady of the house).

Culture Misunderstandings

Serious misunderstandings occur when marketers use stereotypes of their own self-reference criteria for designing strategies. A telephone company commercial portrayed a wife saying to her husband, "Run downstairs and phone Maria. Tell her we'll be a little late." Two serious culture errors were committed. First, it is socially unacceptable for a Latin wife to give her husband orders. Second, Hispanics do not normally call to say they will not be on time; it is customary to arrive a little late. Misunderstandings about the meaning of time may be one of the reasons Mexican-Americans have more complaints about the delivery service of retailers than do other consumers.[51]

A radio station ran a contest in which the prize was two tickets to Disneyland, but few Hispanics were interested. Giving away two tickets was not enough for the family-oriented Hispanic. When the number was increased, much more interest was generated.

Hispanic Idiosyncrasies

Marketing blunders sometimes occur from failure to understand the idiosyncrasies of each segment of the total Hispanic market. Just as British, Canadians, South Africans, and Americans have major differences even though English is the common language, so there are differences between Mexican-Americans, Puerto Rican-Americans, Cuban-Americans, and other Hispanics. A radio advertisement in Miami used the term *banditas,* which is a Puerto Rican term for Band-Aids. The ad failed because Miami's largely Cuban population did not recognize the term. Domino planned to add papaya flavor into its line of tropical-flavored drinks but dropped the idea because of the vulgar connotations papaya has for Cubans in Miami. A beer company filmed a Hispanic advertisement using the *Paseo del Rio* (Riverwalk) in San Antonio, Texas, as a background. The ad was well received among Hispanics living on the West Coast, who liked the Spanish atmosphere. In San Antonio itself, Hispanics did not like the ad because they considered the *Paseo del Rio* to be an attraction for non-Hispanic white tourists rather than for Hispanic residents.

The Hispanic market is being assimilated into older non-Hispanic markets, and many assumptions—such as higher brand loyalty, lower coupon usage, and more shopping enjoyment—are increasingly questionable or need to be qualified.[52] Brand loyalty is increasingly questioned as typical of Hispanics, although price, product quality, and shopping ease appear to be important attributes to Hispanics.[53] Research findings about Hispanic or other ethnic groups are often confusing because they fail to consider the strength or weakness of identification with the ethnic group.[54] Consumer in Focus 18.4 shows, however, how Kodak has incorporated an understanding of the Hispanic market into its marketing and public relations strategy.

An additional reason for interest in Hispanic culture is the impact it is having on the majority culture. Ethnic foods, including Hispanic, have become popular mainstream offerings — ranging from Taco Bell, a division of PepsiCo, Inc. — to Cantina del Rio — a division of Bob Evans. Cantina del Rio collected recipes from Mexico and sent trucks to search the countryside bringing back artifacts and enlisted the help of local Hispanic culture groups in designing the restaurants to

18.4   Consumer in Focus

Kodak Develops Family Theme via Cultural Tie-ins

Kodak reaches Hispanic consumers via tie-ins with local cultural events, museums, and festivals. Kodak's "family fun" outings encourage picture-taking and provide fun activities and thematic photo backdrops. Family members can also borrow a Kodak camera for the day.

In 1989, the company tied in with a large Hispanic cultural festival in Miami. Since then, Kodak has refined its cultural tie-in approach to concentrate more on activities, workshops, and picture-taking opportunities for Hispanic families with young children. Kodak also supports the California Museum of Latino History, said to be the largest repository of Hispanic-American documents and artifacts in the United States.

To provide a picture-taking opportunity that celebrated Hispanic performing arts, Kodak involved Telemundo (Spanish TV) soap opera stars and performances at Nuanu's Festival of the Americas, culminating in a fireworks display provided by Kodak. Festival-goers had the chance to have photos taken with stars of Hispanic TV and other celebrities.

Kodak ethnic marketing efforts are coordinated by UniWorld Group, Inc., a New York City-based communications company. For ethnic festivals, Kodak has developed a backdrop where families can pose for pictures. There is a kiosk where Kodak film is sold and cameras are demonstrated and loaned to consumers for the day. On a single day in Miami, Kodak sold more than 1,000 rolls of film.

Source: Summarized from Susan L. Fry, "Reaching Hispanic Publics with Special Events," *Public Relations Journal 47* (February 1991), 12–13ff.

Figure 18.8   Hispanic Appeals for Both Majority and Minority Markets

gain as much cultural authenticity as possible when bringing Mexico to the Midwest.[55] Another attempt at appealing to majority market segments as well as Hispanic market segments is shown in Figure 18.8. Pepsi not only owns Taco Bell but has been aggressive in reaching ethnic markets. PepsiCo, Inc. advertises its soft drink brands in colors and words that make a special appeal to the Hispanic market but are probably also understood by English-speaking consumers (Figure 18.9).

North America is a multicultural society — composed of basic core values in the macroculture as we saw in the previous chapter and of many microcultures as we saw in this chapter. Many marketers are becoming more aware of the need to understand these microcultures. Figure 18.10 shows two ads that reflect these themes. Avon has built much of its business on understanding cultures within North America, and increasingly, the focus is on global cultures. Figure 18.10 also shows the need to bring cultural diversity into the work force serving the Federal Bureau of Prisons.

Figure 18.9   Appeals to Hispanic and Majority Markets

French-Canadian Culture

One of the largest and most distinct cultures in North America is the French-Canadian area of Canada, mostly in Quebec. This might be considered a nationality group or a geographic culture. The province of Quebec accounts for more than 27 percent of the Canadian population and about 25 percent of income and retail sales.[56] For years, the French culture was somewhat ignored by English-oriented advertisers, thereby creating a social problem as well as limiting the potential effectiveness of communications to the French market. Some of the differential treatment may have been caused by different social class groupings compared with Anglo markets.[57]

Figure 18.10 Appeals to Cultural Diversity

Marketing strategists should be concerned with whether advertising is transferable between the French-Canadian (FC) culture and the English-Canadian (EC) or Anglophone culture. Some marketers believe that separate advertising material must be developed to be effective in the FC microculture. Others believe materials can be developed that are effective with both groups. A minimum of verbal material is used, with emphasis on the visual.

Tamilia's research,[58] which compared communications with FC and EC consumers on a cross-cultural basis, indicated the potential for increasing effectiveness in advertising communications. This is built on some previous research by Tigert that indicated the French are more responsive to people-oriented than to message-oriented advertisements. Tamilia's research led to the conclusion that FCs do react more to the source of the advertisement than do ECs who are more message-oriented. Consumer in Focus 18.5 discusses other differences in marketing to FCs and ECs.

Because of the size and importance of the FC market, it has attracted the attention of many marketers. The process of understanding communications in

| 18.5 | **Consumer in Focus** |

Marketing Information Sources in French Canada

Market information can come from various sources including friends, family members, and the mass media. Where do French Canadians obtain their information? A recent study on the purchase of a car showed that, contrary to expectations, English Canadians used personal sources to a greater extent than French Canadians. Other interesting findings showed that French Canadians considered fewer cars than did English Canadians; French Canadians devoted less time to search; English Canadians made three times as many test drives as French Canadians. Overall, English Canadians generally seem to conduct a more extensive information search than French Canadians, at least as it applies to the purchase of a new car.

French Canadians traditionally have showed affinity for mass media preferences quite unlike their English counterparts. As a result, brand images, brand attitudes, product attributes, and positioning strategies in general may not achieve similar response patterns among the two groups. Language affects media choice, and obviously the marketing information contained therein impacts on the quantity and quality of the information received. For example, Quebec lags behind all other provinces and the United States in newspaper production per capita. The daily newspaper is not standard reading material for French Canadians as it is for the rest of Canadians. Television viewing is also heaviest among French Canadians, the heaviest in the world according to a source. Radio listening is also heaviest in Canada, with listening and television viewing habits showing marked contrast between Montreal and Quebec City, as an example, or between French Canadians working versus nonworking viewers and listeners, or between business executives living in Quebec City and Montreal. There is no doubt that media buying in Quebec is a complex decision process.

Source: Robert D. Tamilia, "The Duality of Canadian Culture: Toward an Understanding of the Quebec and French Canadian Markets," Working Paper No. 01-88 (Montreal: University of Quebec, Department of Administrative Sciences, 1988), 59–60.

a cross-cultural setting, however, is applicable to other situations in which diverse ethnic groups are the target for marketing programs.

Summary

Marketing to consumers in North America must be done in an environment of multicultural diversity. The norms and values of specific groups are called *microcultures*, in contrast to the macroculture of the nation. Ethnic groups may be formed around nationality, religion, physical attributes, or geographic location. Ethnicity is a process that may be defined objectively, based on sociocultural characteristics, or subjectively, based on identification that a person makes for self or others.

Major microcultures in North America include Native Americans, Asian-Americans, African-Americans, Hispanics, and FCs as well as religious and geographic microcultures. African-American or black consumers currently are the largest market segment, but Asian-Americans are the most affluent—more so even than majority segments. Hispanic or Latino segments are growing fast and are expected to eventually be larger than the African-American segment because of high fertility and immigration rates.

Review and Discussion Questions

1. "There are no more mass markets; there are only variations in the size of segments." How would you evaluate this statement, considering the material in this chapter?

2. Do many Americans live in "tribes"? Considering the material in Consumer in Focus 18.1, what are the marketing implications of tribes in America?

3. What are some of the practical considerations that a marketer should consider in developing products for religious ethnic groups?

4. What are the most important structural influences on African-American values and consumer behavior?

5. Are there really differences between black and white consumption patterns? Explain your answer.

6. Asian-Americans are a small proportion of the total population of the United States. Why should they be given much importance in marketing strategies? What adaptations in a marketing plan should be made to reach Asian-Americans?

7. Assume that a soft drink marketer wanted to increase penetration into the Hispanic market. Prepare a set of recommendations for doing so.

8. Assume that a major retailer of shoes was considering a market program to make a special appeal to African-American consumers. Would you suggest such an approach? If so, what would be your recommendations?

9. Assume that a French manufacturer of women's apparel is seeking to expand markets by exporting to Canada. What marketing program should be recommended for maximum effectiveness?

10. How would you suggest a firm organize itself to understand and market its products to culturally diverse markets?

Endnotes

1. Leon E. Wynter, "Double Whammy Hinders 'Double Minorities,'" *Wall Street Journal* (January 19, 1994), B1.

2. Rohit Deshpande, Wayne D. Hoyer, and Naveen Donthu, "The Intensity of Ethnic Affiliation: A Study of the Sociology of Hispanic Consumption," *Journal of Consumer Research* 13 (September 1986), 214–219.

3. Elizabeth C. Hirschman, "An Examination of Ethnicity and Consumption Using Free Response Data," in AMA *Educators' Conference Proceedings* (Chicago: American Marketing Association, 1982), 84–88.

4. Johanna Zmud and Carolos Arce, "The Ethnicity and Consumption Relationship," in John F. Sherry, Jr., and Brian Sternthal, eds., *Diversity in Consumer Behavior* (Provo, UT: Association for Consumer Research, 1992), 443–449.

5. Leon E. Wynter, "Multiculturalism Stalls at the National Divide," *Wall Street Journal* (January 19, 1994), B1.

6. Dan Fost, "American Indians in the 1990s," *American Demographics* 13 (December 1991), 26–34.

7. Edith McArthur, "What Language Do You Speak?" *American Demographics* 6 (October 1984), 32–33.

8. Nathan Caplan, John K. Whitmore, and Marcella H. Choy, *The Boat People and Achievement in America: A Study of Family Life, Hard Work, and Cultural Values* (Ann Arbor, Mich.: University of Michigan Press, 1989).

9. Brad Edmondson, "Bringing in the Sheaves," *American Demographics* 10 (August 1988), 28–32.

10. Findings in this paragraph are summarized from Elizabeth C. Hirschman, "American Jewish Ethnicity: Its Relationship to Some Selected Aspects of Consumer Behavior," *Journal of Marketing* 45 (Summer 1981), 102–109; and Elizabeth C. Hirschman, "Ethnic Variation in Leisure Activities and Motives," in AMA *Educators' Conference Proceedings* (Chicago: American Marketing Association, 1982), 93–98.

11. Joel Garreau, *The Nine Nations of North America* (Boston: Houghton Mifflin, 1981).

12. Lynn R. Kahle, "The Nine Nations of North America and the Value Basis of Geographic Segmentation," *Journal of Marketing* 50 (April 1986), 37–47.

13. Reynolds Farley and Suzanne M. Bianchi, "The Growing Gap between Blacks," *American Demographics* 5 (July 1983), 15–18.

14. Cyndee Miller, "Research on Black Consumers," *Marketing News* 27 (September 13, 1993), 1ff.

15. Mark Green, *Invisible People: The Depiction of Minorities in Magazine Ads and Catalogs* (New York: City of New York Department of Consumer Affairs, 1991).

16. Tommy E. Whittler, "The Effects of Actors' Race in Commercial Advertising: Review and Extension," *Journal of Advertising* 20 (1991), 54–60; Tommy E. Whittler and Joan DiMeo, "Viewers' Reactions to Racial Cues in Advertising Stimuli," *Journal of Advertising Research* 31 (December 1991), 37–46.

17. Jerome D. Williams, "Reflections of a Black Middle-Class Consumer: Caught between Two Worlds or Getting the Best of Both?" in Sherry and Sternthal, *Diversity in Consumer Behavior*, 850–855.

18. U.S. Department of Commerce, *Current Population Reports*, Series P-60-181 (Washington, D.C.: U.S. Government Printing Office, 1993).

19. William O'Hare, "Blacks and Whites: One Market or Two?" *American Demographics* 9 (March 1987), 44–48.

20. William J. Qualls and David J. Moore, "Stereotyping Effects on Consumers' Evaluation of Advertising: Impact of Racial Difference between Actors and Viewers," *Psychology and Marketing* 7 (Summer 1990), 135–151.

21. Nancy Ten Kate, "Black Children More Likely to Live with One Parent," *American Demographics* 13 (February 1991), 11.

22. A collection of articles on this topic is found in Harriette Pipies McAdoo, ed., *Black Families* (Newbury Park, Calif.: Sage Publications, 1988).

23. Frank McCoy, "Rethinking the Cost of Discrimination," *Black Enterprise* 24 (January 1994), 54–59.

24. Marilyn K. Foxworth, "Celebrating Black History," *Public Relations Journal* 47 (February 1991), 16–21.

25. Adrienne S. Harris, "Hot Kidpreneur Programs," *Black Enterprise* 24 (February 1994), 177–182.

26. "Black and White in Color," *American Demographics* 14 (November 1992), 9–10.

27. Parke Gibson, *$70 Billion in the Black* (New York: Macmillan, 1978); B. G. Yovovich, "The Debate Rages On: Marketing to Blacks," *Advertising Age* (November 29, 1982), M-10; David Astor, "Black Spending Power: $140 Billion and Growing," *Marketing Communications* (July 1982), 13–18; P. A. Robinson, C. P. Rao, and S. C. Mehta, "Historical Perspectives of Black Consumer Research in the United States: A Critical Review," in C. T. Tan and J. Sheth, eds., *Historical Perspectives in Consumer Research* (Singapore: National University of Singapore, 1985), 46–50.

28. Raymond A. Bauer and Scott M. Cunningham, *Studies in the Negro Market* (Cambridge, Mass.: Marketing Science Institute, 1970). Also Donald Sexton, "Black Buyer Behavior," *Journal of Marketing* 36 (October 1972), 36–39.

29. Thomas E. Ness and Melvin T. Stith, "Middle-Class Values in Blacks and Whites," in Robert E. Pitts, Jr., and Arch G. Woodside, *Personal Values and Consumer Psychology* (Lexington, Mass.: Lexington Books, 1984), 255–270.

30. Alphonziz Wellington, "Traditional Brand Loyalty," *Advertising Age* (May 18, 1981), S-2.

31. Michelle Healy, "Consumers 'Hunger' for New Products," *USA Today* (December 10–12, 1993), 1A.

32. Cyndee Miller, "Cosmetics Firms Finally Discover the Ethnic Market," *Marketing News* 27 (August 30, 1993), 2.

33. Wendy Manning and William O'Hare, "Asian-American Businesses," *American Demographics* 10 (August 1988), 35–39.

34. Thomas G. Exter, "Middle-Aging Asians," *American Demographics* 14 (November 1992), 67.

35. Dan Fost, "California's Asian Market," *American Demographics* 12 (October 1990), 34–37.

36. Cyndee Miller, "Hot Asian-American Market Not Starting Much of a Fire Yet," *Marketing News* 25 (January 21, 1991), 12.

37. William O'Hare, "Reaching for the Dream," *American Demographics* 14 (January 1992), 32–36.

38. Ivan Light and Edna Bonacich, *Immigrant Entrepreneurs: Koreans in Los Angeles, 1965–1982* (Los Angeles: University of California Press, 1988).

39. Joel Kotkin, "Selling to the New America," *Inc.* (July 1987), 46–47.

40. Humberto Valencia, "Hispanic Values and Subcultural Research," *Journal of the Academy of Marketing Science* 17 (Winter 1989), 23–28. Van R. Wood and Roy Howell, "A Note on Hispanic Values and Subcultural Research: An Alternative View," *Journal of the Academy of Marketing Science* 19 (Winter 1991), 61–67.

41. Geraldine Fennel, Joel Saegert, Francis Piron, and Rosemary Jimenez, "Do Hispanics Constitute a Market Segment?" in Sherry and Sternthal, *Diversity in Consumer Behavior*, 28–33.

42. "Quandry over One Term to Cover Myriad People," *Wall Street Journal* (January 18, 1994), B1.

43. Daniel Yankelovich, *Spanish USA* (New York: Yankelovich, Skelly & White, Inc., 1981). Also see reports on a repetition in 1984 of the same study in "Homogenized Hispanics," *American Demographics* 7 (February 1985), 16.

44. Yankelovich, *Spanish USA.*

45. Jim Sondheim, Rodd Rodriquez, Richard Dillon, and Richard Parades, "Hispanic Market: The Invisible Giant," *Advertising Age* (April 16, 1979), S-20. Also see Martha Frase-Blunt, "Who Watches Spanish Language TV?" *Hispanic* (November 1991), 26–27.

46. Cynthia Webster, "The Effects of Hispanic Subcultural Identification on Information Search Behavior," *Journal of Advertising Research* 32 (September–October 1992), 54–62.

47. Miller, "Cosmetics Firms Finally Discover the Ethnic Market."

48. Examples are from Luiz Diaz-Altertini, "Brand-Loyal Hispanics Need Good Reason for Switching," *Advertising Age* (April 16, 1979), SX-23.

49. Lisa Penaloza Alaniz and Marcy C. Gilly, "The Hispanic Family-Consumer Research Issues," *Psychology and Marketing* (Winter 1986), 291–303.

50. Humberto Valencia, "Point of View: Avoid Hispanic Market Blunders," *Journal of Advertising Research* 23 (January 1984), 19–22.

51. T. Bettina Cornewell and Alan David Bligh, "Complaint Behavior of Mexican-American Consumers to a Third-Party Agency," *Journal of Consumer Affairs* 25 (Summer 1991), 1–18.

52. Robert E. Wilkes and Humberto Valencia, "Shopping-Related Characteristics of Mexican-Americans and Blacks," *Psychology and Marketing* 3 (Winter 1986), 247–259.

53. Joel Saegert, Robert J. Hoover, and Marye Tharp Hilger, "Characteristics of Mexican American Consumers," *Journal of Consumer Research* 12 (June 1985), 104–109.

54. Deshpande, Hoyer, and Donthu, "The Intensity of Ethnic Affiliation."

55. Roger D. Blackwell, Kristina S. Blackwell, and W. Wayne Talarzyk, *Contemporary Cases in Consumer Behavior* (Forth Worth, Tex.: Harcourt Brace Jovanovich, 1993).

56. Clarkson Gordon, *Tomorrow's Customers in Canada* (Toronto: Woods Gordon, 1984).

57. Pierre C. Lefrancois and Giles Chatel, "The French-Canadian Consumer: Fact and Fancy," in J. S. Wright and J. L. Goldstrucker, eds., *New Ideas for Successful Marketing* (Chicago: American Marketing Association, 1966), 705–717; Bernard Blishen, "Social Class and Opportunity in Canada," *Canadian Review of Sociology and Anthropology* 7 (May 1970), 110–127.

58. Robert Tamilia, "Cross-Cultural Advertising Research: A Review and Suggested Framework," in Ronald C. Curhan, ed., *1974 Combined Proceedings of the AMA* (Chicago: American Marketing Association, 1974), 131–134.

CHAPTER 19

Social Class and Status

▲▲▲▲▲▲▲▲▲▲▲▲▲▲▲▲▲▲▲▲▲▲▲▲▲▲▲▲▲▲▲▲▲▲▲▲

A New Approach to Familiar Goals

The complexities of status symbols have helped muddy the waters for many Americans trying to find their place in the new hierarchy. At the same time, most of us would like to avoid being seen as striving too hard to appropriate the right symbols. We make cartoons of those hapless middle-class strivers, grasping at the next rung, who name their children Chauncey or Dierdre, keep temperamental pets with long pedigrees, and take up ruinously expensive sports like sailing.

And just watch out for the next shift in tastes: If the Eighties were about greed and ostentation for the uppers, the Nineties are about value and self-fulfillment. The experts observe that affluent tastes now run more toward the utilitarian: A Range Rover or Ford Explorer, rather than a Mercedes, is the vehicle of choice, and a bank credit card with frequent-flier miles attached seems to make more sense than American Express Platinum with a high annual fee. Dressing down seems more practical as well—loafers instead of lace-ups for men, one-inch pumps rather than high heels for women. Those $115 Hermes ties may come off as a little foppish these days, and top executives even at GM have taken to wearing open collars to work on Friday.

Clothing, of course, has always been a peculiarly resonant class symbol. Writes Alison Lurie, in her book *The Language of Clothes:* "The man who goes to buy a winter coat may simultaneously want it to shelter him from bad weather, look expensive and formidable, announce that he is sophisticated and rugged, attract a certain sort of sexual partner, and magically invest him with the qualities of Robert Redford."

On the job, your wardrobe goes to the heart of class status. Many a regiment in the vast army of blue-collar workers, everyone from postal employees to the kids behind the counter at McDonald's, are issued uniforms that let the world know they are in the subservient service role. Most of the rest of us have more latitude about our business wardrobe but are limited by our sense of status and appropriateness. Particularly amusing are men who spend enormous sums on their clothes but cannot master the casual elegance of the upper classes.

Source: Excerpts from Kenneth Labich, "Class in America," Fortune (February 7, 1994), 114–126.

Social Class and Consumer Behavior

Social class affects consumer behavior—how people spend their time, the products they buy, and where and how they shop. Magazines such as *Town & Country, Architectural Digest, Connoisseur,* and *Avenue* are read by certain consumers because the contents reflect the interests of the affluent social classes to which the readers belong or to which they aspire. The magazines advertise upscale products for affluent consumers and contain articles that reflect the themes and motivations of special significance to affluent social classes—articles about arts and craftsmanship, interior decoration, dominance of nature, the triumph of technology, fashions, and the ideology of affluence.[1]

Consumers associate brands of products and services with specific social classes. For instance, Heineken and Amstel Light are considered to be upper middle-class drinks, whereas Old Style is perceived as a beer for "every person" and is consumed mainly by middle- and lower-class drinkers. In the United States early in this century, beer was perceived as a lower-class beverage, but today it is popular with all classes—perhaps as a result of heavy marketing efforts and the introduction of light beers.

Stores such as Bloomingdale's and Marshall Field once had reputations as stores primarily for the upper or upper middle classes, while Kmart was mainly where the lower classes shopped. Target achieved much of its success as a discount department store positioned as more upscale than Kmart. Among restaurants, Wendy's is considered more upscale than Burger King or Denny's.[2]

You may find this chapter unsettling because American traditions emphasize equality. In the United States and Canada, in one generation a family can rise from the lowest social/economic level to almost the highest; yet few could deny that there are enormous variations between the homeless of America and the individuals described in Consumer in Focus 19.1.

In England, citizens can rarely change class rapidly and can never be royalty unless born into it. In India, the family can never change class, but individuals may do so through reincarnation. In countries such as Russia and others such as China and Hungary, consumers formerly subscribed to the common person ideology of communism and socialism. Today, there are new stirrings and the emergence of a consumer culture that is demonstrated in homes, electronic

Consumer in Focus   19.1

The Social Ladder

Consider the following biographies:

When Henry Ross Perot was a boy growing up in Texarkana, his mother tacked a Norman Rockwell print above his desk—"Boy Scout at Prayer." Perot became much more than the reverent boy above his desk; he became an Eagle Scout, a midshipman, a computer services entrepreneur worth $2.5 billion, a builder of modern Dallas, and a candidate for U.S. president.

John Kluge is tied for second place, with H. Ross Perot, on the *Forbes* list of the 400 richest Americans. He is a self-made man. His entrepreneurial instincts seemed to have surfaced first at Columbia University where in addition to studying economics and working three shifts in the dining hall, he began to run small enterprises out of his dormitory room. Kluge decided to express his taste in consumption through his residence. He and his wife Patricia have spent five years creating Albemarle House, an immense English-style estate, out of more than 6,000 acres of rolling farmland in Virginia. In addition to their forty-five room Georgian country house, the Kluges have built a Gothic-style chapel, a glass conservatory, a stables and antique carriage house, a golf-course designed by Arnold Palmer, a tournament croquet lawn, several staff cottages and barns, a log cabin, and a helicopter landing pad.

Descended from one of the immortal entrepreneurs, Jennifer Rockefeller led the Columbia University Marching Band in front of the Rockefeller Center. Jennifer is devoted to The Fund for Animals, especially its project to save America's wild horses. Her suit is Oscar de la Renta. Her stockings are Fogal. She wears Petrochi and Gorevic jewels with perfume by Oscar de la Renta. She is photographed in front of Rockefeller Center, one of her ancestor's notable secular monuments.

Source: Excerpts from Elizabeth C. Hirschman, "Secular Immortality and the American Ideology of Affluence," Journal of Consumer Research 17 (June 1990), 31–42.

equipment, cars, number of bodyguards, and clothes that no longer reflect the stereotyped view of a person as a cog in the societal mechanism.[3]

Even if it is uncomfortable for you to think about social status and inequality, it is necessary because both buying and consumption are directly affected by such divisions in society. In this chapter, we first analyze the basic concept of status and consider how to study it and then examine the effects of status on consumer behavior.

Social Stratification

Social classes and status systems exist in every country of the world. In Europe, the concept is so important to understanding consumer behavior that the European

Society for Opinion and Marketing Research (ESOMAR) devised questions so that social-class research would be comparable between countries. Japan is a country with rigid expectations about social class, even though a large proportion of consumers are middle class. In Latin America, many countries have huge numbers of poorer classes struggling for existence, while the small but wealthy classes purchase a wide array of products that serve as visible symbols of class membership. Even in formerly Marxist societies, which were officially classless, the best of available consumer products went to privileged classes, based on party affiliation, athletic ability, or educational attainment. Americans sometimes believe social class is unimportant but act as if class were quite important. Research indicates that Americans perceive effects of social class even more than in England, a country known for class importance.[4]

Even animals other than humans divide themselves into stratified societies. One famous study described a barnyard society in which each hen maintained a definite position in the pecking order of the group.[5] This is where the term *pecking order* apparently originated. Ries and Trout,[6] in their influential book on positioning, extend this principle: "Consumers are like chickens. They are much more comfortable with a pecking order that everybody knows and accepts." Brand names and stores also have a pecking order by which they seek to lure customers whose values and beliefs will lead them to say, "This brand (or store) is for me."

Beer advertisements illustrate how social-class positioning is achieved. Despite recent inroads into the upper middle classes, beer is still purchased mostly by middle and lower social classes, in contrast to wine. Miller once positioned its brand as "the champagne of bottled beer," but later Miller changed to the slogan, "When you've got the time, we've got the beer," to target the busy, active leisure activities of the upper middle class. More recently, Miller switched to "the workingman's beer" to try to emulate Budweiser's success with less affluent drinkers. Budweiser ads feature people who don't have much fun in their jobs, but who relax with "The King of Beers" to forget their jobs. Budweiser's symbol of Clydesdale horses also ties in to the strong, physical demands on lower- and middle-class workers.

Few constructs are better documented in sociological literature than social inequality and the differential prestige or **deference** (granting of social honor) paid by some in society to members of higher classes. Most sociologists accept class inequality as a proven fact based on the empirical evidence. Americans may hope that every person has equal opportunity to gain access to products and services. Yet, the empirical evidence indicates otherwise. Social class determines *life chances*, a term used by Max Weber to emphasize the fundamental aspects of an individual's future possibilities. Life chances range from the infant's chances for decent nutrition to the adult's opportunities to purchase the goods and services that marketers constantly urge her or him to buy.

Understanding the development of social class is important in understanding consumption, for lifestyles of the upper middle class tend to filter down and become generally accepted by the rest of society. Although most of us cannot afford Jennifer Rockefeller's clothes or jewels described in Consumer in Focus 19.1, we can, for $10 an hour, have our picture taken skating on the ice at Rockefeller Center.

What Is Social Class?

Social class is defined as relatively permanent and homogeneous divisions in a society into which individuals or families sharing similar values, lifestyles, interests, and behavior can be categorized. It refers to a grouping of people who are similar in their behavior based on their economic position in the marketplace. Class membership exists and can be described as a statistical category whether or not individuals are aware of their common situation. **Status groups** reflect a community's expectations for style of life among each class as well as the positive or negative social estimation of honor given to each class. Max Weber,[7] who along with Karl Marx might be regarded as the father of social-class theory, clarified the distinction:

> With some over-simplification, one might thus say that "classes" are stratified according to their relations in the production and acquisition of goods, whereas "status groups" are stratified according to the principles of their consumption of goods as represented by special "styles of life."

For marketers, status systems are of primary interest because they exert a major influence on what people buy and consume. However, what consumers are able to buy is determined by social class—namely, the income or wealth of the consumer—and thus, our empirical emphasis in marketing research is on social-class variables. For practical purposes, it is usually adequate in the study of consumer behavior to treat the terms *status* and *class* interchangeably, as we do in this chapter, although recognizing that status may be used in other contexts to describe differential respect given to an individual within a group. Some scholars separate the patterns of behavior associated with a social class as having separate benefits of class, prestige, and power.[8]

Inequality Systems

All countries, except the smallest and most primitive, are stratified or have formal systems of inequality, known as social classes, castes, or estates. Regardless of the specific system, stratification occurs to develop and preserve collective social identity in a world characterized by pervasive economic inequality.[9] Social identity is achieved by establishing boundaries on interactions between people of unequal status.

Social class systems rank families rather than individuals. A family shares many characteristics among its members that affect relationships with outsiders, such as the same house, the same income, the same values, and thus much of the same buying behavior. When a large group of families are approximately equal in rank to each other and clearly differentiated from other families, they form a social class.

The *caste* system is more rigid. Only relatively controlled interaction is permitted between castes, and mobility between groups is limited. Caste is based on hereditary status and, especially as it was practiced in India, on religion.

The *estate* system was founded on power and alliances—mainly, the power of the lords and their warriors to offer protection from violence in earlier eras. Force was often the basis of power, status, and a share of the land's produce. An extension of this system of inequality in contemporary societies is the power and deference given to people in the media, in professional athletics, and in organizations such as labor unions, political parties, and government agencies. Giant corporations, such as Rubbermaid, which was ranked as the most admired American firm in America in 1994, General Electric, and Mitsubishi, convey such status. People who work for "status corporations" have more prestige in society and perhaps more ability to achieve better jobs in other firms because of the status of the "estate" in which they serve.

What Determines Social Class?

What causes your social status? The variables that determine social class have been identified in social stratification studies that began in the 1920s and 1930s. Early studies were descriptions of social classes in small towns of New England and the South. Today, social-class research includes thousands of studies dealing with the measurement of social class in large cities; movement between social classes; interactions of social class with gender, race, ethnicity, and education; and the effects of social class on poverty and economic policy.

From extensive research on social class, nine variables have emerged as most important in determining social class. These nine variables were identified by Gilbert and Kahl in three categories as shown in the following table:[10]

Economic Variables	Interaction Variables	Political Variables
Occupation	Personal prestige	Power
Income	Association	Class consciousness
Wealth	Socialization	Mobility

Some of these are more important than others in the study of consumer behavior just described.

Your social class is influenced mostly by the family in which you were raised. Your father's occupation probably had a significant effect on your social class because a man's occupation historically has been the most important determinant, followed closely by the wife's occupation.[11] The primary role of the father may be less true in the future, especially among families in which wives have better paying or more prestigious careers than their husbands.

For consumer analysts, six variables of the nine listed on the previous are especially useful in understanding a consumer's social class. These are based on the original research of sociologist Joseph Kahl[12] and include occupation, personal performance, interactions, possessions, value orientations, and class consciousness.

Do not make the mistake of thinking of equating social class with income. Social class is not determined by income, even though there may be a correlation due to the relationship between income and other variables that determine social class. A senior garbage collector, for example, might earn more than an assistant professor of history. The professor typically would be ascribed higher social class, however. You can probably think of more examples of how income and social class differ.

Occupation

Occupation is the best single indicator of social class in most consumer research. You probably have had the experience of meeting someone, quickly followed by the question, "What do you do?" The answer provides a good clue to the social class of the individual. The work consumers perform greatly affects their lifestyles and is the single most important basis for according prestige, honor, and respect. Consumption varies considerably between occupations. Blue-collar workers spend a greater proportion of their income on food, whereas managers and professionals spend a higher share of their income on eating out, clothing, and financial services.[13]

In most cultures of the world, physicians historically have been accorded respect and usually high financial reward. In more recent years, some of the information occupations have gained status, such as television anchors, computer programmers, and logistics managers. Capitalist or entrepreneur is one of the occupations that offers the potential of "secular immortality" or more lasting effect on the family's social class because of the possibility of building a store of capital that will continue the income for future generations.

Personal Performance

A person's status can also be influenced by her or his success relative to that of others in the same occupation—by an individual's personal performance.

Statements such as "She is the finest trial lawyer in town," or "Frank is the only programmer that I trust to do it right," or "That professor is doing the most significant research in the field" are examples of evaluations of personal performance. Even though income is not a good indicator of overall social class, it may serve as a gauge of personal performance within an occupation. The top 25 percent of income producers in any occupation are also likely to be the most highly respected and personally competent in their field.

Personal performance also involves activities other than job-related pursuits. Perhaps your father has a low-status occupation. Your family may still achieve more status if your father is perceived as one who helps others in need, is unusually kind and interested in fellow workers, or is a faithful worker in civic or religious organizations. The president of a corporation who serves as chairperson of the United Way or a trustee of a university may achieve higher social status than the president of a similar corporation not involved in such activities. A reputation as a good mother or a good father may contribute to one's status.

Interactions

People feel most comfortable when they are with people of similar values and behavior. Sociologists who emphasize analyses of social interactions are sometimes called the "who-invited-whom-to-dinner" school. In such an approach, group membership and interactions are considered a primary determinant of a person's social class.

The interaction variables of personal prestige, association, and socialization are the essence of social class. People have high **prestige** when other people have an attitude of respect or deference to them. **Association** is a variable concerned with everyday relationships, with people who like to do the same things they do, in the same ways, and with whom they feel comfortable. **Socialization** is the process by which an individual learns the skills, attitudes, and customs to participate in the life of the community. Social-class behavior and values are clearly differentiated in children by the time they have reached adolescence, in variables that vary by social class such as self-esteem.[14] Interactions are the best validity check in social-class research but are not used extensively in consumer research because they are difficult and expensive to measure.

Social interactions ordinarily are limited to one's immediate social class, even though opportunities exist for broader contact. Most marriages occur within the same or adjacent social classes. In public schools, open contact may be encouraged by the institution, but children usually reveal definite patterns of restricted association. Sometimes these groups have their own names—the "straights," the "grubbies," the "cheerleaders," and so forth. One of the most obvious examples of restricted social interaction is the *Social Register,* which contains rigid criteria for gaining and maintaining admission. Recently, it was changed from a series of local editions to a national edition listing socially prominent people throughout the United States.

Possessions

Possessions are symbols of class membership—not only the number of possessions, but the nature of the choices made. Thus, a middle-class family may choose wall-to-wall carpeting, whereas an upper-class family is more likely to choose Oriental rugs, even if the prices are equal. Thornston Veblen referred to such symbols as "conspicuous consumption." Consumption of products such as cars, homes, causes, and clothing is affected because the ideology of affluence promotes seeking personal "secular immortality" through the cultural celebration of achievement, wealth, and the accumulation of possessions.[15]

Possessions and wealth are closely related. Wealth is usually a result of an accumulation of past income. In certain forms, such as ownership of a business or of stocks and bonds, wealth is the source of future income that may enable a family to maintain its (high) social class from generation to generation. Thus, possessions that indicate the family's wealth are important in reflecting social class.

The most important possession decision reflecting a family's social class is the choice of where to live. This includes both the type of home and the neighborhood. Notice the description of John and Patricia Kluge's house in Consumer in Focus 19.1 (page 679). Another important "possession" is the university one attends. Upper-class individuals select the "best" schools, which in turn reinforces class consciousness and cohesion.[16] Other possessions that serve as indicators of social status include club memberships (which also reflect interactions), preferred furniture styles, clothing, appliances, and types of vacations chosen. People who lack the possessions or knowledge of them but who aspire to a higher social class may study diligently to learn more about the possessions of that class. Business students and others interested in making it "to the top," for example, are prime prospects for books and courses that teach how to "dress for success" or the secrets "they didn't teach you in business school."

Products and brands often seek to be positioned as symbols of status—as the products used by upper middle or upper classes. For people who are striving to become associated with those classes, the purchase of such brands may be partially based on the desire for such affiliation or identification. Consumer in Focus 19.2 describes such status symbols, based on a list prepared for consumers who may have been raised in social classes lower than their improved status.

Value Orientations

Values—shared beliefs about how people should behave—indicate the social class to which one belongs. When a group of people share a common set of abstract convictions that organize and relate many specific attributes, it is possible to categorize an individual in the group by the degree to which he or she possesses these values. Some observers believe that in countries other than the United States, values are more important than possessions. Class is indicated

| **19.2** | **Consumer in Focus** |

Brands to Buy to Reflect Increasing Social Status

THE WATCH: Rolex, for its Swiss accuracy, respectable name, and gold-link band. THE RAINCOAT: Burberry. Check the coatroom where the rich and powerful lunch and you'll find a sea of Burberry trench coats. THE SUIT: Armani. While the traditional status-conscious male may continue to have suits tailor-made, the new breed will plunk down as much as $1,500 for one of Giorgio Armani's couture suits. THE ATTACHE CASE: Mark Cross, because what's on the outside can be as important as what's on the inside. THE PEN: Montblanc. This top-dollar writing utensil starts at $12 for the ballpoint and reaches the $6,500 mark for a solid-gold fountain pen. THE CAR: Porsche, for those who are serious about power, performance and being out in front on the road. THE SUNGLASSES: Porsche, an extension of the car. THE SNEAKERS: Reeboks. Averaging about $55 a pair, these leather aerobic shoes are gracing the most graceful to work out in the trendiest health spas. THE GOOD SOUND: Front row orchestra seats at a Wynton Marsalis or Sade concert. THE SWEET SMELL OF SUCCESS: For women, Giorgio, at $150 an ounce; for men, Lagerfeldt, at $30 for the four-ounce spray cologne. MAN'S BEST FRIEND: The Akita. They resemble German shepherds, but they're really Japanese guard dogs who will be your constant companion if you're willing to pay $750 to $2,000 for one.

Source: Monique Greenwood, "Status Symbols," Black Enterprise (May 1986), 65.[16]

more by merit derived from expressions in art, science, and religion and even in such mundane things as dressing and eating properly rather than defined in pecuniary terms. In contrast to Europe, people in the United States are believed to make a religion of money or using money as a "votive offering and pagan ornament."[17]

Consumer analysts need to answer the question, "What values characterize specific market segments?" These beliefs may refer to general values abut political ideals, religious practices, work motivation, the capitalistic economic system, and so forth. Also included are more specific activities such as child rearing, family structure, sexual behavior, abortion, and impulsiveness in decision making.

Figure 19.1 shows ads that might appeal to upper social classes. Notice how Movado appeals to the interests of the upper classes in art and museums. Similarly, Martini & Rossi speaks of Pavarotti, Tintoretto, and Tuscany. Both ads use a minimum of words and a maximum of image.

Class Consciousness

One of the important political variables of social class is class consciousness. Class consciousness refers to the degree to which people in a social class are aware of themselves as a distinctive group with shared political and economic

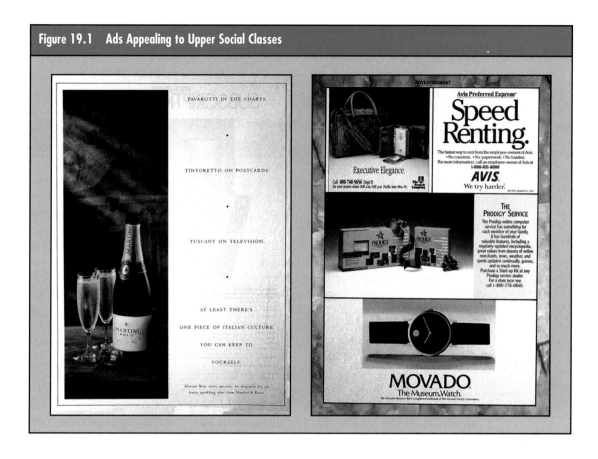

Figure 19.1 Ads Appealing to Upper Social Classes

interests. As people become more group-conscious, they are likely to organize political parties, trade unions, and other associations to advance their group interests.[18]

Americans often state they are not class-conscious. To some extent, a person's social class is indicated by how conscious that person is of social class. Lower social class individuals may recognize the reality of social class but may not be as sensitive to specific differences. Thus, advertising for goods selling to upper-class market targets are often rich with social-class symbols, but ads to middle and lower social class targets may not be well received if they use a direct class appeal.

Other political variables that are sometimes useful in understanding social class include power and mobility. Power is the potential of individuals or groups to carry out their will over others. Mobility and succession is a dual concept related to the stability or instability of stratification systems. Succession refers to the process of children inheriting the class position of their parents. When mobility occurs in an upward direction, consumers may need to learn a new set of consumption behaviors—products and brands that are consistent with their new status, the kind of advice described in Consumer in Focus 19.2.

How to Measure Social Class

Consumer researchers have developed and borrowed a variety of methods to measure and describe social class. These methods have been developed to relate dependent variables, such as product usage, brand preference, attitudes, store image, and patronage, to the independent variable of social class. With such research, it may be possible to define market segments on the basis of social class and to understand consumption and buying patterns of those segments.

Social-class research methods are used for two purposes: theoretical or validity research and practical marketing research. A specific method might be used for either purpose, but the theoretical methods are often so costly and time-consuming that market researchers do not use them on a day-to-day basis. They help develop the theory of social class and serve as a validity check on practical methods.

Research methods may also be classified as **objective** when they involve quantitative variables of socioeconomic status (SES) measures such as occupation, education, and income. Methods may also be **subjective** when they involve reports by individuals of their perceptions of other people. Research methods may be described as **interpretive**, in which researchers "read" society as a "text" by using novels, autobiographies, ads, and other materials much like literary criticism.[19]

Marketing researchers like objective methods because of the availability of census and survey data adapted to micromarketing segments using computerized, quantitative analytical techniques. Richer insights and understanding may be provided, however, by subjective or interpretive methods.

Theoretical and Validity Methods

Reputational methods involve asking people to rank the social position or prestige of other people. The reputational method was developed by Lloyd Warner, one of the pioneers in the study of social class in the United States.[20] This work was extended by Burleigh Gardner and associates in the Deep South[21] and in the Midwest by Hollingshead.[22]

These studies also include *association or sociometric measures*, which count the number and nature of personal contacts of people in their informal relationships. These studies are also called *evaluative participation studies* because researchers add to the data they collect from respondents their own observations gained from living in the community and participating in the informal networks and formal organizations of the community.

Warner and colleagues developed the *Index of Status Characteristics* based on the need for more objective and less laborious research techniques. After years of work with reputational, associational, and evaluative participation methods, which established the validity of social class, researchers concluded that, once the evaluated rankings were established, they could accurately predict such rankings on the basis of a family's *occupation, source of income, house type,* and *residential area.* By establishing the validity of these objective measures in social-class research, marketing researchers can use updated and readily quantifiable methods.

The theoretical research provided a stream of empirical data and concepts that are central to our present efforts to relate social class to consumption. It was Warner, Gardner, and their colleagues who described the six basic social classes found in the United States, which are detailed in Table 19.1.

Marketing Research Methods for Measuring Social Class

Marketing researchers measure social class as an independent variable to determine its association with dependent variables of interest in marketing. Objective methods assign status on the basis of respondents' possessing some value of a stratified variable. The most often used variables are occupation, income, education, size and type of residence, ownership of possessions, and organizational affiliations. Objective methods can be divided into those that are single indexes and those that are multiple indexes.

Subjective or self-reporting methods ask respondents to rate themselves on social class. These methods, although occasionally used, are of limited value to consumer analysts for two reasons: (1) respondents tend to overrate their own class position, and (2) respondents avoid the connotative terms of upper and lower classes and, thus, exaggerate the size of the middle class.

Single-Item Indexes

Occupation is the best single proxy indicator of social class. People who have similarly ranked (in prestige) occupations often share similar access to the means of achieving a lifestyle. Leisure time, income independence, knowledge, and power are often common to occupational categories. They interact with one another and generally agree with each other concerning the types of activities, interests, and possessions that are important and how family resources should be allocated to implement the achievement of these goals.

Occupation is used in consumer research by asking respondents to write in their exact occupation, which can later be coded numerically according to its social class or status value. These values are established in one of two ways. One method is to use surveys of people asked to rank the prestige of people in various occupations or of the occupations themselves. A second method is

Table 19.1   Traditional Social Class Behavior in America

Upper Upper. Upper uppers are the social elite of society. Inherited wealth from socially prominent families is the key to admission. Children attend private preparatory schools and graduate from the best colleges.

Consumers in the upper upper class spend money as if it were unimportant, not tightly but not with display either, for that would imply that money is important. For some products, a trickle-down influence may exist between social classes. The social position of these individuals is so secure that they can deviate from class norms if they choose to without losing status.

Lower Upper. Lower uppers include the very high-income professional people who have earned their position rather than inherited it. They are the *nouveaux riches,* active people with many material symbols of their status. They buy the largest homes in the best suburbs and the most expensive automobiles, swimming pools, and other symbols of conspicuous consumption, making them innovators and good markets for luxury marketing offerings.

Upper Middle. The key word for upper middles is *career.* Careers are based on successful professional or graduate degrees for a specific profession or the skill of business administration. Members of this class are demanding of their children in educational attainment.

The quality market for many products is the upper middle class, and gracious living in a conspicuous but careful manner characterizes the family's lifestyle. The home is of high importance and an important symbol of the family's success and competence.

Lower Middle. Lower middle-class families are typical Americans, exemplifying the core of respectability, conscientious work habits, and adherence to culturally defined norms and standards. They believe in attending church and obeying the law and are upset when their children are arrested for law violations. They are not innovators.

The *home* is very important to the lower middle-class family, and they want it to be neat, well painted, and in a respected neighborhood. They may have little confidence in their own tastes and adopt standardized home furnishings—perhaps from Levitz or similar furniture stores. This is in contrast to the upper middle-class consumer who feels freer to experiment with new styles and new arrangements and with the upper lower-class consumer who is not very concerned about the overall plan for furnishing the home: The lower middle-class consumer reads and follows the advice of the medium-level shelter and service magazines in an attempt to make the house pretty.

The lower middle-class consumer works more at shopping than others and considers purchase decisions demanding and tedious. He or she may have a high degree of price sensitivity.

Upper Lower. Upper lower social classes exhibit a routine life, characterized by a day-to-day existence of unchanging activities. They live in dull areas of the city, in small houses or apartments. The hard hats are included in this class, with many members working at uncreative jobs requiring manual activity or only moderate skills and education. Because of unions and security, many may earn incomes that give them considerable discretionary income.

The purchase decisions of the working class are often impulsive but at the same time may show high brand loyalty to national brands. Buying them is one way to prove knowledge as a buyer, a role in which he or she thinks (probably correctly) that he or she has little skill. This consumer has little social contact outside the home and does not like to attend civic organizations or church activities. Social interaction is limited to close neighbors and relatives. If he or she takes a vacation, it will probably be to visit relatives in another city. Upper lowers are concerned that they not be confused with the lower lowers.

Lower Lower. The lower lower social class contains people who may try to rise above their class but usually fail to do so. An individual in the lower lower class often rejects middle-class morality and gets pleasure wherever possible—and this includes buying impulsively. This lack of planning causes purchases that cost too much and may result in inferior goods. This person pays too much for products, buys on credit at a high interest rate, and has difficulty obtaining quality or value. This group includes highly distressed families, some who have habitual legal problems, and the homeless.

to use objective measures, such as ranking of the average educational level and/or income of occupational groups.

There is a long history of studies of occupational prestige. They disclose stability of prestige ratings over time. High correlations between nations are also found. The key variables causing occupations to have prestige are the amount of education required as a prerequisite for entering the occupation and the reward (typically income) that society bestows on the occupation.

Government data relating to occupations are classified using the Standard Occupational Classification (SOC).[23] The classification provides a coding system and nomenclature for identifying and classifying occupations in a system that can be used for marketing purposes as well as standard categories used by diverse governmental agencies. Information is included about the company and type of business in which the individual works; the kind of work and job duties as well as occupational title; and the classification of work as public, private, or self-employed.

One of the easiest scales for marketing researchers to use was developed by Nam and Powers[24] and provides a precise, numerical status score for 589 occupations. An example of some of the scores that are assigned to occupations using the Nam and Powers scale is shown in Table 19.2 on page 694.

Multiple-Item Indexes

Multiple-item indexes combine several indicators of social class into one index to provide a richer measure of social status. These indexes start with a single index, such as the Nam and Powers scores shown in Table 19.2, but are combined with additional scores for variables such as education and income of the consumer. The three scores (occupation, education, income) are then summed and divided by 3 to provide a multiple-item SES score. This provides an easy-to-use, numerical score of social class that can then be related to product purchase, brand preference, media processing, or other variables of interest to marketing researchers.

Coleman's Computerized Status Index

Coleman's Computerized Status Index (CSI) is an index developed by Social Research, Inc., and is extensively used in commercial consumer research. Figure 19.2 shows the format for administering the CSI. In this particular version, occupation is weighted double when computing the total scale. Other versions include an occupation scaling specifically for employed women, to be used whether they are the spouse or the household head. The status for conventional married couples with a male household head between 35 and 64 years of age is as follows: upper American, 37 to 53; middle class, 24 to 36; working class, 13 to 23; and lower American, 4 to 12. Additional refinements beyond updating income include adjustment for unusual income levels or abnormalities in occupation or neighborhood ratings.[25]

Figure 19.2   Example of a Computerized Status Index (CSI)

Interviewer circles code numbers (for the computer) which in his/her judgment best fit the respondent and family. Interviewer asks for detail on occupation, then makes rating. Interviewer then asks the respondent to describe neighborhood in own words. Interviewer asks respondent to specify income—a card is presented to the respondent showing the eight brackets—and records R's response. If interviewer feels this is overstatement or under, a "better-judgment" estimate should be given, along with explanation.

Education	Respondent	Respondent's Spouse
• Grammar school (8 yrs or less)	− 1 *R's*	− 1 *Spouse's*
• Some high school (9 to 11 yrs)	− 2 age:	− 2 age:
• Graduated high school (12 yrs)	− 3	− 3
• Some post high school (business, nursing, technical, one yr college)	− 4	− 4
• Two, three years of college—possibly Associate of Arts degree	− 5	− 5
• Graduated four-year college (B.A./B.S.)	− 7	− 7
• Master's or five-year professional degree	− 8	− 8
• Ph.D. or six/seven-year professional degree	− 9	− 9

Occupation Prestige Level of Household Head

Interviewer's judgment of how head of household rates in occupational status. (Respondent's description—ask for previous occupation if retired, or if R. is widow ask husband's: _____)

• Chronically unemployed—"day" laborers, unskilled: on welfare	− 0
• Steadily employed but in marginal semiskilled jobs: custodians, minimum-pay factory help, service workers (gas attendants, etc.)	− 1
• Average-skill assembly-line workers, bus and truck drivers, police and firefighters, route deliverymen, carpenters, brickmasons	− 2
• Skilled craftsmen (electricians), small contractors, factory foremen, low-pay salesclerks, office workers, postal employees	− 3
• Owners of very small firms (2–4 employees), technicians, salespeople, office workers, civil servants with average level salaries	− 4
• Middle management, teachers, social workers, lesser professionals	− 5

Continued

Figure 19.2   Continued

- Lesser corporate officials, owners of middle-sized businesses
  (10–20 employees), moderate-success professionals
  (dentists, engineers, etc.) 7
- Top corporate executives, "big successes" in the professional
  world (leading doctors and lawyers, "rich" business owners) 9

Area of Residence

Interviewer's impressions of the immediate neighborhood in terms of its reputation in the eyes of the community.
- Slum area: people on relief, common laborers...1
- Strictly working class: not slummy but some very poor housing 2
- Predominantly blue-collar with some office workers 3
- Predominantly white-collar with some well-paid blue-collar...4
- Better white-collar area; not many executives, but hardly any blue-collar either 5
- Excellent area: professionals and well-paid managers..7
- "Wealthy" or "society"-type neighborhood..9

Total Family Income per Year

Under $5,000	– 1
$5,000 to $9,999	– 2
$10,000 to $14,999	– 3
$15,000 to $19,999	– 4
$20,000 to $24,999	– 5
$25,000 to $34,999	– 6
$35,000 to $49,999	– 7
$50,000 and over	– 8

Total Score _____

Estimated Status _____

(Interviewer's estimate: _____ and explanation: _____)
Married _____ Divorced/Separated _____ Widowed _____ Single _____ (Code____)

Source: Richard P. Coleman, "The Continuing Significance of Social Class to Marketing," Journal of Consumer Research 10 (December 1983), 265–280.

Table 19.2 Occupational Status Scores of Occupations

Occupation	Status Score
Accountants	89
Architects	97
Engineers	
Aeronautical	96
Industrial	93
Mechanical	93
Librarians	75
Physicians	
Chiropractors	95
Medical and osteopathic	99
Registered nurses	66
Clergymen	77
Social scientists	
Economists	96
Sociologists	94
Social workers	82
Teachers	
Chemistry	97
Business and commerce	95
Elementary school, public	80
Secondary school, public	86
Sales managers, retail trade	74
Sales managers, except retail	94
Bank tellers	49
Cashiers	29
Keypunch operators	49
Typists	46
Mechanics	
Aircraft	72
Automotive	45
Office machine	69
Bottling and canning operatives	22
Dry wall installers	51
Coal mine operatives	35
Bus drivers	40
Taxicab drivers	35
Farm managers	52
Farm laborers, wage workers	04
Bartenders	42
Busboys	12

Source: Excerpts from Table A1 of Charles B. Nam and Mary G. Powers, The Socioeconomic Approach to Status Measurement (Houston: Cap and Gown Press, 1983). See this source for a complete list of occupations.

Commercial marketing research firms and other organizations sometimes develop their own scales to measure social status or other variables such as lifestyles. These scales assign a status value to the postal zip code or other geographic designation of a respondent's residence. The values reflect geodemographic data based on the distribution of occupations, educational characteristics, income, condition of housing, and so forth, in zip code areas.

Zip methods are valuable because of their ability to measure status without the need to collect additional data from respondents beyond their addresses. This information can then be related to variables such as the class of customers that will be attracted to a shopping center or a specific store or the type of people that may respond to types of merchandise offered by a direct-mail organization.

The marketing research firm Claritas uses zip code information to classify households into segments such as the "Suburban Elites" who live in Scarsdale (New York), Winnetka (Illinois), or similar locations. This segment is likely to own a new convertible, read business magazines, and have a full-service brokerage account. People classified as "Urban Gold" are likely to live in places such as the Upper East Side of Manhattan or on Michigan Avenue in Chicago. Their leisure is likely to be sailing and their media tastes information TV.[26]

One further complexity in measuring social class, as if any more were needed, is the problem of status inconsistency or consideration of people who rate high on one variable but low on another. Highly paid athletes and popular musicians often fit this category. The other end of the spectrum of status inconsistency would include some professors who have little income but much education and cultural advantages. These people do not fit into many of the generalizations about social class.

Lenski developed an index of status crystallization and concluded that some people have a low degree of status crystallization. An example might be Dave Thomas, founder of Wendy's, who is wealthy, powerful, and well known because of his frequent TV ads but possesses the language patterns and characteristics of a person with little formal education or family foundation.[27] Lenski[28] found, among other things, that people with low-status crystallization are more willing to support programs of social change.

Are Social Classes Changing?

Are social classes as prevalent as they once were? Maybe social class is vanishing among working-class and middle-class people. This theory is sometimes called the embourgeoisment of society or the massification theory. Perhaps the prevalence of mass media and increasing income as well as the dissemination of economic and political power on a wider basis have eliminated many of the differences between working-class and middle-class people. A major controversy exists concerning whether the middle class is shrinking in America.[29] This issue is usually addressed by examining economic indicators of income and wealth such as those in Chapter 10.

An extensive review of factors such as power, income, wealth, status, and participation in the political process caused Kriesberg[30] to conclude that personal wealth has probably become more equally distributed in the past 50 years, but wealth in the form of corporate shares has become more concentrated with the decline of self-employment. Bottomore's[31] studies also indicate that corporate wealth is more powerful than ever as a result of large, multinational corporations but that due to a growth of state intervention and other factors, the middle class has increased in numbers and in its social and political importance.

The Duncan studies at the University of Michigan indicate much more economic mobility than was generally thought to be true in the past.[32] These studies are based on analysis of movement between quintiles of income and show that in a decade only about half of those who started out in the lowest-income quintile ended up there. Conversely, of the individuals in families in the highest quintile, fewer than half stayed there. Thus, "riches to rags" is about as common in the United States as "rags to riches."

Perhaps most surprising in the Duncan studies—and important for consumer researchers—is the finding that consumers below the poverty line do not stay there. In the 10-year period of the study, with average poverty levels about 12 percent, about 25 percent of Americans were below the poverty line for at least 1 year, but only 2.6 percent stayed there. In their book *Years of Poverty, Years of Plenty*, Duncan and fellow researchers reported that the 2 percent chronically below the poverty level tend to be heavily dependent on welfare; to live in rural areas; and to be black, elderly, disabled, or in households headed by women with limited job opportunities. For most consumers, economic mobility is as probable as geographic mobility.

Marketers must realize that except for the 2 to 3 percent who are chronically poor, poor consumers who have little purchasing power in one year may be individuals whom marketers may seek as valued customers in later years. Firms such as Wal-Mart have policies to treat all customers well, even poor ones. Many of the poor ones become affluent and contribute to the reason Wal-Mart became the largest retailer in the United States. Social class has not been eliminated in the United States; it has just changed a little.

How Likely Are You to Change Your Social Class?

You may change your occupation and income, but can you change them enough to attain a social class different from your parents? How often are changes such as those in Consumer in Focus 19.3 likely to occur? These are issues of intergenerational mobility.

The answer seems to be that, although it is possible to climb upward (or downward) in the social order, the probabilities of this actually happening are not very high.[33] Both men and women are affected by the low probability of change in social class, although women may have a bit more mobility through marriage than do men through occupations, because a man is more likely to inherit his father's status.[34] Women are also more likely to be lowered in status by divorce than are men. Upper-class people are more likely to believe that poverty is a result of equity or wasting money, whereas lower-class people tend to believe that the rich resist social change that might end poverty.[35] Parental wealth is very important in determining the social class of the next generation, not only because of its direct effect but also because parental wealth has such a strong effect on the quality of education an individual receives.[36]

Consumer in Focus   **19.3**

Overcome Your Upbringing

It is often overlooked that most Americans who are born in the ghetto aren't destined to die there. According to researchers at the University of Michigan, 56 percent of teenagers whose family income put them in the nation's lowest fifth of all families in the 1970s had climbed out of the basement a decade later. Indeed, 12 percent were among the country's top 40 percent of earners. Seattle attorney Jose Gaitan, 39, was one of them.

Gaitan grew up in the city's rough central neighborhood, the son of an illegal Salvadoran immigrant father, who was deported when Jose was five, and an American-born, heroin-addicted mother. Today Gaitan is co-owner of the law firm Gaitan & Cusak and an adjunct professor at the University of Washington's law school. He earns more than $100,000 a year and lives in a $225,000 house with his wife, Olive.

Growing up on welfare, Gaitan remembers that food was so scarce that he shared two turkey TV dinners with his mother and younger brother on Thanksgiving. He found the path to a better life at Seattle First Baptist Church, where a minister, a Boy Scout leader, and a Boeing engineer encouraged him to work hard in school.

His grades won him scholarships at Linfield College and later he worked his way through the University of Washington's School of Law. He worked as a county and federal prosecutor until he and a partner opened a private practice. Today his firm counts Nabisco and the Federal Deposit Insurance Corporation among its clients and employs 13 lawyers. Says Gaitan, "Social and economic mobility is a function of hard work, a can do attitude and being good to people."

Source: Excerpted from "Overcome Your Upbringing," Money (October 1991), 153.

After reviewing the literature, Snarey and Vaillant[37] concluded:

> Children's social class is a stubborn predictor of their social class as adults. Only 1.8% of the children of manual laborers, for instance, entered the professions. Research to date has impressively documented factors that derail lower- and working-class individuals from upward social mobility. Among these are restricted access to educational and employment opportunities; high school tracking; class-biased career counseling; residential segregation by social class; class-biased achievement and IQ tests; lower teacher expectations for lower-class youth; and, perhaps most serious of all, racial prejudice.

How Large Are Social Classes?

There is no unqualified answer to the question of how large specific social classes are. Table 19.3 shows generally accepted estimates.[38] The Gilbert and Kahl definitions shown in Table 19.3 emphasize economic distinctions, especially the recent emphasis on capitalism and entrepreneurship, whereas the Coleman-Rainwater approach emphasizes how people interact with each other as equals, superiors, or inferiors, especially in their work relationships.

Social-Class Dynamics

Social-class behavior is dynamic because it reflects the changing environment. Some people think a lot about upholding their social class; others actively rebel against it by becoming part of the "counterculture."

Parody display is a term used to describe the mockery of status symbols and behavior, such as when the well-to-do wear blue jeans, even ones with holes in the knees, to proclaim their distaste for class or their own security in the social status system.

Social-class symbols are dynamic for other reasons. Some of these reasons relate to insecurity about the economic environment. Other reasons relate to the broad egalitarian interest that characterizes American history and culture. Some of the differences between status symbols of the 1980s and 1990s are described in Table 19.4. Today, there is also more individualism or "doing your own thing" among the middle social classes. Coleman[39] describes this situation:

> Through the 1960s and 1970s, the lifestyles and self-conceptions of people identified with the upper sixth of the nation appear to have changed more than those of people in the classes below. The lifestyle variations that have emerged exist vertically within Upper America, crossing the substrata and combining people from several status layers into one consumer group with common goals that are differentiated internally mainly by income. . . . The result is that Upper America is now a vibrant mix of many lifestyles, which may be labeled post-preppy, sybaritic, countercultural, conventional, intellectual, political, and so on. Such diversions are usually of more importance for targeting messages and goods than are the horizontal, status-flavored, class-named strata.

Table 19.3 Social Classes in America

Two Recent Views of the American Status Structure

The Gilbert-Kahl New Synthesis Class Structure: A situations model from political theory and sociological analysis[a]

The Coleman-Rainwater Social Standing Class Hierarchy: A reputational behavioral view in the community study tradition[b]

Upper Americans

Capitalist Class (1%) — Their investment decisions shape the national economy, income mostly from assets earned inherited, prestige university connections

Upper Middle Class (14%) — Upper managers, professionals, medium businessmen; college educated; family income ideally runs nearly twice the national average

Upper Americans

Upper Upper (0.3%) — "Capital S society" world of inherited wealth, aristocratic names

Lower Upper (1.2%) — Newer social elite drawn from current professional corporate leadership

Upper Middle (12.5%) — Rest of college graduate managers and professionals; lifestyle centers on private clubs, causes, and the arts

Middle Americans

Middle Class (33%) — Middle-level white-collar, top-level blue-collar; education past high school typical; income somewhat above the national average

Working Class (32%) — Middle-level blue-collar; lower-level white-collar; income runs slightly below the national average; education is also slightly below

Middle Americans

Middle Class (32%) — Average-pay white-collar workers and their blue-collar friends; live on "the better side of town," try to "do the proper things"

Working Class (38%) — Average-pay blue-collar workers; lead "working class lifestyle" whatever the income, school background, and job

Marginal and Lower Americans

Working Poor (11–12%) — Below mainstream America in living standard but above the poverty line; low-paid service workers, operatives; some high school education

Underclass (8–9%) — Depend primarily on welfare system for sustenance; living standard below poverty line; not regularly employed; lack schooling

Lower Americans

"A lower group of people but not the lowest" (9%) — Working not on welfare; living standard is just above poverty; behavior judged "crude," "trashy"

"Real lower lower" (7%) — On welfare, visibly poverty-stricken, usually out of work (or have "the dirtiest jobs"); "bums," "common criminals"

[a] *Abstracted by Coleman from Dennis Gilbert and Joseph A. Kahl, "The American Class Structure: A Synthesis," Chapter 11. The American Class Structure: A New Synthesis (Homewood, Ill.: The Dorsey Press, 1982).*
[b] *This condensation of the Coleman-Rainwater view is drawn from Chapters 8, 9, and 10 of Richard P. Coleman and Lee P. Rainwater, with Kent A. McClelland, Social Standing in America: New Dimensions of Class (New York: Basic Books, 1978).*

| Table 19.4 | Changing Consumption Symbols |

Class Distinctions: You Are What You Choose

		Lower Middle	Middle	Upper Middle
Car	1980s	Hyundai	Chevrolet Celebrity	Mercedes
	1990s	Geo	Chrysler minivan	Range Rover
Business shoe (men)	1980s	Sneakers	Wingtips	Cap toes
	1990s	Boots	Rockports	Loafers
Business shoe (women)	1980s	Spike-heel pumps	Mid-heel pumps	High-heel pumps
	1990s	High-heel pumps	Dressy flats	One-inch pumps
Alcoholic beverage	1980s	Domestic beer	White wine spritzer	Dom Perignon
	1990s	Domestic lite beer	California Chardonnay	Cristal
Leisure pursuit	1980s	Watching sports	Going to movies	Golf
	1990s	Playing sports	Renting movies	Playing with computers
Hero	1980s	Roseanne Barr	Ronald Reagan	Michael Milken
	1990s	Kathie Lee Gifford	Janet Reno	Rush Limbaugh

Source: Kenneth Labich, "Class in America," Fortune (Februatry 7, 1994), 116.

Marketing to Social-Class Segments

After reading the preceding pages, you should have a good grasp of what is meant by social stratification—how it is measured, how it is changing (both for individual consumers and in the society as a whole), and some reasonably specific descriptive ideas of how people in one social stratum differ in their behavior from people in higher or lower strata. Now it is time to bring this all together and ask, "How are buying and consumption decisions affected by social class? What does this mean for a marketing organization?"

Market Segmentation

Segmentation, as you remember from Chapter 2, focuses on variations in behavior between divisions of the whole. Social class has been useful in analysis of these variations since the pioneering work of people such as Pierre Martineau (marketing researcher at the *Chicago Tribune*), Sidney Levy of Northwestern University, and Richard Coleman of Social Research Inc.[40] The procedures for market segmentation include the following steps:

1. Identification of social-class usage of product
2. Comparison of social-class variables for segmentation with other variables (income, life cycle, etc.)
3. Description of social-class characteristics identified in market target
4. Development of marketing program to maximize effectiveness of marketing mix based on consistency with social-class attributes

Analysis of market segments by socioeconomic profile helps in the development of a comprehensive marketing program to match the preferences and behavior of the market target. This would include product attributes, media strategy, creative strategy, channels of distribution, and pricing. Notice in Table 19.5 the differences between social classes both in general statements about fashion and comfort as well as product-specific statements such as how telephone design should coordinate with the room.

Need Recognition and Evaluative Criteria

Consumer decision making is influenced by a person's social class, especially in the determination of needs and evaluative criteria. Look closely at Table 19.5 and you will see much more emphasis on form among upper classes than the functional needs of the lower social class. (Higher agreement with fashion than comfort, for example.) These influences can be observed in product decisions of consumers.

Clothing

The kind, quality, and style of clothing a person wears is closely linked to that person's social class, as Consumer in Focus 19.4 so vividly describes. Clothing furnishes a quick, visual cue to the class culture of the wearer. It serves well as a symbol of social differentiation because of its high visibility. When adolescent girls are asked to describe the characteristics of the popular girls, "dressed well" is the response most frequently given—that is, linked to social-class characteristics.

A 14-year-old student, attending a private high school in an upper middle-class suburb, described the other students in the following manner:

> There are three types of kids in our school. The rich kids wear Guess Jeans or clothes from The Limited. They have their parents' credit cards or their own, so they are used to getting what they want. They have to go to the bathroom after lunch to put on their makeup. They have seven Swatch watches, one for each day of the week. Their hair is curly or bobbed in a wave. At home, they have waterbeds. The lower-class kids don't dress as well. They don't hang around the cooler groups. They get made fun of a lot. They may have styles from The Limited but you know

Table 19.5 Descriptions of Socioeconomic Market Segments

General Psychographic Profile of Customer's Socioeconomic Status

Style/Color Statements	Lower-Class Agreement (%) (*n*=25)	Lower Middle-Class Agreement (%) (*n*=108)	Upper Middle-Class Agreement (%) (*n*=202)	Upper-Class Agreement (%) (*n*=105)
I am generally willing to try even the most radical fashion at least once.	32	25	42	37
When I must choose between the two, I usually dress for fashion, not for comfort.	9	15	24	29
Our home is furnished for comfort, not style.	96	87	79	79
I have more modern appliances in my home than most people.	17	23	41	48
I prefer colored appliances.	57	73	87	92
I enjoy the better things in life and am willing to pay for them.	36	70	70	82

Product-Specific Psychographic Profile of Customer's Socioeconomic Status

Style/Color Statements	Lower-Class Agreement (%) (*n*=25)	Lower Middle-Class Agreement (%) (*n*=108)	Upper Middle-Class Agreement (%) (*n*=202)	Upper-Class Agreement (%) (*n*=105)
Phones should come in patterns and designs as well as colors.	60	80	63	58
A telephone should improve the decorative style of a room.	47	82	73	77
Telephones should be modern in design.	58	85	83	89
A home should have a variety of telephone styles.	8	46	39	51
You can keep all those special phones. All I want is a phone that works.	83	67	68	56
The style of a telephone is unimportant to me.	86	54	58	51

Note: All significant levels are based on x2 with p=.05, 3 d.f.
Source: A. Marvin Roscoe, Jr., Arthur LeClaire, Jr., and Leon G. Schiffman, "Theory and Management Applications of Demographics in Buyer Behavior," in Arch G. Woodside, Jagdish N. Sheth, and Peter D. Bennett, eds., Consumer and Industrial Buying Behavior (Amsterdam: North-Holland, 1977), 74–75.

Consumer in Focus | **19.4**

Social Class Influences on Appearance Product: You Are What You Wear

There is an elite look in this country. It requires women to be thin, with a hairstyle dating back eighteen or twenty years or so. (The classiest women wear their hair for a lifetime in exactly the same style they affected in college.) They wear superbly fitting dresses and expensive but always understated shoes and handbags, with very little jewelry. They wear scarves—these instantly betoken class, because they are useless except as a caste mark. Men should be thin. No jewelry at all. No cigarette case. Moderate-length hair, never dyed or tinted, which is a middle-class or high-prole sign. . . . Never a hairpiece, a prole usage. Both women's and men's elite looks are achieved by a process of rejection—of the current, the showy, the superfluous. Thus the rejection of fat by the elite. It pays to be thin.

"Layering" is obligatory. It has generally been true that the more clothes someone has on, the higher his or her status; it is a fine way of displaying a large wardrobe. The upper-middle-class woman will appear almost invariably in a skirt of gray flannel, Stuart plaid, or khaki; a navy-blue cardigan, which may be cable stitched; a white blouse with Peter Pan collar; hose with flat shoes; hair preferably in a barrette. When it gets cold, she puts on a blue blazer, or for business, a gray flannel suit. But the color toward which everything aspires is really navy.

If navy is the upper-middle-class color, purple is the prole equivalent. The purple polyester pantsuit offends two principles that determine class in clothes: the color principle and the organic-materials principle. Navy blue aside, colors are classier the more pastel or faded, and materials are classier the more they consist of anything that was once alive. That means wool, leather, silk, cotton, and fur. Only. All synthetic fibers are prole, party because they're cheaper than natural ones, partly because they're not archaic, and partly because they're entirely uniform and hence boring—you'll never find a bit of straw or sheep excrement woven into an acrylic sweater. (The organic principle also determines that in kitchens wood is classier than Formica, and on the kitchen table a cotton cloth "higher" than plastic or oilcloth.)

Source: Paul Fussell, Class (New York: Ballatine Books, 1983).

they bought them at T. J. Maxx. The lower class (at this school) have more money than the kids at public schools, but they don't dress well or act right. The middle-class kids have money and dress nice, but they are not really cool, and they don't talk about themselves as much as the upper-class kids.

Home Furnishings

The criteria used by consumers to furnish a home are closely related to social class. Higher social classes tend to feel most comfortable with worn Oriental rugs on parquet floors, middle classes love wall-to-wall carpeting, and lower classes have vinyl floors. Originals—paintings, Tiffany lamps, or exhibits of ancient languages—are favorites of upper classes. Lower classes buy reproductions of these things or display collections of various items. The contents of the home can be identified so closely by social class that a scale has been developed for calculating social class on the basis of such items as furniture, venetian blinds, periodicals displayed, and family photographs present.[41]

Leisure

Social class affects leisure in a variety of ways. The type of leisure preferred is based on activities that occur primarily with people in the same or closely adjacent status levels. The influence to adopt new leisure activities will be from people with the same or slightly higher status than the adopters.[42]

The proportion of family income spent on leisure may not vary a great deal between social classes, but the type of recreation varies greatly. Polo is upper class; bridge is a middle- to upper-class game; bingo is lower class. Squash is upper class; tennis and racquetball are middle to upper class; boxing is predominantly lower class. Opera is upper class; professional wrestling is lower class.

Prestige leisure-time activities (jogging, swimming, tennis, and so on) involve fairly rapid movement, with extreme use of arms and legs, suggesting a compensatory form of leisure for the otherwise sedentary life of many prestige occupations. Most of these pursuits do not require much time to the degree that activities such as hunting, fishing, or boating would—typical leisure-time pursuits of lower social classes. Time is a critical element in the prestige classes' use of leisure. Members of lower social classes tend to participate in team sports, whereas people of higher socioeconomic status tend to participate in individual or dual sports.[43] The heaviest users of both commercial leisure and public facilities (such as parks, museums, and swimming pools) are the middle classes, because upper classes frequently have their own facilities and the lower classes often cannot afford them or do not have the propensity to participate in them.

Chief executives of major corporations may have little time for leisure because of their long hours, typically 59 hours a week at work and increasing. Most senior managers enjoy leisure pursuits on a daily basis, however. Many take part in recreational sports; others paint, play musical instruments, photograph nature and family, or escape into the world of literature. Reading work-related books and listening to music are among the favorite pursuits of highest-ranking executives, with social-class backgrounds reflected in their preferences. Executives with middle-class backgrounds prefer classical music more than do those with upper-class backgrounds.[44]

Information Processing

The amount and type of search undertaken and information processing by an individual varies by social class. Unfortunately, the lowest social classes often have limited information sources and may be at a disadvantage in filtering out misinformation and fraud in a complex, urbanized society. To compensate, working-class consumers often rely on relatives or close friends for information about consumption decisions. Middle-class consumers rely more on media-acquired information and actively engage in an external search of information from the media. As the level of social classes increases, usually so does access to media information.

Media and messages can be tailored to specific social classes. The language and appearance, as well as how the product is used, communicate to each social class whether or not "this product is for me." At times, some TV networks have had stronger appeal in some social classes than in others, and many firms forgo direct commercial messages for the soft sell of "Funding provided by . . . " that can be placed on the Public Broadcasting Service stations directed to upper-class audiences.

Magazines and newspapers have more appeal to upper classes than lower, and media may influence how social classes perceive social reality.[45] Magazines also offer excellent potential for detailed positioning to social-class segments. When the usage of a brand is correlated with purchases in these groups, zip code information can provide measures of the strength of various magazines in reaching each group.[46] If you subscribe to *Guns & Ammo* and drive a Dodge, for example, you are more likely to be on the list for direct mail from Sears than more upscale stores.

Social Language

The language patterns of individuals are closely correlated with their social class. In one set of experiments, the social classes of respondents were first measured before they were asked to make a 40-second reading of the fable, "The Tortoise and the Hare." These short recordings were played to groups of 15 to 30 regionally diverse college students who served as judges. The average ratings of social class by these judges correlated 0.80 with the speakers' social classes.[47]

When speakers were asked in role playing to alter their voices to sound upper class, the student judges' correlation with measured actual class was still 0.65. All the subjects used proper grammar, but their choice of vocabulary, sentence length, sentence structure, and fluency varied by social class. In still another approach, speakers were asked to count from 1 to 20, and even in this situation, college students' rankings correlated 0.65 with social class of speakers.

The importance of language can be understood by analysis of the copy used in advertisements. Ads for expensive cars such as Mercedes and Infiniti typically use longer words, fewer euphemisms, and more abstract language or visual materials. Lower- and middle-class car ads speak more of physical attributes, emphasize pictures rather than words, and are more likely to use slang or street language. These principles are often found in clothing and accessory ads.

Notice in Figure 19.3 how two companies—Boss and Fendi—use almost no words at all except the company name.

Purchasing Processes

Social status influences where and how people think they should shop. Lower-status people prefer local, face-to-face places where they get friendly service and easy credit—often in the neighborhood. Upper middle consumers feel more confident in their shopping ability. They will venture to new places to shop and will range throughout a store to find what they want.

The discount store traditionally appeals to the middle classes because they are careful and economy-minded in their buying. In their early years, discount stores frequently did not carry prestige or designer brands, but as the middle classes' income grew and information influences broadened, firms such as J. C.

Figure 19.3   Social Language in Upper-Class Advertisements

BOSS
HUGO BOSS

FENDI
720 FIFTH AVENUE
NEW YORK

Penney, Kmart, and Target have added more designer brands. Major retail organizations such as The Limited need a portfolio of stores ranging from Lerner to Henri Bendel to appeal to the variety of social classes and lifestyles that exist in industrialized societies such as Canada and the United States.[48]

Consumers have an image of what social class a store attracts and have an understanding of what shopping should be like in a store that appeals to their own social class. People in upper classes want a pleasant store atmosphere featuring exciting displays and excellent service. Lower classes emphasize acquiring household items or clothing as the enjoyable part of shopping. Historically, upper classes shop more frequently than middle or lower classes but may be shopping more in the future with catalogs, videotex offerings such as CompuServe, or interactive CD-ROM "catalogs" because of the time pressures felt by dual-income families. The greatest propensity for family members to shop together is among lower, white-collar, skilled, and semiskilled occupational classes. Shopping for many middle-class families, however, is a form of recreation. They are the ones willing to visit regional shopping malls. They are also most likely to experiment with store brands and respond most to variations in price offerings. Brand loyalty may be higher or lower among higher social class, depending on intervening variables such as purchase experience and perceived risk.[49]

A Concluding Note

Social class is an important concept in developing positioning strategies—the creating of perceptions in consumers' minds about the attributes of a product or organization. To accomplish positioning effectively requires a good understanding of the class characteristics of the target market and the class attributes desired for the product. If you are marketing products or services to social-class targets different from your own, be sure you do your homework to understand well the social-class characteristics of your market target. Sometimes the process is uncomfortable, but it is essential. The concepts and methods discussed in this chapter will be helpful to you in accomplishing the process.

Remember also that the number of consumers who aspire to higher social classes is much larger than those who are in them. Many of the middle class can buy products with the symbols and allure of higher social classes—and often do for products as diverse as those of Russell Athletic, shown in Figure 19.4, or Godiva. Market researchers at Grey Advertising estimate only a few million Americans have incomes that enable them to live affluent or rich lives. But far more—perhaps 10 times as many—partake of the good life some of the time, treating themselves to Godiva chocolates, Armani cologne, or Hermes scarves.

Figure 19.4   Appeals to the Upwardly Mobile

Source: Courtesy Russell Athletic.

Wanting it all is a hallmark of the middle class. Buying the best on at least a few occasions is a way to set themselves apart and bolster their self-image. Ads for premium-priced products need to be sensual, provocative, and elegant for these products.[50]

Summary

Social classes are relatively permanent and homogeneous groupings of people in society, permitting groups of people to be compared with one another. These groups are recognized as having inferior or superior positions by other people, often based on economic position in the marketplace.

Social class is determined by three types of variables: economic, interaction, and political. For marketers, the most important determinants of social class are usually considered to be occupation, personal performance, interactions, possessions, value orientations, and class consciousness.

Measures of social class may be based on single variables or multiple variables. Multiple-variable measures provide the best theoretical information, but occupation is the best single proxy indicator of social class.

Social classes in the United States are traditionally divided into six groups: upper upper, lower upper, upper middle, lower middle, upper lower, and lower lower or marginal classes. Newer classification systems emphasize the enlarged capitalist or professional classes in the upper middle or lower lower classes. Social classes are always in transition, however, causing status and its symbols to be dynamic. Each group displays characteristic values and behaviors that are useful to consumer analysts in designing marketing programs. Social-class analysis helps understand need recognition of consumers, search processes and information processing, evaluative criteria, and purchasing patterns of actual and aspiring social classes.

Review and Discussion Questions

1. What variables determine an individual's social class? In what order of importance should they be ranked?

2. In what way does income relate to social class? Why is it used so little as an indicator of social class? What should be its proper value as an indicator?

3. Prepare an outline of the major problems involved in the measurement of social classes. How would your outline differ for academic researchers as compared with business practitioners?

4. Some observers of contemporary America believe that social classes have declined in importance and presence, but others disagree. Outline your analysis of what has happened in recent years to social classes in the United States or in other countries.

5. A marketing researcher is speculating on the influence of upper classes on the consumption decisions of the lower classes for the following products: automobiles, food, clothing, and baby care products. What conclusions would you expect for each of these products? Describe a research project that could be used to answer this question.

6. The leisure products group of a large conglomerate is constantly seeking additional products for expanding markets and additional penetration for existing products. What conclusions that would be helpful in the design of marketing strategy might be reached concerning social class and leisure?

7. The operator of a large discount chain is contemplating a new store in an area of upper lower-class families. He asks for a consulting report defining the precautions he should take to ensure patronage among this group. What would you place in

such a report? Assume that the area is mostly lower lower-class families. Would you recommend entry?

8. Prepare a research report comparing the search process of the main social classes of consumers in the United States or other countries.

9. Assume that you are preparing the advertisements for a home furnishings store. How would you vary the ads if the target segments are lower middle rather than upper middle?

10. In what social class would you place professional athletes? Actors and actresses?

Endnotes

1. Elizabeth C. Hirschman, "Secular Immortality and the American Ideology of Affluence," *Journal of Consumer Research* 17 (June 1990), 31–42.

2. Kjell Gronhaug and Paul S. Trapp, "Perceived Social Class Appeals of Branded Goods," *Journal of Consumer Marketing* 5 (Fall 1988), 25–30.

3. Natalya Prusakova, "Dress to Impress," *Business in the USSR* (December 1991), 90–93.

4. Robert V. Robinson, "Explaining Perceptions of Class and Racial Inequality in England and the United States of America," *British Journal of Sociology* 34 (1983), 344–363.

5. T. Schjelderup-Ebbe, "Social Behavior of Birds," in C. Murchison, ed., *A Handbook of Social Psychology* (Worcester, Mass.: Clark University Press, 1935).

6. Al Ries and Jack Trout, *Positioning: The Battle for Your Mind* (New York: McGraw-Hill, 1981), 53.

7. Max Weber, in H. H. Gard and C. Wright Mills, *From Max Weber: Essays in Sociology* (New York: Oxford University Press, 1946), 193.

8. Daniel W. Rossides, *Social Stratification* (Englewood Cliffs, N.J.: Prentice-Hall, 1990).

9. Max Haller, "Marriage, Women, and Social Stratification: A Theoretical Critique," *American Journal of Sociology* 86 (1981), 766–795.

10. Reprinted with permission of Wadsworth, Inc. From *The American Class Structure: A New Synthesis,* 3rd ed., Dennis Gilbert and Joseph A. Kahl, 1982. Although not cited in each instance, this excellent book has influenced the content of this chapter in numerous other points.

11. Stephen L. Nock, "Social Origins as Determinants of Family Social Status" (paper presented to the Mid-South Sociological Association, 1980).

12. Joseph A. Kahl, *The American Class Structure* (New York: Holt, Rinehart and Winston, 1957), 8–10. A more recent emphasis centers on the ownership of capitalistic assets and the role of occupations. See Gilbert and Kahl, *The American Class Structure.*

13. Robert Cage, "Spending Differences across Occupational Fields," *Monthly Labor Review* 112 (December 1989), 33–43.

14. David H. Demo and Ritch C. Savin-Williams, "Early Adolescent Self-Esteem as a Function of Social Class," *American Journal of Sociology* 88 (1983), 763–773. Viktor Gecas and Monica A. Seff, "Social Class and Self-Esteem: Psychological Centrality, Compensation, and the Relative Effects of Work and Home," *Social Psychology Quarterly* 53 (1990), 165–173.

15. Hirschman, "Secular Immortality and the American Ideology of Affluence."

16. Lewis H. Lapham, *Money and Class in America* (Weidenfeld & Nicholson, 1988).

17. Michael Useem and S. M. Miller, "The Upper Class in Higher Education," *Social Policy* 7 (January–February 1977), 28–31.

18. Reeve Vanneman and Lynn Weber Cannon, *The American Perception of Class* (Philadelphia: Temple University Press, 1987).

19. Barbara B. Stern, "Literary Criticism and Consumer Research: Overview and Illustrative Analysis," *Journal of Consumer Research* 16 (December 1989), 322–334. See also Russell W. Belk, Melanie R. Wallendorf, and John Sherry, Jr., "The Sacred and the Profane in Consumer Behavior: Theodicy on the Odyssey," *Journal of Consumer Research* 16 (June 1989), 1–38.

20. W. Lloyd Warner and Paul S. Lunt, *The Social Life of a Modern Community* (New Haven, Conn.: Yale University Press, 1941). See also the classic book by W. Lloyd Warner, *Yankee City* (New Haven, Conn.: Yale University Press, 1963).

21. Allison Davis, Burleigh B. Gardner, and Mary R. Gardner, *Deep South: A Social-Anthropological Study of Caste and Class* (Chicago: The University of Chicago Press, 1941).

22. August B. Hollingshead, *Elmtown's Youth* (New York: John Wiley & Sons, 1949).

23. U.S. Department of Commerce, *Standard Occupational Classification Manual* (Washington, D.C.: U.S. Government Printing Office, 1980).

24. Charles B. Nam and Mary G. Powers, *The Socioeconomic Approach to Status Measurement* (Houston: Cap and Gown Press, 1983).

25. Richard P. Coleman, "The Continuing Significance of Social Class to Marketing," *Journal of Consumer Research* 10 (December 1983), 265–280.

26. Kenneth Labich, "Class in America," *Fortune* (February 7, 1994), 114–126.

27. R. Dave Thomas, *Dave's Way: A New Approach to Old-Fashioned Success* (New York: G. P. Putnam's Sons, 1991).

28. Gerhard E. Lenski, "Status Crystallization: A Non-Vertical Dimension of Social Status," *American Sociological Review* 21 (August 1956), 458–464.

29. Dick Stevenson, "The Middle Class Comes Undone," *Ad Forum* 5 (June 1984), 32–39; Neal H. Rosenthal, "The Shrinking Middle Class: Myth or Reality?" *Monthly Labor Review* 108 (March 1985), 3–10; McKinley L. Blackburn and David F. Bloom, "What Is Happening to the Middle Class?" *American Demographics* 7 (January 1985), 19–25; Patrick J. McMahon and John H. Tschetter, "The Declining

Middle Class: A Further Analysis," *Monthly Labor Review* 109 (September 1986), 22–26.

30. Louis Kriesberg, *Social Inequality* (Englewood Cliffs, N.J.: Prentice-Hall, 1979), 77–78.

31. Tom Bottomore, *Classes in Modern Society* (London: HarperCollinsAcademic, 1991).

32. Greg J. Duncan, ed., *Years of Poverty, Years of Plenty* (Ann Arbor, Mich.: Institute for Social Research, 1984).

33. Andrea Tyree and Robert W. Hodge, "Five Empirical Landmarks," *Social Forces* 56 (March 1978), 761–769. Some of the methodological issues in these studies are discussed in C. Matthew Snipp, "Occupational Mobility and Social Class: Insights from Men's Career Mobility," *American Sociological Review* 50 (August 1985), 475–492.

34. Ivan D. Chase, "A Comparison of Men's and Women's Intergenerational Mobility in the United States," *American Sociological Review* 40 (August 1975), 483–505.

35. Robert L. Leahy, "Development of the Conception of Economic Inequality: Explanations, Justifications, and Concepts of Social Mobility and Change," *Developmental Psychology* 19 (1983), 111–125.

36. Russell W. Rumberger, "The Influence of Family Background on Education, Earnings, and Wealth," *Social Forces* 61 (March 1983), 755–770.

37. John R. Snarey and George E. Vaillant, "How Lower- and Working-Class Youth Become Middle-Class Adults: The Association between Ego Defense Mechanisms and Upward Social Mobility," *Child Development* 56 (1985), 904–908.

38. The Gilbert-Kahl estimates are also accepted in Daniel W. Rossides, *Social Stratification* (Englewood Cliffs, N.J.: Prentice-Hall, 1990), 406–408.

39. Richard P. Coleman, "The Continuing Significance of Social Class in Marketing," *Journal of Consumer Research* 10 (December 1983), 263–280.

40. Class publications that in the 1990s are still valuable reading for consumer analysts include Pierre Martineau, "Social Classes and Spending Behavior," *Journal of Marketing* 23 (October 1958), 121–130; Sidney Levy, "Social Class and Consumer Behavior," in Joseph W. Newman, ed., *On Knowing the Consumer* (New York: John Wiley & Sons, 1966), 146–160; Richard P. Coleman and Bernice L. Neugarten, *Social Status in the City* (San Francisco: Jossey-Bass, 1971).

41. Paul Fussell, *Class* (New York: Ballantine Books, 1983), 230–233.

42. Patrick C. West, "Status Differences and Interpersonal Influence in the Adoption of Outdoor Recreation Activities," *Journal of Leisure Research* 16 (1984), 350–354.

43. Susan L. Greendorfer, "Social Class Influence on Female Sport Involvement," *Sex Roles* 4 (August 1978), 619–625.

44. Louis E. Boone, David L. Kurtz, and C. Patrick Fleenor, "Games CEOs Play," *American Demographics* 11 (January 1989), 43–45.

45. Richard L. Allen and Leah Waks, "The Social Reality Construction of Attitudes toward the Social Roles of Women and African Americans," *Howard Journal of Communications* 2 (Spring 1990), 170–191.

46. Hugh M. Canon and Gerald Linda, "Beyond Media Imperatives: Geodemographic Media Selection," *Journal of Advertising Research* 22 (June–July 1982), 31–36.

47. Dean S. Ellis, "Speech and Social Status in America," *Social Forces* 45 (March 1967), 431–437.

48. Roger Blackwell and Wayne Talarzyk, "Lifestyle Retailing: Competitive Strategies for the 1980's," *Journal of Retailing* 59 (December 1983), 7–27.

49. Rajesh Kanwar and Notis Pagiavlas, "When Are Higher Social Class Consumers More and Less Brand Loyal than Lower Social Class Consumers?" in John F. Sherry, Jr., and Brian Sternthal, eds., *Diversity in Consumer Behavior* (Provo, Utah: Association for Consumer Research, 1992), 589–595.

50. Jaclyn Fierman, "The High-Living Middle Class," *Fortune* 115 (April 13, 1987), 27.

CHAPTER 20

Personal Influence

▲▲

SATURN — Breaking the Mold in New Car Advertising

General Motors Corporation more or less bet its future on its Saturn brand introduced in 1991. America's slumping automotive giant had to prove once again that it could compete on the world market. It did this in part by redefining the whole process of automotive engineering, and the outcome was a potent new world-class competitor.

What really stands out in the Saturn story, however, is the genius of its advertising designed by Hal Riney & Partners. The mold of new car advertising was totally broken. "A different kind of company, A different kind of car" personifying the best of American human values became the advertising theme line. People, assembly line workers, management, and owners told the simple story of their love for a great car.

"Spring in Spring Hill," a 26-minute film and infomercial was the kickoff in 1989. It told the story of a team of managers and workers who, in near cult-like fashion, had an incredible emotional involvement at Saturn. "Spring" was built around the simple idea of letting Saturn team members explain, often emotionally, just what the project was all about and what it meant to them.

A 1991 commercial showed a Saturn representative traveling to Alaska to fix the seat in the Saturn owned by Robin Millage, a real customer who had ordered her car sight unseen from a dealer in the continental United States.

And a 1993 commercial is based on a letter from a third grade teacher who has ordered a Saturn. "To let you know who you're building that blue-green car for, I've enclosed my school picture," she writes. In that spot, as in real life, an employee at the factory tapes the photo to the rear-view mirror of the car on the assembly line. In that one commercial, it's all there, the essence of the brand Saturn and Riney have built: the enthusiastic customer, the caring employee, the bond between them and the pride in a job well done.

Source: Ramond Serafine, "The Saturn Story," Advertising Age (November 16, 1992), 13–15. Reproduced by special permission.

General Motors rediscovered a basic human principle—personal influence, direct or indirect, is one of the very best forms of persuasion. This is because the input from people with whom we can identify and relate can attain remarkable credibility. Indeed, it is common for that personal influence to be the key to success or failure.

You learn in this chapter that personal influence takes two main forms. First, other people often are used as a **reference group**—a mirror, if you will, reflecting which choices are acceptable and which are not. Sometimes, this input is viewed as binding, in which case it is referred to as **normative** influence. At other times, it is only **comparative** and serves as yet another source of information to be weighed.

Personal influence also can come through word-of-mouth communication initiated or supplied by a person known as an opinion leader. Information from this source usually is viewed as being highly credible and often has the power to make or break a marketing campaign.

You will discover that the impact of personal influence varies directly with the degree of involvement. Involvement increases when the choices made are perceived as affecting one's social status and acceptance. It follows under these circumstances that personal input will be assigned high importance.

Reference Group Influence

A reference group is any "person or group of people that significantly influences an individual's behavior."[1] Reference groups provide standards (norms) and values that can become the determining perspective for how a person thinks and behaves.

Solomon Asch undertook a seminal study in 1951[2] that has been widely cited as demonstrating beyond doubt that most people are averse to behavior that contradicts group consensus.[3] In this experiment, subjects were required to choose which of three lines differing in length matched the length of a fourth line. Each person was seated with a group of confederates, all strangers, who were instructed to make an incorrect choice. When exposed to these incorrect choices, experimental subjects made a substantial number of errors consistent with group consensus. This was not the case, however, when other people were not present.

A similar study demonstrated the same personal influence pattern within a consumer behavior context. Venkatesan[4] presented subjects with three identical suits and asked them to select the one they considered to be of highest quality. Confederates always chose the suit labeled "B," and the experimental subjects were influenced to give the same response. Suit B was chosen least often, however, when other people were not present.

Types of Reference Groups

Social groups can take many forms. The classifications introduced here reflect standard terminology, but no category is mutually exclusive. It is possible, for example, for a person to be part of a formal, primary group.

Primary versus Secondary

The greatest influence and impact usually is exerted by *primary* groups, defined as a social aggregation that is sufficiently small to permit and facilitate unrestricted face-to-face interaction. They exist because "like attracts like." There is cohesiveness and motivated participation. As a result, members exhibit marked similarities in beliefs and behavior.[5] The family is the most obvious example of a strongly influential primary group.

Secondary groups also have face-to-face interaction, but it is more sporadic, less comprehensive, and less influential in shaping thought and behavior.[6] Examples are professional associations, trade unions, and community organizations.

Aspirational versus Dissociative

Aspirational groups exhibit a desire to adopt the norms, values, and behavior of others with whom the individual aspires to associate. On occasion, there is anticipation of acceptance into membership and motivation to behave accordingly, although membership aspirations are not always present.

The influence of aspirational groups, although often indirect, can play a significant role in product choices. The ad in Figure 20.1 ran in Nairobi, Kenya, a typical non-Western urban center characterized by a predominance of families living at or only slightly above the poverty line. The lifestyle depicted here accurately reflects the dreams and aspirations of many, and it is not surprising that products such as Clear-tone have achieved significant market penetration.

Influence also can be exerted by **dissociative groups** when the individual is motivated to avoid association. Certainly, this has been the case among most baby boomers with respect to the Yuppies whose lifestyles have been increasingly discredited in their eyes.

Figure 20.1   Capitalizing on Consumer Dreams and Aspirations in a Non-Western Market

Formal versus Informal

Formal groups are characterized by a defined, known list of members, and the organization and structure are codified in writing. Examples are churches, fraternal bodies, and community service organizations. The influence exerted on behavior varies, depending on the motivation of the individual to accept and comply with the group's standards. Also, there are wide latitudes in the degree to which specific conformity is expected and enforced.

However, **informal groups** have far less structure and are likely to be based on friendship or collegial association. Norms can be stringent, but they seldom appear in writing. The effect on behavior can be strong if individuals are motivated by social acceptance. There also is a high degree of intimate, face-to-face interaction, which further strengthens the power with which expectations and sanctions are expressed and enforced.

Three Forms of Reference Group Influence

Reference groups affect consumer choice in three principal ways: (1) normative compliance, (2) value-expressive influence, and (3) informational influence.

Normative Compliance

When reference groups affect behavior through pressure for conformity and compliance, this is referred to as **normative influence**. Appeal to conformity is most effective when these conditions are met: (1) strong normative pressures exist; (2) social acceptance is a strong motivation; and (3) the product or service is *conspicuous* in its purchase and/or use.

Presence of Normative Pressure

Sociologist George Homans has shed useful light on the dynamics of normative compliance.[7] He has put forth an equation of human exchange that is built on the relationship between the rewards of compliance as compared with the costs. Symbols of esteem or approval can provide rewards and incentives, thereby reinforcing that behavior and encouraging its repetition. There also are costs, however, such as association with certain undesirable people, lost time, or restriction on freedom of choice.

The outcomes will be determined by an individual's perception of the profit inherent in the interaction (that is, rewards minus costs). Examples would be a college fraternity member who perceives that the rewards of acceptance outweigh the costs of not wearing a high school letter jacket, or the marketing manager who willingly endures the sometimes abusive responses of dissatisfied customers knowing full well that future advancement is based on high customer retention.

Strong Motivation for Social Acceptance

There is growing evidence that susceptibility to normative influence is a general characteristic that extends across situations.[8] You will remember our discussion of *self-monitoring* in Chapter 12.[9] High self-monitors show the following characteristics:

- Concern for the social appropriateness of actions.

- Attention to social comparison as a guide for appropriate self-expression. This is expressed in willingness to learn about products and services by observing others or actively seeking information from them.

- Willingness to modify self-presentation and self-expression as needed. High self-monitors will be especially willing to conform by making the "right" product and brand choices.

This motivation functions even when others do not control tangible outcomes through reward or punishment. Mason Haire's classic 1950 study is a case in point.[10] Haire showed that perceptions of users of regular coffee were evaluated favorably, whereas purchasers of instant coffee (a new product at that time) were perceived as lazy and incompetent.

Conspicuousness

Several other studies over the years have demonstrated that motivation to conform and conformity pressures are not sufficient to induce behavior unless the product or service is *publicly conspicuous* in its purchase and use.[11] Furthermore, luxuries are more susceptible to social influence than necessities.[12] Nothing is more public than clothing. Therefore, it should not be surprising to learn that fashion-conscious women receive clear signals from their peers, which makes further information search unnecessary.[13]

Conspicuousness is not a fixed product characteristic but depends on the situation and the ways in which the product is used. Miniard and Cohen[14] found,

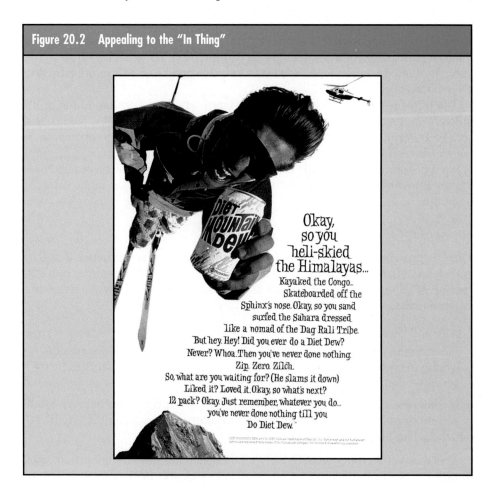

Figure 20.2   Appealing to the "In Thing"

for example, that normative influence on brand choice is important when beer is to be served to friends but not when it is consumed privately.

Appealing to Normative Influence in Marketing Strategy

Marketers have learned the potency of appealing to the "in thing," as the ad in Figure 20.2 demonstrates. But such appeals can backfire unless it can be demonstrated that both susceptibility to normative influence and product/service visibility interact to affect buying action. Bearden and Etzel[15] undertook a direct-mail survey of 800 households in which respondents were asked to consider 16 products that differed along the private–public and necessity–luxury dimensions. For each product, they rated the extent of reference group influence on both the choice of the product class and a brand. A summary of these results appears in Figure 20.3.

Figure 20.3 Reference Group Influence as a Function of Product Type and Consumption Situation

		Publicly consumed	
	Product Brand	Weak reference group influence (−)	Strong reference group influence (+)
		Public necessities	*Public luxuries*
	Strong reference group influence (+)	Influence: Weak product and strong brand Examples: Wristwatch, automobile, man's suit	Influence: Strong product and brand Examples: Golf clubs, snow skis, sailboat
Necessity		*Private necessities*	*Private luxuries*	Luxury
	Weak reference group influence (−)	Influence: Weak product and brand Examples: Mattress, floor lamp, refrigerator	Influence: Strong product and weak brand Examples: TV game, trash compactor, icemaker

Source: William O. Bearden and Michael J. Etzel, "Reference Group Influence on Product and Brand Purchase Decisions," *Journal of Consumer Research 9* (September 1982), 185.

Figure 20.3 contains some interesting findings. Look at the upper left quadrant, for example. Here we encounter public consumption of a necessity in which there is weak reference group influence on choice of the product but strong influence on selection of the brand. A wristwatch is worn out of necessity, and it is of little consequence what others do. But brand choice is quite different, an example being the high social acceptability in some quarters signified by wearing a Rolex. As you read through these four quadrants, you gain helpful insights into the ways in which social influence becomes expressed.

We cannot overlook the fact, however, that normative compliance seems to be declining in its impact in much of the Western world.[16] Consumer in Focus 20.1 makes the strong case that today's baby boomers are putting personal needs ahead of group loyalty.

A main factor in this decline, we believe, is the worldwide growth of urbanization, which leads to greater social isolation and individualism. Grandparents, uncles, aunts, and other members of the extended family have far less face-to-face influence. Also, urban living arrangements, often in high-rises, minimize

---

20.1 Consumer in Focus

Baby Boomer Individualism: The Master Trend of Our Time

It's more than a coincidence that America's social fabric began to tear just as the baby-boomer generation, born between 1946 and 1964, came of age in the late 1960s. Boomers' attitudes and values are profoundly different from those of older Americans. At the root of these differences is a strong sense of individualism instilled in baby boomers by their parents.

Baby boomers' parents raised their children to think for and of themselves. Studies of child-rearing practices show that parents of the 1950s and 1960s consistently ranked "to think for themselves" as the number-one trait they wanted to nurture in their children. They encouraged their children to succeed in a job market that rewarded competitive drive more than cooperative spirit, and individual skills more than teamwork.

In turn, the sheer size of the generation encouraged businesses to promote the emerging individuality of baby boomers. Businesses offered individualistic boomers a growing array of customized products and services. The houses, cars, furniture, appliances, clothes, vacations, jobs, leisure time, and even beliefs of boomers became increasingly unique.

Some social observers decry this individualism. They blame young people for their selfishness and demand that Americans show more concern for community needs. But the individualistic perspective is not something baby boomers can turn on and off like a faucet. It is not a simple choice, like buying a new pair of jeans. It is not even something they consciously pursue. Instead, it is the way they see and relate to the world. For better and for worse, individualism is here to stay. It is the master trend of our time.

Source: Cheryl Russell, "The Master Trend," American Demographics (October 1993), 30.

the social interaction that takes place much more readily when living in the country or the bush.

Finally, television and other mass media open windows to the world and thereby broaden horizons and interests beyond normal social circles. In fact, a case can be made that television and other media represent social reality with such power that the media themselves are becoming a major normative influence on beliefs and behavior.[17]

Another consideration leading to diminished normative compliance is a weakened respect for social norms rather than a complete denial of their existence or impact. This is referred to by sociologists as anomie.[18] People so affected are apt to conform grudgingly or, in certain instances, to engage in motivated evasion and failure to conform. The ad in Figure 20.4 by Raymond's of India speaks effectively to the man who is unwilling to fit into a rigid mold and is motivated to "be me."

Figure 20.4   Raymond's of India Fights Normative Social Influence

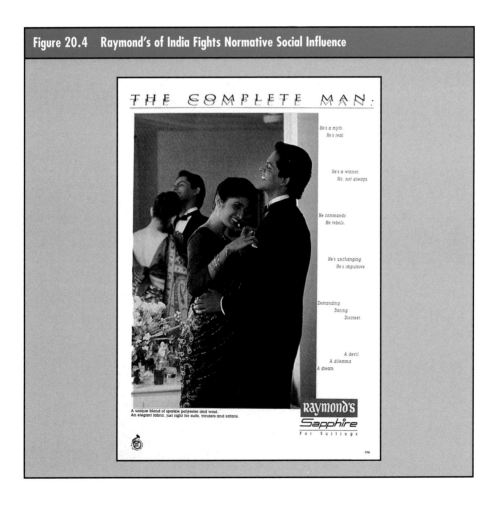

Value-Expressive Influence

Reference groups also can perform a value-expressive function, whereby a need for psychological association with a group is evidenced by acceptance of its norms, values, or behavior and a conforming response is made, even though there may be no motivation to become a member. One desired outcome is enhanced image in the eyes of others. Another is identification with people who are admired and respected. Certainly, this explains the burgeoning growth of Western brands throughout the world (Figure 20.5). See Consumer in Focus 20.2 for an interesting discussion of why Western brands are achieving such impact.

Figure 20.5 is a good example of aspirational impact of Western brands worldwide, and that impact can be negative as well as positive. The picture says it all—"smoking is cool for everybody, young and old alike." What a contrast to the warning from the Ministry of Health about the dangers of smoking!

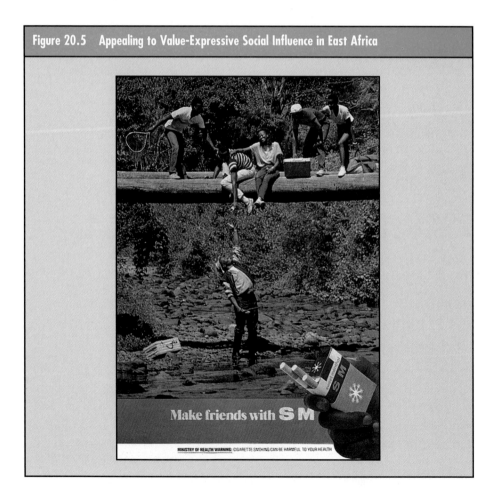

Figure 20.5   Appealing to Value-Expressive Social Influence in East Africa

Make friends with **S M**

MINISTRY OF HEALTH WARNING: CIGARETTE SMOKING CAN BE HARMFUL TO YOUR HEALTH

Consumer in Focus	**20.2**

Asia, Where the Big Brands Are Blooming

Brand equity may be buffeted at home, but across Asia, from Beijing to Bombay, American brands are commanding big premiums over inferior hometown competitors. Says Al Ries, chairman of Trout-Ries, a marketing strategy firm: "Countries, like companies, have positions in the minds of the buyer. The U.S. is seen as a country that produces high-quality consumer brands."

The growing popularity and reach of American culture in Asia provide the perfect backdrop for a global commercialism. Says Richard Barnet, author of the forthcoming *Global Dreams:* "People will buy branded products because they are seen as an embodiment of the American Dream."

Demand for branded goods in Asia is rising even faster than the frenetic growth of those economies would suggest. Says Manu Bamni, director of PSi Inc., a New York consulting firm: "Frustrated consumers in Asia are ready and willing to move to premium brands."

Source: Rahul Jacob, "Asia, Where the Big Brands Are Blooming," Fortune (August 23, 1993), 55.

Such an appeal would face immediate boycott pressures in the United States for what we consider to be good and proper reasons. Unfortunately, many businesses are adopting the principle that says take it to the Third World if you can't get away with it here. What does this say about observance of the consumer's right to safety?

Informational Influence

Consumers often accept the opinions of others as providing credible and needed evidence about reality.[19] This is most apparent when it is difficult to assess product or brand characteristics by observation. Under these circumstances, it is more likely that usage or recommendation by others will be perceived as thoughtful and valid.[20] This is what Cialdini[21] refers to as the *principle of social proof*. We have more to say about this principle in the next section of this chapter.

Word-of-Mouth Influence

As we have already stated, consumers frequently turn to others, especially friends and family members, for opinions about products and services. The transmitter of this information is referred to as an influential. Over the years, the influential also has been labeled as an **opinion leader**, but we prefer to avoid this term because of the connotation that the transmitter has a dominant position over a so-called follower. As you will see, word-of-mouth influence usually is not expressed in such a hierarchical pattern.

When are consumers most likely to accept and respond to word-of-mouth communication? Based on more than 30 years of research, it is safe to conclude that personal influence in the form of opinion leadership is most likely when one or more of these conditions and situations are present:

- The consumer lacks sufficient information to make an adequately informed choice. When, however, internal search for information proves to be adequate, word of mouth has less impact.[22]

- The product is complex and difficult to evaluate using objective criteria. Hence the experience of others serves as "vicarious trial."[23]

- The person lacks ability to evaluate the product or service, no matter how information is disseminated and presented.

- Other sources are perceived as having low credibility.

- An influential person is more accessible than other sources and hence can be consulted with a saving of time and effort.

- Strong social ties are in existence between transmitter and receiver.[24]

- The individual has a high need for social approval.

Models of the Personal Influence Process

Personal influence has been theorized as working in three different ways: (1) trickle down, (2) a two-step flow, or (3) multistage interaction.

Trickle-Down Theory

The oldest theory of personal influence alleges that lower classes often emulate the behavior of their higher-class counterparts.[25] In other words, influence is transmitted vertically through social classes, especially in the area of new fashions and styles. Presumably those in the higher classes express wealth through "conspicuous consumption," and their behavior is copied, when possible, by those in lower social strata.

The trickle-down theory is rarely seen demonstrated today in economically developed countries. The reason is that new fashions are disseminated overnight through mass media and quickly copied on a mass-merchandise basis. It still is observed, however, in underdeveloped economies when access to the mass media is restricted or absent altogether. Even here, however, it is rapidly disappearing as media access increases.

It is far more common for this type of influence to occur among peers. This has come to be known as **homophilous influence**, a term that refers to information transmission between those who are similar in social class, age, education, and other demographic characteristics.[26] As we have demonstrated, reference group impact is often greatest when there is at least some degree of prior association and relationship.

Two-Step Flow

In 1948, Lazarsfeld and his colleagues[27] observed that new ideas and other influences flow from the mass media to influentials who, in turn, pass them on through word of mouth to others who are more passive in information seeking and far less exposed to the mass media and other sources.

Although this model was a historic breakthrough for its time, there is ample reason now to question its accuracy. The primary reason is the audience is not as passive as the theory assumes. It is apparent, first of all, that the mass media have a widespread impact that is not confined to the influential. Furthermore, the initiative does not necessarily lie with the influential, as the theory assumed. Word-of-mouth communication is equally, if not more often, initiated by the receiver who is seeking the advice of a credible friend or relative.

Multistage Interaction

Extensive reasearch on the diffusion of innovations has largely invalidated the two-step flow model by demonstrating that both influential and seeker are affected by the mass media. In fact, mass media can motivate the seeker to approach someone else for advice rather than vice versa. Rarely does the influential mediate the flow of mass media content, as the two-step theory assumes.

At one time, it was accepted that advertisers and other commercial persuaders would achieve greatest impact by concentrating only on the influential. It was assumed that they would pass on what they learned from the media. Current understanding shows that both the influential and the seeker are legitimate targets.

The Influential

How do we find the influentials? What type of people are they? What motivates them to share their experience? These questions have stimulated extensive research over the years in many countries of the world,[28] and it now is possible to advance some valid generalizations.

Research Methods

There are three basic ways to identify the influential through research:

1. *Sociometric* — people are asked to identify the other people they seek out for advice or information in making a particular type of decision.
2. *Key informant* — knowledgeable people are used to identify the influentials within a social system.
3. *Self-designation* — people are asked to evaluate the extent to which they are sought out for advice.

The first two methods do not find widespread use in marketing research because of the focus on a specific, identifiable existing group. There are times, however, when a high-rise apartment complex or a neighborhood is the focus. When that is the case, the key-informant method is usually preferred because of greater ease of administration.

When many groups are targeted, the self-designation method is preferred. It is designed to be used on a wide scale, and it appears to have acceptable validity. The objective is to identify whether certain types or categories of people serve as influentials and not to designate the individuals themselves by name. If they can be identified and isolated from others as a distinct market segment, it is possible to direct marketing efforts their way. An example of a multi-item scale designed for this purpose appears in Table 20.1.

Characteristics

Extensive research on the characteristics of the influential is summarized in Table 20.2. It is safe to conclude that source and receiver are similar to one another in terms of demographic characteristics and lifestyle (that is, they are *homophilous*).[29] Evidence also shows that the person who provides the information also is a seeker in other situations.

One issue of importance is whether the influence process is product-specific (**monomorphic**) or overlapping into the other product areas (**polymorphic**). Although much of the earlier literature supported the monomorphic hypothesis, there now is evidence that word-of-mouth influence is quasi-generalized, in that most serve as influentials for related products but not for all products in general.[30]

Motivations

Generally speaking, people will not share their experience with products or services unless the conversation produces some type of gratification. The motivations that drive such interactions fall into one or more of the following categories: (1) involvement, (2) self-enhancement, (3) concern for others, (4) message intrigue, and (5) dissonance reduction.

Involvement

First, the tendency to initiate conversations is directly proportional to the extent of interest or involvement in the topic under consideration.[31] A young executive is the first among his or her peers to have a new high-resolution television set complete with a built-in VCR. Telling others can serve as an outlet for pleasure or excitement caused by or resulting from its purchase and use.

Self-Enhancement

Many years ago, Dichter[32] suggested that word-of-mouth initiation can perform such functions as gaining attention, showing connoisseurship, suggesting status,

Table 20.1 Self-Designating Scale Used for Isolating an Influential Person

(1) In general, do you like to talk about _____ with your friends?
   Yes _____ −1   No _____ −2

(2) Would you say you *give very little information, an average amount of information,* or *a great deal of information* about _____ to your friends?
   You give very little information   _____ −1
   You give an average amount of information   _____ −2
   You give a great deal of information   _____ −3

(3) During the *past six months,* have *you told anyone* about some _____ ?
   Yes _____ −1   No _____ −2

(4) Compared with your circle of friends, are you *less likely, about as likely,* or *more likely* to be asked for advice about _____ ?
   Less likely to be asked   _____ −1
   About as likely to be asked   _____ −1
   More likely to be asked   _____ −3

(5) If you and your friends were to discuss _____ , what part would *you* be most likely to play?
   Would you *mainly listen* to your friends' ideas or would you *try to convince them* of your ideas?
   You mainly listen to your friends' ideas   _____ −1
   You try to convince them of your ideas   _____ −2

(6) Which of these happens more often? Do *you tell your friends* about some _____ , or do *they tell you* about some _____ ?
   You tell them about   _____ −1
   They tell you about   _____ −2

(7) Do you have the feeling that you are generally regarded by your friends and neighbors as a good source of advice about _____ ?
   Yes _____ −1   No _____ −2

Source: Charles W. King and John O. Summers, "Generalized Opinion Leadership in Consumer Products: Some Preliminary Findings," paper no. 224 (Lafayette, Indiana: Institute for Research in the Behavioral, Economic and Management Sciences, Krannert Graduate School of Industrial Administration, January 1969), 16.

giving the impression of possessing inside information, and asserting superiority. For example, it is not uncommon for this to take the form of "insider information" — "I've just discovered the greatest Ethiopian restaurant."

Concern for Others

Conversation also is precipitated simply by a genuine desire to help a friend or relative make a better purchase decision. This is especially likely when the influential has experienced high satisfaction in consumption of a product or service that is of interest to another person.[33] In other words, old-fashioned altruism still plays a role, especially when social ties are strong.

> ### Table 20.2 Characteristics of the Influential
>
> *Demographic*
> There is wide variation from one product category to another:
> Young women dominate for fashions and movie-going.
> Women with many children are consulted about self-medication.
> Demographics usually show low correlation and are not a good predictor.
>
> *Social Activity*
> Gregariousness is the most frequently found predictor of opinion leadership.
>
> *General Attitudes*
> Opinion leaders are innovative and positive toward new products.
>
> *Personality and Lifestyle*
> Personality measures generally do not correlate with opinion leadership.
> Opinion leaders tend to be more socially active, fashion conscious, and independent.
>
> *Product Related*
> Opinion leaders are more interested in the topic under discussion than others are. Fashion is an example.
> They are active searchers and information gatherers, especially from the mass media.

Message Intrigue

Some people find it entertaining to talk about certain ads or selling appeals. Who can deny the word of mouth that occurs when jokes are made of the Jolly Green Giant or the person who squeezes the Charmin?

Dissonance Reduction

Finally, research suggests that word of mouth is sometimes used to reduce cognitive dissonance (doubts) after a major purchase decision.[34] As we discussed in Chapter 8 and elsewhere, dissatisfied customers can be dangerous. It is not unusual for them to vent anger by disparaging the product or brand. Marketers worldwide are discovering that negative information of this type can have a decided impact on potential buyers.

Impact of Word-of-Mouth Communication

Here is what we know about the effects of personal influence on consumer behavior.

Comparison with Other Media

First, research consistently demonstrates that personal influence generally has a more decisive role in influencing behavior than advertising and other marketer-dominated sources.[35] The issue of greater perceived credibility is most often the deciding factor. It is common to assume that another consumer has no ulterior or commercially motivated reasons for sharing information.

Source- versus Seeker-Initiated Conversation

Word of mouth can be initiated by either the source or the receiver, and the impact usually is strongest when the receiver plays this role.[36] The difference no doubt arises from the fact that a seeker is motivated to attend to and process the information, whereas that may not be the case when the source is the initiator.

Negative versus Positive Information

More than a third of all word-of-mouth information is negative in nature, and evidence indicates that it usually is given higher priority and assigned a greater weight in decision making.[37] No doubt this occurs because marketer-dominated communication will be uniformly positive, thus making the potential buyer all the more alert to anything that provides a different perspective. Also, the dissatisfied buyer is more motivated to share.[38]

Verbal versus Visual Information

Information can be passed interpersonally in either verbal or visual form. To the extent that information can be given visually, through observation or actual product demonstration, the greater will be the impact in terms of awareness and stimulation of interest. However, verbally communicated information has a stronger effect on thinking and evaluation.[39] Ideally, both visual and verbal will work in combination.

Using Personal Influence in Marketing Strategy

Positive word of mouth can be one of the marketer's greatest assets, whereas the opposite can be true when the content is negative. Personal influence cannot be directly controlled by a business firm, but it can be stimulated and channeled in many ways.

Monitoring the Content of Word of Mouth

At the very least, it is necessary to monitor whether word-of-mouth communication is occurring and the impact it is having. For example, Coca-Cola examined the communication patterns undertaken by those who had complained to the company.[40] Here are some of the main conclusions:

- More than 12 percent told 20 or more people about the response they had received from the company.
- Those who were completely satisfied with the response told a median of four to five others about their positive experience.

- Nearly 10 percent who were completely satisfied increased their purchases of company products.

- Those who thought they were not treated adequately communicated this fact to a median of nine to ten other people.

- Nearly a third who thought their complaints were not dealt with adequately refused to buy any more company products, and another 45 percent reduced their purchases.

Although involvement is usually a predisposing factor for social influence, this example shows how extensive word of mouth can be, even for a low-involvement product such as a soft drink. This was further demonstrated during the now legendary "cola war," in which consumers overwhelmingly rejected "New Coke" and expressed their feelings negatively in the marketplace.

Focus-group research is often the best method for monitoring influence. When personal influence is taking place, its nature and impact quickly become evident because most people are willing to talk about products and their experiences. This is especially true when involvement is high.

Primary Reliance on Word of Mouth

On some occasions, it is possible to rely on word-of-mouth communication as a substitute for advertising. This was done by Anheuser-Busch when a new ultrapremium beer was introduced into test market.[41] Admittedly, it is highly unusual to omit advertising and sales efforts entirely, and few would risk this step. Wal-Mart Stores, however, has demonstrated that advertising can be sharply reduced when word of mouth is strong.[42]

Using the Influential as a Market Target

Although the two-step flow has largely been abandoned, it cannot be denied that influentials are sensitive to various sources of information, including advertising.[43] It is at least theoretically feasible to view them as a distinct market segment if they can be identified. You will recall that identification can present quite a research challenge because of the similarity (homophily) between sender and receiver.

Even if they can be identified, however, their media exposure patterns often do not differ in any meaningful ways from those of receivers. Hence, it may be impossible to mount strategies that reach only this segment. The only exception is when certain types of social or organizational leaders are known to play the role of influentials. Examples are coaches, physicians, pharmacists, and pastors.

When identification is feasible, there are several possible strategies. One of the most common is to establish them as the target of space advertising, direct mail, and publicity releases aimed at them. It is possible to buy mailing lists for coaches, teachers, and other specialized professions. Another option is to use the general media, knowing full well that there will be waste resulting from the large number of nonprospects. Sometimes, there is no other option.

Stimulating Word of Mouth

At times, there is benefit in either loaning or giving known influentials a product to display and use. The Ford Motor Co. used this approach as part of its strategy to promote the 1984 Thunderbird.[44] Invitations were mailed to more than 406,000 executives and professional people, giving them the opportunity to drive the car for a day, and about 15,000 took advantage. Although only 10 percent became buyers, 84 percent indicated they would recommend the Thunderbird to a friend.

Another familiar option is to induce the influential to open his or her home for product presentations. The classic example is the "Tupperware Party" described in Consumer in Focus 20.3.

Creating Influentials

Next, it is sometimes possible to hire or directly involve those who seem to have the characteristics of an influential. Department stores and other clothing retailers, for example, have experimented with hiring the most popular young people, who then receive substantial discounts on clothing they purchase. Hospitals have coped with excess capacity by forming alliances with physicians, who often hold the key to which hospital is chosen.

Yet another possible approach is to provide incentives for new customers to attract others to the point of sale. Sometimes this is done by offering attractive product premiums or even outright financial rebates.

At times, it also is possible to activate information seeking through word of mouth. This can be done through ads that capture imagination and intrigue, especially through phrases or characters that become part of the everyday vernacular. A famous early example is the "thousands of tiny time pills" theme used when Contac was first introduced as a cold remedy. This phrase in itself stimulated a great deal of conversation. More recently, Wendy's Clara Peller and the bucolic spokespersons for Bartle & Jaymes wine coolers have frequently been the subject of amused conversations.

Another tactic is to use ads asking consumers to seek information. "Ask the person who owns one" is an example of this approach.

Finally, demonstrations, displays, and trial usage can be helpful. For example, color television manufacturers sell their sets to hotels and motels at low prices partly because it can help generate consumer interest and information seeking. And automobile manufacturers make deals with rental companies on cars such as the Lincoln Continental featured at Budget Rent-a-Car.

Curbing Negative Word of Mouth

You have started your car and suddenly it surges, out of control, forward or backward. This is exactly what happened with the 1986 Audi 5000S, according to more than 500 complaints made to the National Highway Traffic Safety Administration. Audi management initially refused to acknowledge any

| 20.3 | **Consumer in Focus** |

Using Friends to Close the Sale

"Hello, Robyn? This is Liz."

"Liz, how are you? It's been awhile since we have talked."

"Yes, and that's exactly why I called, Robyn. I'm inviting a few of the girls over on the 15th for dessert, and I wondered if you could come. Also, my new friend Mary Anne, will be there to show you the latest in the Tupperware line."

(Pause) "Ok, let's see. Yes. . . . (pause) . . . I think I can be there."

"Great, we'll have dessert at 7:30, and we will end around 9:30. See you then."

Sound familiar? Certainly, most women in North America have experienced a call of this type, if not from Tupperware Home Parties Corp., then from Mary Kay Cosmetics or a host of others. Smart marketing? You bet. A Tupperware party starts somewhere every 2.7 seconds, and it is estimated that Tupperware sales now exceed $2.5 million per day.

The simple reason is that most of us are inclined to say yes to a request made by a person whom we know and like. And here is how the formula goes:

- *Reciprocity.* Everybody is a winner. Through games or grabbags, everybody gets a gift before the sales presentation begins.

- *Commitment.* Everybody is urged to give public testimony about the uses and benefits from the Tupperware (or Mary Kay or . . .) products they already own.

- *Social proof.* Once the buying process begins, it is made very clear that other people who you know and like want these products. Therefore, they have to be good.

Customers seem to be fully aware of the friendship pressures that are being used, and yet they come. Some are favorable, but others feel trapped and voice resentments. But there is no denying that it works. Careful consumer research has shown that adding the social tie to the pitch about the product doubles product purchases.

Sources: Robert B. Cialdini, Influence Science and Practice, 3rd ed. (New York: HarperCollins, 1993), 136–137; J. H. Frenzen and H. L. Davis, "Purchasing Behavior in Embedded Markets," Journal of Consumer Research 17 (March, 1990), 1–12; and "Mary Kay Cosmetics, Inc.," in James F. Engel and W. Wayne Talarzyk, eds., Cases in Promotional Strategy, rev. ed. (Homewood, Ill.: Richard D. Irwin, 1984), 3–10.

culpability for this problem, even after a "60 Minutes" exposé on television activated public outrage.

It took a drastic drop in sales to induce acknowledgement of a problem, product recall, and remedial repair.[45] It later turned out that Audi management was vindicated in their claims of innocence, but the company never has fully recovered from this unfortunate attitude of public insensitivity.

What can be done in an instance like this? Certainly, stonewalling (denying the problem) is not the answer. The Toshiba Corp. found out that resignation and public disgrace of top management did little to mitigate U.S. public outrage over the release of important military secrets in product sales to Russia. The company decided to take the major face-losing step of running ads in several major papers that were headlined, "Toshiba Corporation Extends Its Deepest Regrets to the American People." This was a step in the right direction, but it may have been too little and too late.

The best strategy usually is an immediate acknowledgement of a problem by a credible company spokesperson. It is important to recognize that negative word of mouth rarely goes away by itself. If matters are not dealt with promptly, the financial results could be immediate and catastrophic.

Summary

Personal influence often plays an important role in consumer decision making, especially when there are high levels of involvement and perceived risk and the product or service has public visibility. This is expressed both through reference groups and through word-of-mouth communication.

Reference groups are any type of social aggregation that can influence attitudes and behavior, including primary (face-to-face) groups, secondary groups, and aspirational groups. The influence occurs in three ways: (1) utilitarian (pressures to conform to group norms in thinking and behavior), (2) value-expressive (reflecting a desire for psychological association and a willingness to accept values of others without pressure), and (3) informational (beliefs and behaviors of others are accepted as evidence about reality). When there is motivation to comply with group norms, it is important to make this a feature in marketing appeals.

Personal influence also is expressed through what has traditionally been referred to as "opinion leadership." What this means is that a credible person, referred to as an "influential," is accepted as a source of information about purchase and use. Usually, the influential and the seeker are similar in characteristics, and both are influenced by mass media. The greater the credibility of the influential, the greater his or her impact on other people.

Marketers can capitalize on personal influence by monitoring word of mouth and attempting to curb it when it is negative. Other strategies include creating new influentials, stimulating information seeking through this source, relying entirely on interpersonal influence to promote products, and combating negative word of mouth.

Review and Discussion Questions

1. For which of the following products would you expect personal influence to be a factor in buying decisions: soft drinks, motor oil, designer jeans, eyeliner, house paint, breakfast cereals, wine, carpeting, a dishwasher, and a 35mm camera? What are your reasons in each case?

2. Regarding each product listed in Question 1, do you think there could be a variation between personal influence on product choice and on brand name? Why do you say this?

3. Would any of the products in Question 1 be subject to personal influence coming from normative compliance? From value expression? From informational influence?

4. Assume that you are a consultant for a manufacturer of men's clothing. How would you go about identifying influentials on the college campus?

5. Recall the last time you volunteered information to someone about a brand or product that you purchased. What caused you to share in this way? How does your motivation compare with the motivations mentioned in the text?

6. In what ways do influentials differ from those who are information seekers?

7. Defend the conclusion mentioned in the text that influentials, as a rule, have a greater impact on consumer decision than advertising or personal selling.

8. Your company manufactures a full line of mobile homes in all price ranges. Several studies have indicated that word-of-mouth communication plays a role in the buying decision. Prepare a statement indicating the alternative strategies that can be used to harness and capitalize on this source of consumer influence. Which strategy do you think would be most effective?

9. Assume that you are a public relations consultant for a state medical society concerned about public attitudes toward malpractice claims. The problem is to counteract a point of view, picked up through word-of-mouth monitoring, that filing a malpractice claim against a doctor is an easy way to pay medical bills or to get something for nothing. What can be done to attack this way of thinking?

Endnotes

1. William O. Bearden and Michael J. Etzel, "Reference Group Influence on Product and Brand Purchase Decisions," *Journal of Consumer Research* 9 (September 1982), 184.

2. Solomon E. Asch, "Effects of Group Pressure on the Modification and Distortion of Judgments," in H. Guetzkow, ed., *Groups, Leadership, and Men* (Pittsburgh, Pa.: Carnegie Press, 1951).

3. Lee Ross, Gunter Bierbrauer, and Susan Hoffman, "The Role of Attribution Processes in Conformity and Dissent: Revisiting the Asch Situation," *American Psychologist* (February 1976), 148–157.

4. M. Venkatesan, "Experimental Study of Consumer Behavior Conformity and Independence," *Journal of Marketing Research* 3 (November 1966), 384–387.

5. Robert E. Witt and Grady D. Bruce, "Group Influence and Brand Choice," *Journal of Marketing Research* 9 (November 1972), 440–443.

6. James C. Ward and Peter H. Reingen, "Sociocognitive Analysis of Group Decision Making among Consumers," *Journal of Consumer Research* 17 (December 1990), 245–262.

7. George Homans, *Social Behavior: Its Elementary Forms* (New York: Harcourt, 1961).

8. See William O. Bearden and Randall L. Rose, "Attention to Social Comparison Information: An Individual Difference Factor Affecting Consumer Conformity," *Journal of Consumer Research* 16 (March 1990), 461–472; and William O. Bearden, Richard G. Netemeyer, and Jesse E. Teel, "Measurement of Consumer Susceptibility to Interpersonal Influence," *Journal of Consumer Research* 15 (March 1989), 473–481.

9. William O. Bearden, F. Kelley Shuptrine, and Jesse E. Teel, "Self-Monitoring and Reactions to Image Appeals and Claims about Product Quality," in Thomas K. Srull, ed., *Advances in Consumer Research* 16 (Provo, Utah: Association for Consumer Research: 1989), 703–710; and Jacques A. Nantel and William Strahle, "The Self-Monitoring Concept: A Consumer Behavior Perspective," in Richard J. Lutz, ed., *Advances in Consumer Research* 13 (Provo, Utah: Association for Consumer Research, 1986), 83–87.

10. Mason Haire, "Projective Techniques in Marketing Research," *Journal of Marketing* 14 (April 1950), 649–656.

11. Gwen Rae Bachmann, Deborah Roedder John, and Akshay R. Rao, "Children's Susceptibility to Peer Group Purchase Influence: An Exploratory Investigation," in Leigh McAllister and Michael L. Rothschild, eds., *Advances in Consumer Research* 20 (Provo, Utah: Association for Consumer Research, 1992), 463–468; Stephen A. LaTour and Ajay K. Manrai, "Interactive Impact of Information and Normative Influence on Donations," *Journal of Marketing Research* 26 (August 1989), 327–335; Paul W. Miniard and Joel E. Cohen, "Modeling Personal and Normative Influences on Behavior," *Journal of Consumer Research* 10 (September 1983), 169–180; C. Whan Park and V. Parker Lessig, "Students and Housewives: Differences in Susceptibility to Reference Group Influence," *Journal of Consumer Research* 4 (September 1977), 102–109.

12. Bearden and Etzel, "Reference Group Influence."

13. David F. Midgley, Grahame R. Dowling, and Pamela D. Morrison, "Consumer Types, Social Influence, Information Search and Choice," in Srull, *Advances*, 137–143.

14. Miniard and Cohen, "Modeling Personal and Normative Influences."

15. Bearden and Etzel, "Reference Group Influence."

16. "31 Major Trends Shaping the Future of American Business," *The Public Pulse* 2 (1986), 1; Park and Lessig, "Students and Housewives"; and Robert E. Burnkrant and Alan Cousineau, "Informational and Normative Social Influence in Buyer Behavior," *Journal of Consumer Research* 2 (December 1975), 206–215.

17. L. J. Shrum, Thomas C. O'Guinn, Richard J. Semenik, and Ronald J. Faber, "Processes and Effects in the Construction of Normative Consumer Beliefs: The Role of Television," in Rebecca H. Holman and Michael R. Solomon, eds., *Advances in Consumer Research* 18 (Provo, Utah: Association for Consumer Research, 1991), 755–763.

18. Emile Durkheim, *Suicide,* trans. by George Simpson (New York: Free Press, 1951). For a cultural perspective, see Robert Merton, "Anomie, Anomia, and Social Interaction: Contexts of Deviate Behavior," in M. B. Clinard, ed., *Anomie and Deviate Behavior* (New York: Free Press, 1964).

19. Burnkrant and Cousineau, "Informational and Normative Social Influence."

20. Bobby Calder and Robert Burnkrant, "Interpersonal Influence on Consumer Behavior: An Attribution Theory Approach," *Journal of Consumer Research* 4 (June 1977), 29–38.

21. Robert B. Cialdini, *Influence Science and Practice,* 3rd ed. (New York: HarperCollins, 1993), Chapter 4.

22. Paul M. Herr, Frank R. Kardes, and John Kim, "Effects of Word-of-Mouth and Product-Attribute Information on Persuasion: An Accessibility-Diagnosticity Perspective," *Journal of Consumer Research* 17 (March 1991), 458–462.

23. William L. Wilkie, *Consumer Behavior* (New York, Wiley, 1986), 160.

24. Jacqueline Johnson Brown and Peter H. Reingen, "Social Ties and Word-of-Mouth Referral Behavior," *Journal of Consumer Research* 14 (December 1987), 350–362.

25. Thorstein Veblen, *The Theory of the Leisure Class* (New York: Macmillan, 1899); and George Simmel, "Fashion," *International Quarterly* 10 (1904), 130–155.

26. Paul F. Lazarsfeld and Robert K. Merton, "Friendship as Social Process: A Substantive and Methodological Analysis," in Monroe Berger et al., eds., *Freedom and Control in Modern Society* (New York: Octagon, 1964).

27. Paul F. Lazarsfeld, Bernard R. Berelson, and Hazel Gaudet, *The People's Choice* (New York: Columbia University Press, 1948), 151.

28. See, especially, Everett M. Rogers, *Diffusion of Innovations,* 3rd ed. (New York: Free Press, 1983). Also, most of the pertinent references have been cited in the first seven editions of this book.

29. See Brown and Reingen, "Social Ties and Word-of-Mouth Referral Behavior."

30. James H. Myers and Thomas S. Robertson, "Dimensions of Opinion Leadership," *Journal of Marketing Research* 9 (February 1972), 41–46; Charles W. King and John O. Summers, "Overlap of Opinion Leadership across Consumer Product Categories," *Journal of Marketing Research* 7 (February 1970), 43–50; and Edwin J. Gross, "Support for Generalized Marketing Leadership Theory," *Journal of Advertising Research* (November 1969), 49–52.

31. Meera P. Venkatraman, "Opinion Leadership: Enduring Involvement and Characteristics of Opinion Leaders: A Moderating or Mediating Relationship," in Marvin E. Goldberg, Gerald Gorn, and Richard W. Pollay, eds., *Advances in Consumer Research* 17 (Provo, Utah: Association for Consumer Research, 1990), 60–67.

32. Ernest Dichter, "How Word-of-Mouth Advertising Works," *Harvard Business Review* (November–December 1966), 147–166.

33. Paula Fitzgerald Bone, "Determinants of Word-of-Mouth Communications During Product Consumption," in John F. Sherry and Brian Sternthal, eds, *Advances in Consumer Research* 19 (Provo, Utah: Association for Consumer Research, 1992), 579–583.

34. Hubert Gatignon and Thomas S. Robertson, "A Propositional Inventory for New Diffusion Research," *Journal of Consumer Research* 11 (March 1985), 849–867.

35. For a review of relevant research, see Herr, Kardes, and Kim, "Effects of Word-of-Mouth"; Linda L. Price and Lawrence F. Feick, "The Role of Interpersonal Sources and External Search: An Informational Perspective," in Thomas C. Kinnear, ed., *Advances* 11 (Provo, Utah: Association for Consumer Research, 1984), 250–255; and Theresa A. Swartz and Nancy Stephens, "Information Search for Services: The Maturity Segment," in Kinnear, ed., *Advances*, 244–249.

36. Gatignon and Robertson, "A Propositional Inventory."

37. Herr, Kardes, and Kim, "Effects of Word-of-Mouth"; Marsha L. Richins, "Word of Mouth Communication as Negative Information," in Kinnear, ed., *Advances*, 697–702; and Richard W. Mizerski, "An Attribution Explanation of the Disproportionate Influence of Unfavorable Information," *Journal of Consumer Research* 9 (December 1982), 301–310.

38. John H. Holmes and John D. Lett, Jr., "Product Sampling and Word of Mouth," *Journal of Advertising Research* 17 (October 1977), 35–40.

39. Gatignon and Robertson, "A Propositional Inventory."

40. *Measuring the Grapevine: Consumer Response and Word-of-Mouth.* The Coca-Cola Co., 1981.

41. Scott Hume, "Anheuser Beer Arrives without Ads," *Advertising Age* (July 6, 1987), 2.

42. Christy Fisher, "Wal-Mart's Way," *Advertising Age* (February 18, 1991), 3.

43. Jonathan Gutman and Michael K. Mills, "Fashion Lifestyle and Consumer Information Usage: Formulating Effective Marketing Communications," in Bruce J. Walker et al., eds., *An Assessment of Marketing Thought and Practice* (Chicago: American Marketing Association, 1982), 199–203.

44. Meg Cox, "Ford Pushing Thunderbird with VIP Plan," *Wall Street Journal* (October 17, 1983), 37.

45. John E. Pluennecke and William J. Hampton, "Can Audi Fix a Dented Image?" *Business Week* (November 17, 1986), 81–82.

CHAPTER 21

FAMILY AND HOUSEHOLD INFLUENCES

▲▲

Diet Coke Adjusts to Changing Roles

Family, changing female—male roles, and sex. These were all some of the new messages in advertising introduced in 1994 by Diet Coke. For more than a decade, Diet Coke had great success with "Just for the Taste of It" featuring stars such as Elton John and Paula Abdul, along with film classics Humphrey Bogart and Louis Armstrong. In 1993, the company introduced a glitzy campaign with surfing ministers and speeding insurance agents built on a fame-and-fortune theme of having it all. The slogan "Taste It All" created little excitement among anyone except Coke bottlers who distinctly disliked the campaign. After 6 weeks, the campaign was discontinued and Coke fired Lintas, the advertising agency it had employed since Diet Coke was introduced in 1982.

Diet Coke's new campaign, created by Lowe & Partners, is heavily targeted toward women. Creative appeals rely on sex, humor, and hit songs. Some are blatantly sexy. One spot shows female office workers whispering to one another that it's time for their Diet Coke break. They rush to a window where they can stare at a well-chiseled construction worker taking off his shirt. He's on a break, guzzling down the soft drink and the women are enjoying the view greatly. Another ad shows a woman pulling up to a billiard hall, unloading her boyfriend's possessions, chugging a Diet Coke, and triumphantly speeding away. A third spot shows a bellhop knocking on the door of a honeymoon suite with a delivery of two cans of the soft drink on ice. He makes the trip four times, each time to be greeted just by the hands of a man grabbing the soda. Each spot ends with the slogan: "This is refreshment."

Nancy Gibson, Diet Coke's world-wide brand director, is responsible for the ads and says, "The focus now is on the simpler pleasures with families and friends." The new campaign will be in all English-speaking countries, although in some countries, the diet product is called Coke Light. Ms. Gibson says Diet

Coke tested the new commercials with audiences, including on-air testing in two cities, and received favorable response. The tests show that men like the spots as much as women.

Sources: Media accounts including "New Diet Coke Ads Pour on the Bubbly," Columbus Dispatch (January 14, 1994), 2c; and Kevin Goldman, "Refreshment Bears Weight for Diet Coke," Wall Street Journal (January 13, 1994, B6.

Families and the Study of Consumer Behavior

The importance of the family/household unit in consumer behavior arises for two reasons:

1. Many products are purchased by a family unit.
2. Buying decisions of individuals may be heavily influenced by other members of the family.

Homes and cars are examples of products purchased by both spouses, perhaps with involvement from children or other members of the extended family. Visits to shopping malls often involve multiple family members buying a variety of household items, clothing, and perhaps groceries. Such trips may also involve all members in selecting a restaurant at which to spend the family's money.

Family influences on an individual's purchase can be seen when children buy clothing paid for and perhaps sanctioned by parents. Teenagers may also influence the clothing purchases of a parent. The person responsible for buying and preparing family meals may act as an individual in the supermarket but be influenced by the preferences and power of the other family members. Even when people are "on their own" as individual households, they may prefer the same furniture style as (or perhaps the opposite of) the family in which they were raised.

The study of family consumer decisions is less common than that of individuals because of the difficulty of researching and studying the family as a unit. Administering a questionnaire simultaneously to an entire family requires accessing all members (difficult in today's hectic environment), using language that has the same meaning to all family members (difficult with discrepancies in age or education), and interpreting results when members of the same family report conflicting opinions about family purchases or influences on decisions (a common finding in family research).

What Is a Family?

A family is a group of two or more persons related by blood, marriage, or adoption who reside together. The nuclear family is the immediate group of father, mother, and child(ren) living together. The extended family is the nuclear family, plus other relatives, such as grandparents, uncles and aunts, cousins, and in-laws. The family into which one is born is called the family of orientation, whereas the one established by marriage is the family of procreation.

What Is a Household?

The term **household** is used to describe all persons, both related and unrelated, who occupy a housing unit. There are significant differences between the terms *household* and **family** even though they are sometimes used interchangeably. It is important to distinguish between these terms when examining data.

Household is becoming a more important unit of analysis for marketers because of the rapid growth in nontraditional families and nonfamily households. Among nonfamily households, the great majority consist of people living alone. The remaining nonfamily households include those consisting of elderly people living with nonfamily members and the relatively new census category POSSLQ, "Persons of Opposite Sex Sharing Living Quarters." Families are the largest category of households, but nonfamily households are growing faster. One way to avoid the problem of whether to study families or households is to simply use the term *consumer unit* (CU) or *minimal household unit* (MHU). It is easier and sometimes just as useful to avoid the distinctions between each group and refer to CU or MHU buying behavior.[1]

Variables Affecting Family/Household Purchases

Consumer purchasing is affected by family or household variables. Structural variables include the age of head of household or family, marital status, presence of children, and employment status. For example, families have higher median incomes than do households because of the greater number of employed individuals in families.

Families are like corporations; they are organizations formed to accomplish particular functions more effectively than individuals could. The most obvious of these functions is having children. Consumer analysts have enormous interest in whether families have children and how many they have. Economically, children in a family create demand for clothing, food, furniture, homes, medical care, and education, while they decrease demand for products such as travel, some restaurants, adult clothing, and many discretionary items.

Sociological Variables Affecting Families

The family is a "buying center" and reflects the activities and influences of the individuals in the family. Individuals often buy products for the family as well as their own use. Marketers can sometimes understand these decisions better by focusing on sociological dimensions of how families make consumer decisions.

Three variables that help explain how families function include cohesion, adaptability, and communication.

Cohesion is the emotional bonding between family members. It measures how close to each other family members feel on an emotional level. Cohesion reflects a sense of connectedness to or separateness from other family members.

Adaptability measures the ability of a family to change its power structure, role relationships, and relationship rules in response to situational and developmental stress. The degree of adaptability shows how well a family can meet the challenges presented by changing needs.

Communication is a facilitating dimension, critical to movement on the other two dimensions. Positive communication skills (such as empathy, reflective listening, supportive comments) enable family members to share their changing needs and preferences as they relate to cohesion and adaptability. Negative communication skills (such as double messages, double binds, criticism) minimize the ability to share feelings, thereby restricting movement in the dimensions of cohesion and adaptability. Understanding whether family members are satisfied with family purchases may require understanding communication within the family.[2]

Some of the sociological research on how families function can be helpful in the development of marketing programs. For example, sociological research in recent years has increasingly focused on "resilient" families — those that are better able to negotiate their way through transitions and tragedies. Families that place more importance on family celebrations, family time and routines, and family traditions are more likely to develop resilient families.[3]

Marketers recognize that family celebrations are not only important to helping families survive crises, but they are also critically important to creating consumer demand for many products. More than 50 percent of retail sales and an even higher percentage of profits are normally generated by the Hanukkah and Christmas holidays. Understanding gift giving and family holidays has become an important area of study by Belk, Hirschman, and others.[4] A family's holiday spirit can also be seen in other non-gift-giving consumer behaviors such as decorating homes for the holidays.[5] Advertising attempts to relate a family's holiday celebrations to consumption as do store and shopping mall decorations. Duracell and Absolut relate to the holidays in their ads seen in Figure 21.1.

Who Determines What the Family Buys?

Families use products even though individuals usually buy them. Determining what and where products should be bought, how and when products are used, and who should buy them is a complicated process involving a variety of roles and actors. Before discussing who purchases what in a family, you might want to review what families buy as listed in Table 21.2 (page 754).

Figure 21.1 Appealing to Families' Holiday Celebrations

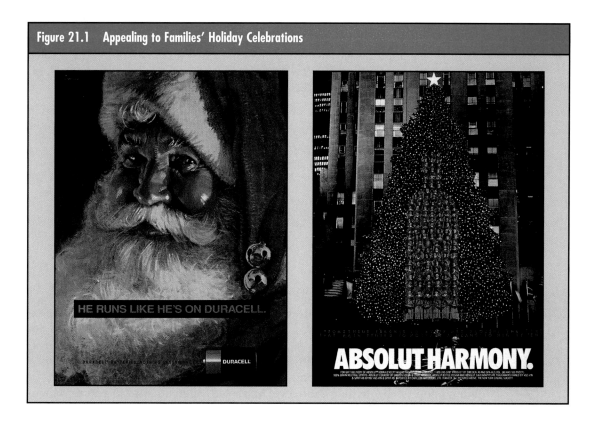

Role Behavior

Families and other groups exhibit what sociologist Talcott Parsons called instrumental and expressive role behaviors. Instrumental roles, also known as functional or economic roles, involve financial, performance, and other "functional" attributes such as conditions of purchase. Expressive roles involve supporting other family members in the decision-making process and expressing the family's aesthetic or emotional needs, including upholding family norms. Choosing the color, product features, and retailer that fit most closely to the family's needs is the outcome of role performance.

Marketing communications are usually directed to individuals, but Childers and Rao[6] warn that marketers should consider the consumption circumstances and the family structure before deciding on specific communication or advertising methods, such as use of spokespersons, to attract their segment. Individuals are often influenced by other family members. For example, as Davis[7] explains, "A husband may buy a station wagon, given the reality of having to transport four children, despite his strong preference for sports cars." A father may choose to ask his daughter and son about color and style of the car before he and his wife venture out to make the purchase.

Individual Roles in Family Purchases

Family consumption decisions involve at least five definable roles. These roles may be assumed by a husband, wife, children, or other members of a household. Both multiple roles and multiple actors are normal.

1. *Initiator/gatekeeper:* Initiator of family thinking about buying products and gathering information to aid the decision.
2. *Influencer:* Individual whose opinions are sought concerning criteria the family should use in purchases and which products or brands most likely fit those evaluative criteria.
3. *Decider:* The person with the financial authority and/or power to choose how the family's money will be spent and on which products or brands.
4. *Buyer:* The person who acts as the purchasing agent by visiting the store, calling suppliers, writing checks, bringing products into the home, and so on.
5. *User:* The person(s) who uses the product.

Marketers need to communicate with occupants of each role. Children, for example, are users of cereals, toys, clothing, and many other products but may not be the buyers. One or both of the parents may be the decider and the buyer, although the children may be important as influencers and as users. Parents may act as gatekeepers by preventing children from watching some TV programs or attempting to negate their influence. Marketers often attempt to get agreement between parents and kids about products. Kix cereal uses the tag line "Kid tested, Mother approved." Figure 21.2 shows how pediatricians approve of Yoplait yogurt while kids like the taste.

Influencer roles may be taken by those with the most expertise. For example, a parent may be the decider about which car to purchase, but teenagers often play a major role as gatekeepers of information and as influencers because of greater knowledge about performance, product features, or social norms. Consumer in Focus 21.1 looks at U.S. and Italian children as influencers in family purchasing decisions.

Family marketing focuses on the relationships between the purchaser and the family consumer rather than just the purchase decision maker. It creates a relationship between individuals and products, as does individual marketing. The family purchase decision-making process can be complex, but answering the following questions helps identify different purchase/consumer relationships:

1. Who's buying for whom?
2. Who are the principal characters?
3. What's the plot for the purchase?
4. Who wants what when?
5. What can we assume?[8]

Figure 21.2   Yoplait Appeals to Parents and Kids

Although these answers may not identify all essential relationships marketers should consider, they do identify a family marketing plan. Family marketing identifies scenarios where some purchases might have more than one decision maker, whereas some have more than one consumer. Sometimes the purchaser and consumer are the same person; sometimes they are different people. The Family Marketing Model, as seen in Table 21.1, represents nine cells describing various purchaser/consumer relationships. Depending on where in the matrix various products fall, marketers can advertise and position products differently according to their purchaser/consumer relationships.

Spousal Roles in Buying Decisions

Which spouse is most important in family buying decisions? How does this vary by product category? How does this vary by stage of decision making? Generally, the following role-structure categories are used to analyze these questions:

| 21.1 | **Consumer in Focus** |

Children as Influencers

Marketers have followed children as buyers and influencers for many years. According to Children's Market Research Inc., U.S. youngsters aged 6 to 14 years spend an estimated $7 billion and influence another $120 billion on items ranging from groceries to cars. According to the 1993 Simmons Kids Study conducted by the Simmons Market Research Bureau, "45.2% of kids influence the choice of sneaker brands bought for them; 38.6% help decide what kind of jeans they buy; 38.2% pick shirts; 34% choose casual pants; and 32.8% select sweats."

Now with the globalization of business, marketers are conducting more research into the patterns of youth purchasing behaviors in other countries. According to a survey by DOXA, Italy's leading polling firm, Italian children (5 million of them) have both money to spend (approximately $150 billion on any given day) and influence on how their parents spend money. Italian children display independence on purchasing snack items such as chewing gum, chocolate, and ice cream — their favorite items to buy — with carbonated drinks and video games ranking far behind.

Italian children, 70% of whom are only children, also have a lot of influence on family purchasing decisions. Most of their influence is on items parents buy for them such as sneakers, jeans, sweatshirts, jackets, and most important, school backpacks, with Italian maker Invicta dominating the market. Although parents have the most influence on where the family takes its summer vacation, children still have strong influence on family movie choices.

Children had the most influence on items they bought for themselves and high-tech products of which they might be a likely user. Some specific product purchases children influence are listed in the accompanying chart. You might want to ask yourself how, as a marketer, information such as this might influence how you would market these products in Italy.

Durable	Indication of Child's Influence (1–10 scale)
Television	1.6
VCR	1.9
Personal computer	3.6
Automobile	1.5
Walkman	5.0
Bicycle	6.3
Camera	2.3

Sources: Todd Ebitz, "Italian Children May Be the Influencers," Market: Europe (January 1994), 5–7; "Youth Marketing Isn't Dismissed as Kid Stuff," Columbus Dispatch (March 4, 1993), 2E; Gary Levin, "Teens Reveal Clout in Buying Decisions; Take Note of Ads," Advertising Age (January 10, 1994), 28.

Table 21.1   Family Marketing Model

Family purchases fall into 9 categories, depending on who makes the purchase decision and who uses the item purchased.

	A Purchase Decision Maker		
A Consumer	**One Member**	**Some Members**	**All Members**
One Member	1	2 Tennis Racket	3
Some Members	4 Sugar Pops	5	6
All Members	7	8	9 Refrigerator

For Example:

1. Mom and Dad go to buy a new tennis racket for Mom. Dad advises Mom on her purchase. Some members are decision-makers and one member is a consumer: cell 2.

2. Mom goes to the grocery store to buy Sugar Pops cereal for her children. She'll never eat the stuff. One member is a decision-maker and some members are consumers: cell 4.

3. Mom, Dad, and the kids go to the department store to buy a refrigerator. All members are decision-makers and all are consumers: cell 9.

Source: Robert Boutilier, "Pulling the Family's Strings," *American Demographics* (August 1993), 46.

1. Autonomic, when an equal number of decisions is made by each spouse, but each decision is individually made by one spouse or the other

2. Husband dominant

3. Wife dominant

4. Joint (syncratic), when most decisions are made by both husband and wife

These categories are sometimes simplified to "husband more than wife," "wife more than husband," "both husband and wife," or simply "husband only," "wife only," or "children only." The type of product, stage in the decision process, and nature of the situation surrounding the decision influence which situation exists.

A landmark study investigating husband–wife influences was conducted by Harry Davis and Benny Rigaux.[9] Their findings are usually presented in the familiar triangular configuration shown in Figure 21.3 and have greatly influenced thinking about the relative influence of husbands and wives on decision making and the extent of role specialization. This study was recently updated by Management Horizons, a division of Price Waterhouse, for use by businesses selling a wide variety of goods.[10]

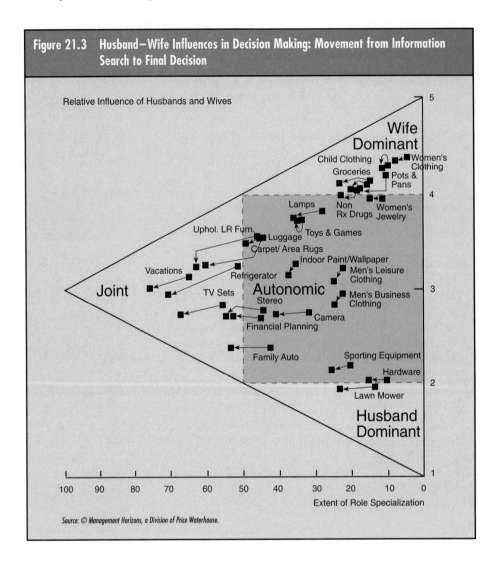

Figure 21.3 Husband–Wife Influences in Decision Making: Movement from Information Search to Final Decision

Source: © Management Horizons, a Division of Price Waterhouse.

Overall Influence

Figure 21.3 displays measures of husbands' and wives' perceptions of their relative influence on decision making across decision stages. Some product/service categories are wife-dominant. They include women's clothing, children's clothing, and groceries. Two categories that are husband-dominant include lawn mowers and hardware. Joint decisions tend to be made about vacations, televisions, refrigerators, and upholstered living room furniture. Autonomic decision making tends to be present in decisions about categories that include women's jewelry, men's leisure clothing, men's business clothing, sporting equipment, lamps, toys and games, indoor paint/wallpaper, and luggage.

Influence by Decision Stage

Figure 21.3 shows variation in the influence of spouses by stages in the decision-making process. This is indicated by the direction of the arrow, which shows movement from information search to final decision. This movement may be minimal in the case of many low-involvement goods but more pronounced for goods that are risky or have high involvement for the family. The decision process tends to move toward joint participation and away from autonomic behavior as a final decision nears. Movement is most pronounced for refrigerators, family autos, upholstered living room furniture, and carpets/rugs. Vacations are perhaps the most democratic of a family's purchase decisions.

The information-search stage is more autonomic than joint when compared with final decisions. Marketing plans thus require specialized use of media, such as magazines or other media having a strong appeal to either husbands or wives rather than both. Product or store design must reflect the evaluative criteria of both, however, as consensus on these must be achieved in the final decision. Separate campaigns may be timed to coincide with specialized interests, especially for products with a long planning cycle.

Influence of Employment

In the past, marketers were able to refer to the traditional role-structure categories to determine which family member was most likely to purchase a specific product. Lavin[11] states that in recent years because of the high number of women working outside of the home and the questioning of traditional spousal roles, marketers must focus on the new ways contemporary couples divide their buying responsibilities. "Husbands in dual-income marriages may be willing to stop at the grocery store to pick up a few items, and working wives may drop the family car at the service station for an oil change, but these occurrences need not be evidence of the erosion of traditional buying roles." Yet Lavin points out that contemporary couples—many from the baby boomer segment—are not inclined to shift traditional joint buying responsibilities to only one spouse, but they are willing to shop jointly for major items that might have been the responsibility of one spouse in traditional families.

Decline of Gender Differences

Changes in family structure over time are causing husband and wife decisions increasingly to be made jointly (syncratically). Qualls[12] studied family decisions concerning vacations, automobiles, children's education, housing, insurance, and savings. All these products had been studied extensively in prior decades and generally were reported to involve a minority of joint decisions. Qualls found overwhelmingly that joint decisions are now the norm for children's education and housing in 80 percent or more households. The majority shared decisions for the other products as well, although not as dramatically. The

Management Horizons Family Purchasing Study found that increasing resources of women and shifts toward egalitarianism are producing more joint decision making in product/service categories of perceived high risk. In contrast, however, time pressures, brought about by larger numbers of dual-worker families, may produce more autonomic decisions in categories of perceived low risk. Notice in Consumer in Focus 21.2 the changing roles of men and women when it comes to grocery shopping.

Because of declining gender differences and the waning of gender identification of products, many marketers are researching issues such as how to market products that have traditionally been gender-dependent to dual-gender positioning.[13] Yet consumer researchers must recognize that gender differences, despite movement away from sex-role dominance, still exist for some products and in some situations.[14] Also, advertising still includes sex-role dominance, perhaps by companies insensitive to such issue. Literature reviews of these areas are available in Jenkins[15]; Burns and Granbois[16]; and Gupta, Hagerty, and Myers.[17] But psychological gender differences in household decision making today is a low-yield area of research. Roberts explains: "It has never been very productive, and it will be even less productive in the future."[18]

There are many causes for the demise of gender differences in family buying decisions, many related to the changing employment status and roles of women. The resource-contribution theory suggests that the greater the relative contribution of an individual, the greater the influence in decision making. A variation of this theory is called the "least interested partner" hypothesis, which states that the greater the value of one partner relative to the other as valued by society,

---

| **21.2** | **Consumer in Focus** |

Spousal Roles in the Supermarket

Men who have to ask a woman what's for dinner are on the way out. Women still do most of the food shopping. But men are getting more involved. Thirty-five percent of couples claim both the man and the woman are equally responsible for food shopping, according to a telephone survey of nearly 1,000 adults conducted by the Opinion Research Corporation for *Men's Health* magazine. Only 8 percent of couples say that the man does all or most of the food shopping, whereas 56 percent say the woman does all the shopping.

Some experts say that men are helping take the burden off their overworked working wives and that men and women want egalitarian relationships. Peter Stein of William Paterson College in New Jersey says that a man might even experience a hunter-like feeling when he's shopping—like the primordial male coming home with the catch. Herb Goldberg, an L.A.-based psychologist, agrees: "I see food shopping as a latter-day version of food gathering. Instead of going into the woods, we go to the supermarket."

Source: Excerpted from "Tarzan of the Foodmart," American Demographics 12 (May 1990), 13.

the greater influence that partner will have. Gender-related consumer behavior still exists and is even pervasive in some types of purchasing decisions. Such roles are not determined by biological sex so much as the socialization experiences a person is likely to have and thus the consumer activities that will be learned by men and women.[19]

Family Life Cycles

Families change over time, passing through a series of stages. This process historically has been called the family life cycle (FLC). The concept may need to be changed to household life cycle (HLC) or consumer life cycle (CLC) in the future to reflect changes in society, but we will use the term *FLC*, popularized in marketing research by Wells and Gubar[20] and later in a book by Reynolds and Wells[21] showing how the life cycle affects consumer behavior.

Traditional FLC

The traditional FLC describes family patterns as they marry, have children, leave home, lose a spouse, and retire. These stages are described in Table 21.2, along with consumer behavior associated with each stage. Other versions, such as that of Murphy and Staples,[22] recognize contemporary developments of divorce, smaller sizes of families, and delayed age of marriage.

Modified FLC Matrix

Marketing organizations may need to modify the traditional FLC to make it more specific to their analytical needs. Adding socioeconomic data, especially income, improves predictions about product choices such as clothing and helps in using the traditional FLC to explain consumer behavior.[23]

An example of a modified model reflecting contemporary lifestyles is the Consumer Market Matrix developed by Management Horizons, a division of Price Waterhouse. This matrix of consumer markets analyzes the interaction of income and lifestages on consumer behavior. It recognizes the increasing importance of aging of the population as well as the increased tendency for women either to delay having children to a later age or to choose not to have children.[24]

The main lifestages of households represent important market segments and are described as follows:

Younger singles: Head of household single and younger than 45 years with no children present

Younger couples: Married couple with head of household younger than 45 years and no children present

Table 21.2 Traditional Life Cycles and Buying Behavior

Single Stage
Although earnings are relatively low, they are subject to few rigid demands, so consumers in this stage typically have substantial discretionary income. Part of this income is used to purchase a car and basic equipment and furnishings for their first residence away from home—usually an apartment. They tend to be more fashion- and recreation-oriented, spending a substantial proportion of their income on clothing, alcoholic beverages, food away from home, vacations, leisure time pursuits, and other products and services involved in the mating game.

Newly Married Couples
Newly married couples without children are usually better off financially than in the past and even better in the near future because many become dual-income families. Families at this stage also spend a substantial amount of their income on cars, clothing, vacations, and other leisure time activities. They also have the highest purchase rate and highest average purchases of durable goods, particularly furniture and appliances, and appear to be more susceptible to advertising.

Full Nest I
With the arrival of the first child, often one parent stops working outside the home, and consequently family income declines. Simultaneously, the young child creates new needs that change the way the family spends its income. The couple is likely to move into its first home; purchase furniture and furnishings for the child; buy a washer, dryer, and home maintenance items; and purchase such products as baby food, cough medicine, vitamins, toys, wagons, sleds, and skates. These requirements reduce family savings, and the husband and wife are often dissatisfied with their financial position.

Full Nest II
At this stage the youngest child is 6 years or older, the employed spouse's income has improved, and the other often returns to work outside the home. Consequently, the family's financial position usually improves. Consumption patterns continue to be heavily influenced by the children as the family tends to buy large-sized packages of food and cleaning supplies, bicycles, pianos, and music lessons.

Full Nest III
As the family grows older, its financial position usually continues to improve because the primary wage earner's income rises, the other spouse returns to work or enjoys a higher salary, and the children earn money from occasional employment. The family typically replaces several pieces of furniture, purchases another automobile, buys several luxury appliances, and spends a considerable amount of money on dental services and education for the children.

Empty Nest I
At this stage, the family is most satisfied with their financial position and the amount of money saved because income has continued to increase, and the children have left home and are no longer financially dependent on their parents. The couple often make home improvements, buy luxury items, and spend a greater proportion of their income on vacations, travel, and recreation.

Empty Nest II
By this time, the household head has retired and so the couple usually suffers a noticeable reduction in income. Expenditures become more health-oriented, centering on such items as medical appliances; medical care products that aid health, sleep, and digestion; and perhaps a smaller home, apartment, or condominium in a more agreeable climate.

The Solitary Survivor
If still in the labor force, solitary survivors still enjoy a good income. They may sell their home and usually spend more money on vacations, recreation, and the types of health-oriented products and services mentioned above.

The Retired Solitary Survivor
The retired solitary survivor follows the same general consumption pattern except on a lower scale because of the reduction in income. Also, these individuals have special needs for attention, affection, and security.

Younger parents: Head of household younger than 45 years with child(ren)

Midlife families: Head of household between the ages of 45 and 64 years with child(ren) either present in or financially supported by the household

Midlife households: Head of household between the ages of 45 and 64 years with no child(ren) either present in or financially supported by the household

Older households: Head of household aged 65 years or older or retired

The lifestage segments in the matrix are divided by income into

Down market: The lower quartile of household income for a specific lifestage

Middle market: The two middle quartiles of household income for a specific lifestage

Up market: The upper quartile of household income for a specific lifestage

This type of contemporary FLC matrix permits a quantitative analysis of market sizes. Additional data are collected concerning preferences, expenditures, and shopping behavior of each segment. The objective is to attract core customers in the lifestage most profitable as the firm's target market. Close examination of the firm's marketing mix might reveal, for example, lack of a clearly defined offer, suggesting that the current marketing mix may be aimed at fringe rather than core customers.

The FLC helps explain how a specific family changes over time whereas modified forms are useful to identify core market targets. But the basic structure of families and households is changing in the United States, Canada, and other industrialized countries. In the next section, we examine trends in family and household structure. Many of these changes greatly affect marketing strategies and tactics.

Changing Family and Household Structure

What is the structure of contemporary families? How is that structure changing? How does structure affect consumption? Are the developing realities of family structure a problem or an opportunity for marketing organizations? These are some of the questions that consumer researchers try to answer. Many of the answers involve data from the decennial census and interim reports by the Bureau of Census. Figure 21.4, an ad for an insurance company, addresses the need recognition stage of the changing family. There are other topics relating to the family that could be mentioned, such as the effects on families caused by the aging of the population as covered in Chapter 2.

Figure 21.4 Need Recognition Stage in the Changing Family

1 home,
1 husband,
1 career,
2 daughters,
3 savings accounts ...and 1 State Farm agent.

Agent Karen Blosser

Cherie Frost has a loving husband and two sweet little girls. But she also has a thriving business she runs out of their home. So Kevin takes care of Mallory and Kelsey as often as Cherie does. As a working mother, Cherie took on a full load of responsibilities, including sitting down with State Farm Agent Karen Blosser to talk about life insurance for herself and her husband.

Karen listened to Cherie and Kevin as they talked about their careers, their dreams for the girls, and all their financial commitments. Then, together, they designed a life insurance plan that could help make those dreams come true.

Life insurance, like careers, used to be just for men. State Farm agents like Karen Blosser know how much the world has changed, and how much women have changed along with it.

State Farm sells life insurance.

State Farm Life Insurance Company
State Farm Life And Accident Assurance Company
(New York and Wisconsin)
Home Offices: Bloomington, IL.

Source: Courtesy of State Farm.

Married or Single?

Marriage: To be or not to be? That is the question. The answer is that marriage is in the cards for most consumers, although they are delaying the age of first marriage. Consumer in Focus 21.3 describes the latest marriage patterns among Americans. Although most adults marry at some time in their lives, the proportion of consuming households composed of nonmarried individuals is increasing rapidly because of the delay in marriage and remarriage.

Smaller Households

Average household size is falling in most industrialized countries. In the United States, it dropped from to 2.63 in 1990, down from 2.76 in 1980 and 3.14 in 1970. One-person households are now about 24 percent of the total, compared with

Consumer in Focus **21.3**

Marriage, American Style

Americans are waiting longer and longer to get married these days, the Census Bureau reports. The average first-time bride is older than at any time in the past century. Postponing nuptials is one way to cope with the increasing complexity of U.S. life. People are delaying marriage because their lives have become more entangled with school, career, and other things, said Martha Farnsworth Riche, a sociologist with the Population Reference Bureau in Washington, D.C.

According to the Census Bureau, in 1992 the average age for first-time bridegrooms was 26.5 years and for first-time brides was 24.4 years. In the 1950s, men on average were about 22 years when they tied the knot for the first time; women were almost 20 years.

The Census Bureau survey also found the proportion of women in their early thirties who had never walked down the aisle nearly tripled to 16 percent in 1990 from 6 percent in 1970. There were 2.9 million unmarried couples living together, up 80 percent from 10 years earlier.

Eventually, however, by their early forties, 91 percent of all men and 92 percent of all women do get married. It is interesting to note that only 78 percent of men and 74 percent of women in that age bracket are currently married. One area in which the statistics have not changed much over the past 100 years is the over-65-years age bracket. As in previous years, 5 percent of men and 4 percent of women older than 65 years have never been married.

Sources: "People Are Waiting Longer to Get Married, Study Shows," Columbus Dispatch (June 7, 1991), 3A; "Almost All Get Around to Getting Married," Wall Street Journal (March 5, 1993), B1.

18 percent in 1970, and households with six or more persons dropped from 19.5 percent of all households to less than 6 percent today. Recent census surveys disclose that only 26 percent of American households consist of a married couple with a child younger than 18 years, compared with 31 percent in 1980 and 40 percent in 1970. Table 21.3 estimates changes in number of households by type in 1990 and 2000 and shows how rapidly the nonfamily households are increasing.

Marketers are increasingly interested in single-parent households. About 11 million of these are headed by a female with no husband present and about 3 million by a male householder with no wife present. Women without husbands maintain 13 percent of all white family households, 44 percent of all black family households, and 23 percent of all Hispanic family households. The rate of increase in single black parenthood slowed during the past decade to 3.8 percent per year, while the rate for Hispanics more than doubled to 7 percent per year, the highest rate of increase for any ethnic group. About 24 percent of all American children, and about 55 percent of all black children, live in a single-parent household. Table 21.4 shows how the number of single-parent households is changing in the United States.

Table 21.3 Households by Type: 1990–2000 Projections

	1990	2000	% Change 1990–2000
All households	95.2ᵃ	110.2	15.8
Family households	65.9	70.0	13.8
Married couples	51.7	52.3	1.1
Male householder	2.7	3.8	40.7
Female householder	11.5	13.9	20.9
Nonfamily households	29.3	40.2	37.2
Male householder	13.0	19.5	50.0
Female householder	16.3	20.7	27.0

ᵃ *Numbers refer to millions.*
Source: U.S. Bureau of the Census, Current Population Reports, Series P-25, No. 986, Series A Assumptions (reflecting recent changes in marriage and divorce trends).

Table 21.4 Single Mothers and Single Fathers to 2010

Single Mothers

	1990 Number	1990 Percent	1995 Number	2000 Number	2000 Percent	2005 Number	2010 Number	2010 Percent	Percent Change 1990–2000	Percent Change 2000–2010
Total	6,599	100.0	7,238	7,473	100.0	7,607	7,779	100.0	13.2	4.1
Younger than 25	786	11.9	831	931	12.5	1,091	1,234	15.9	18.4	32.5
25 to 34	2,625	39.8	2,721	2,605	34.9	2,637	2,834	36.4	−0.7	8.8
35 to 44	2,341	35.5	2,800	2,966	39.7	2,852	2,675	34.4	26.7	−9.8
45 to 54	707	10.7	769	851	11.4	891	879	11.3	20.4	3.3
55 to 64	99	1.5	92	93	1.2	109	127	1.6	−6.0	36.6
65 to 74	31	0.5	18	17	0.2	17	20	0.3	−43.9	13.9
75 and older	8	0.1	7	9	0.1	10	10	0.1	7.7	16.8

Single Fathers

	1990 Number	1990 Percent	1995 Number	2000 Number	2000 Percent	2005 Number	2010 Number	2010 Percent	Percent Change 1990–2000	Percent Change 2000–2010
Total	1,153	100.0	1,366	1,523	100.0	1,598	1,660	100.0	32.1	9.0
Younger than 25	96	8.3	90	102	6.7	113	120	7.2	6.7	17.3
25 to 34	349	30.2	437	482	31.6	511	571	34.4	38.1	18.5
35 to 44	458	39.7	554	604	39.7	600	576	34.7	31.8	−4.6
45 to 54	193	16.7	220	259	17.0	283	286	17.2	34.0	10.7
55 to 64	38	3.3	48	55	3.6	68	81	4.9	44.7	46.6
65 to 74	13	1.1	12	11	0.7	12	13	0.8	−12.5	16.4
75 and older	7	0.6	7	10	0.6	11	12	0.8	38.5	28.6

Note: Numbers may not add to total due to rounding.
(Numbers in thousands and percent of households, by age of householder, 1990–2010, and percent change 1990–2000 and 2000–2010)
Source: American Demographics (December 1993), 37.

The U.S. Bureau of the Census reports that the annual incomes for 1991 per household type are reported to be:

Household Type	1991 Median Income	Percentage Change 1980–1991
Total families	$36,404	3.9
Married couples	41,075	7.1
Female householder, no spouse present	17,961	0.2
Male householder, no spouse present	31,010	–0.2
Nonfamily households	17,774	13.6

The median income levels of married couples and nonfamily households grew substantially from 1980 to 1990, yet the annual incomes of families headed by single women or men barely changed.[25]

Later Marriages

The median age at which people get married has increased substantially as described in Consumer in Focus 21.3. In older marriages, consumers may have to buy fewer of the basic furnishings and products needed for housekeeping but are able to buy better merchandise: higher-quality furniture, designer services, and so forth. Older marriages produce more extensive travel capabilities — perhaps a honeymoon in Grenada; a higher probability of owning two cars; and firmer preferences for styles, colors, and product designs because both the bride and the groom are likely to bring more housekeeping experience into the marriage.

Divorce and Consumer Behavior

The number of divorces increased for many years in the United States and in most other countries. A slight decrease in the rate has begun to occur attributed to various causes, such as marriage at later ages or the possibility that the pent-up demand for divorce of previous decades has simply been satisfied. Divorce contributes an added dimension to analyzing consumer decision making. Consumers who have been previously married, sometimes called the "single again" market, carry with them preferences and shopping patterns learned in a family situation. They often carry financial problems that restrict their ability to buy the things that married couples or never-married singles might buy.[26]

Despite recent declines in divorce rate, 51.6 percent of today's marriages end in divorce.[27] If a couple completes 10 years of marriage, the odds of divorce fall to 30 percent. Thus, although most people live most of their lives married, about half live part of their lives divorced.

Divorce creates markets. One family becomes two—with two households and two sets of household equipment. There are fewer divorced men because more men than women remarry and men remarry sooner. Studies show that on the average a man's income usually rises after a divorce whereas a woman's income usually falls, especially if she gets custody of children. For this reason, some divorced adults spend freely whereas others are forced into frugality. Both parties learn new patterns of consumer behavior.[28]

Remarriages and Redivorce

Most divorced people remarry. Markets in total, therefore, remain mostly married. Once-divorced couples are more likely, however, to be redivorced than are couples who have been married only once. Consumers who remarry, however, are more complex to analyze because they are often subject to the family influences from stepchildren. Also, there is potential conflict between siblings of the multiple families as well as continuing influences from former spouses on the children of their own households.

The problem of analyzing resource distribution and other consumption problems can make analysis of consumer behavior complex:

> When a person enters into a remarriage, financial decision-making becomes more complex. After having spent some time in independent households, remarried partners must find some compatible way to handle their two economies. This may necessitate incorporating people from two separate households and two different generations who have different and/or opposing earning, spending, and saving habits. An additional factor complicates the family economy . . . financial responsibilities after remarriage may involve three or four adults across several households. In addition, the remarried family may be experiencing several different family stages simultaneously (for example, the newly married couple stage and the adolescent child stage). These two stages may conflict in their demands for resource distribution. That means problems may arise over whether to spend money for new household items versus a teenage child's request for a used car.[29]

Cohabiting Singles

Another category exists that is difficult to categorize as either family or single. Legally composed of singles, but functioning more as a family, cohabiting singles are the fastest-growing segment of the singles market. Although their numbers are small in proportion to the total number of households, the number of unmarried couples increased from 523,000 in 1970 to 1.6 million in 1980 to 2.9 million in 1990. Most are young and likely to have less income than married couples, but nearly one-third have at least one child. One study found that 8 percent are married to someone other than the person with whom they are cohabiting.[30]

A study financed by the National Institute of Health found that almost half of all Americans aged 25 to 35 years have lived with an individual of the opposite sex outside of marriage, with a prediction that in the 1990s this practice will be a majority experience.[31]

Marketing to Singles

Some singles maintain their own households. Others live with their families or with other singles. Regardless of where they live they are a major target for marketing organizations and increasing in importance every year. Consumer in Focus 21.4 describes some of the ways companies seek to attract singles.

Singles Boom

There are more singles in the United States than ever before. Nearly 73 million adult Americans are not in married relationships, according to Census Bureau reports, an increase of 35 million from just 20 years ago. When those who are single due to death or divorce are included, the percentage leaps from 28 percent in 1970 to 41 percent today. About one-fourth of men aged 30 to 34 years have never been married, and one in six aged 35 to 39 years has never been married. The number of never-married women, although slightly smaller, has tripled in 20 years. The number of single men will increase 20.4 percent from 1990 to 2000 whereas the number of single women will increase 16.7 percent in the same decade.[32] About one of every four occupied dwelling units has only one person in it. The notion that people must be married to be happy and productive is fading away in American society.

Another reason for more singles is the increasing time between divorce and remarriage. Divorced women wait an average of 3.6 years before remarrying and divorced men wait an average of 3.2 years, figures that are both more than a year longer than in prior decades.[33]

Older Singles

Most singles (61 percent) are women, and of the 12 million women who live alone, the median age is 66 years. For the men, the median age is 45 years. The demographics of single men and women are dramatically different because they are single for different reasons. Women live alone more because their husbands have died, and nearly half of all women older than 75 years are widows. Men live alone because they have not yet married or they are divorced. In the next 20 years, the wild and crazy single guys of the 1990s will become the tired and

21.4	**Consumer in Focus**

Marketing to Singles

Reaching Younger Singles

Mary Kowalski dug into her savings account and packed her bags recently for 2 months in Italy and France. At 46, Mary has been divorced for years, with no relationship on the horizon, and travels with her two best women friends. Mary may be the perfect consumer for the 1990s. Free of the costs of braces, Nintendos, and college tuition, singles such as Mary Kowalski are an increasingly important market for products from furs and jewelry to real estate and foreign travel.

Marketing successfully to singles means straddling traditional values and speaking about buying cars and whipping up dinner without talking down. Campbell Soup, for example, introduced "Soup for One," a single-serve portion. Singles liked the soup but they hated the name. They called it "The Lonely Soup" in focus groups. Campbell corrected the problem by expanding the line but dropped the reference to being for singles.

Honda invested heavily in ads in women's magazines and created a how-to guide for first-time women buyers. Today, women account for more than half the sales of some Honda models. Similarly, in the single male market, Drano is running spots of an obviously single young man bouncing in the tub to the strains of "Splish, Splash" and then, after discovering the drain's clogged, pouring in a slug of Drano without skipping a beat. A generation ago, you would've had a guy saying, "Honey, I can't fix the drain," says Ann Clurman of Grey Advertising, the agency that created the spot.

Reaching the Older Singles Market

The older singles market is one of increasing size and thus important in the eyes of many marketers. Companies such as Levi Strauss and Hyatt are focusing on expansion in this market. Levi Strauss & Co. launched a line of comfortable pants for women aged 50 to 60 years who would rather wear pants than dresses. The line, Travelers, is an extension of Levi's successful brand Bendover, a line of pants for women older than 60 years. Bendover has a loyal following among its customers because of its comfort features. Levi Strauss has provided clothing for baby boomer women throughout their lives and plans following them to the next stages of their lives.

Travel Companion Exchange understands the needs of older singles when it comes to traveling. Many women want to travel even if single but often don't because they don't have anyone to accompany them. Travel Companion Exchange has a dating service–like list of thousands of singles, many of whom are older than 60 years, looking for a travel companion. Because the mature single man is a rarity, cruise lines often hire such men as "hosts" to dance and interact with single older women. Customers say it is not just romance they seek, it is safety, friendship, and shared travel expenses that make companies like Travel Companion Exchange so popular.

Sources: Jon Berry, "Forever Single," Adweek's Marketing Week 31 (October 15, 1990), 20–24; Paula Mergenhagen, "All the Lonely People," American Demographics (April 1992), 44–47; and Patricia Braus, "Women of a Certain Age," American Demographics (December 1992), 44–48.

pudgy older guys.[34] The time, money, and energy of women, especially elderly women, is creating a new kind of singles market.

The gap in life expectancy between men and women means that the largest fraction of singles in the foreseeable future will be elderly widows—with a median income of $8,000. Single men have a median annual income of $14,000, which is more likely to be from wages and salaries, whereas single women are more likely to receive monies from Social Security, pensions, interest, and dividends. Consumer analysts will find most of this part of the "booming singles market" buying home-security devices, treatment for chronic health problems, congregate care facilities, and perhaps a sedate Caribbean cruise. Consumer in Focus 21.4 shows how marketers are targeting the older singles market.

Younger Singles

Specialized media and products are often directed to the younger portions of the singles market with magazines such as *Living Single.* Resorts such as Club Med started out directed mostly to young singles, but in recent years have broadened their appeal. There are miniaturized appliances for the condominium-size kitchen, and Corning Glass Works' small microwaveproof bowls for the cook who eats alone. Singles can list preferred birthday gifts in the Bloomingdale's Self-Registry, which works as any bridal registry does.

Home builders are also adapting because singles account for one-fourth of first-time home buyers. Design changes include fewer bedrooms; less dining room space; and more kitchen space, which is becoming a living room to the single. Master bedrooms are more luxurious, bathrooms more spa-like, and living space better equipped for high-tech entertainment.[35]

Gay Markets

Gay or lesbian consumers represent a segment of the market receiving increasing attention by marketing organizations. Most are classified as singles, although some jurisdictions may recognize the married status of some gay households and some gay individuals live in traditional family settings at least part of their lives. Reliable data concerning the size of the market are not available, although it is estimated that as few as 6 percent or as high as 16 percent of adult Americans may be part of this market.[36] This raises the questions: Is the market size 5 million or 18.5 million, and is the gay market purchasing power $394 billion or $514 billion?[37] To add even more confusion to the subject, in 1993 the Alan Guttmacher Institute released findings of a recent study that only 1 percent of men considered themselves exclusively homosexual.[38]

The difficulty believed to exist for some marketers is how to target effectively the gay market without alienating their heterosexual customers. The risk may be worthwhile, however, because gay consumers are above average in income, relatively well-educated, and are likely to have higher proportions of disposable income. Gay and lesbian consumers are likely to be urban, travel extensively, spend considerable money on clothing, and express more interest in the arts. Often they are more aware of current social issues and politically active than their heterosexual counterparts. But targeting all gay men is like targeting all heterosexual men. Although there are characteristics to define the homosexual market, as with all other markets, there exist differences between the individuals.

For the first time in history, the 1990 Census provides information on the number of same-sex couples and included a question in which gay couples had the opportunity to designate each other as an "unmarried partner" as opposed to "housemate/roommate." While this does not directly measure sexual orientation, the National Gay and Lesbian Task Force hopes to use the data to influence policy making in the areas of corporate health benefits, probate, adoption law, and AIDS treatment and prevention. Some private companies, such as Overlooked Opinions, Inc., conduct ongoing panels reporting data on homosexual consumers.[39]

Targeting gay and lesbian markets can be accomplished in a variety of ways. Understanding their needs is the preface to each. Commercial research firms such as Overlooked Opinions have created a panel of 12,000 gay men, lesbians, and bisexuals, representing every state and all major markets. Research from this panel indicates that the gay market is not only very affluent but is very image-conscious. An ad targeting gays, for example, might show a refrigerator stocked with Beck's Dark and brie instead of an ad targeted to straights that would show a mass-market beer and Cheez Whiz.

The primary marketing technique in reaching the gay market is simply to recognize that the market exists and to be willing to establish a relationship with this segment of the market. This can be done by participation in or sponsorship of activities considered important by gay consumers, such as sponsorship of AIDS research or community events relating to AIDS. Corporations can also create considerable awareness among the gay community by sponsorship of operas, ballets, classical concerts, and museums that attract high participation among the gay community, while at the same time also reaching the wider community.

Marketers may also advertise in gay-oriented media that exist at both the local and national levels. Many publications, such as *The Advocate, Out, Overlooked Opinions, Genre,* and *Deneuve,* have become strong national advertising mediums and have attracted advertisers such as Banana Republic, Benetton, Benson & Hedges, and Calvin Klein. It is believed that advertisers generate high loyalty among gay readers for advertising in those media without alienating homophobic consumers who do not read such media.[40] Carillon Importers began advertising Absolut vodka in *The Advocate* in 1979. After many years of clever Absolut ads and years of targeting the gay market in addition to its traditional straight market, patrons of gay bars tend to ask for Absolut rather than just vodka.

Other advertisers use the straight media but design ads with a sensitivity that attract gays. An ad for Paco Rabanne cologne, for example, has an ad that shows a man sprawled on a bed. The copy makes no specific mention of gender, which sends a message to gay men without offending straight customers.[41]

Changing Roles of Women

Marketing managers have always been interested in women because female consumers buy so many products. Interest in female consumers has intensified in recent years because of greater numbers of women, improved purchasing and employment status, and changed roles of women.

The female population is growing faster than the male population due to a higher survival rate for women. Life expectancy has increased more for women than for men. Controversy exists about why women live so much longer than men, but whatever the reasons, females now outnumber males by 6.5 million. This figure is expected to be 7.5 million by the year 2000.

More women attend colleges or universities than do men, contrary to the past. The principal reason females outnumber males on college campuses today is the greater number of women older than 25 years returning to campus. Some other differences between men and women are culturally determined and some genetically determined. Although women are more sensitive to smell, men are more sensitive to bright lights. This might explain differences in the greater purchase of perfume by women.

Feminine roles are of great concern today to consumer analysts and marketers. A role specifies what the typical occupant of a given position is expected to do in that position in a particular social context.[42] Consumer analysts are especially concerned with gender roles of women in the family and in their position as purchasing agents for the family.

Female Employment

Women today have much higher rates of employment outside the home than in past eras. Women have left hearth and home to bring home some of the bacon. Today, more than 58 percent of women are employed, in contrast to less than 25 percent in 1950. This trend is occurring on a global scale as well, with the percentages of women who work reaching 52 percent in Canada, 49 percent in Japan, 47 percent in Great Britain, 46 percent in Australia, and 39 percent in Western Germany.[43] When movement in and out of the labor force is considered, the proportion of women working outside the home within a 2-year period may be as high as 80 percent.[44] In 1995, more than 80 percent of all mothers with children at home are expected to be working outside the home.[45] Figure 21.5 shows how American Express targets women who have broken into nontraditional job areas and supports their efforts to become entrepreneurs.

How does female employment status affect buying? The most important impact is caused by income. Analysis of the employment variable sometimes uses the following nomenclature:

NWW: The wife is not employed outside the home

FWW: The wife works full time, 35 hours or more per week

PWW: The wife works part time, less than 35 hours per week

Figure 21.5   Women Breaking into Nontraditional Roles

FWW families average more than $10,000 additional income than NWW families. Today, the wife's work status is less of a determinant to how a family spends its income than is the total amount of net income the family has to spend.[46]

Other than differences caused by income, some other variation occurs caused by employment. Child care is a primary example with both PWW and FWW families spending 17 percent more than NWW families, although the gap narrows as the age of the family increases. Families in which the wife is employed also spend significantly more on food away from home, gasoline, and motor oil than do NWW families, although not more on vehicles. FWW families spend more on shelter than do one-earner families.[47]

A major limitation in the purchasing power of women is that they face a "dual labor market," the term used to describe the situation in which women receive less for the same work than do men. This condition occurs across all industries and almost all jobs, including marketing. In a recent study, the incomes of males in marketing management exceeded females by $18,300, by $12,000 in marketing research, and by $25,200 in advertising management. Some of the gap can be attributed to factors other than gender, such as years of business experience (5 years more for males), older age, higher corporate rank, more likely to work in manufacturing, and more education, but gender discrimination is still the underlying problem.[48]

Some change is occurring. Women in some occupations are perceived by young consumers more positively than are men,[49] and among dual-income families, more than 6 million women earn more than their husbands.[50] One of the factors most frequently cited as important in equalizing incomes of women and men is the availability of good, reasonably priced child care. For marketers, such factors are not only a social responsibility but increasingly an entrepreneurial opportunity. Figure 21.6 is an ad for Mercedes-Benz that is directed toward women, presumably highly paid professionals, who have enough money to buy a Mercedes motor car for the man in her life.

Career Orientation

Employed individuals are sometimes classified by orientation toward their careers. Rena Bartos finds two groups of working women: those who think of themselves as having a career and those to whom work is "just a job." There are also housewives who prefer to stay at home and those who plan to work in the future. For marketers, this may be important because homemakers and just-a-job women are more likely to read traditional women's magazines, whereas professional women are more likely to read general interest and business-oriented magazines and newspapers.[51] But Schaninger, Nelson, and Danko[52] point out that neither working nor nonworking wives should be treated as homogeneous segments. Differences between stay-at-home and plan-to-work wives and between career and just-a-job wives account for different purchasing behaviors.

For example, convenience and "junk food" ads might best be targeted to plan-to-work and just-a-job wives but not career wives, whereas marketers of take-out foods and alcoholic beverages might best be targeted toward both classes of working wives.

The primary reason women and men work are similar—for the income. A growing proportion of women regard their work as a career rather than "just a job." Today, 45 percent of women think of their work as career, up from 41 percent in 1985. About 57 percent of men regard their work as a career, a level that has remained constant in recent years.[53]

Women and Time

Married working women experience many time pressures. They often have two jobs: household responsibilities, including children, plus their jobs in the mar-

Figure 21.6   Mercedes-Benz Targets Professional Women

He may give you
diamonds
this holiday season.

You can give him
a star.

ENGINEERED LIKE NO OTHER
CAR IN THE WORLD

© 1991 Mercedes-Benz of N.A., Inc., Montvale, N.J.

ketplace. Studies show they have significantly less leisure time than either their husbands or full-time homemakers.[54] This would suggest that working wives would buy more time-saving appliances, use more convenience foods, spend less time shopping, and so forth. Figure 21.7 shows how Quaker Oatmeal is positioned toward working women who might be short on time but want to be good mothers. Actually, Weinberg and Winer[55] found that working and nonworking wives are similar in such behavior if income, life cycle, and other situational variables are held constant. Bellante and Foster[56] report that, although understanding employment effects is complex, working-wife families appear to spend more on food away from home, child care, and some services.

Today's retail facilities must be open longer hours because of working women and because they frequently work different shifts than their spouses. One study found that among mothers who work full time, 45 percent work different shifts than their spouse. Among part-time working women, 57.4 percent

Figure 21.7 Quaker Understands that Working Mothers May Not Have a Lot of Time

work different shifts than their husbands.[57] Split shifts may force retailers to be open longer hours. They may also increase use of "800" numbers for catalogs as well as time-flexible, interactive television and computer shopping networks. Carlisle, a direct marketer of upscale women's clothing, adapts to women's busy schedules and hectic lifestyles by showing all its products in the comfort of associates' homes. Clients can make appointments during their lunch hours, evening hours, or weekends to view and try on clothing in the comfort of a nice home. Figure 21.8 shows an ad for Carlisle clothing.

Role Overload

Role overload exists when the total demands on time and energy associated with the prescribed activities of multiple roles are too great to perform the roles

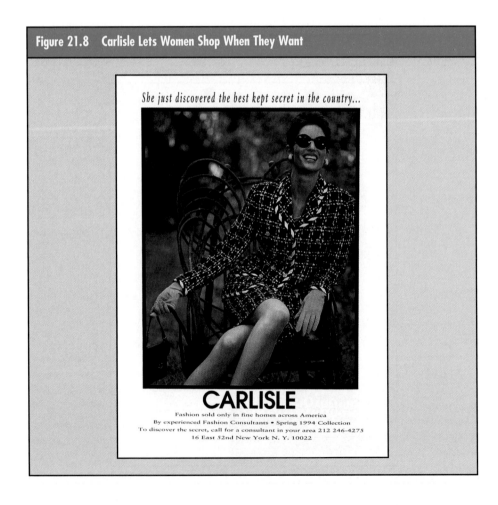

Figure 21.8   Carlisle Lets Women Shop When They Want

adequately or comfortably.[58] Sex-role ideology, especially found in feminism, and other forces are creating pressures toward more equality in work loads between men and women. Data from three main studies of families, classified by gender and employment, examined paid work versus family work and disclosed that employed women work more hours each day than husbands who are employed and wives who are not employed, resulting in role overload felt by many contemporary women.[59] This creates the notion of solving overload problems with products or services from marketing organizations.[60]

The 1990 Virginia Slims Opinion Poll found that the most tangible way for women to balance jobs and family is for men to take on more household work. Token help with the dishes or children no longer inspires women's gratitude. As women contribute more to the family income, they expect in return a more equal division of the household responsibilities.[61] There is evidence, especially among younger families, of a shift in attitudes toward work and housework that is causing a move toward more household equality between the sexes.[62]

Marketers must find ways of communicating with women who feel role overload. Recent Whirlpool ads recognize the increasing number of employed women and lives that are busier than ever in its "Whirlpool Makes Homes Run" campaign. Yet they avoid referring to employed women specifically. To do so might alienate nonemployed women. Whirlpool makes products of high quality, targeted especially to families with the income to purchase quality—a situation most likely to occur among families with employed women. The ads are positioned to this target market, both in copy and illustration as seen in Fig. 21.9.

Feminist Roles

Consumer researchers are interested in measuring the multiple roles of women, which may provide clues to the development of effective marketing programs. The extent to which women hold feminist attitudes and values, for example, may be related to consumer behavior.

A typical method used to divide women into feminist or traditionalist categories is the Smith and Self scale.[63] The scale consists of 21 items, such as the achievements of women in history, whether women or men tend to have more common sense, and a biological drive for sex. Using the Smith and Self scale with more specific behaviors than other studies, Koch[64] found that attitudes toward clothing and the way a woman dresses are significantly related to feminist orientation.

With such information, marketers can become sensitive to the topics that can be the same or must be different for different female segments. An ad appearing in a magazine appealing to feminists might show boys playing with dolls, but the same illustration would have little appeal in magazines whose readers were mostly traditionalists. Concerning fashion, however, about 90 percent of all types of women say, "I like to feel attractive." Ads with such appeal are likely to cut across almost all types of women.

Women's attitudes about men have changed in the past decades for a variety of reasons. After an era of accomplishments and growth, women feel more negative toward men today than they did in the 1970s as seen in Table 21.5. An early Jeep ad showed a race between a man and a woman to the top of the mountain. The woman won. Advertisers and marketers who understand attitudes of women or men can develop ads that appeal to specific issues of importance such as that of equality between men and women shown in the Toyota ad in Figure 21.10.

Women's Roles in Marketing

Advertising has often portrayed women in limited, stereotyped roles. Generally, women were shown as purchasers of low-unit-price items and as homemakers rather than career persons. Contemporary women are increasingly oriented toward self-realization, self-expression, and personal fulfillment. In Figures 21.10 and 21.11, you can see how two firms have translated these needs into ads. Asics plays on the phrase that indicates that the country would be better if it were run by women, and Bailey's implies that our supreme being might be a woman.

Women's roles in the purchase of major durable products are very important in contemporary society. Women may represent about half the automobile buy-

Table 21.5 Women's Attitudes toward Men		
Women have a more negative attitude toward men today than they did in 1970. Most women think men want to keep women down.		
(Percent of women holding selected attitudes toward men, 1990 and 1970)	1990	1970
Most men think only their own opinions about the world are important.	58%	50%
Most men find it necessary for their egos to keep women down.	55	49
Most men look at a woman and immediately think how it would be to go to bed with her.	54	41
Most men are interested in their work and life outside the home and don't pay much attention to things going at home.	53	39
Most men are basically kind, gentle, and thoughtful.	51	67
Most men are more interested in their own, rather than a woman's, sexual satisfaction.	50	40
Most men are basically selfish and self-centered.	42	32

Source: The 1990 Virginia Slims Opinion Poll, conducted by The Roper Organization, New York City, 1990.

Figure 21.9   A Play on Words to Appeal to Important Women's Issues

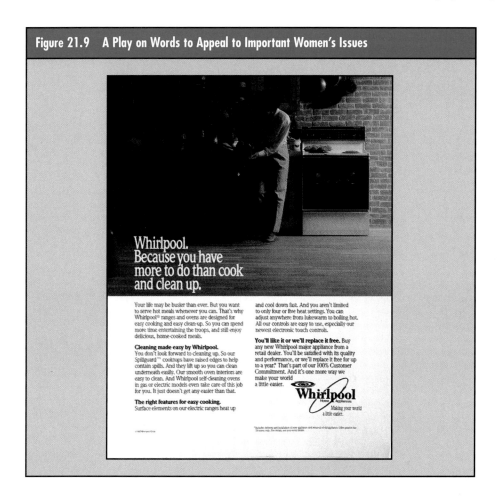

ers in this country, according to the Motor Vehicle Manufacturers Association. Marketers are responding to these roles by targeting women in their ads. Training programs, among others, are being conducted to help dealers better attract and service the female market. Training videotapes teach dealers how to attract and work with women customers, and individual dealers are sponsoring special events to bring women into their showrooms. Automakers are also offering mail-in credit applications in print ads to counteract discrimination women have felt in relation to financing.[65]

The *new traditionalist* is a term used by some advertisers to describe the career woman of the 1990s. *Good Housekeeping* used this concept to redesign its magazine. After examining Yankelovich Monitor studies, *Good Housekeeping* concluded that the American contemporary woman feels strongly about building a

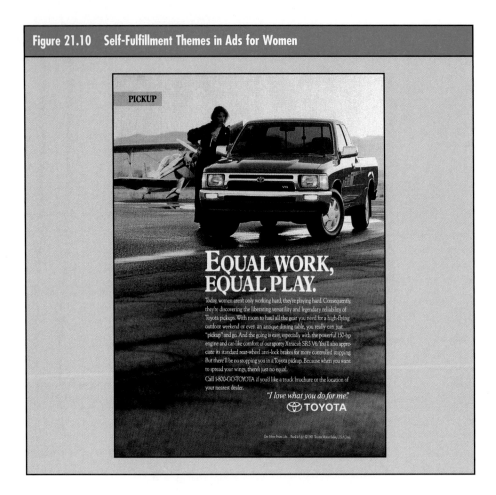

Figure 21.10   Self-Fulfillment Themes in Ads for Women

strong family and has a strong commitment to her husband, her home, and the values her mother had. These traditional values are synthesized with an emphasis on individuality and on tolerance for diverse ideas, lifestyles, and beliefs. Although many marketers have accepted this concept of the "new traditionalist," other observers and women's scholars see the repetition of "traditional values" as reviving former stereotypes of the dependent housewife. Feminist Betty Friedan warns that this new "feminine mystique" defines a woman once again in terms of her husband, family, and home. Other feminists see such efforts of marketers as antifreedom, antiliberty, and anti-self-actualizing.[66]

The reality facing marketers in the period between now and 2000 is that there is no mass market of women anymore, if there ever was. New options, economic realities, and changes in the family structure have torn stereotypes to bits. A review of how marketers are responding to new roles reveals six core groups of

Figure 21.11   Self-Fulfillment Themes in Ads for Women

women, even though there is great variation within each category. Consumer in Focus 21.5 describes these market segments and some of the ways marketers are reaching them.

Changing Masculine Roles

Roles of men in families are changing substantially. As men's share of family income decreases and as values shift in society, men are free to participate more fully in family functions and are taking on new roles in consuming and purchasing products.[67] In a survey of 1,000 American men by the advertising agency Cunningham & Walsh, more and more men could be observed as househusbands. The privately published survey disclosed that 47 percent of men vacuum the house, 80 percent take out the garbage, 41 percent wash dishes, 37 percent make beds, 33 percent load the washing machine, 27 percent clean the

| 21.5 | **Consumer in Focus** |

Reaching Six Female Market Segments

New Moms

Whether to work or stay at home is a raging debate among new mothers. Some 49 percent of mothers said preschool kids need their mothers' full-time care; another 49 percent said it didn't make any difference so long as the care they got was loving. Marketers need to approach the "nurturers,"or stay-at-home mothers, as women who will try new products and pay a premium price if the products show value in what they do for the baby. Working mothers are more realistic and respond best to appeals that help control their time. Instead of the picture-perfect mom whipping up a pitcher of Kool-Aid for kids, a new spot shows a group of parents hanging around a comfortably disheveled kitchen talking about life and Kool-Aid.

50-Plus

Older women want to be connected to their wisdom and abilities, not their limitations and disabilities, according to George Moschis at Georgia State University. Johnson & Johnson introduced Affinity shampoo with ads claiming, "the first shampoo created for hair over 40." The product failed because consumers did not want to be reminded that they had old hair. More successful approaches show attractive, silver-haired women riding with their husbands on motorcycles to a softball game. Models such as Cybill Shepherd, 40, appear in ads for L'Oreal and Linda Evans, 47, sells for Clairol.

By the year 2000, women will own at least half of 30 million businesses in the United States, up from 5 percent a few decades earlier. These businesses purchased over half of PBX equipment, copiers, telephones, fax machines, and personal computers. Female entrepreneurs have been overlooked in the past, but marketers are targeting them for a wide variety of business and personal goods and services, often in a variety of new magazines targeted to working women.

Continued

bathroom, 23 percent dust, 23 percent dry dishes, 21 percent sort laundry, 16 percent clean the refrigerator, and 14 percent clean the oven. More than 50 percent of men take part in regular shopping trips, suggesting that men are important targets for marketing activity for many types of household products.

Men not only participate in household and consumption activities but are increasing their rate of participation. Men now do one-fifth of the cooking, cleaning, and laundry, and married men now do more housework than unmarried men. Fathers are doing more than they once did, and mothers are doing less than previously (although still more than men).[68]

Consumer in Focus, Continued 21.5

Blue/Pink Collars

Working-class women are still the keepers of the family dinner, and they want products that are satisfying, convenient, and most important, fast. This women is 31 years old on average, has a young family, annual household earnings of about $34,000, a husband in the industrial labor force, and works outside the home to help pay the bills. Marketers often ignored this prime target by focusing on more affluent segments. These generally patriotic families began buying Toyotas because American cars weren't giving them what they wanted: a quality product at an affordable price. Shows like "Roseanne" and "The Simpsons" demonstrated the influence of this market segment and firms such as Sears, Roebuck & Co. and Kmart are working hard to regain this customer by stressing both quality and reasonable prices.

Teenagers

Today's teenagers are searching a little less for personal excellence and a little more for clean air. Marketers are forced to recognize their thirst for information. They're talking to them rather than at them. They are savvier shoppers with a new sense of materialism, believing that only "dumb" kids will spend $40 for a T-shirt at Benetton when they could buy it for $10 at The Gap. They are willing to pay more for "green" products at the Body Shop, a pricy British cosmetics company that promises none of its products have been tested on animals.

Homemakers

Once a homogeneous American segment, this group is diverse and demanding. Marketers are only beginning to recognize and contend with the unexpected diversity among this consumer group with some 43 million people who control billions in spending power. Advertising should replace the bonbon-eating, soap-opera-watching female stereotype with an intelligent and economically powerful woman at home. Although still rare, a more intellectual approach was used by Dakin toys. Instead of purely emotional and visual approaches, its ads included an intellectual discussion about what stimulates a child's imagination. Cathi Mooney, a principal at the ad agency that created the ads, said, "I don't think we would have done an ad like this 8 years ago, but there is now a growing respect for women who stay at home."

Source: Excerpts from "The Many Faces of Eve," Adweek's Marketing Week (June 25, 1990), 44–49.

Not all researchers accept the finding that the "new father" is widespread nor even beneficial.[69] Much literature, however, is focusing on new roles of men.[70] One of the primary contributors to this literature, Joseph Pleck,[71] concludes that while some of these images reflect hype, there is also much of substantive change:

A new image, summed up in the term "the new father," is clearly on the rise in print and broadcast media. This new father differs from older images of involved fatherhood in several key respects: he is present at the birth; he is involved with his children as infants, not just when they are older; he participates in the actual day-to-day work of child care, and not just play; he is involved with his daughters as much as his sons.

Men in the 1990s see themselves as being more sensitive. They are more like Kevin Costner than John Wayne, according to Roper poll studies for male-oriented magazines.[72] Men remain interested in romance, but they also express a high interest in fitness, health, helping raise the children, helping out with household chores, and finding a better balance between work and leisure. These new roles appear to be creating a male market that is more interested in products and brands and therefore more brand loyal than in earlier decades. Johnson's Baby Shampoo appeals to the "new father's" desire to take a more active role in caring for children in Figure 21.12. Some of the methods, as well as the controversies, of how to market to men are illustrated in Consumer in Focus 21.6.

Figure 21.12   Johnson's Baby Shampoo Ads Appeal to the New Father

As economic conditions and men's roles in the home change, men are having to redefine themselves. According to Kimmel, the organization man of the 1950s wanted a settled, stable, suburban existence, whereas in the 1970s he cared more about power than fitting in. "Today's organization man carries a briefcase in one hand and pushes a baby carriage with the other . . . and while he considers his career important, he doesn't want to sacrifice time with his family."[73] Businesses will have to adapt to the changes that men are facing, such as having to stay

---

Consumer in Focus **21.6**

How to Market to Men

The macho man is nearing extinction on the advertising landscape. Even after being "sensitized" to sexual stereotypes, Madison Avenue hasn't decided who should replace him. A peculiar set of fellows is showing up in commercials: from hypernurturing single dads to goofy, tongue-tied bachelors to menopausal men to artistic "animals."

Hulk Hogan, the huge and well-sculpted professional wrestler, was captured painting a sunset at the beach in a spot for Right Guard antiperspirant designed to reach a "rough-and-tumble audience" of men.

The infantile husband is portrayed in a commercial for Robitussin: He can't manage the house and kids for even one day while his wife is sick. In contrast, the rare, enlightened dad is used to appeal to female consumers' fantasies as much as to men themselves in Motrin ads. The ad features a man who, upon arriving home from the office, immediately gives his wife the pain reliever and then gives their child a bath. The ad is actually targeted to 24- to 44-year-old women, the primary purchasers of Motrin.

Marketers nevertheless cannot lose sight of the "man thing" — that guys respond to sports, sex, and grooming no matter how sensitive they strive to be. For Procter & Gamble's Old Spice, the "Mariner Man" cruises through port, whistling a familiar jingle and attracting stares from lovely lasses. As he escorts one away, he tosses an Old Spice bottle to an envious nerd.

Bugle Boy Industries targets 16- to 20-year-old men with ads featuring sexy women trying on men's Bugle Boy jeans. The message reads, "Attention all guys. First the bad news. Bugle Boy is demanding we show their new Color Denims in this commercial. Now the good news. Nobody said we had to put them on men." The same company targets men 25 or older with a spot that pokes fun at male bonding and makes the married, domestic guy look cool. Three golf buddies pity a fourth who "has to" stay home with his wife. Yet steamy shots of the couple frolicking seductively at home show they're having a fine time without the boys. The spot is a poke at Bugle Boy's archrival, Dockers from Levi Strauss, whose ads turned male bonding into a fashion occasion.

"During research men will spout all kinds of stuff," says Simon Silvester. When a woman leads an automobile focus group, men talk about wanting safety features and leg room, he says. But when a man leads the discussion, they say, "I just want something I can accelerate at traffic lights." He concludes: "A lot of men are going in for this New Man image, but deep down they're all the same."

Source: Excerpted from Laura Bird, "Madison Avenue Stalks Today's Archetypal Male," Wall Street Journal (March 5, 1992), B1–3.

home with a sick child. The compromises today's organization man is making are very similar to the ones made by working women, and Kimmel predicts that if companies do not address the needs of the 1990s family, they will lose some of their best and brightest female and male employees.

Childhood Socialization and Influence

Much of consumer behavior is learned as a child. Consumer socialization is the process by which young people acquire skills, knowledge, and attitudes relevant to becoming consumers in the marketplace.[74] Family communication about purchases and consumer behavior is the key in children's consumer socialization process. Socialization occurs similarly to the way the cultural transfusive triad passes values from one generation to the next through nuclear and extended family. Single consumers, more than others, tend to be loyal to the brands they learned to buy as children.

Co-shopping, or shopping done together by parent and child, is a direct influence on a person's consumer decisions. Studies by Grossbart, Carlson, and Walsh[75] indicate some of the influences that can be expected. Their studies indicate co-shoppers have more concern with children's development as consumers. They also place more value on children's input in family consumer decisions—even decisions on products not encountered on typical co-shopping trips such as automobiles, major appliances, life insurance, and vacations. Co-shoppers explain more to their children why they don't buy products and discuss the role of advertising, which to some extent may mediate the influence of advertising.

Different types of mothers communicate consumer skills and knowledge to their children in different ways. Carlson, Grossbart, and Stuenkel[76] found that mothers who are restrictive and warm in their relationships with their children tend to monitor and control children's consumption activities more, whereas mothers who respect and solicit children's opinions use messages that promote purchasing and consumption decision-making abilities.

Retailers can also benefit from understanding the role of children in buying. Some retailers may consider children as an interference with parents' shopping time. Retailers such as Ikea provide play areas for children while parents shop. A more proactive approach is found in Japanese department stores, which encourage children and parents, principally mothers, to interact with toys found in the store. This approach is shown in Figure 21.13 in which Japanese children are encouraged to become involved in creative arts and computers while mothers are in the stores, thus making the store a fun place for children to visit.

Many changes in family structure directly affect how marketers communicate to children and their families. For example, delayed marriage and higher education is increasing the number of families with only one child. The increasing

Figure 21.13　Involving Children in Shopping in a Japanese Department Store

number of "only child" consumers creates families with children who are accustomed to communicating with adults more than with siblings or peers. Their preferences may be much more "adult" than marketers traditionally expected. Effective communications must take into consideration the higher verbal and creative skills associated with only children. Understanding children's information processing skills may require analysis of their developmental process as well as the use of research methodologies such as observational techniques, play behavior and storytelling, and specialized questioning techniques.[77]

Families in which both parents are employed may have little time to spend with children. They may be willing to spend more money on consumer products for children (and certainly, they have more money available than single-earner families) to compensate for the lack of time to spend with their children. Studies based on Canadian data indicate that young children cause less participation in the labor force, change how families spend their money, and reduce the amount of time and money available for leisure.[78]

Research Methodology for Family Decision Studies

When you prepare an analysis of family influences on buying or the consumption decisions of families, most of the research techniques will be similar to other marketing research studies. There are a few unique aspects of family decisions that should be considered, however, in these final pages of the chapter.

Decision-Process Framework

Role-structure studies have often viewed purchasing as an act rather than a process and have based findings on questions such as "Who usually makes the decision to purchase?" or "Who influences the decision?" Yet, the role and influence of family members vary by stage in the decision process. An example of process methodology is provided by Wilkes[79] who found the following types of questions useful for measuring family influence:

1. Who was responsible for initial need recognition?
2. Who was responsible for acquiring information about the purchase alternatives?
3. Who made the final decision as to which alternative should be purchased?
4. Who made the actual purchase of the product?

Better results using this methodology were obtained than with more global measures. Husbands and wives are more likely to hold similar perceptions about their relative influence for a given phase than when questioning fails to ask about decision stages.

Role-Structure Categories

The relevant role-structure categories in a research project depend on the specific product or service under consideration, but in many product categories, only the husband or wife is involved. In other categories, it is useful to measure the amount of influence in different roles. Spiro[80] found that influence strategies or persuasion depend on several variables, especially stage in the life cycle and lifestyles. Children are involved in many types of purchase situations, but the nature of their influence has often been ignored.

Interviewer Bias

The sex of the interviewer or observer may influence the roles husbands and wives say they play in a purchase situation. To overcome this bias, either self-administered questionnaires should be used or the sex of the observer should be randomly assigned to respondents.

Respondent Selection

In measuring family buying, it is necessary to decide which member(s) of the nuclear family should be asked about the influence of family members. Results often vary considerably depending on which family members are interviewed. Most often wives are the ones interviewed, but the percentage of couples whose responses agree is often so low as to make interviewing only one member unacceptable.

Granbois and Summers[81] found husbands' responses concerning purchase intentions to be better than those of their wives as predictors of total planned cost and number of items planned from joint responses, although wives predicted better for certain products such as appliances, home furnishings, and entertainment equipment plans. The researchers concluded that joint responses are more likely to uncover more plans of the family. Multiple roles in the influence and purchase process are illustrated in a study of vacation decisions by Filiatrault and Ritchie,[82] in which they found substantial differences in influence of each parent and of the children on different stages of decisions. This study also shows that differences exist in the perceptions that people have about their influence on others in the family.

Demise of the Family?

Since former Vice President Quayle commented on the famous "Murphy Brown" episode when she decides to become a single mother, the phrase *family values* has taken a position in the minds of mainstream Americans. We have all asked ourselves how the family can survive in the next decades without strong family values. After reading about all the changes in family and household structure, you may have concluded that the family is finished, but don't conclude that. It is true that dramatic changes are taking place in family life in many industrialized countries. Urie Bronfenbrenner,[83] one of the most influential analysts of family patterns, concludes that the underlying dynamics and ultimate effects of family change are occurring in many countries and are strikingly similar around the globe.

The demise of the family is not imminent, at least in the foreseeable future. A Roper poll of U.S. consumers indicates that being a good spouse and parent is the most common measure of success for many people, even more important than being true to oneself, to God, or to wealth. Table 21.6 shows the top 12 family values as identified and ranked in a recent study released by the Massachusetts Mutual American Family Values Study.

Table 21.6 The 12 Commandments	
Most Americans agree that being happily married is an important family value. But more and more Americans never achieve this goal.	
(Percent of adults by the things they define as important family values, for values that captured at least 50 percent of responses, 1989)	
Family Values	**Percent**
Respecting your parents	70
Providing emotional support for your family	69
Respecting people for who they are	68
Being responsible for your actions	68
Communicating your feelings to your family	65
Respecting your children	65
Having a happy marriage	64
Having faith in God	59
Respecting authority	57
Living up to your potential	54
Being married to the same person for life	54
Leaving the world in better shape	51

Source: Massachusetts Mutual American Family Values Study, quoted in Norval D. Glenn, "What Does Family Mean?" American Demographics (June 1992), p. 36.

Summary

Families or households are CUs of critical importance in the study of consumer behavior for two reasons. First, families or households are the unit of usage and purchase for many consumer products. Second, the family is a major influence on the attitudes and behavior of individuals. As consumers, we are the creation of our families to a large extent.

A family is a group of two or more persons related by blood, marriage, or adoption who reside together. A household differs from a family by describing all the persons, both related and unrelated, who occupy a housing unit. Thus, households outnumber families and are smaller in size; the average income is higher for families than households.

Family (or household) members occupy various roles, which include initiator (gatekeeper), influencer, decider, buyer, and user. The influence of spouses, children, or other family members varies depending on the resources of family members, the type of product, the stage in the life cycle, and the stage in the buying decision. These variables are more important in understanding family decisions than traditional roles ascribed to one gender or the other.

The FLC describes how families change over time. Traditional approaches of analyzing FLC have been updated with a consumer market matrix of lifestages that emphasizes the relative income of a family in each stage. This matrix is built upon six stages: younger singles, younger couples, younger parents, midlife families, midlife households, and older households.

Families and households are changing in their structure and composition. Among more important recent changes are increases in the number of single households, smaller average family size, later marriages, divorce, remarriage and redivorce, cohabiting singles, and the existence of the gay market. The increasing number of employed women has created role overload for employed women who work more hours (combining paid work and family work) each week than their husbands or nonemployed women.

Marketers are concerned with the roles performed by women, men, and children. Advertising to women increasingly reflects themes of increasing income and responsibility and drives for self-fulfillment and self-enhancement. Masculine roles increasingly reflect shared performance of household activities. Children learn much of their consumption and buying behavior from parents and exert considerable influence on family purchases.

Marketing research techniques useful in studying families and households give special consideration to the decision-process framework, questioning techniques, role-structure categories and relative influence, interviewer bias, and respondent selection. A methodological problem is created because husbands and wives often differ in their responses to questions about how their families buy consumer goods and services.

Review and Discussion Questions

1. What is meant by the term *family?* What is the importance of studying families to the understanding of consumer behavior?

2. Some studies of consumer behavior maintain that the family rather than the individual should be the unit of analysis in consumer behavior. What

are the advantages and disadvantages of using the family as the unit of analysis?

3. Do husbands or wives have the most influence on buying decisions? Outline your answer.

4. How might an advertisement be designed that would appeal to the differences in instrumental and expressive roles within families?

5. Will there be more or fewer women employed outside the home in the future? What variables should be considered in answering this question? How does the answer affect demand for consumer products?

6. Analyze the statement, "Working women buy products and services essentially the same as nonworking women."

7. What is meant by the "singles" market? How would a food company appeal to the singles market?

8. Assume that an airline has asked for a research project to understand how families make vacation decisions. You are asked to prepare a research design for the project. What would you suggest?

9. Assume that you are the marketing manager for a clothing firm that wishes to attract the gay market. How would you assess the size of this market? Outline the marketing program you would recommend.

10. Children do not have much purchasing power. Yet, they are believed to be important in the understanding of consumer behavior. Why? What might firms do to be more profitable as a result of understanding the role of children in family buying?

Endnotes

1. For a discussion of these issues on a global perspective, see Nico Keilman, Anton Kuitsten, and Ad Vossen, eds., *Modeling Household Formation and Dissolution* (New York: Oxford University Press, 1988).

2. David H. Olson et al., *Families: What Makes Them Work?* (Beverly Hills, Calif.: Sage Publications, 1983).

3. Hamilton I. McCubbin and Marilyn A. McCubbin, "Typologies of Resilient Families: Emerging Roles of Social Class and Ethnicity," *Family Relations* 37 (July 1988), 247–254.

4. Russell Belk, "A Child's Christmas in America: Santa Claus as Deity, Consumption as Religion," *Journal of American Culture* 10 (Spring 1987), 87–100; David Cheal, *The Gift Economy* (London: Routledge, 1988); Elizabeth Hirschman and Priscilla LaBarbera, "The Meaning of Christmas," in Elizabeth Hirschman, ed., *Interpretative Consumer Research* (Provo, Utah: Association for Consumer Research), 136–147.

5. Russell Belk and Gregory Coon, "Gift Giving as Agapic Love: An Alternative to the Exchange Paradigm Based on Dating Experiences," *Journal of Consumer Research* 20 (December 1993), 393–417.

6. Terry Childers and Akshay Rao, "The Influence of Familial and Peer-based Reference Groups on Consumer Decisions," *Journal of Consumer Research* 19 (September 1992), 198–221.

7. Harry L. Davis, "Decision Making within the Household," *Journal of Consumer Research* 2 (March 1976), 241–260.

8. Robert Boutilier, "Pulling the Family's Strings," *American Demographics* (August 1993), 44–48.

9. Harry L. Davis and Benny P. Rigaux, "Perception of Marital Roles in Decision Processes," *Journal of Consumer Research* 1 (June 1974), 5–14.

10. Mandy Putnam and William R. Davidson, *Family Purchasing Behavior: II Family Roles by Product Category* (Columbus, Ohio: Management Horizons, Inc., a Division of Price Waterhouse, 1987).

11. Marilyn Lavin, "Husband-Dominant, Wife-Dominant, Joint: A Shopping Typology for Baby Boom Couples?" *Journal of Consumer Marketing* 10 (1993), 33–42.

12. William J. Qualls, "Changing Sex Roles: Its Impact upon Family Decision Making," in Andrew Mitchell, ed., *Advances in Consumer Research* 9 (Ann Arbor: Association for Consumer Research, 1982), 267–270.

13. Joseph Bellizzi and Laura Milner, "Gender Positioning of a Traditionally Male-Dominated Product," *Journal of Advertising Research* 31 (June–July 1991), 72–79.

14. For research on this topic from a wide variety of disciplines, see Beth B. Hess and Myra Marx Ferree, *Analyzing Gender* (Newbury Park, Calif.: Sage Publications, 1987).

15. Roger Jenkins, "Contributions of Theory to the Study of Family Decision-Making," in Jerry Olson, ed., *Advances in Consumer Research* 7 (Ann Arbor, Mich.: Association for Consumer Research, 1980), 207–211.

16. Alvin Burns and Donald Granbois, "Advancing the Study of Family Purchase Decision Making," in Olson, *Advances in Consumer Research*, 221–226.

17. Sunil Gupta, Michael R. Hagerty, and John G. Myers, "New Directions in Family Decision Making Research," in Alice M. Tybout, ed., *Advances in Consumer Research* 10 (Ann Arbor, Mich.: Association for Consumer Research, 1983), 445–450.

18. Mary Lou Roberts, "Gender Differences and Household Decision-Making: Needed Conceptual and Methodological Developments," in Thomas C. Kinnear, ed., *Advances in Consumer Research* 11 (Provo, Utah: Association for Consumer Research, 1984), 276–278.

19. Eileen Fischer and Stephen J. Arnold, "More than a Labor of Love: Gender Roles and Christmas Gift Shopping," *Journal of Consumer Research* 17 (December 1990), 333–343.

20. William D. Wells and George Gubar, "The Life Cycle Concept," *Journal of Marketing Research* 2 (November 1966), 355–363.

21. Fred D. Reynolds and William D. Wells, *Consumer Behavior* (New York: McGraw-Hill, 1977).

22. Patrick E. Murphy and William Staples, "A Modernized Family Life Cycle," *Journal of Consumer Research* 6 (June 1979), 12–22.

23. Janet Wagner and Sherman Hanna, "The Effectiveness of Family Life Cycle Variables in Consumer Expenditure Research," *Journal of Consumer Research* 10 (December 1983), 281–291.

24. Mandy Putnam, Sharyn Brooks, and William R. Davidson, *The Expanded Management Horizons Consumer Market Matrix* (Columbus, Ohio: Management Horizons, a Division of Price Waterhouse, 1986).

25. Bureau of the Census, *Current Population Reports, Money Income of Households, Families, and Persons in the United States: 1991,* Series P-60, No. 180, 1992.

26. For a thorough analysis of the financial and other decision-making capabilities of these families, see Frank Furstenbert and Graham B. Spanier, *Recycling the Family* (Beverly Hills, Calif.: Sage Publications, 1984).

27. "The Life of a Marriage," *American Demographics* 11 (February 1989), 12.

28. Kathryn A. London and Barbara Foley Wilson, "Divorce," *American Demographics* 10 (October 1988), 23–26.

29. Marilyn Ihinger-Tallman and Kay Pasley, *Remarriage* (Newbury Park, Calif.: Sage Publications, 1987), 70.

30. Graham B. Spanier, "Living Together in the Eighties," *American Demographics* 4 (November 1982), 17–31.

31. Alan A. Otten, "People Patterns," *Wall Street Journal* (June 14, 1988), 33.

32. "The Future of Households," *American Demographics* (December 1993), 39.

33. Martha Farnsworth Riche, "The Postmarital Society," *American Demographics* 10 (November 1988), 23–26ff.

34. "The Future of Households," 38.

35. "Living Alone and Loving It," *U.S. News and World Report* (August 3, 1987).

36. W. Wayne Delozier and C. William Roe, "Marketing to the Homosexual (Gay) Market," in Robert L. King, ed., *Marketing: Toward the Twenty-First Century* (Richmond, Va.: Southern Marketing Association, 1991), 107–109.

37. Bradley Johnson, "The Gay Quandary," *Advertising Age* (January 18, 1993), 29–30.

38. Felicity Barringer, "Sex Survey of American Men Finds 1% Are Gay," *New York Times* (April 15, 1993), section A, column 1, 1.

39. "Gay Community Looks for Strength in Numbers," *American Marketplace* (July 4, 1991), 134.

40. Richard V. Weekes, "Gay Dollars," *American Demographics* 10 (October 1989), 45ff.

41. Cyndee Miller, "Gays Are Affluent but Often Overlooked Market," *Marketing News* 24 (December 24, 1990), 2.

42. David Wilson, "Role Theory and Buying–Selling Negotiations: A Critical Review," in Richard Bagozzi, ed., *Marketing in the 1980s* (Chicago: American Marketing Association, 1980), 118–121.

43. Salah Hassan and Roger Blackwell, *Global Marketing Perspectives and Cases* (Fort Worth: Dryden Press, 1994), 122.

44. Elizabeth Waldman, "Labor Force Statistics from a Family Perspective," *Monthly Labor Review* (December 1983), 16–20.

45. Bureau of National Affairs, *Work and Family: A Changing Dynamic* (Washington, D.C.: Bureau of National Affairs, 1986).

46. Rose M. Rubin, Bobye J. Riney, and David J. Molina, "Expenditure Pattern Differentials between One-Earner and Dual-Earner Households: 1972–1973 and 1984," *Journal of Consumer Research* 17 (June 1990), 43–52.

47. Eva Jacobs, Stephanie Shipp, and Gregory Brown, "Families of Working Wives Spending More on Services and Nondurables," *Monthly Labor Review* 112 (February 1989), 15–23.

48. Pamela L. Kiecker, Shelby D. Hunt, and Lawrence B. Chonko, "Gender, Income Differences, and Marketing: Examining the 'Earnings Gap' in Three Areas of Marketing," *Journal of the Academy of Marketing Science* 19 (Spring 1991), 77–82.

49. Mary M. Brabeck and Karen Weisgerber, "College Students' Perceptions of Men and Women Choosing Teaching and Management: The Effects of Gender and Sex Role Egalitarianism," *Sex Roles* 21 (1989), 841–857.

50. Suzanne M. Bianchi, "Wives Who Earn More than Their Husbands," *American Demographics* 6 (July 1984), 18–23.

51. Rena Bartos, *The Moving Target: What Every Marketer Should Know about Women* (New York: Free Press, 1982).

52. Charles Schaninger, Margaret Nelson, and William Danko, "An Empirical Evaluation of the Bartos Model of Wife's Work Involvement," *Journal of Advertising Research* 33 (May–June 1993), 49–63.

53. Bickley Townsend and Kathleen O'Neil, "American Women Get Mad," *American Demographics* 12 (August 1990), 26–32.

54. Marianne Ferber and Bonnie Birnbaum, "One Job or Two Jobs: The Implications for Young Wives," *Journal of Consumer Research* 8 (December 1980), 263–271.

55. Charles B. Weinberg and Russell S. Winer, "Working Wives and Major Family Expenditures: Replication and Extension," *Journal of Consumer Research* 7 (September 1983), 259–263.

56. Done Bellante and Ann C. Foster, "Working Wives and Expenditure on Services," *Journal of Consumer Research* 11 (September 1984), 700–707.

57. Alan Otten, "People Patterns," *Wall Street Journal* (June 14, 1988), 33.

58. Patricia Voydanoff, *Work and Family Life* (Newbury Park, Calif.: Sage Publications, 1987), 83.

59. Joseph Pleck, *Working Wives/Working Husbands* (Beverly Hills, Calif.: Sage Publications, 1985), 30.

60. Alvin C. Burns and Ellen Foxman, "Role Load and Its Consequences on Individual Consumer Behavior," in Terence A. Shimp et al., eds., *1986 AMA Educators' Proceedings* (Chicago: American Marketing Association, 1986), 18.

61. Townsend and O'Neil, "American Women Get Mad."

62. F. Thomas Juster, "A Note on Recent Changes in Time Use," In F. Thomas Juster and Frank P. Stafford, eds., *Time, Goods, and Well-Being* (Ann Arbor, Mich.: Institute for Social Research, 1985), 313–332.

63. M. D. Smith and G. D. Self, "Feminists and Traditionalists: An Attitudinal Comparison," *Sex Roles* 7 (1981), 182–188.

64. Kathryn E. Koch, "Dress-Related Attitudes of Employed Women Differing in Feminist Orientation and Work Status: Emphasis on Career Apparel" (unpublished Ph.D. dissertation, The Ohio State University, Columbus, 1985).

65. Frieda Curtindale, "Marketing Cars to Women," *American Demographics* 10 (November 1988), 29–31.

66. Connie Koenenn, "New Women's Ad Causes Stir," from the *Los Angeles Times,* in the *Columbus Dispatch* (January 15, 1989), 5F.

67. Linda Jacobsen and Brad Edmondson, "Father Figures," *American Demographics* (August 1993), 22–27.

68. John P. Robinson, "Who's Doing the Housework," *American Demographics* 10 (December 1988), 24–28ff.

69. Charlie Lewis and Margaret O'Brien, eds., *Reassessing Fatherhood* (Newbury Park, Calif.: Sage Publications, 1987).

70. Michael S. Kimmel, ed., *Changing Men: New Directions in Research on Men and Masculinity* (Newbury Park, Calif.: Sage Publications, 1987).

71. Joseph H. Pleck, "American Fathering in Historical Perspective," in Kimmel, *Changing Men,* 93.

72. Laurie Freeman, "America's Man Has Gone Domestic," *Advertising Age* (April 15, 1991), S4.

73. Michael Kimmel, "What Do Men Want?" *Harvard Business Review* (November– December 1993), 50–63.

74. Scott Ward, "Consumer Socialization," in Harold Kassarjian and Thomas Robertson, eds., *Perspectives in Consumer Behavior* (Glenville, Ill.: Scott Foresman).

75. Sanford Grossbart, Les Carlson, and Ann Walsh, "Consumer Socialization and Frequency of Shopping with Children," *Journal of the Academy of Marketing Science* 19 (Summer 1991), 155–163.

76. Les Carlson, Sanford Grossbart, and J. Kathleen Stuenkel, "The Role of Parental Socialization Types on Differential Family Communication Patterns Regarding Consumption," *Journal of Consumer Psychology.*

77. James Garbarino et al., *What Children Can Tell Us* (San Francisco: Jossey-Bass Publishers, 1990).

78. Robin A. Douthitt and Joanne M. Fedyk, "Family Composition, Parental Time and Market Goods: Life Cycle Trade-Offs," *Journal of Consumer Affairs* 24 (Summer 1990), 110–133.

79. Robert E. Wilkes, "Husband–Wife Influence in Purchase Decisions: A Confirmation and Extension," *Journal of Marketing Research* 12 (May 1975), 224–227.

80. Rosann L. Spiro, "Persuasion in Family Decision-Making," *Journal of Consumer Research* 9 (March 1983), 393–401.

81. Donald H. Granbois and John O. Summers, "Primary and Secondary Validity of Consumer Purchase Probabilities," *Journal of Consumer Research* 1 (March 1975), 31–38.

82. Pierre Filiatrault and J. R. Brent Ritchie, "Joint Purchasing Decisions: A Comparison of Influence Structure in Family and Couple Decision-Making Units," *Journal of Consumer Research* 6 (September 1980), 131–140.

83. Urie Bronfenbrenner, "What Do Families Do?" *Family Affairs* 4 (Winter–Spring 1991), 1–6.

CHAPTER 22

Situational Influences

▲▲▲▲▲▲▲▲▲▲▲▲▲▲▲▲▲▲▲▲▲▲▲▲▲▲▲▲▲▲▲▲▲▲▲▲▲

Smells That Sell

It's beginning to smell a lot like . . . money. Next time you go holiday shopping, keep your sniffer open. At a growing number of stores, retailers are counting on specially designed scents to entice you to spend.

"It's not that common yet, but I think it will be used in a very wide way. By the year 2000, this will be as common as Muzak or neon lights are today," said researcher Alan Hirsch of the Smell and Taste Treatment and Research Foundation Ltd. in Chicago.

Experiments have shown that scents affect how people shop. In Philadelphia, jewelry store customers lingered longer at perfumed counters. In Chicago, people were more likely to buy and to pay more for sneakers when the room was scented. In Las Vegas, gamblers at a scented bank of slot machines spent 33 percent to 53 percent more.

Studies using college students as subjects show smells affect brain wave frequencies, even at levels so low the students were not aware of the scents, Hirsch said. Even smells that can be detected might affect shoppers without them noticing, said Susan Knasko of the Monell Chemical Sense Center in Philadelphia. "It's often something that people don't pay much attention to. It's just like when you come out of a store humming a song and you don't know where you heard it," Knasko said. However, Louise Kosta of the Human Ecology Action League in Atlanta thinks otherwise: "I think it's insulting. If people know about it, I think people will be pretty miffed at what is a blatant attempt to pick their pocket."

Source: Excerpted in part from "Retailers Try Selling 'Inscentives,'" The State (December 7, 1992), 3A.

Our opening examples provide a rather compelling demonstration of how situational influences within the purchase environment can shape consumer behavior. This chapter focuses on the role of situational influences as a determinant of consumer behavior and therefore marketing strategy. Indeed, situations exert some of the most pervasive influences on consumer behavior for one simple reason—behavior always occurs within some situational context. This is not to say that behavior is always shaped by situational influences. Die-hard Budweiser drinkers, for instance, might always buy a Bud regardless of whether they are out partying with friends or sitting home alone watching TV. In many, if not most, cases, however, situational factors will exert important influences.

Before proceeding any further, let us define what we mean by the term **situational influence**. Because consumer situations also involve people and objects (such as a product or advertisement), it is necessary to distinguish between influences due to consumers and objects from those that are unique to the situation itself. Accordingly, situational influence can be viewed as the influence arising from factors that are particular to a specific time and place that are independent of consumer and object characteristics.[1]

What are these situational factors or characteristics? Belk[2] has suggested that consumer situations may be defined along the lines of five general characteristics, which are summarized in Table 22.1. Although you probably can remember how each of these factors has, at one time or another, affected your own behavior as a consumer, additional examples of their influence can be found throughout the chapter.

Types of Consumer Situations

The examples described in the chapter opening centered around a very important type of consumer situation—namely, the purchase situation. Consumer situations can, in fact, be separated into three main types: communication, purchase, and usage situations.[3] Each of these is discussed in the following sections.

Communication Situations

Communication situations can be defined as those settings in which the consumer is exposed to either personal or nonpersonal communications. Personal communications would encompass conversations consumers might have with others, such as salespeople or fellow consumers. Nonpersonal communications would involve a broad spectrum of stimuli, such as advertising and consumer-oriented programs and publications (for example, *Consumer Reports*).

To illustrate the potential impact of the communication situation, let us consider how it might determine the effectiveness of television advertising. We fo-

Table 22.1   **Characteristics of Consumer Situations**
1. *Physical surroundings:* the tangible properties comprising the consumer situation. These features include geographical location, decor, sounds, aromas, lighting, weather, and visible configurations of merchandise or other material surrounding the stimulus object.
2. *Social surroundings:* the presence or absence of other people in the situation.
3. *Time:* the temporal properties of the situation such as the particular moment when behavior occurs (e.g., time of day, weekday, month, season). Time may also be measured relative to some past or future event for the situational participant (e.g., time since last purchase, time until payday).
4. *Task:* the particular goals or objectives consumers have in a situation. For instance, a person shopping for a wedding gift for a friend is in a different situation than when shopping for one's own personal use.
5. *Antecedent states:* the temporary moods (e.g., anxiety, pleasantness, excitement) or conditions (e.g., cash on hand, fatigue) that the consumer brings to the situation. Antecedent states are distinguished from those momentary states that occur in response to a situation as well as from more enduring individual traits (e.g., personality).
Source: Russell W. Belk, "Situational Variables and Consumer Behavior," Journal of Consumer Research 2 (December 1975), 157–164.

cus on this particular form of communication for two reasons. First, expenditures on TV advertising often receive a significant share of the promotion budget. Moreover, TV ads have often been used in empirical investigations of the influences arising from the communication setting.

In the context of television advertising, several situational characteristics are likely to surface as potential determinants of an ad's effectiveness. The presence of others during message exposure may easily undermine the likelihood that the ad will receive much, if any, attention. Viewers often use commercial breaks as a time to interact with others in the immediate audience. Similarly, factors such as an ad's position within a commercial "string" (that is, a series of consecutive ads) or program might also be important. Reductions in audience size have been found to be greater for commercials in the middle of a string versus ads at the beginning or end.[4]

The sheer number of ads that are processed during television viewing can have an adverse impact on a given ad's effectiveness.[5] Given the trend toward shorter commercials (the industry standard has been shifting from 30 seconds to 15 seconds), which permits broadcasting more messages in a given time period, marketers have become increasingly concerned about the potential effects of **advertising clutter**.[6] Clutter refers to the problem of simply too many ads in the viewing environment. This increase in the number of ads can interfere with the consumer's ability to process and remember advertising messages.[7]

Situational influences may also arise from the particular program in which an ad appears. Sometimes a program may be so involving that consumers become preoccupied with the program (such as avid football fans watching the Super Bowl), thus making them rather oblivious to anything that appears during the commercial breaks.[8] Programs can also alter how consumers feel, and these feelings may affect how they respond to advertising contained within the program. In one investigation, viewers' mood states while watching commercials were affected by the surrounding program. Happy programs induced happier moods during commercial exposure compared with sad programs. This more favorable mood state led subjects to have more positive thoughts while processing the ads, as well as better recall of the commercial information.[9] Note, however, that some ads may be more sensitive to their surrounding program than others.[10]

In print advertising, the reputation, credibility, and content of the magazine or newspaper carrying the ad may influence the ad's effectiveness. Such is the message carried by the ad for the *Wall Street Journal* appearing in Figure 22.1, which extols the virtues of the publication as an advertising vehicle. For outdoor advertising, billboards must be designed to accommodate the fact that exposure will be quite brief in most instances. This communication situation is quite different from, say, being exposed to ads while seated in a theater. In the latter

Figure 22.1   This Ad Emphasizes the Importance of the Communication Situation in Print Advertising

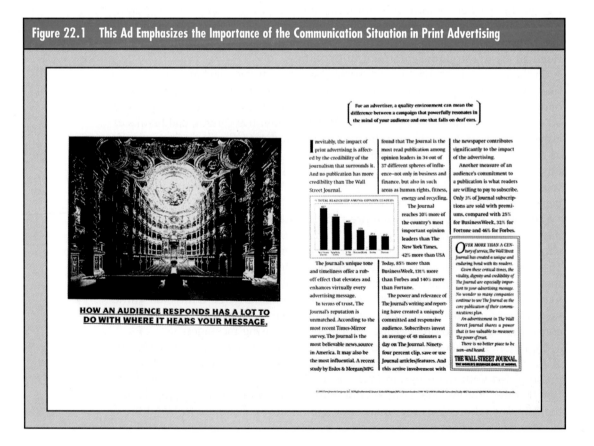

setting, consumers have far less stimuli competing for their attention, thereby diminishing the need for including attention-getting elements within the advertisement such as those described earlier in Chapter 14.

Companies are very aware of the potential influences that the communication situation may exert on the effectiveness of their advertising. Coca-Cola, for instance, avoids advertising during TV news programs because "there's going to be some bad news in there and Coke is an upbeat, fun product."[11] Similar concerns led to Chrysler's withdrawal of its advertising from ABC's miniseries "Amerika," which portrayed the life of an American family living in the United States after it had been peacefully taken over by the Soviet Union. Although Chrysler had initially purchased about $7 million of air time, it decided that "the subject matter and its portrayal are so intense and emotional that our upbeat product commercials would be both inappropriate and of diminished effectiveness in that environment."[12] Read Consumer in Focus 22.1 for more information on how companies try to deal with these concerns.

Consumer in Focus 22.1

How Companies Try to Avoid Unfriendly Communication Situations

Because an ad's effectiveness may be diminished in certain viewing environments, advertisers often try to minimize the potential damage through informal agreements. Magazine publishers have an unspoken agreement with tobacco companies to pull cigarette ads from issues that include a report on lung cancer. Newspaper and TV stations routinely pull airline ads after a plane crash. In addition, dozens of companies have started their own publications in recent years to ensure ad-friendly editorial content.

Recently, Mercedes-Benz of North America attempted to go one step further by formalizing the policy rather than trusting a magazine's judgment and then threatened punishment for non-compliance. Mercedes, through its New York ad agency, mailed letters to about 30 magazines insisting its ads be pulled from issues that carried any negative stories about the company — or, incredibly, about Germany itself. If magazines failed to comply with the tough policy, Mercedes said it would refuse to pay for the ad or seek a free make-good ad.

Although Mercedes said about half of the publications contacted returned signed copies of the letter to indicate agreement, several major magazines apparently refused to sign. Worse yet, a barrage of negative newspaper stories hit the automaker and questioned whether the company was trying to control the editorial content of the magazines in which its ads appear. Facing a public relations nightmare and criticism that it was trying to censor the U.S. media, the German automaker rescinded the policy on placing ads that had caused the uproar. One leading magazine editor said, "They made a big mistake in putting this in writing. They should have just done what the Japanese companies did and what the cigarette companies do, and they would have been all right."

Source: Adapted from Scott Donaton, "Mercedes in Full Retreat on Ad Placement Order," Advertising Age (September 20, 1993), 2.

Purchase Situations

Purchase situations refer to those settings in which consumers acquire products and services. Situational influences are very prevalent during purchasing. As a simple example, consider the tremendous change in consumers' price sensitivity across purchase situations. A grocer would find it extremely difficult to charge the prices that consumers pay for soda and snacks at a movie theater or ballpark.

In examining how the purchase situation can affect consumer behavior, we first consider those influences arising from the information environment followed by a discussion of situational influences stemming from the retail environment in which purchase occurs.

The Information Environment

Information environment refers to the entire array of product-related data available to the consumer.[13] Some of the main characteristics of this environment include the availability of information, the amount of information load, and the modes in which information is presented and organized.

Information Availability

Information may be either externally available in the marketplace or internally available within the consumer's memory. Of course, available information may not be utilized during decision making, such as when consumers do not exert the effort during external search necessary to acquire certain pieces of information. Similarly, as we noted in the Chapter 15 discussion of forgetting, not all of the information available in memory need be accessible at a particular point in time.

Research suggests that consumers' choices may depend on the extent to which product information is externally present during decision making versus being available only in memory (such as the consumer at Sears trying to decide whether to buy the microwave in front of him or her or the one he or she examined yesterday at a competitive store). In one study, subjects were more likely to select the "best" brand when information about the brand was externally available than when they had to rely on their ability to recall this information, which had been presented previously but removed at the time of choice.[14]

Note that the issue of information availability is particularly relevant to those concerned with providing an information environment that allows consumers the opportunity to make reasoned and informed choices. In this regard, researchers have considered the potential value of providing consumers with information such as the energy consumption costs of appliances,[15] a product's life-cycle cost (purchase price plus operating costs),[16] unit price information,[17] and nutritional information.[18]

Information Load

The information load of a choice environment is determined by the number of choice alternatives and the number of attributes per alternative. Increases in the number of choice alternatives can alter the type of decision rule (see Chapter 6) consumers use during decision making.[19] Some have also argued that, beyond a certain level, information load may exceed consumers' ability to process accurately the information (that is, they become "overloaded") and, consequently, reduce their accuracy during decision making (see Chapter 9).[20]

Information Format

Information format, representing the manner in which information is organized, can also influence the behavior of consumers.[21] Consumers' use of unit price information, for example, may depend on how it is organized or presented in the retail environment. Consumers have shown greater use of unit price information when presented in the form of a list, which ranks the relative cost of competing brands on a single piece of paper, than when the unit price of each brand was posted on separate tags.[22] Format can also influence the order in which information is acquired or processed and the amount of time taken to reach a decision .[23]

Information Form

Even information form can play an important role. For some attributes (gas mileage, nutritional properties), product information can be presented either numerically (30 miles per gallon) or semantically (excellent, good, average, and so on). Numerical product ratings enable consumers to estimate more easily differences among products. Consequently, consumers are more inclined to compare brands on an attribute-by-attribute basis when brand information is presented in numerical rather than semantic form.[24]

The Retail Environment

The physical properties of the retail environment, often referred to as **store atmospherics**, are of particular interest to companies for two fundamental reasons. First, unlike situational influences that are beyond the marketer's control, marketers have the ability to create the retail environment. Second, this influence is brought to bear on consumers at just the right place—inside the store. Consumer in Focus 22.2 provides testimony to the importance of the retail environment.

From the marketer's perspective, a store's atmospherics can have several desirable effects on consumers.[25] First, it can help shape both the direction and duration of consumers' attention, thereby enhancing the odds of purchase for

22.2	**Consumer in Focus**

Store Atmospherics and Retail Stores

Retailers are finding that spiffing up their stores not only makes them look boffo, but pays off in increased sales. Ann Erickson, marketing director at Retail Planning Associates, said a new look can boost a store's sales anywhere from 10% to 300%.

Such was the case for the Sears store in Mexico City. Sears was ready to close down the place, but when it talked to customers it found they didn't want the store to move. They were just disappointed with the look and feel of the store. Working with Retail Planning Associates, Sears ended up gutting the store and putting in new colors, lighting, and signage. Consumers liked what they saw. Overall sales soared 175%, and in certain key departments, they jumped a whopping 300%.

Source: Excerpted from Cyndee Miller, "Glitzy Interiors Transform Stores into 'Destinations,' Boost Sales," Marketing News 27 (August 30, 1993), 1, 6.

products that otherwise might go unnoticed. Second, the retail environment can express various aspects about the store to consumers, such as its intended audience and positioning (for example, the clothing store wishing to attract upscale customers with a fashion image). Finally, the store setting can also elicit particular emotional reactions, such as pleasure and arousal, from consumers. These feelings can influence the amount of time and money consumers spend while shopping.[26]

The retail environment is composed of a variety of elements, including store layout, aisle space, placement and form of displays, colors, lighting, presence and volume of in-store music, smells, and temperature. Although much of the research documenting the influence of these factors is of a proprietary nature, published studies have gradually accumulated in this area.

Music

Some of the more interesting demonstrations of situational influence have used music.[27] In an early study, the volume of music played by supermarkets was varied from loud to soft. Consumers exposed to the loud music took less time shopping but spent the same amount of money relative to those exposed to the soft music.[28] The effect of music tempo (slow versus fast) has also been examined in a supermarket setting. Slow-tempo music increased both shopping time and expenditures compared with fast-tempo music.[29] Similar effects caused by tempo have also been observed in a restaurant setting. Patrons spent nearly 25 percent more time and nearly 50 percent more on bar purchases when the tempo was slow rather than fast.[30] To learn about how music can affect consumer behavior within a department store, read Consumer in Focus 22.3.

Consumer in Focus **22.3**

When the Music Plays, the Customer Pays

The next time you hear music in the air while shopping, there is a good chance that it was provided by Muzak. Muzak specializes in providing retailers the "right kind" of music for their customers. Retailers can choose among different types of music such as adult contemporary, light classical, Top 40, and New Age.

What is the "right kind" of music? The kind that sells. To demonstrate this payoff, Muzak conducted a test at a major department store. The company varied the presence and type of music played throughout the day. Shoppers, interviewed as they left the store, reported how long they were in the store and the number of purchases they made.

The effect of the music depended on whether it matched the shopper's demographic characteristics. When they matched, consumers shopped an average of 18 percent longer. Longer shopping time could mean more buying. In this case, it did. The number of purchases rose by 17 percent.

Source: Cyndee Miller, "The Right Song in the Air Can Boost Retail Sales," Marketing News 25 (February 4, 1991), 2.

Layout and In-Store Location

Store layout and product location can be used to enhance the likelihood of consumers coming into contact with products. A supermarket might design a layout that encourages a traffic flow that guides shoppers into particular areas. Similarly, the bakery department might be located close to the entrance and/or cash registers so that the aromas of fresh-baked items will entice shoppers. Department stores will place product displays in high-traffic areas, such as at the end of an escalator. Vendors are extremely sensitive to a product's location because they recognize the incremental sales that can result from shelf position. And convenience stores strategically place impulse items near the check-out in the hope that consumers will succumb to the buying urge.

Colors

The colors within the store are sources of potential influence on both consumers' perceptions and behavior. Warm colors, such as red and yellow, appear more effective in physically attracting people, relative to the cooler colors of green and blue. In one study in which subjects were allowed to determine how close they sat to a colored wall, the distance was much shorter for warm than cool colors. Nonetheless, subjects rated retail interiors using cool colors as more positive, attractive, and relaxing than those using warmer colors. The researchers concluded that warm colors were most suitable for a store's exterior color or display windows as a means of drawing customers into the store.[31] Additional support of color's behavioral impact comes from the finding that the shade of brown used in coloring walls altered the speed at which people moved through a museum.[32]

Point-of-Purchase Materials

Point-of-purchase (POP) materials can serve as very powerful stimuli. Displays and signs can enhance the odds of capturing the consumer's attention, and thereby stimulate purchasing. Consistent with this, POP materials have been shown to increase sales.[33] It is likely that marketers will place greater emphasis on POP materials given that they are relatively inexpensive compared with other forms of promotion. Also, informative and easy-to-use POP materials can partly help offset declines in the quantity and quality of retail salespeople.[34] One example is the POP unit called Y.E.S. (which stands for "Your Extra Salesman"). This unit, which hangs on the shelf where the product is located, works like a window shade. Product information is printed on a self-retracting shade that rolls down from the canister unit.[35]

Salespeople

Although our discussion of the retail environment thus far has focused on non-personal stimuli, it is important to recognize the role of salespeople. The potential to influence consumers during shopping can be strongly affected by the retailer's front line staff. Indeed, a store's image and ability to build loyalty can heavily depend on the availability and characteristics (such as the attentiveness, expertise, friendliness, and appearance) of salespeople.

Crowding

Another aspect of the retail setting that may affect shopping behavior is the perceived level of crowding caused by the density of shoppers within the store. High levels of crowding can lead to reductions in shopping time, postponement of unnecessary purchases, and less interaction with sales personnel.[36]

Influence of Time

As noted in Table 22.1 (page 795), time represents an important aspect of situational influence. This is particularly true for purchase situations. The demand for many products is highly time sensitive. The Christmas season is vitally important for many products, especially toys. Consumers' purchase of soft drinks, which peak during the summer, slow down considerably during the winter months (with the exception of the temporary spurts brought on by holidays such as Christmas and New Year). Moreover, products may be positioned differently depending on the time of year. As reflected by the promotional piece

Figure 22.2   Time-Dependent Product Positioning: An Example of Off-Season Selling

appearing in Figure 22.2, Sanka attempted to overcome the sales lag typically experienced during warmer months by promoting a different way of consuming coffee.

The amount of time available for decision making can also be an important situational influence. A consumer whose refrigerator has broken down beyond repair will typically experience greater pressure to make a speedy decision than consumers shopping to replace an old but still working refrigerator.

Time pressure can affect consumer decision making in a couple of ways. First, it may lead consumers to rely on existing knowledge and experience in making their decisions, rather than collecting additional information. Even if time pressures are not so great as to preclude some use of external information during decision making, they can still lead consumers to adopt simpler product evaluation strategies, such as relying on fewer attributes in comparing alternatives.[37]

Time pressure has been found to reduce both the purchasing of products that consumers had initially planned to buy before time pressure manifested itself and the frequency of unplanned purchases (products that are acquired even though they are not on the shopping list).[38]

Time relative to prior events can also affect purchase behavior. A classic example is the effect of food deprivation on grocery shopping. The food expenditures of many consumers grow larger as the time since their last meal increases.[39] For this reason, home economists often recommend food shopping on a full stomach to decrease the impulse buying hunger often motivates.

Finally, evidence suggests that advertising effectiveness can be affected by the particular time of day when consumers encounter an advertisement.[40] Shoppers at a suburban mall were shown a segment of a television news program containing six new 30-second TV commercials. Sessions were conducted in either the morning, afternoon, or early evening. When ad retention was measured immediately after the program, learning was best for the morning sessions and worst in the evening sessions. However, just the opposite pattern was observed when learning was not tested until nearly 2 hours had elapsed since viewing the commercials.

Usage Situations

The remaining type of consumer situations considered here are **usage situations**, which refer to those settings in which consumption occurs. In many instances, purchase and usage situations are virtually the same, such as when consumers eat their meals at a fast-food restaurant. But product consumption often occurs in settings that are quite removed, both physically and temporally, from the setting in which the product is acquired.

Even when purchase and usage situations are distinct, the latter can still have a powerful influence as consumers take into account the "intended" usage situation during decision making.[41] Consider consumers purchasing rice, who might choose a brand based on whether they were planning to serve the rice as a stand-alone side dish, as an ingredient in recipes, or both.

The social surroundings that characterize a usage situation can have an important influence on consumer behavior.[42] In today's increasingly anti-smoking environment, the presence of nonsmokers will often serve as an impediment to smokers' "lighting up." Beer sales are particularly sensitive to whether consumption occurs in public versus private settings. Between 80 and 90 percent of import beer sales are "on premise" (for example, in bars and restaurants) where others can see the type of beer one consumes. In contrast, 70 percent of domestic brands' sales are generated by in-home consumption.[43]

The time at which usage occurs may also affect consumer behavior. For example, food consumption depends very heavily on the time of day. We rarely eat spaghetti for breakfast or cereal for dinner. Figure 22.3 shows how college students' preferences for various fruits depended on the time of day and context in

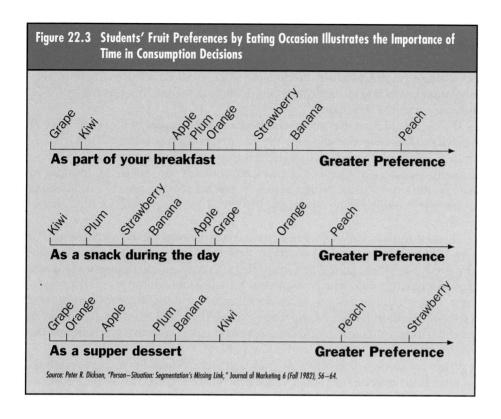

Figure 22.3 Students' Fruit Preferences by Eating Occasion Illustrates the Importance of Time in Consumption Decisions

Source: Peter R. Dickson, "Person–Situation: Segmentation's Missing Link," Journal of Marketing 6 (Fall 1982), 56–64.

which consumption occurred. Peaches were the most preferred fruit for breakfast or a daytime snack but were replaced by strawberries for a supper dessert.

To understand why behavior is affected by usage situations, it is useful to examine how the importance consumers attach to product attributes and their beliefs about a product's performance may change across various settings. Consider, for instance, Miller and Ginter's[44] findings that patronage of a particular fast-food restaurant often depended on the usage situation. Although McDonald's had a market share of nearly 40 percent for leisurely evening meals with the family, its share of weekday lunches was less than 30 percent. This fluctuation in share was driven by two factors. First, consumers gave McDonald's its lowest convenience ratings when it was to be used for a weekday lunch. Second, convenience was viewed as more important in this situation.

Usage Situations and Marketing Strategy

Marketing strategy and tactics are affected by usage situations in several ways. First, it may often be vital that market segmentation schemes reflect the variety of usage situations. The apparel market, for instance, can be segmented in terms of the situation in which clothing is to be worn (for example, formal dinners, work, sports, casual). Targeting each of these segments will obviously necessitate changes in the product offering. Another more detailed example of segmentation based on the usage situation involving suntan lotion is presented in the next section of the chapter.

The usage situation may often assume an important part in the positioning of a product. The advertising campaign that promotes the theme "The night belongs to Michelob" represents an attempt to position this beer as the one to use in nighttime social settings. Wet Ones, a premoistened towelette, introduced itself to the marketplace with a series of ads showing a variety of situations (at the beach, in the car, on a camping trip) in which the product would come in handy.

The discovery or development of new usage settings can be a vital source of new sales and often represents an important strategic option for revitalizing mature products.[45] Perhaps the best example of a company doing this is Arm and Hammer baking soda, which has successfully broadened its appeal by promoting a variety of uses, ranging from dental care to a deodorizer for carpets and refrigerators. Refrigerator manufacturers have benefited from an expansion of potential usage situations by producing very small models that easily fit into the office.

When consumers narrowly perceive a product as limited to a single usage situation, efforts may be warranted to alter such perceptions. The ad for Pop-Tarts appearing in Figure 22.4 tells consumers that the product is "not just for breakfast." This same basic theme was reflected in an advertising campaign developed for orange juice producers that claimed "It isn't just for breakfast anymore." Similarly, as shown in Figure 22.5, Swiss Miss uses its product packaging to convey the variety of settings in which consumption may occur. Not all such efforts will be successful, as reported in Consumer in Focus 22.4.

Sometimes opportunities arise for one product because of changes in usage situations for another product. Wrigley's gum, for example, has capitalized on recent restrictions on smoking in certain situations by promoting itself as something smokers can consume when they can't light up (see Figure 22.6, page 810).

Person–Situation Interactions

Thus far, our discussion has implicitly assumed that all consumers respond in the same manner to a particular situation. Yet, this may not be the case. Although consumers may be highly influenced by situational variations, others may often prove to be rather insensitive.

Figure 22.4 Pop-Tarts Wants More Than Just Breakfast Consumption of Its Product

As an illustration of person–situation interactions, let us return to the previously discussed finding that consumers' grocery purchases escalated as the time since their last meal increased.[46] Whereas this effect was observed for average-weight consumers, it did not occur for overweight consumers. Thus, the situational influence of time since their last meal depended on the type of consumer.[47]

The notion that consumers are not homogeneous in their response to situational factors has important implications for market segmentation. Because different consumers may seek different product benefits, which can change across different usage situations, Dickson[48] has argued that marketers may often need to use person–situation segmentation. An example of this form of segmentation in the context of suntan lotions appears in Figure 22.7 (page 811). The columns represent different types of people who are consumers of

Figure 22.5 Swiss Miss Uses Its Packaging to Illustrate Different Usage Situations

suntan lotion. The rows identify various settings in which the product may be used. The benefits desired by a particular group or sought within a given usage situation are listed at the bottom of the column and at the end of the row. These are the benefits that the product should deliver in courting a specific person–

Consumer in Focus **22.4**

Pepsi's Courting of the Morning Market

What did you have to drink with breakfast this morning? Chances are it was not a soft drink. Coffee dominates the morning market with a 47 percent share of morning beverages sold. Soft drinks register a meager 4 percent share. During most other times of the day, however, soft drinks typically outsell most other beverages.

Soft drink manufacturers are fully aware of this untapped potential. Less obvious is the most effective strategy for enhancing consumption within this particular usage situation. Should the positioning of current offerings be expanded to incorporate morning consumption? Or would a new offering positioned specifically for morning use be more effective?

Pepsi has sought answers to these questions by test marketing a new brand extension called Pepsi A.M., which contains a higher-caffeine, low-carbonation flavor formula. The accompanying ad campaign centered around the theme: "The taste that beats coffee cold." In another test market, a similar ad campaign was launched that encouraged morning consumption of the regular Pepsi brand. A year later, Pepsi A.M. terminated the test market. Sluggish sales were attributed to the new formulation having a flat taste. According to a Pepsi spokeswoman, the test showed that "we don't need to introduce a reformulated [product] to encourage morning consumption." The company does intend to continue promoting morning consumption of their regular Pepsi brand.

Sources: Michael J. McCarthy, "Test Shows that Pepsi's Rival to Coffee So Far Isn't Most People's Cup of Tea," Wall Street Journal (March 30, 1990), B1–B2; "PepsiCo Discontinues Test of Higher-Caffeine A.M.," Wall Street Journal (October 15, 1990), B7.

situation segment. Also, some person–situation segments seek unique benefits (female skiers wanting a scented winter lotion) that are listed within that cell of the matrix. A suntan lotion manufacturer interested in targeting dark-skinned adult women who use the product while snow skiing, for instance, should include ingredients that will provide special protection from the light rays and weather, an antifreeze formula, and a winter perfume scent that appeals to women.

Unexpected Situational Influences

Marketers sometimes ask target consumers their purchase intentions to forecast future demand for products. Although purchase intentions can, under the right conditions, be predictive of future behavior (see Chapter 11), one main threat to their predictive power is the disruption caused by unexpected situational

Figure 22.6   Changes in the Usage Situations for One Product Can Lead to New Opportunities for Another Product

influences.[49] For example, a consumer may fully anticipate buying a particular brand of potato chips during the next visit to the grocer. Yet, this purchase intention may not be fulfilled if the product is out of stock or if another brand of similar quality is on sale. Conversely, a consumer may lack any interest in buying a product when surveyed at a particular point in time. Nonetheless, purchase may occur subsequently because of some unanticipated event (the noncoffee drinker who buys coffee for her visiting, coffee-drinking parents).

The important point here is simply that one must recognize the potential for unexpected situational influences to undermine the accuracy of forecasts based on purchase intentions. Although it is often hoped that such effects will tend to be counterbalancing (that is, the number of customers lost because of unexpected situational influences will be offset by the number gained due to unanticipated situational influences), this may not be the case.

Figure 22.7   Person–Situation Segmentation Matrix for Suntan Lotion

Situations	Young Children		Teenagers		Adult Women		Adult Men		Situation Benefits/Features
	Skin								
	Fair	Dark	Fair	Dark	Fair	Dark	Fair	Dark	
Beach/boat sunbathing	Combined insect repellant				Summer perfume				a. Windburn protection b. Formula and container can stand heat c. Container floats and is distinctive (not easily lost)
Home-poolside sunbathing					Combined moisturizer				a. Large pump dispenser b. Won't stain wood, concrete, or furnishings
Sunlamp bathing					Combined moisturizer and massage oil				a. Designed specifically for type of lamp b. Artificial tanning ingredient
Snow skiing					Winter perfume				a. Special protection from special light rays and weather b. Antifreeze formula
Person Benefits/Features	Special protection a. Protection critical b. Non-poisonous		Special protection a. Fit in jean pocket b. Used by opinion leaders		Special protection Female perfume		Special protection Male perfume		

Source: Peter R. Dickson, "Person–Situation: Segmentation's Missing Link," *Journal of Marketing 6 (Fall 1982), 56–64.*

Summary

This chapter has focused on the influences that may arise from situational properties. The physical and social surroundings, time, task, and antecedent states are the main characteristics that comprise a given consumer situation.

In consumer behavior, it is useful to consider the potential impact of environmental factors in three main areas: communication, purchase, and usage situations. The effectiveness of marketing messages may often depend on the communication setting. The impact of a TV ad, for example, may in part be determined by the program in which it appears.

The purchase situation can have a strong influence on consumer behavior. Properties of the information environment, such as the availability, amount, format, and form of information, can affect decision making. Similarly, features of the retail environment, including music, layout, colors, POP materials, and crowding, will influence shopping and purchase behaviors.

The situation in which product consumption occurs can exert a major influence on consumer behavior. Consumers may often alter their purchasing patterns depending on the usage situation. What is an acceptable brand of beer in one setting may be unacceptable in another. An understanding of the usage situation can be invaluable for segmenting markets and developing appropriate product positionings.

Review and Discussion Questions

1. What are the five basic characteristics of a consumer situation?

2. What are the three main types of consumer situations?

3. A recent test of advertising effectiveness has revealed that your television advertising was more effective when shown during program A than program B. How could you explain this finding?

4. A grocery chain has recently developed a set of private-label brands. These brands are comparable in product quality with their competition but offer the consumer a substantial price savings. How might this grocer structure the information environment to best convey this price differential to consumers?

5. What is meant by "store atmospherics"? Why is it important to marketers?

6. Many consumers will switch from one brand of rice to another depending on the usage situation. What explanations can you offer as to why this switching may occur?

7. Describe how the concept of the usage situation could be useful to a snack food manufacturer.

8. A manufacturer has discovered a new usage situation that offers considerable market potential. One strategy for tapping this potential is to broaden the positioning of the company's current products (for example, by showing consumption of their existing brands in the new situation). An alternative strategy is to develop a new brand positioned specifically for the new usage situation. Which strategy would you recommend? Why?

9. Returning to Figure 22.7, suppose a suntan lotion manufacturer was interested in targeting fair-skinned teenagers who use the product while sunlamp bathing. What benefits and features should the product deliver in courting this segment?

Endnotes

1. Russell W. Belk, "An Exploratory Assessment of Situational Effects in Buyer Behavior," *Journal of Marketing Research* 11 (May 1974), 156–163.

2. Russell W. Belk, "Situational Variables and Consumer Behavior," *Journal of Consumer Research* 2 (December 1975), 157–164.

3. Flemming Hansen, *Consumer Choice Behavior: A Cognitive Theory* (New York: Free Press, 1972), 53.

4. Burke Marketing Research Inc., "Viewer Attitudes toward Commercial Clutter on Television and Media Buying Implications" (paper presented at the 18th Advertising Research Foundation Conference, New York, 1972).

5. Peter H. Webb, "Consumer Initial Processing in a Difficult Media Environment," *Journal of Consumer Research* 6 (December 1979), 225–236.

6. See, for example, "Emotional Impact Can Cut Clutter of 15-Second Spots," *Marketing News* 20 (December 5, 1986), 13; Michael L. Ray and Peter H. Webb, "Three Prescriptions for Clutter," *Journal of Advertising Research* 26 (February–March 1986), 69–77.

7. Interestingly, adverse effects due to clutter may not always occur. See Tom J. Brown and Michael L. Rothschild, "Reassessing the Impact of Television Clutter," *Journal of Consumer Research* 20 (June 1993), 138–146.

8. Gary F. Soldow and Victor Principe, "Response to Commercials as a Function of Program Context," *Journal of Advertising Research* 21 (April 1981), 59–65. Also see Punam Anand and Brian Sternthal, "The Effects of Program Involvement and Ease of Counterarguing on Advertising Effectiveness," *Journal of Consumer Psychology* 1 (1992), 225–238; Kenneth R. Lord and Robert E. Burnkrant, "Television Program Elaboration Effects on Commercial Processing," in Michael J. Houston, ed., *Advances in Consumer Research* 15 (Provo, Utah: Association for Consumer Research, 1988), 213–218; C. Whan Park and Gordon W. McClung, "The Effect of TV Program Involvement on Involvement with Commercials," in Richard J. Lutz, ed., *Advances in Consumer Research* 13 (Provo, Utah: Association for Consumer Research, 1986), 544–548.

9. Marvin E. Goldberg and Gerald J. Gorn, "Happy and Sad TV Programs: How They Affect Reactions to Commercials," *Journal of Consumer Research* 14 (December 1987), 387–403. Also see John P. Murry, Jr., John L. Lastovicka, and Surendra N. Singh, "Feeling and Liking Responses to Television Programs: An Examination of Two Explanations for Media-Context Effects," *Journal of Consumer Research* 18 (March 1992), 441–451. For an arousal explanation of programming effects, see Surendra N. Singh and Gilbert A. Churchill, Jr., "Arousal and Advertising Effectiveness," *Journal of Advertising* 16 (1987), 4–10.

10. Robert E. Burnkrant, H. Rao Unnava, and Kenneth R. Lord, "The Effects of Programming Induced Mood States on Memory for Commercial Information,"

(Working Paper Series, The Ohio State University, Columbus, Ohio, October 1987).

11. "GF, Coke Tell Why They Shun TV News," *Advertising Age* (January 28, 1980), 39.

12. Peter J. Boyer, "Chrysler Pulls Ads from 'Amerika,'" *New York Times* (January 28, 1987), C26.

13. James R. Bettman, "Issues in Designing Consumer Information Environments," *Journal of Consumer Research* 2 (December 1975), 169–177.

14. Gabriel Biehal and Dipankar Chakravarti, "Information Accessibility as a Moderator of Consumer Choice," *Journal of Consumer Research* 10 (June 1983), 1–14.

15. Dennis L. McNeill and William L. Wilkie, "Public Policy and Consumer Information: Impact of the New Energy Labels," *Journal of Consumer Research* 6 (June 1979), 1–11.

16. R. Bruce Hutton and William L. Wilkie, "Life Cycle Cost: A New Form of Consumer Information," *Journal of Consumer Research* 6 (March 1980), 349–360.

17. J. Edward Russo, "The Value of Unit Price Information," *Journal of Marketing Research* 14 (May 1977), 193–201; J. Edward Russo, Gene Krieser, and Sally Miyashita, "An Effective Display of Unit Price Information," *Journal of Marketing* 39 (April 1975), 11–19.

18. Bettman, "Issues in Designing Consumer Information Environments"; J. Edward Russo, Richard Staelin, Catherine A. Nolan, Gary J. Russell, and Barbara L. Metcalf, "Nutrition Information in the Supermarket," *Journal of Consumer Research* 13 (June 1986), 48–70. Also see Christine Moorman, "The Effects of Stimulus and Consumer Characteristics on the Utilization of Nutrition Information," *Journal of Consumer Research* 17 (December 1990), 362–374.

19. Denis A. Lussier and Richard W. Olshavsky, "Task Complexity and Contingent Processing in Brand Choice," *Journal of Consumer Research* 6 (September 1979), 154–165.

20. Jacob Jacoby, Donald Speller, and Carol Kohn, "Brand Choice as a Function of Information Load," *Journal of Marketing Research* 11 (February 1974), 63–69. See Chapter 9 for additional citations on this subject.

21. Display format, representing the manner in which products are displayed, can affect consumer behavior. See Itamar Simonson and Russell S. Winer, "The Influence of Purchase Quantity and Display Format on Consumer Preference for Variety," *Journal of Consumer Research* 19 (June 1992), 133–138.

22. J. Edward Russo, "The Value of Unit Price Information," *Journal of Marketing Research* 14 (May 1977), 193–201; J. Edward Russo, Gene Krieser, and Sally Miyashita, "An Effective Display of Unit Price Information," *Journal of Marketing* 39 (April 1975), 11–19. See also Valarie A. Zeithaml, "Consumer Response to In-Store Price Information Environments," *Journal of Consumer Research* 8 (March 1982), 357–369.

23. James R. Bettman and Pradeep Kakkar, "Effects of Information Presentation Format on Consumer Information Acquisition Strategies," *Journal of Consumer*

Research 3 (March 1977), 233–240; James R. Bettman and Michael A Zins, "Information Format and Choice Task Effects in Decision Making," *Journal of Consumer Research* 6 (September 1979), 141–153. See also Scott Painton and James W. Gentry, "Another Look at the Impact of Information Presentation Format," *Journal of Consumer Research* 12 (September 1985), 240–244.

24. J. Edward Russo and Barbara Dosher, "Strategies for Multiattribute Binary Choice," *Journal of Experimental Psychology: Learning, Memory, and Cognition* 9 (1983), 676–696.

25. Philip Kotler, "Atmospherics as a Marketing Tool," *Journal of Retailing* 49 (Winter 1973–1974), 48–65.

26. Robert J. Donovan and John R. Rossiter, "Store Atmosphere: An Environmental Psychology Approach," *Journal of Retailing* 58 (Spring 1982), 34–57; Elaine Sherman and Ruth Belk Smith, "Mood States of Shoppers and Store Image: Promising Interactions and Possible Behavioral Effects," in Melanie Wallendorf and Paul Anderson, eds., *Advances in Consumer Research* 14 (Provo, Utah: Association for Consumer Research, 1987), 251–254.

27. For a review and analysis of music's usefulness to marketers, see Gordon C. Bruner II, "Music, Mood, and Marketing," *Journal of Marketing* 54 (October 1990), 94–104.

28. Patricia Cane Smith and Ross Curnow, "Arousal Hypotheses and the Effects of Music on Purchasing Behavior," *Journal of Applied Psychology* 50 (June 1966), 255–256.

29. Ronald E. Milliman, "Using Background Music to Affect the Behavior of Supermarket Shoppers," *Journal of Marketing* 46 (Summer 1982), 86–91.

30. Ronald E. Milliman, "The Influence of Background Music on the Behavior of Restaurant Patrons," *Journal of Consumer Research* 13 (September 1986), 286–289.

31. Joseph A. Bellizzi, Ayn E. Crowley, and Rondla W. Hasty, "The Effects of Color in Store Design," *Journal of Retailing* 59 (Spring 1983), 21–45.

32. Rajendra K. Scrivastava and Thomas S. Peel, *Human Movement as a Function of Color Stimulation* (Topeka: Environmental Research Foundation, 1968).

33. V. Kumar and Robert P. Leone, "Measuring the Effect of Retail Store Promotions on Brand and Store Substitution," *Journal of Marketing Research* 25 (May 1988), 178–185; Gary F. McKinnon, J. Patrick Kelly, and E. Doyle Robison, "Sales Effects of Point-of-Purchase In-Store Signing," *Journal of Retailing* 57 (Summer 1981), 49–63; Arch G. Woodside and Gerald L. Waddle, "Sales Effects of In-Store Advertising," *Journal of Advertising Research* 15 (June 1975), 29–33.

34. John A. Quelch and Kristina Cannon-Bonventre, "Better Marketing at the Point of Purchase," *Harvard Business Review* 61 (November–December 1983), 162–169.

35. Howard Schlossberg, "P-O-P Display Designer Wants to Keep Shoppers Shopping Longer," *Marketing News* 25 (November 11, 1991), 15.

36. Gilbert D. Harrell, Michael D. Hutt, and James C. Anderson, "Path Analysis of Buyer Behavior under Conditions of Crowding," *Journal of Marketing Research* 17 (February 1980), 45–51. See also Michael K. Hui and John E. G. Bateson, "Perceived Control and the Effects of Crowding and Consumer Choice on the Service Experience," *Journal of Consumer Research* 18 (September 1991), 174–184.

37. Peter L. Wright and Barton Weitz, "Time Horizon Effects on Product Evaluation Strategies," *Journal of Marketing Research* 14 (November 1977), 429–443.

38. C. Whan Park, Easwar S. Iyer, and Daniel C. Smith, "The Effects of Situational Factors on In-Store Grocery Shopping Behavior: The Role of Store Environment and Time Available for Shopping," *Journal of Consumer Research* 15 (March 1989), 422–433.

39. R. E. Nisbett and D. E. Kanouse, "Obesity, Food Deprivation, and Supermarket Shopping Behavior," *Journal of Personality and Social Psychology* 12 (August 1969), 289–294.

40. Jacob Hornik, "Diurnal Variation in Consumer Response," *Journal of Consumer Research* 14 (March 1988), 588–591.

41. John L. Stanton and P. Greg Bonner, "An Investigation of the Differential Impact of Purchase Situation on Levels of Consumer Choice Behavior," in Jerry C. Olson, ed., *Advances in Consumer Research* 7 (Ann Arbor, Mich.: Association for Consumer Research, 1980), 639–643.

42. For an interesting demonstration of how social situations may affect the relationships between consumer ethnicity and food choices, see Douglas M. Stayman and Rohit Deshpande, "Situational Ethnicity and Consumer Behavior," *Journal of Consumer Research* 16 (December 1989), 361–371.

43. Kevin T. Higgins, "Beer Importers Upbeat about Future, Despite Warning Signs," *Marketing News* (October 25, 1985), 1ff.

44. Kenneth E. Miller and James L. Ginter, "An Investigation of Situational Variation in Brand Choice Behavior and Attitude," *Journal of Marketing Research* 16 (February 1979), 111–123.

45. Jagdish Sheth and Glenn Morrison, "Winning Again in the Marketplace: Nine Strategies for Revitalizing Mature Products," *Journal of Consumer Marketing* 1 (1984), 17–28.

46. Nisbett and Kanouse, "Obesity, Food Deprivation, and Supermarket Shopping Behavior."

47. The manner in which situational influences vary across consumers and products has been examined in several studies. A review of this literature can be found in Belk, "Situational Variables and Consumer Behavior." See also Girish N. Punj and David W. Stewart, "An Interaction Framework of Consumer Decision Making," *Journal of Consumer Research* 10 (September 1983), 181–196.

48. Peter R. Dickson, "Person–Situation: Segmentation's Missing Link," *Journal of Marketing* 6 (Fall 1982), 56–64.

49. For an empirical demonstration of how unexpected situations affect the intention–behavior relationship, see Joseph A. Cote, James McCullough, and Michael Reilly, "Effects of Unexpected Situations on Behavior–Intention Differences: A Garbology Analysis," *Journal of Consumer Research* 12 (September 1985), 188–194.

Retailing

Diffusion of
Innovations

Consumerism
and Ethical
Responsibility

PART VI

Marketing Strategies and Ethical Responsibility

▲▲

This section highlights two areas in which consumer research has had unique and powerful impacts—**retailing** (Chapter 23) and **diffusion of innovations** (Chapter 24). You will quickly grasp the impact of this research on marketing strategy worldwide.

No study of consumer behavior would be complete, however, without careful reflection from the broader perspective of ethics and consumer rights. Therefore, Chapter 25 focuses on **consumerism** and **ethical responsibility**. It reviews the basic consumer rights that must be guaranteed and affirmed by any economic system and its agencies that take consumer interests seriously.

This final chapter has many implications. We challenge you to think seriously about your own code of ethics and moral values. The choices you make can have far-reaching implications

CHAPTER 23

Retailing

▲▲▲▲▲▲▲▲▲▲▲▲▲▲▲▲▲▲▲▲▲▲▲▲▲▲▲▲▲▲▲▲▲▲▲▲▲▲▲

Retailers Coming Out of Dream World

Harris Gordon, a partner in the retail and distribution group of Deloitte & Touche, gave the following response to the question, "How would you describe the present state of retailing?"

The 1970s and 1980s were a "field of dreams" for retailing. The industry went from eight square feet per capita in the early 1970s to more than 18 square feet at the end of the 1980s. But while the store space was more than doubling, retail sales dropped from about $190 per square foot to $160. Over-building, a flat population growth rate, and decreasing disposable income all contributed to this. Shoppers' trips to the mall have fallen from 12 hours per month to four, and they're only visiting about half the stores they used to—3.5 stores per trip as opposed to seven.

How will these pressures affect retailing? The answer comes down to three concepts that will dominate the industry this decade: They are building a market intelligence culture, developing a rapid response organization, and creating a low-cost infrastructure.

Source: "The Changing Face of Retail," The Retailer (Winter 1994), 6–15.

Retailing: Ultimate Test of Consumer Research

The retailing environment is changing fast, as the opening scenario indicates and earlier chapters of this book have documented. You remember, we hope, that in Chapters 6 and 7, we examined the conceptual foundations of the purchase process—the final stage of decision making and decisions that occur in stores and in some of the new non-store retailing formats. This chapter "brings it home" with an applied analysis of retailing adaptation to consumer behavior in a changing environment. Here we examine the question of how consumers make decisions about retailers and retailing, and how this affects marketing strategy. Both are core components of a "market intelligence culture."

Retailing is called the ultimate test of consumer research because the material you learned in previous chapters will be wasted unless it meets the ultimate test: Will retailers stock, price, service, and sell effectively a manufacturer's product? "Nothing happens of any value until someone sells something," the adage states. And it's true. The best designed, produced, and advertised product is worthless unless retailers make it available to consumers in the rapid response format and at costs that will create satisfied consumers.

Some retailers know how to do it all and do it right, as Consumer in Focus 23.1 indicates. The Gap produces annual sales of more than $2 billion with a return on equity averaging more than 25 percent over the past 10 years in its more than 1,000 stores, even during the tough recession years of the early 1990s. The Gap started out as a mostly jeans store with cluttered racks jammed with unrelated pants and shirts. Today, The Gap reflects the disciplined management that understands its customers and how to please them. The firm is absolutely fastidious about the style and quality of its merchandise, and it doesn't play games with phony sales or messy stores.

23.1	**Consumer in Focus**

Filling a Gap

Would you be able to take control of a company and triple its sales and increase profits sixfold in just a few years? Mickey Drexler did. By age 47, he turned The Gap into the most popular and profitable specialty clothing chain in American retailing. When other firms were stuck in recession and retailing retrenchment, sales at The Gap and its sibling stores, GapKids and Banana Republic, blasted up to $2.5 billion, an average earnings growth of 43 percent. The formula behind The Gap's rise is invoked by Drexler almost as a mantra: "Good style, good quality, good value."

That's good enough as far as it goes, but The Gap is a lot more than nice-looking T-shirts and denim jackets. It's a network of sites that have been shrewdly chosen by its founder. It's a carefully tended vision of a store that is a clean, well-lighted place where harried consumers can shop easily and quickly. It's a culture that fusses over the most mundane details, from cleaning store floors to rounding counter corners at GapKids stores for safety's sake. And it's a high tech distribution network that keeps 1,200 Gap stores constantly stocked with fresh merchandise. Buttressed by its acclaimed advertising, The Gap look is accepted equally by tots, teenagers, young adults, and graying baby boomers.

Source: Excerpted from Russell Mitchel, "The Gap," Business Week (March 9, 1992), 58–65.

The Gap is just one of many retailers who know how to win, even in the face of a tough environment and fierce competition. Other notable winners include The Limited, Wal-Mart, Ikea, Dillard's, Nordstrom, Home Depot, Circuit City, and the Disney Store. Have you ever noticed that when companies are successful, they attribute it to good management, but when they are unsuccessful, they attribute it to problems beyond the control of management? In good times and in bad, in industries as diverse as discount stores, department stores, and specialty retailers, some win even when most lose. The purpose of this chapter is to help you sort out what it takes to win—that unique combination of understanding consumers and knowing how to delight them at the retail level.

Retailing and Your Career in Consumer Behavior

As you approach the end of this book, you may be asking how the study of consumer behavior will have an effect on your career. Some students find careers in product management. A few find jobs in advertising and marketing research. But most firms recruiting students in consumer behavior or marketing are looking for people who understand sales or retailing. Increasingly, good jobs are found in the retailing sector rather than manufacturing. The wealthiest person in America was Sam Walton, founder of Wal-Mart, with personal assets of more than $10 billion before his death. Or maybe you prefer the career pattern of Les Wexner, chairman of The Limited, who made the list of the top billionaires, with assets of more than $2 billion.

Even if you work for a manufacturing organization, you will find understanding retailing and gaining the acceptance of distribution channels increasingly your keys to success. Marketing budgets are being shifted from media advertising to promotional programs that provide a direct or indirect incentive to retailers to put the product where it can be bought. As the major retailers' market share expands, so does their power to dictate terms.[1] If you do not understand retailing, your chances for success are greatly diminished in a consumer-related career.

Relationship Retailing

Relationship marketing is important when developing effective strategies. One type of relationship marketing is the enduring relationship that goods or service retailers seek with their customers.[2] This type of relationship marketing was introduced in Chapter 1 and is illustrated in Figure 23.1. Notice how Paine Webber invests in a customer for life—or at least 20 years. In this chapter, our concern is to understand changes in channel relationships and how to build strong retailing relationships.

Figure 23.1 Relationship Marketing with Consumers

"...so I pick up the phone and it's my PaineWebber guy... He asked about my retirement plans. I said, c'mon, you're about 20 years too soon.

And I didn't think anymore about it. Until I happened to visit my old boss. What an eye-opener. He's sure not living like he used to ...you know, when he was working.

Next day I called my broker back and said, 'What were those questions again, about retirement?'

And we figured out how I should be putting something away now.

I know I'm not going to need that money for a long time. But it sure feels good—dealing with a company that'll be there when I'm ready...and knowing I'll have the kind of retirement I want. Because I have a broker who asked."

PaineWebber
We invest in relationships.

Changing Channel Power

A massive power struggle is occurring between manufacturers and retailers in the development of a relationship with consumers. Power is the ability of one channel member to influence the actions of other channel members. Increasingly, retailers are winning the power struggle.

The struggle for channel power is not new. Only the winner is new. The period after the Revolutionary War was the era of the traders, the forerunners of today's wholesalers. The wealthy and powerful businesses were those that could find manufacturers (mostly small, cottage industry firms) and match their goods with the small, decentralized retailers of the nation. The most important relationships often centered around the wholesaler. After the Civil War, the locus of power changed to large manufacturers, a condition that accelerated during the post–World War I era and continued until recently.

The emergence of massive mass merchants put retailers in the driver's seat. When "power retailers" such as The Limited, Wal-Mart, or Toys "R" Us speak, manufacturers and distributors listen. Buyers at such firms know their customers well and buy in such volume that when they tell suppliers "Change it," the suppliers do!

Internal power is also becoming more concentrated at the best retailers, as they seek more efficient infrastructures. In the past, department organizations such as Federated, Macy's, and May were highly decentralized. Today centralized buying, national promotions, and sophisticated data-base and logistics systems are common, forcing manufacturers to conform to retailer requirements to achieve low costs and rapid response. Vendors may have their national brands in Wal-Mart stores, but the orders are probably entered and controlled through RetailLink, Wal-Mart's EDI and MIS system. Retailers such as The Gap and The Limited do more than just put their own label on products. They control nearly every aspect of what manufacturers do from design through physical distribution, ending in advertising, merchandising, and in-store selling under the control of power retailers. An example of the strength of retailers is the growing sales of store brands, both basic and "premium" store brands. Look at Consumer in Focus 23.2 to see how retailers are grabbing power for their own brands.

Another reason for power shifting to retailing organizations is that retailers today are hiring the best students on campus. Retailers often can provide better career opportunities than manufacturers. When salespeople sit across from buyers and managers of the best retailers, manufacturers are dealing with highly competent buyers backed with the power that arises from comprehensive information systems, often tied to scanner data.

Relationship Retailing with Process Partners

It is not surprising that retailers and vendors are joining with other firms to become process partners united to establish a strong relationship with consumers. Four requirements for a quality buyer–seller relationship are identified by Martin and Sohi[3] as (a) trust, (b) frequency of communication, (c) quality of communication, and (d) norms of relationship. Effectiveness in relationship marketing is similar in structure and function with good marriages.[4] Just as with good marriages, values must be shared for relationships to be effective and continuing. Trust appears to be the core variable in the emerging understanding of effective relationships.

Relational Product Development

Relationship marketing requires new approaches to the development of new products. In the conventional approach, new product development was the responsibility of manufacturers, with new products originated in market research

| 23.2 | **Consumer in Focus** |

Retailer Brands Arise among Giants Coke and Pepsi

Sales of store-brands are rising twice as fast as overall soda pop sales in supermarkets, according to Nielsen Marketing Research. The emergence of store brands is likely to affect pricing and product strategies at Coke and Pepsi more than ever before. And though store beverages normally thrive in recessions, they may now be building long-term staying power because of big improvements in taste and graphics, as well as increasingly powerful retailers and more value-conscious shoppers.

At Wal-Mart, Sam's American Choice colas have red-and-white cans that resemble those of Coke and the message, "We believe these products . . . offer better value than the leading national brands." Even though store brands sell at an average discount of 35 percent compared with regular-priced national brands, they are more profitable with margins of 30 percent compared with about 21 percent for Pepsi and Coke.

In Canada, Loblaw Co. grocery chain introduced its President's Choice cola and boosted its cola market share in its 135 stores to more than 50 percent from about 10 percent. David Nichol, president of Loblaw's product-development division, says, "When there is no difference form a performance point of view, people aren't willing to pay the premium for Coke and Pepsi."

A *Consumer Reports* study recently found that store brands tasted just about as good as the Big Two. Private-label companies are betting that the cola leaders' traditional strengths—image and brand loyalty—are weakening amid price cutting and consumers' focus on value.

Source: Excerpted from Michael J. McCarthy, "Soft-Drink Giants Sit Up and Take Notice as Sales of Store Brands Show More Fizz," Wall Street Journal (March 6, 1992), B1ff.

or R & D shown in Figure 23.2a. In the relational approach process, partners are linked together in a relationship between consumers and distribution supply chain firms as shown in Figure 23.2b. Conventional organizations develop products "top down" compared with the contemporary approach in which process partners jointly form a business team that seeks to solve consumer problems with new products and integrated marketing programs as Figure 23.2c shows. Relational product teams may evolve into joint ventures and other close relationships for product expansion and market penetration.

An example of relationship marketing is Manco, known for tape, packaging, and other products marketed under the logo of its wide-eyed bright-yellow duck. Perhaps less known is how rapidly it responds to the needs of major customers such as Wal-Mart, Kmart, and Ace Hardware. The development of Kids-Craft described in Consumer in Focus 23.3 (page 830) followed the process outlined in Figure 23.2. Success in relationship marketing was one of the reasons its CEO, Jack Kahl, was named one of America's most admired executives along with CEOs of much larger firms such as GE, Whirlpool, Microsoft, AT&T, Intel, and Emerson Electric.[5]

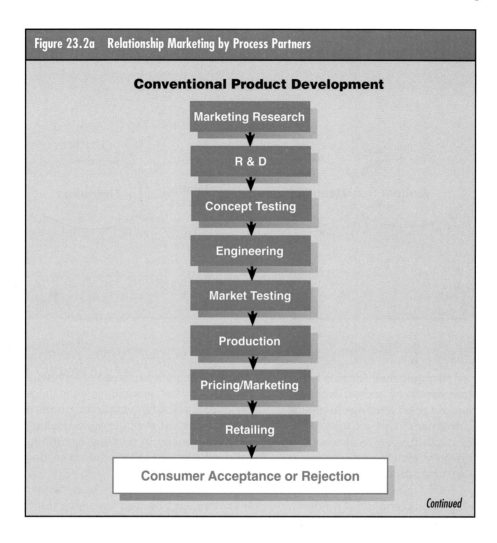

Figure 23.2a   Relationship Marketing by Process Partners

Conventional Product Development

Marketing Research

R & D

Concept Testing

Engineering

Market Testing

Production

Pricing/Marketing

Retailing

Consumer Acceptance or Rejection

Continued

Multichannel Retailing Revolution

Retailing is in a state of revolution as profound and pervasive in its effects as the industrial revolution of the previous century. The twenty-first century seems likely to usher in a new millennium in which retailers are pursuing innovations in productivity and customer satisfaction with aggressiveness and competitive fervor unmatched in history.

In the past, many of these innovations focused on supply side improvements, usually initiated by producers of products. Today, retailers increasingly

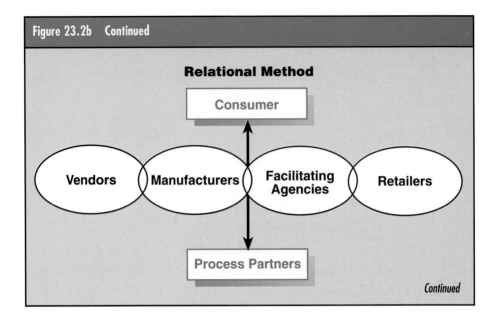

Figure 23.2b   Continued

Relational Method

Consumer

Vendors · Manufacturers · Facilitating Agencies · Retailers

Process Partners

Continued

are changing their formats to fit the lifestyles of consumers instead of relying on merchandising and mark-downs to move goods. Lifestyle retailing is the tailoring of a retail offering closely to the lifestyles of specific target market groups of consumers.[6] This contrasts with what might be called supplier-style retailing, in which the key to success is a focus on homogeneity in retailing operations. Lifestyle retailing usually involves the necessity of knowing a lot about how consumers buy.

Attracting consumers to buy more from a particular supply-chain partnership (a retailer and its vendors), process partners increasingly are using multichannel retailing formats. Multichannel retailing includes many formats classified as in-store and nonstore or out-of-store. In-store retailing includes both traditional stores and new formats. Specialty stores, mass merchants, and factory direct stores dominate the in-store part of the retailing revolution. Out-of-store formats include direct selling, direct-marketing, and electronic retailing.

Retailing Is a Many Splendored Thing

Two trends are especially dramatic among in-store retailing formats. The first is the growth of the **limited-line specialty store**, which features narrow product lines but wide assortments. Firms such as The Body Shop, H2O, Nature Company, and Paul Harris stores serve as examples. In these formats, the service needs of customers can be met on a personalized basis. This is often tailored to specific lifestyle segments.

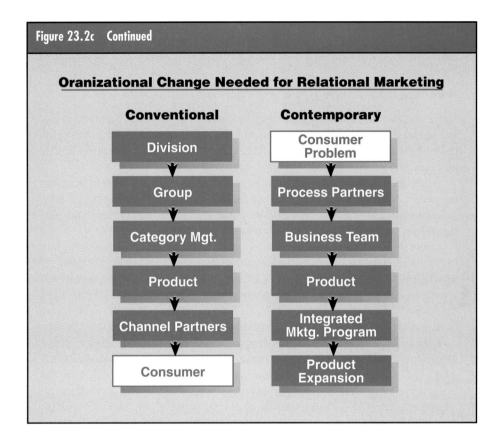

Figure 23.2c   Continued

Oranizational Change Needed for Relational Marketing

A second trend is the growth of **mass merchandisers**. They provide strong price appeal based on economies associated with self-service and operational efficiencies based on cost reductions in the infrastructure. They may also offer wide assortments to consumers. Caught in the middle are conventional outlets, which have increasing trouble competing and surviving.

Successful retailing firms often build portfolios of retailing chains that may include many formats, each positioned to specific lifestyle segments. Companies such as Dayton-Hudson, Melville Co., Woolworth, and The Limited are examples of portfolio retailers. The Limited, which operates more than 4,600 stores in carefully selected locations, maintains an ongoing program of consumer research to determine product and store criteria used by its market segments and creates an exciting in-store atmosphere for presentation of fashion merchandise in a portfolio of specialty stores including Express, Structure, Abercrombie & Fitch, Cacique, and Bath & Body Works. The appeal of these specialty stores is that each store in the portfolio can be carefully tailored to meet lifestyle or other segments with a unique product mix.

| 23.3 | **Consumer in Focus** |

From Tape to KidsCraft: A Duck Leads the Way

Long before Disney's Michael Eisner took his Mighty Ducks off the marquee and put them on the ice rink, Jack Kahl was leading a flock of his own mighty ducks. As CEO, Kahl is top duck at Manco, a company producing weatherstripping, mailing supplies, and other products found in the nation's best retailers. Most visible among these products is duct tape—a product with a myriad of uses.

Kahl rejected a consultant's opinion that a smiling duck caricature would never sell items such as duct tape. Instead, Kahl commissioned an artist to create the ducks that are the company's image and brand name, Duck Tape. At the grand opening of a Wal-Mart, Kmart, or other store, giant costumed Manco ducks often attract a parade of customers—especially kids—into the stores.

Because of their constant contact with consumers in the stores of their leading customers, Manco team members observed that these retailers needed products to attract parents and grandparents seeking creative, involving products that were fun, not messy, and safe. Manco worked closely with its process partners to create KidsCraft. One of the products is unique water paints in a tube. The paints smell like their colors, and they don't run like ordinary paints. They look and feel like markers but don't dry out readily. They can be easily washed from surfaces, such as walls, that kids might think nice to paint, but parents might not.

Manco worked closely with kids, retailers, technologists, artists, and art teachers but still developed the new product in record time. Major retailers were involved from the very beginning of the process. They contributed ideas about consumer preferences, display sizes, and ideal inventories, practically ensuring that product design, packaging, displays, promotion, and other elements of the marketing mix would precisely meet the requirements of both retailers and the target consumer market. This relationship marketing process developed a win-win-win solution to consumer needs better than if Manco had used a conventional product development approach and then attempted to sell the new product to retailers and consumers.

This fun, new product category is totally consistent with the approach of Manco, a household supplies company with a duck for its symbol. Perhaps it should not be surprising that many of the process partners celebrate their success each October with a gala event in which Manco team members, vendors, and retailers jump into the company's duck pond for an annual duck race.

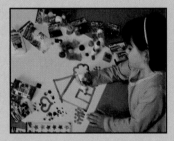

At the other end of the spectrum are the **mass merchants**. These include Wal-Mart, one of the most successful retailers in the world, with a portfolio of Wal-Mart, Sam's Club, and superstores that include groceries. Some stores have relationships with McDonald's and other retailers to provide a portfolio of formats within Wal-Mart stores. Another example is Target, a division of Dayton-Hudson, which also operates major department stores.

Superstores are becoming major participants in the retailing revolution. Mass merchants such as Home Depot, Circuit City, Toys "R" Us, and Incredible World concentrate on specific product lines in ways that make them commodity supermarkets. They meet consumer needs in much the way that Kroger, Winn-Dixie, Food Lion, Publix, and others do for food products.

One of the most dramatic and innovative of mass-merchandising forms is the **hypermarket**. These are stores in the 60,000- to 200,000-square-foot range that carry both convenience and shopping goods, with a heavy emphasis on general merchandise as well as on food. They incorporate breakthrough technology in materials handling in a warehouse operating profile that provides both a warehouse feel for consumers as well as strong price appeal. The hypermarket has been most successful in countries other than the United States. Carrefour in France and Cara in Benelux are examples that use massive amounts of merchandise, total store graphics (graphics coordinated throughout the store), and classification dominance, all of which create excitement and price appeal. Hypermarkets also take advantage of operating economies involved in the technology of palletized product display and storage and the latest in scanning equipment at the cash registers.

The largest single hypermarket in the world is probably Pick 'n Pay, in a suburb of Johannesburg selling as much as R2–3 million (about $1 million in U.S. currency) in a single day.[7] In Figure 23.3, you can see some elements of hypermarkets that cause them to be destination stores for consumers. Classification, dominance, and disciplined merchandise is a characteristic of the best. Pick 'n Pay has its own line of products that reflect graphics and packaging and sensitivity to environmental trends and value that are highly attractive to consumers. Unfortunately, photos cannot capture the full excitement created by the best of the hypermarkets. Their size and scope of activities illustrate the principle that great retailers provide theater for consumers.

Direct stores are one of the fastest growing forms of in-store retailing. Two forms predominate. One form is factory outlet stores, in which the emphasis is on name brand merchandise at discount prices. Liz Claiborne, Mikasa, Anne Klein, and Dansk are typical of such firms. Often, they are clustered in factory outlet or "value malls" containing so many of these stores that customers are attracted from a wide area. The direct stores provide the greatest competitive challenge to department stores because of the name brands involved as well as the prices. For the manufacturers, the net profit margin is often larger by selling in their direct stores, even at discounted prices, than from wholesale transactions to conventional retailers. Direct stores have grown so rapidly that some

Figure 23.3   Hypermarkets Provide Theater in Retailing

manufacturers, such as Van Heusen shirts, now make more sales through their direct stores than through department stores.

Another form of direct stores is operated by manufacturers as *exemplars* of customer service and selection rather than discount prices. Examples of such stores include Nike and Sony, both of which operate stores on Michigan Avenue in Chicago, as well as other locations. The Nike store provides more selection than would be found at other retailers, expert salespeople backed up by computerized data bases throughout the store, and merchandising excitement so innovative that it includes a basketball court and goal inside the store for customers to "test drive" potential purchases.

Nonstore Retailing

A portion of the retailing revolution that stimulates high interest to most consumer analysts is out-of-store or nonstore retailing. This includes direct selling, direct marketing, and electronic marketing. You studied these methods in detail in Chapters 7 and 8. The purpose in mentioning them again is to emphasize that marketing channels are multichannel. When you design a strategy for reaching consumers, many forms of retailing may be used.

Direct selling includes methods of directly selling goods and services to consumers by means of personal selling, often in consumers' homes. Examples include Avon, World Book, Amway, and Tupperware. The best of these firms are members of the Direct Selling Association and subscribe to a set of ethical standards designed to protect consumers and sales representatives of the firms. Longaberger baskets, as an example, failed to sell baskets effectively through retailers, but after developing a direct sales program, the firm skyrocketed in sales of hand-made baskets direct to consumers through a channel employing 25,000 representatives selling in the homes of consumers.[8]

Direct marketing involves direct contact with consumers through media other than by salespersons. In a sense, direct selling could be considered part of direct marketing but usually a distinction is made between the two forms. Direct marketing normally involves direct response to media such as advertisements, catalogs, and direct mail. Direct marketing offers the possibility of selecting specific target markets through the use of specialized mailing lists, data bases, or media. This permits customized appeals and creative strategy based on the lifestyles and needs of the target market segments. Direct marketers are also heavy users of predictive modeling, mailing list enhancement, lifetime value analysis, and advanced forms of cross-selling or up-selling. They are heavy users of controlled testing and experimentation.

Examples of direct marketing help clarify its advantages. Executive Gallery markets a wide variety of products designed to increase business and personal productivity. Should these products be directed to individuals or organizations? By placing its ads in airline magazines, such as those shown in Figure 23.4, Executive Gallery reaches both types of persons—individuals who use the

Figure 23.4   Executive Gallery—Direct Marketer to Frequent Fliers

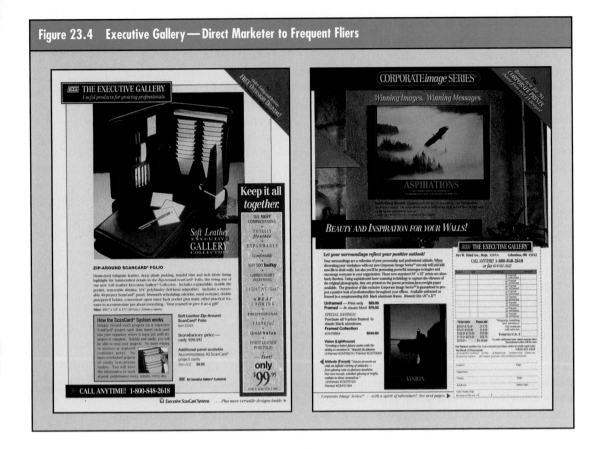

products as well as individuals who may initiate such purchases for organizations. Another example is Spiegel, a direct marketer with busy career women as its target market. Figure 23.5 shows a catalog cover for this firm, which has experienced rapid growth and profitability by knowing its customer base well, targeting products specifically to their needs, and making it simple to buy. Keep in mind that Spiegel is a multichannel retailer that recently opened its own direct retail stores. It even sells its catalogs in the stores of other retailers!

Electronic retailing is a special form of direct marketing using electronic media to sell to customers. There are many forms of this rapidly growing way of reaching consumers, as you read in Chapter 7. The most visible is Home Shopping Network and other television programming. Others include the "Electronic Mall" on CompuServe and Prodigy, and the newest forms involve CD-ROM versions that combine catalogs from L. L. Bean, Lands' End, and other leading direct marketers that allow consumers to browse many retailers on a

Figure 23.5   Spiegel—Successful Direct Marketer

computer. For years, marketers have categorized home shoppers as junk-jewelry-buyers with overextended credit cards, but new studies indicate that most shoppers are women in their peak earning years, socially active, married, working outside the home, and generally better educated than the average store shopper.[9]

Can in-store retailing survive the massive challenge provided by electronic retailing and other forms of nonstore or direct marketing? That question is hotly debated. It appears that electronic marketing is about 5 percent of total retail sales now, and some industry analysts project about 15 percent by the year 2000.[10] When you evaluate the future of in-store retailing, consider factors such as convenience, efficiency of operations, and the "theater" or drama that characterizes the most successful retailers. If you work for a producer of consumer goods, it is obvious that you will want to consider a multichannel strategy. If you work for a retailer, you may also want to reach consumers through some of the new media, as many leading retailers are already doing. If you work for an in-store retailer, there are ways to compete effectively against the new electronic media, however, as Consumer in Focus 23.4 shows.

Innovations in the retailing revolution underscore the rapidity of change in consumer buying and the consequent need for retailers to have a keen understanding of consumer research issues. Retailers and their suppliers need a market intelligence culture. How do consumers choose stores in which to shop? How important is location? How important is a store's image in determining store patronage? What factors determine image? What can be done to build store loyalty and to reduce shopper switching? These topics are discussed in the remaining pages of this chapter.

23.4 | **Consumer in Focus**

How to Compete with the Home Shopping Challenge

Jump into the Fray: In order to expand their base, many retailers such as Neiman-Marcus, Bloomingdale's, and Saks are extending their mail order business. Saks and Macy's are experimenting with home shopping.

Bring Back the Entertainment: Customers are bored with the typical shopping experience. They want fun and games as well as merchandise. The success of Warner Bros. and the Disney Store bear out the fact that shoppers like to have fun.

Rethink Value: Price alone isn't good enough anymore. Customers are balancing price and quality. Too often retailers try to lure customers by slashing prices. That, unfortunately, erodes profits, too. By delivering top quality, retailers can still be perceived as a value outlet.

Define What You Are: The cookie cutter approach to retailing is dead. Retailers need to decide what kind of outlet they choose to be and then deliver on that promise. If you want to market to the less affluent, make sure you have the right brands and prices. If fantasy is your game, ensure that the environment delivers on that fun.

Try Cohort Merchandising: It may be against retailers' grain to duplicate merchandise throughout the store. But it can make shopping more efficient and that's what today's customer craves.

Stress Human Contact: Make sure sales staffs are well-trained and knowledgeable. They can make the difference between a sale and a no sale. Interactive computers can be used to assist sales personnel.

Stress Unique Labels: Customers will go out of their way for something they can't find everywhere. Retailers who build strong private label programs can benefit from this trend.

Make It Worth the Trip: People appear willing to invest time and energy into events that pay off. Make shopping a pleasurable experience and customers will come back.

Source: Meet the New Competition: Emerging Home Shopping Alternatives, MasterCard (1994).

Consumer Decisions about Store Patronage

Answering questions about which stores consumers will patronize involves several issues. How far will they travel to a retail location? Will they prefer regional shopping malls, neighborhood strip centers, or downtown shopping areas? After answering these questions, we can address the issue of which stores they will choose within acceptable categories. The strengths of individual stores will also influence consumer decisions about which shopping center may be chosen.

Number of Locations

Location strategies of retailers are one of the most important determinants of consumer behavior. More consumers buy fast food from McDonald's than any other organization, partially because McDonald's has two or three times more stores than its closest competitors. Attitude research may indicate consumers prefer Wendy's or taste tests may indicate consumers prefer Burger King's Whopper, but McDonald's, with more than 12,000 stores, sells twice as much as the combined sales of both of its rivals. It is pretty difficult to find a place in the United States (and many other countries) where consumers are not close to a McDonald's.

Retailers with too few or too many stores often fail. So do retailers that locate on the wrong street, in the wrong shopping center, in the wrong city, or have the wrong parking spaces. An adage says the three most important variables associated with retail success are location, location, and location. More modern theories say more important variables involve services that produce customer satisfaction, but it is still location that determines whether a retailer gets the chance to satisfy customers. In this chapter, strategic issues relating to consumer choice of retail locations are discussed. For information about how to make such decisions, you may want to read a reference source on this topic.[11]

Retailer Strategies

Three levels of location decisions face marketing strategists: market selection, area analysis, and site evaluation. This process is shown in Figure 23.6. Understanding how consumers decide where to buy is a critical input in each of these levels. Retailers need a clear understanding of the value platform of the firm—the manner in which the firm differentiates itself from its competitors in the minds of the consumers it intends to serve, allowing it to achieve a sustainable differential advantage over competitors.[12]

This strategic approach relates location issues to the overall marketing plan of the firm. Management Horizons, a division of Price Waterhouse, concluded that location decisions for retailers and suppliers should be as follows:

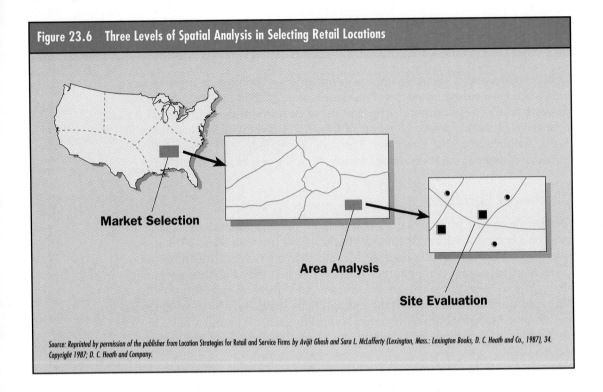

Figure 23.6   Three Levels of Spatial Analysis in Selecting Retail Locations

Market Selection

Area Analysis

Site Evaluation

Source: Reprinted by permission of the publisher from Location Strategies for Retail and Service Firms by Avijit Ghosh and Sara L. McLafferty (Lexington, Mass.: Lexington Books, D. C. Heath and Co., 1987), 34. Copyright 1987; D. C. Heath and Company.

1. broad-based—incorporating the exploration of new markets, the penetration of existing markets, and other long-term growth issues

2. proactive—helping to meet long-term corporate goals

3. ongoing—occurring at all levels of the strategic planning process, from the development of corporate objectives to the monitoring of store location performance

4. consumer-oriented—based on a thorough knowledge of the target market population, including its desire for convenience in time and space

5. whole-market—maximizing market coverage within a market

6. functionally integrated—providing input for merchandising, customer communications, and especially market share management[13]

In Figure 23.6, the process of spatial analysis appears sequential. First, markets are selected, then areas within those markets, and finally specific sites. In actual practice, the process is interactive. Site selection may affect market selection as much as the converse.

As an example, a successful computer retailer based in one city wanted to expand its success to other cities. During the market selection process, it identified 15 cities with the geodemographic and competitive conditions that corresponded to the conditions of its current successful market. The firm did further analysis of the areas within those cities most likely to support the sales of personal computers. After completing the competitive and shopping center analysis, however, some cities contained much more attractive sites than did others. The final selection was made in the cities that ranked seventh, tenth, and eleventh on the original ranking of 15 cities but were the best locations when specific sites and competitors were considered.

Cognitive Mapping

Cognitive maps or consumer perceptions of store locations and shopping areas are more important than actual location.[14] Cognitive maps refer both to cognized distances and cognized traveling times. Consumers generally overestimate both functional (actual) distance and functional time.

Variations between cognitive and actual distance are related to factors such as ease of parking in the area, quality of merchandise offered by area stores, and display and presentation of merchandise by stores and ease of driving to an area. Other factors affecting the cognitive maps of consumers include price of merchandise and helpfulness of salespeople.[15]

Computer Mapping

Location decisions must be made not only well but they must be made quickly. This process is made easier with computer access to data bases. Proposed sites are evaluated by constructing computer maps that measure the number of target consumers around the site. Demographic data are updated frequently that indicate the number of consumers by age, income, education, ethnicity, and other variables within a ring drawn around a distance of 1.5 miles, 3 miles, or 5 miles. A refinement of this process is to compute the circles on the basis of 5, 10, or 20 minutes driving time to the store. Access to these data bases is available through commercial research firms specializing in demographic analysis and through networking services such as CompuServe. A market analyst with a personal computer, a modem, and an account can obtain data quickly with which to make retail location decisions. Discriminant analysis or multiple regression models can be used to assess the probability of success of a specific site based on comparisons with other sites of the firm.

Individual Site Location

The success of a location is influenced by very specific details of the retail site. For example, two restaurants may have similar offerings but the selection of a site a block or so away from the main artery may cause as much as 10 to 20 percent variation in sales between the otherwise identical restaurants. Retailers sometimes fail because they succumb to a short-term strategy of leasing cheaper space, with the consequence of long-term reduced profitability.

Some of the more important components of a site evaluation include the following items[16]:

1. site description (size, shape, etc.)
2. lease requirements/land costs
3. parking ratio
4. pedestrian flow
5. traffic flow (numbers and average speed)
6. egress/ingress
7. public transportation access
8. visibility, signage, ambience
9. affinities (neighbors)
10. access to trade area

Competitive Battle between Shopping Areas

A war is raging to decide which shopping area consumers will choose. The major competitors include regional shopping malls, neighborhood strip centers, or downtown central business district (CBD) shopping centers. Currently, regional malls are under heavy attack. A "flanking action" by some retailers is to locate stores in free-standing locations, usually near regional shopping malls. Innovative hybrids also arise such as "power centers" combining the convenience of neighborhood centers and the selection and attractiveness (although smaller) of regional malls.

Malling of America

Regional shopping malls have progressed dramatically since J. C. Nichols built the first one, Country Club Plaza, in Kansas City in 1922. Updating over the years, the Plaza is still one of the most exciting collections of upscale retailers in the nation. The ultimate progression of the original shopping center is West Edmonton Mall in Edmonton, Alberta, Canada. The West Edmonton Mall is generally recognized as the largest in the world and was the first mega-mall, with 5.2 million square feet and 800 stores and services. One of the features is a 5-acre World Waterpark, the largest indoor waterpark in the world. Other features include 19 movie theaters, a hotel, 110 food outlets, dozens of amusement rides,

Figure 23.7　The Evolution of Malls

an ice rink, a miniature golf course, a chapel, a car dealership, and a zoo. Consumers arrive not only from nearby to shop; they arrive from all over North America to shop and play for a few days. West Edmonton Mall is a "destination shopping center."

A somewhat similar mega-mall opened in 1992 in suburban Minneapolis, as the Mall of America, which occupies a 78-acre site in suburban Minneapolis, with more than 400 retail stores. Four major anchors include Bloomingdale's, Macy's, Nordstrom's, and Sears, Roebuck and Co. The 4.2 million-square-foot mall includes an 18-hole miniature golf course; a 14-unit theater; more than 50 restaurants; and Camp Snoopy (Figure 23.7), an amusement park operated by Knott's Berry Farm.[17]

There are more than 28,500 shopping centers in America, compared with only 2,000 in 1957. This has produced a serious overbuilding problem described in the opening scenario of this chapter. As a consequence, very few regional malls are being built today in sharp contrast with an average of 14 per year in the 1980s and a high of 30 per year in the mid-1970s. The competitive reality is that shopping centers are working as hard to attract consumers from other centers as are individual retailers competing with each other. Regional malls compete by adding the entertainment, merchandise, food, services, and ambience required to be the new "Main Streets" of America.

Mini-Malls and Strip Centers

The fastest growing shopping areas are small- and medium-sized centers of various formats, usually with less than 100,000 square feet. Some "strip" centers are still being built, containing mostly mom-and-pop stores. Some are neighborhood shopping centers with a variety of convenience merchandise stores accompanied also by substantial traffic flow problems, with concerns of the effects on neighboring residential areas. They emerged to serve homemakers who need basic items from the grocery store, dry cleaner, and drugstore. Most are street-oriented and pedestrian and car friendly and account for 87 percent of all shopping malls and 51 percent of total shopping center retail sales in 1990.

Most were not designed to be architecturally "important," but a few of these are well planned and designed, sometimes in an enclosed or all-weather format, and are called mini-malls or "power" malls. Many older shopping centers have been "reformatted" by enclosing them and giving them a more contemporary appearance. Some have recaptured or maintained consumer patronage because of convenient location and density of population in the surrounding neighborhood.

Consumers in mini-malls and strip centers differ from others. Eighty-nine percent of adult Americans shop in these malls and 24 percent of Americans shop only at small shopping centers compared with just 5 percent who shop only at large regional centers. Small mall shoppers are more likely to be women, to have children, to be married, and to be homemakers. They usually have a specific purpose in mind. They are more likely to see shopping as a chore rather than a leisure activity as do the regional mall shoppers.[18]

Stores typically found in mini-malls or power strips include Blockbuster Video, Circuit City, and Pier One, or one of Mickey Drexler's Gaps or Banana Republics. Stores in strip malls have an edge over regional malls; stores in smaller malls have more opportunity to build relationships with individual consumers rather than relying on price or selection. Point-of-sale technology allows such stores to keep track of what's hot and what's not in their neighborhood. Combined with survey research, these stores can have a clear idea of exactly who their customer is and what he or she wants. Figure 23.8 shows how one of these, Loehman's Plaza in Norwalk, Connecticut, succeeds with careful analysis of its market.

CBD Centers

A major question about where consumers will shop is whether they will return downtown — to the CBD. There are many efforts to revitalize the downtown area as a place to shop as well as a place to work. One of the most successful is Faneuil Hall Marketplace in Boston. The "flats" is an area of restaurants and shops in Cleveland that has brought people downtown, along with a new baseball stadium for the Indians and the nearby Galleria Shopping Center. In Columbus, Ohio, City Center is a development that proves that public and private sectors

Figure 23.8   Mining the Neighborhood

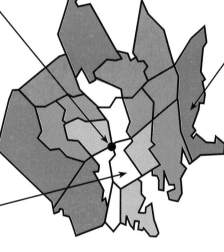

MINING
the NEIGHBORHOOD

**(census tracts within 2.5 miles of
Loehman's Plaza, Norwalk, Connecticut)**

Loehman's Plaza in Norwalk, Connecticut, is an upscale shopping center on the shabby side of town. Its nearest competition is the Salvation Army Thrift Store. How can this neighborhood support a strip mall that has BMWs, Jaguars, and Mercedes all over the parking lot? The answer is in the demographic map of the area, provided by the Claritas Corporation's COMPASS desktop marketing system.

Loehman's Plaza is strategically located near several pockets of wealth. That's why the area's retail sales potential for women's apparel is more than adequate to keep The Gap's cash registers ringing. The four most affluent tracts contain 5,528 households, and Claritas estimates that they spend a total of $5.4 million a year on women's clothes. But the 5,854 households in the five least affluent tracts have a market potential of only $3.4 million. The five tracts are shown here in white.

A visit to several Loehman's Plaza stores confirms that this mini-mall attracts upscale shoppers in droves. In The Gap, well-dressed suburban mothers lay down gold cards to pay for khakis and polo shirts. At the electronics store Sam Goody, pipe-smoking tweedy-looking gentlemen purchase stacks of classical CDs. These people don't come from the four census tracts bordering on Loehman's, where the median household income is as low as $19,826. They come from the 16 other tracts within a 2.5-mile radius, four of which have median household incomes greater than $73,000. The four tracts are shown here in dark blue.

Retailers at Loehman's can use this kind of information to target advertising and promotions to individual households. The demographic map shows them the individual block groups most likely to produce customers; other databases provide mailing lists of each block group. The next big advance in demographic systems is even more precise: a satellite link that can provide a current aerial photo of the area in question. With these photos, retailers can examine the houses on each street in more detail. It sure beats driving around.

**Retail Sales Potential
for Women's Apparel**

Highest
Above-average
Average
Below-average
Lowest

Source: Chip Walker, "Strip Malls: Plain but Powerful," *American Demographics* 13 (October 1991), 48–52.

can cooperate to create a successful environment to bring people to the CBD for shopping and entertainment. Retailers such as Marshall Field, Jacobson's, Max & Erma's, and The Limited have found City Center to be the location for some of their most successful stores.

Why Consumers Go Shopping

Consumers shop for many reason, as you read in Chapter 7. The landmark study described in Table 23.1 identified both personal and social motives for shopping. Examination of these motives indicates many things retailers can do to attract consumers. Consider, for example, the motive of "sensory stimulation" described in Table 23.1. Successful grocery stores place a bakery near the front of the store, greeting people with the aroma of fresh-baked products. The Limited has been a leader in attracting consumers with visual and auditory stimuli, and in its Victoria's Secret stores, attractive scents whiff through the store, enhancing the appeal of entering and lingering in the store.

The Store-Choice Decision Process

The process of choosing a specific store is a function of consumer characteristics and store characteristics. Consumers in each market segment form images of various stores based on their perceptions of the attributes they consider important. This process is shown in Figure 23.9. Consumers sort out or compare perceived characteristics of stores with evaluative criteria of the core customers. Store choice is thus a function of four variables shown in Figure 23.9: (1) evaluative criteria, (2) perceived characteristics of stores, (3) comparison process, and (4) acceptable and unacceptable stores. These processes are complex but understandable.

Automatic cognitive processing of these variables determines which stores will be the primary choice of consumer segments. Research conducted by Woodside and Trappey[19] indicates that customers can quickly name a store (that is, retrieve from long-term memory) when asked what store comes to mind for specific attributes such as "lowest overall prices," "most convenient," and so forth and that these top-of-mind responses are associated strongly with customers' primary store choices. Automatic cognitive processes, distinguished from those that are based more on conscious thinking, are based on an attitude accessibility model that views behavior as a function of an individual's immediate perceptions of the object in the context of the situation in which the object is encountered.

Retail Image

The overall perception of a store is referred to as store image. This concept has been defined in various ways,[20] but no one has improved much on Martineau's

Table 23.1   Why Do People Shop?

Personal Motives

Role Playing

Many activities are learned behaviors, traditionally expected or accepted as part of a certain position or role in society—mother, housewife, husband, or student.

Diversion

Shopping can offer an opportunity for diversion from the routine of daily life and thus represents a form of recreation.

Self-Gratification

Different emotional states or moods may be relevant for explaining why (and when) someone goes shopping. Some people report that often they alleviate depression by simply spending money on themselves. In this case, the shopping trip is motivated not by the expected utility of consuming, but by the utility of the buying *process* itself.

Learning about New Trends

Products are intimately entwined in one's daily activities and often serve as symbols reflecting attitudes and lifestyles. An individual learns about trends and movements and the symbols that support them when the individual visits a store.

Physical Activity

Shopping can provide people with a considerable amount of exercise at a leisurely pace, appealing to people living in an urban environment. Some shoppers apparently welcome the chance to walk in centers and malls.

Sensory Stimulation

Retail institutions provide many potential sensory benefits for shoppers. Customers browse through a store looking at the merchandise and at each other; they enjoy handling the merchandise, the sounds of background music, the scents of perfume counters or prepared food outlets.

Social Motives

Social Experiences outside the Home

The marketplace has traditionally been a center of social activity, and many parts of the United States and other countries still have market days, country fairs, and town squares that offer a time and place for social interaction. Shopping trips may result in direct encounters with friends (e.g., neighborhood women at a supermarket) and other social contact.

Communications with Others Having a Similar Interest

Stores that offer hobby-related goods or products and services such as boating, collecting stamps, car customizing, and home decorating provide an opportunity to talk with others about their interests and with sales personnel who provide special information concerning the activity.

Peer Group Attraction

The patronage of a store sometimes reflects a desire to be with one's peer group or a reference group to which one aspires to belong. For instance, record stores may provide a meeting place where members of a peer group may gather.

Status and Authority

Many shopping experiences provide the opportunity for an individual to command attention and respect or to be waited on without having to pay for this service. A person can attain a feeling of status and power in this limited master–servant relationship.

Pleasure of Bargaining

Many shoppers appear to enjoy the process of bargaining or haggling, believing that with bargaining, goods can be reduced to a more reasonable price. An individual prides himself in his ability to make wise purchases or to obtain bargains.

Source: Excerpted from Edward M. Tauber, "Why Do People Shop?" Journal of Marketing 36 (October 1972), 46–59. Reprinted from the Journal of Marketing published by the American Marketing Association.

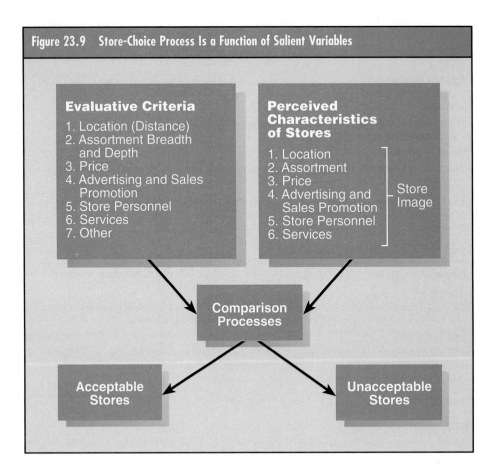

Figure 23.9 Store-Choice Process Is a Function of Salient Variables

idea of store personality as "the way in which a store is defined in the shopper's mind, partly by its functional qualities and partly by an aura of psychological attributes."[21] Because image is the perceptual reality on which consumers rely when making choices, image measurement is an essential tool for consumer analysts.

Retail Image Measurement

Retail image is measured across several dimensions reflecting salient attributes. Not surprisingly, almost the entire gamut of attitude-research methods is used, including semantic differential,[22] customer prototypes,[23] the Q-sort,[24] the Guttman scale,[25] multidimensional scaling,[26] and psycholinguistics.[27] Attitude-measurement techniques you've learned are equally applicable for retail measurement, including multiattribute approaches.[28]

An example of a multiattribute approach in retailing is presented in Table 23.2 for men's clothing stores. Potential customers were asked to list attributes, characteristics, or terms that come to mind when one thinks of men's clothing stores. From that list, the attributes perceived as having the most salience were found to be assortment, personnel, atmosphere, service, quality, and price. Then stores were rated on a 1-to-7 scale along with each attribute, providing useful information for diagnostic purposes.[29] Store C, for example, rated poorly on quality, the most salient attribute that could be a major cause of low patronage.

Determinants of store-choice decision vary by market segment and by product class. Salient or determinant attributes usually fall into the following categories: (1) location, (2) nature and quality of assortment, (3) price, (4) advertising and promotion, (5) sales personnel, (6) services offered, (7) physical store attributes, (8) nature of store clientele, (9) store atmosphere, and (10) post-transaction service and satisfaction. Location, as we have already seen, may be perceived by consumers in terms of time and hassle as well as actual distance.

Nature and Quality of Assortment

Depth, breadth, and quality of assortment are often determinants of store choice. This is especially true for department stores and other stores in shopping centers.[30] One reason specialty stores have risen rapidly in the retailing revolution is their ability to assemble and present dominant assortments, whether defined on the basis of classification, end-use, or lifestyle.[31]

The importance of dominant assortments of merchandise is also critical to the success of mass merchandisers known as "category killers," which carry a dominant assortment in one category of merchandise. An example is Toys "R" Us,

---

Table 23.2   Belief and Importance Scores for Retail Stores

Attribute	Importance Scores	Store A	Store B	Store C	Store D	Store E	Store F	Store G	Store H
Price	6.13	3.71	3.91	4.48	5.14	3.93	4.11	3.92	4.06
Assortment	6.11	4.79	4.56	4.21	4.68	4.33	4.23	4.39	4.46
Personnel	5.15	4.70	4.56	4.31	4.40	4.39	4.34	4.34	4.43
Atmosphere	4.84	4.86	4.64	4.24	4.56	4.50	4.35	4.42	4.53
Service	5.63	4.89	4.67	4.23	4.47	4.62	4.47	4.49	4.50
Quality	6.37	5.15	5.02	3.97	4.35	4.80	4.65	4.71	4.69

Source: Don L. James, Richard M. Durand, and Robert A. Dreves, "The Use of a Multi-Attribute Model in a Store Image Study," *Journal of Retailing 52 (Summer 1976)*, 23–32.

with hundreds of stores spread from Germany to Hong Kong. Other category killers include Tower Records, Circuit City, Blockbuster Video, Lenscrafters, Home Depot, and Office Depot. Other retailers, such as The Gap and The Limited, dominate on the merchandise attribute but in a more limited niche. They have narrow but deep assortments.

Category killers and niche retailers compete effectively with department stores, which used to be the place for quality and quantity of assortments, because of the effect that narrow lines and disciplined merchandising have on turnover. In contrast, department stores typically have slower inventory turns along with higher operating expenses, lower sales per square foot, and larger inventory losses.

Price

The importance of price as a determinant of store patronage varies by type of product. Supermarkets have placed great emphasis on price since the 1930s when King Kullen on Long Island, New York, pioneered the concept. Aldi's has built a worldwide supermarket chain based on merciless price competition backed by similar emphasis on cost reduction.

At one time, price was less important in consumer selection of department stores, which built their consumer franchise on product selection and service. Because of intense competition and often because of deterioration in service levels, price has become more important for some department stores. Some department stores—generally the least successful ones—develop "sales mania" in their attempt to buy back market share from competitors. Constant sales may have undermined the credibility of department stores and the confidence of customers in store prices. The importance of price depends on the nature of the buyer. Some customers preferring other factors, such as convenience, will, in effect, trade off that consideration against higher prices.[32] Keep in mind that it is cognitive processing or the consumer's perception of price that is usually more important than actual price.[33]

Price may be the most misunderstood variable in retailing. When Wal-Mart overtook Sears as the largest retailer in the United States, Sears cut its prices. What Sears may have failed to understand is that Wal-Mart not only has the policy of "Everyday Low Prices (ELP)," it also has highly disciplined policies to enforce the policy "Treat every customer as a guest."

Advertising and Promotion

Advertising and promotion can be used in at least two ways in retailing. One way is to communicate information about price or other attributes of the store. The second way is in positioning—creating perceptions about attributes or overall image of the store.

Price Advertising

The effectiveness of price promotions is questionable, despite their widespread use.[34] Price promotion may only shift demand from one time period to another for a store. Price cuts may only shift from one brand to another without increasing a store's total sales, or they may shift market share from one competitor to the next without increasing total demand. Nevertheless, price advertising is frequently done to maintain competitive parity. Apparently, a segment of the population—as large as a third or more—is affected by price advertising. But loyalty may last only until the next set of advertised prices attracts that segment elsewhere.

Questions about the relative effectiveness of price promotions, advertising, sales promotion, and so forth are increasingly answered more reliably by scanner data in the research of Allenby[35] and others. Specifically, retailers who are equipped to do so can examine brand and store substitution effects with sophisticated scanner data analysis. Research by Kumar and Leone[36] indicated that price promotions and to a lesser degree displays have brand substitution effects but also store substitution effects on a retailer and its competitors.

The effects of price advertising are filtered by recipients through the dimensions of their overall image. Keiser and Krum[37] concluded that "other information cues besides advertised low price would seem to influence consumer choice of retailers. These information cues are received from personal shopping experience, from friends, and from many other sources besides newspaper advertisements."

Positioning

The new role of advertising for retailers appears to be for positioning in contrast to the traditional role of advertising by retailers for communication of the price attribute. An example is the use of TV advertising by Home Depot, one of America's most successful retailers, featuring an associate who is asked to define his job at Home Depot. He replies, "To help customers make their dreams come true."

A change is occurring in retailing that might be described as the evolution from merchandising to marketing. Major retail firms traditionally put great emphasis on merchandising—buying the right merchandise, displaying and stocking it correctly, pricing and taking markdowns at the right time. The career path to the top of major department stores was always as a "merchant." Most retailers gave little attention to marketing activities outside of the store environment, such as media advertising, except for price advertising that was closely connected to merchandising decisions.

Today, retailers are starting to put more emphasis on advertising and other marketing activities that communicate with consumers outside the store environment, in an effort to create changed perceptions of the store and to attract consumers to the store.[38] Stores are adding special hours and services for "preferred customers," communicating with segments through computerized data bases, often related to credit card transactions. And the nation's largest retailers are beginning to make more extensive use of advertising for positioning objectives. Figure 23.10 shows an example by Wal-Mart, in which the objective is to position the retailer as offering a large selection of videos. Figure 23.11 shows how Sears is attempting to reposition itself to a position of strength in soft goods as well as hard lines with the new slogan "Come see the softer side of Sears." Figure 23.12 is an ad from *People* magazine for Express—a firm that rarely used media advertising for more than decade.

Advertising, along with other forms of sales promotion, can affect store choice, but its impact is difficult to assess. It depends on the type of purchase and the nature of the store itself. Its effectiveness varies by product category be-

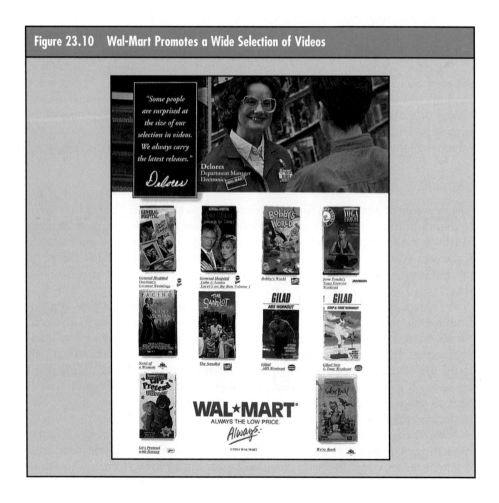

Figure 23.10   Wal-Mart Promotes a Wide Selection of Videos

cause some products and services are inherently more appealing than others. Men find restaurant ads and ads about tires and batteries most attention-getting, for example, whereas women look most at ads for restaurants, women's shoes, and women's apparel.[39]

Sales Personnel

You Win with People! Coach Woody Hayes titled his book. It is as true in retailing as in football. Knowledgeable and helpful salespeople were rated as an important consideration in choice of a shopping center by more than three-quarters of those interviewed in five major metropolitan areas.[40] The necessity of skillful personal selling was discussed in Chapter 7, so this finding may not be surprising. Retailer performance, unfortunately, does not always match consumer expectations.

Figure 23.11   Sears Promotes Its "Softer Side" by Advertising Soft Goods in Addition to Its Traditional Hard Goods Offerings

Figure 23.12 Express Advertising in People Magazine

Consumer confidence in retail salespeople is often low. But Home Depot has become the most successful do-it-yourself, home improvement store. Part of its success is its policy of 4 weeks or more training for people walking the floors to help consumers—a rarity among most retailers. Before salespeople start, they must learn about every item in their aisle and in two aisles adjacent. Salespeople, often recruited from the ranks of carpenters and electricians, are encouraged to spend all the time needed with customers, even if it takes hours.[41]

Perhaps no retailer is more successful at winning with personnel than Nordstrom, the West Coast-based specialty department store. The secret of Nordstrom's success may be tied to a story, possibly apocryphal, about a retailer who asked a salesperson at Nordstrom, "What can you be fired for?" The person replied: "Number one, for not taking care of the customer. Number two, for stealing." Nordstrom can afford to provide good service because its sales per square foot is $350, compared with about $150 for similar competitors, and it employs large numbers of employees that earn twice as much as if they worked for competitors—often more than $60,000 a year. Bruce Embree, a manager at

Nordstrom explains the secret, "It's not like brain surgery. You just have to be nice."[42]

Many people believe that no retailer has a handle on customer service as well as Nordstrom. Perception or fact? Most likely, a halo effect has developed around the company's outstanding service. But the fact is, its service is excellent and is provided by highly trained and motivated sales personnel enmeshed in a culture that defines success as personal service to customers. It is a consistent philosophy that gets communicated when hiring people, and it is constantly reinforced.

You might be asking if these policies only apply to large retailing chains. Frankly, these policies are probably the reason these organizations are large, because they all started out small and most of them relatively recently. Suppose you were given the responsibility for managing a single store, the smallest in the market and previously unsuccessful. Would you know how to turn it around to become the largest in the nation? Fred Ricart did, as Consumer in Focus 23.5 shows. The success story includes a major emphasis on training of personnel.

People are also at the center of the strategy of Starbucks Coffee Co., a company growing at greater than 80 percent over several years. The firm provides stock options even for its part-time workers and tremendous training programs and achieves employee turnover half or less than other food operations. The company operates on the philosophy that every dollar invested in employees shows up—and then some—on the bottom line. CEO Howard Schultz explains,[43] "Our only sustainable competitive advantage is the quality of our work force. We're building a national retail company by creating pride in—and a stake in—the outcome of our labor."

Services Offered

Convenient self-service facilities, ease of merchandise return, delivery, credit, and overall good service have all been found to be considerations affecting store image.[44] This varies depending on the type of outlet and consumer expectations. For instance, the 90 Giant supermarkets in the Washington, D.C., area began a nutrition education program in cooperation with the National Heart, Lung, and Blood Institute with good results. The program is called "Foods for Health," and various tips are presented through shelf-talkers, posters, and other forms of display.[45] Similarly, a *Chain Store Age Executive* survey of managers revealed that the presence of in-store banking facilities such as automated teller machines raised traffic levels by 10 to 15 percent annually.[46] In-store restaurants increase sales in the range of 5 to 6 percent. Hardware and home supply stores that service their products increase sales. Grocery stores sell products such as stamps as a service because of the increase in traffic. Other stores add technology, personnel, and training to increase service and decrease the time consumers spend in waiting at the checkout or other places in the store.[47] These are just a few examples of the variety of services that may influence which stores consumers choose.

| 23.5 | **Consumer in Focus** |

#1 Auto Dealer in the Nation

Auto Age magazine and *Automotive News* have both reported that Ricart Ford is the #1 Ford dealer in the world and the #1 Ford dealer in retail sales for multiple years. With annual sales of more than $232 million and 22,000 cars in 1992, it might be expected that the #1 dealership would be in a major market such as New York or Los Angeles. Ricart Ford is in Canal Winchester, Ohio. In May 1994, international quality authority J. D. Powers convened an international conference at the dealership so other auto executives could understand how Ricart does it.

Ricart Ford was not always that successful. The average dealer in the United States sells about 500 cars in a year, and in 1983, Ricart was below average. But during the 1980s, Ricart began to experiment with new forms of selling, training, and advertising. The firm conducted more than 500 consumer experiments, carefully observing the results of each.

Experiments involving careful observation and analysis to evaluate causation were nothing new to the president of the dealership, Fred Ricart. Ricart studied at Case Western Reserve University, earning a bachelor's degree in biochemistry. During graduate study, he became a lab scientist, spending years researching the light-sensitive chemical necessary to transmit light patterns from the retina to the brain for translation into a visual image. Working hours in a darkened laboratory with only a dim safelight bulb for illumination, he turned to music to pass the time, singing to himself and playing the guitar. When the family business ran into a crisis, Fred Ricart left the lab to help his father but brought his scientist's approach to understanding consumer behavior — and his guitar — to the Ford dealership.

He spent years, along with his younger brother Rhett, who is the accountant and information systems expert of the team, finding what works and what doesn't. They developed a training system for sales personnel that involves weeks of learning how "to sell yourself, instead of cars." They experimented with advertising media, learning what response could be expected if an ad was on the Bill Cosby show instead of Wheel of Fortune and the difference in response between ten commercial run-of-schedule (ROS) on

Continued

Physical Store Attributes

Facilities such as elevators, lighting, air conditioning, convenient and visible washrooms, layout, aisle placement and width, carpeting, and architecture have been found to be factors in and of themselves in store image and choice.[48] In a recent study, 61 percent of shoppers said convenient parking and 52.8 percent of shoppers said quick checkout would influence their decision about where to shop. Another physical store attribute of great importance was women's restrooms, rated by 50.7 percent of the women in the study as a factor influencing where they shop.[49] Crowding in a store often causes people to be less satisfied, and widening aisles may help to increase consumer willingness to buy. If this is not physically possible, allowing consumers to have some

Consumer in Focus, continued **23.5**

one channel versus more expensive commercials carefully placed on channels selected to match market targets.

They developed a system of selling whereby all visitors to the dealership are met with a parking plan as carefully orchestrated as parking at Disney World. Visitors are introduced to the well-trained salespersons, and the information system starts. At the beginning of each day, the computer displays the "close ratio" for each of the more than 100 salespersons. The results: While the national average of 17 percent is considered good in many dealerships, Ricart Ford achieves a close ratio over 50 percent. You can afford to spend more on advertising to get a potential customer into the store when you are well prepared for them when they arrive.

With information systems that permit management to identify what every person in the firm is accomplishing, it is no wonder that independent rating services report the customer satisfaction with Ricart's service area one of the highest of all dealerships in the nation. For both sales and service, as well as other areas of the business, the Ricarts have detailed reports on the precise accomplishments of each person the preceding day. They don't threaten or intimidate employees with such information. Fred Ricart explains, "The advantage is derived simply from the fact that I know what our people are doing—and they know that I know."

Consumers are drawn from as far as Cleveland and Cincinnati. They see a friendly dealer having fun on TV, playing the guitar he picked up as a student and laboratory scientist, singing "We're dealing." The consumers may not see one of the most advanced training programs in the business, the careful design for the store and surrounding area, the cost-effective media plan, the computerized TV studio that allows changes in advertising (such as rebates or special service contracts) 2 to 3 weeks earlier than competitors, or the state-of-the-art information system by which the firm is managed.

Advertising is the tip of the iceberg. It's the rest of the story that explains why Ricart Ford is the #1 dealer in America.

Source: Excerpted from media accounts including "Entrepreneur of the Year Awards," Inc. (January 1991), 51, and company interviews.

choice about handling the crowded conditions may cause them to be more positive about the store.[50]

Store Clientele

The type of person who shops in a store affects choice because of the pervasive tendency to match one's self-image with that of the store. The clientele of a restaurant makes it attractive or not-so-attractive to customers who want to see or be seen by others. Some customers may avoid a restaurant because of the type of people who are generally there, such as an instance when adults avoid restaurants that are believed to attract children.

Store Atmosphere

An important determinant of store choice is store atmosphere. Its importance is recognized in the term **store atmospherics,** the conscious designing of space to create certain effects in buyers.[51] Intense competition between stores for young, upscale consumers has caused stores to discard their dowdy old formats for colorful, well-designed, image-enhanced selling environments. Even the masses of consumers want some class in their stores.

Supermarkets such as Byerly's in Minneapolis delight customers with the atmospherics of their attractive stores. In Canada, Loblaws is an outstanding example of a store with coordinated graphics. The exterior signing invites people to come inside. When inside, customers are faced with super graphics and signing, clean and contemporary displays, and lighting and colors that encourage people to stay and shop. Products as ordinary as cookies can be exciting with the right atmospherics. Figure 23.13 shows a retail outlet for Cheryl & Co., a company that started with Cheryl Krueger making cookies in her kitchen for friends. The firm evolved into a successful entry in regional shopping malls, exciting not only because of the excellent taste of its cookies and other products but because of the bright red colors with designer-developed accents of black and

Figure 23.13   Atmospherics of Cheryl & Co.: The Conscious Design of Space to Attract Consumers

Source: Courtesy of Cheryl & Co.

white and carefully coordinated displays. While competitors sell cookies in "plain vanilla" stores, Cheryl & Co. has used atmospherics to make the store much more than just a "cookie store."

Atmospherics can be managed to achieve desired effects. Music played in a store at a low volume may encourage more social interaction between shoppers and sales staff. Faster or slower music may affect perceptions of time spent in the store, and classical music may give a more upscale or higher-priced image than other music.[52] Color can affect perceptions of the store. Crowley's[53] research indicates that short wavelength colors (red and blue) are more activating and may stimulate impulse buying, whereas moderate wavelength colors such as green should be avoided except in consumer behavior contexts such as waiting in line where a lower level of activation may be more desirable. Perceptions of merchandise quality do not seem to be affected by color, but merchandise displayed in a red environment is perceived as especially "up-to-date."

Post-transaction Service and Satisfaction

Customers want service and satisfaction after the sale. This is especially true for those who purchase such high-involvement products as furniture, appliances, and automobiles. More and more retailers and service firms are providing comment cards and other forms of feedback to ensure that consumers are satisfied. Marriott Hotels go to great efforts to serve consumers well and to find out about unmet expectations through questionnaires in every room as well as additional questionnaires sent to some guests after their stay. In an era of slow growth in the total market, the best source of new business usually is current customers. In such times, it is cheaper to implement programs that will satisfy present customers than to spend money to obtain new customers. Growing profits require more attention to meeting customer expectations for service.[54] The president and CEO of McDonald's says, "Customers are very special to us; serving them is the reason we are in business. We know our customers have many choices and we want to be their first choice every time. Making them want to come back is the key to continued success and growth in the coming years."[55]

Developing Comprehensive Retailing Strategies

The key to long-term sustainable competitive advantage for retailers, vendors, and other partners in the retailing process is a comprehensive strategy for maximum consumer impact. This usually involves core decisions and definition of a value platform, achieving an efficient infrastructure and implementing an integrated marketing communications program. This process is described in Figure 23.14.

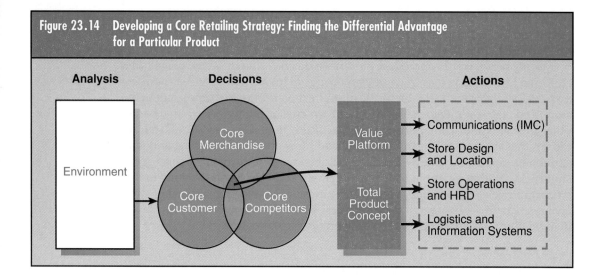

Figure 23.14 Developing a Core Retailing Strategy: Finding the Differential Advantage for a Particular Product

Core Decisions

The first step in developing a long-term retailing strategy is analysis of the environment—all the types of information discussed in previous chapters of this book as well as the development of a market intelligence culture for the firm.

The second step is to make decisions. These decisions are fundamental. Who will be our core customer? What will be our core merchandise? Who is likely to be among core competitors? Focusing on the really important or core aspects of the situation is more likely to produce a differential advantage than trying to be all things to all people. From the intersection of these core concepts should evolve the total product concept and the value platform that serves to make it specific and observable to the consumer.

Efficient Infrastructure

Long-term strategy also rests on an efficient infrastructure, including such variables as store design and location, provision for effective store operations and human resources development (HRD), and development of logistics and information systems.

Re-engineering the retailing operation is often needed. The objective of re-engineering is to align processes, people, and technology with customer needs. Re-engineering may require shifting resources from nonvalue added activities to those that provide value to customers. Customer service needs (friendliness, information, convenience) and merchandise needs (quality, selection, price, dependability) may be met at higher levels and lower costs through changing inventory management processes, supply chain processes, and support processes. For example, if inventory records indicate high shrink levels (because of theft) for some merchandise, existing processes might cause the retailer to place high shrink merchandise (jewelry, electronics, CDs) locked under glass. A re-engineering approach might add "impulse tagging" — tiny, postage stamp electronic signatures made by firms such as CheckPoint that sound an alarm when merchandise makes an unauthorized exit from the store. By re-engineering the control process, "open" merchandising can be achieved with results of higher satisfaction and sales to customers at lower costs and "out-of-stock" problems (because stolen goods are not recorded out of inventory by computers).

Once a firm "has it right," does that mean it can relax and reap the profits? Hardly. It is the best stores that keep changing things — that strive for continual improvement. "If it ain't broken, don't fix it," says an old adage. It is a false adage. It is the unsuccessful retailers that stay the same. The ones at the top are continually modifying their operations, experimenting with new products, new training programs, and new operating procedures.

When Sam Walton opened the first Wal-Mart discount store in Rogers, Arkansas, in 1962, the retail industry didn't notice. Shortly before his death in 1992, he wished his new store, also in Arkansas, would likewise escape attention because of the design and innovations built into the new prototype. Wal-Mart thinks its customers of the future will be as concerned about service as about low prices. With wide aisles and classy displays, it looks more like an upscale department store than a spartan discounter. One of the biggest distinctions between discount and department stores — self-service vs. full service — is blurred at this store; new technology provides information about products and helps customers locate them. The new store even has some designer names typically found only at upscale department stores, such as Estée Lauder and Calvin Klein. Unlike department stores, however, the Wal-Mart store has the same bargain basement prices found in all its outlets.

Wal-Mart, long a leader in computerizing the distribution side of retailing, is putting technology in the hands of customers at this store. Consumerscan, found throughout the store, gives customers their own bar code scanners to check prices. The Wal-Mart Arts Report has a TV screen to let customers preview movies and music videos. Shoppers also can use the device to order titles that aren't in stock. Wal-Mart is becoming a leader in providing improved consumer information through technology, different from most self-service stores that provide little information.[56]

Integrated Marketing Communications

The final step in taking actions to implement strategies is developing integrated marketing communications (IMC). IMC[57] involves shared meanings between retailing organizations and persons, with exchange as their objective, achieved with more efficiency than fragmented or partial attempts at communication. IMC of retailers or other organizations differs from traditionally programmed communications in several ways:

1. IMC programs are comprehensive. Advertising, personal selling, retail atmospherics and in-store programs, behavioral modification programs, public relations, investor relations programs, employee communications, and other forms are all considered in the planning of an IMC.

2. IMC programs are unified. The messages delivered by all media, including such diverse influences as employee recruiting and the atmospherics of retailers, are the same or supportive of a unified theme.

3. IMC programs are targeted. The public relations program, advertising programs, in-store and point-of-purchase programs, all have the same or related target markets.

4. IMC programs have coordinated execution of all the communications components of the organization.

5. IMC programs emphasize productivity in reaching the designated targets when selecting communication channels and allocating resources to marketing media.

Information-Based Strategies

Changing demographics, especially more education, have created a consumer responsiveness to information-based marketing strategies. Understanding this can lead to higher margins as part of the IMC. As the ratio of information increases relative to the physical mass of the product, the potential increases for higher margin selling of goods by retailers. Higher margins are possible because information increases the value of products and services to consumers. Higher margins are possible, assuming that the marginal cost of producing the information is less than the marginal value created for consumers.[58]

Information-based strategies take many forms. Some include more information on packaging; special inserts or hangtags accompanying products; more attention to information contained in advertising; special training programs for salespeople and other workers who have contact with customers; enhanced point-of-purchase materials, including videotapes and computerized displays; and seminars or training programs for customers and potential customers. One of the appeals of catalogs compared with in-store retailing is the higher ratio of information than is found in most self-service stores. Crate & Barrel is an example of an in-store retailer that provides signs alongside products that provide high levels of information about how products are made and used.

Globalized Retailing

Discussion of long-term strategies for retailers should not end, nor should this chapter, without mentioning the increasing importance of globalized retailing. Some firms are well established as global retailers. Examples include the Body Shop (U.K.), Benetton (Italy), and Eskada (Germany). From the United States, McDonald's has circled the world, with its largest stores in Moscow and Beijing. Toys "R" Us does well in the United States, but even better in countries such as

Germany and Japan, where children are given more care and concern by parents. Swedish retailer Ikea operates massive home furnishings from New Jersey to Hong Kong.

Global thinking involves global sourcing and global marketing as well as global selling, as you may remember from Chapter 3. Many retailers have been good at global sourcing for decades, but more are now recognizing the need for global selling. Nordstrom is studying a joint venture in China. Dillard Department Stores is entering Mexico and Wal-Mart is already there and headed for Canada and other countries. Consumer in Focus 23.6 provides a fitting close to this chapter and prelude to the future of retailing by describing how quickly JC Penney is becoming a globalized retailer.

Consumer in Focus 23.6

A Globalized Penney

Penney's recent foray into foreign markets began less than 3 years ago. Given Penney's traditional caution, management faced some opposition, but with U.S. opportunities dwindling, the company had to take the foreign gamble to stay competitive and keep growing. Company studies indicated that the United States was "really overstored" and that at the 22 Penney stores near the Mexican border, as much as 60 percent of sales were to Mexicans traveling north to shop.

Unlike most mass merchants, the repositioning of Penney in recent years has created such strong house brands that Penney has a big competitive advantage in overseas markets. Its own brands include Hunt Club, Worthington, Stafford, St. John's Bay, and Arizona jeans.

Penney management traveled the world to understand consumers and their cultures. They found that in Chile, men consider short pants suitable only for children and that Abu Dhabi women, despite wearing full-length robes outdoors, like party dresses. And it tailored stores to the customs of each country, hiring nationals from those countries but bringing them to Dallas to learn Penney merchandising methods.

In "understored" countries where real estate was affordable and laws allowed for foreign ownership, Penney opened and operates stores itself. Where problems make it too tough to own stores, Penney licenses local retailers to sell its branded apparel. In still tougher markets such as Singapore and Japan, where high property costs and regulations make it almost impossible to build large stores, Penney licenses other retailers to operate in-store shops selling specific branded lines, such as the Hunt Club shop in Robinson's Department Store in Singapore.

Penney's biggest entry is into Mexico, where it constructed and owns its own stores, which are expected to generate higher sales volume than U.S. stores. It has been scouting sites in Chile after surveys showed that many Chileans are so eager to buy American goods that they regularly fly to the United States to shop. Licensed Penney shops are racking up impressive sales in the United Arab Emirates and Singapore. It is selling goods in Portugal and Greece and considering anchoring a new regional mall in Taiwan and is looking into Thailand and Indonesia. It offers catalogs in Iceland, Brazil, and Russia.

Source: Excerpted from Bob Ortega, "Penney Pushes Abroad in Unusually Big Way as It Pursues Growth," Wall Street Journal (February 1, 1994), A1.

Summary

Retailing is important in the study of consumer behavior because it provides the ultimate test of consumer research and strategy: Will consumers buy the product? That question is decided in retail stores. Retailing also offers one of the fastest growing career opportunities for students of consumer behavior.

A massive power struggle is occurring between manufacturers and retailers in the development of a relationship with consumers. Power is the ability of one channel member to influence the actions of other channel members. Increasingly, retailers are winning the power struggle.

Changing channel power is being resolved among the best firms by relationship or partnership marketing. Retailers and vendors are forming close linkages among a variety of firms, to become process partners united to establish a strong relationship with consumers. Trust appears to be the core variable in the emerging understanding of effective relationships.

Attracting consumers to buy more from a particular supply-chain partnership (a retailer and its vendors), process partners increasingly are using multichannel retailing formats. Multichannel retailing includes many formats classified as in-store and nonstore or out-of-store. In-store retailing includes both traditional stores and new formats. Specialty stores, mass merchants, and factory direct stores dominate the in-store part of the retailing revolution. Out-of-store formats include direct selling, direct marketing, and electronic retailing.

The fundamental question facing retailers concerns which stores consumers will chose. Store choice is a complex process consisting of four variables: (1) evaluative criteria, (2) perceived characteristics of stores, (3) comparison process, and (4) acceptable and unacceptable stores. In general, the variables involved in this process are location, nature and quality of assortment, price, advertising and promotion, sales personnel, services offered, physical attributes, store clientele, store atmosphere, and post-transaction service. Many retailers are developing globalized retailing strategies.

Review and Discussion Questions

1. Why is retailing important in the study of consumer behavior?

2. Why is power in distribution channels changing between retailers and manufacturers?

3. What is the difference between relationship marketing as it was described in Chapter 1 of this book compared with this chapter?

4. What differences in product development and organization form can be expected in relationship marketing compared with conventional approaches?

5. Assume that a restaurant chain is considering expansion. What factors should be considered in selecting locations for new restaurants?

6. Why is the number of new regional malls declining? Why are strip shopping centers increasing in importance for some retailers?

7. Suppose that a large city is seeking to build a major new shopping mall in its CBD. What factors should be considered to make it a success?

8. Define the term *store image* and explain why it is important as a concept for retail management.

9. Think of the last time you bought a product. How did you decide which store to patronize? How does your behavior compare with the conceptualization of the process as presented in this chapter?

10. Assume that you are asked to measure the image of the dominant grocery chain in your area. How would you recommend this be done? Why?

11. Describe the importance of price in the patronage decision for supermarkets.

Endnotes

1. Leo Bogart, James Webb Young Fund Address, University of Illinois, April 7, 1988.

2. Kristy L. Ellis, Jungki Lee, and Sharon E. Beatty, "Relationships in Consumer Marketing: Directions for Future Research," in David Cravens and Peter Dickson, *Enhancing Knowledge Development in Marketing* (Chicago: American Marketing Association, 1993), 225–229.

3. Mary C. Martin and Raviprett S. Sohi, "Maintaining Relationships with Customers: Some Critical Factors," in Cravens and Dickson, *Enhancing Knowledge Development in Marketing,* 21–127.

4. Jeffrey J. Stoltman, James W. Gentry, and Fred Morgan, "Marketing Relationships: Further Consideration of the Marriage Metaphor with Implications for Maintenance and Recovery," in Cravens and Dickson, *Enhancing Knowledge Development in Marketing,* 28–35.

5. Joseph F. McKenna, "America's Most Admired CEOs," *Industry Week* (December 6, 1993), 22–30.

6. Much of the following material is based on Roger D. Blackwell and W. Wayne Talarzyk, "Life-Style Retailing: Competitive Strategies for the 1980's," *Journal of Retailing* 59 (Winter 1983), 7–27.

7. Additional details of this innovative retail chain can be found in Roger D. Blackwell, Kristina V. Blackwell, and Wayne Talarzyk, *Contemporary Cases in Consumer Behavior,* 4th ed. (Fort Worth, Tex.: Dryden Press, 1993).

8. See Longaberger Basket cases, in Blackwell, Blackwell, and Talarzyk, *Contemporary Cases.*

9. Patrick M. Reilly, "TV Shopping Hooks High-Toned Viewers," *Wall Street Journal* (November 16, 1993), B1.

10. Robert Kahn, "Direct Retailing," *Retailing Today* (March 1994), 4.

11. Barry Berman and Joel R. Evans, *Retail Management: A Strategic Approach* (New York: Macmillan Publishing Co., 1992), Chapters 7 and 8.

12. Avijit Ghosh and Sara L. McLafferty, *Location Strategies for Retail and Service Firms* (Lexington, Mass.: Lexington Books, 1987), 16.

13. Peter A. Doherty, *Location Strategies to Support the Marketing Management Function* (Columbus, Ohio: Management Horizons, 1984), 4.

14. David B. Mackay and Richard W. Olshavsky, "Cognitive Maps of Retail Locations: An Investigation of Some Basic Issues," *Journal of Consumer Research* 2 (December 1975); and Edward M. Mazze, "Determining Shopper Movements by Cognitive Maps," *Journal of Retailing* 50 (Fall 1974), 43–48.

15. R. Mittelstaedt et al., "Psychophysical and Evaluative Dimensions of Cognized Distance in an Urban Shopping Environment," in R. C. Curhan, ed., *Combined Proceedings* (Chicago: American Marketing Association, 1974), 190–193.

16. For additional details on store location decisions, see William R. Davidson, Daniel J. Sweeney, and Ronald W. Stampfl, *Retailing Management*, 5th ed. (New York: John Wiley & Sons, 1984), 179–197.

17. Kate Fitzgerald, "Mega Malls," *Advertising Age* (January 27, 1992), S-1.

18. Chip Walker, "Strip Malls: Plain but Powerful," *American Demographics* 13 (October 1991), 48–51.

19. Arch G. Woodside and Randolph J. Trappey III, "Finding Out Why Customers Shop Your Store and Buy Your Brand: Automatic Cognitive Processing Models of Primary Choice," *Journal of Advertising Research* 32 (November–December 1992), 59–78.

20. See Jay D. Lindquist, "The Meaning of Image," *Journal of Retailing* 50 (Winter 1974–1975), 29–38; Robert A. Hansen and Terry Deutscher, "An Empirical Investigation of Attribute Importance in Retail Store Selection," *Journal of Retailing* 53 (Winter 1977–1978), 59–72; Leon Arons, "Does Television Viewing Influence Store Image and Shopping Frequency?" *Journal of Retailing* 37 (Fall 1961), 1–13; Ernest Dichter, "What's in an Image," *Journal of Consumer Marketing* 2 (Winter 1985), 75–81.

21. Pierre Martineau, "The Personality of the Retail Store," *Harvard Business Review* 36 (January–February 1958), 47.

22. G. H. G. McDougall and J. N. Fry, "Combining Two Methods of Image Measurement," *Journal of Retailing* 50 (Winter 1974–1975), 53–61.

23. W. B. Weale, "Measuring the Customer's Image of a Department Store," *Journal of Retailing* 37 (Spring 1961), 40–48.

24. See, for example, William Stephenson, "Public Images of Public Utilities," *Journal of Advertising Research* 3 (December 1963), 34–39.

25. Elizabeth A. Richards, "A Commercial Application of Guttman Attitude Scaling Techniques," *Journal of Marketing* 22 (October 1957), 166–173.

26. Peter Doyle and Ian Fenwick, "How Store Image Affects Shopping Habits in Grocery Chains," *Journal of Retailing* 50 (Winter 1974–1975), 39–52.

27. Richard N. Cardozo, "How Images Vary by Product Class," *Journal of Retailing* 50 (Winter 1974–1975), 85–98.

28. See, for example, Don L. James, Richard M. Durand, and Robert A. Dreves, "The Use of a Multi-Attribute Model in a Store Image Study," *Journal of Retailing* 52 (Summer 1976), 23–32; and Hansen and Deutscher, "An Empirical Investigation."

29. For a useful discussion, see Eleanor G. May, "Practical Applications of Recent Retail Image Research," *Journal of Retailing* 50 (Winter 1974–1975), 15–20.

30. Hansen and Deutscher, "An Empirical Investigation"; Lindquist, "The Meaning of Image"; Gentry and Burns, "How Important"; and John D. Claxton and J. R. Brent Ritchie, "Consumer Prepurchase Shopping Problems: A Focus on the Retailing Component," *Journal of Retailing* 55 (Fall 1979), 24–43.

31. Walter K. Levy, "Department Stores: The Next Generation," *Retailing Issues Letter* 1 (1987), 1.

32. Robert H. Williams, John J. Painter, and Herbert R. Nicholas, "A Policy-Oriented Typology of Grocery Shoppers," *Journal of Retailing* 54 (Spring 1978), 27–42.

33. Kent B. Monroe, "Buyers' Subjective Perceptions of Price," *Journal of Marketing Research* 10 (February 1973), 73–80.

34. Joseph N. Fry and Gordon H. McDougall, "Consumer Appraisal of Retail Price Advertisements," *Journal of Marketing* 38 (July 1974); V. Kumar and Robert P. Leone, "Measuring the Effect of Retail Store Promotions on Brand and Store Substitution," *Journal of Marketing Research* 25 (May 1988), 178–185.

35. Greg Allenby, "Reassessing Brand Loyalty, Price Sensitivity, and Merchandising Effects on Consumer Brand Choice," working paper, 1993.

36. Kumar and Leone, "Measuring the Effect of Retail Store Promotions.

37. Stephen K. Keiser and James R. Krum, "Consumer Perceptions of Retail Advertising with Overstated Price Savings," *Journal of Retailing* 452 (Fall 1976), 27–36.

38. "Limited Expands Marketing Chief's Job," *Columbus Dispatch* (January 3, 1994), 6.

39. Leo Bogart and B. Stuart Tolley, "The Search for Information in Newspaper Advertising," *Journal of Advertising Research* 28 (April–May 1988), 9–19.

40. "Service: Retail's No. 1 Problem," *Chain Store Age Executive* (January 1987), 19.

41. Gav Christopher Power and Laura Power, "Their Wish Is Your Command," *Business Week/Quality 1991* (January 15, 1992), 126–127.

42. Gavin Power, "The Secrets behind Nordstrom's Service," *Positive Impact* 4 (February 1993), 7.

43. Matt Rothman, "Into the Black," *Inc.* 15 (January 1993), 59–65.

44. Lindquist, "The Meaning of Image."

45. Jo-Ann Zbtniewski, "Just-the-Facts-Ma'am on Health and Nutrition Posted in Giant Stores," *Progressive Grocer* (February 1979), 29.

46. "Retailers Asking: Is There Money in In-Store Banking?" *Chain Store Age Executive* 54 (October 1978), 35–39.

47. John V. Hummell and Ronald Savitt, "Customer Service in Retailing: A Temporal Approach," in Robert L. King, ed., *Retailing: Its Present and Future* (Charleston, S.C.: Academy of Marketing Science, 1988), 50–55.

48. "Retailers Asking: Is There Money in In-Store Banking?"

49. "Service: Retail's No. 1 Problem."

50. Michael K. Hui and John E. G. Bateson, "Perceived Control and the Effects of Crowding and Consumer Choice on the Service Experience," *Journal of Consumer Research* 18 (September 1991), 174–184.

51. Philip Kotler, "Atmospherics as a Marketing Tool," *Journal of Retailing* 49 (Winter 1973–1974), 48–63.

52. Richard Yalch and Eric Spangenberg, "Effects of Store Music on Shopping Behavior," *Journal of Consumer Marketing* 7 (Spring 1990), 55–63.

53. Ayn E. Crowley, "The Two-Dimensional Impact of Color on Shopping," *Marketing Letters* 4:1 (1993), 59–69.

54. For expansion of this concept, see Roger D. Blackwell, "The Consumer Affairs Role in an Era of Slow Growth Markets," *Mobius: Journal of Consumer Affairs Professionals in Business* 7 (Fall 1988), 1–7.

55. *McDonald's Fourth Quarter Report 1991*, cover.

56. Kevin Helliker, "Wal-Mart's Store of the Future Blends Discount Prices, Department-Store, Feel," *Wall Street Journal* (May 17, 1991), B1.

57. This section is based on Roger D. Blackwell, "Integrated Marketing Communications," in Gary L. Frazier and Jagdish N. Sheth, eds., *Contemporary Views on Marketing Practice* (Lexington, Mass.: Lexington Books, 1987), 237–250.

58. Paul Hawken, *The New Economy* (New York: Ballantine Books, 1983).

CHAPTER 24

Diffusion of Innovations

▲▲▲

French Fries at 55-mph

Do you enjoy eating pizza while you drive to work but cringe when the boss notices the pepperoni on your lapel? Do you reach in your pocket for a pen and pull out a french fry instead? Are you a mess at 55 miles an hour? Worry no more: American inventors may have solved your problem.

An article in the *Wall Street Journal* about eating in the car inspired 33-year-old Edwins Arthurs Spulgis to invent the Original CatchMaster, which he hopes to sell for $10. It features a soft vinyl lap cover with a trough-like spillway, complete with a large plastic clip meant to hold beverages securely between the wearer's thighs. The clip can be removed to hold french fries and works like a charm. Mr. Spulgis estimates he has spent at least $15,000 for prototypes but has yet to manufacture the product in quantity, and he is uncertain how to market the product.

Source: Based on Kathleen Deveny, "Neat Tricks: Inventors Tidy Up Automotive Dining," Wall Street Journal *(February 1, 1994), B1.*

New Products in the Marketplace

As the opening scenario to this chapter indicates, consumers are bombarded with new products to buy or reject and marketers are often perplexed about how to stimulate the buying decision. In Naples, New York, there is an art gallery exhibiting some of the 75,000 new products introduced in recent years.

Some new products succeed, bought by enough customers to achieve profitability. Most new products fail. This chapter discusses why some succeed and why some fail. The chapter also shows how to increase the number that succeed.

Sony is an example of a company that has experienced both success and failures. The Walkman personal stereo and other new products diffused successfully around the world. But Sony is the company that also invented the Betamax VCR. With Beta, Sony tried to keep the technology proprietary. Its competitor, Matsushita, licensed its VHS format widely, and as VHS spread, Betamax was doomed. Sony learned from its mistake with Beta and licensed its 8-mm camcorders and components to big names such as Fuji, Sharp, and Canon. A big new push by Sony is the electronic book. This innovative product is designed as a replacement for an old, old product—books in a library.[1] See Figure 24.1 for another innovative product, a strap-on wrist telephone from AT&T.

Consumers are bombarded with new products of every form. In Tokyo, nearly every street is lined with vending machines selling everything from iced coffee and beer to underwear. In Vienna, visitors from around the world can insert their dollars, yen, francs, or pounds into a cash machine and change them

Figure 24.1   Positioning of a New Product as Replacement for an Old Product

into marks. Will such machines be as common in North America in the future as they are now in Tokyo and Vienna?

A pharmaceutical firm is testing a new product that allows people to sleep only 4 hours a night and keep, at least for short time periods, the energy and alertness of a night with 8 hours of sleep. If the company introduces the product to the market, will consumers buy it? Or would they rather stay in bed?

Embryo implants are a product developed in England and now diffused throughout the world, allowing hundreds of thousands of couples to give birth to children who previously could not do so. Researchers are now experimenting with a process that would implant embryos in men. The embryos would attach to an intestine for blood supply and be delivered by cesarean section. If the medical service is perfected to allow men to give birth, will any do so? How many would adopt this new service? If men, as well as women, can have babies, what will happen to the world's birthrate?

Criticality of New Product Management

Successful introduction of new products is a critical component of contemporary marketing programs requiring careful coordination between marketing, engineering, and other parts of firms.[2] It is also one of the most misunderstood. About 5,000 new products appear each year on supermarket shelves, but as many as 80 percent are commercial duds. Both macromarketing and micromarketing reasons exist for concern about this situation.

Macromarketing

First, at the macromarketing level, much of the nation's technological and other resources are devoted to developing new products that are rejected. This causes two concerns:

1. Valuable resources are wasted that might have been channeled toward more productive uses

2. Products that might have helped people do things more productively or attain higher levels in their quality of life fail to be used

Perhaps the rejected products should never have been developed because they were inferior to existing products and benefits. Perhaps the rejected products failed because of ineffective communication and diffusion processes. In either instance, society is harmed by the failure to understand why and how people adopt new products. Some of the research about diffusion has produced mathematical models that can be used cross-culturally to predict the rate of adoption of products such as television.[3]

Second, at the moral or ethical level, the introduction of new products involves the attempt to change the behavior of human beings, often in rather fundamental ways. The changes usually involve more than simply switching from one brand to another, as is true in much of the material you have studied in this book. Sometimes the changes have profound effects on the people who buy the new product—as was true when some tampons produced adverse effects compared with the existing form of sanitary napkins or when silicon breast implants later created major problems. Sometimes the changes have profound effects on the people who do not adopt the product—as may be true among those who fail to adopt usage of personal computers or vaccines. More than any other area of marketing, perhaps, the ability to introduce new products effectively is the ability to change how society is organized, a direct influence on consumption behavior.

The desire in most diffusion research is to persuade people to accept new products or practices. Successful products are those that become *culturally anchored*—so inextricably a part of a consumer's life and sociocultural surroundings that the person–product interface is an important part of the individual's self-concept.[4] Culturally anchored products are almost addictive. Imagine doing without personal computers, fax machines, or microwave ovens with today's values and lifestyles. The "products" have been as diverse as birth control methods, sanitation techniques, computers, and hybrid seed corn. The motivation for research on these topics stems from the notion that people should change to what is good for them or society. With personal computers, as an example, the technology has often been urged on consumers with little concern about the underlying value of the benefit or the information that consumers would derive from microcomputers.[5] People and organizations are agents for change in the behavior of other people. In a market economy, consumers are sovereign in their acceptance or rejection of products and practices, but there remain important moral and ethical questions about who should have the ability to be effective change agents.

Micromarketing

Concern about new products also exists at the microeconomic level, which is the main focus of this chapter. New products are the lifeblood of many firms. In past decades, firms could grow profits by selling the same products to an increasing number of customers. In the slow-growing populations you read about in Chapters 2 and 3, firms often must depend on marketing new products to a slow-growing or declining number of customers.

A second reason for new product development is the role market leadership plays in a firm's profitability. Research indicates that firms that are market leaders, as measured by market share, generally have the highest return on investment (ROI) and enhanced shareholder value (ESV). The *profit impact of market strategy (PIMS)* research indicates that market leaders achieve average rates of return three times greater than firms with low market share.[6] The PIMS data also indicate that perceived product quality is highly associated with ROI and ESV. Successful new product development is an important element in achieving long-term competitive superiority and profitability and is one of the keys to making

Rubbermaid the most admired firm in America, as you can read in Consumer in Focus 24.1.

A successful new product can also be the beginning of a whole new company. Edison's invention of electricity was the beginning of GE. Today, new entrepreneurial activity is often based on new products rather than on attempts to compete with marketers of existing products. Thus, the path to asset accumulation for individuals often stems from a single new product. Examples include computer products of Silicon Valley entrepreneurs, new packages such as Softsoap, and new services such as the automatic debit service of CheckFree that allows people to pay bills without writing checks each month. Being one of the first firms to market a product successfully in an emerging market often leads to what is called the *pioneering advantage*. Extremely favorable evaluations may be formed toward the pioneer that lead not only to a high level of penetration but because these favorable evaluations are bolstered by a large amount of information stored in long-term memory, they persist over time and often resist competitors' tactics used against the pioneer.[7]

Large corporations usually require a portfolio of products, some of which are new but many of which are not so new. Such a portfolio often derives the most

---

Consumer in Focus **24.1**

Product Innovation at America's Most Admired Company

Rubbermaid introduces a new product, on average, every day of the year, creating a reputation for the company as "the new product machine." The company will not accept a "business-as-usual" attitude. It seeks change and reinvents itself consistently through initiatives such as Creative Innovation, a thinking process involving technology, business development, new product breakthroughs, strategic thinking, and planning for each business. The goals include entering a new product category every 12 to 18 months, getting 33% of sales from products introduced in the past five years, and by the year 2000 getting 25% of total revenues from outside the U.S. (18% currently). To do this, Rubbermaid depends on small improvements to its 5,000 products that include mailboxes, window boxes, storage boxes, toys, mops, and many others. The results: 9 out of 10 of the new products are profitable and Rubbermaid earns an average 20% return on shareholders' equity, with 41 consecutive years of sales records, 55 years of profitable performance, and 38 consecutive years of dividends-per-share gains. In 1994, Rubbermaid was named by *Fortune* magazine as the most admired firm in America, after achieving second place for five of the previous six years.

Even Rubbermaid's top management looks for new product ideas everywhere. When CEO Wolf Schmidt and Senior VP Richard Gates visited the British Museum in London, they came away with 11 product ideas from an exhibit of Egyptian antiquities. They concluded about the Egyptians, "They used a lot of kitchen utensils, some of which were very nice. Nice designs."

Sources: Rubbermaid Annual Report; and Alan Farnham, "America's Most Admired Company," Fortune (February 7, 1994), 50–54.

sales not from new products but from rapid growth from products that are recent introductions. Although the Boston Consulting Group (BCG) matrix of "cash cows," "dogs," and other barnyard animals has been challenged as overly simplistic,[8] most corporations do maintain a variety of products at various life cycle stages and with varying rates of growth and return on investment.

Existing products sometimes can be changed so they are perceived as new. Tom Peters, in lectures to business executives, makes the point that no marketing manager should accept the premise that he or she markets a "commodity." If you think such a goal is unrealistic, consider the case of Frank Perdue in Consumer in Focus 24.2. He changed consumer perceptions of "dead chickens" into a highly profitable, billion-dollar corporation. Even today, Perdue continues this

---

24.2 **Consumer in Focus**

Perdue: Changing a Commodity into a New Product

Before Frank Perdue took over the chicken business from his father it was the quintessential commodity business. Chickens had as strong a claim to commodity status as pork bellies or crude oil. The performance of each competitor was the same on each product and service attribute. This placed Perdue and his representative competitor at the 50th percentile on relative quality, neither ahead nor behind. With no differences in performance on product and service attributes, the customer bought basically on price.

After Frank Perdue took over the chicken business, he pulled ahead on almost every nonprice attribute that counts in the purchase decision. His research showed that customers in his served market prefer their chickens plump and yellow. Careful breeding and the judicious use of feed additives enabled Frank to produce meatier, yellower chickens than competitors. His actions also produced a higher, more consistent meat-to-bone ratio.

To prevent wet pinfeathers from slipping past the torching process that's supposed to burn them off, he purchased a turbine engine to blow-dry his chickens just before they reach the torching station. This didn't get him to zero defects, but it did mean that fewer pinfeathers wound up in supermarkets or in family dining rooms. Notice that his particular investment in capital equipment did not expand capacity and it did not take out labor costs. It just improved the perceived quality of Perdue's chickens! Most capital appropriation requests have difficulty quantifying the justification for expenditures to improve perceived quality.

To make sure that the customer perceived and remembered his quality improvements, Perdue utilized catchy slogans in audacious media advertising: "It takes a tough man to make a tender chicken"; "Buy Perdue chickens—you get an extra bite in every breast." (Would you have spent millions trying to differentiate chickens?) Perdue developed a favorable difference, he made sure that it was perceived, and as a result he gets a substantial premium for what certainly had been a commodity. As Perdue himself says, "Customers will go out of their way to buy a superior product, and you can charge them a toll for the trip." Is your product, with all its potential associated services, really harder to differentiate than a dead chicken?

Source: Robert D. Buzzell and Bradley T. Gale, The PIMS Principles (New York: Free Press, 1987), 119–120.

progression with new packages, new methods of cooking, and new species of poultry.

Product quality in mature products is often linked to product innovation. Polaroid introduced instant photography and was, for decades, one of the nation's most innovative and successful companies. But without breakthrough products to replace the maturing instant photography, the company stagnated and quality fell behind Japanese competitors. The CEO of the company reported that this lack of innovative products led to Polaroid being "asleep at the switch for 20 years."[9]

Product Life Cycle

The product life cycle (PLC) is a key concept for understanding the criticality of new products. You probably studied the PLC similar to that shown in Figure 24.2 in a basic marketing course. This figure shows that just as products grow and mature, so do they decline and fail. As the process evolves, major changes are necessary in the marketing strategies and mix: price, product, place, and promotion. For the consumer as well as for marketing managers, the role of advertising may be different at varying stages of the life cycle.[10]

Profit margins vary greatly during the product life cycle, usually peaking during the latter stage of the growth phase and declining during subsequent stages. Firms need a portfolio of products in various stages of the PLC to achieve the growth, profitability, and capital objectives of the firm. The problem increases because of what Olshavsky and others show to be an increasing rate of adoption of innovations, causing a rapidly shortened product life cycle,[11] although this view has been challenged by others such as Bayus.[12] Shortened PLCs, caused by rapidly changed technologies and improved mass communications, create the need for shorter amounts of time in management approval of movement between phases of product introduction.[13]

The diffusion of innovations and the acceptance (and rejection) of new products are some of the most researched topics in marketing. Research by the consulting firm of Booz-Allen & Hamilton shows that major obstacles in introducing new products include lack of attention by management and delays in making decisions, as well as inadequate market research.[14] Ideally, a firm and its managers would have plenty of time to perform new product research. Instead, managers must often rely on what is already known about how new products are accepted, based on other products and theory. Fortunately, there is a great deal of both. That is why this chapter may be extremely relevant to you. As you make quick decisions about new products, you will have a thorough, immediate information base of concepts and principles to help guide your decisions.

In addition to formal research, marketing managers need grass roots ways of understanding consumer reaction to new products. Sony requires that its

Figure 24.2   Impact of the Product Life Cycle on Marketing

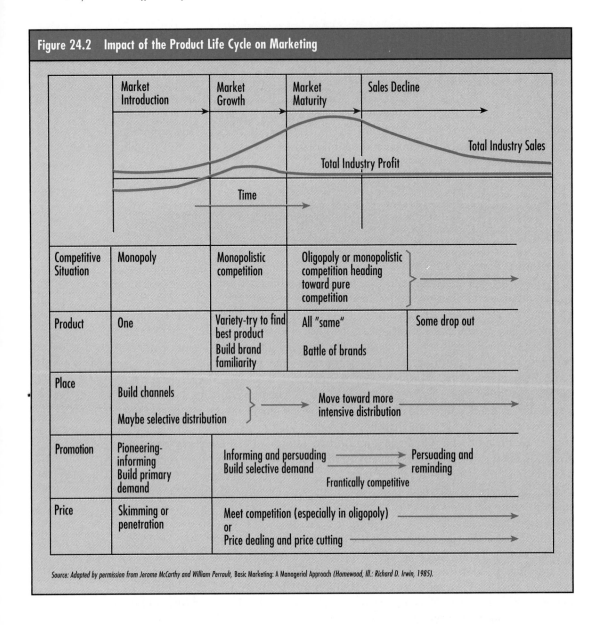

	Market Introduction	Market Growth	Market Maturity	Sales Decline
Competitive Situation	Monopoly	Monopolistic competition	Oligopoly or monopolistic competition heading toward pure competition	
Product	One	Variety-try to find best product Build brand familiarity	All "same" Battle of brands	Some drop out
Place	Build channels Maybe selective distribution	Move toward more intensive distribution		
Promotion	Pioneering-informing Build primary demand	Informing and persuading Build selective demand Frantically competitive	Persuading and reminding	
Price	Skimming or penetration	Meet competition (especially in oligopoly) or Price dealing and price cutting		

Source: Adapted by permission from Jerome McCarthy and William Perrault, Basic Marketing: A Managerial Approach (Homewood, Ill.: Richard D. Irwin, 1985).

managers talk with dealers and consumers constantly to get their reactions to new products from Sony and its competitors. Campbell Soup Co. insists that managers do their own grocery shopping and the Campbell board of directors meets in the back room of a supermarket after roaming the store aisles and probing shoppers for comments on Campbell products.[15] Even though you will find many useful principles in the following pages, the best understanding will probably occur because of the time you spend in the marketplace, talking to customers and reflecting on their comments.

Growing Competitive Challenge

Contemporary firms are being attacked competitively on every dimension and from every direction. The only way to survive this onslaught, Porter[16] has convincingly argued, is to create a "value chain" to serve the customer, which will serve to differentiate the successful firm from its competitors and will provide competitive superiority on the critical attributes of importance to the customer. A product that will "delight the customer" is the foundational variable of marketing strategy. The challenge is to understand which new products will do that.

Innovation is not limited to new products. Innovative ideas, innovative people, and innovative processes are characteristic of the business firms and other organizations that are surviving and thriving. After careful research of more than 115 innovations in major corporations, Kanter[17] concluded that winners generate "idea power" that provides the competitive advantage, not only in new products but also in new ideas in every area: better packaging, more efficient invoicing techniques, new planning systems, and lower-cost manufacturing. The winners today are better users, adaptors, and incorporators of technology.

Diffusion Process

The diffusion process helps explain how new ideas or cultural practices spread through a society, as well as how new products are diffused. The criticality of new product adoption is clear, but, you might be asking, why should consumer decisions about new products be studied any differently from decisions about other products? Why not simply consider the elements of decision making and psychological and environmental variables that have been discussed in the text previously as they apply to new products rather than existing products?

The main distinction in traditional analyses of the diffusion of innovations is the emphasis on communications within the social structure rather than individual information processing. The *relational approach* analyzes communication networks and how social-structural variables affect diffusion flows in the system, in contrast to a *monodic approach*, which focuses on the personal and social characteristics of individual consumers.

Major Research Stream

A reason for a separate chapter on new product diffusion is the great quantity of research on the topic and the diversity of disciplines from which the research is drawn. More than 3,000 studies and discussions of diffusion processes have been published in at least 12 identifiable disciplines. These include anthropology, sociology, rural sociology, education, marketing, psychology, and geography.

The most important contribution to the study of diffusion of innovations was a book of the same name, written by Everett Rogers in 1962 and updated in later years.[18] According to Rogers, diffusion is defined as the *process by which an innovation (new idea) is communicated through certain channels over time among the members of a social system.* Under this definition, a product might be around for a long time but still be perceived as new and be an innovation in a given market.

Consumer researchers and marketing analysts have been important contributors to the study of diffusion of innovations, along with the disciplines of general sociology, anthropology, geography, and public health as well as rural sociology, communication, and education. The bulk of consumer behavior research, however, is on the adoption process of consumers rather than on the social structure and process variables.

Marketing strategists should use care when applying diffusion research. Many of the studies were conducted in primitive societies where government or some other agency had the ability to contact every member of the community. In marketing programs, effective communication with all members of the community is much more limited. Also, many of the products involved in sociologic or anthropologic studies have been high-involvement and more personal products. The consistency between disciplines is one of the basic reasons, however, for the impact diffusion research has achieved. This chapter emphasizes findings with marketing applications.[19]

Diffusion Variables

The critical determinants of success for a new product have been identified in thousands of diffusion studies. From these studies, the main elements in the diffusion of innovations include

1. innovation (new product, service, idea, and so on)
2. communication (through certain channels)
3. time (at which certain individuals decide to adopt the product relative to others)
4. social system (interrelated people, groups, or other systems)

Each of these topics is discussed in the following pages.

The result of this process shows that some members of the social system are **adopters**—people who have made a decision to continue using a new product. Other people are **nonadopters**, and their decision not to adopt may occur for many reasons. Some will not be exposed to information about the product or will wait until other people have tried the product before doing so themselves. Some consumers will quickly decide a new product is not what they want, perhaps because of brand loyalty and satisfaction with current products. Other consumers may want a product but may not buy it for a variety of reasons.[20]

An early decision not to adopt is apparently what occurred when Gerber brought out a new product called Singles, small servings of beef burgundy and other foods that should appeal to the growing number of single households. The product was targeted to people such as college students who need a simple-to-fix, inexpensive, nutritious meal without cooking or other complications. Gerber placed the product in the same type of glass jar in which consumers had purchased baby food and identified the manufacturer as Gerber. The product was a bomb. Apparently, many consumers did not like to be identified as singles eating alone. They also associated the product with baby food even though it tasted good and was very convenient. Years later, another company successfully introduced SmartOnes, also a single serving product offering the benefits of good nutrition and convenience but with no reference to the singles market.

In the following pages, let us look closely at the four elements of diffusion that cause some people to be early adopters, late adopters, or nonadopters.

The Innovation: Which Products Are Winners?

An innovation can be defined in a variety of ways. The most commonly accepted definition is that an innovation is *any idea or product perceived by the potential adopter to be new.* This is a *subjective definition* of innovation, because it is derived from the thought structure of a particular individual.

Innovations can also be *defined objectively,* based on criteria external to the adopter. According to this definition, new products are *ideas, behaviors, or things that are qualitatively different from existing forms.* This definition also has its problems because of disagreement about what constitutes a qualitative difference. Certainly, TV is qualitatively different from existing communication forms, but is Liquid Tide a new product compared with the existing form of Tide? Does the addition of "blue crystals" or an improved package make a product new?

Marketing studies often define new products in relation to market acceptance. A simple approach is to call any product that has recently become available in a market "new." The Federal Trade Commission sanctions such an approach but limits the use of "new" in advertising to products available in the marketplace for less than 6 months.

Academic researchers have often defined a new product as any recently introduced product that has achieved less than x percent of market penetration. Innovations frequently are operationally defined as recently introduced products that have not attained 10 percent of their ultimate market share. All these definitions have problems, pointing to the need for a classification system for various types of innovations.

Types of Innovations

One system of classifying innovations is based on the impact of the innovation on behavior in the social structure. This taxonomy was described by Robertson[21] and has been used extensively in marketing. It classifies innovations as (1) continuous, (2) dynamically continuous, and (3) discontinuous.

A **continuous innovation** is the modification of an existing product rather than the establishment of a totally new one. It has the least disrupting influence on established patterns of behavior. Examples include adding fluoride to toothpaste, introducing new-model automobile changeovers, adding menthol to cigarettes or changing their length, and replacing dot matrix printers with laser printers. Figure 24.3 describes an example called Zima, a nonbeer beer that's made like beer but doesn't taste like beer.

A **dynamically continuous innovation** may involve the creation of either a new product or the alteration of an existing one but does not generally alter established patterns of customer buying and product use. Examples include electric toothbrushes, front-wheel-drive cars, compact discs, natural foods, Post-it Notes, and many forms of interactive media.

Figure 24.3 Zima: Example of a Continuous Innovation

Zima Clearmalt is an alcoholic malt-based beverage that is brewed like beer but has none of beer's taste or color, the first of a new category called clear malt. Zima has the same alcoholic content and calories of a full-bodied beer but tastes like a lightly flavored mixed drink. Some have described it as a gin and tonic with a twist.

Coors brews the product with malt, but Zima is filtered to remove the beer taste, color, and foam, having a clear base to which citrus and other flavors are added. It is priced about the same as super premium Canadian imports. Zima is targeted primarily at drinkers in the 21- to 34-year age group looking for a nonsweet lighter alternative. The secondary market is 35- to 49-year-olds who are moderate drinkers.

Among the criteria Coors used to develop it are drinkability and refreshment, adult taste that is not sweet or fruity, and light with no aftertaste. Research indicates that 59 percent of the adult population has an orientation toward light products, including white wine, wine coolers, spritzers, light beer, and white-based mixed drinks.

Sources: Media accounts including Christopher A. Amatos, "Coors' Zima Clearmalt Clearly Not Same Ol' Brew," Columbus Dispatch (February 8, 1994), 1D.

A **discontinuous innovation** involves the introduction of an entirely new product that causes buyers to alter their behavior patterns significantly. Examples include television, computers, cars, videocassette recorders, and microwave ovens. Some of the emerging forms of interactive media may prove to be discontinuous if they fundamentally change shopping behavior, transferring it from stores to homes. Most new products are of the continuous form. Often, the most successful are just modifications or extensions of existing products, with little change in basic behavior patterns required by consumers.

Products Most Likely to Succeed

New products most likely to be adopted by consumers have some common basic characteristics. Innovations include both a hardware component and a software component. Hardware refers to the physical or tangible aspects of a product. Software is the information base that accompanies the hardware component. Just as with computers, a new product that is functionally excellent in its hardware may fail to be adopted because of inadequate software or information base. A frequent mistake is spending resources on research and development to perfect the physical attributes of the product but failing to provide adequate resources for the software necessary for success with the product. Understanding consumers' values and lifestyles in developing the software may determine success of the new product just as much as the technical R&D.

As an example, RCA devoted millions to technical perfection of the video disc, which delivered a picture quality superior to that of videocassettes. RCA later wrote off the entire new product costs (reportedly more than $150 million) because the product was never accepted by consumers. For consumers, the software component of the activity—the ability to copy materials from TV or other videocassettes—apparently was more valued than the hardware component of the product.

Total Product Concept

New products are often rejected because of failure to adopt a total product concept. Ted Levitt[22] makes the point that products have little opportunity for profit when viewed only as tangible attributes or attributes (generic products). The total product concept defines the expectations of consumers about tangible and other attributes such as delivery conditions and post-purchase service. The augmented product includes what the customer perceives the product to do to provide more than what is expected (and thereby provides extra "value" beyond what would be justified to pay the price of the product). All these produce the product potential or everything potentially feasible that will attract and hold customers. The total product concept is shown graphically in Figure 24.4. When

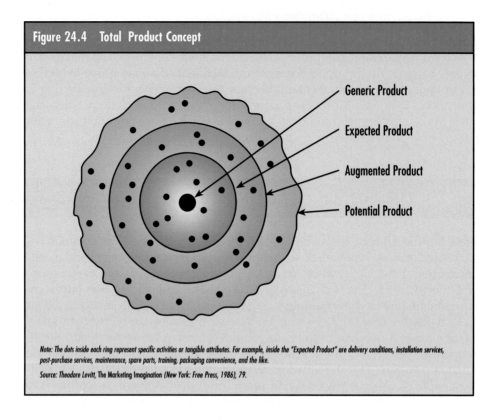

Figure 24.4   Total Product Concept

Generic Product

Expected Product

Augmented Product

Potential Product

Note: The dots inside each ring represent specific activities or tangible attributes. For example, inside the "Expected Product" are delivery conditions, installation services, post-purchase services, maintenance, spare parts, training, packaging convenience, and the like.

Source: Theodore Levitt, The Marketing Imagination (New York: Free Press, 1986), 79.

introducing new products, marketers may be so enamored with the "new" qualities of the product (tangible attributes) that they ignore the success requirements identified by understanding the total product concept.

Some products are winners and others are losers. Others may eventually be adopted but take much longer than expected. For example, Knight-Ridder lost about $50 million in a failed home-shopping service, and Citicorp has watched $200 million go down the drain in failed services such as one aimed at grocery shoppers. For every success story such as compact discs or Nintendo, there are fizzles such as picture phones and home banking.[23]

Why are some winners and some losers? What are some of the attributes or expectations and augmentations of a total product? Research by Rogers and other investigators indicated five characteristics that are associated with success with new products. These variables may not apply uniformly to all types of innovation adoption decisions. Hassan[24] has developed an elaborate list of attributes that may be used by potential adopters to assess a particular innovation for a given situation. Here we look at the five primary attributes proposed by Rogers. They include

1. relative advantage
2. compatibility
3. complexity
4. trialability
5. observability

Relative Advantage

The most important question to ask in evaluating the potential success of a new product is, "Will it be perceived to offer substantially greater advantage than the product it supersedes?" The issue is not whether the product is objectively better than the existing product but whether consumers are likely to perceive a relative advantage. To what degree will the new product be a substitute for existing ones or complementary with the array of products already in consumers' inventories?

New products most likely to succeed are those that appeal to strongly felt needs. One marketer asked consumers about their problems around home and found that many people perceive problems with collection of their garbage. Existing garbage bags were too small and too easily broken. The company brought out a new line of strong, large garbage bags, and the product was diffused quickly. Garbage disposals appeal to similar felt needs and have been one of the most widely diffused new products for homes.

Campbell, however, introduced a new instant soup consisting of single servings of highly concentrated soup. The consumer merely added boiling water. Response by consumers was tepid. They perceived it to be scarcely more instant than Campbell's regular soup, to which consumers simply add water and then boil. Although the dry product was physically quite different from liquid soup and offered many advantages to the marketers (because dry products are more efficient to ship and store than liquid ones), the product failed because it lacked perceived relative advantage to consumers.

In banking, ATMs diffused through the social system quickly because they offer high perceived advantage to consumers who want 24-hour availability. Debit cards, in contrast, have been slow to diffuse. Although debit cards and point of sale (POS) may offer advantages to banks and retailers, consumers perceive little relative advantage over checks or credit cards.

Compatibility

Compatibility is an important determinant of new product acceptance. Compatibility refers to the degree to which the product is consistent with existing values and past experiences of the potential adopters. Clairol introduced a new shampoo called A Touch of Yogurt. It was unsuccessful, apparently because people found the idea of putting yogurt in their hair incompatible with their value systems, despite the fact that yogurt may be good for hair. Perhaps if the product had been called A Touch of Glamour, with yogurt as an ingredient, it might have succeeded. Glamour is a part of the norm of the target market even though yogurt in the hair is not.

Radio Shack, in contrast, was successful in introducing personal computers to America because of its existing distribution system of thousands of stores. Customers whose normal behavior favored technologically innovative products were already in the stores buying products. Computers, although technically different in function, were related to consumers' product interests. The combination of distribution, personal service, and related product interests was compatible with the existing values and experiences of early adopters of computers.

Manco is an example of a firm that has been highly successful in introducing new products that provide high relative value but are also compatible with existing consumer usage patterns. Look at Figure 24.5 to see some of the new products they introduced at a trade show in 1994 for retailers such as Wall-Mart, Kmart, and Ace Hardware. The company's basic product is Duck Tape, but it has created a wide range of related innovative products. One of these is Kids-Craft water paints that do not drip, are washable, and smell like their color. Other products include CareMail, an innovative line of convenient mailing products. The company has addressed consumers' chronic lack of space with DuraClear storage products as well as the rising green concern about recycling with reusable lunch and school storage pouches. Perhaps one of the reasons for the company's success is how closely its new products conform to the variables described in this section as those correlated with why products succeed.

Complexity

Complexity is the degree to which an innovation is perceived as difficult to understand and use. The more complex the new product, the more difficult it will be to gain acceptance. Microwave ovens represent a discontinuous or dynamically continuous innovation, but they diffused rapidly because they are easy to use. The complexity principle makes it advantageous to build products as simple as possible during initial introduction to achieve simplicity in understanding and operation for consumers.

Apple Computer followed such a strategy with great success. Even the apple as a symbol communicates simplicity and a product that can be understood by all ages. IBM also used a symbol—"Charlie"—to personalize its technologic image. Charlie bridged the gap to consumers who might have perceived "International Business Machines" as too complex for personal use, even though the IBM personal computer is relatively simple to use. IBM chose readily accessible software in the introduction of its personal computers, rather than less well-known software of its own. Software that is "user-friendly" is initially more successful, even though complex software might be more efficient.

Figure 24.5   Innovative Products Compatible with Consumer Usage Patterns

Source: Courtesy of Manco, Inc.

Products can be designed to minimize perceived complexity. When consumers read instructions for assembly or use of a new product, will such instructions be perceived as simple or complex? The more complex, the less likely the product is to succeed.

Trialability

New products are more apt to succeed when consumers can experiment with or try the idea on a limited basis. Sampling is an effective method of inducing trial of new products. Companies such as Procter & Gamble and General Foods give millions of new products away each year to make trial easy without economic risk to the consumer.

Enhancing the trialability of new products can be accomplished through sampling in continuous innovations, especially for low-unit-value, consumer-packaged goods. How can marketers do something similar for expensive, complex, and high-involvement, discontinuous innovations? The same principles apply, but it takes more creativity.

Leasing is a strategy for such products, widely used by auto manufacturers in the 1990s. Auto manufacturers often make special offers to rental car companies on substantially changed models or cars equipped with innovative features. They know this gives consumers, especially those likely to be good prospects for new cars, an opportunity to try the new product or new feature. When computers were first introduced, IBM and other firms used leases to reduce the perceived risk for innovators. New recipes and products are introduced in supermarkets through programs that demonstrate how to prepare these products. They also offer taste samples. Even communication programs can enhance the trailability of products by urging people to "Try it—you'll like it!"

The effectiveness of such programs is greatest when the trial is induced in settings likely to contain innovative consumers. An example was the introduction of Eagle Snacks, a new type of snack food consisting of nuts coated with honey. Anheuser-Busch introduced Eagle Snacks by providing small packages of the product on airlines. This setting contained large numbers of upscale consumers able to afford the relatively expensive snack food.

Observability

Observability and communicability reflect the degree to which results from using a new product are visible to friends and neighbors. It influences the acceptance of new products. For instance, when room air conditioners were first introduced, it was found that adoption often occurred within concentrated areas rather than throughout the city. Neighbors from next door or across the back fence saw the results of an air-conditioned room and wanted one for themselves.

Marketers can sometimes use strategies to enhance the visibility of products by inducing celebrities to use them. Thus, the visibility of the celebrity makes the new product visible. Nike used this strategy with its tennis shoes and sporting goods. It gave them to celebrities, such as Andre Agassi, for their own use. Visible use of a new product in popular movies, TV shows, or sports events can also be an effective device for obtaining the adoption of new products. Gangster Rap, Hip Hop, and Grunge clothing styles are combined to use the visibility of recording stars to influence adoption of new clothing styles and other products among some segments of the population.

Researching New Product Attributes

Developing a new product that will be a winner requires attention to the details of the total product concept. The complication with new products, compared with researching attributes of existing products, is the difficulty consumers have in thinking about products with which they have no experience. Often, new product research investigates only tangible attributes and market segmentation variables rather than the lifestyle or other software details that determine the success or failure of the product.

Focus groups are a technique that can be helpful in the investigation of specific details that determine the fate of the products. Focus groups can even be used to spot the trends that indicate needs that lead to new product development. Products most likely to succeed are those that solve consumers' problems. Where do problems come from? From life; therefore consumer analysts need good methods to study lifestyles. New products, however, often must be based on emerging lifestyles, and these are difficult to measure with quantitative techniques. Emerging lifestyles and trends usually are uncovered through qualitative research. A popular method of qualitative research is focus groups to indicate consumer acceptance of items that adapt to their wants, needs, and behavior. Two approaches are inferred insights and cross-study insights.[25]

Inferred insights are observations drawn from product-specific studies, revealing whether consumers feel certain products fit their lives. Cross-study insights are observations based on a wide variety of product-specific studies. They help uncover demographic groups, psychographic groups, changing values, and shopping habits, as well as feelings about advertising, service, and health.

Judith Langer, president of a New York research firm, usually begins lifestyle studies by asking consumers this question: "Thinking about yourself and the people you know, how is your lifestyle different today from a few years ago?" Focusing on change by having respondents describe ways in which their lives have been altered gives clues about where they are heading and the types of products they will take with them.

Communications about New Products

Communication is the process by which consumers and marketing organizations share information with one another to reach a mutual understanding. Communication is critical to the widespread acceptance of new products, just as it is to other products discussed throughout this book. Some principles are especially applicable to new product decisions of consumers, however, and are described subsequently.

Two models have been used by marketers in attempts to gain acceptance of new products. One is called the **hypodermic needle model**. It proposes that media have direct, immediate, and powerful effects on the acceptance of new products by a mass audience. Mass media are especially important in the acceptance of continuous innovations. As new products approach higher levels of discontinuity (that is, more fundamental behavioral changes are required of adopters), however, the media appear to be limited in effectiveness. For innovations, the media are considered to be less important than interpersonal communications, especially those of opinion leaders.

The **two-step flow model** or **multistage flow model** provides another view of the role of media and personal communications. In this model of innovation communication, ideas flow from the media to opinion leaders and from those opinion leaders to the mass market. The mass media accomplish the transfer of information to opinion leaders, but influence is transferred by opinion leaders to the rest of the population.

Word of Mouth: Key to Success for New Products

Word of mouth (WOM), or interpersonal communications, plays a critical role in the adoption of new products. WOM is most important when the product is perceived to have substantial social, psychological, or economic risk involved in its purchase. WOM is also important when the choice between products is ambiguous. At later stages of the decision process to buy a new product—when people are evaluating products or confirming their decision—and when consumers have substantial experience with a product category, they may be more willing to rely on the media. But the more innovative the product, the more likely consumers will be influenced by an existing user of the product or someone they consider an "expert" on the subject.

Speed of Diffusion

Although WOM is very important to the innovation diffusion process, marketers have little control over this variable. Marketers have more control over some factors, such as product characteristics, pricing, and resource allocations, which contribute to the speed of diffusion. Robertson and Gatignon[26] compiled the diffusion literature into the following propositions that affect the speed of diffusion.

The greater the **competitive intensity** of the supplier, the more rapid the diffusion and the higher the diffusion level. Highly competitive firms have more aggressive pricing strategies and allocate greater resources to the product introduction. Intense competition frequently leads to price wars and an increase in demand due to the more price-sensitive customers entering the market. High competitive intensity is likely to reduce the market penetration level for any given firm within an industry, however.

The better the **reputation of the supplier** (breeding confidence among potential adopters), the faster the initial diffusion, even though the final shape of the diffusion curve may depend on the actual technology incorporated into the product. A good reputation leads to source credibility, which in turn may reduce uncertainty and risk in the purchase decision.

Products diffuse more rapidly when **standardized technology** is used. This is particularly true with products dependent on auxiliary components, such as personal computers. Consumers may believe a purchase to be more risky if they are unsure which technology will become standard. When this risk is reduced or avoided, more consumers are likely to adopt the product. High-resolution television (HRT), for example, offers readily perceived benefits to consumers but was delayed until the 1990s in the United States because of difficulty in agreeing on either the European or Japanese standards.

Vertical coordination, which refers to a high degree of vertical dependence and an interlocking relationship among channel members, is also related to diffusion. As coordination increases, the information flow from supplier to consumer increases. As a result, diffusion increases. A corollary to this idea is that as information flows back up the channel—from consumer to supplier—innovative customers and opinion leaders can help identify new product opportunities.

Resource commitments are also important to the diffusion process. Greater research and development expenditures are positively related to innovations. As technologies become enhanced and more alternatives become available, diffusion will become broader and more rapid. As advertising, personal selling, sales promotion activities, and distribution support increase, diffusion also increases. Marketing research allocations can help guide R&D expenditures as well as develop a positioning strategy for the new technology; both of these areas are instrumental in the diffusion process.

Homophily-Heterophily: Whom Do You Trust?

Consumers tend to trust a homophilous person when they need information about new products. **Homophily** is the degree to which pairs of individuals who interact are similar in important attributes such as beliefs, education, and social status. When people share common meanings, beliefs, and a mutual language, communication between them is more likely to be effective. **Heterophilous communications** may cause cognitive dissonance because individuals are exposed to messages that are inconsistent with their own beliefs and values. Homophily and effective communication, in contrast, breed each other.

Perhaps you are beginning to understand why so many new products fail. Marketing strategies rely heavily on advertising and personal selling—messages transmitted with a definite bias in their opinion ("buy our product") from people and organizations who exist outside the interpersonal communications network. Keep in mind that the homophily principle also means that people tend to trust people of similar socioeconomic status to themselves when deciding to buy new products. Many times, advertising spokespeople and sales personnel are heterophilous with the potential buyers of the new products.

Everett Rogers reviewed thousands of empirical studies concerning the diffusion of innovations, and many of these dealt with the issue of effective communications. He summarized his conclusions from this research in 17 generalizations. These, along with the number and percentage of studies that support each, are presented in Table 24.1. Although this and later tables in this chapter

Table 24.1   Summary of Research Evidence Supporting and Not Supporting Generalizations about Opinion Leadership and Diffusion Networks

Generalization	Support for the Generalization (Number of Research Studies)		Percentage of Research Studies Supporting the Generalization
	Supporting	Not Supporting	
8-1: Interpersonal diffusion networks are mostly homophilous.	22	13	62
8-2: When interpersonal diffusion networks are heterophilous, followers seek opinion leaders of higher socioeconomic status.	11	0	100
8-3: When interpersonal diffusion networks are heterophilous, followers seek opinion leaders with more education.	6	2	75
8-4: When interpersonal diffusion networks are heterophilous, followers seek opinion leaders with greater mass media exposure.	5	0	100
8-5: When interpersonal diffusion networks are heterophilous, followers seek opinion leaders who are more cosmopolitan.	1	0	100
8-6: When interpersonal diffusion networks are heterophilous, followers seek opinion leaders with greater change agent contact.	2	0	100
8-7: When interpersonal diffusion networks are heterophilous, followers seek opinion leaders who are more innovative.	10	1	91
8-8: Opinion leaders have greater exposure to mass media than their followers.	9	1	90
8-9: Opinion leaders are more cosmopolitan than their followers.	10	3	77
8-10: Opinion leaders have greater change agent contact than their followers.	10	3	77
8-11: Opinion leaders have greater social participation than their followers.	11	4	73
8-12: Opinion leaders have higher socioeconomic status than their followers.	20	7	74
8-13: Opinion leaders are more innovative than their followers.	24	4	86
8-14: When a social system's norms favor change, opinion leaders are more innovative, but when the norms do not favor change, opinion leaders are not especially innovative.	7	2	78
8-15: The interconnectedness of an individual in a social system is positively related to the individual's innovativeness.	4	0	100
8-16: The information-exchange potential of communication network links is negatively related to their degree of (1) communication proximity, and (2) homophily.	2	0	100
8-17: Individuals tend to be linked to others who are close to them in physical distance and who are relatively homophilous in social characteristics.	9	0	100

Source: Everett M. Rogers, Diffusion of Innovations, 3rd ed. (New York: Free Press, 1983), 308–309.

may seem complicated, as you study them you will see they provide excellent insights to understanding diffusion and how to encourage it.

Marketing Management of WOM

Marketing organizations function as change agents—stimulating the diffusion of the new product. Change agents need to manage WOM. Public relations and sales promotion are examples of programs that accomplish the goal of stimulating WOM.

Among business or industrial firms, there is an increasing practice of bringing the key opinion leaders in an industry together for a party, seminar, laser show, or other event in which these leaders become aware of, experience, and evaluate the new product. They return home and tell opinion followers about it. This has become standard practice when firms such as IBM, Xerox, and Apple introduce new products. As methods of managing WOM such mega events not only are effective ways of introducing new products but they may also be used to revitalize existing products to generate positive affective response and a new vitality.

Stimulating Opinion Leadership

When LaCoste was a small, unknown marketer of premium shirts, it developed a new concept of selling quality sports apparel for everyday usage. To achieved diffusion of this concept, LaCoste gave shirts bearing its logo—a distinctive alligator—to tennis and media celebrities. After the careful placement of these shirts with key opinion leaders who were encouraged to wear them in places other than the tennis courts, there was widespread diffusion of the concept of wearing "Alligators" in settings far removed from tennis courts. Mass media can create awareness and even interest in new products, but personal communications are more effective in persuading people to try new products.

Sales Promotion

When Owens-Corning introduced a new drapery fabric made of Fiberglas, the company developed a total promotional program that emphasized the interpersonal communications that might occur among homeowners. Among other things, the company knew that the people in the "back rooms" of fabric departments often talked with customers when they measured and installed the draperies. To ensure that even these people said good things and supported good WOM, Owens-Corning promoted a contest featuring a luxurious vacation for the "back room" that installed the most draperies made of the new Fiberglas product.

Public Relations

Managing WOM well often involves public relations as an important marketing function. Too often, public relations has been considered a function of finance, industrial relations, or other areas of the firm. Publicity and public relations, however, should be viewed as a major communications priority, especially among marketing managers working on new product introduction. WOM can be stimulated by well-placed publicity in the media, for example. Trade shows can be made more effective in introducing new products because of media presence and interest in the "latest and newest." Consumer electronics shows, toy shows, and clothing fashion shows are typical examples of events where firms make extensive use of publicity to stimulate WOM about their new products.

There are also cases in which unfavorable interpersonal communications can kill a new product. As an example, Anheuser-Busch introduced a soft drink called Chelsea, which contained a very small amount of alcohol, so low that labeling requirements did not even require mention of the alcohol. The word got around about the alcohol, however, and even though teenagers could drink two cases without becoming intoxicated, they would drink two or three bottles and pretend to be drunk. Parents went through the roof, forcing the withdrawal of the product from the market. The advertising was great, but that was irrelevant. WOM killed the product. Years later, the Gulf War created a situation in which members of the U.S. military drank Sharp's and O'Doul's nonalcoholic beer, and when they returned to civilian life, the brands experienced a sharp increase in sales due to both publicity about and usage of a product perceived as "new" by many consumers.

Adoption-Decision Process over Time

Adoption of a new product is a decision process, in many ways similar to the general decision process described throughout this book. Not only does an individual consumer move through the stages of adopting the product through time, but other consumers are also moving through the process, probably at different rates and with different starting points in time. Thus, adoption of new products must be understood in a temporal context. Avoid any illusion that acceptance occurs instantly, either for an individual or a society. The rate of diffusion will vary between societies based on cultural values. If a marketer can determine the degree to which a society is futuristic, normal, or tradition-oriented, timing and expectations of the diffusion will be modified for each market.[27]

Understanding the temporal process of adoption is very important. Otherwise, a firm might introduce a product, advertise it heavily, and commit large amounts of resources to the project, only to see it "fail." In actuality, the product may not have had enough time to move through the early stages that must inevitably be passed before arriving at the action—purchase—desired by the marketer. Frequently, firms fail when introducing new products because they underestimate the time required for new products to diffuse through the market.

Business firms sometimes act as if individual consumers or markets simply decide to buy or not buy. When this fallacious assumption is made, the firm is likely not to budget properly, not to calculate return correctly, or not to plan promotional activity effectively. A further complication may arise because of confusing adoption of the physical product with the product concept or idea. People may move through the entire process of adoption but, due to situations such as their current inventory of goods or inadequate income, not buy the product until later. All elements of the firm's marketing program may have been well designed and executed, but the firm will fail if it does not understand the time and situations required for new product adoption.

Understanding the time and process required for adoption to occur may help explain why so many new products fail, especially when they are discontinuous innovations. Too many firms appear to believe that if they just develop a new product that fits an important need recognized by consumers and promote, price, and distribute it well, sales should result. Unfortunately, it does not work that way.

Marketing analysts have examined the process of both adoption and diffusion for many years. Models that have been used to depict the process are shown in Figure 24.6. An early conceptualization of adoption was called **AIDA** (awareness, interest, desire, action). Alternative conceptualizations of this process use different terminology but are attempts to describe the same process, as Figure 24.6 shows.

The most widely adopted model is that of Rogers, in which stages are described as knowledge, persuasion, decision, implementation, and confirmation. The Rogers model of innovation decisions is compared with alternatives in Figure 24.6, and the variables associated with movement through the process are elaborated in Figure 24.7.

Knowledge

The knowledge stage begins when a consumer receives physical or social stimuli that give exposure and attention to the new product and how it works. In this stage, consumers are aware of the product but have made no judgment concerning the relevance of the product to a problem or a recognized need. Knowledge of the new product is usually thought to be a result of selective perception. It is more likely to occur through the mass media than in later stages, which are more influenced by opinion leaders.

Persuasion

Persuasion, in the Rogers paradigm, refers to the formation of favorable or unfavorable attitudes toward the innovation. The consumer may mentally imagine how satisfactory the new product might be in some anticipated future-use situation, perhaps giving the product a "vicarious trial" in the consumer's mind.

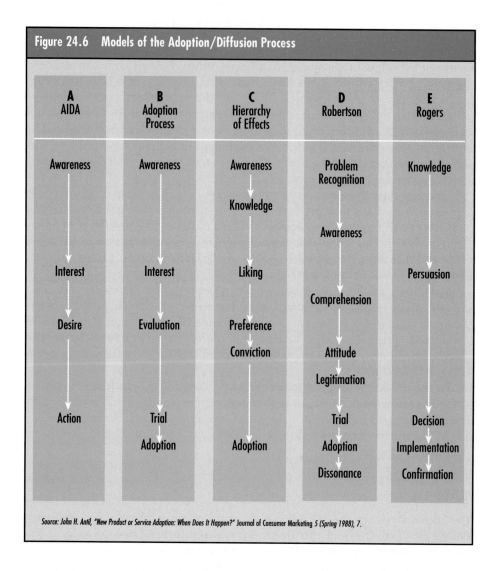

Figure 24.6   Models of the Adoption/Diffusion Process

A AIDA	B Adoption Process	C Hierarchy of Effects	D Robertson	E Rogers
Awareness	Awareness	Awareness	Problem Recognition	Knowledge
		Knowledge		
			Awareness	
Interest	Interest	Liking		Persuasion
			Comprehension	
Desire	Evaluation	Preference		
		Conviction	Attitude	
			Legitimation	
Action	Trial		Trial	Decision
	Adoption	Adoption	Adoption	Implementation
			Dissonance	Confirmation

Source: John H. Antil, "New Product or Service Adoption: When Does It Happen?" Journal of Consumer Marketing 5 (Spring 1988), 7.

Persuasiveness is related to perceived risk in the new product or an evaluation of the consequences of using the product. When an individual considers a new product, she or he must weight the potential gains from adopting the product against the potential losses of switching from the product now used. If the new product is adopted, it may be inferior to a present product or the cost may be greater than the increased value gained by using the new product. Consumer in Focus 24.3 shows how perceived risk plays a role in the process of consumers adopting a new breakfast cereal.

Knowledge and persuasion are necessary conditions for adoption but not necessarily sufficient. Potential adopters, may be persuaded of the advantages

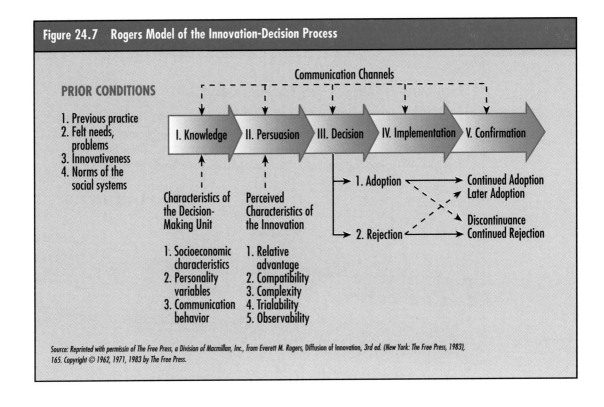

Figure 24.7   Rogers Model of the Innovation-Decision Process

Communication Channels

PRIOR CONDITIONS

1. Previous practice
2. Felt needs, problems
3. Innovativeness
4. Norms of the social systems

I. Knowledge   II. Persuasion   III. Decision   IV. Implementation   V. Confirmation

Characteristics of the Decision-Making Unit

Perceived Characteristics of the Innovation

1. Adoption
2. Rejection

Continued Adoption
Later Adoption
Discontinuance
Continued Rejection

1. Socioeconomic characteristics
2. Personality variables
3. Communication behavior

1. Relative advantage
2. Compatibility
3. Complexity
4. Trialability
5. Observability

Source: Reprinted with permissin of The Free Press, a Division of Macmillan, Inc., from Everett M. Rogers, Diffusion of Innovation, 3rd ed. (New York: The Free Press, 1983), 165. Copyright © 1962, 1971, 1983 by The Free Press.

and the importance of accepting an innovation (see Fig. 24.7). Some will not do so, however, because of a variety of person and/or situation-specific factors. Consumers may not have the economic resources to buy or try it. Perhaps their current technology, as in the case of many computer and communication products, may cause significant constraint on adoption.

Consumers can reduce perceived risk in adopting new products—and consequently, the uncertainty that retards buying—by acquiring additional information. A person may seek out news stories, pay particular attention to advertising for the product, subscribe to product-rating services, talk with individuals who have already tried the product, talk with experts on the subject, or in some instances, try the product on a limited basis. Adopters of new health care products, for example, are most likely to rely on medical experts, but nonadopters may rely more on interpersonal sources.[28] Each of these information-search and evaluation strategies has a financial and/or psychological cost. Moreover, they are unlikely to yield information that will completely reduce uncertainty.

Catalogs are often used to introduce new products because they can solve many problems. One reason for their effectiveness includes the ability to provide more information than the typical retail setting. Figure 24.8 (page 896)

24.3 | **Consumer in Focus**

How Consumers Adopt a New Breakfast Cereal

New breakfast cereals are constantly entering the market. About half of consumers are brand loyal but others adopt new brands, with 23 percent changing monthly. One reason for reluctance to adopt new brands is a consumer perception of more risk with new products. Not liking the taste and a waste of money (financial risk) are the most common risks. Providing free samples or small, trial sizes as well as low intro-

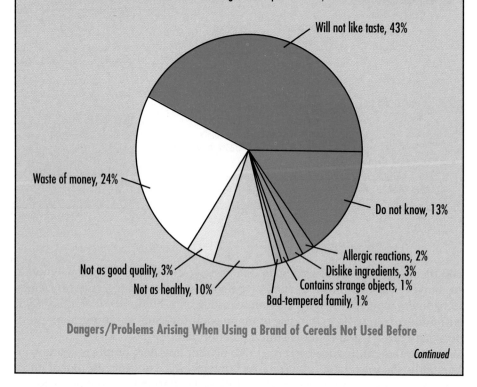

Will not like taste, 43%

Waste of money, 24%

Do not know, 13%

Allergic reactions, 2%
Dislike ingredients, 3%
Contains strange objects, 1%

Not as good quality, 3%
Not as healthy, 10%
Bad-tempered family, 1%

Dangers/Problems Arising When Using a Brand of Cereals Not Used Before

Continued

provides an example for an innovative product called ScanCard. Notice how the left side of this ad addresses many of the problems that consumers have in organizing their time for maximum productivity. The ad is also graphic and large enough to gain attention. The copy addresses several needs and attempts to show the relative advantages over present solutions to productivity problems. The endorsement in the bottom of the left page includes references to opinion leaders such as AT&T and Procter & Gamble. Attempts are made to reduce perceived financial risk by full refund if the product does not increase productivity. This quantity of information would not be available in a retail store nor would consumers have the time to read the information in most advertising media, but

Consumer in Focus, continued **24.3**

ductory prices are ways to reduce financial risk. Given that the main risk is that of taste, the market could be segmented by taste. For example, when aiming the product at children, sweeter cereals could be developed, concentrating on packaging, advertising and endorsements. Nutritional value might be used as a segmentation tool when targeting the cereal at the female market, since this is more important for female purchasers. Clearly, the most important attribute to emphasize is taste. The vast majority of consumers are almost never certain that a new brand of cereal they have not tried before will be as good as their brand. About 24 percent of consumers are very willing to try a familiar brand of a new product but only 1 percent are willing to try a new product with an unfamiliar brand. This confirms the efficiency of introducing new products with well-accepted brands.

Not influenced

Husband/wife, 37%

Advertising, 2%

Doctor's advice, 2%

Influenced Children, 49%

Friends/relatives, 10%

26%

Purchaser

Influences on the Purchaser

Source: V. W. Mitchell and P. Boustani, "Market Development Using New Products and New Customers: A Role for Perceived Risk," *European Journal of Marketing* 27 (1993), 17–32.

this ad is in flight magazines when potential consumers have considerable free time for studying such information. Using an "800" number and bank cards also makes the decision as easy as possible.

Decision

The decision stage involves activities that lead to a choice between adopting or rejecting the innovation. Adoption can be defined as a decision to make full use of an innovation as the best course of action. Adoption involves both psychological and behavioral commitment to a product over time.[29] Ordinarily, this

Figure 24.8   Providing Knowledge to Potential Consumers for a New Product

Source: Courtesy of Executive Gallery.

means continued use of the product unless situational variables (lack of availability, and so on) prevent usage. Rejection is a decision not to adopt an innovation. Active rejection consists of considering adoption of an innovation, perhaps even a trial, but then deciding not to adopt it. Passive rejection (or nonadoption) consists of never really considering use of the innovation.

Implementation

Implementation occurs when the consumer puts an innovation into use. Until the implementation stage, the process has been a strictly mental exercise, but now behavioral change is required. The strength of the marketing plan may be the critical determinant in whether a good product that has been communicated effectively actually results in a sale.

The marketing mix should make purchase easy. To do so requires careful coordination of the channels of distribution with the new product information and communication process. Price is also an important ingredient. In the introduction of microcomputers, software availability, sales demonstrations in nonthreatening environments, price concessions, and educational seminars may be as important in the success of the innovation as the product itself—perhaps more so. Often consumers find ways of implementing a new product not even considered by the change agent. An example is illustrated by Post-it Notes, a new product consisting of simple notepaper with a special adhesive strip on the back. The product was introduced by 3M and has diffused throughout the world as a replacement for paper clips, notepads, and loose pieces of paper. 3M made extensive use of sampling and because the samples were "free," office workers took the Post-it Notes home. Family members began using them for many purposes, creating rapid diffusion of the product.

Confirmation

Confirmation is the process through which consumers seek reinforcement for the innovation decision. Consumers sometimes reverse previous decisions, especially when exposed to conflicting messages about the innovation, causing dissonance.

Discontinuance is a serious concern to marketers. The rate of discontinuance may be as important as the rate of adoption, with a corresponding need for marketing strategies to devote attention to preventing its occurrence. Pringles was introduced by Procter & Gamble as a new potato snack and was successful in attracting many adopters. The product eventually failed in its original form, however, because the level of discontinuers was so high, a condition the company did not observe until too late.

People who adopt the product later than early adopters may be more likely to discontinue adoption. Marketing organizations must work hard, therefore, with follow-up service and feedback as sales of a new product expand.

Discontinuance is likely to occur when the new product is not integrated into the practices and ways of life of the purchasers or when the new product conflicts with some aspects of consumer lifestyles.

Consumers Most Likely to Buy New Products

Which consumers are most likely to buy new products? If you knew the answer to that question, consider how helpful it would be in concentrating the firm's resources on those people as primary targets for the marketing program of new products. Although the following discussion is based on research about individuals, keep in mind that family and other influences can be very important. Burns[30] found evidence

> . . . to support the premise that a wife is the primary force behind the expression of innovative behavior in a family structure that includes a husband and a wife. It further appears that wives' needs may be the driving factor behind much of the innovative behavior decision making that occurs in such families today, and the evidence suggests that this influence extends to several product categories.

Adopter Classes

Consumers can be classified according to the time they adopt a new product relative to other consumers. In the decision to buy a specific new product, some people are innovators. Others are early adopters. Others can be classified as early or later majority. The ones who are last to adopt the product are called laggards. The distribution of people has been described as a normal distribution or, when describing the cumulative total of adopters, as an S curve. These distributions are shown in the top portion of Figure 24.9. Both curves represent the same data. The S-shaped curve represents the adoption of the innovation over time by the members of a social system, whereas the bell-shaped curve presents these data in terms of individuals adopting each year. The shaded area marks the time period during which the S curve of diffusion "takes off"—the critical interval between failure or success for most marketers.

The pattern shown in Figure 24.9 displays what is sometimes described as an imitation effect. That is, the rate of adoption increases as the number of adopters increases.[31] An idea is transmitted to a few innovators who must pass through various stages to acceptance or rejection. After some innovators have adopted the product, others may follow, depending on the value of the innovation and other characteristics of the product.

The lower portion of Figure 24.9 vividly emphasizes the point that acceptance of a new product does not come all at once in a social system. Usually, it comes much slower than marketers wish it did. The process continues throughout the

Figure 24.9 Classifying Adopter Categories

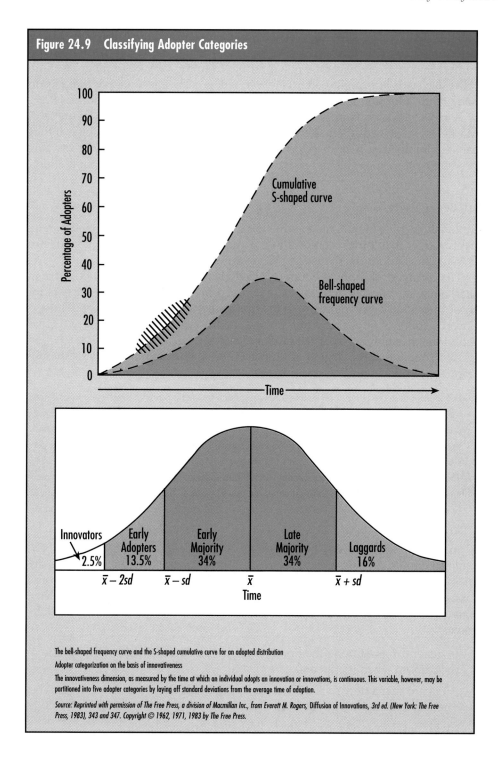

The bell-shaped frequency curve and the S-shaped cumulative curve for an adopted distribution

Adopter categorization on the basis of innovativeness

The innovativeness dimension, as measured by the time at which an individual adopts an innovation or innovations, is continuous. This variable, however, may be partitioned into five adopter categories by laying off standard deviations from the average time of adoption.

social system, and its speed as well as eventual penetration of the system will be determined by many factors. Not everyone falls into these categories. Some consumers may actively reject the new product from the very beginning. They are called laggards but might better be described as early rejectors. For that reason and others, adoption may be less than the 100 percent shown in Figure 24.9.

A key conclusion is possible from the phenomena expressed in Figure 24.9. Marketers must focus their attention on the innovators and early adopters if they can be identified. If marketers do not succeed in winning adoption of the new product by these people, there is not much hope for the rest of the population.

Innovativeness

Innovativeness is the degree to which an individual adopts an innovation relatively earlier than other members in the system. A goal of marketing strategies is to understand innovativeness to target innovators.

The construct of innovativeness typically is measured in one of two ways in marketing studies. The first measure is based on time of adoption, such as for those individuals who purchase in the first x weeks, months, and so on. The second is a count of how many of a prespecified list of new products a particular individual has purchased at the time of the study.

Everyone has some degree of innovativeness. Hirschman[32] explains the importance of understanding this principle:

> Few concepts in the behavioral sciences have as much immediate relevance to consumer behavior as innovativeness. The propensities of consumers to adopt novel products, whether they are ideas, goods, or services, can play an important role in theories of brand loyalty, decision making, preference, and communication. If there were not such characteristics as innovativeness, consumer behavior would consist of a series of routine buying responses to a static set of products. The inherent willingness of a consuming population to innovate is what gives the market place its dynamic nature. On an individual basis, every consumer is, to some extent, an innovator; all of us over the course of our lives adopt some objects or ideas that are new in our perception.

Innovativeness can also be measured with self-reporting instruments. The scale should be domain-specific or refer to new products within a specific domain of interest. An example is provided for interest in rock music records and tapes in the research of Goldsmith and Hofacker.[33] It asks people to indicate their agreement (or disagreement to negatives, in parenthesis) to the following statements:

> In general, I am among the first (last) in my circle of friends to buy a new rock album when it appears.

> If I heard that a new rock album was available in the store, I would (not) be interested enough to buy it.

> I will (not) buy a new rock album if I haven't heard it yet.

> I (do not) know the names of new rock acts before other people do.

Three main types of variables have been studied to determine their correlation with innovativeness: socioeconomic, personality, and communication behavior. These variables and the conclusions about their relationships (positive, negative, or not related) are described below, based on Rogers,[34] who has summarized years of research on the diffusion process.

Socioeconomic Variables

Most studies that analyze socioeconomic variables show the following variables to be positively related to innovativeness:

Education

Literacy

Higher social status

Upward social mobility

Larger-sized units

Commercial, rather than a subsistence orientation

More favorable attitude toward credit

More specialized operations

Studies have been mixed in their conclusions about the effect of age on innovativeness. Remember that nearly all the above conclusions have been modified or contradicted in some studies, indicating that these relationships must always be interpreted in the context of specific products and buying situations.

For most situations, however, marketing programs for innovative products are most likely to succeed if they are directed to people of high social status, who are upwardly mobile, educated and/or literate, and who are privileged relative to others in the social system. Income is almost always useful in profiling innovativeness. Higher-income people not only have the ability to buy more new products, but they also have the ability to take the risk of trying new products.

Personality and Attitude

Personality and attitudinal variables associated with innovativeness in consumers include positive relationships with the following:

Empathy

Ability to deal with abstractions

Rationality

Intelligence

Favorable attitude toward change

Ability to cope with uncertainty

Favorable attitude toward education

Favorable attitude toward science

Achievement motivation

High aspirations

Negative relationships between innovativeness and personality variables have generally been found for the following:

Dogmatism

Fatalism

Consumers also may react to new products based on their cognitive style of problem solving. Kirton[35] indicated people can be placed on a continuum between two extremes: adaptors or innovators. Extreme adaptors will adopt solutions that improve technical efficiency but involve practices and objects similar to those previously used for the same purpose. Innovators are less likely to seek solutions within the context of previous solutions to the problem. They tend to produce different ways of organizing, deciding, and behaving that entail radical change and the incorporation of novel activities, techniques, and objects. Using the Kirton Adaption-Innovation Inventory (KAI), Foxall and Hawkins[36] found relationships between this measure of personality and innovative brand choice. Behavior varies by stage of the consumer decision process.[37] Examples are shown in Table 24.2.

Innovators can be segmented into cognitive innovators and sensory innovators. **Cognitive innovators** have a strong preference for new mental experiences. **Sensory innovators** have a strong preference for new sensory experiences. Some innovators prefer both. Cognitive innovators enjoy thinking, problem solving, puzzling over issues, and other mental exertions whereas sensory innovativeness involves new experiences such as fantasy and daydreaming and externally available new thrilling and adventurous activities.[38]

Advertising and other communication messages can be targeted to cognitive and sensory innovators. For cognitive innovators, communications should emphasize the relative advantages of the innovation in comparison with other existing products and services and deemphasize the enjoyment risk. For sensory innovators, communications should emphasize the uniqueness of the product and reduce its complexity, performance, and economic risks. For sensory innovators, marketers should reduce complexity and risk with long warranties, manufacturer-supported service centers, toll-free lines, and easy-to-read and understand instructions. For cognitive innovators, product manuals and other product information can be comprehensive and detailed, including sections on the technology and advanced applications. For sensory innovators, it is important to make the set-up and operating instructions very simple. Sensory innovators typically are younger males; cognitive innovators have higher educations. This makes it possible to select the media to reach these segments with the communication messages that can be tailored to the attributes they are seeking.[39]

Table 24.2   Decision Styles of Market Segments Based on Adaption-Innovation and Personal Involvement

Adoption decision-process stage	Less-involved adaptors	Innovators	More-involved adaptors
Problem recognition Search	Passive, reactive Minimal, confined to resolution of minor anomalies caused by current consumption patterns	Active Superficial but extensively based within and across product class boundaries	Proactive Extensive within relevant product category; assiduous exploration of all possible solutions within that framework
Evaluation	Meticulous, rational, slow and cautious; objective appraisal using tried and tested criteria	Quick, impulsive, based on currently accepted criteria; personal and subjective	Careful, confined to considerations raised by the relevant product category but executed confidently and (for the Adaptor) briskly within that frame of reference
Decision	Conservative selection within known range of products, continuous innovations preferred	Radical; easily attracted to discontinuously new product class and able to choose quickly within it. Frequent trial, followed by abandonment	Careful selection within a product field that has become familiar through deliberation, vicarious trial, and sound and prudent pre-purchase comparative evaluation
Post-purchase evaluation	Meticulous, tendency to brand loyalty if item performs well	Less loyal; constantly seeking novel experiences through purchase and consumption	Loyal if satisfied but willing to try innovations within the prescribed frame of reference; perhaps tends toward dynamically continuous innovations

Source: Gordon Roxall and Seema Bhate, "Cognitive Style and Personal Involvement as Explicators of Innovative Purchasing of 'Healthy' Food Brands," European Journal of Marketing 27 (1993) 13.

Communication Variables

Communication behavior variables that are positively associated with innovativeness include the following:

Social participation

Interconnectedness with the social system

Cosmopoliteness

Change agent contact

Mass media exposure

Exposure to interpersonal communication channels

Knowledge of innovations

Opinion leadership

Belonging to highly interconnected systems

Some of these variables—such as cosmopoliteness—are ones in which the marketing program must be adapted. Others—such as mass media exposure—may be influenced directly by marketing. In the past, it was thought that innovators and early adopters use the mass media more but that later adopters use interpersonal sources more. Some research indicates that earlier adopters use both mass media and interpersonal sources more than later adopters.[40]

Polymorphism

Polymorphism is the degree to which the innovators and early adopters for one product are likely to be innovators for other products. Consumers who are innovators for many products are said to be polymorphic, whereas those who are innovators for only one product are **monomorphic.** If innovativeness is monomorphic, the process of finding innovators for a specific new product may not be worth the cost. If it is polymorphic, however, the search would be justified more.

Findings are conflicting in this area, but a position may be emerging that identifies categories of products that have the same innovators. For example, some people tend to be technophiles and are easy to sell a wide range of the latest techno-toys, whereas other people are technophobes and would not touch a computer if you paid them. Technology is to them as snakes, spiders, and heights are to other fear-filled people. These types of consumers are described in Consumer in Focus 24.4. The people who are likely to be innovators for microcomputers or a wide range of consumer electronics are unlikely, however, to be innovators for fashion clothing, food, or other products.

Predicting Diffusion and Adoption Success

Marketing strategies often have a need for predicting the ultimate sales that will be achieved for new products in future time periods. Several mathematical approaches are used for this purpose.[41]

Fundamental diffusion models are called *penetration* models. These predict the level of penetration by a new product in a given time period based on early sales results. *Epidemiologic* models predict acceptance based on the view that new product diffusion is a process of social interaction in which the innovators and early adopters "infect" the rest of the people, similar to disease epidemics that move through a population. These models are stochastic in nature. Analy-

| **Consumer in Focus** | **24.4** |

Technophiles and Technophones

The original personal computer is like an abacus when compared with new technologies on the horizon. Consumers will soon have the chance to buy interactive television, virtual-reality toys, and wireless communications. The world is divided into those who will eagerly await these new products, those who will shrug at them, and a large group who actively fear them. Understanding what makes each group tick is vital to selling any new technology and the services that go with them.

Technophones

Technophones are people who can program their VCRs. But more than that, they are "early adopters," people whose interest extends beyond the practical use of technology. They get excited about technology itself, whatever its purpose. One in five American adults is a "techthusiast" according to a study by Backer Spielvogel Bates (BSB) of New York. These 37 million adults are younger, more affluent, and better-educated than the average American. Despite their technical bent, they watch less television than average and read more magazines and newspapers. With a median household income of $56,500, techthusiasts can afford to take a chance on new gadgets.

Technophobes

One-fourth of American adults have never used a computer or programmed a VCR. A similar share are not comfortable using a computer on their own. More striking is the nearly one-third of adults who are so intimidated by computers that they are afraid they will break them. Nearly one-fourth of the phones, or about 8 percent of all adults, are uncomfortable setting a digital alarm clock. The age gap shows up here. Nine in ten teenagers are comfortable using a range of technical devices, from answering machines and VCRs to compact-disc players and computers. Only 74 percent of older adults can claim this level of ease. Auto manufacturers would never try to sell a car that requires drivers to understand the workings of an internal combustion engine. Yet many businesses that sell new technologies still do not realize that many consumers just want to turn it on and go.

For evidence of the generational technology gap, look no further than the nation's capital. When boomer president Bill Clinton moved in, he found a White House frozen in time. Telephone operators had to plug cords into the switchboard to connect callers. There was one lonely fax machine in the communications department. Clinton could barely grasp how anyone could work in an environment so low-tech that it didn't have e-mail. Clinton's young staffers quickly brought in new technologies. Now, if you want to reach the president, you can send an e-mail message to *president@whitehouse.gov*.

Source: Excerpts from Susan Mitchell, "Technophiles and Technophobes," American Demographics 16 (February 1994), 36.

sis in the marketing literature has generally focused on the structural or mathematical properties of the models rather than on a comparison of their ability to generate forecasts of new product sales in empirical studies. An excellent review of these models is available in Mahajan and Peterson.[42]

Adoption models are deterministic. They include internal variables that describe consumer decision making concerning the new product and the effects of external variables that may affect the penetration rates and timing of acceptance. These models, and hybrids that relate external variables to diffusion models, can be useful to show effects of marketing mix variables. Horsky and Simon,[43] for example, showed that advertising can accelerate the diffusion process. Optimal effects on profitability occur when a firm advertises heavily when the product is introduced and reduces advertising as the product moves through its life cycle and interpersonal communications take effect.

Many adoption models, incorporating market structure variables, are used by advertising agencies and other organizations involved in new product introductions. They use test-market data and simulation models, which when combined with early returns in the marketplace can help forecast future sales and profitability of the new product as well as understand why consumers consider or reject new products.[44] These proprietary models have evolved from the academic research of management scientists to become standard practice in many good marketing organizations.[45] The increasing availability of scanner data in some markets will allow more development of models that predict ultimate market acceptance based on early information about the new product.

Diffusion of Diffusion

Information about the diffusion process has been circulated widely through academic and business organizations. Perhaps no topic of discussion has been affected by, and affected, so many diverse disciplines. Marketing managers could greatly improve the introduction of new products by simply reviewing plans on the basis of principles that are well established in the diffusion literature as it has been described in this chapter.

There is still room for improvement. Much of the diffusion research was conducted in social systems that are much more controlled than those faced by marketing managers. Many of the studies were conducted with discontinuous, high-involvement products that are different from the more mundane products marketing managers often must introduce. There is much more to be learned about diffusion research,[46] but few topics you can study in consumer behavior may be as directly applicable to marketing problems as the study of the diffusion of new products. Management of the innovation process is often hampered by the pressure for quick volume sales, which encourage low-utility new products as well as a system of rewards and promotion in many firms that encourage a custodial approach to management, rather than a higher-risk entrepreneurial approach.[47]

Consumer in Focus **24.5**

Ford Taurus Copycat Stuff? Hardly!

When Ford Motor Co. set out to design the Taurus, it looked hard at the competition: Let's see what we can learn from those guys. But the way they went about it was different, intriguing, and a focus forcer.

Under Vice President Lew Veraldi's direction, Team Taurus identified some 40 cars in the rough class category they were examining (midsize, four door). The idea was to pick the best cars they thought they could learn from—the "best of class"—and see what rival companies and vehicles from all over the world had to teach Ford.

Of the 40, they selected about a dozen cars (most of them foreign), which were then subjected to the indignity of what they call the "layered stripdown." They took them apart piece by piece to see how the cars were made.

They learned a lot. The stripdown helped them identify 400 features that went on their Taurus wish list—items they thought they might be able to beat, or at least emulate. The feature might be something as visible to the customer as a better lumbar support system in the seats, or as innocent and invisible as an engine part designed to be more accessible to the mechanic.

Of the 400, Ford reckons it either met or bettered the competition in 360 of them. It sounds like copycat stuff. Maybe that's why companies don't look at competition in this way more often. But Ford will tell you that this is the first time in a long while that they haven't felt like imitators following a me-too strategy. It's a paradox—by taking little pieces of others, you become a better version of yourself. Ford continued to improve the product with driver's and passenger's air bags and a top of the line Taurus—the SHO, capable of speeds in excess of 150 miles an hour. The result of all this: By 1993, the innovative Taurus beat out Honda to become the best selling car in America.

Sources: Based on Robert H. Waterman, Jr., The Renewal Factor: How the Best Get and Keep the Competitive Edge (New York: Bantam Books, 1987); and Roger D. Blackwell, Kristina S. Blackwell, and W. Wayne Talarzyk, Contemporary Cases in Consumer Behavior (Fort Worth, Tex.: Dryden Press, 1993) 2–16.

New Product Diffusion and ESV

As a concluding perspective to this chapter, study Consumer in Focus 24.5. It provides a realistic application of many of the materials in this chapter. Perhaps it will suggest some things that must be done to manage the development of new products, a topic that space does not permit discussion of here.[48]

Ford Taurus was the most successful introduction of a new car by an American manufacturer in recent years. When it was first introduced, it received little mass acceptance. The innovators and early adopters who first bought it were probably thought a bit weird. The car was thought to be a bit weird—a jelly bean, some called it. Yet, advertising communicated the idea to a relatively upscale, educated market target augmented by favorable publicity in consumer and auto magazines. The innovators "tried" it, and their decisions were confirmed sufficiently that they became opinion leaders, evangelizing others about the relative advantages, simplicity, and other attributes of the car.

Market research in the auto industry often asks consumers what they want (attitudes), but Taurus research asked consumers about their behavior—what they liked and disliked about their present behavior in buying and using cars. The success took time to build, but Taurus (and its Mercury sister, Sable) increased in sales until it beat out traditional rival Chevrolet and became the profit leader for Ford. The result was ESV; the cause was successful management of a new product that diffused through society just the way the textbooks say it should!

Summary

The diffusion of innovations, a topic of study and research that has grown rapidly in the past few decades, deals with how a new product is adopted in a society. It is of high importance to marketing organizations because new products must be brought out continuously for firms to survive.

The elements of the diffusion process include the innovation, the communication of the innovation, time, and the social system. The most commonly accepted definition of an innovation is any idea or product perceived by the potential innovator to be new.

Everett Rogers is the most influential change agent in the diffusion of the diffusion research. He has identified the types of consumers adopting a new product classified by the time of adoption as innovators, adopters, early majority, late majority, and laggards. Consumers who have a high amount of innovativeness can be identified in terms of socioeconomic (privileged), personality (venturesome), and communication behavior (contact with the mass media and other people) variables.

Review and Discussion Questions

1. What are the main differences in perspective on diffusion of innovations of those who are studying macromarketing issues compared with micromarketing issues?

2. Sun Tzu, the famous Chinese strategist, once said, "He who occupies the field of battle first and awaits his enemy is at ease; he who comes later to the scene and rushes into the fight is weary." Does this quotation apply to the study of diffusion of innovations? Explain.

3. How would you define innovation? How does the choice of your definition affect research that might be conducted on the topic?

4. Explain as precisely as possible the differences between continuous, dynamically continuous, and discontinuous innovations. Give some examples of each, other than those mentioned in the text.

5. What are the main competitive challenges facing firms in which understanding of diffusion of innovations might be helpful?

6. Prepare a short easy that explains how to pick winners from the many candidates for new product introduction.

7. Assume that a firm is introducing a new car. How would you suggest they manage word of mouth for this introduction?

8. The manufacturer of a new product is attempting to determine who the innovators for the product might be. The product is a game that requires players to answer each other with phrases from various foreign languages. Whom would you identify as the most likely innovators? What appeals would you suggest to be used in promoting the product?

9. A large manufacturer of drug and personal grooming products wants to introduce a new toothpaste brand in addition to the three already marketed. Evaluate for the firm what information might be used for innovation studies to guide introduction of the product.

10. How would you justify enhanced shareholder value as a firm's primary financial goal? What should be the role of new product development in this goal?

Endnotes

1. Andrew Tanzer, "Sharing," *Forbes* 149 (January 20, 1992), 82.

2. John P. Workman, Jr., "Marketing's Limited Role in New Product Development in One Computer Systems Firm," *Journal of Marketing Research* 30 (November 1993), 405–421.

3. Grahame R. Dowling and Paul K. Walsh, "Describing the New Product Adoption Behavior of Countries Using a New Product Growth Model," *Behavioral Science* 35 (October 1990), 259–280.

4. Michael S. Latour and Scott D. Roberts, "Cultural Anchoring and Product Diffusion," *Journal of Consumer Marketing* 9 (Fall 1991), 29–34.

5. Douglass K. Hawes, "The Role of Marketing in Facilitating the Diffusion of Microcomputers and the Information Society," *Journal of the Academy of Marketing Science* 15 (Summer 1987), 83-89.

6. Robert D. Buzzell and Bradley T. Gale, *The PIMS Principles* (New York: Free Press, 1987).

7. Frank R. Kardes and Gurumurthy Kalyanaram, "Order-of-Entry Effects on Consumer Memory and Judgment: An Information Integration Perspective," *Journal of Marketing Research* 29 (August 1992), 343–357; and Peter N. Golder and Gerald J. Tellis, "Pioneer Advantage: Marketing Logic or Marketing Legend," *Journal of Marketing Research* 30 (May 1993), 158–170.

8. Buzzell and Gale, *The PIMS Principles.*

9. "Where Did They Go Wrong?" *Business Week Quality Imperative* (January 1992), 34–38.

10. Gerald J. Tellis and Claes Fornell, "The Relationship between Advertising and Product Quality over the Product Life Cycle: A Contingency Theory," *Journal of Marketing Research* 25 (February 1988), 64–71.

11. Richard Olshavsky, "Time and the Rate of Adoption of Innovations," *Journal of Consumer Research* (March 1980), 425–428.

12. Barry L. Bayus, "Have Diffusion Rates Been Accelerating over Time?" *Marketing Letters* 3 (1992), 215–226.

13. Milton D. Rosenau, Jr., "Speeding Your New Product to Market," *Journal of Consumer Marketing* 5 (Spring 1988), 23–35.

14. *New Products Management for the 1980's* (New York: Booz-Allen & Hamilton, Inc., 1982).

15. Christopher S. Eklund, "Campbell Soup's Recipe for Growth: Offering Something for Every Palate," *Business Week* (December 14, 1984), 66–67.

16. Michael E. Porter, *Competitive Advantage* (New York: Free Press, 1985).

17. Rosabeth Moss Kanter, "Highlights," in *The Change Masters: Innovation and Entrepreneurship in the American Corporation,* Kanter, ed. (New York: Free Press), 1987.

18. Everett M. Rogers, *Diffusion of Innovations,* 3rd ed. (New York: Free Press, 1983), 5.

19. An excellent source for application materials is Thomas Robertson, *Innovative Behavior and Communication* (New York: Holt, Rinehart, and Winston, 1971).

20. John O'Shaugnessy, *Why People Buy* (New York: Oxford University Press, 1987), 25–38.

21. Thomas S. Robertson, "The Process of Innovation and the Diffusion of Innovation," *Journal of Marketing* (January 1967), 14–19.

22. Theodore Levitt, *The Marketing Imagination* (New York: Free Press, 1986), 74–93.

23. Thomas McCarroll, "What New Age?" *Time* (August 12, 1991), 44–45.

24. Salah Hassan, "Attributes of Diffusion Adoption Decisions," Proceedings of the Academy of Marketing Science, 1990.

25. The information in this and the next two paragraphs is adapted from "Researcher: Focus Groups Are the Best Way to Spot Trends," *Marketing News* 24 (March 28, 1988).

26. Thomas S. Robertson and Hubert Gatignon, "Competitive Effects on Technology Diffusion," *Journal of Marketing* 50 (July 1986), 1–12.

27. James Wills, A. C. Samli, and Laurence Jacobs, "Developing Global Products and Marketing Strategies: A Construct and a Research Agenda," *Journal of the Academy of Marketing Science* 19 (Winter 1991), 1–10.

28. H. David Strutton and James R. Lumpkin, "Information Sources Used by Elderly Health Care Product Adopters," *Journal of Advertising Research* 32 (July–August 1992), 20–30.

29. John M. Antil, "New Product or Service Adoption: When Does It Happen?" *Journal of Consumer Marketing* 5 (Spring 1988), 5–15.

30. David J. Burns, "Husband-Wife Innovative Consumer Decision Making: Exploring the Effect of Family Power," *Psychology and Marketing* 9 (New York: John Wiley & Sons, Inc., 1992), 175–189.

31. Ram C. Rao and Frank M. Bass, "Competition, Strategy, and Price Dynamics: A Theoretical and Empirical Investigation," *Journal of Marketing Research* 24 (August 1985), 283–296.

32. Elizabeth C. Hirschman, "Innovativeness, Novelty Seeking, and Consumer Creativity," *Journal of Consumer Research* (December 1980), 283–295.

33. Ronald E. Goldsmith and Charles F. Hofacker, "Measuring Consumer Innovativeness," *Journal of the Academy of Marketing Science* 19 (Summer 1991), 209–222.

34. Rogers, *Diffusion of Innovations.*

35. M. J. Kirton, "Adaptors and Innovators: A Theory of Cognitive Style," in K. Gronhaug and M. Kaufman, eds., *Innovation: A Crossdisciplinary Perspective* (New York: John Wiley & Sons, 1986).

36. Gordon Foxall and Christopher G. Hawkins, "Cognitive Style and Consumer Innovativeness: An Empirical Test of Kirton's Adaption-Innovation Theory in the Context of Food Purchasing," *European Journal of Marketing* 20 (1986), 63–80.

37. Gordon R. Foxall and Seema Bhate, "Cognitive Style and Personal Involvement as Explicators of Innovative Purchasing of 'Healthy' Food Brands," *European Journal of Marketing* 27 (1993), 5–16.

38. Hirschman, "Innovativeness, Novelty Seeking, and Consumer Creativity"; and M. P. Venkatraman and L. P. Price, "Differentiating between Cognitive and Sensory Innovativeness: Concepts, Measurement and Their Implications," *Journal of Business Research* 20 (1990), 293–315.

39. Meera P. Venkatraman, "The Impact of Innovativeness and Innovation Type on Adoption," *Journal of Retailing* 67 (Spring 1991), 51–67.

40. Linda Price, Lawrence Feick, and Daniel Smith, "A Re-Examination of Communication Channel Usage by Adopter Categories," in Richard Lutz, ed., *Advances in Consumer Research* 13 (Provo, Utah: Association for Consumer Research, 1986), 409–412.

41. Space does not permit more detailed discussion of these models. If you are interested, you will find them described, along with appropriate citations to source materials, in earlier editions of this text. See James Engel and Roger Blackwell, *Consumer Behavior,* 4th ed. (Homewood, Ill.: Dryden Press, 1982), 401–409. For a review of these models, see C. Naqrasimhan and S. K. Sen, "Test Market Models

for New Product Introduction," in Yoram Wind, Vijay Mahjan, and Richard Cardozo, eds., *New Product Forecasting: Models and Applications* (Lexington, Mass.: Lexington Books, 1981).

42. Vijay Mahjan and Robert A. Peterson, *Innovation Diffusion: Models and Applications* (Beverly Hills, Calif.: Sage Publications, 1985). Also see Vijay Mahjan, Eitan Muller, and Frank M. Bass, "New Product Diffusion Models in Marketing: A Review and Directions for Research," *Journal of Marketing* 54 (January 1990), 1–26.

43. Dan Horsky and Leonard S. Simon, "Advertising and the Diffusion of New Products," *Marketing Science* 2 (Winter 1983), 1–17.

44. Glen L. Urban, John S. Hulland, and Bruce D. Weinberg, "Premarket Forecasting for New Consumer Durable Goods: Modeling Categorization, Elimination, and Consideration Phenomena," *Journal of Marketing* 57 (April 1993), 47–63.

45. Robert S. Shulman and Kevin J. Clancy, "Refinements Improve New Product Models' Predictions," *Marketing News* (August 31, 1984), 15.

46. Also see Hubert Gatignon and Thomas S. Robertson, "A Propositional Inventory for New Diffusion Research," *Journal of Consumer Research* 11 (March 1985), 849–867.

47. Rick Brown, "Managing the 'S' Curves of Innovation," *Journal of Consumer Marketing* 9 (Winter 1991), 61–72.

48. This topic is addressed well in William E. Souder, *Managing New Product Innovations* (New York: Lexington Books, 1987).

CHAPTER 25

Consumerism and Ethical Responsibility

▲▲

The Fat Is in the Fire

The Food and Drug Administration (FDA) under a new commissioner, David A. Kessler, launched an all-out assault in the early 1990s on food labeling that was judged to be false and misleading. An early target on the hit list was companies that trumpeted the "no-cholesterol" properties of such high-fat foods as potato chips, margarine, and salad dressing. Agency studies showed that as many as 40 percent of all shoppers believed that a no-cholesterol label also signified "no fat." But that definitely is not the case with 100 percent fat vegetable oils. Three companies, including Procter & Gamble, Great Foods of America, and CPC International, were ordered to remove "no-cholesterol" claims under the threat of seizure of all products labeled in this way.

Source: Adapted from John Carey and Zachary Schiller, "The FDA Is Swinging 'A Sufficiently Large Two-by-Four,'" Business Week (May 17, 1991), 44.

The rumor of this FDA action found its way throughout food industry ranks long before the order was issued. And quite a controversy emerged in some quarters.

Let's listen in on one coffee break discussion:

BETH: This is disgusting and makes me ashamed to be in this business. We are guilty as charged, and it's about time that the Feds caught up with us.

MARK: Wait a minute—get off your high horse. This kind of thing is done every day.

BETH: That's my point exactly. It is done every day, and it's tarring us all with a bad brush.

MARK: Yeah, what makes you so high and mighty?

BETH: I can't believe what I'm hearing. We've made it look like our corn oil is fat-free, and that's an outright lie.

MARK: Oh, come on. Get down out of the heavenlies. All we said was "no cholesterol." And that's not a lie — it's the absolute truth.

BETH: Look, hot shot, that claim has a lousy double meaning when so many people believe that no cholesterol also means no fat. They will believe that our product reduces the risk of heart disease when it doesn't. A lie is a lie no matter how you try to cover it up. And that's wrong!

MARK: So, Ms. Lily White, you're one of those purists, huh? Show me what law was violated. After all, anyone with common sense would look at the label, and the fat content is clearly indicated there.

BETH: For crying out loud, who looks at the box? Don't all consumers, including you and me, have a right to expect the truth? I'm glad at least one of us around here pays attention to ethics. It ticks me off plenty that they cheated me in this way. I'm not about to pull such a trick on someone else.

MARK: I'm sick of moralists like you. Don't swing your personal code of ethics at me. You won't last long here if you keep that up. We've got just one duty to the company — to make as much money as possible as long as we don't break the law. We'll do what the Feds tell us to do, but it's a darn shame!

A real hot potato, isn't it? And who's right? On what basis can we decide? Our concern in this chapter lies with ethical responsibility to the consumer — managerial behavior that is consistent with accepted standards of what is right and what is wrong.

Lantos puts it this way:

> Ethics can be defined as the study of morality, i.e., standards that determine what is right and wrong, good and evil, helpful or harmful, acceptable or unacceptable. It is the name given to the attempt to think through the moral implications of human actions. Ethics is concerned with any situation where there is actual or potential harm to any individual or group from a particular course of action.[1]

Although such eminent management authorities as Peter Drucker[2] have long stressed the central role of social responsibility and ethics, most evidence indicates that this has not been taken especially seriously until recently. Fortunately, business enterprises are facing a consumer uprising they cannot ignore. A movement that has become known as consumerism has grown from a small voice to a formidable outcry for consumer interests.

It is necessary to tackle the issues of consumerism head on because public pressure does not allow any enterprise to rest for long on its ethical haunches. If we are to do this, however, we must put in place a framework to guide ethical thinking and reasoning, and that's how the chapter begins. This is followed by an overview of the historical and sociological context in which consumerism has arisen. Then we discuss the basic dimensions of a proper ethical response to consumer interests. The subject of corporate and individual ethics is basic in this context.

Ethical Thinking and Reasoning*

As Mark and Beth talked, you saw that there was little real common ground between them regarding the alleged violation by three food companies of the second consumer right focusing on the question of truthfulness in advertising. Although many, perhaps most, readers will side with Beth and her ethical perspective, we will also see that Mark has an ethical perspective—a different and contradictory one based on a set of different standards and reasoning.

Which ethical perspective is best? To answer this question with any degree of clarity and objectivity, we must delve a bit into the nature and premises of ethical reasoning. We recognize that some readers who have extensive background in philosophy will find our discussion unduly brief. For others, however, it hopefully will provide sufficient foundation for you to grapple with where you stand on such issues.

Three Ethical Perspectives

There are many bases or principles for ethical reasoning that have relevance for our discussion, but space limits us to only three: (1) utilitarianism, (2) justice and fairness, and (3) personal rights.

Utilitarianism

Utilitarianism has its roots in the eighteenth century thinking of Adam Smith, Jeremy Bentham, and John Stuart Mill. The objective is to produce the greatest good for the greatest number as opposed to the concerns of a single individual or enterprise. Moral worth is determined by the consequences of an act, making use of these two criteria:

1. Is there a net increase in the well-being or welfare within a society?

2. Have the means used to achieve this end been efficient—that is, has optimal use been made of productive resources from the perspective of both the enterprise and society as a whole?

---

*The authors gratefully acknowledge the significant contribution of Van B. Weigel, Professor of Ethics and Economic Development at Eastern College. We also have been influenced by Geoffrey Lantos of Stonehill College. Many of his perspectives are reflected here (see Endnote 1).

In other words, has there been a positive impact in terms of pleasure, satisfaction, and well-being in terms of a societal cost-benefit ratio?

This ethical perspective requires the following steps in reasoning[3]:

- Identify all relevant stakeholders (those who are impacted in any way — consumers, workers, stockholders, and so on).
- Identify alternative strategies.
- Estimate the cost and benefit impact on each stakeholder group.
- Select the option that gives the best cost-benefit outcome.

In our scenario, Mark was, at least in part, thinking as a utilitarian. He was contending that the consequences of this advertising claim were not especially harmful. Why get uptight just because the truth was stretched a bit? Furthermore, it worked and increased the profit bottom line. Isn't that worthwhile?

Beth, however, was using the standard that the consumer has a right to the absolute truth. To her, the act is immoral in its own right regardless of utilitarian consequences.

So who is right and who is wrong in this argument? Utilitarian theory probably will not provide a clear answer. Costs and benefits are extraordinarily hard to compute. Furthermore, it focuses only on the interests of the majority and does not explicitly take individual rights into account. Nevertheless, it provides a way of thinking that often proves helpful.

Justice and Fairness

Aristotle and Plato are traditionally considered to be the fathers of this influential perspective, which holds that impartiality and fairness are the criteria for ethical decision making. Justice is attained when the benefits and burdens of society are distributed fairly to stakeholders unless there are clear and defensible reasons for differential treatment. Everyone has a right to equal opportunity and treatment. Many legal codes are rooted in this philosophy. Rules for fair treatment are established and enforced as the norms and methods of restitution.

Beth also is using justice as a criterion in her reasoning when she contended that she and others were cheated by not having full information up front. From her perspective, this action is a moral violation. Mark was not in the least bit motivated by such an argument.

Theory of Personal Rights

From the earliest recorded times, there has been a recognition that individuals have rights ensuring their dignity, respect, and autonomy. These are inherent within the great religions of the world and also appear in the writings of such seventeenth century philosophers as Hobbes, Locke, and Kant.

A right implies that an individual, ourself or others, is entitled to something. Often, rights are captured in legal documents such as a national constitution.

But they also exist in moral codes that exist apart from any legal system. Velasquez put it this way:

> Rights are powerful devices whose main purpose is that of enabling the individual to choose freely whether to pursue certain interests or activities and of protecting those choices.[4]

Personal rights and the accompanying ethical responsibilities are expressed eloquently in the Judeo-Christian tradition in the form of the familiar Golden Rule—"Love your neighbors as you love yourself" (often rephrased as "Do unto others as you would have them do unto you"). It also is widely attested to in other religious traditions. At its heart, the Golden Rule calls for moral and ethical reasoning to be based on the highest principle that the rights of others should be paramount to our own.

One also finds a very similar expression in the writings of philosopher Immanuel Kant (1724–1804). His reasoning was based on a moral principle he referred to as the "Categorical Imperative" and was worded in this way in its original formulation: "I ought never act except in such a way that I can also will that my maxim become a universal law."[5] For Kant, the word *maxim* designated the basis of reasoning that shapes behavior in a particular situation. A maxim, in turn, would become a universal law if everyone based their choices on it in a similar situation.

Here is a rephrasing that may make this principle easier to understand:

> An action is morally justifiable if and only if a person's rationale for carrying out that action in a given situation is one that the person would be willing to have everyone else use in a similar situation.

Kant amplified his imperative by a second formulation worded in this way: "Act in such a way that you always treat humanity, whether in your own person or in the person of any other, never simply as a means, but always at the same time as an end."[6] In other words, don't use others only to advance your own interests but also develop their capacity to choose for themselves.

Can the teachings of Kant and Christ be synthesized? Many contend that they touch a common theme—*the principle of equal regard.* In other words, the rights of others are to be viewed, at the very least, as equal to your own. Traditional Christian teaching would take this even a step farther and affirm that the highest principle is to put others' rights above your own. No matter how this is interpreted, the rights of others will be affirmed and protected.

Beth is straightforward in her assertion that consumers have individual rights. Her ethical code embraces these rights and the necessity to protect them in all she does. Mark may not disagree explicitly, but it's obvious that he takes the issue of consumer rights less seriously. What will he do when profit considerations contradict the consumer's best interests? It is likely that profit maximization will be the determining criterion. Now he finds himself on ethical thin ice from this perspective.

Issue of Relativism

In approaching ethical dilemmas such as the one discussed here, there always will be three standards to use in the process of reasoning regardless of the ethical perspective you embrace: (1) legal codes, (2) cultural norms and behavioral codes, and (3) moral absolutes.

Legal statutes, cultural norms, and behavioral codes are closely related. They arise through a process of regulation or consensus and are often situation- and context-specific—what applies in one situation will not necessarily apply elsewhere. Moral absolutes, however, are universal and transcend context. They may be reflected in the law and cultural norms, but this is by no means a certainty.

Many are uneasy when moral absolutes are introduced into ethical reasoning, contending that they fall into the category of philosophical and religious moralizing, which has no place in a pluralistic world. Those who reason this way are referred to as **relativists**. They will fall back to a conviction that holds that morality is relative to or dependent on some cultural, social, or personal standard—there cannot be an absolute.[7]

Certainly, Mark is a moral relativist. First, he justified an action that skirts the borderline of many people's ethical standards by referring to "our profit interests." Also, he made it quite clear that "what's right for you may not be right for me."

In one sense, relativism legitimately recognizes complexity and affirms individual diversity in ethical matters. But it also can have consequences that stifle moral reasoning because, first, it cuts off rational moral discourse. If "it all depends," what basis is there for any kind of serious discussion on ethics? This becomes an especially acute problem in transcultural situations.

The Nestle Corp., for example, unexpectedly found itself enmeshed in a problem when its marketing of baby formula to Third World nations began to prove successful. It could argue, on the one hand, that there are some undeniable benefits brought about through better nutrition. On the other hand, minimization of breast feeding goes against cultural mores in many societies, and there has been a strong outcry that acceptance of this product only contributes to impoverished conditions among the poor. If everything is relative, there is no ultimate basis to determine ethical validity.

Some relativists argue that we should be tolerant of everyone as long as they are acting sincerely and in accord with their own belief or role expectations. In making such a statement, however, the relativist says always be tolerant—*it all depends.* Strangely enough, tolerance now becomes expressed as an absolute moral view in and of itself.

Individual, social, and cultural diversity does not require us to conclude that there are no universal norms and values to guide morality. If there are no universals, ethical questions all-too-often can only be resolved on the shifting basis of arbitrary whims, biases, or traditions.

It was, in our opinion, perfectly fair game for Beth to push Mark on his dictum that the company's primary role is to make a profit as long as one lives somewhere within the broad confines of the law. After all, she was not denying the validity of the profit motivation but suggested that there might be boundaries. He ventured into troublesome territory when he put her down and ruled out further deliberation of right and wrong. In effect, he set himself up as having the "highest standard."

Tension between Ethics and Bottom-line Business Realities

"Is it possible to be ethical and still come out on top?" This was the title of a Management Focus editorial in *The Economist* in 1993,[8] and it raises the very question that will trouble any thoughtful reader. Moral issues, especially when phrased in the lofty terms of the ethicist, often seem very far removed from the day-to-day realities of the managerial world. We must remove what seems to be a fundamental conflict between an inherent sense of doing what is right while, at the same time, producing an acceptable financial return for stockholders and owners.

First, each of us must clarify what we believe to be right and what we believe to be wrong. If there is no sound rationale, our ethics will quickly become vaporous moral platitudes. Personal values must, of necessity, be an essential part of moral dialogue. Van Weigel[9] offered good counsel:

> Bare ethical principles are rarely able to inspire the energy and devotion necessary for carrying them out. Just actions thrive upon the religious and moral ideals that belong to the human heritage.

Probably no one can be ethically spotless in an environment that blurs differences between right and wrong. We agree with Laura Nash of Boston University that ethical dilemmas should be resolved on the basis of covenants with employees, customers, suppliers, and other stakeholders.[10] According to Nash, "All parties in a commercial endeavor should prosper on the basis of created value and the *voluntary* exchange of resources." In other words, all parties have legitimate expectations that should be kept at the forefront and honored in a voluntary relationship. Compromises will be required in a process of give and take, but the rights of all parties are taken seriously.

Now, to the central question once again: Can you be ethical and thrive on the job? Goolsby and Hunt[11] come to our aid here through their landmark study on the state of cognitive moral development (CMD) among marketing practitioners and its impact on ethical behavior. CMD refers to the level of maturity in the process of moral reasoning. Their main conclusions are worthy of note:

- Marketers compare favorably with other comparable professional groups in CMD levels.
- The higher the level of CMD, the greater the ethical sensitivity and behavior exhibited in the business environment.

Advancement and success are *not* jeopardized by managerial integrity. In fact, just the opposite may be true.

Training in CMD can be fruitful in developing skills to reason through troublesome ethical issues and to encourage ethical behavior.

It is not our intent in this all-too-short ethical overview to endorse any point of view, let alone any religion or school of philosophical thought. Nevertheless, it is our hope that you will be challenged to reason more deeply as we explore the Consumer Bill of Rights.

Ultimately, it all comes down to the individual. We have given you much to think about here and affirm your integrity in arriving at your personal code of ethics. You will soon discover that application of any ethical code is difficult. Terms, concepts, and outcomes must be defined precisely. Often, there will be no clear answer at all. We like the way in which Peter Dickson has fleshed out a personal ethics checklist for managers and present it to you for your consideration in Figure 25.1.

Understanding and Responding to Consumer Rights

The consumerist voice was given its marching orders in 1962, as you may recall from Chapter 1, by President John F. Kennedy, who proclaimed four basic consumer rights, which since have been expanded to six[12]:

1. *The right to safety*—protection against products or services that are hazardous to health and life.

2. *The right to be informed*—provision of facts necessary for an informed choice; protection against fraudulent, deceitful, or misleading claims.

3. *The right to choose*—assured access to a variety of products and services at competitive prices.

4. *The right to be heard (redress)*—assurance that consumer interests receive full and sympathetic consideration in formulation and implementation of regulatory policy; prompt and fair restitution.

5. *The right to enjoy a clean and healthful environment.*

6. *The right of the poor and other minorities to have their interests protected.*

Historic Perspective

Consumerism has roots reaching far beyond the past two decades, when this name was assigned to the activities of such well-known leaders as Ralph Nader. The Bible, especially the Book of Proverbs, has many references to deceptive and irresponsible business practices. In their time, Thomas Aquinas, Martin Luther,

| Figure 25.1 | **Personal Ethics Checklist** |

1. Am I violating the law? If yes, why?
2. Are the values and ethics that I am applying in business lower than those I use to guide my personal life? If yes, why?
3. Am I doing to others as I would have them do to me? If not, why not?
4. Am I willfully risking the life and limb of consumers and others by my action? If yes, why?
5. Am I willfully exploiting children, the very elderly, the illiterate, the feeble minded, naive, or the poor? If yes, why?
6. Am I keeping my promises? If not, why not?
7. Am I telling the truth—all the truth? If not, why not?
8. Am I exploiting a confidence or a trust? If yes, why?
9. Am I misrepresenting my true intentions to others? If yes, why?
10. Am I loyal to those who have been loyal to me? if not, why not?
11. Have I set up others to take responsibility for any negative consequences of my action? If yes, why?
12. When it comes to a marginal call am I fair and considerate or ruthless and greedy ? If yes, why?
13. Am I prepared to redress wrongs and fairly compensate for damages? If not, why not?
14. Are my values and ethics as expressed in my strategy offensive to certain groups? If yes, why?
15. Am I being as efficient as I can? If not, why not?

Source: Peter Dickson (Unpublished manuscript. The Ohio State University, Columbus, 1988).

John Calvin, and other reformers also represented a kind of consumerism. Specific attacks were made on deceptive selling practices.

An historic analysis reveals that consumerism increases most sharply when an era of rapidly rising income is followed by a decrease in real purchasing power coming from rising prices.[13] Also, the environment must be conducive to the rise of leadership for the movement, which normally centers among those with greater-than-average wealth and income.

Alienation is another major triggering factor. It arises when the basic causes fueling consumer discontent are not dealt with satisfactorily or relief is only transitory. Feelings of powerlessness, alienation, and isolation lead essentially to defensive responses in the forms of boycotts, pressures for legislation, and so on.

Consumerism as it is known today generally is attributed to President John F. Kennedy's message to Congress on March 15, 1962, in which he put forth the original version of the Consumer Bill of Rights quoted at the beginning of this section. Kennedy was explicit that government is the ultimate guarantor of these rights and hence built the foundation for much of the role the federal government plays today.

Other well-known issue advocates galvanized a movement that was to have many facets: women's liberation, Gray Panthers, and so on. Ralph Nader was one major catalyst with his book on the automobile industry, *Unsafe at Any Speed*. Rachel Carson polarized the pollution issue with *Silent Spring*. And these are only two examples from a large group.

Government took Kennedy seriously and began an activist role. False and misleading advertising was a main target of the Federal Trade Commission (FTC). Product safety also became a major issue, especially in the automobile industry, which became characterized by government-ordered recalls. Products were withdrawn from the market because of pollution and public health danger — DDT being a leading example.

History often records a moderating trend or pendulum swing after a period of extensive activism. Many came to believe that governmental regulation was more of a hindrance than a help. This conservatism was expressed in the election of Ronald Reagan and George Bush, although it was to achieve its fullest expression under Reagan. Thus far, the Clinton administration is more middle of the road.

The outcome has been substantial deregulation in many industries or, more precisely, a return to reliance on regulation by the marketplace through its own corrective influences. The jury is still out on the impact of President Clinton's policies on consumer interests. One should not assume, however, that consumerism concerns have abated, for that is not the case. Among the greatest worries are low product quality and deficient after-sale service,[14] indiscriminate use and resale of private information in data bases,[15] and business indifference to environmental issues.[16]

Taken together, studies show that public attitudes toward consumerism in general are favorable and should remain strong.[17] Moreover, there is a trend toward more rigorous enforcement by regulatory agencies.

What does the future hold? There is one helpful clue to use in making such a prognosis. Do not fail to grasp the essential lesson: *Consumerism arises because of the failure of business or other organizations in the exchange relationship to meet and respond to legitimate consumer demands*. Business as a whole has yet to clean its house. Socially responsive business practices could have anticipated these movements and responded before alienation became widespread. Unfortunately, however, one basic law of history seems to be that its lessons are not heeded until it is too late.[18]

Importance of a Research Perspective

Consumer research is essential if disparate views of diverse groups are to be resolved. All parties, especially business and government, need the objectivity that well-designed research can provide in problem identification, problem clarification, and evaluation of proposed solutions.[19]

Few disagree with the need for objectivity, but there are inevitable difficulties in the use and interpretation of research. Differing values and resulting self-interest can lead to varying agendas from one party to the next.

How, for example, do we interpret and use a finding that 11 percent of consumers misunderstood an ad and formed beliefs about the advertised product that contradict actual fact? An ardent consumer advocate could label this as a blatant indication of deception. The advertiser, however, could contend, with some merit, that a certain amount of misperception will occur regardless of the wording that is used. It is precisely at this point that the propositions developed over the years in consumer research as a discipline and field of study find fruitful application.

As you have seen throughout this book, it is now possible to state with a fairly high degree of confidence how consumers process and use information. Therefore, there is an increasingly firm basis of theory and evidence on which to resolve disagreements more objectively. The resolution now relies less on theories of what consumers ought to do and shifts instead to actual responses to current or contemplated strategies.

Consumer research also offers the benefit of test marketing proposed consumerism programs, just as it is used in all phases of marketing practices. Often, there is need for sophisticated experimental designs.[20] Agencies such as the FTC are increasingly research-sensitive, and this is an encouraging trend.

Right to Safety

ISSUE: One of the models of a popular automobile make can be purchased with a hatchback design. This allows much more interior space. The lid on the hatchback is automatically self-supporting. It was recognized in design that the pneumatic self-support mechanisms will fail in 11 of 5,000 cars, potentially resulting in serious or even fatal injury. The actual incidence of failure is 39 of 5,000. Should there be a product recall? Thus far, sales are below the breakeven point. It will cost $500 for each repair, and the total costs required will drive losses up significantly.

How would you approach this issue? The first plank in the Consumer Bill of Rights reads, *"Consumers have the right to be protected against products or services that are hazardous to health and life."*[21] The right to safety has been made specific under the Consumer Product Safety Act, which established the Consumer Product Safety Commission (CPSC).[22]

The CPSC has the mandate to protect consumers against unreasonable risk of injuries caused by hazardous household products. Manufacturers have always had some safety liability under common law, but now the manufacturer must assume explicit responsibility for designing the product in accordance with safety considerations.

Since 1980, however, the activity of the CPSC has been cut back, reflecting the move toward voluntary industry self-regulation. When enforcement and redress are necessary, increasing use has been made of cost-benefit criteria, assessing whether the benefits of a proposed remedial action are justified by its costs. This is not an easy issue to resolve.[23]

Using Consumer Research

Consumer research has two specific functions here. The first is to document product-usage patterns, especially unexpected safety hazards. The second is to establish the expected probability of injuries or levels of safety.

A particular doctrine, **foreseeability**, is often a matter of contention between manufacturer and government. This doctrine holds that the manufacturer should be able to foresee (anticipate and evaluate) risks inherent in product use and find out ways to avoid them.

Complaints about safety and poor performance often arise because of incorrect consumer usage. The real difficulty, however, lies in anticipating and minimizing the problems arising when so-called normal people use the product in a distinctly abnormal way. The manufacturer often is held liable in such situations. Therefore, extensive usage testing may be required.

Issue of Costs versus Benefits

What would your solution be in the automotive safety issue discussed at the beginning of this section? Everyone feels uneasy when a monetary value is placed on human life. Many would not hesitate to recommend the change, regardless of its cost, because of the consumer's right to safety. If this is your position, you have reasoned **deontologically**. This term comes from the Greek word *deon*, which refers to right or duty. You have reasoned that rightness or wrongness is inherent within the act itself.

Others would be more hesitant, because matters of this type are never as simple as they seem. What effect will this have on lower-income buyers? Is a potential increased price because of the recall justified if it is demonstrated that potential buyers with lower incomes are, in effect, priced out of the market? Those raising this type of issue are reasoning *teleologically* — you are placing emphasis on rightness or wrongness of ends *(teleos)* or consequences.

Frankly, this creates an almost unavoidable dilemma for anyone attempting to make use of the *Principle of Equal Regard* (Categorical Imperative or Golden Rule). One could build a reasonable case from either side, thus making absolute certainty elusive. Our position here is strictly deontological — everything possible should be done to build a zero defect policy that attempts to eliminate accidents resulting from foreseeable product failure even if it causes low-income people to not be able to afford cars. Diminished profitability, although never to be dismissed, should not be the determining criterion.

Unfortunately, Dow Chemical Co. and others have discovered it is one thing to establish a deontological philosophy on product safety and quite another to enforce it throughout the company ranks. Be sure to read Consumer in Focus 25.1, which tells the story of how Dow's widely lauded ethics system

Consumer in Focus   25.1

Faulty Breast Implants — A Nightmare That Eluded Dow's Ethics System

Dow Corning Corp. has long been recognized as a pioneer in corporate ethics. It was among the first to establish an ethics program, which many believe to be the most elaborate in Corporate America. Yet, even the best plans are no guarantee against lapses.

In 1976 Dow Corning's chairman at that time, John S. Ludington, sought to create a corporate culture that emphasized high ethical standards. He launched a Business Conduct Committee, made up of company executives who report directly to a board committee. From the beginning it was an ambitious effort. The company immediately began a series of audits to monitor compliance and communicate with employees about ethics. These sessions were to take place at every operation every three years. Two company training programs included segments on the subject, and Dow Corning's semiannual employee opinion surveys had an ethics section.

The system that so impressed others, however, seemingly failed to pick up any signs of controversy over the safety of breast implants during four separate audits since 1983, the most recent being 1990. Yet as far back as 1976 the engineer who sounded an early alarm on the product's safety quit the company in protest. A Dec. 15, 1977, memo from employee Frank Lewis recounted reports by four doctors that 52 of 400 implant procedures had resulted in ruptures. These and other internal documents suggest that Dow Corning was aware of problems for years and tried to keep the public from learning of them — although the company maintains that it has done nothing wrong.

Why did the ethics system fail? For the most part, ethics programs aren't designed to deal directly with complex problems. Instead they are there only to help cultivate an overall environment of proper conduct. The fact is that few managers are likely to speak openly about moral issues in a room filled with many employees, including one's boss.

Likewise you won't get many red flags when top managers believe concerns about product safety are unwarranted. Dow Corning still argues that the product does not pose an unreasonable risk, and Keith R. McKennon, who recently succeeded Ludington as chairman, vigorously defends the conduct of the company's managers. "I have a high regard for their sincerity and integrity, and I don't ascribe bad motives to anyone," he says.

Source: John A. Byrne, "The Best-Laid Ethics Programs . . . ," Business Week (March 9, 1992), 67–69.

failed to detect flagrant abuse in its Corning Wright Div., which produced faulty breast implants.

Multicultural Ethical Dilemma

It has been illegal for more than two decades to advertise cigarettes on TV in the United States. Print ads are allowed only if there is a prominent warning, also appearing on each package, that cigarette smoking may be dangerous for your health. Growing antipathy toward smoking has led to a decrease in the number of smokers, except on college campuses where it has been increasing since 1986.

Manufacturers are more than making up for these lost sales, however, by turning to Africa, Asia, and elsewhere.[24] Figure 25.2 shows that Joe Camel has become as common in parts of Asia as he has in North America.

The cigarette manufacturers are not alone in pursuing such marketing policies; cosmetics and self-medication products now abound. "So what's the problem?" is the frequent response. "After all, there is no law against it, and people are just exercising their freedom when they make the purchase."

Eminent consumer researcher Elizabeth C. Hirschman pulls no punches on this issue and raises this question: "Whose interests are being served? Those of the consumer or those of the business enterprise?"[25] She correctly labels as dysfunctional this type of practice that draws scarce economic resources away from meeting crucial survival necessities. We agree that these examples represent little more than blatant attempts at profit maximization with little regard shown for consumer interest.

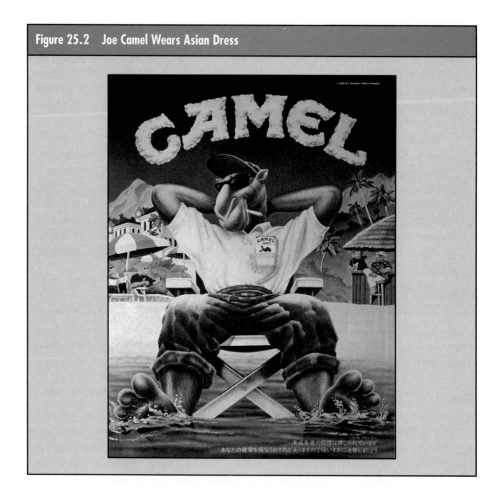

Figure 25.2   Joe Camel Wears Asian Dress

Right to Be Informed

We started the chapter with an example of questionable advertising veracity. Here's another example for you:

> ISSUE: For months, the FDA had been writing letters to Procter & Gamble Co., complaining that it was misleading to use the word "fresh" on Citrus Hill packages because the orange juice is made up of concentrate. And despite a long day of meetings between agency and company representatives, Procter & Gamble would not back down and remove the offending word.[26]

Procter & Gamble management played "hardball" here with the FDA. Were they right in what they did? What would your decision have been? Ultimately, Procter & Gamble lost in a big way. The FDA immediately confiscated a shipment of Citrus Hill and won the battle in having the questionable wording removed from all packaging and promotional material. Furthermore, management was tarred with the brush of playing free and easy with consumer rights.

The Consumer Bill of Rights advocates that the consumer has the right "to be protected against fraudulent, deceitful, or grossly misleading information, advertising, labeling, or other practices, and to be given the facts he [or she] needs to make an informed choice."[27] How do we tackle this issue? First, we need to clarify what the phrase *informed choice* means. Even more important is to determine when a message is misleading. Both of these issues are more difficult than they might seem.

What Is an "Informed Choice"?

Hans Thorelli has this to say on information adequacy: "Informed consumers are protected consumers—more than that, they are liberated consumers."[28] But how much information does the consumer want and need? How should it be provided? Can we provide too much information?

When Is an Appeal Informative?

As you might expect, there is disagreement on what the word *informative* means. Contrast the two ads appearing in Figure 25.3. The Colgate ad was aimed at middle-class Kenyan families, whereas the China Airlines ad was designed for English speakers in Asian countries. Which do you think is most informative?

Most readers probably will vote for the Colgate ad because of the product-feature demonstration and endorsement by the Kenya Dental Association. Empirical studies show, however, that less than half of all ads are informative in the sense that focus is on such objective features as price, quality, performance, and availability.[29]

But what about the China Airlines appeal? Would you say that it is noninformative because of its decidedly subjective (that is, more emotional) message? We would seriously caution against such an interpretation because the focus on Chinese tradition and ambience is a benefit in and of itself, even though it

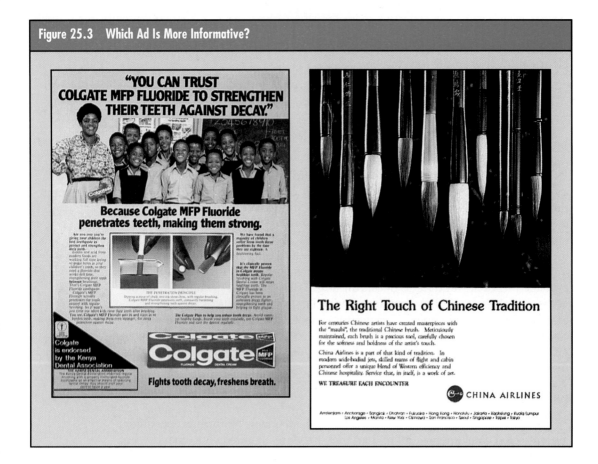

Figure 25.3   Which Ad Is More Informative?

cannot be quantified or objectified. It is entirely possible that the decision process of an Asian consumer is enhanced far more by the psychological and emotional associations than in any other way.

The issue comes down to this important point: Only the consumer can decide whether useful information has been provided. It can be a serious mistake to allege, following some consumerists, that valid information is confined only to the factual and objective.

How Much Is Enough?

It has been made clear in many chapters that both the amount and type of information needed will depend on the degree of involvement and resulting extended problem solving. Furthermore, there are individual differences in desire to search and willingness to act on limited information.

The problem is further complicated by information overload. You will remember from our discussion of information processing that provision of too much information can impair decision making. There are distinct limits on information-processing capacity. Many well-meaning consumer advocates mistakenly assume that "more is better" and wind up hindering rather than helping the consumer.

Therefore, it is impossible to give a simple answer to the question of how much is enough. It can only be resolved on the basis of research that verifies actual information acquisition and use. If there are deficiencies resulting in unwise buying decisions, action can be taken in the form of revamped promotion or consumer education efforts.

Day's conclusion regarding well-intended consumerism efforts on this dimension has stood the test of time:

> What is clear . . . is that it is not enough to simply provide consumers with more information. That is simply the first step in a major educational task of getting consumers to understand the information, and persuading them to use it. Consumer researchers can make a significant contribution to both these tasks.[30]

Information Veracity

No issue has given rise to greater concern over the years than deception and misrepresentation because such practices materially interfere with the consumer's legitimate rights.

What Represents Deception?

As you can well imagine, Procter & Gamble's contention with the FDA was that their claim of freshness was not deceptive or misleading, even though the product comes from reconstituted juice. How can the question of deception be decided?

First, what is deception? Definitional issues are of central importance here, because nuances of wording can have great significance. According to Gardner and Leonard,[31] the following points comprise the common elements in all definitions used since 1970:

- The consumer has a set of experiences, beliefs, and attitudes.

- The advertisement as stimulus interacts with the experiences, beliefs, and attitudes of the consumer.

- The impressions, beliefs, or attitudes that follow from the advertisement/ consumer interaction are the basis for the determination of deception.

In its 1983 policy statement, the FTC defined deception as "a representation, omission, or practice that is likely to mislead the consumer acting reasonably in the circumstances, to the consumer's detriment."[32] Its current standard of deception requires that the representation, omission, or practice be "material." The representation becomes "material," in turn, when it is likely to affect consumer decision processes.[33]

The issue thus becomes resolved on the basis of the effect on consumers. In recent actions, courts have ruled that this impact comes from what can be reasonably inferred by the consumer, as well as what is literally said.[34] Also, for a claim to be judged misleading, there generally must be evidence that more than 22 percent of actual or prospective buyers have been misled.[35]

Further, an evaluation of whether deception has occurred also must take into account that all forms of mass media content will be misperceived at times. Jacoby and Hoyer[36] undertook a national study of consumer perception of 54 magazine ads and 54 editorials. Their findings showed that 21.4 percent of the material, on the average, was miscomprehended, and an additional 15.5 percent said they didn't know what it meant.

A standard that can be used is provided by Shimp and Preston,[37] who conclude that the following conditions should be demonstrated before arriving at a conclusion that deception has taken place:

1. The claim is attended to by the consumer.

2. The claim (or its implication) affects beliefs.

3. The claim (or its implication) is important to the consumer.

4. The claim (or its implication) becomes represented in long-term memory.

5. The claim (or its implication) is objectively false.

6. Behavior is influenced as a result of either the claim itself or implications that can reasonably be derived from it.

Impact of Antideception Efforts

During the 1960s and 1970s, the FTC was vigorous in its pursuit of advertising truthfulness. This abated substantially under the Reagan administration in the belief that a free market will provide correctives if left alone. The FTC also relaxed its standards for ad substantiation in that less evidence now is required to prove the veracity of claims.

Traditionally, the FTC and other agencies have performed the function of providing a "well-lighted street." The theory is that the threat of enforcement will deter violations. Fortunately, this light is becoming much brighter recently due to stepped-up enforcement efforts.[38] Also, much greater lip service is paid to voluntary enforcement efforts, which, frankly, have had a mixed record of success.[39]

But can we make a case that the consumer's right to honest and verifiable information is being better met at this point in history? The safest conclusion is that the brighter legal streetlight is making potential offenders more cautious.

It may be premature, however, to give an affirmative answer to this question. Consider these specific instances:

1. Volvo Cars of North America reinforced the cars that were used in an ad to demonstrate how the Volvo withstands unusual crushing because of its strength.

2. Adolph Coors Co. was sued for improperly claiming that it uses Rocky Mountain spring water as its source for its popular beers.

3. Quaker Oats Co. faced the charge over untrue claims that its oat bran cereals cut the risk of heart attack.

We could go on and on about the charges brought against supposedly reputable marketers. This doesn't say much about ethics and self-regulation, does it? It all comes down to this question: Do consumers have a right to receive truthful information?

The definitional and interpretation problems mentioned above need to be considered fully. However, far too many decision makers today use the shoddy ethical standards of Mark mentioned at the opening of this chapter. Is it asking too much to expect everyone to show the ethical integrity displayed by Beth? A deontological (literal) view would require consumer analysts to stand up and be counted!

Right to Choose

ISSUE: The question of lowering trade barriers against other North American countries (NAFTA) and against competitors in other continents (GATT) has been divisive in the United States. On the one hand, free trade advocates claim that the benefits from open markets between trading countries far outweigh the costs. Their chief argument is that the consumer is the beneficiary. Opponents, on the other hand, often allege that subsidies and unfair competitive methods provide advantages to foreign enterprises that are proving ruinous to manufacturers and service providers here. Therefore, barriers should be in place to preserve market share and employment levels in this country.

Free trade advocates frequently cite the third plank in the Consumer Bill of Rights:

Consumers have the right to assured access, whenever possible, to a variety of products and services at competitive prices. In those industries in which competition is not workable, government regulation is substituted to assure satisfactory quality and service at fair prices.[40]

Would you call for restrictions on trade? Would you advise saving jobs of some workers or protecting certain corporations if the result is to restrict choice or raise prices for the consumer? To tackle this issue, first we must explore the problem of monopoly and the ways in which this has been dealt with legally. Then we can begin to assess whether restrictions are in the consumer's best interests. We also will tackle the question of responsibility, if any, to those who choose "unwisely."

Monopoly Power and Barriers to Entry

Traditionally, the laws of market-based economies embody the principle of laissez-faire, which contends that the consumer is best served when firms freely compete, offering an unrestrained choice. Antitrust legislation has long been a potent weapon against monopolies that allegedly curb this freedom—hence, the well-publicized breakup of AT&T into smaller, independent competitive units.

Consumerists usually have not made monopoly power into an issue because of the adequacy of both legislation and enforcement machinery. However, there has been pressure from many quarters other than consumerists for deregulation in certain industries and greater freedom for firms to compete.

Deregulation became a main theme of both the Reagan and Bush administrations. But has this had a discernible influence on consumer interest? Those who have looked at this question most thoroughly cannot come to a conclusion one way or the other, but there is some hope that consumers ultimately will be the beneficiaries.[41]

There is growing concern as of this writing, however, about the impact of corporate takeovers in some industries. Admittedly, the numbers of competing firms have been reduced, but this does not necessarily imply consumer disadvantage. Even if there is no evidence of intent to create a monopoly, there is no denying the fact that entrenched firms with marketing muscle are often difficult and even impossible to dislodge.

As a case in point, how many upstart airlines have been absorbed by the "big four" in the past few years? We no longer see Pan American, Midway, People Express, or Braniff; and others are either in chapter 11 or are close to bankruptcy. The price of being competitive simply proved to be too high.

Fortunately, such barriers to entry rarely are permanent because of competitive counterattack. Just compare the lists of the top firms in any product field from one decade to the next and you will see substantial variation. The crumbling of the General Motors empire and the diminished market share of each of its divisions is ample evidence of competitive vulnerability.

In fact, there is growing evidence that smaller and more aggressive marketers often gain a competitive edge over their larger and more inflexible counterparts. Who would have believed that upstarts such as Dell or Compaq could reach a position from which they could challenge mighty IBM for world leadership? Many other examples can be given.

Trade Restrictions

Consumerists usually are not found among those advocating trade restrictions. Dardis explains why:

> Trade restraints impose high costs on consumers and the economy. The direct costs are higher prices paid by consumers and the reduction in consumer choice due to product upgrading. The indirect costs include the lack of incentive for the domestic industry to respond to changes in production and consumption and the pervasive effects of protectionist measures on economic efficiency and economic growth.[42]

Let's face it—any attempt to restrict competition seldom benefits the consumer. You can be sure that the right of freedom of choice played no role in those who opposed the lowering of North American trade restrictions in the deliberations on NAFTA or GATT.

Problem of Unwise Choice

Here is a challenging question: Does the buyer have a right to choose even if there is evidence that actions are unwise? Should choice be regulated and restricted in such situations? This has been an unresolved issue since the very onset of consumerism nearly a century ago.

Some have doubts that people can make a sound, reasoned choice given the plethora of product alternatives and promotional claims. Others would go even further and contend that consumers should be forced to do what is best for them, regardless of personal preferences. Both points of view, if enacted, inevitably lead to some restriction of choice.

Unfortunately, this is a "no-win" issue. On the one hand, certain clearly unwise and destructive behaviors, such as heroin or cocaine use, must be regulated. Few would have any quarrel with this position, given extensive documentation of disastrous personal and social outcomes of addiction. But what if similar legal limits were placed on the consumption of whole milk, which is known to produce allergies in some adults? Or chocolate? Now we have entered into the domain where any position taken inevitably will be arbitrary. In other words, how can a line be drawn between wise and unwise buying and consumption behavior? In its most general sense, the principle of unrestrained free choice must remain at the bedrock of a market economy except in clear cases of public health or safety dangers.

But, interestingly enough, many marketers are joining in the call to reduce consumer options but from an entirely different point of view. Their contention documented in Consumer in Focus 25.2 is that brand proliferation has passed the limit where it offers advantages to either a manufacturer or distributor.

A more defensible and increasingly popular approach is to move away from regulation and restriction toward education designed to bring about a more

25.2	**Consumer in Focus**

Brand Proliferation Is Attacked

A new study sponsored by Frito-Lay and presented at the Food Marketing Institute's annual meeting will give the strongest ammunition yet to supermarkets aiming to cut back the number of brands and line extensions in stores. The year-long study, conducted by William Bishop Consulting, discovered that consumers prefer branded products but believe there are too many — meaning too many sizes or too many "me-too" products.

Increasingly, marketers are looking at their brand lineups and questioning the need for brands that aren't leaders in their categories. In one recent example, Procter & Gamble Co. is turning White Cloud toilet tissue into a Charmin extension called Charmin Ultra, completely discontinuing the White Cloud brand.

The FMI "product variety" study shows retailers can reduce stock-keeping units by 5% to 25% without hurting sales or consumer perception of the variety offered by the store. "We created a process to help understand when variety becomes duplication and to challenge the theory that more items means more sales," says Doug Adams, Frito-Lay director of sales information. "Variety is good and variety adds to sales if it provides something unique to consumers, while duplication adds to the cost of distribution. Consumers don't consider variety having 16 barbecue chip products."

Source: Ira Teinowitz and Jennifer Lawrence, "Brand Proliferation Attacked," Advertising Age (May 10, 1993), 1.

intelligent choice.[43] The goal is to enhance the ability to cope with complex choice processes in a mass consumption society. Such educational programs should cover these elements:

- Formal knowledge about criteria used to evaluate complex technical products, and ways to choose logically
- Consumer managerial and decision-making skills comparable with those developed in professional education
- Increased consumer knowledge of the workings of business, government, and the marketplace
- Values and consciousness that will encourage respect and concern for others in their pursuit of collective consumption

Right to Be Heard (Redress)

ISSUE: A person has bought an electric range with a 1-year warranty against defective parts. Several repairs were required during the first year and were done at no charge. Problems continued unabated, however, after the warranty expired, and the buyer appealed, asking for replacement of a product that has become a "lemon." The manufacturer declined, pointing to the fact that all liability ceased once the warranty expired.

Does the consumer have a right of redress in such situations? The fourth plank of the Consumer Bill of Rights, as originally stated, is somewhat ambiguous:

> Consumers have the right to be assured that consumer interests will receive full and sympathetic consideration in the formulation of government policy and fair and expeditious treatment in its administrative tribunals.[44]

Its focus as written was entirely on regulatory behavior, although its application has been broadened to encompass the responsibility of the enterprise for redress.

Legislative Protection

There is a substantial body of federal legislation controlling restitution and punishment, and this is detailed in Figure 25.4. The main avenues of redress are summarized in Figure 25.5. Despite these legal remedies, many authorities are not convinced that consumer interests are fully protected.[45] Fortunately, there is constant consumerist activity in this arena. Our greater concern lies with prevention, for it is here that ethics plays its greatest role.

Prevention

Ideally, the consumer voice needs to be heard before problems develop and redress becomes necessary.

One means of prevention can be found in industry codes of ethics, an example of which is presented in Figure 25.6 (page 938). Such creeds are often little more than window dressing because of the lack of enforcement mechanisms. Nonetheless, there is growing consensus that consumerism problems would diminish sharply if such standards were internalized and enforced by top management.[46]

A strong focus on product quality accompanied by meaningful guarantees is another form of prevention. There is no question that levels of consumer dissatisfaction are increasing. In fact, one consumer researcher sees "almost the Naderistic feel of the '60s" in a "fight-back trend" that is making consumers "more conscious about getting ripped off."[47]

Consumer rebellion inevitably will be felt in lost sales and bad word of mouth. The business solution lies in recognition that quality is a marketing problem, not just a production problem. When quality levels are improved and backed by stringent guarantees, it is possible to regain or solidify market position while, at the same time, contributing to legitimate consumer interests.

Restitution

Legal restitution can be made many ways, as Figure 25.5 indicates. Among the most visible is the almost daily incidence of mandatory automobile recalls ordered to remedy safety defects.

Figure 25.4   Selected Federal Consumer Protection Laws

Act	Year	Purposes
Pure Food and Drug Act	1906	Prohibits adulteration and misbranding of foods and drugs sold in interstate commerce
Food, Drug, and Cosmetic Act	1938	Prohibits the adulteration and sale of foods, drugs, cosmetics, or therapeutic devices that may endanger public health; allows the Food and Drug Administration to set minimum standards and to establish guides for food products
Wool Products Labeling Act	1940	Protects producers, manufacturers, distributors, and consumers from undisclosed substitutes and mixtures in all types of manufactured wool products
Fur Products Labeling Act	1951	Protects consumers and others against misbranding, false advertising, and false invoicing of furs and fur products
Flammable Fabrics Act	1953	Prohibits interstate transportation of dangerously flammable wearing apparel and fabrics
Automobile Information Disclosure Act	1958	Requires automobile manufacturers to post suggested retail prices on all new passenger vehicles
Textile Fiber Products Identification Act	1958	Guards producers and consumers against misbranding and false advertising of fiber content of textile fiber products
Cigarette Labeling Act	1965	Requires cigarette manufacturers to label cigarettes as hazardous to health
Fair Packaging and Labeling Act	1966	Declares unfair or deceptive packaging or labeling of certain consumer commodities illegal
Child Protection Act	1966	Excludes from sale potentially harmful toys; allows the FDA to remove dangerous products from the market
Truth-in-Lending Act	1968	Requires full disclosure of all finance charges on consumer credit agreements and in advertisements of credit to allow consumers to be better informed regarding their credit purchases
Child Protection and Toy Safety Act	1969	Protects children from toys and other products that contain thermal, electrical, or mechanical hazards
Fair Credit Reporting Act	1970	Ensures that a consumer's credit report will contain only accurate, relevant, and recent information and will be confidential unless requested for an appropriate reason by a proper party
Consumer Product Safety Act	1972	Created an independent agency to protect consumers from unreasonable risk of injury arising from consumer products; agency is empowered to set safety standards
Magnuson-Moss Warranty-Improvement Act	1975	Provides for minimum disclosure standards for written consumer product warranties; defines minimum content standards for written warranties; allows the FTC to prescribe interpretive rules and policy statements regarding unfair or deceptive practices

Source: William M. Pride and O. C. Ferrell, Marketing: Basic Concepts and Decisions, 4th ed., 481. Copyright © 1985 by Houghton Mifflin Company.

Figure 25.5   Remedies for Consumer Protection

Prevention	Restitution	Punishment
Codes of conduct	Affirmative disclosure	Fines and incarceration
Disclosure of information requirements	Corrective advertising	Loss of profits
Substantiation of claims	Refunds	Class action suits
	Limitations on contracts	
	Arbitration	

Source: Dorothy Cohen, "Remedies for Consumer Protection: Prevention, Restitution, or Punishment," Journal of Marketing (October 1975), 25. Reprinted from the Journal of Marketing published by the American Marketing Association.

You may recall our previous discussion in Chapter 8 of the initial reluctance of management to act when such an order was issued to rectify engine surge problems with the Audi 5000 model. Many would classify this as a clear case of ethical disregard. Issues of restitution should not have to reach the point where legal authorities must step in. The consumer has every right to expect response from the manufacturer or retailer when complaints are made. History has proven time and time again that the gains in consumer loyalty far offset costs. But this type of lesson does not seem to sink in as it should, if complaint levels are any indication.[48]

Ethical Response

Now, back to the issue that opened this section of the chapter—Would you refund the buyer's money in this situation? Or would you enforce the guarantee? If you are using the Categorical Imperative or the Golden Rule, you probably would swallow your profit and make restitution. Where this becomes tough is when it impinges on the bottom line, threatening the survival of the firm. But what is the higher concern here? It all depends on your values (and your courage). Our opinion is that unquestioned and immediate refund is the only policy that reflects both ethical sensitivity and sound business judgment. What is to be gained by losing a customer?

Right to Enjoy a Clean and Healthful Environment

ISSUE: The so-called green movement is pressuring business firms to lessen the extent to which their products pollute the environment. McDonald's agreed to let an advocacy group, The Environmental Defense Fund, put together a plan for recycling and cutting waste. The company has

---

Figure 25.6   Advertising Code of American Business

1. **Truth.** Advertising shall tell the truth, and shall reveal significant facts, the concealment of which would mislead the public.
2. **Responsibility.** Advertising agencies and advertisers shall be willing to provide substantiation of claims made.
3. **Taste and Decency.** Advertising shall be free of statements, illustrations, or implications which are offensive to good taste or public decency.
4. **Disparagement.** Advertising shall offer merchandise or service on its merits, and refrain from attacking competitiors unfairly or disparaging their product, services, or methods of doing business.
5. **Bait Advertising.** Advertising shall offer only merchandise or services which are available for purchase at the advertised price.
6. **Guarantees and Warranties.** Advertising of guarantees and warranties shall be explicit. Advertising of any guarantee or warranty shall clearly and conspicuously disclose its nature and extent, the manner in which the guarantor or warrantor will perform and the identity of the guarantor or warrantor.
7. **Price Claims.** Advertising shall avoid price or savings claims which are false or misleading, or which do not offer provable bargains or savings.
8. **Unprovable Claims.** Advertising shall avoid the use of exaggerated or unprovable claims.
9. **Testimonials.** Advertising containing testimonials shall be limited to those of competent witnesses who are reflecting a real and honest choice.

Note: This code was part of a program of industry self-regulation pertaining to national consumer advertising announced jointly on September 18, 1971, by the American Advertising Federation, the American Association of Advertising Agencies, the Association of National Advertisers, and the Council of Better Business Bureaus, Inc.

---

agreed to test 42 initiatives that will reduce waste by 80 percent. Among these are reusable lids for salad containers and pump-style dispensers for condiments.[49]

Environmental pollution is an unfortunate byproduct of a high and rising standard of living in a technological age, thus necessitating an addition to the Consumer Bill of Rights—*the right to enjoy a clean and healthful environment.* The "green movement" is an outgrowth of this need.

Would you have agreed with the above steps if you had been a member of the McDonald's executive team? Keep several factors in mind as you make this judgment:

- Remember that they, along with other companies, have been the targets of tremendous consumer pressure for change.

- Also, remember that there are some firms who have given in to pressure, only to discover that their actions boomeranged seriously. The most notable case in point is Mobil's Hefty brand plastic trash bag.[50] It was reissued in a biodegradable form at great cost, but it later turned out that it would biodegrade only if it remains exposed to air, a condition that does not happen in most disposal situations. They and others have discovered that the "definition of what's good keeps changing,"[51] thus making this a "Catch-22" situation.

- Consumers, 80 percent or more, are quick to say that they place primary importance on buying environmentally safe products.[52] But other desires such as convenience may overwhelm their idealism.[53] Therefore, their response may be quite different from their voiced convictions.

If we were acting on ethical considerations alone, most of us probably are willing to apply the Principle of Equal Regard here and respond affirmatively. After all, pollution affects us all in increasingly direct ways. Even our friend Mark, whom we met early in the chapter, most likely would agree with the steps taken by McDonald's to answer their critics. But he would be more likely to acquiesce simply because "doing so is good business—ethics has nothing to do with it."

Environmentalism is a fairly recent phenomenon, and scientific knowledge is changing rapidly. In our opinion, we must, of necessity, become more *teleological* and consider seriously the consequences of any proposed step, no matter how good it seems on the surface. All that can be asked is that this consumer right be taken seriously and not subjugated to self-centered profit considerations.

It becomes more difficult when environmental necessity compels such dramatic steps as eliminating internal combustion engines to reduce pollutants to levels that are not life-threatening. At this point, many firms will face the unmistakable necessity of engaging in demarketing—deliberate attempts to induce consumers to buy less or cease consumption altogether.

Take time to read Consumer in Focus 25.3, which describes how Procter & Gamble Co. responded when it faced an uproar over the environmental impacts of its disposable diaper line. Its answer—"Turn them into mulch." Should they drop this profitable line if no realistic recycling method can be found? If this worst-case scenario becomes reality, the conflicting desires of various stakeholder groups will require the wisdom of Solomon to sort out.

Here is where governments may have no other choice but to force demarketing. Yet, such agencies often are greater polluters than anyone else, prompting

25.3	**Consumer in Focus**

Making the Greens See Red

Feel guilty when you toss out your kids' disposable diapers? Then compost them into rich mulch in your garden. That was the message behind an ad campaign that Procter & Gamble, maker of Luvs and Pampers, ran in several national magazines. The ads were another salvo in the company's seemingly endless battle to defend its disposable diaper business—and 18% or about $4 billion of its total sales.

The ad made a lot of greens see red. The objection: There aren't enough recycling facilities in the U.S. capable of making mulch out of the some 15.8 billion disposables Americans discard a year. New York City consumer affairs commissioner Mark Green blasted P&G for creating the impression that city dwellers could compost their disposable diapers and other garbage when there are no such facilities in the entire state.

The company has invested $20 million to learn more about what a spokesman calls "composting technology." P&G hopes to encourage communities to set up compost plants that will accept used diapers. At present, only ten such facilities exist. These plants mulch the diapers along with other garbage like food.

The need to mulch disposable diapers exposes P&G's weak flank. Says Richard Denison, senior scientist at the Environmental Defense Fund in Washington, D.C.: "What makes these diapers appealing in the first place is that you don't have to think about putting them in a special bin and taking them somewhere. You just throw them out." Disposable diehards couldn't agree more.

Source: Jaclyn Fierman, "The Big Muddle in Green Marketing," Fortune (June 3, 1991), 100.

suits by the U.S. Environmental Agency against the Corps of Engineers, state governments, and other offending agencies.

Protection of the Interests of Special Interest Groups and the Poor

> ISSUE: From 1987 to 1990, R. J. Reynolds Tobacco Co. saw its sales of Camel filter cigarettes take a sharp jump, largely because of its campaign featuring Joe Camel (see Figure 25.2, page 926). One research study showed that Camel's share of the under-age children market who smoke increased from less than 1 percent to 33 percent. Other evidence shows that children as young as 3 years identify the cartoon with the Camel logo.[54]

There has been a marked increase in efforts to determine whether a unique set of problems exists among special interest groups and the poor toward which special regulative and informational efforts should be directed. This has given rise to the last component of the Consumer Bill of Rights—*protection of the interests of the poor and other interest groups that have experienced oppression.*

Insensitivity to Special Interest Groups

Antismoking crusaders have leveled their big guns at R. J. Reynolds for going after the under-aged smoker and have mounted a campaign to have its advertising banned if necessary. The company's response? Don't blame us—the average Camel smoker is over 21. But the rebuttal went further than that. Consider these words from James W. Johnston, chairman-CEO:

> The fact that children see and recognize tobacco advertising is not a justification for eliminating those ads or for depriving a company of its right to advertise a legal product. If advertising were the true culprit, then perhaps all ads should be banned.[55]

Free speech, then, is the banner of protection that is raised against such charges. A broader *teleological* ethical perspective, however, would focus on consequences. Does free speech give license to offend or directly hurt another party? Historic precedent and case law supports the fundamental right of free speech but places limits when the consequences are unacceptable.

There also is the strong rebuttal that this kind of advertising sells the product—what's good for the profit bottom line is what counts. And we are only poking fun. Why would anybody be offended? But here is the standard we would impose as a guideline: "Is this the way you would talk to your husband [wife] or kids?" Or, put differently, "How would you feel if the shoe were on the other foot and you were parodied or appealed to with such tactics?

A quick scan of the Letters to the Editor pages of *Advertising Age* and journals will show that many observers plus marketing insiders are up in arms about this kind of unwarranted abuse of free speech. You may get away with it legally, but you will fail from the perspective of consumer rights and common decency.

Dilemma of the Poor

Potentially even more serious are the problems of poverty. These become especially acute in urban areas that are burgeoning around the world. Nairobi, Kenya, for example, must generate 1,000 new jobs each day to cope with urban population growth.[56] Certainly, the former Communist countries are now facing poverty in massive and perhaps unexpected ways, and it is entirely likely that this problem will be all the more aggravated by unethical free-enterprise practices.

Businesses in general and consumer researchers specifically cannot avoid playing a role in determining the kind of urban environment to be built for the future and the ways in which greater equality can be achieved.

Consumer researchers have investigated the problems of how those who have been most subject to discrimination can more efficiently allocate their limited resources. A second contribution is improvement of marketing efficiency among firms and organizations that serve disadvantaged segments. Minority-owned businesses, for example, are being helped to achieve greater market penetration.

A third contribution is made when research evidence documents the ways in which those who are not disadvantaged enhance the problems of those who are. A case in point is the potent curb on upward mobility when those who are white rapidly sell their homes as blacks move in. Legitimate corrective action can be taken on such a foundation.

Organizational Ethics and Consumerism

There is no question that contemporary enterprises—business and nonbusiness—are faced with changing realities. The need is for preventive approaches to these issues of consumerism rather than reactive ones. Consumerism, after all, is not antibusiness per se. It is, as we have stressed, a natural countervailing force in response to alienation. If abuses were not present, it would not exist.

Any market-controlled free-enterprise system is built on the assumption that profit and material gain will be the guiding motive with the constraint that the market must be truly served with a focus on long-run consumer interest.

This doctrine presupposes a set of managerial ethics, a code of right and wrong, that is both workable and actively followed. We have seen at many points what can happen when short-term financial gain becomes the guiding consideration. Ethical mandates quickly fall by the wayside, as economic history (and indeed, the entire history of humankind) so amply reveals. Unfortunately, the public only becomes aware of the most flagrant instances of resulting compromise behavior. Small wonder that 90 percent of business schools teach ethics today[57] and that "businesses are signing up for Ethics 101 in the workplace."[58]

The ultimate dilemma faced in constructing any ethical philosophy is determining what is right and what is wrong. Company-wide codes of ethics such as IBM's Guidelines for Business Conduct can be helpful (Figure 25.7). If these are to work, however, they must be endorsed consistently by top management and find their way into job descriptions, standards of performance, and managerial evaluation. Corporate values of profit and efficiency will dominate, however, unless there is the addition of counterbalancing ethical values. Robin and Reidenbach diagrammed how this might look (Figure 25.8).

Consumerism obviously is not going away, and it must be managed in the same way as every other environmental challenge. Here are the steps in a management system designed to cope with this challenge:

1. Orienting top management to the consumer's world
2. Organizing for responsive action

Figure 25.7   IBM's Guidelines for Business Conduct

- Do not make misrepresentations to anyone you deal with.
- Do not use IBM's size unfairly to intimidate or threaten.
- Treat all buyers and sellers equitably.
- Do not engage in reciprocal dealing.
- Do not disparage competitors.
- Do not make premature disclosure of unannounced offerings.
- Do not engage in further selling after competitor has the firm order.
- Contact with the competition must be minimal
- Do not make any illegal use of confidential information.
- Do not steal or obtain information by willfull deceit.
- Do not engage in violation of patents or copyrights.
- No bribes, gifts, or entertainment that might be seen as creating an obligation should be accepted or given.

Source: Gene R. Laczniak and Patrick E. Murphy, Marketing Ethics: Guidelines for Managers (Lexington, Mass.: Lexington Books, 1985), 117–123.

3. Improving customer contact

4. Redressing grievances

5. Providing consumer information and education

Top Management Orientation

There now is a consensus that the first step is to ensure that both the board of directors and top management are acquainted with the realities of the consumer world, including economic and financial fears, negative attitudes toward business practice, and perceived grievances. This level of knowledge also must be backed consistently by a commitment to take responsible action when needed.

The number one managerial productivity problem in America is, quite simply, managers who are out of touch with their people and out of touch with the customers. And the alternative, "being in touch," does not come via computer printouts or the endless stream of overhead transparencies viewed in the endless darkened meeting rooms stretching across the continent. Being in touch means being informed via tangible, visceral ways.[59]

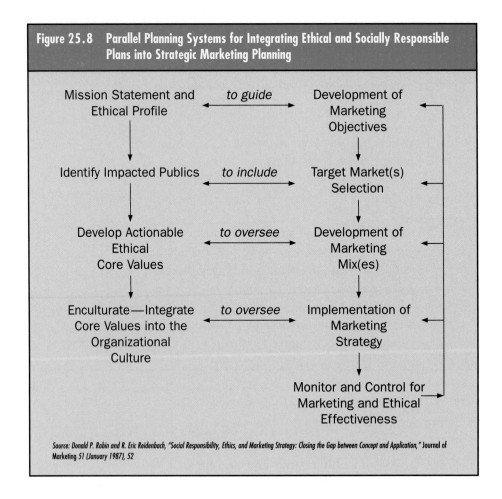

Figure 25.8   Parallel Planning Systems for Integrating Ethical and Socially Responsible Plans into Strategic Marketing Planning

Mission Statement and Ethical Profile — *to guide* → Development of Marketing Objectives

Identify Impacted Publics — *to include* → Target Market(s) Selection

Develop Actionable Ethical Core Values — *to oversee* → Development of Marketing Mix(es)

Enculturate—Integrate Core Values into the Organizational Culture — *to oversee* → Implementation of Marketing Strategy

Monitor and Control for Marketing and Ethical Effectiveness

Source: Donald P. Robin and R. Eric Reidenbach, "Social Responsibility, Ethics, and Marketing Strategy: Closing the Gap between Concept and Application," Journal of Marketing 51 (January 1987), 52

Organizing for Responsible Action

A logical starting point is a written consumer rights policy specifying in detail what the company is prepared to do in the way of implementation when shortcomings arise. We also recommend the establishment of a consumer affairs department that is empowered to have a real voice in marketing decision making and responsibility to provide redress.

The head person of the consumer affairs department, in turn, should be a member of top management assigned the responsibility and authority to assure that product quality and safety are maintained, that promotional strategies are truthful and not misleading, and that there is no deception in other phases of the marketing program. If this position is seen as merely advisory without management power and sanctions, it will be little more than window dressing.

Improving the Quality of Customer Contact

One of the greatest challenges for any management team is to create customer credibility. Some logical steps include community involvement, soft-sell institutional ads, and just plain human friendliness and decency in all dealings. The intent is to break down and hopefully eliminate barriers.

One of the best strategies is a continual customer satisfaction monitoring program following our discussion in Chapter 8. This provides an ongoing evaluation of service as opposed to an occasional "snapshot," thus allowing immediate remedial action when needed.

Providing for Redress

It is essential to respond to grievances and injuries. This requires prompt and direct means of reacting to complaints and inquiries through a consumer affairs department. There must be a clear recognition that commitment to information feedback and post-sale communication is an ethical mandate, to say nothing of the extent to which this response is significant in building long-term consumer loyalty, a phenomenon that is becoming increasingly rare.

Providing for Customer Education

There is a true consumer education movement in some firms, and we find such responses to be encouraging indeed. The focus lies on moving beyond the usual forms of promotion, as important as these are, to efforts that clearly are designed to help the consumer buy wisely.

Conclusion

We have noticed a disturbing trend since the first edition of this book in 1968 that, hopefully, may be abating somewhat at the present time. Most students in the 1960s and 1970s developed a high sense of moral outrage over political and economic shortcomings. For a period, this was expressed through campus protest, but a large percentage carried a commitment to ethically responsible action into their professional lives. Consumerism is a central part of the social agenda of many in that generation of business managers, and many of the most laudable corporate actions have come from their initiative.

It seems, however, that this moral outrage gave way to a sense of individualistic opportunism. Social and moral issues are not seen negatively; rather, such concerns are at the distinct periphery of life. We have tried to make a case that each of us can live responsibly only by focusing on the best interests of consumers as well as the financial bottom line. It's time for a pendulum swing back once again to moral and ethic responsibility.

Summary

The consumer has the right to safety, the right to be informed, the right to choose, and the right to be heard. These tenets have been expanded and reaffirmed by decree and administrative action ever since they were declared in 1962 by President John F. Kennedy. Yet, there is ample evidence that these rights are consistently violated, creating a rising interest in consumerism.

Consumerism is not a recent phenomenon. A historic review showed some ancient antecedents as well as specific activity that began in the United States around the turn of the century. Consumerism as we now know it, however, received its greatest impetus from the Kennedy declarations. The 1960s and 1970s were characterized by a frenzy of activity on many fronts, but there has been a pendulum swing toward a return to market forces as opposed to regulation as a corrective during the 1980s.

Our focus throughout has been twofold: (1) use consumer research to help assure consumer rights, and (2) undertake responsible ethical action that puts consumer interests above such bottom-line concerns as profitability.

We saw that consumer research can play the unique role of providing facts for responsible policy and activity. Otherwise, there often is recourse to normative authoritarianism based on opinion and arbitrary fiat. In a sense, then, a research approach has the potential of becoming a boundary-spanning agent between the conflicting interests of business, government, and consumer advocacy groups.

Research is of no value, however, unless our corporate and individual response is governed by ethics. We reviewed the nature of ethical thinking and put forth the principle that all decision makers need to be guided by the Golden Rule or other philosophical axioms that place primary focus on the best interests of another.

Each of the six consumer rights was evaluated comprehensively from both a research and an ethical perspective. Unfortunately, it becomes apparent that these rights are often treated in a cavalier manner, and this underscores the need for serious attention once again to the integration of ethics into strategy.

Consumerism is just an interesting textbook topic, however, unless recognized as a legitimate force and responded to by business accordingly. Several suggestions were given in the spirit that responsible action is needed if a free-market economy is to function in the best interest of all parties.

Review and Discussion Questions

1. As you learned in this chapter, Dow-Corning has just abandoned a product line for which it had been the world leader — silicone breast implants. Such products are unusual outside of the West. In brief, their primary use is after breast surgery to restore normal feminine appearance. Others use them to enhance breast size. Dow-Corning took this step because of scathing public attack for allegedly having concealed damaging safety information regarding the use of its silicone breast implants. If indeed these charges are justified, what would your verdict be?

2. What if further legal inquiry sustains that Dow-Corning executives indeed withheld safety information but that there was no evidence of intentional legal violation. Assume further that all evidence collected largely affirms the danger if these implants rupture, even though some serious scientists disagree that consumer injury actually has resulted. What responsibility do you feel Dow-Corning has, if any, to women who believe their health was demonstrably damaged by defective implants? Clarify the reasons for your conclusion.

3. You have been charged with writing ad copy that has been charged in court as being false and misleading. The question now is the nature of the defense that you will undertake: (a) What definitional standard(s) should be used to determine whether the appeal truly is false and misleading? (b) You can make a clear case, based on written memoranda, documenting that senior management directed you to write the copy you did. It is clear that you could have lost your job had you not acquiesced. Would you use this in your defense? Is it ethical to do so?

4. Examine your own experiences as a consumer in the past year. Have you experienced feelings of alienation? From what sources? What might have been done by the offending organizations to have prevented this?

5. *Unsafe at Any Speed* was the title of Ralph Nader's book castigating the automobile industry, and he alleges that things have not improved to any degree. Following a research approach, how would you go about substantiating his claim? What types of safety standards could legitimately be proposed, taking cost-benefit analysis into account?

6. William Lazer, a former president of the American Marketing Association, advocated during the 1960s that marketing should work toward the end of helping the consumer to accept self-indulgence, luxurious surroundings, and nonutilitarian products. Do you agree?

7. A former president of Hunt-Wesson Foods proposed several years ago that business must divert some of its profits to help solve social problems and issues such as consumerism. Many today are making similar statements. However, such a practice might adversely affect financial returns, thus giving rise to potential conflict of interest. Can this be resolved?

8. "Get government out of the business of regulating automotive safety. The industry will police itself." What is your response?

9. This is not the typical end-of-chapter question, but we leave it with you anyway. You are selling a name brand headache remedy containing only pure aspirin. You are fully aware that generic brands containing exactly the same ingredients sell for half the price or less. Yet, your brand is marketed with such claims as "purity," "a name you can trust," "speed of relief." Examine your own code of ethics carefully, and answer this question: Can you justify this marketing strategy? What would your answer be to the charge that the advertising is deceptive from a belief–claim interaction perspective? Is it justifiable to continue selling as long as people keep buying? Try to make explicit the ethical principles underlying your initial responses.

Endnotes

1. Geoffrey P. Lantos, "Arthur Andersen & Co. Business Ethics Overview: A Summary and Critique," Stonehill College working paper.

2. See, for example, Peter F. Drucker, *An Introductory View of Management* (New York: Harper & Row, 1977), Part. 4.

3. Lantos, "Business Ethics Overview," 4.

4. Manuel G. Velasquez as quoted in Van B. Weigel, *Business Ethics and Transitional Economies.* Unpublished manuscript, Eastern College 1992.

5. Kant's Categorical Imperative as cited in Manuel G. Velasquez, *Business Ethics: Concepts and Cases,* 2nd ed. (Englewood Cliffs, N.J.: Prentice-Hall, 1988), 196.

6. From Weigel, *Business Ethics and Transitional Economies.*

7. See Nancy Gifford, *When in Rome: An Introduction to Relativism and Knowledge* (Albany, N.Y.: SUNY Albany Press, 1983).

8. "How to Be Ethical, and Still Come Out on Top," *The Economist* (June 5, 1993), 71.

9. Weigel, *Business Ethics and Transitional Economies.*

10. Laura Nash, as quoted in "How to Be Ethical, and Still Come Out on Top."

11. Jerry R. Goolsby and Shelby D. Hunt, "Cognitive Moral Development and Marketing," *Journal of Marketing* 56 (January 1992), 55–68.

12. Robert J. Lampman, "JFK's Four Consumer Rights: A Retrospective View," in E. Scott Maynes, ed., *The Frontier of Research in the Consumer Interest* (Columbia, Mo.: American Council on Consumer Interests, 1988), 19–36.

13. Robert O. Herrman, "Consumerism: Its Goals, Organizations and Future," *Journal of Marketing* 35 (October 1970), 55–60.

14. "Detroit May Be Missing the Market that Matters Most—Business Week/Harris Poll," *Business Week* (October 22, 1990), 91.

15. Scott Hume, "Consumers Target Ire at Data Bases," *Advertising Age* (May 6, 1991), 3.

16. "Americans Favor a Tight Leash on Business," *American Demographics* (August 1991), 20.

17. Darlene Brannigan Smith and Paul N. Bloom, "Is Consumerism Dead or Alive? Some New Evidence," in Thomas C. Kinnear, ed., *Advances in Consumer Research* 11 (Provo, Utah: Association for Consumer Research, 1984), 469–473.

18. For a sobering analysis on this point, see Will and Ariel Durant, *The Lessons of History* (New York: Simon & Schuster, 1968).

19. For helpful examples on the role of consumer research, see William L. Wilkie, *Consumer Behavior* (New York: John Wiley & Sons, 1986), Chapter 21.

20. See, for example, Lynn Phillips and Bobby Calder, "Evaluating Consumer Protection Laws, Promising Methods," *Journal of Consumer Affairs* 14 (Summer 1980), 9–36.

21. "The Consumer Bill of Rights," in *Consumer Advisory Council, First Report* (Washington, D.C.: U.S. Government Printing Office, 1963).

22. For a thorough review of product safety issues, see Jennifer L. Gerner, "Product Safety: A Review," in Maynes, *The Frontier of Research*, 37–60.

23. See Robert W. Crandall, "The Use of Cost-Benefit Analysis in Product Safety Regulation," in Maynes, *The Frontier of Research*, 61–76. Also Eric B. Ault, "CPSC'S Voluntary Standards: An Assessment and a Paradox," in Maynes, *The Frontier of Research*, 77–82.

24. Mike Levin, "U.S. Tobacco Firms Push Eagerly into Asian Market," *Advertising Age* (January 21, 1991), 2, 14.

25. Elizabeth C. Hirschman, "Marketing as an Agent of Change in Subsistence Cultures: Some Dysfunctional Consumption Consequences," in Richard J. Lutz, ed., *Advances in Consumer Research* 13 (Provo, Utah: Association for Consumer Research, 1986), 99–104.

26. "Procter & Gamble: On a Short Lease," *Business Week* (July 22, 1991), 76.

27. "The Consumer Bill of Rights."

28. Hans Thorelli, "The Future for Consumer Information Systems," in Jerry C. Olson, ed., *Advances in Consumer Research* 8 (Ann Arbor, Mich.: Association for Consumer Research, 1980), 222.

29. Alan J. Resnik and Bruce L. Stern, "An Analysis of Information Content in Television Advertising," *Journal of Marketing* (January 1977), 50–53.

30. See George S. Day, "Assessing the Effects of Information Disclosure Requirements," *Journal of Marketing* (April 1976), 42–52.

31. David M. Gardner and Nancy H. Leonard, "Research in Deceptive and Corrective Advertising: Progress to Date and Impact on Public Policy," in James H. Leigh and Claude R. Martin, Jr., eds., *Current Issues & Research in Advertising* 12 (Ann Arbor, Mich.: Division of Research, School of Business Administration, University of Michigan, 1991), 278.

32. Resnik and Stern, "An Analysis of Information Content."

33. Dorothy Cohen, "Legal Interpretations of Deception Are Deceiving," *Marketing News* (September 26, 1986), 12.

34. Ibid.

35. Cyndee Miller, "Ads Must Back up Their Claims — or Pay the Legal Price," *Marketing News* (February 1, 1988), 22.

36. Jacob Jacoby and Wayne D. Hoyer, "The Comprehension/Miscomprehension of Print Communication: Selected Findings," *Journal of Consumer Research* 15 (March 1989), 434–443.

37. Terence A. Shimp and Ivan L. Preston, "Deceptive and Nondeceptive Consequences of Evaluative Advertising," *Journal of Marketing* (Winter 1981), 22–32.

38. Howard Schlossberg, "The Simple Truth: Ads Will Have to Be Truthful," *Advertising Age* (December 24, 1990), 6.

39. For a helpful review of voluntary regulation practices, see Gordon E. Miracle and Terence Nevett, *Voluntary Regulation of Advertising* (New York: Lexington Books, 1987).

40. "The Consumer Bill of Rights."

41. John E. Kushman, "Increasing Competition through Deregulation: Do Consumers Win or Lose?" in Maynes, *The Frontier of Research*, 413–439.

42. Rachel Dardis, "International Trade: The Consumer's Stake," in Maynes, *The Frontier of Research*, 355.

43. See, for example, Marilyn Kourilsky and Trudy Murray, "The Use of Economic Reasoning to Increase Satisfaction with Family Decision-Making," *Journal of Consumer Research* 15 (September 1981), 183–188.

44. "The Consumer Bill of Rights."

45. See George L. Priest, "The Disappearance of the Consumer from Modern Products Liability Law," in Maynes, *The Frontier of Research*, 771–791.

46. Shelby D. Hunt, Van R. Wood, and Lawrence B. Chonko, "Corporate Ethical Values and Organizational Commitment in Marketing," *Journal of Marketing* 53 (July 1989), 79–90.

47. Faith Popcorn as quoted in Janet Neiman, "Values-Added Marketing," *ADWEEK* (April 6, 1987), 19.

48. Claes Fornell and Robert A. Westbrook, "The Vicious Cycle of Consumer Complaints," *Journal of Marketing* 48 (Summer 1984), 68–78.

49. Jaclyn Fierman, "The Big Muddle in Green Marketing," *Fortune* (June 3, 1991), 92.

50. Ibid., 91.

51. Ibid., 92–102.

52. Howard Schlossberg, "Americans Passionate about the Environment? Critic Says That's Nonsense," *Advertising Age* (September 16, 1991), 8.

53. Rose Gutfield, "Eight of 10 Americans Are Environmentalists, at Least So They Say," *Wall Street Journal* (August 2, 1991), 1.

54. Walecia Konrad, "I'd Toddle a Mile for a Camel," *Business Week* (December 23, 1991), 34.

55. James W. Johnston, "For Old Joe: Free Speech Is the Issue," *Advertising Age* (January 27, 1992), 22.

56. Comments made by the Hon. B. L. Kiplagat, Permanent Secretary of State, The Republic of Kenya, March 6, 1988.

57. "How to Be Ethical, and Still Come Out on Top."

58. John A. Byrne, "Businesses Are Signing Up for Ethics 101," *Business Week* (February 15, 1988), 56–57.

59. Tom Peters and Nancy Austin, *A Passion for Excellence* (New York: Random House, 1985), 8.

Glossary

▲▲▲

absolute standards categorical moral revelations and religious laws used as the basis for ethical decision making.

absolute threshold the amount of stimulus energy or intensity necessary for sensation to occur.

abstract elements intangible elements of culture, such as values, attitudes, ideas, personality types, and summary constructs, such as religion.

abstract words those that express a quality apart from an object (e.g., justice, equality)

acceptance a stage of information processing representing the degree to which a stimulus influences the person's knowledge and/or attitudes.

accessibility the likelihood that information can be retrieved from memory.

active rejection the decision not to adopt an innovation.

Actual State Types consumers in whom need recognition results from changes in actual state.

adaptation level the level at which an individual becomes so habituated to a stimulus that it is no longer noticed.

adopter one who makes the decision to continue using a new product.

adoption the decision to make full use of an innovation.

advertising clutter refers to the problem of too many ads in the viewing environment; it can interfere with the consumer's ability to process and remember advertising messages.

advertising wearout the reduction of advertising effectiveness as a result of excessive ad repetition.

affect feeling states that influence consumer behavior.

affective attitude the attitude component that represents a person's feelings about the attitude object.

affective responses the feelings and emotions that are elicited by a stimulus.

affect referral a decision rule that assumes that a consumer has previously formed overall evaluations of each choice alternative, rather than judging them on various evaluative criteria.

AIDA an early conceptualization of the adoption process, including Awareness, Interest, Desire, and Action.

aided recall measures measures that provide cues for retrieving learned information.

AIO measures measures of activities, interests, and opinions.

alienation feelings of powerlessness and isolation that, when experienced in regard to the business world, often result in consumerism.

alternative evaluation the third stage of the nonhabitual decision-making process in which a choice alternative is evaluated and selected to meet consumer needs.

analytical cross-cultural studies studies that attempt to deduce general principles of behavior that apply in one or more cultures.

anomie social instability resulting from a weakened respect for social norms and values.

approach in motivation, the theory that some forces promote or produce movement toward a goal object.

a priori segmentation analysis defining the segmentation base in advance.

Area of Dominant Influence an area for which advertising media is purchased, usually in cities or areas surrounding them.

argument a message element relevant to forming a rational, reasoned opinion.

arousal a person's degree of alertness along a continuum ranging from extreme drowsiness to extreme wakefulness

aspirtional group a reference group whose numbers wish to adopt the norms, values, and behaviors of others.

association a variable of social class concerned with everyday relationships between people.

association measures (see evaluated participation studies)

associative network a conceptualization according to which memory consists of a series of nodes (representing concepts) and links (which represent associations between nodes)

attention a stage of information processing representing the allocation of cognitive capacity. (see also direction of attention and intensity of attention).

attitude an overall evaluation that can range from extremely positive to extremely negative.

attitude change a term used to characterize conditions under which a person holds a preexisting attitude that is changed subsequently.

attitude formation a term used to characterize conditions under which a person has yet to develop an attitude.

attraction effect a phenomenon in which a given alternative's attractiveness is enhanced when an inferior alternative is added to the set of choice alternatives.

attribute a characteristic or property of a product; generally refers to a characteristic that serves as an evaluative criterion during decision making.

attribute evaluation measures measures used to assess the goodness or badness of an attribute.

attribute importance measures measures used to assess the concept of salience or potential influence of product attributes.

attribute search sequence brand information is collected on an attribute-by-attribute basis.

attribute theory a theory stating that an individual encountering a situation is motivated to ascertain whether the casual influence on the person is internal or external (e.g., if a product fails, is the failure in the product or in an adjunct system such as wiring?)

augmented product the tangible attributes of a product plus its additional value to the consumer.

avoidance in motivation, the theory that some forces promote or produce movements away from a goal object.

awareness analysis a technique for assessing brand awareness by asking consumers to recall or recognize brand names.

awareness set a set of brands familiar to a consumer.

baby boomer one of the cohort of 77 million Americans born between 1946 and 1964.

background noise a description of the way in which advertising may strike the consumer.

back-translation a procedure in which a message is translated from its original to the translated language and back to the original by a number of translators.

backward conditioning classical conditioning in which the conditioned stimulus follows the unconditioned stimulus.

behavioral consistency a phenomenon that exists when the purchase behavior of individuals in a submarket remains constant over time.

behavioral intention measures measures of the perceived likelihood that a particular behavior will be undertaken by the person.

behaviorist approach an approach to learning in which learning is demonstrated by changes in behavior and the role of mental processes is ignored.

behavioristic variables variables used for segmentation, including extent of use, loyalty, benefit, and usage situations.

belief a link between two nodes in an associate network, such as "IBM is an expensive brand."

benefit segmentation a marketing strategy oriented toward meeting a benefit or felt need in a target market segment.

birthrate the number of live births per 1,000 population in a given year.

brand interest represents the inquisitiveness or curiosity a consumer has about a particular brand.

brand loyalty a motivated, difficult-to-change habit of purchasing the same item or service, often rooted in high involvement.

brand personality the attributes of a product and the profile of perceptions received by consumers about a specific brand.

brand search sequence brand information is collected on a brand-by-brand basis.

breaking point in location analysis, the point at which 50 percent of the market trade is attracted to each of two locations.

Bureau of Economic Analysis Economic Area an area of geographic analysis designated by the Bureau of Economic Analysis and consisting of an "economic node" and the surrounding counties.

buyer's regret a feeling of remorse following a purchase decision with high involvement.

cancellation rate the proportion of customers who do not repurchase.

cannibalization a new product reduces the market share of another product by the same company.

capacity the cognitive resources that an individual has available at any given time for processing information.

category killer a retailer that carries a broad assortment in one category of merchandise.

causal differences consumer differences that represent motivating influences or other factors that define and shape behavior.

Censal-Ratio method a population estimate method comparing an area's population from the most recent census with a variable that changes as the size of the population changes.

Central Business District the traditional "downtown" shopping district.

central route a form of persuasion in which issue relevant thinking is high and message elements or arguments relevant to forming a reasoned opinion are influential.

chunk a grouping or combination of information that can be processed as a unit.

classical conditioning a form of learning in which a conditioned stimulus (e.g., the sound of a bell) is paired with an existing unconditioned stimulus (e.g., the sight of food) until the conditioned stimulus alone is sufficient to elicit a previously unconditioned response (e.g, salivation) which is now a conditioned response.

classification dominance the state a retailer achieves when giving the customer the impression that the merchandise assortment contains virtually any item that could be desired.

closure the tendency to develop a complete picture or perception even when elements in the perceptual field are missing.

cognitive approach an approach to learning in which learning is seen as reflected in changes in knowledge, and emphasis is on understanding the mental processes that determine how people learn information.

cognitive attitude the attitude component that refers to a person's knowledge and beliefs about an attitude object.

cognitive consistency theories theories, such as balance theory and congruity, that propose that people strive to maintain a consistent set of beliefs and attitudes.

cognitive map consumer perceptions of store locations and shopping areas, as opposed to actual locations.

cognitive responses the thoughts that occur to an individual during the comprehension stage of information processing.

cognitive resources refers to the mental capacity available for undertaking various information-processing activities.

cohesion the emotional bonding that family members have toward one another.

cohort any group of individuals linked in some way, usually by age.

cohort analysis a method of investigating the changes in patterns of behavior or attitudes of groups called cohorts.

commodity product status a status when different brands offer essentially the same features and compete mostly on price; no brand has a competitive edge.

communicability the degree to which results from using a new product are visible to friends and neighbors.

communication a facilitating dimension, critical to movement on the other family dimensions of cohesion and family adaptability.

communication situation the setting in which the consumer is exposed to either personal or non-personal communications.

comparative advertising advertising that makes comparisons between products.

compatibility the degree to which a product is consistent with the existing values and past experiences of a potential adopter.

compensatory strategy a strategy in alternative evaluation in which a perceived weakness on one attribute may be compensated for or offset by strength on others.

competitive intensity the degree of a firm's competition.

completed fertility rate the total number of children ever born to women of a specific age group.

complexity the degree to which an innovation is perceived as difficult to understand and use.

component method a population estimate method that divides population into its components of change: births, deaths, and migration.

comprehension a stage of information processing in which interpretation of a stimulus occurs.

compulsive consumption those practices that, although undertaken to bolster self esteem, are inappropriate, excessive, and disruptive to the live of those involved.

conative attitudes the attitude component that refers to a person's action or behavioral tendencies toward an attitude object.

concentrated marketing marketing in which the primary focus is on one segment.

concrete words those than name a real thing or class of things.

conditioned response (see classical conditioning)

conditioned stimulus (see classical conditioning)

confidence the degree of conviction with which an attitude is held.

confirmation the process through which consumers seek reinforcement for the innovation decision.

conjunctive decision rule a non-compensatory decision rule involving processing by brand in which cutoffs are established for each salient attribute and each brand is compared to this set of cutoffs.

consideration set the set of alternatives from which choice is made.

Consolidated Metropolitan Statistical Area a grouping of closely related PMSAs.

constructive decision rule a decision rule that a consumer builds using elementary processing operations (fragments of rules) available in memory that can accommodate the choice situation.

consumer behavior those actions directly involved in obtaining, consuming, and disposing of products and services, including the decision processes that precede and follow these actions.

consumerism policies and activities designed to protect consumer interests and rights as they are involved in an exchange relationship with any type of organization.

consumer knowledge information relevant to the functioning of consumers in the marketplace.

consumer satisfaction/dissatisfaction (CS/D) a judgement as to whether purchase outcomes meet expectations.

consumer socialization the acquisition of consumption-related cognitions, attitudes, and behavior.

content analysis a technique for determining the values, themes, role prescriptions, norms of behavior, and other elements of culture.

contextualized marketing a marketing strategy designed to take into account cultural differences in consumer motivation and behavior by adapting marketing efforts in such a way that they are perceived as culturally relevant.

continuous innovation the modification of an existing product.

core merchandise the basic group of products essential to a store's traffic, customer loyalty, and profits.

core values values that are basic to understanding human behavior.

corrective advertising advertising used to rectify deception that occurred in previous advertising.

counterargument a cognitive response that opposes the claims made in a communication.

credence claims claims that a consumer cannot evaluate or verify (e.g., "Millions of research dollars are behind this project").

credit an amount or sum placed at a person's disposal by a bank or other financial institution that extends the income resource, at least temporarily.

cross-cultural analysis the systematic comparison of similarities and differences in the material and behavioral aspects of cultures.

crude birthrate (see birthrate)

CUBE (Comprehensive Understanding of Buyer Environment) post-hoc segmentation analysis identifying eight primary segments.

cultural analysis studies whose goal is to create the ability to understand and be effective in addressing the core values of a society.

cultural artifacts (see material components)

cultural empathy the ability to understand without judging the inner logic and coherence of other ways of life.

cultural functionalist an anthropologist holding the view that culture is an entity that serves humans in their efforts to meet the basic biological and social needs of the society.

culture the values, ideas, artifacts, and other meaningful symbols that help individuals communicate, interpret, and evaluate as members of society.

customer satisfaction monitoring program a policy of using ongoing customer surveys to continually monitor and evaluate service.

cutoff a restriction or requirement for acceptable attribute values, used in alternative evaluation.

decay theory a theory positing that the strength of a memory trace will fade over time.

decision rule a strategy that a consumer uses to make a selection from the choice alternatives.

declarative knowledge knowledge of information facts, which are subjective in that they need not correspond to objective reality.

defensive marketing marketing that encourages and resolves consumer complaints.

deference the granting of social honor.

degree of search a dimension of search indicating the total amount of search.

demarketing a deliberate attempt to induce consumers to buy less in a product class.

demographics the characteristics of human populations, such as size, growth, density, distribution, and vital statistics; used in consumer research to describe segments of consumers in such terms as age, income, and education.

demographic segmentation directing marketing efforts toward differing segments as defined by demographic characteristics.

demography the study of demographics

demonstrated recall measure a measure utilizing a survey to determine what percentage of viewers can recall the name of the advertised product and one point from the advertising copy.

deontologically reasoning based on one's right or duty or the inherent morality within the act itself.

depth interview the interviewing of a small sample (50 or fewer), one at a time, in a lengthy, unstructured session.

descriptive cross-cultural studies studies that describe structural components and are used to contrast or compare societies.

descriptive differences consumer differences that are merely descriptive, as opposed to casual.

Designated Marketing Area (see Area of Dominant Influence)

desired state types consumers in whom need recognition results from changes in the desired state.

determinant attribute a salient attribute on which choice alternatives differ in their performance.

dialectical materialism the view that culture moves in a determined direction through a process of exchange and social interaction in competition for scarce resources.

difference threshold the smallest change in stimulus intensity that will be noticed by an individual.

differentiated marketing marketing that concentrates on two or more segments, offering a differing marketing mix for each.

diffusion the process by which an innovation is communicated through certain channels over time among the members of a social system.

direct marketing activities by which products and services are offered for information purposes or to solicit a direct response from a present or prospective customer or distributor by mail, telephone, or other access.

direct selling any form of face-to-face contact between a salesperson and a customer away from a fixed retail location.

direct stores a fast- growing form of in-store retailing that provides a great challenge to department stores. One form is factory outlet stores that emphasize brand name merchandise at discount prices. Another form is operated by manufacturers as exemplars of customer service and selection rather than discount prices.

directed learning learning that occurs when learning is the primary objective during information processing (i.e., motivation is high)

direction of attention a dimension of attention representing the focus of cognitive capacity.

direction of search a dimension of search representing the specific content of search.

discontinuance ceasing to use a previously adopted innovation.

discontinuous innovation an entirely new product that causes buyers to significantly alter their behavior patterns.

discrimination in classical conditioning, the process whereby an organism learns to emit a response to one stimulus but avoids making the same response to a similar stimulus.

discriminitive stimuli stimuli that serve as cues about the likelihood that performing a particular behavior will lead to reinforcement.

dissatisfaction the outcome of purchase when the consumer perceives the choice as falling short of expectations.

dissociative group a reference group whose members are motivated to avoid association.

door-in-the-face a multiple-request procedure under which compliance with a critical request is increased if this request is preceded by an even more demanding request which is refused.

doubling rate the length of time required for the population to double in size based on current birth rates.

drive a condition of arousal that occurs when there is sufficient discrepancy between a present state and a desired or preferred state of being.

dyadic interaction a retailing situation where the buyer and seller become involved in a face-to-face exchange.

dynamically continuous innovation either the creation of a new product or the alternation of an existing one; either way, there is no alteration in established patterns of customer buying and product use.

early adopter a consumer who adopts an innovation later than innovators.

early majority consumers who adopt an innovation after early adopters.

echoic the term used to describe auditory processing at the sensory-memory stage.

economic demographics the study of the economic characteristics of a nation's population.

economic node a metropolitan or similar area that serves as center of economic activity.

economic role (see instrumental role)

elaboration the amount of integration between new information and existing knowledge stored in memory (or, the number of personal connections made between the stimulus and one's life experiences and goals).

Elaboration Likelihood Model the theory of persuasion which proposes that the influence exerted by various communications elements will depend on the elaboration that occurs during processing.

electronic retailing a special form of direct marketing using electronic media to sell customers (e.g., the Home Shopping Network).

elimination by aspects decision rule a noncompensatory decision rule involving processing by attribute in which cutoffs are established for each salient attribute and brands are compared on the most important attribute; if several brands meet the cutoff, the next most important attribute is selected until the tie is broken.

empty-nester an older adult whose children have left home and the university.

enhanced shareholder value long-term, consistent appreciation of shareholder value.

enthography a research method, borrowed from cultural anthropology, which includes a guided interview supplemented by participant observation of buying and consumption behavior.

entrepreneurship organizing, managing, and assuming the risks of a business enterprise. Refers not only to the traditional small business, but also to the value of individual effort and accomplishment in large corporations.

environmental scanning analysis of the current environment and projected trends, including internal and external variables.

epidemiological model a diffusion-prediction model assuming that diffusion is a process of social interaction in which innovators and early adopters "infect" other consumers.

episodic knowledge knowledge involving information that is bound by the passage of time (e.g., knowing when one last purchased clothing).

equitable performance in purchase expectations, a normative judgement reflecting the performance one ought to receive.

ergonomics the study of the human factors involved with product design.

ethnic patterns the norms and values of specific groups within the larger society.

ethnocentricity an attitude that one's own group, race, or nationality is superior.

ethnographic research research in which researchers place themselves in the culture or its artifacts in order to "soak up" meaning.

evaluation the measure used to assess the "goodness-badness" of an attribute or product.

evaluative criteria the standards and specifications used by consumers to compare different products and brands.

evaluative participation studies studies in which researchers count the number and nature of personal contacts in people's informal relationships, using data collected from respondents as well as their own observations of the community and its formal and informal networks.

event marketing creating events at which opinion leaders are brought together to experience and evaluate a new or existing product.

evoked set (see consideration set)

executional elements elements in a communication other than the message content, such as visuals, sounds, colors, and pace.

expectancy disconfirmation model a theory of the process by which performance of a product or service is evaluated and a satisfaction/dissatisfaction outcome is reached.

expected performance in purchase expectations, a normative judgement reflecting what the performance probably will be.

experience claims claims that a consumer can fully evaluate only after product consumption

experiential benefits the symbolic value of a consumption object in terms of emotional response, sensory pleasure, daydreams, or aesthetic considerations.

exposure physical proximity to a stimulus that allows the opportunity for one or more senses to be activated.

expressive role role behavior involving support to other family members in the decision-making process and expression of the family's aesthetic or emotional needs.

extended family nuclear family plus such other relatives as grandparents, uncles and aunts, cousins, and in-laws.

extended problem solving detailed and rigorous decision-making behavior including need recognition, search for information, alternative evaluation, purchase, and outcomes. Often used in making major or critical purchases.

external search a stage of the consumer decision process in which relevant information is acquired.

extinction in classical conditioning, when the conditioned stimulus no longer evokes the conditioned response.

extremity the intensity of liking or disliking in an attitude.

exurbs areas beyond the suburbs.

family a group of two or more persons related by blood, marriage, or adoption who reside together.

family adaptability the ability of a family or marital system to change its power structure, role relationships, and relationship rules in response to situational and developmental stress.

family life cycle (FLC) the stages a family passes through during its lifetime.

family of orientation the family into which an individual is born.

family of procreation the family which is established by marriage.

favorability the degree of negativeness or positiveness of an attitude.

fertility rate the number of live births per 1,000 women of childbearing age.

festival marketplace a large complex of shops and restaurants, such as Boston's Faneuil Hall Marketplace or New York City's South Street Seaport.

figure those elements within a perceptual field that receive the most attention (see also ground)

first-order child first-born child

focus direction of attention

focus group a group of about 10 individuals, brought together with a trained leader for about one hour to discuss motivations and behavior.

foot-in-the-door a multiple-request procedure under which compliance with a critical request is increased if the person first agrees to an initial smaller request.

forced-choice recognition measures measures that require respondents to choose among a set of fixed answers (as in a multiple-choice instrument) to demonstrate their memory of specific ad and brand elements.

foreseeability the doctrine that a manufacturer should be able to anticipate and evaluate risks inherent in product use and find ways to avoid them.

formal group a reference group characterized by a defined, known list of members and an organization and structure codified in writings.

forward conditioning conditioning in which the conditioned stimulus precedes the unconditioned stimulus.

framed ad an ad in which the message relates the picture to the product.

fully planned purchase a purchase in which both the product and the brand are selected as intended.

functionality the degree to which a product's features meet a consumer's needs.

functional role (see instrumental role)

general fertility rate (see fertility rate)

generalization a classical conditioning when a new stimulus similar to the existing one elicits the same response.

generational change a societal change that suggests that there will be a gradual replacement of existing values by those young people who form the leading generation in value terms.

generic branding descriptive labeling of products that sell at lower prices than nationally advertised brands

generic need recognition the activation of a need for a particular product category; the need is not brand specific as in selective need recognition.

gentrification a process in which people move back to revitalized city neighborhoods, often displacing low-income families.

geodemography the analysis of demographic lifestyle profiles for areas as small as a neighborhood

geographic segmentation analysis of geographic differences in terms of region, size of metropolitan area, and density.

Gestalt psychology a theory that focuses on how people organize or combine stimuli into a meaningful whole.

global marketing the technique of using the same marketing strategy in all cultural contexts.

global thinking the ability to understand markets beyond one's own country of origin with respect to sources of demand, sources of supply, and methods of effective management and marketing.

Gross Domestic Product (GDP) a measure of goods and services produced in the United States, including those produced or provided by foreign companies operating in the United States.

gross national product GNP an economic measurement that analyses the total goods and services produced or provided by the U.S. economy, valued at market prices.

ground the elements, other than figure, that comprise the background in a perceptual field.

group norms stable expectations arrived at by consensus concerning behavioral rules for individual members.

growth rate the increase in population due to natural increase and net migration, expressed as a percentage of base population.

habitual decision making decision making based on habits of repeat purchasing, often formed to simplify decision-process activity.

hardware the physical or tangible aspects of a product.

heavy half the heavy users of a product.

hedonic benefits (see experiential benefits)

heterophilous communications a situation in which individuals are exposed to messages that are inconsistent with their own beliefs and values, which may cause cognitive dissonance and be a less effective method of communicating.

higher-order child any child born after a first-born child.

highspot a strategy in which a salesperson focuses only on hot prospects to secure a sale.

homophilous influence influence brought about by information transmission between people similar in social class, age, education, and other demographic characteristics.

homophily the degree to which pairs of individuals who interact are similar in important attributes, such as beliefs, education, and social class.

household all the persons, related and unrelated, who occupy a housing unit.

housing-unit method a population estimate method that multiplies occupied housing units buy the average of the household size.

hypermarket a retail store in the 60,000-to-200,000-square-foot range that carries both convenience and shopping goods with a heavy emphasis on general merchandise as well as on food.

hypodermic needle model a theory of marketing communications proposing that media have direct, immediate, and powerful effects on new product acceptance.

iconic the terms used to describe visual processing at the sensory-memory stage

ideal performance in purchase expectations, a normative judgement reflecting the optimum or ideal performance level.

ideology of consumption the social meaning attached to and communicated by products.

image analysis the examination of consumers' knowledge or beliefs about a product's properties.

imagery a process by which sensory information and experiences are represented in working memory.

imitation effect a phenomenon in which the rate of adoption increases as the number of adopters increases.

implementation the process by which a consumer puts a product into use.

importance the measure used to perationalize the concept of salience.

impulse purchase a spur-of-the-moment purchase triggered by product display or point-of-sale promotion.

inbound telemarketing use of the telephone to place order for goods or services.

incentive an anticipated reward from a course of action that offers need-satisfying potential.

incidental learning learning that occurs even when learning is not the primary objective during information processing.

in-depth (or guided) interview a research method, borrowed from clinical psychology, using a small sample (50 or less), one at a time in a lengthy, unstructured interview session.

individualized marketing a marketing strategy that recognizes, acknowledges, appreciates and serves the interests and needs of selected groups or consumers whose individual identities are or become known to the marketer.

individualized standards situational or individual ethic strategies used as the basis for ethical decision making.

inertia a motivation that leads to habitual decision making due to a lack of sufficient incentive to consider alternative brands.

influential a transmitter of opinions about products and services.

infommercials 30-60 minute television time purchases.

informal group a loosely structured reference group based on friendship or collegial associations. Norms, even when strigent, seldom appear in writing.

informational advertising advertising that attempts to influence consumers' product knowledge and attitudes by providing information that elicits favorable cognitive responses.

information environment the entire array of product-related data available to the consumer.

informational influence the influence of friends or spokespeople, which consumers often accept as providing credible and needed evidence about reality.

information overload a situation that occurs when the amount of information in a choice environment exceeds cognitive capacity.

information processing the process by which a stimulus is received, interpreted, stored in memory, and later retrieved.

information veracity the degree to which advertising is free of deception and misrepresentation.

inner-directed consumers consumers whose lives are directed

more toward their individual needs than toward values oriented to externals.

innovation any idea or product perceived by the potential adopters to be new.

innovativeness the degree to which an individual adopts an innovation relatively earlier than other members in the system do.

innovator a consumer who adopts a new product early.

instrumental learning a form of learning in which the consequences of a behavior affect the frequency or probability of the behavior being performed again.

instrumental role role behavior based on knowledge of functional attributes, such as financial aspects, performance characteristics, or conditions of purchase.

Integrated Marketing Communications (IMC) a comprehensive, unified marketing program emphasizing the same theme or themes in advertising, public relations, investor relations, and other communications, with a targeted market.

intensity the strength of an attitude.

intensity of attention the amount of attention focused in a particular direction.

interactive picture one in which both the product class and brand name are represented visually.

interactive electronic media cable television home shopping featuring two-way communication and providing access to virtually unlimited worldwide sources of programming, information, communication, and so on.

integrated marketing campaign broad-based strategy that involves components ranging from packaging, price, advertising, sales promotion, and so on.

inter-environmental considerations the concept, important in global marketing strategy, of considering the characteristic ways a culture responds to marketing.

interference theory according to this theory, forgetting is due to the learning of new information.

internal search retrieval of knowledge from memory.

intra-environmental considerations the methods of marketing that are characteristic of a firm in its own culture.

involvement strong motivation, as reflected in high perceived personal relevance of a stimulus in a particular context.

key-informant method a research method in which knowledgeable people are used to identify the influentials within a social system.

knowledge the information stored within memory.

knowledge stage the first Rogers innovation-decision stage, in which a consumer receives physical or social stimuli that give exposure and attention to the new product.

labeling a behavior modification technique in which attaching a label or description to a person increases the likelihood of her or him behaving in a manner that is consistent with the label.

laddering in-depth probing directed toward uncovering higher-level meanings both at the benefit (attribute) level and at the value level.

laggard consumers who are the last to adopt a new product.

later majority consumers who adopt an innovation after the early majority.

learning the process by which experience leads to changes in knowledge, attitudes, and/or behavior resulting from experience.

leisure discretionary or uncommitted time.

lexicographic decision rule a noncompensatory rule involving processing by attribute in which brands are compared on the most important attribute; if more than one brand qualifies, the next most important attribute is selected until the tie is broken.

life chances   the fundamental aspects of a person's future possibilities.

life cycle explanation   the concept that changes in a society's values can be forecast by noting that as individuals grow older, their values change.

lifestyle   patterns by which people live and spend time and money.

lifestyle retailing   the policy of tailoring a retail offer closely to the lifestyles of specific target market groups of consumers.

limited line specialty store   an in-store retailing outlet that features narrow product lines but wide assortments.

limited problem solving   limited decision-making behavior using a reduced number and variety of information sources, alternatives, and evaluation criteria.

lowballing   the behavior modification technique of citing a low price to gain customer commitment, then raising the price.

lower threshold   (see absolute threshold)

macroculture   the set of values and symbols that apply to an entire society.

macromarketing   macroanalysis of consumer behavior focused on determining the aggregate performance of marketing in society.

Management by Wandering Around   the practice of keeping open channels of communication with subordinates and customers by direct personal contact.

market-driven   a firm using a strategy that involves identifying high-growth opportunities in consumer, merchandise, and geographic markets, and having well-defined marketing strategies geared to some form of dominance.

marketing   the process of planning and executing the conception, pricing, promotion, and distribution of ideas, goods, and services to create

exchanges that satisfy individual and organizational objectives.

marketing communications   shared meanings between retailing organizations and persons, with exchange as their objective.

marketing mix   a marketing strategy integrating product, price, promotion, and distribution.

market segment   one of various groupings of buyers who expect benefits from a given transaction.

market segmentation   a marketing strategy involving viewing each segment as a distinct target with its own requirements for product, price, distribution, and promotion.

market types   classification of products, including consumer package goods, consumer durable goods, industrial support consumables, industrial process consumables (commodities), make-or-buy consumables, and industrial capital goods.

massification theory   the theory that social class distinction among the working and middle classes is disappearing

material components   the physical components of culture, such as books, computers, tools, buildings, and specific products.

meaning transfer   an advertising strategy whereby the meaning of one object is transferred to another, so consumers may come to see a product as more desirable because it is associated with endorsers having those meanings.

measurement correspondence   the degree to which a measure captures the action, target time, and/or contextual elements that make up the to-be-predicted behavior.

megalopolis   (see Consolidated Metropolitan Statistical Area)

me-too product   one whose packaging mimics that of a highly successful brand.

Metropolitan Statistical Area   a freestanding metropolitan area, surrounded by nonmetropolitan counties and not closely related with other metropolitan areas.

microculture   the set of values and symbols of a restrictive group, such as a religious, ethnic, or other subdivision of the social whole.

micromarketing   microanalysis of consumer trends and demographics that focuses on the marketing programs of specific organizations.

microspecialization   the identification of specific market targets and the development of specialized retailing formats that provide a high level of satisfaction to those market targets.

mid-range problem solving   decision-making behavior falling between extended problem solving and limited problem solving on the problem-solving continuum.

mini-mall   small and medium-size shopping centers of various formats, usually with less than 100,000 square feet. Some are fully enclosed or have an all-weather format.

misperception   inaccurate knowledge.

mobility and succession   a dual concept related to the stability or instability of stratification systems.

modeling   a form of learning in which an individual observes the behaviors of others and the consequences of those behaviors.

monochronic time   the concept of consumers performing only one activity at a time.

monodic approach   in innovation-diffusion research, a focus upon the personal and social characteristics of industrial consumers.

monomorphic   describes consumers who are innovative for only one product.

monomorphic influence   influence that relates to one product only.

motivation research   research into the classification of consumer motives and whether they are conscious or unconscious.

motive   an enduring predisposition that arouses and directs behavior toward certain goals. Motives can be rational (utilitarian) or emotional (hedonic).

multiattribute attitude models models that propose that overall attitude depends on beliefs about the attitude object's attributes weighted by the salience of these attributes.

multi-stage interaction a theory of personal influence that holds that both influentials and information seekers are affected by the media.

multi-state flow model a model of innovation communication where ideas flow from the media to opinion leaders and from those opinion leaders to the mass market.

natural increase the surplus of births over deaths in a given time period.

need a perceived difference between an ideal state and the present state, sufficient to activate behavior.

need-driven consumers consumers who exhibit spending driven by need rather than preference.

need for cognition a personality trait representing an individual's tendency to undertake and enjoy thinking.

need recognition perception of a difference between the desired state of affairs and the actual situation, sufficient to arouse and activate the decision process; the first stage of the decision-making process.

negative disconfirmation a CS/D judgement that performance is worse than expected.

negative reinforcement in operant conditioning, a behavior leading to the removal of some adverse stimulus which increases the odds of the behavior being repeated.

network marketing the development of a firm's marketing mix in close relationship to the marketing program of other firms.

new consumerism contemporary consumerism, generally thought to have begun with President Kennedy's 1962 address on the consumer bill of rights.

niche retailer a retailer offering a narrow but deep assortment, such as Banana Republic.

nonadopter one who makes the decision not to adopt a new product.

nonadoption (see passive rejection)

no-name brand (see generic branding)

noncumpensatory strategy a strategy in alternative evaluation in which a brand's weakness on one attribute cannot be offset by a strength on another attribute.

noninteractive pictures pictures in which either product class or brand name, but not both, are shown visually.

normative influence (see utilitarian influence)

norms beliefs held by consensus of a group concerning the behavior rules for individual members.

nuclear family immediate group of father, mother, and children living together.

objective claims claims that focus on factual information that is not subject to individual interpretations.

objective knowledge measures measures that assess the knowledge actually stored in memory.

objective research methods assigning status to respondents on the basis of a stratified variable such as occupation, income, or education.

observability (see communicability)

observation a measure for observing consumer search based on how much people seek information before making a decision.

one-sided message a communication presenting only the pros of the advocated position.

ongoing search a type of external search in which information acquisition occurs on a relatively regular basis regardless of sporadic purchase needs.

operant conditioning (see instrumental learning)

opinion leader person from whom a consumer seeks consumer-related advice.

order effects the differences in consumption between families caused by birth order (first-order babies generate more economic impact that higher-order babies).

outbound telemarketing marketing telephone contact by the seller to the consumer.

outcomes the fifth stage in decision making in which the consumer evaluates whether or not the chosen alternative meets needs and expectations once it is used.

outer-directed consumers consumers who generally buy with awareness of what other people will attribute to their consumption of the purchased product.

outshopper a consumer who shops outside a local trading area.

PAD paradigm a categorization of emotional responses including the dimensions of pleasure, arousal, and dominance.

parody display the mockery of status symbols and behavior, as in the wearing of "work clothes" by upper-class youth.

partially planned an intention to buy the product but brand choice is deferred until shopping.

partial reinforcement a schedule of reinforcement in which the desired response is reinforced only part of the time; it may be systematic (e.g, every third response) or random.

passive rejection never really considering use of an innovation.

penetration model model that predicts the level of penetration by a new product in a given time period based on early sales results.

pension elite three million older adults, mostly between 65 and 74, with enough income from multiple sources to support an active, independent, and healthy lifestyle.

perceived behavioral control represents a person's belief about how easy it would be to perform a particular behavior.

peripheral cues elements in a communication that are irrelevant to developing a reasoned opinion.

peripheral route a form of persuasion in which issue relevant thinking is low and peripheral cues become influential.

persistence a property or attitude that reflects the notion that attitudes may gradually erode simply due to the passage of time.

personal determinants of attention the characteristics of an individual that influence attention.

personality the consistent responses of an individual to environmental stimuli.

person-situation segmentation a segmentation strategy that takes into account the fact that different consumers seek different product benefits, which can change across different usage situations.

persuasion the formation of favorable or unfavorable attitudes toward an innovation.

phased decision strategy a process using one decision rule as a screening device to help narrow the choice set to a more manageable number, and a different rule or rules to make the final choice.

piece part and tooling costs a reflection of whether a product is designed to be produced with processes and materials suited to the manufacturer's product levels and target costs as well as the product's actual purpose.

polychronic time involves combining activities simultaneously such as eating while watching television, or working on a laptop computer while on an airplane.

polymorphic influence influence that relates to several product areas.

polymorphism describes consumers who are innovators for many products.

positive disconfirmations a CS/D judgement that performance is better than expected.

positive reinforcement in operant conditioning, a behavior leading to

receiving some positive stimulus which increases the odds of the behavior being repeated.

post-hoc segmentation analysis defining the segmentation base as an outcome of analysis.

positivism the research theory in which rigorous empirical techniques are used to discover generalized explanations and laws.

postmodernism a form of inquiry that embraces different goals and methods.

power potential of individuals or groups to carry out their will over others.

power mall (see mini-mall)

preattentive processing the constant monitoring of the cognitive system of sensory inputs at a preconscious level.

prepotency the theory that needs are organized in such a way as to establish priorities and hierarchies of importance.

prepurchase alternative evaluation the third stage of the decision-making process whereby a choice alternative is evaluated and selected to meet consumer needs.

prepurchase search a type of external search that is motivated by an upcoming purchase decision.

prestige a variable of social class reflecting other people's attitudes of respect or deference to a person.

primacy an order effect wherein stimuli appearing at the beginning of a sequence are given more weight in the resulting interpretation.

primary group a social aggregation (reference group) sufficiently small to permit and facilitate unrestricted face-to-face interaction.

primary metropolitan statistical area a metropolitan area closely related to another city.

principle of reciprocity the principle of trying to repay what others have done for us.

proactive inhibition a form of interference in which prior learning

hinders the learning and retrieval of new information.

problem solving thoughtful, reasoned action undertaken to bring about need satisfaction.

procedural knowledge the understanding of how the facts of declarative knowledge can be used.

processing by attribute (see attribute search sequence)

processing by brand (see brand search sequence)

producibility the degree to which a product can be made with a firm's normal capabilities.

product category the category of goods (e.g., clothing, appliance)

product knowledge information stored in memory about a product category, such as the brands within it, product terminology, product attribute, and beliefs about the product category and specific brands.

product life cycle the cycle of introduction, growth, and decline of a product. Marketing strategy and mix must be adapted to the changing stages of the life cycle.

product positioning the ways in which consumers identify a product with a defined set of attributes such as power, sportiness, caffeine, or color.

product potential the tangible attributes, augumented product, and consumer expectations for the product, all combined to incorporate every factor that might attract and hold customers.

product semantics (see semiotics)

Profit Impact of Market Strategy Research research into how market strategy affects practitioners economically; it indicates that market leaders achieve average rates of return three times greater than firms with low market share.

programmed resource relationship a retailer-supplier relationship in which the retailer is a powerful controlling factor.

projective set a questioning technique that allows the respondent to reply in the third person.

prompting a behavior modification technique in which consideration of product purchase is gained by a simple request (e.g., offering or suggesting a side dish in a restaurant).

proposition (see belief)

proxy variable a variable that stands in for another (eg., demographic data can serve as a proxy variable for motivation and interests).

psychoanalytic theory a personality theory that posits that the human personality system consists of the id (the source of psychic energy), the super-ego (representing societal or personal norms), and the ego (which mediates the hedonistic demands of the id and the moralistic prohibitions of the superego.

psychographcis research into psychological profiles of groups or individuals, especially regarding personality traits, values, beliefs, preferences, and behavior patterns.

psychographic segmentation analysis of lifestyle factors for segmentation purposes.

psycholinguistics the study of psychological factors involved in the perception of and response to linguistic phenomena.

pull strategy a marketing strategy for creating product demand by appealing to the ultimate consumers, who, in turn, encourage the channel to carry the product.

purchase the fourth stage in the decision-making process, in which the consumer acquires the preferred alternative or an acceptable substitute.

purchase knowledge information stored in memory that is germane to acquiring products.

purchase situation those settings in which consumers acquire products and services.

push strategy a marketing strategy that involves focusing selling efforts on the channel, which is then responsible for attracting consumers.

Quality Function Deployment the use of customer input throughout the design, engineering, manufacturing, and distribution of a product.

ratio-correlation method a population estimation method that uses multiple regression to mathematically compute a population estimate.

rational decision making problem solving based on the careful weighing and evaluation of utilization or functional product attributes.

recall measures measures of cognitive learning that do not provide cues to prompt memory.

recency an order affect wherein stimuli appearing at the end of a sequence are given more weight in the resulting interpretation.

reciprocity a principle that states that we should try to repay what others have done for us.

recognition measures measures of cognitive learning that provide cues to prompt memory.

reference group a person or group of people that significantly influences an individual's behavior and attitudes.

rehearsal the mental repetition of information (i.e., the recycling of information through short-term memory).

rejection the decision not to adopt an innovation.

relational approach in innovation-diffusion research, a focus on communication networks and how social-structural variables affect diffusion flows in the system.

relationship marketing a time-tested concept of more intimate, one-on-one relationship between the buyer and seller.

relative advantage the degree to which consumers perceive a relative advantage of a new product over the existing product.

relativism a belief that morality is relative to or dependent on some cultural, social, or personal standard. There cannot be an absolute moral standard.

relativists people who do not believe in moral absolutes, but instead believe that morality depends on cultural, social, and personal standards.

remarketing the practice of the sale of used items.

repeated problem solving decision-making dynamics that lead the consumer to buy a different brand than previously purchased.

replacement rate the fertility rate required to replace the current population, with allowances for some infant mortality.

reputational research methods methods utilizing people's ranking of the social position or prestige of other people.

resource commitments the degree to which research and development, advertising, personal selling, sales promotion, and distribution support are devoted to the diffusion process.

retail image the way a store is defined in a shopper's mind, partly by its functional qualities and partly by an aura of psychological attributes.

retail image measurement measures of image include many attitude-measurement techniques, including semantic differential and psychololinguistics.

retailing portfolio a group of specialty stores, each programmed for a specific lifestyle, owned by one retailer.

retention the transfer of information to long-term memory.

retrieval the process by which knowledge stored in long-term memory is activated.

retrieval set a consideration set obtained by recall of alternatives from memory.

retroactive questioning a measure for consumer search based on recall of search activities during decision making.

role what the typical occupant of a given position is expected to do in that position in a particular social context.

role overload a situation in which the total demands on time and energy associated with the prescribed activities of multiple roles are too great to allow an individual to perform the roles adequately or comfortably.

salience the potential influence that a criterion exerts during the alternative evaluation process, often measured in terms of importance.

satisfaction a postconsumption evaluation that a chosen alternative meets or exceeds expectations.

sales promotion those marketing activities other than personal selling, advertising, and publicity that stimulate consumer purchasing and dealer effectiveness.

schema a high-order knowledge structure made up of a combination of propositions or beliefs.

script one type of schema, which contains knowledge about the temporal action sequences that occur during an event.

search the motivated activation of knowledge stored in memory or acquisition of information from the environment; the second stage of the decision-making process.

search claims claims that a consumer can accurately evaluate before purchase through external search.

secondary group a reference group exhibiting face-to-face behavior that is more sporadic, less comprehensive, and less influential in shaping thought and behavior than that of a primary group.

selective need recognition the activation of a need for a specific brand within a product category.

self-actualization the desire to know, understand, systematize, prioritize, and construct a system of values.

self concept an organized configuration of perceptions of the self which are admissible to awareness, including perceptions of one's characteristics, values, and relationships.

self-designation method a research method by which people are asked to evaluate the extent to which they are sought out for advice.

self monitoring a personality trait representing the degree of sensitivity to situational and interpersonal considerations.

self-perception theory a theory stating that individuals come to know their own attitudes, emotions, and other internal states by inferring them from observations of their own behavior.

self-referencing relating information to one's own self and experiences.

self-serving strategy a technology-development strategy in which a firm develops innovations but waits to introduce them until sales of its current products decline.

semantic knowledge generalized knowledge that gives meaning to an individual's world.

semiotics the study of the symbolic qualities of products in the context of their use.

sensation the activation of sensory receptors, following which the encoded information about the stimulus is transmitted along nerve fibers to the brain.

sensation seeker an individual motivated by the need for continued high-level stimulation.

shaping the reinforcement of successive approximations of a desired behavior pattern or of behaviors that must be performed before the desired response can be emitted.

shelf talker an ad placed on the shelf or within the product display in such a way that the brand name stands out.

simple additive decision rule a compensatory decision rule under which the consumer counts the number of times each alternative is judged favorably in terms of the set of salient evaluative criteria.

simple confirmation a CS/D judgement that performances equal expectations.

simple recognitive measures measures that involve presenting ads to people and asking whether they remember seeing them previously.

simultaneous conditioning classical conditioning in which the conditioned stimulus and unconditioned stimulus are presented at the same time.

situational influence the influence arising from factors that are particular to a specific time and place and are independent of consumer and object characteristics.

situational influence the influence arising from factors that are particular to a specific time and place and are independent of consumer and object characteristics.

slotting allowances premium fees paid to acquire prime, eye-level display space.

social class divisions within society composed of individuals sharing similar values, interests, and behavior.

socialization the process of absorbing a culture and all of its values and symbols.

sociometric measures (see evaluative participation studies)

sociometric method a research method in which individuals are asked to identify others they seek out for advice or information for decision making.

socio-psychological theory a personality theory that posits that social variables (not biological instincts) shape personality and that behavioral motivation is directed to shape those needs created by the social variables.

software the information base that accompanies a product's hardware component.

stability a dimension of one's attitude determining its endurance and longevity.

standardized technology technology that has become standardized among firms; its presence encourages diffusion.

Standard Metropolitan Statistical Area the old term for Metropolitan Statistical Area.

status group a group that reflects a community's expectations for style of life among each class as well as the positive or negative social estimation of honor given each class.

stimulus categorization the classifying of stimulus during the comprehension stage of information processing using concepts stored in memory.

stimulus determinants of attention the characteristics of a stimulus that influence attention.

store atmospherics the physical properties of the retail environment.

store image (see retail image)

structuralist an anthropologist who believes that culture follows a logic based on the patterns of the human mind.

subjective claims claims that evoke different responses from individual to individual.

subjective knowledge measures measures that assess a person's perception of the amount of knowledge he or she possesses, which may or may not correspond to her or his actual knowledge.

subjective research methods methods assigning status to individuals based on the perceptions of other people and the subjective insights or theories of the researchers.

subliminal persuasion the theory that stimuli below the lower or absolute threshold can influence attitudes and behavior.

superstores new, major retailers, such as Home Depot and Circuit Toys, that concentrate on specific product lines that make them commodity supermarkets.

supplier-style retailing in contrast to lifestyle retailing, supplier-side retailing emphasizes homogeneity and gives little or no recognition to customer differences.

support argument a cognitive response that is favorable to the claims of a communication.

surrogate shopping list a list of products obtained in response to product display rather than through cognitive planning.

telogically reasoning based on the morality of the consequences of one's actions.

terminal threshold the point at which additional increases in stimulus intensity have no effect on sensation.

time goods products and services classified by their time properties.

time guarantee a promise by the seller that the customer will not have to devote an unreasonable amount of time in getting product and service problems resolved.

total fertility rate the average number of children that would be born alive to a woman if she were to pass through all her childbearing years conforming to the age specific fertility rates of a given year.

total product concept the combination of the generic product, expected product, augmented product, and potential product; successful introduction of new products requires understanding of this concept.

total reinforcement a schedule of reinforcement in which the desired response is always reinforced.

trait any distinguishable, relatively enduring way in which one individual differs from another.

trait-factor theory a personality theory that postulates that an individual's personality is composed of definite predispositional attributes called traits.

transformational advertising advertising that attempts to influence consumers' perceptions of a product's emotional and symbolic features by eliciting favorable affective responses.

trend analysis the analysis of marketing opportunities that arise as a result of changes in the environment

trend following a technology-development strategy in which a firm capitalizes on the developments of other firms in the industry while minimizing its own research and development expenses.

trend setting a technology-development strategy in which a firm continuously develops innovations for current and future product developments, and introduces these innovations as soon as feasible.

trickle-down theory a theory of personal influence that holds that lower classes emulate the behavior of their high-class counterparts.

two-sided message a communication presenting the pros and cons of the advocated position.

two-step flow model a theory of personal influence that holds that new ideas first flow to influentials, who then pass them on to the rest of the population.

unaided recall measures measures that do not provide cues for retrieving information from memory.

unconditioned response (see classical conditioning).

unconditioned stimulus (see classical conditioning).

undifferentiated marketing marketing that targets all available segments.

unframed ad an ad in which the message does not relate the picture to the product.

unplanned purchase a purchase for which a conscious intention was not articulated in advance.

usage knowledge information in memory about how a product can be used and what is required to actually use it.

usage situation the setting where consumption occurs.

usage situation segmentation segmentation derived from information on product usage.

utilitatian benefits benefits resulting from purchase or other consumer decisions that are objective, functional product attributes.

utilitarian influence pressure that the reference group applies to the individual to comply with group norms.

valence refers to whether an attitude is positive, negative, or neutral.

value an enduring belief that a specific mode of conduct or end-state of existence is personally or socially preferable to an opposite or converse mode of conduct or end-state of existence.

value-expressive influence the pressure to experience psychological association with a group by conforming to its norms, values, or behaviors, even if membership is not sought.

value-oriented retailer a retailer who offers low prices and basic levels of product selection, and appeals to the economic shopper.

value platform the manner in which a firm differentiates itself from its competitors in the minds of the consumers it intends to service.

values shared beliefs or group norms that have been internalized by individuals.

variety seeking switching of brands simply in the interest of variety; often used when many similar alternatives are available.

vertical coordination the flow of information from supplies to consumer that affects the diffusion of information.

vicarious learning (see modeling)

videotex interactive electronic media used for in-home shopping and information.

volitional control represents the degree to which a behavior can be performed at will.

wants behavior patterns recognized as more effective than others for need satisfaction.

waverer a consumer whose commitment to the product is diminishing.

wealth net worth or assets, in consumer terms correlated with income.

Weber's Law a rule stating that the amount of change necessary to reach the difference threshold will depend on the initial starting point; e.g., as stimulus intensity increases, a greater amount of change is required to produce a just noticeable difference.

weighted additive decision rule a compensatory decision rule in which judgements about an alternative's performance on evaluative criteria are weighted by the relative salience of the evaluative criteria.

Credits

▲▲

PHOTO CREDITS

Page 20 Courtesy of Armour Food Company.

Page 139 © 1994, The Stock Yard.

Page 206 © 1994, The Stock Yard.

Page 526 © 1994, The Stock Yard.

Page 542 ©1994, The Stock Yard.

Page 734 Courtesy of Tupperware US, Inc.

Page 841 © 1993, Kax Mori/The Image Bank.

Page 856 Courtesy of Cheryl and Co.

MISCELLANEOUS CREDITS AND COPYRIGHTS

Page 20 (CF 1.3) "Never Underestimate the Power of a Hot Dog," by Roger D. Blackwell, James F. Engel, David T. Kollat, *Cases in Consumer Behavior* (New York: Holt, Rinehart & Winston, 1969), 75-81. © Holt, Rinehart & Winston.

Page 98 (Table 3.4) "Outlook 1994," *The Futurist*, 27, No. 6 (November-December 1993). © *Futurist Magazine*.

Page 107 (Figure 3.5) Cross Cultural Questionaire for Holiday Inn, "The Faces Game." © Holiday Inns.

Page 108–109 (text) "Strategic Implications of a Cross-Cultural Comparison of Attribute Importance: Automobiles in Japan and the United States," in Proceedings of the American Marketing Association Educators' Conference (Chicago: American Marketing Association, 1983), 327–332. © American Marketing Association.

Page 108 (Table 3.6) ESOMAR Seminar Seminar, 1993. ESOMAR Central Secretariat, J.J. Viottastratt 29, 1071 JP Amsterdam, The Netherlands. © ESOMAR.

Page 119 (Table 3.7) Americans and Japanese; How They See Each Other. "Japan in the Mind of American, American in the Mind of Japan," *Time* 139 (February 10, 1992), 16–23. © *Time*.

Page 169 (Figure 4.12) Judith L. Zaichowsky, "Measuring the Involvement Construct," *Journal of Consumer Research* 12 (December 1985), 350. © Journal of Consumer Research.

Page 196 (Figure 5.6). William L. Wilkie and Peter R. Dickson, "Shopping for Appliance: Consumers' Strategies and Patterns of Information Search," Marketing Science Institute Working Paper No. 85–108, 1985, Figure 2. © Marketing Science Institute.

Page 212 (CF 6.1) "Why Canadians Like U.S. Food," *American Demographics* (November 1993) 25–26. © *American Demographics*..

Page 215 (Table 6.1). John R. Hauser and Birger Wernerfelt, "An Evaluation Cost Model of Consideration Sets," *Journal of Consumer Research* 16 (March 1990), 393–408. © *Journal of Consumer Research*.

Page 221 (CF 6.3) "Washing Machines," *Consumer Reports* (February 1991), 112–117. © *Consumer Reports*.

Page 241 (Table 7.1) Excerpted from Edward M. Tauber, "Why Do People Shop?" *Journal of Marketing* 36 (October 1972), 46–59. © *Journal of Marketing*, American Marketing Association.

Page 243 (Table 7.2) Business Week/Harris Poll, "Shoppers Are a Dwindling Species," *Business Week* (November 26, 1990), 144. © *Business Week*.

Page 251 (Table 7.3) Source: 1992–1993 Statistical Fact Book. © Statistical Fact Book.

Page 274 (CF 8.3) Joe Peritz, "Retailers Who Keep Score Know What Their Shoppers Value," *Marketing News* (May 24, 1993), 9. © *Marketing News*.

Page 298 (Figure 9.2). David Wessel, "Confidence Surveys May Help to Predict Shape of the Recovery," *Wall Street Journal* (March 5, 1992), 1 ff. © *Wall Street Journal*.

Page 314 (Table 9.4) John P. Robinson, "Your Money of Your Time," *American Demographics* 13 (November 1991). © *American Demographics*.

Page 317 (CF 9.3) "Hilton Targets Time-Crunched Consumers," © Hilton Hotels Corporation.

Page 318 (Figure 9.8) John P. Robinson and Franco N. Nicosia, "Of Time, Activity, and Consumer Behavior: An Essay on Findings, Interpretations, and Needed Research," *Journal of Business Research*, 22 (1991), 171–186. © *Journal of Business Research*.

Page 319 (Table 9.5) "Time Savers," *American Demographics* 13 (February 1992), 10 .© *American Demographics*.

Page 339 (Table 10.1) Total Research Corporation, as cited in Diane Crispell and Kathleen Brandenburg, "What's in a Brand?" *American Demographics* (May 1993), 26–32. © *American Demographics*.

Page 361–362 (text) Diane Crispell and Kathleen Brandenburg, "What's in a Brand?" *American Demographics* (May 1993), 26–32. © *American Demographics*.

Page 422 (Figure 12.10) Maslow Hierachy of Needs. A.H. Maslow, *Motivation and Personality* (New York: Harper & Row, 1954). © Harper & Row. (Table 13.1) Kathryn E. A. Villani and Yoram Wind, "On the Usage of 'Modified' Personality Trait Measures in Consumer Research," Journal of Consumer Research 2 (December 1975), 223–228. © Journal of Consumer Research.

Page 441 (Table 13.2) Elizabeth Kendall Sproles and George B. Sproles, "Consumer Decision-Making Styles as a Function of Individual Learning Styles," *Journal of Consumer Affairs*, 24 (Summer 1990), 134–147. © *Journal of Consumer Affairs*.

Page451 (Table 13.3) Lifestyles of the Public and Advertising Agency Employees. "Study: The Customer Ain't Me," *Advertising Age* (January 20, 1992). © *Advertising Age*.

Page 453 (Table 13.4) Joseph T. Plummer, "The Concept and Application of Life Style Segmentation," *Journal of Marketing* 38 (January 1974), 34. © *Journal of Marketing*, American Marketing Association.

Page 457 (Table 13.4) Macmillan Publishing Company from Arnold Mitchell, *Nine American Lifestyles: Who We Are and Where We Are Going* (New York: Macmillan, 1983). Copyright © 1983 by Arnold Mitchell.

Page 460 (Table 13.6) Sheena Ashford and Noel Timms, *What Europe Thinks: A Study of Western European Values* (Aldershot: Dartmouth, 1992). © Dartmouth Publishing Company Ltd.

Page 500 (Table 14.1) Julie A. Edell and Marian Chapman Burke, "The Power of Feelings in Understanding Advertising Effects," J*ournal of Consumer Research* 14 (Decemver 1987), 424, Table 1.©*Journal of Consumer Research*.

Page 540 (Figure 15.11) Three Forms of Operant Conditioning. Adapted from Stanley M. Widrick, "Concept of Negative Reinforcement Has Place in Classroom," *Marketing News* 20 (July 18, 1986), 48–49. © *Marketing News*.

Page 562 (Figure 16.2). Richard E. Petty, John T. Cacioppo, and David Schumann, "Central and Periperal Routes to Advertising Effectivness: The Moderating Role of Involvement," *Journal of Consumer Research* 10 (September 1983), 135–136.©*Journal of Consumer Research*.

Page 564 (Figure 16.3). Marvin E. Goldberg and Jon Hartwick, " The Effects of Advertiser Reputation and Extremity of Advertising Claim on Advertising Effectiveness," *Journal of Consumer Research* 17 (September 1990), 172–179. © *Journal of Consumer Research*.

Page 568 (Table 16.1) Gary T. Ford, Darlene B. Smith and John L. Swasy, "Consumer Skepticism of Advertising Claims: Testing Hypotheses from Economics of Information," *Journal of Consumer Research* 16 (March 1990), 433–441.©*Journal of Comsumer Research*..

Page 590 (Figure 16.13) Chrysler's Rebate Program Boosted Minivan Sales. Neal Templin, "GM Declares War Over Minivans," *Wall Street Journal* (March 23, 1990), B1, B6. © *Wall Street Journal*.

Page 626 (Table 17.2) Source: Summarized from Seymour Martin Lipset, *Continental Divide: The Values and Institutions of the United States and Canada* (New York: Routledge, 1990). © Routeledge.

Page 627 (Table 17.3) Joseph T. Plummer, "Changing Values," *The Futurist* 23 (January–February 1989), 10. © *Futurist Magazine*.

Page 636 (Table 17.4) Institute for Social Research, University of Michigan, quoted in Cheryl Russell, "The Master Trend," *American Demographics*,15 (October 1993), 28–37, at 30. © *American Demographics*.

Page 721 (Figure 20.3) William O. Bearden and Michael J. Etzel, "Reference Group Influence on Product and Brand Purchase Decisions," *Journal of Consumer Research* 9 (September 1982), 185. © *Journal of Consumer Research*.

Page 729 (Table 20.1) Charles W. King and John O. Summers, "Generalized Opinion Leadership in Consumer Products: Some Preliminary Findings," paper No. 224 (Lafayette, Indiana: Institute for Research in thre Behavioral, Economic and Management Sciences, Krannert Graduate School of Industrial Administration, January 1969), 16. © Professor Charles King.

Page 749 (Table 21.1) Robert Boutilier, "Pulling the Family's Strings," *American Demographics* (August 1993), 44. © *American Demographics*..

Page 750 (Figure 21.3) © Management Horizons, A Division of Price Waterhouse.

Page 758 (Table 21.4) American Demographics-Single Mothers and Single Father to 201–, © *American Demographics*.

Page 772 (Table 21.5) The 1990 Virginia Slims Opinion Poll, conducted by The Roper Organization, New York City, 1990, p. 54. © Philip Morris USA.

Page 784 (Table 21.6) Massachusetts Mutual American Family Values Study, quoted in Norval D. Glenn, "What Does Family Mean?" *American Demographics*, June 1992, 30–37. © *American Demographics*.

Page 795 (Table 22.1) Russell W. Belk, "Situational Variables and Consumer Behavior," *Journal of Consumer Research* 2 (December 1975), 157–164. © *Journal of Consumer Research*.

Page 805 (Figure 22.3) Peter R. Dickson, "Person-Situation: Segmentation's Missing Link," Journal of Marketing 6 (Fall 1982), 56–64. © *Journal of Marketing*, American Marketing Association.

Page 811 (Figure 22.7) Peter R. Dickson, "Person-Situation: Segmentation's Missing Link," Journal of Marketing 6 (Fall 1982), 56–64. © *Journal of Marketing*, American Marketing Association.

Page 838 (Figure 23.6) *Location Strategies for Retail and Service Firms* by Avijit Ghosh and Sara L. McLafferty (Lexington, Mass; Lexington Books, D.C. Heath and Company, 1987, 34, Copyright 1987; D.C. Heath and Company).

Page 843 (Figure 23.8) Chip Walker, "Strip Malls: Plain But Powerful," *American Demographics* 13 (October 1991), 48–52. © *American Demographics*.

Page 845 (Table 23.1) Edward M. Tauber, "Why Do People Shop?" *Journal of Marketing* 36 (October 1972), 46–59. Reprinted from the Journal of Marketing published by the American Marketing Association.

Page 847 (Table 23.2) Don L. James, Richard M. Durand, and Robert A. Dreves, "The Use of a Multi-Attribute Model in a Store Image Study," *Journal of Retailing* 52 (Summer 1976), 23–32. © *Journal of Retailing*.

Page 921 (Figure 25.1) Peter Dickson (unpublished manuscript. The Ohio State University, 1988).*f* © Ohio State University.

Page 936 (Figure 25.4) William M. Pride and O.C. Ferrell, *Marketing: Basic Concepts and Decisions*, 4th ed., 481. © Houghton Mifflin Company.

Page 937 (Figure 25.5) Dorothy Cohen, "Remedies for Consumer Protection: Prevention, Restitution, or Punishment," *Journal of Marketing* (October 1975), 25. © *Journal of Marketing*, American Marketing Association.

Page 943 (Figure 25.7) Gene R. Laczniak and Patrick E. Murphy, *Marketing Ethics: Guidelines for Managers* (Lexington, Mass.: Lexington Books, 1985), 117–123. © D.C. Heath and Company, Lexington Books.

Page 944 (Figure 25.8) Donald P. Robin and R. Eric Reidenbach, "Social Responsibility, Ethics, and Marketing Strategy: Closing the Gap between Concept and Application," *Journal of Marketing* 51 (January 1987), 52. © *Journal of Marketing*, American Marketing Association.

Name Index

Subject Index